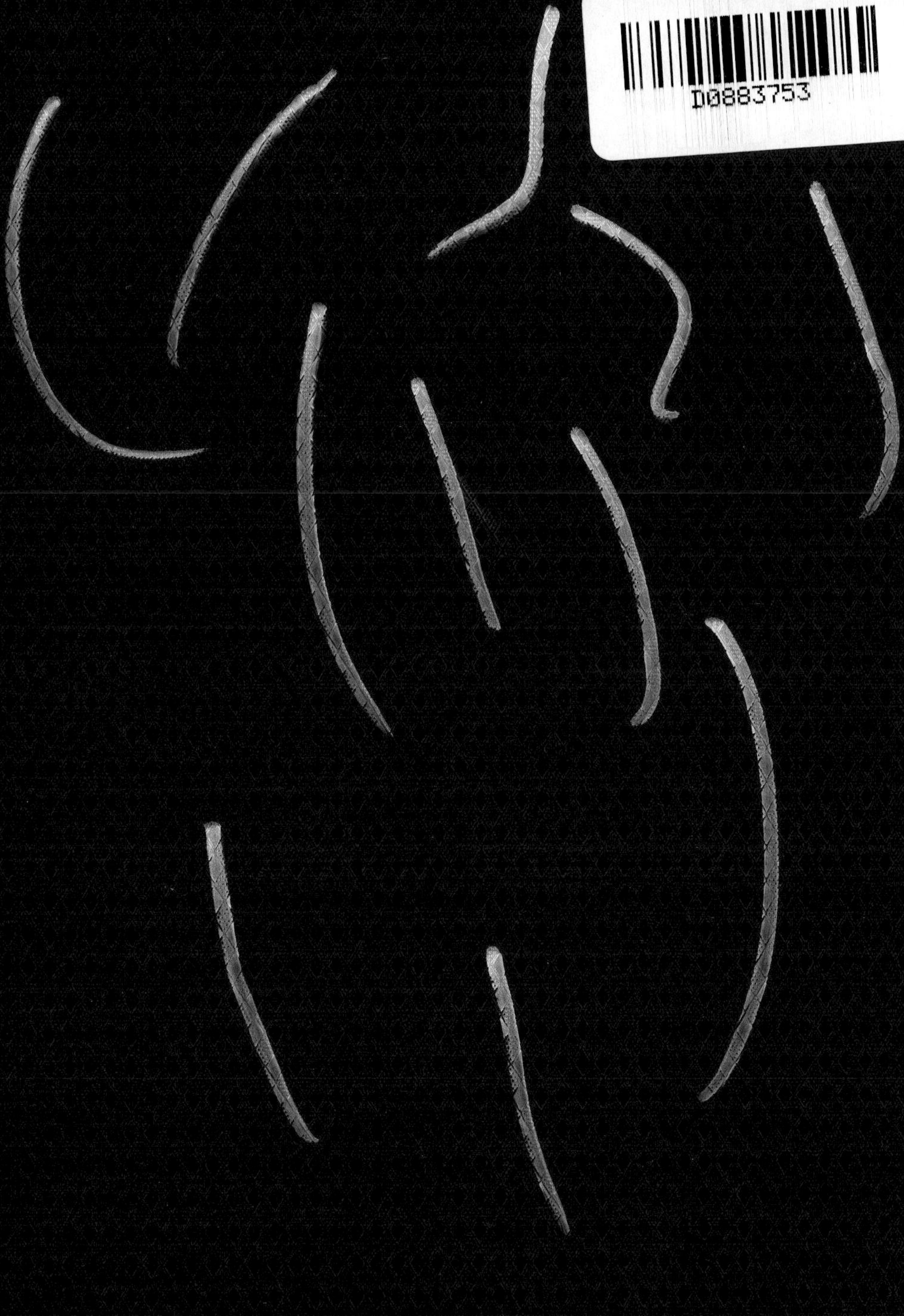

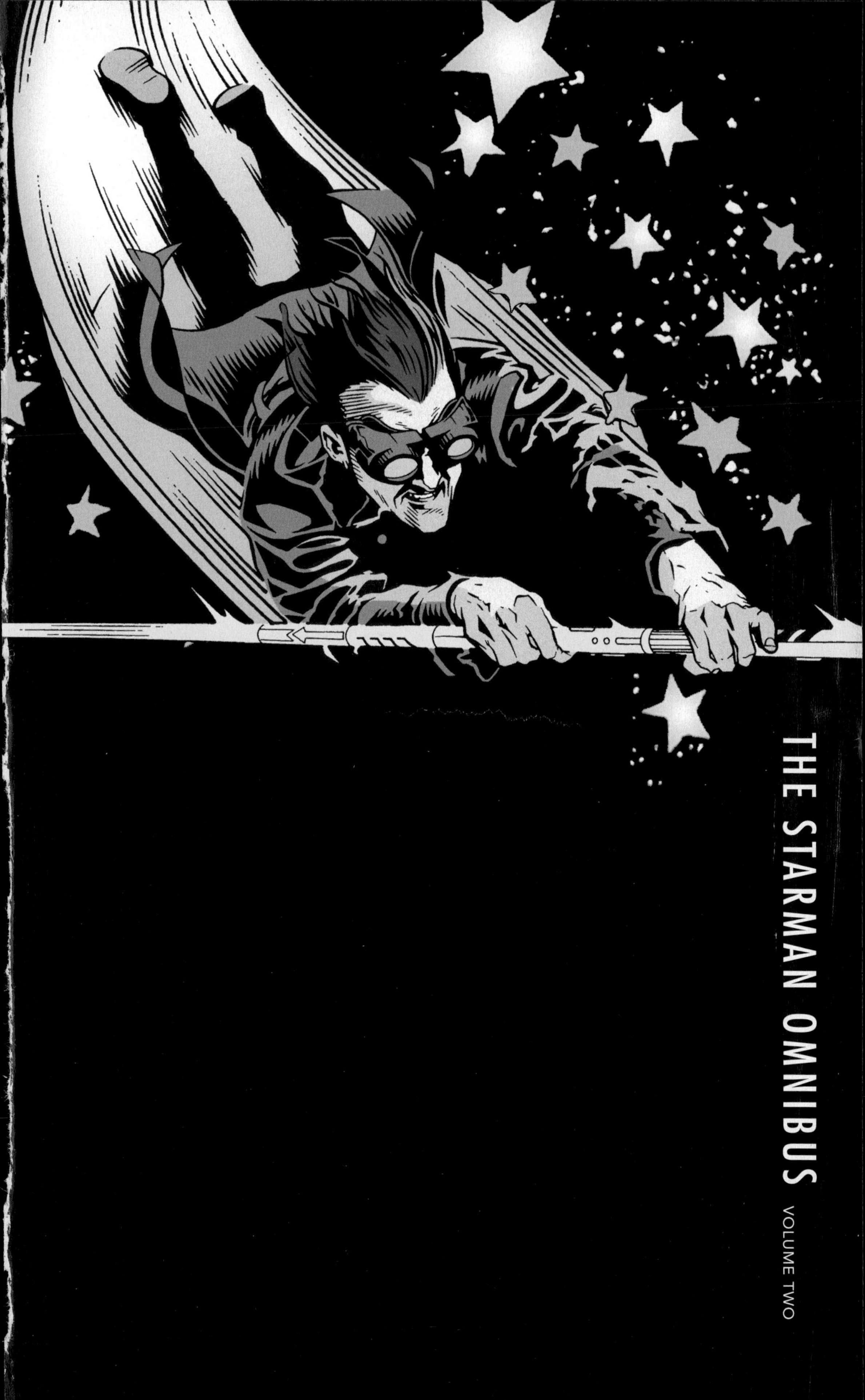

THE STARMAN OMNIBUS

VOLUME TWO

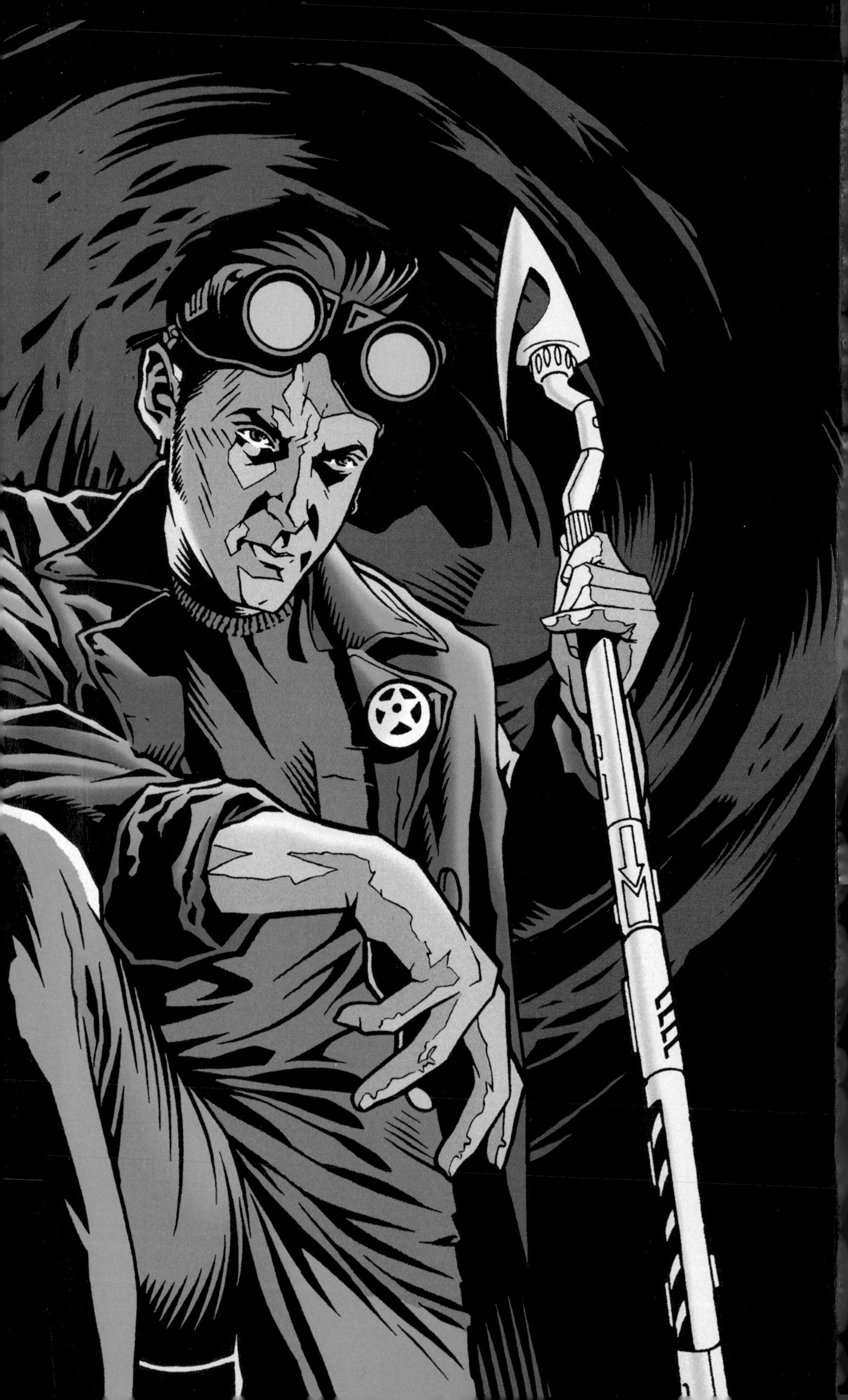

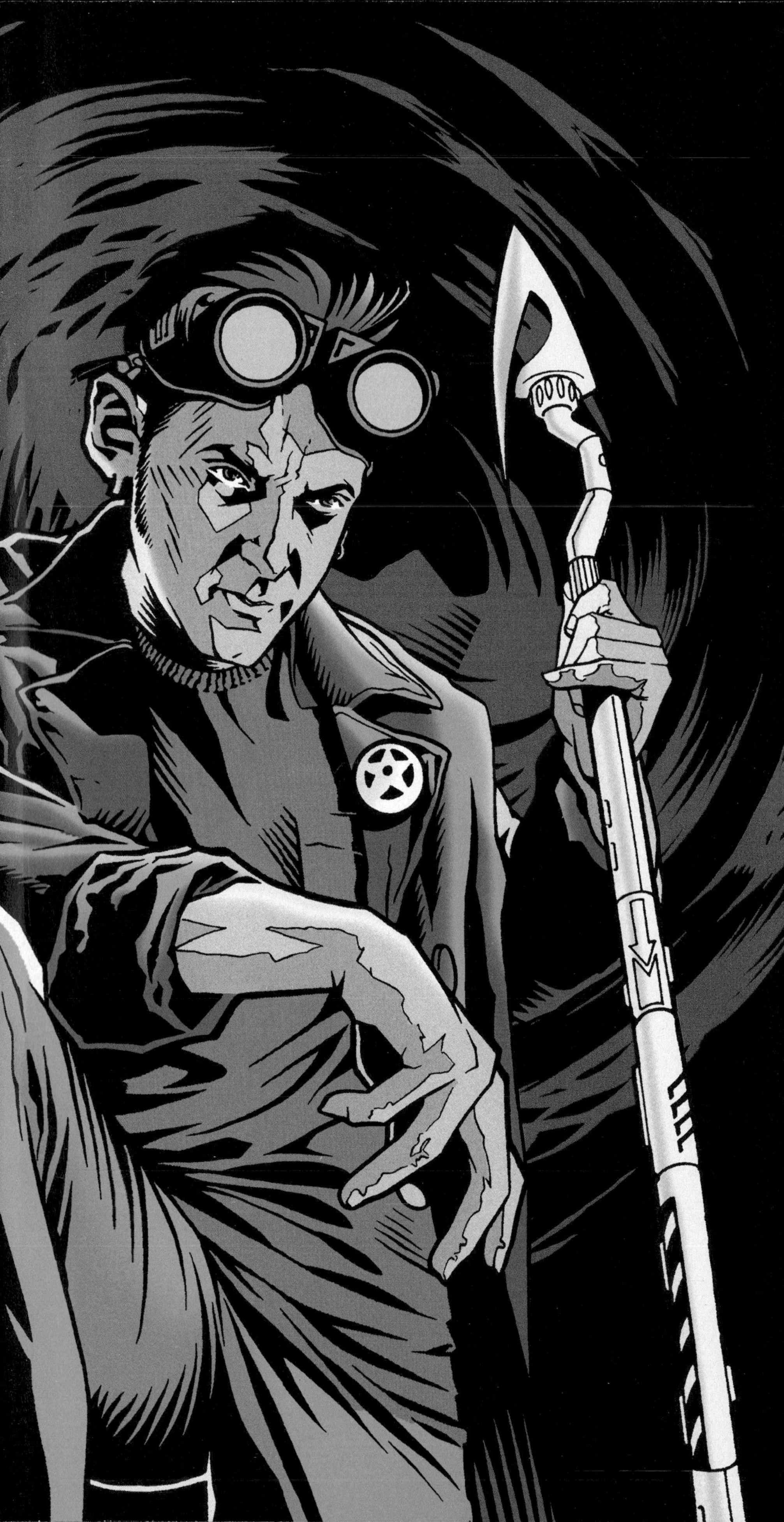

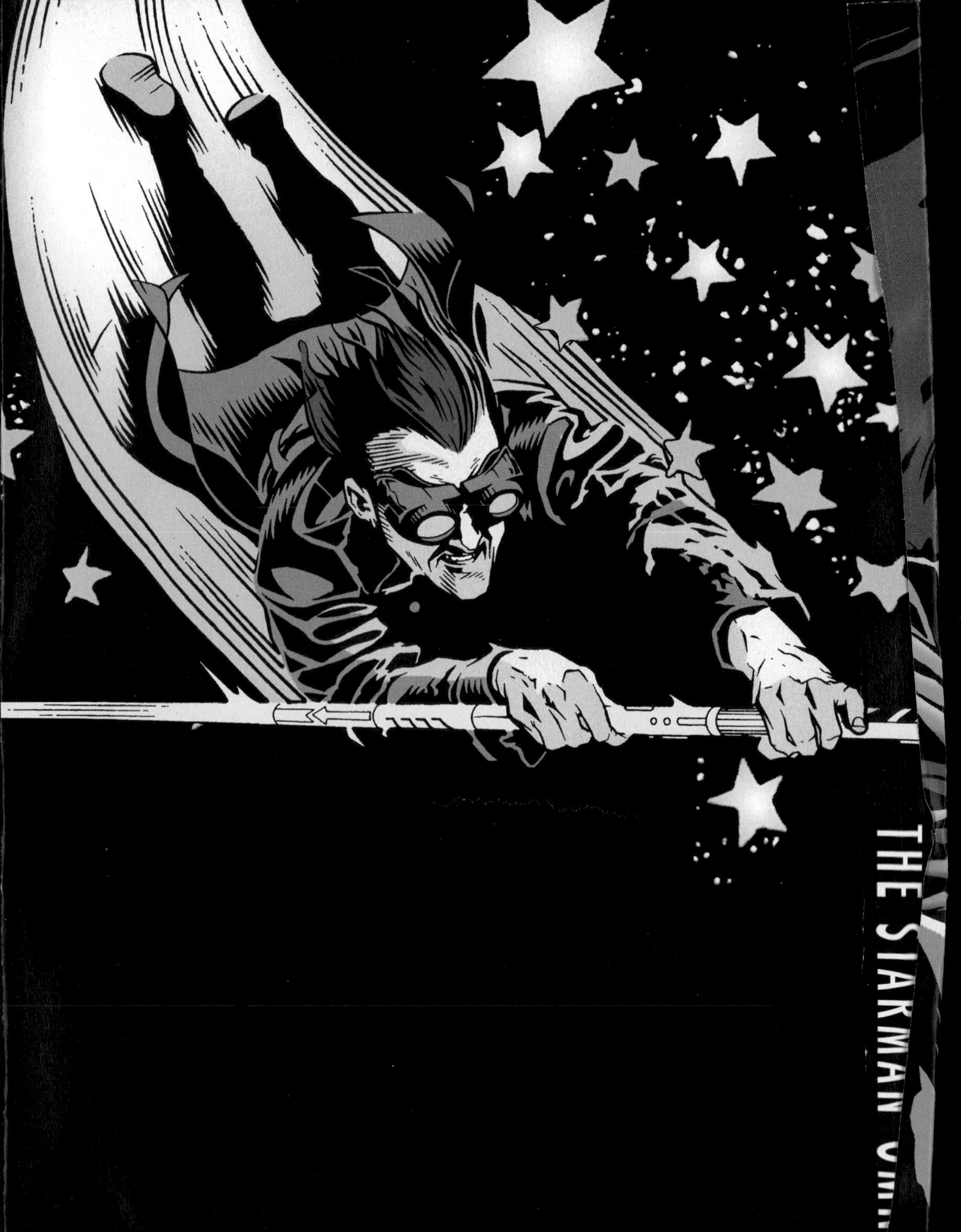
THE STARMAN

THE STARMAN OMNIBUS VOLUME TWO

James Robinson Writer   Tony Harris Penciller   Wade von Grawbadger Inker
Gregory Wright Colorist   Bill Oakley/N.J.Q. Letterers

Craig Hamilton & Ray Snyder   John Watkiss   Steve Yeowell   Matt Smith
J.H. Williams III & Mick Gray   Bret Blevins   Guy Davis   Wade von Grawbadger
Chris Sprouse   Gary Erskine Additional Artists

Kevin Somers   Pat Garrahy   Melissa Edwards   Debbie McKeever
Trish Mulvihill   Dave Hornung Additional Colorists

Chris Eliopoulos Additional Letterer

Tony Harris Original Covers and Sketches

Jack Knight created by James Robinson and Tony Harris

Dan DiDio
Senior VP-Executive Editor

Archie Goodwin
Editor-original series

Chuck Kim
Assistant Editor-original series

Anton Kawasaki
Editor-collected edition

Robbin Brosterman
Senior Art Director

Paul Levitz
President & Publisher

Georg Brewer
VP-Design & DC Direct Creative

Richard Bruning
Senior VP-Creative Director

Patrick Caldon
Executive VP-Finance & Operations

Chris Caramalis
VP-Finance

John Cunningham
VP-Marketing

Terri Cunningham
VP-Managing Editor

Amy Genkins
Senior VP-Business & Legal Affairs

Alison Gill
VP-Manufacturing

David Hyde
VP-Publicity

Hank Kanalz
VP-General Manager, WildStorm

Jim Lee
Editorial Director-WildStorm

Gregory Noveck
Senior VP-Creative Affairs

Sue Pohja
VP-Book Trade Sales

Steve Rotterdam
Senior VP-Sales & Marketing

Cheryl Rubin
Senior VP-Brand Management

Alysse Soll
VP-Advertising & Custom Publishing

Jeff Trojan
VP-Business Development, DC Direct

Bob Wayne
VP-Sales

Cover by Tony Harris

**Special thanks to Stuart Schreck,
Drew R. Moore and Matt Kramer.**

THE STARMAN OMNIBUS
Volume Two

DC Comics, 1700 Broadway,
New York, NY 10019
A Warner Bros. Entertainment Company
Printed in USA. First Printing.

HC ISBN: 978-1-4012-2194-2
SC ISBN: 978-1-4012-2195-9

HOW TO MAKE A PERFECT CUP OF TEA —

TONY HARRIS

There are so many things that come to mind when I think about STARMAN, which is daily. Sometimes it's the work itself, with James, with Wade, with Gary Erskine, who I talked a lot with and liked so much. Or I think about Peter Snejbjerg, who came in to take over the art when I left. He ended up doing as much or more than I did on the series, but fans still tell me how much they missed me after I left, some saying they left the series when I did. But I know the *real* story...that Peter gave as much of himself to Jack and Opal as I did. Other times, and most frequently, about conversations I had with Archie Goodwin. What I should say is that I *try* and remember them. Time has a way of being cruel to your memories, and it hasn't spared mine about Archie. But I do remember lots. *Lots.* But most of those are for me. My private high. Sometimes I think about the art, which I will periodically pull out in trade paperback and look at either by myself or with my 13-year-old son, who is now reading the series for the first time. He has lots of questions — many of which I have never answered at a convention. Questions like...

What is Jack's favorite thing to collect?

How come when you draw him in convention sketches, he doesn't look like himself?

Did he always have the goatee?

How does the rod make him fly?

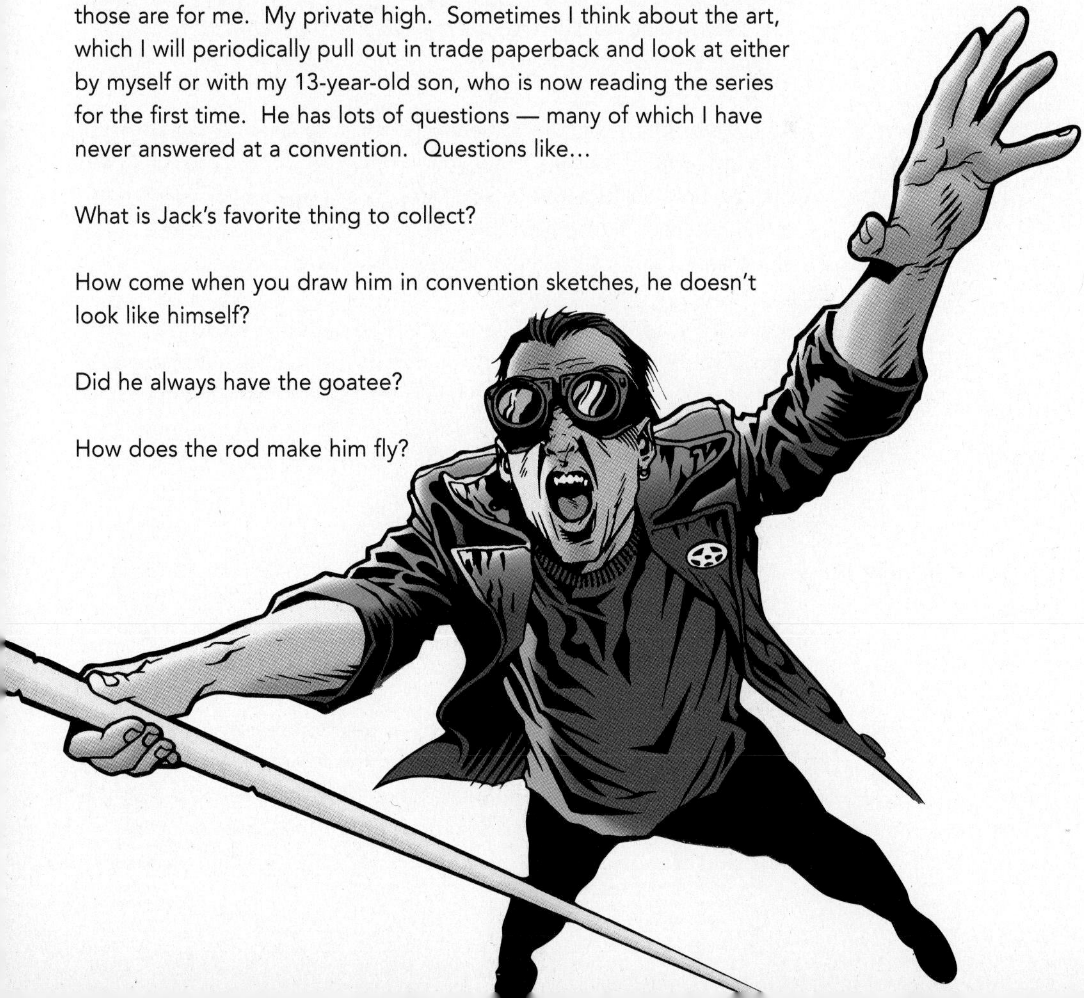

Is Ragdoll ever gonna get a big story of his own?!?!? (He *loves* that character).

Why don't you paint covers any more?

Are you ever gonna draw a Starman book again? (Okay, I get that one a LOT!!)

Needless to say I get to relive the series, and revisit the work, and examine it in a way I never would've these many years later with my son. Wow. Isn't that really what this series was about on so many levels? A father and his sons?

But I think the one thing I think about the most when it comes to Starman is a perfect cup of tea.

James and I were in St. Louis, Missouri, around the launch of the book. We went there to promote, sign, and mingle with the new fans of a new DC title. I can't recall the exact year now, but it was early on. So we arrived in St. Louis, and settled into our rooms, which were these REALLY nice suites. So we had the kitchen thingy, and sitting room, etc... Anyway, I called up James on the hotel phone the next morning and asked if he was ready to go. He replied that he was getting dressed and making a cup of tea and that I should trot over to his suite.

So I gathered my things and headed over. I walk in and was greeted by a jovial Mr. Robinson. Mind you, if I remember correctly, this was the first time we had met face to face, so this was a cool moment for me. I had read James' work on THE GOLDEN AGE, and was a fan. Needless to say, I was excited to be working with him.

So I come in, sit down, and James excuses himself back to the bedroom to finish getting ready. I look over and notice that there is a kettle on the stove that is heating up. We talk through the doorway to the back of the suite about the day ahead, and how excited we are. Exchanging personal information about our lives as we get to know each other.

Then I hear a piercing scream coming from the stovetop. So I get up and head over to turn off the burner and quiet the noise. After all, it was done, right? Wrong. James emerges from the back in a rush and asks me, "What are you *doing*?!" I answer, "It's done, I turned it off."

So James was a bit upset that I turned off the kettle. What I didn't know at the time is that for a perfect cup of tea you have to pour the boiling water over the tea bag (already deposited inside the cup). So James was quick to tell me what I did wrong, and I am fairly sure he did it as politely as was possible. See, I know how important my coffee is to me in the morning. You like your shit the way you like it, dammit!

I can't even tell you why, but that moment has stuck with me. To this day, when I make my wife a cup of tea (which is almost nightly), I wait until the water is boiling, the tea bag is in the cup, and I pull the pot off the flame and pour it over the tea bag. Perfect cup of tea. So my wife tells me. I don't drink tea. Like I said...I'm a coffee man.

So every time I make a cup of tea for my wife, James Robinson, and that day in St. Louis comes back to me. But I also know that our working relationship was a lot like that day in Missouri. I was the new guy. I didn't know squat. James had a reputation. He had done things.

So I stumbled through drawing a monthly comic, learning the ropes, the rules, the do's and the don'ts. And James helped me, along with Archie Goodwin, to become the creator I am today — to find my voice. Through teaching, advice, passion, angst, anger, and love, those two men are probably more responsible for my place in the industry today than anyone else.

I learned how to collaborate with writers when I was working with James. I learned how to speak to editors when I talked with Archie. I learned how to let go of an idea, and when to pursue one, with James. I learned how to be aggressive with Archie, and when to shut the hell up.

So, I know two things. One, that collaboration, a true give-and-take between writer and artist, is absolutely a MUST to make good comics. And Two...

I make a damn good cup of tea.

Tony Harris
Macon, Georgia
November, 2008

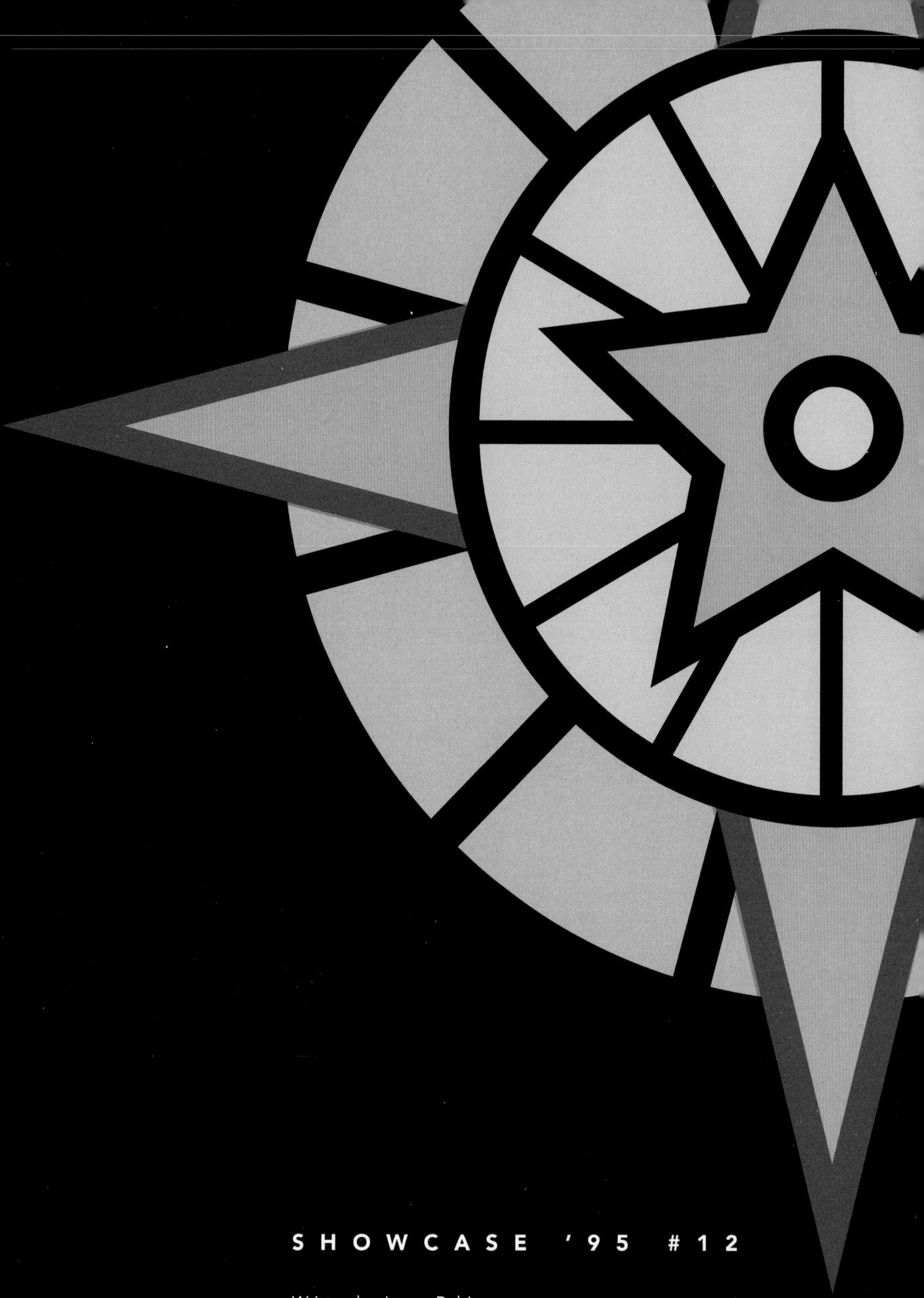

SHOWCASE '95 #12

Written by James Robinson

Art by Wade von Grawbadger

with colors by Debbie McKeever

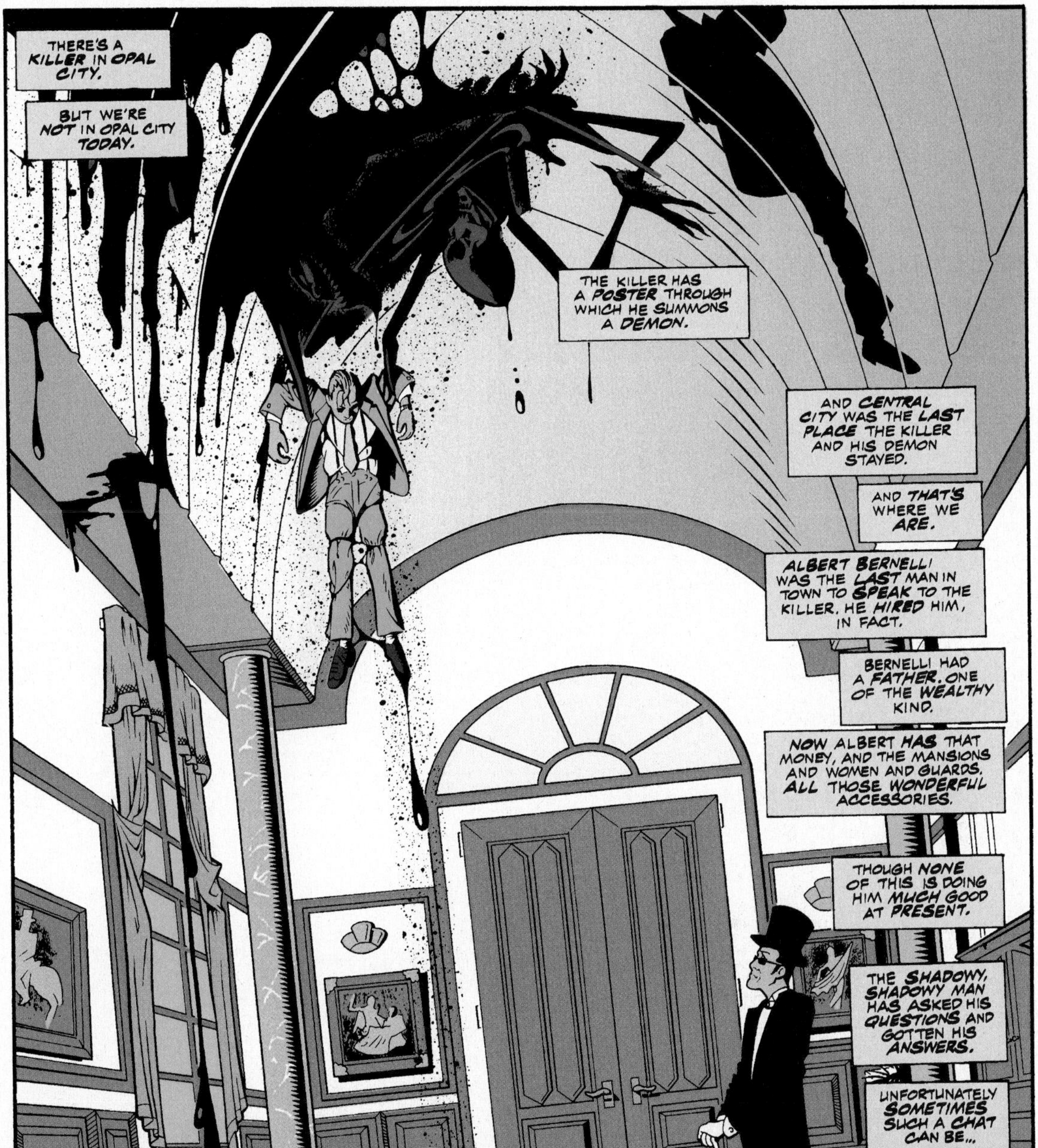
THERE'S A KILLER IN OPAL CITY.
BUT WE'RE NOT IN OPAL CITY TODAY.
THE KILLER HAS A POSTER THROUGH WHICH HE SUMMONS A DEMON.
AND CENTRAL CITY WAS THE LAST PLACE THE KILLER AND HIS DEMON STAYED.
AND THAT'S WHERE WE ARE.
ALBERT BERNELLI WAS THE LAST MAN IN TOWN TO SPEAK TO THE KILLER. HE HIRED HIM, IN FACT.
BERNELLI HAD A FATHER. ONE OF THE WEALTHY KIND.
NOW ALBERT HAS THAT MONEY, AND THE MANSIONS AND WOMEN AND GUARDS. ALL THOSE WONDERFUL ACCESSORIES.
THOUGH NONE OF THIS IS DOING HIM MUCH GOOD AT PRESENT.
THE SHADOWY, SHADOWY MAN HAS ASKED HIS QUESTIONS AND GOTTEN HIS ANSWERS.
UNFORTUNATELY SOMETIMES SUCH A CHAT CAN BE...
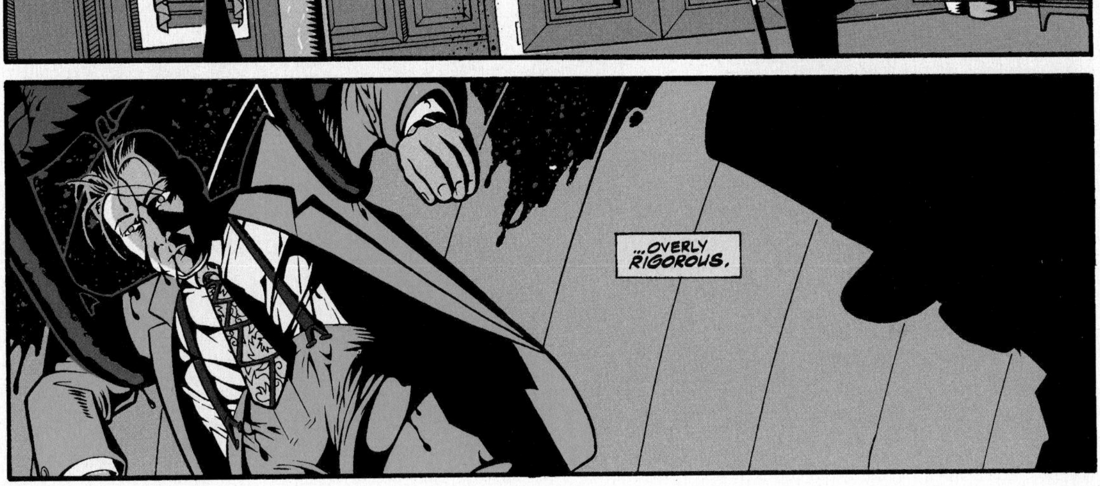
...OVERLY RIGOROUS.

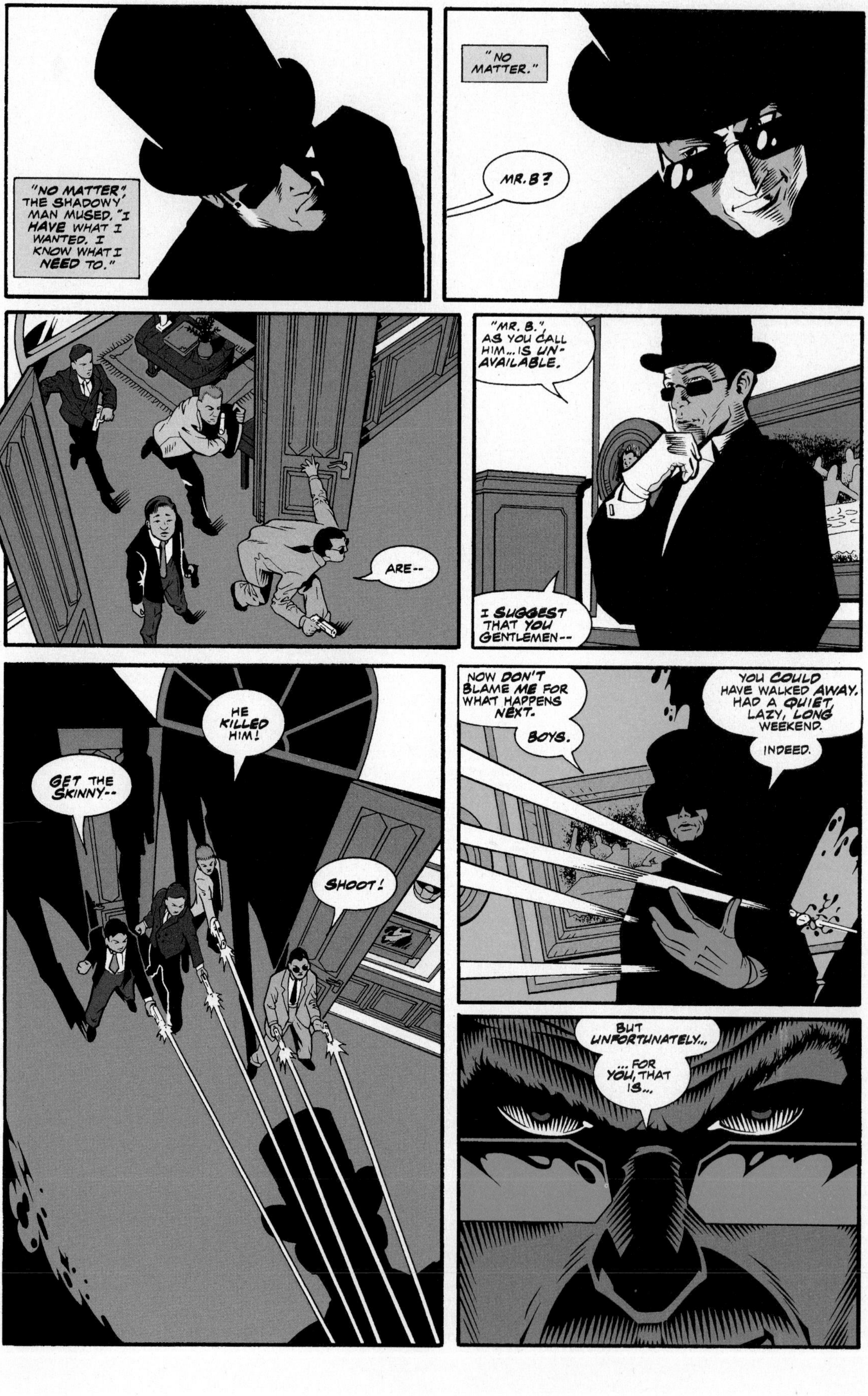
"NO MATTER", THE SHADOWY MAN MUSED. "I HAVE WHAT I WANTED. I KNOW WHAT I NEED TO."
"NO MATTER."
MR. B?
ARE--
"MR. B.," AS YOU CALL HIM... IS UN-AVAILABLE.
I SUGGEST THAT YOU GENTLEMEN--
GET THE SKINNY--
HE KILLED HIM!
SHOOT!
NOW DON'T BLAME ME FOR WHAT HAPPENS NEXT.
BOYS.
YOU COULD HAVE WALKED AWAY. HAD A QUIET, LAZY, LONG WEEKEND.
INDEED.
BUT UNFORTUNATELY...
... FOR YOU, THAT IS...

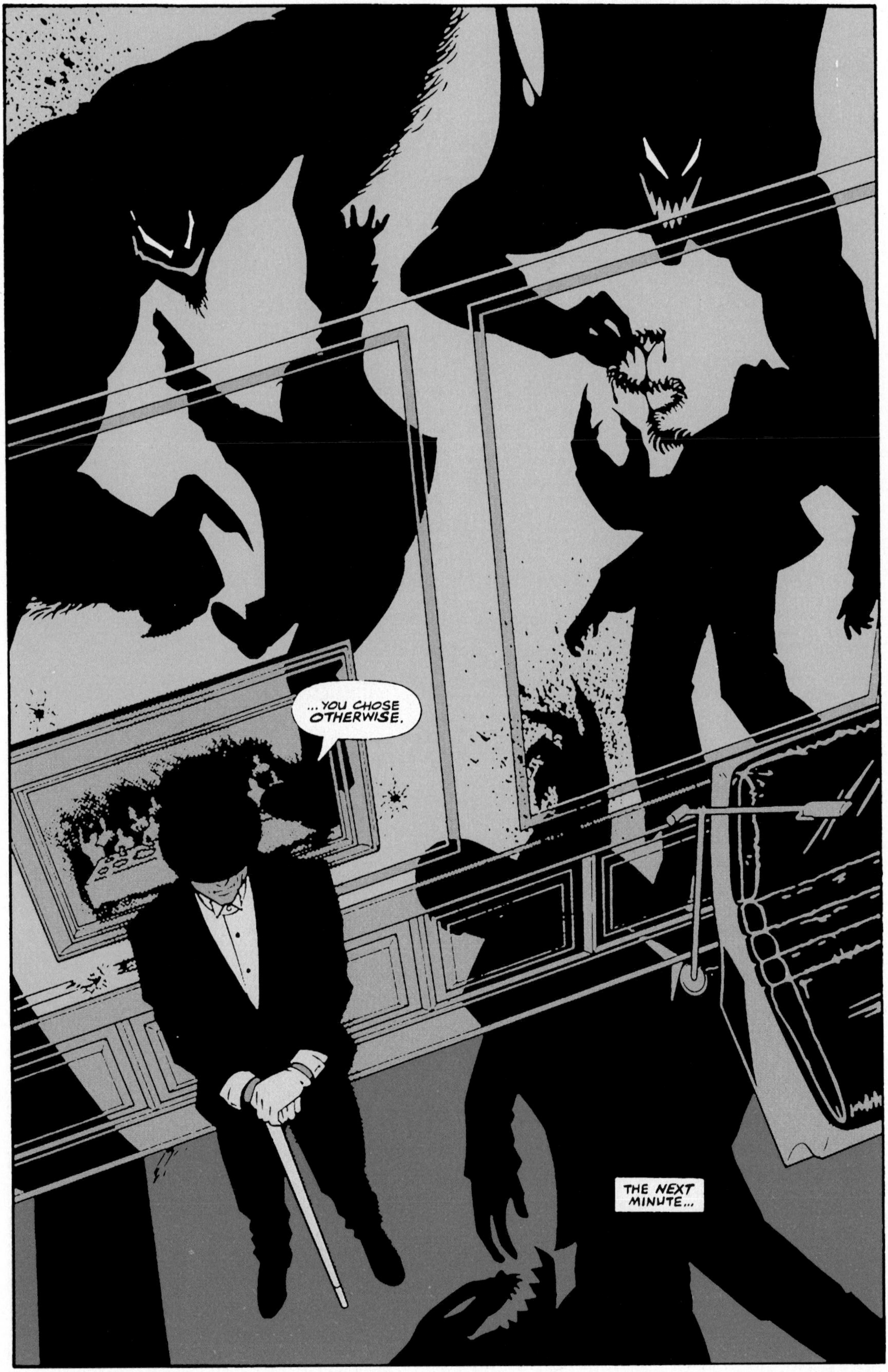
...YOU CHOSE OTHERWISE.
THE NEXT MINUTE...

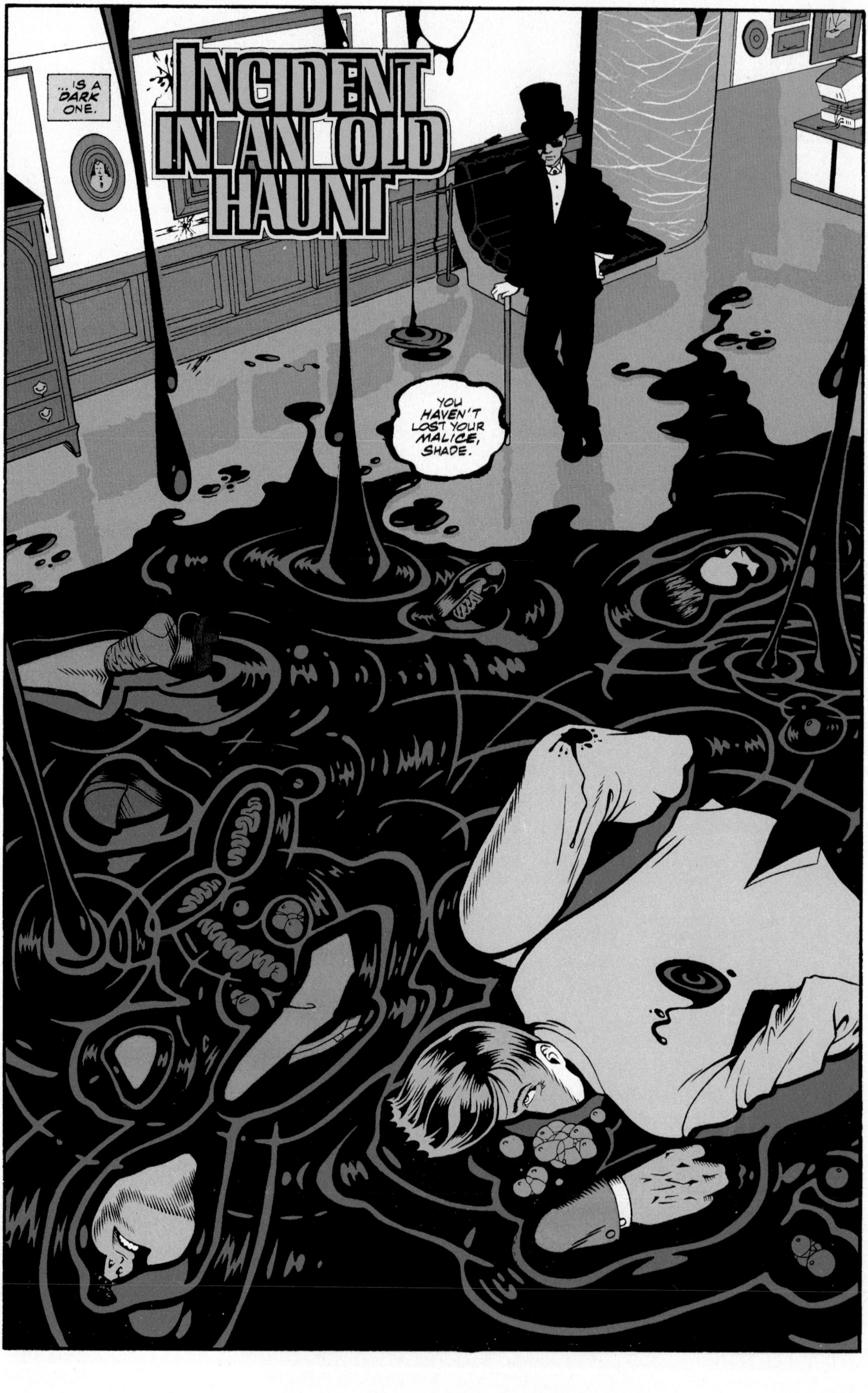
...IS A DARK ONE.
INCIDENT IN AN OLD HAUNT
YOU HAVEN'T LOST YOUR MALICE, SHADE.

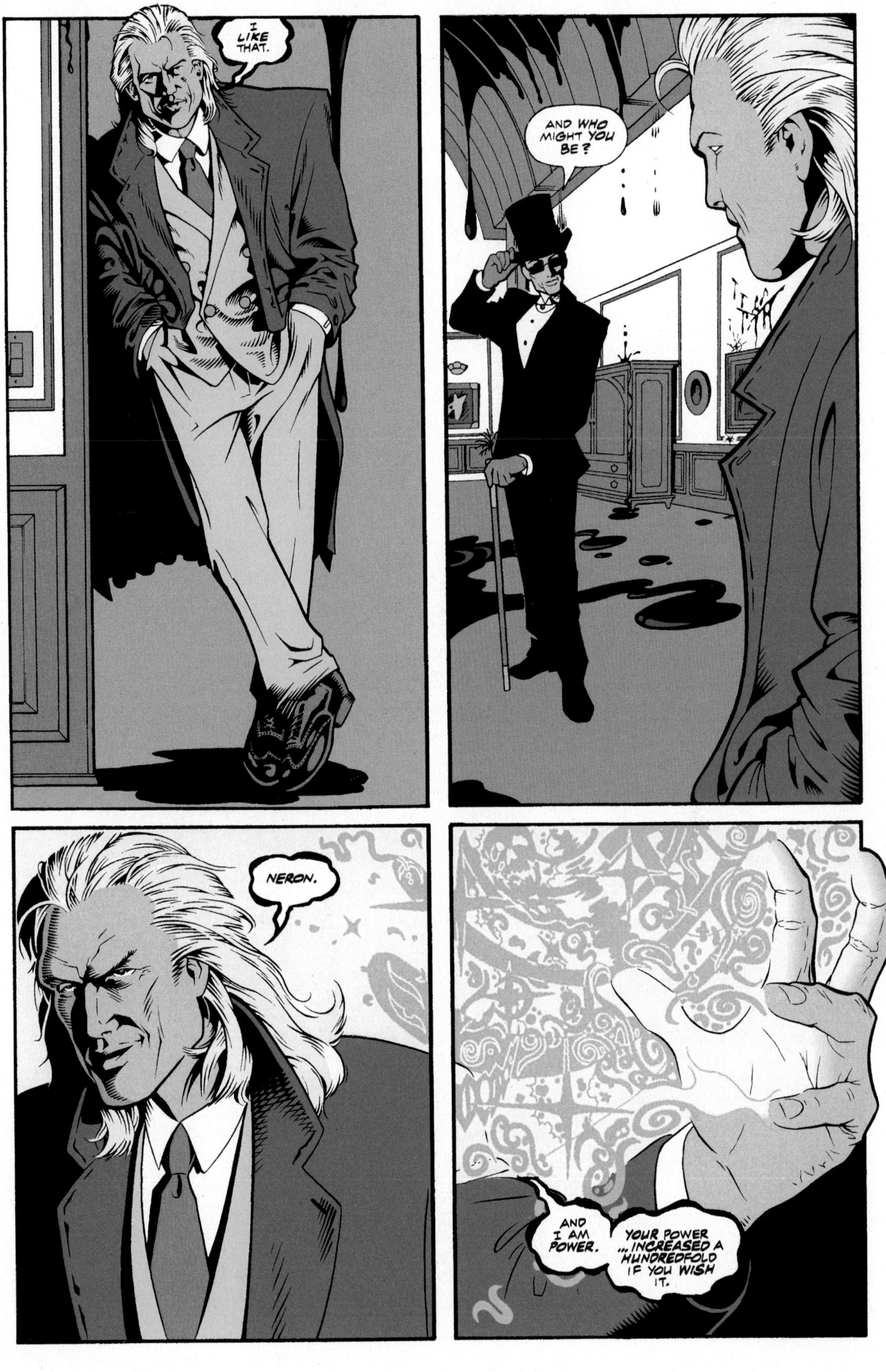

I LIKE THAT.
AND WHO MIGHT YOU BE?
NERON.
AND I AM POWER.
YOUR POWER ...INCREASED A HUNDREDFOLD IF YOU WISH IT.

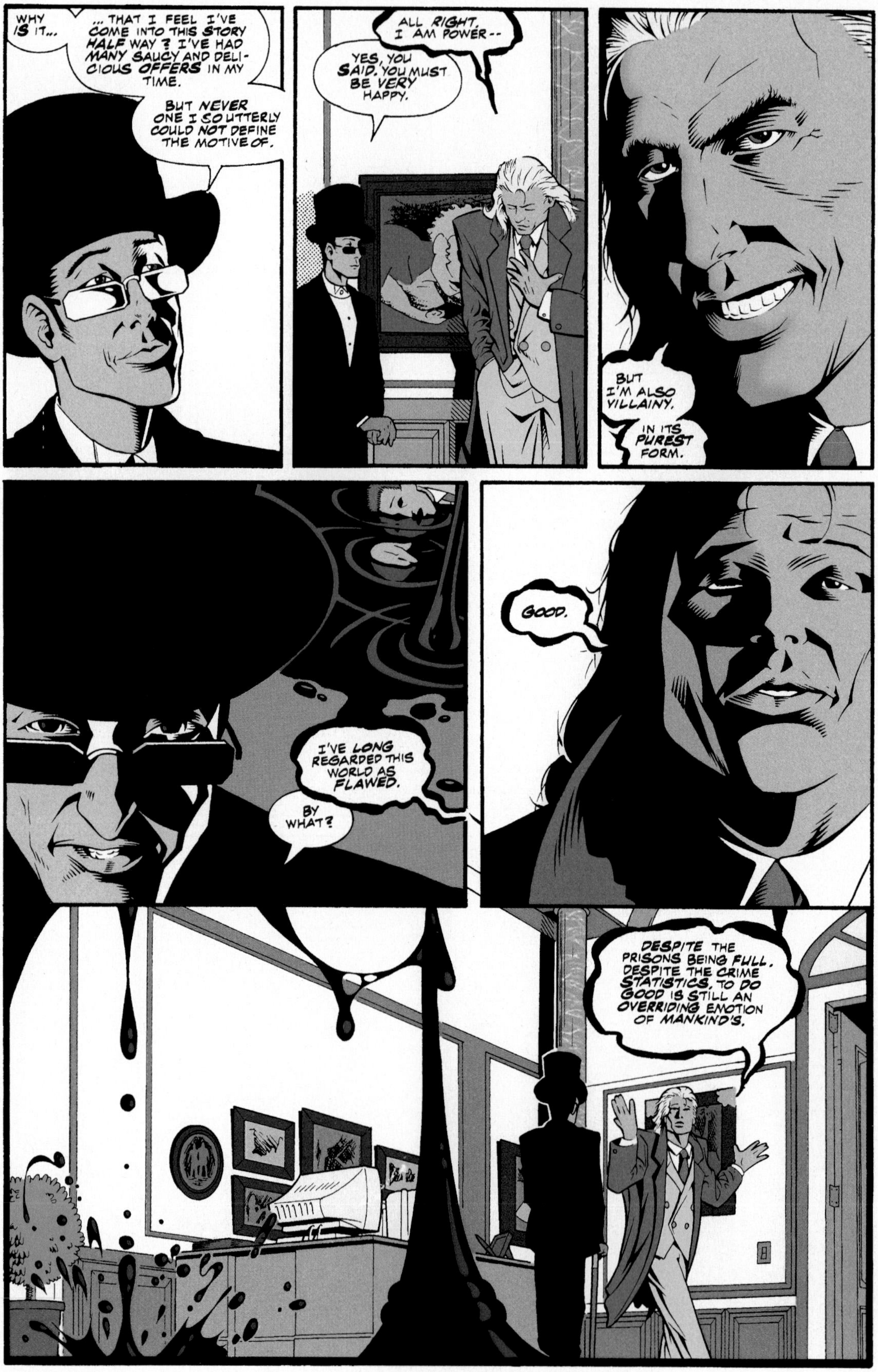
WHY IS IT...
... THAT I FEEL I'VE COME INTO THIS STORY HALF WAY? I'VE HAD MANY SAUCY AND DELICIOUS OFFERS IN MY TIME.
BUT NEVER ONE I SO UTTERLY COULD NOT DEFINE THE MOTIVE OF.
ALL RIGHT. I AM POWER--
YES, YOU SAID. YOU MUST BE VERY HAPPY.
BUT I'M ALSO VILLAINY.
IN ITS PUREST FORM.
GOOD.
I'VE LONG REGARDED THIS WORLD AS FLAWED.
BY WHAT?
DESPITE THE PRISONS BEING FULL, DESPITE THE CRIME STATISTICS, TO DO GOOD IS STILL AN OVERRIDING EMOTION OF MANKIND'S.

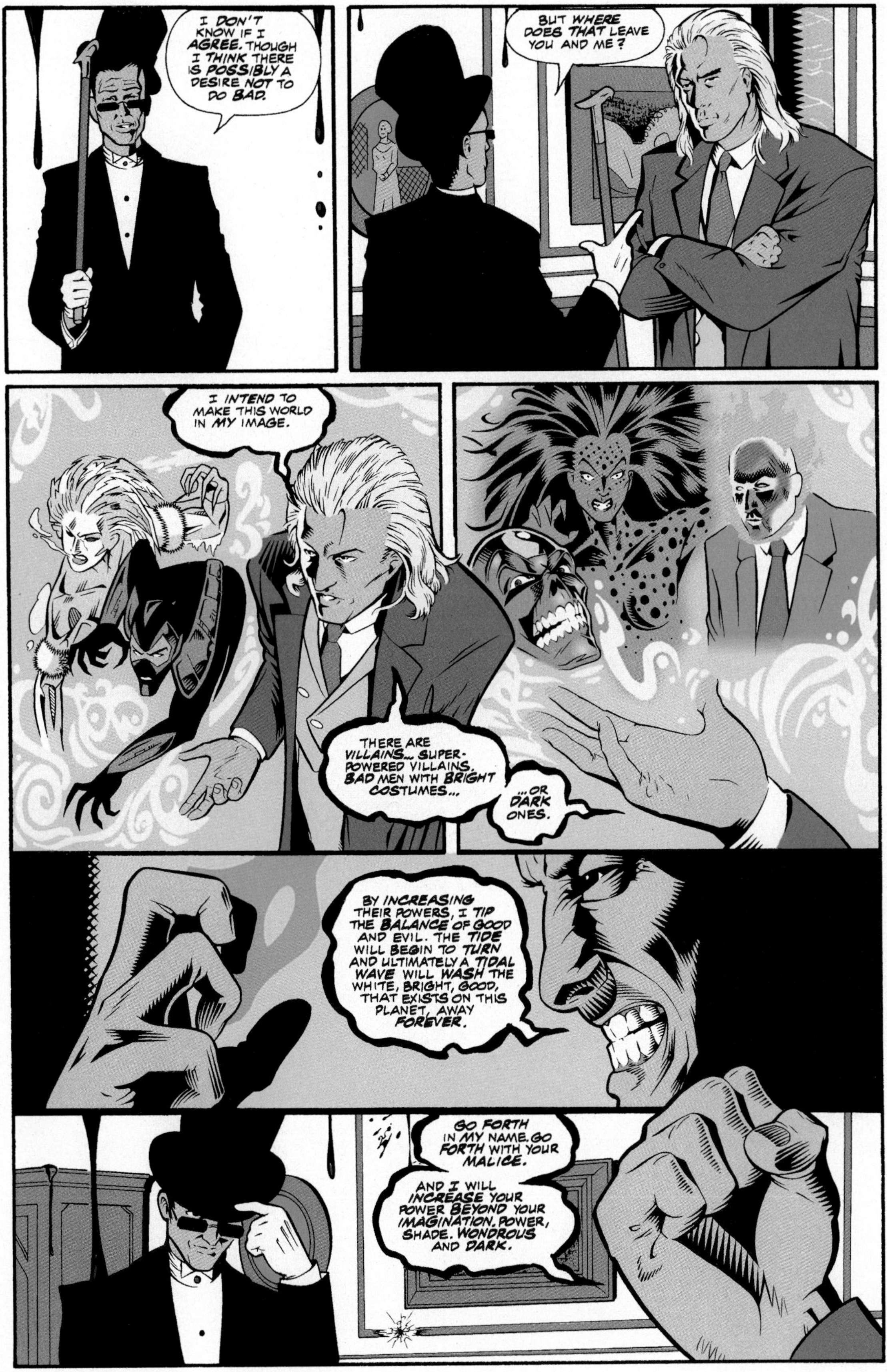

I DON'T KNOW IF I AGREE. THOUGH I THINK THERE IS POSSIBLY A DESIRE NOT TO DO BAD.
BUT WHERE DOES THAT LEAVE YOU AND ME?
I INTEND TO MAKE THIS WORLD IN MY IMAGE.
THERE ARE VILLAINS... SUPER-POWERED VILLAINS. BAD MEN WITH BRIGHT COSTUMES...
...OR DARK ONES.
BY INCREASING THEIR POWERS, I TIP THE BALANCE OF GOOD AND EVIL. THE TIDE WILL BEGIN TO TURN AND ULTIMATELY A TIDAL WAVE WILL WASH THE WHITE, BRIGHT, GOOD, THAT EXISTS ON THIS PLANET, AWAY FOREVER.
GO FORTH IN MY NAME. GO FORTH WITH YOUR MALICE.
AND I WILL INCREASE YOUR POWER BEYOND YOUR IMAGINATION. POWER, SHADE. WONDROUS AND DARK.

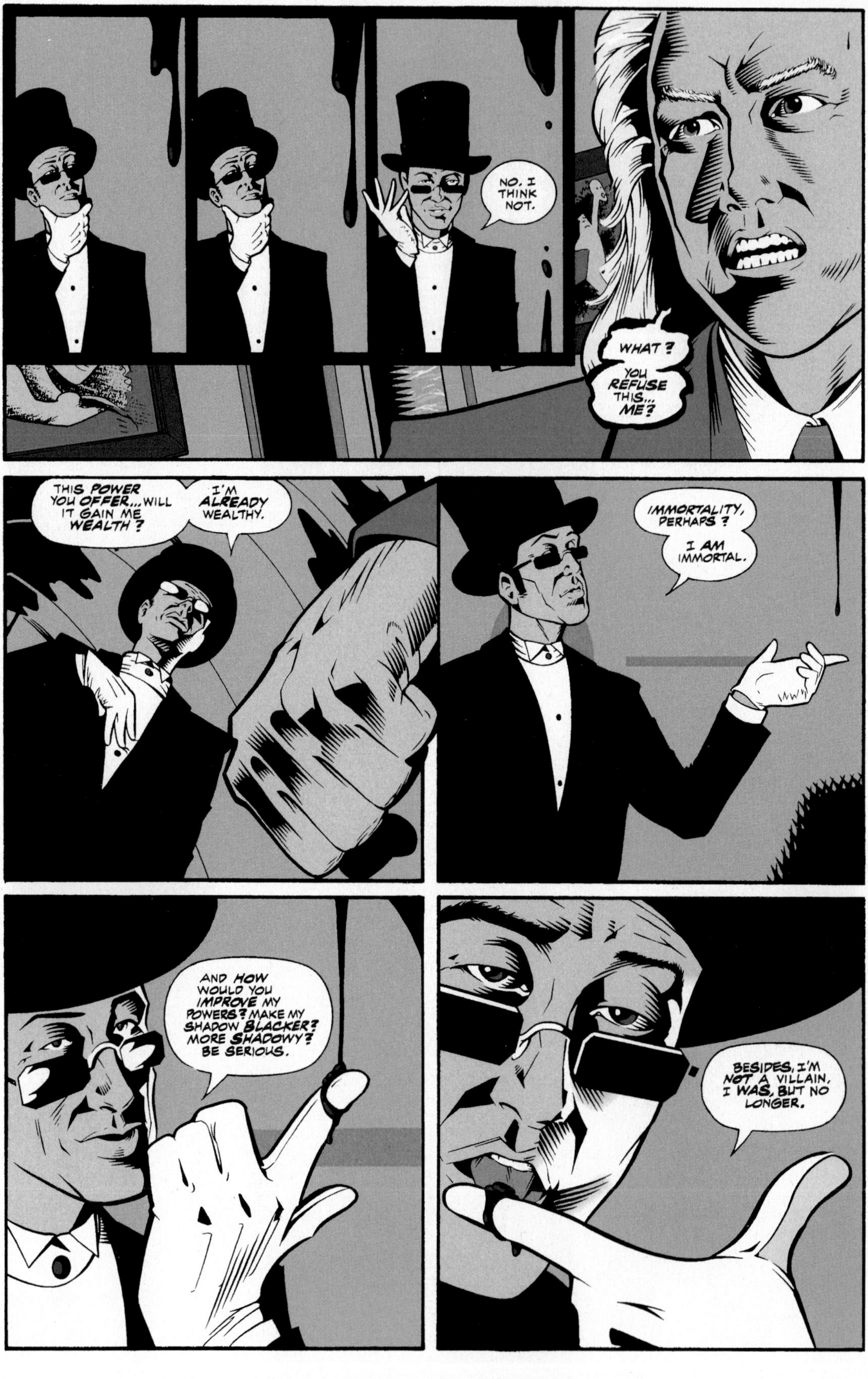
NO, I THINK NOT.
WHAT? YOU REFUSE THIS... ME?
THIS POWER YOU OFFER... WILL IT GAIN ME WEALTH?
I'M ALREADY WEALTHY.
IMMORTALITY, PERHAPS?
I AM IMMORTAL.
AND HOW WOULD YOU IMPROVE MY POWERS? MAKE MY SHADOW BLACKER? MORE SHADOWY? BE SERIOUS.
BESIDES, I'M NOT A VILLAIN. I WAS, BUT NO LONGER.

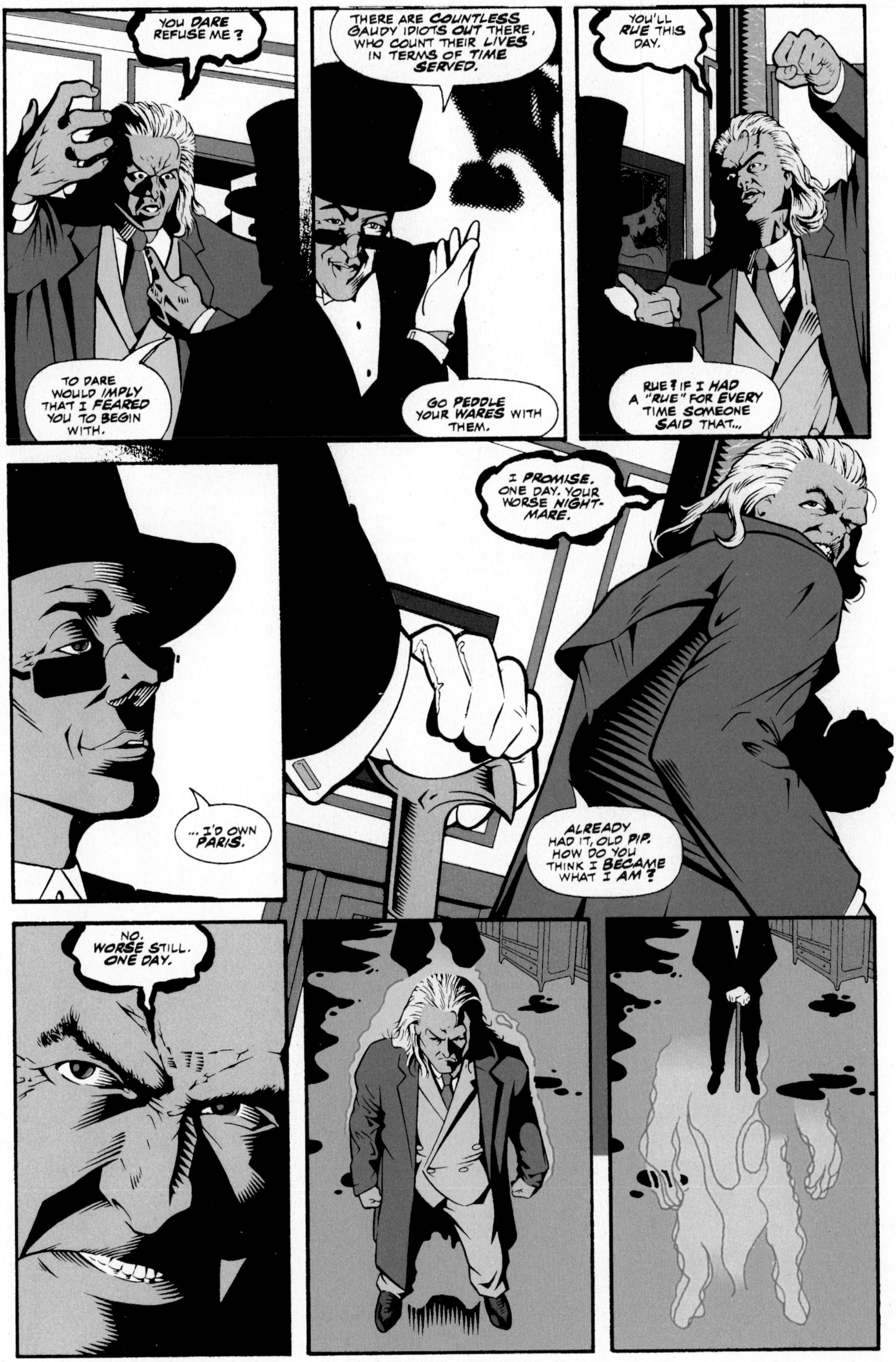
YOU DARE REFUSE ME?
TO DARE WOULD IMPLY THAT I FEARED YOU TO BEGIN WITH.
THERE ARE COUNTLESS GAUDY IDIOTS OUT THERE, WHO COUNT THEIR LIVES IN TERMS OF TIME SERVED.
GO PEDDLE YOUR WARES WITH THEM.
YOU'LL RUE THIS DAY.
RUE? IF I HAD A "RUE" FOR EVERY TIME SOMEONE SAID THAT...
...I'D OWN PARIS.
I PROMISE. ONE DAY. YOUR WORSE NIGHT-MARE.
ALREADY HAD IT, OLD PIP. HOW DO YOU THINK I BECAME WHAT I AM?
NO. WORSE STILL. ONE DAY.

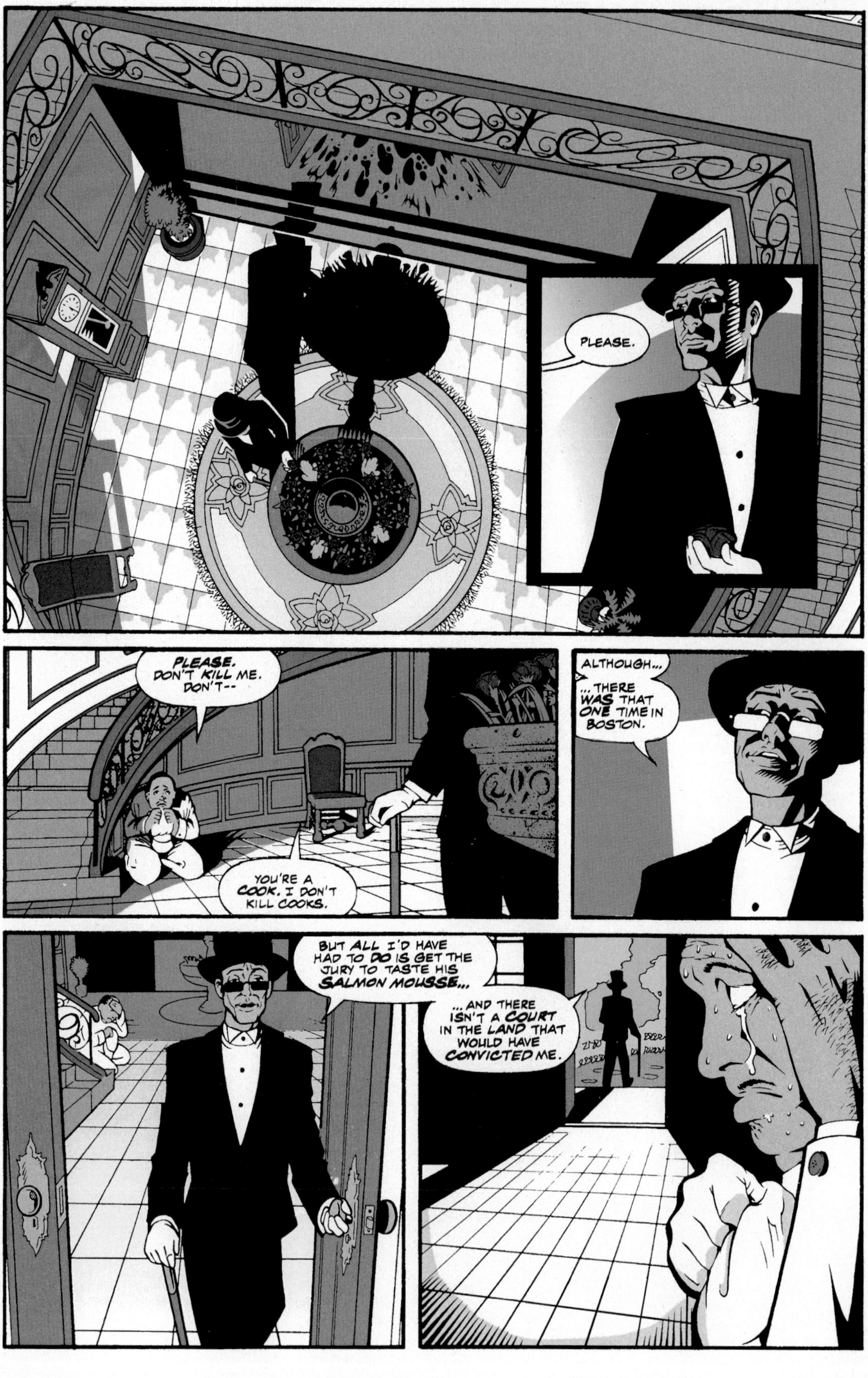
PLEASE.
PLEASE. DON'T KILL ME. DON'T--
YOU'RE A COOK. I DON'T KILL COOKS.
ALTHOUGH...
...THERE WAS THAT ONE TIME IN BOSTON.
BUT ALL I'D HAVE HAD TO DO IS GET THE JURY TO TASTE HIS SALMON MOUSSE...
...AND THERE ISN'T A COURT IN THE LAND THAT WOULD HAVE CONVICTED ME.

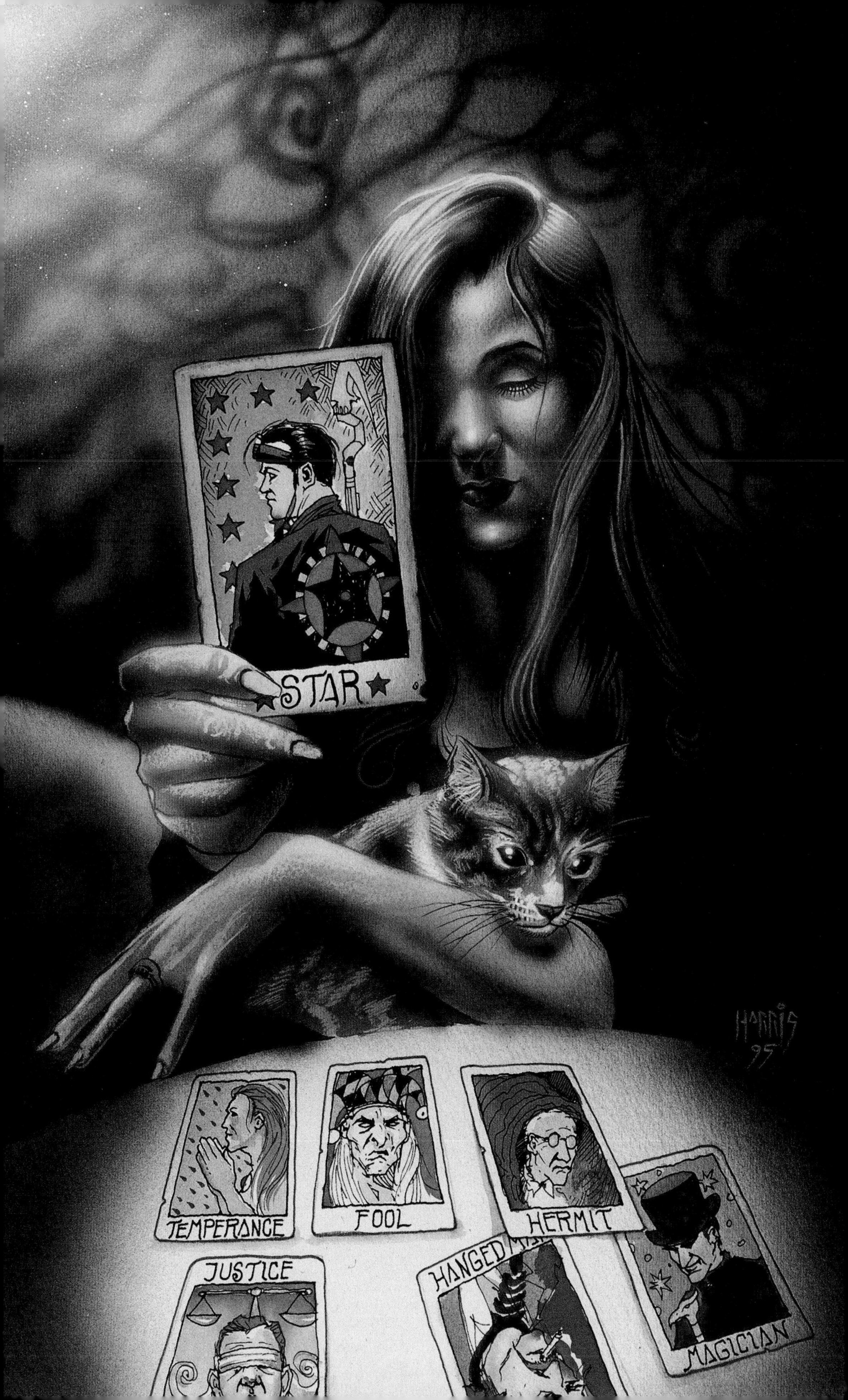
STAR
HARRIS 95
TEMPERANCE
FOOL
HERMIT
JUSTICE
MAGICIAN

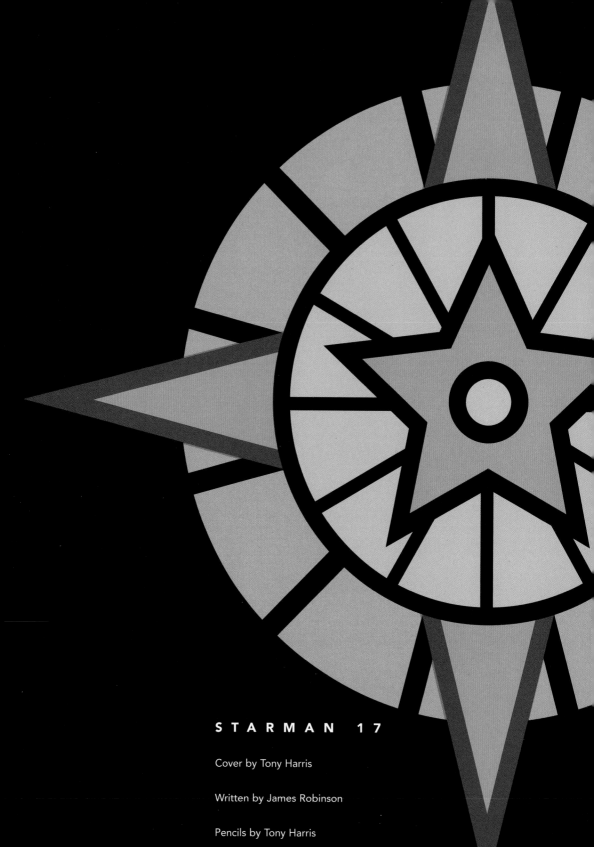

STARMAN 17

Cover by Tony Harris

Written by James Robinson

Pencils by Tony Harris

with inks by Wade von Grawbadger

and colors by Gregory Wright

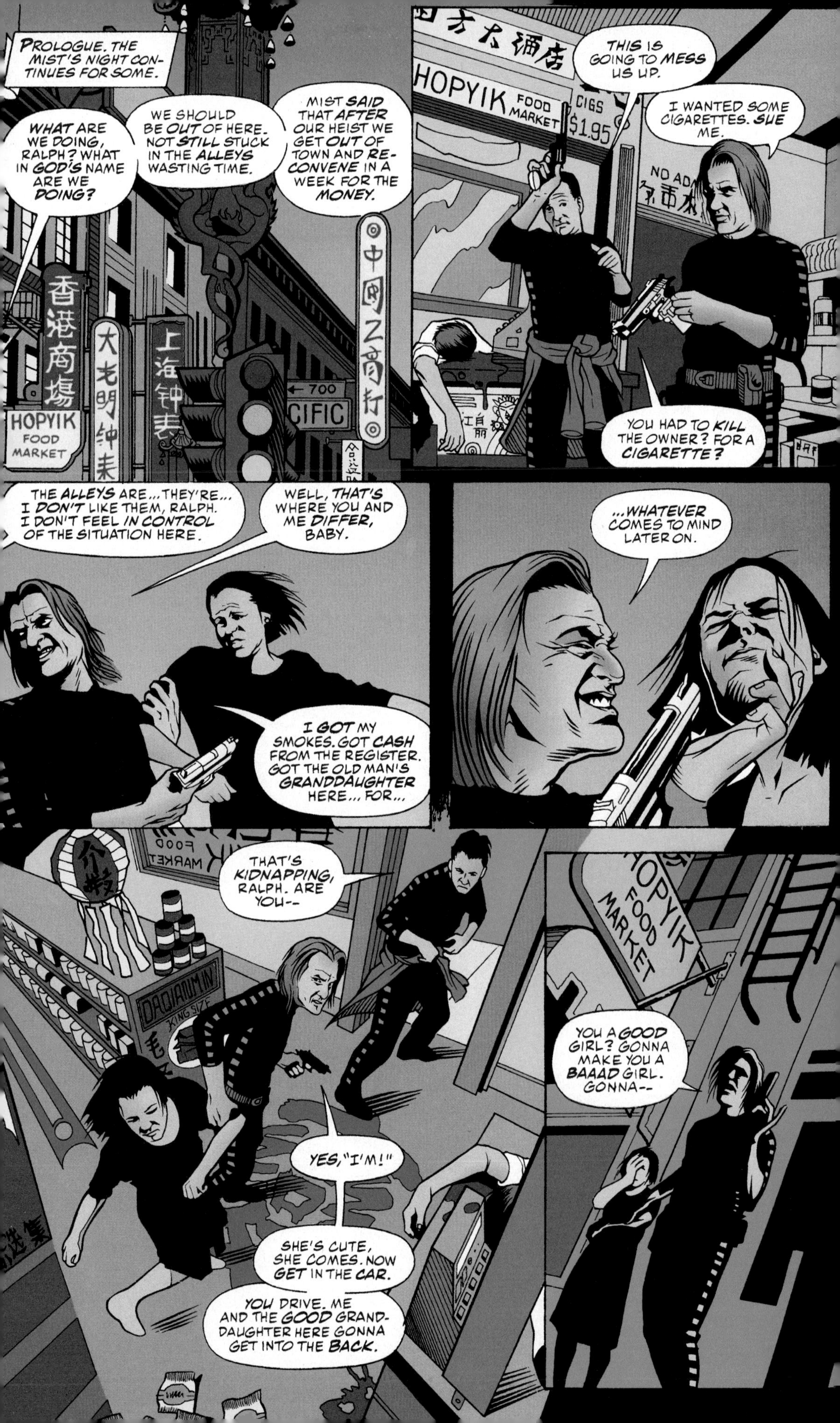
PROLOGUE. THE MIST'S NIGHT CONTINUES FOR SOME.
WHAT ARE WE DOING, RALPH? WHAT IN GOD'S NAME ARE WE DOING?
WE SHOULD BE OUT OF HERE. NOT STILL STUCK IN THE ALLEYS WASTING TIME.
MIST SAID THAT AFTER OUR HEIST WE GET OUT OF TOWN AND RECONVENE IN A WEEK FOR THE MONEY.
HOPYIK FOOD MARKET
← 700
CIFIC
THIS IS GOING TO MESS US UP.
I WANTED SOME CIGARETTES. SUE ME.
HOPYIK FOOD MARKET
CIGS $1.95
NO ADA
YOU HAD TO KILL THE OWNER? FOR A CIGARETTE?
THE ALLEYS ARE... THEY'RE... I DON'T LIKE THEM, RALPH. I DON'T FEEL IN CONTROL OF THE SITUATION HERE.
WELL, THAT'S WHERE YOU AND ME DIFFER, BABY.
I GOT MY SMOKES. GOT CASH FROM THE REGISTER. GOT THE OLD MAN'S GRANDDAUGHTER HERE... FOR...
...WHATEVER COMES TO MIND LATER ON.
THAT'S KIDNAPPING, RALPH. ARE YOU--
YES, "I'M!"
SHE'S CUTE, SHE COMES. NOW GET IN THE CAR.
YOU DRIVE. ME AND THE GOOD GRANDDAUGHTER HERE GONNA GET INTO THE BACK.
HOPYIK FOOD MARKET
YOU A GOOD GIRL? GONNA MAKE YOU A BAAAD GIRL. GONNA--

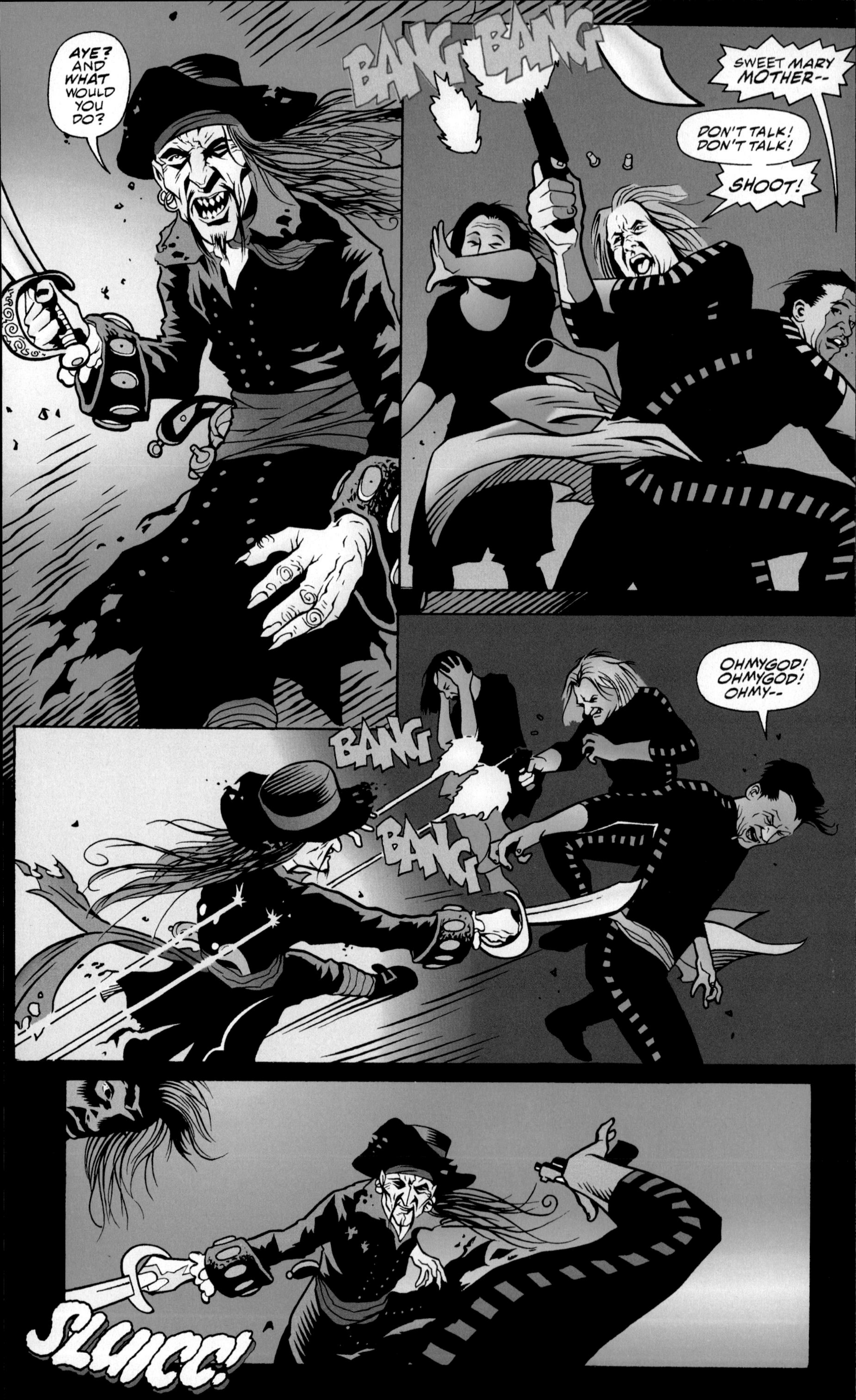
AYE? AND WHAT WOULD YOU DO?
BANG BANG
SWEET MARY MOTHER--
DON'T TALK! DON'T TALK!
SHOOT!
OHMYGOD! OHMYGOD! OHMY--
BANG
BANG
SLUICC!

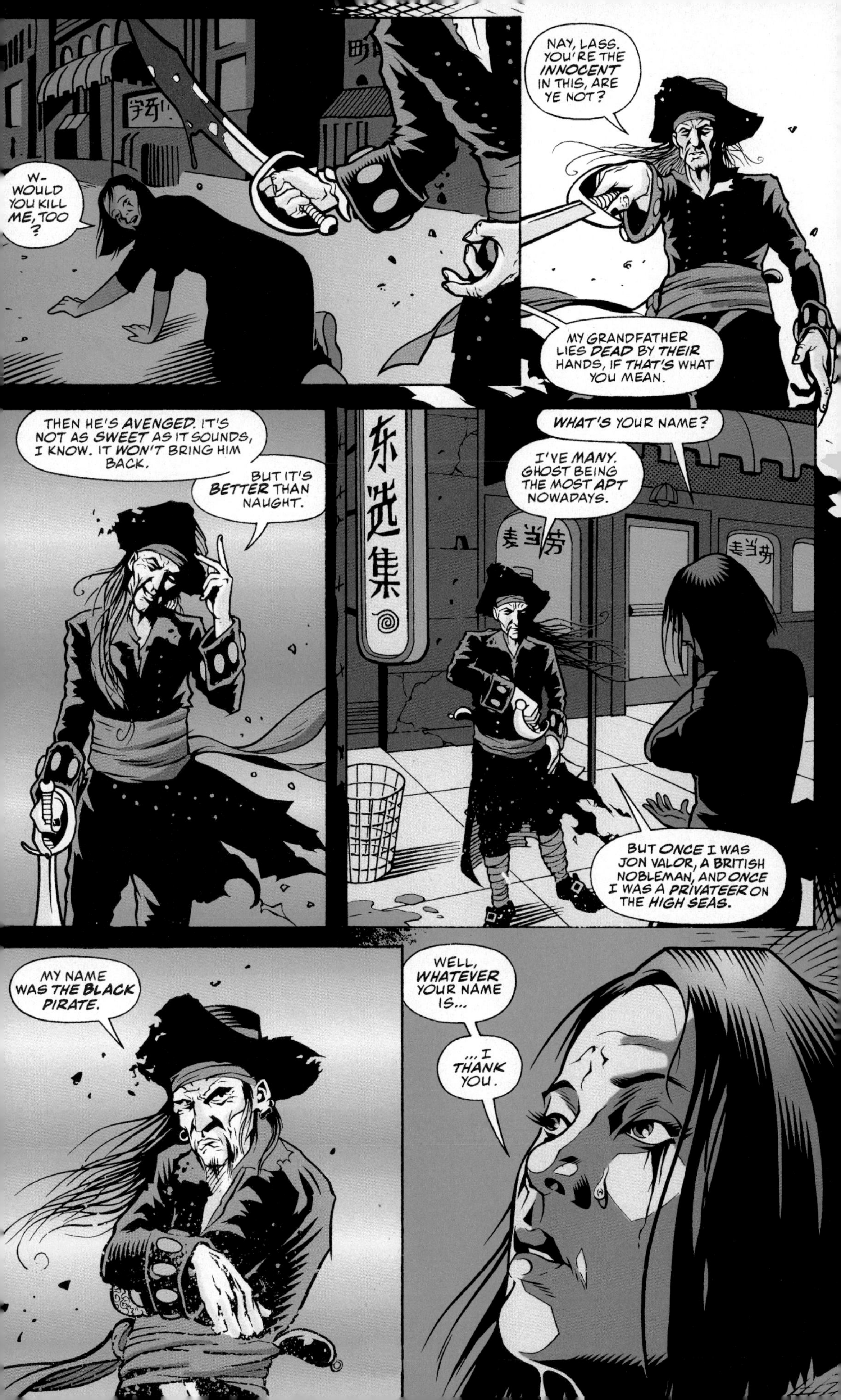
W-WOULD YOU KILL ME, TOO?
NAY, LASS. YOU'RE THE INNOCENT IN THIS, ARE YE NOT?
MY GRANDFATHER LIES DEAD BY THEIR HANDS, IF THAT'S WHAT YOU MEAN.
THEN HE'S AVENGED. IT'S NOT AS SWEET AS IT SOUNDS, I KNOW. IT WON'T BRING HIM BACK.
BUT IT'S BETTER THAN NAUGHT.
WHAT'S YOUR NAME?
I'VE MANY. GHOST BEING THE MOST APT NOWADAYS.
BUT ONCE I WAS JON VALOR, A BRITISH NOBLEMAN, AND ONCE I WAS A PRIVATEER ON THE HIGH SEAS.
MY NAME WAS THE BLACK PIRATE.
WELL, WHATEVER YOUR NAME IS...
...I THANK YOU.

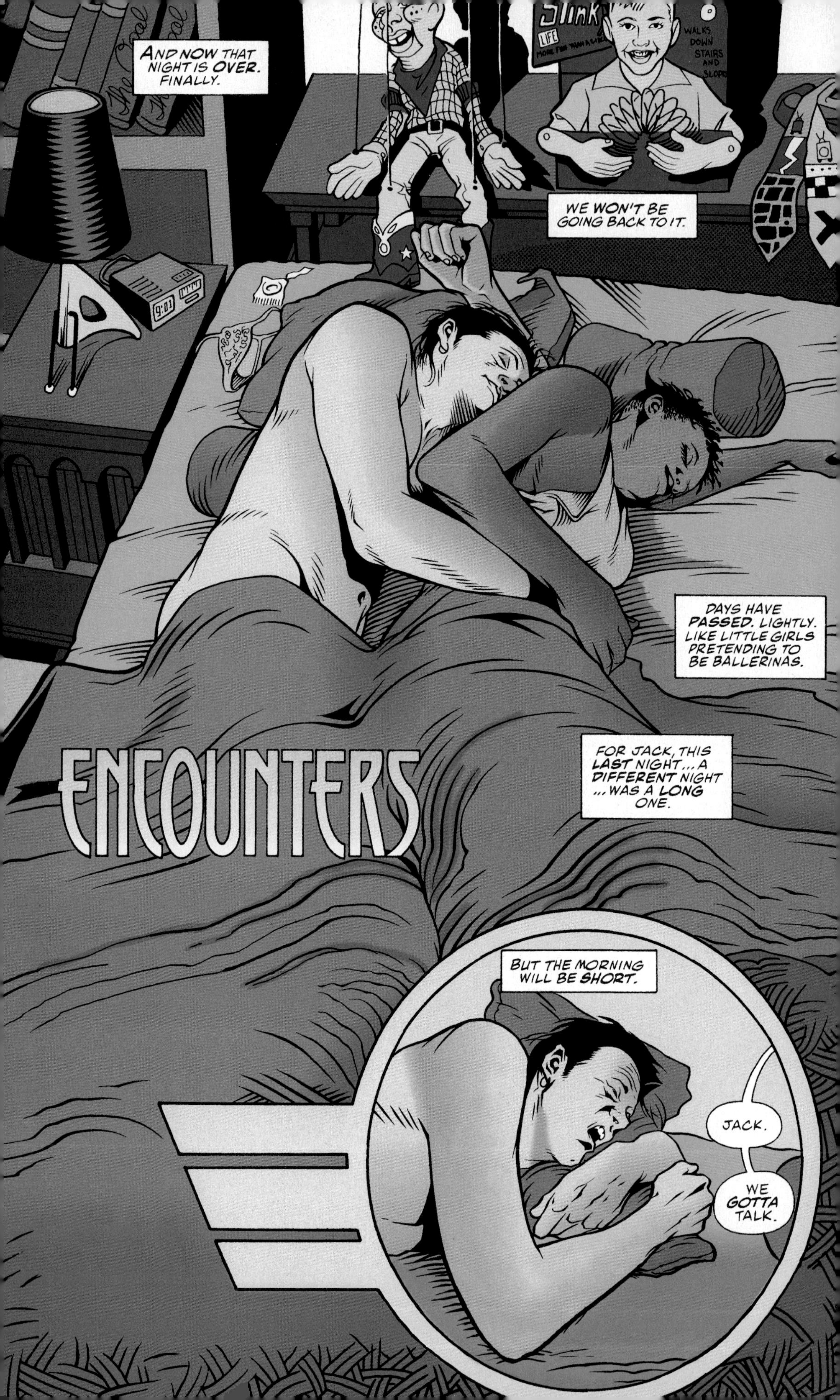
AND NOW THAT NIGHT IS OVER. FINALLY.
WE WON'T BE GOING BACK TO IT.
DAYS HAVE PASSED. LIGHTLY. LIKE LITTLE GIRLS PRETENDING TO BE BALLERINAS.
ENCOUNTERS
FOR JACK, THIS LAST NIGHT... A DIFFERENT NIGHT ...WAS A LONG ONE.
BUT THE MORNING WILL BE SHORT.
JACK.
WE GOTTA TALK.

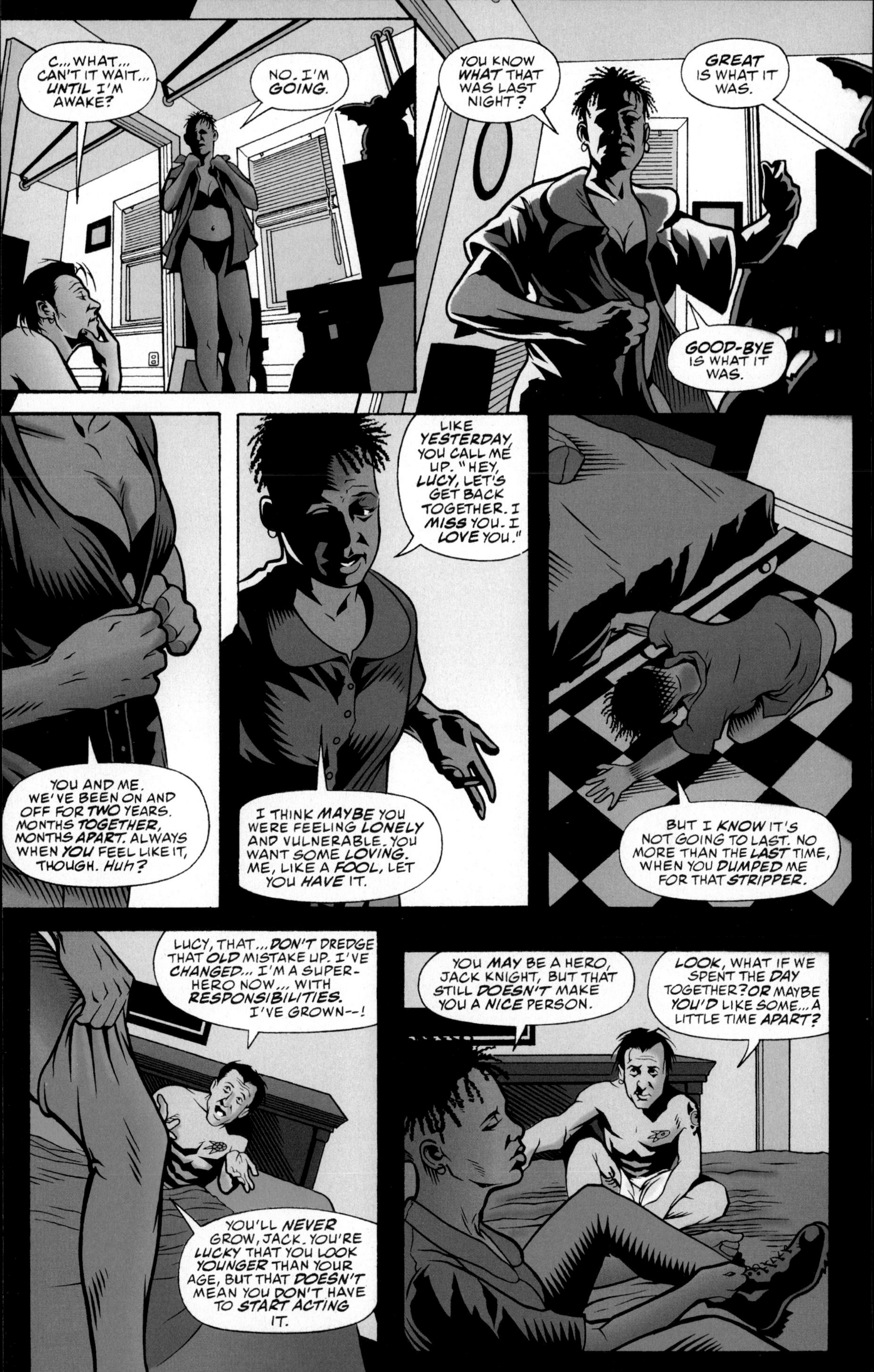
C... WHAT... CAN'T IT WAIT... UNTIL I'M AWAKE?
NO. I'M GOING.
YOU KNOW WHAT THAT WAS LAST NIGHT?
GREAT IS WHAT IT WAS.
GOOD-BYE IS WHAT IT WAS.
YOU AND ME. WE'VE BEEN ON AND OFF FOR TWO YEARS. MONTHS TOGETHER, MONTHS APART. ALWAYS WHEN YOU FEEL LIKE IT, THOUGH. Huh?
LIKE YESTERDAY, YOU CALL ME UP. "HEY, LUCY, LET'S GET BACK TOGETHER. I MISS YOU. I LOVE YOU."
I THINK MAYBE YOU WERE FEELING LONELY AND VULNERABLE. YOU WANT SOME LOVING. ME, LIKE A FOOL, LET YOU HAVE IT.
BUT I KNOW IT'S NOT GOING TO LAST. NO MORE THAN THE LAST TIME, WHEN YOU DUMPED ME FOR THAT STRIPPER.
LUCY, THAT... DON'T DREDGE THAT OLD MISTAKE UP. I'VE CHANGED... I'M A SUPER-HERO NOW... WITH RESPONSIBILITIES. I'VE GROWN--!
YOU'LL NEVER GROW, JACK. YOU'RE LUCKY THAT YOU LOOK YOUNGER THAN YOUR AGE, BUT THAT DOESN'T MEAN YOU DON'T HAVE TO START ACTING IT.
YOU MAY BE A HERO, JACK KNIGHT, BUT THAT STILL DOESN'T MAKE YOU A NICE PERSON.
LOOK, WHAT IF WE SPENT THE DAY TOGETHER? OR MAYBE YOU'D LIKE SOME... A LITTLE TIME APART?

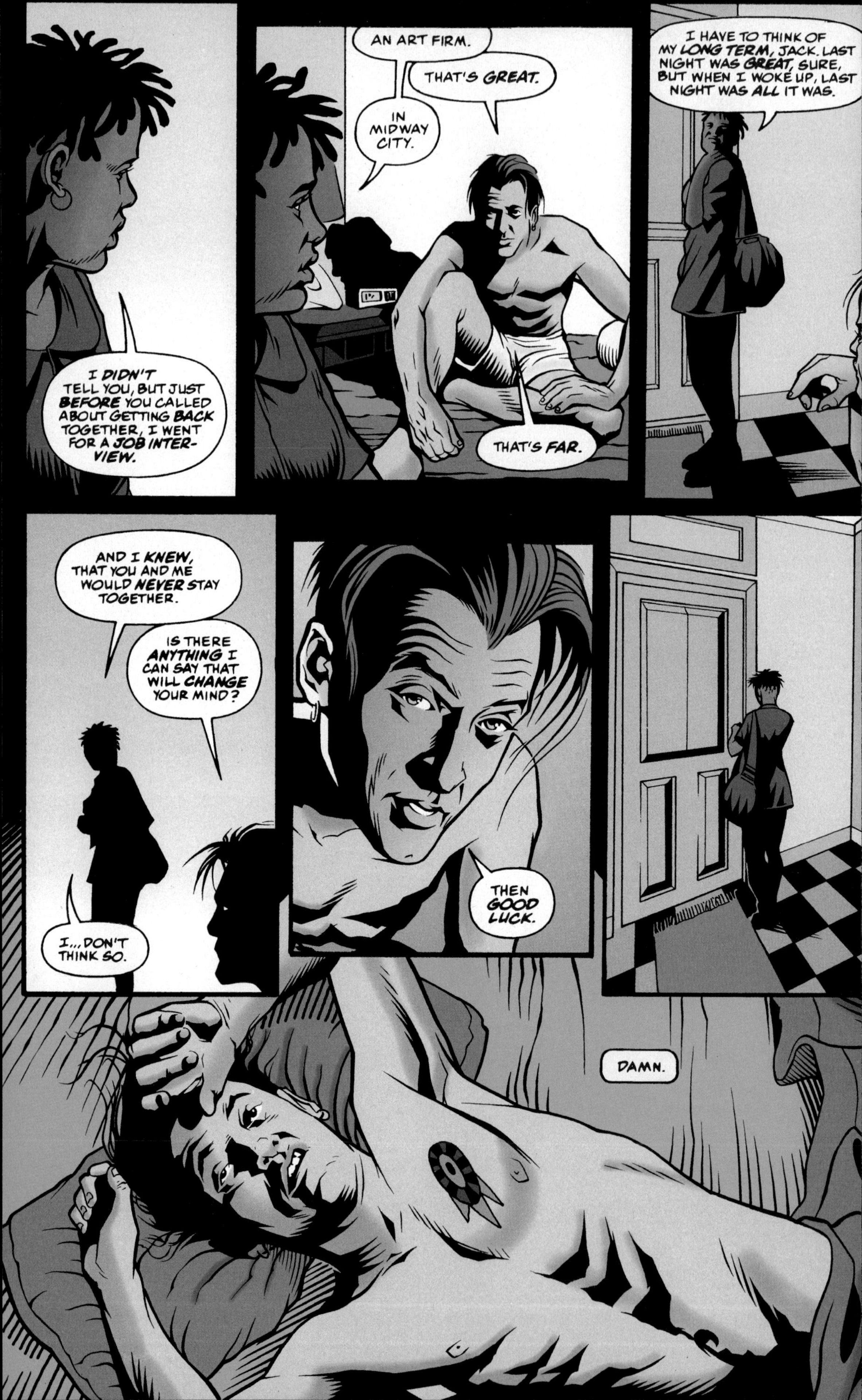
I DIDN'T TELL YOU, BUT JUST BEFORE YOU CALLED ABOUT GETTING BACK TOGETHER, I WENT FOR A JOB INTER-VIEW.
AN ART FIRM.
THAT'S GREAT.
IN MIDWAY CITY.
THAT'S FAR.
I HAVE TO THINK OF MY LONG TERM, JACK. LAST NIGHT WAS GREAT, SURE, BUT WHEN I WOKE UP, LAST NIGHT WAS ALL IT WAS.
AND I KNEW, THAT YOU AND ME WOULD NEVER STAY TOGETHER.
IS THERE ANYTHING I CAN SAY THAT WILL CHANGE YOUR MIND?
I... DON'T THINK SO.
THEN GOOD LUCK.
DAMN.

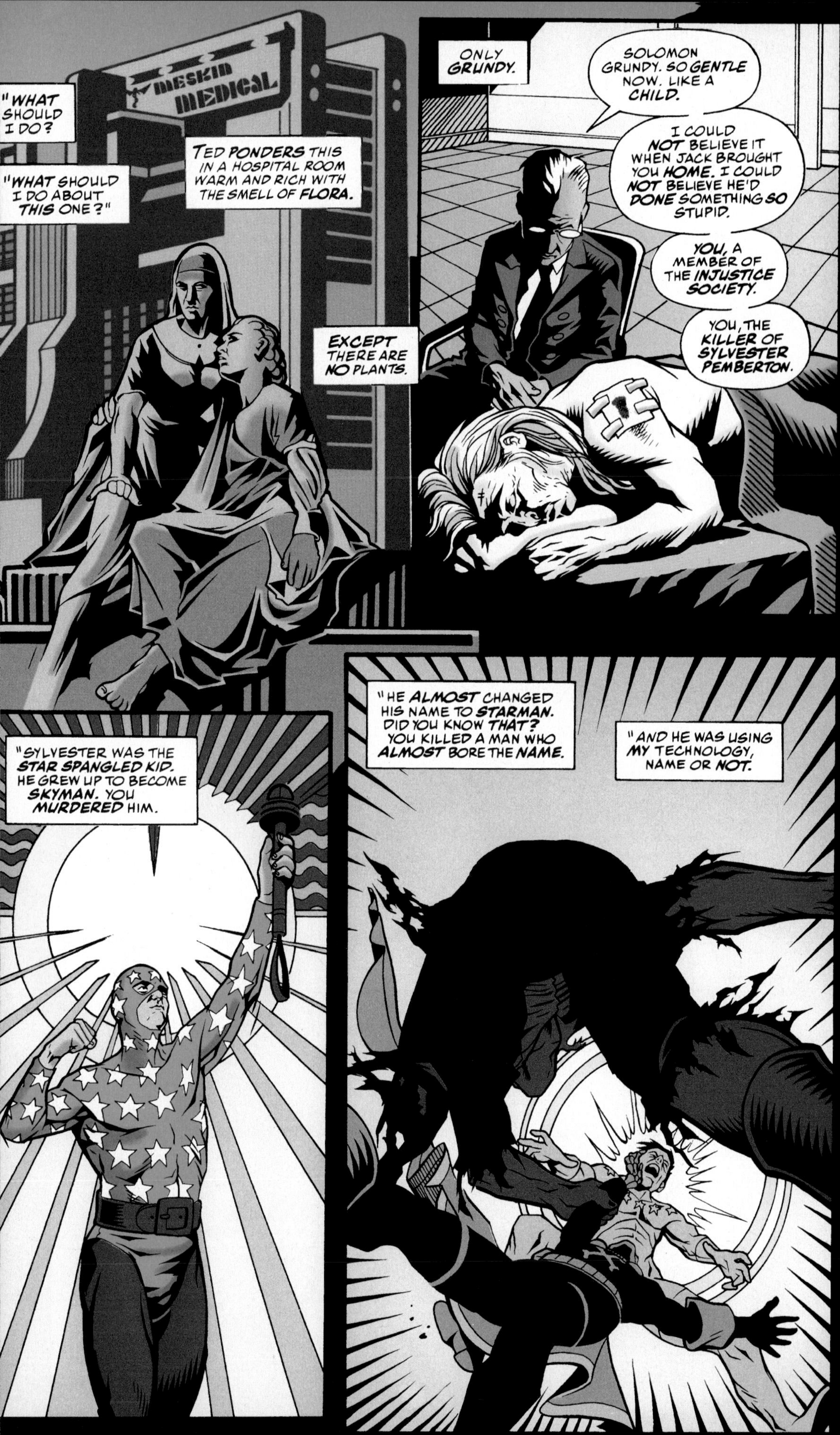

MESKID MEDICAL
"WHAT SHOULD I DO?
"WHAT SHOULD I DO ABOUT THIS ONE?"
TED PONDERS THIS IN A HOSPITAL ROOM WARM AND RICH WITH THE SMELL OF FLORA.
EXCEPT THERE ARE NO PLANTS.
ONLY GRUNDY.
SOLOMON GRUNDY. SO GENTLE NOW. LIKE A CHILD.
I COULD NOT BELIEVE IT WHEN JACK BROUGHT YOU HOME. I COULD NOT BELIEVE HE'D DONE SOMETHING SO STUPID.
YOU, A MEMBER OF THE INJUSTICE SOCIETY.
YOU, THE KILLER OF SYLVESTER PEMBERTON.
"SYLVESTER WAS THE STAR SPANGLED KID. HE GREW UP TO BECOME SKYMAN. YOU MURDERED HIM.
"HE ALMOST CHANGED HIS NAME TO STARMAN. DID YOU KNOW THAT? YOU KILLED A MAN WHO ALMOST BORE THE NAME.
"AND HE WAS USING MY TECHNOLOGY, NAME OR NOT.

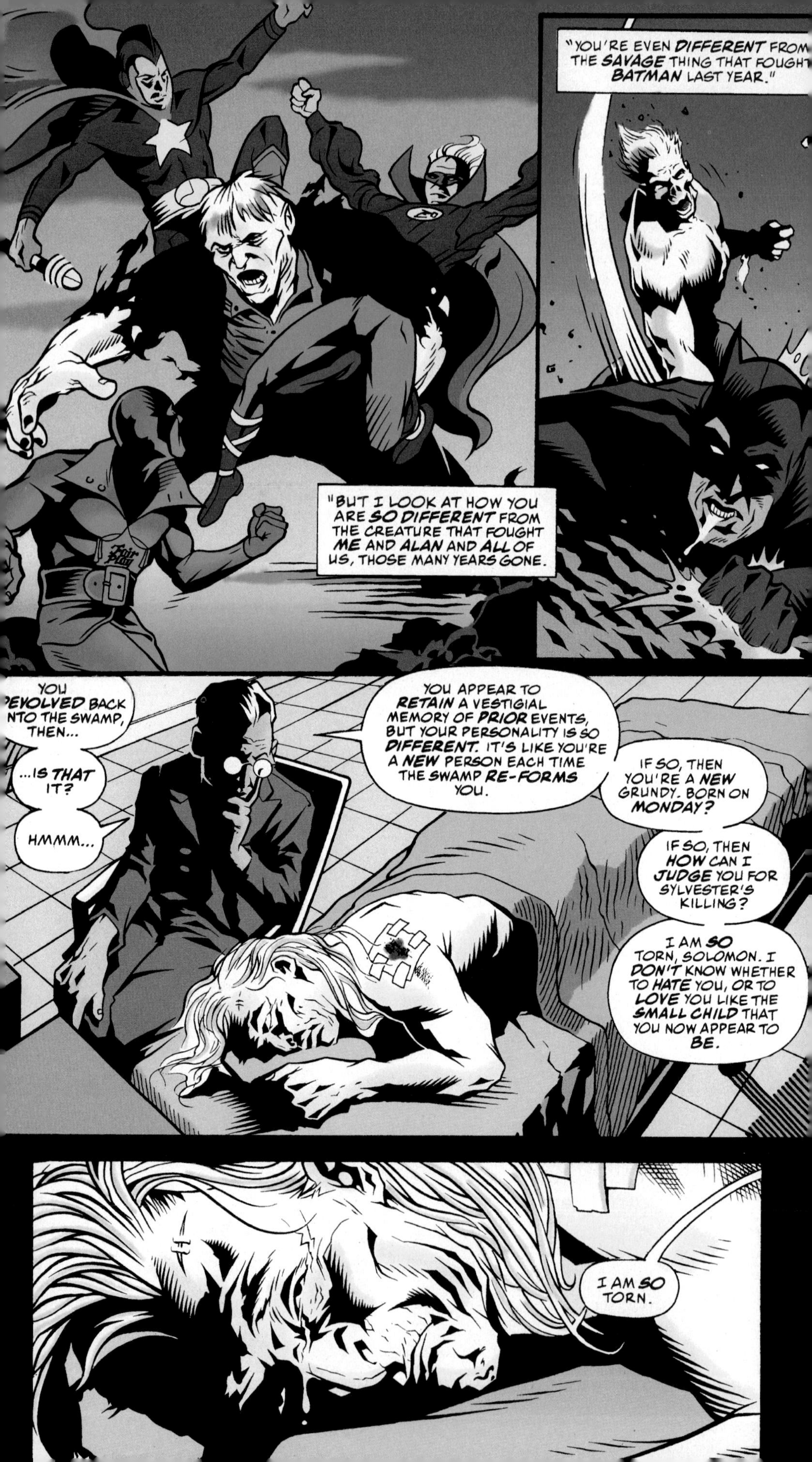

"BUT I LOOK AT HOW YOU ARE SO DIFFERENT FROM THE CREATURE THAT FOUGHT ME AND ALAN AND ALL OF US, THOSE MANY YEARS GONE.
"YOU'RE EVEN DIFFERENT FROM THE SAVAGE THING THAT FOUGHT BATMAN LAST YEAR."
YOU DEVOLVED BACK INTO THE SWAMP, THEN...
...IS THAT IT?
HMMM...
YOU APPEAR TO RETAIN A VESTIGIAL MEMORY OF PRIOR EVENTS, BUT YOUR PERSONALITY IS SO DIFFERENT. IT'S LIKE YOU'RE A NEW PERSON EACH TIME THE SWAMP RE-FORMS YOU.
IF SO, THEN YOU'RE A NEW GRUNDY. BORN ON MONDAY?
IF SO, THEN HOW CAN I JUDGE YOU FOR SYLVESTER'S KILLING?
I AM SO TORN, SOLOMON. I DON'T KNOW WHETHER TO HATE YOU, OR TO LOVE YOU LIKE THE SMALL CHILD THAT YOU NOW APPEAR TO BE.
I AM SO TORN.

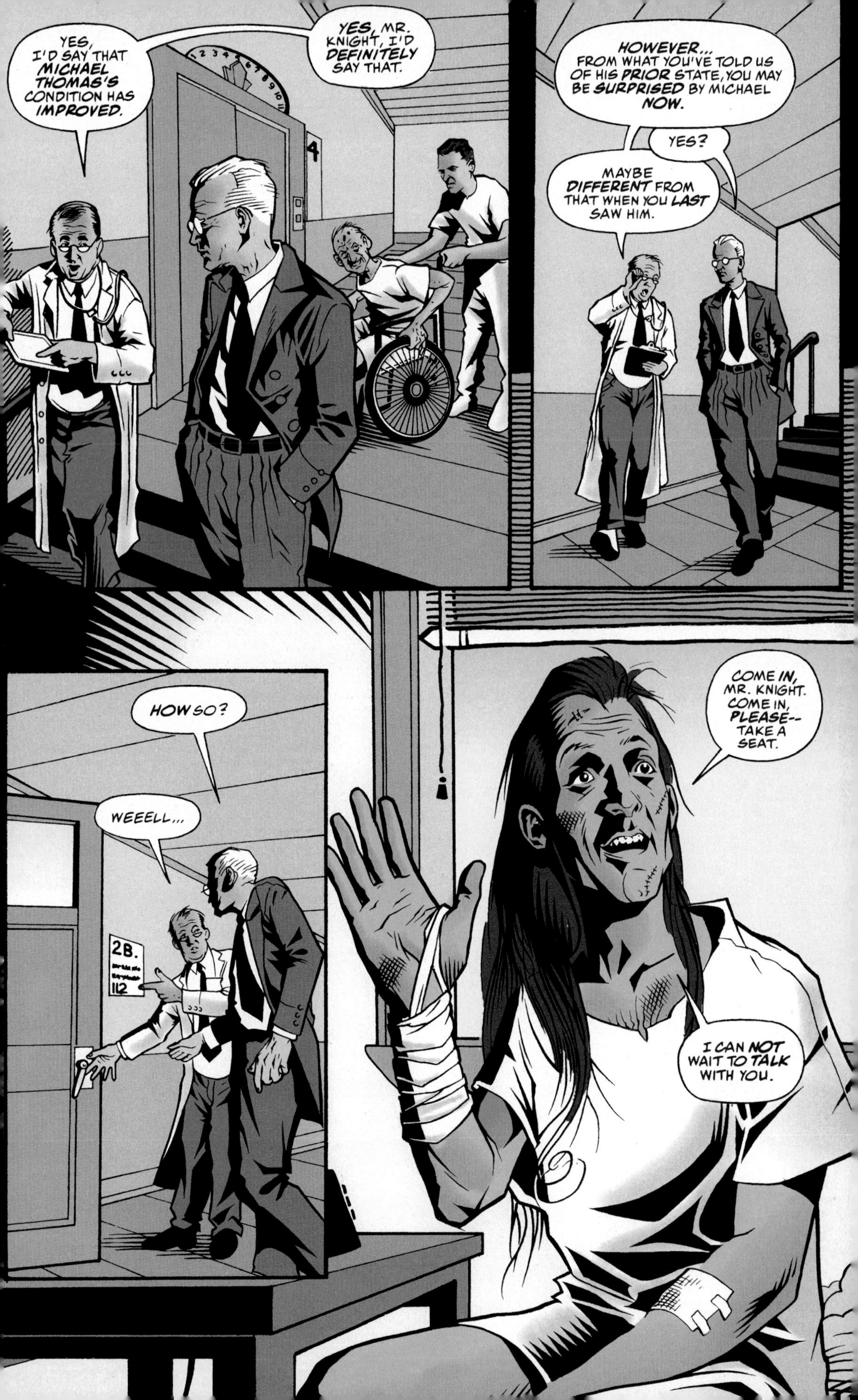
YES, I'D SAY THAT MICHAEL THOMAS'S CONDITION HAS IMPROVED.
YES, MR. KNIGHT, I'D DEFINITELY SAY THAT.
4
HOWEVER... FROM WHAT YOU'VE TOLD US OF HIS PRIOR STATE, YOU MAY BE SURPRISED BY MICHAEL NOW.
YES?
MAYBE DIFFERENT FROM THAT WHEN YOU LAST SAW HIM.
HOW SO?
WEEELL...
2B.
112
COME IN, MR. KNIGHT. COME IN, PLEASE-- TAKE A SEAT.
I CAN NOT WAIT TO TALK WITH YOU.

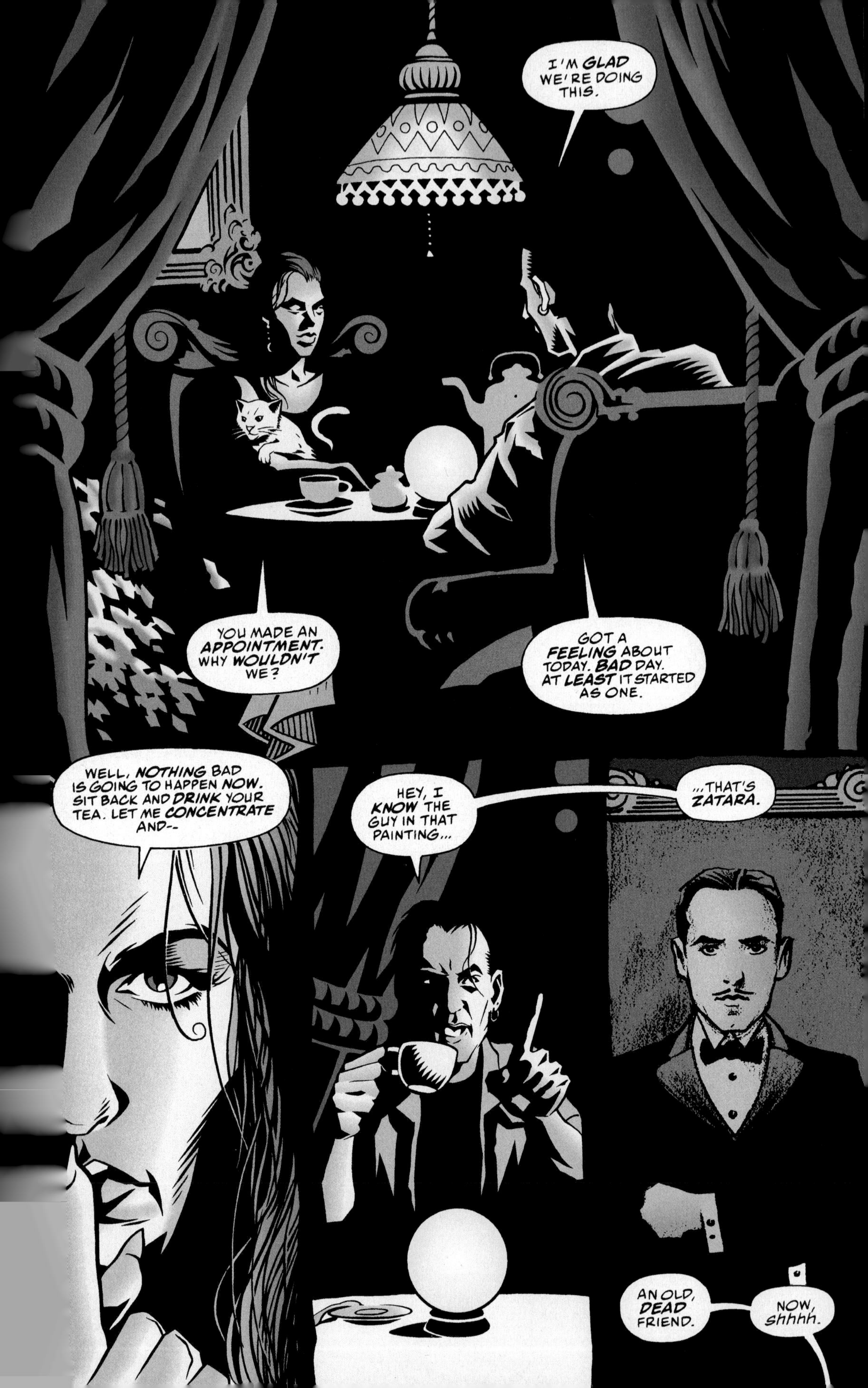
I'M GLAD WE'RE DOING THIS.
YOU MADE AN APPOINTMENT. WHY WOULDN'T WE?
GOT A FEELING ABOUT TODAY. BAD DAY. AT LEAST IT STARTED AS ONE.
WELL, NOTHING BAD IS GOING TO HAPPEN NOW. SIT BACK AND DRINK YOUR TEA. LET ME CONCENTRATE AND--
HEY, I KNOW THE GUY IN THAT PAINTING...
...THAT'S ZATARA.
AN OLD, DEAD FRIEND.
NOW, shhhh.

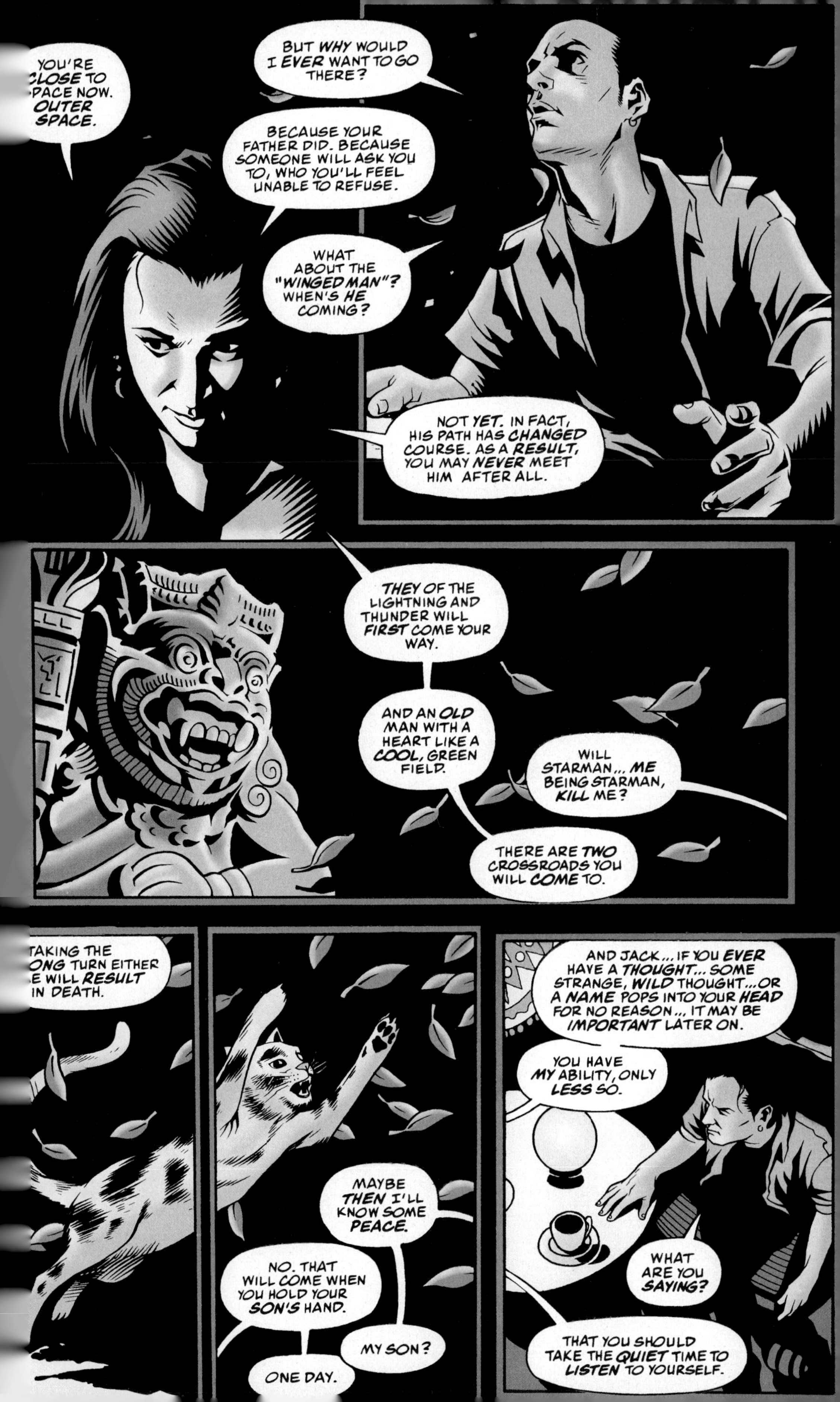

YOU'RE CLOSE TO SPACE NOW. OUTER SPACE.
BUT WHY WOULD I EVER WANT TO GO THERE?
BECAUSE YOUR FATHER DID. BECAUSE SOMEONE WILL ASK YOU TO, WHO YOU'LL FEEL UNABLE TO REFUSE.
WHAT ABOUT THE "WINGED MAN"? WHEN'S HE COMING?
NOT YET. IN FACT, HIS PATH HAS CHANGED COURSE. AS A RESULT, YOU MAY NEVER MEET HIM AFTER ALL.
THEY OF THE LIGHTNING AND THUNDER WILL FIRST COME YOUR WAY.
AND AN OLD MAN WITH A HEART LIKE A COOL, GREEN FIELD.
WILL STARMAN... ME BEING STARMAN, KILL ME?
THERE ARE TWO CROSSROADS YOU WILL COME TO.
TAKING THE ONG TURN EITHER E WILL RESULT IN DEATH.
MAYBE THEN I'LL KNOW SOME PEACE.
NO. THAT WILL COME WHEN YOU HOLD YOUR SON'S HAND.
MY SON?
ONE DAY.
AND JACK... IF YOU EVER HAVE A THOUGHT... SOME STRANGE, WILD THOUGHT... OR A NAME POPS INTO YOUR HEAD FOR NO REASON... IT MAY BE IMPORTANT LATER ON.
YOU HAVE MY ABILITY, ONLY LESS SO.
WHAT ARE YOU SAYING?
THAT YOU SHOULD TAKE THE QUIET TIME TO LISTEN TO YOURSELF.

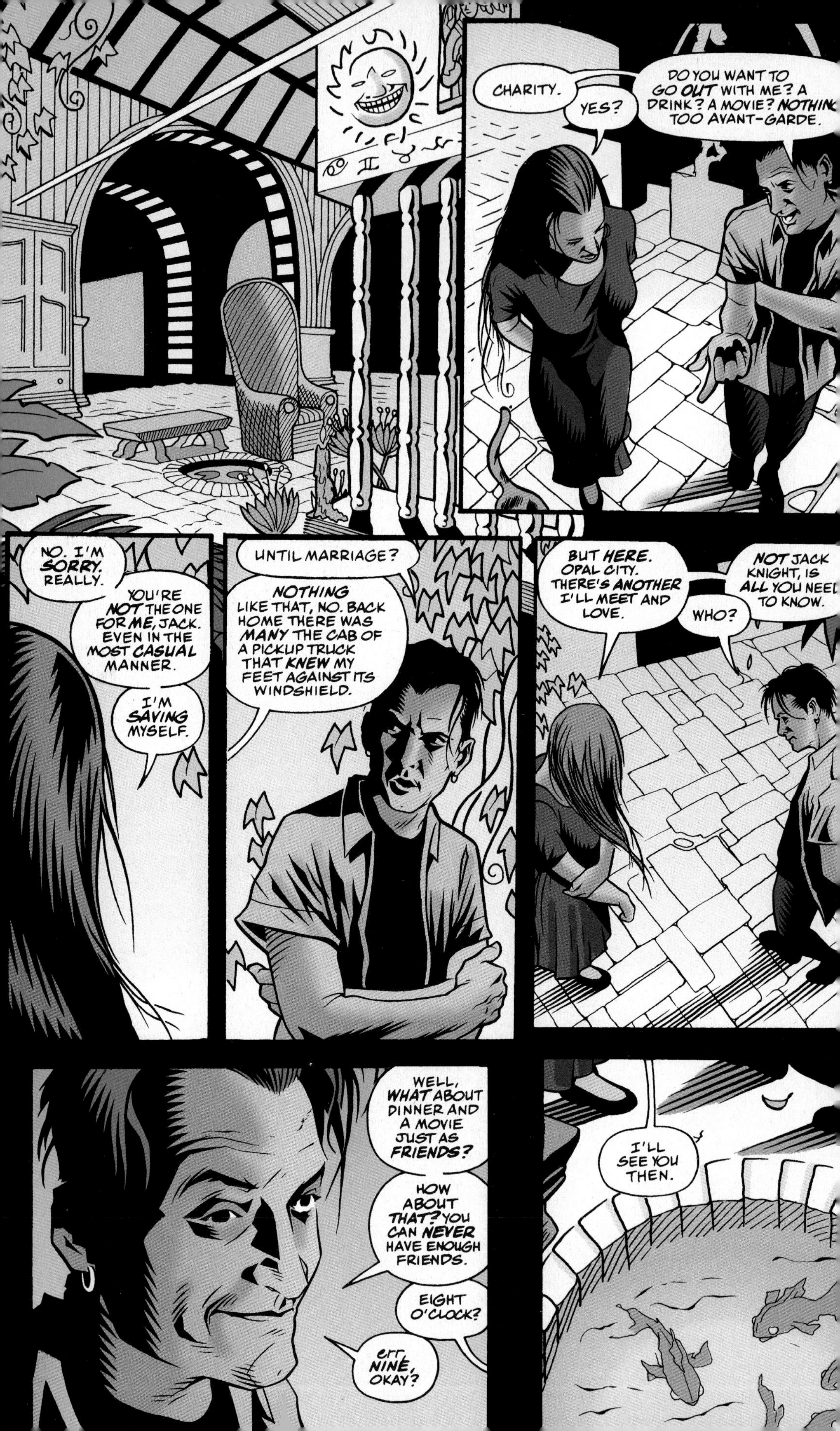
CHARITY.
YES?
DO YOU WANT TO GO OUT WITH ME? A DRINK? A MOVIE? NOTHING TOO AVANT-GARDE.
NO. I'M SORRY. REALLY.
YOU'RE NOT THE ONE FOR ME, JACK. EVEN IN THE MOST CASUAL MANNER.
I'M SAVING MYSELF.
UNTIL MARRIAGE?
NOTHING LIKE THAT, NO. BACK HOME THERE WAS MANY THE CAB OF A PICKUP TRUCK THAT KNEW MY FEET AGAINST ITS WINDSHIELD.
BUT HERE. OPAL CITY. THERE'S ANOTHER I'LL MEET AND LOVE.
WHO?
NOT JACK KNIGHT, IS ALL YOU NEED TO KNOW.
WELL, WHAT ABOUT DINNER AND A MOVIE JUST AS FRIENDS?
HOW ABOUT THAT? YOU CAN NEVER HAVE ENOUGH FRIENDS.
EIGHT O'CLOCK?
err, NINE, OKAY?
I'LL SEE YOU THEN.

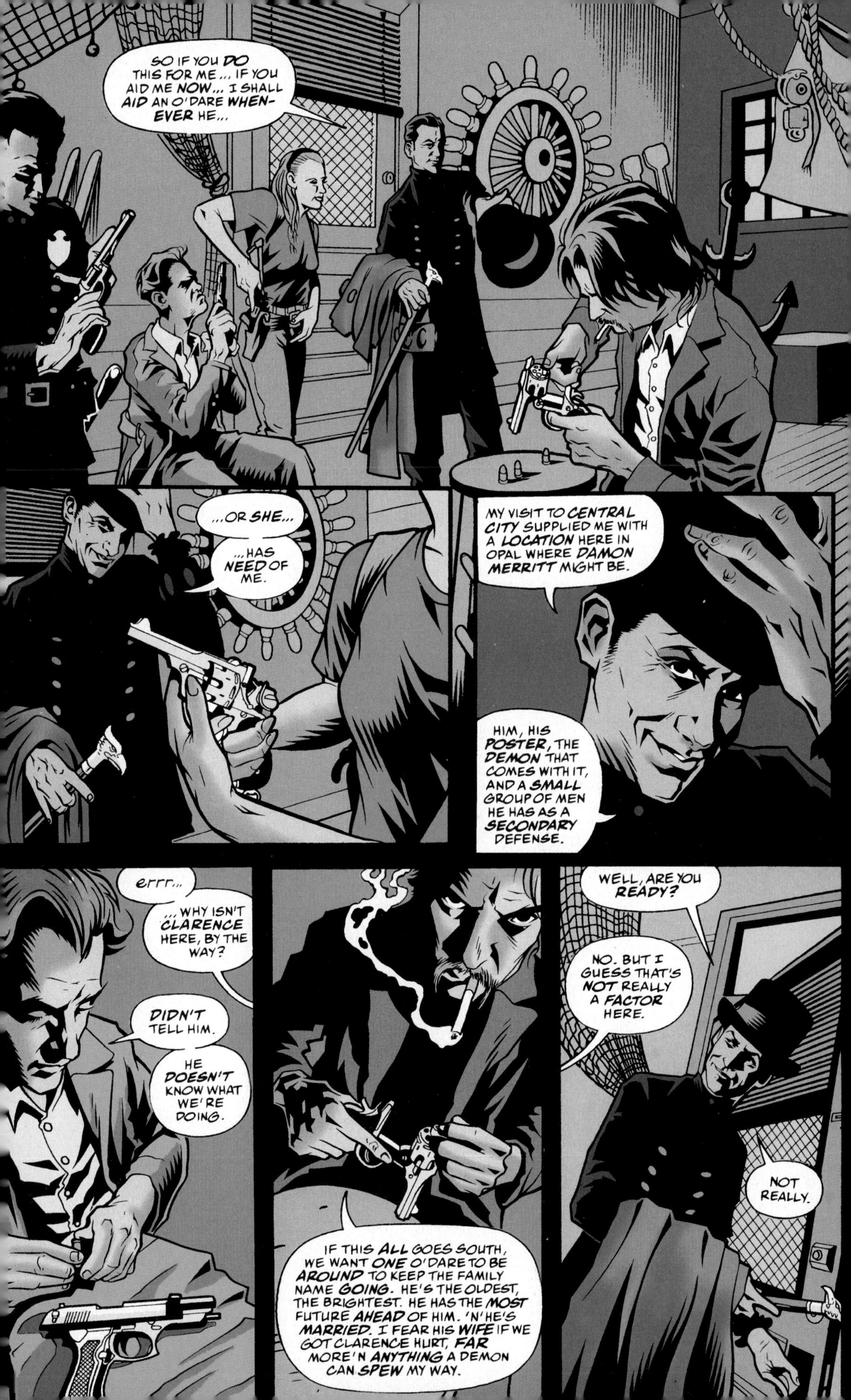

SO IF YOU DO THIS FOR ME... IF YOU AID ME NOW... I SHALL AID AN O'DARE WHENEVER HE...
...OR SHE...
...HAS NEED OF ME.
MY VISIT TO CENTRAL CITY SUPPLIED ME WITH A LOCATION HERE IN OPAL WHERE DAMON MERRITT MIGHT BE.
HIM, HIS POSTER, THE DEMON THAT COMES WITH IT, AND A SMALL GROUP OF MEN HE HAS AS A SECONDARY DEFENSE.
errr...
...WHY ISN'T CLARENCE HERE, BY THE WAY?
DIDN'T TELL HIM.
HE DOESN'T KNOW WHAT WE'RE DOING.
IF THIS ALL GOES SOUTH, WE WANT ONE O'DARE TO BE AROUND TO KEEP THE FAMILY NAME GOING. HE'S THE OLDEST, THE BRIGHTEST. HE HAS THE MOST FUTURE AHEAD OF HIM. 'N' HE'S MARRIED. I FEAR HIS WIFE IF WE GOT CLARENCE HURT, FAR MORE'N ANYTHING A DEMON CAN SPEW MY WAY.
WELL, ARE YOU READY?
NO. BUT I GUESS THAT'S NOT REALLY A FACTOR HERE.
NOT REALLY.

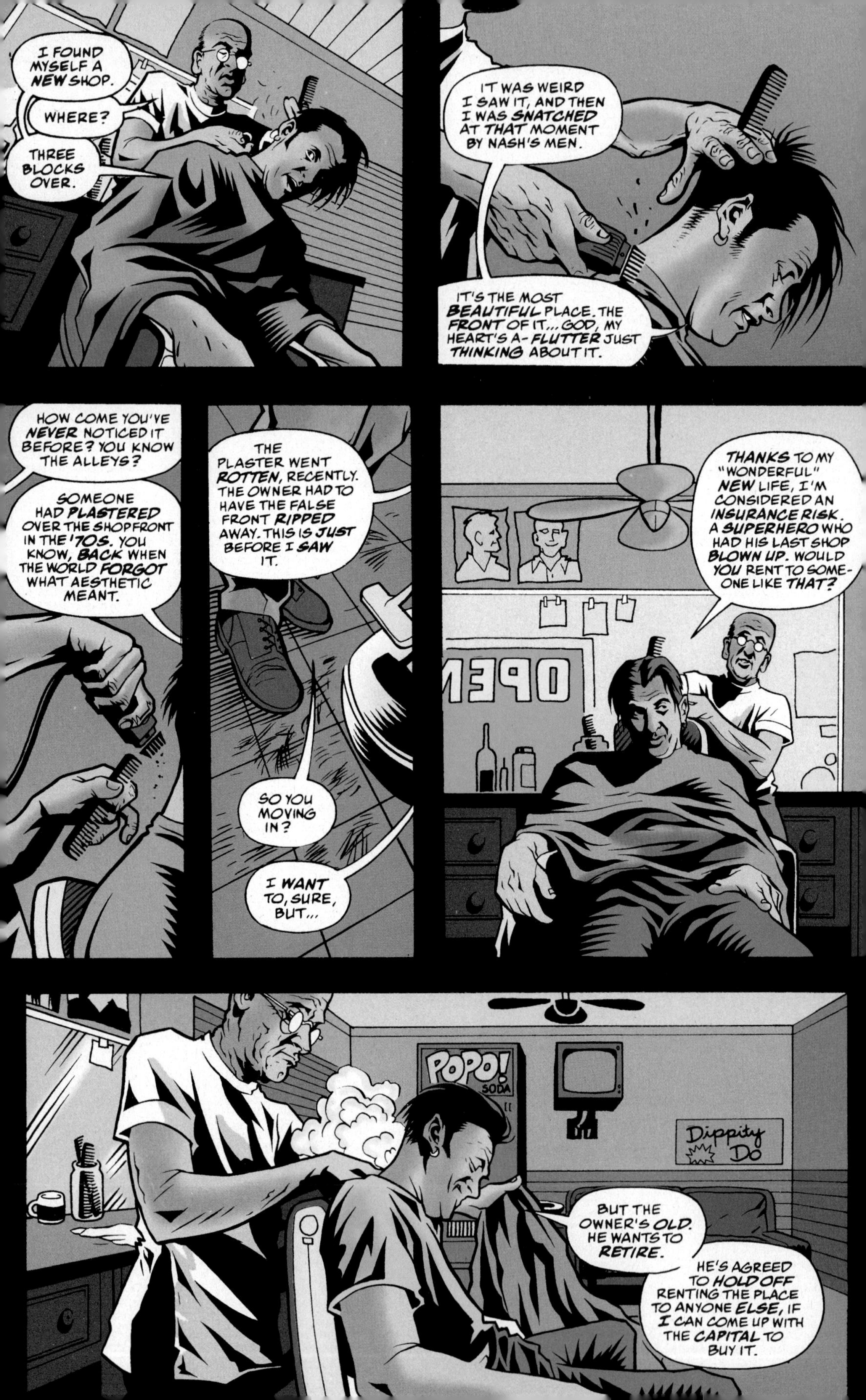
I FOUND MYSELF A NEW SHOP.
WHERE?
THREE BLOCKS OVER.
IT WAS WEIRD I SAW IT, AND THEN I WAS SNATCHED AT THAT MOMENT BY NASH'S MEN.
IT'S THE MOST BEAUTIFUL PLACE. THE FRONT OF IT... GOD, MY HEART'S A-FLUTTER JUST THINKING ABOUT IT.
HOW COME YOU'VE NEVER NOTICED IT BEFORE? YOU KNOW THE ALLEYS?
SOMEONE HAD PLASTERED OVER THE SHOPFRONT IN THE '70S. YOU KNOW, BACK WHEN THE WORLD FORGOT WHAT AESTHETIC MEANT.
THE PLASTER WENT ROTTEN, RECENTLY. THE OWNER HAD TO HAVE THE FALSE FRONT RIPPED AWAY. THIS IS JUST BEFORE I SAW IT.
SO YOU MOVING IN?
I WANT TO, SURE, BUT...
THANKS TO MY "WONDERFUL" NEW LIFE, I'M CONSIDERED AN INSURANCE RISK. A SUPERHERO WHO HAD HIS LAST SHOP BLOWN UP. WOULD YOU RENT TO SOMEONE LIKE THAT?
OPEN
POPO! SODA
Dippity Do
BUT THE OWNER'S OLD. HE WANTS TO RETIRE.
HE'S AGREED TO HOLD OFF RENTING THE PLACE TO ANYONE ELSE, IF I CAN COME UP WITH THE CAPITAL TO BUY IT.

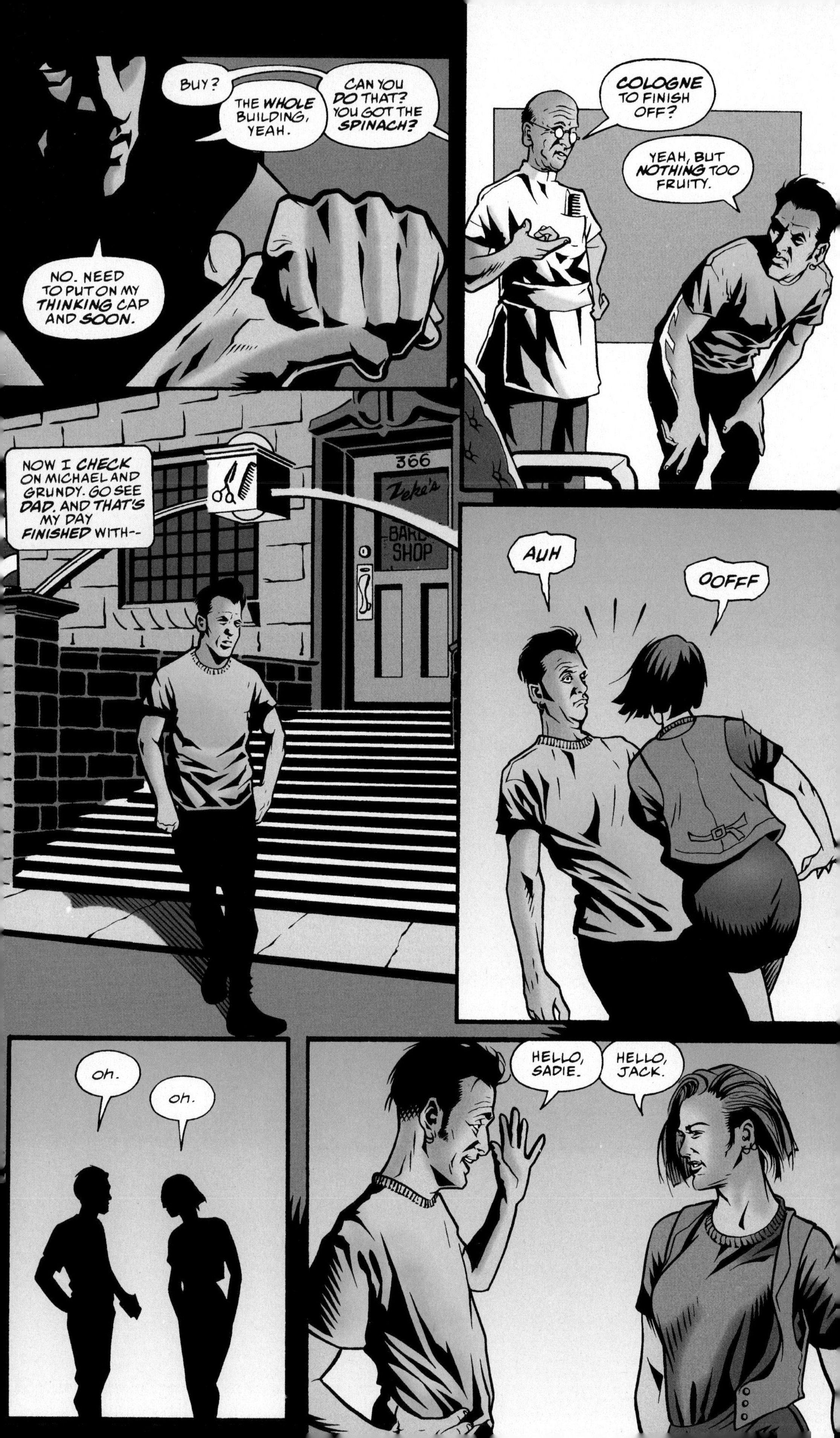
BUY?
THE WHOLE BUILDING, YEAH.
CAN YOU DO THAT? YOU GOT THE SPINACH?
NO. NEED TO PUT ON MY THINKING CAP AND SOON.
COLOGNE TO FINISH OFF?
YEAH, BUT NOTHING TOO FRUITY.
NOW I CHECK ON MICHAEL AND GRUNDY. GO SEE DAD. AND THAT'S MY DAY FINISHED WITH--
366
Zeke's
BARB SHOP
AUH
OOFFF
oh.
oh.
HELLO, SADIE.
HELLO, JACK.

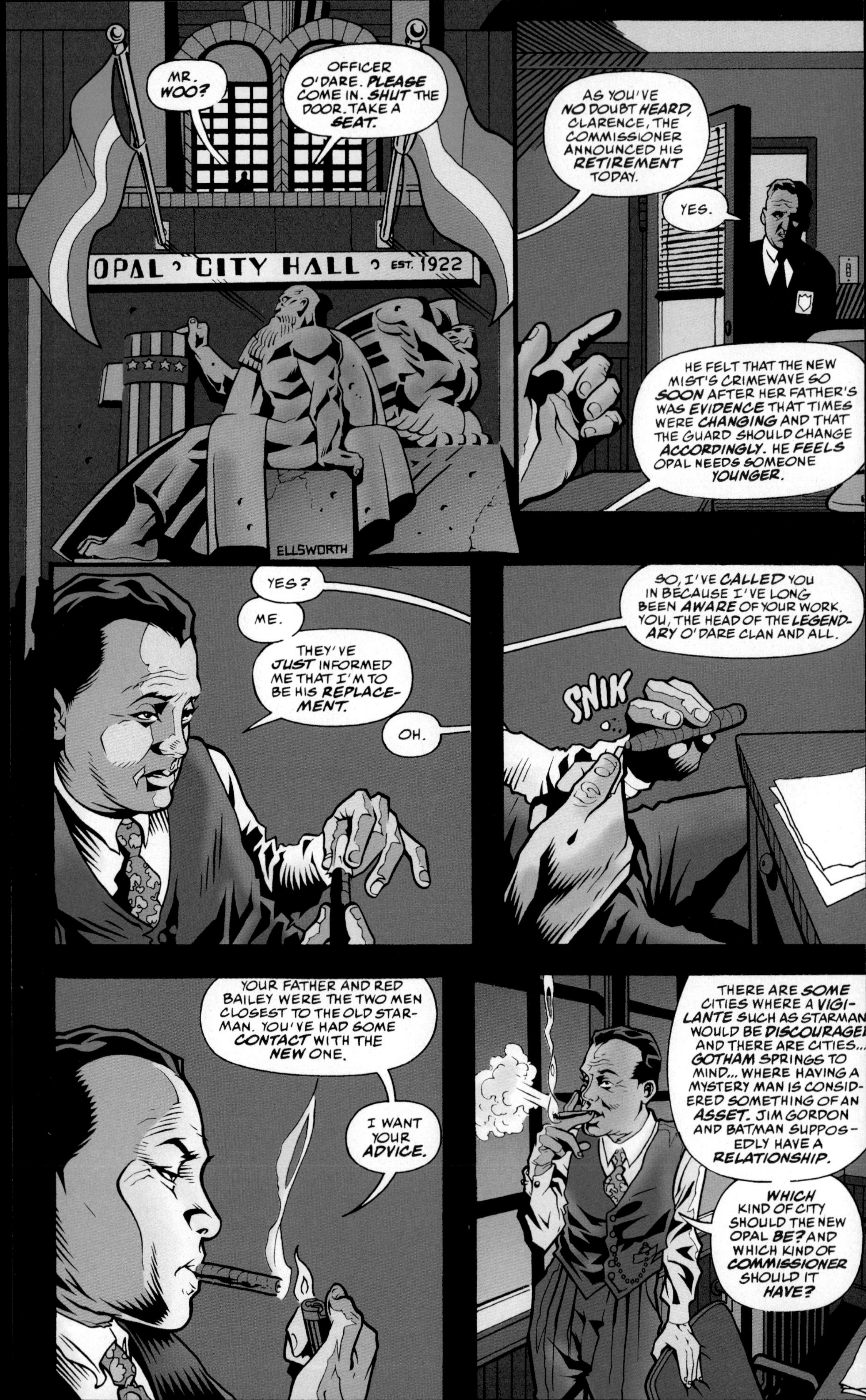
MR. WOO?
OFFICER O'DARE. PLEASE COME IN. SHUT THE DOOR. TAKE A SEAT.
OPAL CITY HALL EST. 1922
ELLSWORTH
AS YOU'VE NO DOUBT HEARD, CLARENCE, THE COMMISSIONER ANNOUNCED HIS RETIREMENT TODAY.
YES.
HE FELT THAT THE NEW MIST'S CRIMEWAVE SO SOON AFTER HER FATHER'S WAS EVIDENCE THAT TIMES WERE CHANGING AND THAT THE GUARD SHOULD CHANGE ACCORDINGLY. HE FEELS OPAL NEEDS SOMEONE YOUNGER.
YES?
ME.
THEY'VE JUST INFORMED ME THAT I'M TO BE HIS REPLACEMENT.
OH.
SO, I'VE CALLED YOU IN BECAUSE I'VE LONG BEEN AWARE OF YOUR WORK. YOU, THE HEAD OF THE LEGENDARY O'DARE CLAN AND ALL.
SNIK
YOUR FATHER AND RED BAILEY WERE THE TWO MEN CLOSEST TO THE OLD STARMAN. YOU'VE HAD SOME CONTACT WITH THE NEW ONE.
I WANT YOUR ADVICE.
THERE ARE SOME CITIES WHERE A VIGILANTE SUCH AS STARMAN WOULD BE DISCOURAGED AND THERE ARE CITIES... GOTHAM SPRINGS TO MIND... WHERE HAVING A MYSTERY MAN IS CONSIDERED SOMETHING OF AN ASSET. JIM GORDON AND BATMAN SUPPOSEDLY HAVE A RELATIONSHIP.
WHICH KIND OF CITY SHOULD THE NEW OPAL BE? AND WHICH KIND OF COMMISSIONER SHOULD IT HAVE?

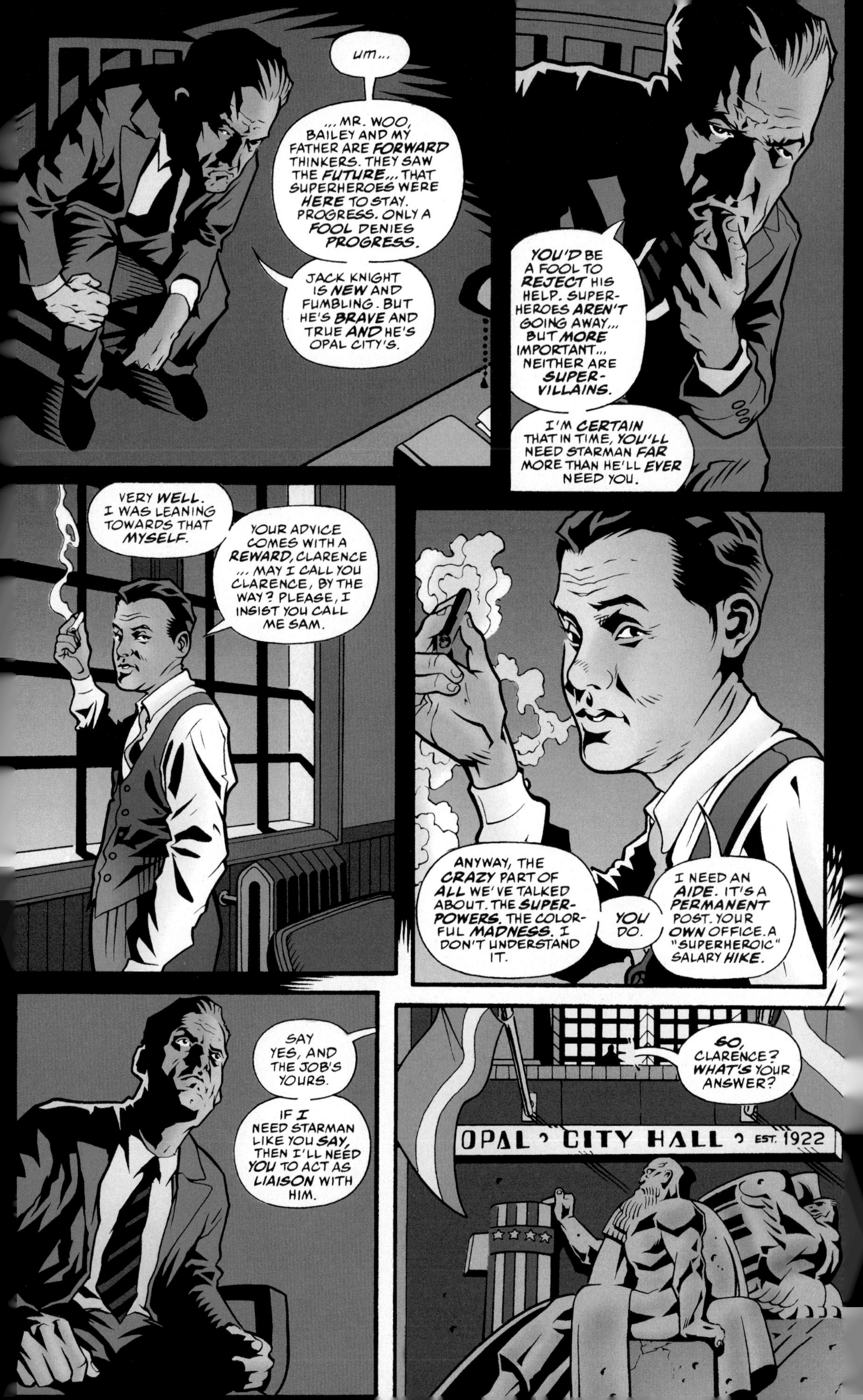
um...
...MR. WOO, BAILEY AND MY FATHER ARE FORWARD THINKERS. THEY SAW THE FUTURE... THAT SUPERHEROES WERE HERE TO STAY. PROGRESS. ONLY A FOOL DENIES PROGRESS.
JACK KNIGHT IS NEW AND FUMBLING. BUT HE'S BRAVE AND TRUE AND HE'S OPAL CITY'S.
YOU'D BE A FOOL TO REJECT HIS HELP. SUPER-HEROES AREN'T GOING AWAY... BUT MORE IMPORTANT... NEITHER ARE SUPER-VILLAINS.
I'M CERTAIN THAT IN TIME, YOU'LL NEED STARMAN FAR MORE THAN HE'LL EVER NEED YOU.
VERY WELL. I WAS LEANING TOWARDS THAT MYSELF.
YOUR ADVICE COMES WITH A REWARD, CLARENCE ... MAY I CALL YOU CLARENCE, BY THE WAY? PLEASE, I INSIST YOU CALL ME SAM.
ANYWAY, THE CRAZY PART OF ALL WE'VE TALKED ABOUT. THE SUPER-POWERS. THE COLOR-FUL MADNESS. I DON'T UNDERSTAND IT.
YOU DO.
I NEED AN AIDE. IT'S A PERMANENT POST. YOUR OWN OFFICE. A "SUPERHEROIC" SALARY HIKE.
SAY YES, AND THE JOB'S YOURS.
IF I NEED STARMAN LIKE YOU SAY, THEN I'LL NEED YOU TO ACT AS LIAISON WITH HIM.
SO, CLARENCE? WHAT'S YOUR ANSWER?
OPAL CITY HALL EST. 1922

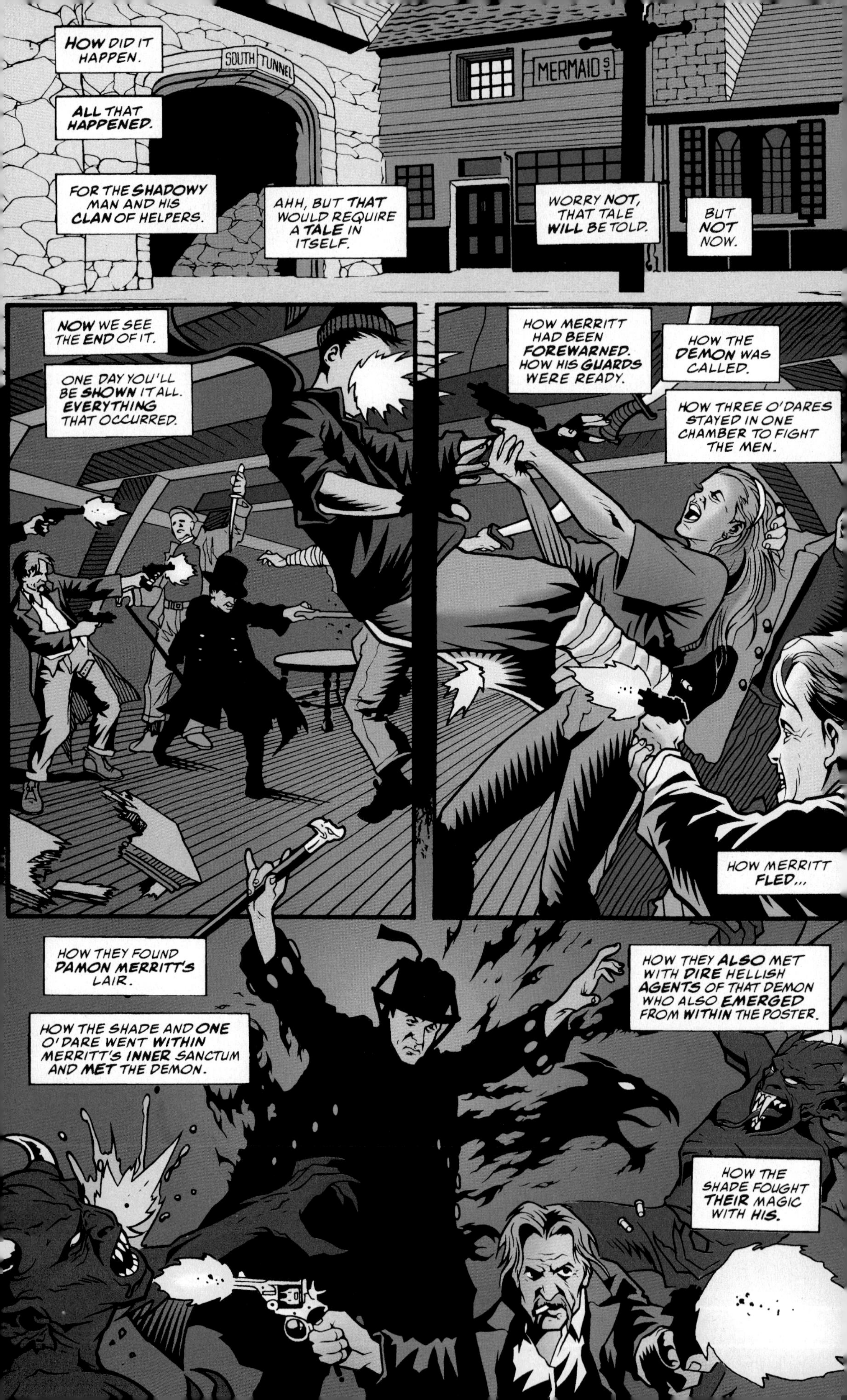
HOW DID IT HAPPEN.
ALL THAT HAPPENED.
SOUTH TUNNEL
MERMAID ST
FOR THE SHADOWY MAN AND HIS CLAN OF HELPERS.
AHH, BUT THAT WOULD REQUIRE A TALE IN ITSELF.
WORRY NOT, THAT TALE WILL BE TOLD.
BUT NOT NOW.
NOW WE SEE THE END OF IT.
ONE DAY YOU'LL BE SHOWN IT ALL. EVERYTHING THAT OCCURRED.
HOW MERRITT HAD BEEN FOREWARNED. HOW HIS GUARDS WERE READY.
HOW THE DEMON WAS CALLED.
HOW THREE O'DARES STAYED IN ONE CHAMBER TO FIGHT THE MEN.
HOW MERRITT FLED...
HOW THEY FOUND DAMON MERRITT'S LAIR.
HOW THE SHADE AND ONE O'DARE WENT WITHIN MERRITT'S INNER SANCTUM AND MET THE DEMON.
HOW THEY ALSO MET WITH DIRE HELLISH AGENTS OF THAT DEMON WHO ALSO EMERGED FROM WITHIN THE POSTER.
HOW THE SHADE FOUGHT THEIR MAGIC WITH HIS.

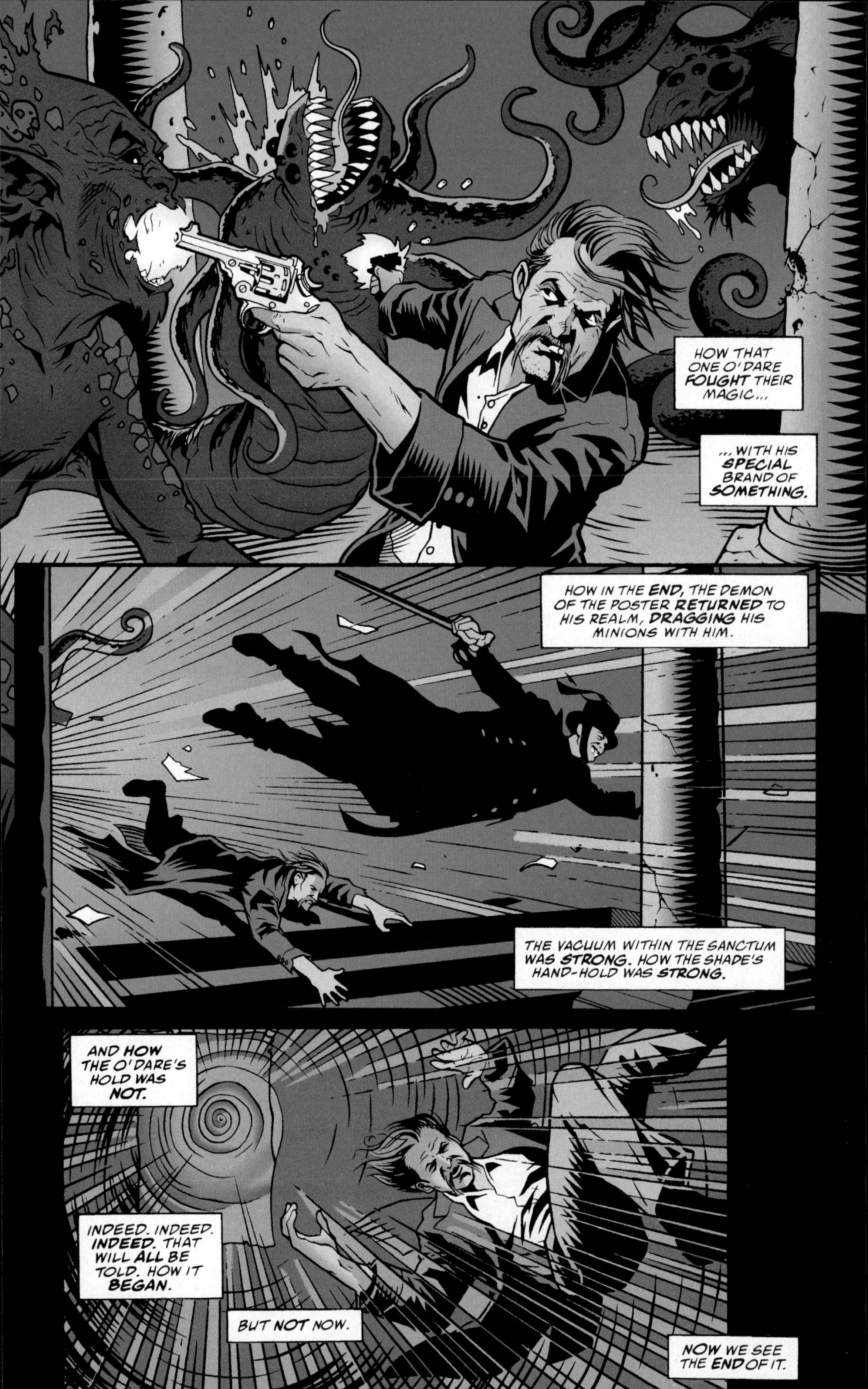
HOW THAT ONE O'DARE FOUGHT THEIR MAGIC...
...WITH HIS SPECIAL BRAND OF SOMETHING.
HOW IN THE END, THE DEMON OF THE POSTER RETURNED TO HIS REALM, DRAGGING HIS MINIONS WITH HIM.
THE VACUUM WITHIN THE SANCTUM WAS STRONG. HOW THE SHADE'S HAND-HOLD WAS STRONG.
AND HOW THE O'DARE'S HOLD WAS NOT.
INDEED. INDEED. INDEED. THAT WILL ALL BE TOLD. HOW IT BEGAN.
BUT NOT NOW.
NOW WE SEE THE END OF IT.

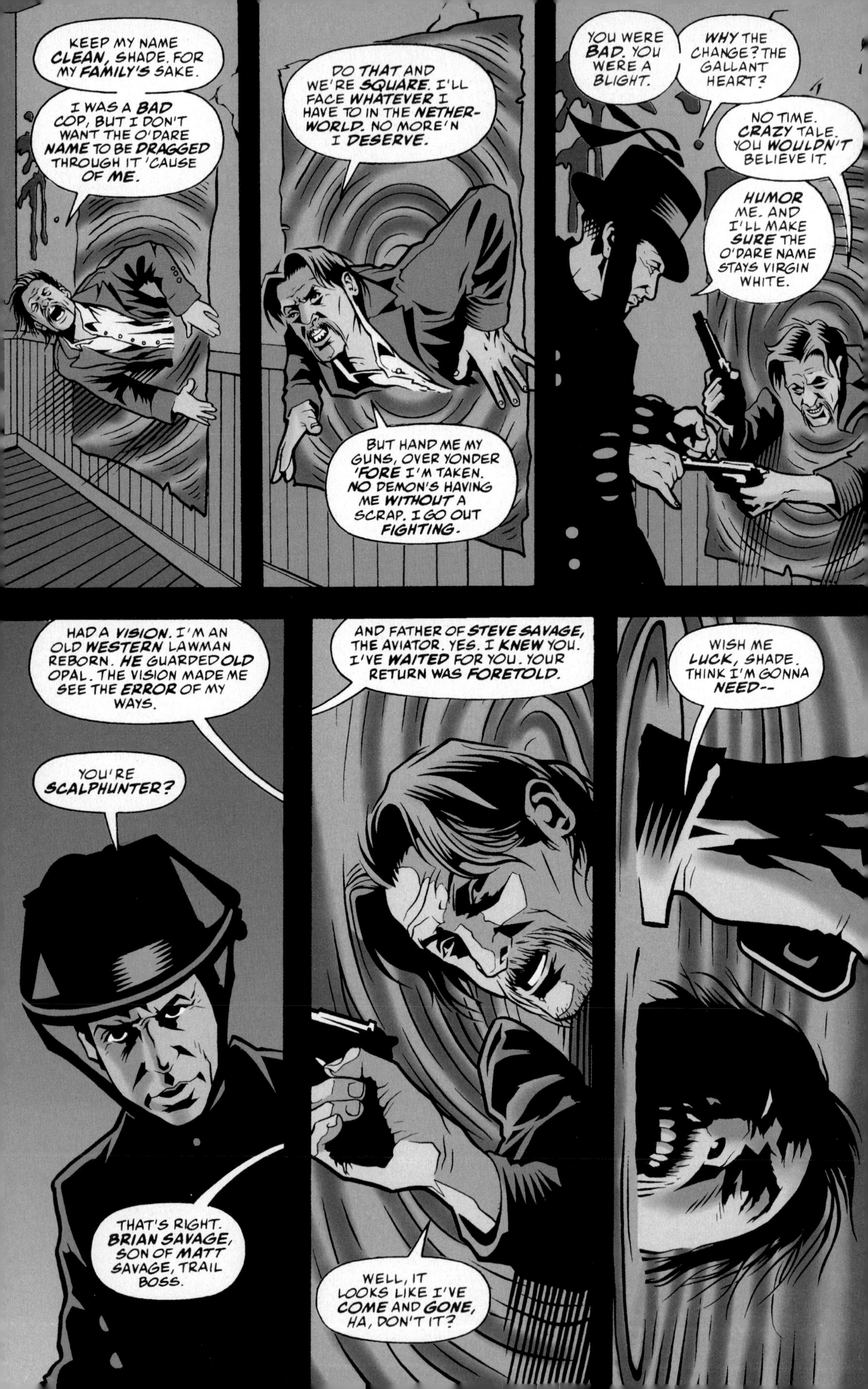
KEEP MY NAME CLEAN, SHADE. FOR MY FAMILY'S SAKE.
I WAS A BAD COP, BUT I DON'T WANT THE O'DARE NAME TO BE DRAGGED THROUGH IT 'CAUSE OF ME.
DO THAT AND WE'RE SQUARE. I'LL FACE WHATEVER I HAVE TO IN THE NETHER-WORLD. NO MORE'N I DESERVE.
BUT HAND ME MY GUNS, OVER YONDER 'FORE I'M TAKEN. NO DEMON'S HAVING ME WITHOUT A SCRAP. I GO OUT FIGHTING.
YOU WERE BAD. YOU WERE A BLIGHT.
WHY THE CHANGE? THE GALLANT HEART?
NO TIME. CRAZY TALE. YOU WOULDN'T BELIEVE IT.
HUMOR ME. AND I'LL MAKE SURE THE O'DARE NAME STAYS VIRGIN WHITE.
HAD A VISION. I'M AN OLD WESTERN LAWMAN REBORN. HE GUARDED OLD OPAL. THE VISION MADE ME SEE THE ERROR OF MY WAYS.
YOU'RE SCALPHUNTER?
THAT'S RIGHT. BRIAN SAVAGE, SON OF MATT SAVAGE, TRAIL BOSS.
AND FATHER OF STEVE SAVAGE, THE AVIATOR. YES. I KNEW YOU. I'VE WAITED FOR YOU. YOUR RETURN WAS FORETOLD.
WELL, IT LOOKS LIKE I'VE COME AND GONE, HA, DON'T IT?
WISH ME LUCK, SHADE. THINK I'M GONNA NEED--

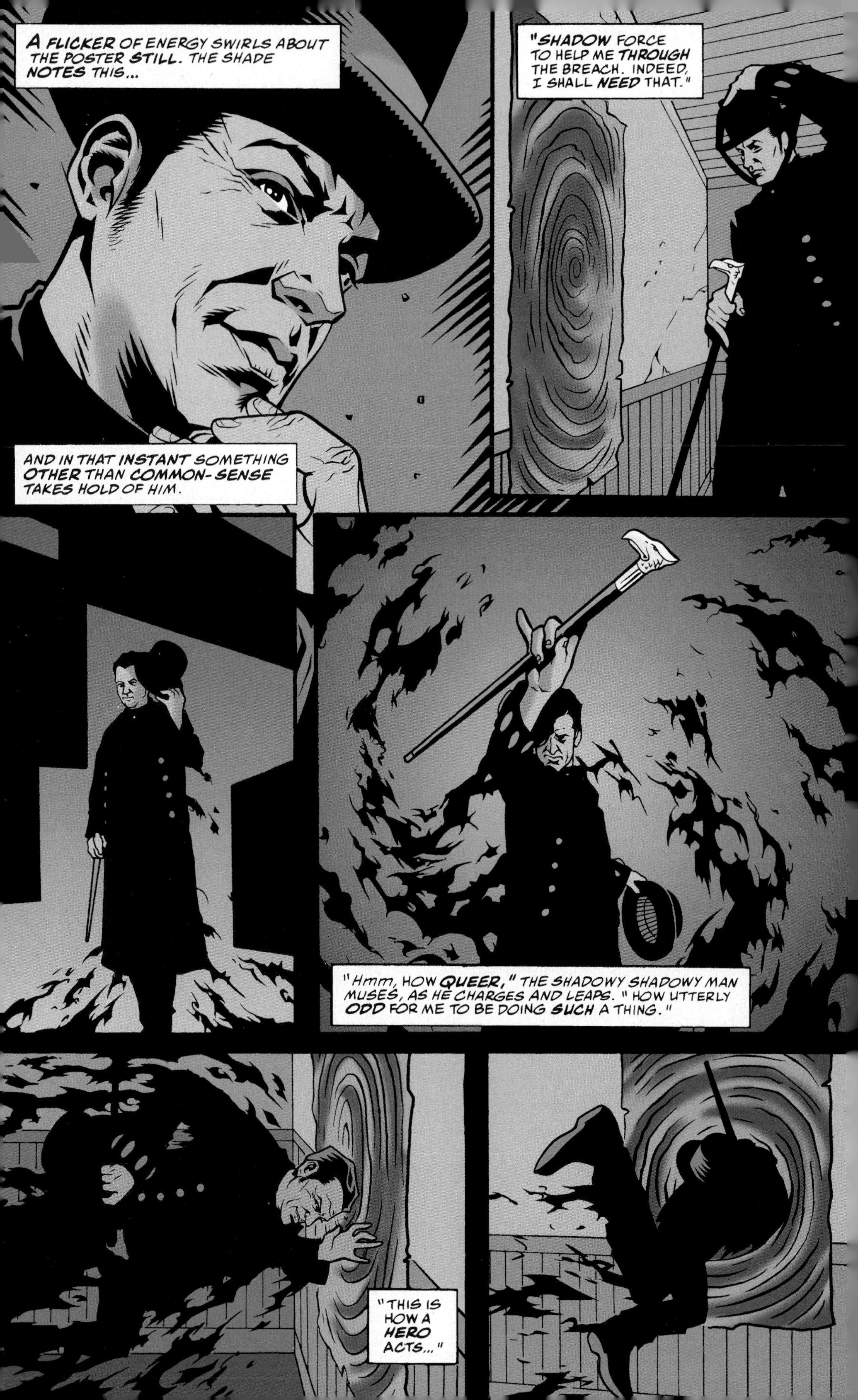
A FLICKER OF ENERGY SWIRLS ABOUT THE POSTER STILL. THE SHADE NOTES THIS...
AND IN THAT INSTANT SOMETHING OTHER THAN COMMON-SENSE TAKES HOLD OF HIM.
"SHADOW FORCE TO HELP ME THROUGH THE BREACH. INDEED, I SHALL NEED THAT."
"Hmm, HOW QUEER," THE SHADOWY SHADOWY MAN MUSES, AS HE CHARGES AND LEAPS. "HOW UTTERLY ODD FOR ME TO BE DOING SUCH A THING."
"THIS IS HOW A HERO ACTS..."

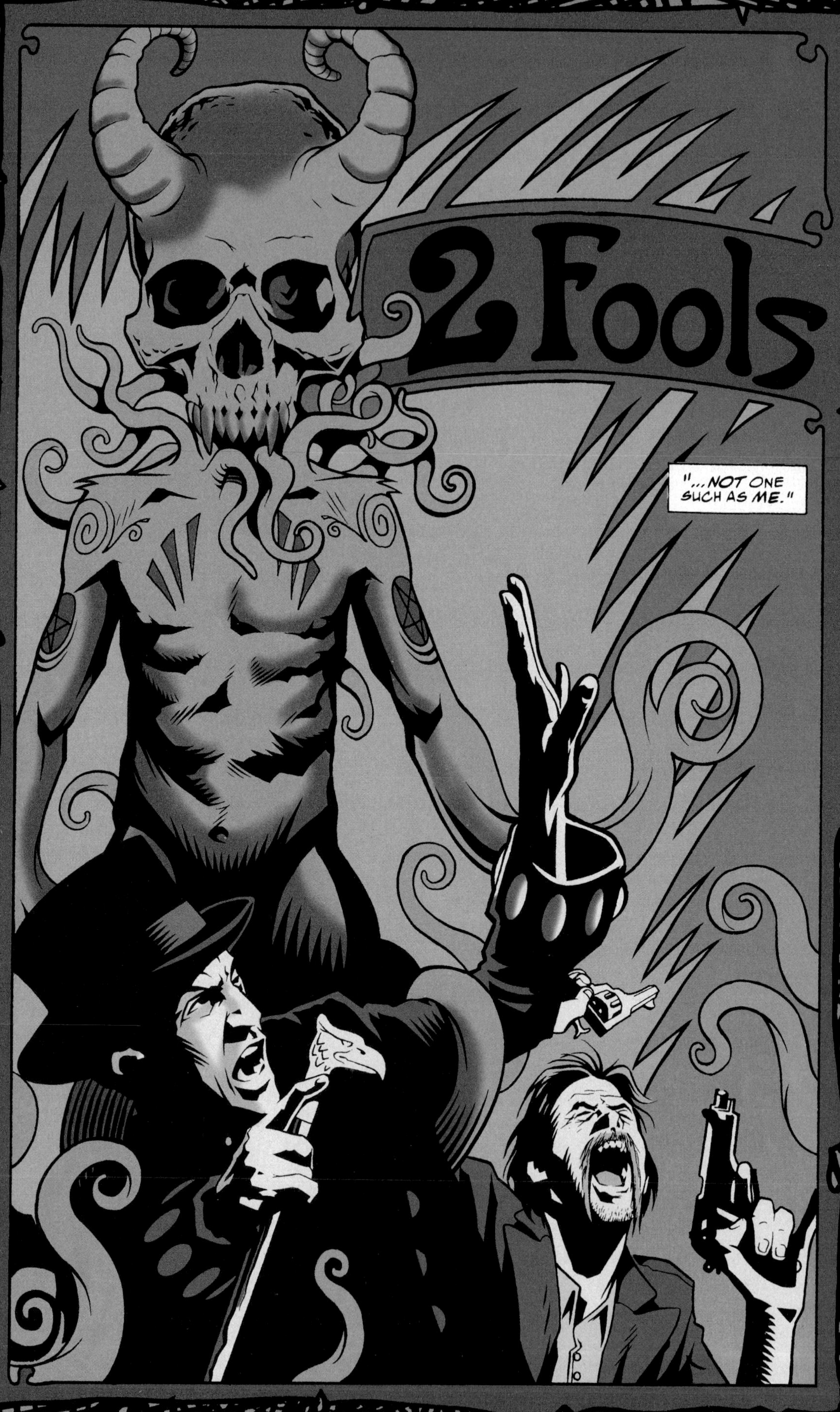
2 Fools
"...NOT ONE SUCH AS ME."

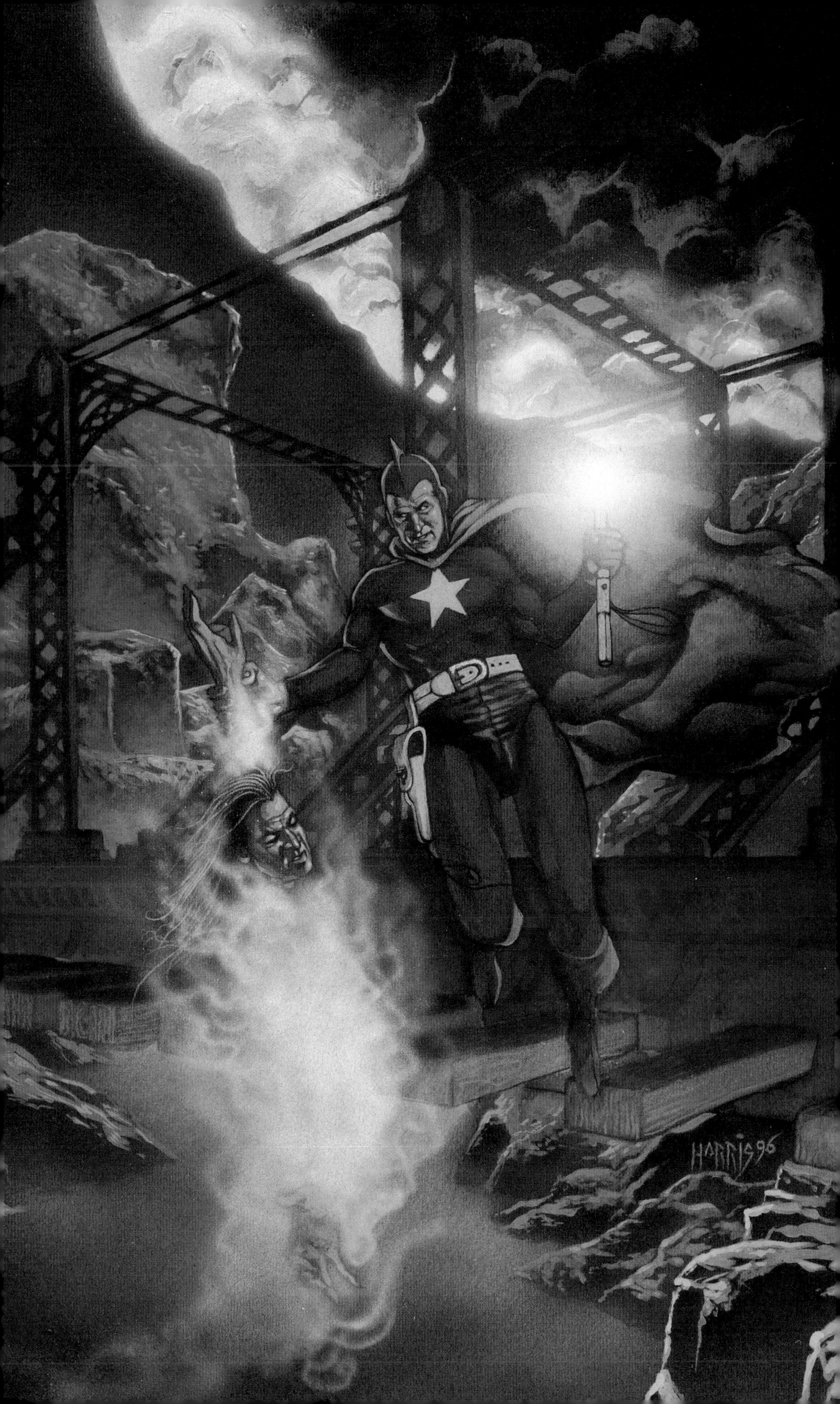
HARRIS 96

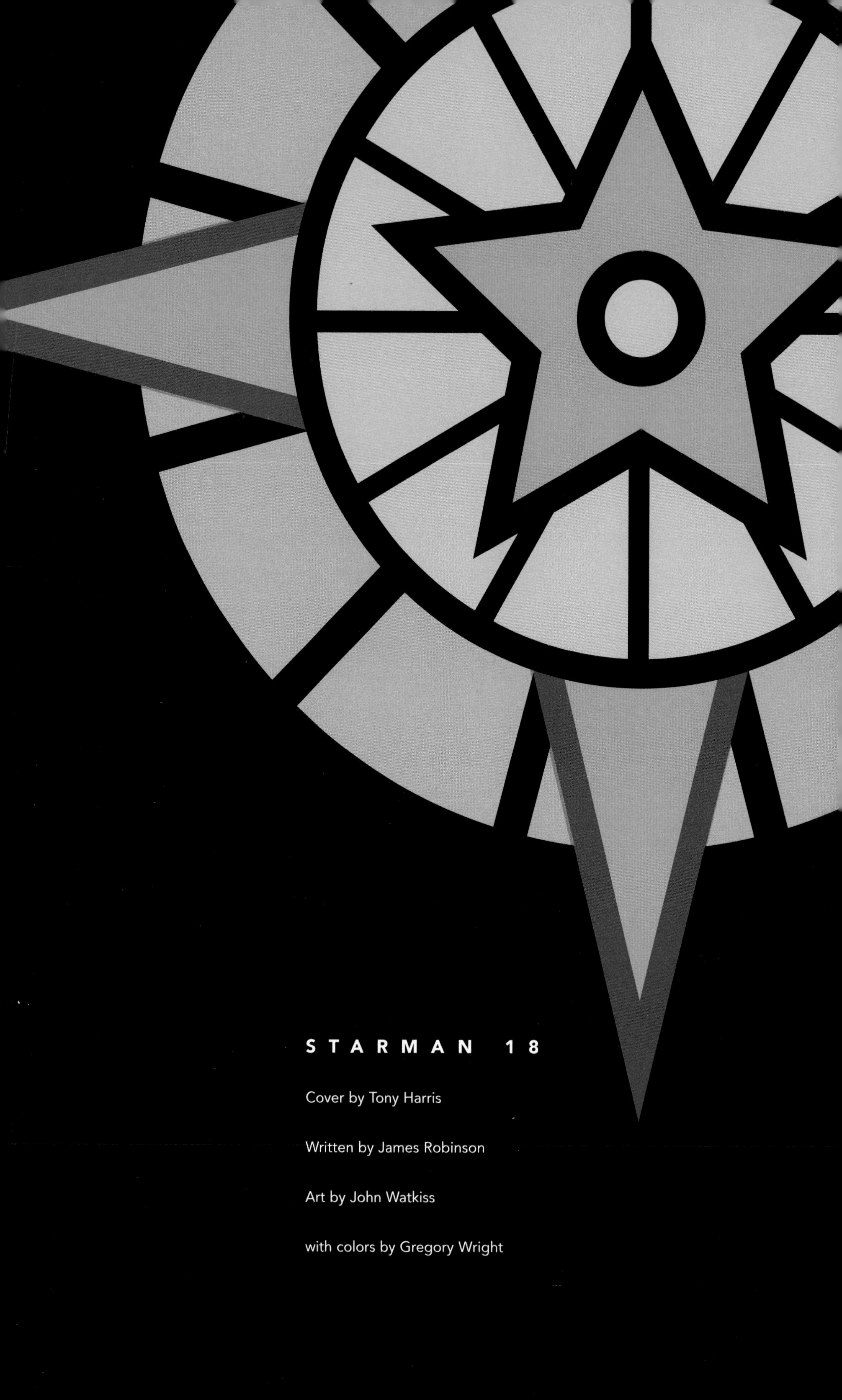

S T A R M A N   1 8

Cover by Tony Harris

Written by James Robinson

Art by John Watkiss

with colors by Gregory Wright

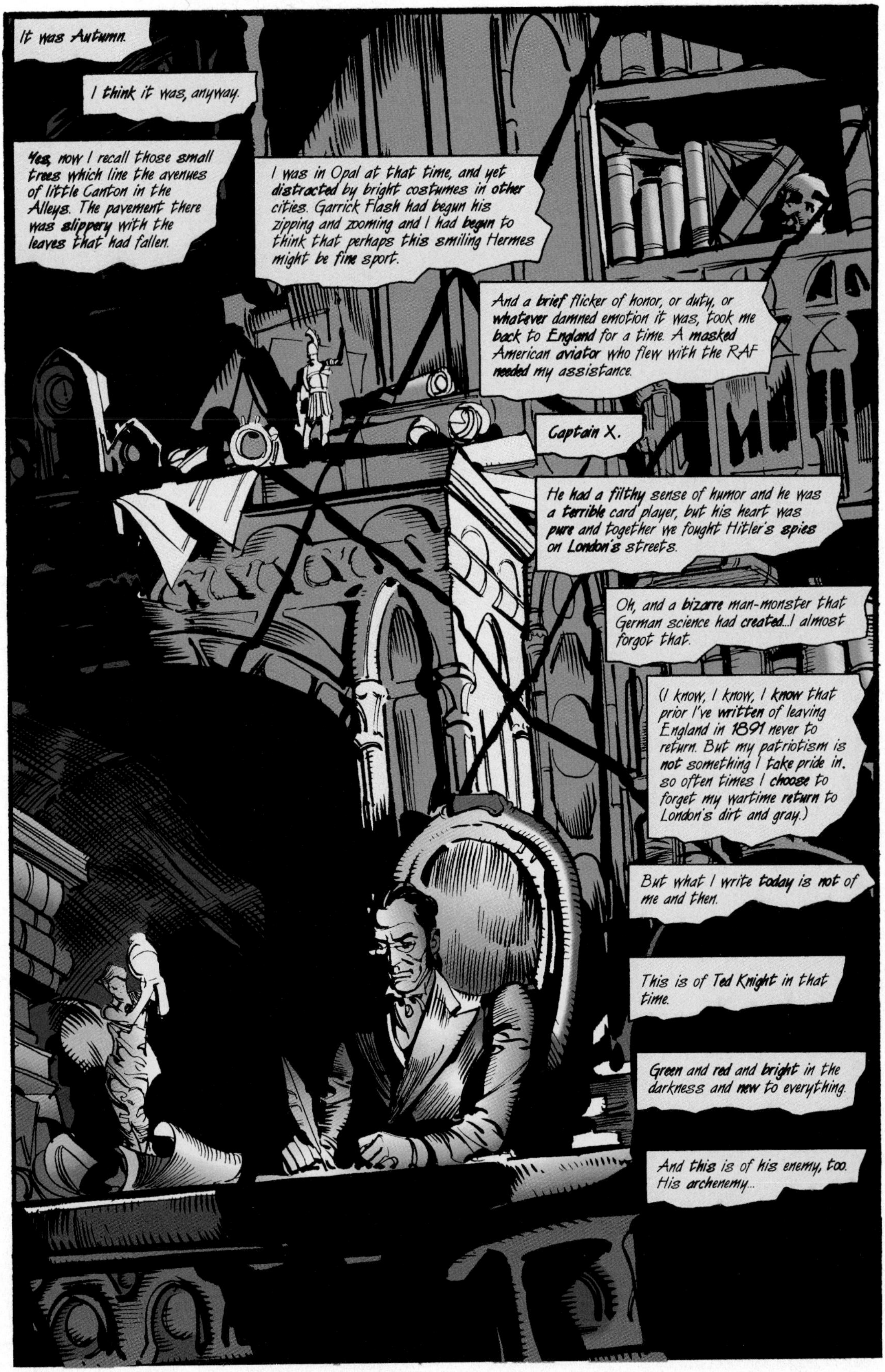
It was Autumn.
I think it was, anyway.
Yes, now I recall those small trees which line the avenues of little Canton in the Alleys. The pavement there was slippery with the leaves that had fallen.
I was in Opal at that time, and yet distracted by bright costumes in other cities. Garrick Flash had begun his zipping and zooming and I had begun to think that perhaps this smiling Hermes might be fine sport.
And a brief flicker of honor, or duty, or whatever damned emotion it was, took me back to England for a time. A masked American aviator who flew with the RAF needed my assistance.
Captain X.
He had a filthy sense of humor and he was a terrible card player, but his heart was pure and together we fought Hitler's spies on London's streets.
Oh, and a bizarre man-monster that German science had created...I almost forgot that.
(I know, I know, I know that prior I've written of leaving England in 1891 never to return. But my patriotism is not something I take pride in. so often times I choose to forget my wartime return to London's dirt and gray.)
But what I write today is not of me and then.
This is of Ted Knight in that time.
Green and red and bright in the darkness and new to everything.
And this is of his enemy, too. His archenemy...

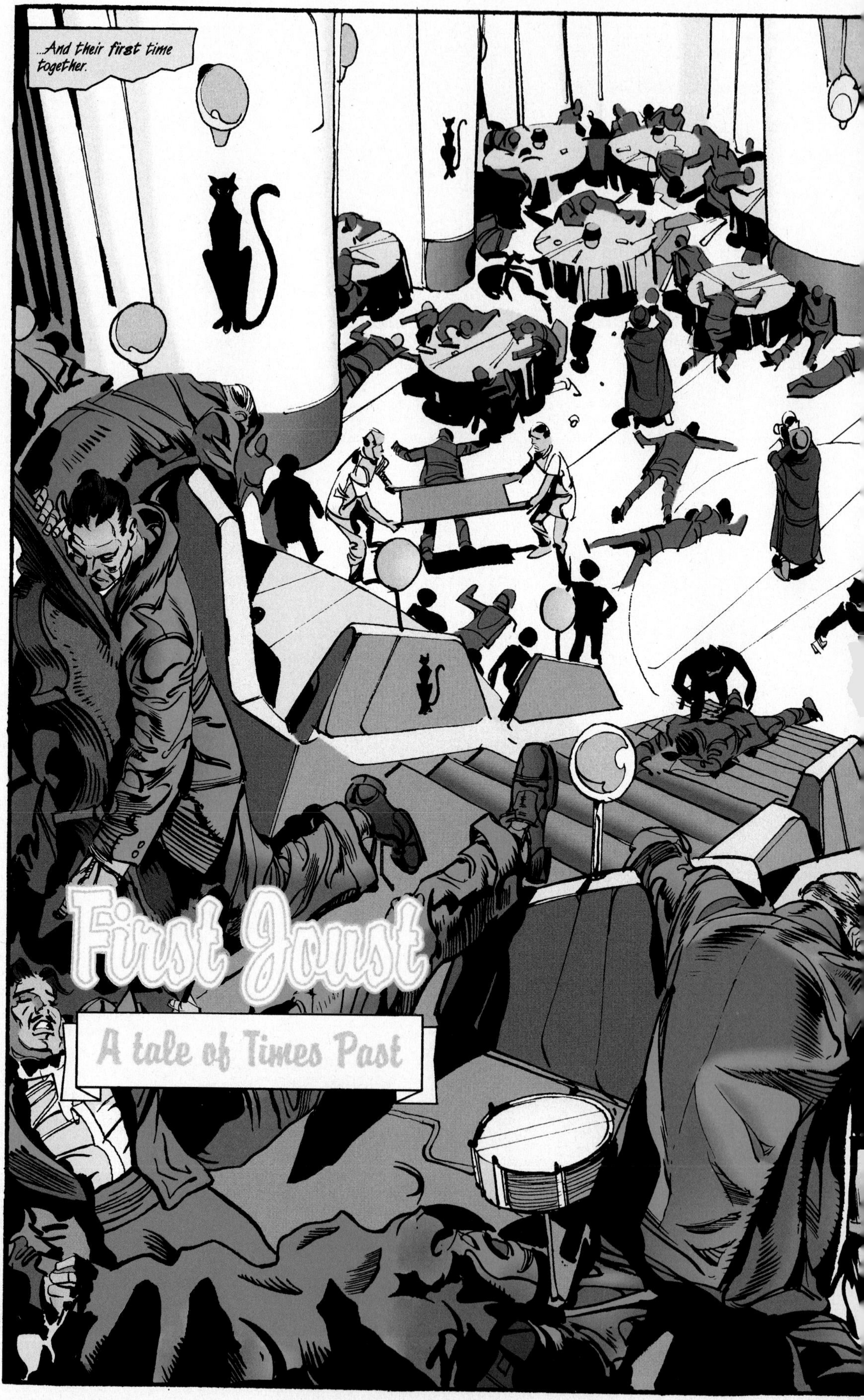

...And their first time together.
First Joust
A tale of Times Past

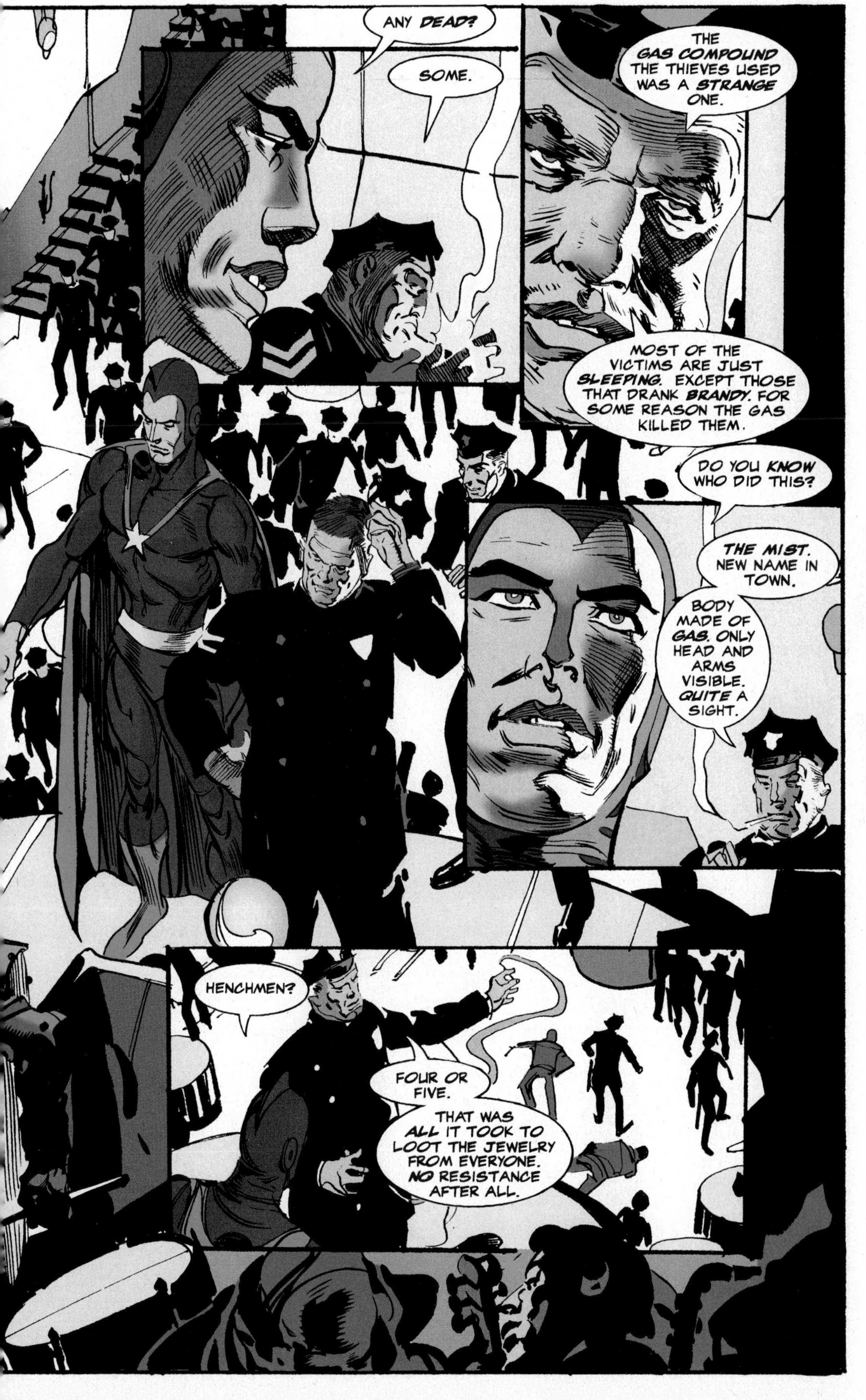
ANY DEAD?
SOME.
THE GAS COMPOUND THE THIEVES USED WAS A STRANGE ONE.
MOST OF THE VICTIMS ARE JUST SLEEPING. EXCEPT THOSE THAT DRANK BRANDY. FOR SOME REASON THE GAS KILLED THEM.
DO YOU KNOW WHO DID THIS?
THE MIST. NEW NAME IN TOWN.
BODY MADE OF GAS. ONLY HEAD AND ARMS VISIBLE. QUITE A SIGHT.
HENCHMEN?
FOUR OR FIVE.
THAT WAS ALL IT TOOK TO LOOT THE JEWELRY FROM EVERYONE. NO RESISTANCE AFTER ALL.

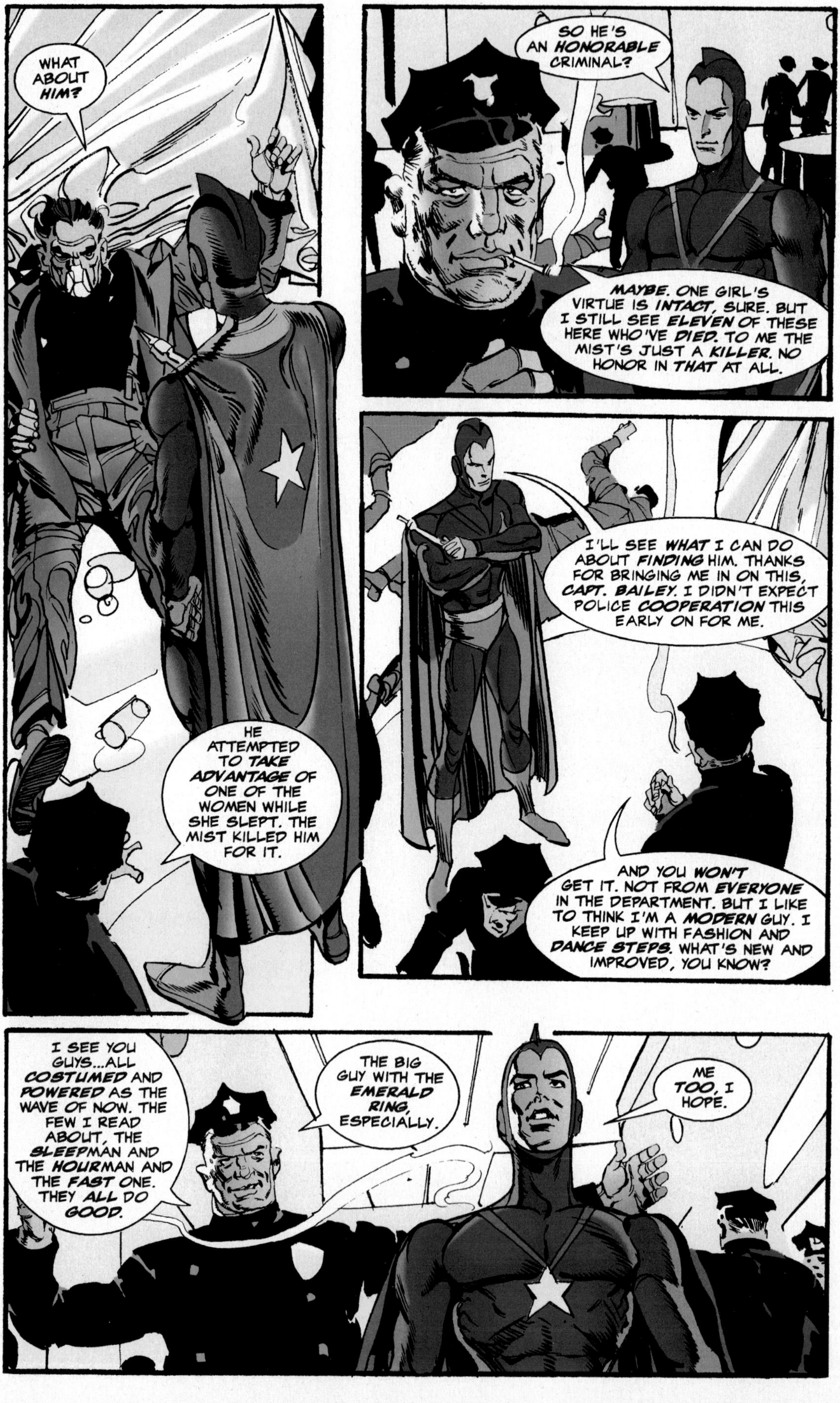
WHAT ABOUT HIM?
HE ATTEMPTED TO TAKE ADVANTAGE OF ONE OF THE WOMEN WHILE SHE SLEPT. THE MIST KILLED HIM FOR IT.
SO HE'S AN HONORABLE CRIMINAL?
MAYBE. ONE GIRL'S VIRTUE IS INTACT, SURE. BUT I STILL SEE ELEVEN OF THESE HERE WHO'VE DIED. TO ME THE MIST'S JUST A KILLER. NO HONOR IN THAT AT ALL.
I'LL SEE WHAT I CAN DO ABOUT FINDING HIM. THANKS FOR BRINGING ME IN ON THIS, CAPT. BAILEY. I DIDN'T EXPECT POLICE COOPERATION THIS EARLY ON FOR ME.
AND YOU WON'T GET IT. NOT FROM EVERYONE IN THE DEPARTMENT. BUT I LIKE TO THINK I'M A MODERN GUY. I KEEP UP WITH FASHION AND DANCE STEPS. WHAT'S NEW AND IMPROVED, YOU KNOW?
I SEE YOU GUYS...ALL COSTUMED AND POWERED AS THE WAVE OF NOW. THE FEW I READ ABOUT, THE SLEEPMAN AND THE HOURMAN AND THE FAST ONE. THEY ALL DO GOOD.
THE BIG GUY WITH THE EMERALD RING, ESPECIALLY.
ME TOO, I HOPE.

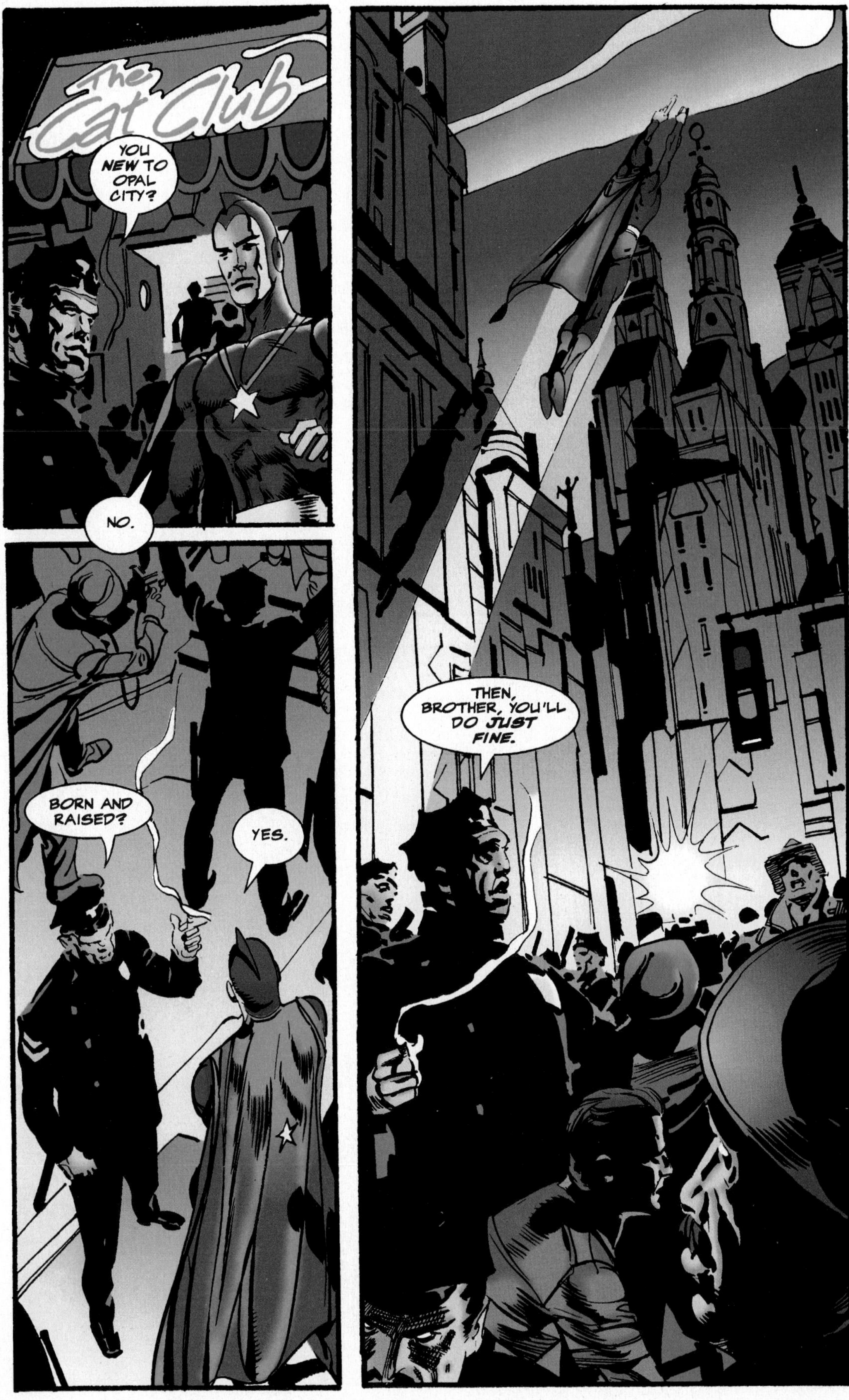
The Cat Club
YOU NEW TO OPAL CITY?
NO.
BORN AND RAISED?
YES.
THEN, BROTHER, YOU'LL DO JUST FINE.

IS *THIS* WHAT MY LIFE SHALL *BE?*

WHAT?

NOTHING. THINKING ALOUD. KEEP SORTING THE LOOT.

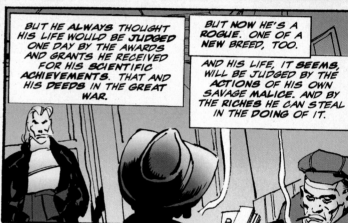

BUT HE ALWAYS THOUGHT HIS LIFE WOULD BE JUDGED ONE DAY BY THE AWARDS AND GRANTS HE RECEIVED FOR HIS SCIENTIFIC ACHIEVEMENTS. THAT AND HIS DEEDS IN THE GREAT WAR.

BUT NOW HE'S A ROGUE. ONE OF A NEW BREED, TOO.

AND HIS LIFE, IT *SEEMS*, WILL BE JUDGED BY THE ACTIONS OF HIS OWN SAVAGE MALICE. AND BY THE RICHES HE CAN STEAL IN THE DOING OF IT.

"IS THIS MY LIFE TO BE?"

HE THINKS IT THIS TIME. IF HIS THOUGHTS WERE *KNOWN*, THEY MIGHT BE PERCEIVED BY HIS MEN AS *WEAKNESS*. AND HE IS FAR FROM WEAK.

I'M A VILLAIN.

err...

...YEAH, WE *KNOW*, BOSS.

I'M *NOT* SURE THAT *I* DID.

NOT UNTIL *THIS* MOMENT, ANYWAY.

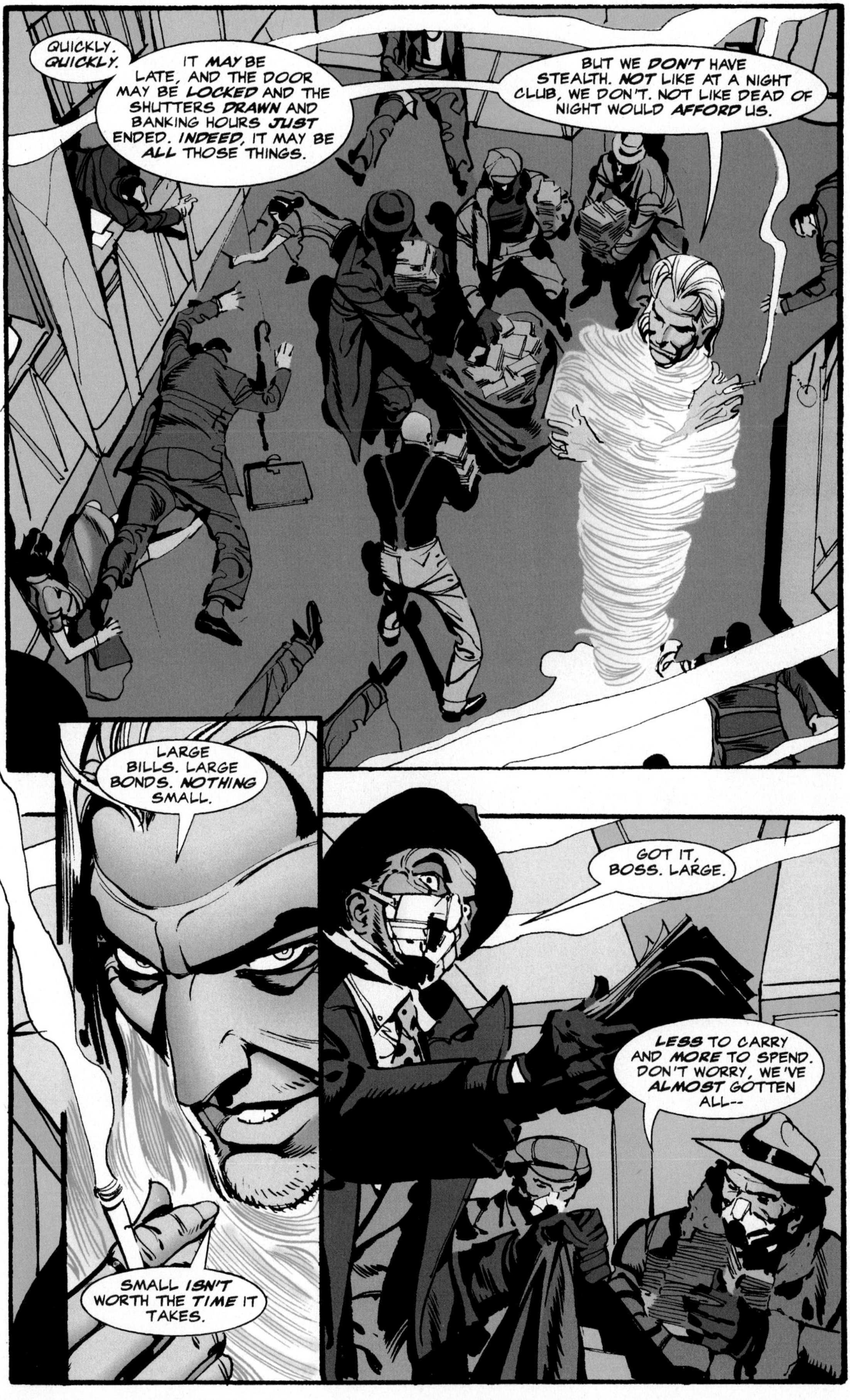
QUICKLY. QUICKLY.
IT MAY BE LATE, AND THE DOOR MAY BE LOCKED AND THE SHUTTERS DRAWN AND BANKING HOURS JUST ENDED. INDEED, IT MAY BE ALL THOSE THINGS.
BUT WE DON'T HAVE STEALTH. NOT LIKE AT A NIGHT CLUB, WE DON'T. NOT LIKE DEAD OF NIGHT WOULD AFFORD US.
LARGE BILLS. LARGE BONDS. NOTHING SMALL.
SMALL ISN'T WORTH THE TIME IT TAKES.
GOT IT, BOSS. LARGE.
LESS TO CARRY AND MORE TO SPEND. DON'T WORRY, WE'VE ALMOST GOTTEN ALL--

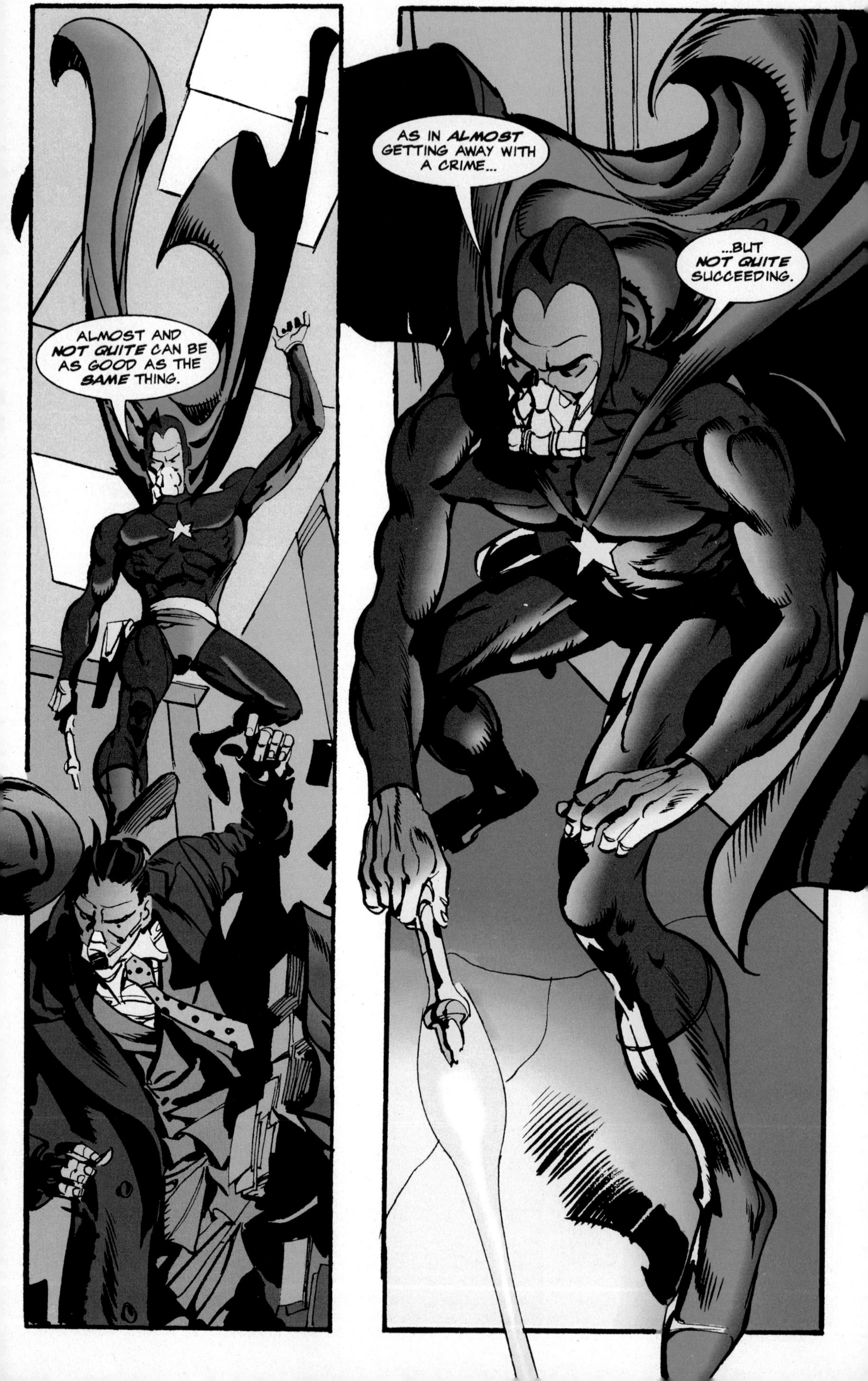
ALMOST AND NOT QUITE CAN BE AS GOOD AS THE SAME THING.
AS IN ALMOST GETTING AWAY WITH A CRIME...
...BUT NOT QUITE SUCCEEDING.

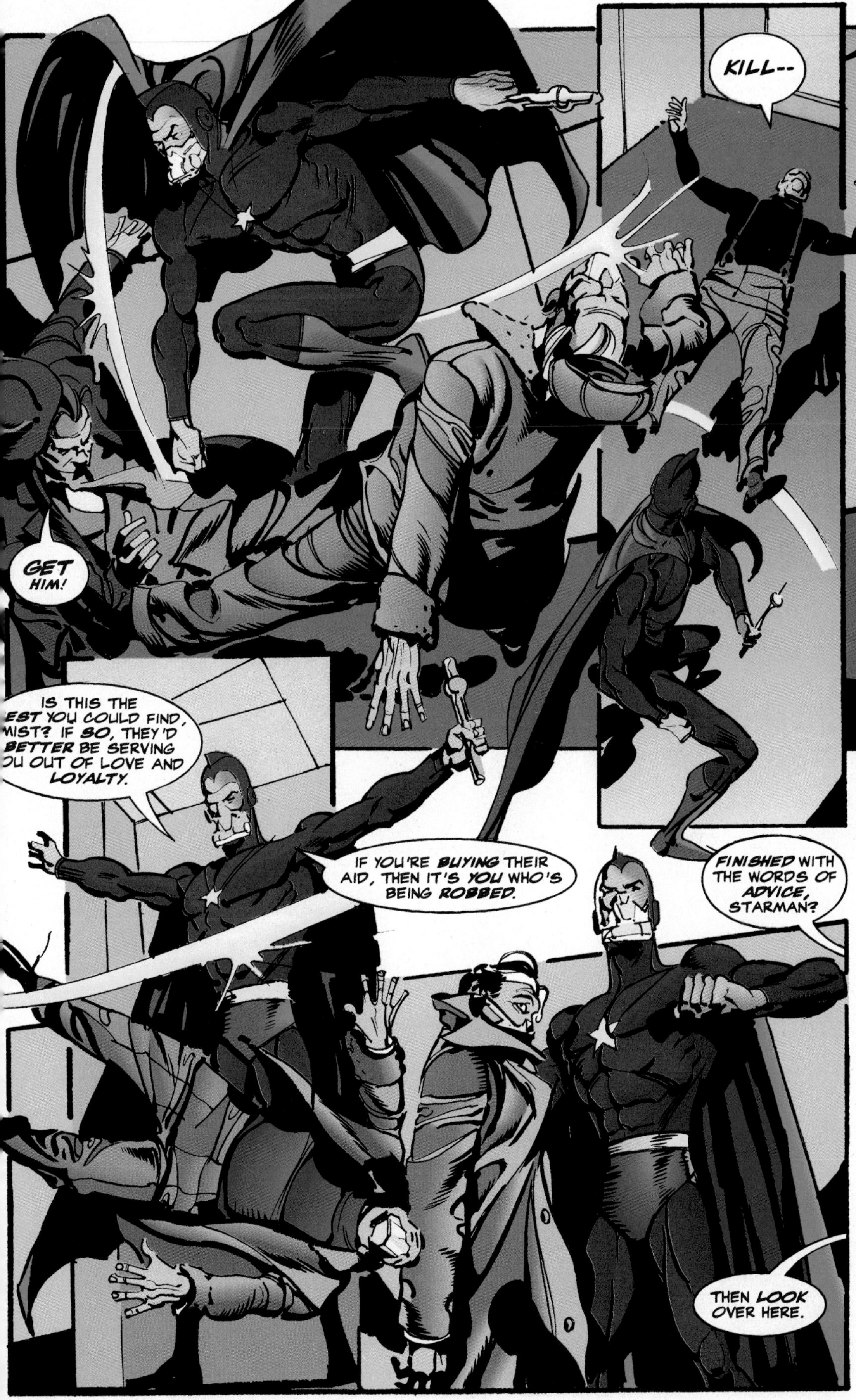
GET HIM!
KILL--
IS THIS THE EST YOU COULD FIND, MIST? IF SO, THEY'D BETTER BE SERVING OU OUT OF LOVE AND LOYALTY.
IF YOU'RE BUYING THEIR AID, THEN IT'S YOU WHO'S BEING ROBBED.
FINISHED WITH THE WORDS OF ADVICE, STARMAN?
THEN LOOK OVER HERE.

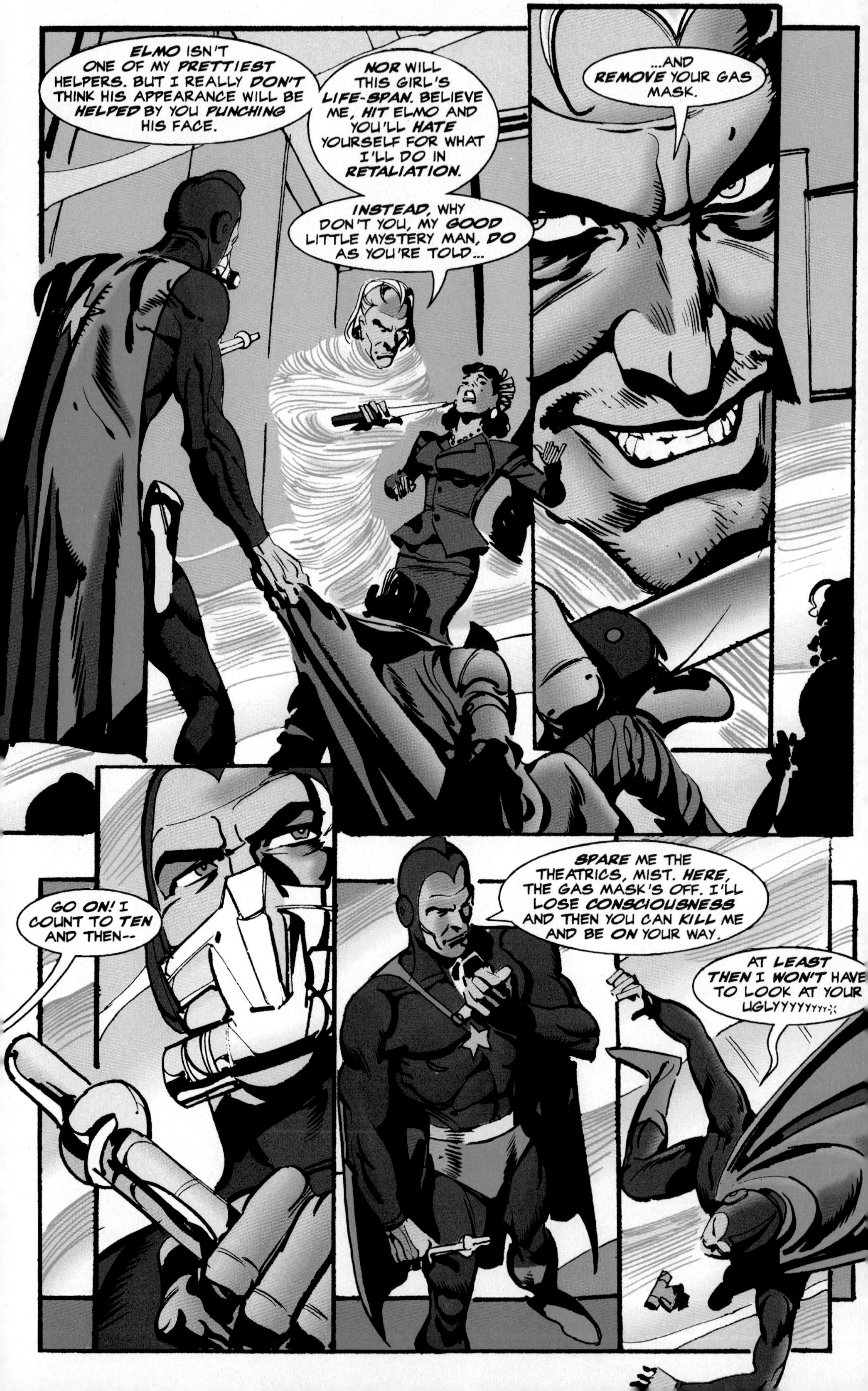
ELMO ISN'T ONE OF MY PRETTIEST HELPERS. BUT I REALLY DON'T THINK HIS APPEARANCE WILL BE HELPED BY YOU PUNCHING HIS FACE.
NOR WILL THIS GIRL'S LIFE-SPAN. BELIEVE ME, HIT ELMO AND YOU'LL HATE YOURSELF FOR WHAT I'LL DO IN RETALIATION.
INSTEAD, WHY DON'T YOU, MY GOOD LITTLE MYSTERY MAN, DO AS YOU'RE TOLD...
...AND REMOVE YOUR GAS MASK.
GO ON! I COUNT TO TEN AND THEN--
SPARE ME THE THEATRICS, MIST. HERE, THE GAS MASK'S OFF. I'LL LOSE CONSCIOUSNESS AND THEN YOU CAN KILL ME AND BE ON YOUR WAY.
AT LEAST THEN I WON'T HAVE TO LOOK AT YOUR UGLYYYYYYYY

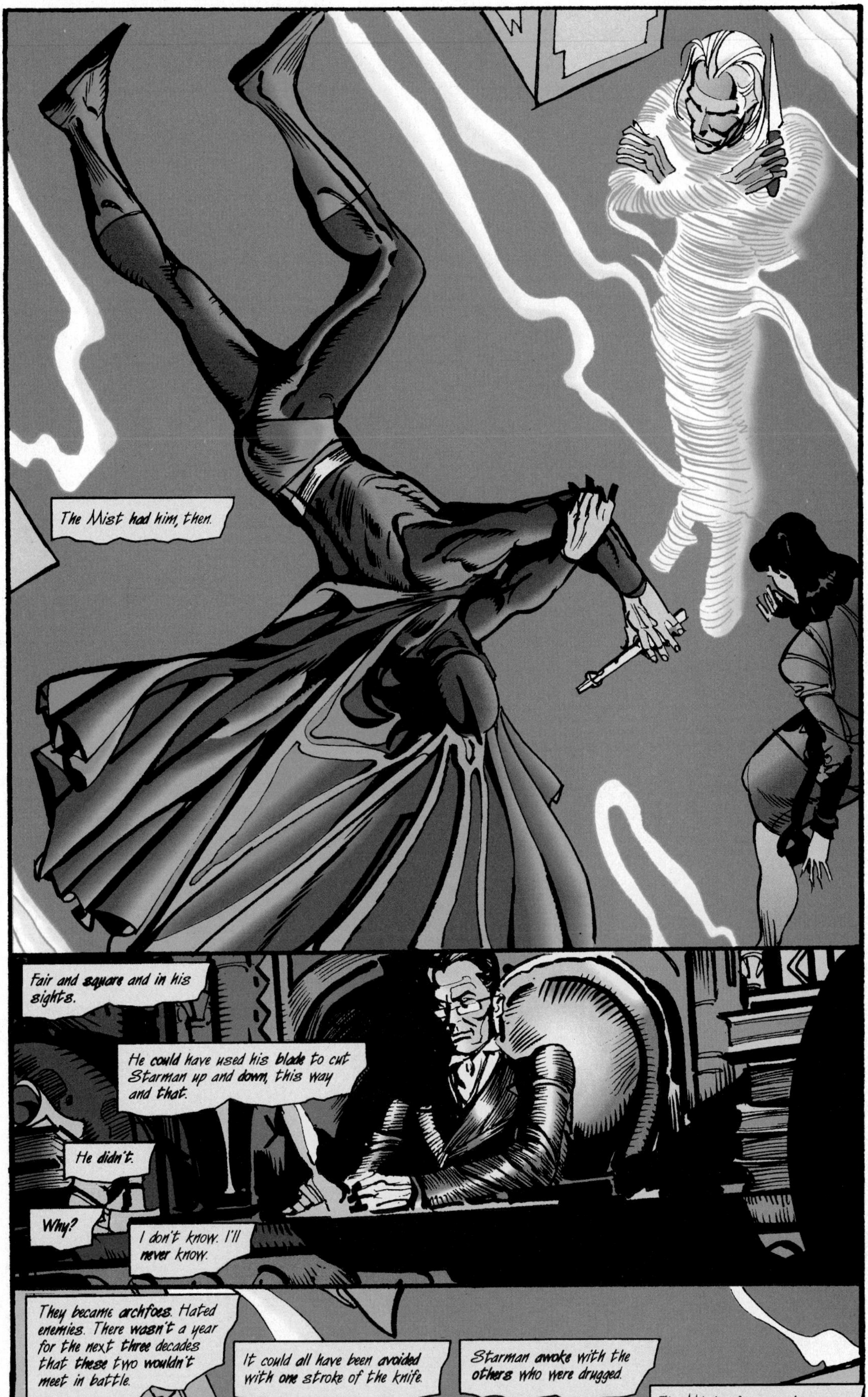

The Mist had him, then.
Fair and square and in his sights.
He could have used his blade to cut Starman up and down, this way and that.
He didn't.
Why?
I don't know. I'll never know.
They became archfoes. Hated enemies. There wasn't a year for the next three decades that these two wouldn't meet in battle.
It could all have been avoided with one stroke of the knife.
Starman awoke with the others who were drugged.
The Mist, of course, long gone.

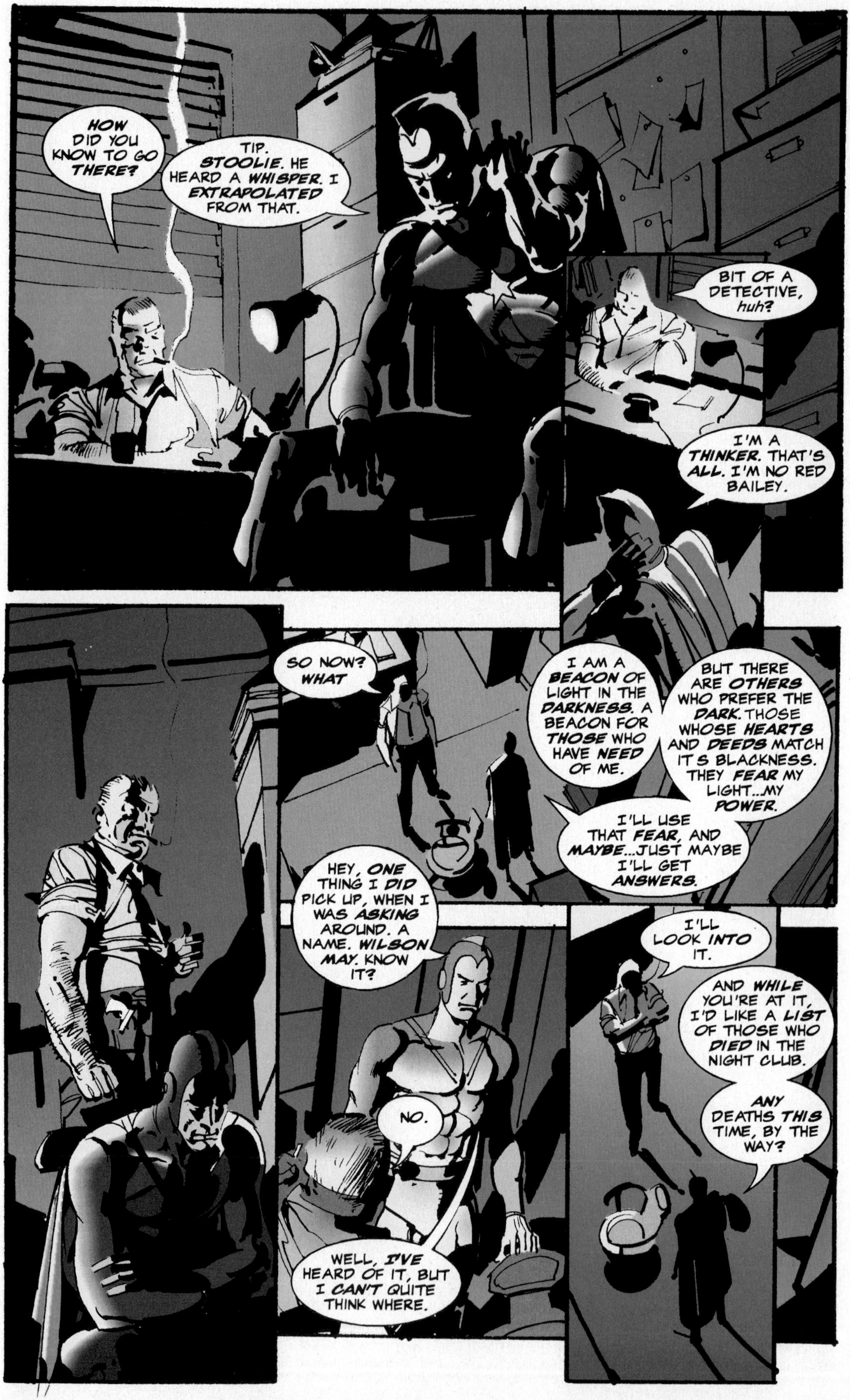
HOW DID YOU KNOW TO GO THERE?
TIP. STOOLIE. HE HEARD A WHISPER. I EXTRAPOLATED FROM THAT.
BIT OF A DETECTIVE, huh?
I'M A THINKER. THAT'S ALL. I'M NO RED BAILEY.
SO NOW? WHAT
I AM A BEACON OF LIGHT IN THE DARKNESS. A BEACON FOR THOSE WHO HAVE NEED OF ME.
BUT THERE ARE OTHERS WHO PREFER THE DARK. THOSE WHOSE HEARTS AND DEEDS MATCH IT'S BLACKNESS. THEY FEAR MY LIGHT...MY POWER.
I'LL USE THAT FEAR, AND MAYBE...JUST MAYBE I'LL GET ANSWERS.
HEY, ONE THING I DID PICK UP, WHEN I WAS ASKING AROUND. A NAME. WILSON MAY. KNOW IT?
NO.
WELL, I'VE HEARD OF IT, BUT I CAN'T QUITE THINK WHERE.
I'LL LOOK INTO IT.
AND WHILE YOU'RE AT IT, I'D LIKE A LIST OF THOSE WHO DIED IN THE NIGHT CLUB.
ANY DEATHS THIS TIME, BY THE WAY?

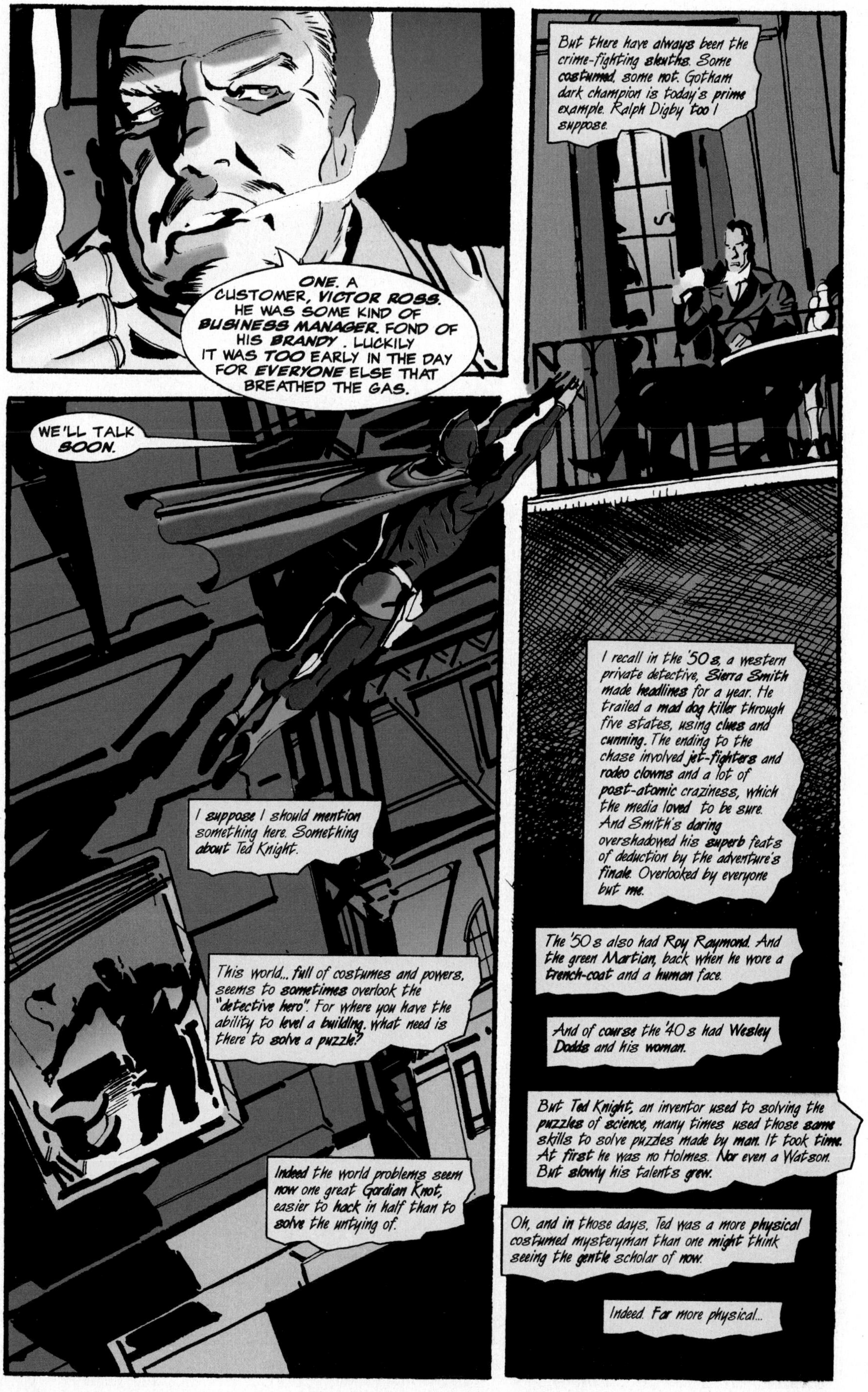
ONE. A CUSTOMER, VICTOR ROSS. HE WAS SOME KIND OF BUSINESS MANAGER. FOND OF HIS BRANDY . LUCKILY IT WAS TOO EARLY IN THE DAY FOR EVERYONE ELSE THAT BREATHED THE GAS.
But there have always been the crime-fighting sleuths. Some costumed, some not. Gotham dark champion is today's prime example. Ralph Digby too I suppose.
WE'LL TALK SOON.
I suppose I should mention something here. Something about Ted Knight.
This world... full of costumes and powers, seems to sometimes overlook the "detective hero". For where you have the ability to level a building, what need is there to solve a puzzle?
Indeed the world problems seem now one great Gordian Knot, easier to hack in half than to solve the untying of.
I recall in the '50 s, a western private detective, Sierra Smith made headlines for a year. He trailed a mad dog killer through five states, using clues and cunning. The ending to the chase involved jet-fighters and rodeo clowns and a lot of post-atomic craziness, which the media loved to be sure. And Smith's daring overshadowed his superb feats of deduction by the adventure's finale. Overlooked by everyone but me.
The '50 s also had Roy Raymond. And the green Martian, back when he wore a trench-coat and a human face.
And of course the '40 s had Wesley Dodds and his woman.
But Ted Knight, an inventor used to solving the puzzles of science, many times used those same skills to solve puzzles made by man. It took time. At first he was no Holmes. Nor even a Watson. But slowly his talents grew.
Oh, and in those days, Ted was a more physical costumed mysteryman than one might think seeing the gentle scholar of now.
Indeed. Far more physical...

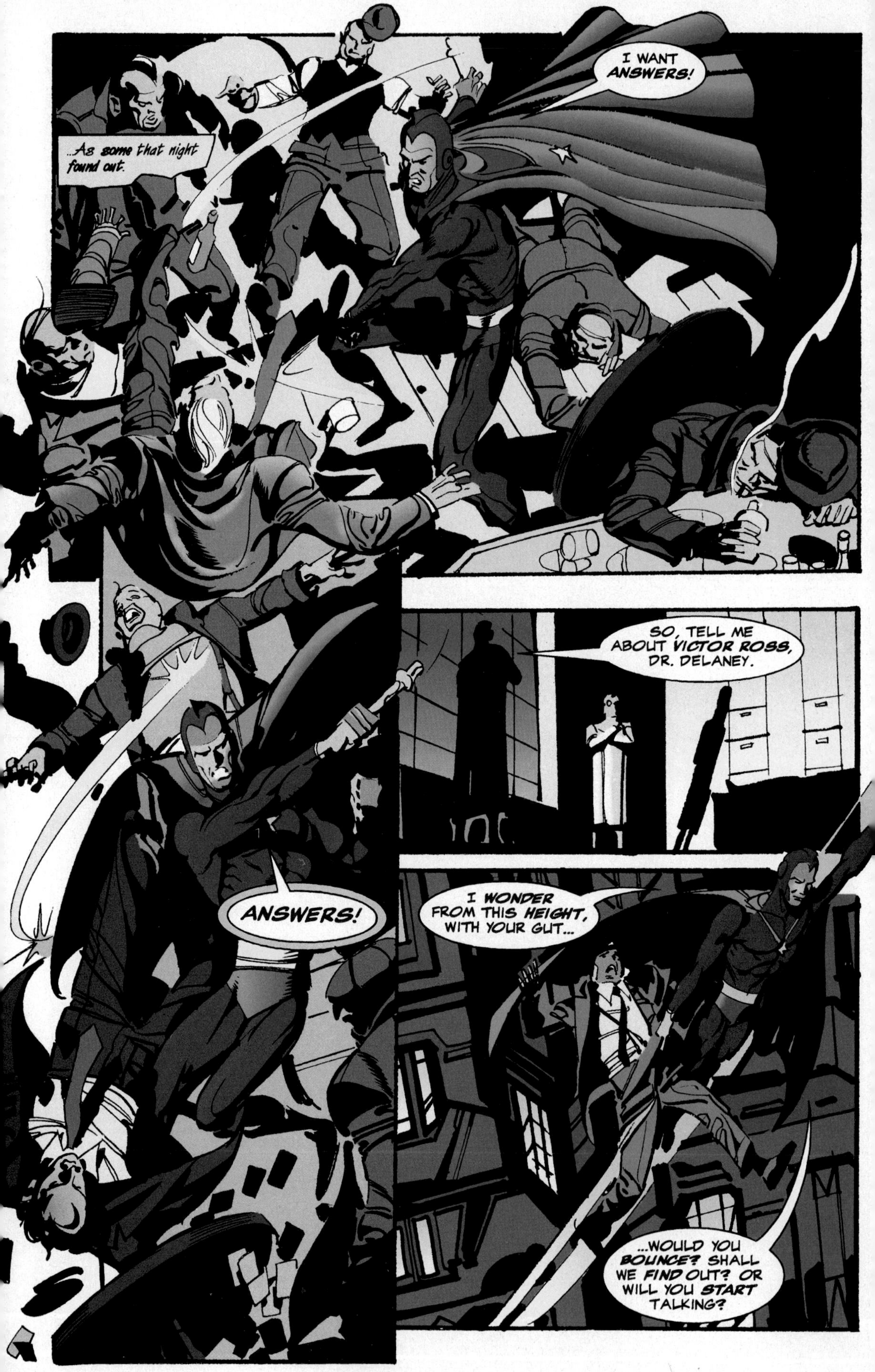

...As some that night found out.
I WANT ANSWERS!
ANSWERS!
SO, TELL ME ABOUT VICTOR ROSS, DR. DELANEY.
I WONDER FROM THIS HEIGHT, WITH YOUR GUT...
...WOULD YOU BOUNCE? SHALL WE FIND OUT? OR WILL YOU START TALKING?

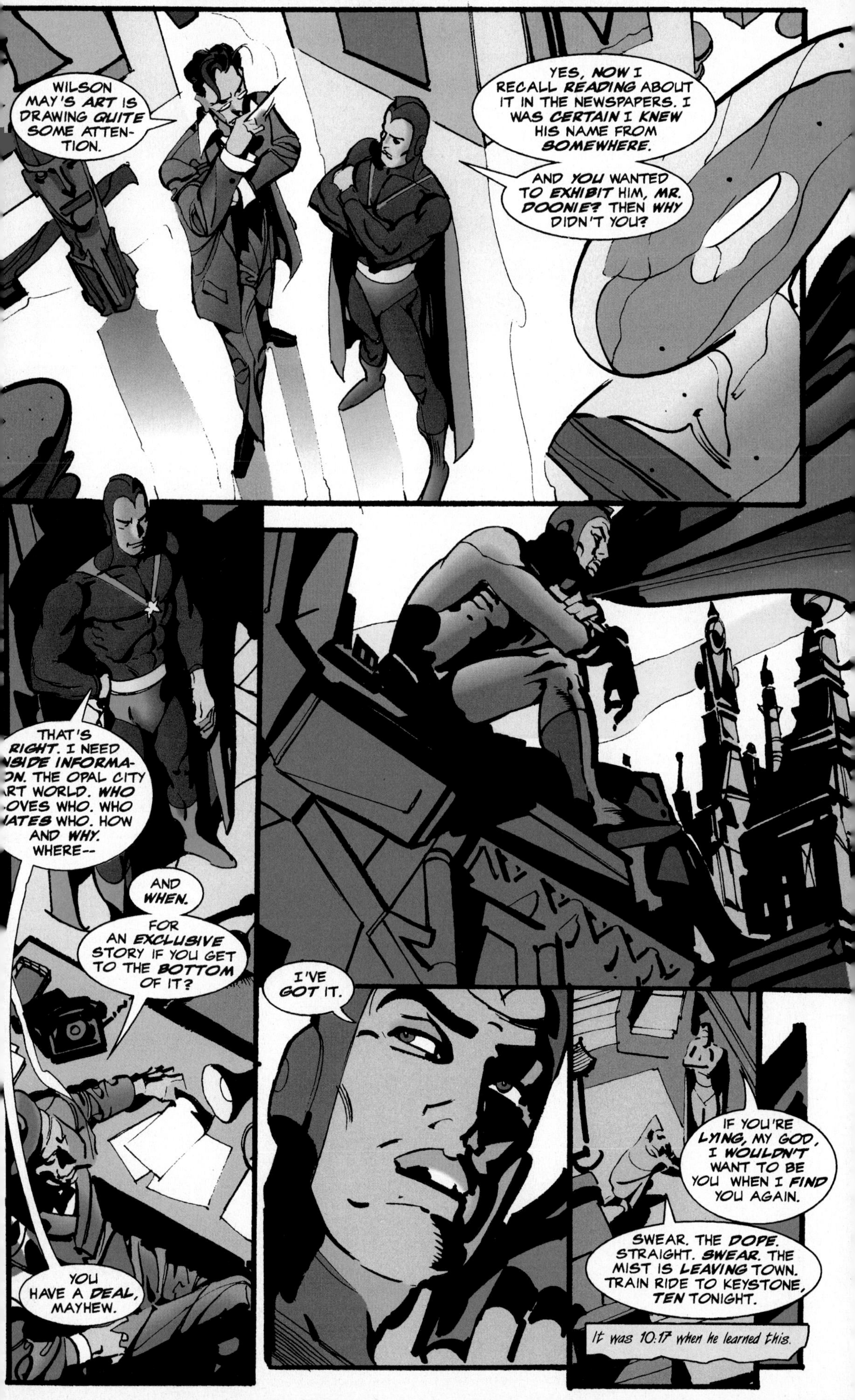
WILSON MAY'S ART IS DRAWING QUITE SOME ATTENTION.
YES, NOW I RECALL READING ABOUT IT IN THE NEWSPAPERS. I WAS CERTAIN I KNEW HIS NAME FROM SOMEWHERE.
AND YOU WANTED TO EXHIBIT HIM, MR. DOONIE? THEN WHY DIDN'T YOU?
THAT'S RIGHT. I NEED INSIDE INFORMATION. THE OPAL CITY ART WORLD. WHO LOVES WHO. WHO HATES WHO. HOW AND WHY. WHERE--
AND WHEN.
FOR AN EXCLUSIVE STORY IF YOU GET TO THE BOTTOM OF IT?
YOU HAVE A DEAL, MAYHEW.
I'VE GOT IT.
IF YOU'RE LYING, MY GOD, I WOULDN'T WANT TO BE YOU WHEN I FIND YOU AGAIN.
SWEAR. THE DOPE. STRAIGHT. SWEAR. THE MIST IS LEAVING TOWN. TRAIN RIDE TO KEYSTONE, TEN TONIGHT.
It was 10:17 when he learned this.

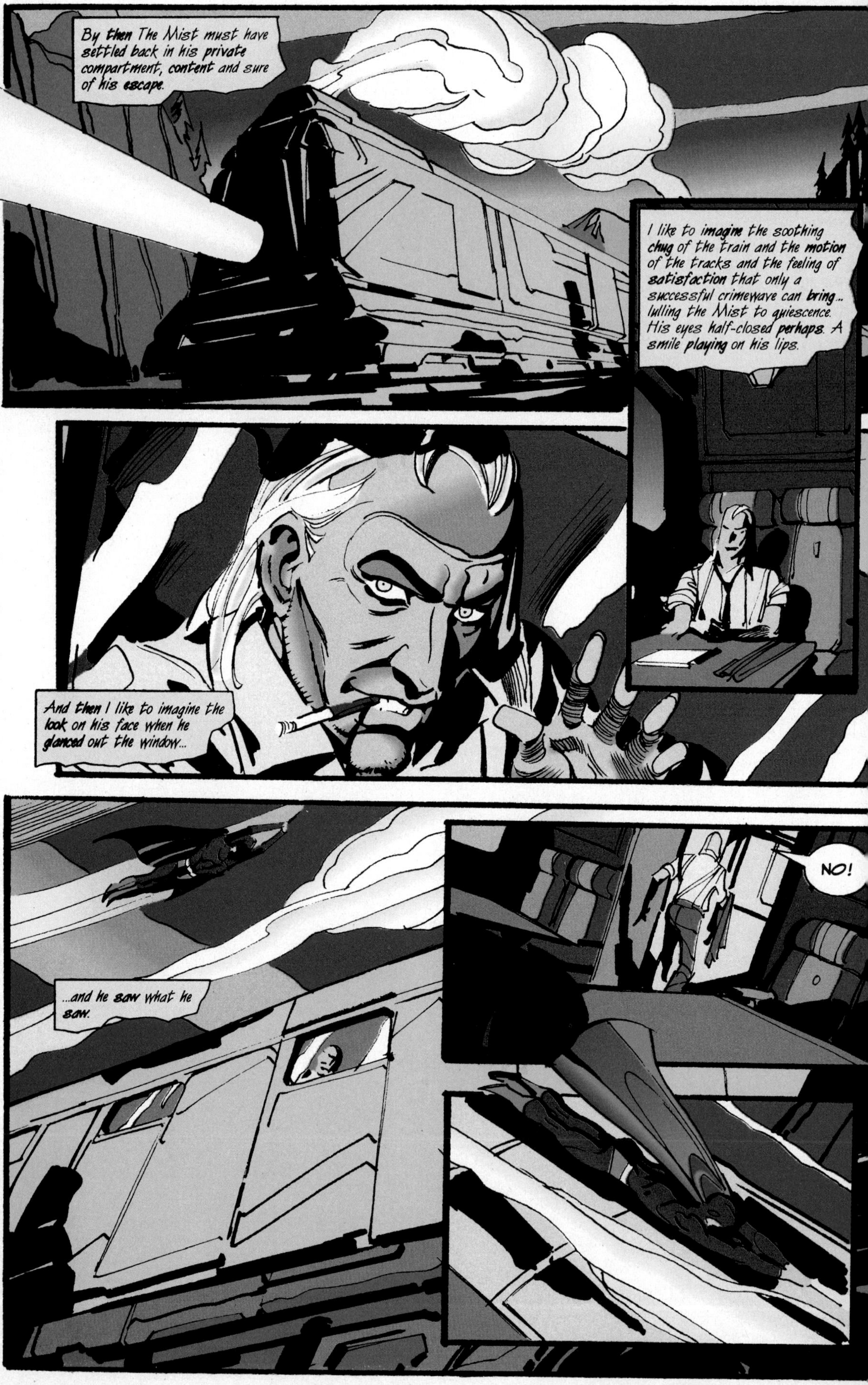

By then The Mist must have settled back in his private compartment, content and sure of his escape.
I like to imagine the soothing chug of the train and the motion of the tracks and the feeling of satisfaction that only a successful crimewave can bring... lulling the Mist to quiescence. His eyes half-closed perhaps. A smile playing on his lips.
And then I like to imagine the look on his face when he glanced out the window...
...and he saw what he saw.
NO!

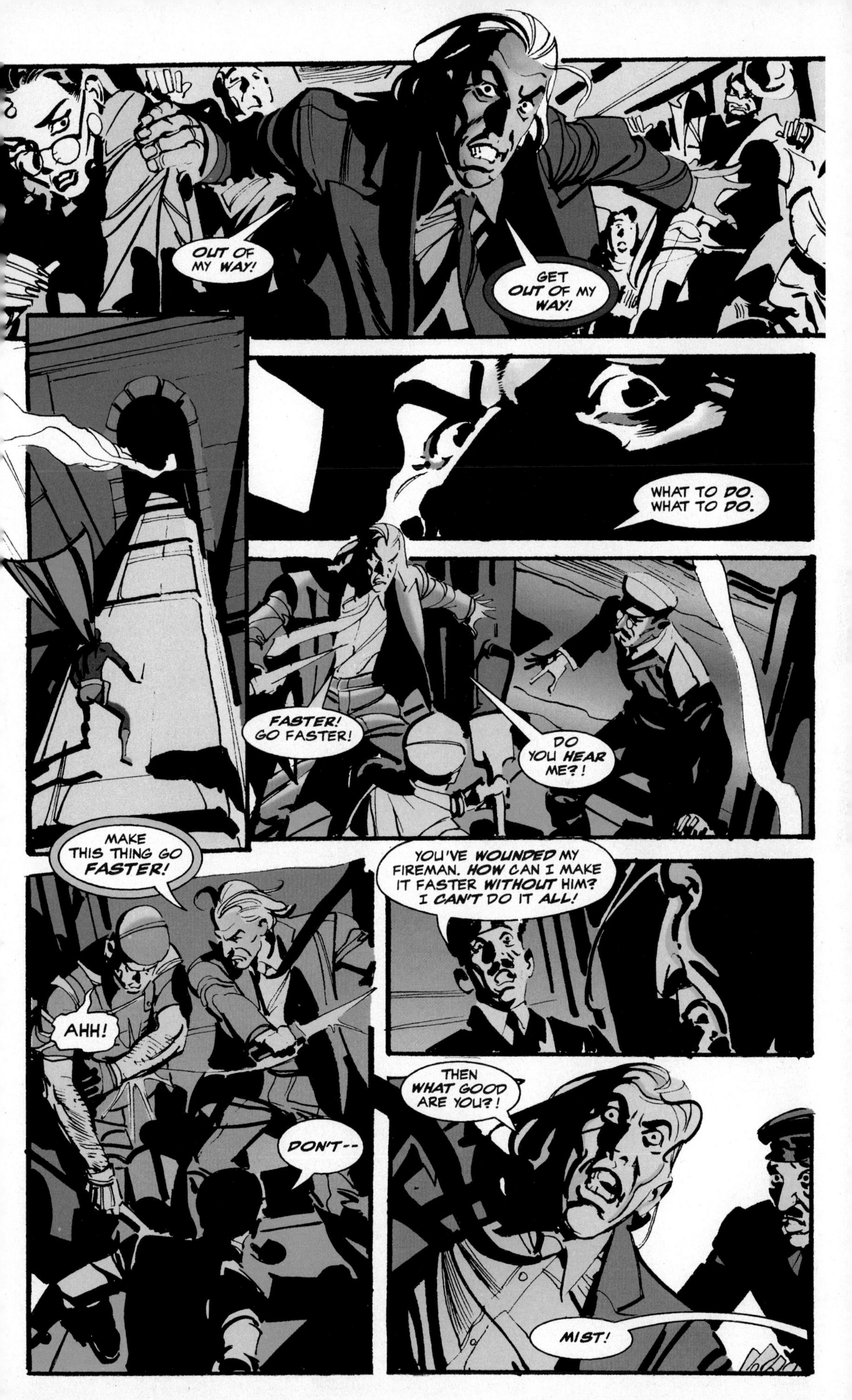
OUT OF MY WAY!
GET OUT OF MY WAY!
WHAT TO DO. WHAT TO DO.
FASTER! GO FASTER!
DO YOU HEAR ME?!
MAKE THIS THING GO FASTER!
AHH!
DON'T--
YOU'VE WOUNDED MY FIREMAN. HOW CAN I MAKE IT FASTER WITHOUT HIM? I CAN'T DO IT ALL!
THEN WHAT GOOD ARE YOU?!
MIST!

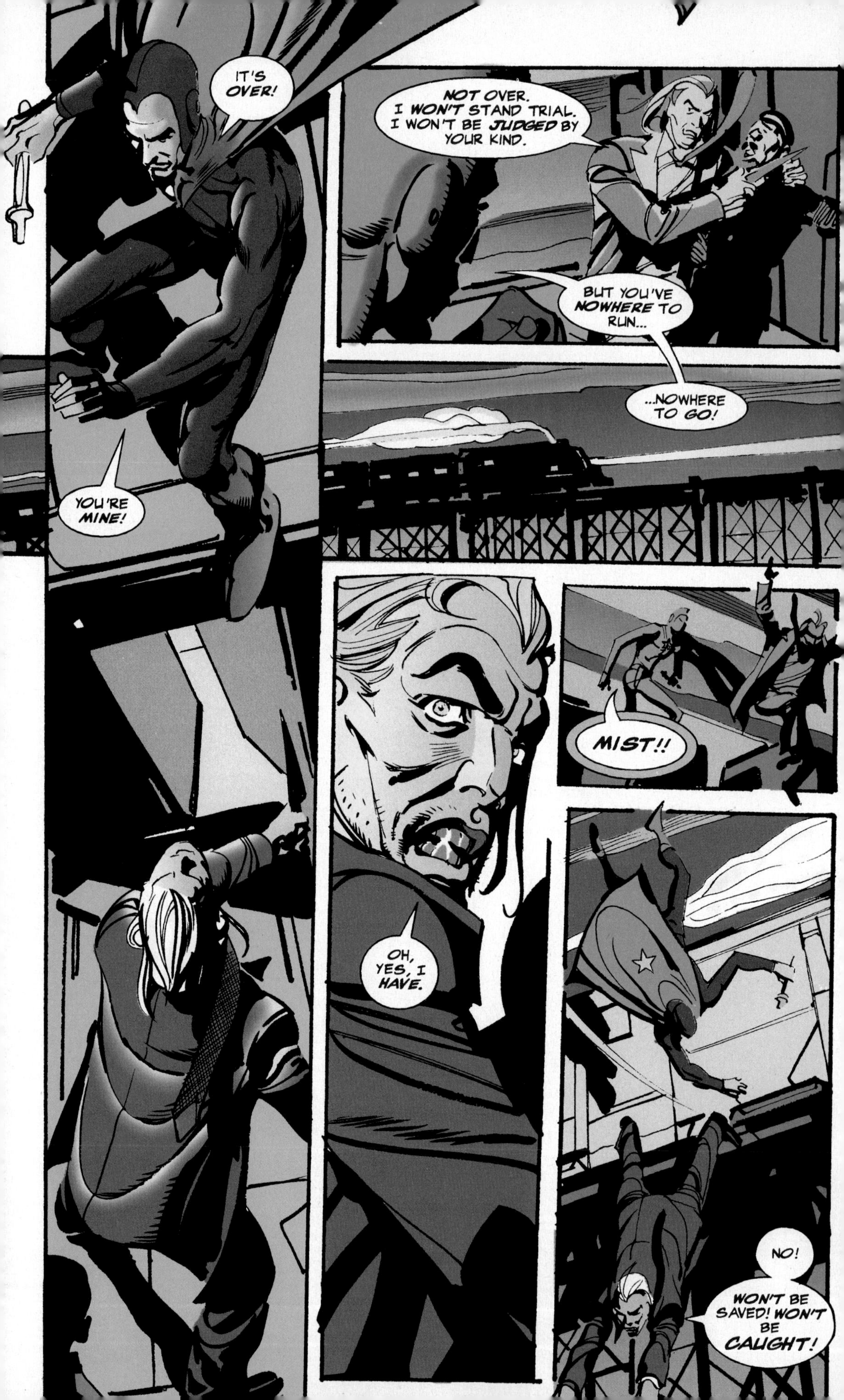
IT'S OVER!
NOT OVER. I WON'T STAND TRIAL. I WON'T BE JUDGED BY YOUR KIND.
BUT YOU'VE NOWHERE TO RUN...
...NOWHERE TO GO!
YOU'RE MINE!
MIST!!
OH, YES, I HAVE.
NO!
WON'T BE SAVED! WON'T BE CAUGHT!

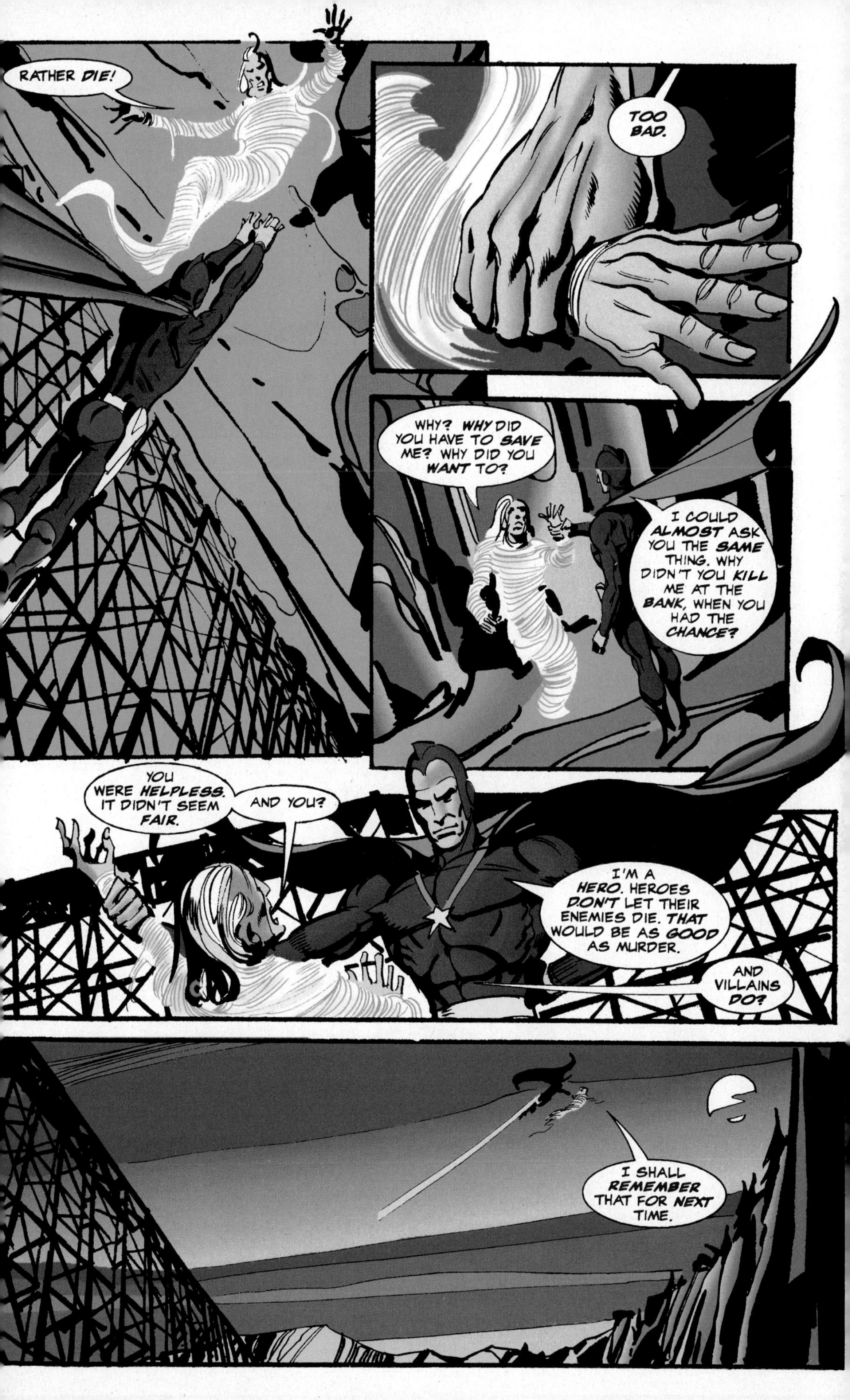
RATHER DIE!
TOO BAD.
WHY? WHY DID YOU HAVE TO SAVE ME? WHY DID YOU WANT TO?
I COULD ALMOST ASK YOU THE SAME THING. WHY DIDN'T YOU KILL ME AT THE BANK, WHEN YOU HAD THE CHANCE?
YOU WERE HELPLESS. IT DIDN'T SEEM FAIR.
AND YOU?
I'M A HERO. HEROES DON'T LET THEIR ENEMIES DIE. THAT WOULD BE AS GOOD AS MURDER.
AND VILLAINS DO?
I SHALL REMEMBER THAT FOR NEXT TIME.

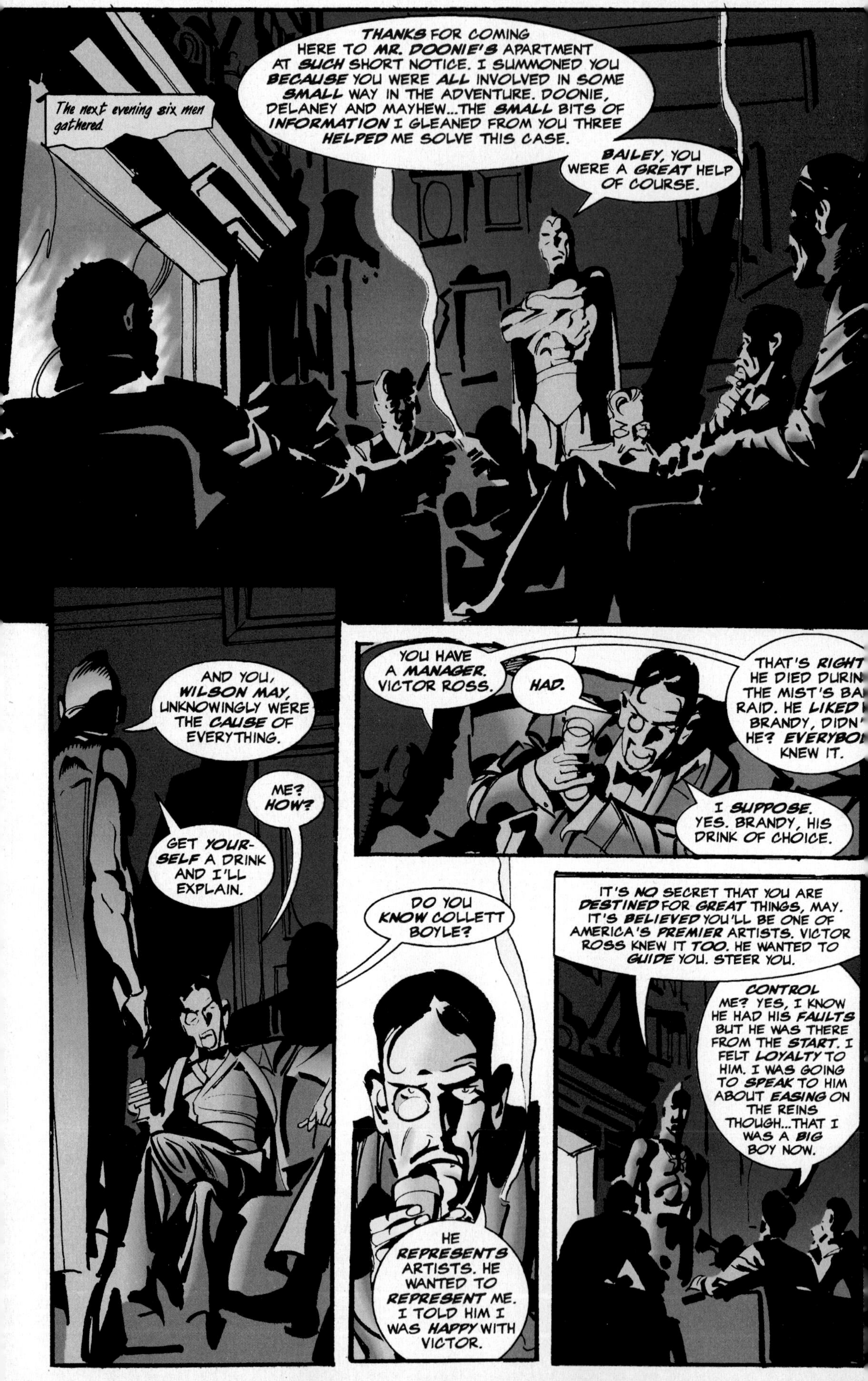

The next evening six men gathered.
THANKS FOR COMING HERE TO MR. DOONIE'S APARTMENT AT SUCH SHORT NOTICE. I SUMMONED YOU BECAUSE YOU WERE ALL INVOLVED IN SOME SMALL WAY IN THE ADVENTURE. DOONIE, DELANEY AND MAYHEW...THE SMALL BITS OF INFORMATION I GLEANED FROM YOU THREE HELPED ME SOLVE THIS CASE.
BAILEY, YOU WERE A GREAT HELP OF COURSE.
AND YOU, WILSON MAY, UNKNOWINGLY WERE THE CAUSE OF EVERYTHING.
ME? HOW?
GET YOURSELF A DRINK AND I'LL EXPLAIN.
YOU HAVE A MANAGER. VICTOR ROSS.
HAD.
I SUPPOSE. YES. BRANDY, HIS DRINK OF CHOICE.
DO YOU KNOW COLLETT BOYLE?
HE REPRESENTS ARTISTS. HE WANTED TO REPRESENT ME. I TOLD HIM I WAS HAPPY WITH VICTOR.
IT'S NO SECRET THAT YOU ARE DESTINED FOR GREAT THINGS, MAY. IT'S BELIEVED YOU'LL BE ONE OF AMERICA'S PREMIER ARTISTS. VICTOR ROSS KNEW IT TOO. HE WANTED TO GUIDE YOU. STEER YOU.
CONTROL ME? YES, I KNOW HE HAD HIS FAULTS BUT HE WAS THERE FROM THE START. I FELT LOYALTY TO HIM. I WAS GOING TO SPEAK TO HIM ABOUT EASING ON THE REINS THOUGH...THAT I WAS A BIG BOY NOW.

VICTOR SAID *NO*. HE SAID I WAS ALREADY *TOO BIG* FOR DOONIE'S GALLERY.

NO OFFENSE, BILL.

DOONIE WANTED TO EXHIBIT *YOU*.

NONE TAKEN.

AND YOU, DOONIE, OFFERED BOYLE A *SMALL* BONUS IF HE *WOOED* WILSON FROM VICTOR ROSS AND ALLOWED WILSON TO EXHIBIT WITH YOU.

YES. I SEE WILSON'S GRAND *FUTURE*, TOO. I WANTED TO BE A *PART* OF THAT.

YOU MAY HAVE BEEN THE *CATALYST*, UNKNOWINGLY. THOUGH PERHAPS BOYLE WOULD HAVE *DONE* WHAT HE DID *ANYWAY*. WHO KNOWS *WHAT DRIVES SOME MEN?*

WHAT HE DID?

HIRE THE MIST, TO *CREATE* A GAS COMPOUND THAT WOULD BE *HARMLESS* TO EVERYONE... EXCEPT *BRANDY DRINKERS*.

LIKE VICTOR.

THE MIST'S CRIME WAVE WAS A *RUSE?*

A SMOKE SCREEN, *EXCUSE* THE PUN? *NO*. HIS CRIMES WERE CRIMES. HE MADE A SMALL *FORTUNE* FROM THEM. BUT HE *ALSO* GOT A PAYMENT FROM COLLETT BOYLE FOR STRIKING AT A BANK WHERE BOYLE *KNEW* VICTOR ROSS WOULD *BE*.

I *KNOW* IT'S FANTASTIC, BUT THE MIST *EXPLAINED* THE *WHOLE* THING TO US. WE ARRESTED BOYLE WHO *CONFIRMED* IT.

ANYWAY, I HAVE ONE MORE SURPRISE FOR YOU. IT'S A *CAR-RIDE* AWAY BUT I *THOUGHT* YOU ALL MIGHT FIND IT INTERESTING.

THE MIST HAD A FEW *DIFFERENT* HIDEOUTS ACROSS TOWN, BUT HE *ALSO* HAD ONE TRUE *LAIR*, WHERE ALL HIS *DEVICES* AND *INVENTIONS* ARE. IF YOU'RE *INTERESTED* AT ALL IN THINGS THAT ARE JUST PLAIN *BIZARRE*, THIS IS A PLACE TO SEE.

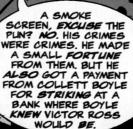

SOUNDS GREAT!

YEAH.

WHEN DO WE *LEAVE?*

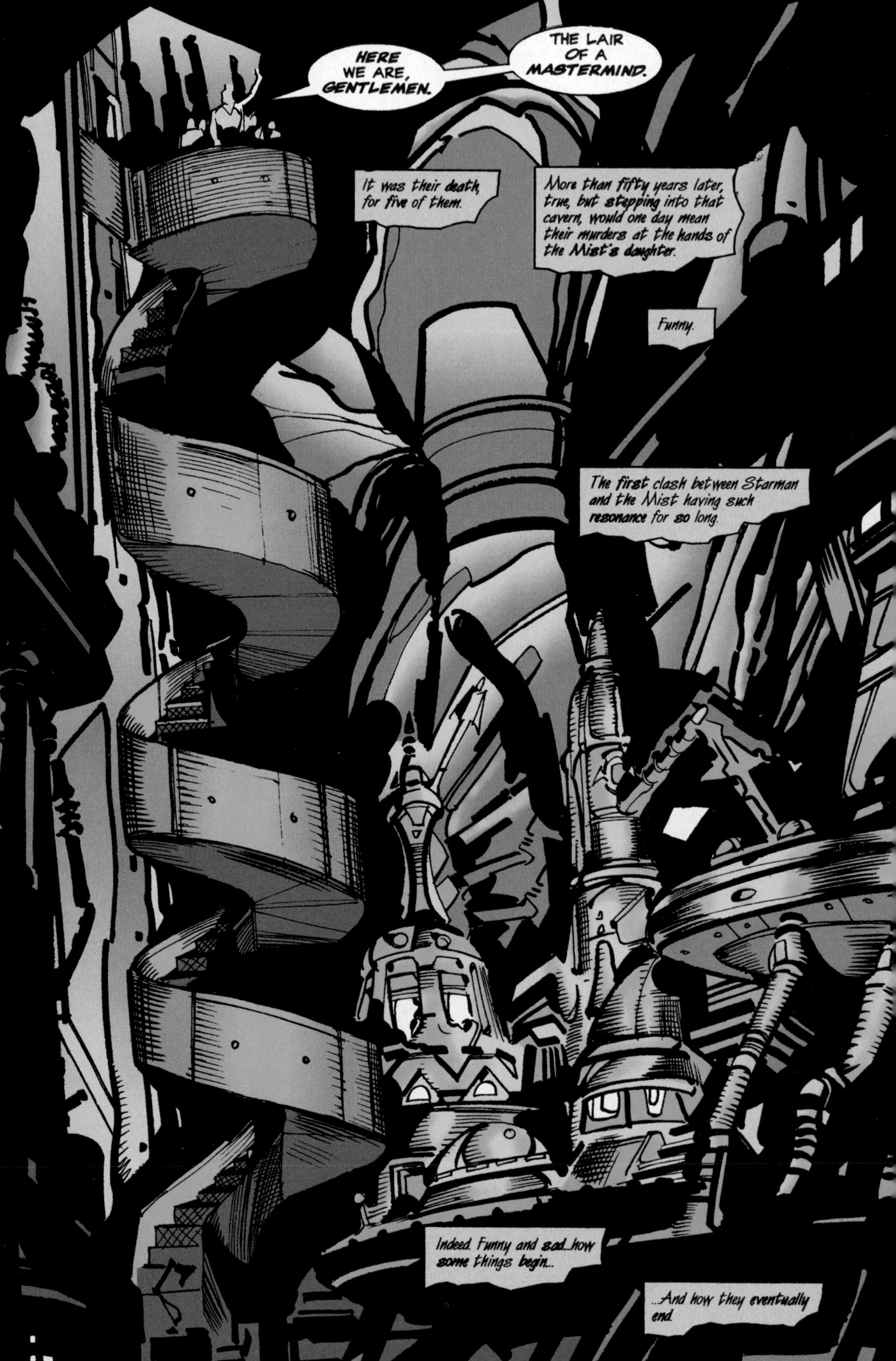
HERE WE ARE, GENTLEMEN.
THE LAIR OF A MASTERMIND.
It was their death, for five of them.
More than fifty years later, true, but stepping into that cavern, would one day mean their murders at the hands of the Mist's daughter.
Funny.
The first clash between Starman and the Mist having such resonance for so long.
Indeed. Funny and sad...how some things begin...
...And how they eventually end.

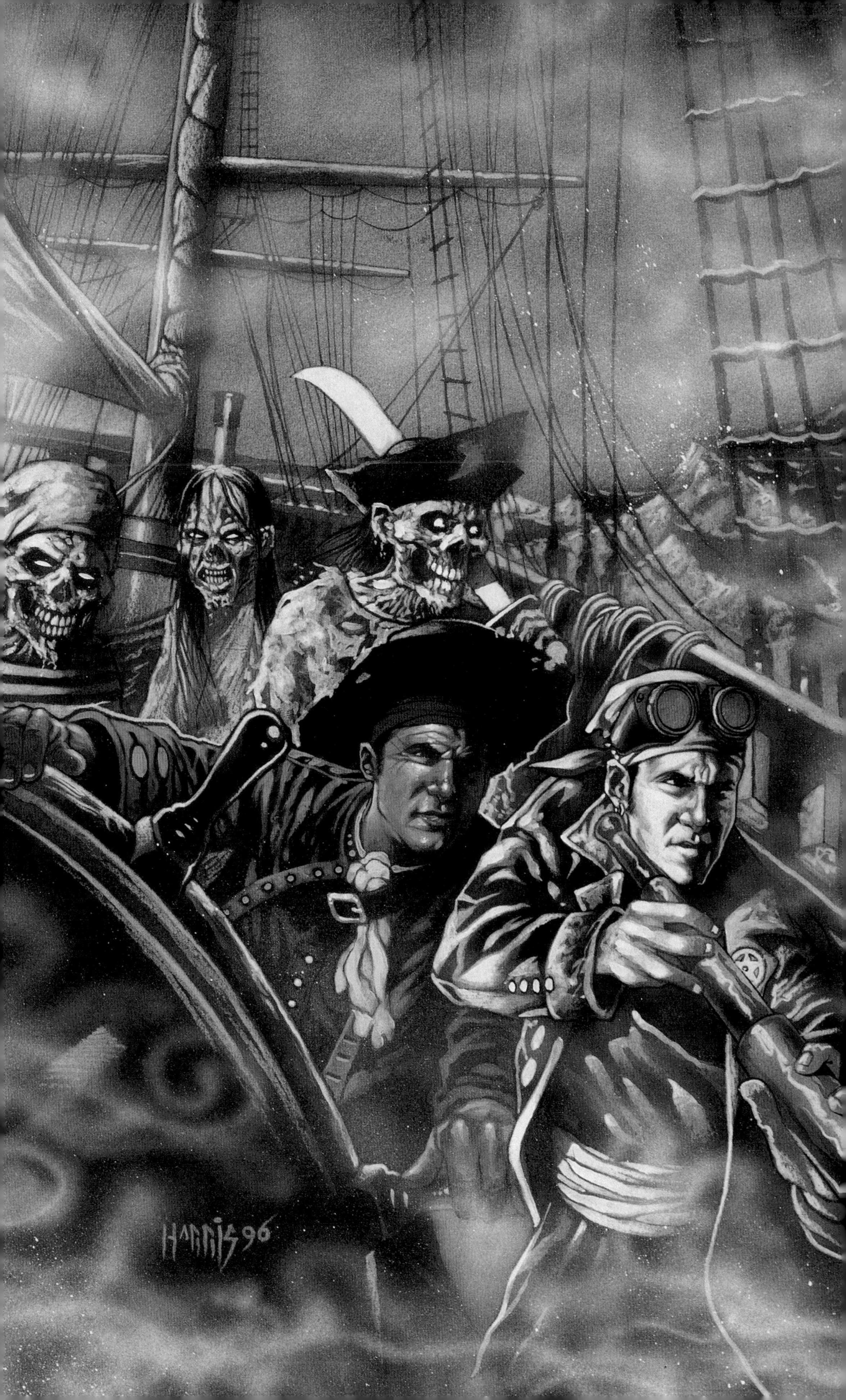
HARRIS 96

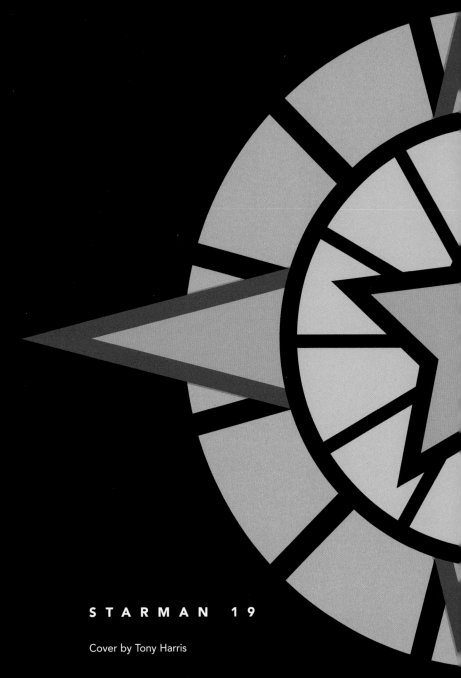

STARMAN 19

Cover by Tony Harris

Written by James Robinson

Pencils by Tony Harris

with inks by Wade von Grawbadger

and colors by Gregory Wright

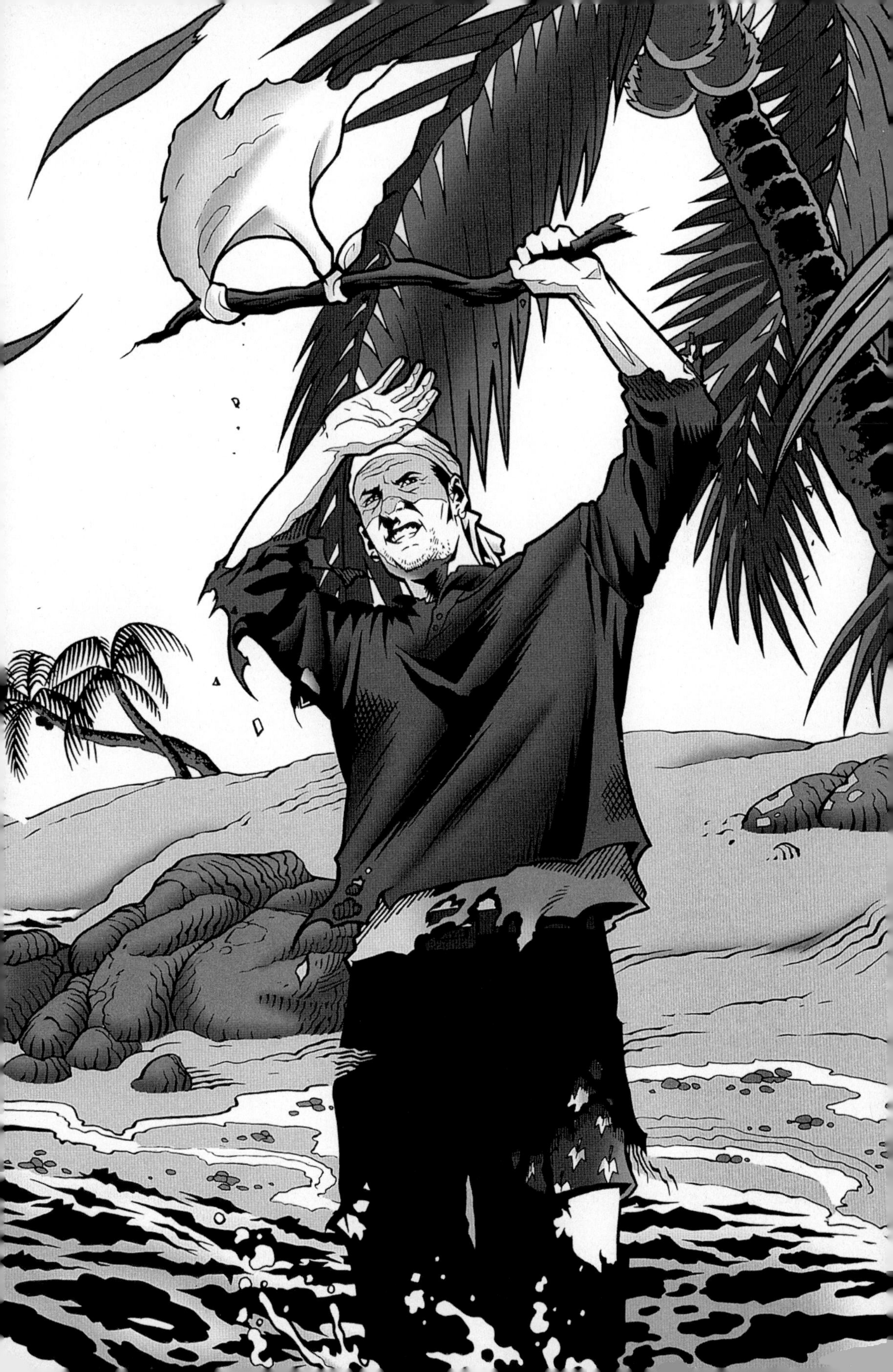

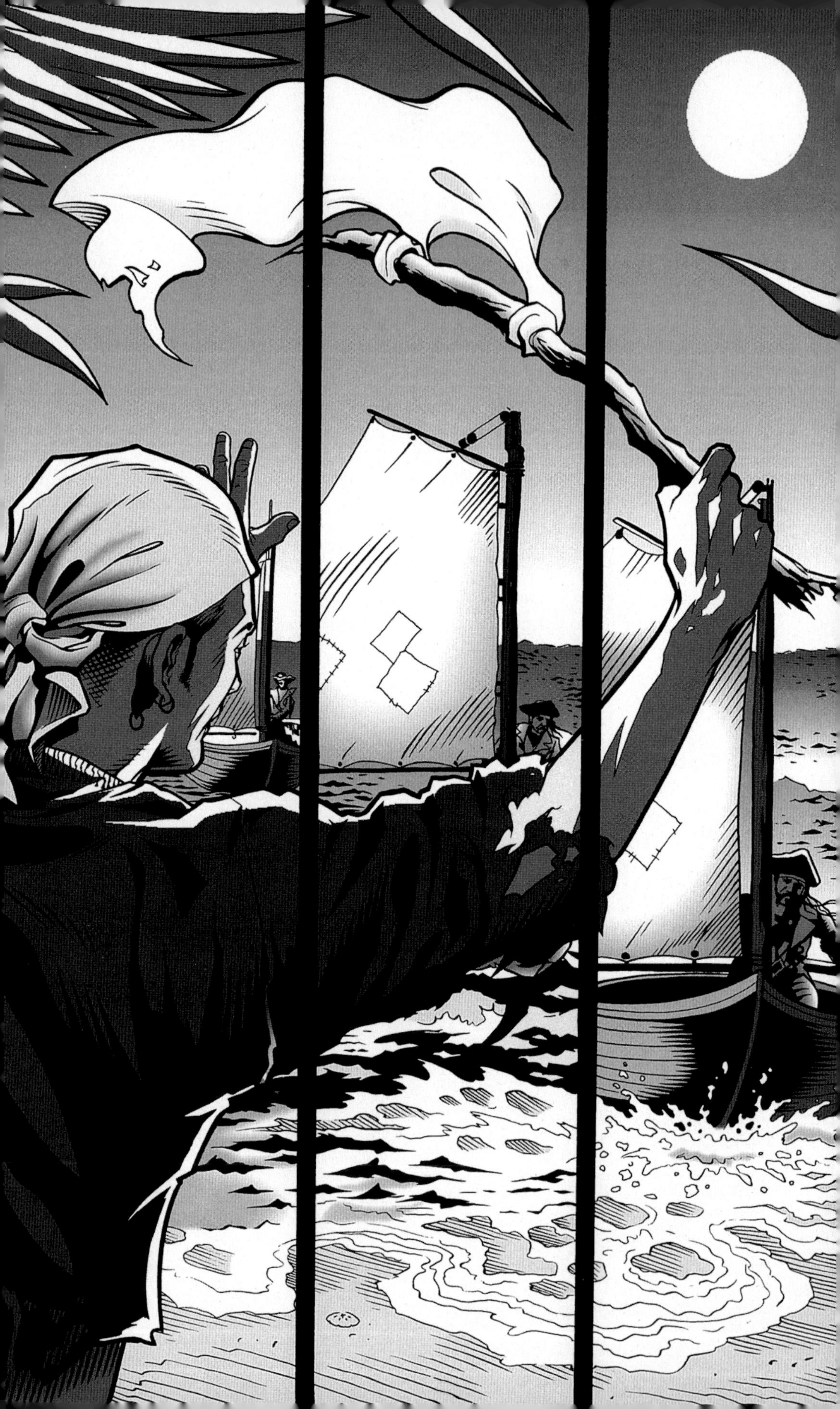

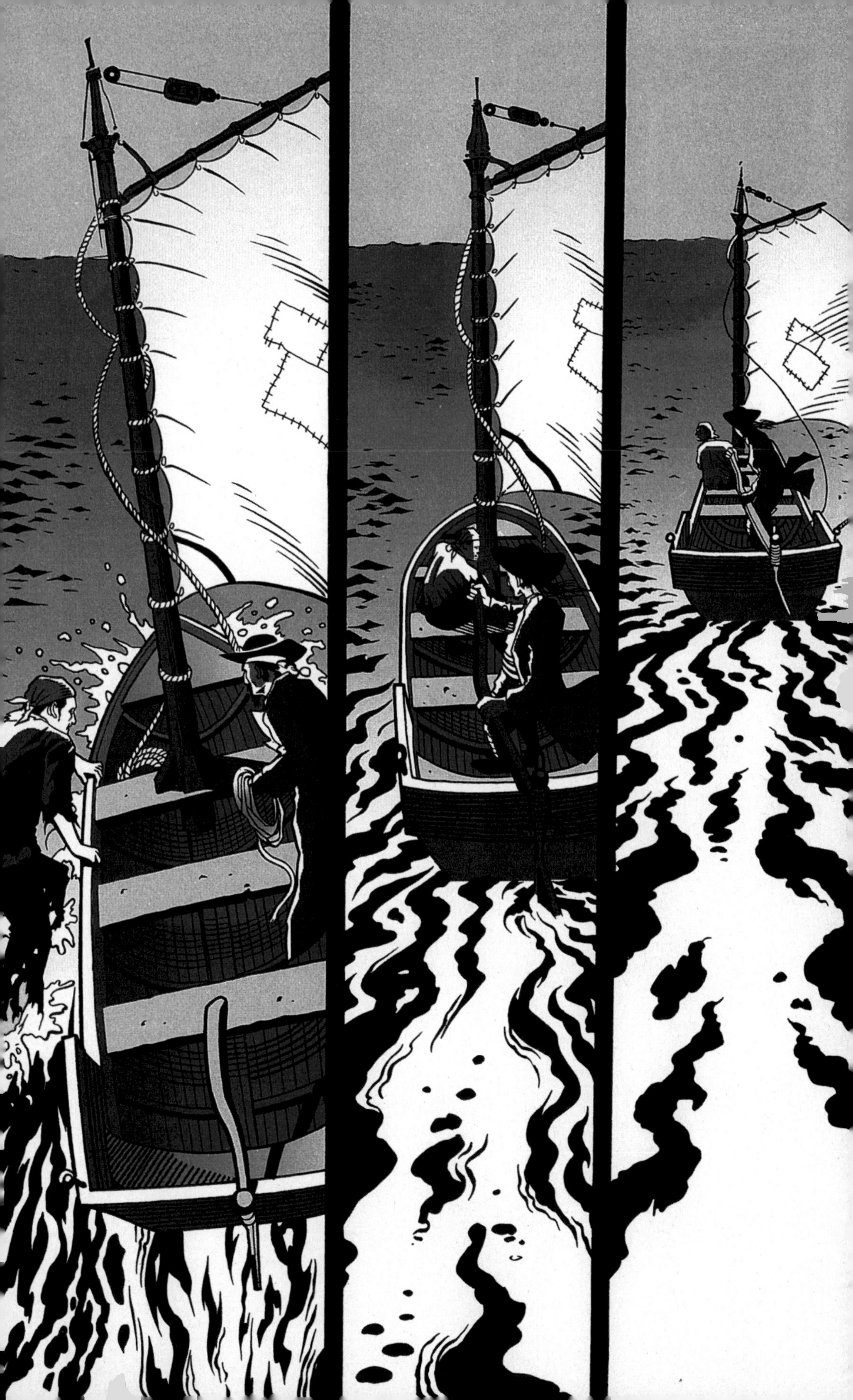

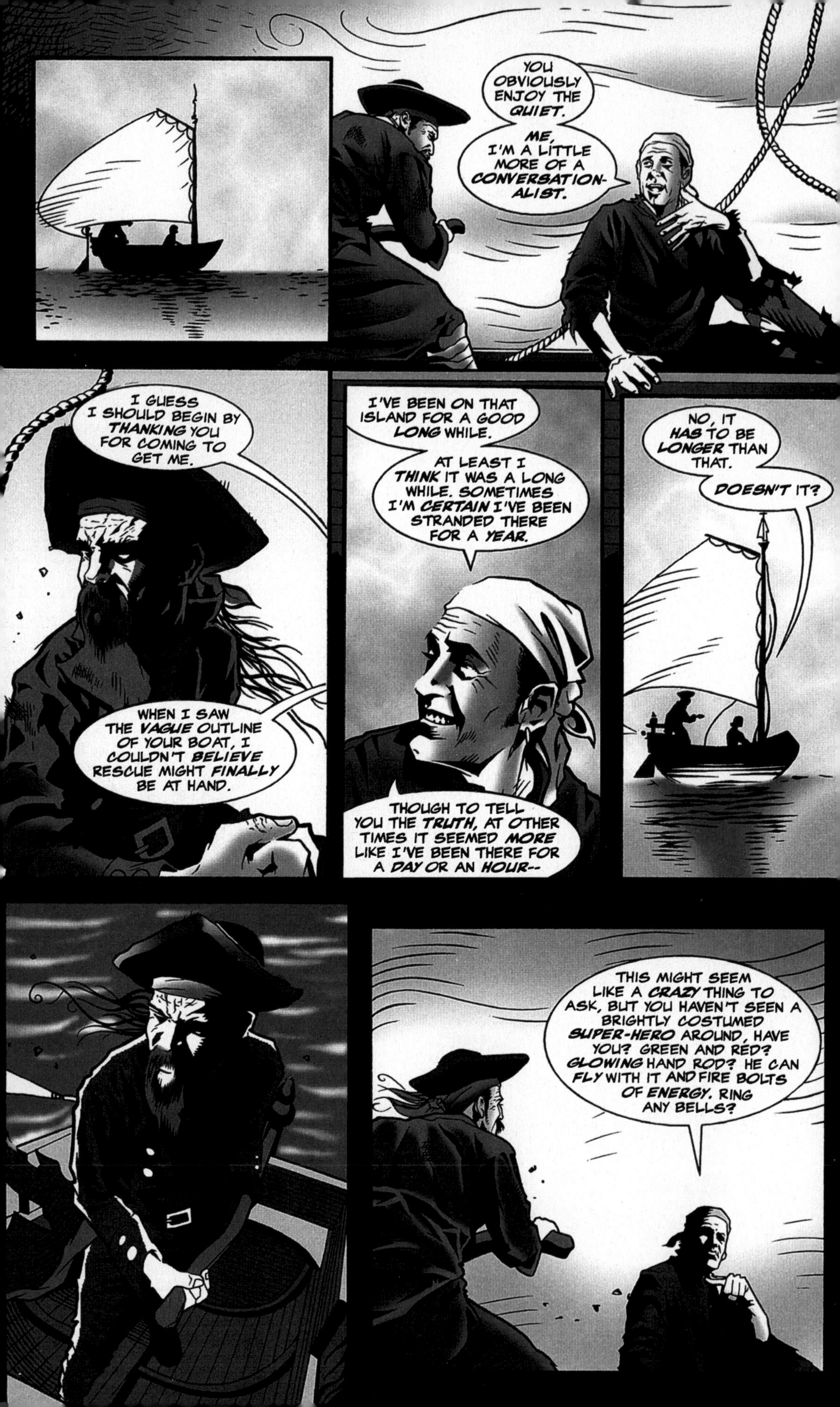
YOU OBVIOUSLY ENJOY THE QUIET.
ME, I'M A LITTLE MORE OF A CONVERSATION-ALIST.
I GUESS I SHOULD BEGIN BY THANKING YOU FOR COMING TO GET ME.
WHEN I SAW THE VAGUE OUTLINE OF YOUR BOAT, I COULDN'T BELIEVE RESCUE MIGHT FINALLY BE AT HAND.
I'VE BEEN ON THAT ISLAND FOR A GOOD LONG WHILE.
AT LEAST I THINK IT WAS A LONG WHILE. SOMETIMES I'M CERTAIN I'VE BEEN STRANDED THERE FOR A YEAR.
THOUGH TO TELL YOU THE TRUTH, AT OTHER TIMES IT SEEMED MORE LIKE I'VE BEEN THERE FOR A DAY OR AN HOUR--
NO, IT HAS TO BE LONGER THAN THAT.
DOESN'T IT?
THIS MIGHT SEEM LIKE A CRAZY THING TO ASK, BUT YOU HAVEN'T SEEN A BRIGHTLY COSTUMED SUPER-HERO AROUND, HAVE YOU? GREEN AND RED? GLOWING HAND ROD? HE CAN FLY WITH IT AND FIRE BOLTS OF ENERGY. RING ANY BELLS?

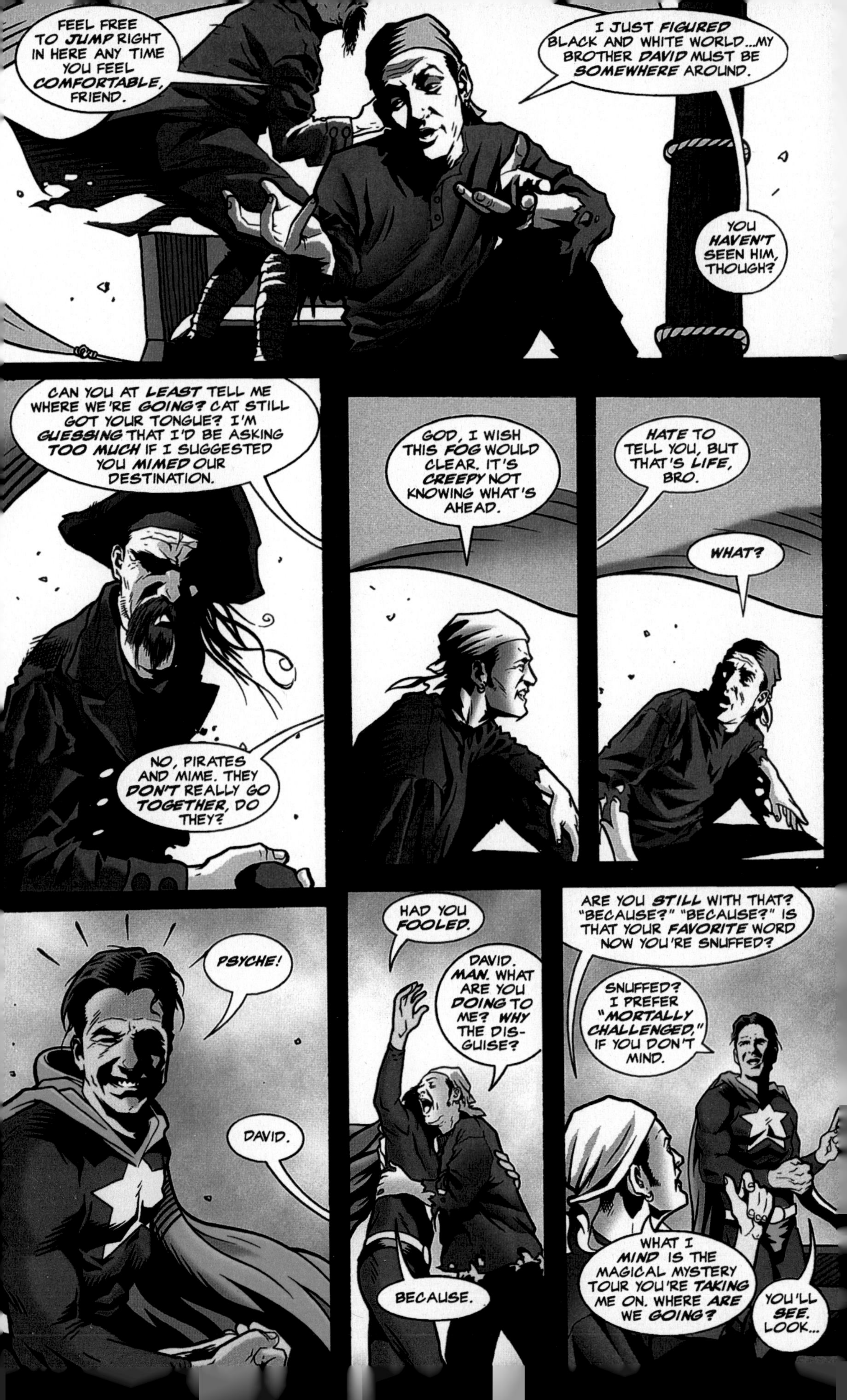
FEEL FREE TO JUMP RIGHT IN HERE ANY TIME YOU FEEL COMFORTABLE, FRIEND.
I JUST FIGURED BLACK AND WHITE WORLD...MY BROTHER DAVID MUST BE SOMEWHERE AROUND.
YOU HAVEN'T SEEN HIM, THOUGH?
CAN YOU AT LEAST TELL ME WHERE WE'RE GOING? CAT STILL GOT YOUR TONGUE? I'M GUESSING THAT I'D BE ASKING TOO MUCH IF I SUGGESTED YOU MIMED OUR DESTINATION.
NO, PIRATES AND MIME. THEY DON'T REALLY GO TOGETHER, DO THEY?
GOD, I WISH THIS FOG WOULD CLEAR. IT'S CREEPY NOT KNOWING WHAT'S AHEAD.
HATE TO TELL YOU, BUT THAT'S LIFE, BRO.
WHAT?
PSYCHE!
DAVID.
HAD YOU FOOLED.
DAVID. MAN. WHAT ARE YOU DOING TO ME? WHY THE DIS-GUISE?
BECAUSE.
ARE YOU STILL WITH THAT? "BECAUSE?" "BECAUSE?" IS THAT YOUR FAVORITE WORD NOW YOU'RE SNUFFED?
SNUFFED? I PREFER "MORTALLY CHALLENGED," IF YOU DON'T MIND.
WHAT I MIND IS THE MAGICAL MYSTERY TOUR YOU'RE TAKING ME ON. WHERE ARE WE GOING?
YOU'LL SEE. LOOK...

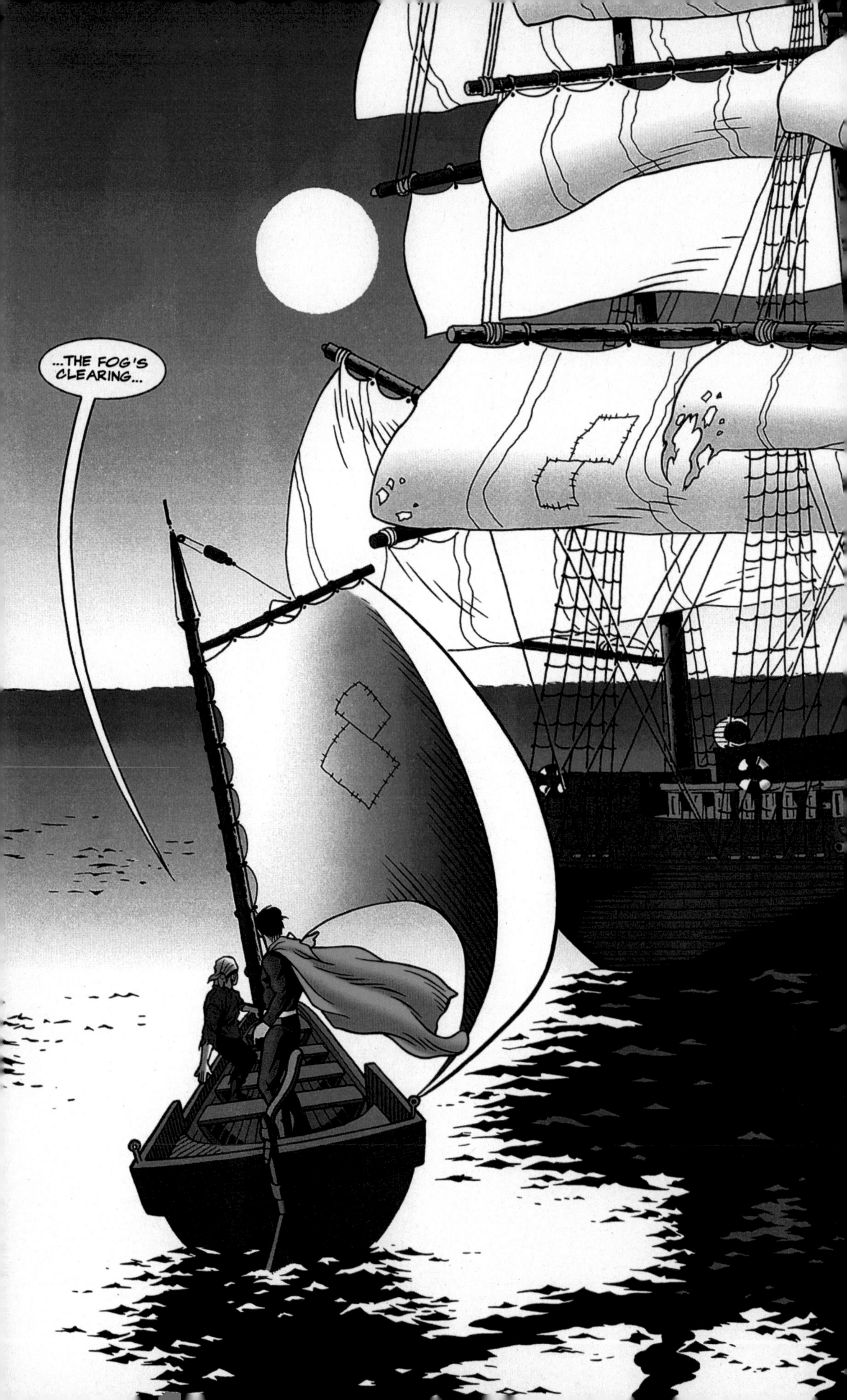
...THE FOG'S CLEARING...

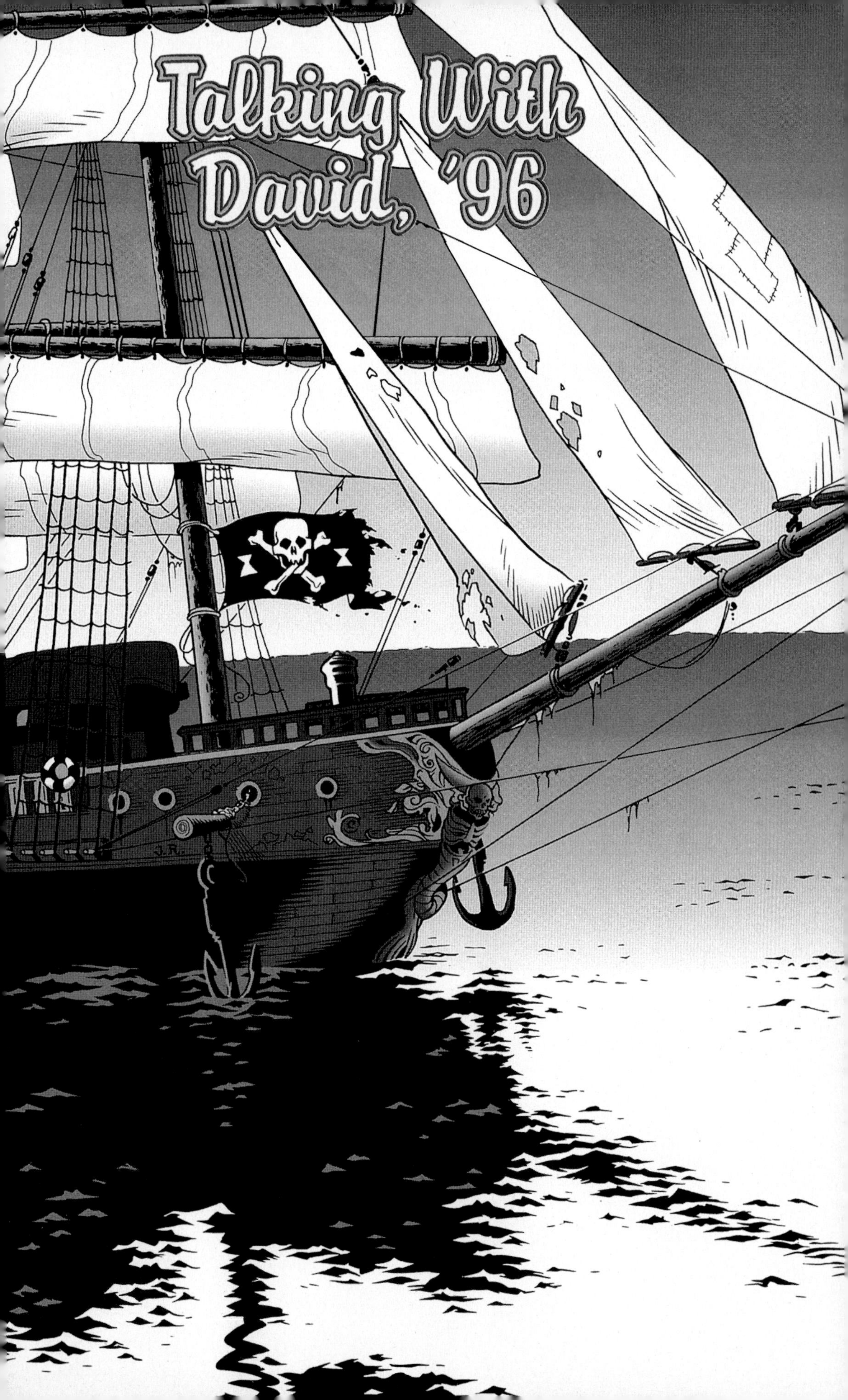
Talking With
David, '96

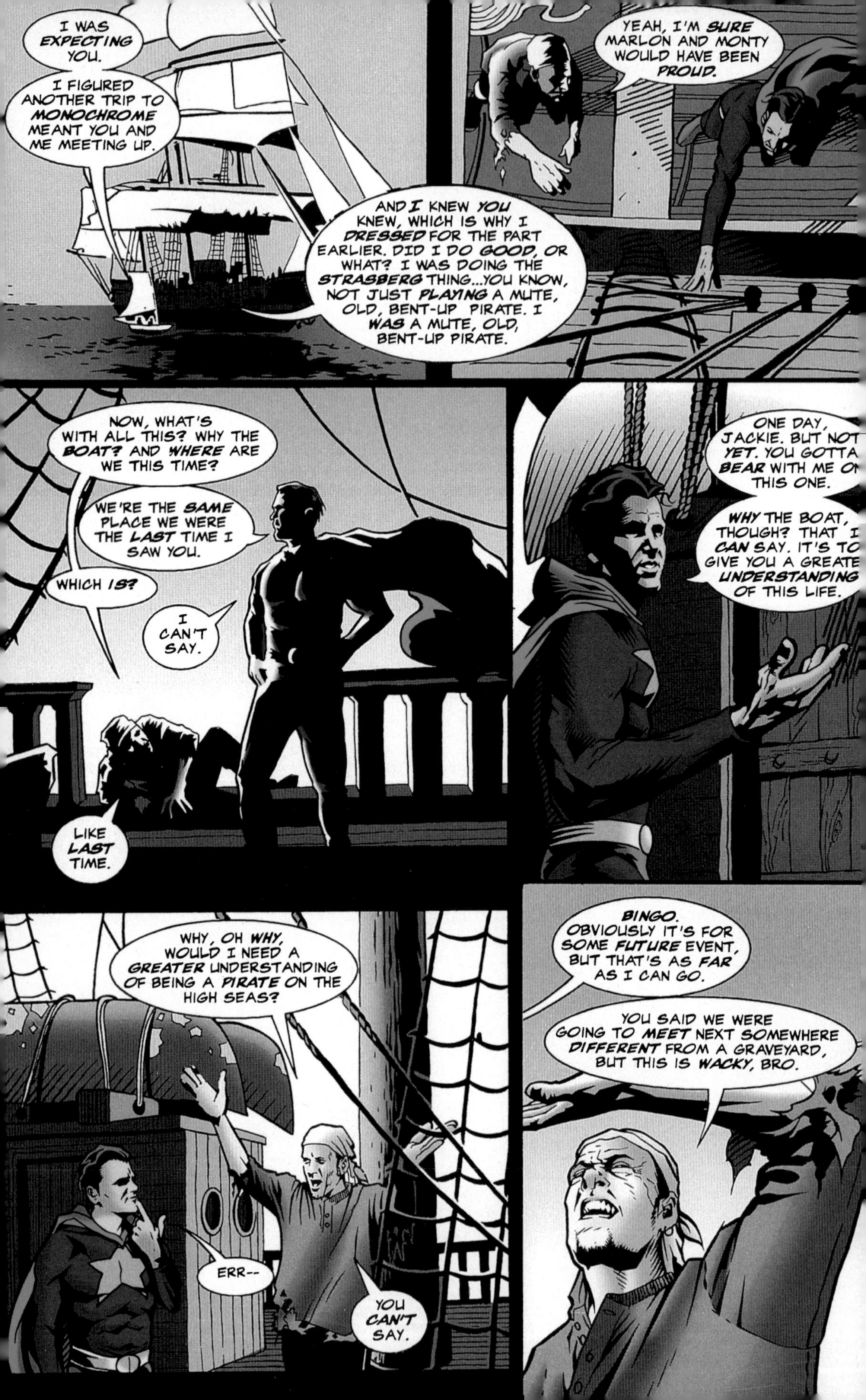
I WAS EXPECTING YOU.
I FIGURED ANOTHER TRIP TO MONOCHROME MEANT YOU AND ME MEETING UP.
YEAH, I'M SURE MARLON AND MONTY WOULD HAVE BEEN PROUD.
AND I KNEW YOU KNEW, WHICH IS WHY I DRESSED FOR THE PART EARLIER. DID I DO GOOD, OR WHAT? I WAS DOING THE STRASBERG THING...YOU KNOW, NOT JUST PLAYING A MUTE, OLD, BENT-UP PIRATE. I WAS A MUTE, OLD, BENT-UP PIRATE.
NOW, WHAT'S WITH ALL THIS? WHY THE BOAT? AND WHERE ARE WE THIS TIME?
WE'RE THE SAME PLACE WE WERE THE LAST TIME I SAW YOU.
WHICH IS?
I CAN'T SAY.
LIKE LAST TIME.
ONE DAY, JACKIE. BUT NOT YET. YOU GOTTA BEAR WITH ME ON THIS ONE.
WHY THE BOAT, THOUGH? THAT I CAN SAY. IT'S TO GIVE YOU A GREATER UNDERSTANDING OF THIS LIFE.
WHY, OH WHY, WOULD I NEED A GREATER UNDERSTANDING OF BEING A PIRATE ON THE HIGH SEAS?
ERR--
YOU CAN'T SAY.
BINGO. OBVIOUSLY IT'S FOR SOME FUTURE EVENT, BUT THAT'S AS FAR AS I CAN GO.
YOU SAID WE WERE GOING TO MEET NEXT SOMEWHERE DIFFERENT FROM A GRAVEYARD, BUT THIS IS WACKY, BRO.

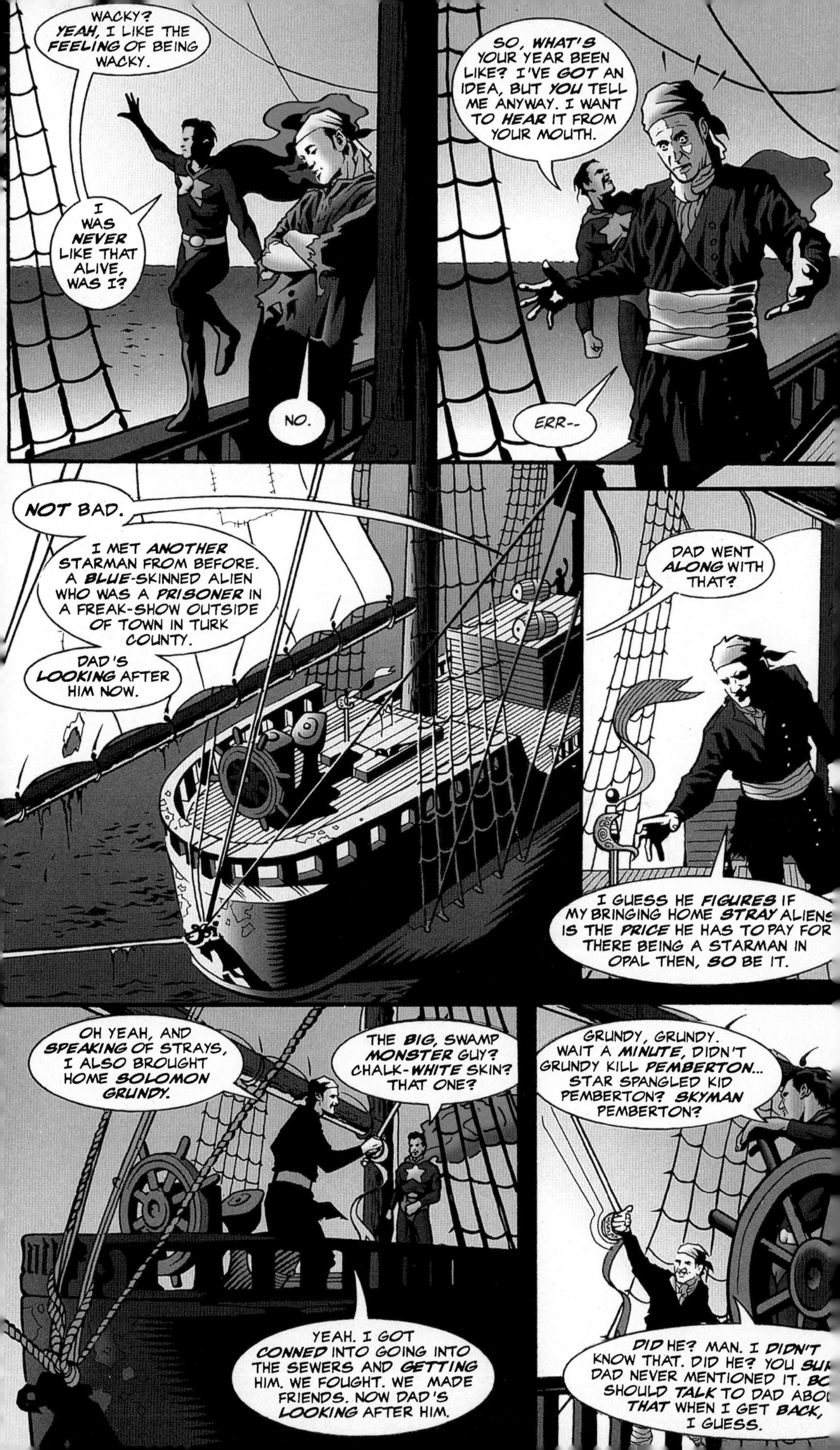
WACKY? YEAH, I LIKE THE FEELING OF BEING WACKY.
I WAS NEVER LIKE THAT ALIVE, WAS I?
NO.
SO, WHAT'S YOUR YEAR BEEN LIKE? I'VE GOT AN IDEA, BUT YOU TELL ME ANYWAY. I WANT TO HEAR IT FROM YOUR MOUTH.
ERR--
NOT BAD.
I MET ANOTHER STARMAN FROM BEFORE. A BLUE-SKINNED ALIEN WHO WAS A PRISONER IN A FREAK-SHOW OUTSIDE OF TOWN IN TURK COUNTY.
DAD'S LOOKING AFTER HIM NOW.
DAD WENT ALONG WITH THAT?
I GUESS HE FIGURES IF MY BRINGING HOME STRAY ALIENS IS THE PRICE HE HAS TO PAY FOR THERE BEING A STARMAN IN OPAL THEN, SO BE IT.
OH YEAH, AND SPEAKING OF STRAYS, I ALSO BROUGHT HOME SOLOMON GRUNDY.
THE BIG, SWAMP MONSTER GUY? CHALK-WHITE SKIN? THAT ONE?
YEAH. I GOT CONNED INTO GOING INTO THE SEWERS AND GETTING HIM. WE FOUGHT. WE MADE FRIENDS. NOW DAD'S LOOKING AFTER HIM.
GRUNDY, GRUNDY. WAIT A MINUTE, DIDN'T GRUNDY KILL PEMBERTON... STAR SPANGLED KID PEMBERTON? SKYMAN PEMBERTON?
DID HE? MAN. I DIDN'T KNOW THAT. DID HE? YOU SUR DAD NEVER MENTIONED IT. BO SHOULD TALK TO DAD ABO THAT WHEN I GET BACK, I GUESS.

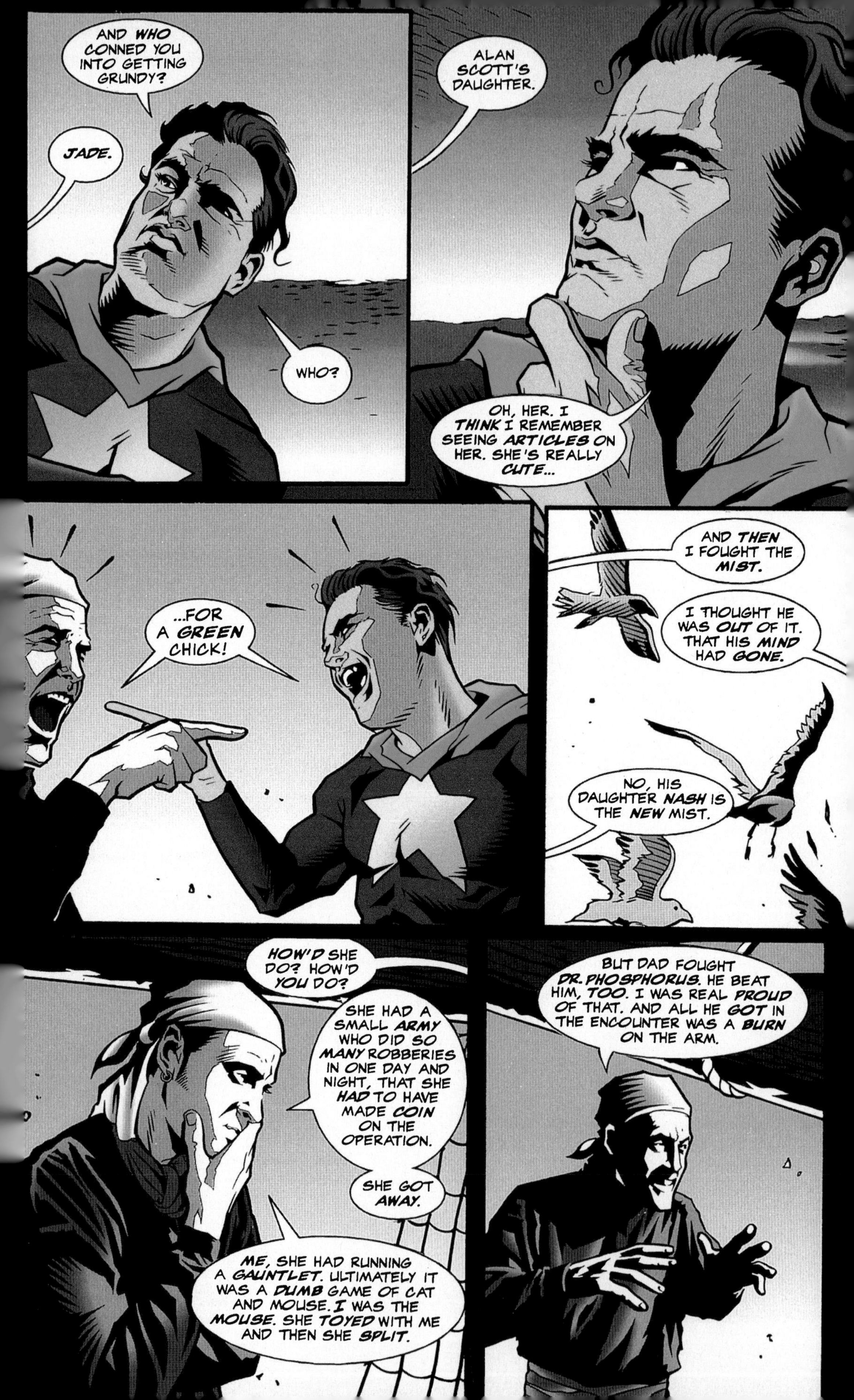
AND WHO CONNED YOU INTO GETTING GRUNDY?
JADE.
ALAN SCOTT'S DAUGHTER.
WHO?
OH, HER. I THINK I REMEMBER SEEING ARTICLES ON HER. SHE'S REALLY CUTE...
...FOR A GREEN CHICK!
AND THEN I FOUGHT THE MIST.
I THOUGHT HE WAS OUT OF IT. THAT HIS MIND HAD GONE.
NO, HIS DAUGHTER NASH IS THE NEW MIST.
HOW'D SHE DO? HOW'D YOU DO?
SHE HAD A SMALL ARMY WHO DID SO MANY ROBBERIES IN ONE DAY AND NIGHT, THAT SHE HAD TO HAVE MADE COIN ON THE OPERATION.
SHE GOT AWAY.
ME, SHE HAD RUNNING A GAUNTLET. ULTIMATELY IT WAS A DUMB GAME OF CAT AND MOUSE. I WAS THE MOUSE. SHE TOYED WITH ME AND THEN SHE SPLIT.
BUT DAD FOUGHT DR. PHOSPHORUS. HE BEAT HIM, TOO. I WAS REAL PROUD OF THAT. AND ALL HE GOT IN THE ENCOUNTER WAS A BURN ON THE ARM.

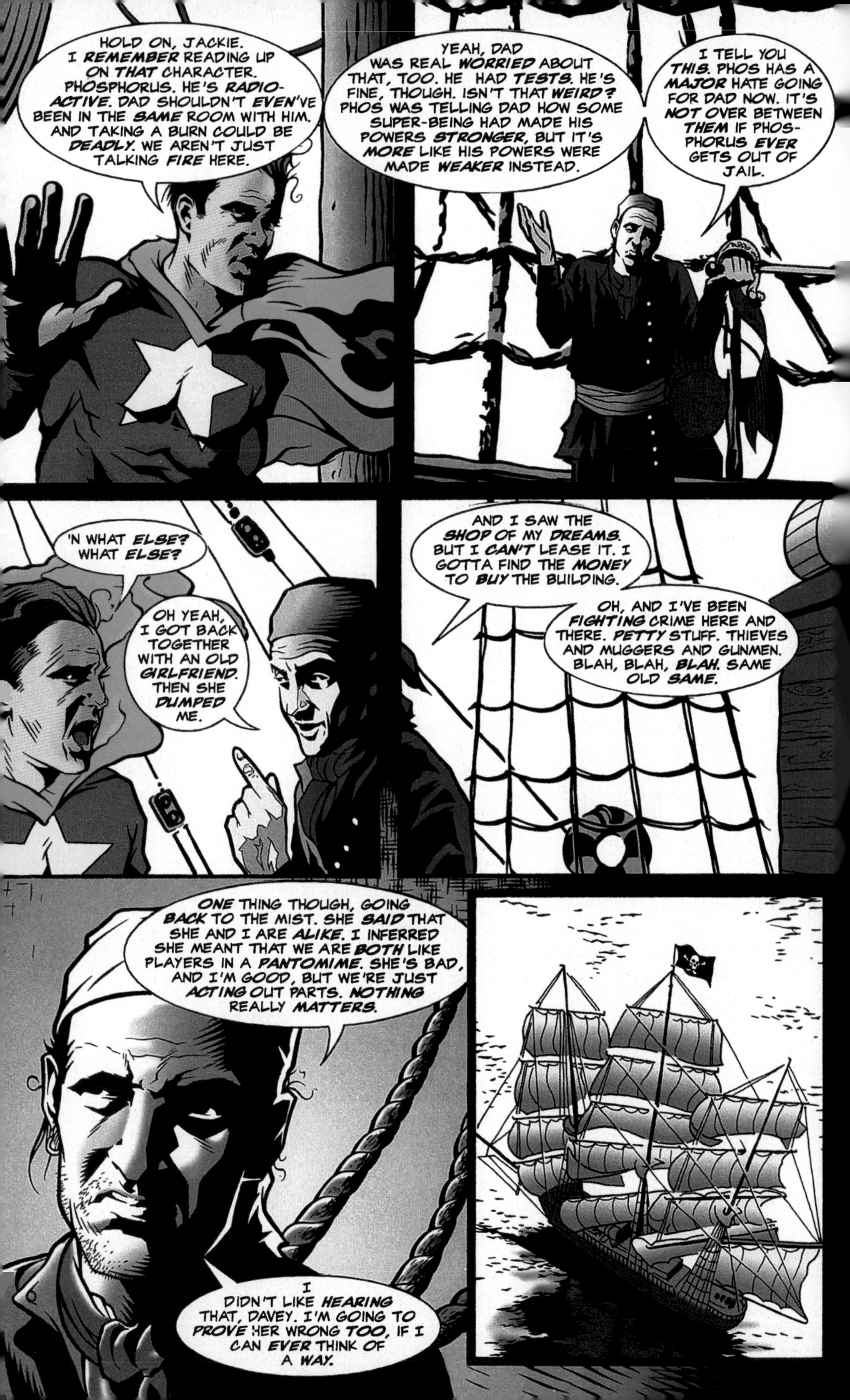
HOLD ON, JACKIE. I REMEMBER READING UP ON THAT CHARACTER. PHOSPHORUS. HE'S RADIO-ACTIVE. DAD SHOULDN'T EVEN'VE BEEN IN THE SAME ROOM WITH HIM. AND TAKING A BURN COULD BE DEADLY. WE AREN'T JUST TALKING FIRE HERE.
YEAH, DAD WAS REAL WORRIED ABOUT THAT, TOO. HE HAD TESTS. HE'S FINE, THOUGH. ISN'T THAT WEIRD? PHOS WAS TELLING DAD HOW SOME SUPER-BEING HAD MADE HIS POWERS STRONGER, BUT IT'S MORE LIKE HIS POWERS WERE MADE WEAKER INSTEAD.
I TELL YOU THIS. PHOS HAS A MAJOR HATE GOING FOR DAD NOW. IT'S NOT OVER BETWEEN THEM IF PHOS-PHORUS EVER GETS OUT OF JAIL.
'N WHAT ELSE? WHAT ELSE?
OH YEAH, I GOT BACK TOGETHER WITH AN OLD GIRLFRIEND. THEN SHE DUMPED ME.
AND I SAW THE SHOP OF MY DREAMS. BUT I CAN'T LEASE IT. I GOTTA FIND THE MONEY TO BUY THE BUILDING.
OH, AND I'VE BEEN FIGHTING CRIME HERE AND THERE. PETTY STUFF. THIEVES AND MUGGERS AND GUNMEN. BLAH, BLAH, BLAH. SAME OLD SAME.
ONE THING THOUGH, GOING BACK TO THE MIST. SHE SAID THAT SHE AND I ARE ALIKE. I INFERRED SHE MEANT THAT WE ARE BOTH LIKE PLAYERS IN A PANTOMIME. SHE'S BAD, AND I'M GOOD, BUT WE'RE JUST ACTING OUT PARTS. NOTHING REALLY MATTERS.
I DIDN'T LIKE HEARING THAT, DAVEY. I'M GOING TO PROVE HER WRONG TOO, IF I CAN EVER THINK OF A WAY.

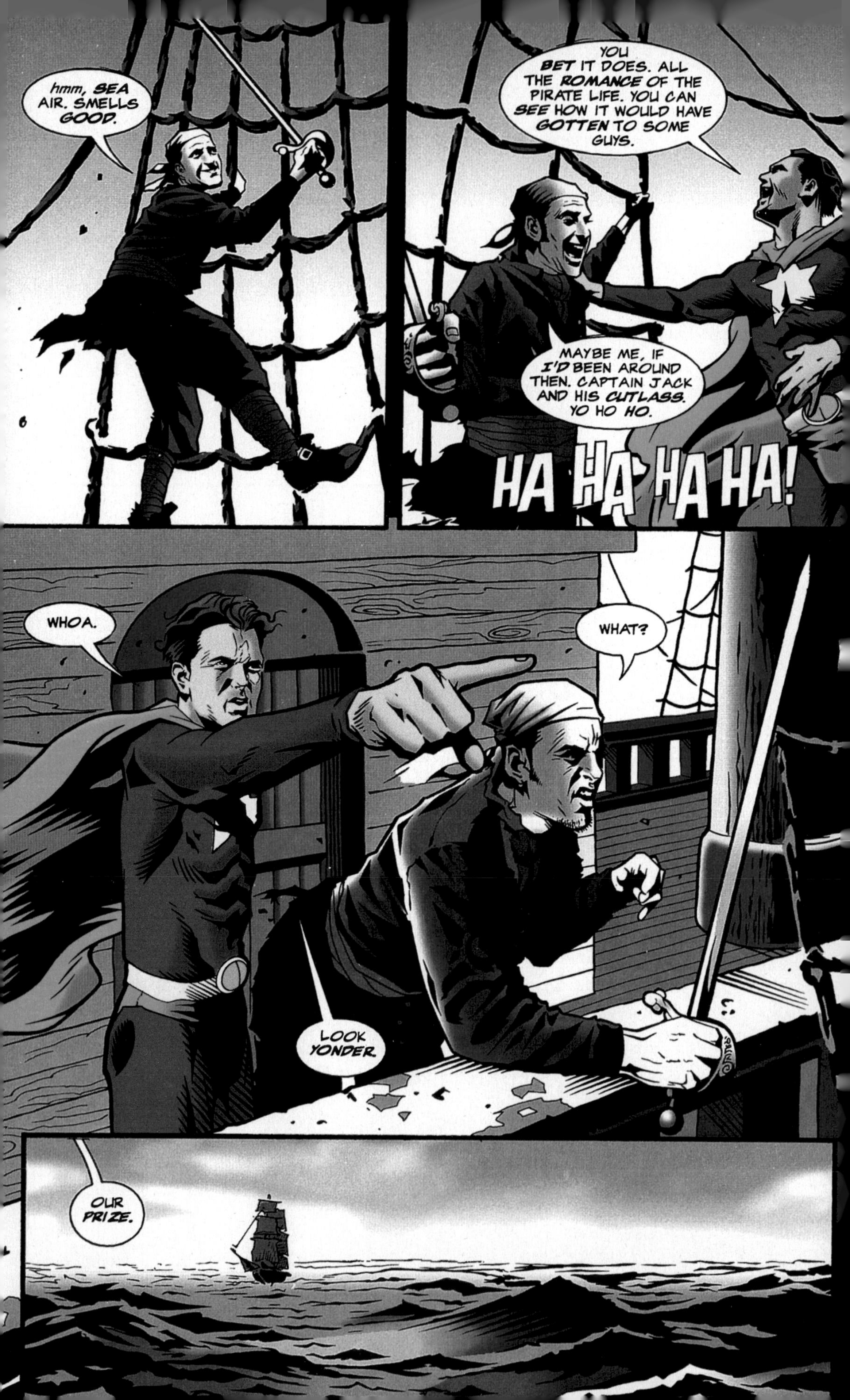
hmm, SEA AIR. SMELLS GOOD.
YOU BET IT DOES. ALL THE ROMANCE OF THE PIRATE LIFE. YOU CAN SEE HOW IT WOULD HAVE GOTTEN TO SOME GUYS.
MAYBE ME, IF I'D BEEN AROUND THEN. CAPTAIN JACK AND HIS CUTLASS. YO HO HO.
HA HA HA HA!
WHOA.
WHAT?
LOOK YONDER
OUR PRIZE.

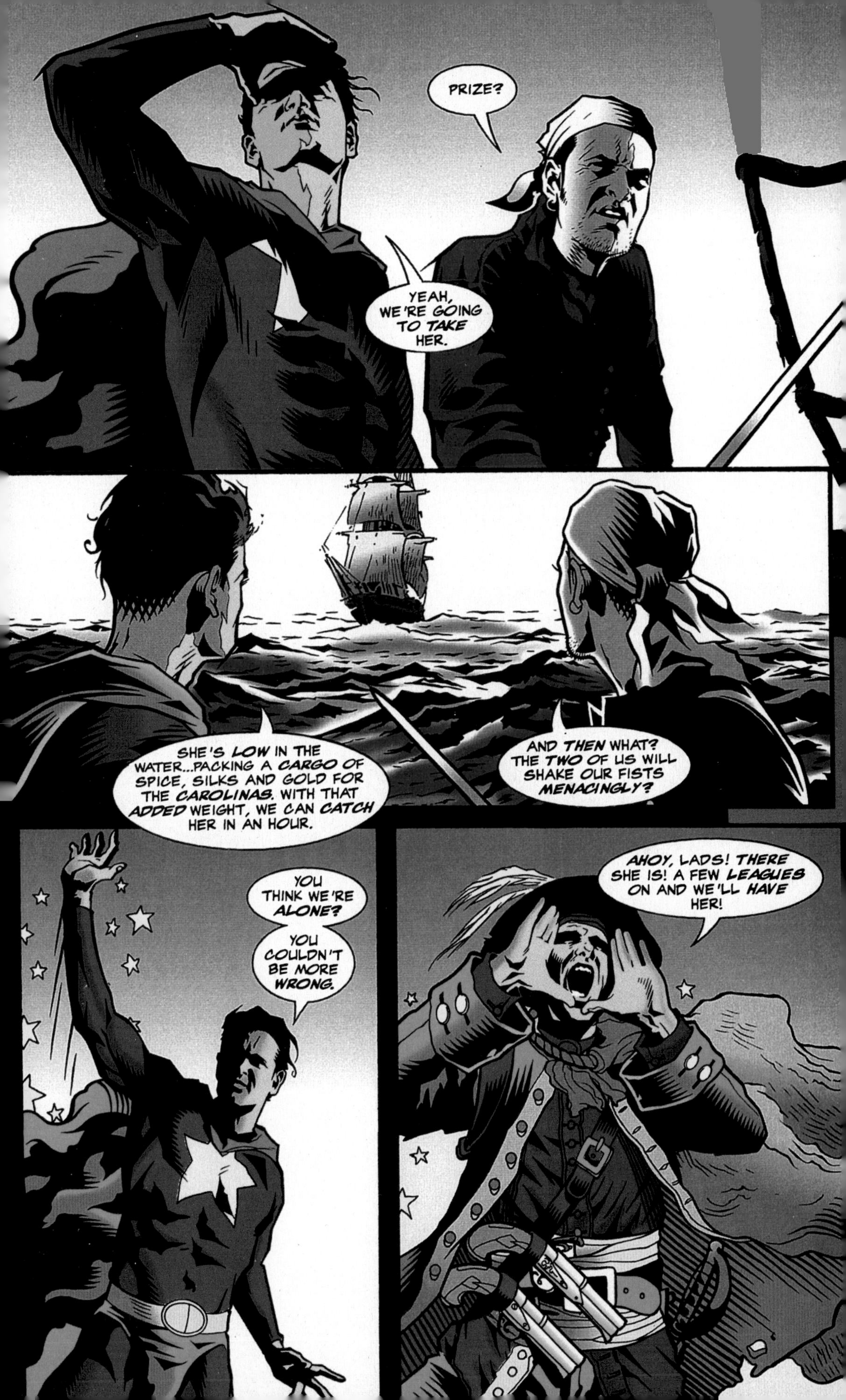
PRIZE?
YEAH, WE'RE GOING TO TAKE HER.
SHE'S LOW IN THE WATER...PACKING A CARGO OF SPICE, SILKS AND GOLD FOR THE CAROLINAS. WITH THAT ADDED WEIGHT, WE CAN CATCH HER IN AN HOUR.
AND THEN WHAT? THE TWO OF US WILL SHAKE OUR FISTS MENACINGLY?
YOU THINK WE'RE ALONE?
YOU COULDN'T BE MORE WRONG.
AHOY, LADS! THERE SHE IS! A FEW LEAGUES ON AND WE'LL HAVE HER!

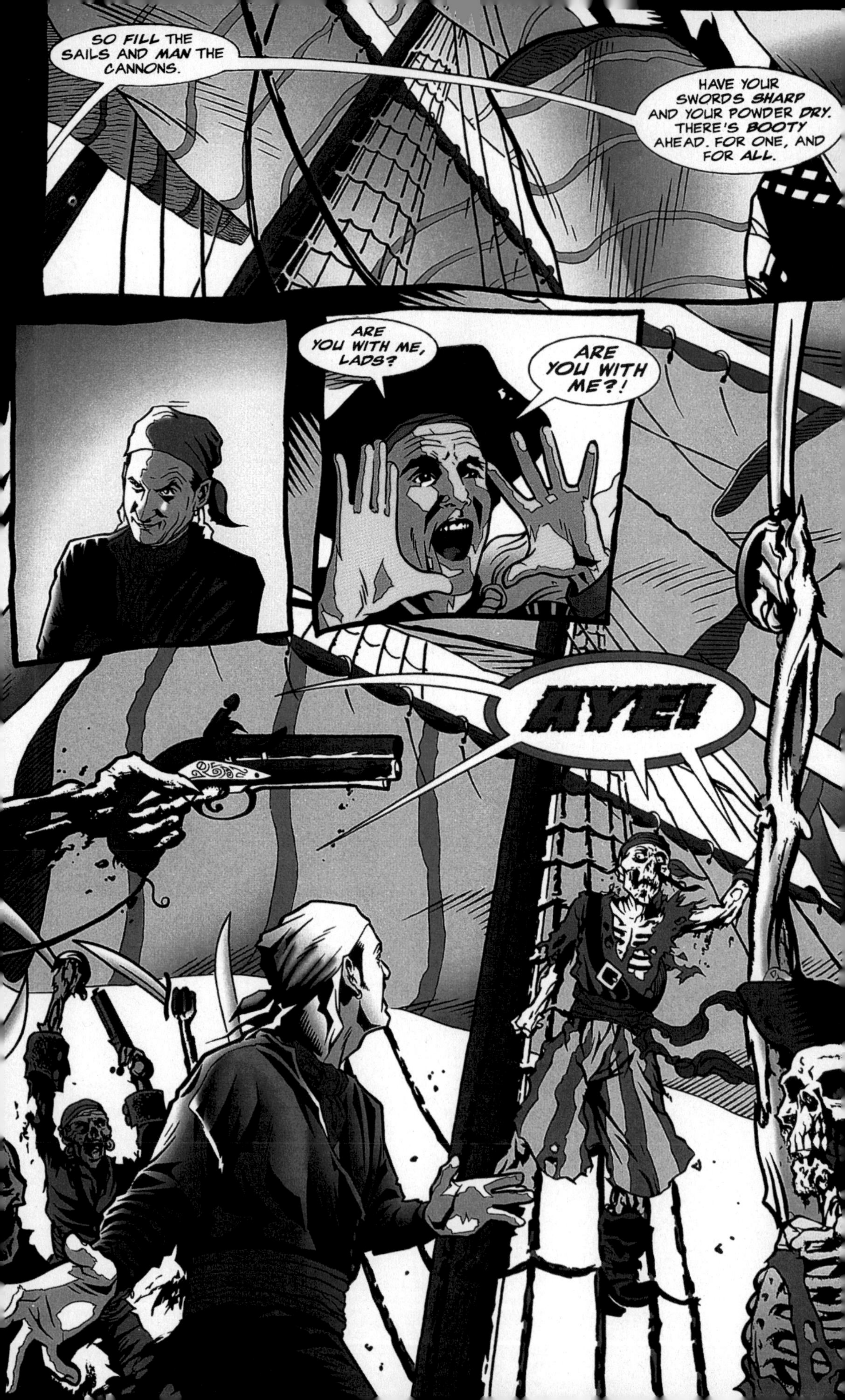
SO FILL THE SAILS AND MAN THE CANNONS.
HAVE YOUR SWORDS SHARP AND YOUR POWDER DRY. THERE'S BOOTY AHEAD. FOR ONE, AND FOR ALL.
ARE YOU WITH ME, LADS?
ARE YOU WITH ME?!
AYE!

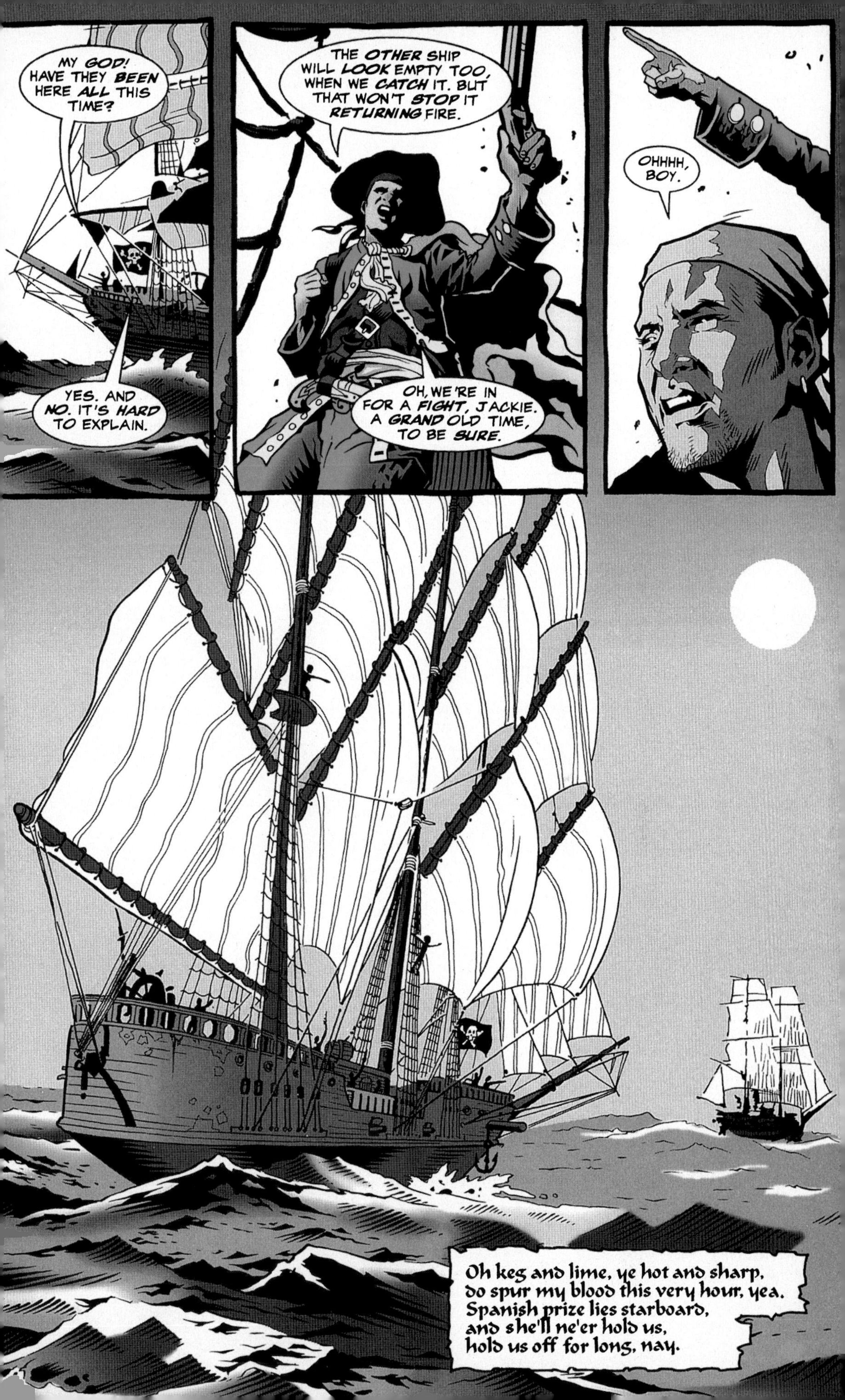
MY GOD! HAVE THEY BEEN HERE ALL THIS TIME?
YES. AND NO. IT'S HARD TO EXPLAIN.
THE OTHER SHIP WILL LOOK EMPTY TOO, WHEN WE CATCH IT. BUT THAT WON'T STOP IT RETURNING FIRE.
OH, WE'RE IN FOR A FIGHT, JACKIE. A GRAND OLD TIME, TO BE SURE.
OHHHH, BOY.
Oh keg and lime, ye hot and sharp,
do spur my blood this very hour, yea.
Spanish prize lies starboard,
and she'll ne'er hold us,
hold us off for long, nay.

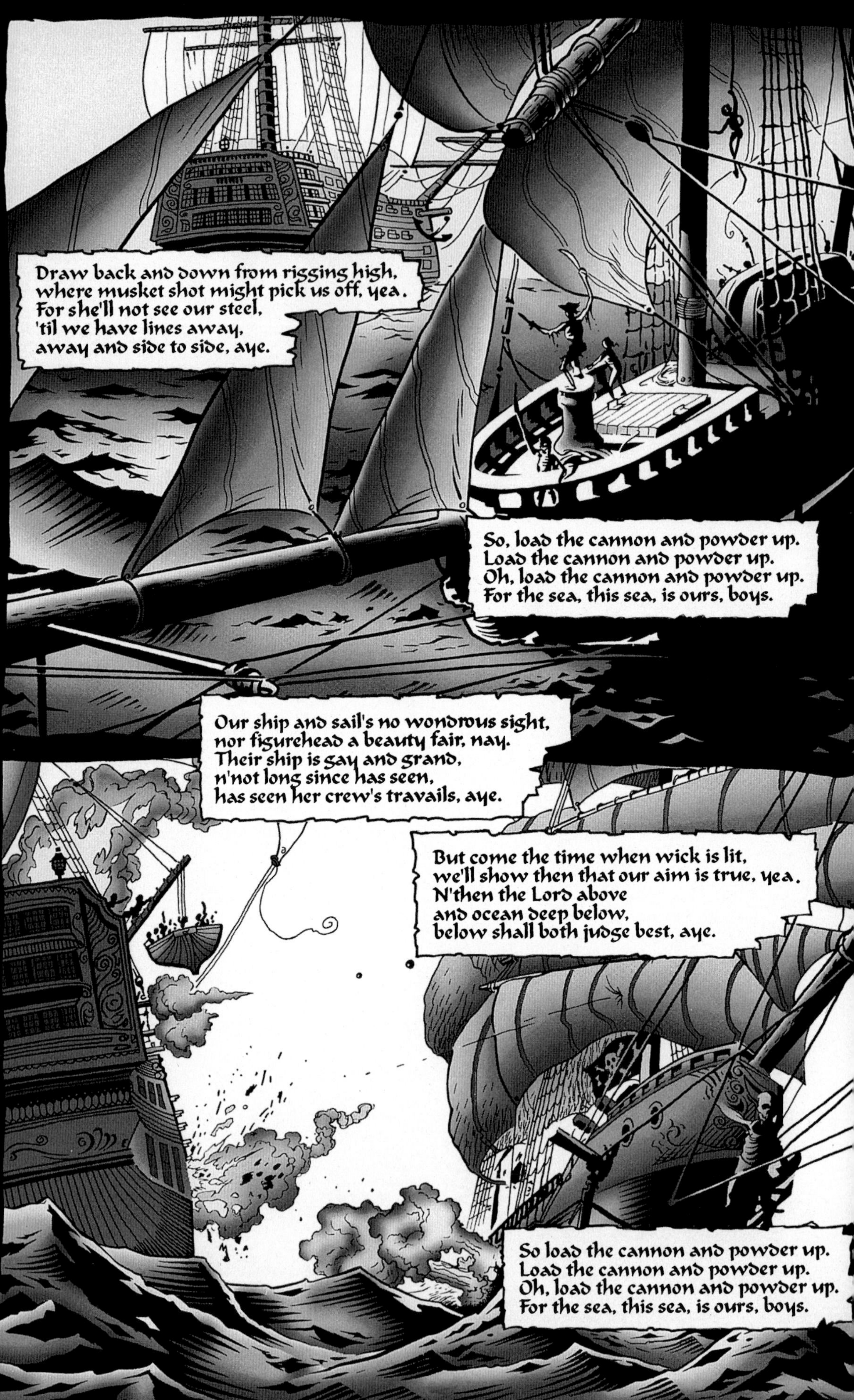
Draw back and down from rigging high,
where musket shot might pick us off, yea.
For she'll not see our steel,
'til we have lines away,
away and side to side, aye.
So, load the cannon and powder up.
Load the cannon and powder up.
Oh, load the cannon and powder up.
For the sea, this sea, is ours, boys.
Our ship and sail's no wondrous sight,
nor figurehead a beauty fair, nay.
Their ship is gay and grand,
n'not long since has seen,
has seen her crew's travails, aye.
But come the time when wick is lit,
we'll show then that our aim is true, yea.
N'then the Lord above
and ocean deep below,
below shall both judge best, aye.
So load the cannon and powder up.
Load the cannon and powder up.
Oh, load the cannon and powder up.
For the sea, this sea, is ours, boys.

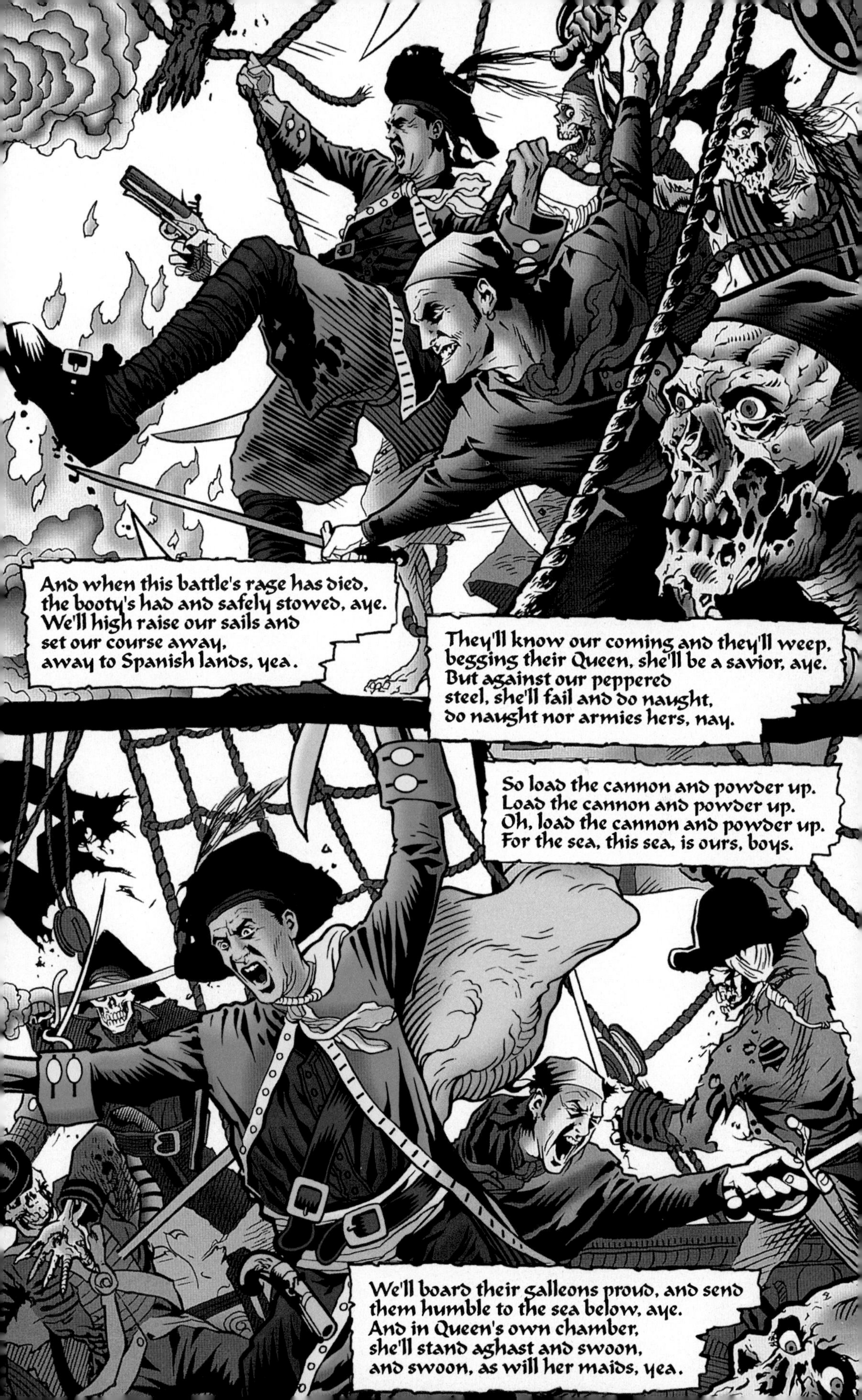
And when this battle's rage has died, the booty's had and safely stowed, aye. We'll high raise our sails and set our course away, away to Spanish lands, yea.
They'll know our coming and they'll weep, begging their Queen, she'll be a savior, aye. But against our peppered steel, she'll fail and do naught, do naught nor armies hers, nay.
So load the cannon and powder up. Load the cannon and powder up. Oh, load the cannon and powder up. For the sea, this sea, is ours, boys.
We'll board their galleons proud, and send them humble to the sea below, aye. And in Queen's own chamber, she'll stand aghast and swoon, and swoon, as will her maids, yea.

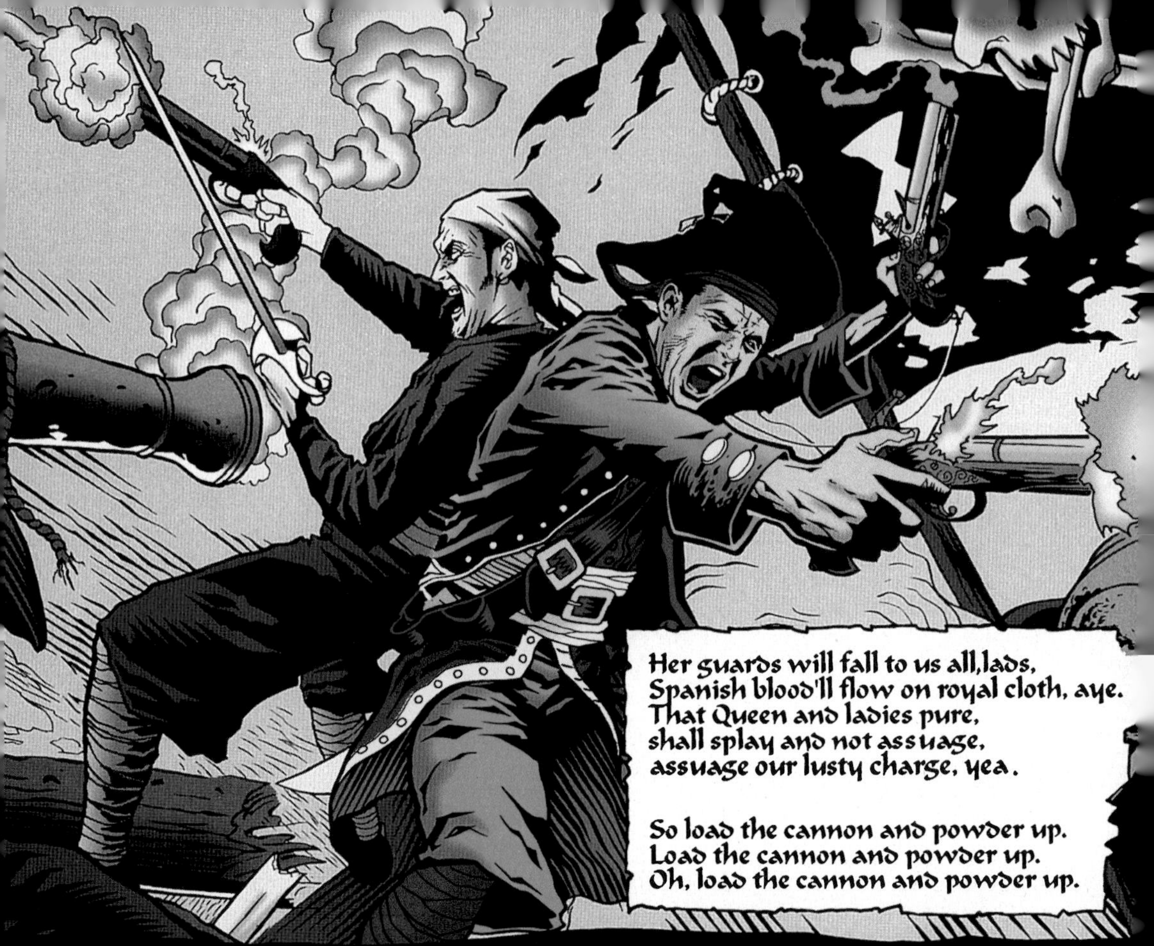
Her guards will fall to us all,lads,
Spanish blood'll flow on royal cloth, aye.
That Queen and ladies pure,
shall splay and not assuage,
assuage our lusty charge, yea.
So load the cannon and powder up.
Load the cannon and powder up.
Oh, load the cannon and powder up.

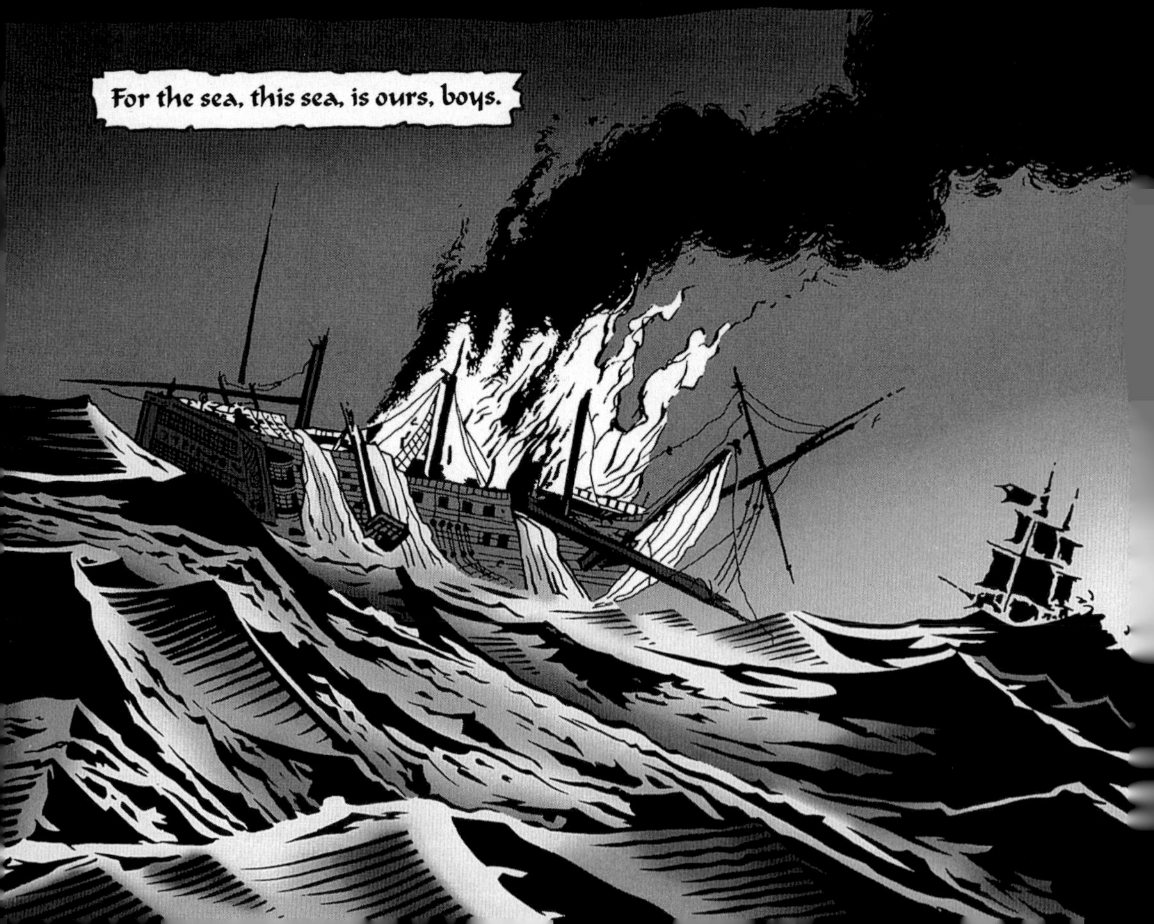
For the sea, this sea, is ours, boys.

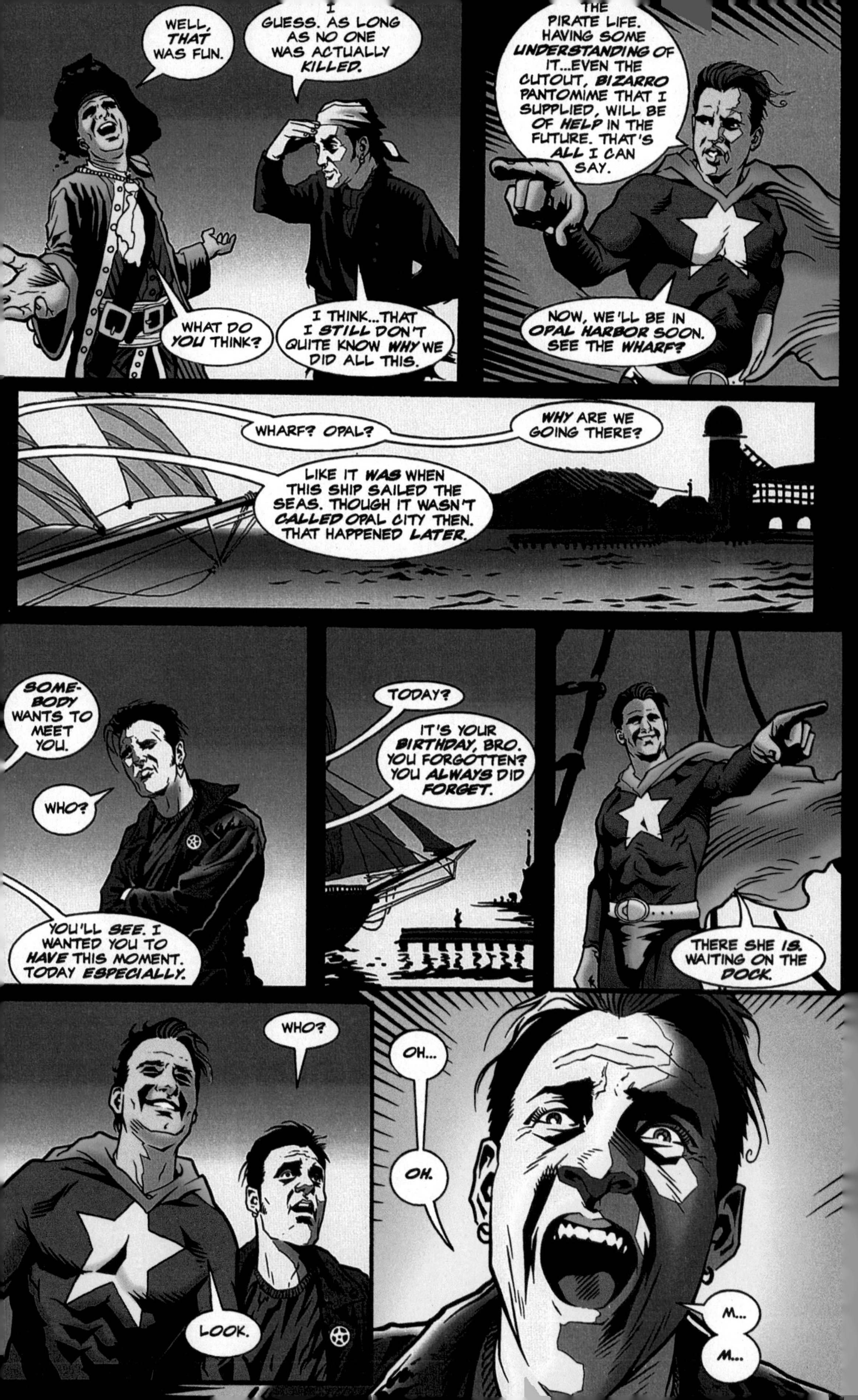
WELL, THAT WAS FUN.
I GUESS. AS LONG AS NO ONE WAS ACTUALLY KILLED.
WHAT DO YOU THINK?
I THINK...THAT I STILL DON'T QUITE KNOW WHY WE DID ALL THIS.
THE PIRATE LIFE. HAVING SOME UNDERSTANDING OF IT...EVEN THE CUTOUT, BIZARRO PANTOMIME THAT I SUPPLIED, WILL BE OF HELP IN THE FUTURE. THAT'S ALL I CAN SAY.
NOW, WE'LL BE IN OPAL HARBOR SOON. SEE THE WHARF?
WHARF? OPAL?
WHY ARE WE GOING THERE?
LIKE IT WAS WHEN THIS SHIP SAILED THE SEAS. THOUGH IT WASN'T CALLED OPAL CITY THEN. THAT HAPPENED LATER.
SOME-BODY WANTS TO MEET YOU.
WHO?
YOU'LL SEE. I WANTED YOU TO HAVE THIS MOMENT. TODAY ESPECIALLY.
TODAY?
IT'S YOUR BIRTHDAY, BRO. YOU FORGOTTEN? YOU ALWAYS DID FORGET.
THERE SHE IS. WAITING ON THE DOCK.
WHO?
LOOK.
OH...
OH.
M...
M...

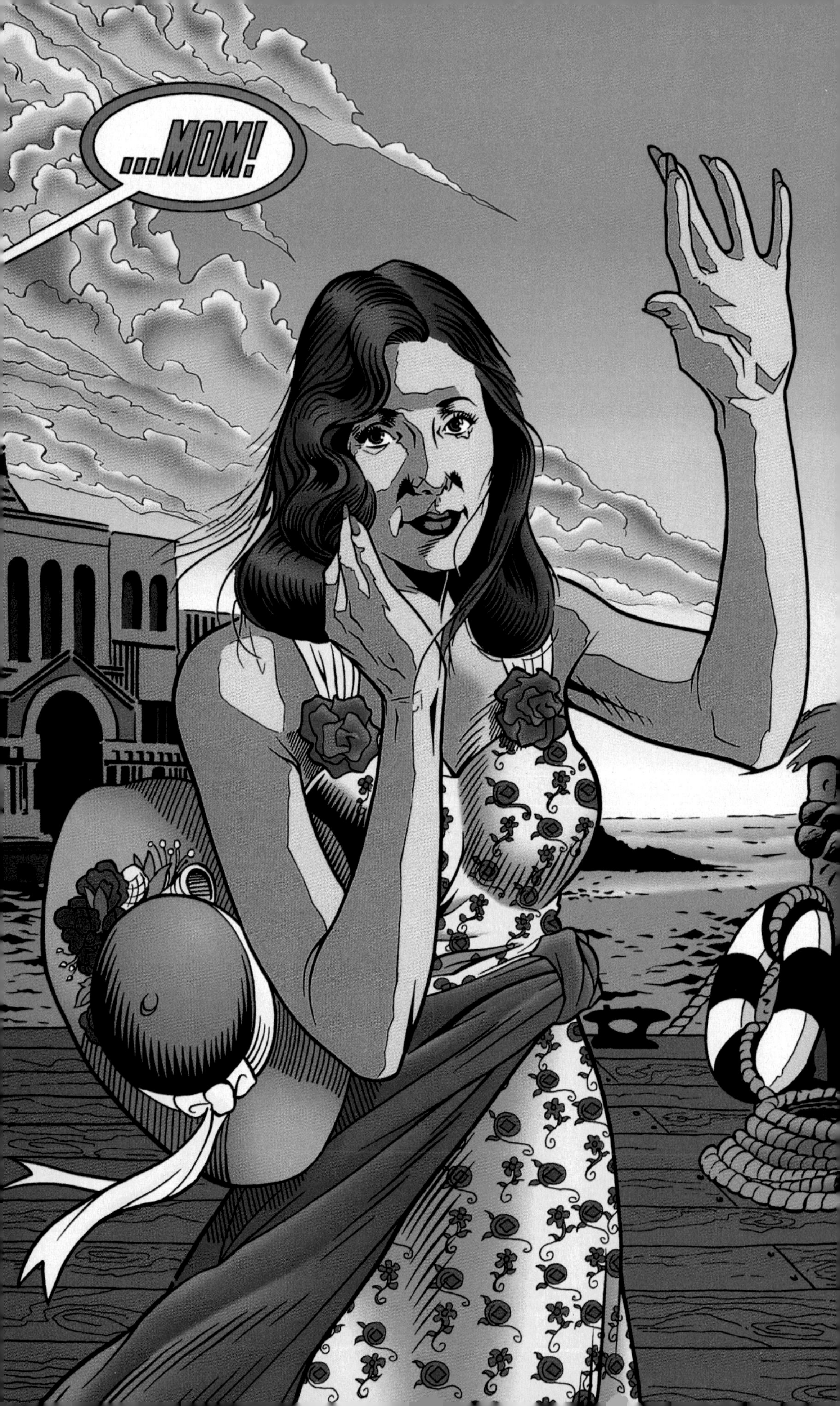
...MOM!

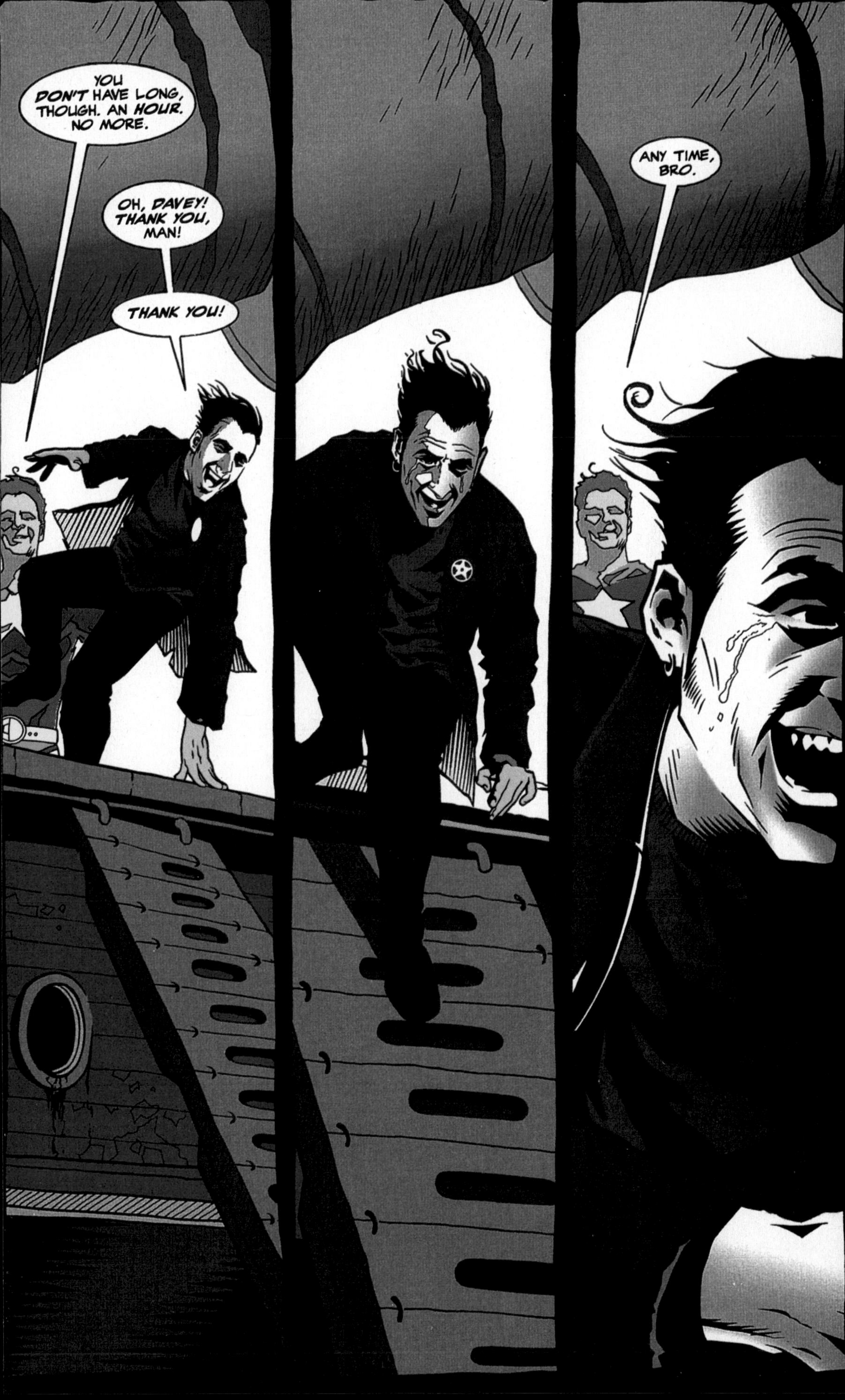
YOU DON'T HAVE LONG, THOUGH. AN HOUR. NO MORE.
OH, DAVEY! THANK YOU, MAN!
THANK YOU!
ANY TIME, BRO.

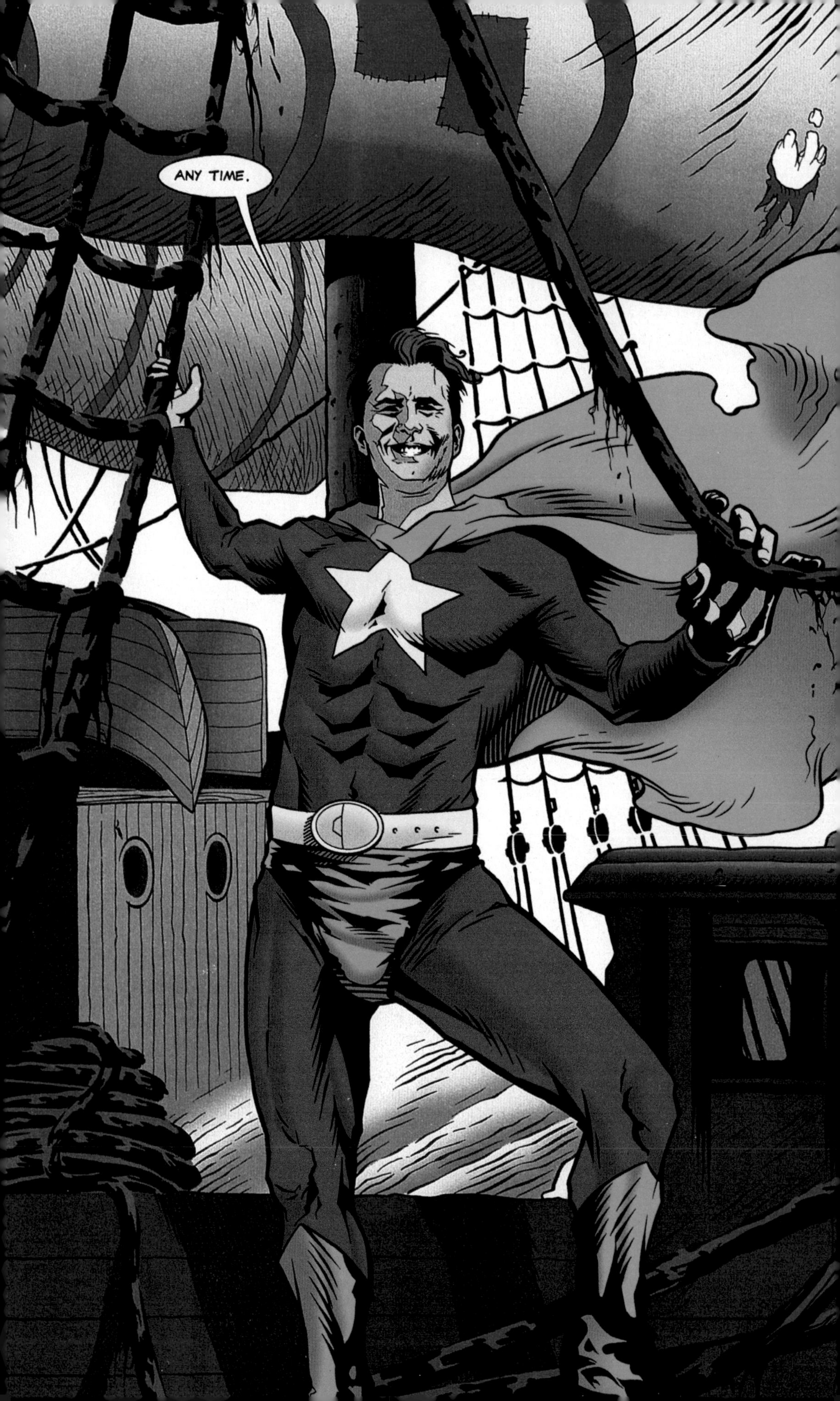
ANY TIME.

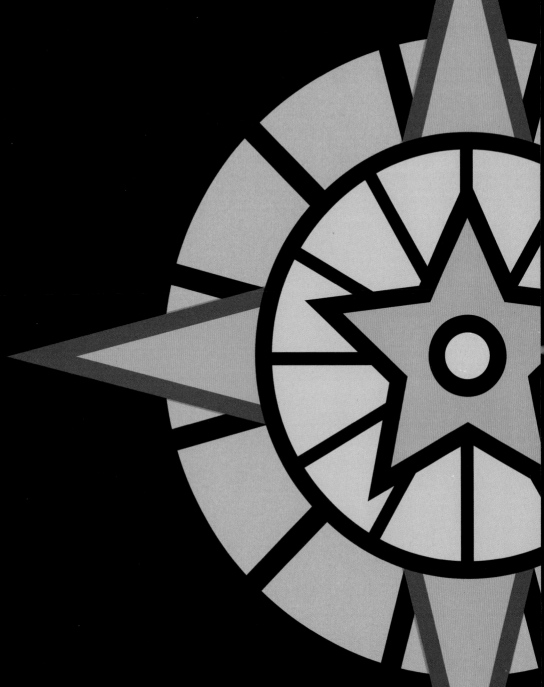

SHOWCASE '96 #4

Written by James Robinson

Art by Matt Smith

with colors by Melissa Edwards

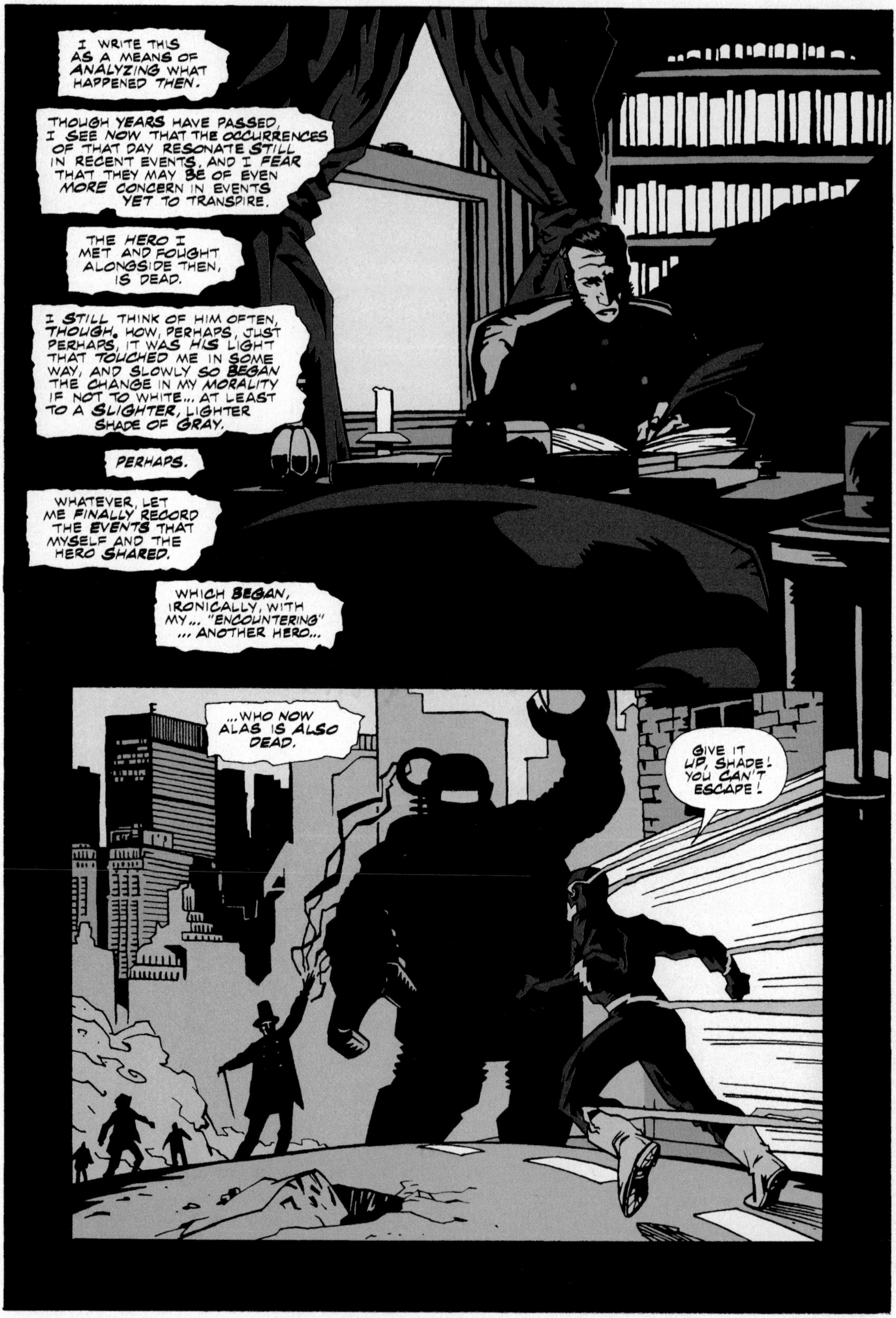
I WRITE THIS AS A MEANS OF ANALYZING WHAT HAPPENED THEN.
THOUGH YEARS HAVE PASSED, I SEE NOW THAT THE OCCURRENCES OF THAT DAY RESONATE STILL IN RECENT EVENTS, AND I FEAR THAT THEY MAY BE OF EVEN MORE CONCERN IN EVENTS YET TO TRANSPIRE.
THE HERO I MET AND FOUGHT ALONGSIDE THEN, IS DEAD.
I STILL THINK OF HIM OFTEN, THOUGH. HOW, PERHAPS, JUST PERHAPS, IT WAS HIS LIGHT THAT TOUCHED ME IN SOME WAY, AND SLOWLY SO BEGAN THE CHANGE IN MY MORALITY IF NOT TO WHITE... AT LEAST TO A SLIGHTER, LIGHTER SHADE OF GRAY.
PERHAPS.
WHATEVER, LET ME FINALLY RECORD THE EVENTS THAT MYSELF AND THE HERO SHARED.
WHICH BEGAN, IRONICALLY, WITH MY... "ENCOUNTERING" ...ANOTHER HERO...
...WHO NOW ALAS IS ALSO DEAD.
GIVE IT UP, SHADE! YOU CAN'T ESCAPE!

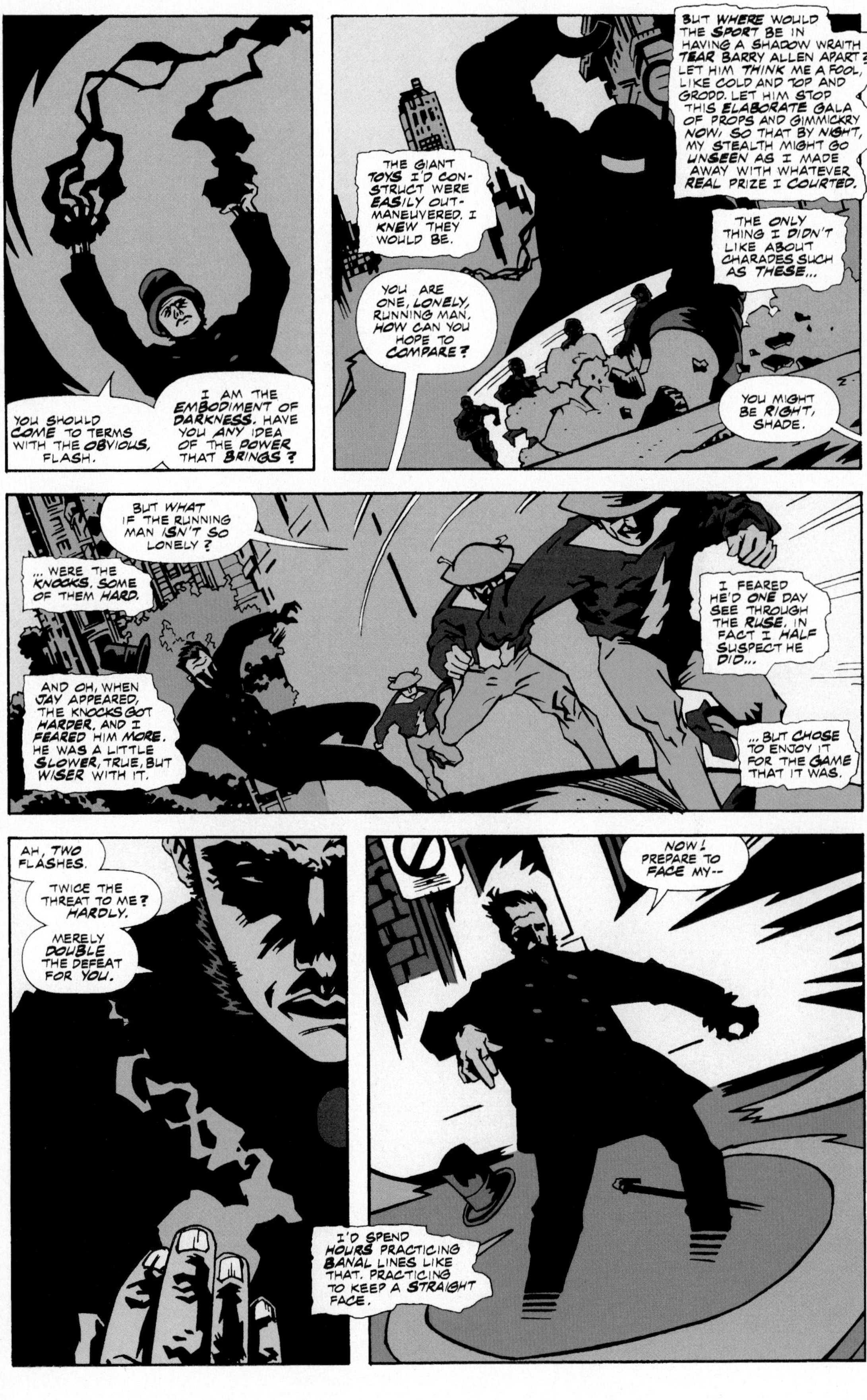
YOU SHOULD COME TO TERMS WITH THE OBVIOUS, FLASH.
I AM THE EMBODIMENT OF DARKNESS. HAVE YOU ANY IDEA OF THE POWER THAT BRINGS?
THE GIANT TOYS I'D CONSTRUCT WERE EASILY OUT-MANEUVERED. I KNEW THEY WOULD BE.
YOU ARE ONE, LONELY, RUNNING MAN. HOW CAN YOU HOPE TO COMPARE?
BUT WHERE WOULD THE SPORT BE IN HAVING A SHADOW WRAITH TEAR BARRY ALLEN APART? LET HIM THINK ME A FOOL, LIKE COLD AND TOP AND GRODD. LET HIM STOP THIS ELABORATE GALA OF PROPS AND GIMMICKRY NOW; SO THAT BY NIGHT, MY STEALTH MIGHT GO UNSEEN AS I MADE AWAY WITH WHATEVER REAL PRIZE I COURTED.
THE ONLY THING I DIDN'T LIKE ABOUT CHARADES SUCH AS THESE...
YOU MIGHT BE RIGHT, SHADE.
BUT WHAT IF THE RUNNING MAN ISN'T SO LONELY?
...WERE THE KNOCKS. SOME OF THEM HARD.
AND OH, WHEN JAY APPEARED, THE KNOCKS GOT HARDER, AND I FEARED HIM MORE. HE WAS A LITTLE SLOWER, TRUE, BUT WISER WITH IT.
I FEARED HE'D ONE DAY SEE THROUGH THE RUSE. IN FACT I HALF SUSPECT HE DID...
...BUT CHOSE TO ENJOY IT FOR THE GAME THAT IT WAS.
AH, TWO FLASHES.
TWICE THE THREAT TO ME? HARDLY.
MERELY DOUBLE THE DEFEAT FOR YOU.
NOW! PREPARE TO FACE MY--
I'D SPEND HOURS PRACTICING BANAL LINES LIKE THAT. PRACTICING TO KEEP A STRAIGHT FACE.

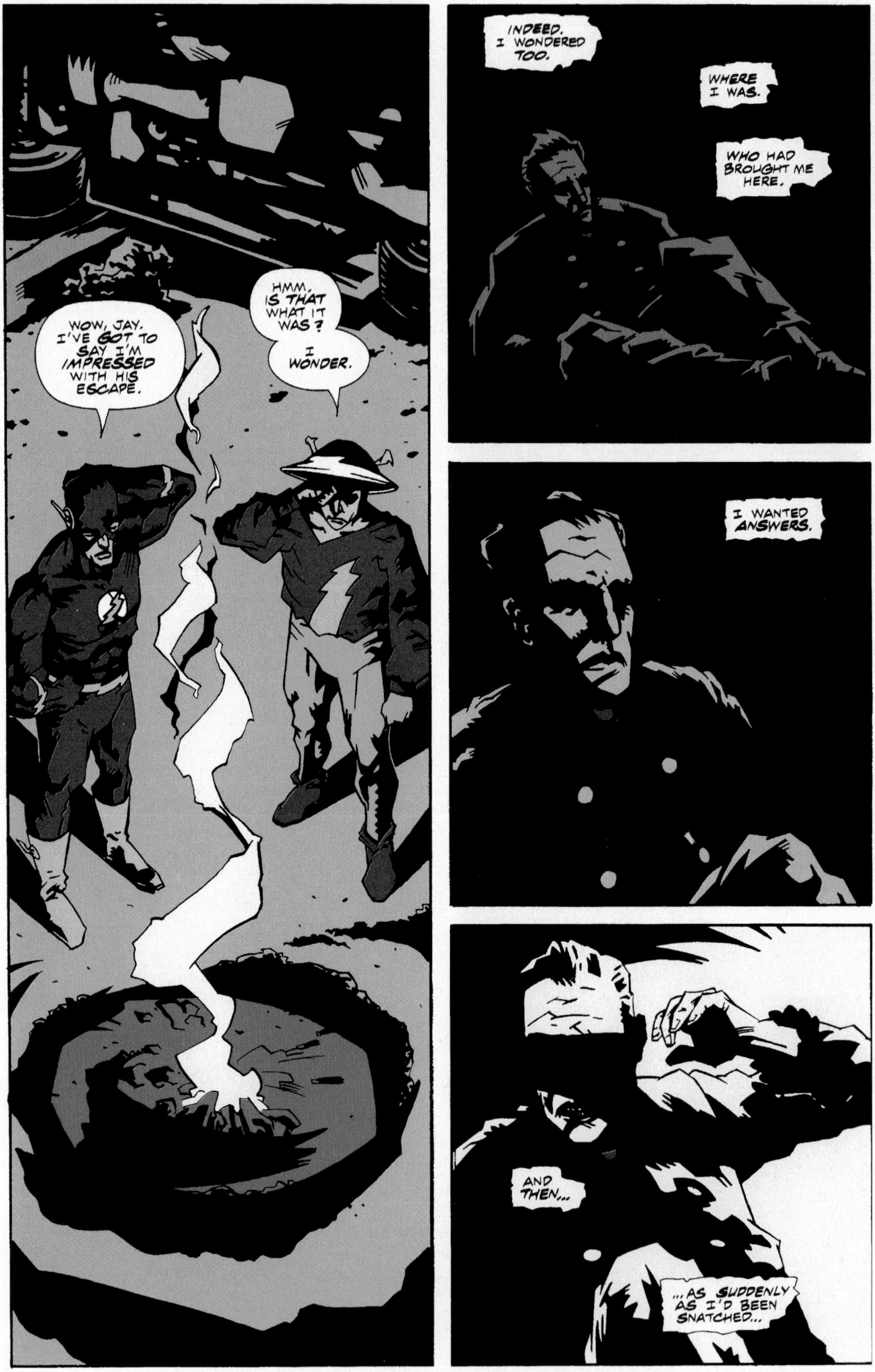
WOW, JAY. I'VE GOT TO SAY I'M IMPRESSED WITH HIS ESCAPE.
HMM. IS THAT WHAT IT WAS?
I WONDER.
INDEED. I WONDERED TOO.
WHERE I WAS.
WHO HAD BROUGHT ME HERE.
I WANTED ANSWERS.
AND THEN...
...AS SUDDENLY AS I'D BEEN SNATCHED...

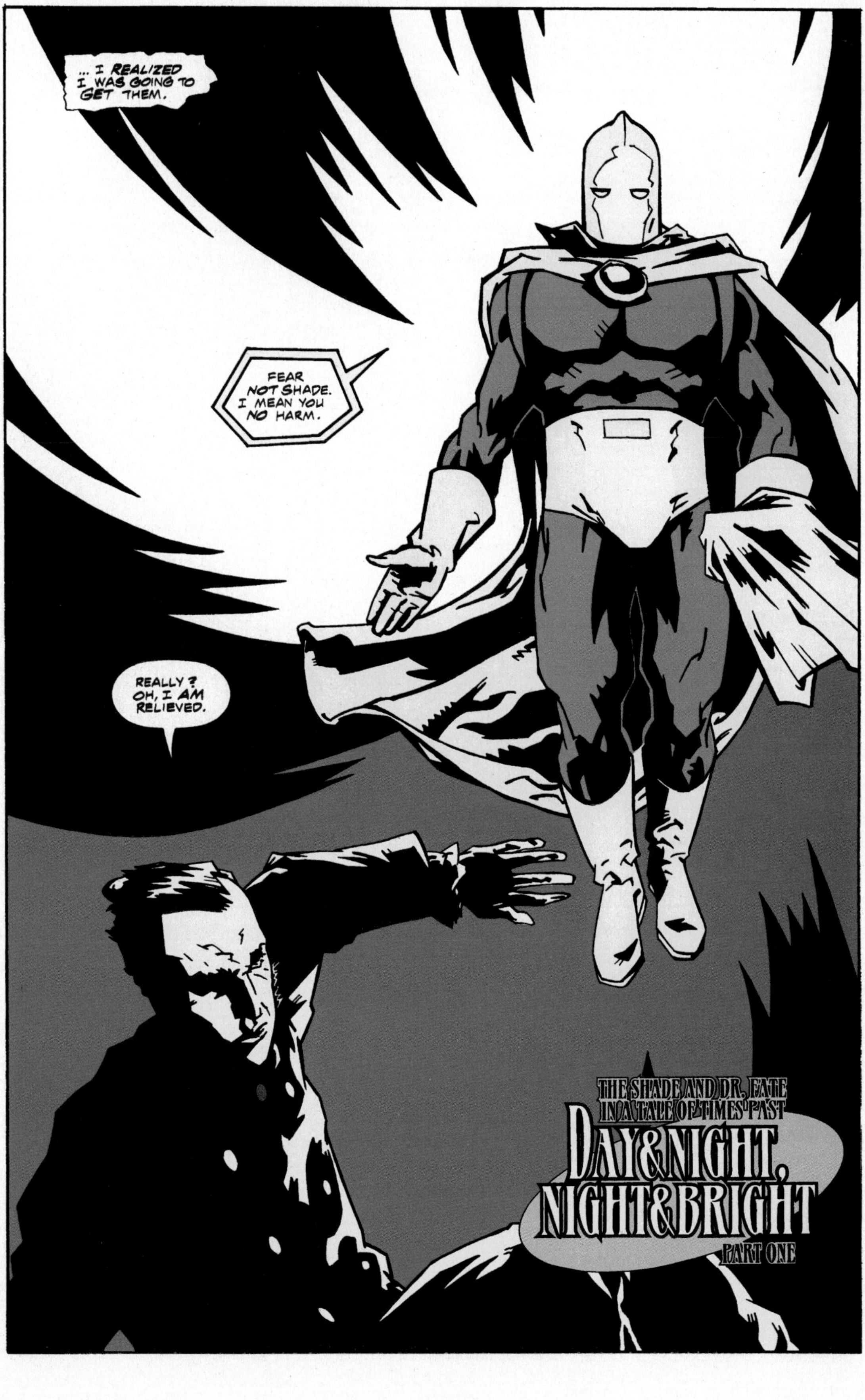
... I REALIZED I WAS GOING TO GET THEM.
FEAR NOT SHADE. I MEAN YOU NO HARM.
REALLY? OH, I AM RELIEVED.
THE SHADE AND DR. FATE IN A TALE OF TIMES PAST
DAY & NIGHT, NIGHT & BRIGHT
PART ONE

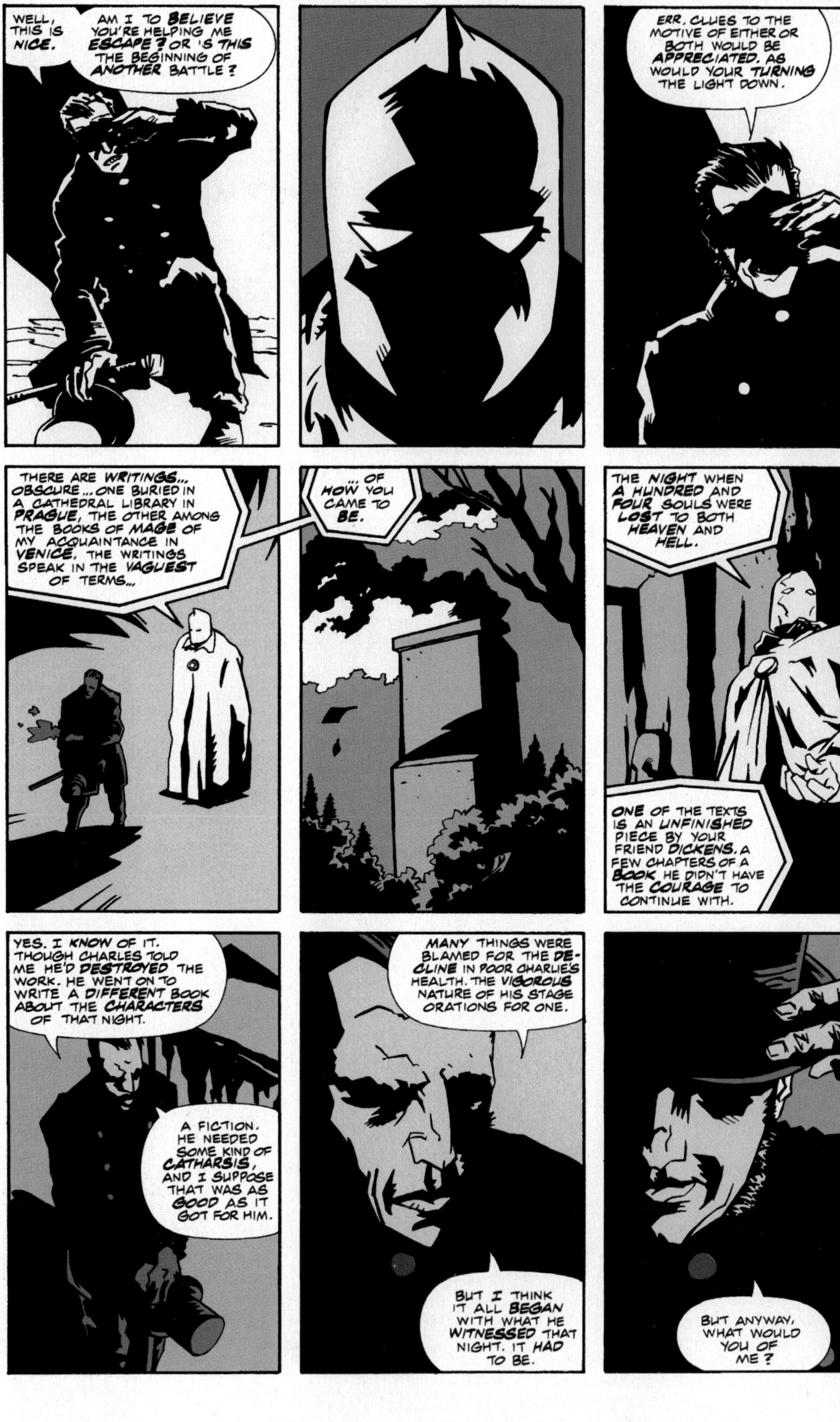

WELL, THIS IS NICE.
AM I TO BELIEVE YOU'RE HELPING ME ESCAPE? OR 'S THIS THE BEGINNING OF ANOTHER BATTLE?
ERR. CLUES TO THE MOTIVE OF EITHER OR BOTH WOULD BE APPRECIATED. AS WOULD YOUR TURNING THE LIGHT DOWN.
THERE ARE WRITINGS... OBSCURE... ONE BURIED IN A CATHEDRAL LIBRARY IN PRAGUE, THE OTHER AMONG THE BOOKS OF MAGE OF MY ACQUAINTANCE IN VENICE. THE WRITINGS SPEAK IN THE VAGUEST OF TERMS...
... OF HOW YOU CAME TO BE.
THE NIGHT WHEN A HUNDRED AND FOUR SOULS WERE LOST TO BOTH HEAVEN AND HELL.
ONE OF THE TEXTS IS AN UNFINISHED PIECE BY YOUR FRIEND DICKENS. A FEW CHAPTERS OF A BOOK HE DIDN'T HAVE THE COURAGE TO CONTINUE WITH.
YES. I KNOW OF IT. THOUGH CHARLES TOLD ME HE'D DESTROYED THE WORK. HE WENT ON TO WRITE A DIFFERENT BOOK ABOUT THE CHARACTERS OF THAT NIGHT.
A FICTION. HE NEEDED SOME KIND OF CATHARSIS, AND I SUPPOSE THAT WAS AS GOOD AS IT GOT FOR HIM.
MANY THINGS WERE BLAMED FOR THE DECLINE IN POOR CHARLIE'S HEALTH. THE VIGOROUS NATURE OF HIS STAGE ORATIONS FOR ONE.
BUT I THINK IT ALL BEGAN WITH WHAT HE WITNESSED THAT NIGHT. IT HAD TO BE.
BUT ANYWAY, WHAT WOULD YOU OF ME?

YOU AREN'T A BEING OF MAGIC, LIKE I AM. YOU AREN'T A BEING OF *SUPERNATURAL* ENERGY. YOUR POWER IS ALMOST *ELEMENTAL*. THE *INVERSE* OF LIGHT.

YOUR POWER WOULD BE *HARD* TO BEAT USING MY MAGIC. EVEN THE *SPECTRE* WOULD HAVE *DIFFICULTY*.

REALLY. HOW *REASSURING*. THOUGH IF THIS IS *YOUR* WAY OF *INTIMIDATING* ME *BEFORE* WE FIGHT, I MIGHT SUGGEST A *SHIFT* IN STRATEGY.

I *DON'T* INTEND TO FIGHT YOU, SHADE. YOU WILL *HELP* ME.

OH, WILL I INDEED. WITHOUT A PLEASE OR THANK YOU. YOU'LL HAVE TO BE *MORE* ALLURING THAN *THAT* IF YOU WANT MY AID.

AND TAKE *OFF* THAT *SILLY* HELMET. I KNOW YOU'RE *KENT NELSON*. I KNOW *ALL* ABOUT YOU.

REALLY? WHAT DO YOU KNOW?

DR. *FATE*, CRIME-FIGHTING *SORCERER*... FOR WANT OF A *BETTER* DESCRIPTION.

KENT NELSON, ON THE *OTHER* HAND, IS AN *ARCHAEOLOGIST* AND WHEN YOU DON THE HELMET YOU'RE *STILL* NELSON SOME OF THE TIME. BUT *SOMETIMES* YOU'RE *NABU*, EGYPTIAN WIZARD, AND MYSTICAL SPIRIT LORD OF *SOME* TYPE OR OTHER.

YOU KNOW MUCH.

I ENJOY *FACTS*. I COLLECT THEM... LIKE *BUTTERFLIES*.

SO WHEN THE HELMET WAS ON JUST *NOW*, WAS I SPEAKING TO NABU?

NO, HIS HOLD ON ME HAS BEEN *LIGHT* THESE PAST FEW MONTHS. IT WAS ME, *NELSON*, UNDER THE HELMET.

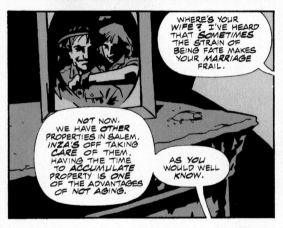

WHERE'S YOUR *WIFE*? I'VE HEARD THAT *SOMETIMES* THE STRAIN OF BEING FATE MAKES YOUR *MARRIAGE* FRAIL.

NOT NOW. WE HAVE *OTHER* PROPERTIES IN SALEM. *INZA'S* OFF TAKING *CARE* OF THEM. HAVING THE TIME TO *ACCUMULATE* PROPERTY IS *ONE* OF THE ADVANTAGES OF NOT AGING.

AS YOU WOULD WELL KNOW.

SO I'VE TOLD YOU WHAT I KNOW. NOW *WHAT DO YOU KNOW?* AND WHY SHOULD I CARE AT *ALL?*

THERE IS A *CULT*, THE *WISE FOOLS*, WHO HAVE COME TO *SALEM*. I WOULD *HAVE* THAT THEY *LEAVE* IT.

THEY PRACTICE *ARCANE RITUAL*, FROM THE *DARK* PAST.

AND THEY WOULD *USE* WHATEVER *NEW* POWER THEY MIGHT *GAIN* FROM IT, FOR *EVIL*.

ALREADY THEY'VE HIRED *ONE* VERSED IN MAGIC. A FELLOW FROM THE *CARIBBEAN* ... *REMY DESHARD*, WHO STAYED WITH THEM *BRIEFLY* AND USED HIS POWERS TO *TRANSFORM* A GROUP OF THE CULT INTO AN *ELITE GUARD*.

DESHARD IS *GONE*. BUT *NOW* THEY'VE BROUGHT IN *ANOTHER*. ONE WHO HAS *KNOWLEDGE* OF YOUR ORIGIN AND THE MAGIC *NEEDED* TO PERFORM IT.

THEY'VE *HIRED* HIM TO IMBUE A *DIFFERENT* GROUP OF THE CULT WITH *YOUR* POWERS.

THE *NEED* FOR THE *ENERGY* OF ONE HUNDRED AND FOUR SOULS THAT IT *TOOK* TO CREATE YOU, HAS BEEN GOTTEN *AROUND* IN THESE *MODERN* TIMES BY A *UNIQUE* TRANSMITTER / RECEIVER THAT *THIS* MAGE CREATED FOR THEM.

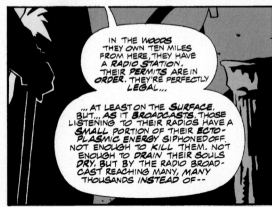

IN THE *WOODS* THEY OWN TEN MILES FROM HERE, THEY HAVE A *RADIO STATION*. THEIR *PERMITS* ARE IN *ORDER*. THEY'RE PERFECTLY *LEGAL*...

... AT LEAST ON THE *SURFACE*. BUT,... AS IT *BROADCASTS*, THOSE LISTENING TO THEIR RADIOS HAVE A *SMALL* PORTION OF THEIR *ECTO-PLASMIC ENERGY* SIPHONED OFF. NOT ENOUGH TO KILL THEM. NOT ENOUGH TO *DRAIN* THEIR SOULS *DRY*. BUT BY THE RADIO BROAD-CAST REACHING MANY, MANY THOUSANDS INSTEAD OF --

EXACTLY! THEY HAVE THE *POWER* TO *RECREATE* THE SPELL THAT MADE YOU. *WITHOUT* THE DEATHS THAT MIGHT DRAW *ATTENTION* TO WHAT THEY'RE *DOING*. IT WILL BE *TOO LATE SOON*, AND NO ONE IS AWARE OF THEIR *INTENT*.

ONE HUNDRED AND FOUR.

EXCEPT *YOU*.

BUT *HOW* DOES THIS MAGE KNOW *SO MUCH* ABOUT MY *CREATION* ?

HOW? WHY, IT WAS *HIS CREATION* TOO.

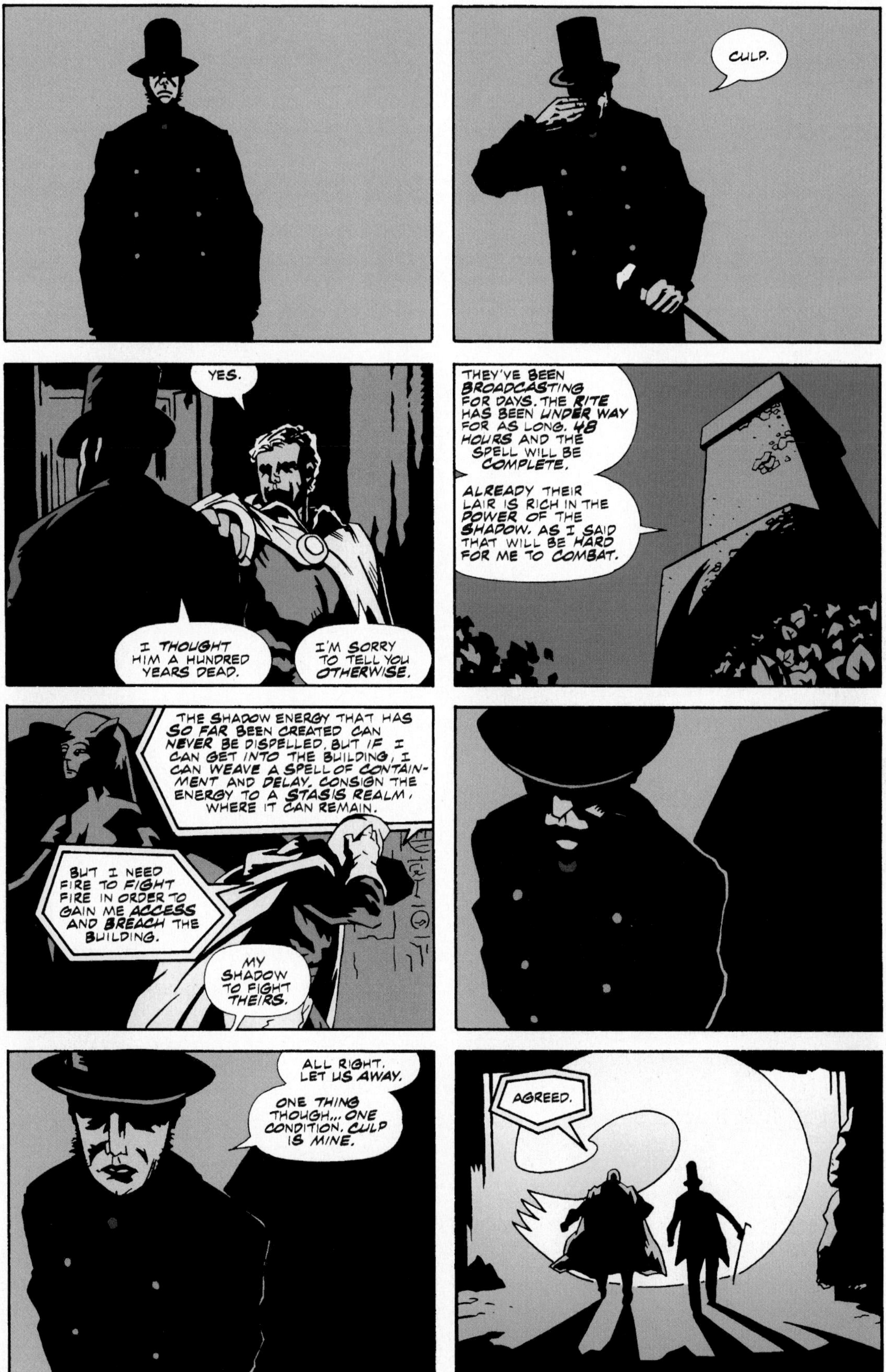
CULP.
YES.
I THOUGHT HIM A HUNDRED YEARS DEAD.
I'M SORRY TO TELL YOU OTHERWISE.
THEY'VE BEEN BROADCASTING FOR DAYS. THE RITE HAS BEEN UNDER WAY FOR AS LONG. 48 HOURS AND THE SPELL WILL BE COMPLETE.
ALREADY THEIR LAIR IS RICH IN THE POWER OF THE SHADOW. AS I SAID THAT WILL BE HARD FOR ME TO COMBAT.
THE SHADOW ENERGY THAT HAS SO FAR BEEN CREATED CAN NEVER BE DISPELLED. BUT IF I CAN GET INTO THE BUILDING, I CAN WEAVE A SPELL OF CONTAINMENT AND DELAY. CONSIGN THE ENERGY TO A STASIS REALM, WHERE IT CAN REMAIN.
BUT I NEED FIRE TO FIGHT FIRE IN ORDER TO GAIN ME ACCESS AND BREACH THE BUILDING.
MY SHADOW TO FIGHT THEIRS.
ALL RIGHT. LET US AWAY.
ONE THING THOUGH... ONE CONDITION. CULP IS MINE.
AGREED.

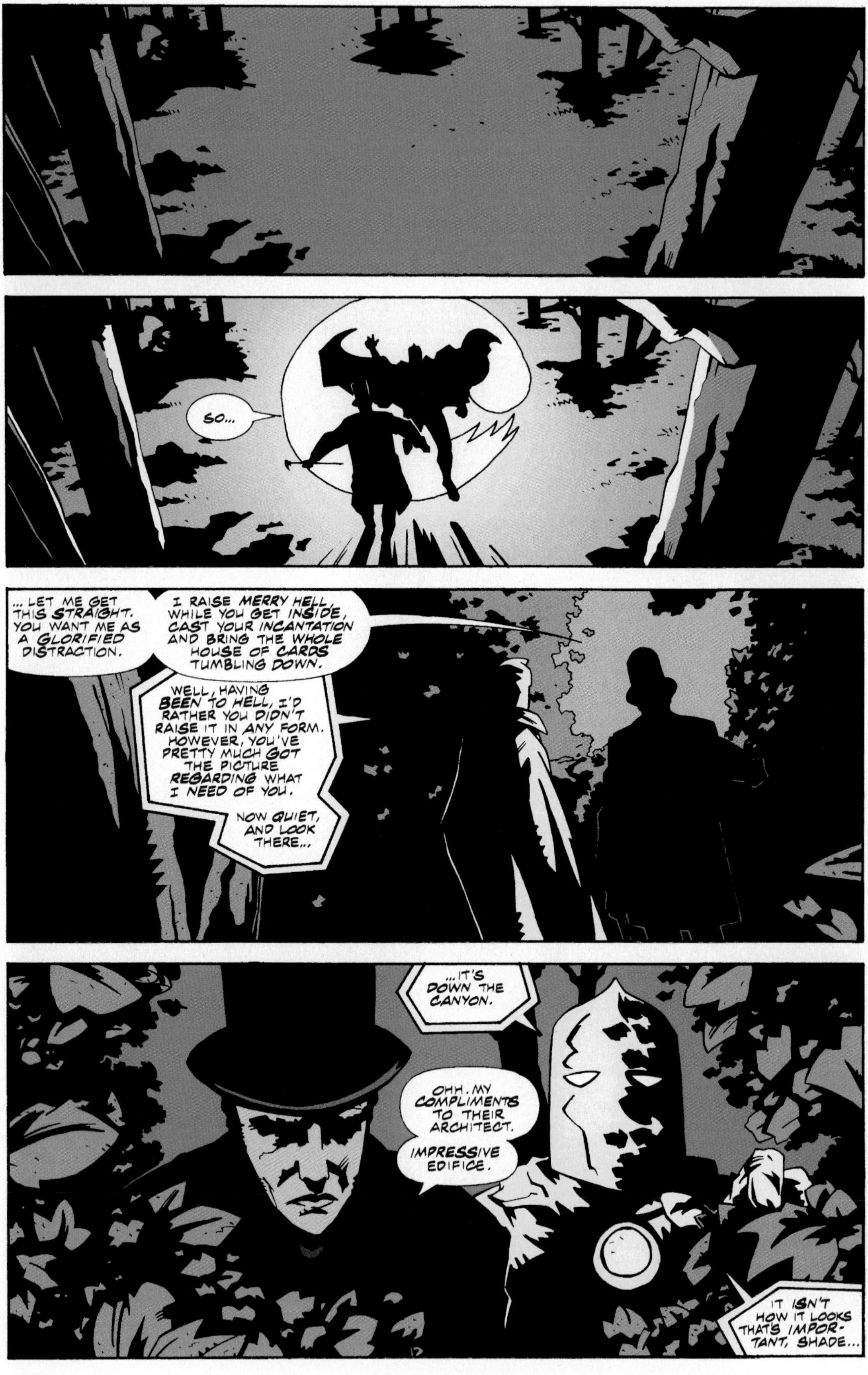
SO...
... LET ME GET THIS STRAIGHT. YOU WANT ME AS A GLORIFIED DISTRACTION.
I RAISE MERRY HELL, WHILE YOU GET INSIDE, CAST YOUR INCANTATION AND BRING THE WHOLE HOUSE OF CARDS TUMBLING DOWN.
WELL, HAVING BEEN TO HELL, I'D RATHER YOU DIDN'T RAISE IT IN ANY FORM. HOWEVER, YOU'VE PRETTY MUCH GOT THE PICTURE REGARDING WHAT I NEED OF YOU.
NOW QUIET, AND LOOK THERE...
...IT'S DOWN THE CANYON.
OHH. MY COMPLIMENTS TO THEIR ARCHITECT.
IMPRESSIVE EDIFICE.
IT ISN'T HOW IT LOOKS THAT'S IMPORTANT, SHADE...

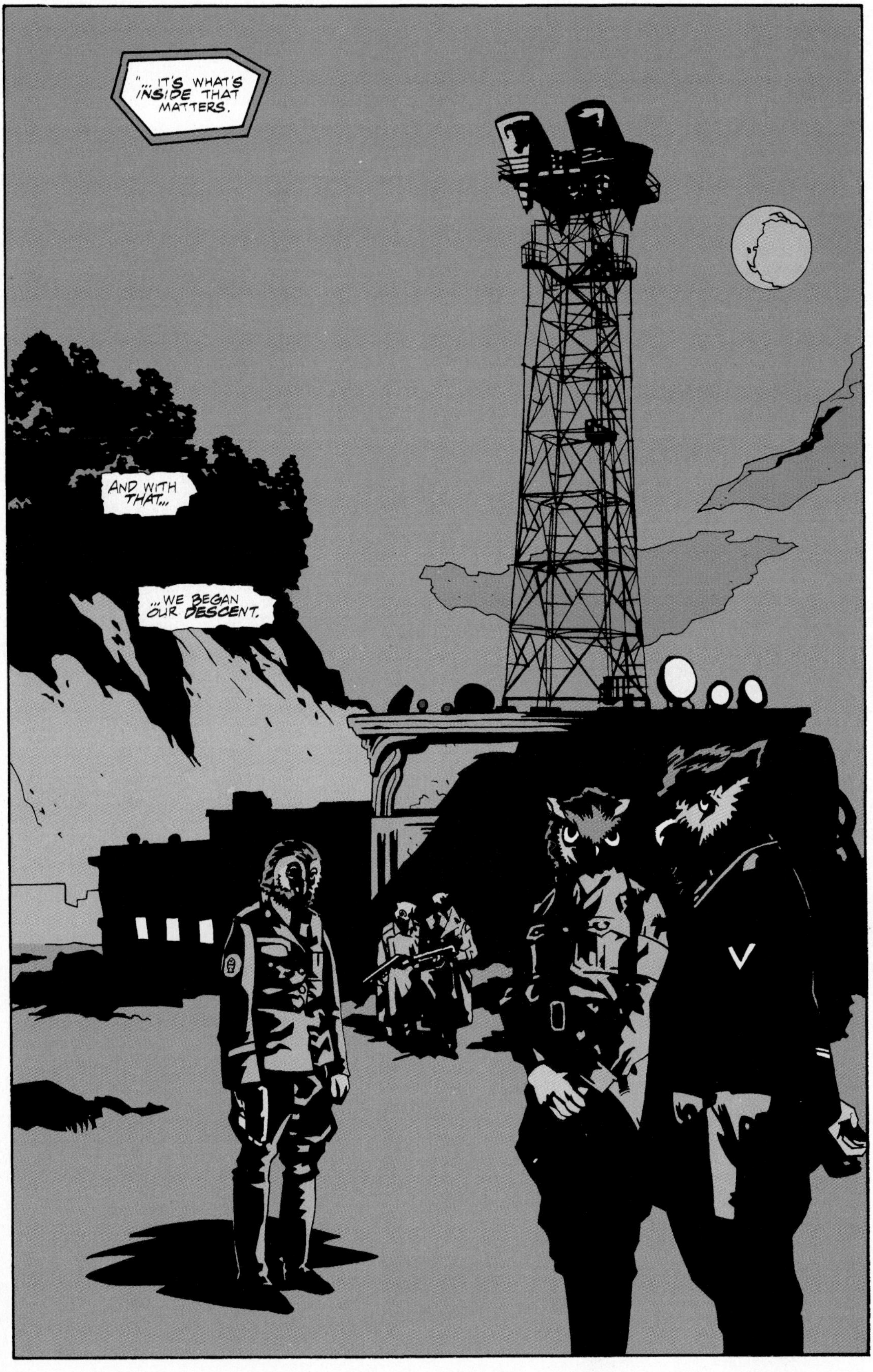
"... IT'S WHAT'S INSIDE THAT MATTERS.
AND WITH THAT...
...WE BEGAN OUR DESCENT.

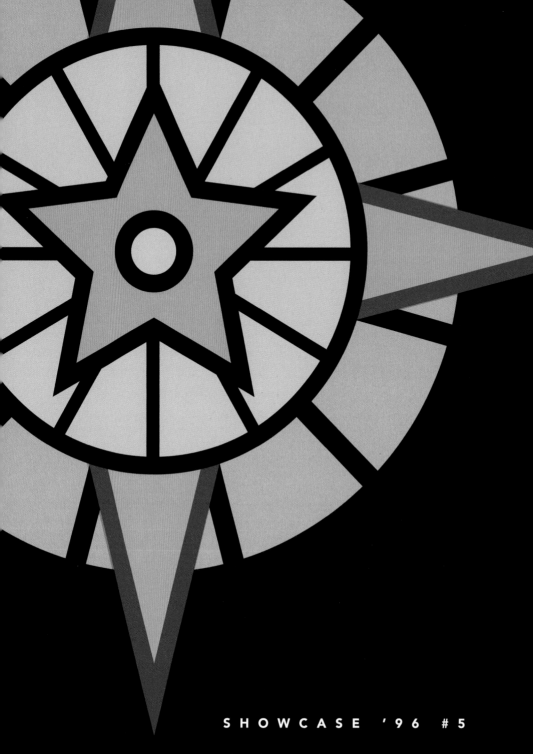

SHOWCASE '96 #5

Written by James Robinson

Art by Matt Smith

with colors by Melissa Edwards

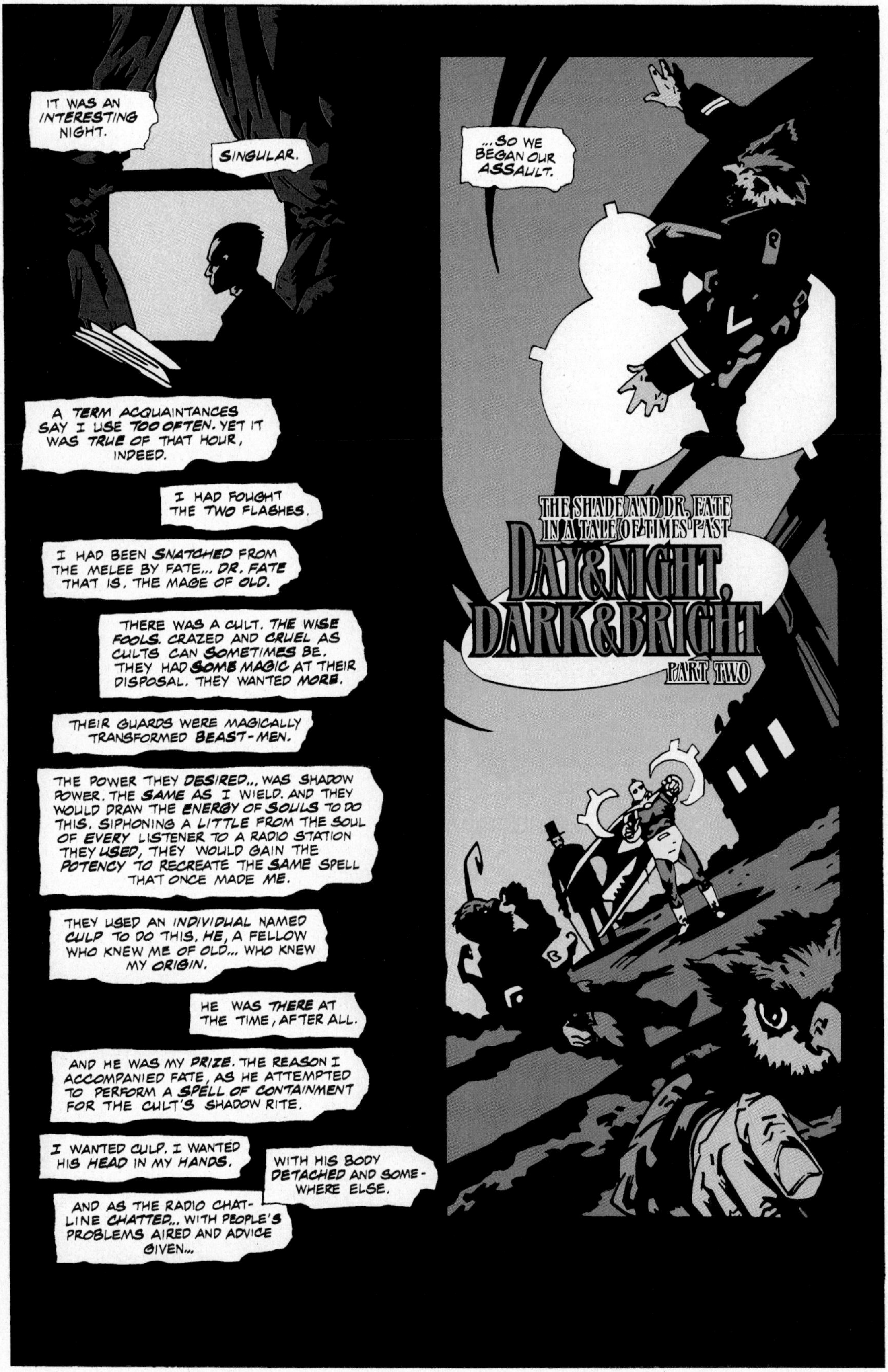
IT WAS AN INTERESTING NIGHT.
SINGULAR.
A TERM ACQUAINTANCES SAY I USE TOO OFTEN. YET IT WAS TRUE OF THAT HOUR, INDEED.
I HAD FOUGHT THE TWO FLASHES.
I HAD BEEN SNATCHED FROM THE MELEE BY FATE... DR. FATE THAT IS. THE MAGE OF OLD.
THERE WAS A CULT. THE WISE FOOLS. CRAZED AND CRUEL AS CULTS CAN SOMETIMES BE. THEY HAD SOME MAGIC AT THEIR DISPOSAL. THEY WANTED MORE.
THEIR GUARDS WERE MAGICALLY TRANSFORMED BEAST-MEN.
THE POWER THEY DESIRED... WAS SHADOW POWER. THE SAME AS I WIELD. AND THEY WOULD DRAW THE ENERGY OF SOULS TO DO THIS. SIPHONING A LITTLE FROM THE SOUL OF EVERY LISTENER TO A RADIO STATION THEY USED, THEY WOULD GAIN THE POTENCY TO RECREATE THE SAME SPELL THAT ONCE MADE ME.
THEY USED AN INDIVIDUAL NAMED CULP TO DO THIS. HE, A FELLOW WHO KNEW ME OF OLD... WHO KNEW MY ORIGIN.
HE WAS THERE AT THE TIME, AFTER ALL.
AND HE WAS MY PRIZE. THE REASON I ACCOMPANIED FATE, AS HE ATTEMPTED TO PERFORM A SPELL OF CONTAINMENT FOR THE CULT'S SHADOW RITE.
I WANTED CULP. I WANTED HIS HEAD IN MY HANDS.
WITH HIS BODY DETACHED AND SOMEWHERE ELSE.
AND AS THE RADIO CHAT-LINE CHATTED... WITH PEOPLE'S PROBLEMS AIRED AND ADVICE GIVEN...
...SO WE BEGAN OUR ASSAULT.
THE SHADE AND DR. FATE IN A TALE OF TIMES PAST
DAY & NIGHT, DARK & BRIGHT
PART TWO

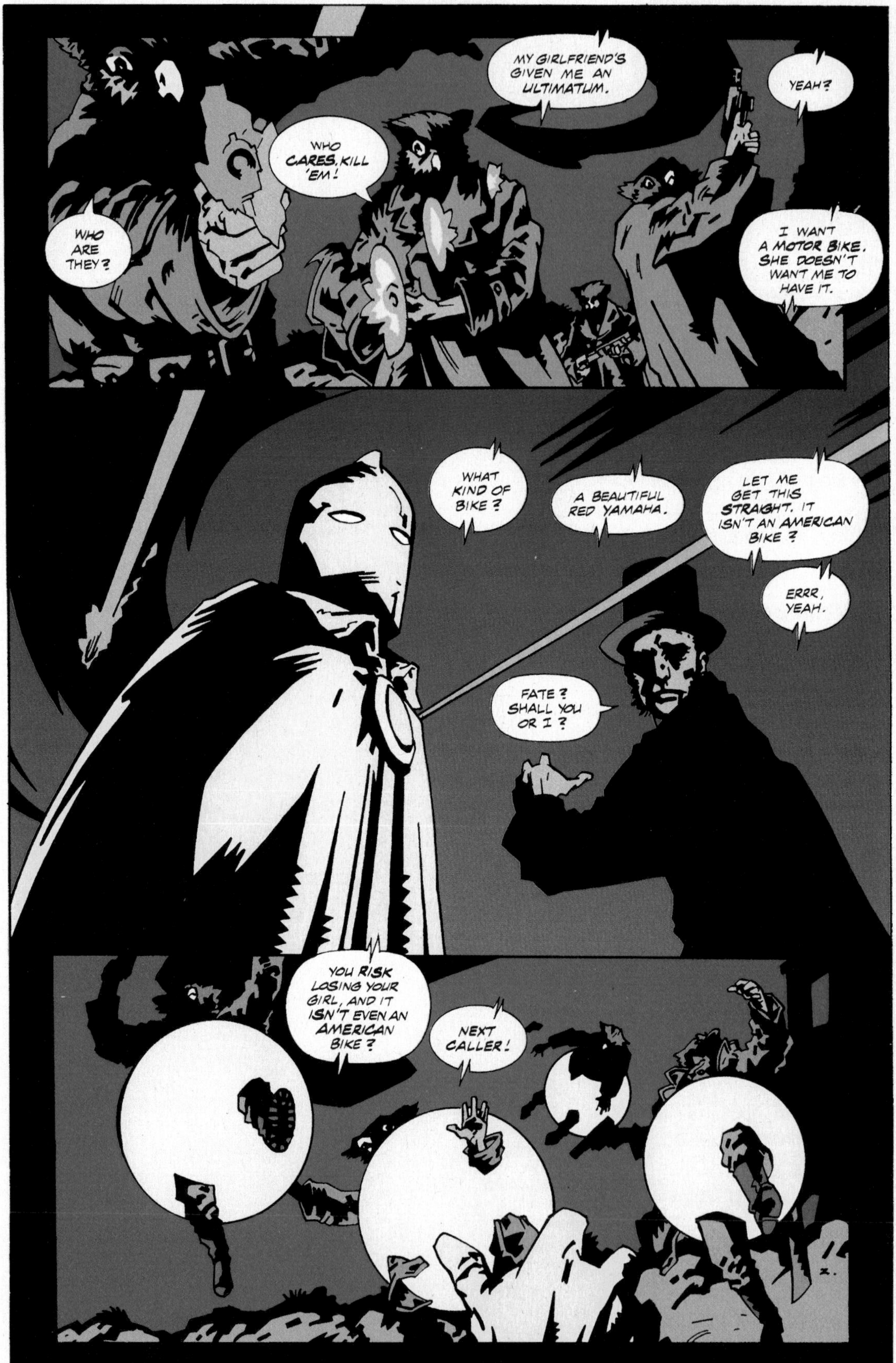
WHO ARE THEY?
WHO CARES. KILL 'EM!
MY GIRLFRIEND'S GIVEN ME AN ULTIMATUM.
YEAH?
I WANT A MOTOR BIKE. SHE DOESN'T WANT ME TO HAVE IT.
WHAT KIND OF BIKE?
A BEAUTIFUL RED YAMAHA.
LET ME GET THIS STRAIGHT. IT ISN'T AN AMERICAN BIKE?
ERRR, YEAH.
FATE? SHALL YOU OR I?
YOU RISK LOSING YOUR GIRL, AND IT ISN'T EVEN AN AMERICAN BIKE?
NEXT CALLER!

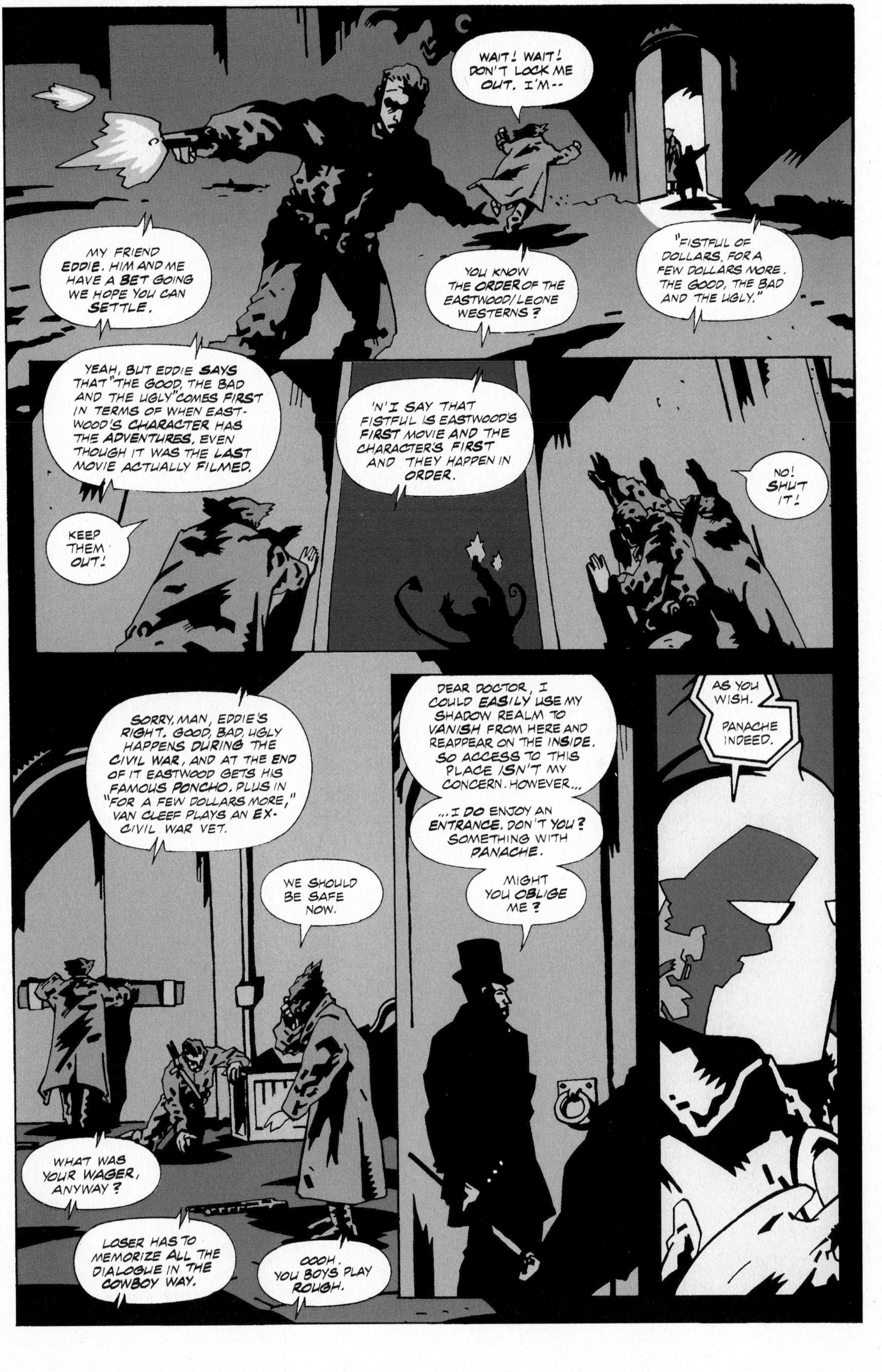
WAIT! WAIT! DON'T LOCK ME OUT. I'M--
MY FRIEND EDDIE. HIM AND ME HAVE A BET GOING WE HOPE YOU CAN SETTLE.
YOU KNOW THE ORDER OF THE EASTWOOD/LEONE WESTERNS?
"FISTFUL OF DOLLARS, FOR A FEW DOLLARS MORE. THE GOOD, THE BAD AND THE UGLY."
YEAH, BUT EDDIE SAYS THAT "THE GOOD, THE BAD AND THE UGLY" COMES FIRST IN TERMS OF WHEN EAST-WOOD'S CHARACTER HAS THE ADVENTURES, EVEN THOUGH IT WAS THE LAST MOVIE ACTUALLY FILMED.
KEEP THEM OUT!
'N' I SAY THAT FISTFUL IS EASTWOOD'S FIRST MOVIE AND THE CHARACTER'S FIRST AND THEY HAPPEN IN ORDER.
NO! SHUT IT!
SORRY, MAN, EDDIE'S RIGHT. GOOD, BAD, UGLY HAPPENS DURING THE CIVIL WAR, AND AT THE END OF IT EASTWOOD GETS HIS FAMOUS PONCHO. PLUS IN "FOR A FEW DOLLARS MORE," VAN CLEEF PLAYS AN EX-CIVIL WAR VET.
WE SHOULD BE SAFE NOW.
WHAT WAS YOUR WAGER, ANYWAY?
LOSER HAS TO MEMORIZE ALL THE DIALOGUE IN THE COWBOY WAY.
OOOH. YOU BOYS PLAY ROUGH.
DEAR DOCTOR, I COULD EASILY USE MY SHADOW REALM TO VANISH FROM HERE AND REAPPEAR ON THE INSIDE. SO ACCESS TO THIS PLACE ISN'T MY CONCERN. HOWEVER...
...I DO ENJOY AN ENTRANCE. DON'T YOU? SOMETHING WITH PANACHE.
MIGHT YOU OBLIGE ME?
AS YOU WISH.
PANACHE INDEED.

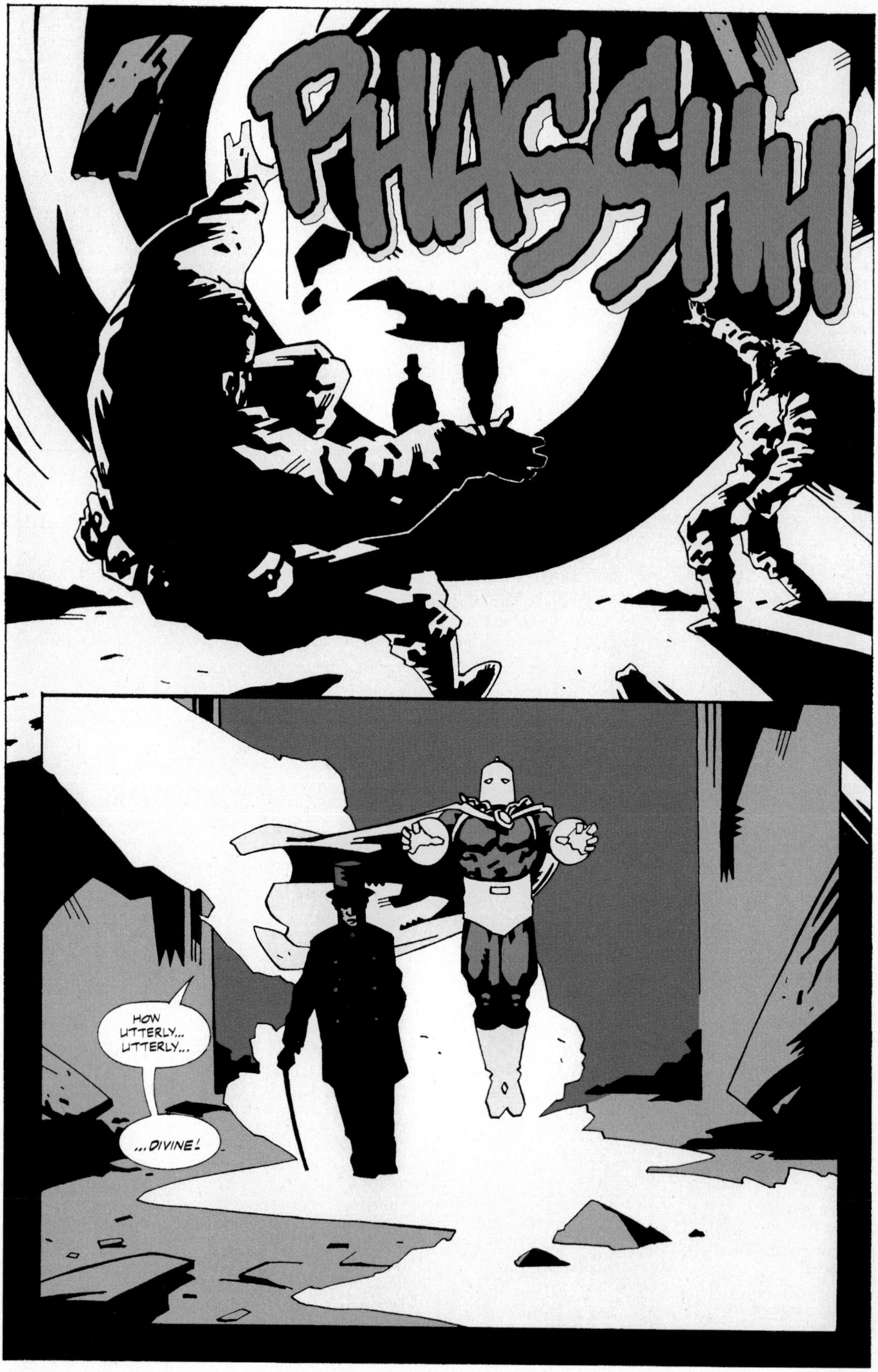
PHASSHH
HOW UTTERLY... UTTERLY...
...DIVINE!

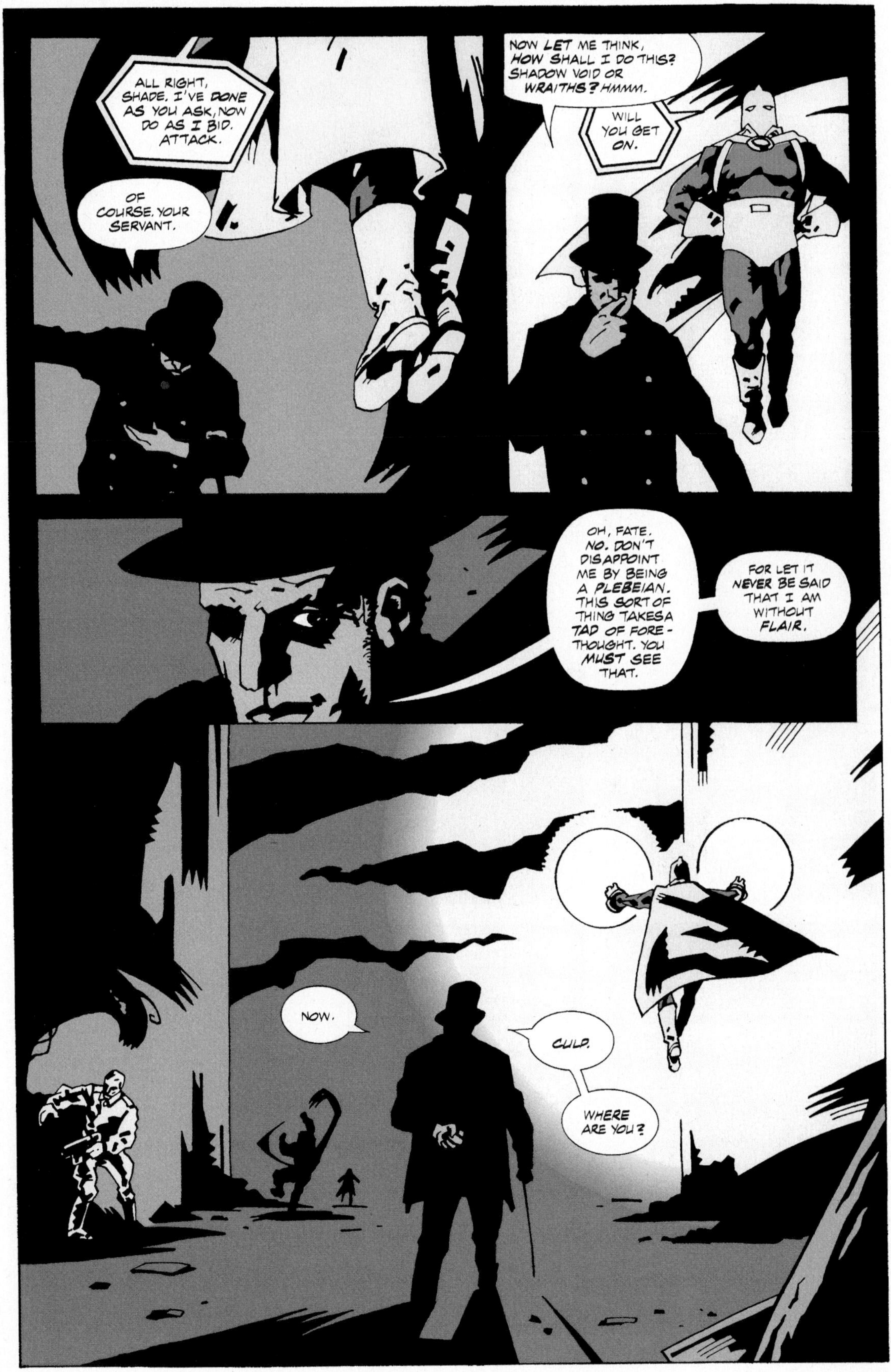
ALL RIGHT, SHADE. I'VE DONE AS YOU ASK, NOW DO AS I BID. ATTACK.
OF COURSE. YOUR SERVANT.
NOW LET ME THINK, HOW SHALL I DO THIS? SHADOW VOID OR WRAITHS? HMMM.
WILL YOU GET ON.
OH, FATE. NO. DON'T DISAPPOINT ME BY BEING A PLEBEIAN. THIS SORT OF THING TAKES A TAD OF FORE-THOUGHT. YOU MUST SEE THAT.
FOR LET IT NEVER BE SAID THAT I AM WITHOUT FLAIR.
NOW.
CULP.
WHERE ARE YOU?

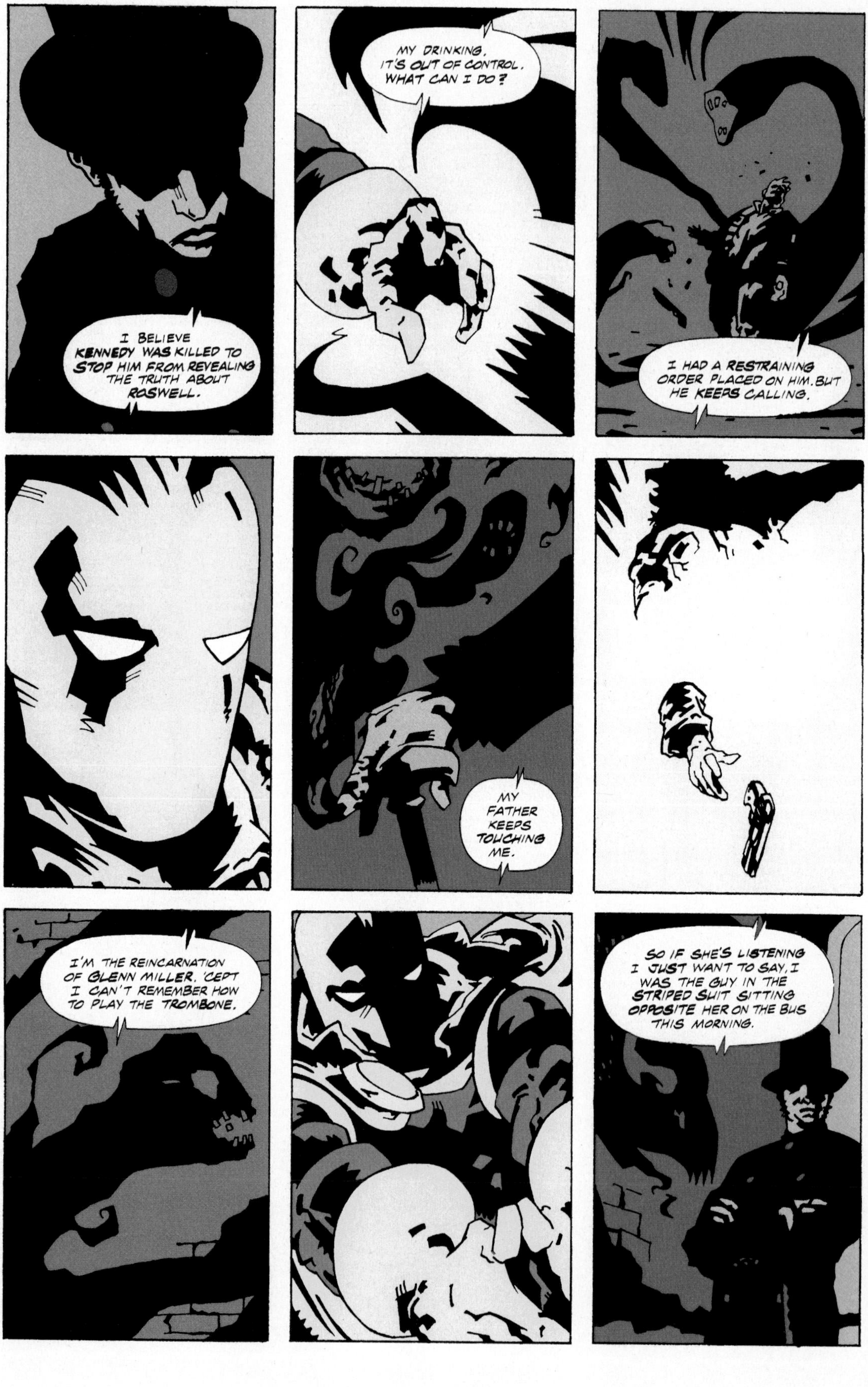
I BELIEVE KENNEDY WAS KILLED TO STOP HIM FROM REVEALING THE TRUTH ABOUT ROSWELL.
MY DRINKING, IT'S OUT OF CONTROL. WHAT CAN I DO?
I HAD A RESTRAINING ORDER PLACED ON HIM. BUT HE KEEPS CALLING.
MY FATHER KEEPS TOUCHING ME.
I'M THE REINCARNATION OF GLENN MILLER, 'CEPT I CAN'T REMEMBER HOW TO PLAY THE TROMBONE.
SO IF SHE'S LISTENING I JUST WANT TO SAY, I WAS THE GUY IN THE STRIPED SUIT SITTING OPPOSITE HER ON THE BUS THIS MORNING.

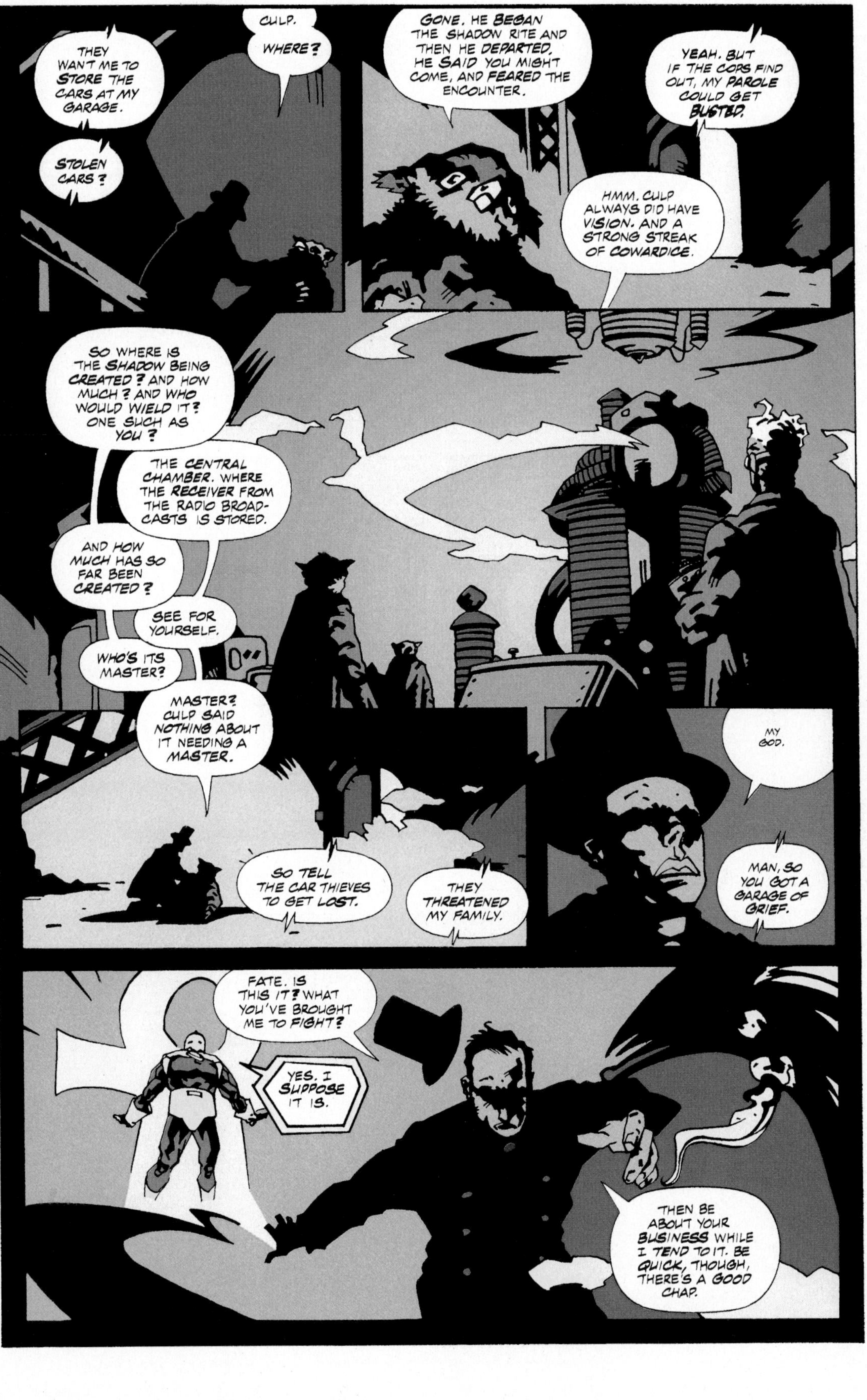
THEY WANT ME TO STORE THE CARS AT MY GARAGE.
STOLEN CARS?
CULP.
WHERE?
GONE. HE BEGAN THE SHADOW RITE AND THEN HE DEPARTED. HE SAID YOU MIGHT COME, AND FEARED THE ENCOUNTER.
YEAH. BUT IF THE COPS FIND OUT, MY PAROLE COULD GET BUSTED.
HMM. CULP ALWAYS DID HAVE VISION. AND A STRONG STREAK OF COWARDICE.
SO WHERE IS THE SHADOW BEING CREATED? AND HOW MUCH? AND WHO WOULD WIELD IT? ONE SUCH AS YOU?
THE CENTRAL CHAMBER. WHERE THE RECEIVER FROM THE RADIO BROAD-CASTS IS STORED.
AND HOW MUCH HAS SO FAR BEEN CREATED?
SEE FOR YOURSELF.
WHO'S ITS MASTER?
MASTER? CULP SAID NOTHING ABOUT IT NEEDING A MASTER.
SO TELL THE CAR THIEVES TO GET LOST.
THEY THREATENED MY FAMILY.
MY GOD.
MAN, SO YOU GOT A GARAGE OF GRIEF.
FATE. IS THIS IT? WHAT YOU'VE BROUGHT ME TO FIGHT?
YES. I SUPPOSE IT IS.
THEN BE ABOUT YOUR BUSINESS WHILE I TEND TO IT. BE QUICK, THOUGH, THERE'S A GOOD CHAP.

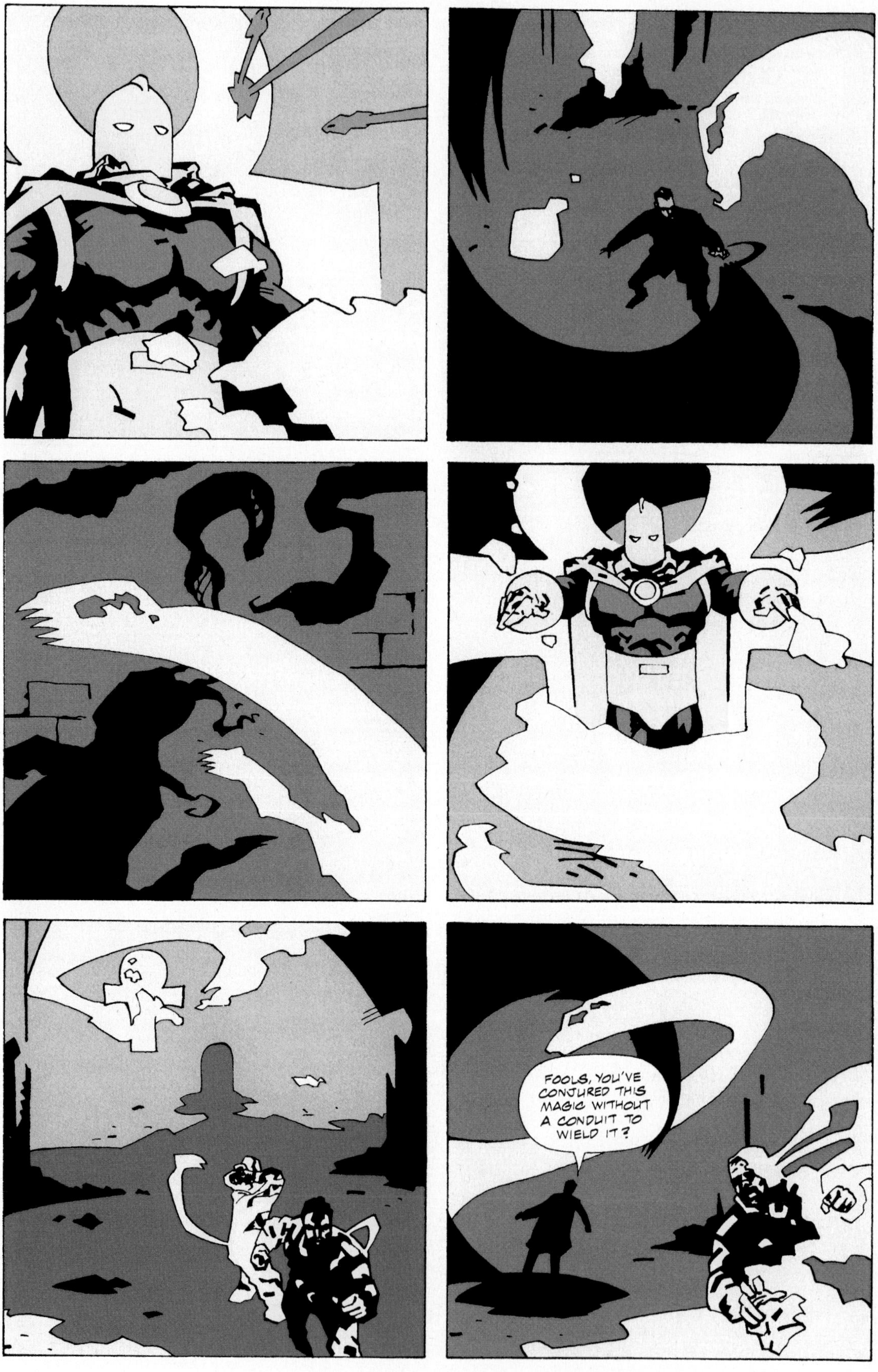
FOOLS, YOU'VE CONJURED THIS MAGIC WITHOUT A CONDUIT TO WIELD IT?

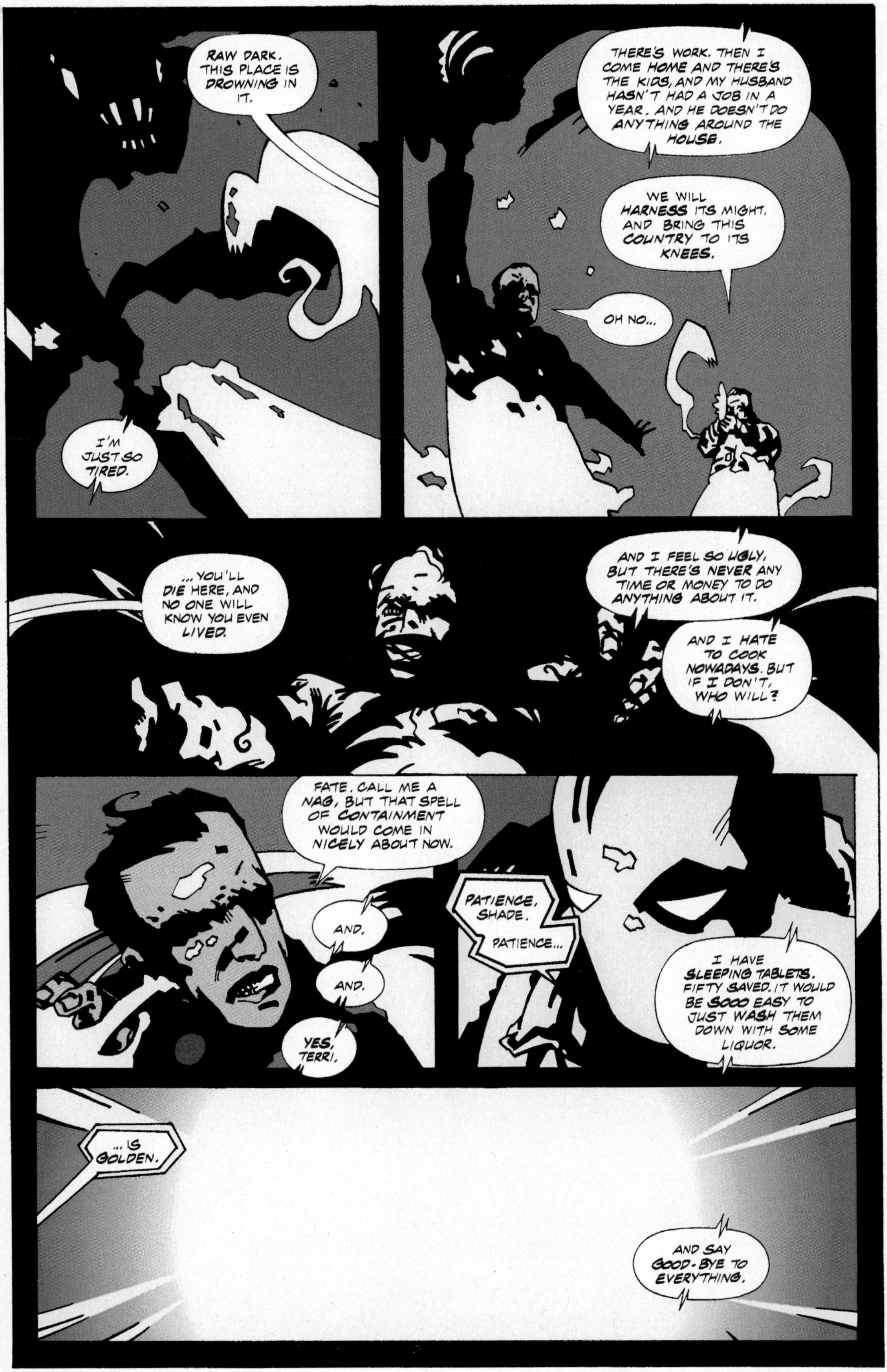
RAW DARK. THIS PLACE IS DROWNING IN IT.
I'M JUST SO TIRED.
THERE'S WORK. THEN I COME HOME AND THERE'S THE KIDS, AND MY HUSBAND HASN'T HAD A JOB IN A YEAR. AND HE DOESN'T DO ANYTHING AROUND THE HOUSE.
WE WILL HARNESS ITS MIGHT, AND BRING THIS COUNTRY TO ITS KNEES.
OH NO...
...YOU'LL DIE HERE, AND NO ONE WILL KNOW YOU EVEN LIVED.
AND I FEEL SO UGLY, BUT THERE'S NEVER ANY TIME OR MONEY TO DO ANYTHING ABOUT IT.
AND I HATE TO COOK NOWADAYS. BUT IF I DON'T, WHO WILL?
FATE, CALL ME A NAG, BUT THAT SPELL OF CONTAINMENT WOULD COME IN NICELY ABOUT NOW.
AND.
AND.
YES, TERRI.
PATIENCE, SHADE.
PATIENCE...
I HAVE SLEEPING TABLETS. FIFTY SAVED. IT WOULD BE SOOO EASY TO JUST WASH THEM DOWN WITH SOME LIQUOR.
...IS GOLDEN.
AND SAY GOOD-BYE TO EVERYTHING.

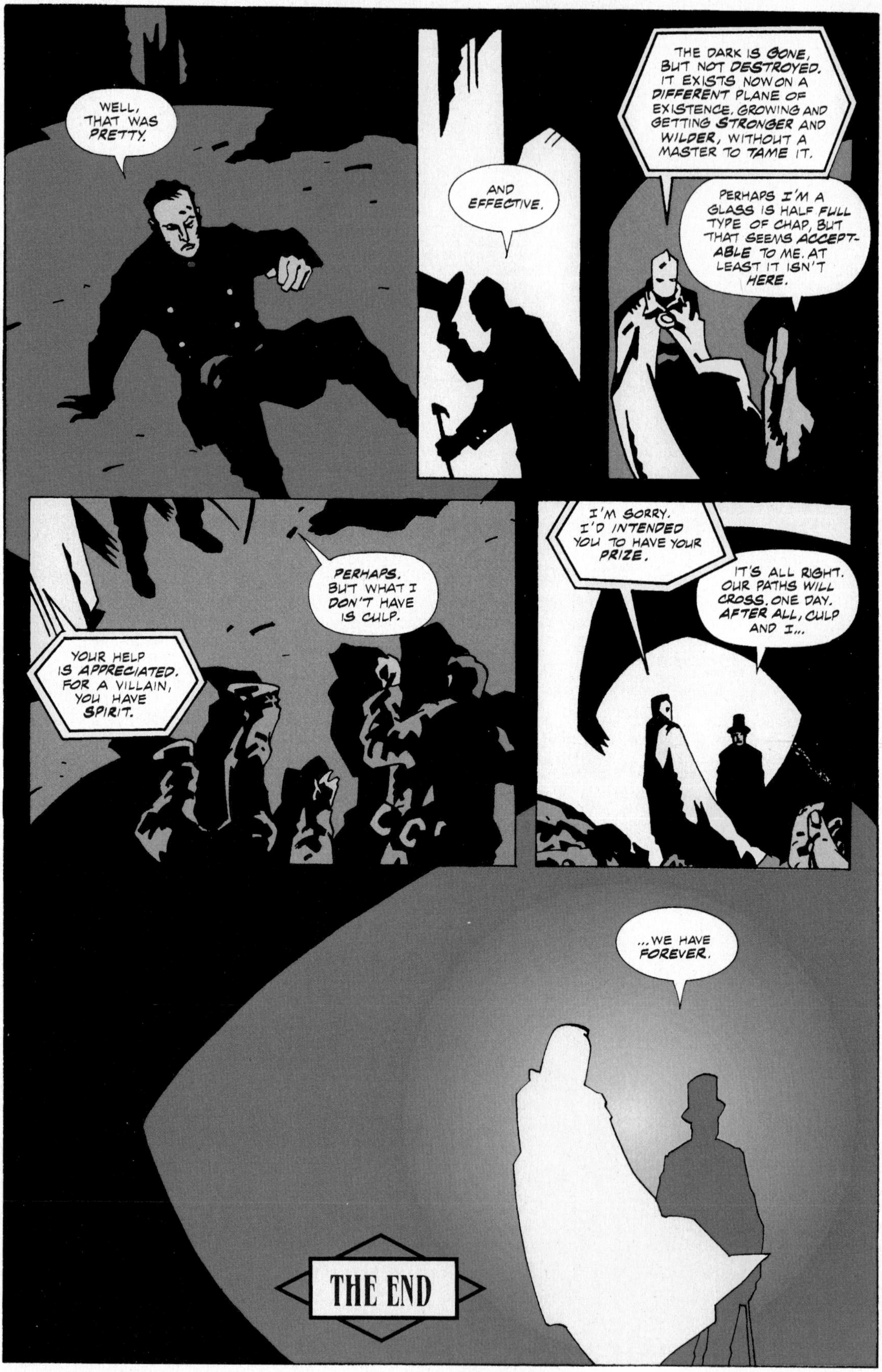
WELL, THAT WAS PRETTY.
AND EFFECTIVE.
THE DARK IS GONE, BUT NOT DESTROYED. IT EXISTS NOW ON A DIFFERENT PLANE OF EXISTENCE, GROWING AND GETTING STRONGER AND WILDER, WITHOUT A MASTER TO TAME IT.
PERHAPS I'M A GLASS IS HALF FULL TYPE OF CHAP, BUT THAT SEEMS ACCEPTABLE TO ME. AT LEAST IT ISN'T HERE.
YOUR HELP IS APPRECIATED. FOR A VILLAIN, YOU HAVE SPIRIT.
PERHAPS. BUT WHAT I DON'T HAVE IS CULP.
I'M SORRY. I'D INTENDED YOU TO HAVE YOUR PRIZE.
IT'S ALL RIGHT. OUR PATHS WILL CROSS. ONE DAY. AFTER ALL, CULP AND I...
...WE HAVE FOREVER.
THE END

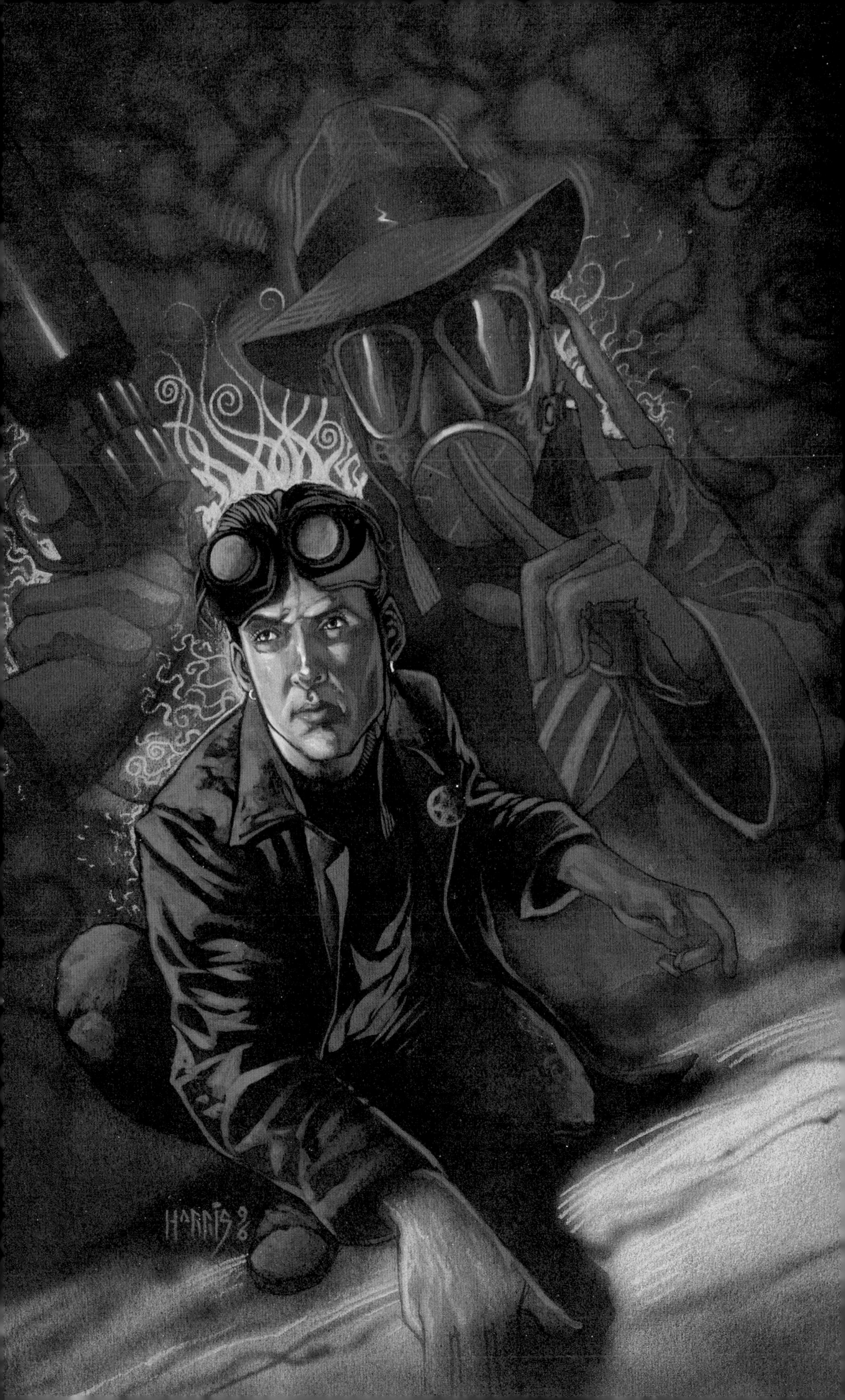

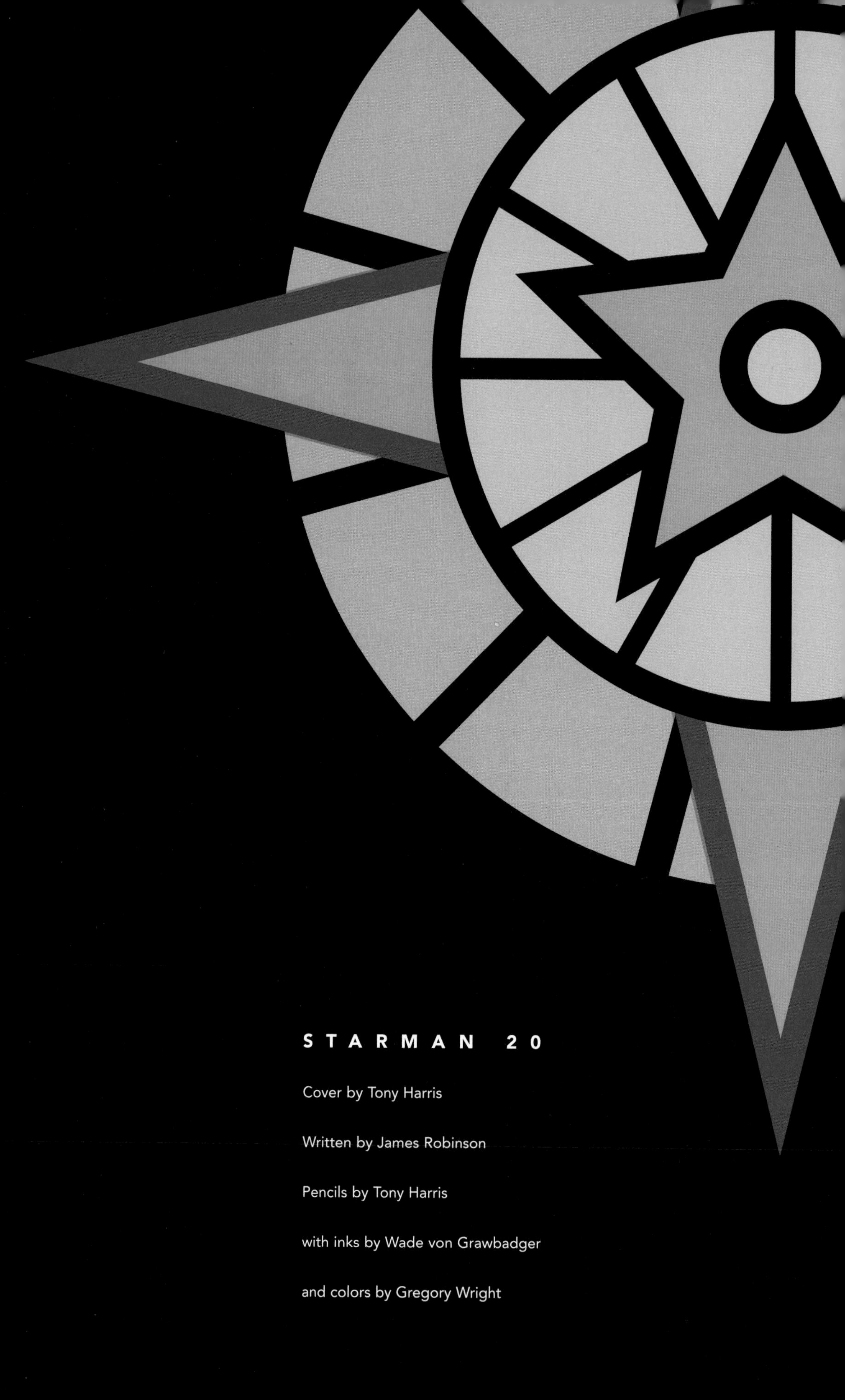

S T A R M A N   2 0

Cover by Tony Harris

Written by James Robinson

Pencils by Tony Harris

with inks by Wade von Grawbadger

and colors by Gregory Wright

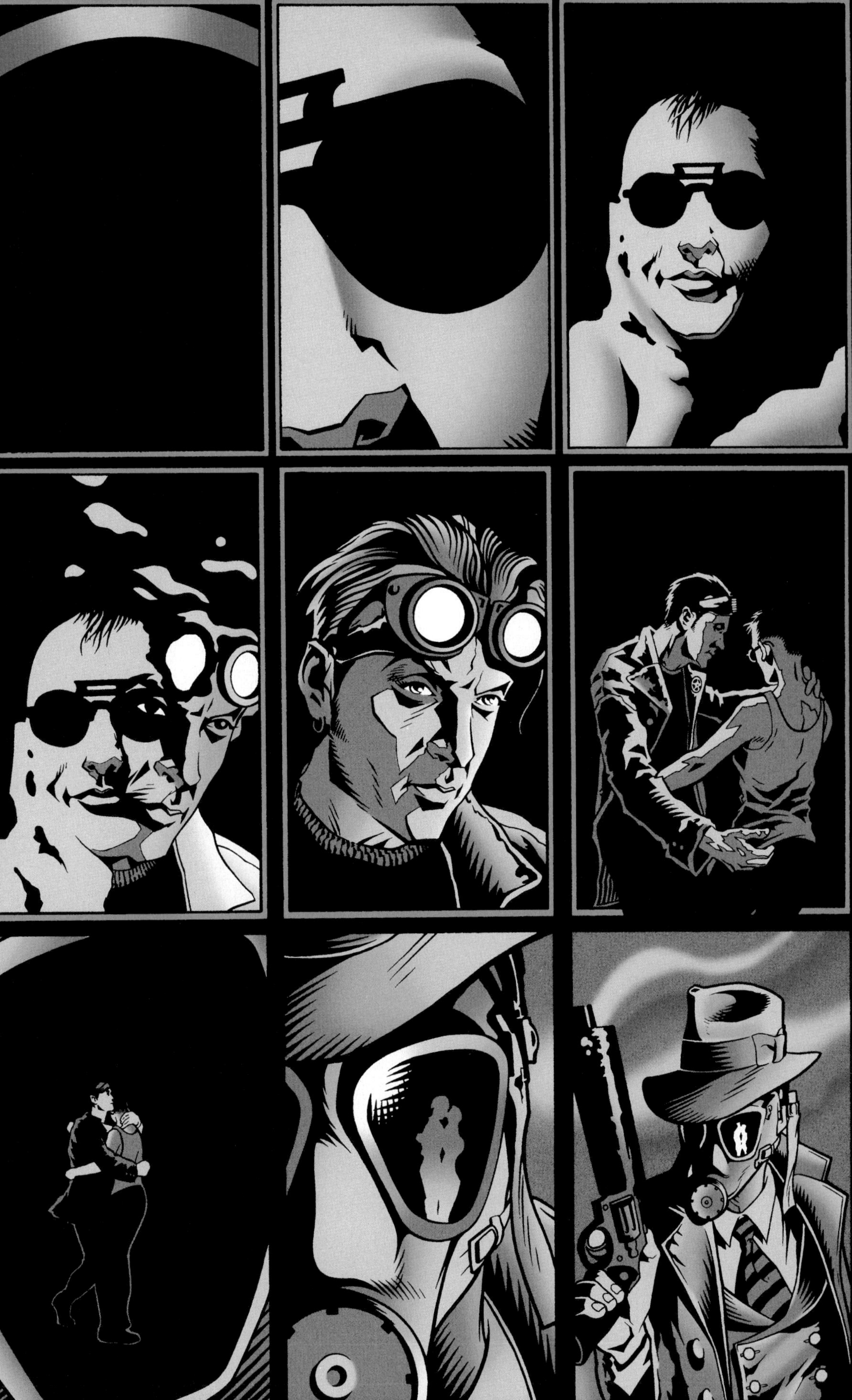

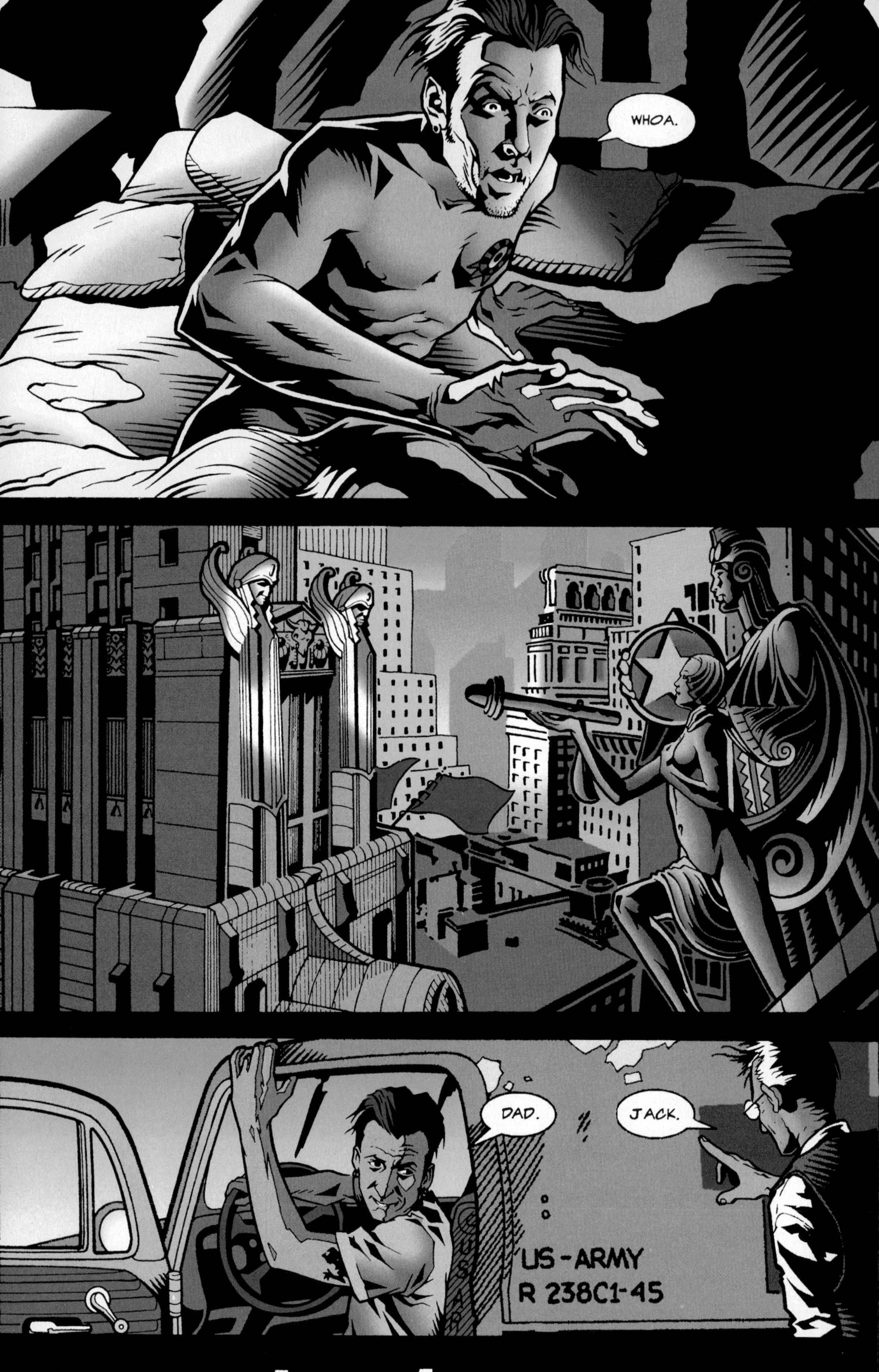
WHOA.
DAD.
JACK.
US-ARMY
R 238C1-45

sand and stars PART ONE

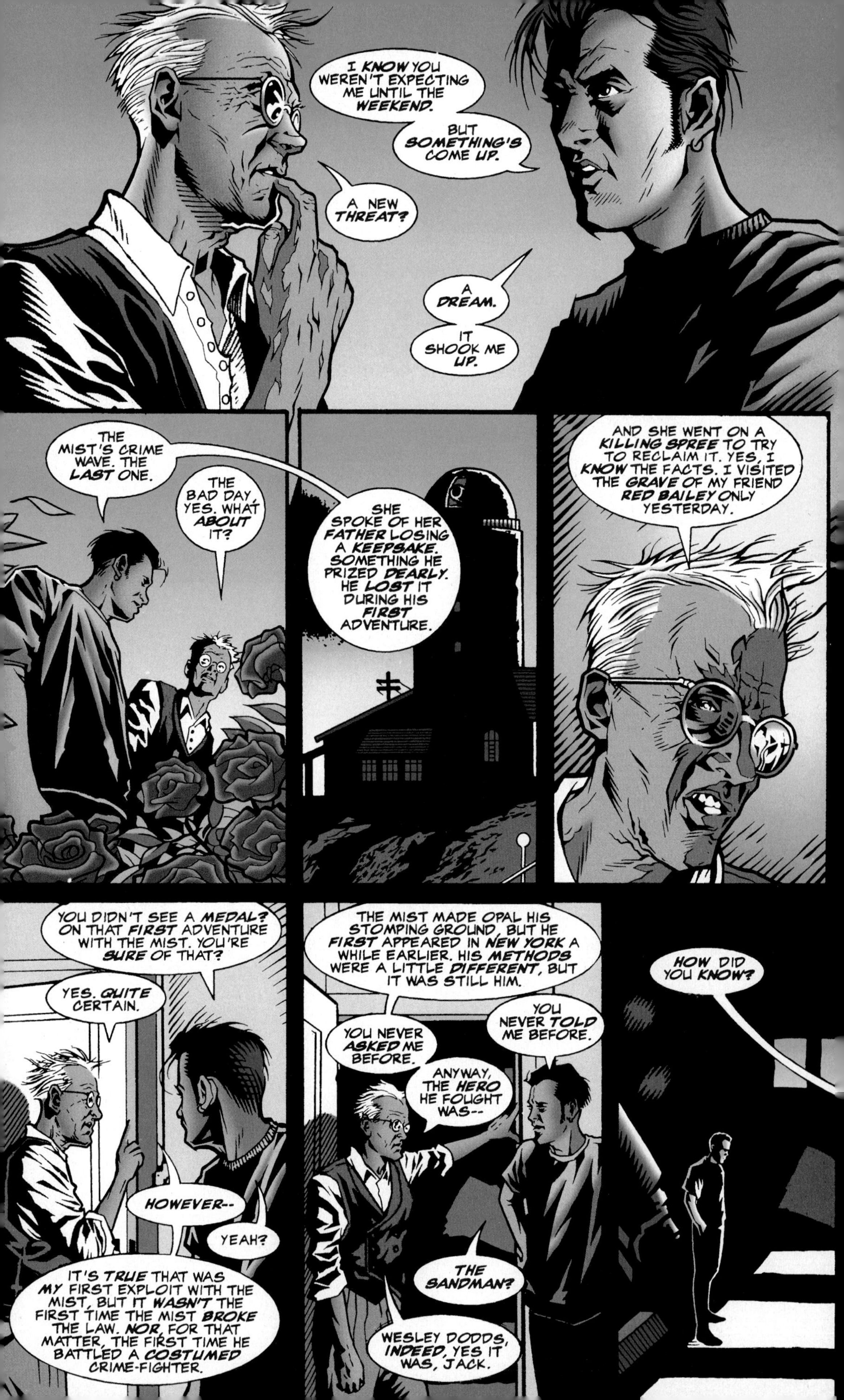
I KNOW YOU WEREN'T EXPECTING ME UNTIL THE WEEKEND.
BUT SOMETHING'S COME UP.
A NEW THREAT?
A DREAM.
IT SHOOK ME UP.
THE MIST'S CRIME WAVE. THE LAST ONE.
THE BAD DAY, YES. WHAT ABOUT IT?
SHE SPOKE OF HER FATHER LOSING A KEEPSAKE. SOMETHING HE PRIZED DEARLY. HE LOST IT DURING HIS FIRST ADVENTURE.
AND SHE WENT ON A KILLING SPREE TO TRY TO RECLAIM IT. YES, I KNOW THE FACTS. I VISITED THE GRAVE OF MY FRIEND RED BAILEY ONLY YESTERDAY.
YOU DIDN'T SEE A MEDAL? ON THAT FIRST ADVENTURE WITH THE MIST. YOU'RE SURE OF THAT?
YES. QUITE CERTAIN.
HOWEVER--
YEAH?
IT'S TRUE THAT WAS MY FIRST EXPLOIT WITH THE MIST, BUT IT WASN'T THE FIRST TIME THE MIST BROKE THE LAW. NOR, FOR THAT MATTER, THE FIRST TIME HE BATTLED A COSTUMED CRIME-FIGHTER.
THE MIST MADE OPAL HIS STOMPING GROUND, BUT HE FIRST APPEARED IN NEW YORK A WHILE EARLIER. HIS METHODS WERE A LITTLE DIFFERENT, BUT IT WAS STILL HIM.
YOU NEVER TOLD ME BEFORE.
YOU NEVER ASKED ME BEFORE.
ANYWAY, THE HERO HE FOUGHT WAS--
THE SANDMAN?
WESLEY DODDS, INDEED, YES IT WAS, JACK.
HOW DID YOU KNOW?

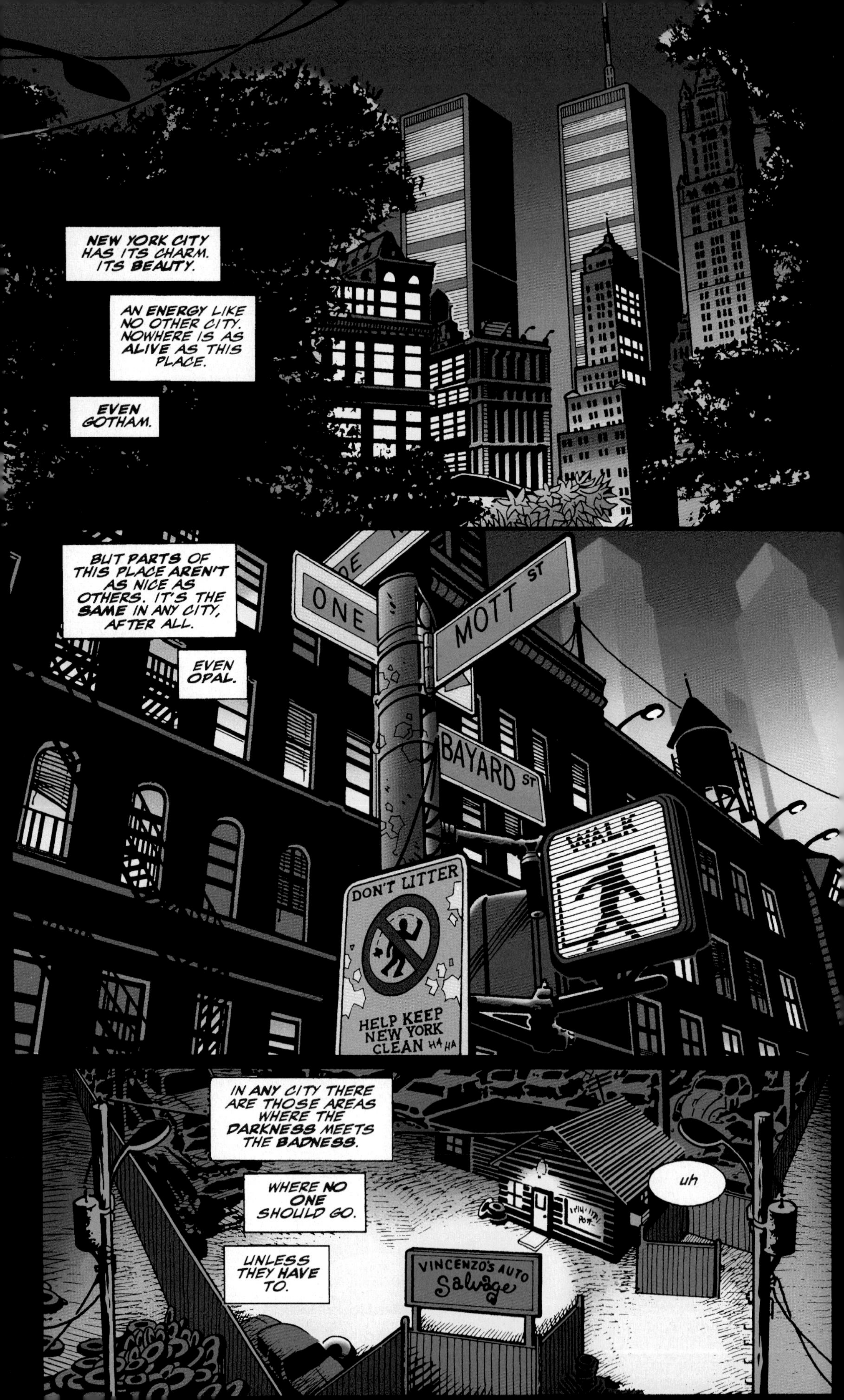
NEW YORK CITY HAS ITS CHARM. ITS BEAUTY.
AN ENERGY LIKE NO OTHER CITY. NOWHERE IS AS ALIVE AS THIS PLACE.
EVEN GOTHAM.
BUT PARTS OF THIS PLACE AREN'T AS NICE AS OTHERS. IT'S THE SAME IN ANY CITY, AFTER ALL.
EVEN OPAL.
ONE
MOTT ST
BAYARD ST
WALK
DON'T LITTER
HELP KEEP NEW YORK CLEAN HA HA
IN ANY CITY THERE ARE THOSE AREAS WHERE THE DARKNESS MEETS THE BADNESS.
WHERE NO ONE SHOULD GO.
UNLESS THEY HAVE TO.
uh
VINCENZO'S AUTO Salvage

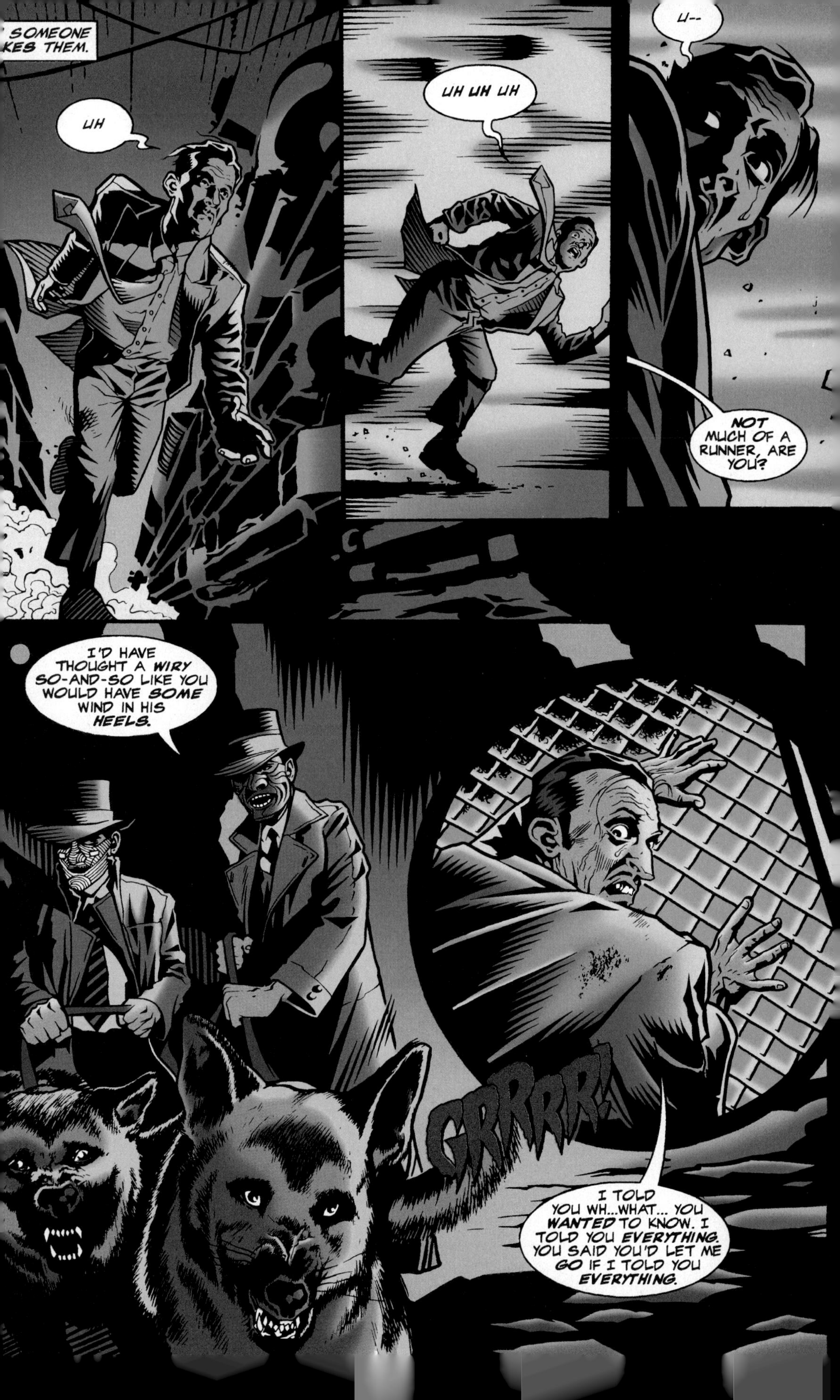
SOMEONE
KES THEM.
UH
UH UH UH
U--
NOT MUCH OF A RUNNER, ARE YOU?
I'D HAVE THOUGHT A WIRY SO-AND-SO LIKE YOU WOULD HAVE SOME WIND IN HIS HEELS.
GRRRR!
I TOLD YOU WH...WHAT... YOU WANTED TO KNOW. I TOLD YOU EVERYTHING. YOU SAID YOU'D LET ME GO IF I TOLD YOU EVERYTHING.

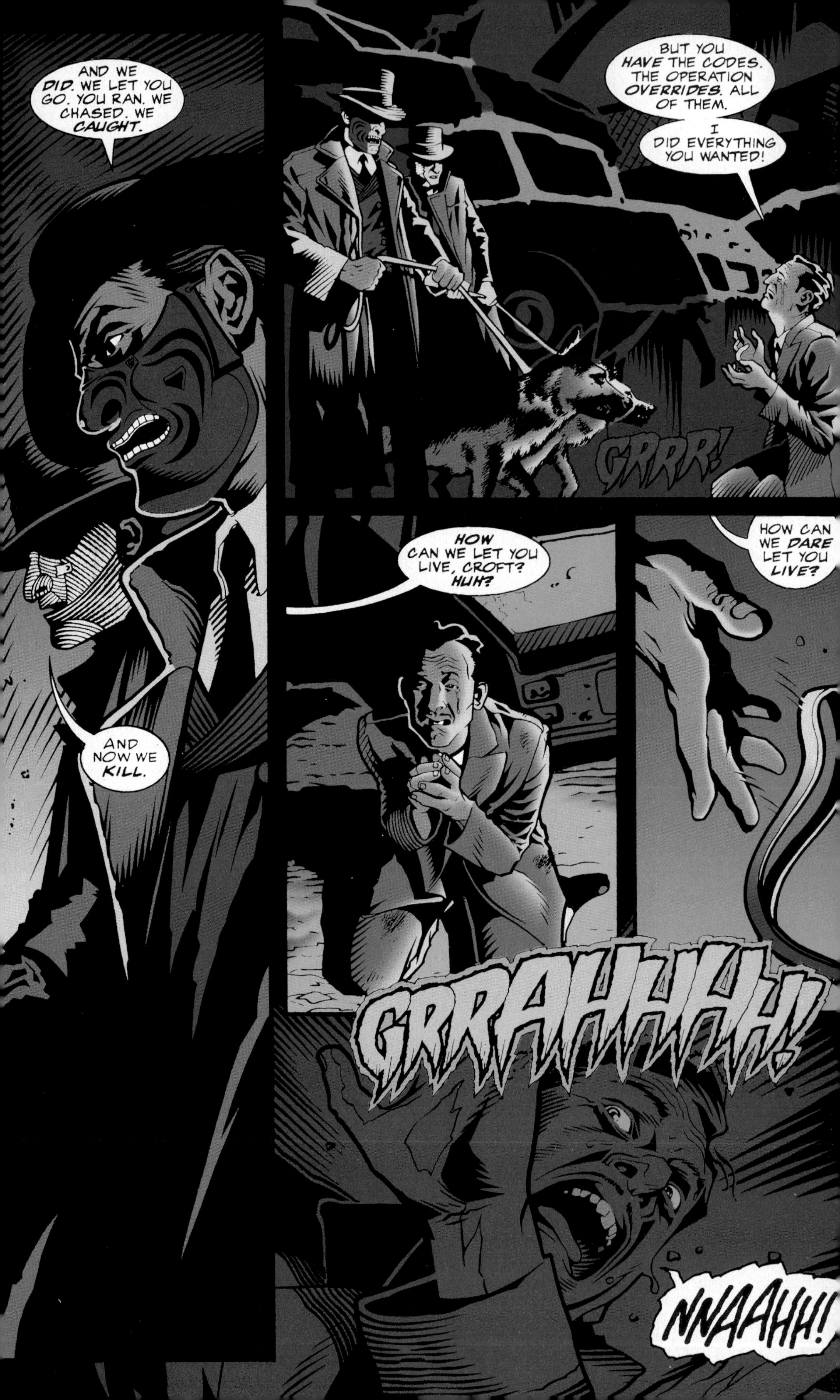
AND WE DID. WE LET YOU GO. YOU RAN. WE CHASED. WE CAUGHT.
AND NOW WE KILL.
BUT YOU HAVE THE CODES. THE OPERATION OVERRIDES. ALL OF THEM.
I DID EVERYTHING YOU WANTED!
GRRR!
HOW CAN WE LET YOU LIVE, CROFT? HUH?
HOW CAN WE DARE LET YOU LIVE?
GRRAHHHH!
NNAAHH!

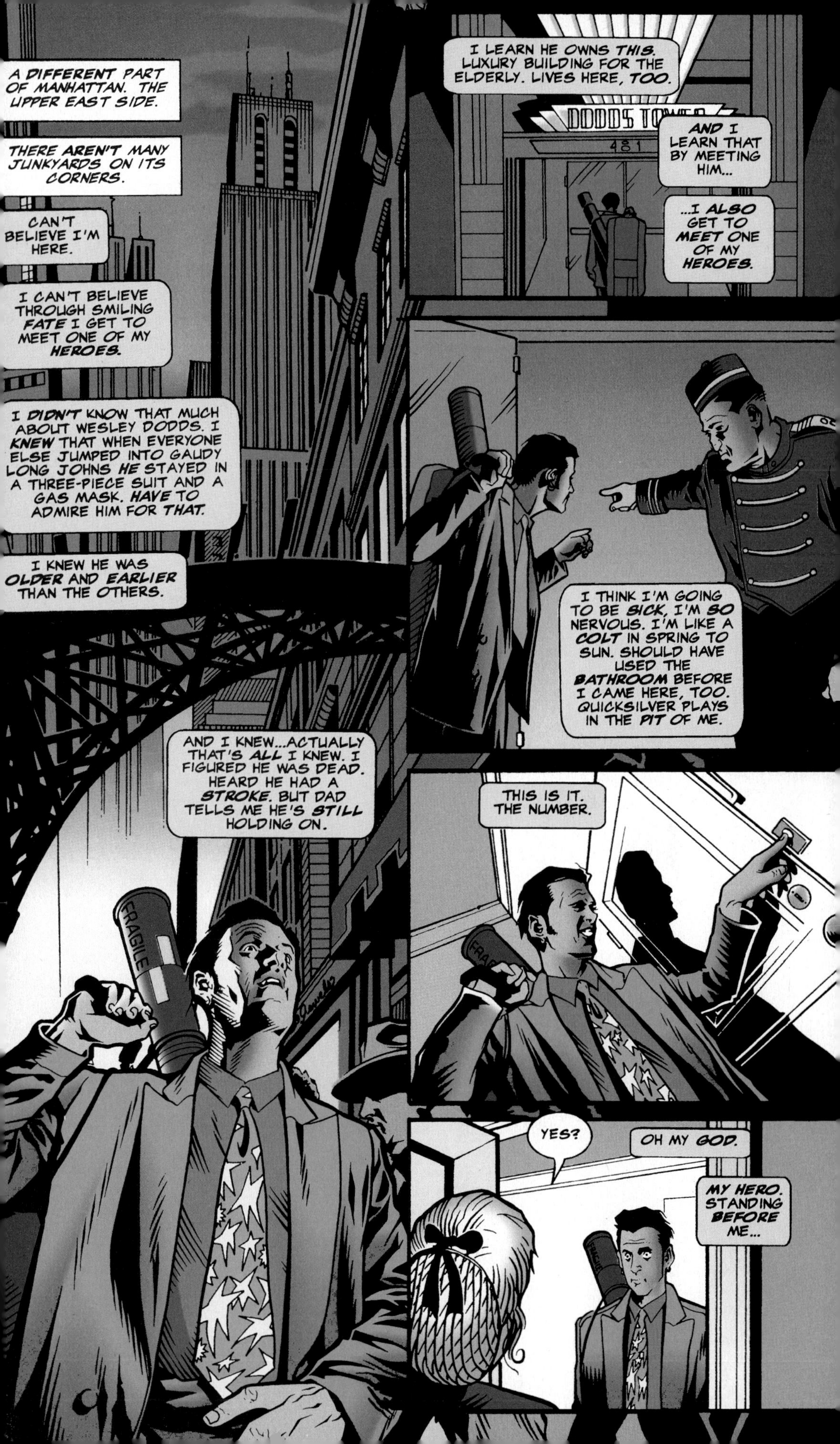
A DIFFERENT PART OF MANHATTAN. THE UPPER EAST SIDE.
THERE AREN'T MANY JUNKYARDS ON ITS CORNERS.
CAN'T BELIEVE I'M HERE.
I CAN'T BELIEVE THROUGH SMILING FATE I GET TO MEET ONE OF MY HEROES.
I DIDN'T KNOW THAT MUCH ABOUT WESLEY DODDS. I KNEW THAT WHEN EVERYONE ELSE JUMPED INTO GAUDY LONG JOHNS HE STAYED IN A THREE-PIECE SUIT AND A GAS MASK. HAVE TO ADMIRE HIM FOR THAT.
I KNEW HE WAS OLDER AND EARLIER THAN THE OTHERS.
AND I KNEW...ACTUALLY THAT'S ALL I KNEW. I FIGURED HE WAS DEAD. HEARD HE HAD A STROKE. BUT DAD TELLS ME HE'S STILL HOLDING ON.
FRAGILE
I LEARN HE OWNS THIS. LUXURY BUILDING FOR THE ELDERLY. LIVES HERE, TOO.
DODDS TOWER
AND I LEARN THAT BY MEETING HIM...
...I ALSO GET TO MEET ONE OF MY HEROES.
I THINK I'M GOING TO BE SICK, I'M SO NERVOUS. I'M LIKE A COLT IN SPRING TO SUN. SHOULD HAVE USED THE BATHROOM BEFORE I CAME HERE, TOO. QUICKSILVER PLAYS IN THE PIT OF ME.
THIS IS IT. THE NUMBER.
YES?
OH MY GOD.
MY HERO. STANDING BEFORE ME...

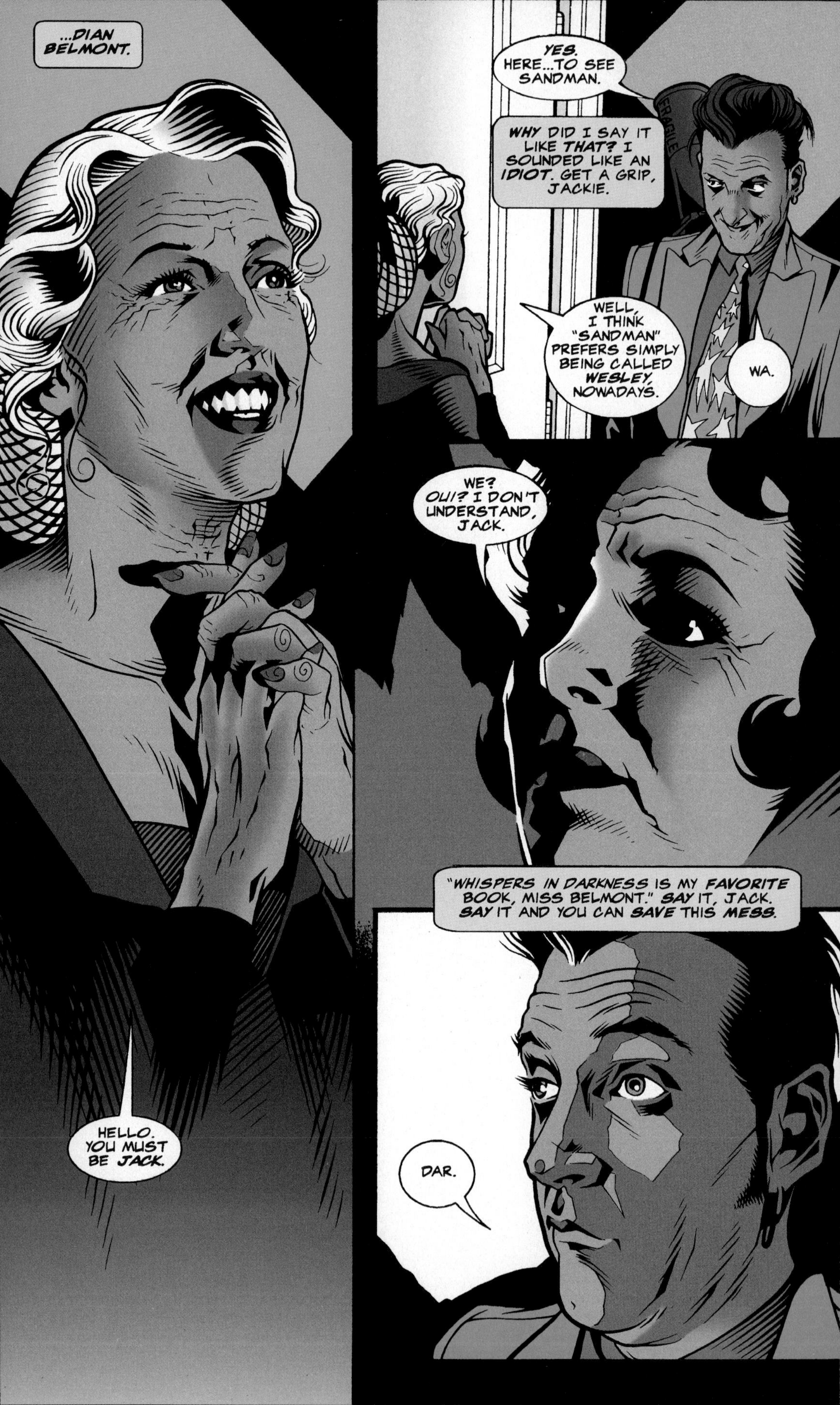
...DIAN BELMONT.
HELLO. YOU MUST BE JACK.
YES. HERE...TO SEE SANDMAN.
WHY DID I SAY IT LIKE THAT? I SOUNDED LIKE AN IDIOT. GET A GRIP, JACKIE.
FRAGILE
WELL, I THINK "SANDMAN" PREFERS SIMPLY BEING CALLED WESLEY, NOWADAYS.
WA.
WE? OUI? I DON'T UNDERSTAND, JACK.
"WHISPERS IN DARKNESS IS MY FAVORITE BOOK, MISS BELMONT." SAY IT, JACK. SAY IT AND YOU CAN SAVE THIS MESS.
DAR.

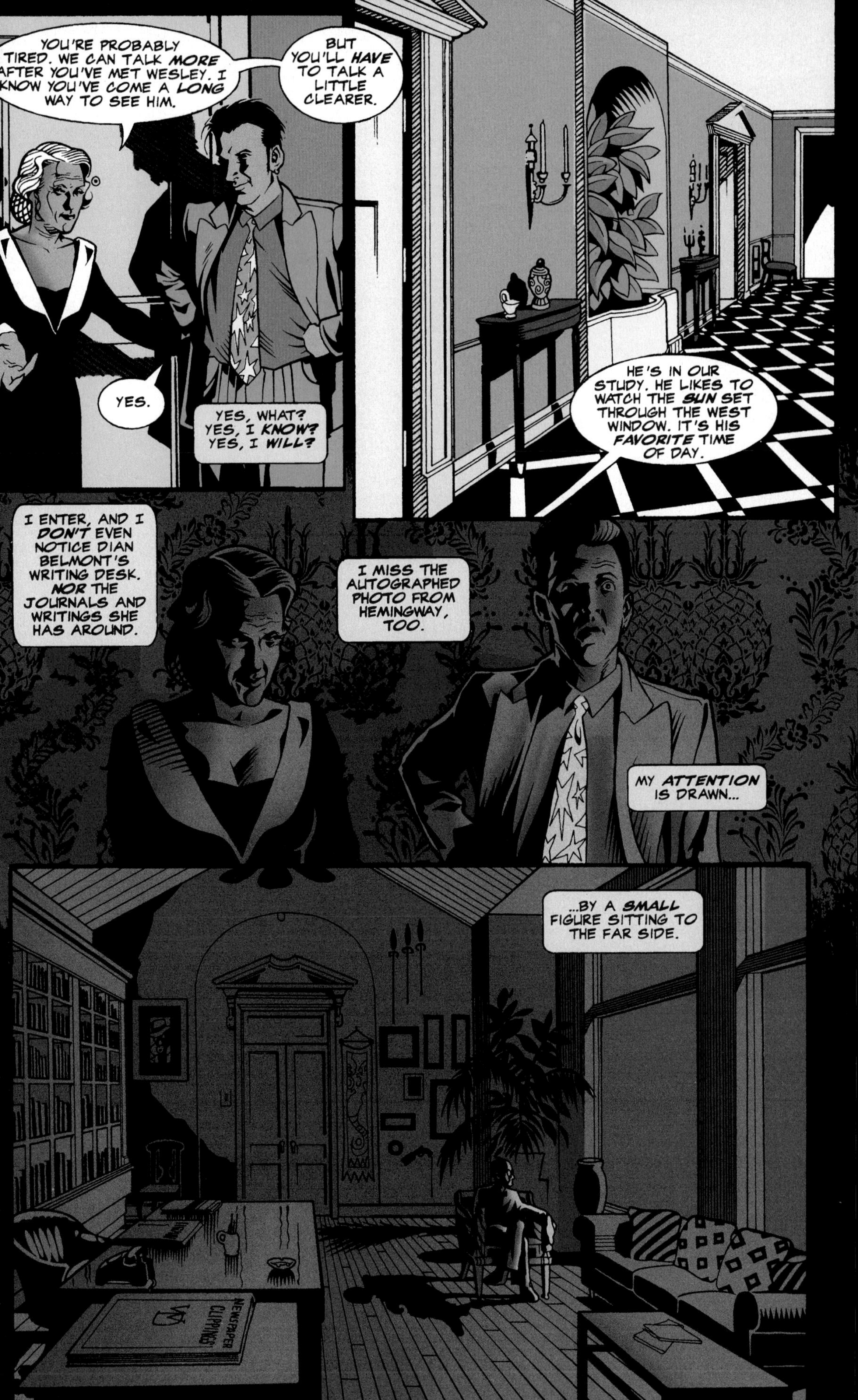
YOU'RE PROBABLY TIRED. WE CAN TALK MORE AFTER YOU'VE MET WESLEY. I KNOW YOU'VE COME A LONG WAY TO SEE HIM.
BUT YOU'LL HAVE TO TALK A LITTLE CLEARER.
YES.
YES, WHAT? YES, I KNOW? YES, I WILL?
HE'S IN OUR STUDY. HE LIKES TO WATCH THE SUN SET THROUGH THE WEST WINDOW. IT'S HIS FAVORITE TIME OF DAY.
I ENTER, AND I DON'T EVEN NOTICE DIAN BELMONT'S WRITING DESK. NOR THE JOURNALS AND WRITINGS SHE HAS AROUND.
I MISS THE AUTOGRAPHED PHOTO FROM HEMINGWAY, TOO.
MY ATTENTION IS DRAWN...
...BY A SMALL FIGURE SITTING TO THE FAR SIDE.
NEWSPAPER CLIPPINGS

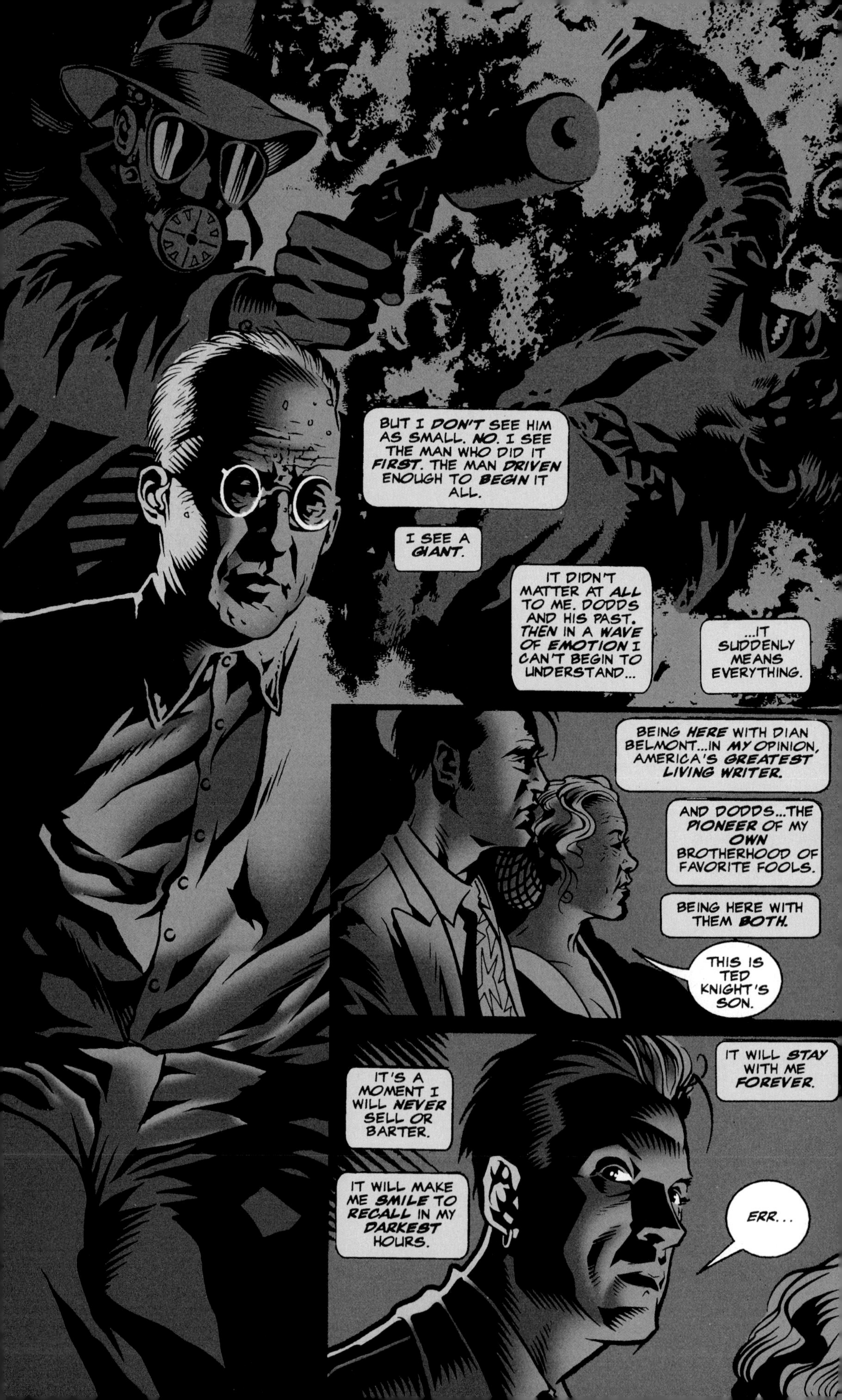
BUT I DON'T SEE HIM AS SMALL. NO. I SEE THE MAN WHO DID IT FIRST. THE MAN DRIVEN ENOUGH TO BEGIN IT ALL.
I SEE A GIANT.
IT DIDN'T MATTER AT ALL TO ME. DODDS AND HIS PAST. THEN IN A WAVE OF EMOTION I CAN'T BEGIN TO UNDERSTAND...
...IT SUDDENLY MEANS EVERYTHING.
BEING HERE WITH DIAN BELMONT...IN MY OPINION, AMERICA'S GREATEST LIVING WRITER.
AND DODDS...THE PIONEER OF MY OWN BROTHERHOOD OF FAVORITE FOOLS.
BEING HERE WITH THEM BOTH.
THIS IS TED KNIGHT'S SON.
IT'S A MOMENT I WILL NEVER SELL OR BARTER.
IT WILL STAY WITH ME FOREVER.
IT WILL MAKE ME SMILE TO RECALL IN MY DARKEST HOURS.
ERR...

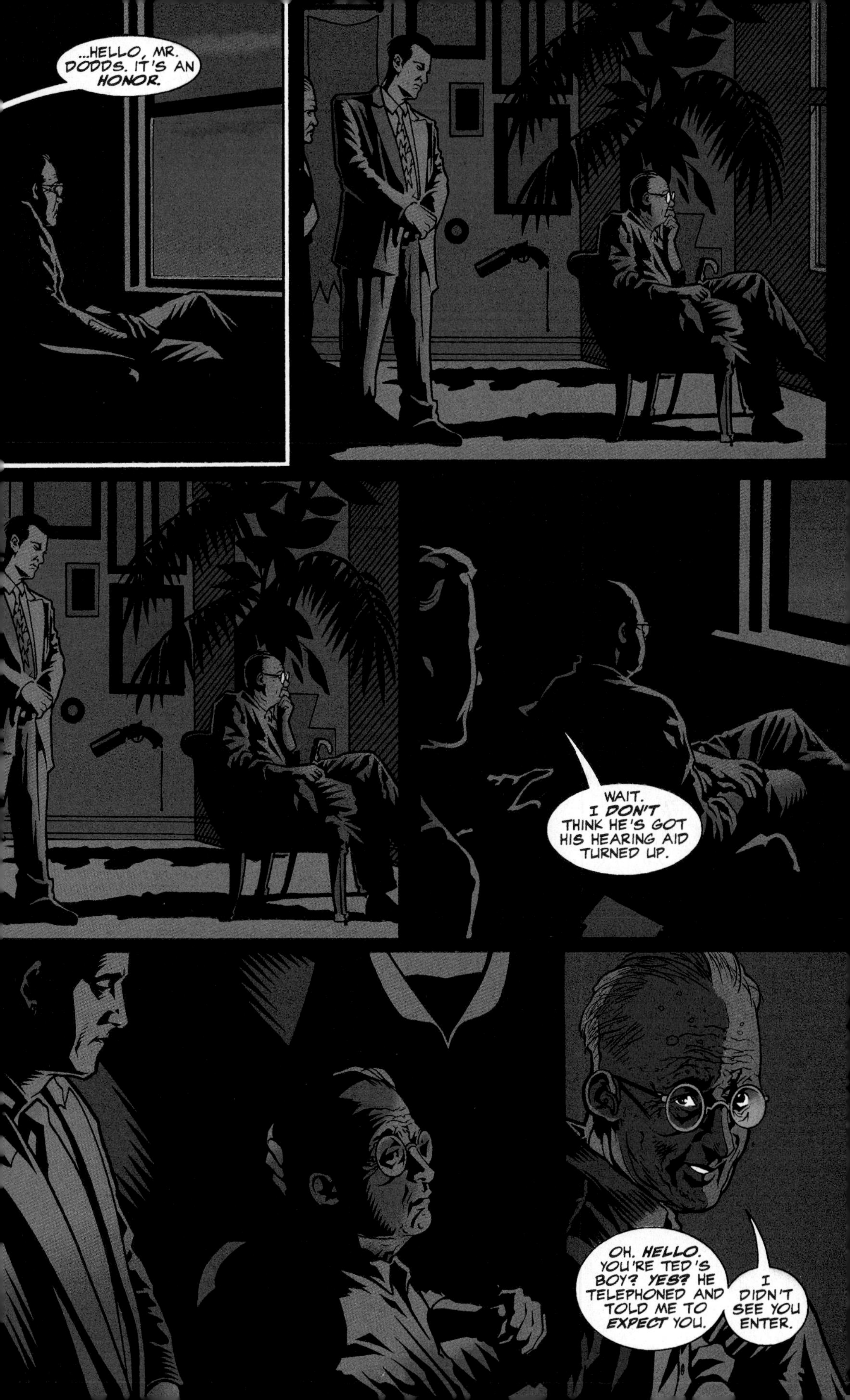
...HELLO, MR. DODDS. IT'S AN HONOR.
WAIT. I DON'T THINK HE'S GOT HIS HEARING AID TURNED UP.
OH. HELLO. YOU'RE TED'S BOY? YES? HE TELEPHONED AND TOLD ME TO EXPECT YOU.
I DIDN'T SEE YOU ENTER.

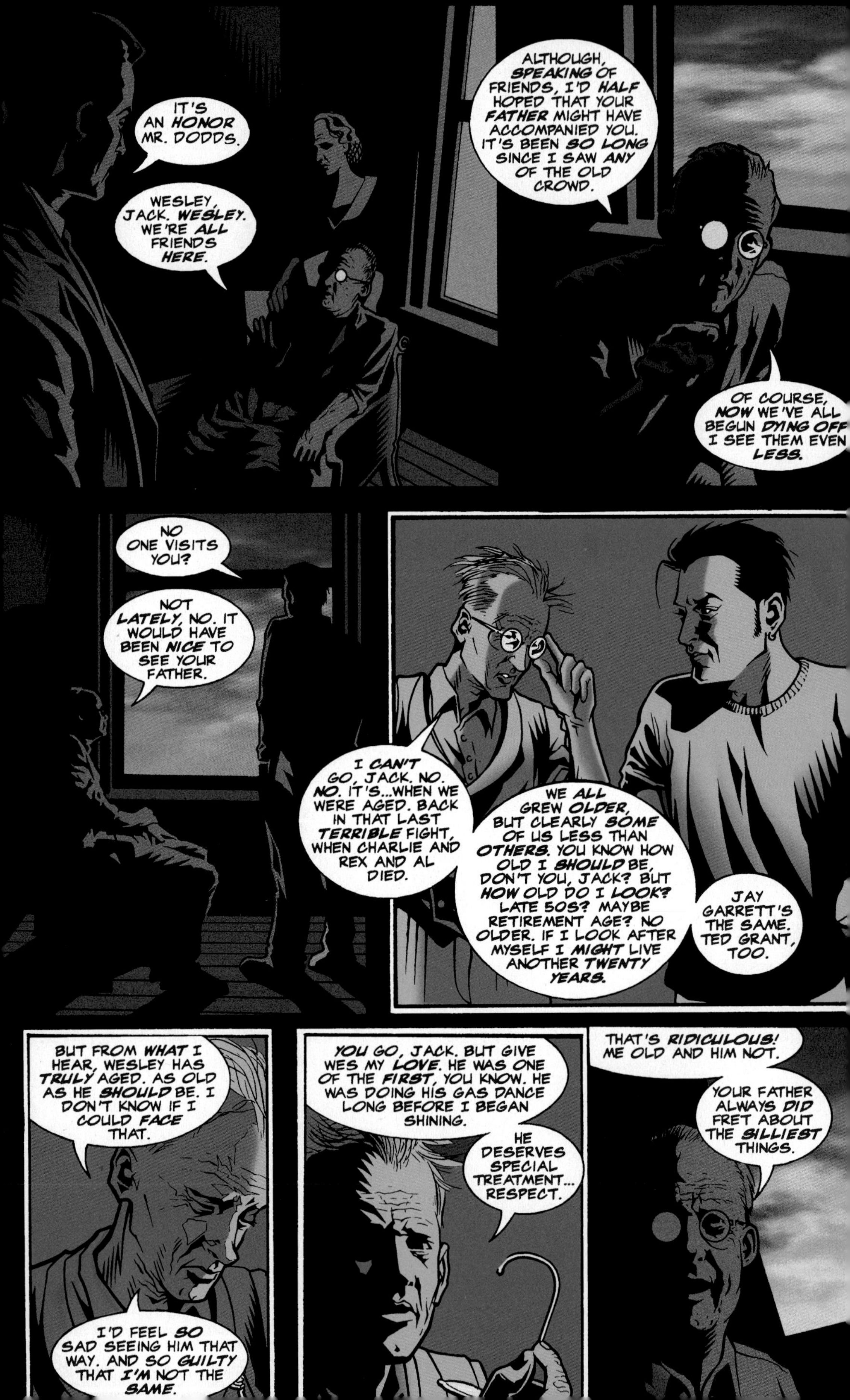
IT'S AN HONOR MR. DODDS.
WESLEY, JACK. WESLEY. WE'RE ALL FRIENDS HERE.
ALTHOUGH, SPEAKING OF FRIENDS, I'D HALF HOPED THAT YOUR FATHER MIGHT HAVE ACCOMPANIED YOU. IT'S BEEN SO LONG SINCE I SAW ANY OF THE OLD CROWD.
OF COURSE, NOW WE'VE ALL BEGUN DYING OFF I SEE THEM EVEN LESS.
NO ONE VISITS YOU?
NOT LATELY, NO. IT WOULD HAVE BEEN NICE TO SEE YOUR FATHER.
I CAN'T GO, JACK. NO. NO. IT'S...WHEN WE WERE AGED. BACK IN THAT LAST TERRIBLE FIGHT, WHEN CHARLIE AND REX AND AL DIED.
WE ALL GREW OLDER, BUT CLEARLY SOME OF US LESS THAN OTHERS. YOU KNOW HOW OLD I SHOULD BE, DON'T YOU, JACK? BUT HOW OLD DO I LOOK? LATE 50S? MAYBE RETIREMENT AGE? NO OLDER. IF I LOOK AFTER MYSELF I MIGHT LIVE ANOTHER TWENTY YEARS.
JAY GARRETT'S THE SAME. TED GRANT, TOO.
BUT FROM WHAT I HEAR, WESLEY HAS TRULY AGED. AS OLD AS HE SHOULD BE. I DON'T KNOW IF I COULD FACE THAT.
I'D FEEL SO SAD SEEING HIM THAT WAY. AND SO GUILTY THAT I'M NOT THE SAME.
YOU GO, JACK. BUT GIVE WES MY LOVE. HE WAS ONE OF THE FIRST, YOU KNOW. HE WAS DOING HIS GAS DANCE LONG BEFORE I BEGAN SHINING.
HE DESERVES SPECIAL TREATMENT... RESPECT.
THAT'S RIDICULOUS! ME OLD AND HIM NOT.
YOUR FATHER ALWAYS DID FRET ABOUT THE SILLIEST THINGS.

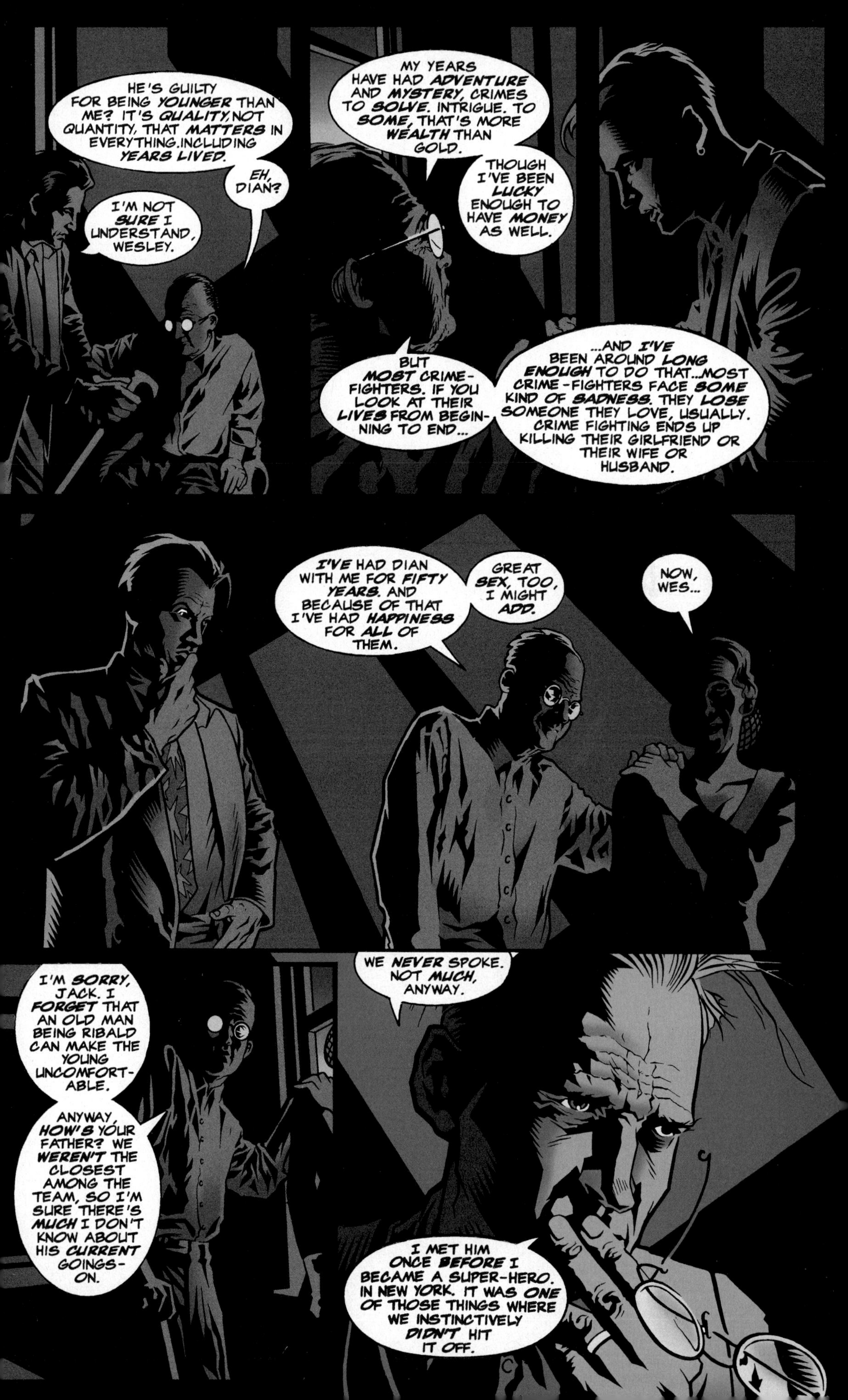
HE'S GUILTY FOR BEING YOUNGER THAN ME? IT'S QUALITY, NOT QUANTITY, THAT MATTERS IN EVERYTHING. INCLUDING YEARS LIVED.
EH, DIAN?
I'M NOT SURE I UNDERSTAND, WESLEY.
MY YEARS HAVE HAD ADVENTURE AND MYSTERY, CRIMES TO SOLVE. INTRIGUE. TO SOME, THAT'S MORE WEALTH THAN GOLD.
THOUGH I'VE BEEN LUCKY ENOUGH TO HAVE MONEY AS WELL.
BUT MOST CRIME-FIGHTERS. IF YOU LOOK AT THEIR LIVES FROM BEGINNING TO END...
...AND I'VE BEEN AROUND LONG ENOUGH TO DO THAT...MOST CRIME-FIGHTERS FACE SOME KIND OF SADNESS. THEY LOSE SOMEONE THEY LOVE, USUALLY. CRIME FIGHTING ENDS UP KILLING THEIR GIRLFRIEND OR THEIR WIFE OR HUSBAND.
I'VE HAD DIAN WITH ME FOR FIFTY YEARS. AND BECAUSE OF THAT I'VE HAD HAPPINESS FOR ALL OF THEM.
GREAT SEX, TOO, I MIGHT ADD.
NOW, WES...
I'M SORRY, JACK. I FORGET THAT AN OLD MAN BEING RIBALD CAN MAKE THE YOUNG UNCOMFORTABLE.
ANYWAY, HOW'S YOUR FATHER? WE WEREN'T THE CLOSEST AMONG THE TEAM, SO I'M SURE THERE'S MUCH I DON'T KNOW ABOUT HIS CURRENT GOINGS-ON.
WE NEVER SPOKE. NOT MUCH, ANYWAY.
I MET HIM ONCE BEFORE I BECAME A SUPER-HERO. IN NEW YORK. IT WAS ONE OF THOSE THINGS WHERE WE INSTINCTIVELY DIDN'T HIT IT OFF.

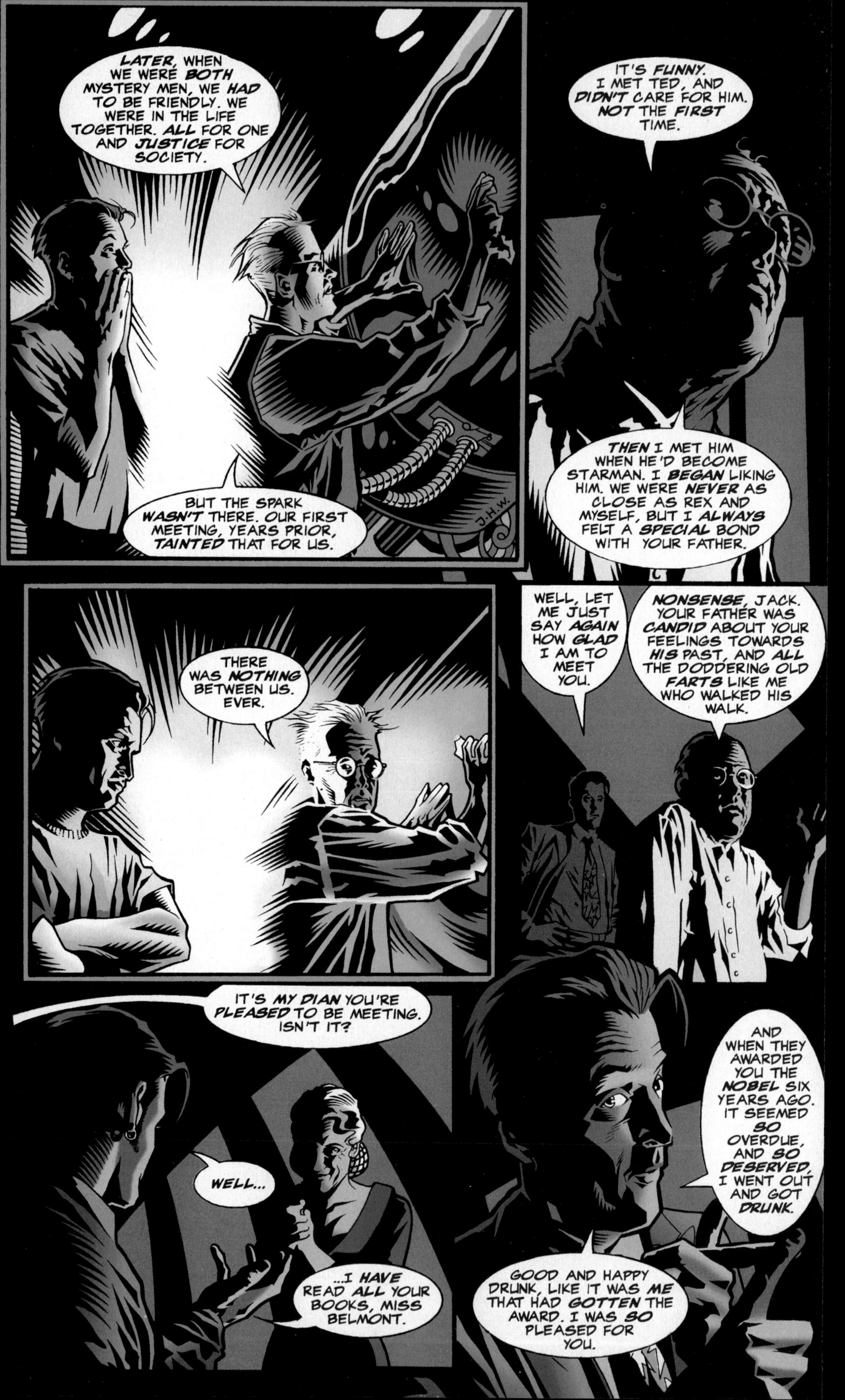
LATER, WHEN WE WERE BOTH MYSTERY MEN, WE HAD TO BE FRIENDLY. WE WERE IN THE LIFE TOGETHER. ALL FOR ONE AND JUSTICE FOR SOCIETY.
BUT THE SPARK WASN'T THERE. OUR FIRST MEETING, YEARS PRIOR, TAINTED THAT FOR US.
J.H.W.
IT'S FUNNY. I MET TED, AND DIDN'T CARE FOR HIM. NOT THE FIRST TIME.
THEN I MET HIM WHEN HE'D BECOME STARMAN. I BEGAN LIKING HIM. WE WERE NEVER AS CLOSE AS REX AND MYSELF, BUT I ALWAYS FELT A SPECIAL BOND WITH YOUR FATHER.
THERE WAS NOTHING BETWEEN US. EVER.
WELL, LET ME JUST SAY AGAIN HOW GLAD I AM TO MEET YOU.
NONSENSE, JACK. YOUR FATHER WAS CANDID ABOUT YOUR FEELINGS TOWARDS HIS PAST, AND ALL THE DODDERING OLD FARTS LIKE ME WHO WALKED HIS WALK.
IT'S MY DIAN YOU'RE PLEASED TO BE MEETING. ISN'T IT?
WELL...
...I HAVE READ ALL YOUR BOOKS, MISS BELMONT.
AND WHEN THEY AWARDED YOU THE NOBEL SIX YEARS AGO, IT SEEMED SO OVERDUE, AND SO DESERVED, I WENT OUT AND GOT DRUNK.
GOOD AND HAPPY DRUNK, LIKE IT WAS ME THAT HAD GOTTEN THE AWARD. I WAS SO PLEASED FOR YOU.

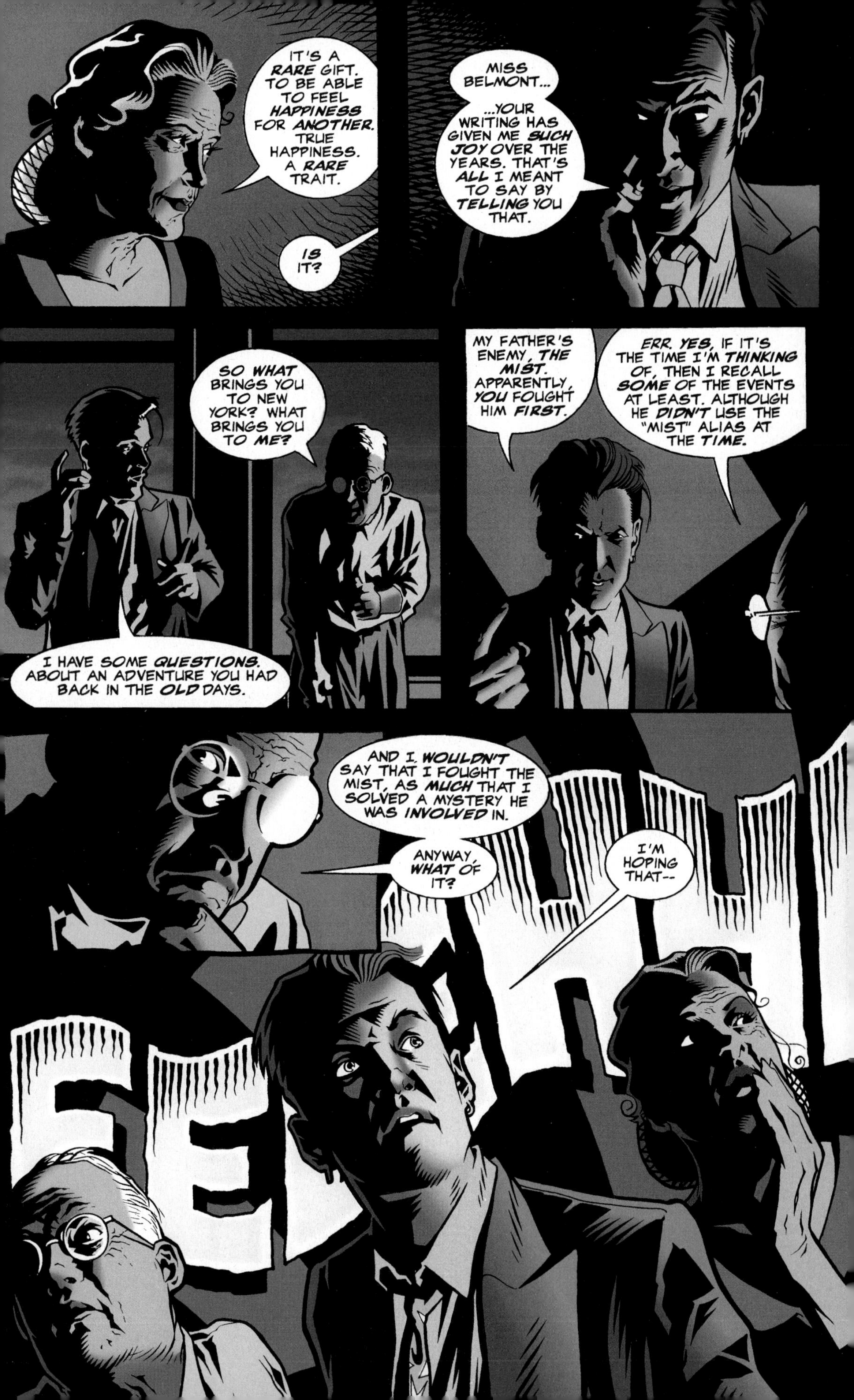
IT'S A RARE GIFT. TO BE ABLE TO FEEL HAPPINESS FOR ANOTHER. TRUE HAPPINESS. A RARE TRAIT.
IS IT?
MISS BELMONT...
...YOUR WRITING HAS GIVEN ME SUCH JOY OVER THE YEARS. THAT'S ALL I MEANT TO SAY BY TELLING YOU THAT.
SO WHAT BRINGS YOU TO NEW YORK? WHAT BRINGS YOU TO ME?
I HAVE SOME QUESTIONS. ABOUT AN ADVENTURE YOU HAD BACK IN THE OLD DAYS.
MY FATHER'S ENEMY, THE MIST. APPARENTLY, YOU FOUGHT HIM FIRST.
ERR. YES, IF IT'S THE TIME I'M THINKING OF, THEN I RECALL SOME OF THE EVENTS AT LEAST. ALTHOUGH HE DIDN'T USE THE "MIST" ALIAS AT THE TIME.
AND I WOULDN'T SAY THAT I FOUGHT THE MIST, AS MUCH THAT I SOLVED A MYSTERY HE WAS INVOLVED IN.
ANYWAY, WHAT OF IT?
I'M HOPING THAT--

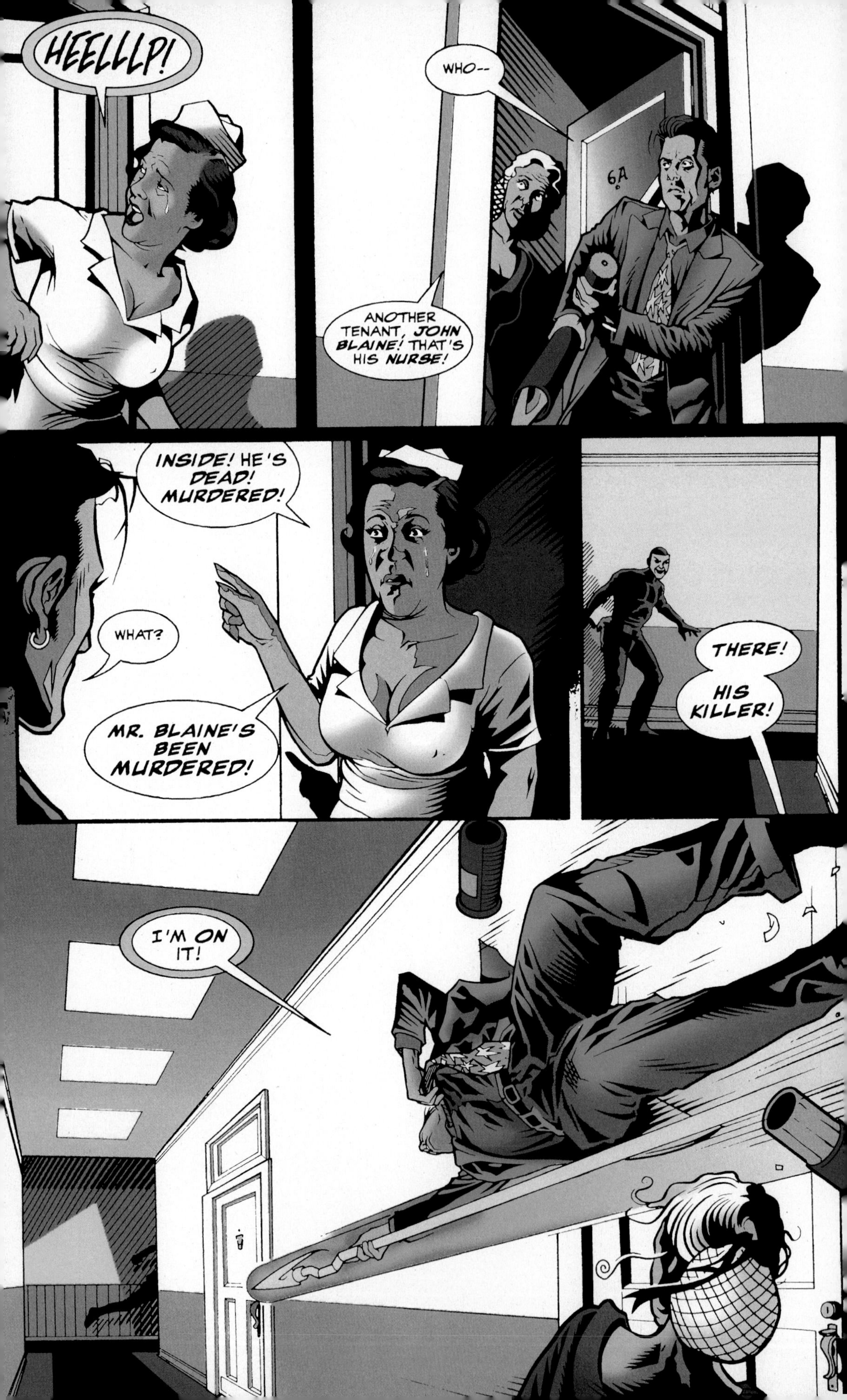
HEELLLP!
WHO--
ANOTHER TENANT, JOHN BLAINE! THAT'S HIS NURSE!
6A
INSIDE! HE'S DEAD! MURDERED!
WHAT?
MR. BLAINE'S BEEN MURDERED!
THERE!
HIS KILLER!
I'M ON IT!

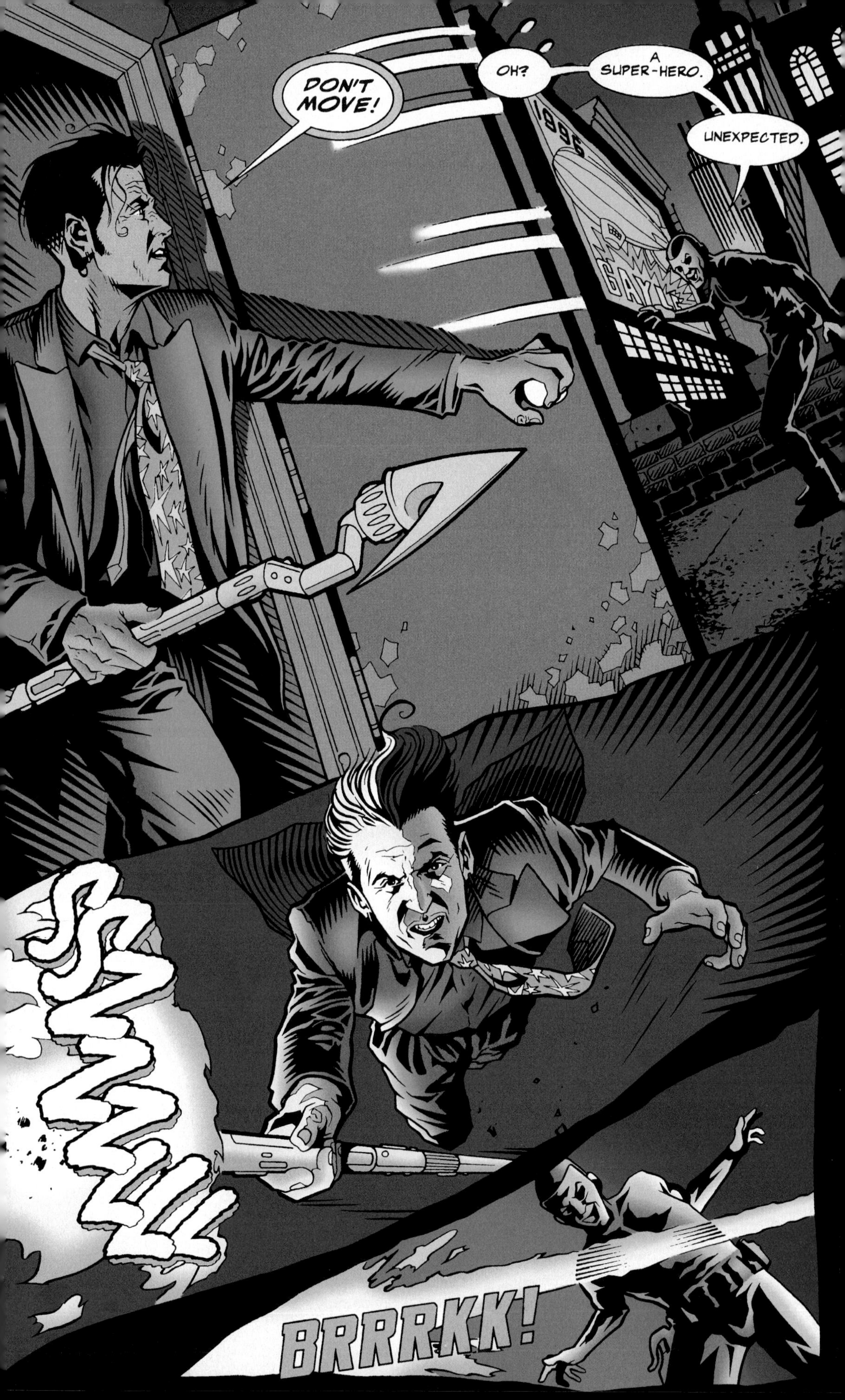
DON'T MOVE!
OH?
A SUPER-HERO.
UNEXPECTED.
BRRRKK!

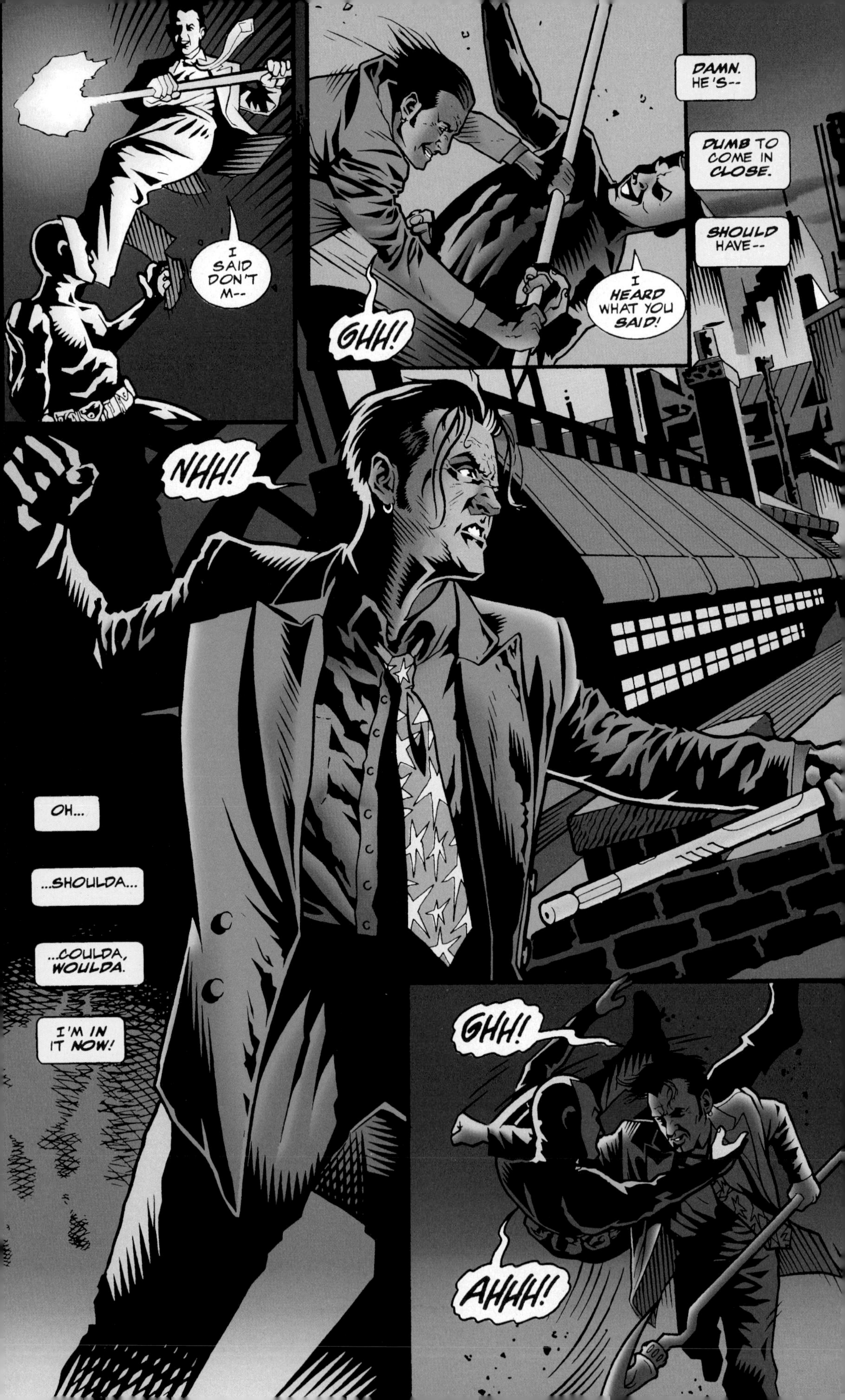
I SAID DON'T M--
GHH!
I HEARD WHAT YOU SAID!
DAMN. HE'S--
DUMB TO COME IN CLOSE.
SHOULD HAVE--
NHH!
OH...
...SHOULDA...
...COULDA, WOULDA.
I'M IN IT NOW!
GHH!
AHHH!

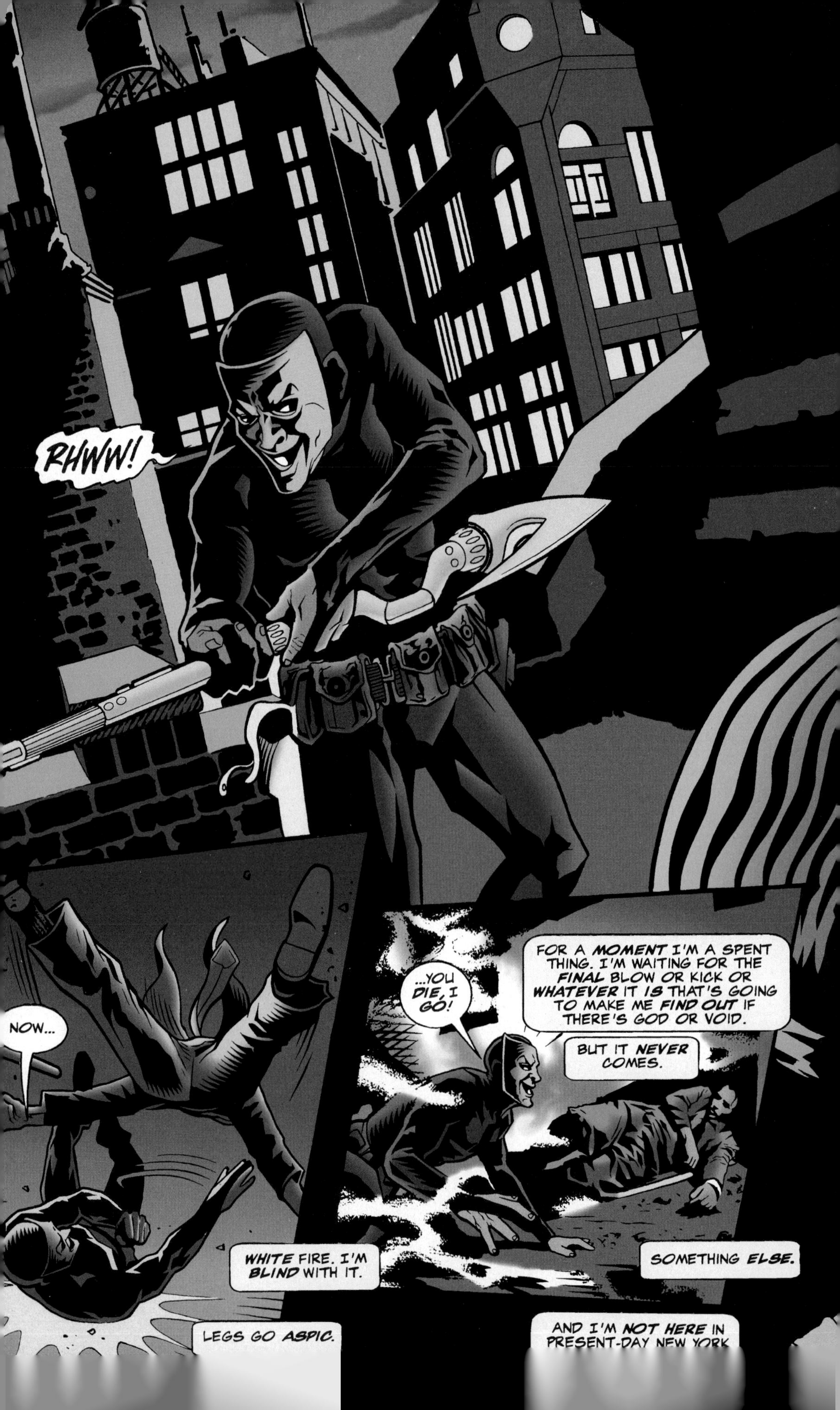
RHWW!
NOW...
WHITE FIRE. I'M BLIND WITH IT.
LEGS GO ASPIC.
...YOU DIE, I GO!
FOR A MOMENT I'M A SPENT THING. I'M WAITING FOR THE FINAL BLOW OR KICK OR WHATEVER IT IS THAT'S GOING TO MAKE ME FIND OUT IF THERE'S GOD OR VOID.
BUT IT NEVER COMES.
SOMETHING ELSE.
AND I'M NOT HERE IN PRESENT-DAY NEW YORK

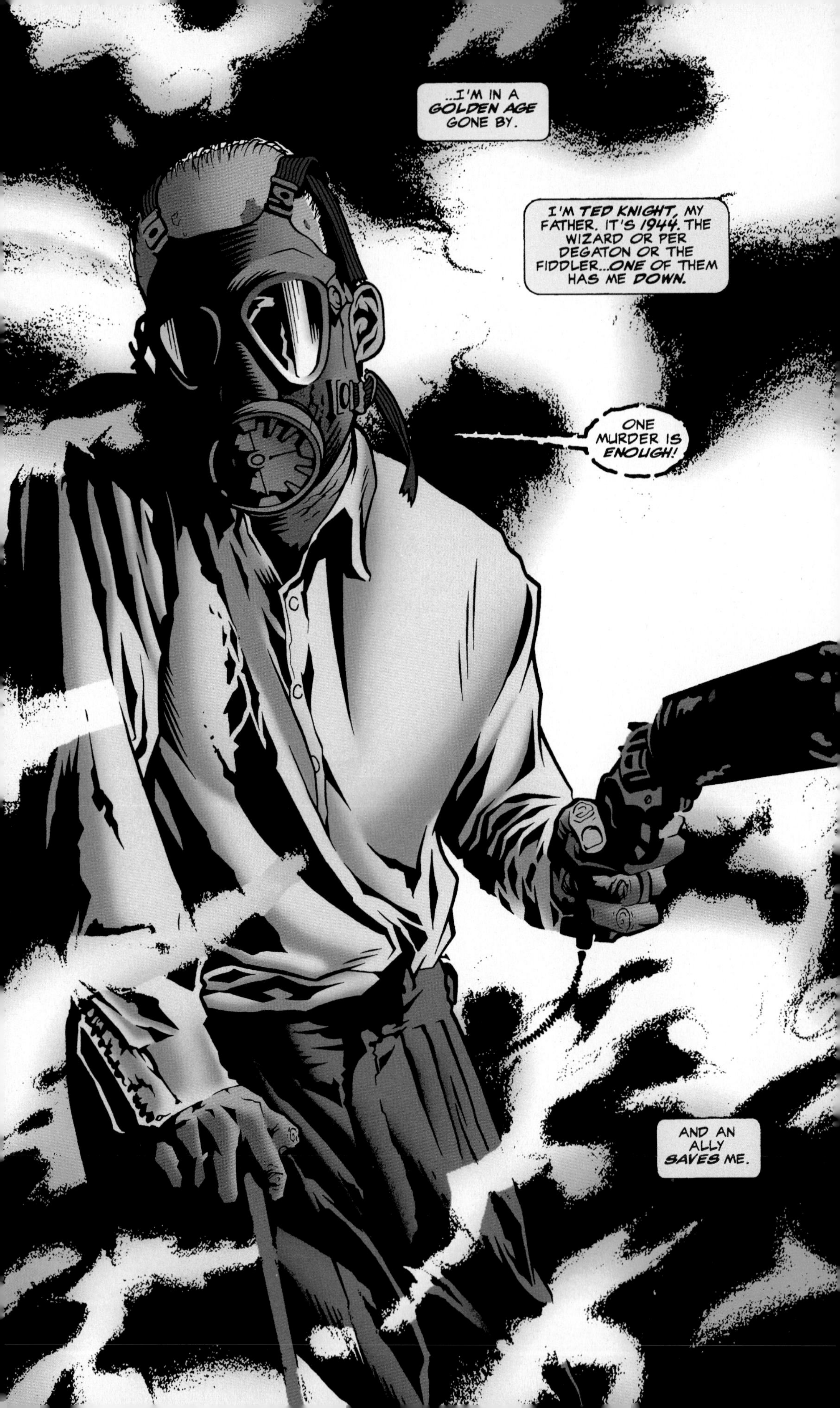
...I'M IN A GOLDEN AGE GONE BY.
I'M TED KNIGHT, MY FATHER. IT'S 1944. THE WIZARD OR PER DEGATON OR THE FIDDLER...ONE OF THEM HAS ME DOWN.
ONE MURDER IS ENOUGH!
AND AN ALLY SAVES ME.

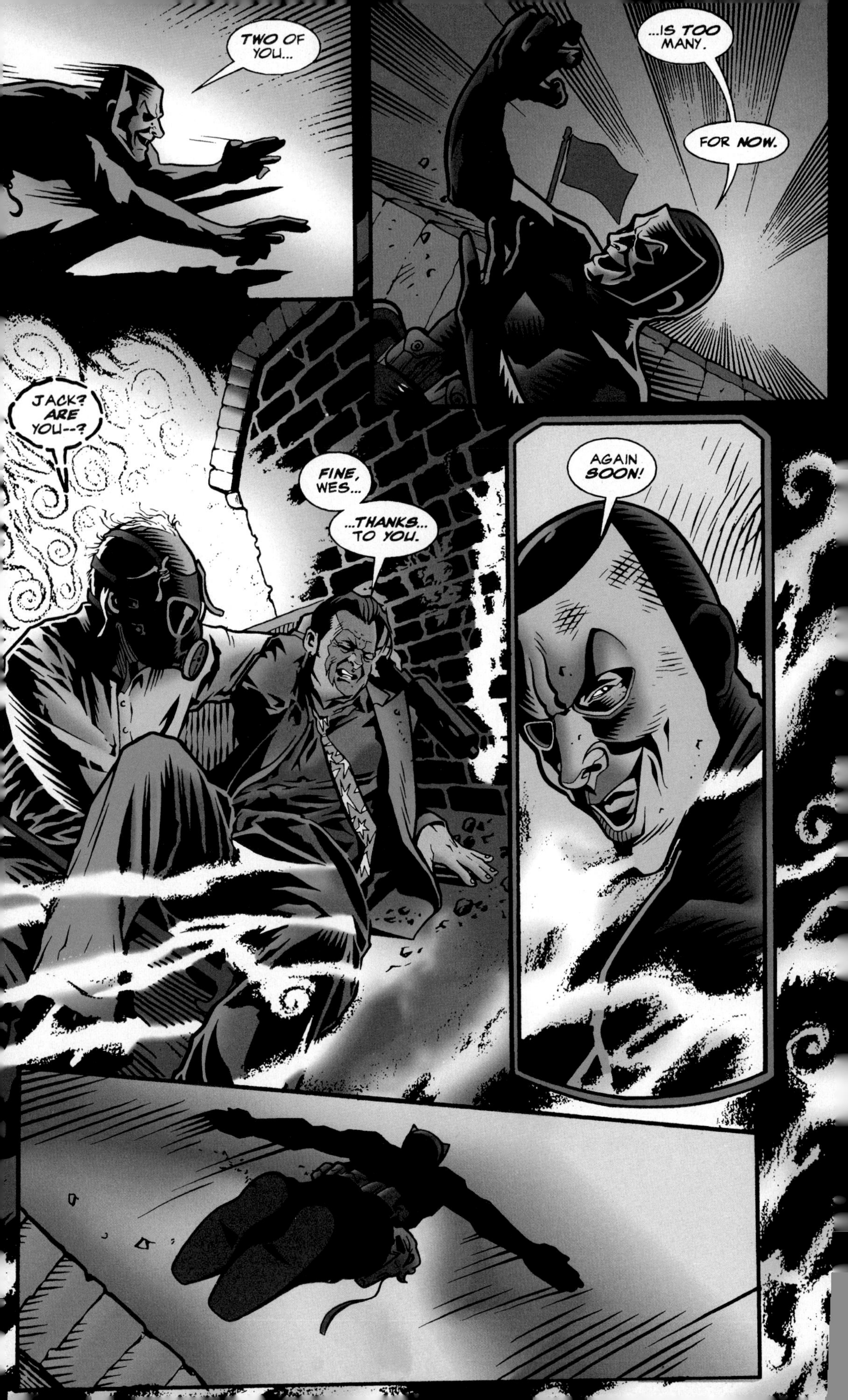
TWO OF YOU...
...IS TOO MANY.
FOR NOW.
JACK? ARE YOU--?
FINE, WES...
...THANKS... TO YOU.
AGAIN SOON!

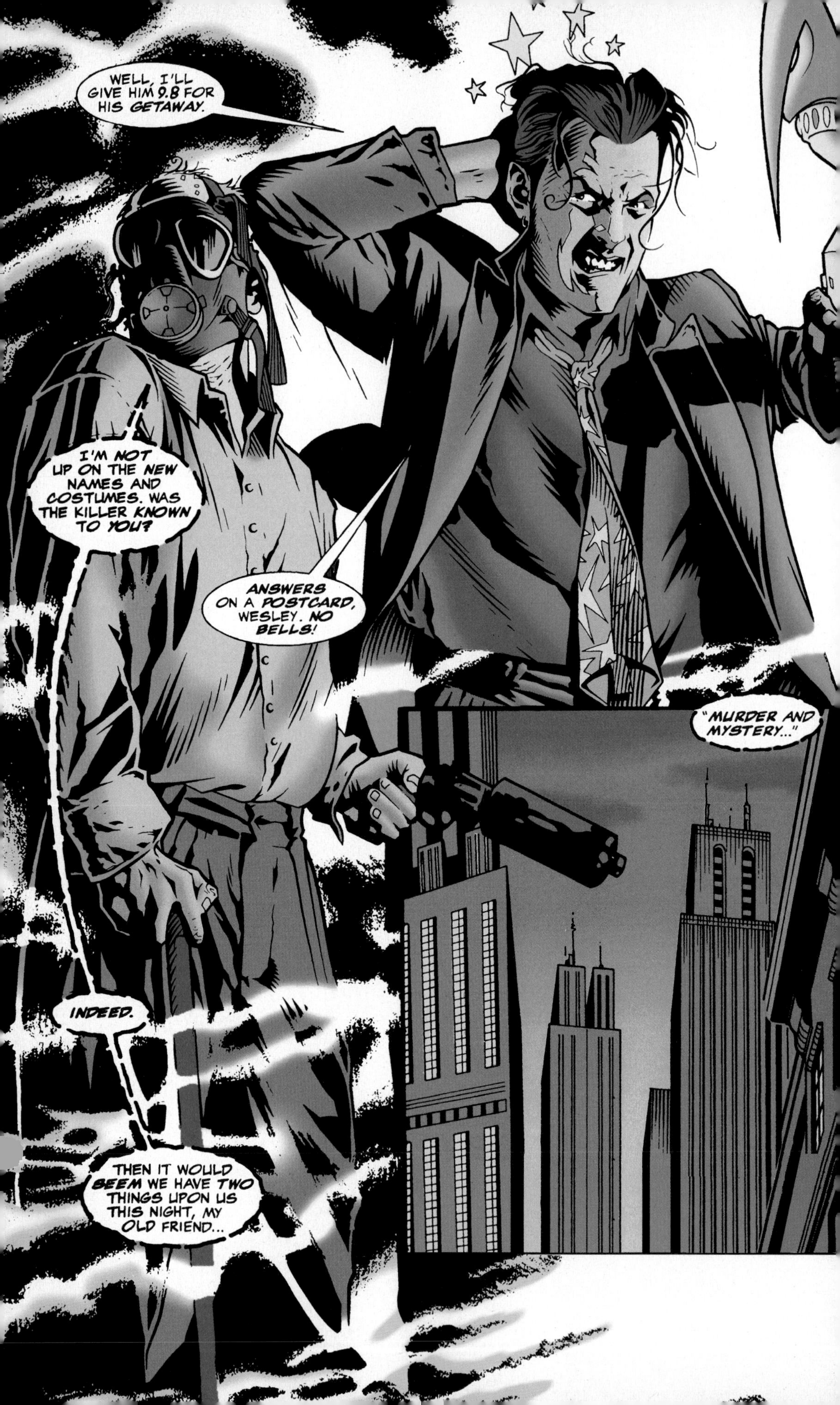
WELL, I'LL GIVE HIM 9.8 FOR HIS GETAWAY.
I'M NOT UP ON THE NEW NAMES AND COSTUMES. WAS THE KILLER KNOWN TO YOU?
ANSWERS ON A POSTCARD, WESLEY. NO BELLS!
INDEED.
THEN IT WOULD SEEM WE HAVE TWO THINGS UPON US THIS NIGHT, MY OLD FRIEND...
"MURDER AND MYSTERY..."

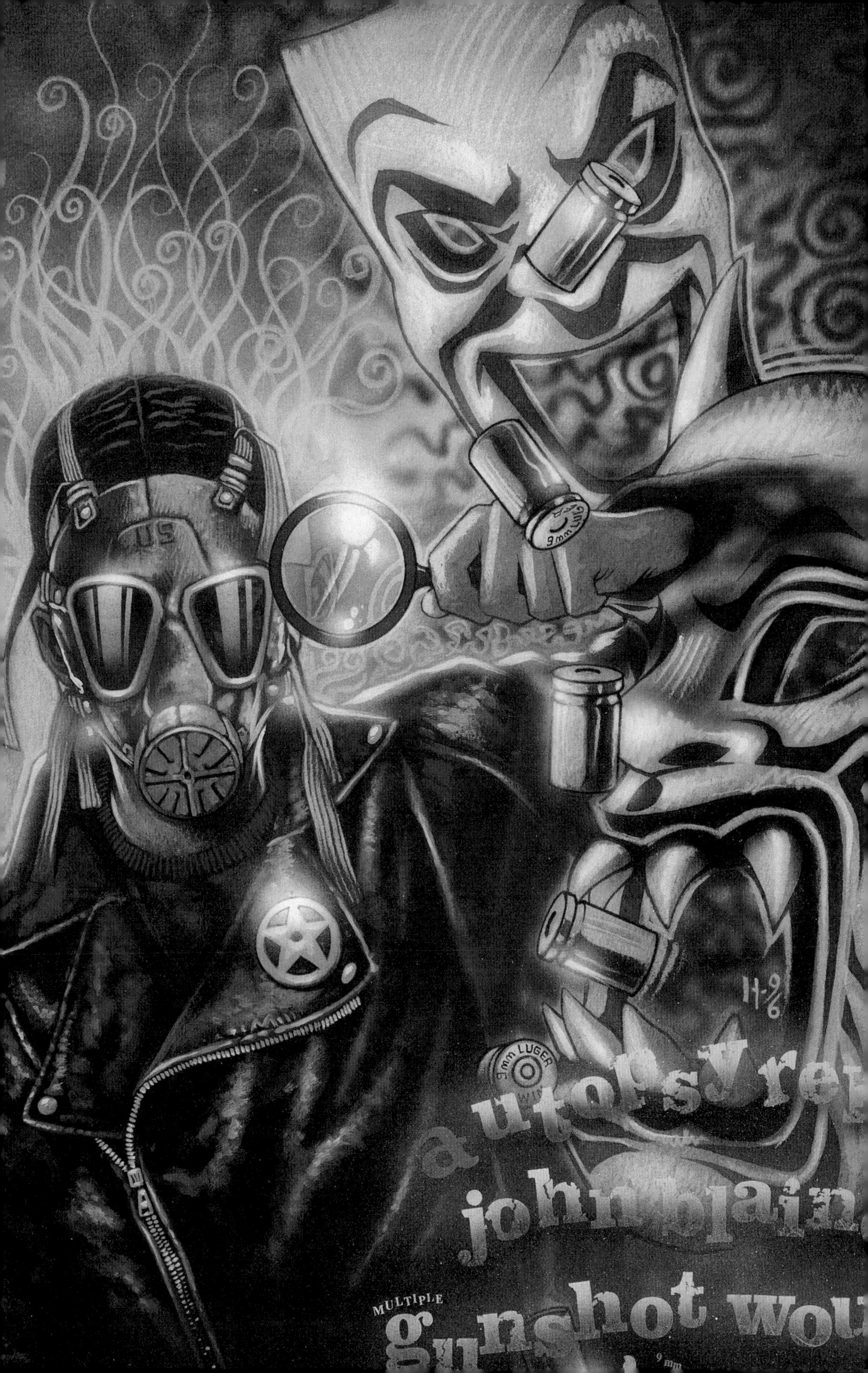
US
9mm LUGER
utopsy re
&
john blain
MULTIPLE
gunshot wou

STARMAN 21

Cover by Tony Harris

Written by James Robinson

Pencils by Tony Harris

with inks by Wade von Grawbadger

and colors by Gregory Wright

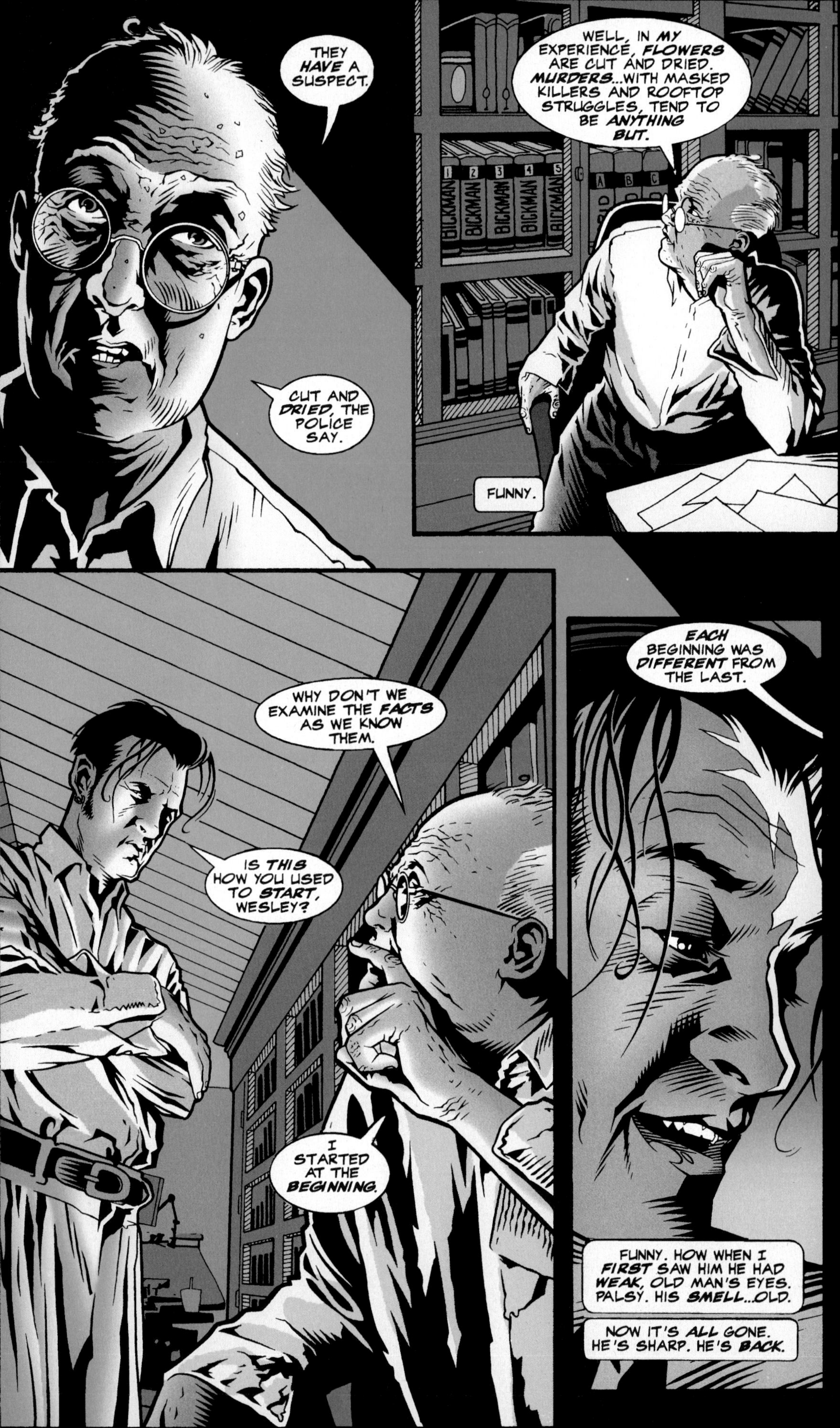
THEY *HAVE* A SUSPECT.
CUT AND *DRIED*, THE POLICE SAY.
WELL, IN *MY* EXPERIENCÉ, *FLOWERS* ARE CUT AND DRIED. *MURDERS*...WITH MASKED KILLERS AND ROOFTOP STRUGGLES, TEND TO BE *ANYTHING BUT*.
FUNNY.
BICKMAN
WHY DON'T WE EXAMINE THE *FACTS* AS WE KNOW THEM.
IS *THIS* HOW YOU USED TO *START*, WESLEY?
I STARTED AT THE *BEGINNING*.
EACH BEGINNING WAS *DIFFERENT* FROM THE LAST.
FUNNY. HOW WHEN I *FIRST* SAW HIM HE HAD *WEAK*, OLD MAN'S EYES. PALSY. HIS *SMELL*...OLD.
NOW IT'S *ALL* GONE. HE'S SHARP. HE'S *BACK*.

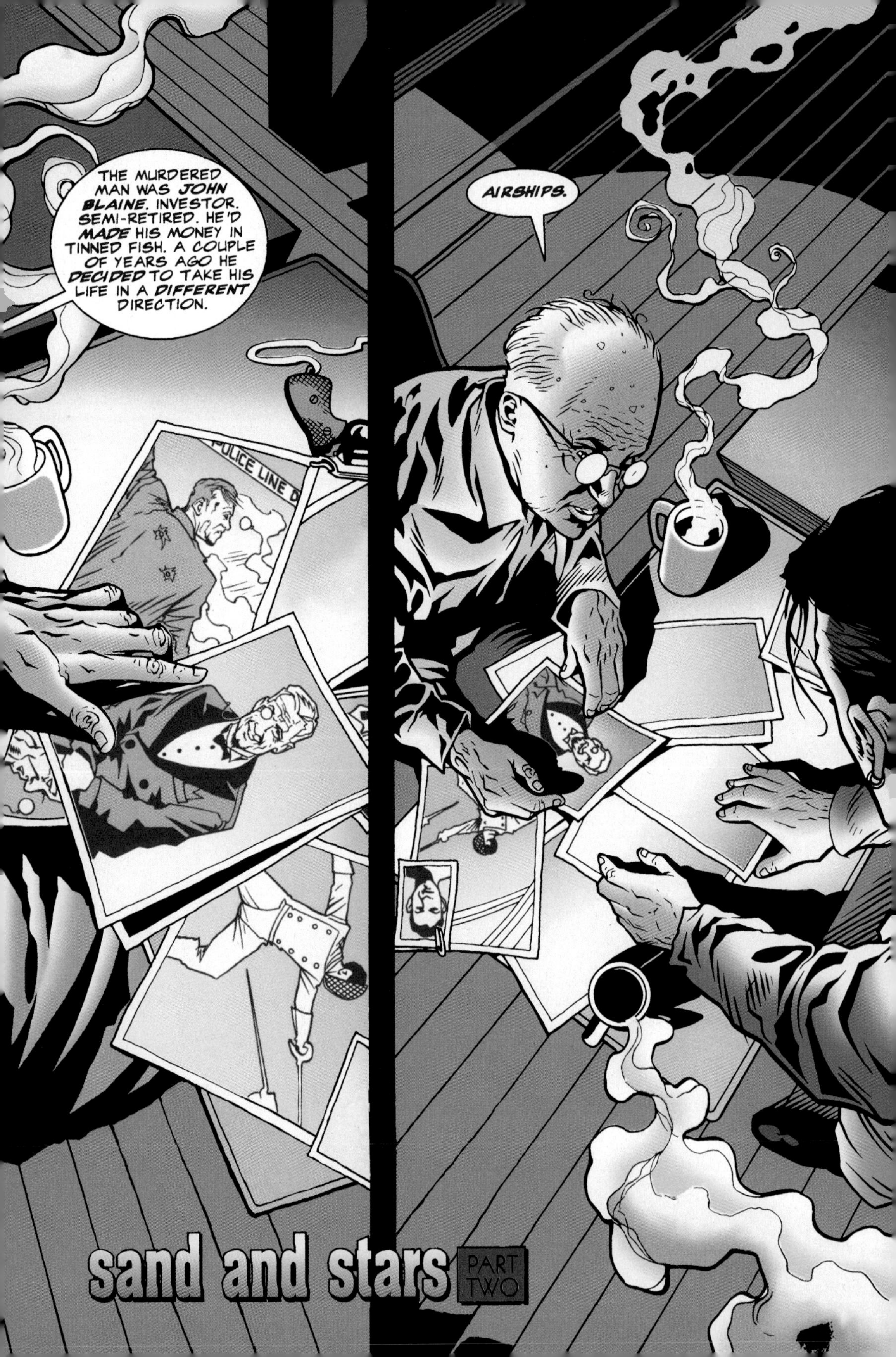
THE MURDERED MAN WAS JOHN BLAINE. INVESTOR. SEMI-RETIRED. HE'D MADE HIS MONEY IN TINNED FISH. A COUPLE OF YEARS AGO HE DECIDED TO TAKE HIS LIFE IN A DIFFERENT DIRECTION.
AIRSHIPS.
POLICE LINE D
sand and stars PART TWO

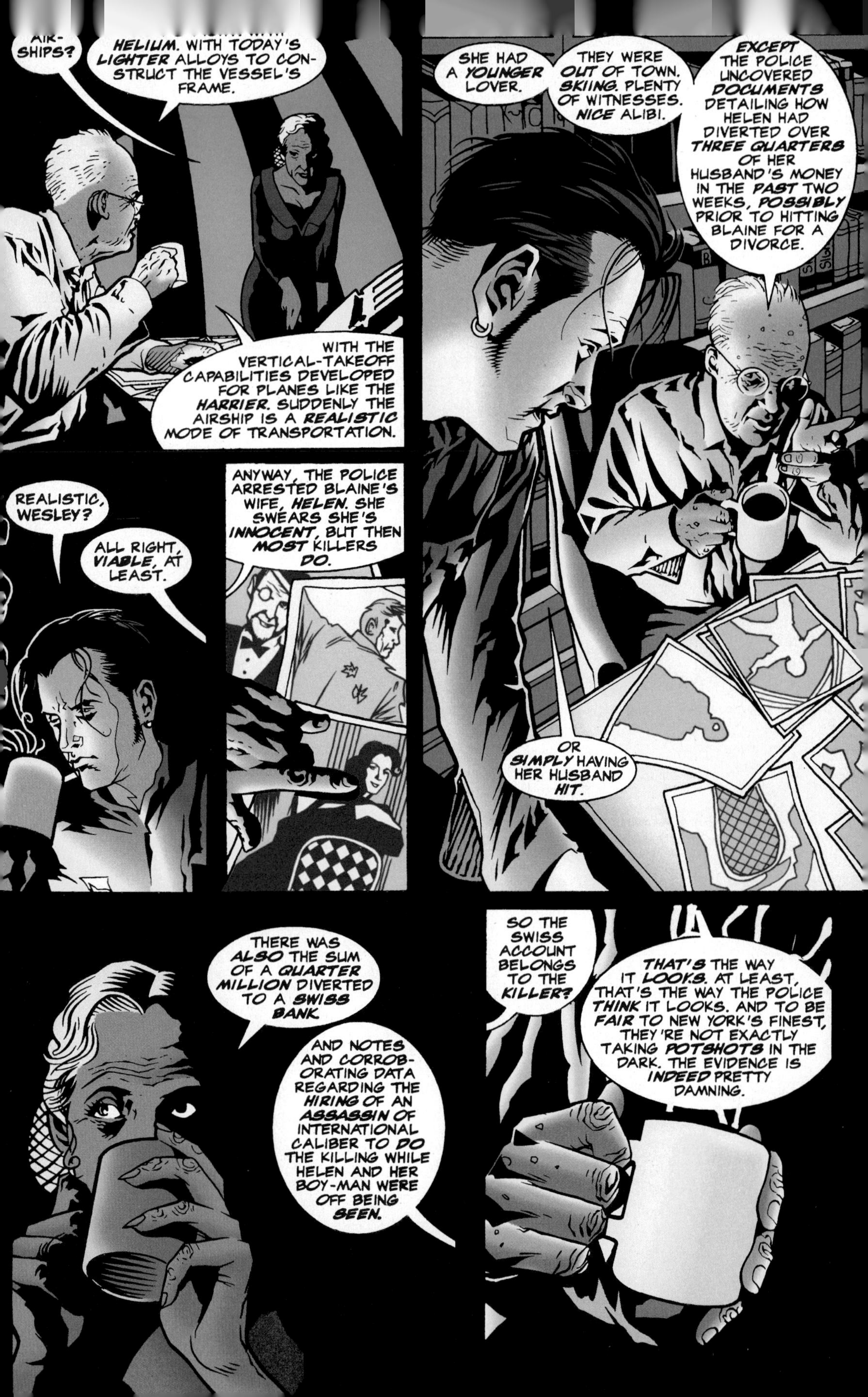

AIR-SHIPS?
HELIUM. WITH TODAY'S LIGHTER ALLOYS TO CON-STRUCT THE VESSEL'S FRAME.
WITH THE VERTICAL-TAKEOFF CAPABILITIES DEVELOPED FOR PLANES LIKE THE HARRIER. SUDDENLY THE AIRSHIP IS A REALISTIC MODE OF TRANSPORTATION.
SHE HAD A YOUNGER LOVER.
THEY WERE OUT OF TOWN. SKIING. PLENTY OF WITNESSES. NICE ALIBI.
EXCEPT THE POLICE UNCOVERED DOCUMENTS DETAILING HOW HELEN HAD DIVERTED OVER THREE QUARTERS OF HER HUSBAND'S MONEY IN THE PAST TWO WEEKS, POSSIBLY PRIOR TO HITTING BLAINE FOR A DIVORCE.
REALISTIC, WESLEY?
ALL RIGHT, VIABLE, AT LEAST.
ANYWAY, THE POLICE ARRESTED BLAINE'S WIFE, HELEN. SHE SWEARS SHE'S INNOCENT, BUT THEN MOST KILLERS DO.
OR SIMPLY HAVING HER HUSBAND HIT.
THERE WAS ALSO THE SUM OF A QUARTER MILLION DIVERTED TO A SWISS BANK.
AND NOTES AND CORROB-ORATING DATA REGARDING THE HIRING OF AN ASSASSIN OF INTERNATIONAL CALIBER TO DO THE KILLING WHILE HELEN AND HER BOY-MAN WERE OFF BEING SEEN.
SO THE SWISS ACCOUNT BELONGS TO THE KILLER?
THAT'S THE WAY IT LOOKS. AT LEAST, THAT'S THE WAY THE POLICE THINK IT LOOKS. AND TO BE FAIR TO NEW YORK'S FINEST, THEY'RE NOT EXACTLY TAKING POTSHOTS IN THE DARK. THE EVIDENCE IS INDEED PRETTY DAMNING.

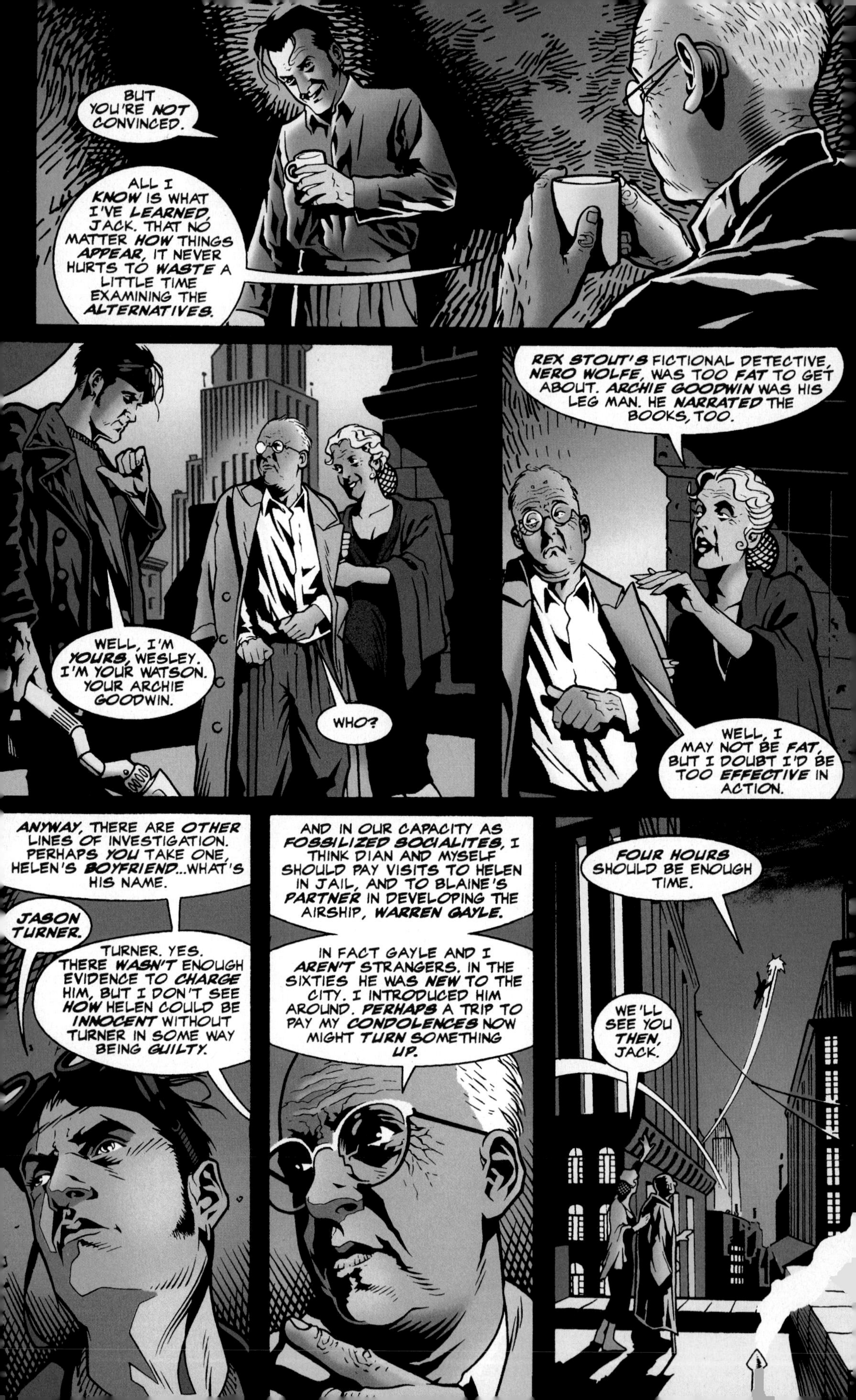
BUT YOU'RE NOT CONVINCED.
ALL I KNOW IS WHAT I'VE LEARNED, JACK. THAT NO MATTER HOW THINGS APPEAR, IT NEVER HURTS TO WASTE A LITTLE TIME EXAMINING THE ALTERNATIVES.
WELL, I'M YOURS, WESLEY. I'M YOUR WATSON. YOUR ARCHIE GOODWIN.
WHO?
REX STOUT'S FICTIONAL DETECTIVE, NERO WOLFE, WAS TOO FAT TO GET ABOUT. ARCHIE GOODWIN WAS HIS LEG MAN. HE NARRATED THE BOOKS, TOO.
WELL, I MAY NOT BE FAT, BUT I DOUBT I'D BE TOO EFFECTIVE IN ACTION.
ANYWAY, THERE ARE OTHER LINES OF INVESTIGATION. PERHAPS YOU TAKE ONE, HELEN'S BOYFRIEND...WHAT'S HIS NAME.
JASON TURNER.
TURNER. YES. THERE WASN'T ENOUGH EVIDENCE TO CHARGE HIM, BUT I DON'T SEE HOW HELEN COULD BE INNOCENT WITHOUT TURNER IN SOME WAY BEING GUILTY.
AND IN OUR CAPACITY AS FOSSILIZED SOCIALITES, I THINK DIAN AND MYSELF SHOULD PAY VISITS TO HELEN IN JAIL, AND TO BLAINE'S PARTNER IN DEVELOPING THE AIRSHIP, WARREN GAYLE.
IN FACT GAYLE AND I AREN'T STRANGERS. IN THE SIXTIES HE WAS NEW TO THE CITY. I INTRODUCED HIM AROUND. PERHAPS A TRIP TO PAY MY CONDOLENCES NOW MIGHT TURN SOMETHING UP.
FOUR HOURS SHOULD BE ENOUGH TIME.
WE'LL SEE YOU THEN, JACK.

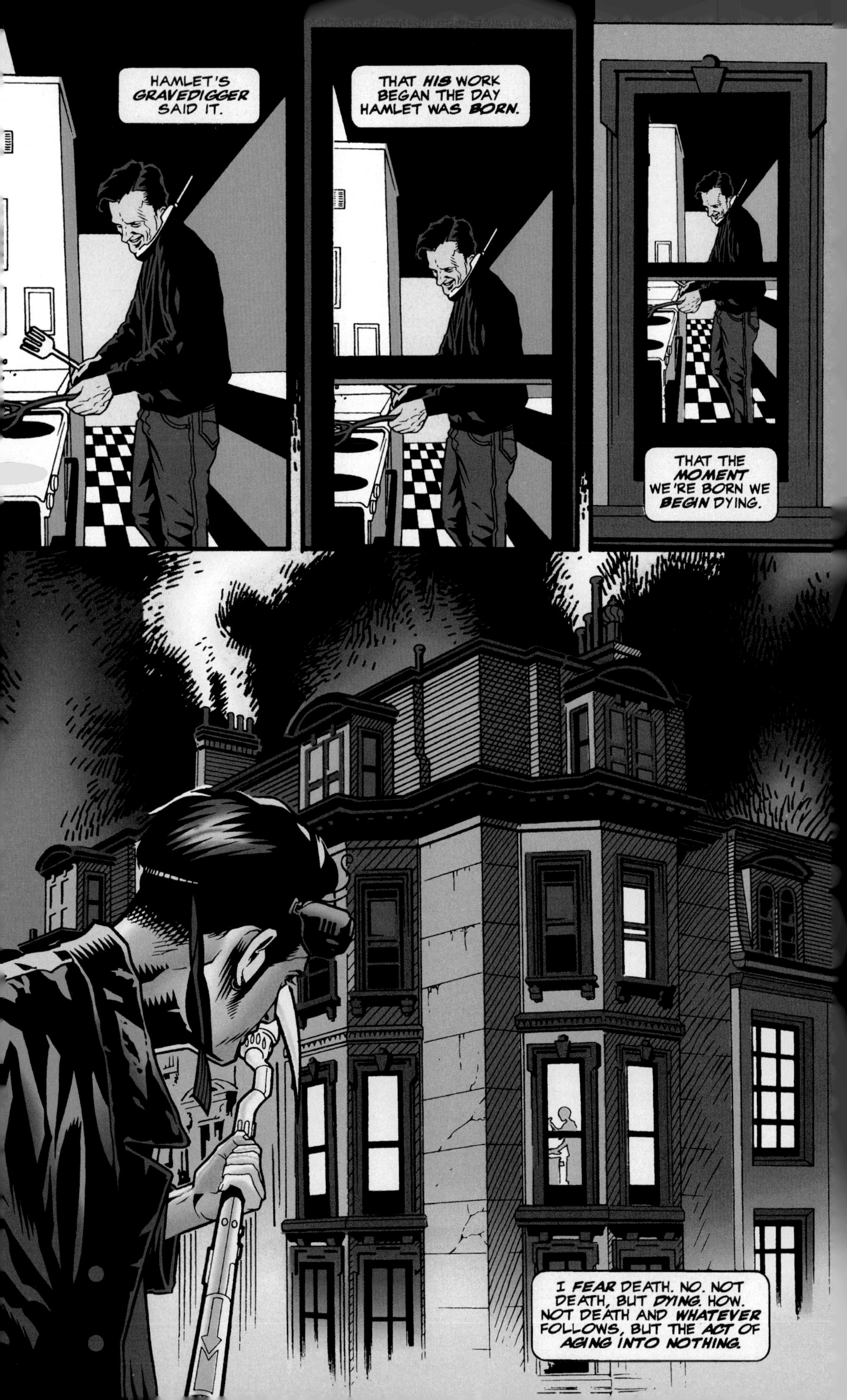
HAMLET'S GRAVEDIGGER SAID IT.
THAT HIS WORK BEGAN THE DAY HAMLET WAS BORN.
THAT THE MOMENT WE'RE BORN WE BEGIN DYING.
I FEAR DEATH. NO. NOT DEATH, BUT DYING. HOW. NOT DEATH AND WHATEVER FOLLOWS, BUT THE ACT OF AGING INTO NOTHING.

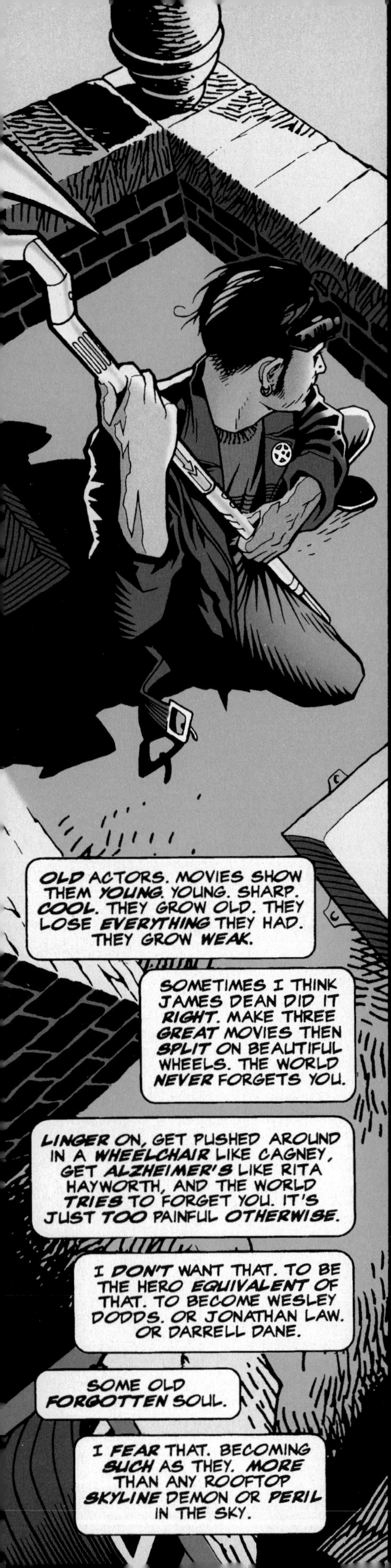
OLD ACTORS. MOVIES SHOW THEM YOUNG. YOUNG. SHARP. COOL. THEY GROW OLD. THEY LOSE EVERYTHING THEY HAD. THEY GROW WEAK.
SOMETIMES I THINK JAMES DEAN DID IT RIGHT. MAKE THREE GREAT MOVIES THEN SPLIT ON BEAUTIFUL WHEELS. THE WORLD NEVER FORGETS YOU.
LINGER ON, GET PUSHED AROUND IN A WHEELCHAIR LIKE CAGNEY, GET ALZHEIMER'S LIKE RITA HAYWORTH, AND THE WORLD TRIES TO FORGET YOU. IT'S JUST TOO PAINFUL OTHERWISE.
I DON'T WANT THAT. TO BE THE HERO EQUIVALENT OF THAT. TO BECOME WESLEY DODDS. OR JONATHAN LAW. OR DARRELL DANE.
SOME OLD FORGOTTEN SOUL.
I FEAR THAT. BECOMING SUCH AS THEY. MORE THAN ANY ROOFTOP SKYLINE DEMON OR PERIL IN THE SKY.
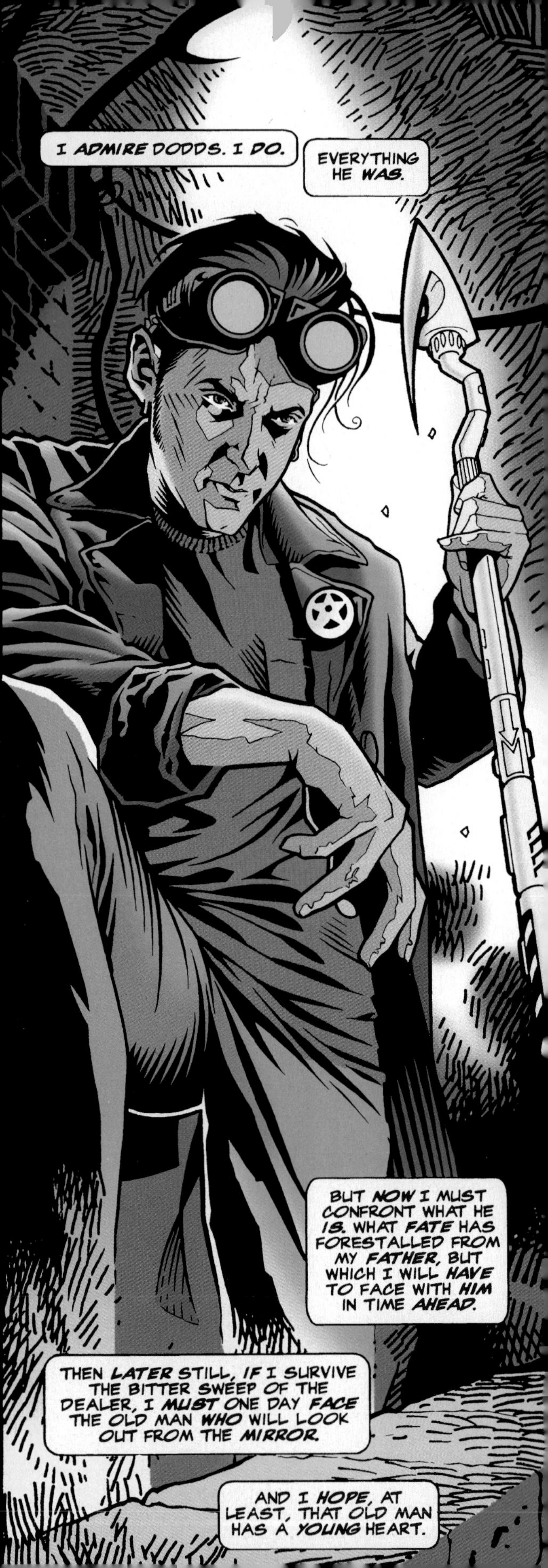
I ADMIRE DODDS. I DO.
EVERYTHING HE WAS.
BUT NOW I MUST CONFRONT WHAT HE IS. WHAT FATE HAS FORESTALLED FROM MY FATHER, BUT WHICH I WILL HAVE TO FACE WITH HIM IN TIME AHEAD.
THEN LATER STILL, IF I SURVIVE THE BITTER SWEEP OF THE DEALER, I MUST ONE DAY FACE THE OLD MAN WHO WILL LOOK OUT FROM THE MIRROR.
AND I HOPE, AT LEAST, THAT OLD MAN HAS A YOUNG HEART.

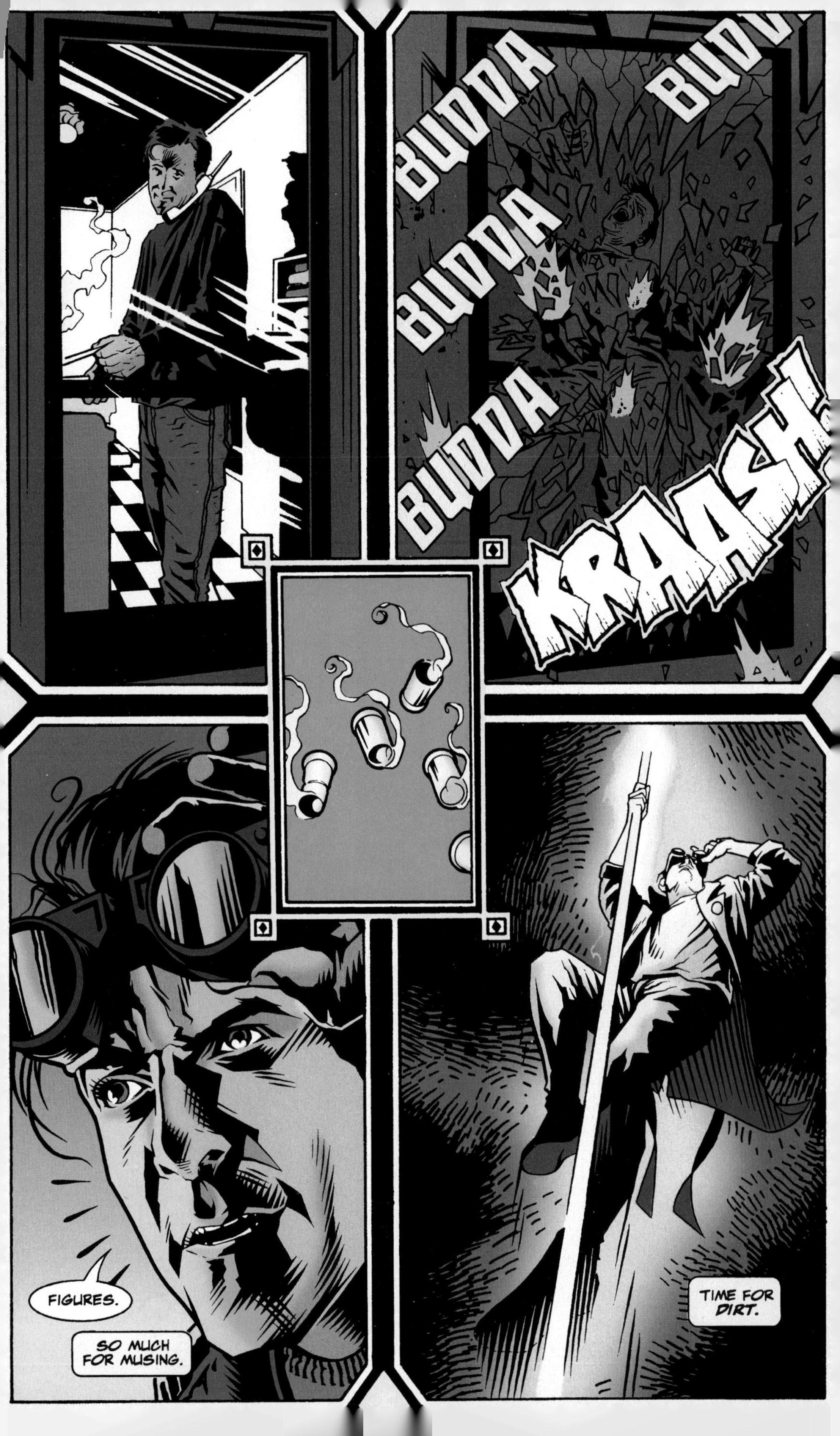

BUDDA
BUDDA
BUDDA
BUDDA
KRAASH!
FIGURES.
SO MUCH FOR MUSING.
TIME FOR DIRT.

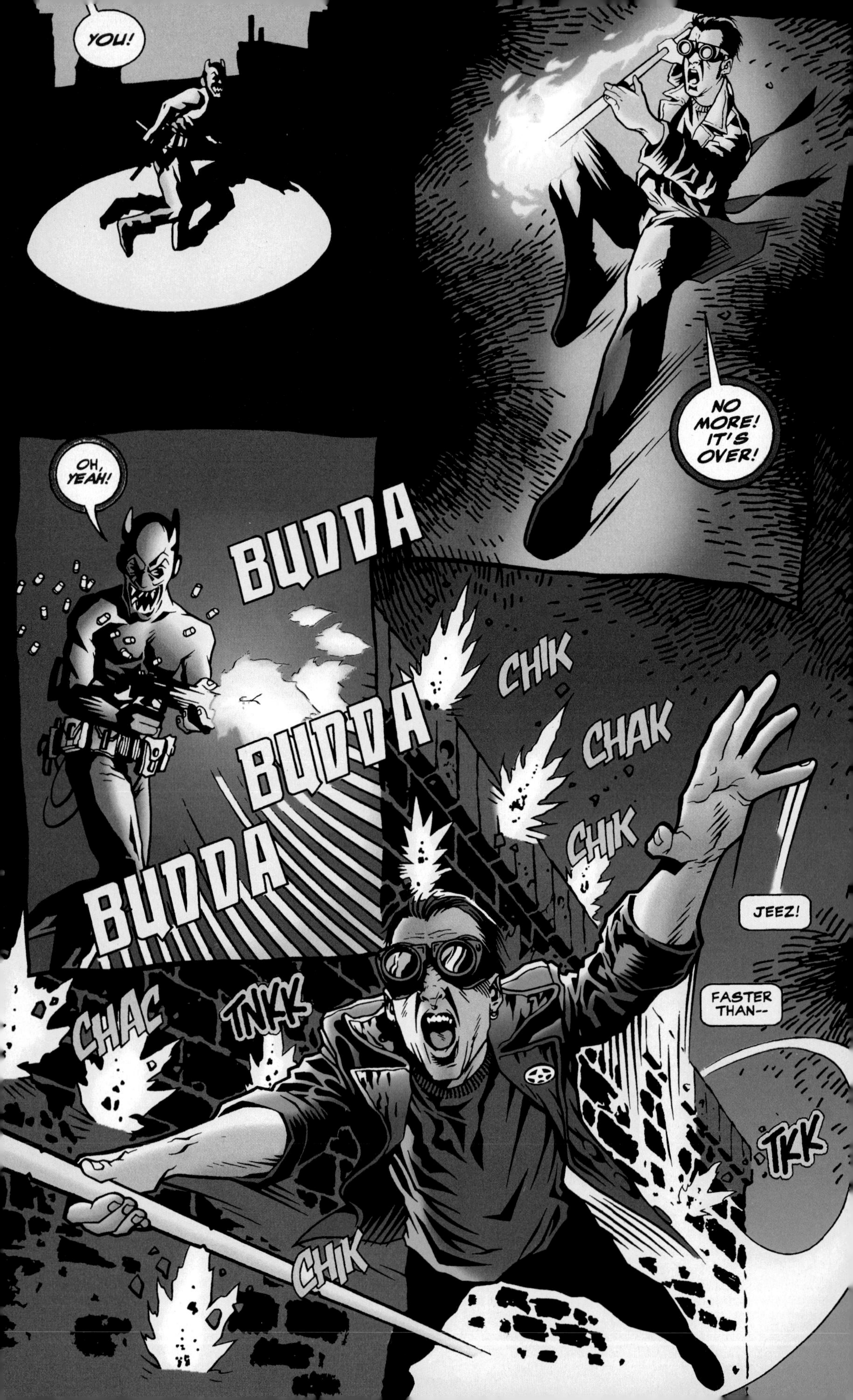
YOU!
NO MORE! IT'S OVER!
OH, YEAH!
BUDDA
BUDDA
BUDDA
CHIK
CHAK
CHIK
JEEZ!
FASTER THAN--
CHAC
TNKK
TKK
CHIK

FASTER THAN I THOUGHT.
--THAN ME.
AND I'LL GIVE HIM 9.9 ON THAT ESCAPE.
SMOOTHER THAN LAST TIME, AND THAT'S SAYING SOMETHING.
TERMINAL HOTEL
GUESS I SHOULD EXAMINE THE DAMAGE.
MAN, I HATE THE SIGHT OF BLOOD.

I WAS *SURPRISED* WHEN YOU OFFERED TO *VISIT*, WESLEY. ALL THE WAY UP HERE TO *ALBANY*. I DIDN'T THINK YOU WENT *OUT* ANY MORE.

I CAME TO PAY MY *RESPECTS*...GIVE MY CONDOLENCES. FOR *BLAINE'S* MURDER.

BESIDES, IT WAS TIME I GOT OUT OF THE HOUSE.

SO MUCH *CONFUSION* AT THIS TIME. HELEN'S *GUILT* SEEMS PRETTY *IRONCLAD*, YET SHE *CLAIMS* SHE'S *INNOCENT*. I DON'T KNOW *WHAT* TO THINK. I'VE KNOWN HELEN PRETTY *CLOSELY* THROUGH THE YEARS, AND TO *THINK* OF HER DOING SOMETHING LIKE *THIS* IS TOUGH.

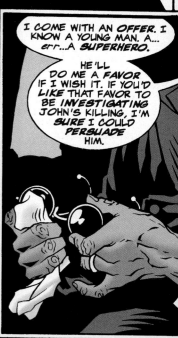

I COME WITH AN *OFFER*. I KNOW A YOUNG MAN. A... err...A *SUPERHERO*.

HE'LL DO ME A *FAVOR* IF I WISH IT. IF YOU'D *LIKE* THAT FAVOR TO BE *INVESTIGATING* JOHN'S KILLING, I'M *SURE* I COULD *PERSUADE* HIM.

ABSOLUTELY NOT.

NO.

MY INVESTORS WOULD...BE *UNPLEASED* BY A BRIGHT COSTUME *FLUTTERING* AROUND IN THEIR PROFIT AND LOSS REPORTS.

ANYWAY, I BROUGHT IN *SECURITY*. HI-TECH. ARMORED. IF I'M IN DANGER, *THEY'LL PROTECT* ME.

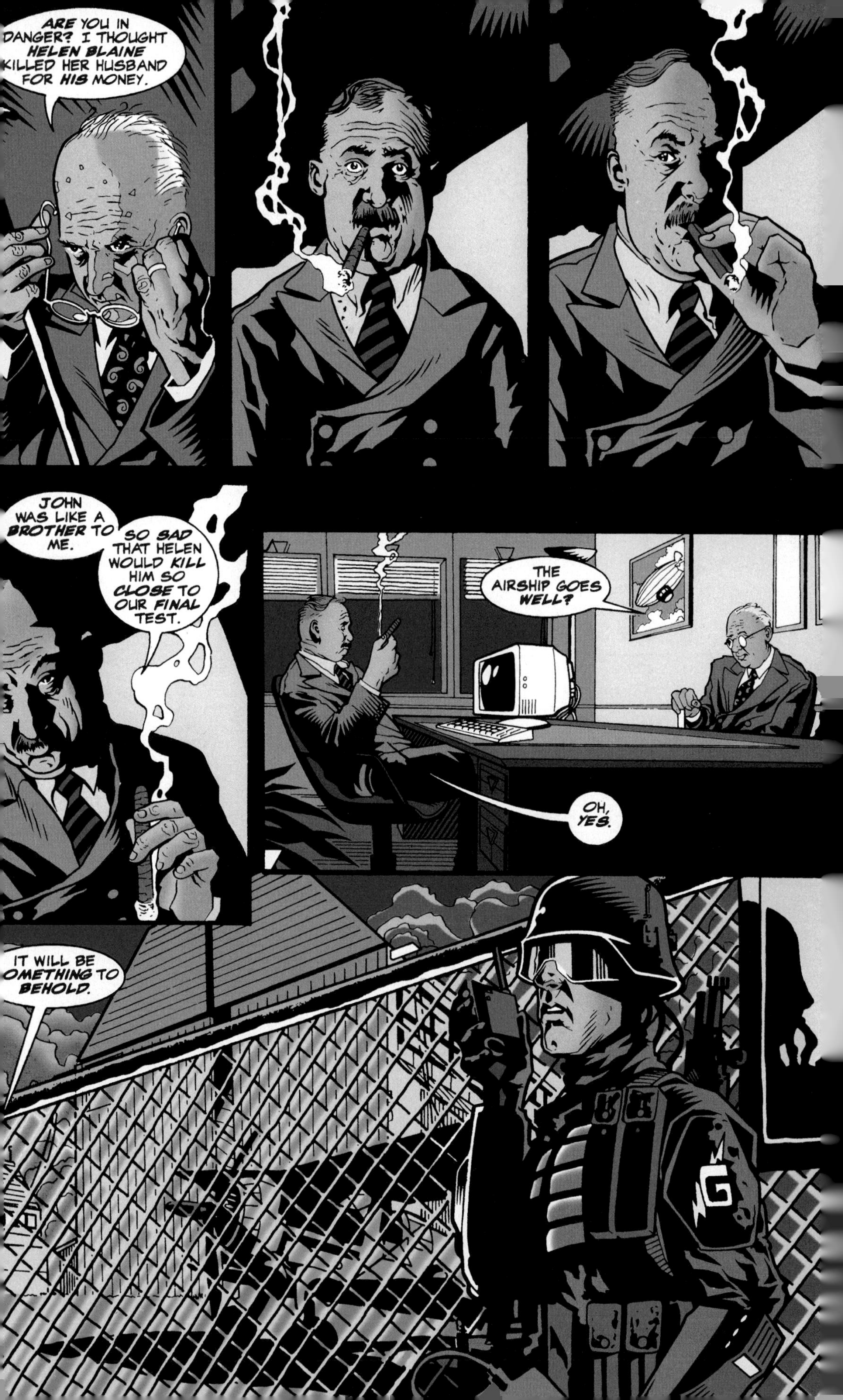
ARE YOU IN DANGER? I THOUGHT HELEN BLAINE KILLED HER HUSBAND FOR HIS MONEY.
JOHN WAS LIKE A BROTHER TO ME.
SO SAD THAT HELEN WOULD KILL HIM SO CLOSE TO OUR FINAL TEST.
THE AIRSHIP GOES WELL?
OH, YES.
IT WILL BE OMETHING TO BEHOLD.

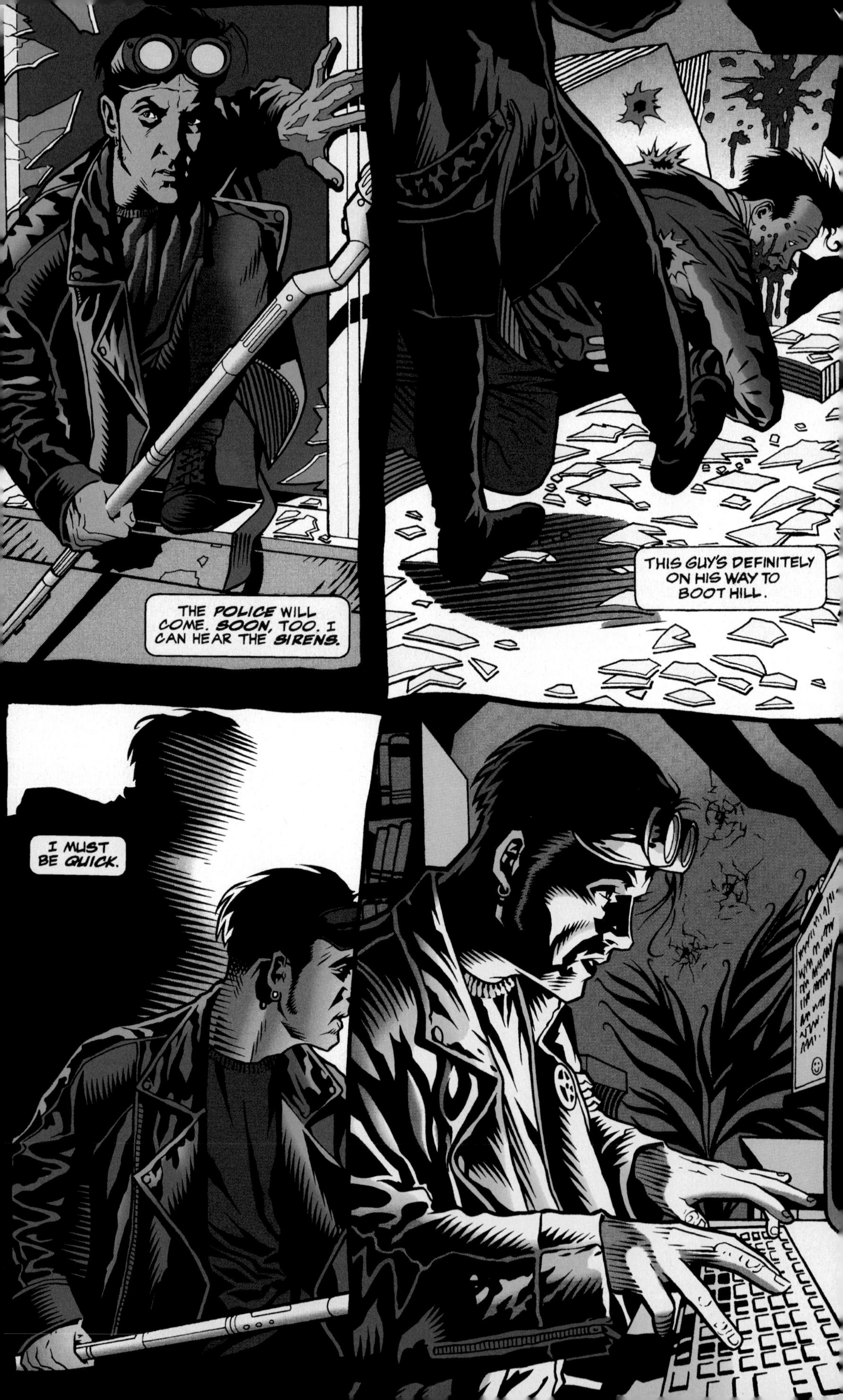
THE POLICE WILL COME. SOON, TOO. I CAN HEAR THE SIRENS.
THIS GUY'S DEFINITELY ON HIS WAY TO BOOT HILL.
I MUST BE QUICK.

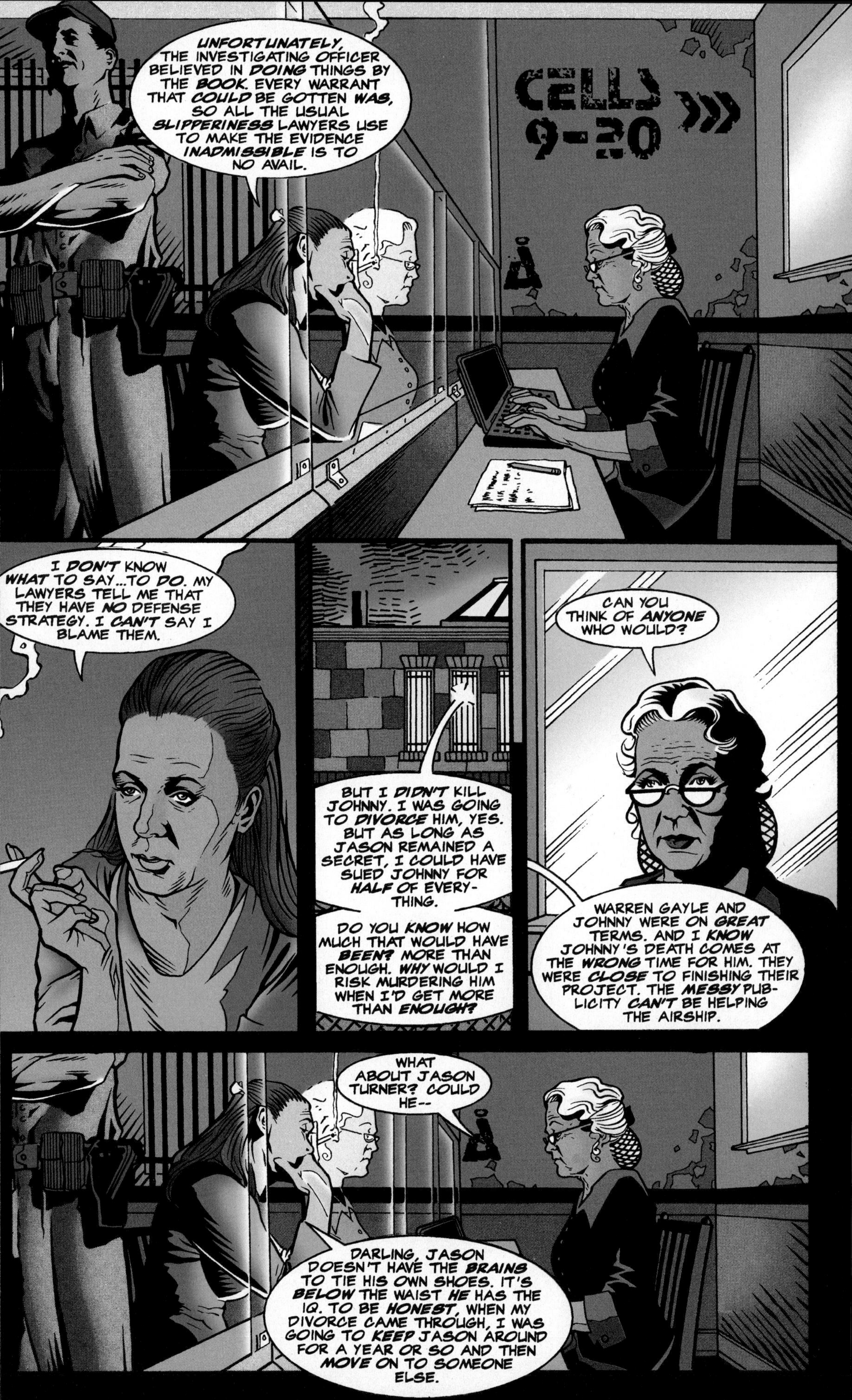

UNFORTUNATELY, THE INVESTIGATING OFFICER BELIEVED IN DOING THINGS BY THE BOOK. EVERY WARRANT THAT COULD BE GOTTEN WAS, SO ALL THE USUAL SLIPPERINESS LAWYERS USE TO MAKE THE EVIDENCE INADMISSIBLE IS TO NO AVAIL.
CELLS 9-20
I DON'T KNOW WHAT TO SAY...TO DO. MY LAWYERS TELL ME THAT THEY HAVE NO DEFENSE STRATEGY. I CAN'T SAY I BLAME THEM.
BUT I DIDN'T KILL JOHNNY. I WAS GOING TO DIVORCE HIM, YES. BUT AS LONG AS JASON REMAINED A SECRET, I COULD HAVE SUED JOHNNY FOR HALF OF EVERY-THING.
DO YOU KNOW HOW MUCH THAT WOULD HAVE BEEN? MORE THAN ENOUGH. WHY WOULD I RISK MURDERING HIM WHEN I'D GET MORE THAN ENOUGH?
CAN YOU THINK OF ANYONE WHO WOULD?
WARREN GAYLE AND JOHNNY WERE ON GREAT TERMS. AND I KNOW JOHNNY'S DEATH COMES AT THE WRONG TIME FOR HIM. THEY WERE CLOSE TO FINISHING THEIR PROJECT. THE MESSY PUB-LICITY CAN'T BE HELPING THE AIRSHIP.
WHAT ABOUT JASON TURNER? COULD HE--
DARLING, JASON DOESN'T HAVE THE BRAINS TO TIE HIS OWN SHOES. IT'S BELOW THE WAIST HE HAS THE IQ. TO BE HONEST, WHEN MY DIVORCE CAME THROUGH, I WAS GOING TO KEEP JASON AROUND FOR A YEAR OR SO AND THEN MOVE ON TO SOMEONE ELSE.

JASON TURNER KEPT A *COMPUTER* DIARY.

HE WAS *SHOWN* HOW TO DIVERT THE *FUNDS* FROM JOHN BLAINE'S ACCOUNT.

TURNER WAS *SELECTED* BECAUSE HIS RELATIONSHIP WITH HELEN HAD *ALREADY* BEGUN. HE WAS *CLOSE* ENOUGH TO HER. HE GAINED *ACCESS* TO *HER* BANK ACCOUNTS AND THROUGH THEM TO *BLAINE'S* MONEY AS WELL.

THE TWO HUNDRED FIFTY THOUSAND WAS *HIS* PAYMENT.

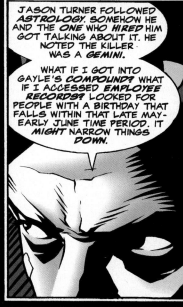

BUT HE WANTED *MORE*. HE THREATENED TO *EXPOSE* THE *WHOLE* SCHEME. THEY *KILLED* HIM.

THEY?

HIS JOURNAL DIDN'T SAY *WHO*. ALL IT SAID WAS THAT THE ONE WHO *HIRED* HIM...ONE OF A *TEAM*...WORKED FOR *WARREN GAYLE*.

GAYLE DOESN'T *KNOW* THOUGH. ALL OF THIS...BLAINE'S MURDER... *EVERYTHING*...IS TO BRING GAYLE *DOWN*. SHOULD WE *TELL* HIM?

HE *DOESN'T* WANT YOU *INVOLVED*, JACK. IF HE *RESISTS* THE INFORMATION...HEARING IT... ALL WE COULD ACCOMPLISH IS *FOREWARNING* THE KILLER.

JASON TURNER FOLLOWED *ASTROLOGY*. SOMEHOW HE AND THE *ONE* WHO HIRED HIM GOT TALKING ABOUT IT. HE NOTED THE KILLER WAS A *GEMINI*.

WHAT IF I GOT INTO GAYLE'S *COMPOUND*? WHAT IF I ACCESSED *EMPLOYEE RECORDS*? LOOKED FOR PEOPLE WITH A BIRTHDAY THAT FALLS WITHIN THAT LATE MAY–EARLY JUNE TIME PERIOD. IT *MIGHT* NARROW THINGS *DOWN*.

WELL, YOU CERTAINLY MIGHT FIND *SOMETHING* OUT. GAYLE KNOWS *MORE* THAN HE LETS ON. HE HIRED *PROTECTION* WHEN *NOTHING* IMPLIES *HE* WAS EVEN IN DANGER.

BUT THE GAYLE COMPOUND DEFENSES ARE PRETTY *ADVANCED*. ARE YOU *PREPARED* FOR THAT?

NO.

BUT...

...WHEN DOES THAT STOP SUCH AS *WE?*

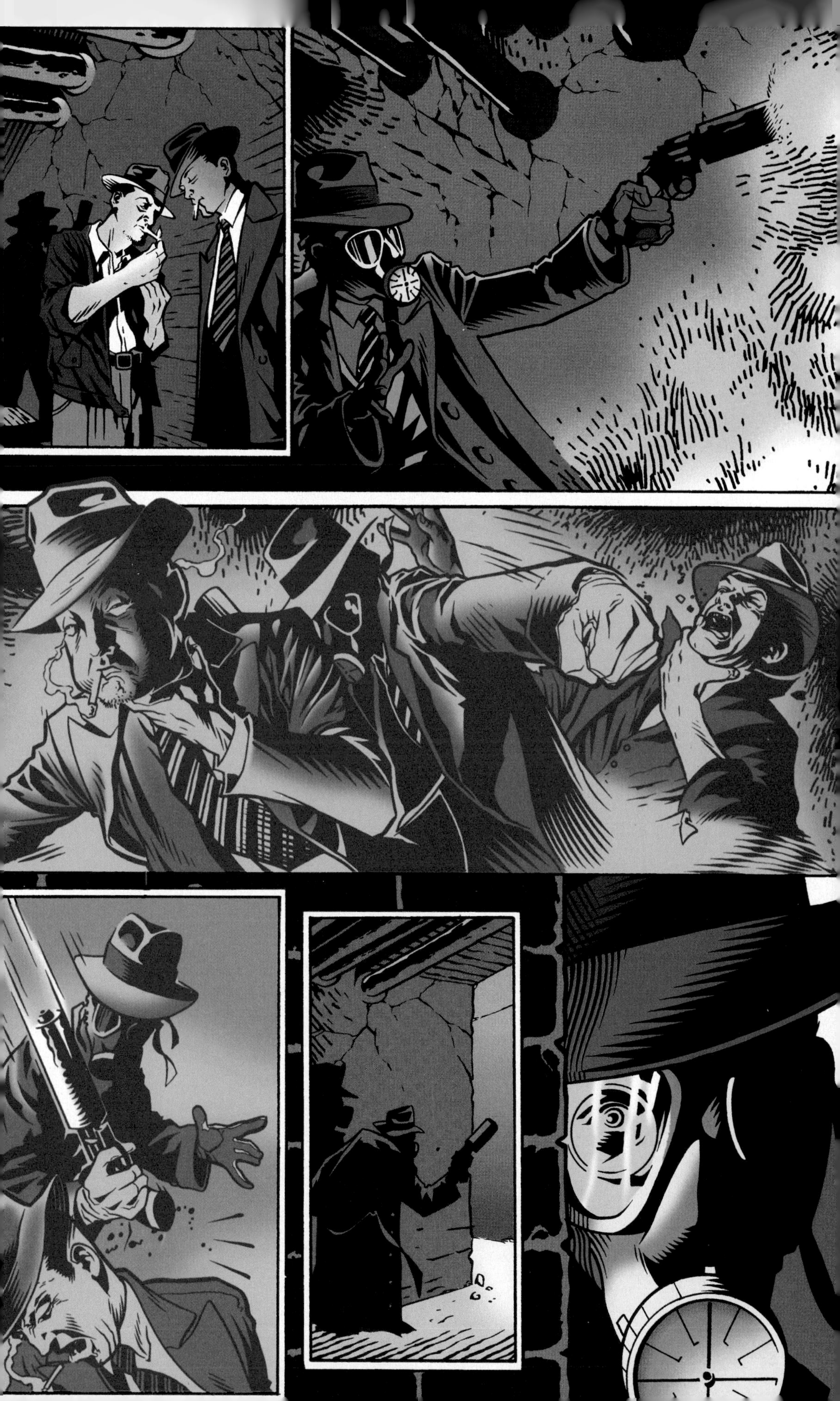

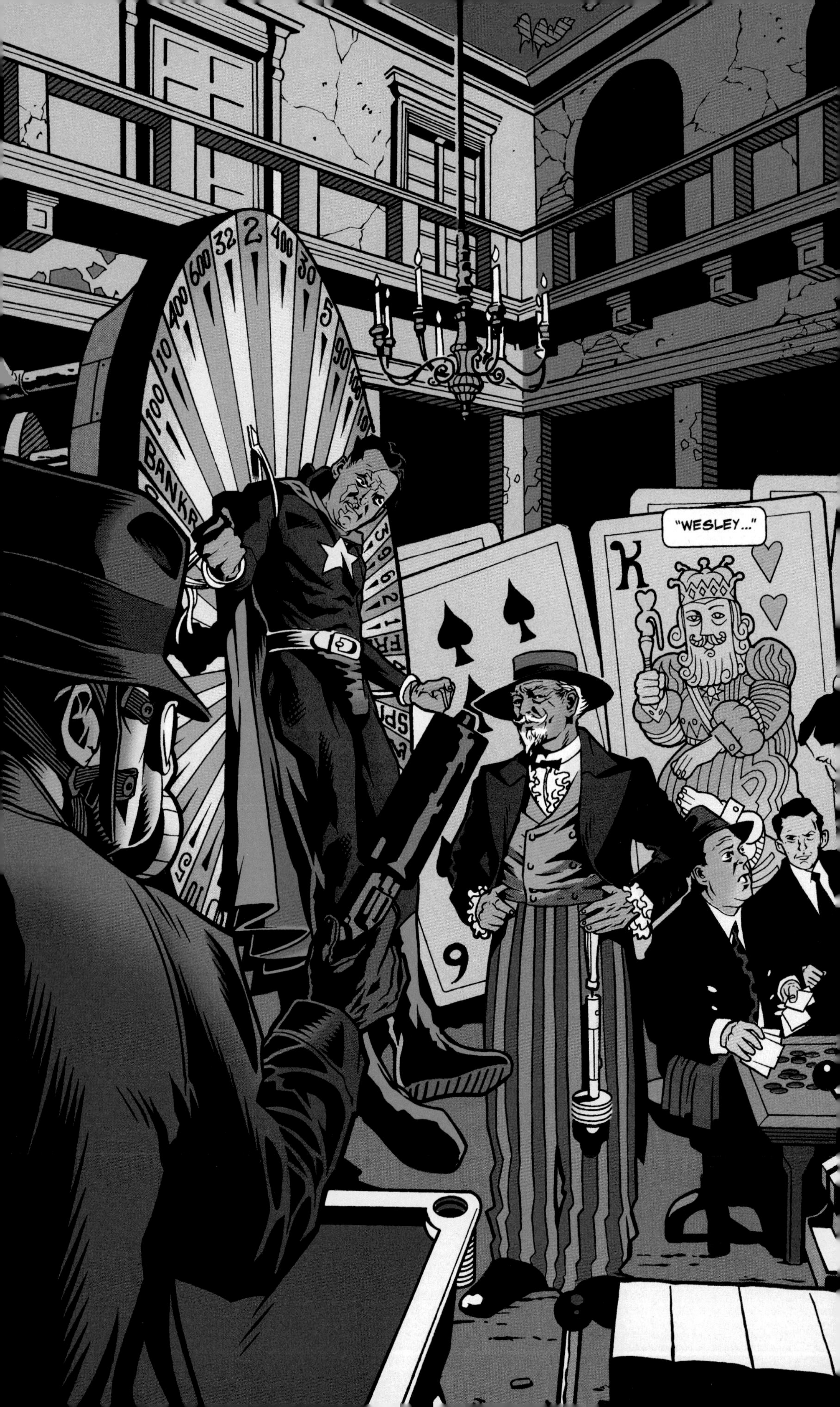
"WESLEY..."

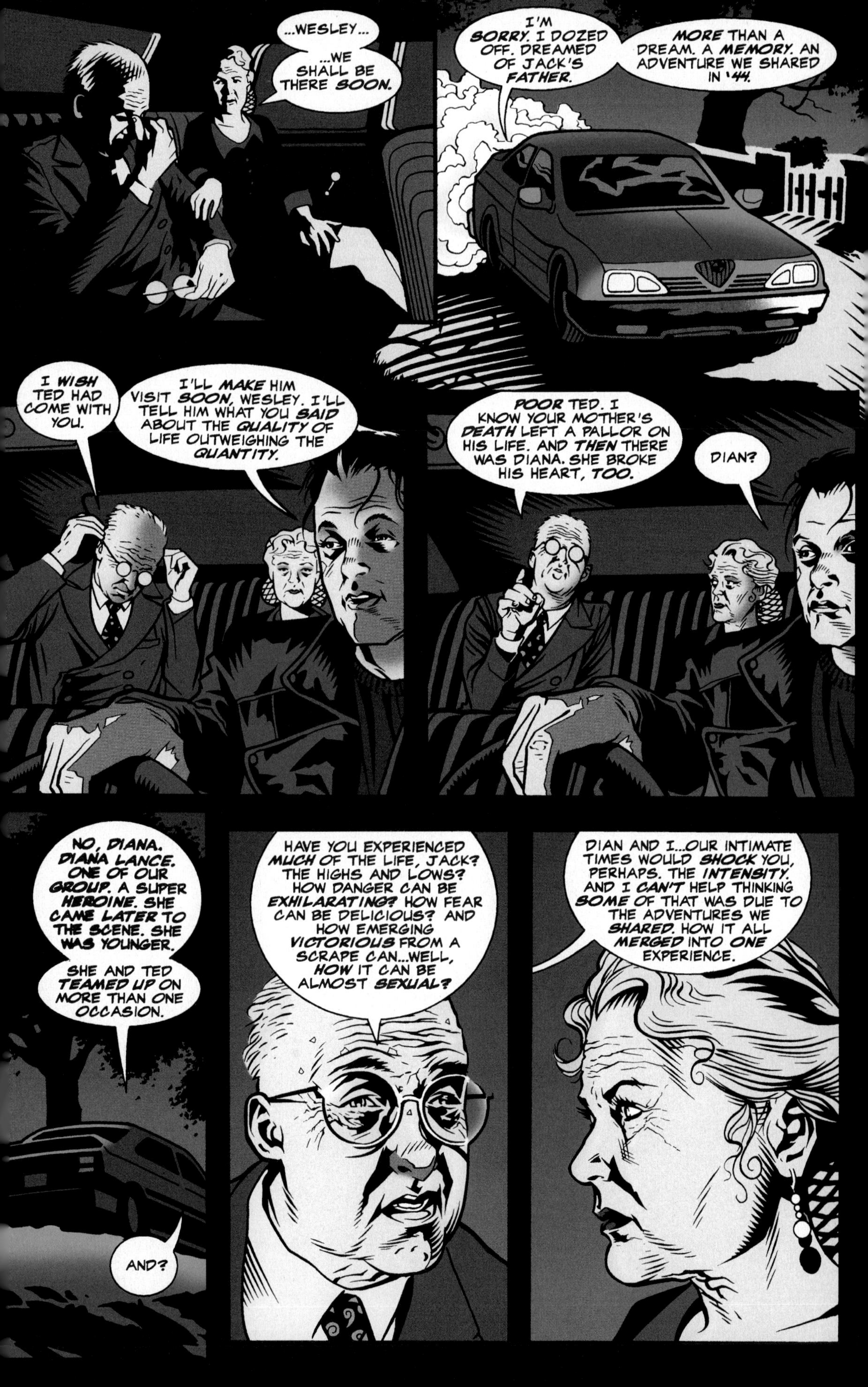
...WESLEY...
...WE SHALL BE THERE SOON.
I'M SORRY. I DOZED OFF. DREAMED OF JACK'S FATHER.
MORE THAN A DREAM. A MEMORY. AN ADVENTURE WE SHARED IN '44.
I WISH TED HAD COME WITH YOU.
I'LL MAKE HIM VISIT SOON, WESLEY. I'LL TELL HIM WHAT YOU SAID ABOUT THE QUALITY OF LIFE OUTWEIGHING THE QUANTITY.
POOR TED. I KNOW YOUR MOTHER'S DEATH LEFT A PALLOR ON HIS LIFE. AND THEN THERE WAS DIANA. SHE BROKE HIS HEART, TOO.
DIAN?
NO, DIANA. DIANA LANCE. ONE OF OUR GROUP. A SUPER HEROINE. SHE CAME LATER TO THE SCENE. SHE WAS YOUNGER.
SHE AND TED TEAMED UP ON MORE THAN ONE OCCASION.
AND?
HAVE YOU EXPERIENCED MUCH OF THE LIFE, JACK? THE HIGHS AND LOWS? HOW DANGER CAN BE EXHILARATING? HOW FEAR CAN BE DELICIOUS? AND HOW EMERGING VICTORIOUS FROM A SCRAPE CAN...WELL, HOW IT CAN BE ALMOST SEXUAL?
DIAN AND I...OUR INTIMATE TIMES WOULD SHOCK YOU, PERHAPS. THE INTENSITY. AND I CAN'T HELP THINKING SOME OF THAT WAS DUE TO THE ADVENTURES WE SHARED. HOW IT ALL MERGED INTO ONE EXPERIENCE.

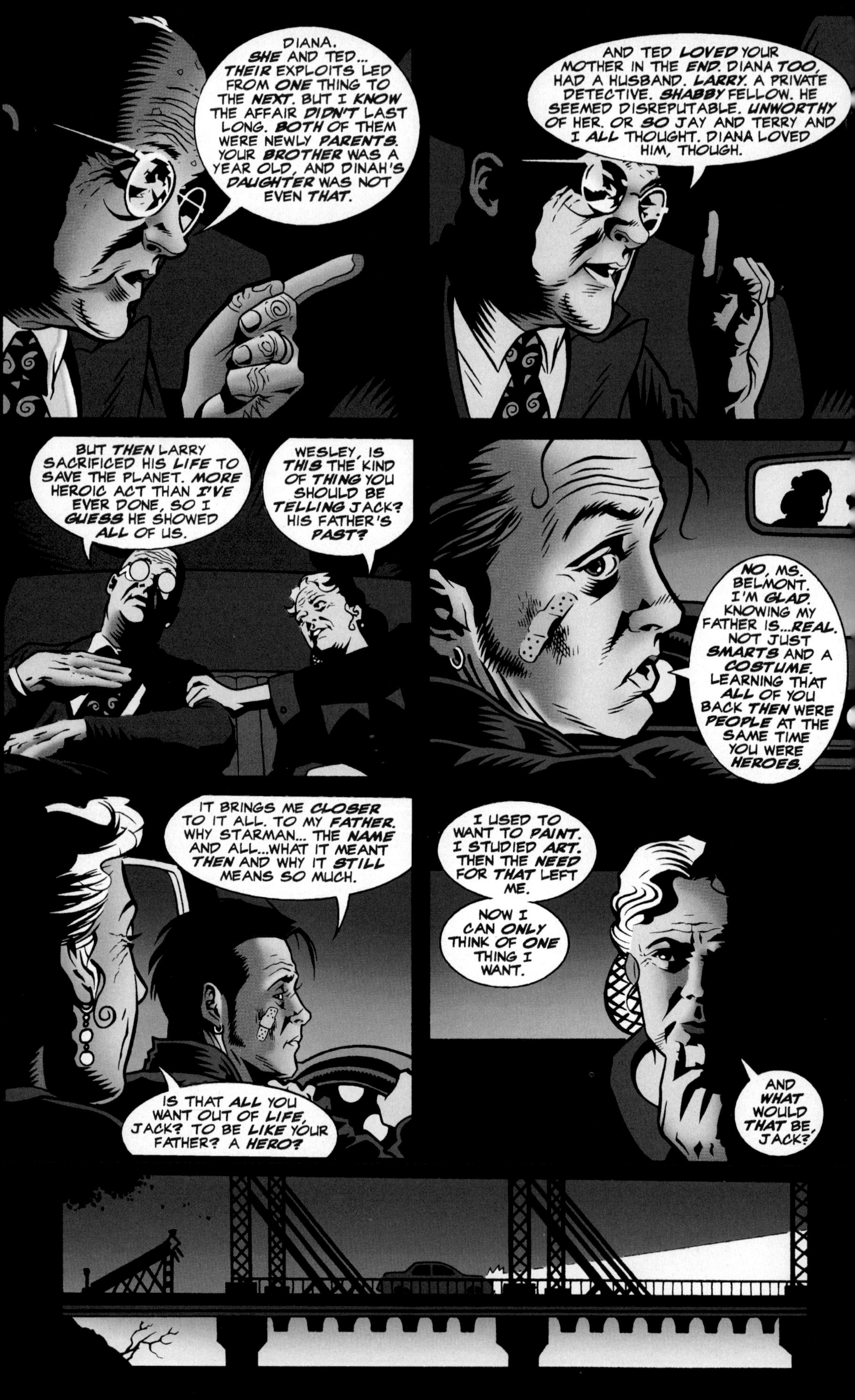
DIANA. SHE AND TED... THEIR EXPLOITS LED FROM ONE THING TO THE NEXT. BUT I KNOW THE AFFAIR DIDN'T LAST LONG. BOTH OF THEM WERE NEWLY PARENTS. YOUR BROTHER WAS A YEAR OLD, AND DINAH'S DAUGHTER WAS NOT EVEN THAT.
AND TED LOVED YOUR MOTHER IN THE END. DIANA TOO, HAD A HUSBAND. LARRY. A PRIVATE DETECTIVE. SHABBY FELLOW. HE SEEMED DISREPUTABLE. UNWORTHY OF HER. OR SO JAY AND TERRY AND I ALL THOUGHT. DIANA LOVED HIM, THOUGH.
BUT THEN LARRY SACRIFICED HIS LIFE TO SAVE THE PLANET. MORE HEROIC ACT THAN I'VE EVER DONE, SO I GUESS HE SHOWED ALL OF US.
WESLEY, IS THIS THE KIND OF THING YOU SHOULD BE TELLING JACK? HIS FATHER'S PAST?
NO, MS. BELMONT. I'M GLAD. KNOWING MY FATHER IS...REAL. NOT JUST SMARTS AND A COSTUME. LEARNING THAT ALL OF YOU BACK THEN WERE PEOPLE AT THE SAME TIME YOU WERE HEROES.
IT BRINGS ME CLOSER TO IT ALL. TO MY FATHER. WHY STARMAN... THE NAME AND ALL...WHAT IT MEANT THEN AND WHY IT STILL MEANS SO MUCH.
IS THAT ALL YOU WANT OUT OF LIFE, JACK? TO BE LIKE YOUR FATHER? A HERO?
I USED TO WANT TO PAINT. I STUDIED ART. THEN THE NEED FOR THAT LEFT ME.
NOW I CAN ONLY THINK OF ONE THING I WANT.
AND WHAT WOULD THAT BE, JACK?

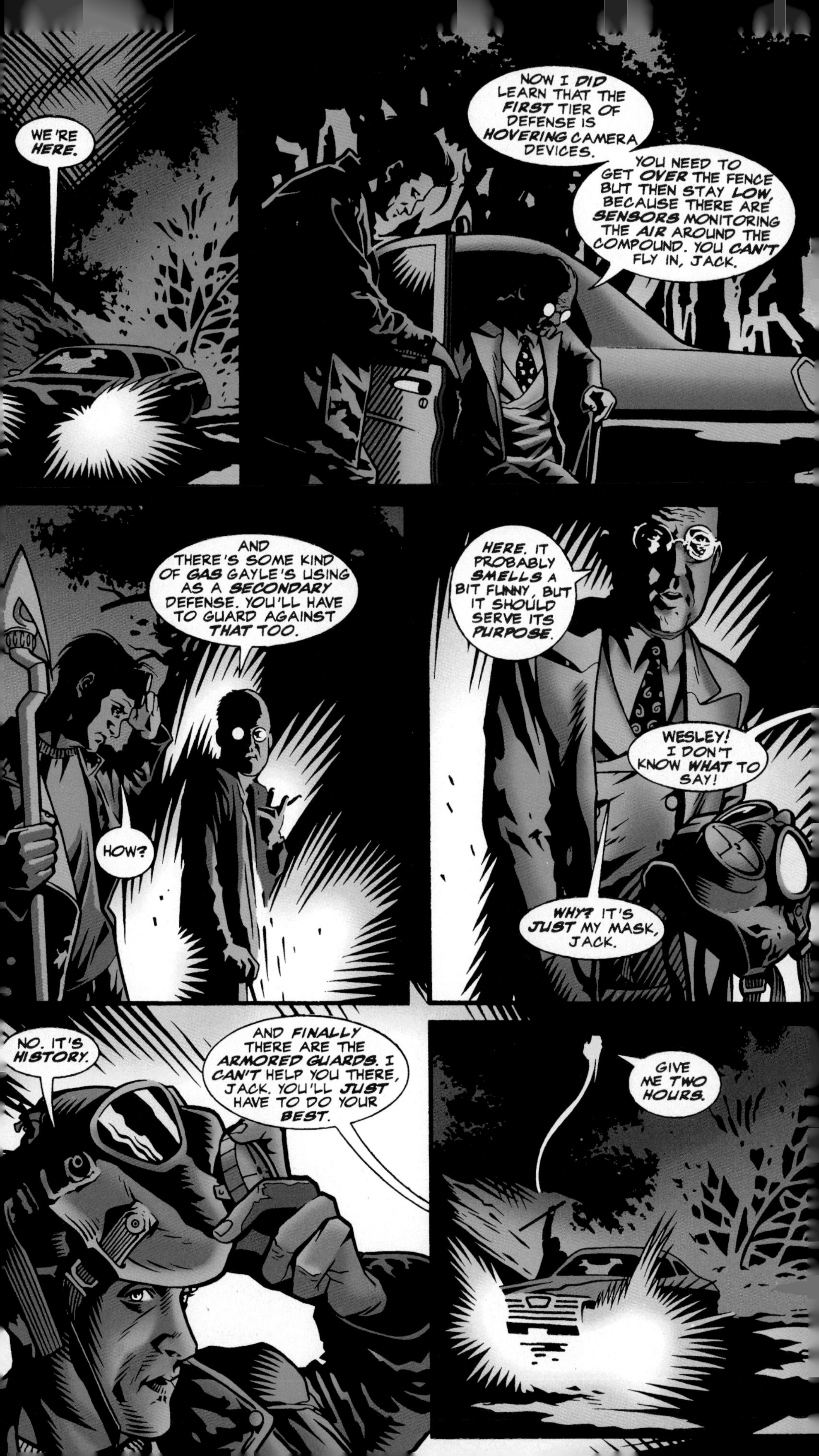

WE'RE HERE.
NOW I DID LEARN THAT THE FIRST TIER OF DEFENSE IS HOVERING CAMERA DEVICES.
YOU NEED TO GET OVER THE FENCE BUT THEN STAY LOW, BECAUSE THERE ARE SENSORS MONITORING THE AIR AROUND THE COMPOUND. YOU CAN'T FLY IN, JACK.
AND THERE'S SOME KIND OF GAS GAYLE'S USING AS A SECONDARY DEFENSE. YOU'LL HAVE TO GUARD AGAINST THAT TOO.
HOW?
HERE. IT PROBABLY SMELLS A BIT FUNNY, BUT IT SHOULD SERVE ITS PURPOSE.
WESLEY! I DON'T KNOW WHAT TO SAY!
WHY? IT'S JUST MY MASK, JACK.
NO. IT'S HISTORY.
AND FINALLY THERE ARE THE ARMORED GUARDS. I CAN'T HELP YOU THERE, JACK. YOU'LL JUST HAVE TO DO YOUR BEST.
GIVE ME TWO HOURS.

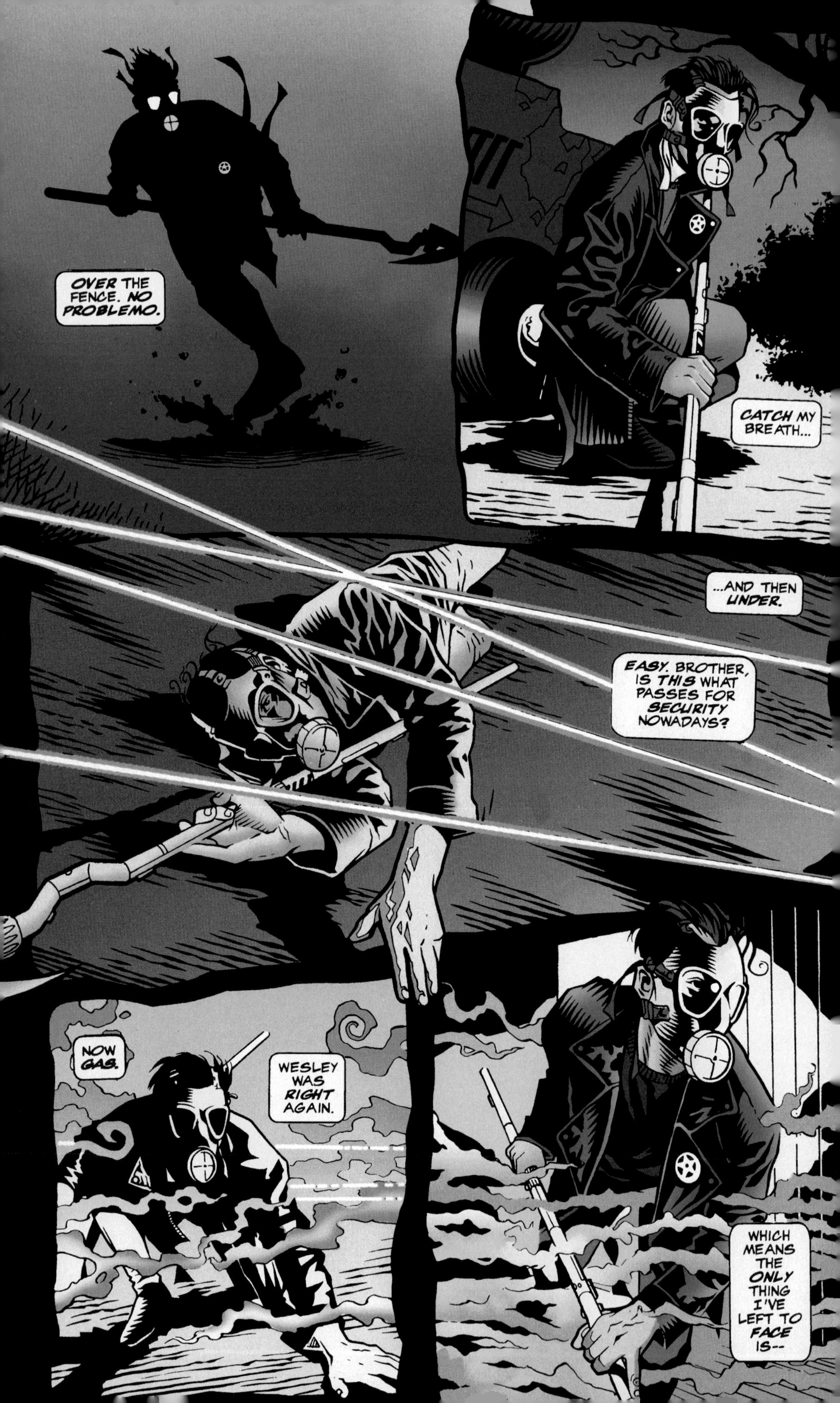
OVER THE FENCE. NO PROBLEMO.
CATCH MY BREATH...
...AND THEN UNDER.
EASY. BROTHER, IS THIS WHAT PASSES FOR SECURITY NOWADAYS?
NOW GAS.
WESLEY WAS RIGHT AGAIN.
WHICH MEANS THE ONLY THING I'VE LEFT TO FACE IS--

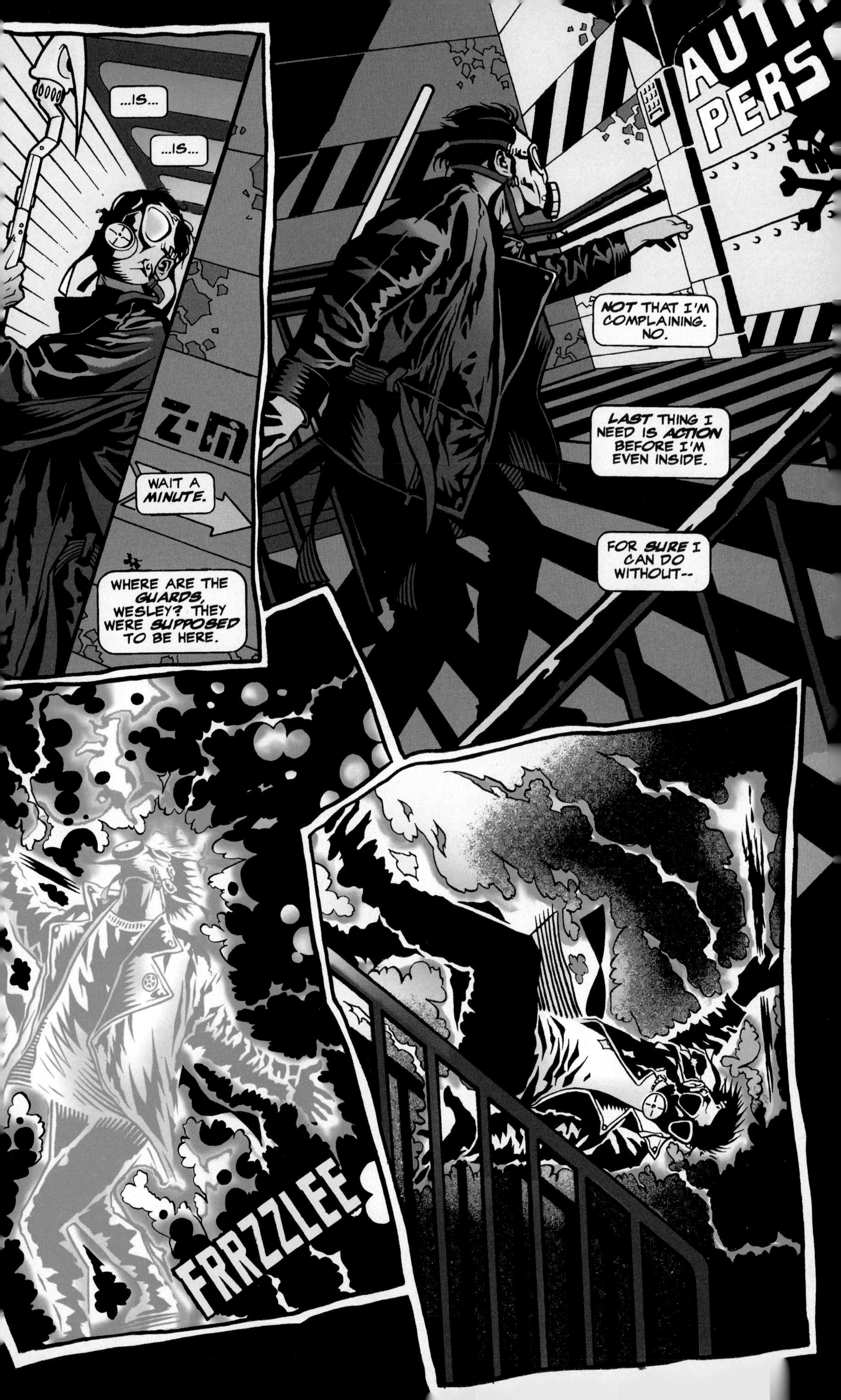

...IS...
...IS...
WAIT A MINUTE.
WHERE ARE THE GUARDS, WESLEY? THEY WERE SUPPOSED TO BE HERE.
NOT THAT I'M COMPLAINING. NO.
LAST THING I NEED IS ACTION BEFORE I'M EVEN INSIDE.
FOR SURE I CAN DO WITHOUT--
FRRZZLEE

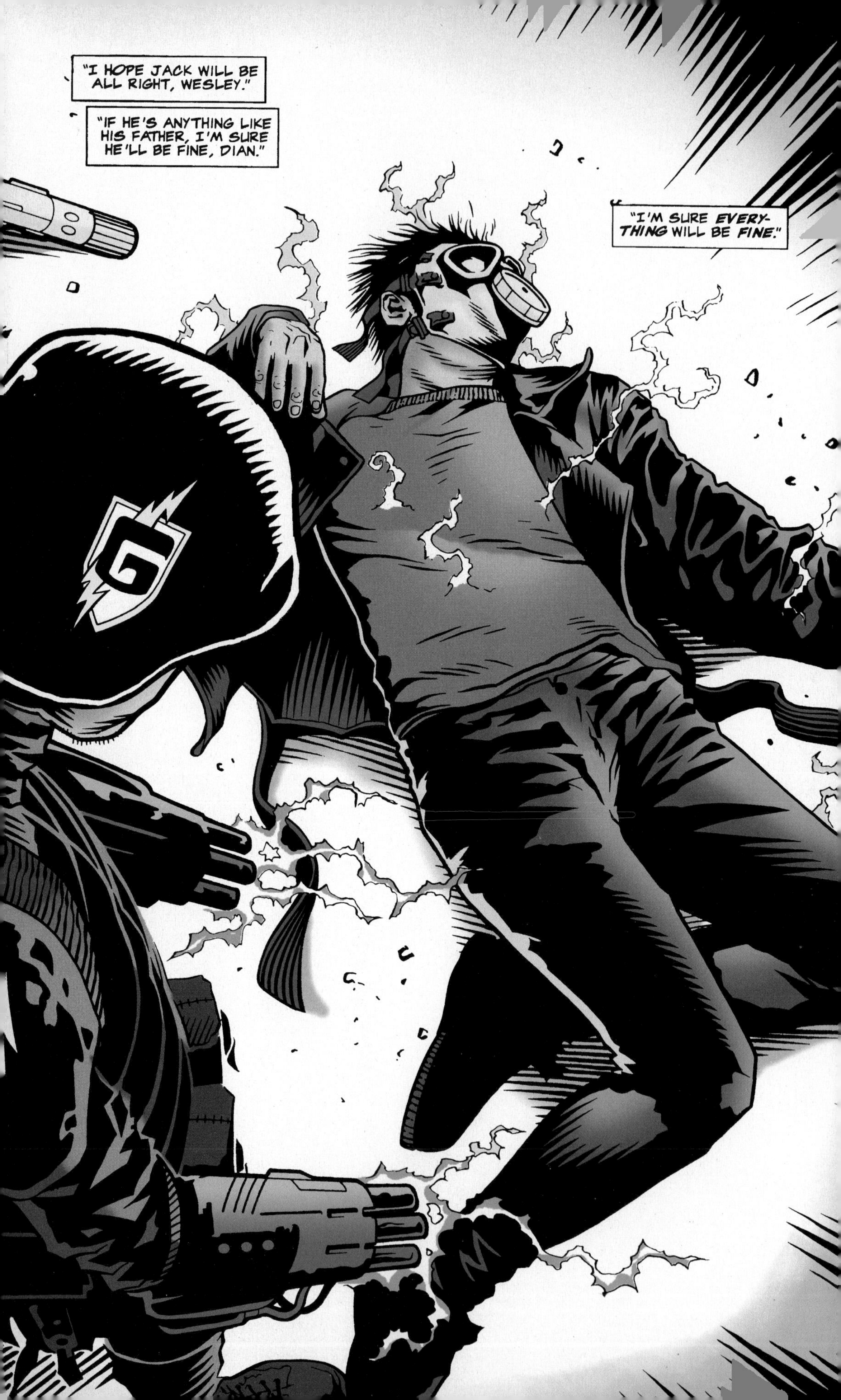
"I HOPE JACK WILL BE ALL RIGHT, WESLEY."
"IF HE'S ANYTHING LIKE HIS FATHER, I'M SURE HE'LL BE FINE, DIAN."
"I'M SURE EVERYTHING WILL BE FINE."

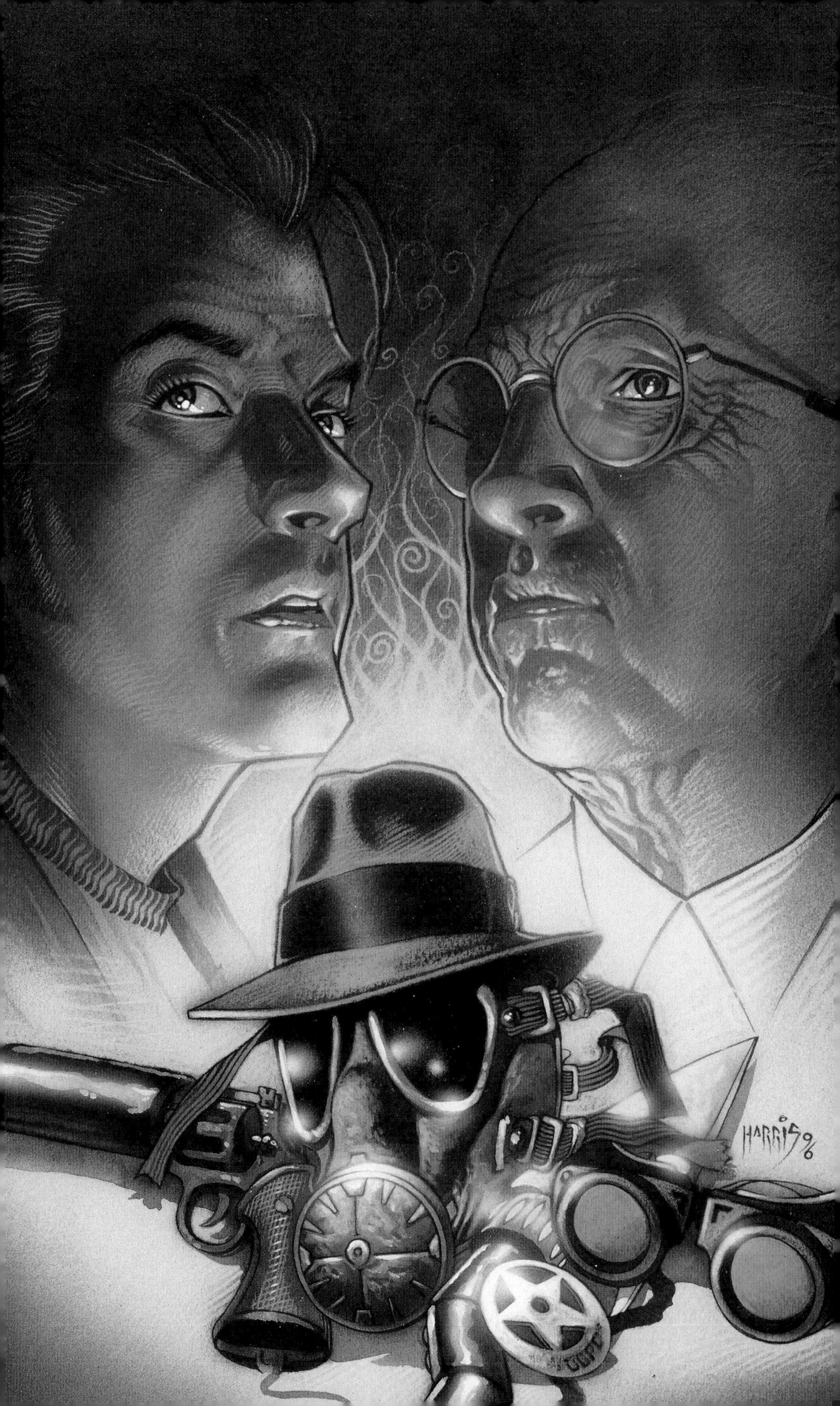
HARRIS

STARMAN 22

Cover by Tony Harris

Written by James Robinson

Art by Tony Harris & Wade von Grawbadger (pgs. 163-171, 183-184)

and Guy Davis (pgs. 172-182)

with colors by Trish Mulvihill & Dave Hornung

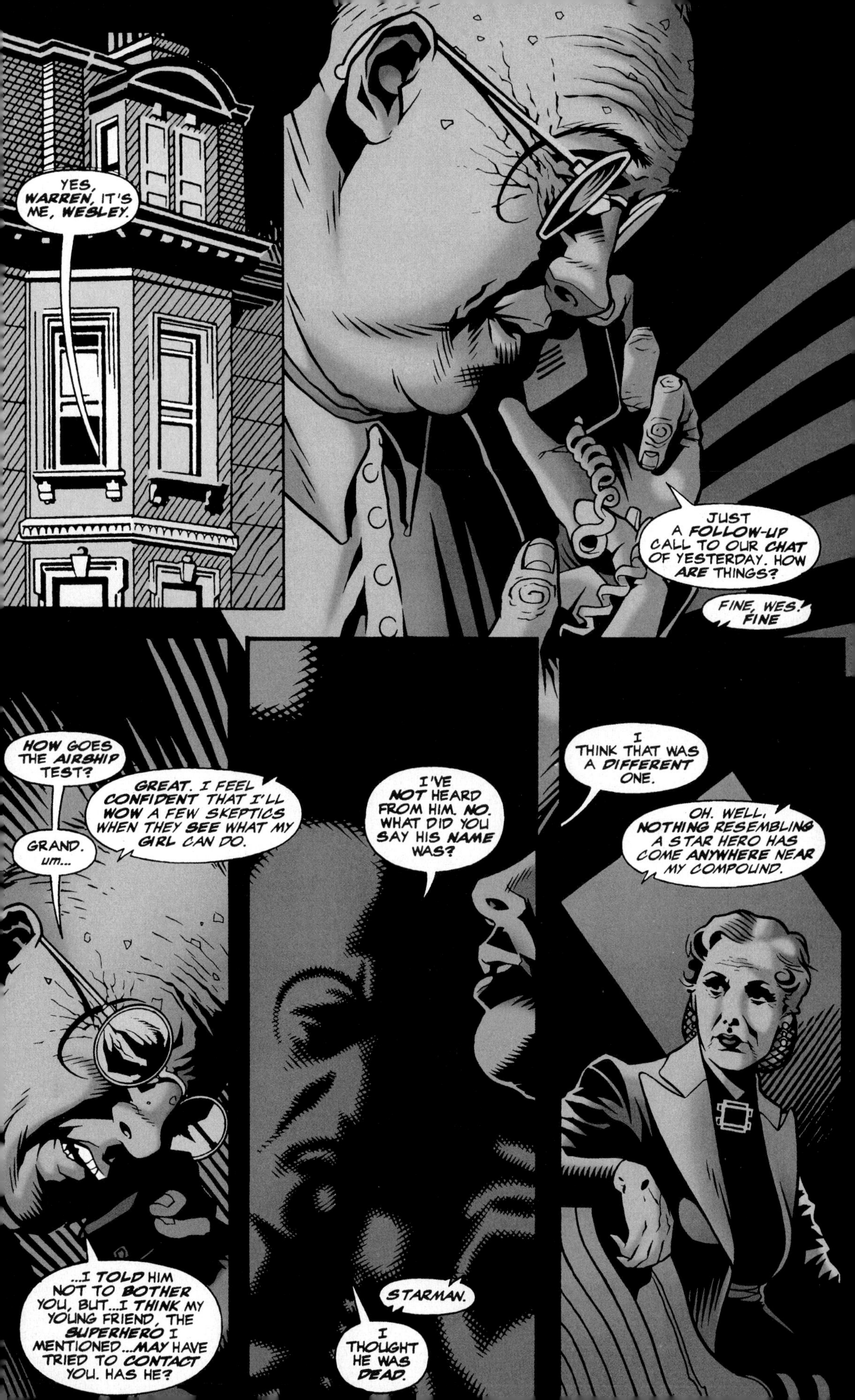
YES, WARREN, IT'S ME, WESLEY.
JUST A FOLLOW-UP CALL TO OUR CHAT OF YESTERDAY. HOW ARE THINGS?
FINE, WES. FINE
HOW GOES THE AIRSHIP TEST?
GREAT. I FEEL CONFIDENT THAT I'LL WOW A FEW SKEPTICS WHEN THEY SEE WHAT MY GIRL CAN DO.
GRAND. um...
...I TOLD HIM NOT TO BOTHER YOU, BUT...I THINK MY YOUNG FRIEND, THE SUPERHERO I MENTIONED...MAY HAVE TRIED TO CONTACT YOU. HAS HE?
I'VE NOT HEARD FROM HIM. NO. WHAT DID YOU SAY HIS NAME WAS?
STARMAN.
I THOUGHT HE WAS DEAD.
I THINK THAT WAS A DIFFERENT ONE.
OH. WELL, NOTHING RESEMBLING A STAR HERO HAS COME ANYWHERE NEAR MY COMPOUND.

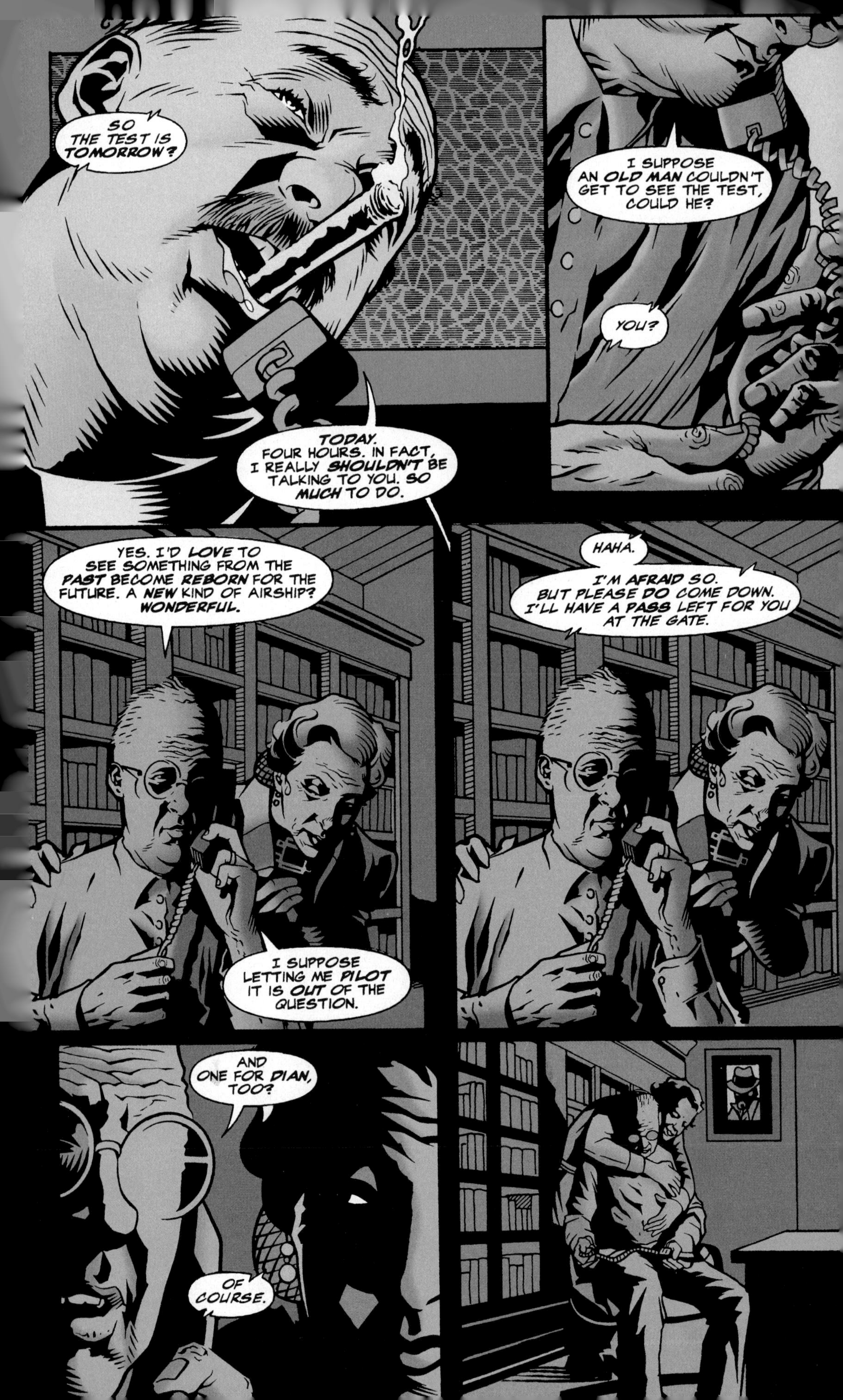
SO THE TEST IS TOMORROW?
I SUPPOSE AN OLD MAN COULDN'T GET TO SEE THE TEST, COULD HE?
YOU?
TODAY. FOUR HOURS. IN FACT, I REALLY SHOULDN'T BE TALKING TO YOU. SO MUCH TO DO.
YES. I'D LOVE TO SEE SOMETHING FROM THE PAST BECOME REBORN FOR THE FUTURE. A NEW KIND OF AIRSHIP? WONDERFUL.
I SUPPOSE LETTING ME PILOT IT IS OUT OF THE QUESTION.
HAHA.
I'M AFRAID SO. BUT PLEASE DO COME DOWN. I'LL HAVE A PASS LEFT FOR YOU AT THE GATE.
AND ONE FOR DIAN, TOO?
OF COURSE.

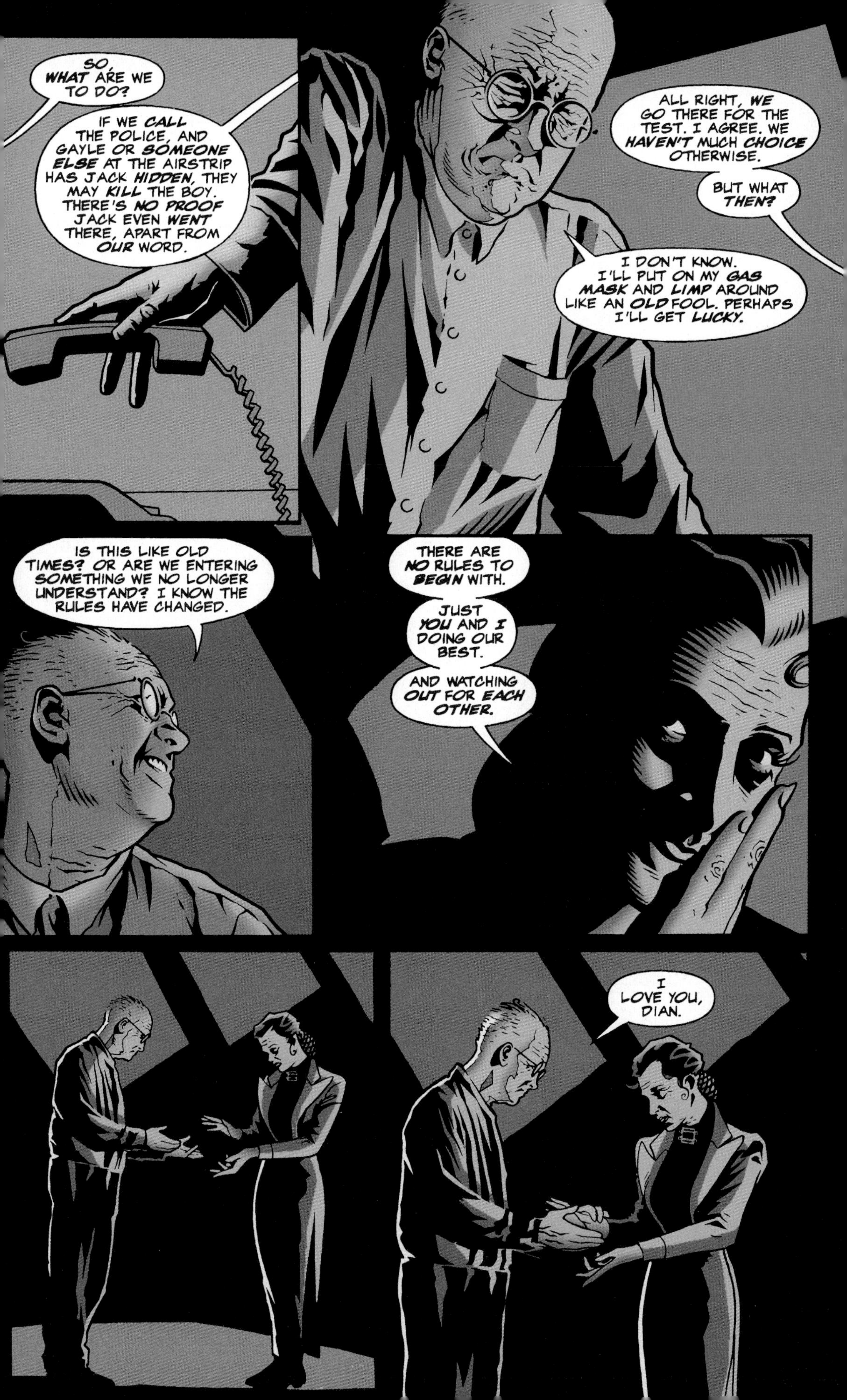
SO, WHAT ARE WE TO DO?
IF WE CALL THE POLICE, AND GAYLE OR SOMEONE ELSE AT THE AIRSTRIP HAS JACK HIDDEN, THEY MAY KILL THE BOY. THERE'S NO PROOF JACK EVEN WENT THERE, APART FROM OUR WORD.
ALL RIGHT, WE GO THERE FOR THE TEST. I AGREE. WE HAVEN'T MUCH CHOICE OTHERWISE.
BUT WHAT THEN?
I DON'T KNOW. I'LL PUT ON MY GAS MASK AND LIMP AROUND LIKE AN OLD FOOL. PERHAPS I'LL GET LUCKY.
IS THIS LIKE OLD TIMES? OR ARE WE ENTERING SOMETHING WE NO LONGER UNDERSTAND? I KNOW THE RULES HAVE CHANGED.
THERE ARE NO RULES TO BEGIN WITH.
JUST YOU AND I DOING OUR BEST.
AND WATCHING OUT FOR EACH OTHER.
I LOVE YOU, DIAN.

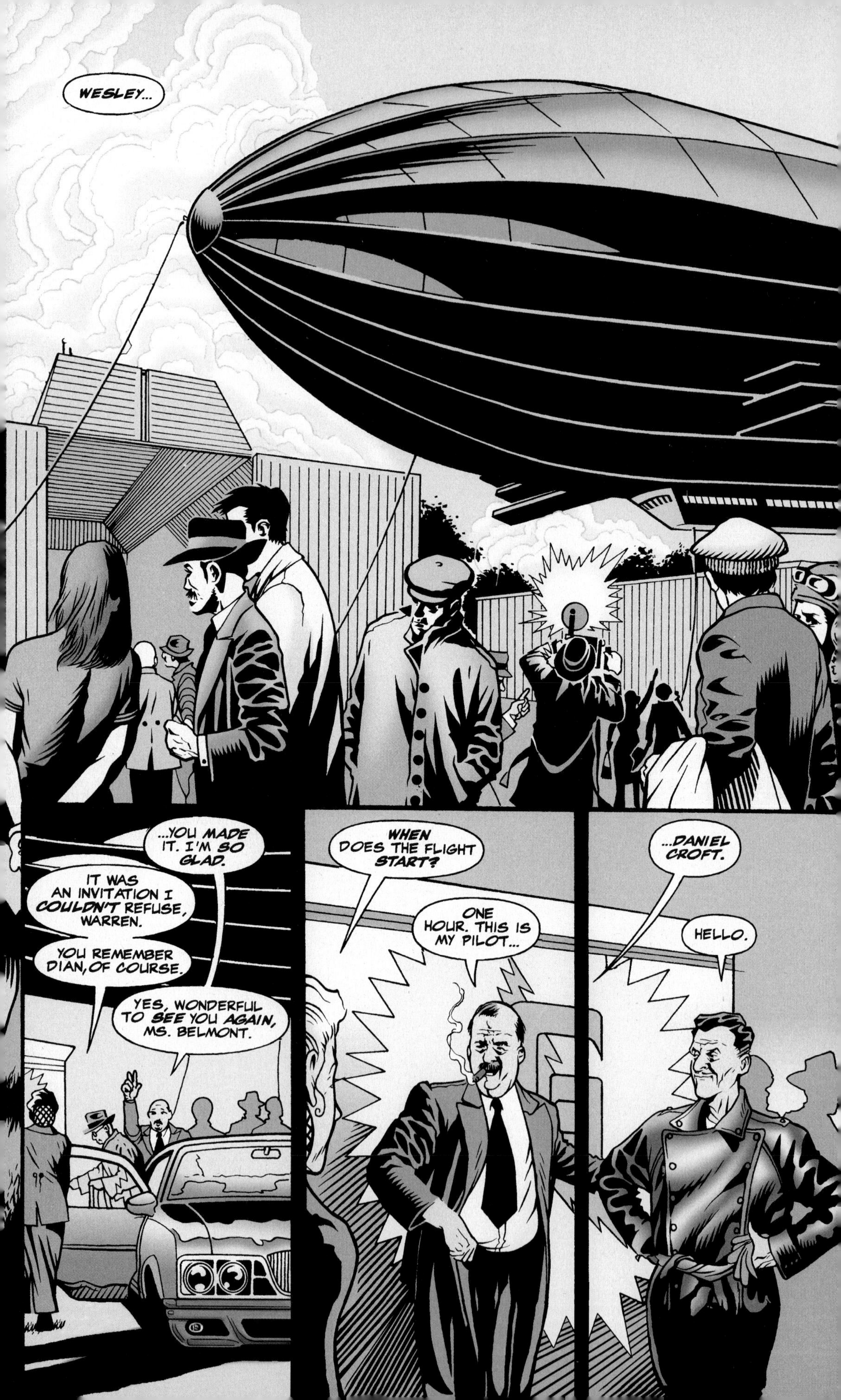
WESLEY...
...YOU MADE IT. I'M SO GLAD.
IT WAS AN INVITATION I COULDN'T REFUSE, WARREN.
YOU REMEMBER DIAN, OF COURSE.
YES, WONDERFUL TO SEE YOU AGAIN, MS. BELMONT.
WHEN DOES THE FLIGHT START?
ONE HOUR. THIS IS MY PILOT...
...DANIEL CROFT.
HELLO.

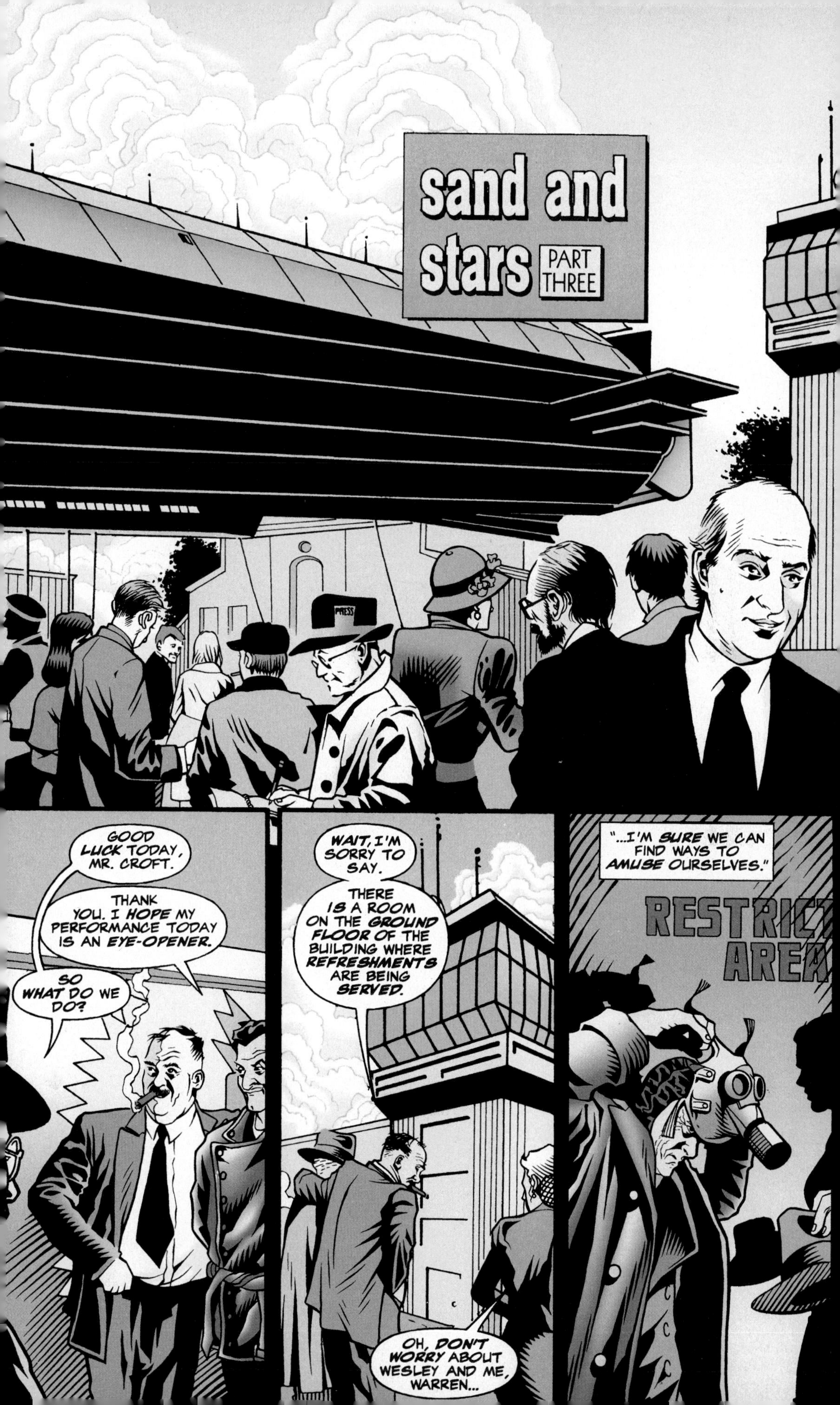

sand and stars PART THREE
PRESS
GOOD LUCK TODAY, MR. CROFT.
THANK YOU. I HOPE MY PERFORMANCE TODAY IS AN EYE-OPENER.
SO WHAT DO WE DO?
WAIT, I'M SORRY TO SAY.
THERE IS A ROOM ON THE GROUND FLOOR OF THE BUILDING WHERE REFRESHMENTS ARE BEING SERVED.
OH, DON'T WORRY ABOUT WESLEY AND ME, WARREN...
"...I'M SURE WE CAN FIND WAYS TO AMUSE OURSELVES."

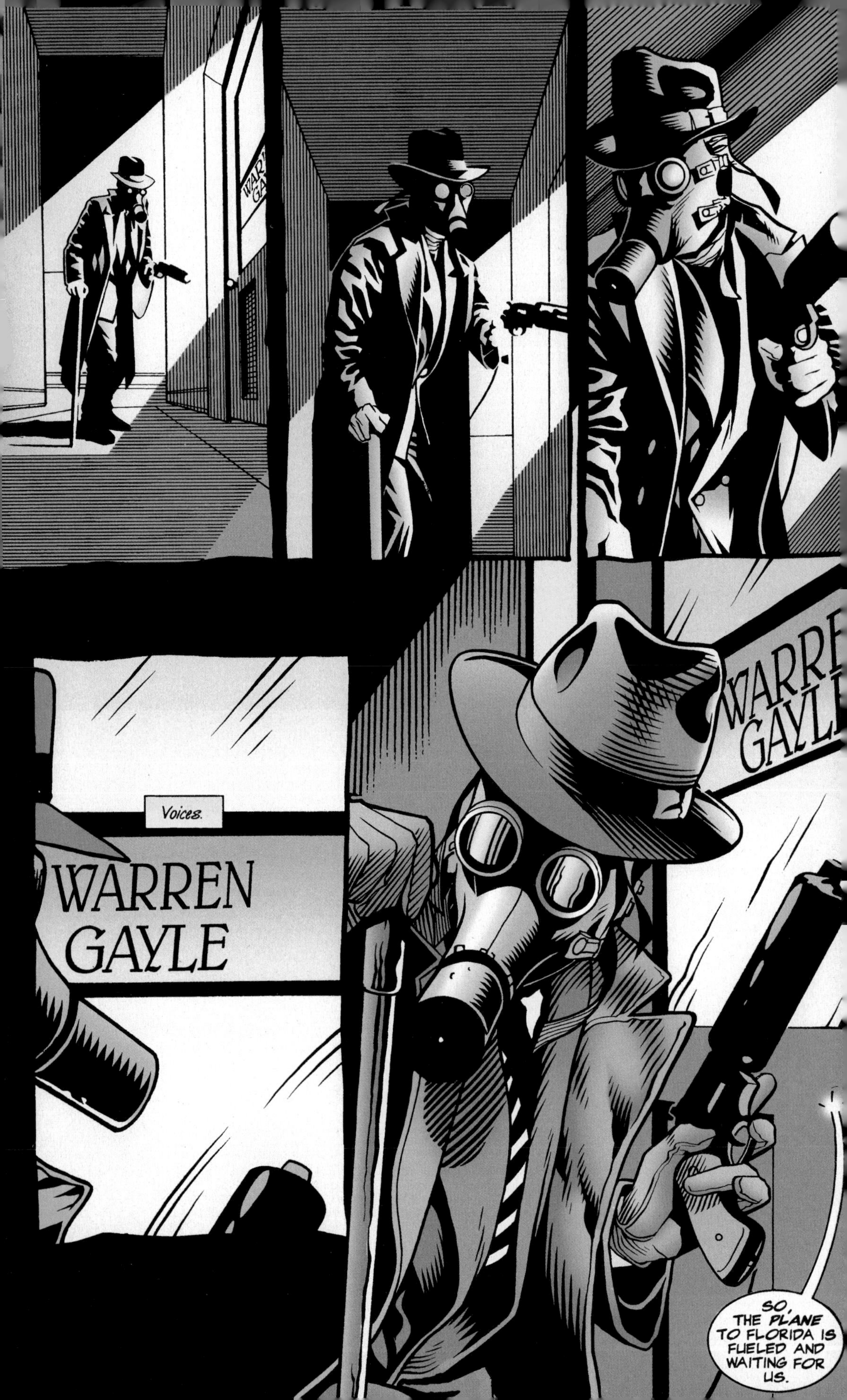

WARREN GAYLE
Voices.
WARREN GAYLE
WARREN GAYLE
SO, THE PLANE TO FLORIDA IS FUELED AND WAITING FOR US.

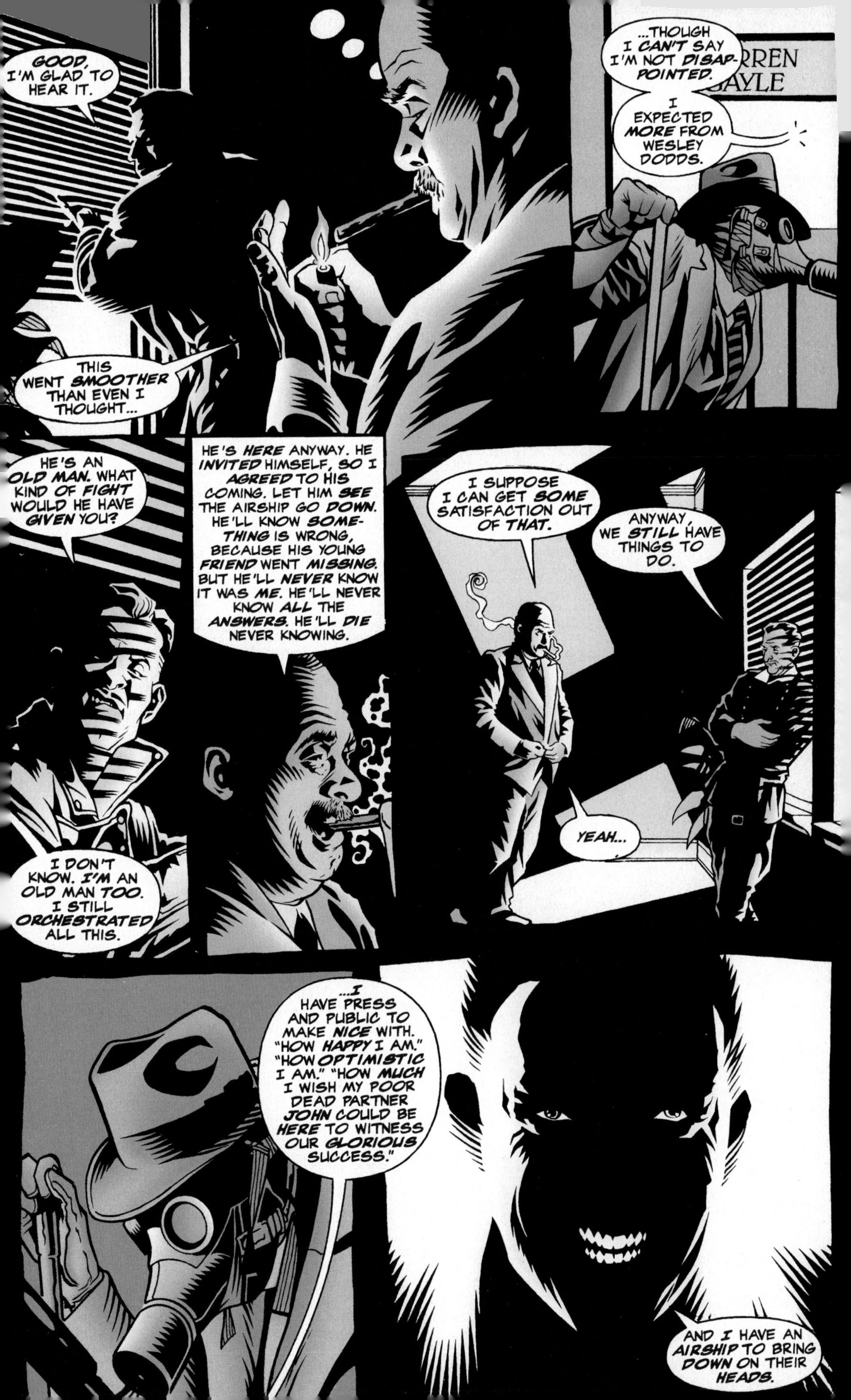
GOOD, I'M GLAD TO HEAR IT.
THIS WENT SMOOTHER THAN EVEN I THOUGHT...
...THOUGH I CAN'T SAY I'M NOT DISAPPOINTED.
I EXPECTED MORE FROM WESLEY DODDS.
RREN AYLE
HE'S AN OLD MAN. WHAT KIND OF FIGHT WOULD HE HAVE GIVEN YOU?
I DON'T KNOW. I'M AN OLD MAN TOO. I STILL ORCHESTRATED ALL THIS.
HE'S HERE ANYWAY. HE INVITED HIMSELF, SO I AGREED TO HIS COMING. LET HIM SEE THE AIRSHIP GO DOWN. HE'LL KNOW SOMETHING IS WRONG, BECAUSE HIS YOUNG FRIEND WENT MISSING. BUT HE'LL NEVER KNOW IT WAS ME. HE'LL NEVER KNOW ALL THE ANSWERS. HE'LL DIE NEVER KNOWING.
I SUPPOSE I CAN GET SOME SATISFACTION OUT OF THAT.
ANYWAY, WE STILL HAVE THINGS TO DO.
YEAH...
...I HAVE PRESS AND PUBLIC TO MAKE NICE WITH. "HOW HAPPY I AM." "HOW OPTIMISTIC I AM." "HOW MUCH I WISH MY POOR DEAD PARTNER JOHN COULD BE HERE TO WITNESS OUR GLORIOUS SUCCESS."
AND I HAVE AN AIRSHIP TO BRING DOWN ON THEIR HEADS.

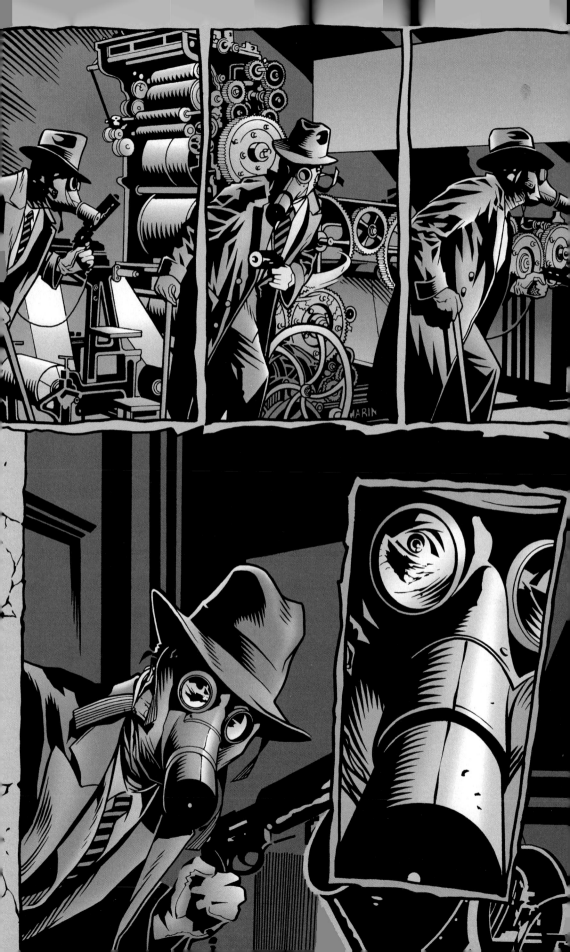

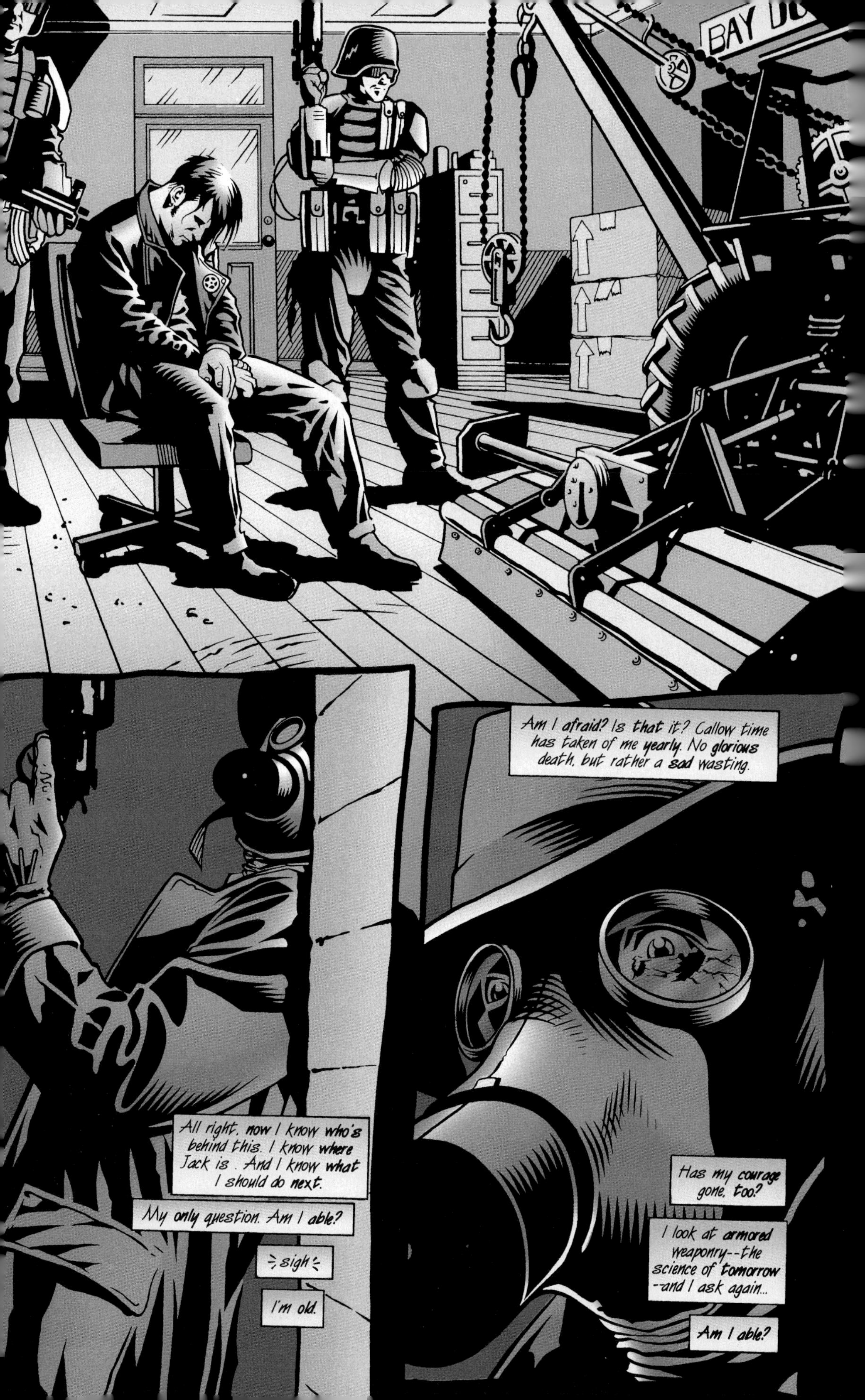
All right, now I know who's behind this. I know where Jack is . And I know what I should do next.
My only question. Am I able?
sigh
I'm old.
Am I afraid? Is that it? Callow time has taken of me yearly. No glorious death, but rather a sad wasting.
Has my courage gone, too?
I look at armored weaponry--the science of tomorrow --and I ask again...
Am I able?

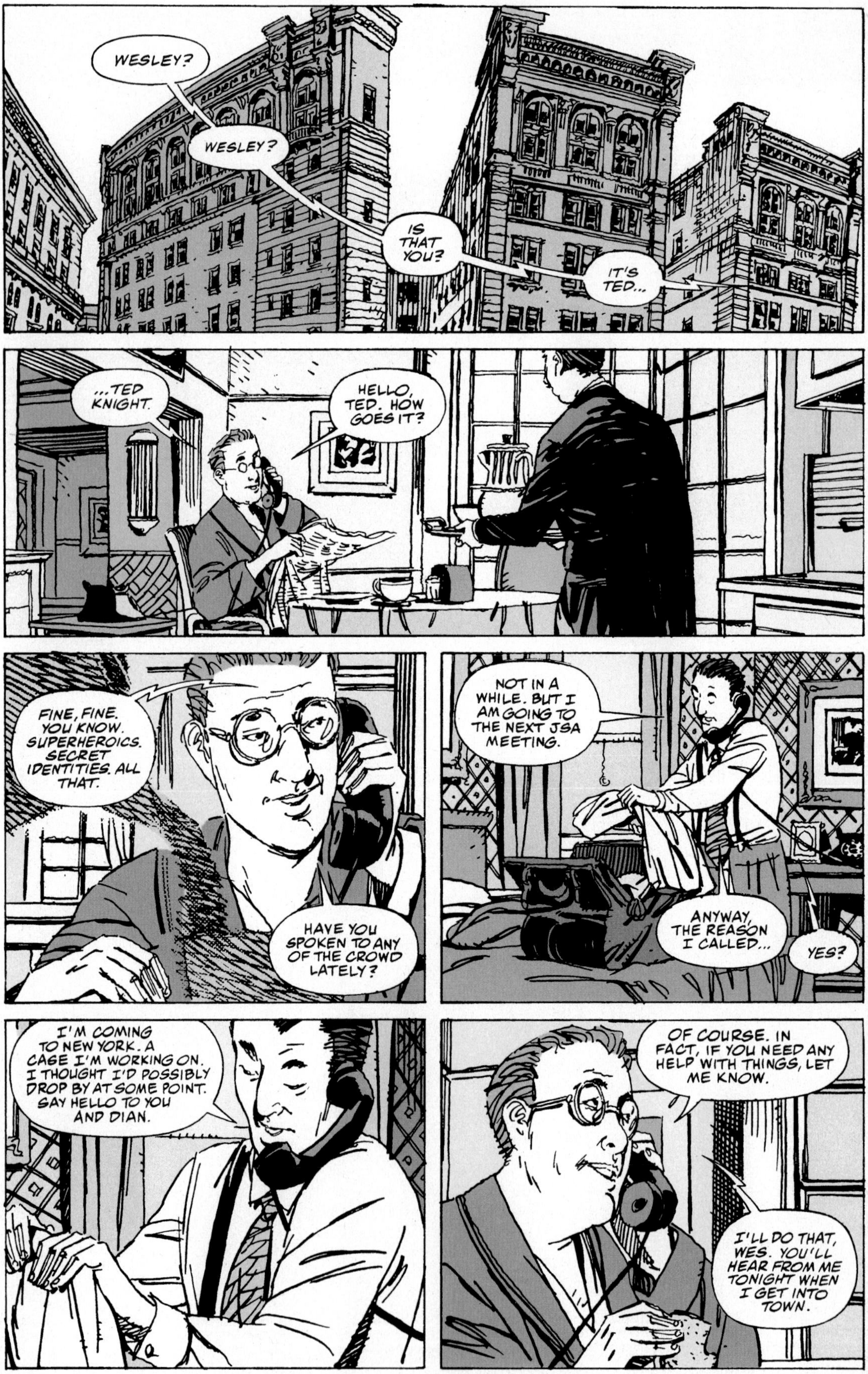
WESLEY?
WESLEY?
IS THAT YOU?
IT'S TED...
...TED KNIGHT.
HELLO, TED. HOW GOES IT?
FINE, FINE. YOU KNOW. SUPERHEROICS. SECRET IDENTITIES. ALL THAT.
HAVE YOU SPOKEN TO ANY OF THE CROWD LATELY?
NOT IN A WHILE. BUT I AM GOING TO THE NEXT JSA MEETING.
ANYWAY, THE REASON I CALLED...
YES?
I'M COMING TO NEW YORK. A CASE I'M WORKING ON. I THOUGHT I'D POSSIBLY DROP BY AT SOME POINT. SAY HELLO TO YOU AND DIAN.
OF COURSE. IN FACT, IF YOU NEED ANY HELP WITH THINGS, LET ME KNOW.
I'LL DO THAT, WES. YOU'LL HEAR FROM ME TONIGHT WHEN I GET INTO TOWN.

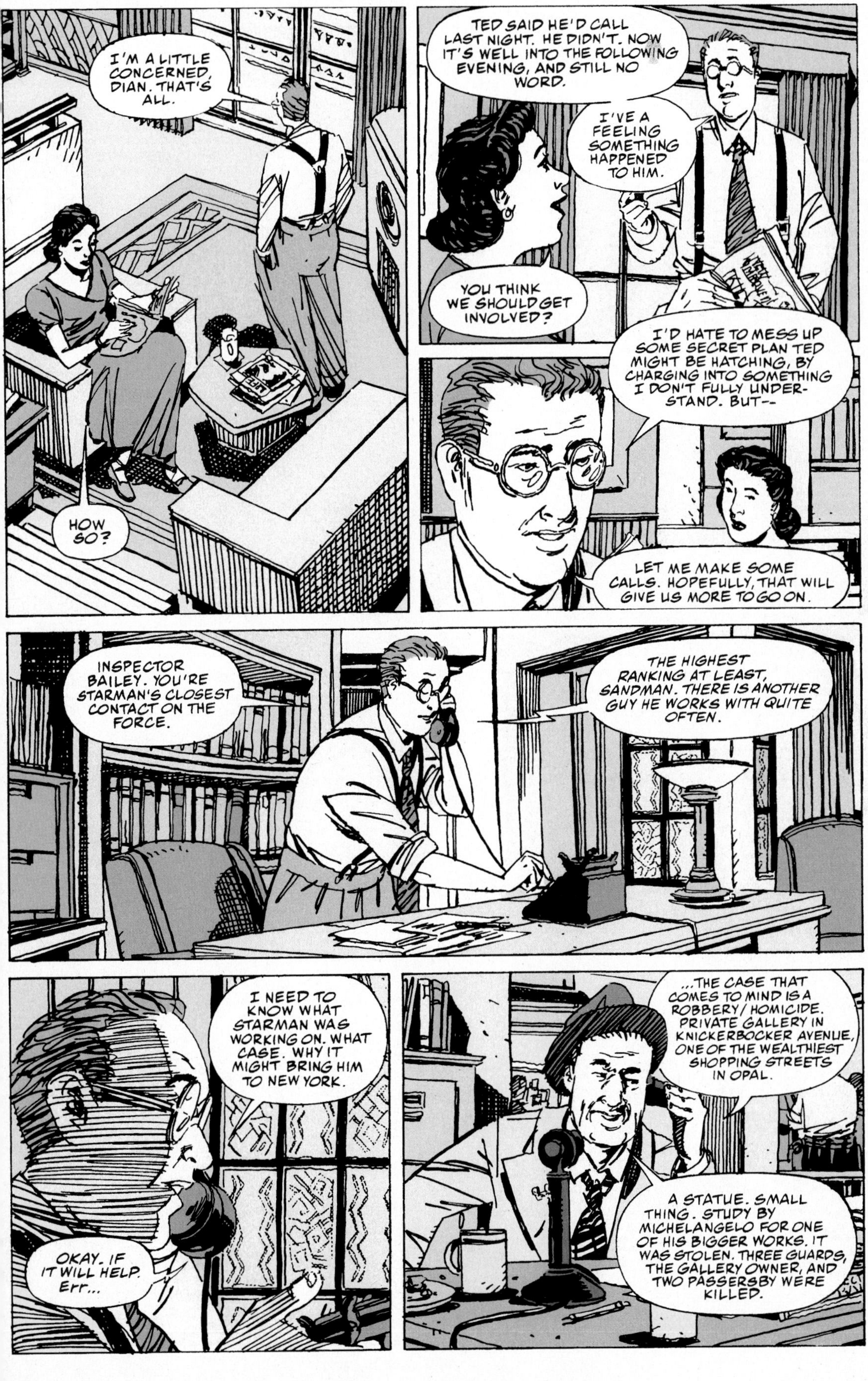
I'M A LITTLE CONCERNED, DIAN. THAT'S ALL.
HOW SO?
TED SAID HE'D CALL LAST NIGHT. HE DIDN'T. NOW IT'S WELL INTO THE FOLLOWING EVENING, AND STILL NO WORD.
I'VE A FEELING SOMETHING HAPPENED TO HIM.
YOU THINK WE SHOULD GET INVOLVED?
I'D HATE TO MESS UP SOME SECRET PLAN TED MIGHT BE HATCHING, BY CHARGING INTO SOMETHING I DON'T FULLY UNDER-STAND. BUT--
LET ME MAKE SOME CALLS. HOPEFULLY, THAT WILL GIVE US MORE TO GO ON.
INSPECTOR BAILEY. YOU'RE STARMAN'S CLOSEST CONTACT ON THE FORCE.
THE HIGHEST RANKING AT LEAST, SANDMAN. THERE IS ANOTHER GUY HE WORKS WITH QUITE OFTEN.
I NEED TO KNOW WHAT STARMAN WAS WORKING ON. WHAT CASE. WHY IT MIGHT BRING HIM TO NEW YORK.
OKAY. IF IT WILL HELP. Err...
...THE CASE THAT COMES TO MIND IS A ROBBERY/ HOMICIDE. PRIVATE GALLERY IN KNICKERBOCKER AVENUE, ONE OF THE WEALTHIEST SHOPPING STREETS IN OPAL.
A STATUE. SMALL THING. STUDY BY MICHELANGELO FOR ONE OF HIS BIGGER WORKS. IT WAS STOLEN. THREE GUARDS, THE GALLERY OWNER, AND TWO PASSERSBY WERE KILLED.

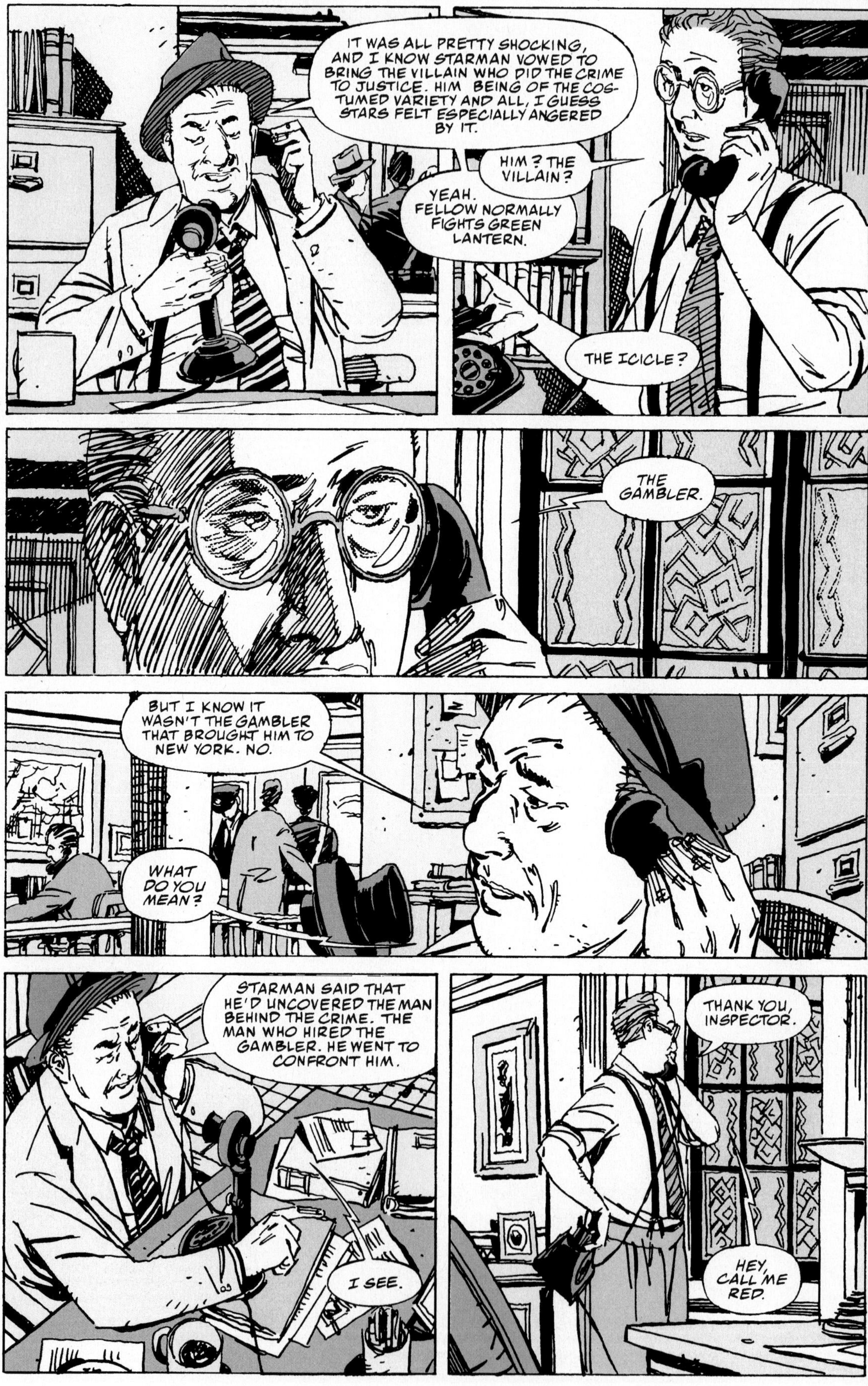
IT WAS ALL PRETTY SHOCKING, AND I KNOW STARMAN VOWED TO BRING THE VILLAIN WHO DID THE CRIME TO JUSTICE. HIM BEING OF THE COSTUMED VARIETY AND ALL, I GUESS STARS FELT ESPECIALLY ANGERED BY IT.
HIM? THE VILLAIN?
YEAH. FELLOW NORMALLY FIGHTS GREEN LANTERN.
THE ICICLE?
THE GAMBLER.
BUT I KNOW IT WASN'T THE GAMBLER THAT BROUGHT HIM TO NEW YORK. NO.
WHAT DO YOU MEAN?
STARMAN SAID THAT HE'D UNCOVERED THE MAN BEHIND THE CRIME. THE MAN WHO HIRED THE GAMBLER. HE WENT TO CONFRONT HIM.
I SEE.
THANK YOU, INSPECTOR.
HEY, CALL ME RED.

WHAT?

WHAT?

TELL ME!

EVERYTHING YOU KNOW!

SO I SUPPOSE YOU HEARD ABOUT THE STATUE THAT WAS STOLEN. THE ONE IN OPAL CITY.

THAT'S JUST WHAT I WANTED TO TALK TO YOU ABOUT, CLARICE. YOU KNOW EVERYONE AND EVERYTHING THAT'S HAPPENING IN TOWN.

I'M SORRY, MADAM. THAT'S ALL I CAN SAY... I MEAN THAT'S ALL I KNOW.

MR. KNIGHT CHECKED IN, MADE ONE PHONE CALL, AND THAT WAS THE LAST MY STAFF AND I SAW OF HIM.

AND, um, YOUR HOTEL OPERATOR WOULDN'T HAVE MADE A NOTE OF THAT TELEPHONE NUMBER, BY ANY CHANCE?

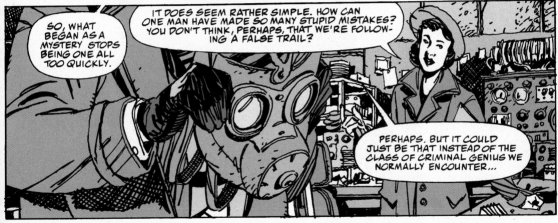

SO, WHAT BEGAN AS A MYSTERY STOPS BEING ONE ALL TOO QUICKLY.

IT DOES SEEM RATHER SIMPLE. HOW CAN ONE MAN HAVE MADE SO MANY STUPID MISTAKES? YOU DON'T THINK, PERHAPS, THAT WE'RE FOLLOWING A FALSE TRAIL?

PERHAPS. BUT IT COULD JUST BE THAT INSTEAD OF THE CLASS OF CRIMINAL GENIUS WE NORMALLY ENCOUNTER...

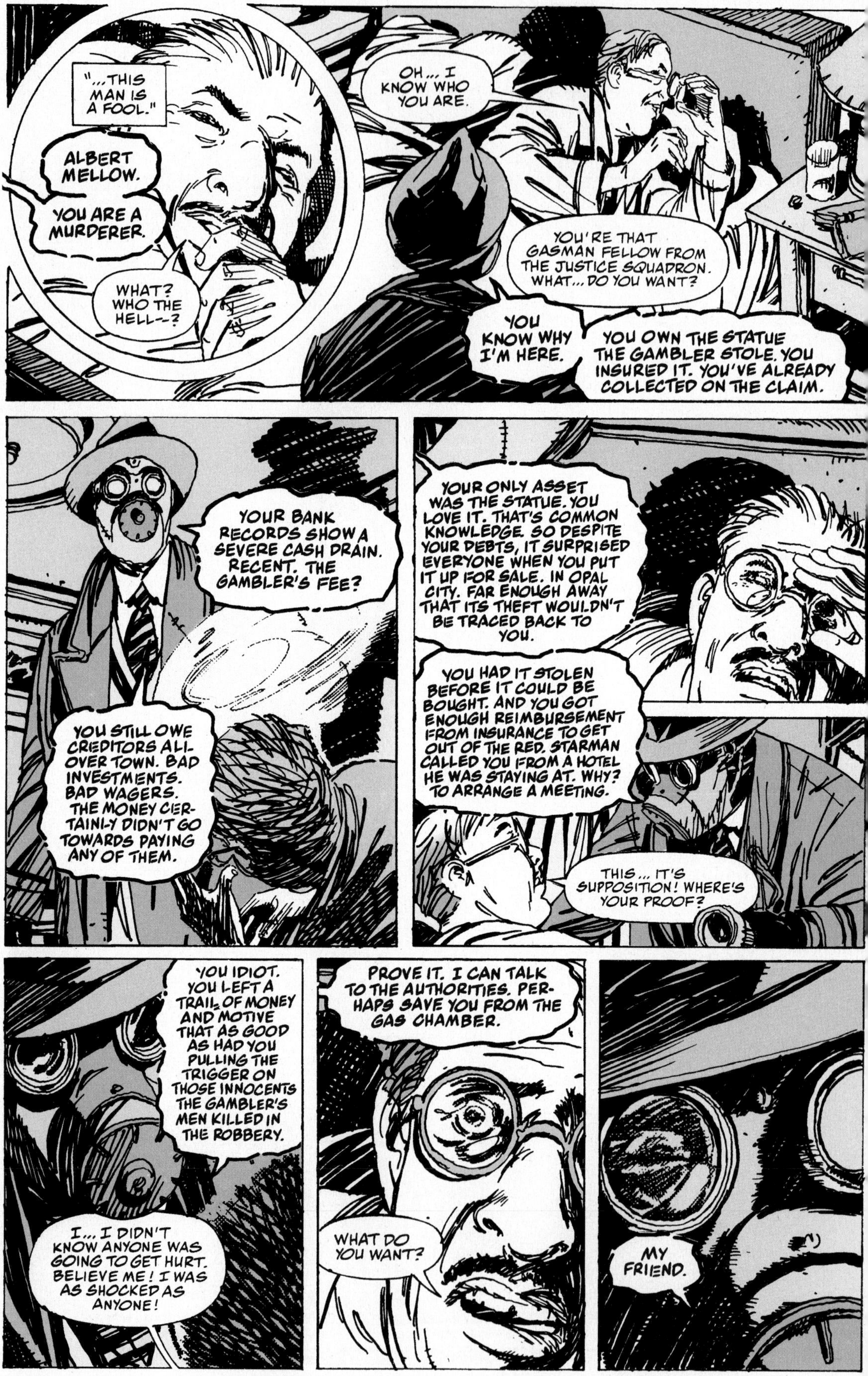
"...THIS MAN IS A FOOL."
ALBERT MELLOW.
YOU ARE A MURDERER.
WHAT? WHO THE HELL--?
OH... I KNOW WHO YOU ARE.
YOU'RE THAT GASMAN FELLOW FROM THE JUSTICE SQUADRON. WHAT... DO YOU WANT?
YOU KNOW WHY I'M HERE.
YOU OWN THE STATUE THE GAMBLER STOLE. YOU INSURED IT. YOU'VE ALREADY COLLECTED ON THE CLAIM.
YOUR BANK RECORDS SHOW A SEVERE CASH DRAIN. RECENT. THE GAMBLER'S FEE?
YOU STILL OWE CREDITORS ALL OVER TOWN. BAD INVESTMENTS. BAD WAGERS. THE MONEY CERTAINLY DIDN'T GO TOWARDS PAYING ANY OF THEM.
YOUR ONLY ASSET WAS THE STATUE. YOU LOVE IT. THAT'S COMMON KNOWLEDGE. SO DESPITE YOUR DEBTS, IT SURPRISED EVERYONE WHEN YOU PUT IT UP FOR SALE. IN OPAL CITY. FAR ENOUGH AWAY THAT ITS THEFT WOULDN'T BE TRACED BACK TO YOU.
YOU HAD IT STOLEN BEFORE IT COULD BE BOUGHT. AND YOU GOT ENOUGH REIMBURSEMENT FROM INSURANCE TO GET OUT OF THE RED. STARMAN CALLED YOU FROM A HOTEL HE WAS STAYING AT. WHY? TO ARRANGE A MEETING.
THIS... IT'S SUPPOSITION! WHERE'S YOUR PROOF?
YOU IDIOT. YOU LEFT A TRAIL OF MONEY AND MOTIVE THAT AS GOOD AS HAD YOU PULLING THE TRIGGER ON THOSE INNOCENTS THE GAMBLER'S MEN KILLED IN THE ROBBERY.
I... I DIDN'T KNOW ANYONE WAS GOING TO GET HURT. BELIEVE ME! I WAS AS SHOCKED AS ANYONE!
PROVE IT. I CAN TALK TO THE AUTHORITIES. PERHAPS SAVE YOU FROM THE GAS CHAMBER.
WHAT DO YOU WANT?
MY FRIEND.

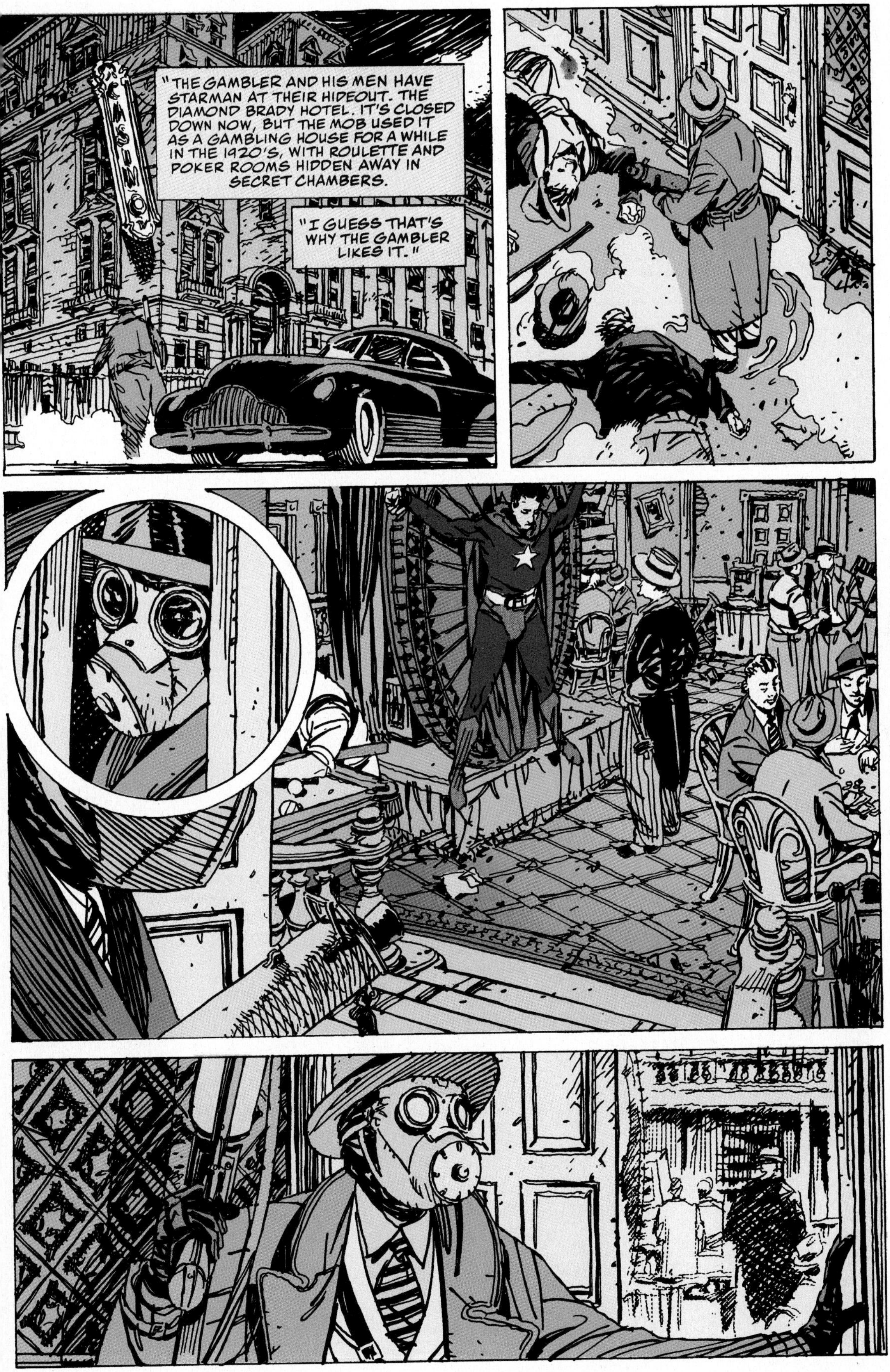
"THE GAMBLER AND HIS MEN HAVE STARMAN AT THEIR HIDEOUT. THE DIAMOND BRADY HOTEL. IT'S CLOSED DOWN NOW, BUT THE MOB USED IT AS A GAMBLING HOUSE FOR A WHILE IN THE 1920'S, WITH ROULETTE AND POKER ROOMS HIDDEN AWAY IN SECRET CHAMBERS.
"I GUESS THAT'S WHY THE GAMBLER LIKES IT."

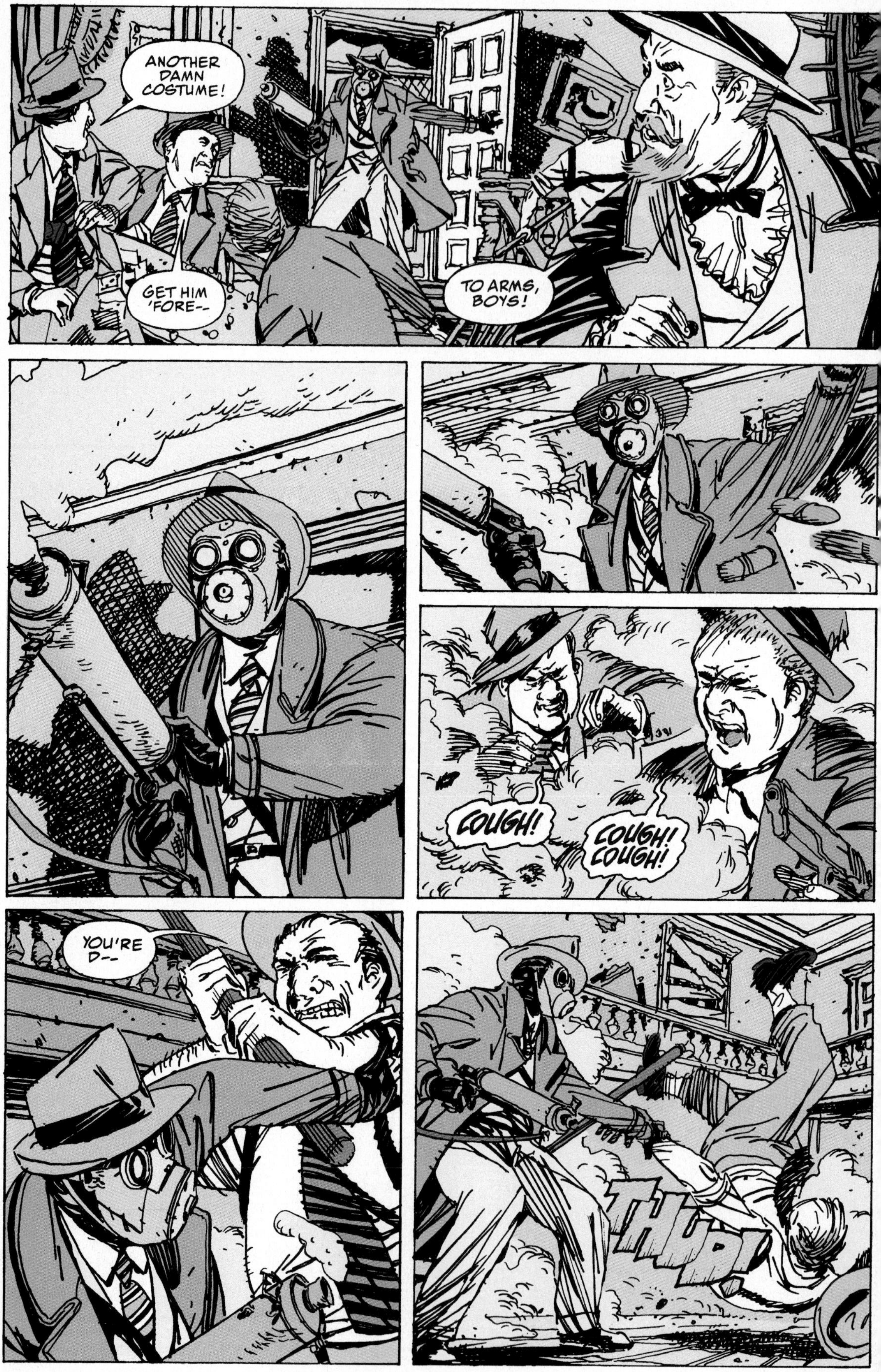
ANOTHER DAMN COSTUME!
GET HIM 'FORE--
TO ARMS, BOYS!
COUGH!
COUGH! COUGH!
YOU'RE D--
THUD!

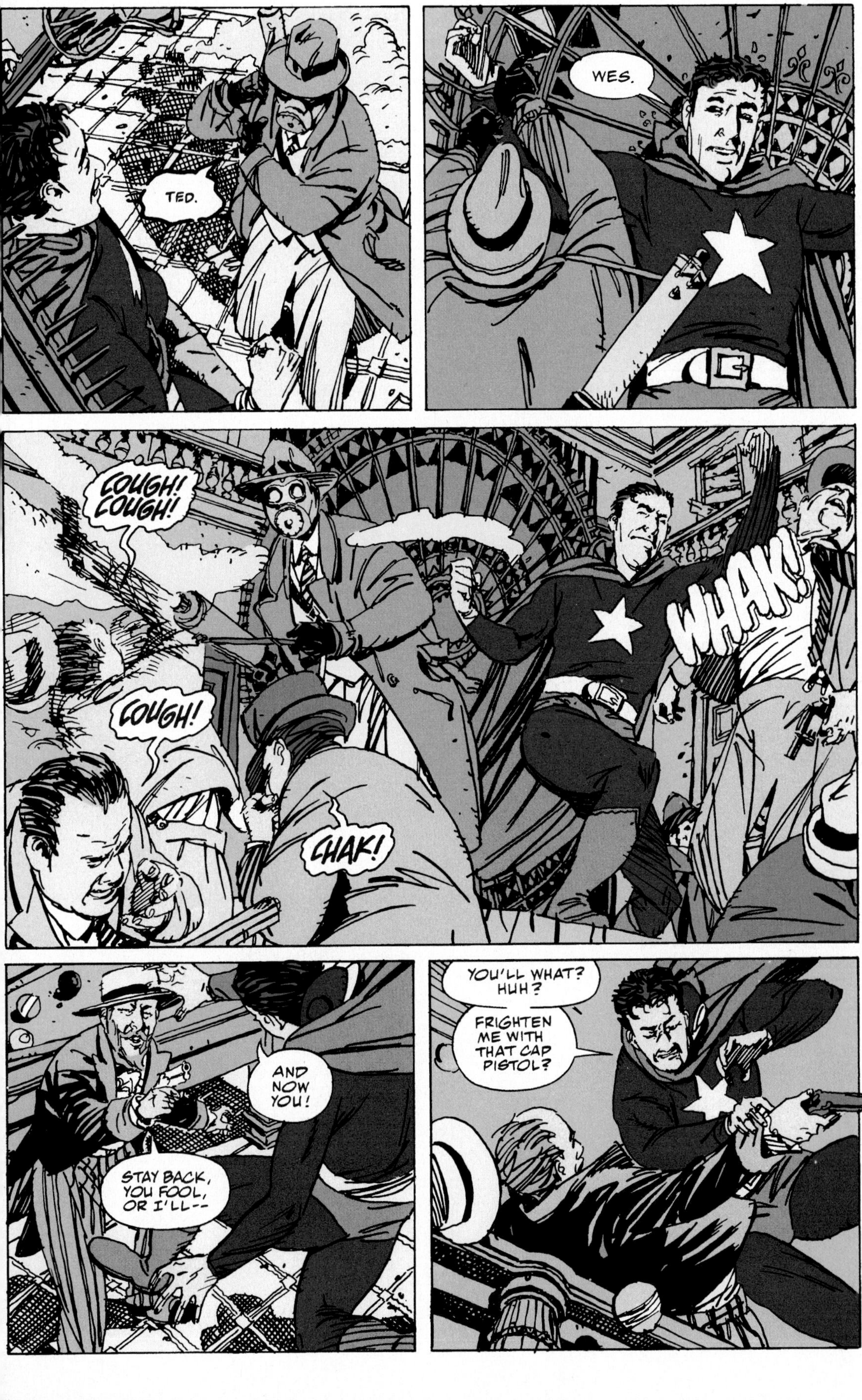
TED.
WES.
COUGH! COUGH!
COUGH!
WHAK!
CHAK!
STAY BACK, YOU FOOL, OR I'LL--
AND NOW YOU!
YOU'LL WHAT? HUH?
FRIGHTEN ME WITH THAT CAP PISTOL?

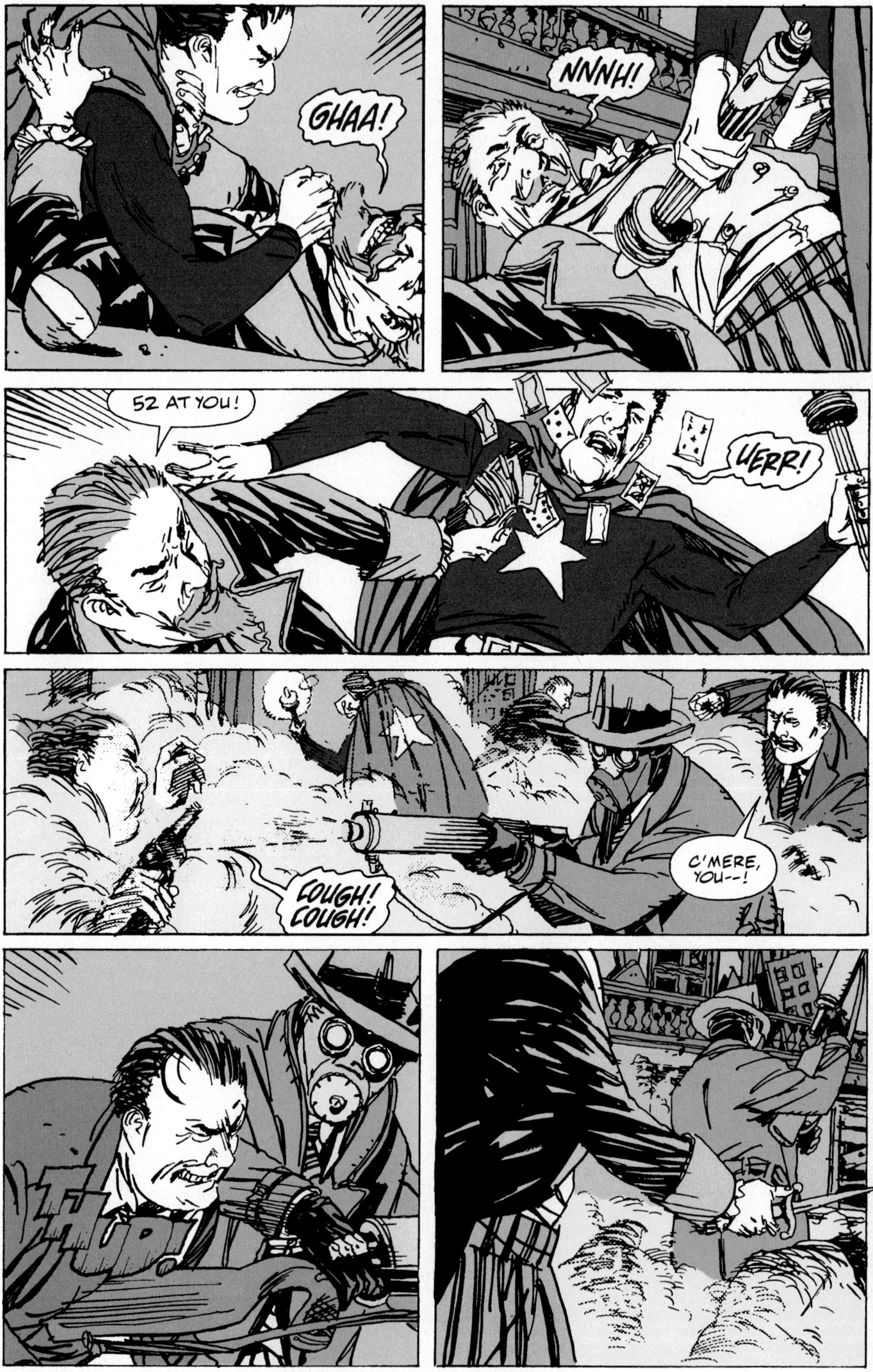
GHAA!
NNNH!
52 AT YOU!
UERR!
COUGH! COUGH!
C'MERE, YOU--!
THUD!

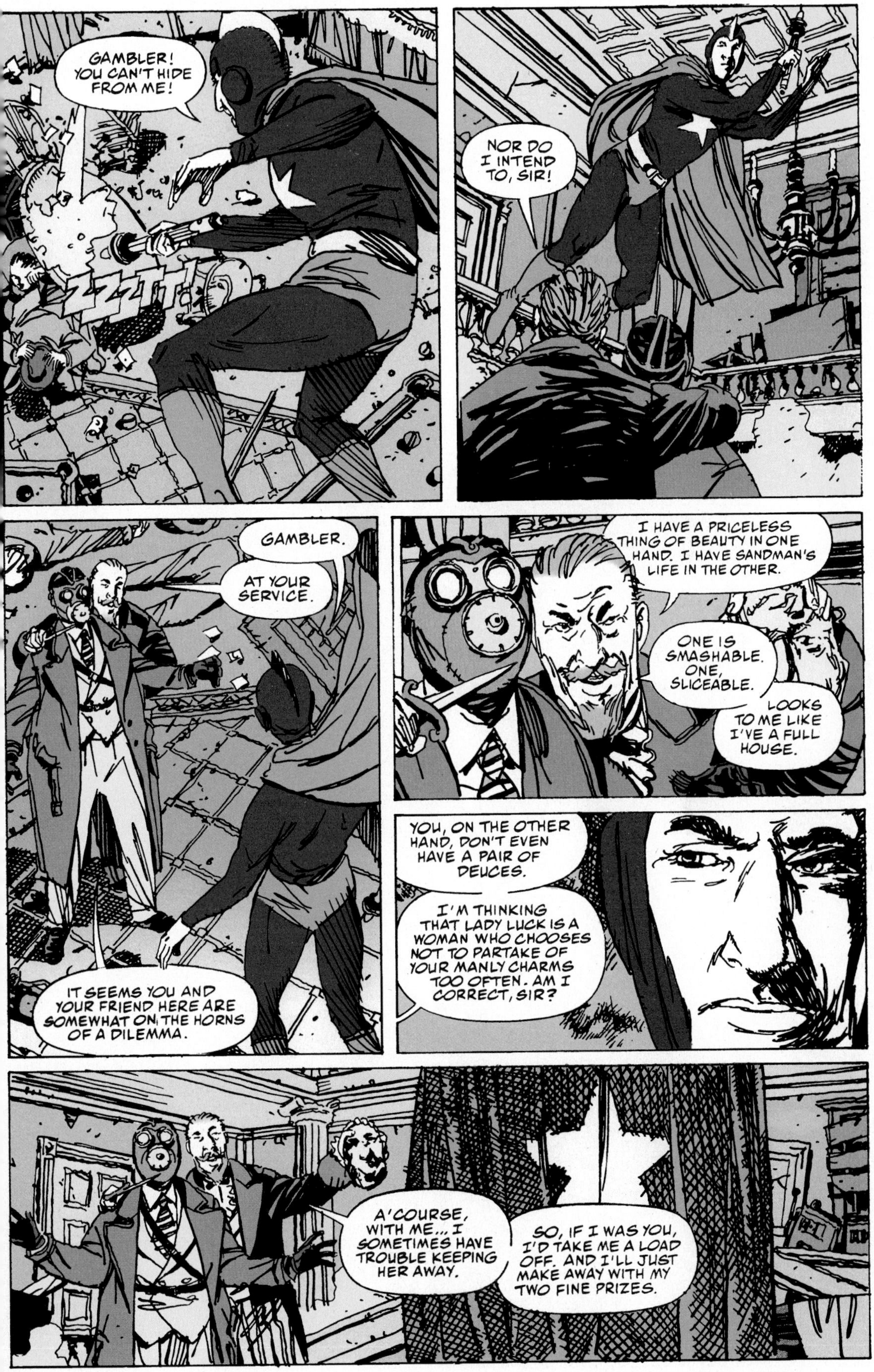
GAMBLER! YOU CAN'T HIDE FROM ME!
ZZZTT!
NOR DO I INTEND TO, SIR!
GAMBLER.
AT YOUR SERVICE.
IT SEEMS YOU AND YOUR FRIEND HERE ARE SOMEWHAT ON THE HORNS OF A DILEMMA.
I HAVE A PRICELESS THING OF BEAUTY IN ONE HAND. I HAVE SANDMAN'S LIFE IN THE OTHER.
ONE IS SMASHABLE. ONE, SLICEABLE.
LOOKS TO ME LIKE I'VE A FULL HOUSE.
YOU, ON THE OTHER HAND, DON'T EVEN HAVE A PAIR OF DEUCES.
I'M THINKING THAT LADY LUCK IS A WOMAN WHO CHOOSES NOT TO PARTAKE OF YOUR MANLY CHARMS TOO OFTEN. AM I CORRECT, SIR?
A'COURSE, WITH ME... I SOMETIMES HAVE TROUBLE KEEPING HER AWAY.
SO, IF I WAS YOU, I'D TAKE ME A LOAD OFF. AND I'LL JUST MAKE AWAY WITH MY TWO FINE PRIZES.

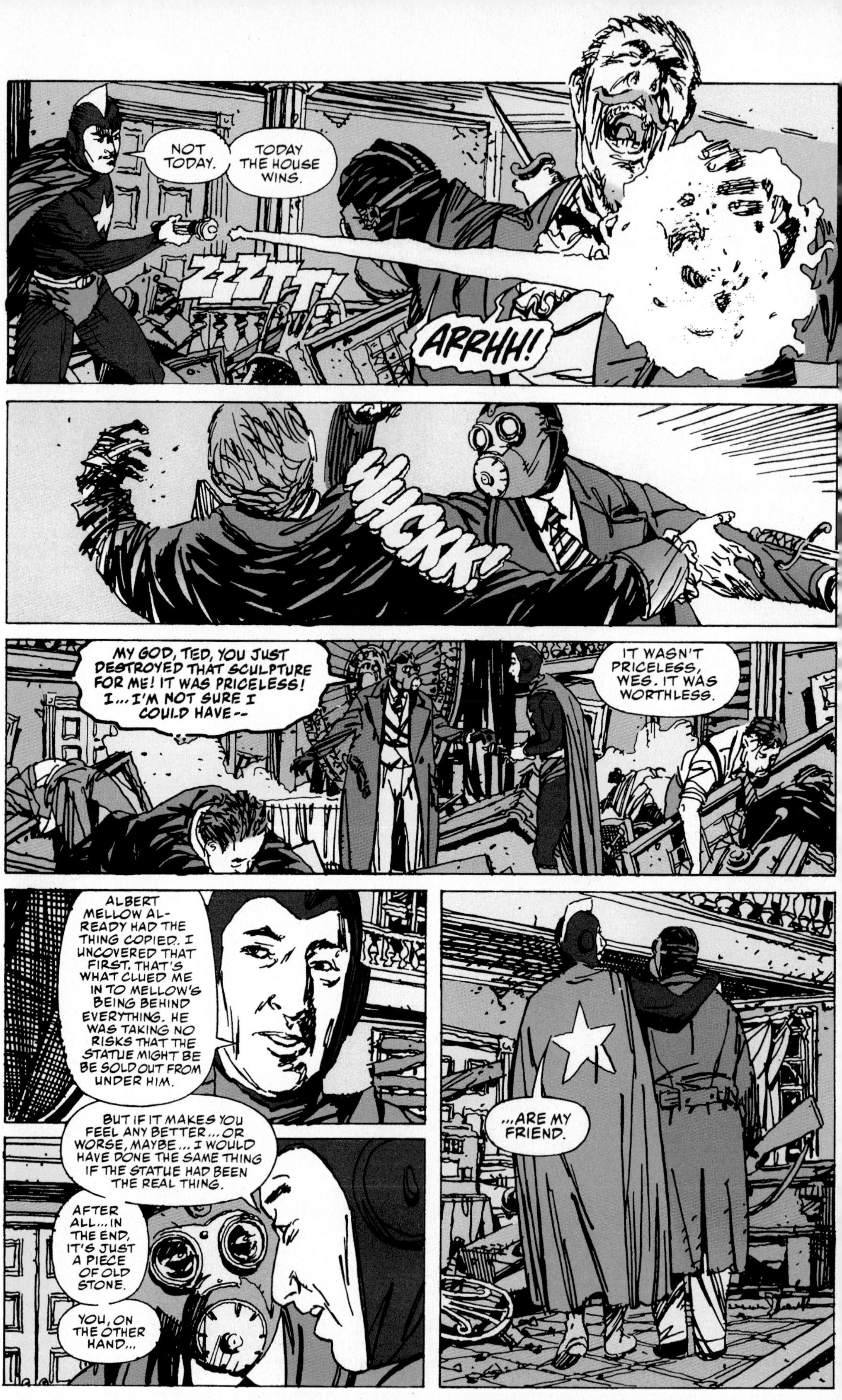
NOT TODAY.
TODAY THE HOUSE WINS.
ZZZTT!
ARRHH!
WHCKK!
MY GOD, TED, YOU JUST DESTROYED THAT SCULPTURE FOR ME! IT WAS PRICELESS! I... I'M NOT SURE I COULD HAVE--
IT WASN'T PRICELESS, WES. IT WAS WORTHLESS.
ALBERT MELLOW ALREADY HAD THE THING COPIED. I UNCOVERED THAT FIRST. THAT'S WHAT CLUED ME IN TO MELLOW'S BEING BEHIND EVERYTHING. HE WAS TAKING NO RISKS THAT THE STATUE MIGHT BE BE SOLD OUT FROM UNDER HIM.
BUT IF IT MAKES YOU FEEL ANY BETTER... OR WORSE, MAYBE... I WOULD HAVE DONE THE SAME THING IF THE STATUE HAD BEEN THE REAL THING.
AFTER ALL... IN THE END, IT'S JUST A PIECE OF OLD STONE.
YOU, ON THE OTHER HAND...
...ARE MY FRIEND.

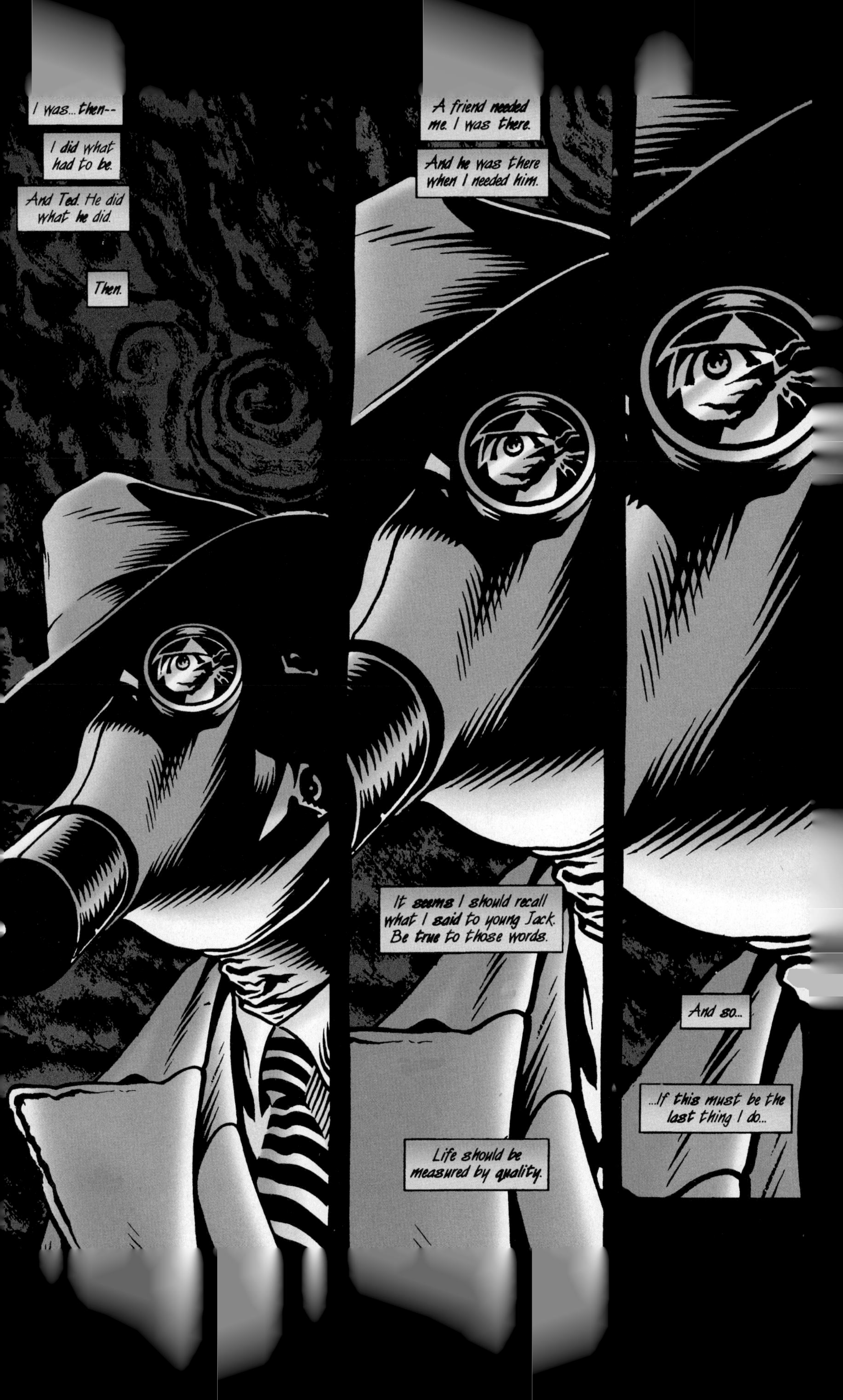
I was... then--
I did what had to be.
And Ted. He did what he did.
Then.
A friend needed me. I was there.
And he was there when I needed him.
It seems I should recall what I said to young Jack. Be true to those words.
Life should be measured by quality.
And so...
...If this must be the last thing I do...

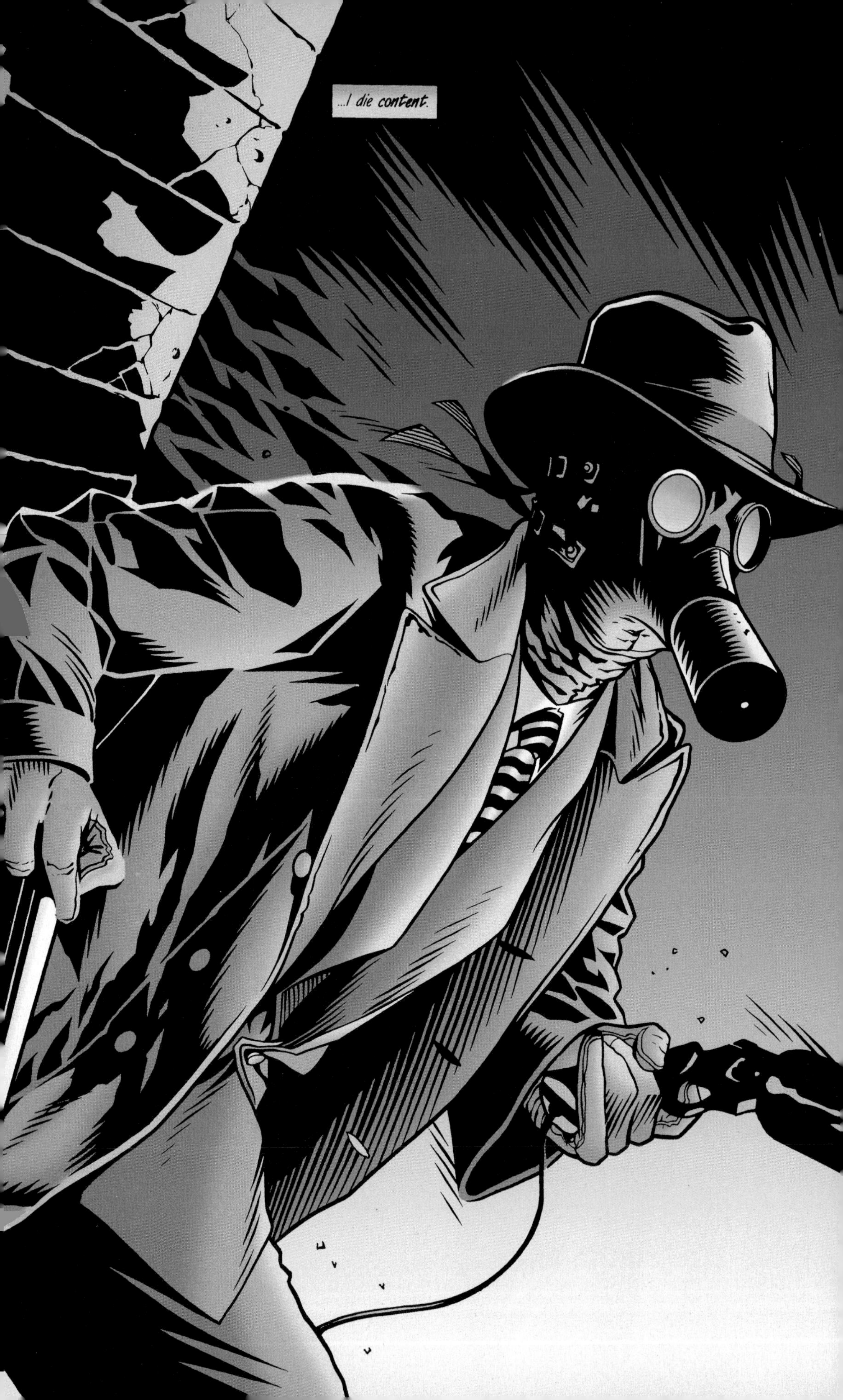
...I die content.

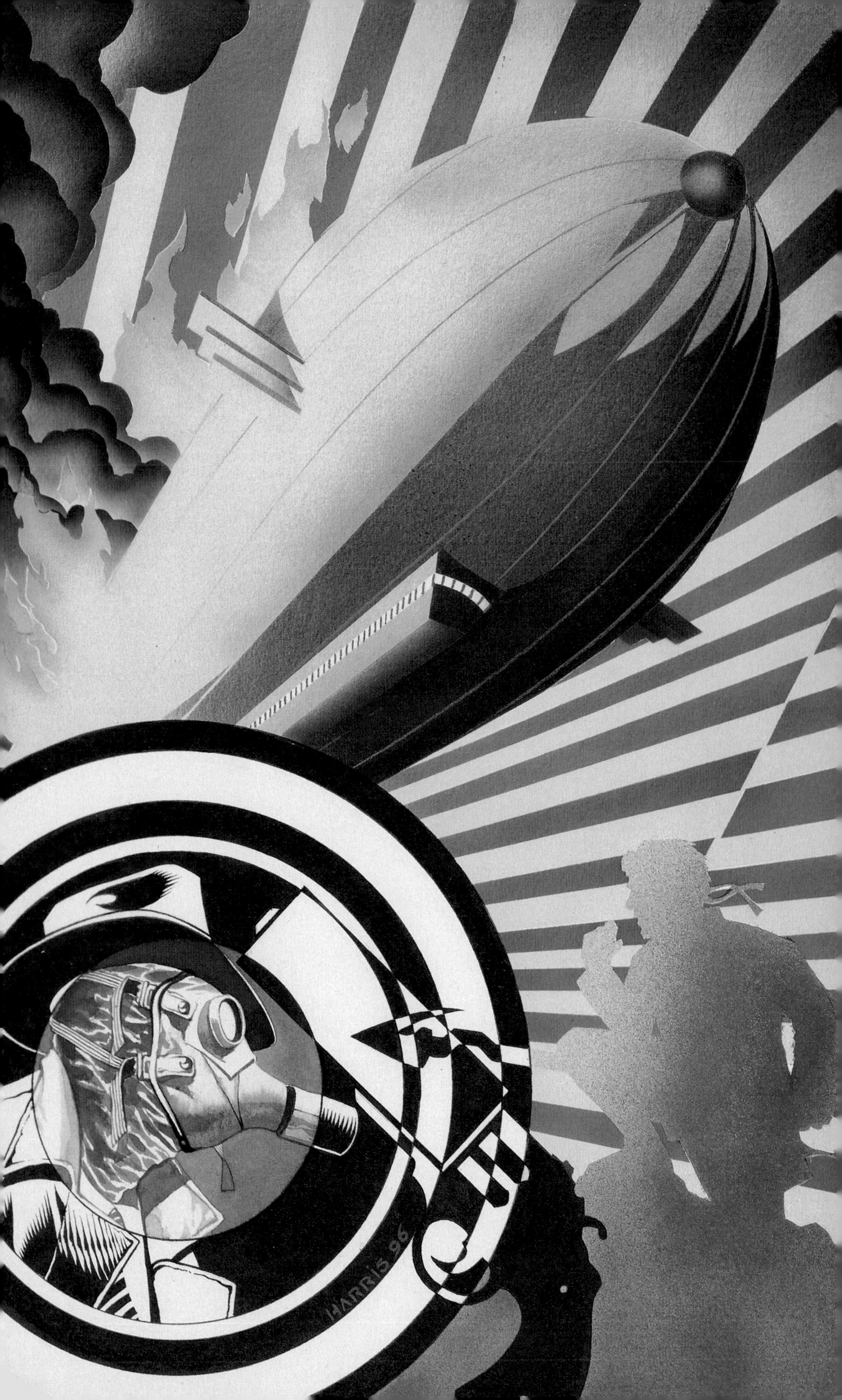
HARRIS 96

STARMAN 23

Cover by Tony Harris

Written by James Robinson

Pencils by Tony Harris

with inks by Wade von Grawbadger

and colors by Kevin Somers

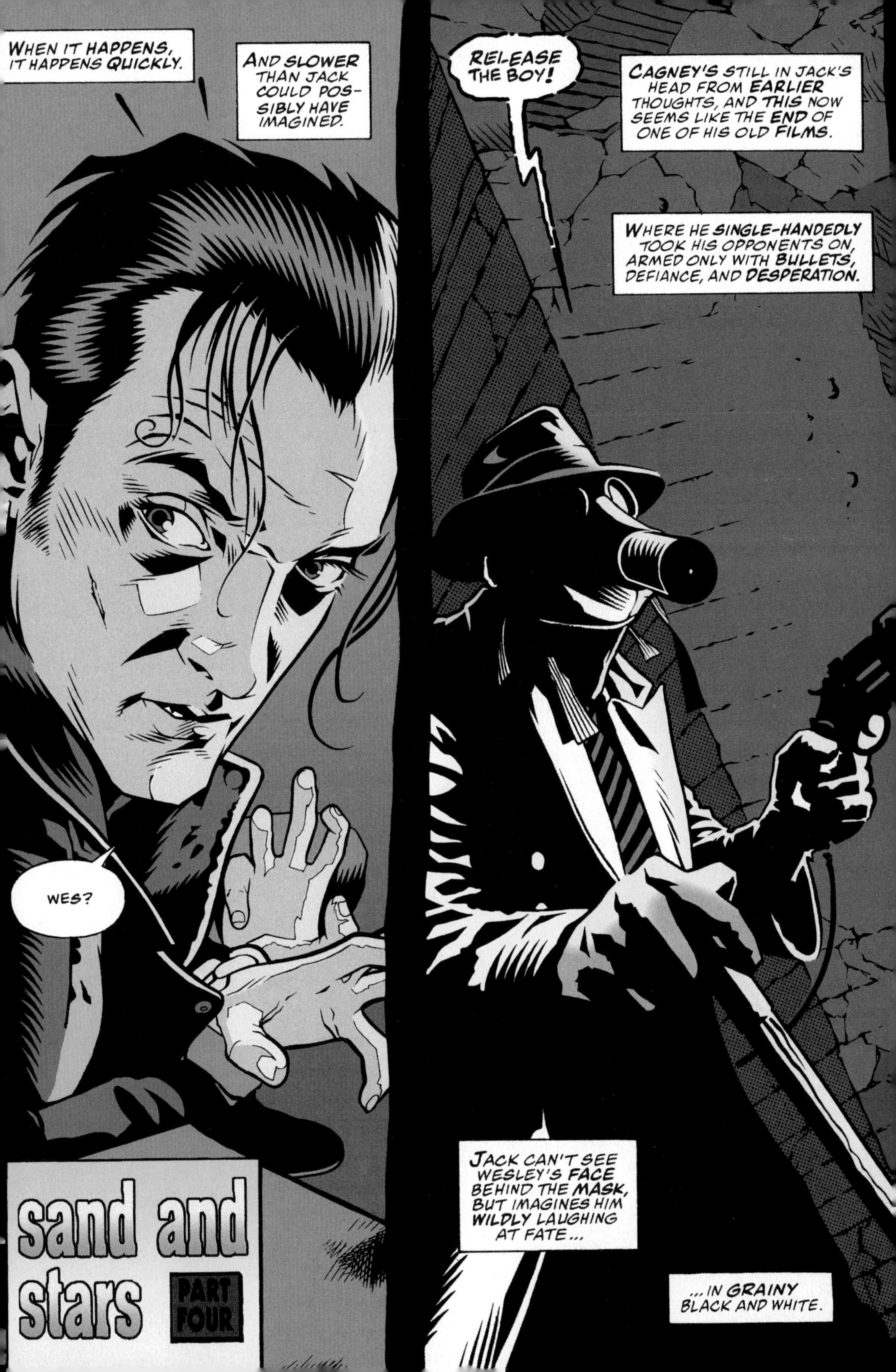

WHEN IT HAPPENS, IT HAPPENS QUICKLY.
AND SLOWER THAN JACK COULD POSSIBLY HAVE IMAGINED.
WES?
sand and stars
PART FOUR
RELEASE THE BOY!
CAGNEY'S STILL IN JACK'S HEAD FROM EARLIER THOUGHTS, AND THIS NOW SEEMS LIKE THE END OF ONE OF HIS OLD FILMS.
WHERE HE SINGLE-HANDEDLY TOOK HIS OPPONENTS ON, ARMED ONLY WITH BULLETS, DEFIANCE, AND DESPERATION.
JACK CAN'T SEE WESLEY'S FACE BEHIND THE MASK, BUT IMAGINES HIM WILDLY LAUGHING AT FATE...
...IN GRAINY BLACK AND WHITE.

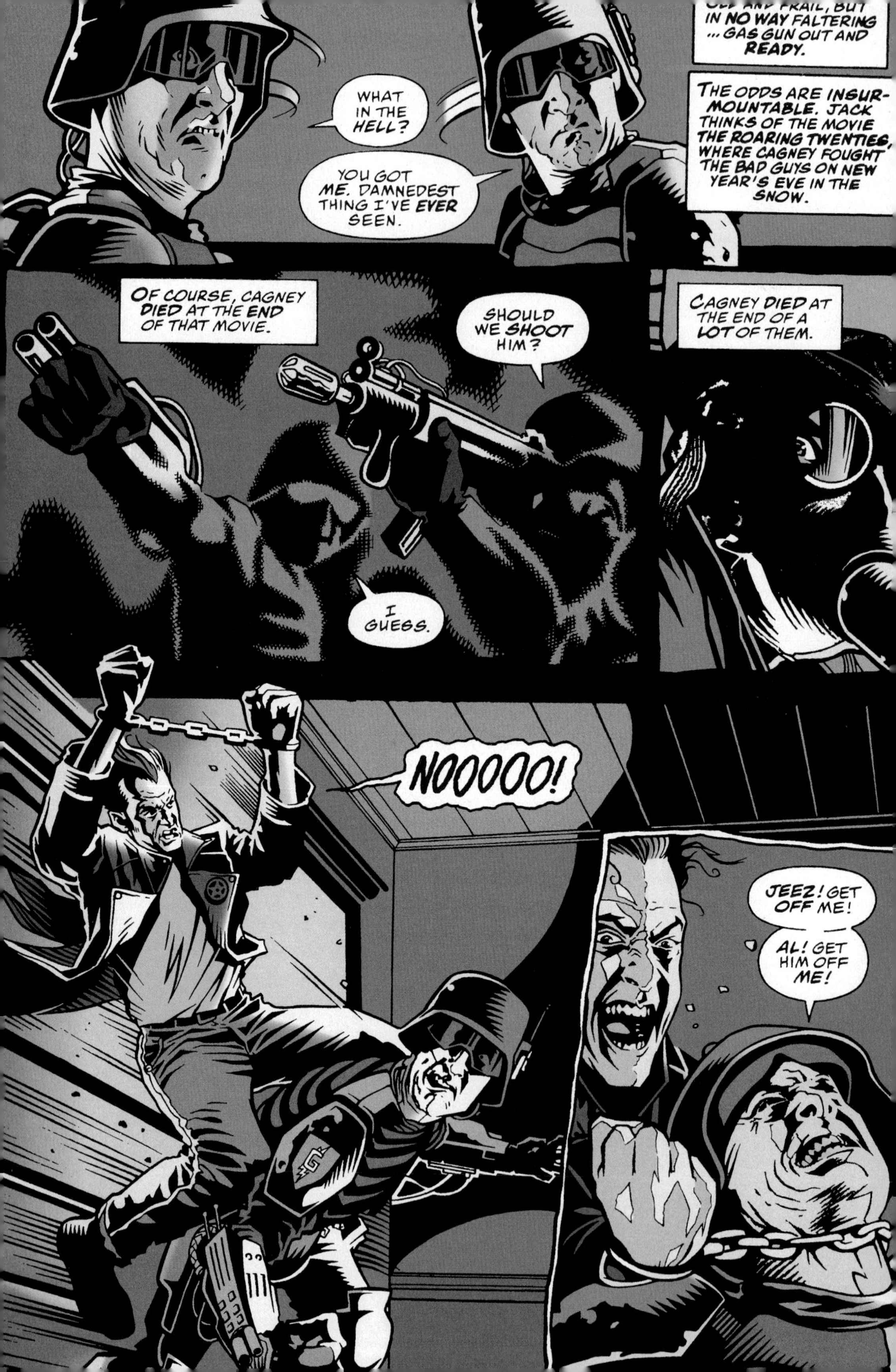

IN NO WAY FALTERING ... GAS GUN OUT AND READY.
WHAT IN THE HELL?
YOU GOT ME. DAMNEDEST THING I'VE EVER SEEN.
THE ODDS ARE INSURMOUNTABLE. JACK THINKS OF THE MOVIE THE ROARING TWENTIES, WHERE CAGNEY FOUGHT THE BAD GUYS ON NEW YEAR'S EVE IN THE SNOW.
OF COURSE, CAGNEY DIED AT THE END OF THAT MOVIE.
SHOULD WE SHOOT HIM?
I GUESS.
CAGNEY DIED AT THE END OF A LOT OF THEM.
NOOOOO!
JEEZ! GET OFF ME!
AL! GET HIM OFF ME!

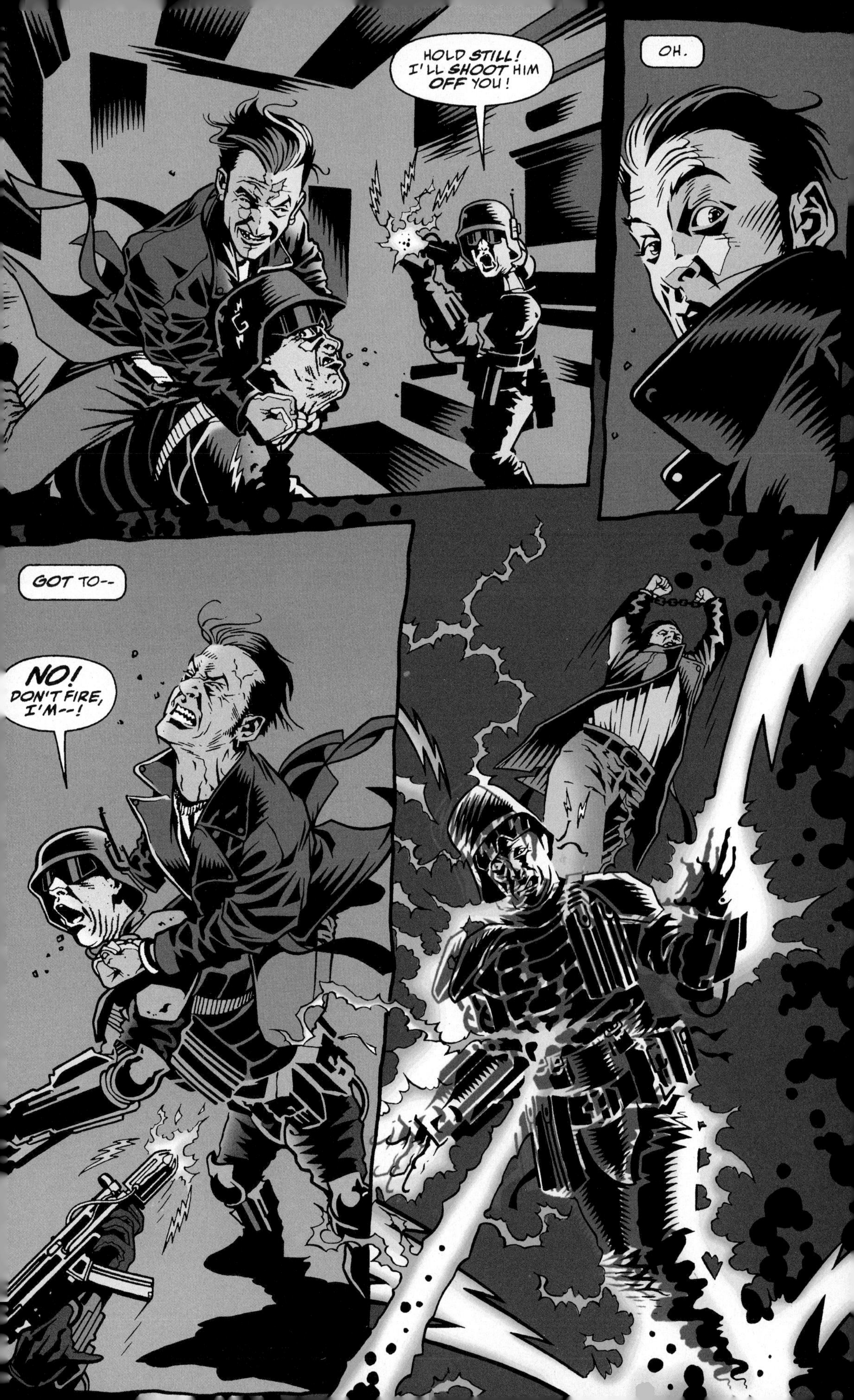

HOLD STILL! I'LL SHOOT HIM OFF YOU!
OH.
GOT TO--
NO! DON'T FIRE, I'M--!

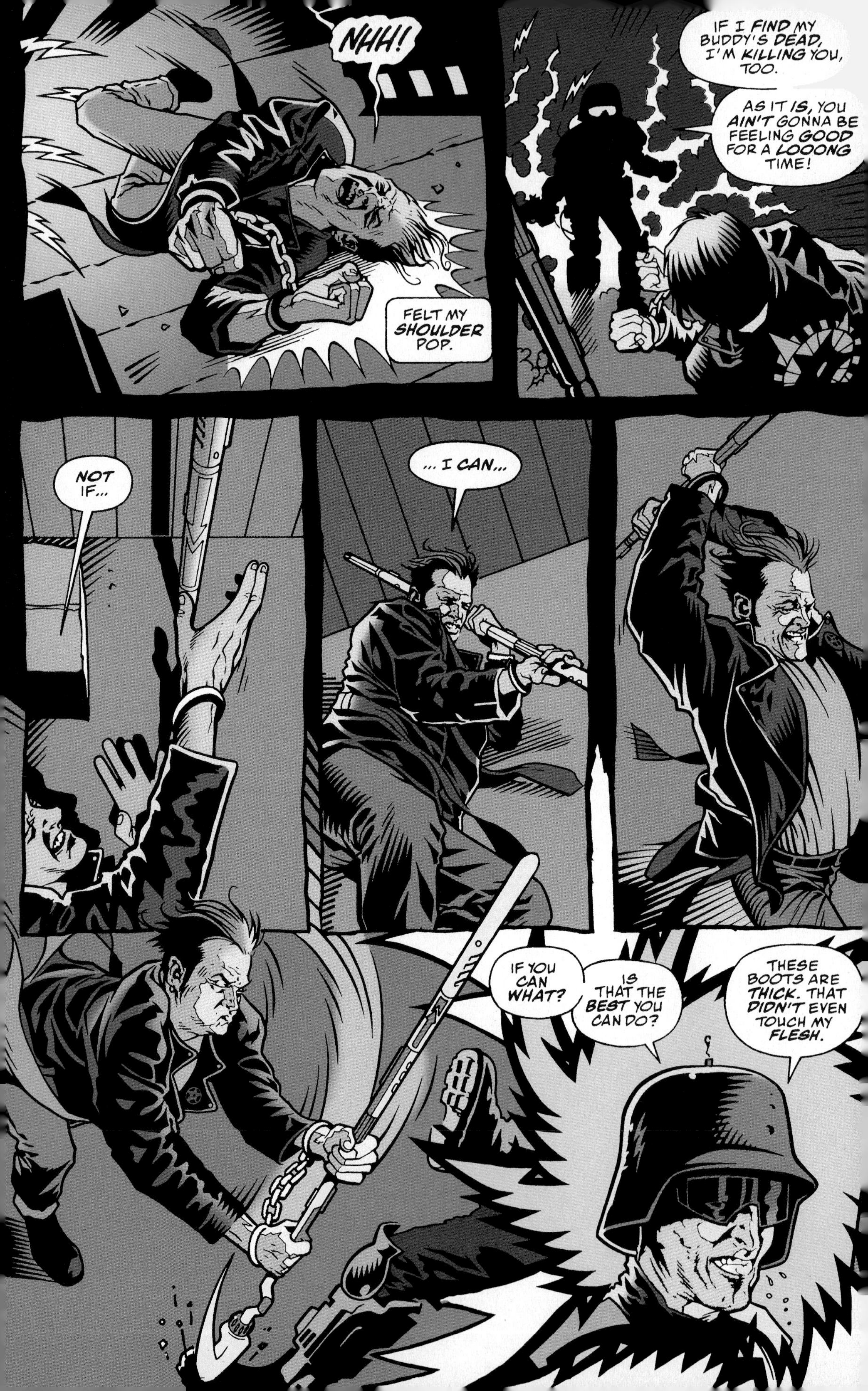
NHH!
FELT MY SHOULDER POP.
IF I FIND MY BUDDY'S DEAD, I'M KILLING YOU, TOO.
AS IT IS, YOU AIN'T GONNA BE FEELING GOOD FOR A LOOONG TIME!
NOT IF...
... I CAN...
IF YOU CAN WHAT?
IS THAT THE BEST YOU CAN DO?
THESE BOOTS ARE THICK. THAT DIDN'T EVEN TOUCH MY FLESH.

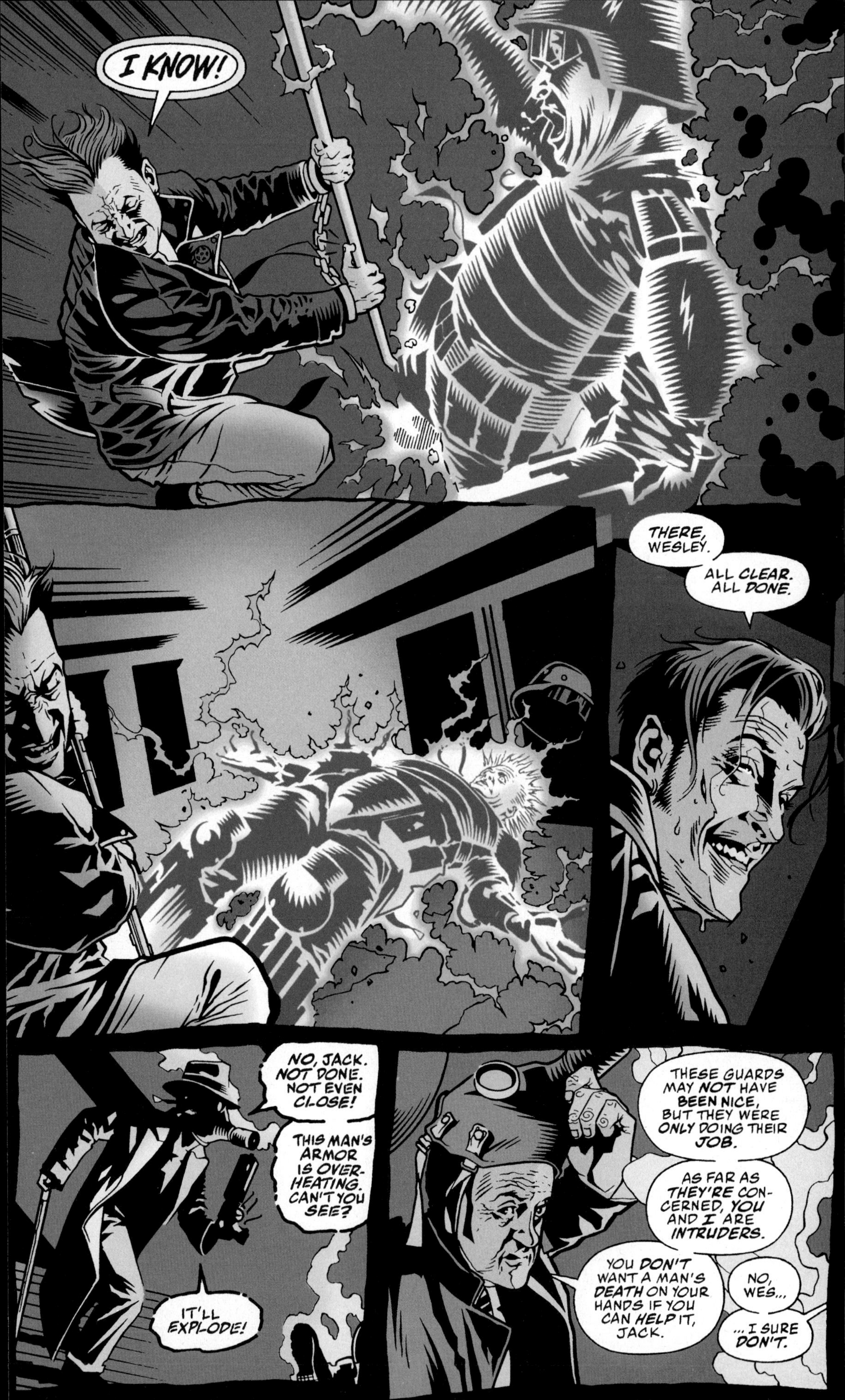
I KNOW!
THERE, WESLEY.
ALL CLEAR. ALL DONE.
NO, JACK. NOT DONE. NOT EVEN CLOSE!
THIS MAN'S ARMOR IS OVER-HEATING. CAN'T YOU SEE?
IT'LL EXPLODE!
THESE GUARDS MAY NOT HAVE BEEN NICE, BUT THEY WERE ONLY DOING THEIR JOB.
AS FAR AS THEY'RE CONCERNED, YOU AND I ARE INTRUDERS.
YOU DON'T WANT A MAN'S DEATH ON YOUR HANDS IF YOU CAN HELP IT, JACK.
NO, WES...
...I SURE DON'T.

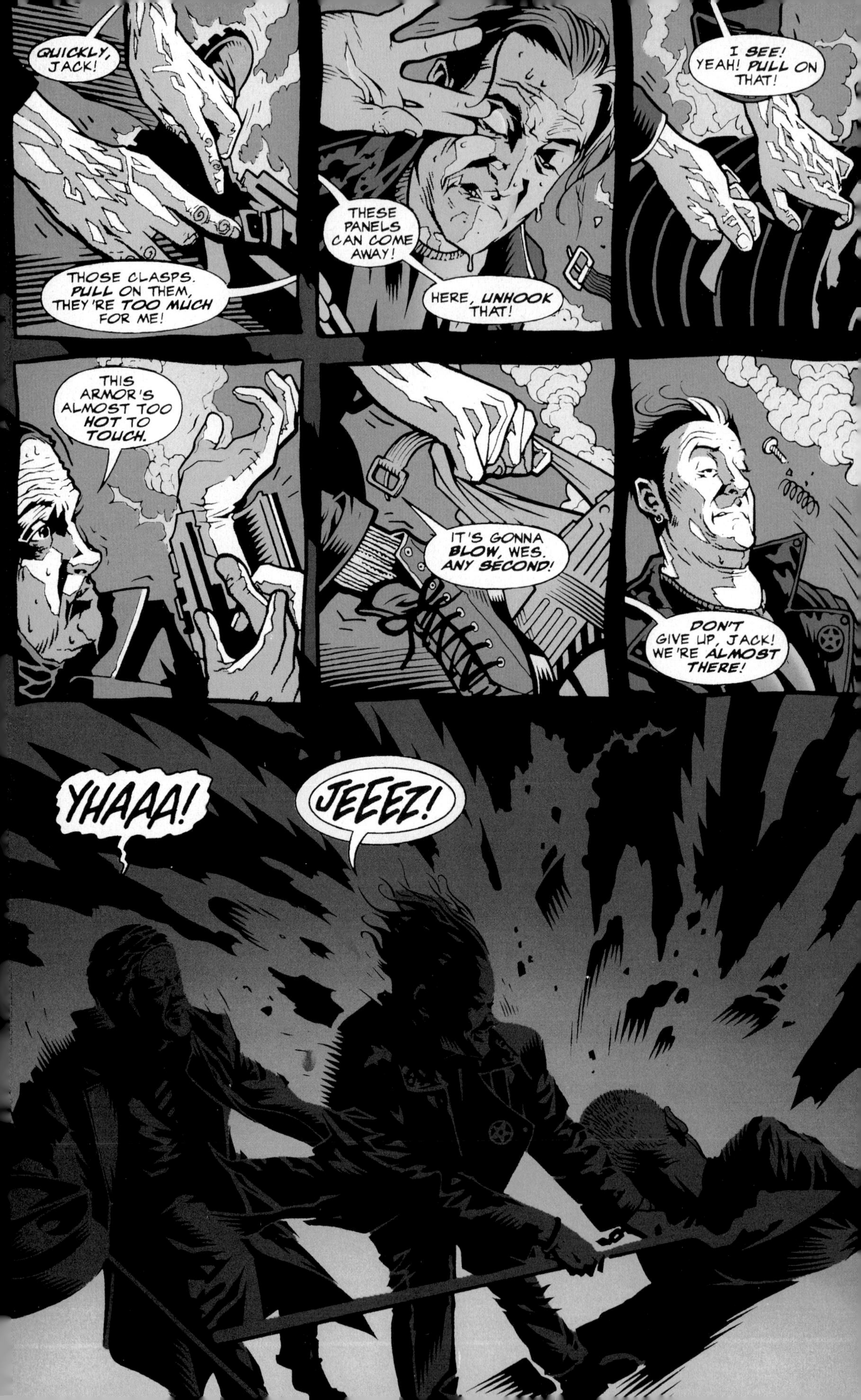
QUICKLY, JACK!
THOSE CLASPS. PULL ON THEM, THEY'RE TOO MUCH FOR ME!
THESE PANELS CAN COME AWAY!
HERE, UNHOOK THAT!
I SEE! YEAH! PULL ON THAT!
THIS ARMOR'S ALMOST TOO HOT TO TOUCH.
IT'S GONNA BLOW, WES. ANY SECOND!
DON'T GIVE UP, JACK! WE'RE ALMOST THERE!
YHAAA!
JEEEZ!

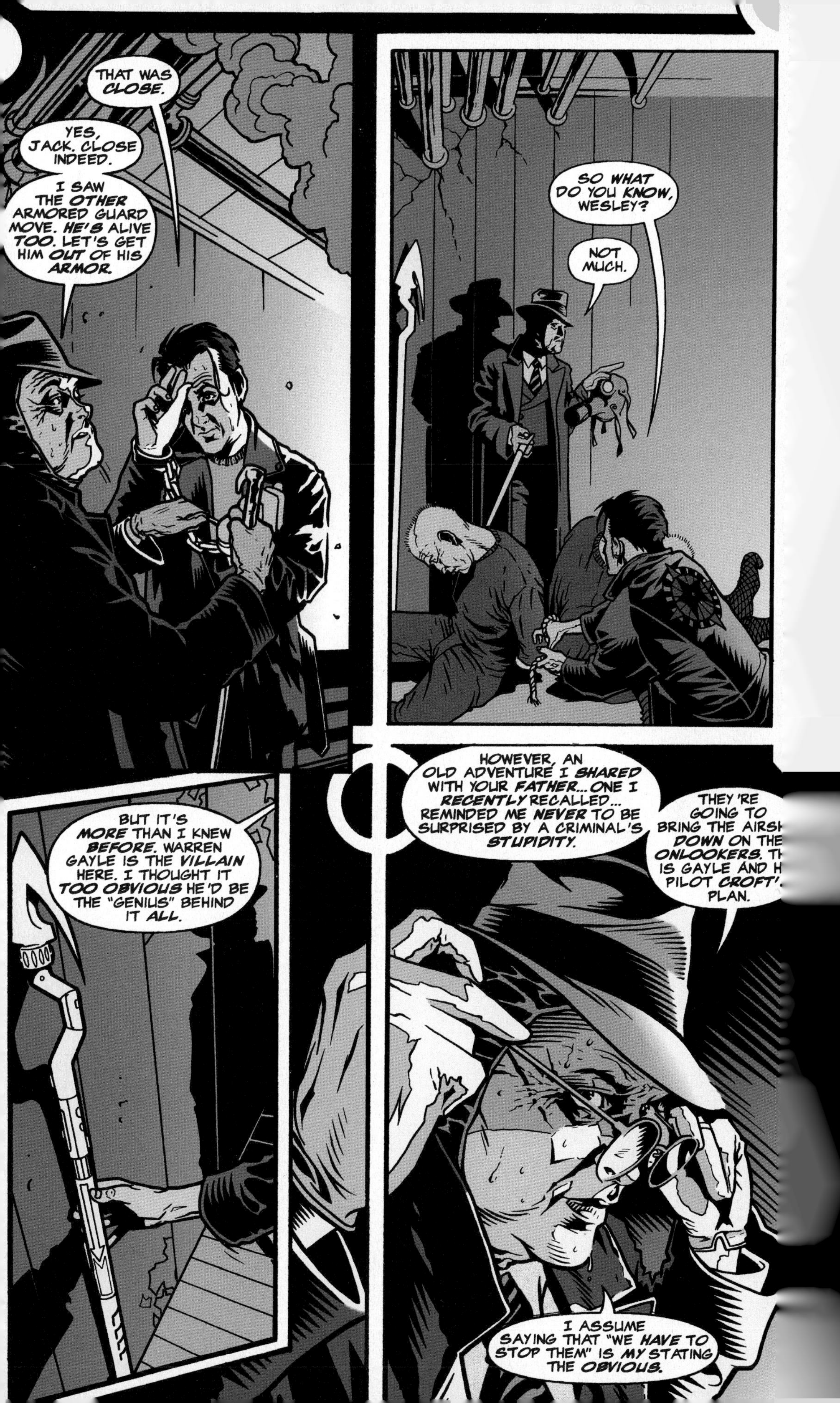

THAT WAS CLOSE.
YES, JACK. CLOSE INDEED.
I SAW THE OTHER ARMORED GUARD MOVE. HE'S ALIVE TOO. LET'S GET HIM OUT OF HIS ARMOR.
SO WHAT DO YOU KNOW, WESLEY?
NOT MUCH.
BUT IT'S MORE THAN I KNEW BEFORE. WARREN GAYLE IS THE VILLAIN HERE. I THOUGHT IT TOO OBVIOUS HE'D BE THE "GENIUS" BEHIND IT ALL.
HOWEVER, AN OLD ADVENTURE I SHARED WITH YOUR FATHER... ONE I RECENTLY RECALLED... REMINDED ME NEVER TO BE SURPRISED BY A CRIMINAL'S STUPIDITY.
THEY'RE GOING TO BRING THE AIRSH DOWN ON THE ONLOOKERS. TH IS GAYLE AND H PILOT CROFT' PLAN.
I ASSUME SAYING THAT "WE HAVE TO STOP THEM" IS MY STATING THE OBVIOUS.

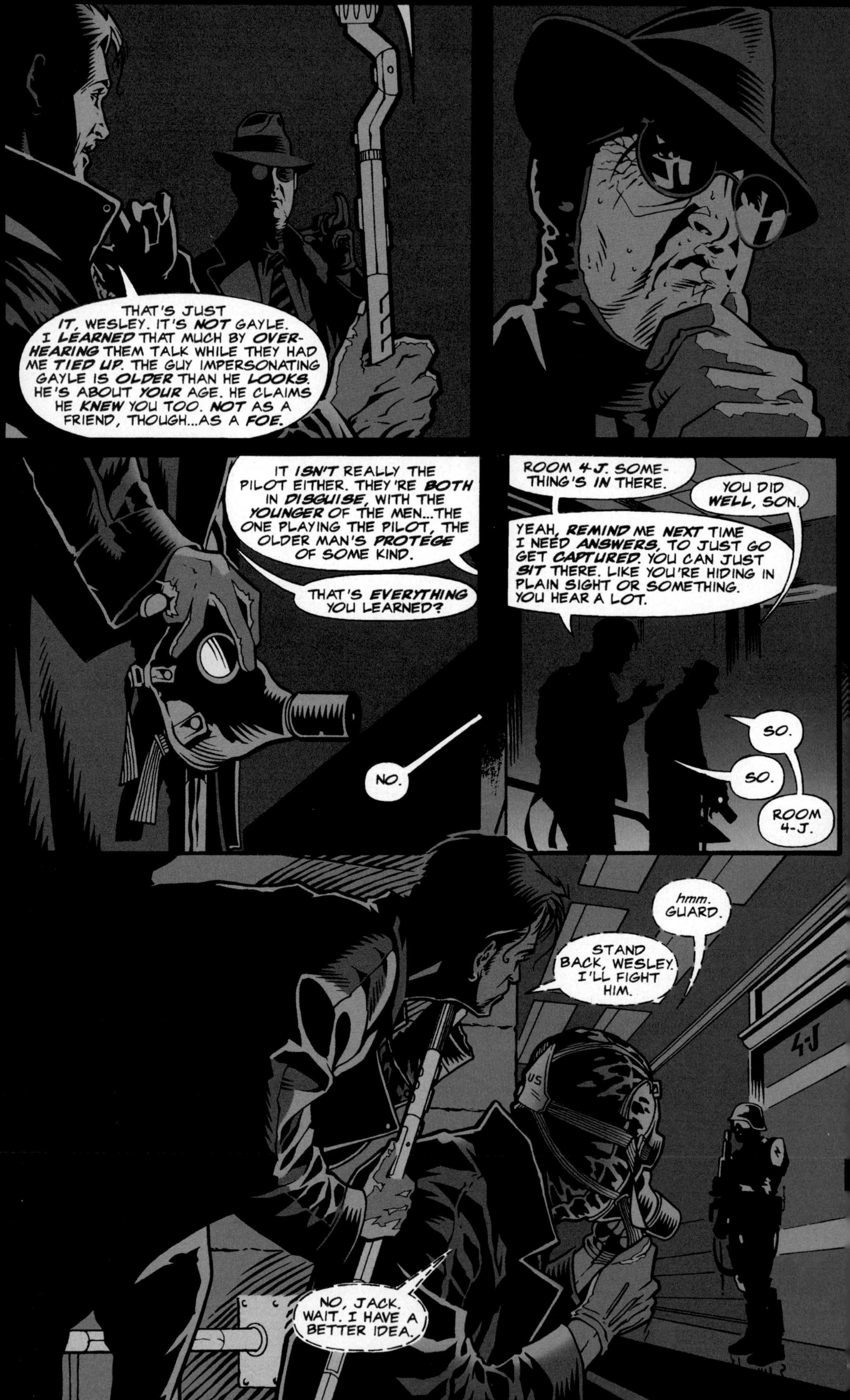

THAT'S JUST IT, WESLEY. IT'S NOT GAYLE. I LEARNED THAT MUCH BY OVER-HEARING THEM TALK WHILE THEY HAD ME TIED UP. THE GUY IMPERSONATING GAYLE IS OLDER THAN HE LOOKS. HE'S ABOUT YOUR AGE. HE CLAIMS HE KNEW YOU TOO. NOT AS A FRIEND, THOUGH...AS A FOE.
IT ISN'T REALLY THE PILOT EITHER. THEY'RE BOTH IN DISGUISE, WITH THE YOUNGER OF THE MEN...THE ONE PLAYING THE PILOT, THE OLDER MAN'S PROTEGE OF SOME KIND.
THAT'S EVERYTHING YOU LEARNED?
NO.
ROOM 4-J. SOME-THING'S IN THERE.
YOU DID WELL, SON.
YEAH, REMIND ME NEXT TIME I NEED ANSWERS, TO JUST GO GET CAPTURED. YOU CAN JUST SIT THERE. LIKE YOU'RE HIDING IN PLAIN SIGHT OR SOMETHING. YOU HEAR A LOT.
SO.
SO.
ROOM 4-J.
hmm. GUARD.
STAND BACK, WESLEY. I'LL FIGHT HIM.
4-J
NO, JACK. WAIT. I HAVE A BETTER IDEA.

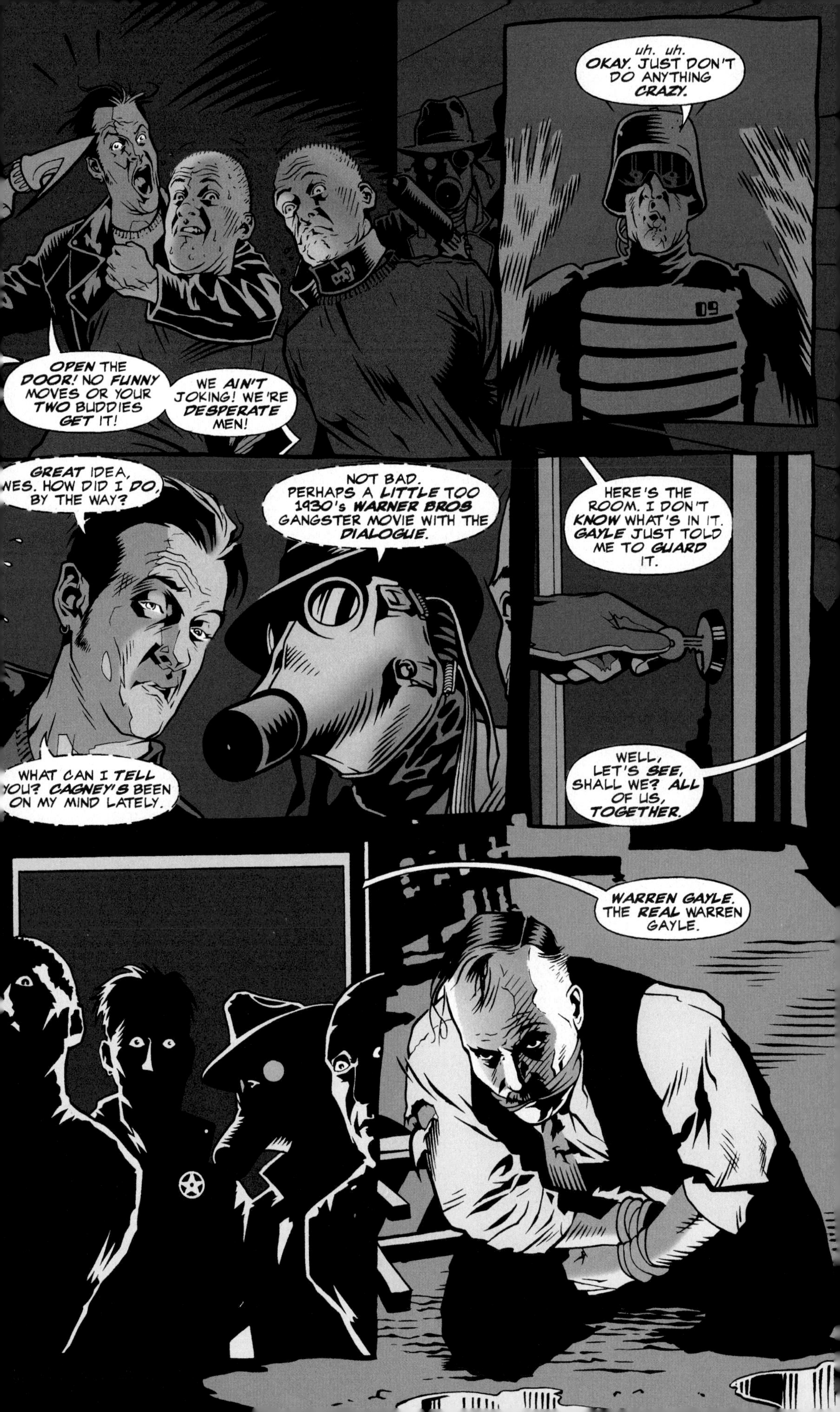
OPEN THE DOOR! NO FUNNY MOVES OR YOUR TWO BUDDIES GET IT!
WE AIN'T JOKING! WE'RE DESPERATE MEN!
uh. uh. OKAY. JUST DON'T DO ANYTHING CRAZY.
09
GREAT IDEA, WES. HOW DID I DO, BY THE WAY?
NOT BAD. PERHAPS A LITTLE TOO 1930's WARNER BROS GANGSTER MOVIE WITH THE DIALOGUE.
WHAT CAN I TELL YOU? CAGNEY'S BEEN ON MY MIND LATELY.
HERE'S THE ROOM. I DON'T KNOW WHAT'S IN IT. GAYLE JUST TOLD ME TO GUARD IT.
WELL, LET'S SEE, SHALL WE? ALL OF US, TOGETHER.
WARREN GAYLE. THE REAL WARREN GAYLE.

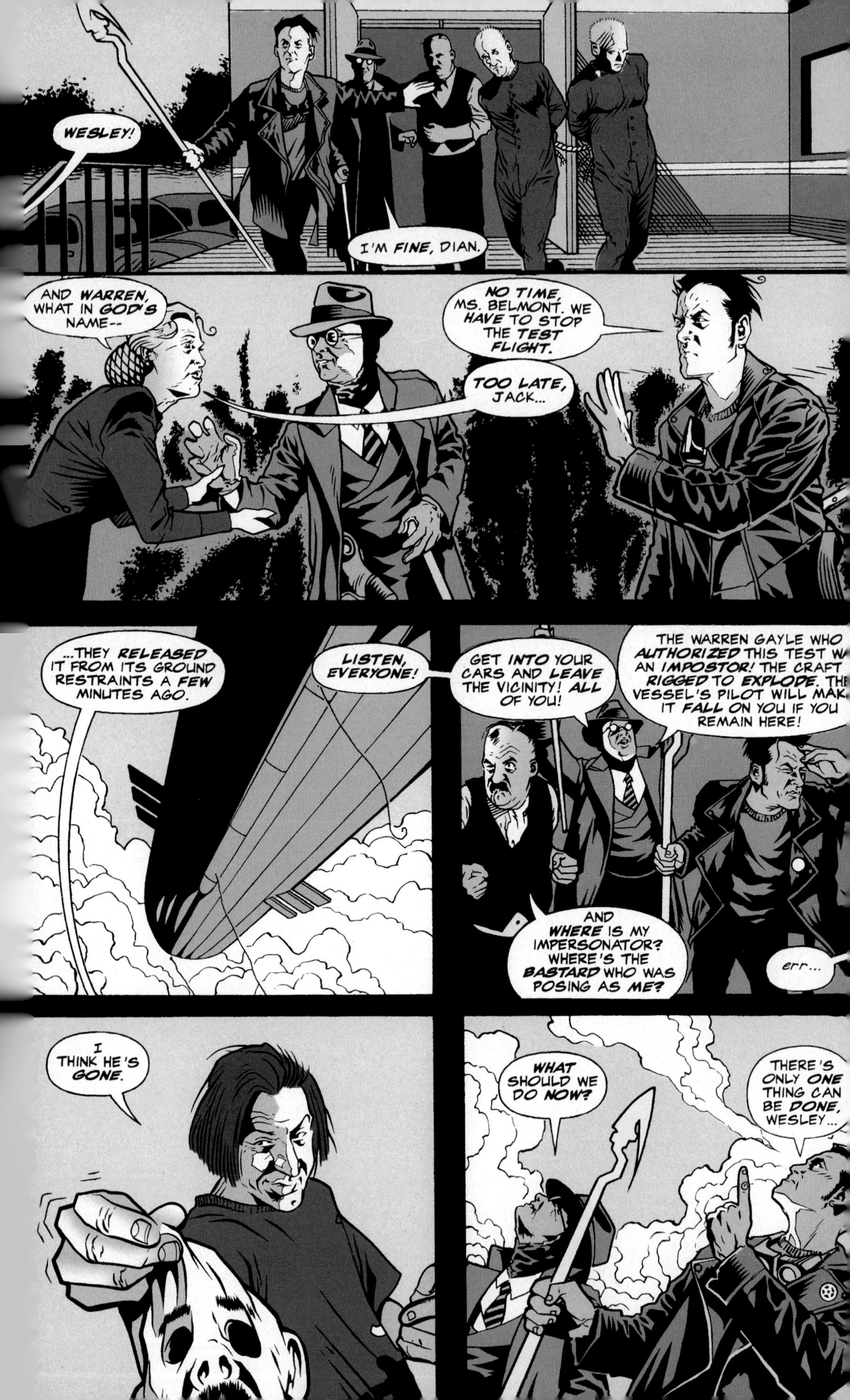
WESLEY!
I'M FINE, DIAN.
AND WARREN, WHAT IN GOD'S NAME--
NO TIME, MS. BELMONT. WE HAVE TO STOP THE TEST FLIGHT.
TOO LATE, JACK...
...THEY RELEASED IT FROM ITS GROUND RESTRAINTS A FEW MINUTES AGO.
LISTEN, EVERYONE!
GET INTO YOUR CARS AND LEAVE THE VICINITY! ALL OF YOU!
THE WARREN GAYLE WHO AUTHORIZED THIS TEST W AN IMPOSTOR! THE CRAFT RIGGED TO EXPLODE. TH VESSEL'S PILOT WILL MAK IT FALL ON YOU IF YOU REMAIN HERE!
AND WHERE IS MY IMPERSONATOR? WHERE'S THE BASTARD WHO WAS POSING AS ME?
err...
I THINK HE'S GONE.
WHAT SHOULD WE DO NOW?
THERE'S ONLY ONE THING CAN BE DONE, WESLEY...

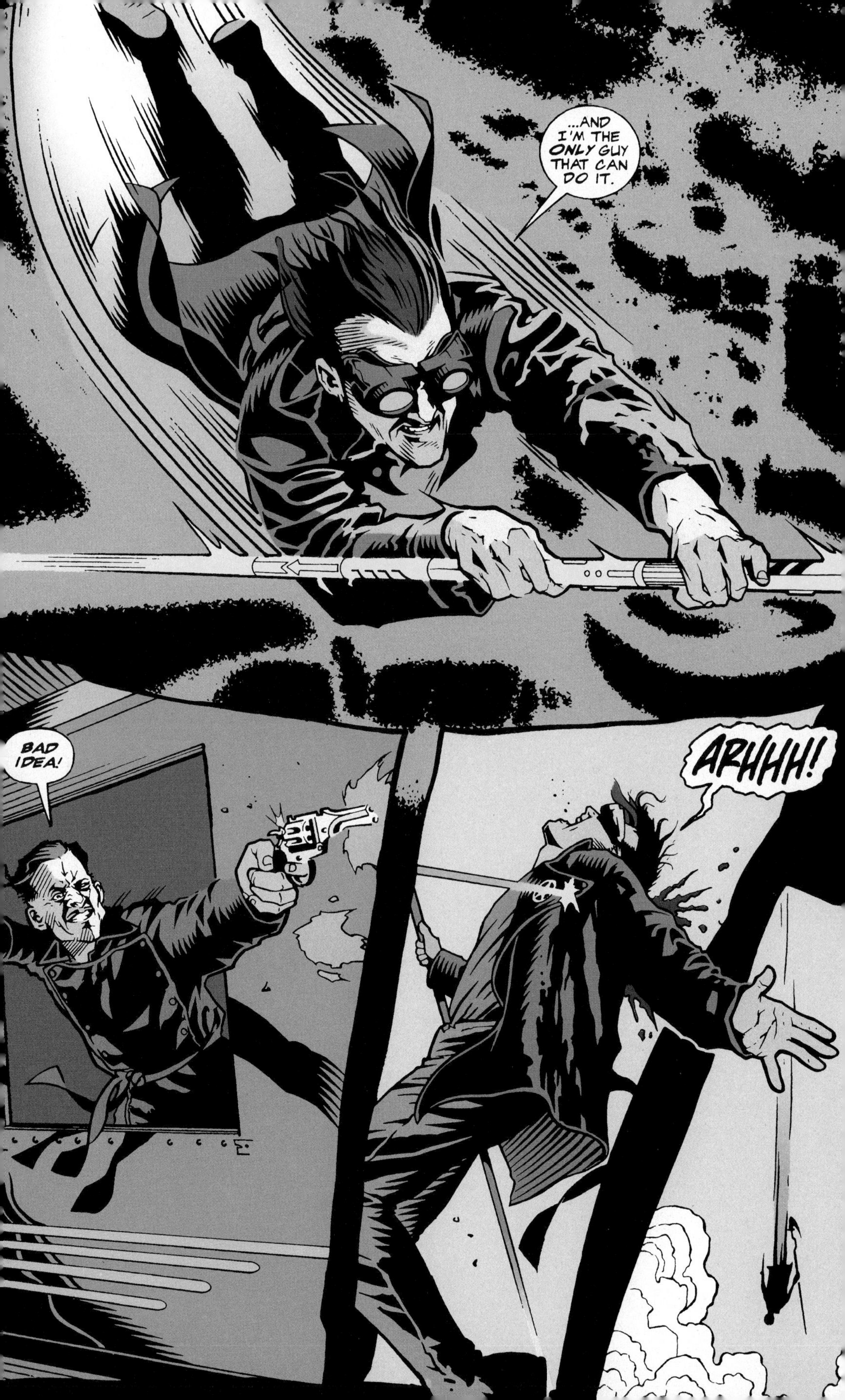
...AND I'M THE ONLY GUY THAT CAN DO IT.
BAD IDEA!
ARHHH!

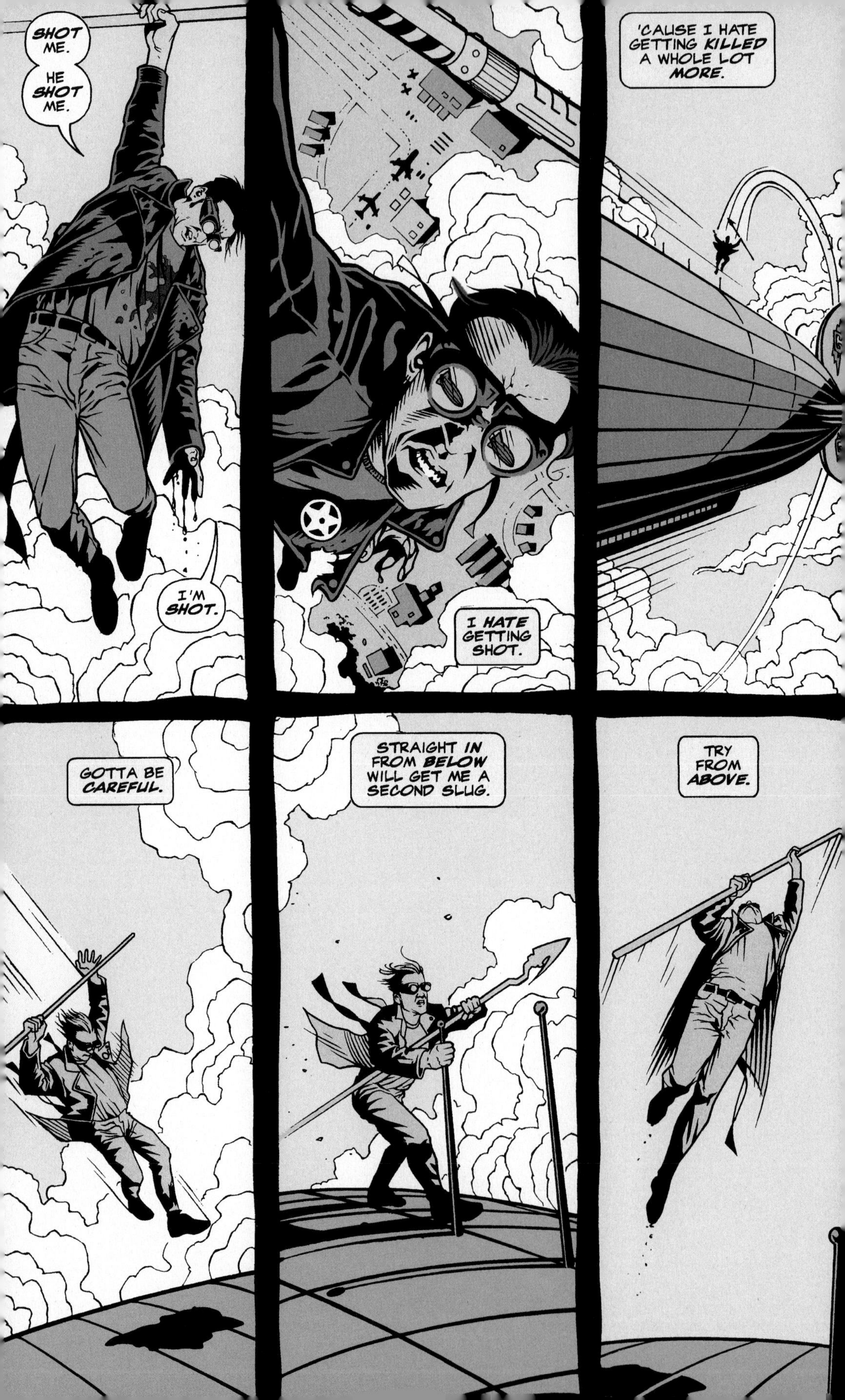
SHOT ME.
HE SHOT ME.
I'M SHOT.
I HATE GETTING SHOT.
'CAUSE I HATE GETTING KILLED A WHOLE LOT MORE.
GOTTA BE CAREFUL.
STRAIGHT IN FROM BELOW WILL GET ME A SECOND SLUG.
TRY FROM ABOVE.

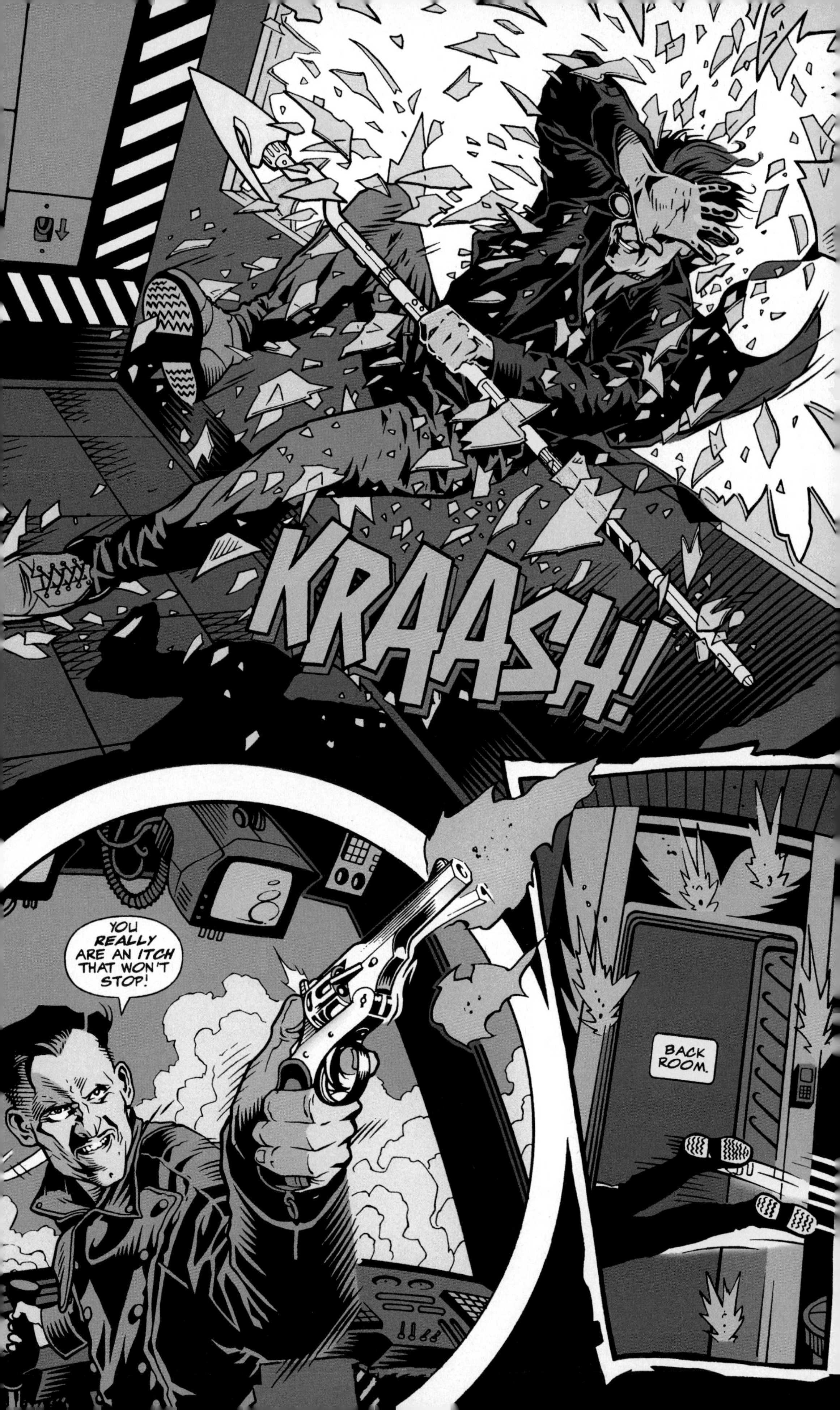
KRAASH!
YOU REALLY ARE AN ITCH THAT WON'T STOP!
BACK ROOM.

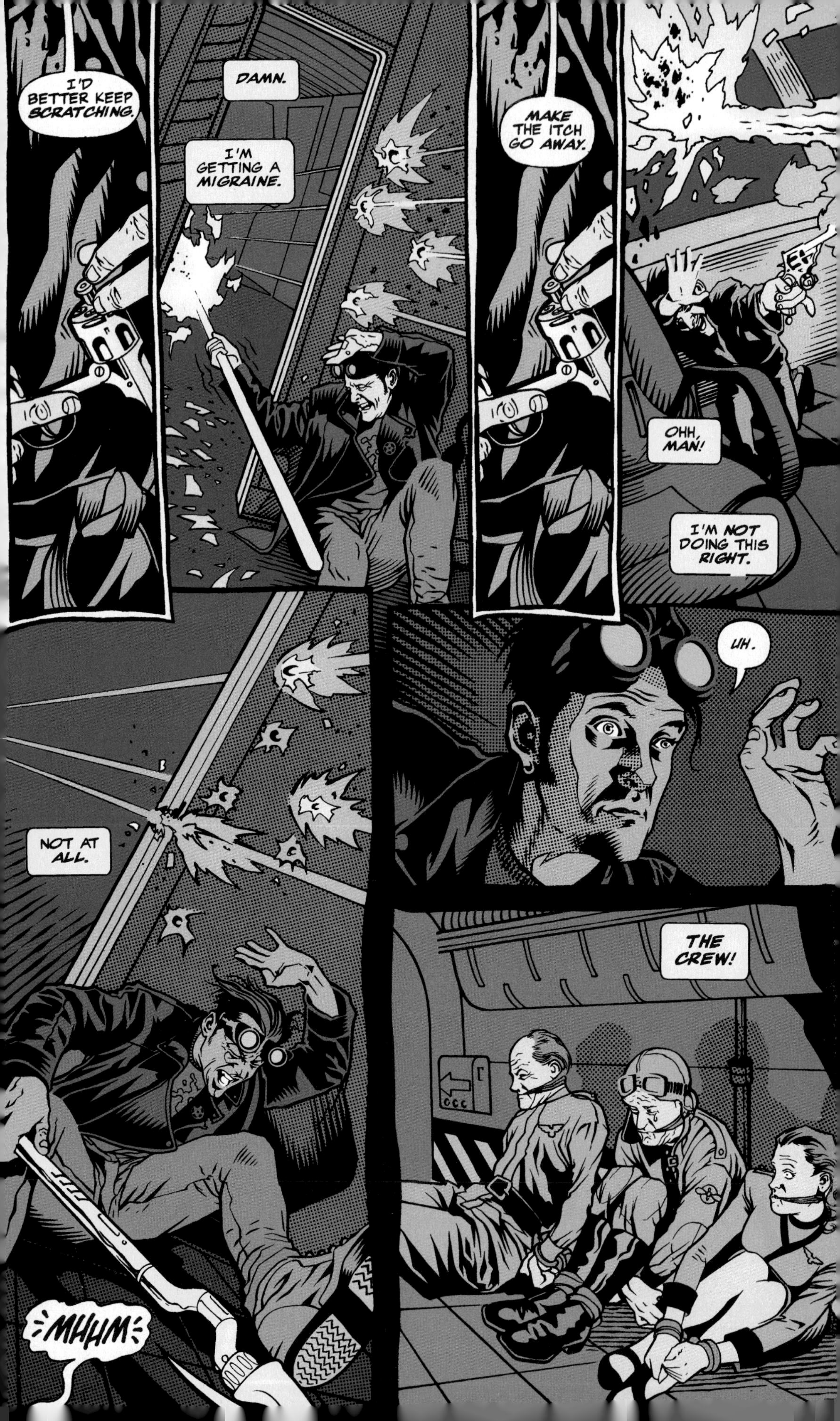
I'D BETTER KEEP SCRATCHING.
DAMN.
I'M GETTING A MIGRAINE.
MAKE THE ITCH GO AWAY.
OHH, MAN!
I'M NOT DOING THIS RIGHT.
NOT AT ALL.
MHUM!
UH.
THE CREW!

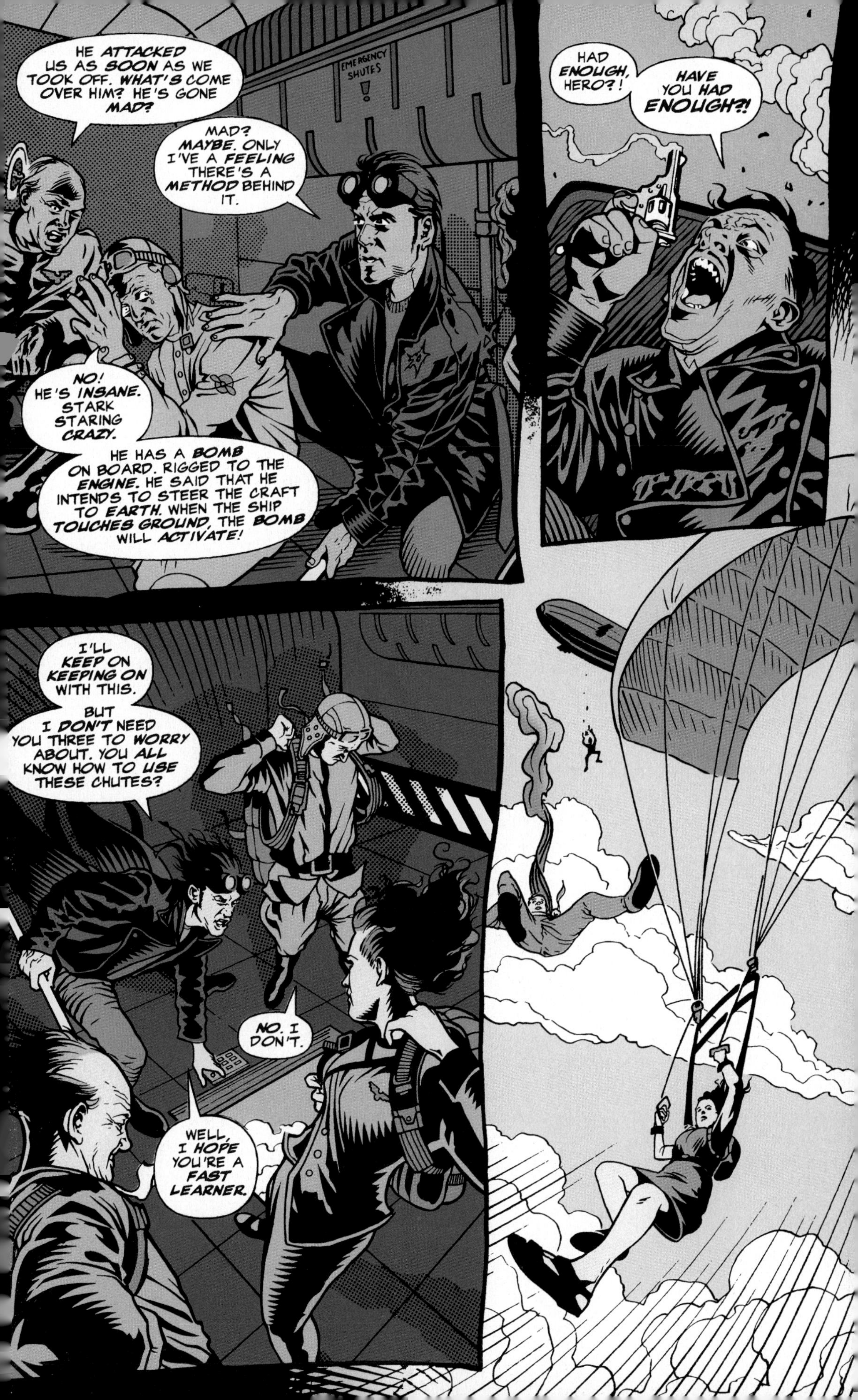

HE ATTACKED US AS SOON AS WE TOOK OFF. WHAT'S COME OVER HIM? HE'S GONE MAD?
EMERGENCY SHUTES
MAD? MAYBE. ONLY I'VE A FEELING THERE'S A METHOD BEHIND IT.
NO! HE'S INSANE. STARK STARING CRAZY.
HE HAS A BOMB ON BOARD. RIGGED TO THE ENGINE. HE SAID THAT HE INTENDS TO STEER THE CRAFT TO EARTH. WHEN THE SHIP TOUCHES GROUND, THE BOMB WILL ACTIVATE!
HAD ENOUGH, HERO?!
HAVE YOU HAD ENOUGH?!
I'LL KEEP ON KEEPING ON WITH THIS.
BUT I DON'T NEED YOU THREE TO WORRY ABOUT. YOU ALL KNOW HOW TO USE THESE CHUTES?
NO. I DON'T.
WELL, I HOPE YOU'RE A FAST LEARNER.

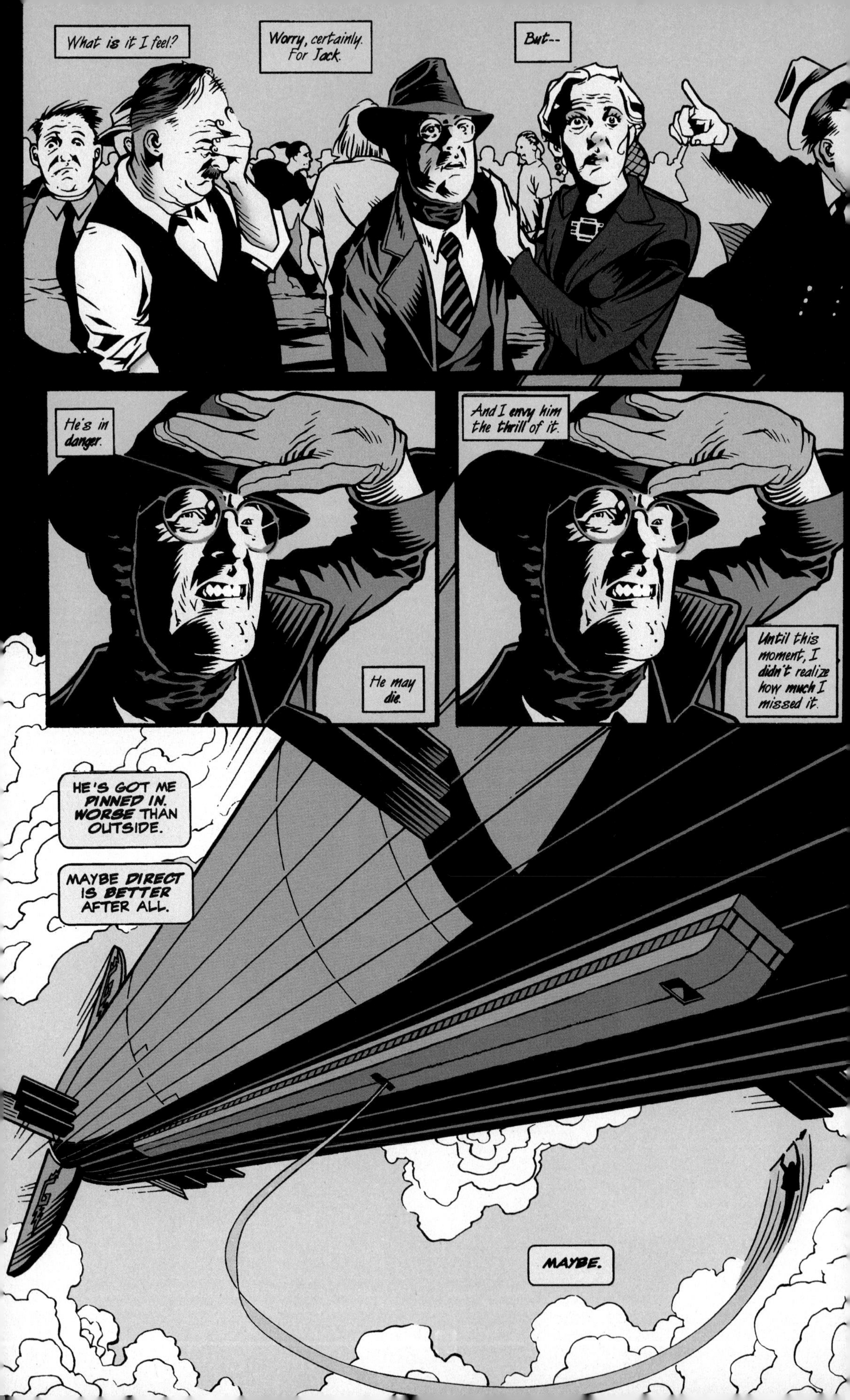
What is it I feel?
Worry, certainly. For Jack.
But--
He's in danger.
He may die.
And I envy him the thrill of it.
Until this moment, I didn't realize how much I missed it.
HE'S GOT ME PINNED IN. WORSE THAN OUTSIDE.
MAYBE DIRECT IS BETTER AFTER ALL.
MAYBE.

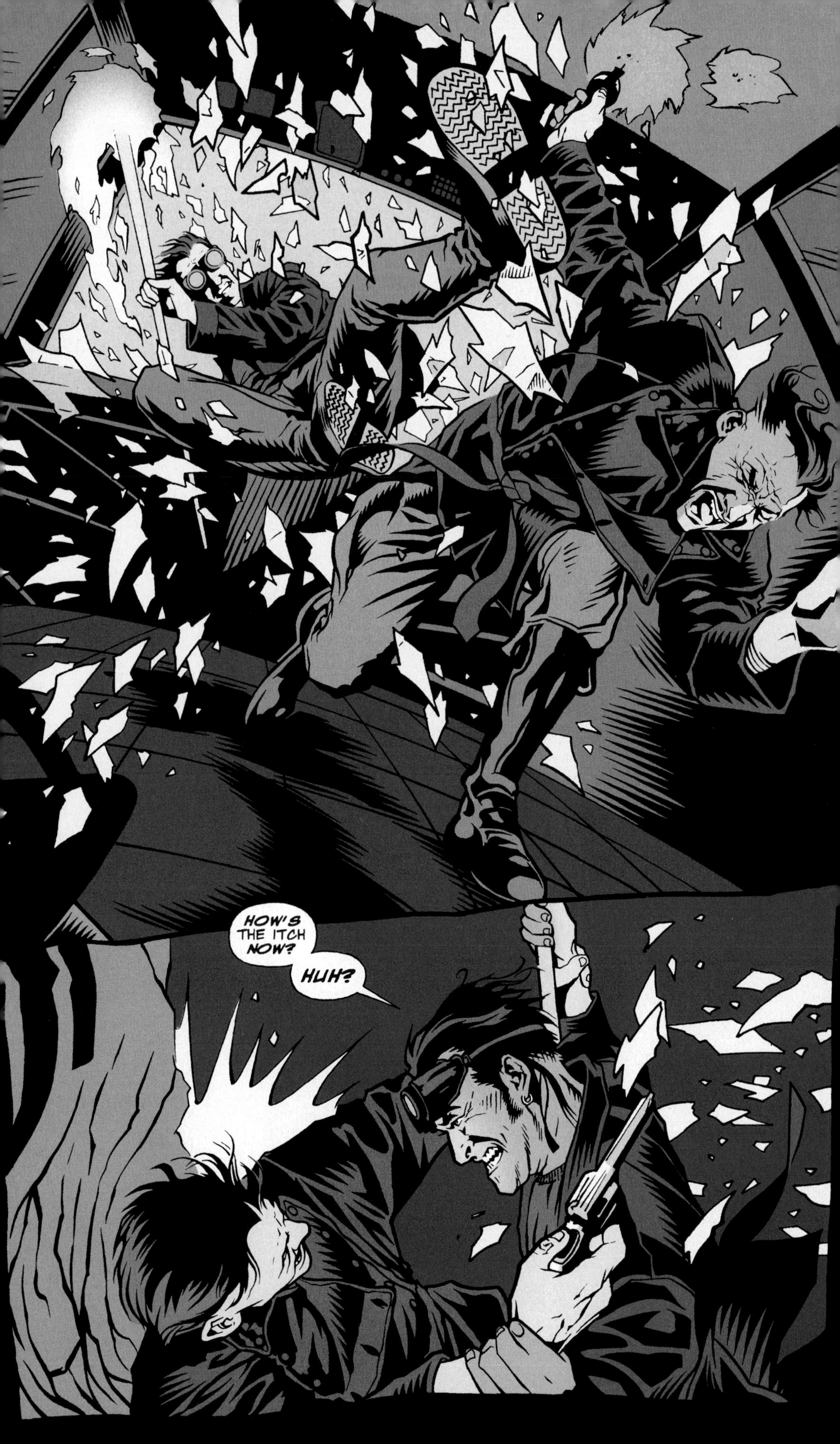
HOW'S THE ITCH NOW?
HUH?

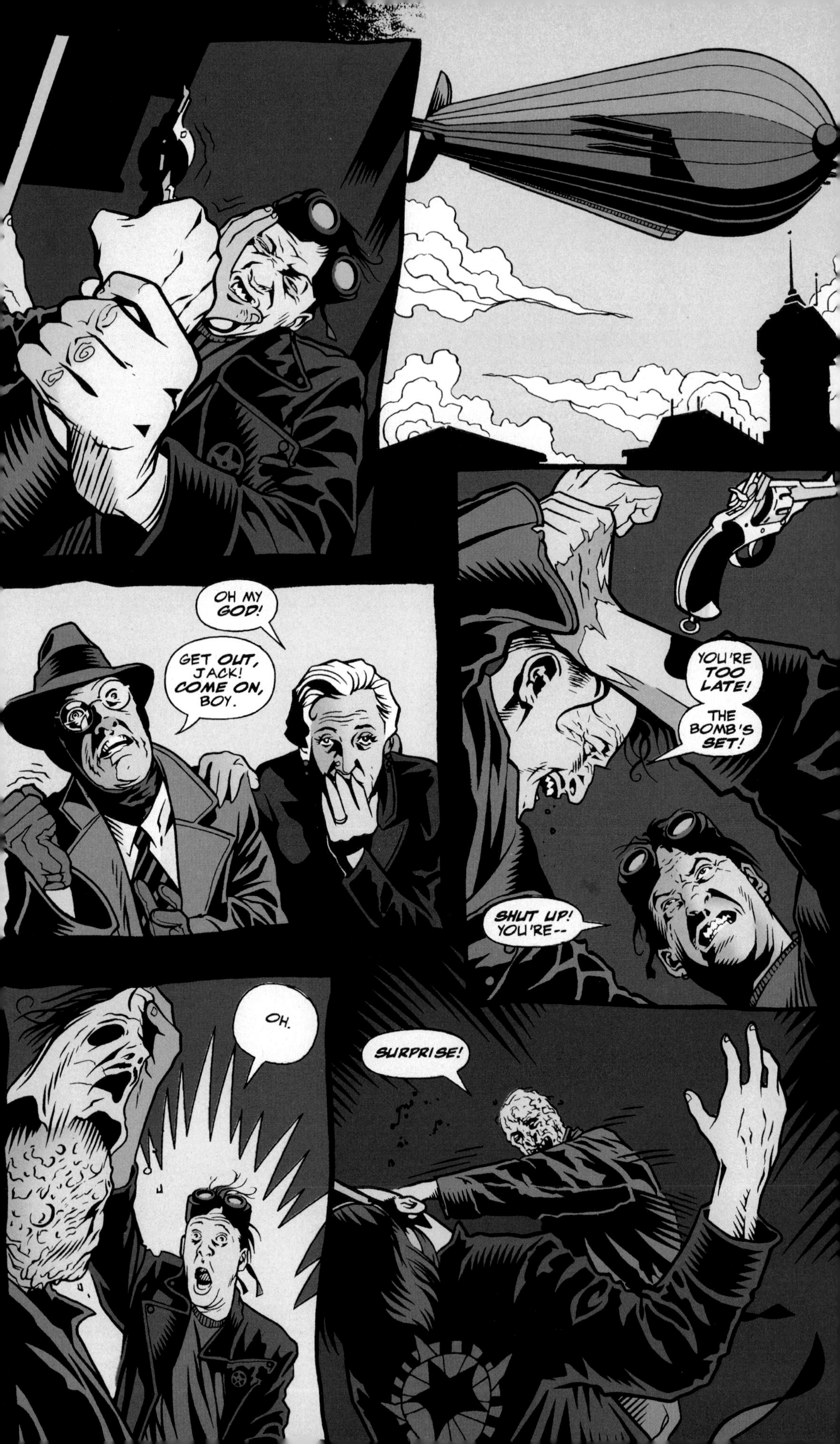
OH MY GOD!
GET OUT, JACK! COME ON, BOY.
YOU'RE TOO LATE!
THE BOMB'S SET!
SHUT UP! YOU'RE--
OH.
SURPRISE!

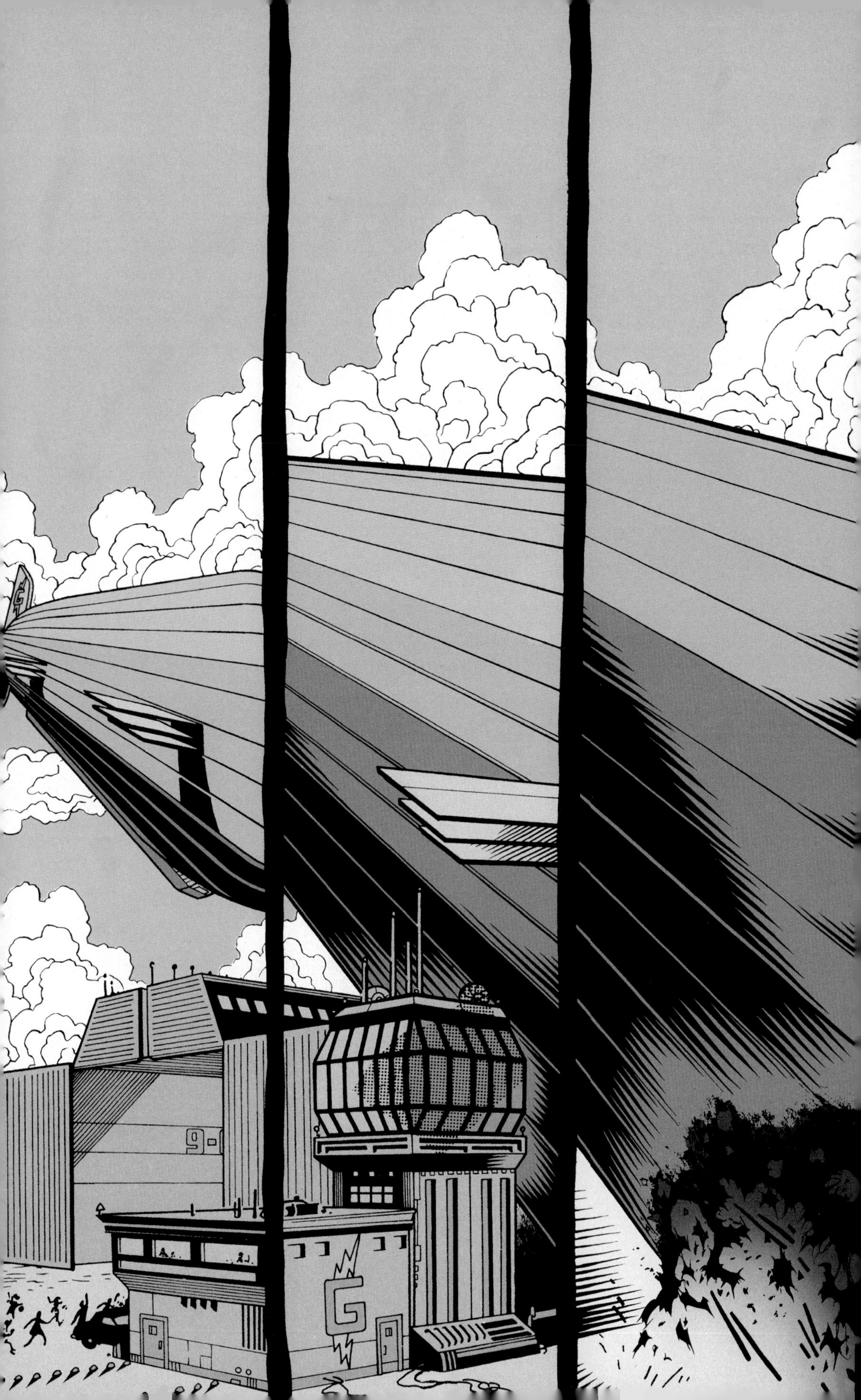

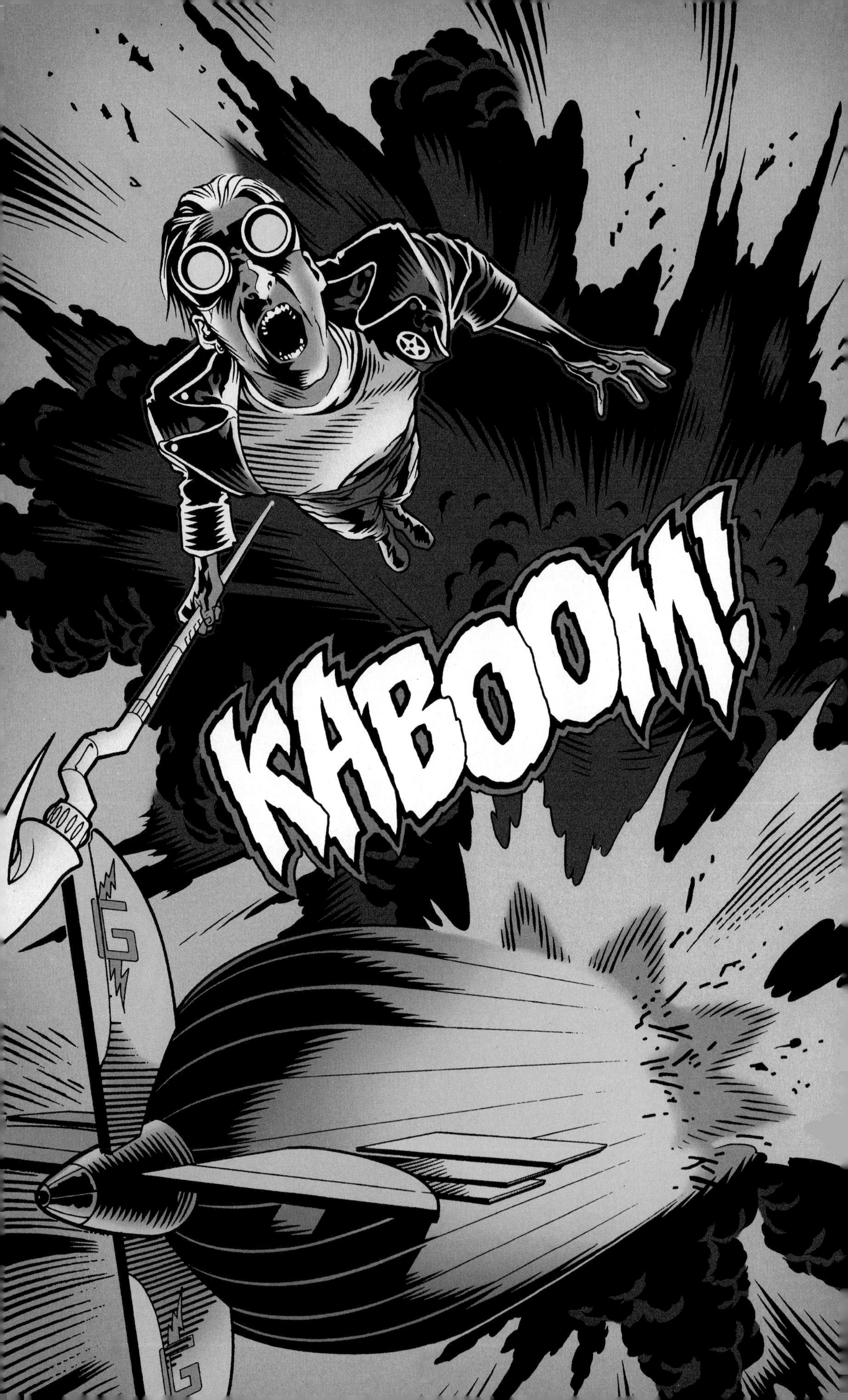
KABOOM!

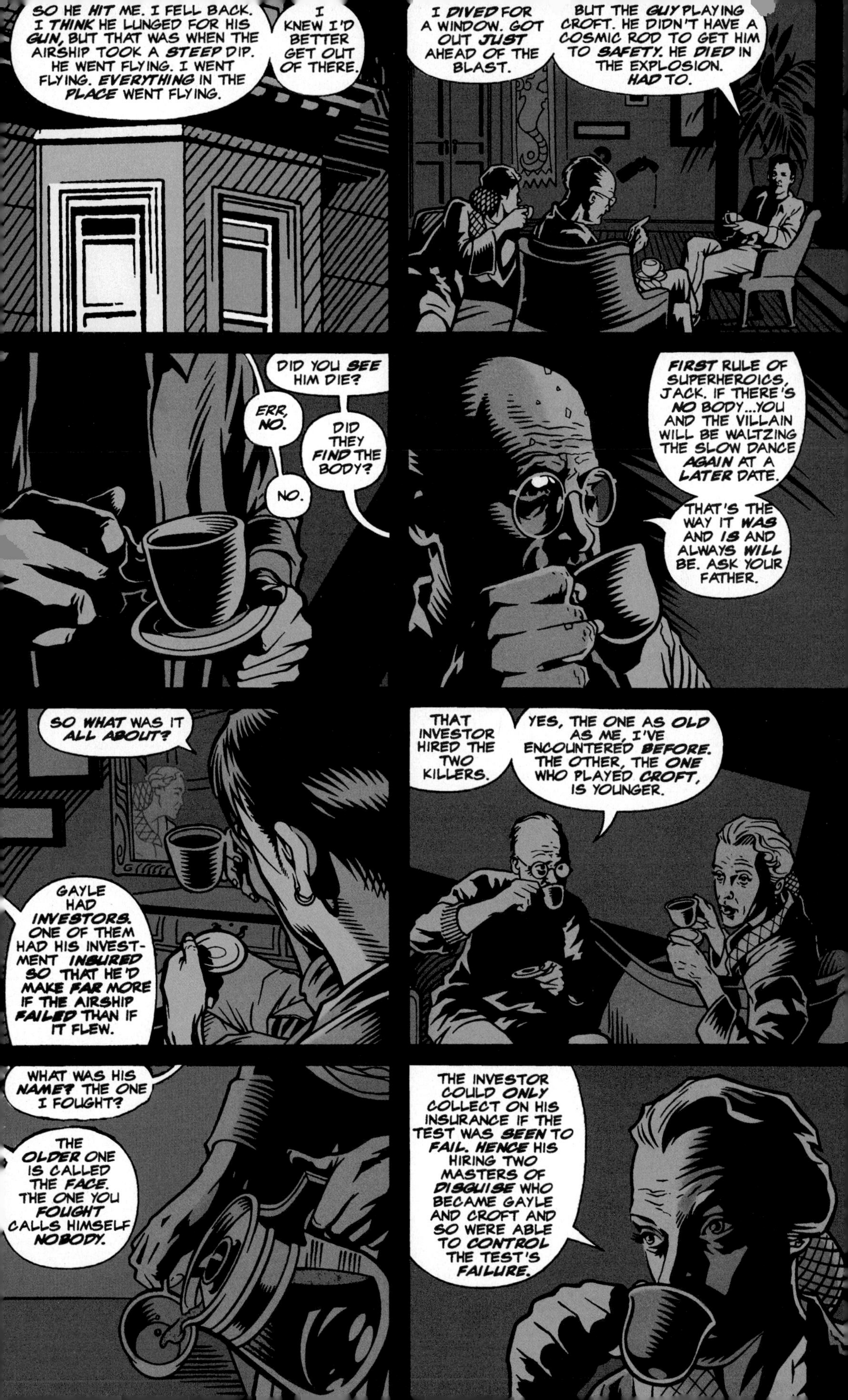
SO HE HIT ME. I FELL BACK. I THINK HE LUNGED FOR HIS GUN, BUT THAT WAS WHEN THE AIRSHIP TOOK A STEEP DIP. HE WENT FLYING. I WENT FLYING. EVERYTHING IN THE PLACE WENT FLYING.
I KNEW I'D BETTER GET OUT OF THERE.
I DIVED FOR A WINDOW. GOT OUT JUST AHEAD OF THE BLAST.
BUT THE GUY PLAYING CROFT. HE DIDN'T HAVE A COSMIC ROD TO GET HIM TO SAFETY. HE DIED IN THE EXPLOSION. HAD TO.
DID YOU SEE HIM DIE?
ERR, NO.
DID THEY FIND THE BODY?
NO.
FIRST RULE OF SUPERHEROICS, JACK. IF THERE'S NO BODY...YOU AND THE VILLAIN WILL BE WALTZING THE SLOW DANCE AGAIN AT A LATER DATE.
THAT'S THE WAY IT WAS AND IS AND ALWAYS WILL BE. ASK YOUR FATHER.
SO WHAT WAS IT ALL ABOUT?
GAYLE HAD INVESTORS. ONE OF THEM HAD HIS INVESTMENT INSURED SO THAT HE'D MAKE FAR MORE IF THE AIRSHIP FAILED THAN IF IT FLEW.
THAT INVESTOR HIRED THE TWO KILLERS.
YES, THE ONE AS OLD AS ME, I'VE ENCOUNTERED BEFORE. THE OTHER, THE ONE WHO PLAYED CROFT, IS YOUNGER.
WHAT WAS HIS NAME? THE ONE I FOUGHT?
THE OLDER ONE IS CALLED THE FACE. THE ONE YOU FOUGHT CALLS HIMSELF NOBODY.
THE INVESTOR COULD ONLY COLLECT ON HIS INSURANCE IF THE TEST WAS SEEN TO FAIL. HENCE HIS HIRING TWO MASTERS OF DISGUISE WHO BECAME GAYLE AND CROFT AND SO WERE ABLE TO CONTROL THE TEST'S FAILURE.

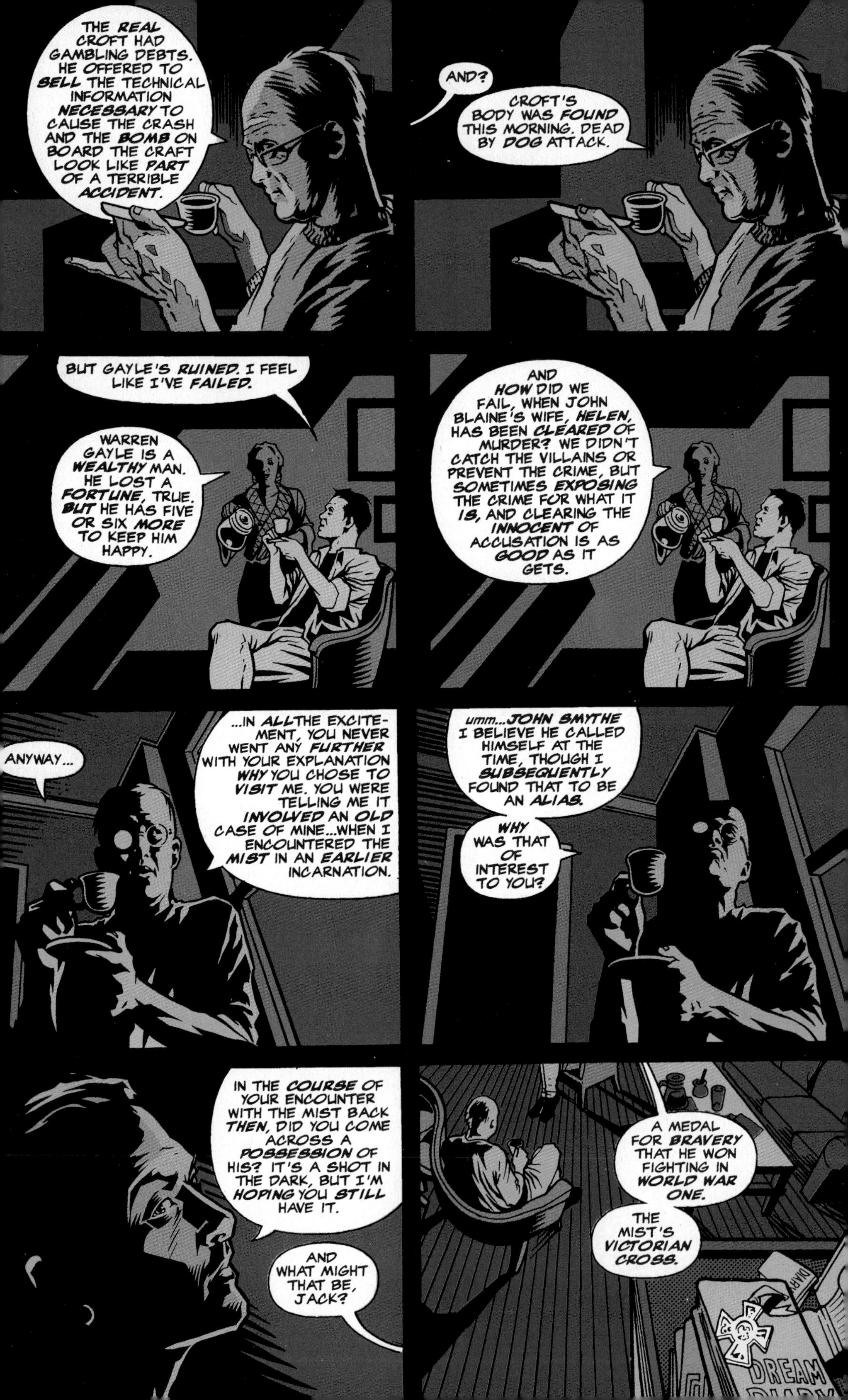
THE REAL CROFT HAD GAMBLING DEBTS. HE OFFERED TO SELL THE TECHNICAL INFORMATION NECESSARY TO CAUSE THE CRASH AND THE BOMB ON BOARD THE CRAFT LOOK LIKE PART OF A TERRIBLE ACCIDENT.
AND?
CROFT'S BODY WAS FOUND THIS MORNING. DEAD BY DOG ATTACK.
BUT GAYLE'S RUINED. I FEEL LIKE I'VE FAILED.
WARREN GAYLE IS A WEALTHY MAN. HE LOST A FORTUNE, TRUE. BUT HE HAS FIVE OR SIX MORE TO KEEP HIM HAPPY.
AND HOW DID WE FAIL, WHEN JOHN BLAINE'S WIFE, HELEN, HAS BEEN CLEARED OF MURDER? WE DIDN'T CATCH THE VILLAINS OR PREVENT THE CRIME, BUT SOMETIMES EXPOSING THE CRIME FOR WHAT IT IS, AND CLEARING THE INNOCENT OF ACCUSATION IS AS GOOD AS IT GETS.
ANYWAY...
...IN ALL THE EXCITEMENT, YOU NEVER WENT ANY FURTHER WITH YOUR EXPLANATION WHY YOU CHOSE TO VISIT ME. YOU WERE TELLING ME IT INVOLVED AN OLD CASE OF MINE...WHEN I ENCOUNTERED THE MIST IN AN EARLIER INCARNATION.
umm...JOHN SMYTHE I BELIEVE HE CALLED HIMSELF AT THE TIME, THOUGH I SUBSEQUENTLY FOUND THAT TO BE AN ALIAS.
WHY WAS THAT OF INTEREST TO YOU?
IN THE COURSE OF YOUR ENCOUNTER WITH THE MIST BACK THEN, DID YOU COME ACROSS A POSSESSION OF HIS? IT'S A SHOT IN THE DARK, BUT I'M HOPING YOU STILL HAVE IT.
AND WHAT MIGHT THAT BE, JACK?
A MEDAL FOR BRAVERY THAT HE WON FIGHTING IN WORLD WAR ONE.
THE MIST'S VICTORIAN CROSS.
DREAM

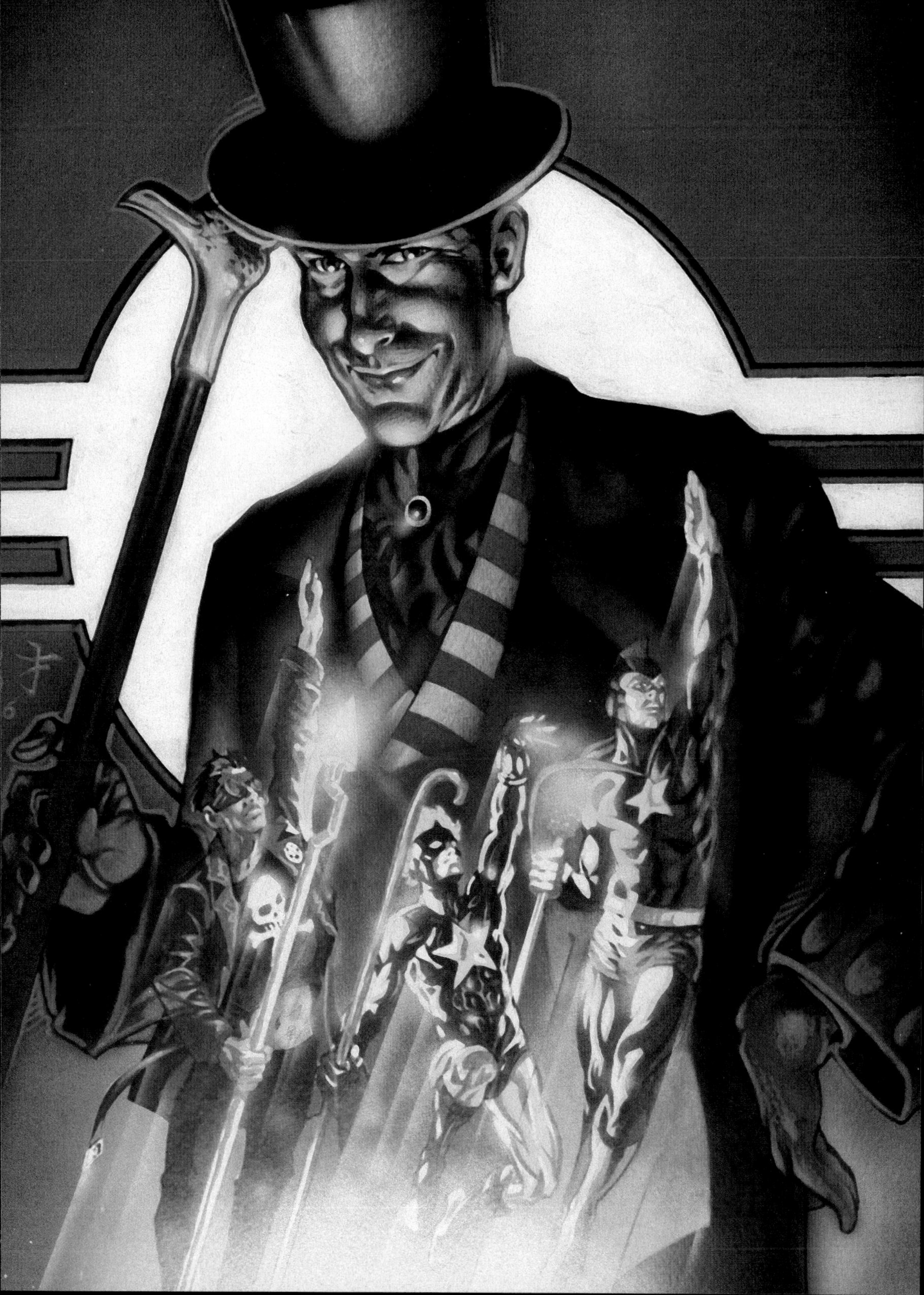

EARTH IS DEAD.

Those who once might have called it home are long scattered

to the endless stars.

But in that scattering, on a thousand different worlds, by a thousand different ways...

Earth's greatest legends live on.

LEGENDS OF THE DEAD EARTH.

STARMAN ANNUAL #1

Cover by Tony Harris & Craig Hamilton

Written by James Robinson

Art by Craig Hamilton & Ray Snyder (pgs. 211-213, 229-230, 246-248)

Bret Blevins (pgs. 214-228) and J.H. Williams III & Mick Gray (pgs. 231-245)

with colors by Kevin Somers

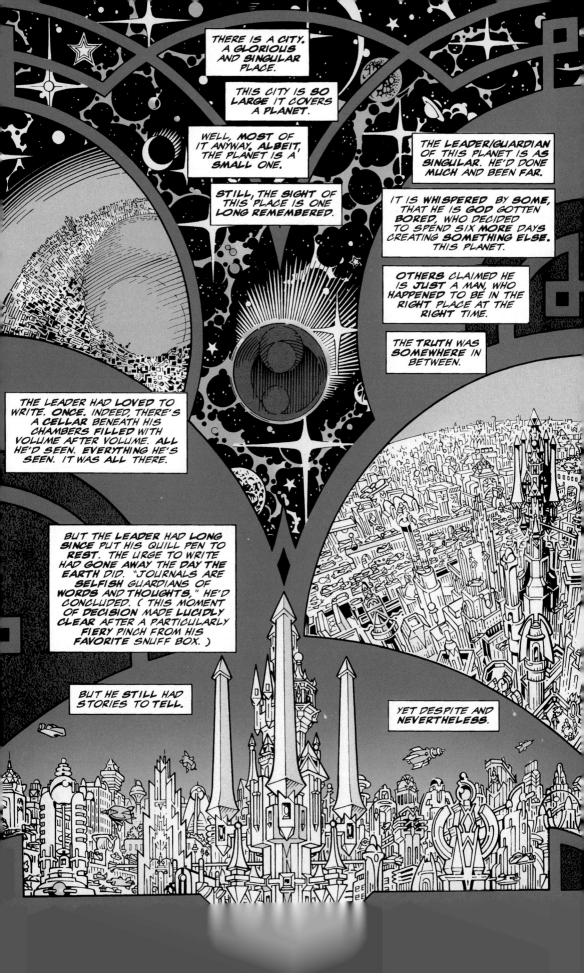

THERE IS A CITY. A GLORIOUS AND SINGULAR PLACE.

THIS CITY IS SO LARGE IT COVERS A PLANET.

WELL, MOST OF IT ANYWAY. ALBEIT, THE PLANET IS A SMALL ONE.

STILL, THE SIGHT OF THIS PLACE IS ONE LONG REMEMBERED.

THE LEADER/GUARDIAN OF THIS PLANET IS AS SINGULAR. HE'D DONE MUCH AND BEEN FAR.

IT IS WHISPERED BY SOME, THAT HE IS GOD GOTTEN BORED, WHO DECIDED TO SPEND SIX MORE DAYS CREATING SOMETHING ELSE. THIS PLANET.

OTHERS CLAIMED HE IS JUST A MAN, WHO HAPPENED TO BE IN THE RIGHT PLACE AT THE RIGHT TIME.

THE TRUTH WAS SOMEWHERE IN BETWEEN.

THE LEADER HAD LOVED TO WRITE. ONCE. INDEED, THERE'S A CELLAR BENEATH HIS CHAMBERS FILLED WITH VOLUME AFTER VOLUME. ALL HE'D SEEN. EVERYTHING HE'S SEEN. IT WAS ALL THERE.

BUT THE LEADER HAD LONG SINCE PUT HIS QUILL PEN TO REST. THE URGE TO WRITE HAD GONE AWAY THE DAY THE EARTH DID. "JOURNALS ARE SELFISH GUARDIANS OF WORDS AND THOUGHTS," HE'D CONCLUDED. (THIS MOMENT OF DECISION MADE LUCIDLY CLEAR AFTER A PARTICULARLY FIERY PINCH FROM HIS FAVORITE SNUFF BOX.)

BUT HE STILL HAD STORIES TO TELL.

YET DESPITE AND NEVERTHELESS.

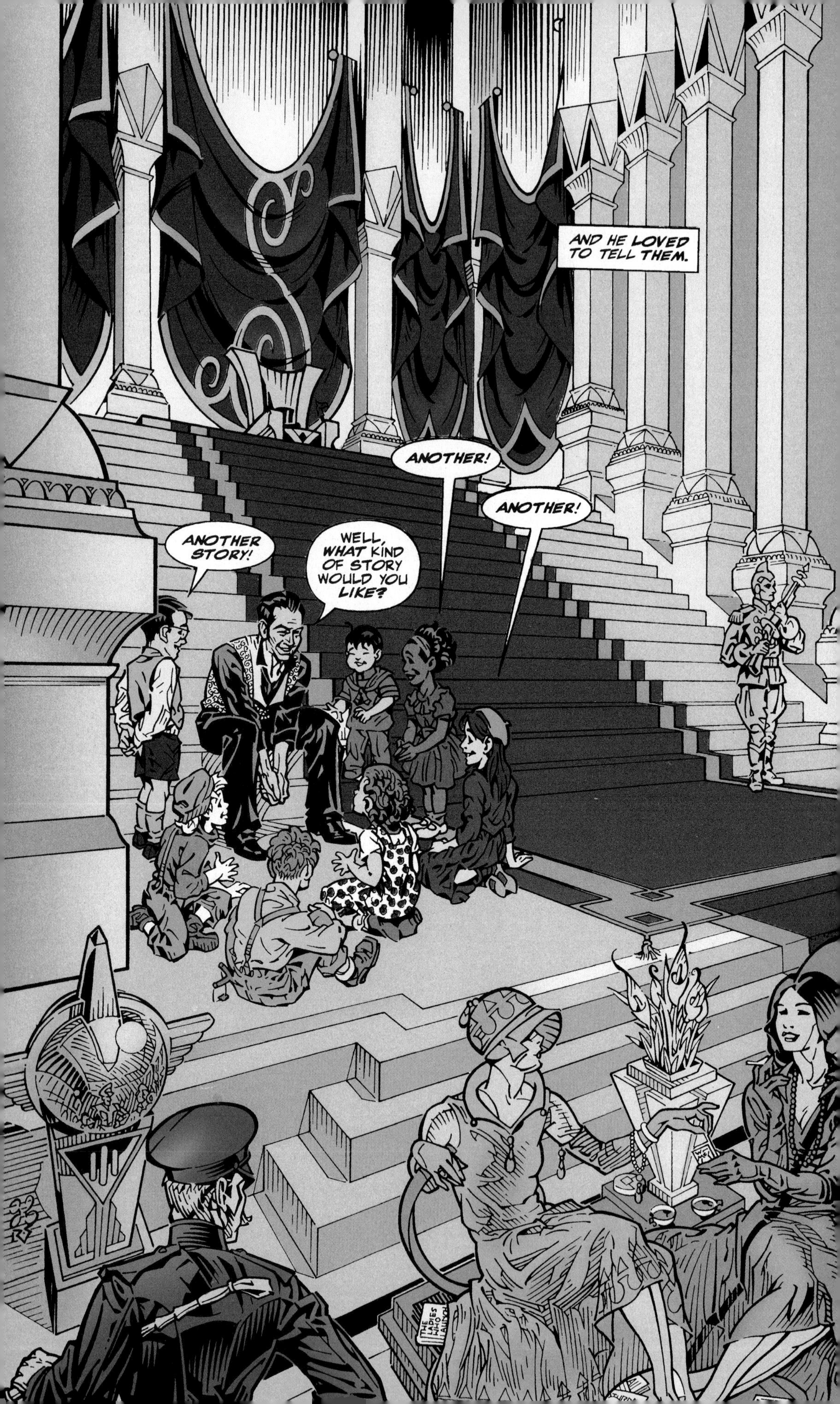
AND HE LOVED TO TELL THEM.
ANOTHER STORY!
WELL, WHAT KIND OF STORY WOULD YOU LIKE?
ANOTHER!
ANOTHER!

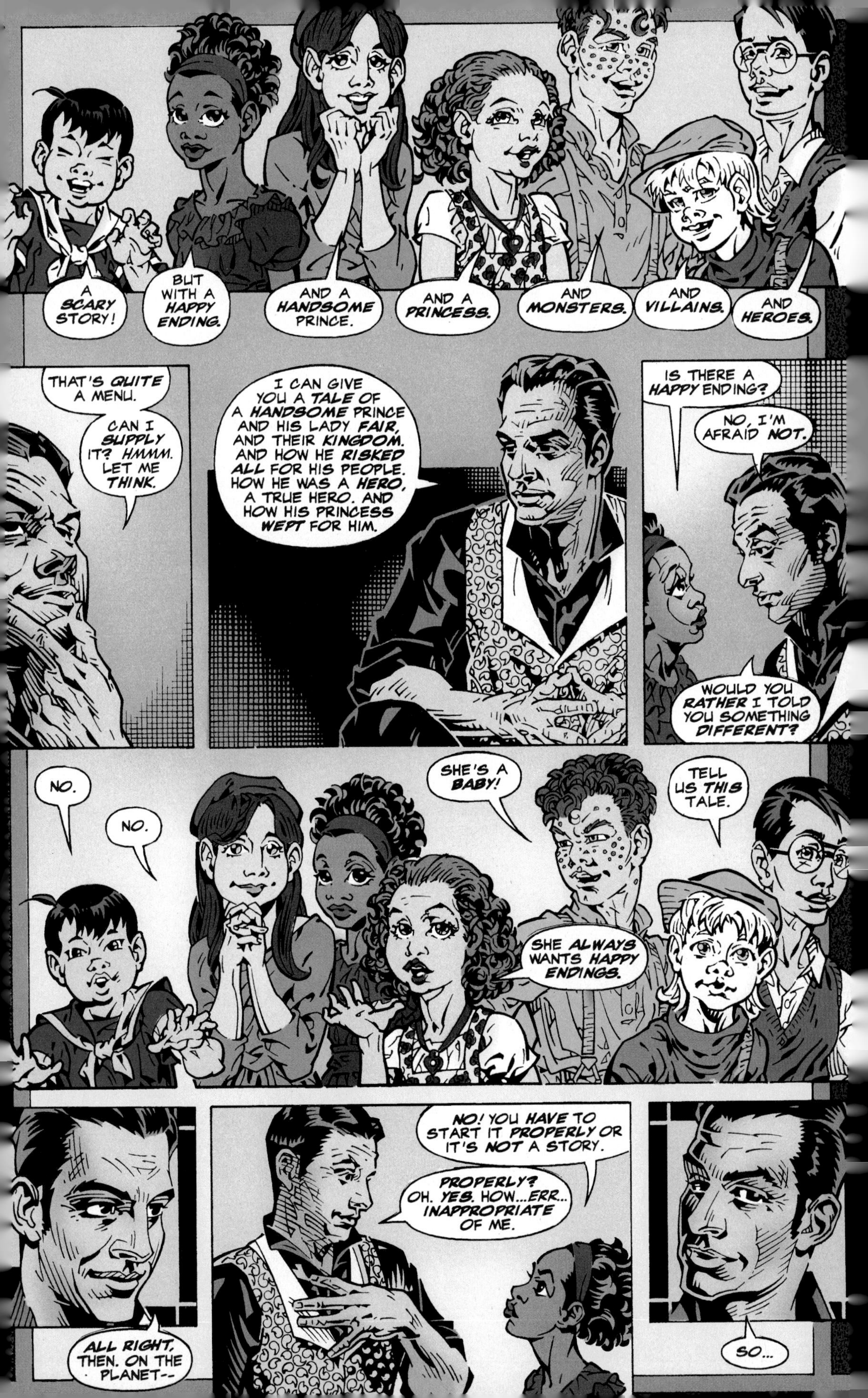

A SCARY STORY!
BUT WITH A HAPPY ENDING.
AND A HANDSOME PRINCE.
AND A PRINCESS.
AND MONSTERS.
AND VILLAINS.
AND HEROES.
THAT'S QUITE A MENU.
CAN I SUPPLY IT? HMMM. LET ME THINK.
I CAN GIVE YOU A TALE OF A HANDSOME PRINCE AND HIS LADY FAIR, AND THEIR KINGDOM. AND HOW HE RISKED ALL FOR HIS PEOPLE. HOW HE WAS A HERO, A TRUE HERO. AND HOW HIS PRINCESS WEPT FOR HIM.
IS THERE A HAPPY ENDING?
NO, I'M AFRAID NOT.
WOULD YOU RATHER I TOLD YOU SOMETHING DIFFERENT?
NO.
NO.
SHE'S A BABY!
SHE ALWAYS WANTS HAPPY ENDINGS.
TELL US THIS TALE.
ALL RIGHT, THEN. ON THE PLANET--
NO! YOU HAVE TO START IT PROPERLY OR IT'S NOT A STORY.
PROPERLY? OH. YES. HOW...ERR... INAPPROPRIATE OF ME.
SO...

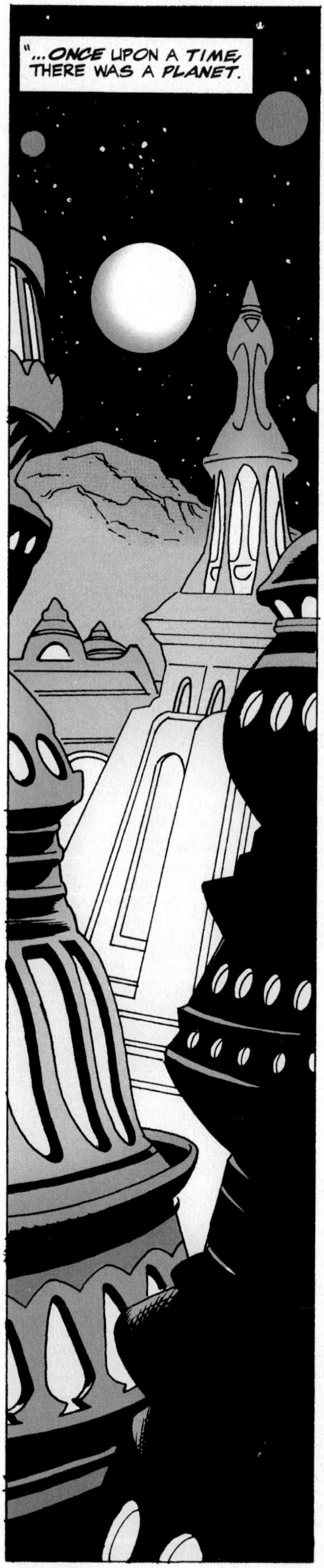
"...ONCE UPON A TIME, THERE WAS A PLANET.

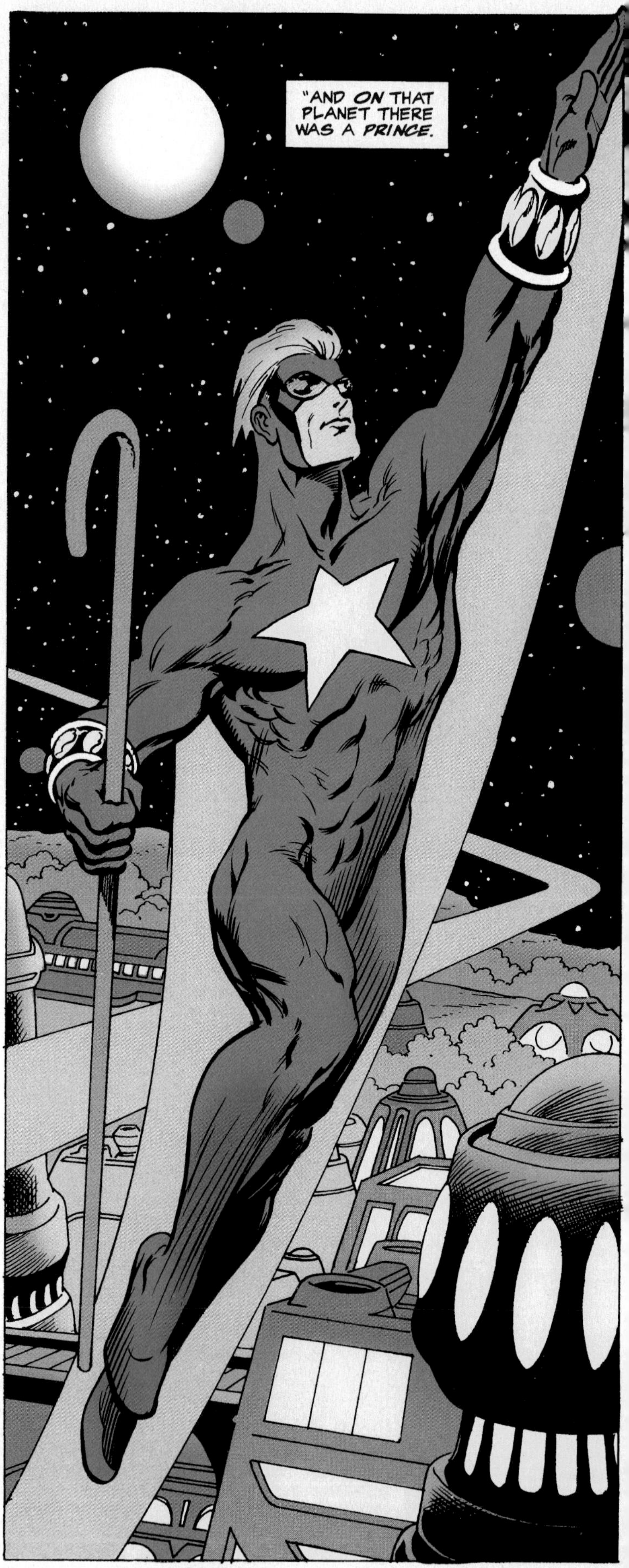
"AND ON THAT PLANET THERE WAS A PRINCE.

"HIS HAD BEEN THE CAPITAL PLANET OF AN *EMPIRE* OF SOME *TWENTY-FOUR* INHABITED ORBS.

"AND HIS TIME AS *HEIR* TO THAT EMPIRE WAS ONE OF *FROLIC.* FOP AND *DANDY* WOULD HAVE BEEN *WORDS* TO DESCRIBE HIM THEN.

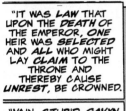

"IT WAS *LAW* THAT UPON THE *DEATH* OF THE EMPEROR, *ONE* HEIR WAS *SELECTED* AND *ALL* WHO MIGHT *LAY CLAIM* TO THE THRONE AND THEREBY CAUSE *UNREST,* BE CROWNED.

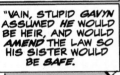

"VAIN, STUPID *GAVYN* ASSUMED *HE* WOULD BE HEIR, AND WOULD *AMEND* THE LAW SO HIS SISTER WOULD BE *SAFE.*

"BUT HIS SISTER WAS ELECTED. *SILLY* LITTLE THING THAT SHE *WAS.* GREEDY FOR THE POWER THAT WAS *HERS.*

"*FEARING* CHANGE, SHE *UPHELD* THE LAW.

"GAVYN WAS *THROWN* INTO SPACE.

"HE *DIED*...

"FOR AN *INSTANT.*

"BEFORE THE *BEING* WHO WOULD BE HIS MAGE, *Mn'TORR* BY NAME, *RETRIEVED* HIM FROM THE VOID.

"GAVYN LEARNED HE WAS A *FREAK.* THAT HE HAD A *POWER* WITHIN HIM. *GREAT POWER* THAT HE DREW FROM THE *STARS.*

"IT'S A *COINCIDENCE* Mn'TORR SOUNDS LIKE THE EARTH WORD *MENTOR,* YET THIS FELLOW DID *INDEED* LIVE UP TO THAT NAME.

"HE *TRAINED* GAVYN. *HARDENED* HIM. MADE HIM *WISE.*

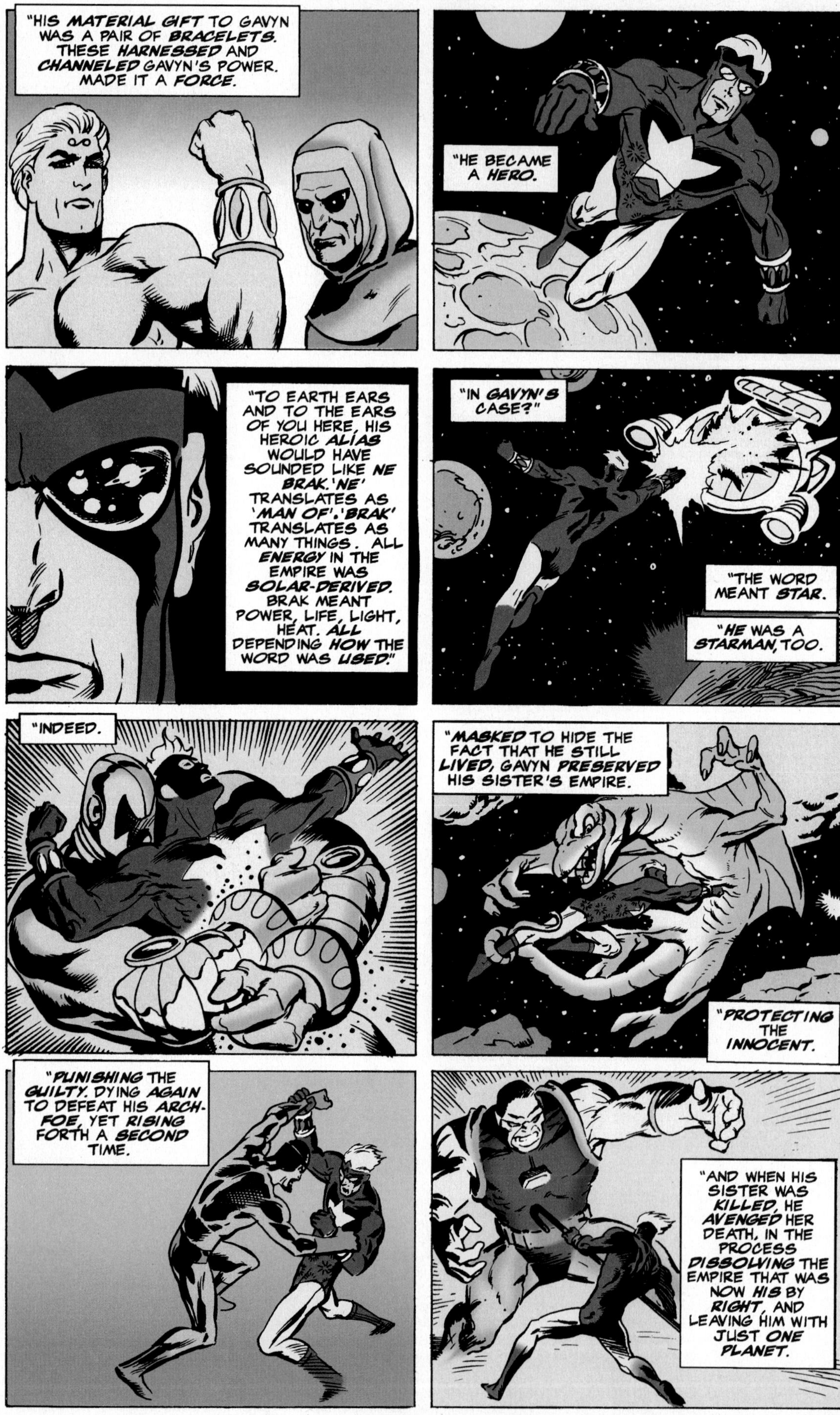
"HIS MATERIAL GIFT TO GAVYN WAS A PAIR OF BRACELETS. THESE HARNESSED AND CHANNELED GAVYN'S POWER. MADE IT A FORCE.
"HE BECAME A HERO.
"TO EARTH EARS AND TO THE EARS OF YOU HERE, HIS HEROIC ALIAS WOULD HAVE SOUNDED LIKE NE BRAK. 'NE' TRANSLATES AS 'MAN OF'. 'BRAK' TRANSLATES AS MANY THINGS. ALL ENERGY IN THE EMPIRE WAS SOLAR-DERIVED. BRAK MEANT POWER, LIFE, LIGHT, HEAT. ALL DEPENDING HOW THE WORD WAS USED."
"IN GAVYN'S CASE?"
"THE WORD MEANT STAR.
"HE WAS A STARMAN, TOO.
"INDEED.
"MASKED TO HIDE THE FACT THAT HE STILL LIVED, GAVYN PRESERVED HIS SISTER'S EMPIRE.
"PROTECTING THE INNOCENT.
"PUNISHING THE GUILTY. DYING AGAIN TO DEFEAT HIS ARCH-FOE, YET RISING FORTH A SECOND TIME.
"AND WHEN HIS SISTER WAS KILLED, HE AVENGED HER DEATH, IN THE PROCESS DISSOLVING THE EMPIRE THAT WAS NOW HIS BY RIGHT, AND LEAVING HIM WITH JUST ONE PLANET.

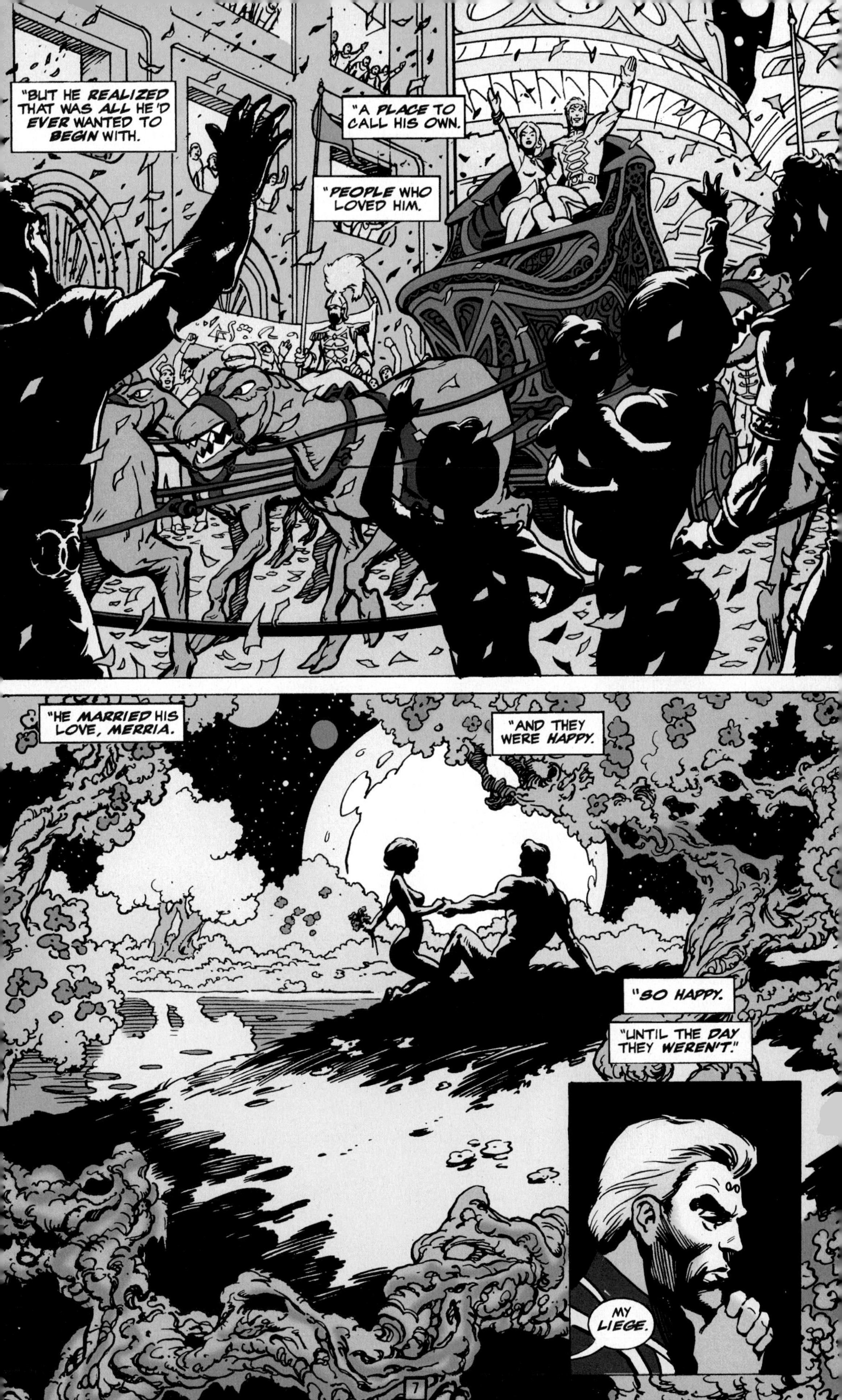
"BUT HE REALIZED THAT WAS ALL HE'D EVER WANTED TO BEGIN WITH.
"A PLACE TO CALL HIS OWN.
"PEOPLE WHO LOVED HIM.
"HE MARRIED HIS LOVE, MERRIA.
"AND THEY WERE HAPPY.
"SO HAPPY.
"UNTIL THE DAY THEY WEREN'T."
MY LIEGE.

I BRING *NEWS.* NOT GOOD, ALAS.

"*JEDIAH RIKANE* WAS GAVYN'S *CLOSEST* AIDE. IT HAD BEEN *LONG* SINCE HIS FRIEND'S *FACE* HAD SEEMED SO *TROUBLED.*"

THERE IS A *THREAT* TO US.

THREAT? TO OUR *PLANET?*

TO EVERY *PLANET.*

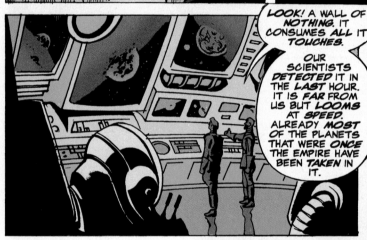

LOOK! A WALL OF *NOTHING.* IT CONSUMES ALL IT *TOUCHES.*

OUR SCIENTISTS *DETECTED* IT IN THE *LAST HOUR.* IT IS FAR FROM US BUT *LOOMS* AT *SPEED.* ALREADY *MOST* OF THE PLANETS THAT WERE *ONCE* THE EMPIRE HAVE BEEN *TAKEN* IN IT.

HOW LONG UNTIL IT IS *UPON* US?

THREE DAYS AT BEST.

AT *BEST?*

WHAT WOULD YOU *SUGGEST,* OLD FRIEND?

THAT WE *SAVE* THE *ROYAL FAMILY.* EVACUATE *YOU* AND THE *LADY MERRIA.*

NO.

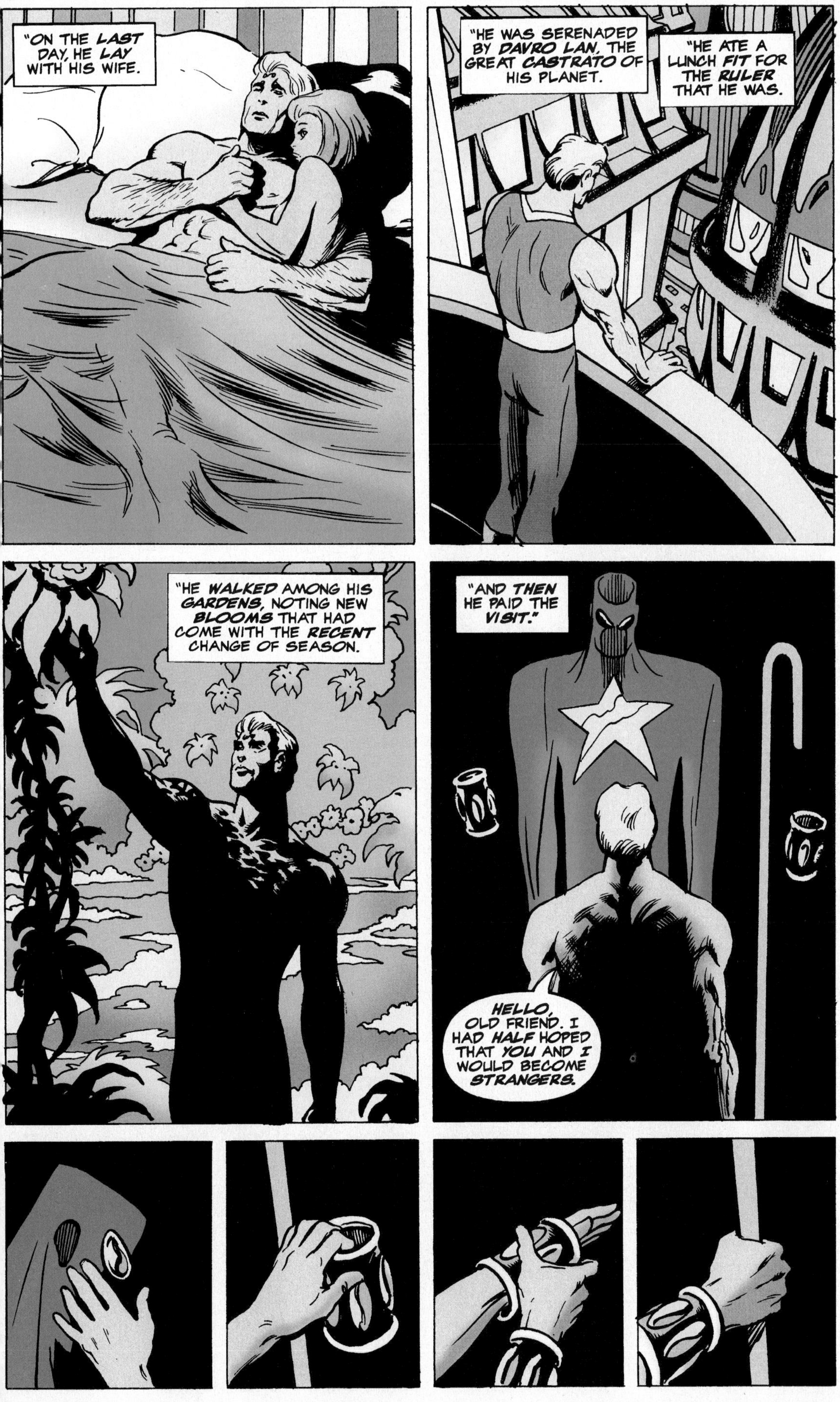
"ON THE LAST DAY, HE LAY WITH HIS WIFE.
"HE WAS SERENADED BY DAVRO LAN, THE GREAT CASTRATO OF HIS PLANET.
"HE ATE A LUNCH FIT FOR THE RULER THAT HE WAS.
"HE WALKED AMONG HIS GARDENS, NOTING NEW BLOOMS THAT HAD COME WITH THE RECENT CHANGE OF SEASON.
"AND THEN HE PAID THE VISIT."
HELLO, OLD FRIEND. I HAD HALF HOPED THAT YOU AND I WOULD BECOME STRANGERS.

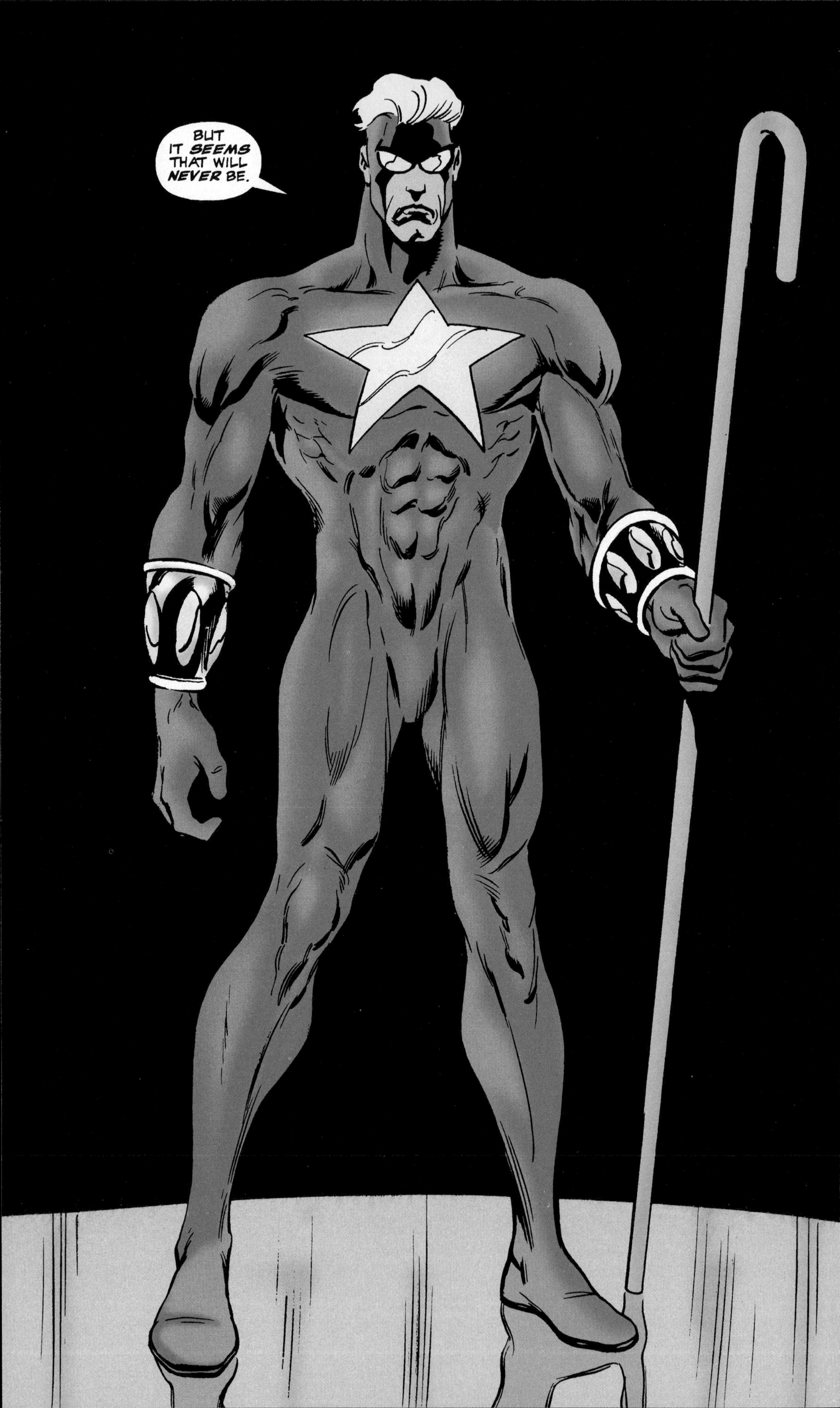
BUT IT SEEMS THAT WILL NEVER BE.

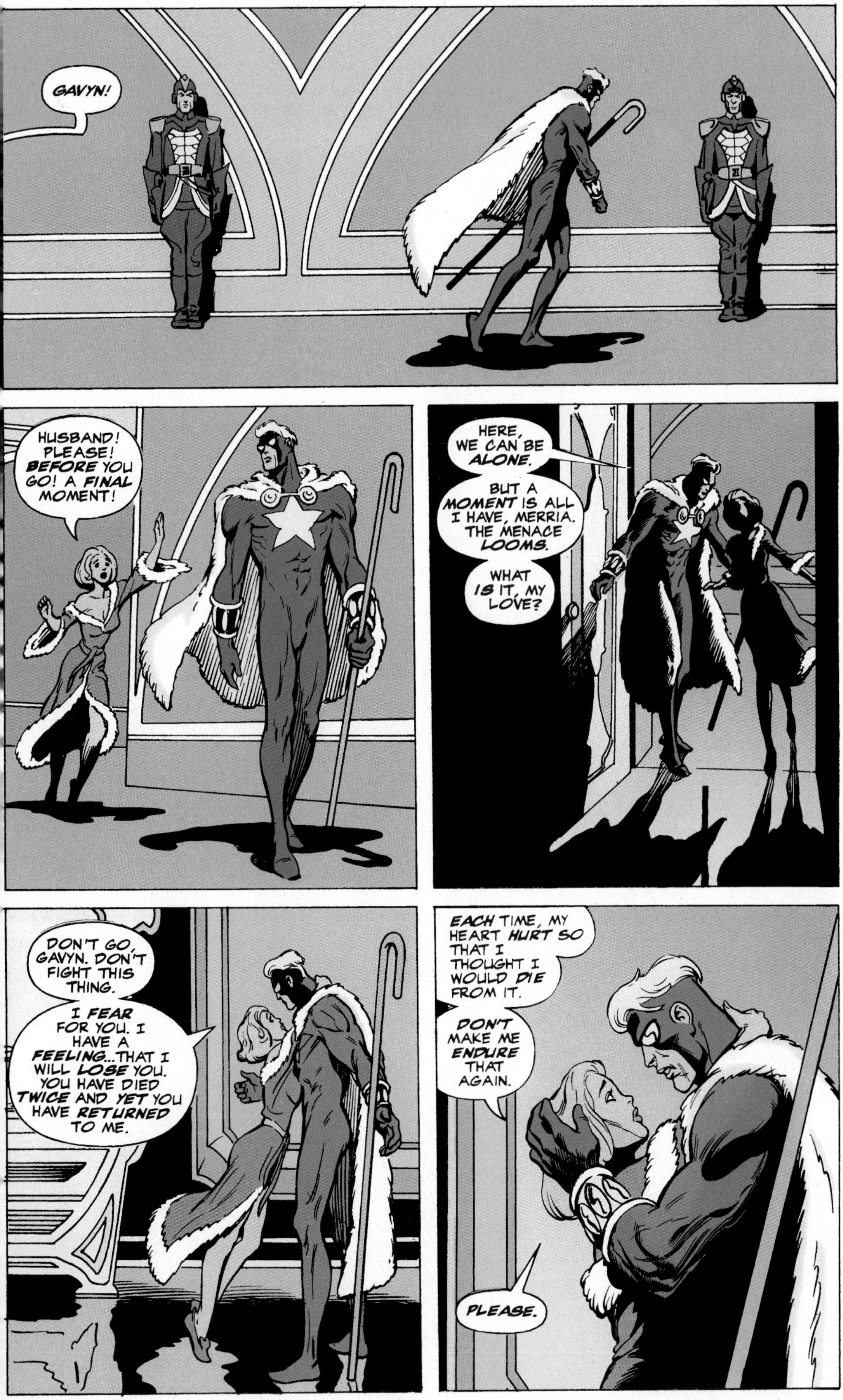
GAVYN!
HUSBAND! PLEASE! BEFORE YOU GO! A FINAL MOMENT!
HERE, WE CAN BE ALONE.
BUT A MOMENT IS ALL I HAVE, MERRIA. THE MENACE LOOMS.
WHAT IS IT, MY LOVE?
DON'T GO, GAVYN. DON'T FIGHT THIS THING.
I FEAR FOR YOU. I HAVE A FEELING...THAT I WILL LOSE YOU. YOU HAVE DIED TWICE AND YET YOU HAVE RETURNED TO ME.
EACH TIME, MY HEART HURT SO THAT I THOUGHT I WOULD DIE FROM IT.
DON'T MAKE ME ENDURE THAT AGAIN.
PLEASE.

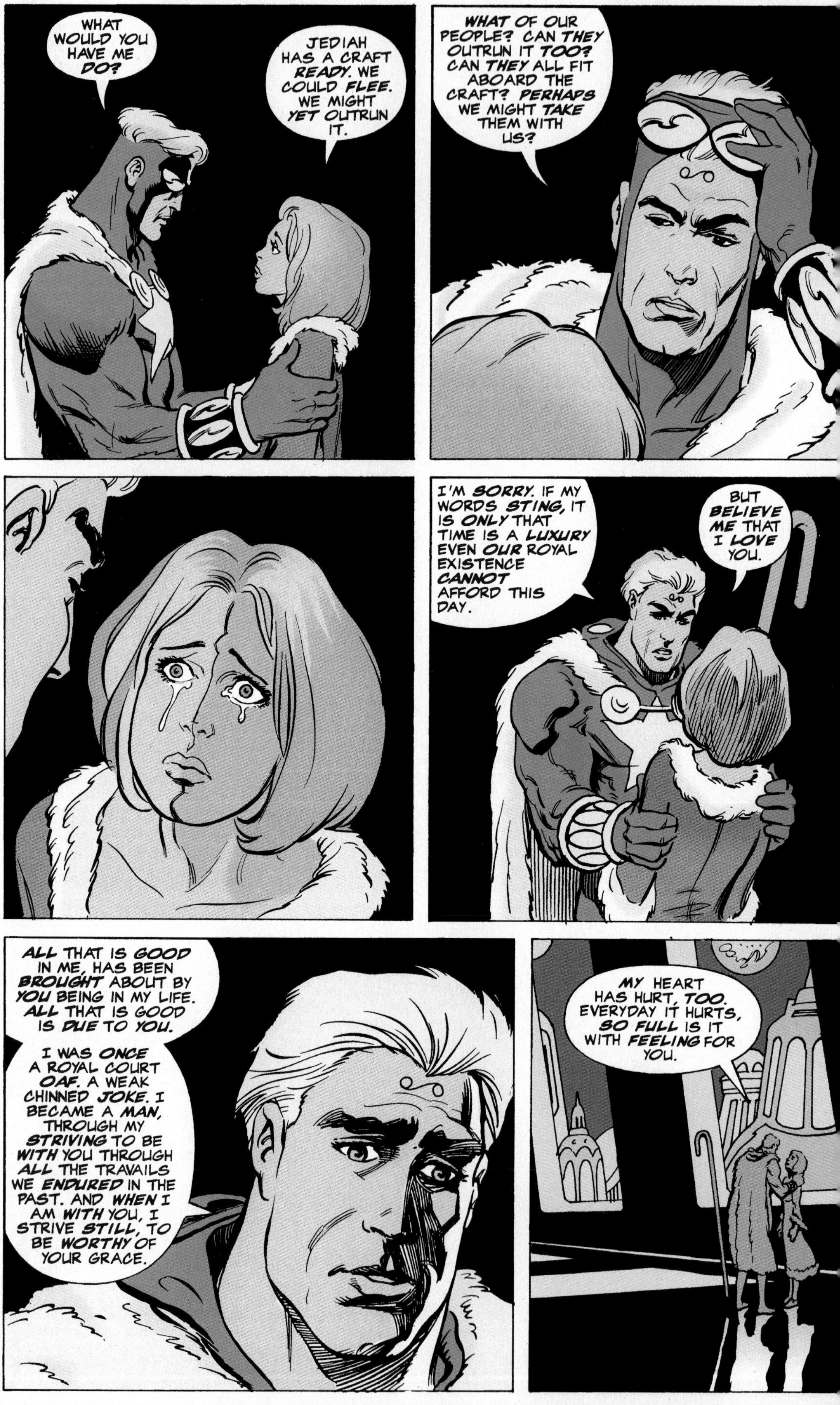
WHAT WOULD YOU HAVE ME DO?
JEDIAH HAS A CRAFT READY. WE COULD FLEE. WE MIGHT YET OUTRUN IT.
WHAT OF OUR PEOPLE? CAN THEY OUTRUN IT TOO? CAN THEY ALL FIT ABOARD THE CRAFT? PERHAPS WE MIGHT TAKE THEM WITH US?
I'M SORRY. IF MY WORDS STING, IT IS ONLY THAT TIME IS A LUXURY EVEN OUR ROYAL EXISTENCE CANNOT AFFORD THIS DAY.
BUT BELIEVE ME THAT I LOVE YOU.
ALL THAT IS GOOD IN ME, HAS BEEN BROUGHT ABOUT BY YOU BEING IN MY LIFE. ALL THAT IS GOOD IS DUE TO YOU.
I WAS ONCE A ROYAL COURT OAF. A WEAK CHINNED JOKE. I BECAME A MAN, THROUGH MY STRIVING TO BE WITH YOU THROUGH ALL THE TRAVAILS WE ENDURED IN THE PAST. AND WHEN I AM WITH YOU, I STRIVE STILL, TO BE WORTHY OF YOUR GRACE.
MY HEART HAS HURT, TOO. EVERYDAY IT HURTS, SO FULL IS IT WITH FEELING FOR YOU.

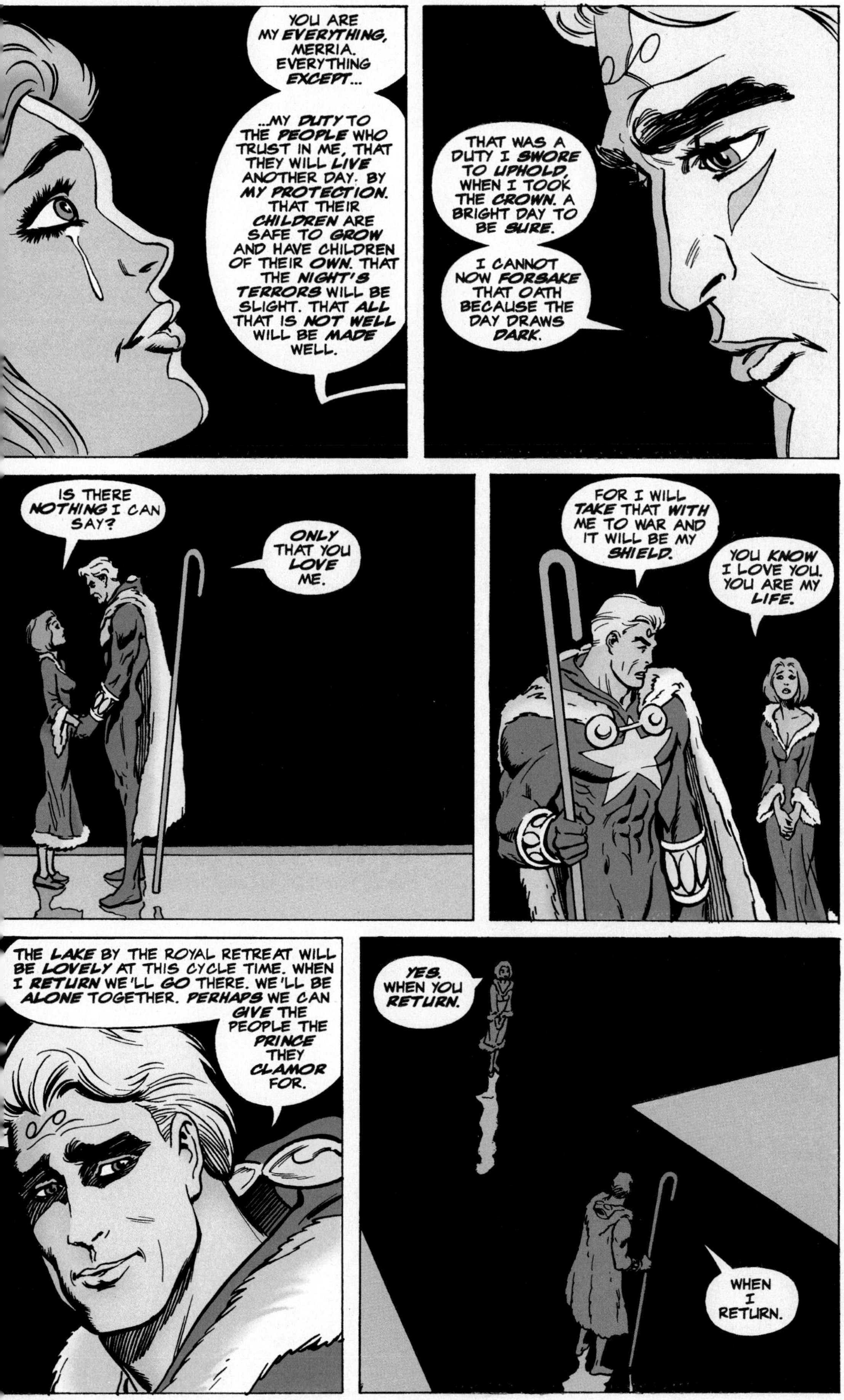

YOU ARE MY EVERYTHING, MERRIA. EVERYTHING EXCEPT...
...MY DUTY TO THE PEOPLE WHO TRUST IN ME, THAT THEY WILL LIVE ANOTHER DAY. BY MY PROTECTION. THAT THEIR CHILDREN ARE SAFE TO GROW AND HAVE CHILDREN OF THEIR OWN. THAT THE NIGHT'S TERRORS WILL BE SLIGHT. THAT ALL THAT IS NOT WELL WILL BE MADE WELL.
THAT WAS A DUTY I SWORE TO UPHOLD, WHEN I TOOK THE CROWN. A BRIGHT DAY TO BE SURE.
I CANNOT NOW FORSAKE THAT OATH BECAUSE THE DAY DRAWS DARK.
IS THERE NOTHING I CAN SAY?
ONLY THAT YOU LOVE ME.
FOR I WILL TAKE THAT WITH ME TO WAR AND IT WILL BE MY SHIELD.
YOU KNOW I LOVE YOU. YOU ARE MY LIFE.
THE LAKE BY THE ROYAL RETREAT WILL BE LOVELY AT THIS CYCLE TIME. WHEN I RETURN WE'LL GO THERE. WE'LL BE ALONE TOGETHER. PERHAPS WE CAN GIVE THE PEOPLE THE PRINCE THEY CLAMOR FOR.
YES. WHEN YOU RETURN.
WHEN I RETURN.

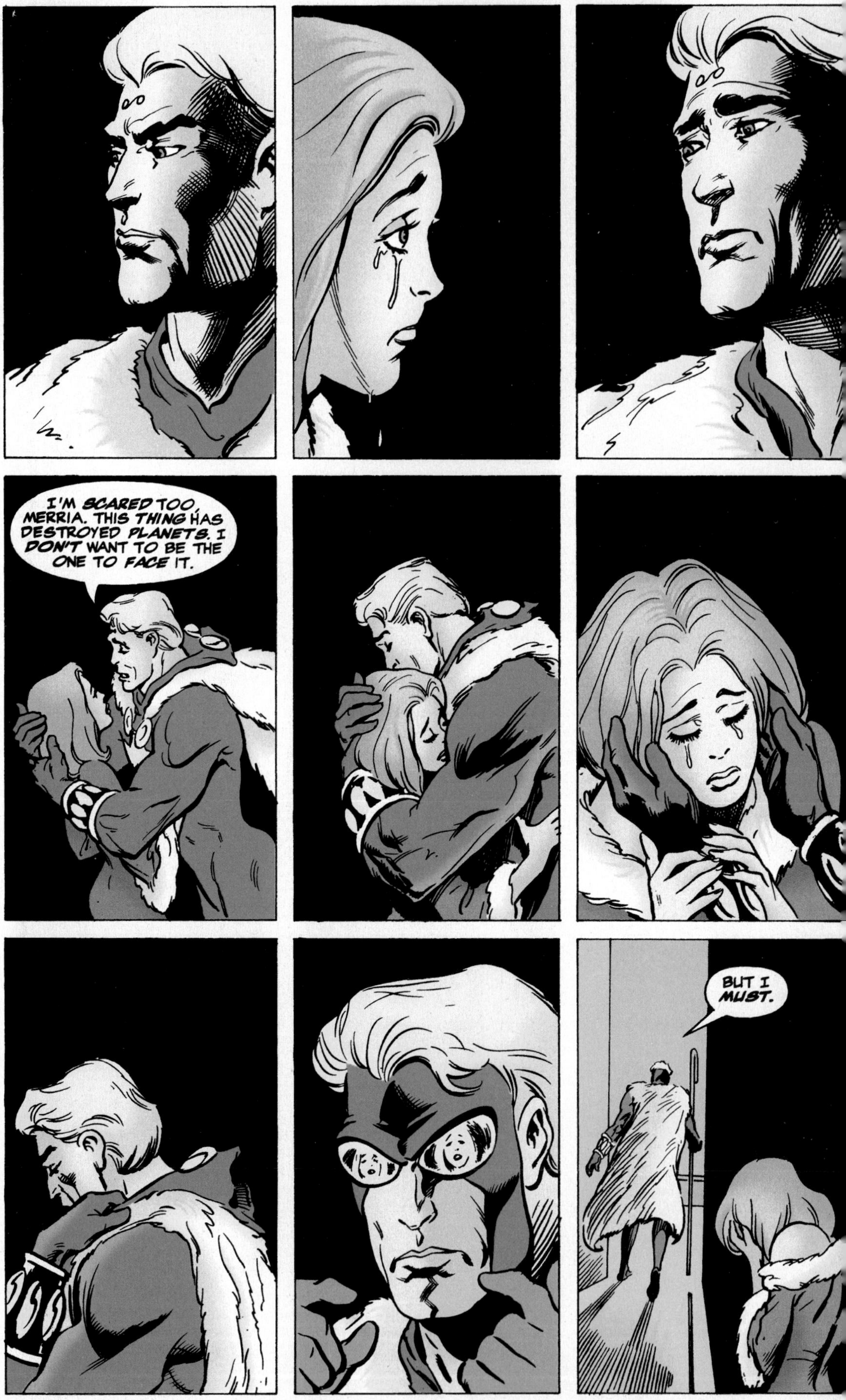
I'M SCARED TOO, MERRIA. THIS THING HAS DESTROYED PLANETS. I DON'T WANT TO BE THE ONE TO FACE IT.
BUT I MUST.

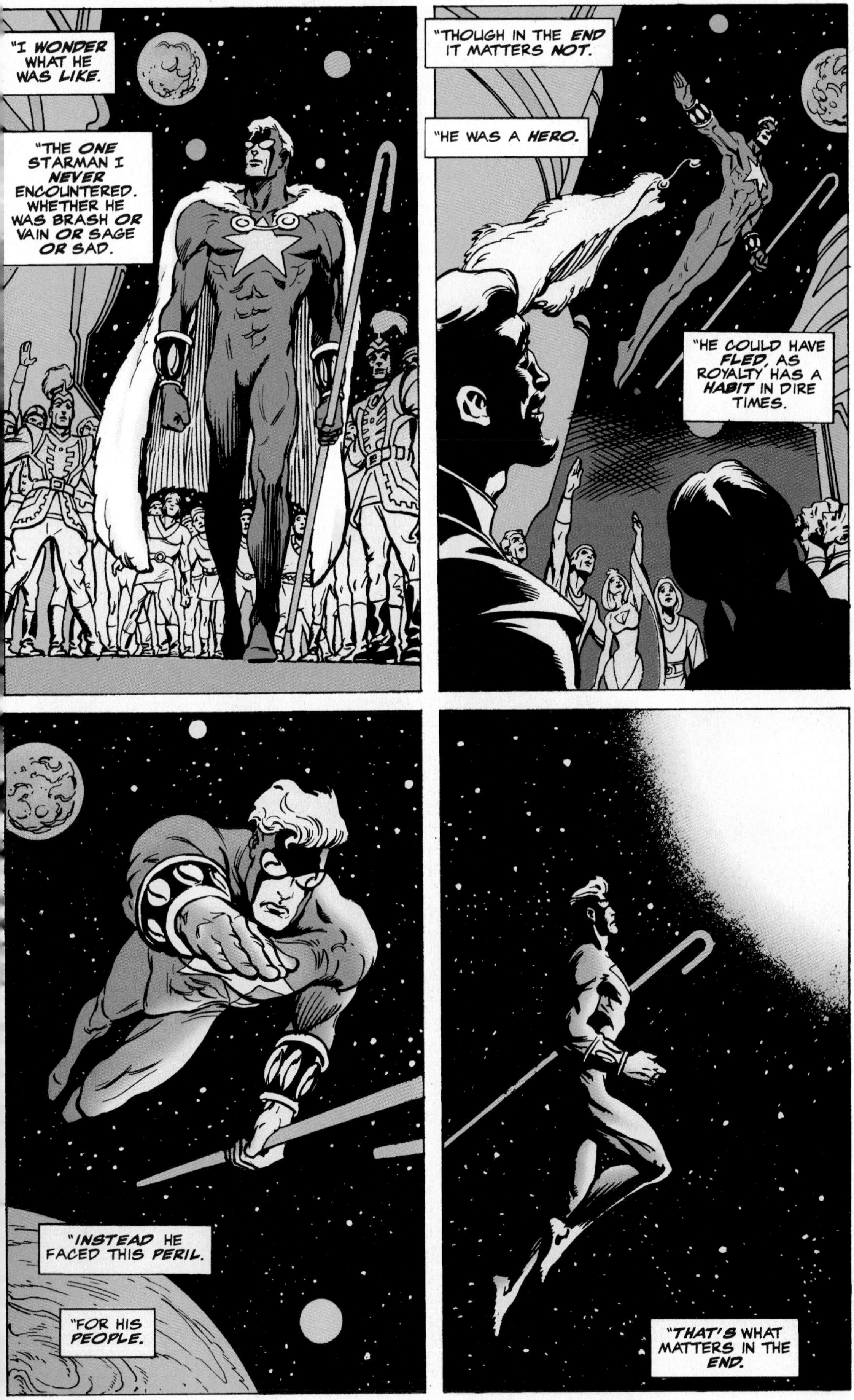
"I WONDER WHAT HE WAS LIKE.
"THE ONE STARMAN I NEVER ENCOUNTERED. WHETHER HE WAS BRASH OR VAIN OR SAGE OR SAD.
"THOUGH IN THE END IT MATTERS NOT.
"HE WAS A HERO.
"HE COULD HAVE FLED, AS ROYALTY HAS A HABIT IN DIRE TIMES.
"INSTEAD HE FACED THIS PERIL.
"FOR HIS PEOPLE.
"THAT'S WHAT MATTERS IN THE END.

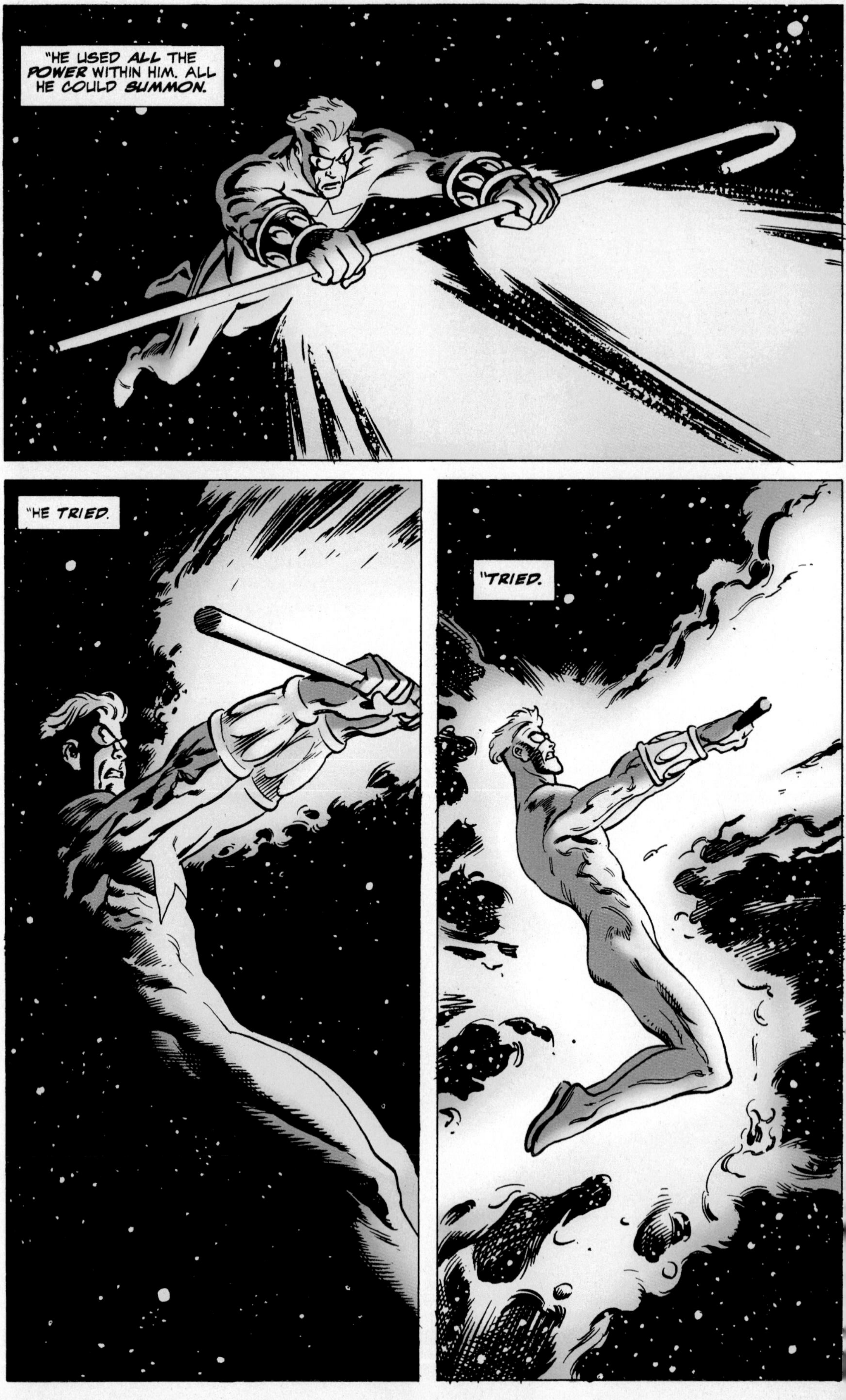
"HE USED ALL THE POWER WITHIN HIM. ALL HE COULD SUMMON.
"HE TRIED.
"TRIED.

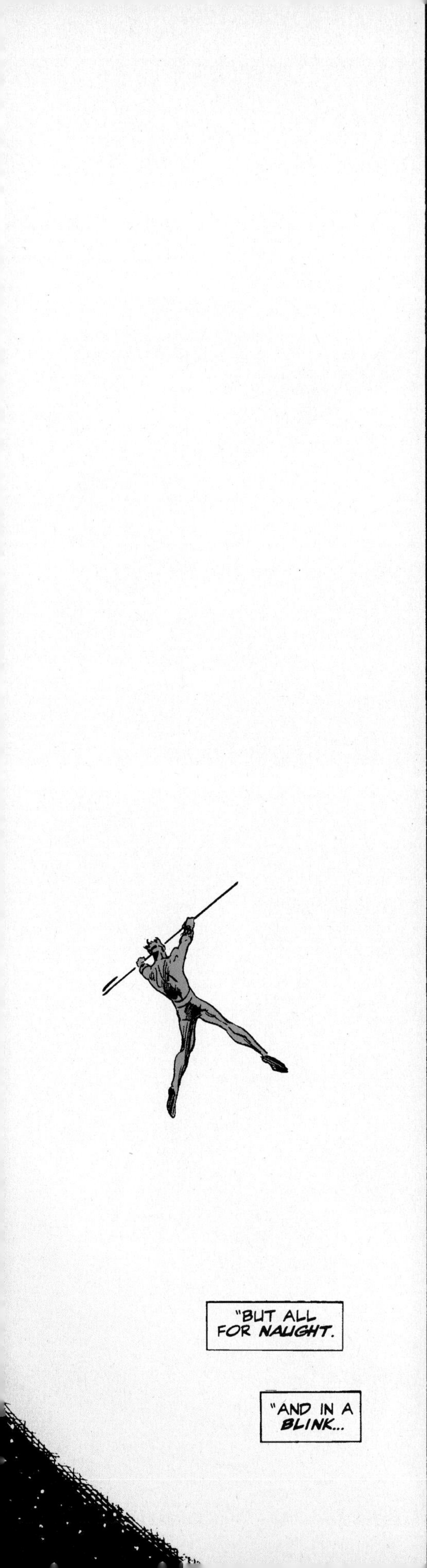
"BUT ALL FOR NAUGHT.
"AND IN A BLINK...
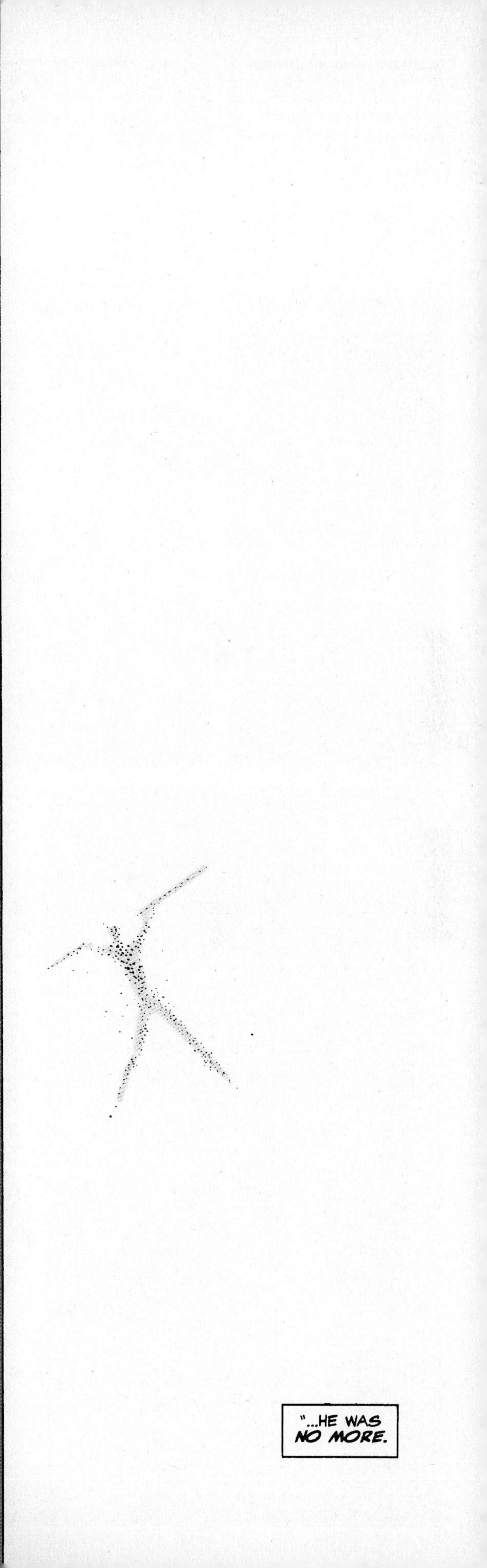
"...HE WAS NO MORE.

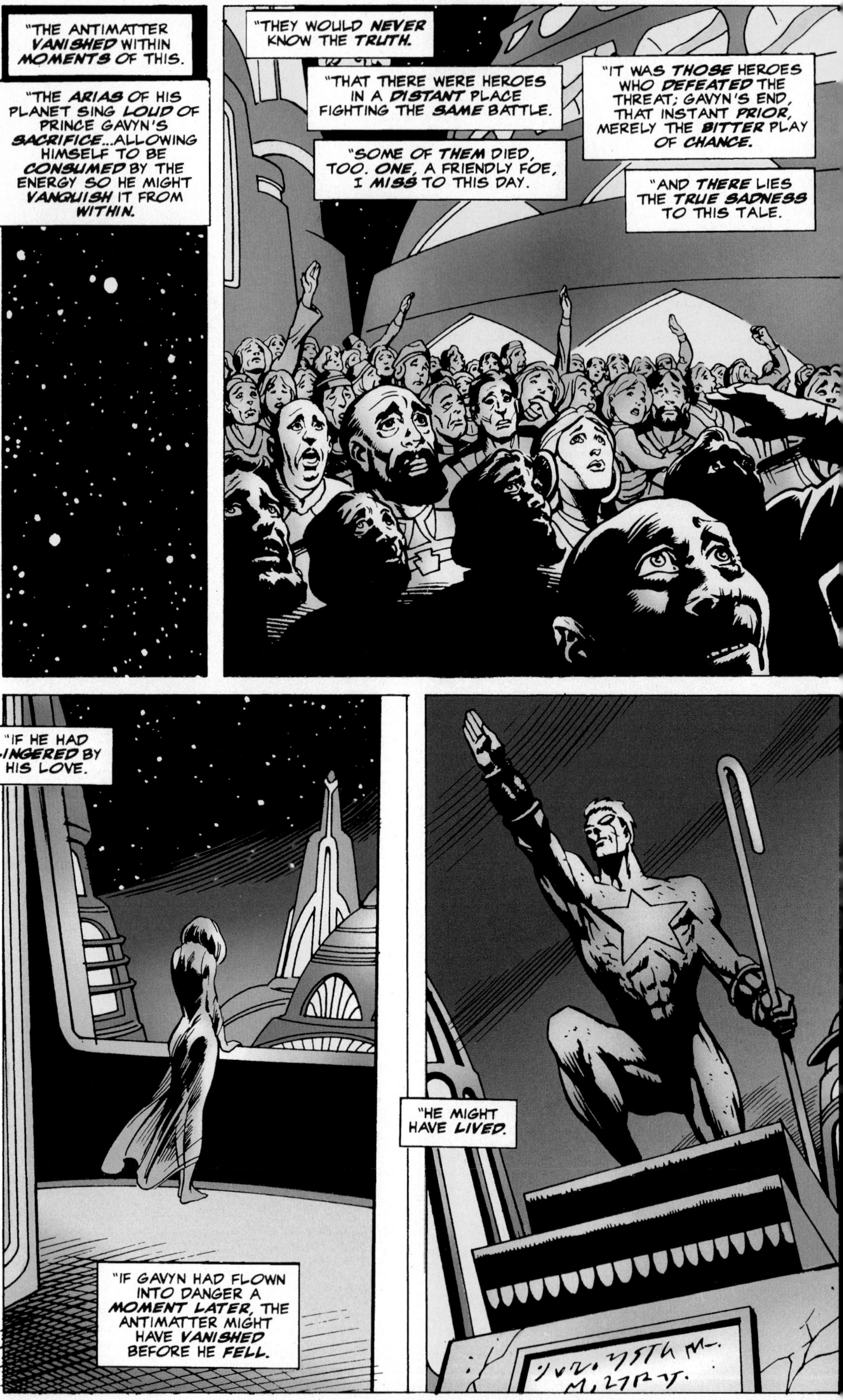
"THE ANTIMATTER VANISHED WITHIN MOMENTS OF THIS.
"THE ARIAS OF HIS PLANET SING LOUD OF PRINCE GAVYN'S SACRIFICE...ALLOWING HIMSELF TO BE CONSUMED BY THE ENERGY SO HE MIGHT VANQUISH IT FROM WITHIN.
"THEY WOULD NEVER KNOW THE TRUTH.
"THAT THERE WERE HEROES IN A DISTANT PLACE FIGHTING THE SAME BATTLE.
"SOME OF THEM DIED, TOO. ONE, A FRIENDLY FOE, I MISS TO THIS DAY.
"IT WAS THOSE HEROES WHO DEFEATED THE THREAT; GAVYN'S END, THAT INSTANT PRIOR, MERELY THE BITTER PLAY OF CHANCE.
"AND THERE LIES THE TRUE SADNESS TO THIS TALE.
"IF HE HAD LINGERED BY HIS LOVE.
"IF GAVYN HAD FLOWN INTO DANGER A MOMENT LATER, THE ANTIMATTER MIGHT HAVE VANISHED BEFORE HE FELL.
"HE MIGHT HAVE LIVED.

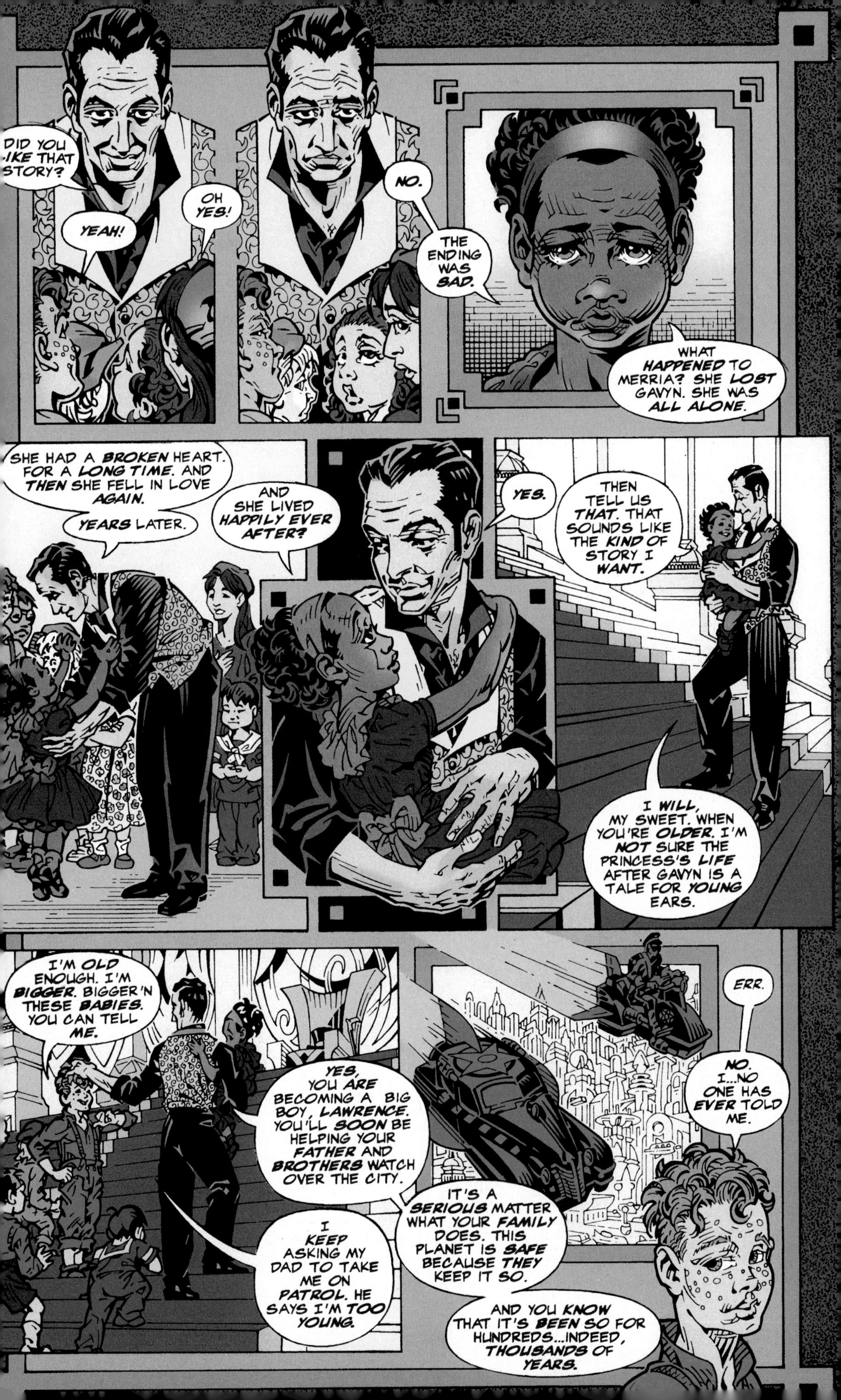

DID YOU LIKE THAT STORY?
YEAH!
OH YES!
NO.
THE ENDING WAS SAD.
WHAT HAPPENED TO MERRIA? SHE LOST GAVYN. SHE WAS ALL ALONE.
SHE HAD A BROKEN HEART. FOR A LONG TIME. AND THEN SHE FELL IN LOVE AGAIN.
YEARS LATER.
AND SHE LIVED HAPPILY EVER AFTER?
YES.
THEN TELL US THAT. THAT SOUNDS LIKE THE KIND OF STORY I WANT.
I WILL, MY SWEET. WHEN YOU'RE OLDER. I'M NOT SURE THE PRINCESS'S LIFE AFTER GAVYN IS A TALE FOR YOUNG EARS.
I'M OLD ENOUGH. I'M BIGGER. BIGGER'N THESE BABIES. YOU CAN TELL ME.
YES, YOU ARE BECOMING A BIG BOY, LAWRENCE. YOU'LL SOON BE HELPING YOUR FATHER AND BROTHERS WATCH OVER THE CITY.
I KEEP ASKING MY DAD TO TAKE ME ON PATROL. HE SAYS I'M TOO YOUNG.
IT'S A SERIOUS MATTER WHAT YOUR FAMILY DOES. THIS PLANET IS SAFE BECAUSE THEY KEEP IT SO.
AND YOU KNOW THAT IT'S BEEN SO FOR HUNDREDS...INDEED, THOUSANDS OF YEARS.
ERR.
NO. I...NO ONE HAS EVER TOLD ME.

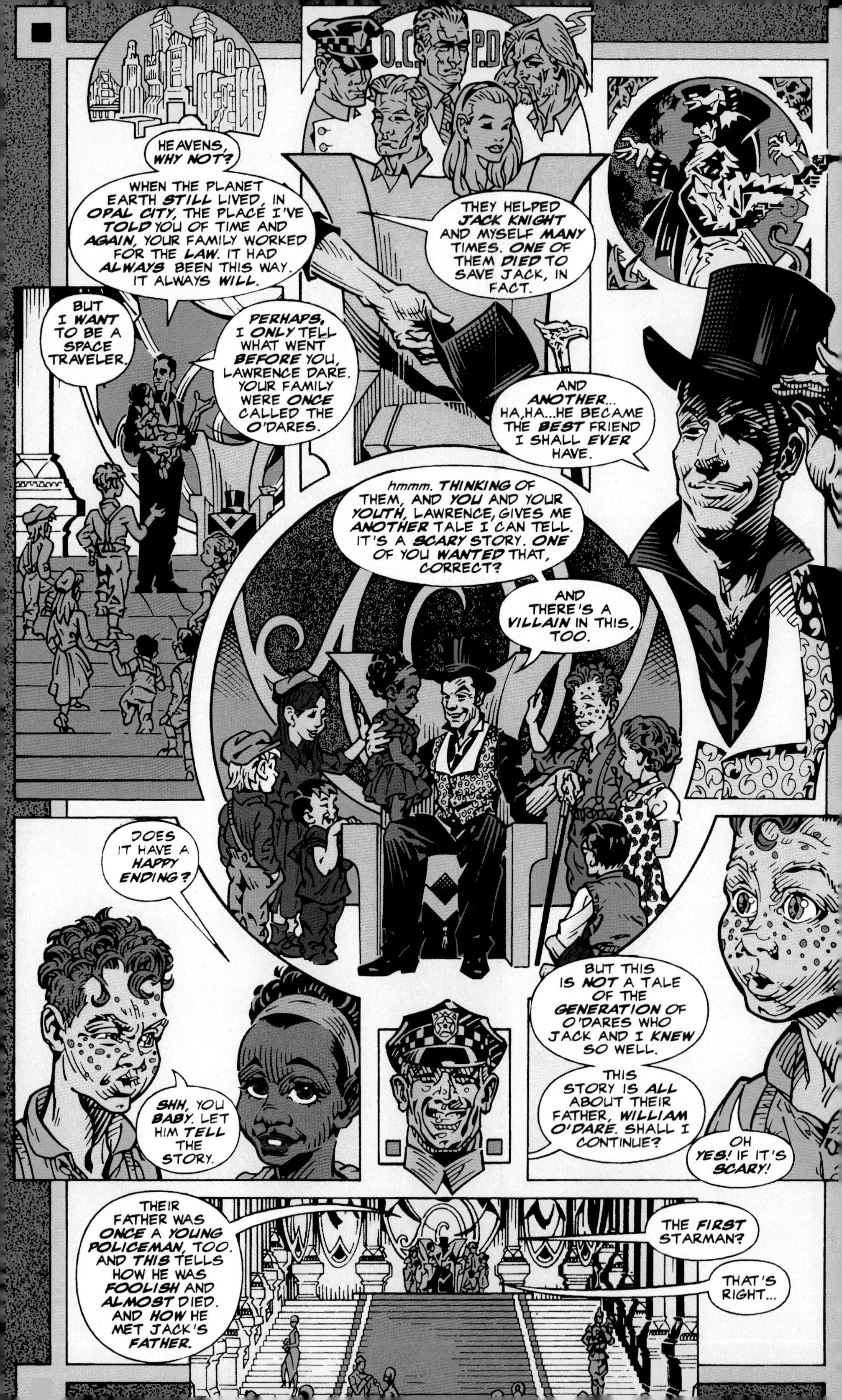
O.C.P.D.
HEAVENS, WHY NOT?
WHEN THE PLANET EARTH STILL LIVED, IN OPAL CITY, THE PLACE I'VE TOLD YOU OF TIME AND AGAIN, YOUR FAMILY WORKED FOR THE LAW. IT HAD ALWAYS BEEN THIS WAY. IT ALWAYS WILL.
THEY HELPED JACK KNIGHT AND MYSELF MANY TIMES. ONE OF THEM DIED TO SAVE JACK, IN FACT.
BUT I WANT TO BE A SPACE TRAVELER.
PERHAPS. I ONLY TELL WHAT WENT BEFORE YOU, LAWRENCE DARE. YOUR FAMILY WERE ONCE CALLED THE O'DARES.
AND ANOTHER... HA,HA...HE BECAME THE BEST FRIEND I SHALL EVER HAVE.
hmmm. THINKING OF THEM, AND YOU AND YOUR YOUTH, LAWRENCE, GIVES ME ANOTHER TALE I CAN TELL. IT'S A SCARY STORY. ONE OF YOU WANTED THAT, CORRECT?
AND THERE'S A VILLAIN IN THIS, TOO.
DOES IT HAVE A HAPPY ENDING?
SHH, YOU BABY. LET HIM TELL THE STORY.
BUT THIS IS NOT A TALE OF THE GENERATION OF O'DARES WHO JACK AND I KNEW SO WELL.
THIS STORY IS ALL ABOUT THEIR FATHER, WILLIAM O'DARE. SHALL I CONTINUE?
OH YES! IF IT'S SCARY!
THEIR FATHER WAS ONCE A YOUNG POLICEMAN, TOO. AND THIS TELLS HOW HE WAS FOOLISH AND ALMOST DIED. AND HOW HE MET JACK'S FATHER.
THE FIRST STARMAN?
THAT'S RIGHT...

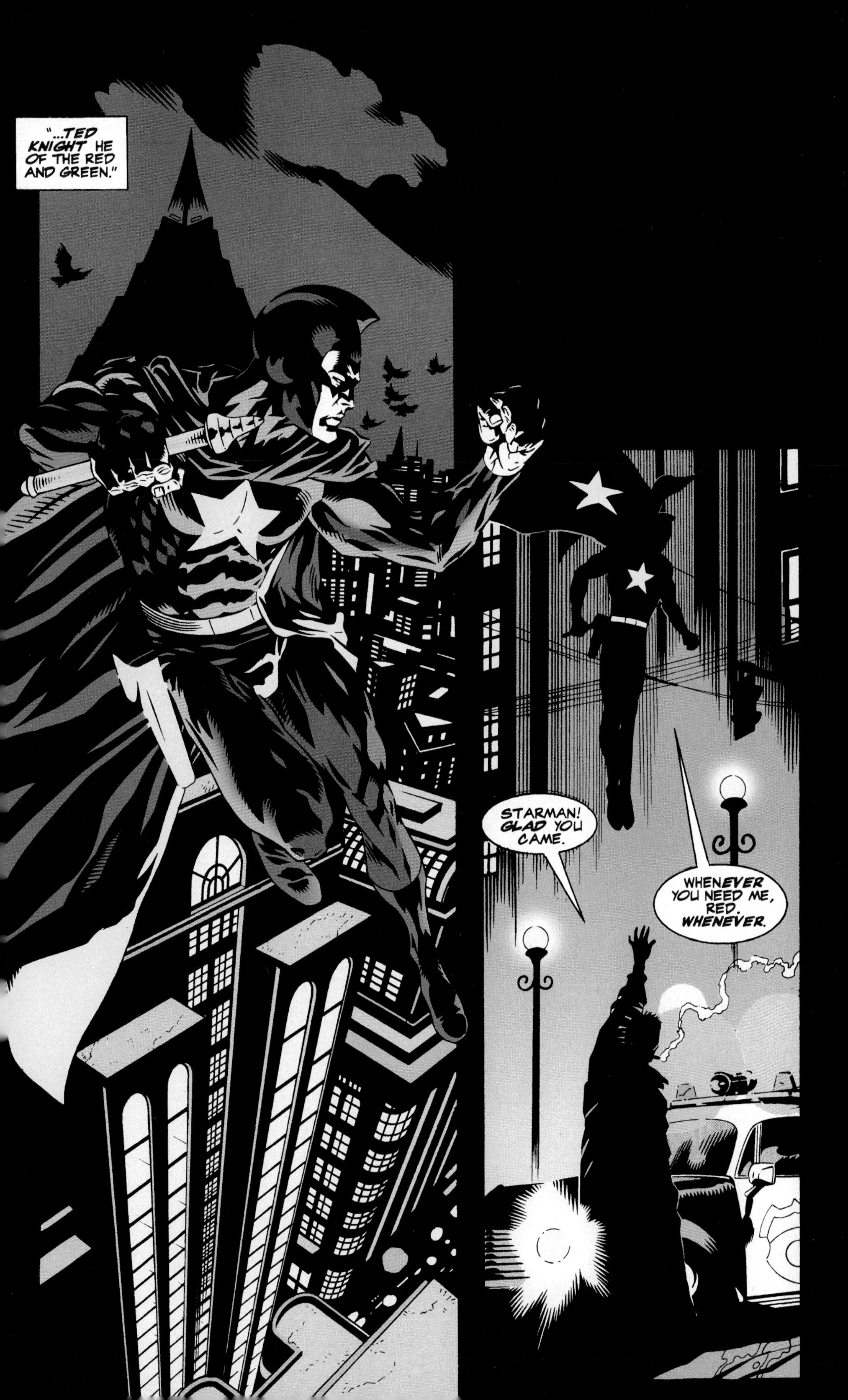
"...TED KNIGHT HE OF THE RED AND GREEN."
STARMAN! GLAD YOU CAME.
WHENEVER YOU NEED ME, RED. WHENEVER.

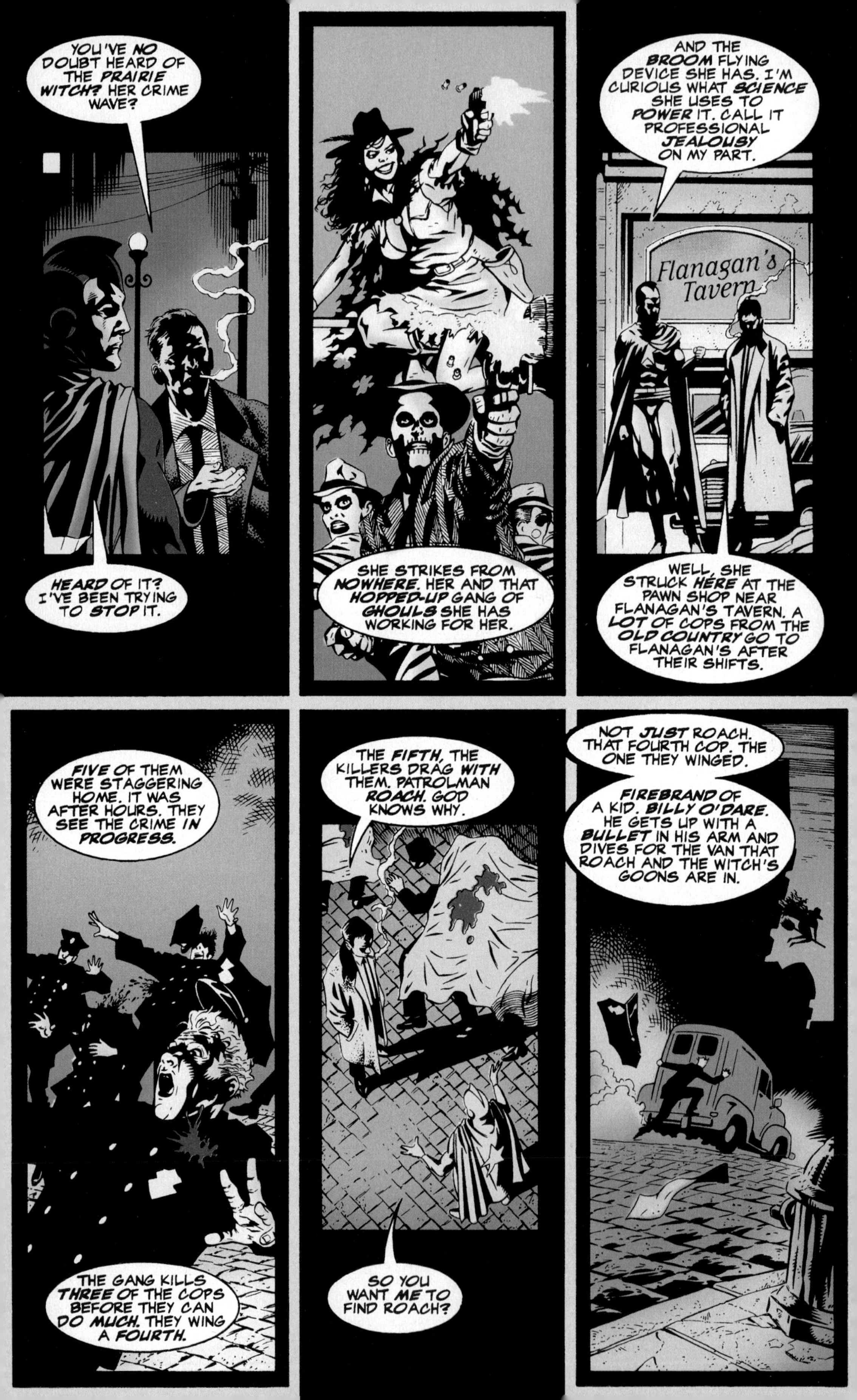
YOU'VE NO DOUBT HEARD OF THE PRAIRIE WITCH? HER CRIME WAVE?
HEARD OF IT? I'VE BEEN TRYING TO STOP IT.
SHE STRIKES FROM NOWHERE. HER AND THAT HOPPED-UP GANG OF GHOULS SHE HAS WORKING FOR HER.
AND THE BROOM FLYING DEVICE SHE HAS. I'M CURIOUS WHAT SCIENCE SHE USES TO POWER IT. CALL IT PROFESSIONAL JEALOUSY ON MY PART.
Flanagan's Tavern
WELL, SHE STRUCK HERE AT THE PAWN SHOP NEAR FLANAGAN'S TAVERN. A LOT OF COPS FROM THE OLD COUNTRY GO TO FLANAGAN'S AFTER THEIR SHIFTS.
FIVE OF THEM WERE STAGGERING HOME. IT WAS AFTER HOURS. THEY SEE THE CRIME IN PROGRESS.
THE GANG KILLS THREE OF THE COPS BEFORE THEY CAN DO MUCH. THEY WING A FOURTH.
THE FIFTH, THE KILLERS DRAG WITH THEM. PATROLMAN ROACH. GOD KNOWS WHY.
SO YOU WANT ME TO FIND ROACH?
NOT JUST ROACH. THAT FOURTH COP. THE ONE THEY WINGED.
FIREBRAND OF A KID. BILLY O'DARE. HE GETS UP WITH A BULLET IN HIS ARM AND DIVES FOR THE VAN THAT ROACH AND THE WITCH'S GOONS ARE IN.

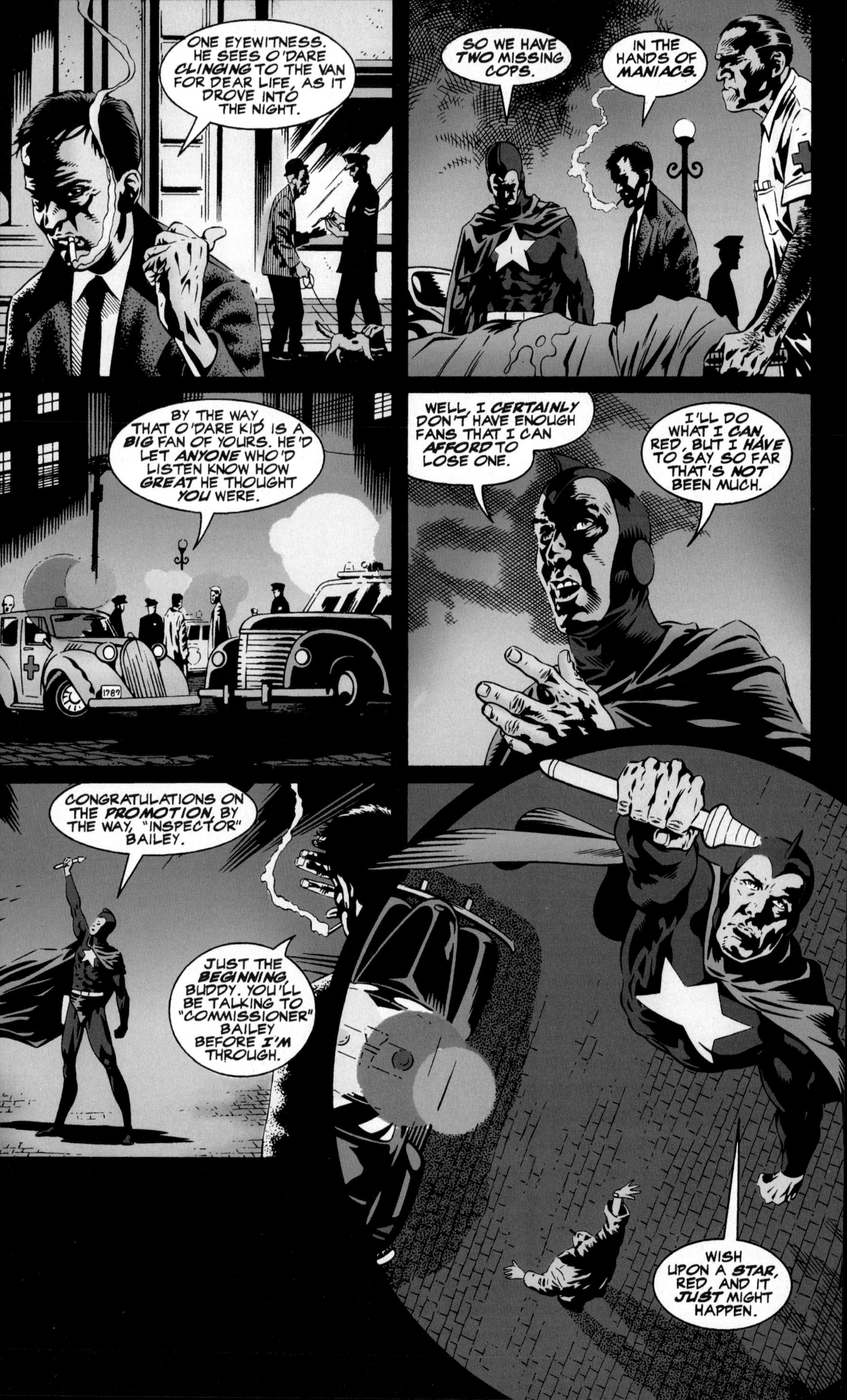

ONE EYEWITNESS. HE SEES O'DARE CLINGING TO THE VAN FOR DEAR LIFE, AS IT DROVE INTO THE NIGHT.
SO WE HAVE TWO MISSING COPS.
IN THE HANDS OF MANIACS.
BY THE WAY, THAT O'DARE KID IS A BIG FAN OF YOURS. HE'D LET ANYONE WHO'D LISTEN KNOW HOW GREAT HE THOUGHT YOU WERE.
WELL, I CERTAINLY DON'T HAVE ENOUGH FANS THAT I CAN AFFORD TO LOSE ONE.
I'LL DO WHAT I CAN, RED, BUT I HAVE TO SAY SO FAR THAT'S NOT BEEN MUCH.
1787
CONGRATULATIONS ON THE PROMOTION, BY THE WAY, "INSPECTOR" BAILEY.
JUST THE BEGINNING, BUDDY. YOU'LL BE TALKING TO "COMMISSIONER" BAILEY BEFORE I'M THROUGH.
WISH UPON A STAR, RED, AND IT JUST MIGHT HAPPEN.

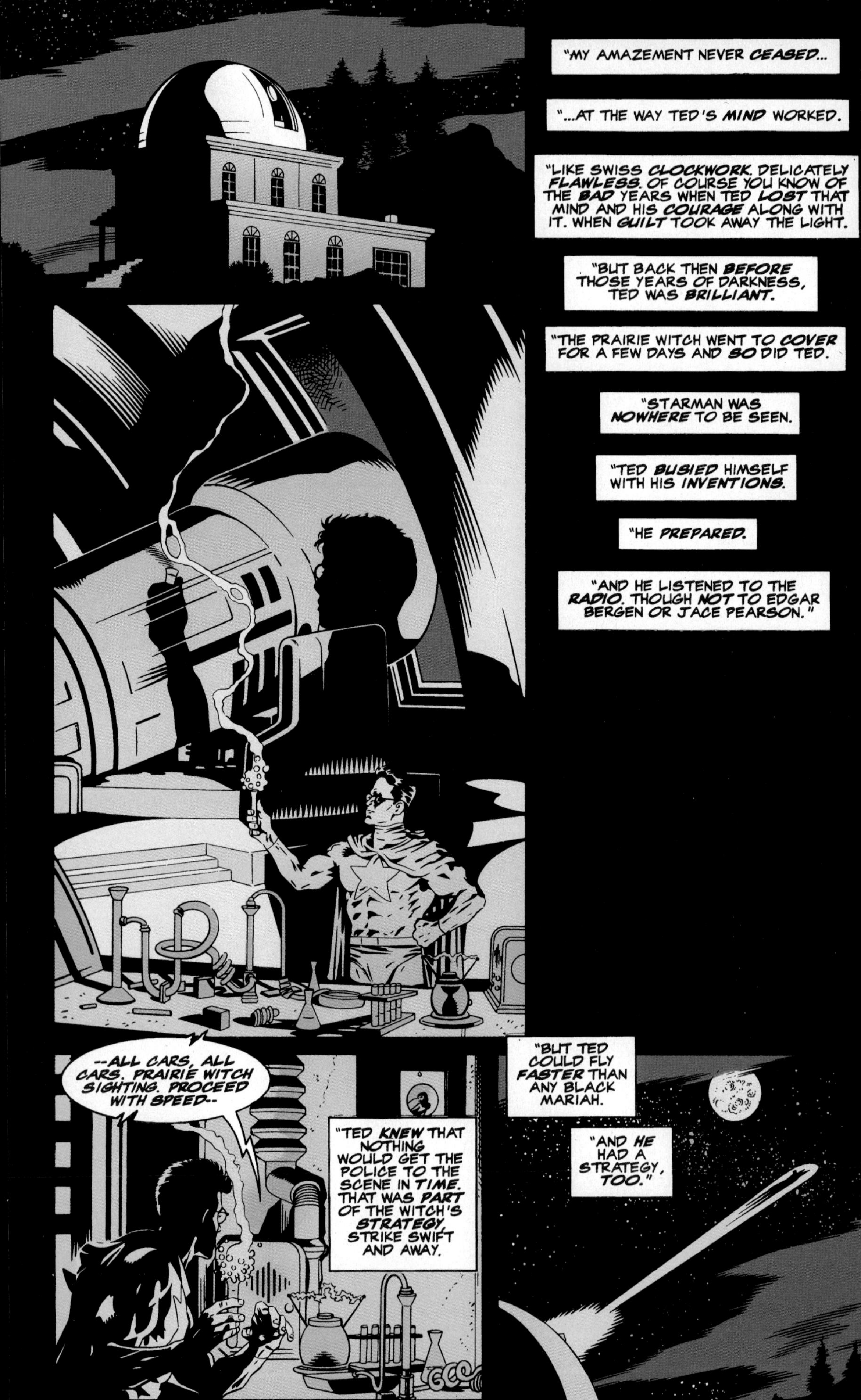
"MY AMAZEMENT NEVER CEASED...
"...AT THE WAY TED'S MIND WORKED.
"LIKE SWISS CLOCKWORK. DELICATELY FLAWLESS. OF COURSE YOU KNOW OF THE BAD YEARS WHEN TED LOST THAT MIND AND HIS COURAGE ALONG WITH IT. WHEN GUILT TOOK AWAY THE LIGHT.
"BUT BACK THEN BEFORE THOSE YEARS OF DARKNESS, TED WAS BRILLIANT.
"THE PRAIRIE WITCH WENT TO COVER FOR A FEW DAYS AND SO DID TED.
"STARMAN WAS NOWHERE TO BE SEEN.
"TED BUSIED HIMSELF WITH HIS INVENTIONS.
"HE PREPARED.
"AND HE LISTENED TO THE RADIO. THOUGH NOT TO EDGAR BERGEN OR JACE PEARSON."
--ALL CARS, ALL CARS. PRAIRIE WITCH SIGHTING. PROCEED WITH SPEED--
"TED KNEW THAT NOTHING WOULD GET THE POLICE TO THE SCENE IN TIME. THAT WAS PART OF THE WITCH'S STRATEGY, STRIKE SWIFT AND AWAY.
"BUT TED COULD FLY FASTER THAN ANY BLACK MARIAH.
"AND HE HAD A STRATEGY, TOO."

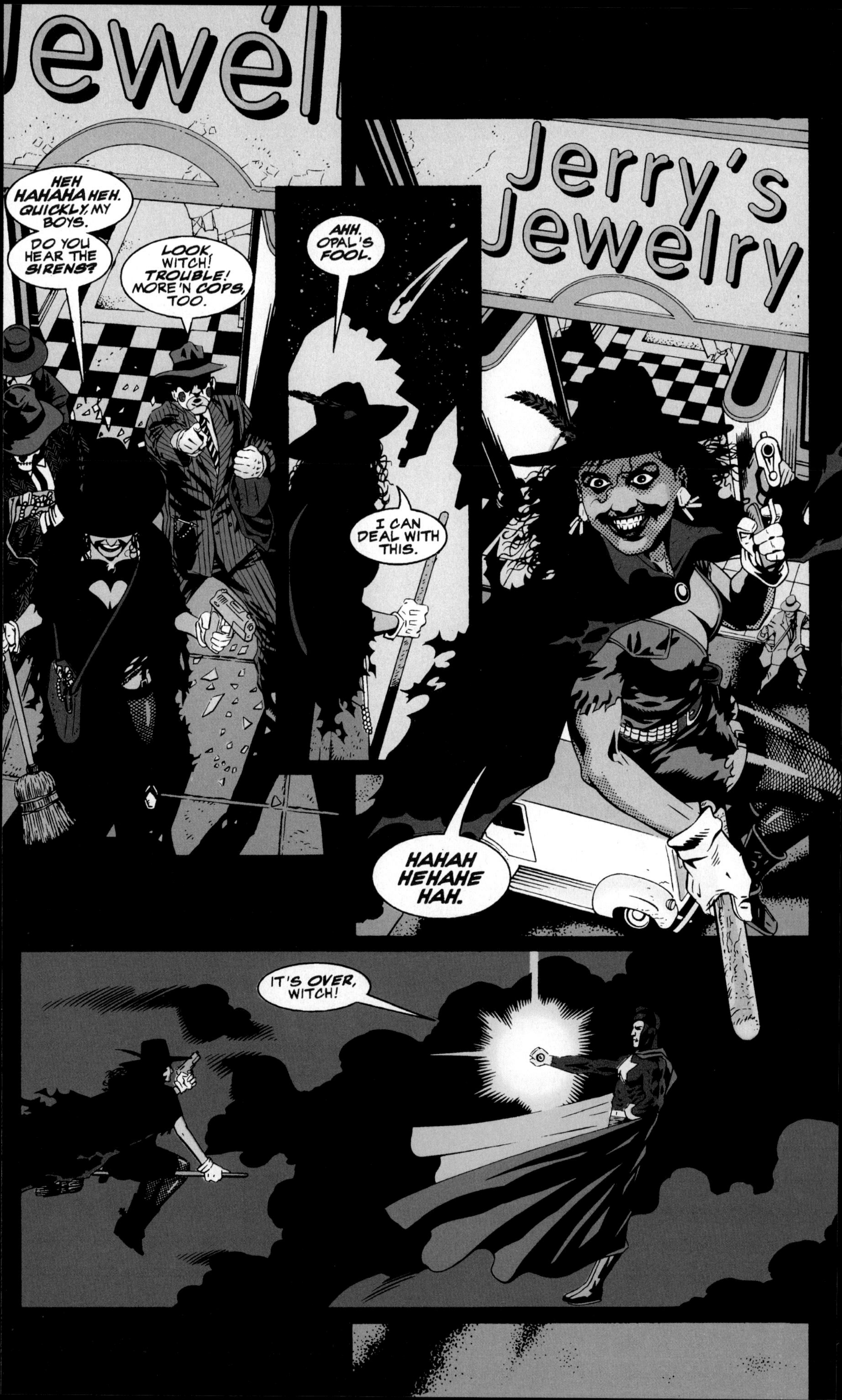
Jewel
HEH HAHAHAHEH. QUICKLY, MY BOYS.
DO YOU HEAR THE SIRENS?
LOOK, WITCH! TROUBLE! MORE'N COPS, TOO.
AHH. OPAL'S FOOL.
I CAN DEAL WITH THIS.
Jerry's Jewelry
HAHAH HEHAHE HAH.
IT'S OVER, WITCH!

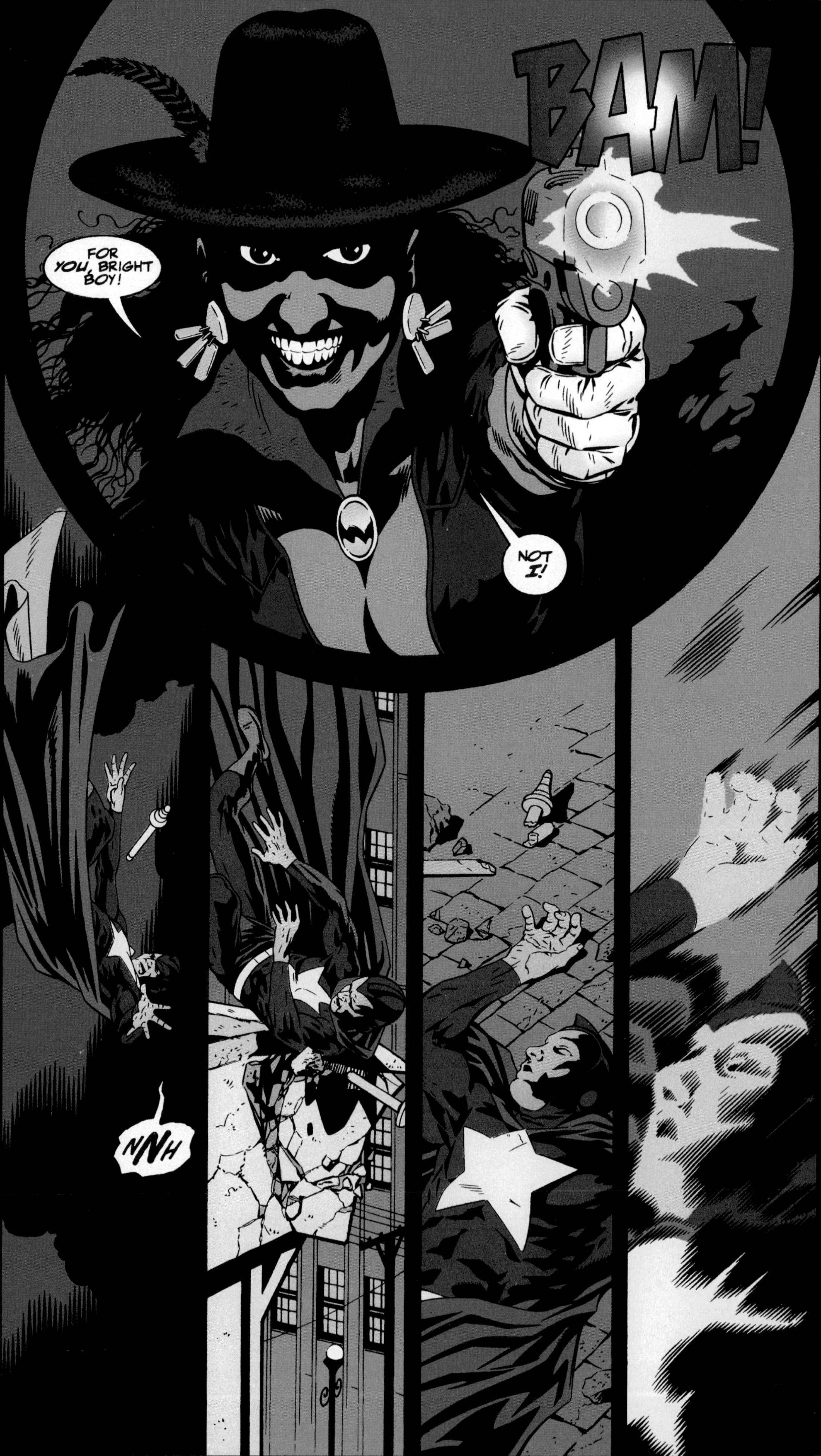
BAM!
FOR YOU, BRIGHT BOY!
NOT I!
NNH

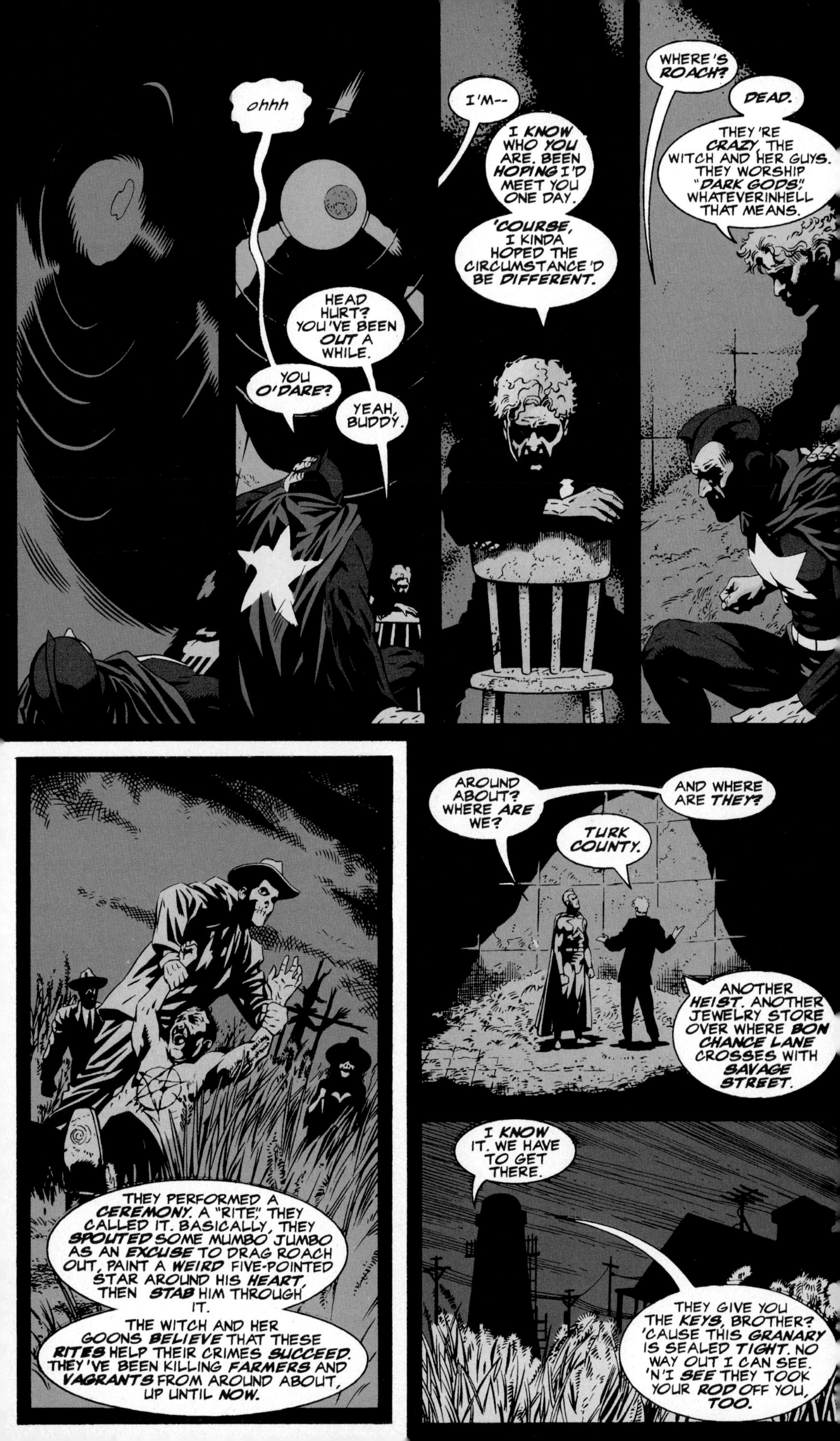

ohhh
HEAD HURT? YOU'VE BEEN OUT A WHILE.
YOU O'DARE?
YEAH, BUDDY.
I'M--
I KNOW WHO YOU ARE. BEEN HOPING I'D MEET YOU ONE DAY.
'COURSE, I KINDA HOPED THE CIRCUMSTANCE'D BE DIFFERENT.
WHERE'S ROACH?
DEAD.
THEY'RE CRAZY, THE WITCH AND HER GUYS. THEY WORSHIP "DARK GODS," WHATEVERINHELL THAT MEANS.
THEY PERFORMED A CEREMONY. A "RITE," THEY CALLED IT. BASICALLY, THEY SPOUTED SOME MUMBO JUMBO AS AN EXCUSE TO DRAG ROACH OUT, PAINT A WEIRD FIVE-POINTED STAR AROUND HIS HEART, THEN STAB HIM THROUGH IT.
THE WITCH AND HER GOONS BELIEVE THAT THESE RITES HELP THEIR CRIMES SUCCEED. THEY'VE BEEN KILLING FARMERS AND VAGRANTS FROM AROUND ABOUT, UP UNTIL NOW.
AROUND ABOUT? WHERE ARE WE?
TURK COUNTY.
AND WHERE ARE THEY?
ANOTHER HEIST. ANOTHER JEWELRY STORE OVER WHERE BON CHANCE LANE CROSSES WITH SAVAGE STREET.
I KNOW IT. WE HAVE TO GET THERE.
THEY GIVE YOU THE KEYS, BROTHER? 'CAUSE THIS GRANARY IS SEALED TIGHT. NO WAY OUT I CAN SEE. 'N'I SEE THEY TOOK YOUR ROD OFF YOU, TOO.

I COULD HAVE STOPPED THEM BACK *THEN*. BUT I FEARED *IF* WE CAUGHT THEM THEY MIGHT *NOT* GIVE YOU UP. I'VE *HEARD* OF PEOPLE BEING TAKEN... *SNATCHED*, WHO WERE *BURIED ALIVE*, AND KEPT THAT WAY *UNTIL* RANSOMS WERE PAID. I *COULDN'T* RISK DELAYING MY *FINDING* YOU.

IT WAS *BROKEN* WHEN I FELL.

OR *SO* THE WITCH *THOUGHT*. OR SO I *WANTED* HER TO THINK. *ACTUALLY* I CONSTRUCTED THAT ROD *ESPECIALLY* SO IT WOULD *SHATTER*.

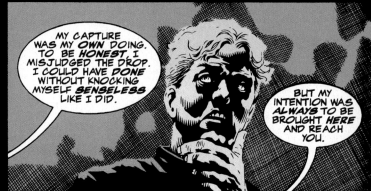

MY CAPTURE WAS MY *OWN* DOING. TO BE *HONEST*, I MISJUDGED THE DROP. I COULD HAVE *DONE* WITHOUT KNOCKING MYSELF *SENSELESS* LIKE I DID.

BUT MY INTENTION WAS *ALWAYS* TO BE BROUGHT *HERE* AND REACH YOU.

BUT *WHAT IF* THEY 'D *KILLED* YOU? YOU TOOK *QUITE* A CHANCE.

YOU TOOK A CHANCE LEAPING FOR THE VAN. YOU *DESERVED* MY EFFORTS.

WITHIN MY *CAPE*, I CONCEALED *FLAT* THE CIRCUITRY TO CREATE *ANOTHER* GRAVITY ROD. ALL I NEED IS A *CYLINDER* OF SOME KIND THAT I CAN *WRAP* THE WIRING AROUND.

HOW ABOUT *THIS*? THEY TOOK MY GUN, BUT I GUESS THEY *FIGURED* MY NIGHT STICK *WASN'T* GONNA HELP ME *MUCH*.

IT LOOKS LIKE THE WITCH WAS *WRONG* AGAIN.

NOW, LET'S GET *OUT* OF HERE.

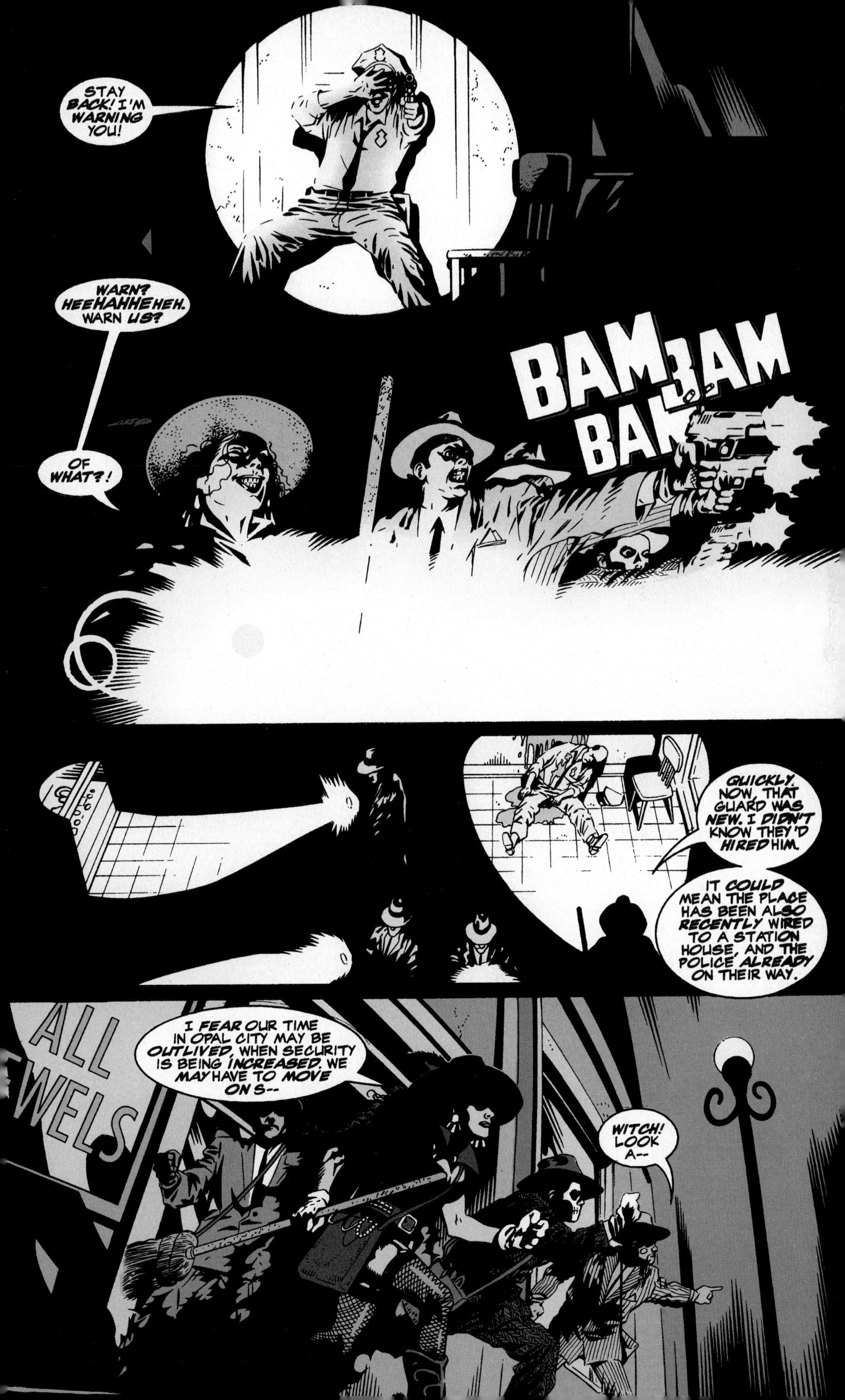
STAY BACK! I'M WARNING YOU!
WARN? HEEHAHHEHEH. WARN US?
OF WHAT?!
BAM BAM BAM BAM
QUICKLY. NOW, THAT GUARD WAS NEW. I DIDN'T KNOW THEY'D HIRED HIM.
IT COULD MEAN THE PLACE HAS BEEN ALSO RECENTLY WIRED TO A STATION HOUSE, AND THE POLICE ALREADY ON THEIR WAY.
ALL
WELS
I FEAR OUR TIME IN OPAL CITY MAY BE OUTLIVED, WHEN SECURITY IS BEING INCREASED. WE MAY HAVE TO MOVE ON S--
WITCH! LOOK A--

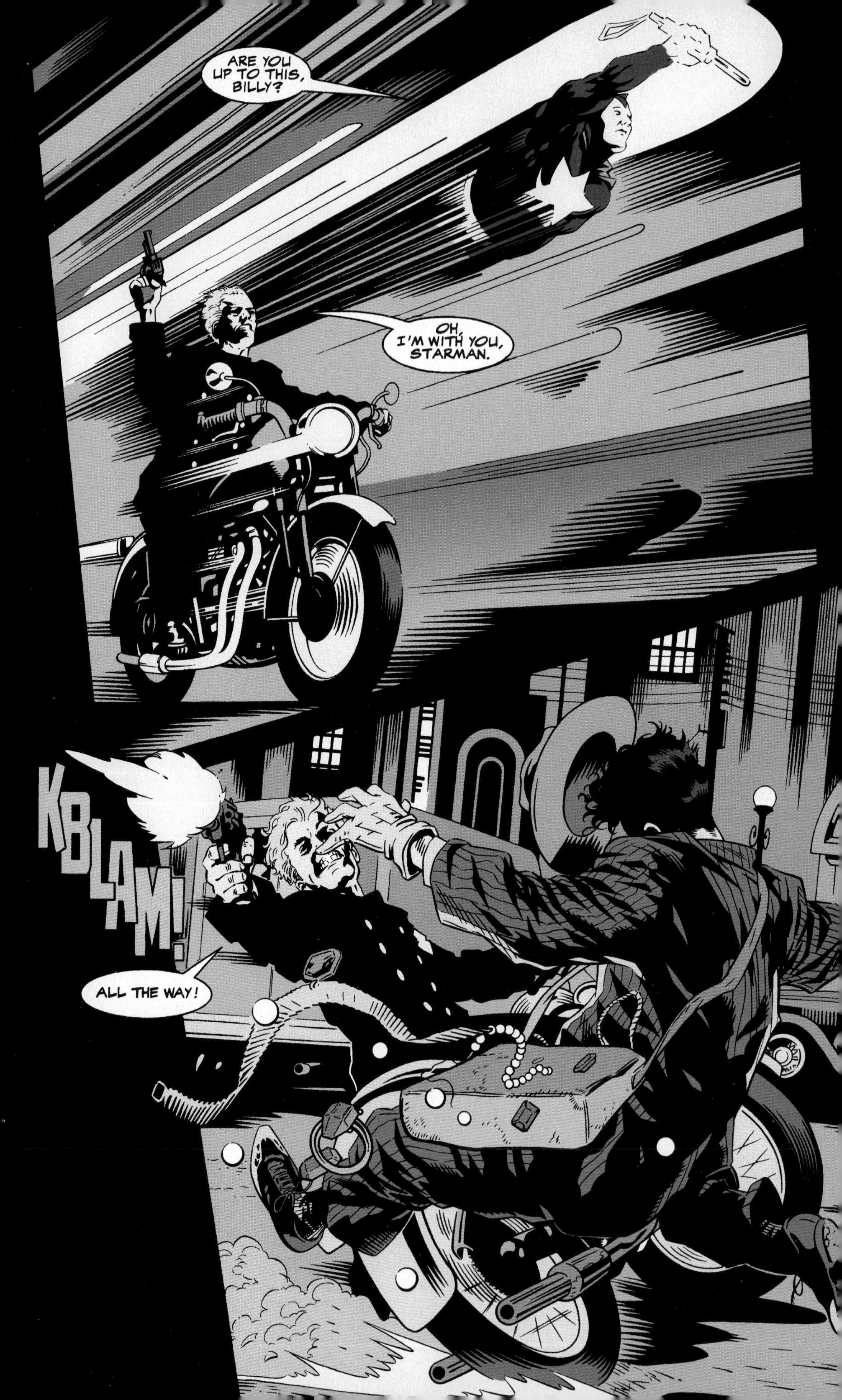

ARE YOU UP TO THIS, BILLY?
OH, I'M WITH YOU, STARMAN.
KBLAM!
ALL THE WAY!

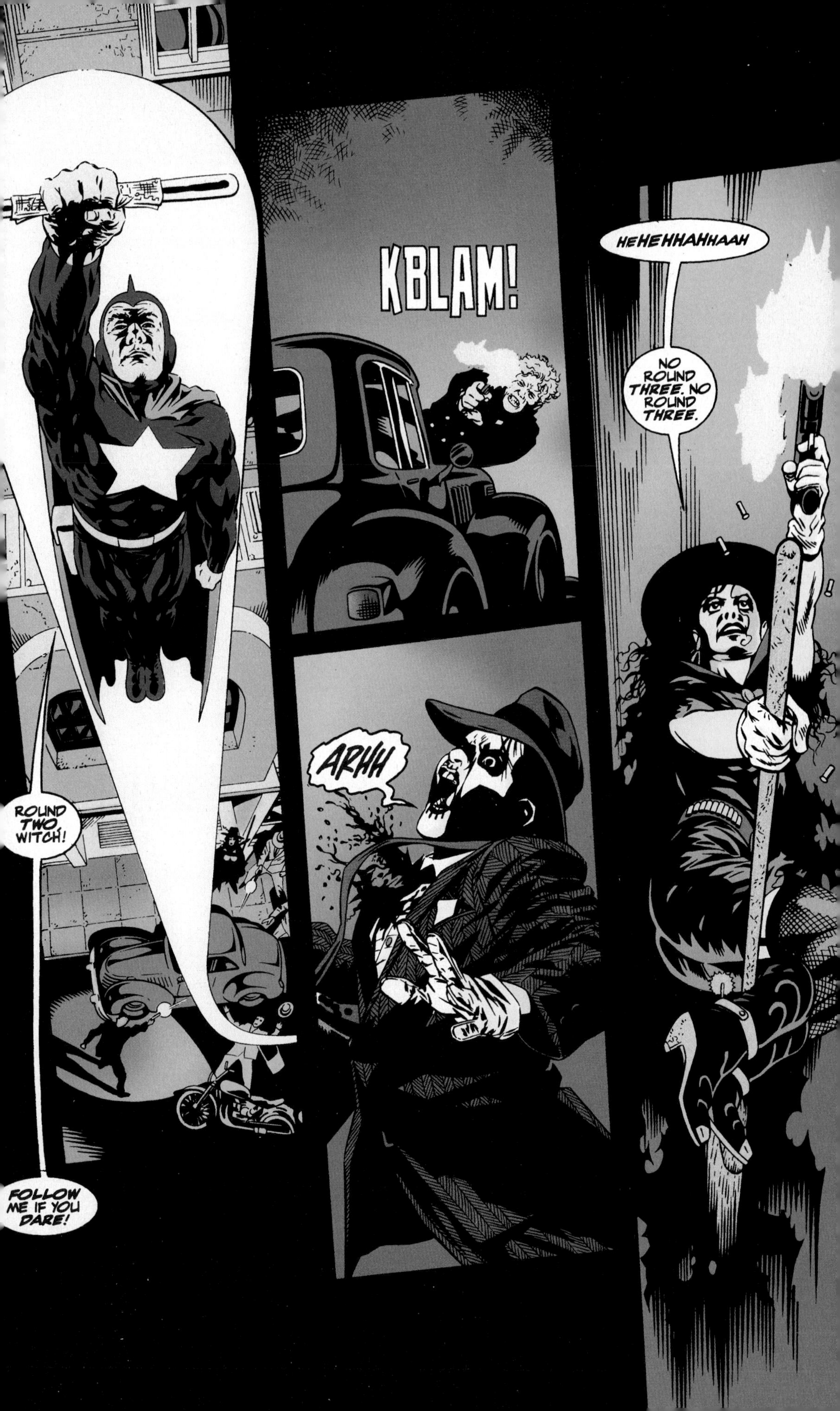
ROUND TWO, WITCH!
FOLLOW ME IF YOU DARE!
KBLAM!
ARHH
HEHEHHAHHAAH
NO ROUND THREE. NO ROUND THREE.

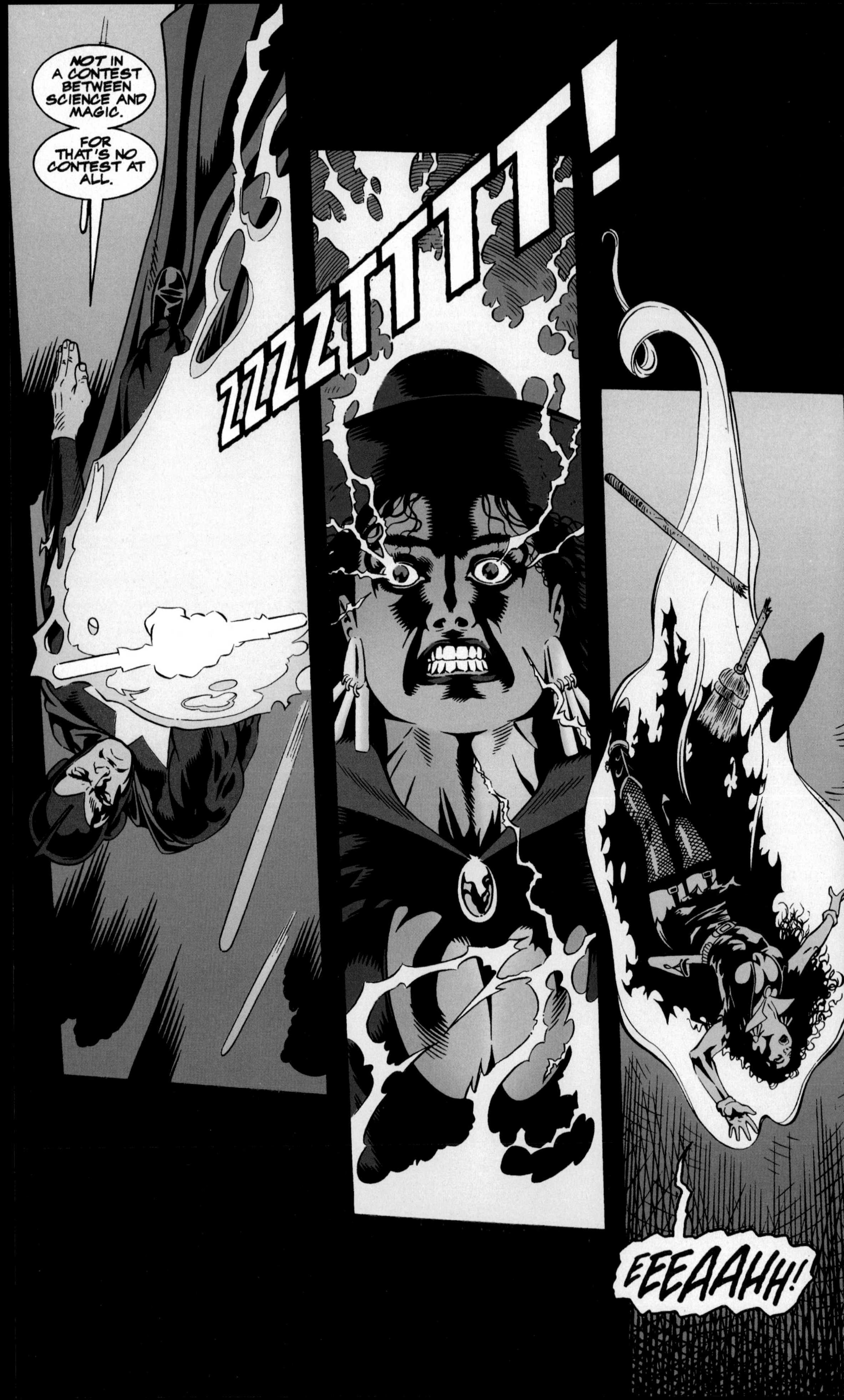
NOT IN A CONTEST BETWEEN SCIENCE AND MAGIC.
FOR THAT'S NO CONTEST AT ALL.
ZZZZTTTTT!
EEEAAHH!

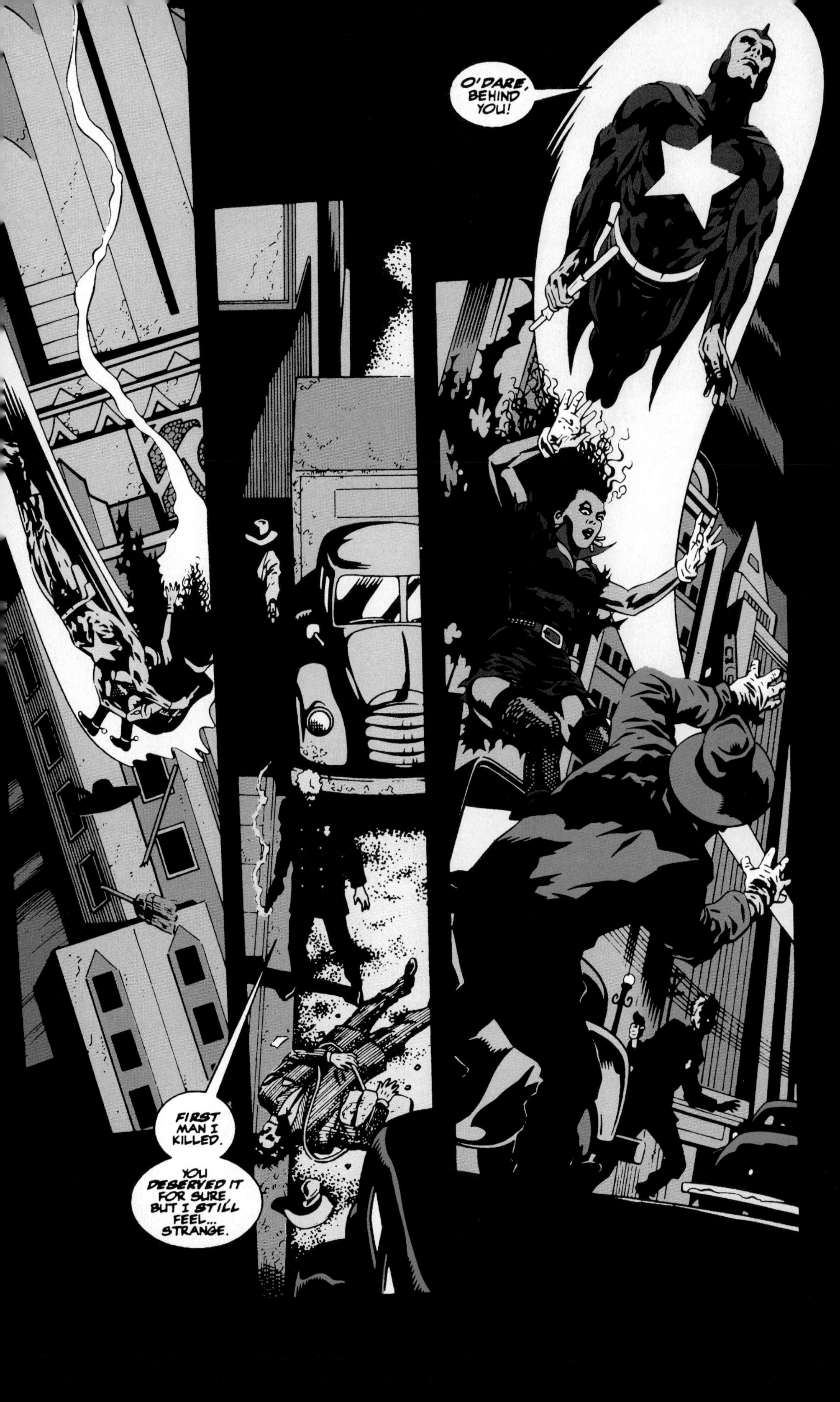
O'DARE, BEHIND YOU!
FIRST MAN I KILLED.
YOU DESERVED IT FOR SURE, BUT I STILL FEEL... STRANGE.

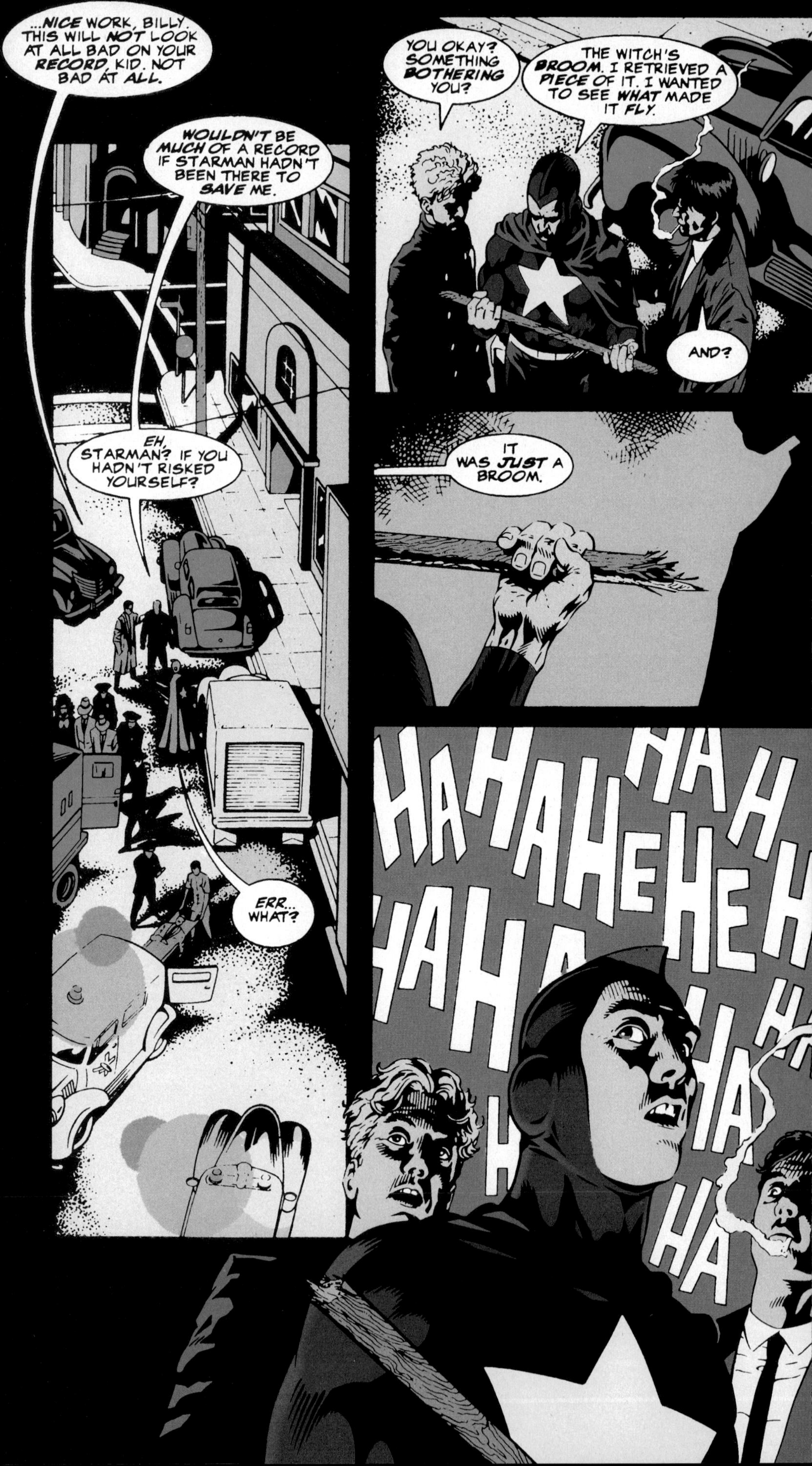

...NICE WORK, BILLY. THIS WILL NOT LOOK AT ALL BAD ON YOUR RECORD, KID. NOT BAD AT ALL.
WOULDN'T BE MUCH OF A RECORD IF STARMAN HADN'T BEEN THERE TO SAVE ME.
EH, STARMAN? IF YOU HADN'T RISKED YOURSELF?
ERR... WHAT?
YOU OKAY? SOMETHING BOTHERING YOU?
THE WITCH'S BROOM. I RETRIEVED A PIECE OF IT. I WANTED TO SEE WHAT MADE IT FLY.
AND?
IT WAS JUST A BROOM.
HA HA HA HA HE HE HE HA HA HA HA HA HA

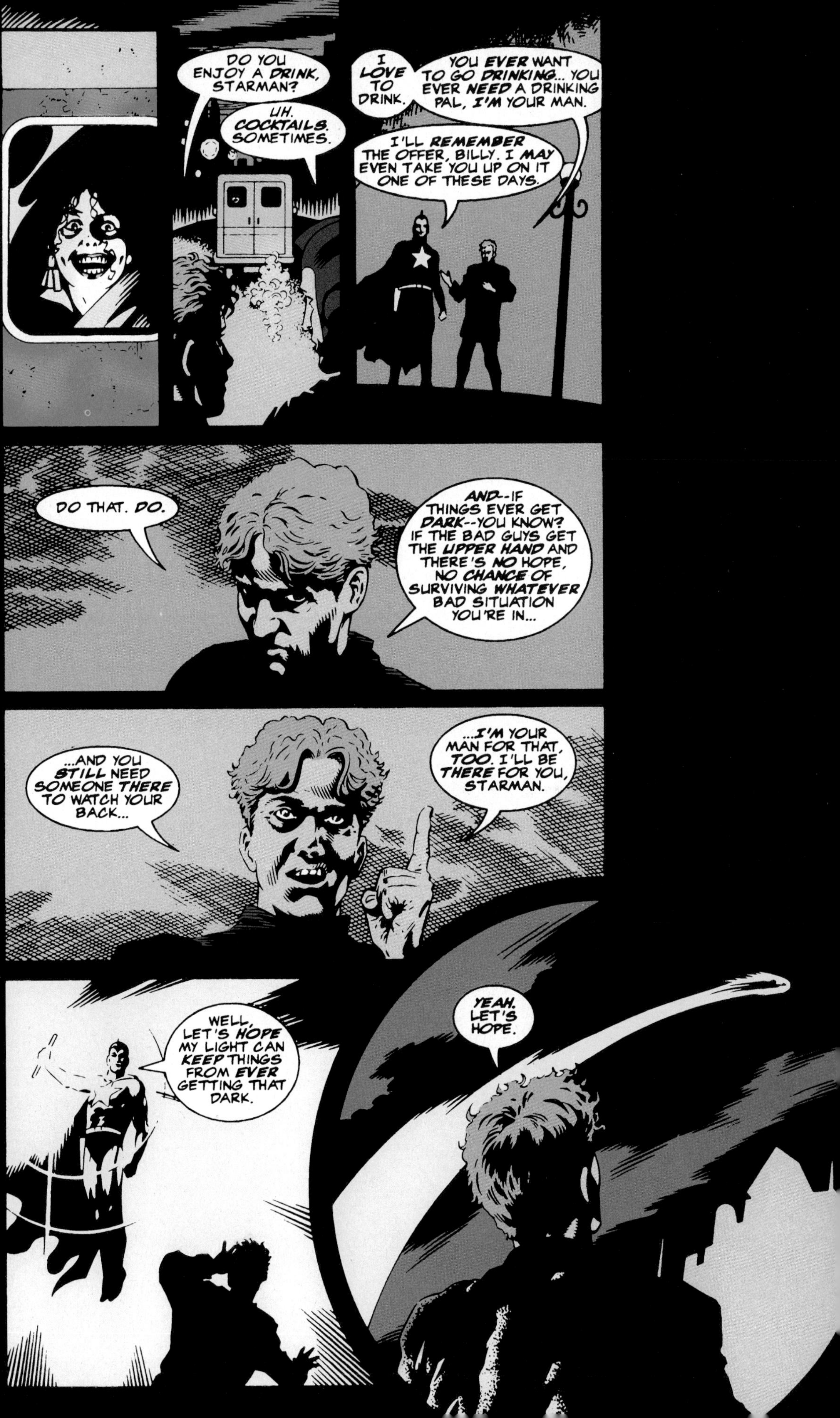
DO YOU ENJOY A DRINK, STARMAN?
UH. COCKTAILS. SOMETIMES.
I LOVE TO DRINK.
YOU EVER WANT TO GO DRINKING... YOU EVER NEED A DRINKING PAL, I'M YOUR MAN.
I'LL REMEMBER THE OFFER, BILLY. I MAY EVEN TAKE YOU UP ON IT ONE OF THESE DAYS.
DO THAT. DO.
AND--IF THINGS EVER GET DARK--YOU KNOW? IF THE BAD GUYS GET THE UPPER HAND AND THERE'S NO HOPE, NO CHANCE OF SURVIVING WHATEVER BAD SITUATION YOU'RE IN...
...AND YOU STILL NEED SOMEONE THERE TO WATCH YOUR BACK...
...I'M YOUR MAN FOR THAT, TOO. I'LL BE THERE FOR YOU, STARMAN.
WELL, LET'S HOPE MY LIGHT CAN KEEP THINGS FROM EVER GETTING THAT DARK.
YEAH. LET'S HOPE.

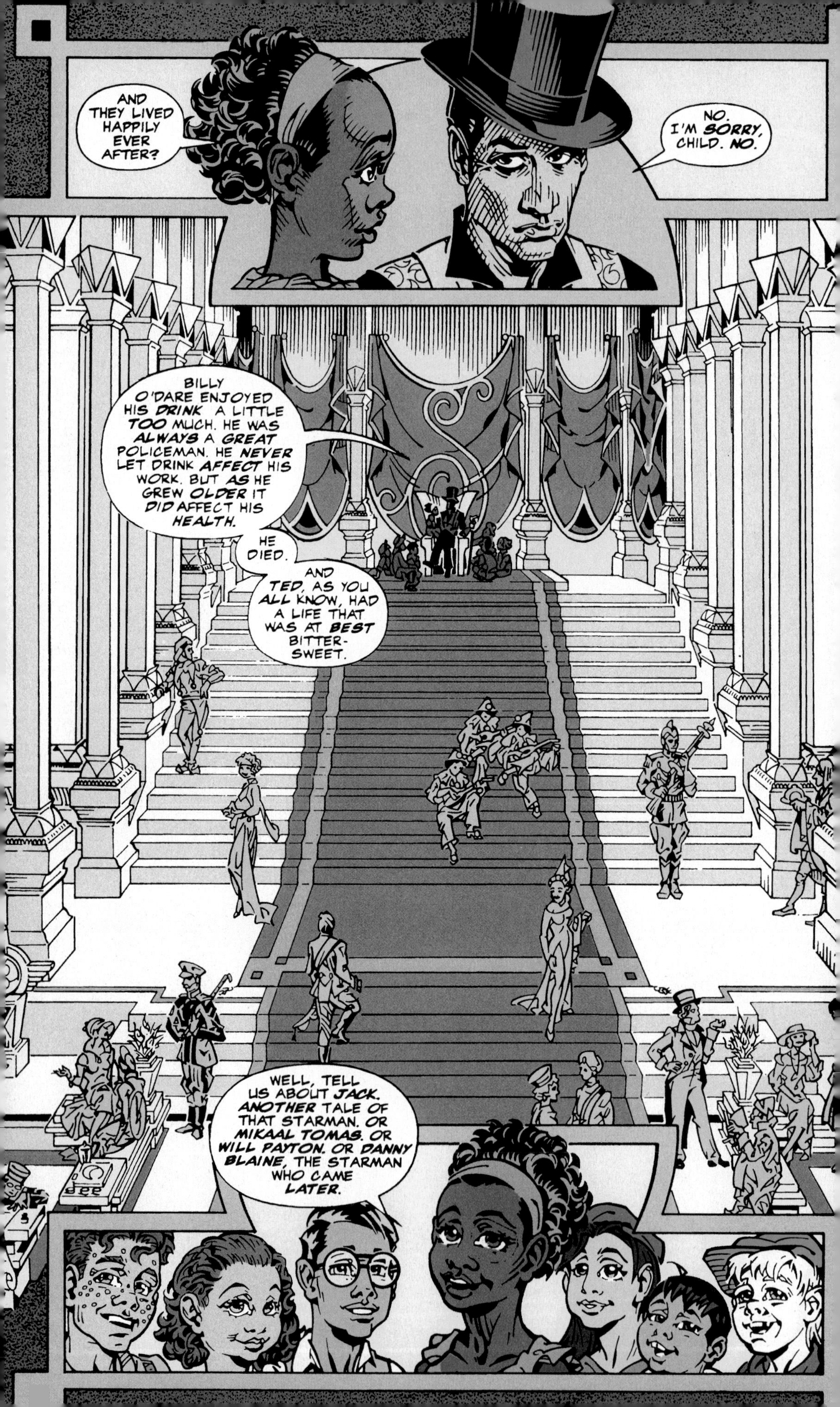
AND THEY LIVED HAPPILY EVER AFTER?
NO. I'M SORRY, CHILD. NO.
BILLY O'DARE ENJOYED HIS DRINK A LITTLE TOO MUCH. HE WAS ALWAYS A GREAT POLICEMAN. HE NEVER LET DRINK AFFECT HIS WORK. BUT AS HE GREW OLDER IT DID AFFECT HIS HEALTH.
HE DIED.
AND TED, AS YOU ALL KNOW, HAD A LIFE THAT WAS AT BEST BITTER-SWEET.
WELL, TELL US ABOUT JACK. ANOTHER TALE OF THAT STARMAN. OR MIKAAL TOMAS. OR WILL PAYTON. OR DANNY BLAINE, THE STARMAN WHO CAME LATER.

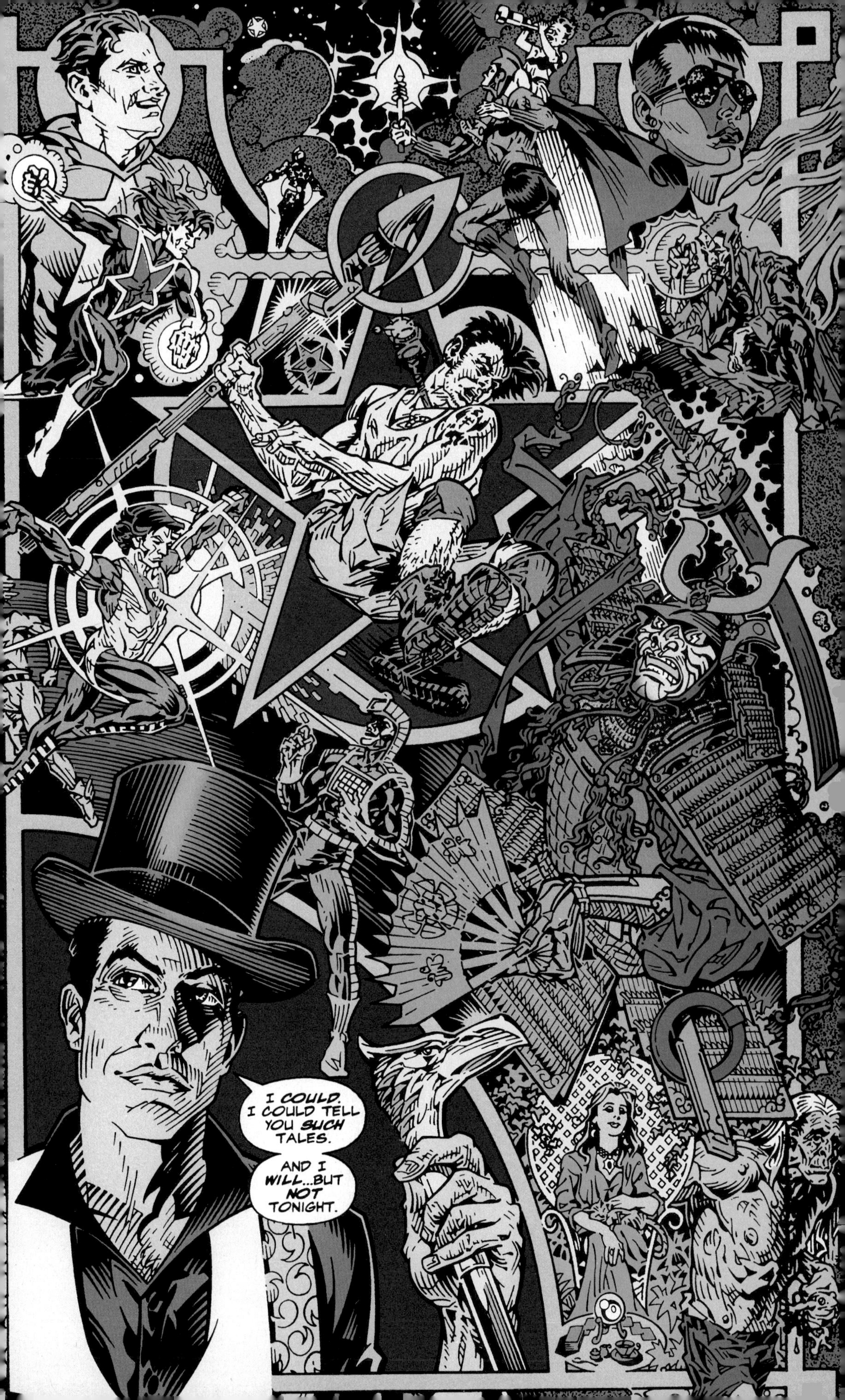
I COULD. I COULD TELL YOU SUCH TALES.
AND I WILL...BUT NOT TONIGHT.

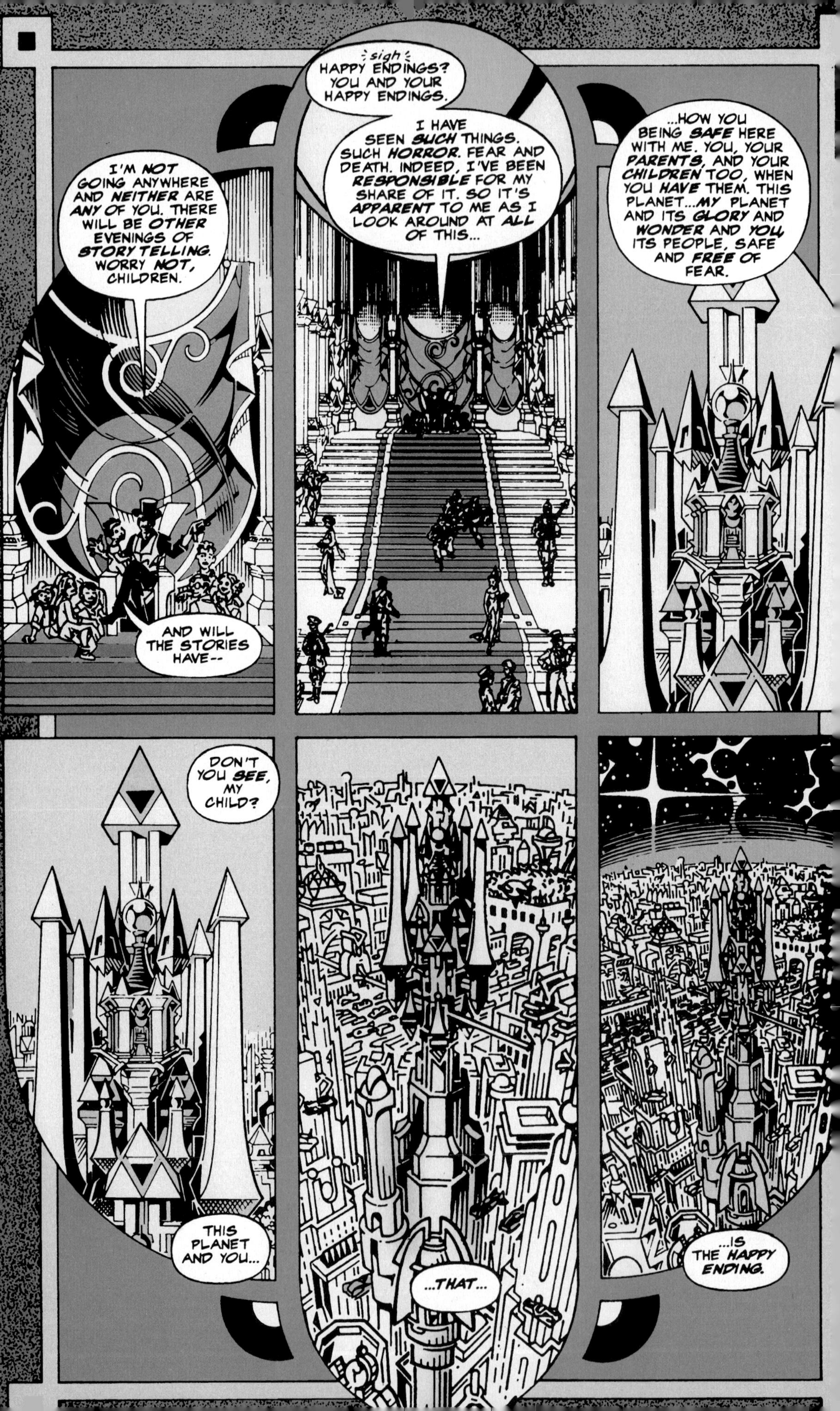
I'M NOT GOING ANYWHERE AND NEITHER ARE ANY OF YOU. THERE WILL BE OTHER EVENINGS OF STORYTELLING. WORRY NOT, CHILDREN.
AND WILL THE STORIES HAVE--
sigh
HAPPY ENDINGS? YOU AND YOUR HAPPY ENDINGS.
I HAVE SEEN SUCH THINGS. SUCH HORROR. FEAR AND DEATH. INDEED, I'VE BEEN RESPONSIBLE FOR MY SHARE OF IT. SO IT'S APPARENT TO ME AS I LOOK AROUND AT ALL OF THIS...
...HOW YOU BEING SAFE HERE WITH ME. YOU, YOUR PARENTS, AND YOUR CHILDREN TOO, WHEN YOU HAVE THEM. THIS PLANET...MY PLANET AND ITS GLORY AND WONDER AND YOU, ITS PEOPLE, SAFE AND FREE OF FEAR.
DON'T YOU SEE, MY CHILD?
THIS PLANET AND YOU...
...THAT...
...IS THE HAPPY ENDING.

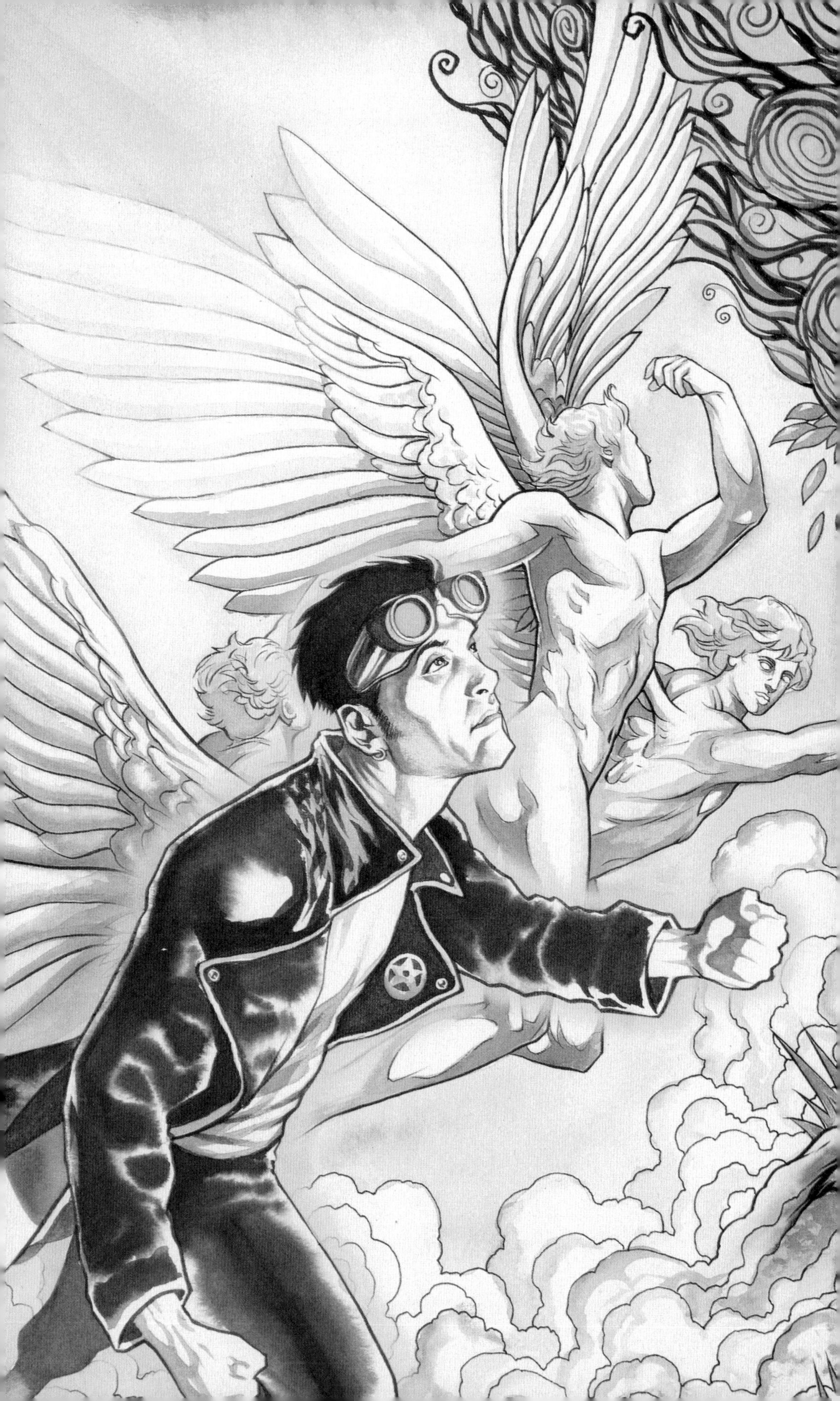

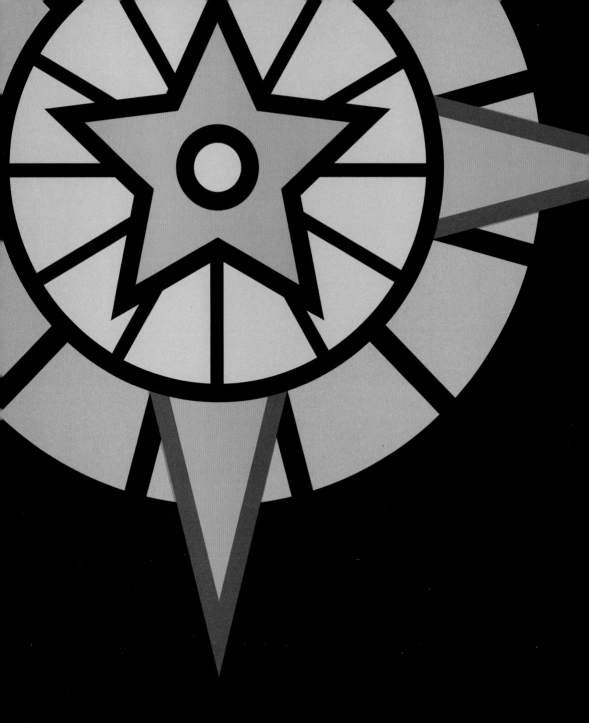

STARMAN 24

Cover by Tony Harris

Written by James Robinson

Pencils by Tony Harris (pgs. 251-259, 261, 263, 266-267, 269, 271-272)

and Chris Sprouse (pgs. 260, 262, 264-265, 268, 270)

with inks by Wade von Grawbadger (251-254, 259-272)

and Ray Snyder (pgs. 255-258), and colors by Gregory Wright.

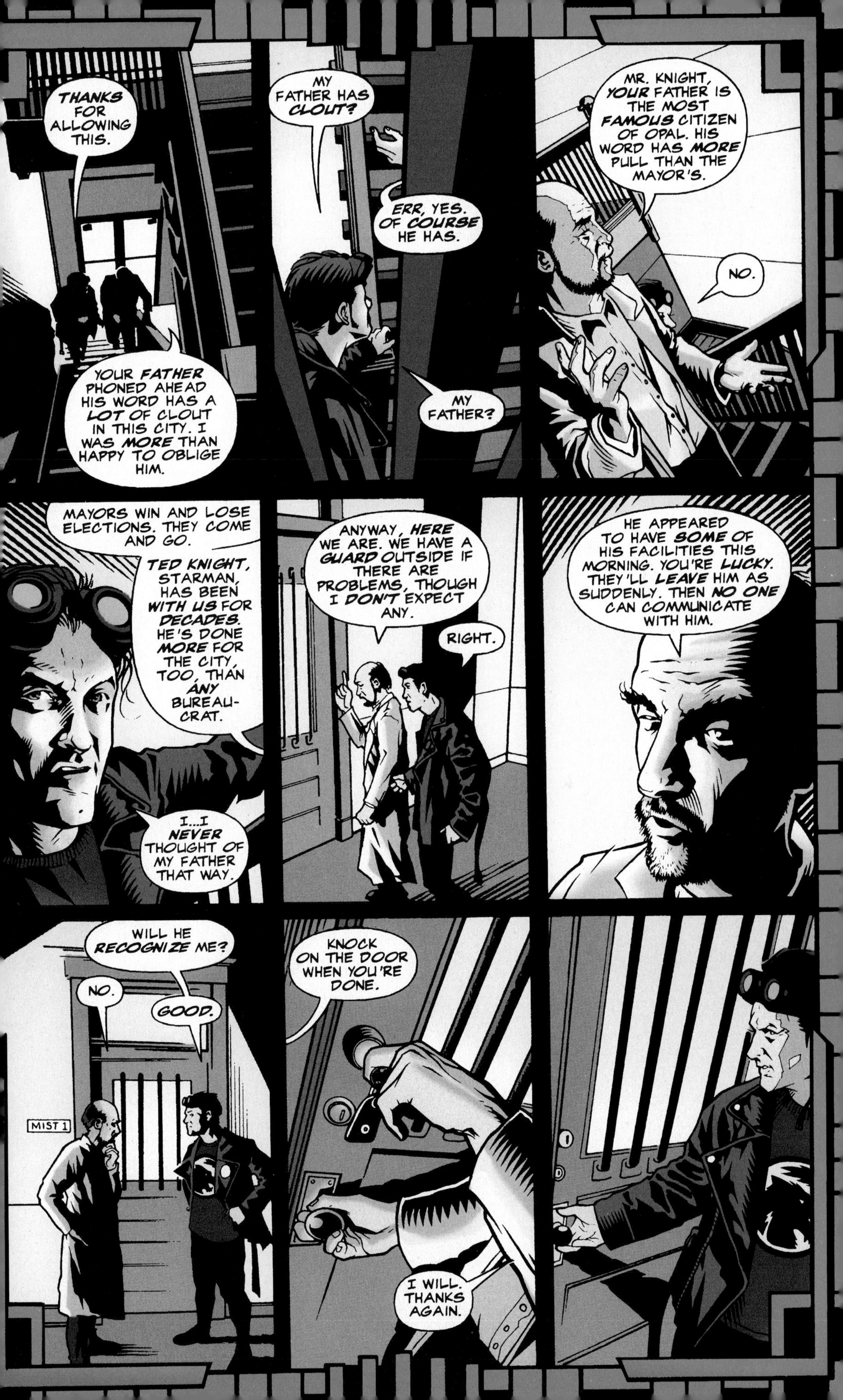
THANKS FOR ALLOWING THIS.
YOUR FATHER PHONED AHEAD HIS WORD HAS A LOT OF CLOUT IN THIS CITY. I WAS MORE THAN HAPPY TO OBLIGE HIM.
MY FATHER?
MY FATHER HAS CLOUT?
ERR, YES. OF COURSE HE HAS.
MR. KNIGHT, YOUR FATHER IS THE MOST FAMOUS CITIZEN OF OPAL. HIS WORD HAS MORE PULL THAN THE MAYOR'S.
NO.
MAYORS WIN AND LOSE ELECTIONS. THEY COME AND GO.
TED KNIGHT, STARMAN, HAS BEEN WITH US FOR DECADES. HE'S DONE MORE FOR THE CITY, TOO, THAN ANY BUREAU-CRAT.
I...I NEVER THOUGHT OF MY FATHER THAT WAY.
ANYWAY, HERE WE ARE. WE HAVE A GUARD OUTSIDE IF THERE ARE PROBLEMS, THOUGH I DON'T EXPECT ANY.
RIGHT.
HE APPEARED TO HAVE SOME OF HIS FACILITIES THIS MORNING. YOU'RE LUCKY. THEY'LL LEAVE HIM AS SUDDENLY. THEN NO ONE CAN COMMUNICATE WITH HIM.
WILL HE RECOGNIZE ME?
NO.
GOOD.
MIST 1
KNOCK ON THE DOOR WHEN YOU'RE DONE.
I WILL. THANKS AGAIN.

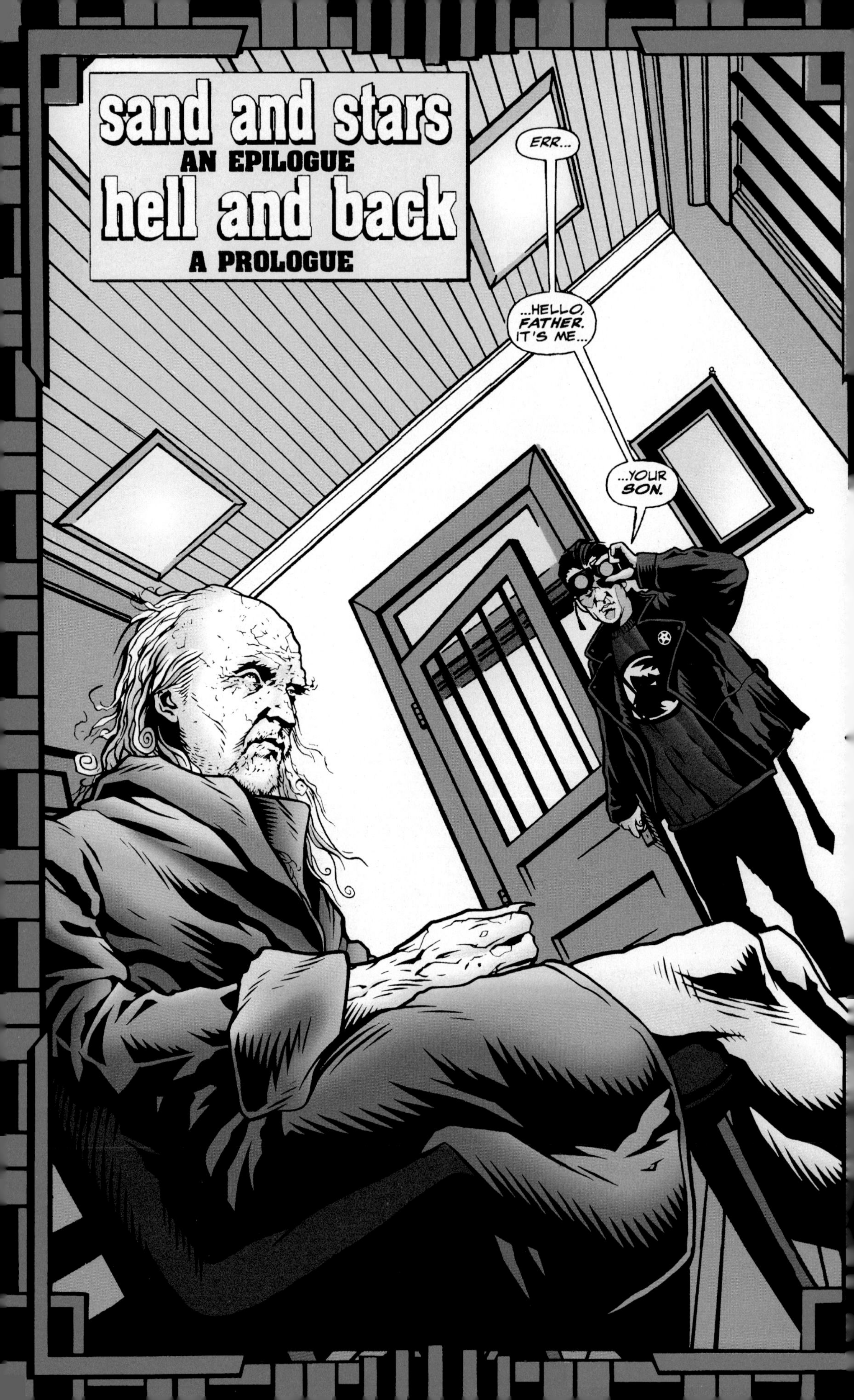
sand and stars
AN EPILOGUE
hell and back
A PROLOGUE
ERR...
...HELLO, FATHER. IT'S ME...
...YOUR SON.

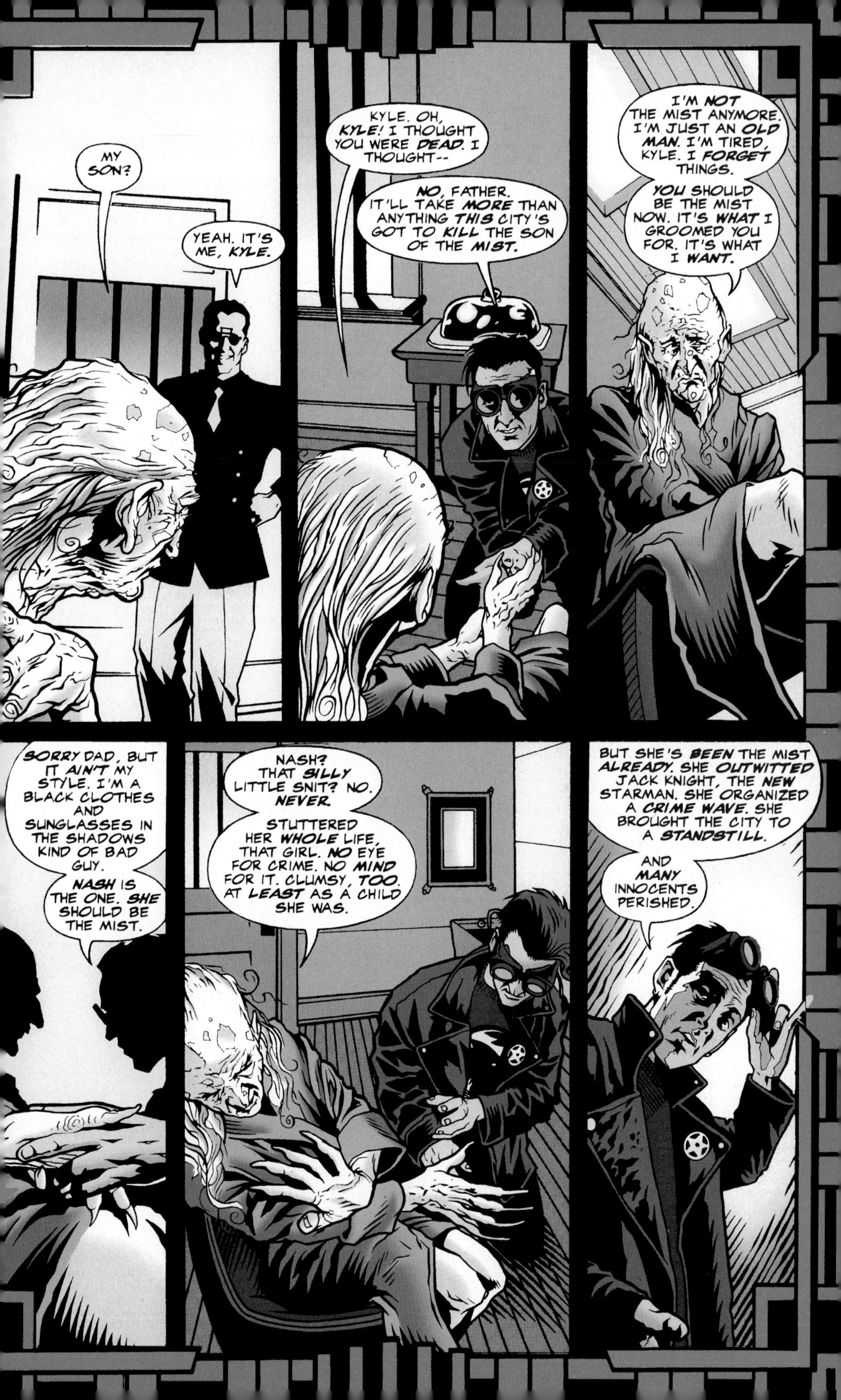
MY SON?
YEAH. IT'S ME, KYLE.
KYLE. OH, KYLE! I THOUGHT YOU WERE DEAD. I THOUGHT--
NO, FATHER. IT'LL TAKE MORE THAN ANYTHING THIS CITY'S GOT TO KILL THE SON OF THE MIST.
I'M NOT THE MIST ANYMORE. I'M JUST AN OLD MAN. I'M TIRED, KYLE. I FORGET THINGS.
YOU SHOULD BE THE MIST NOW. IT'S WHAT I GROOMED YOU FOR. IT'S WHAT I WANT.
SORRY DAD, BUT IT AIN'T MY STYLE. I'M A BLACK CLOTHES AND SUNGLASSES IN THE SHADOWS KIND OF BAD GUY.
NASH IS THE ONE. SHE SHOULD BE THE MIST.
NASH? THAT SILLY LITTLE SNIT? NO. NEVER.
STUTTERED HER WHOLE LIFE, THAT GIRL. NO EYE FOR CRIME. NO MIND FOR IT. CLUMSY, TOO. AT LEAST AS A CHILD SHE WAS.
BUT SHE'S BEEN THE MIST ALREADY. SHE OUTWITTED JACK KNIGHT, THE NEW STARMAN. SHE ORGANIZED A CRIME WAVE. SHE BROUGHT THE CITY TO A STANDSTILL.
AND MANY INNOCENTS PERISHED.

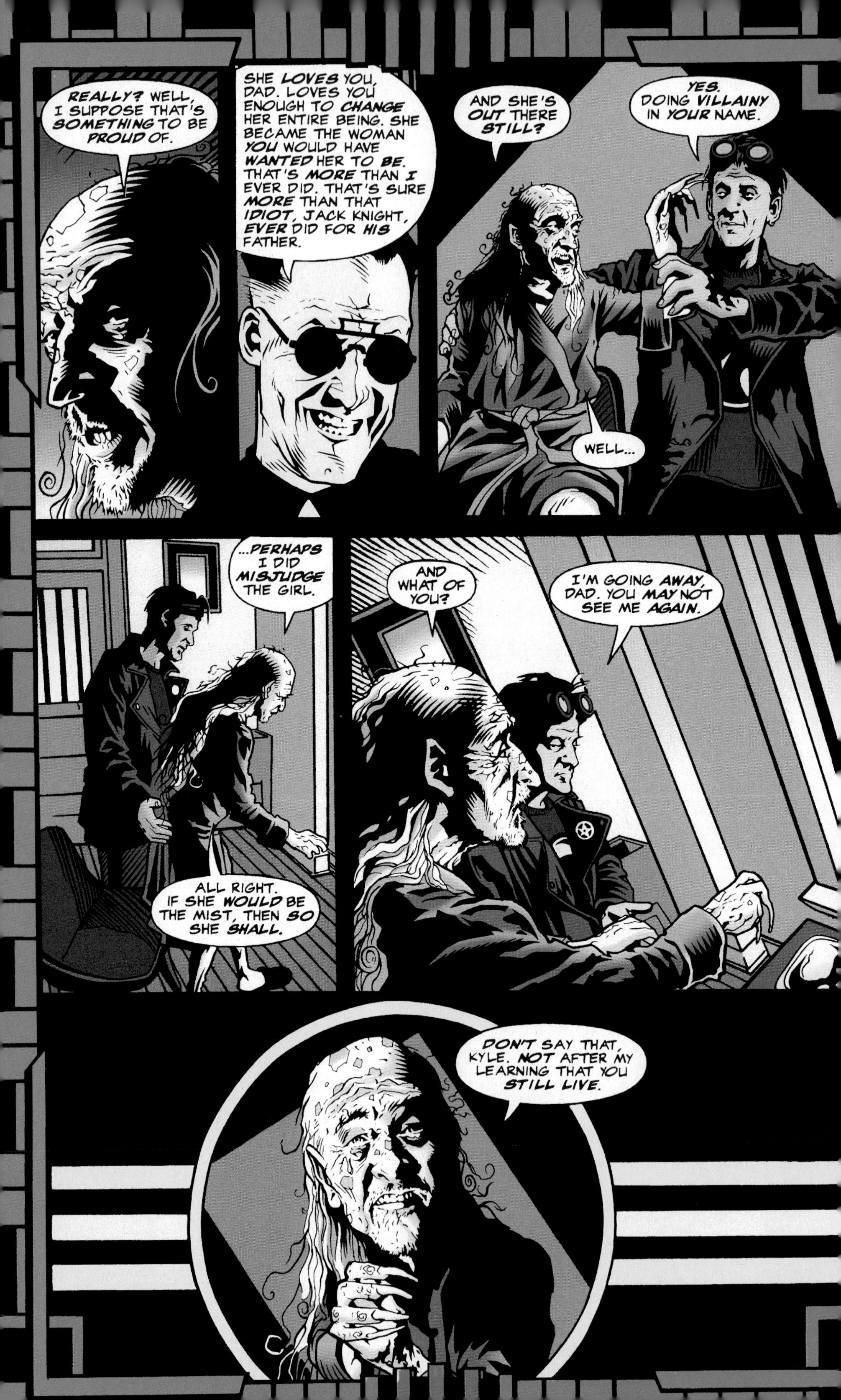
REALLY? WELL, I SUPPOSE THAT'S SOMETHING TO BE PROUD OF.
SHE LOVES YOU, DAD. LOVES YOU ENOUGH TO CHANGE HER ENTIRE BEING. SHE BECAME THE WOMAN YOU WOULD HAVE WANTED HER TO BE. THAT'S MORE THAN I EVER DID. THAT'S SURE MORE THAN THAT IDIOT, JACK KNIGHT, EVER DID FOR HIS FATHER.
AND SHE'S OUT THERE STILL?
YES. DOING VILLAINY IN YOUR NAME.
WELL...
...PERHAPS I DID MISJUDGE THE GIRL.
ALL RIGHT. IF SHE WOULD BE THE MIST, THEN SO SHE SHALL.
AND WHAT OF YOU?
I'M GOING AWAY, DAD. YOU MAY NOT SEE ME AGAIN.
DON'T SAY THAT, KYLE. NOT AFTER MY LEARNING THAT YOU STILL LIVE.

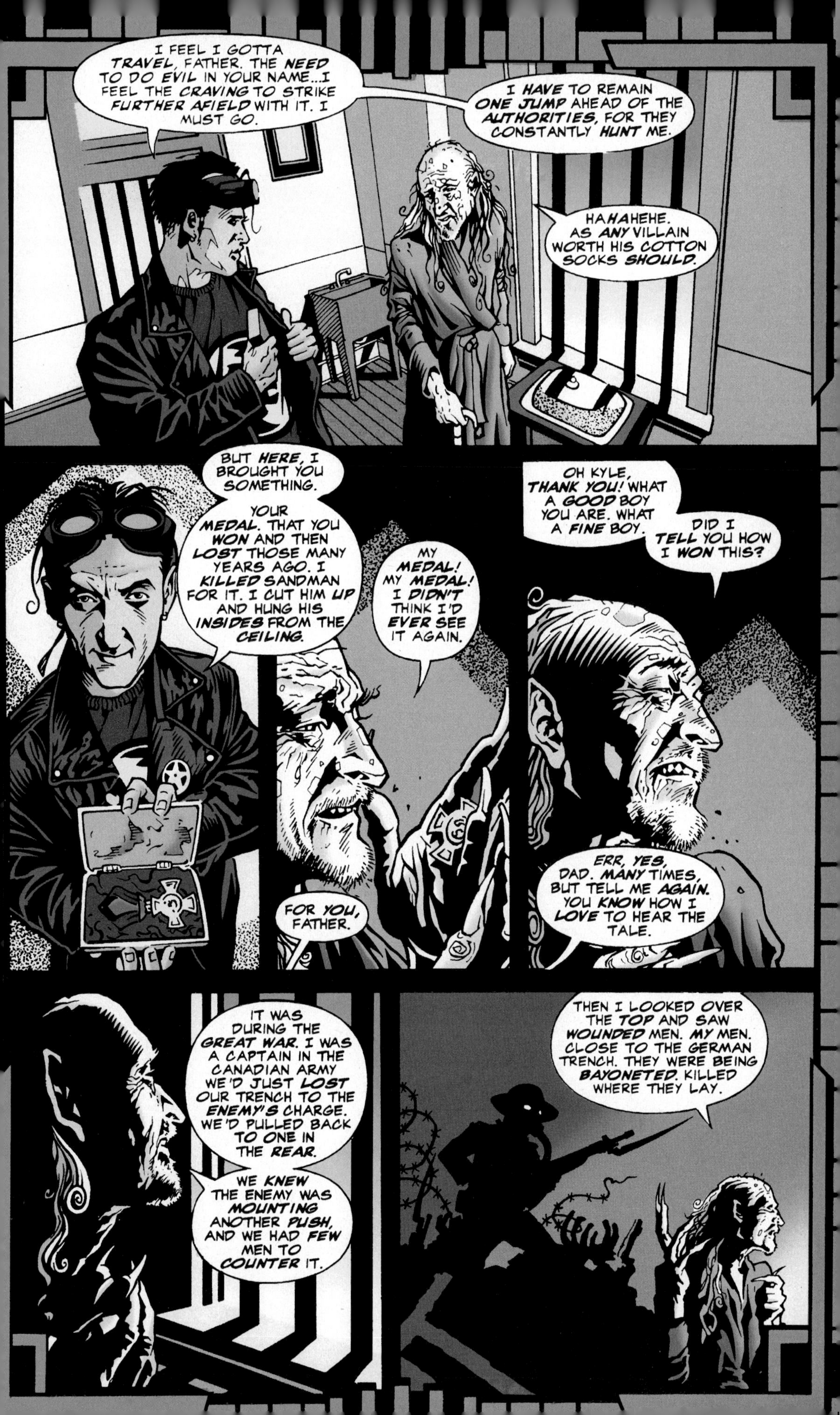
I FEEL I GOTTA TRAVEL, FATHER. THE NEED TO DO EVIL IN YOUR NAME...I FEEL THE CRAVING TO STRIKE FURTHER AFIELD WITH IT. I MUST GO.
I HAVE TO REMAIN ONE JUMP AHEAD OF THE AUTHORITIES, FOR THEY CONSTANTLY HUNT ME.
HAHAHEHE. AS ANY VILLAIN WORTH HIS COTTON SOCKS SHOULD.
BUT HERE, I BROUGHT YOU SOMETHING.
YOUR MEDAL. THAT YOU WON AND THEN LOST THOSE MANY YEARS AGO. I KILLED SANDMAN FOR IT. I CUT HIM UP AND HUNG HIS INSIDES FROM THE CEILING.
MY MEDAL! MY MEDAL! I DIDN'T THINK I'D EVER SEE IT AGAIN.
FOR YOU, FATHER.
OH KYLE, THANK YOU! WHAT A GOOD BOY YOU ARE. WHAT A FINE BOY.
DID I TELL YOU HOW I WON THIS?
ERR, YES, DAD. MANY TIMES, BUT TELL ME AGAIN. YOU KNOW HOW I LOVE TO HEAR THE TALE.
IT WAS DURING THE GREAT WAR. I WAS A CAPTAIN IN THE CANADIAN ARMY WE'D JUST LOST OUR TRENCH TO THE ENEMY'S CHARGE. WE'D PULLED BACK TO ONE IN THE REAR.
WE KNEW THE ENEMY WAS MOUNTING ANOTHER PUSH, AND WE HAD FEW MEN TO COUNTER IT.
THEN I LOOKED OVER THE TOP AND SAW WOUNDED MEN. MY MEN. CLOSE TO THE GERMAN TRENCH. THEY WERE BEING BAYONETED. KILLED WHERE THEY LAY.

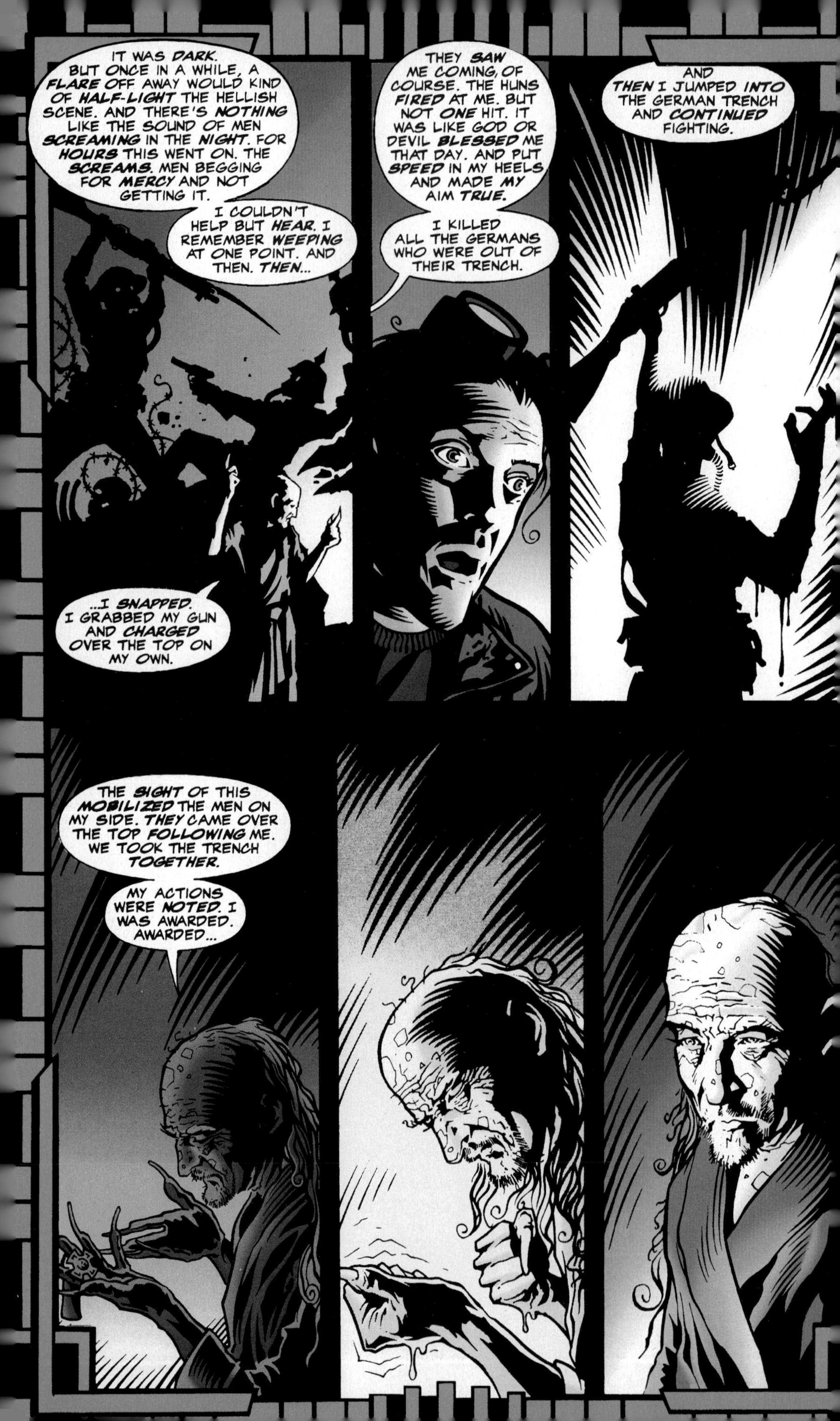
IT WAS DARK. BUT ONCE IN A WHILE, A FLARE OFF AWAY WOULD KIND OF HALF-LIGHT THE HELLISH SCENE. AND THERE'S NOTHING LIKE THE SOUND OF MEN SCREAMING IN THE NIGHT. FOR HOURS THIS WENT ON. THE SCREAMS. MEN BEGGING FOR MERCY AND NOT GETTING IT.
I COULDN'T HELP BUT HEAR. I REMEMBER WEEPING AT ONE POINT. AND THEN. THEN...
...I SNAPPED. I GRABBED MY GUN AND CHARGED OVER THE TOP ON MY OWN.
THEY SAW ME COMING, OF COURSE. THE HUNS FIRED AT ME. BUT NOT ONE HIT. IT WAS LIKE GOD OR DEVIL BLESSED ME THAT DAY. AND PUT SPEED IN MY HEELS AND MADE MY AIM TRUE.
I KILLED ALL THE GERMANS WHO WERE OUT OF THEIR TRENCH.
AND THEN I JUMPED INTO THE GERMAN TRENCH AND CONTINUED FIGHTING.
THE SIGHT OF THIS MOBILIZED THE MEN ON MY SIDE. THEY CAME OVER THE TOP FOLLOWING ME. WE TOOK THE TRENCH TOGETHER.
MY ACTIONS WERE NOTED. I WAS AWARDED. AWARDED...

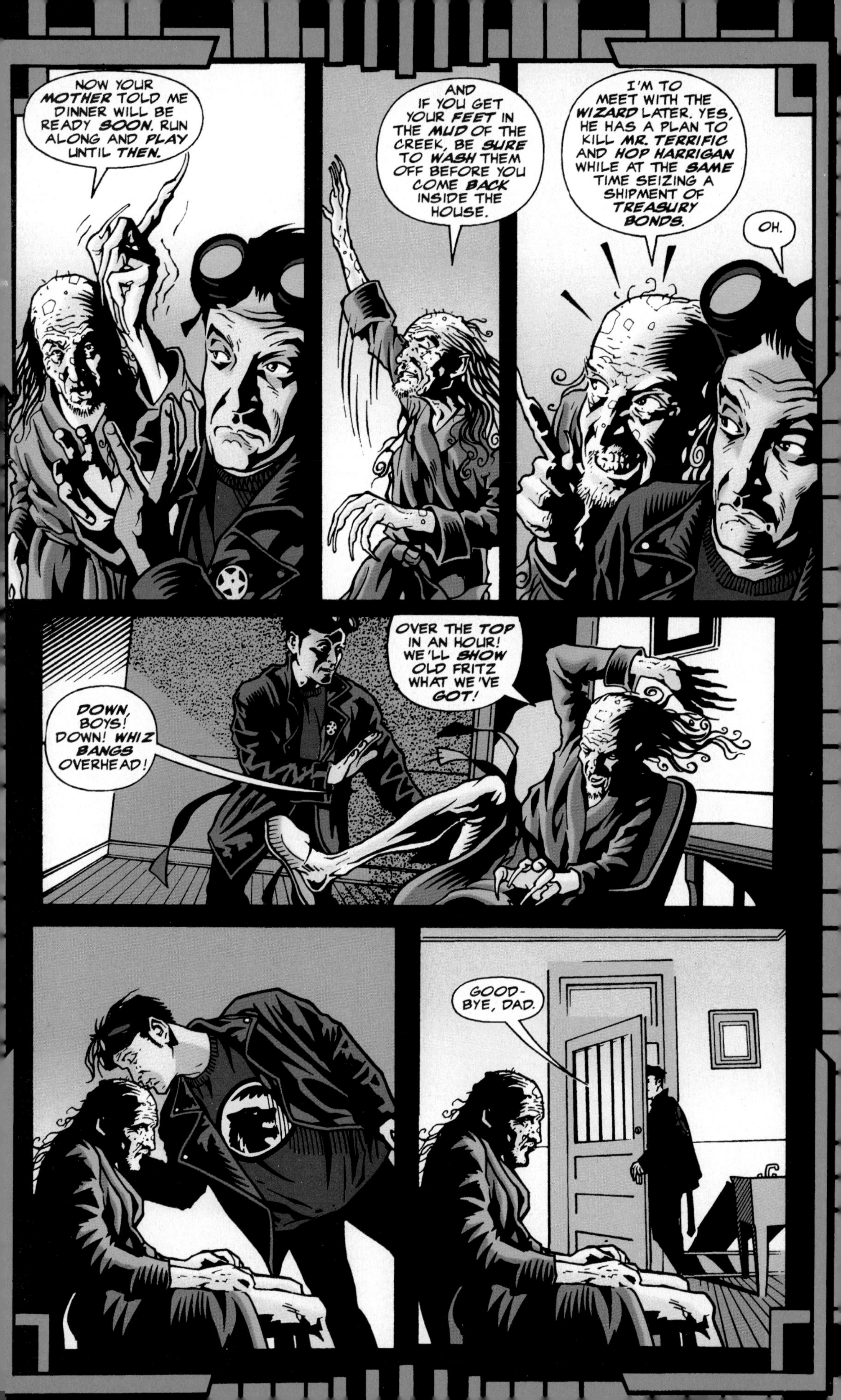
NOW YOUR MOTHER TOLD ME DINNER WILL BE READY SOON. RUN ALONG AND PLAY UNTIL THEN.
AND IF YOU GET YOUR FEET IN THE MUD OF THE CREEK, BE SURE TO WASH THEM OFF BEFORE YOU COME BACK INSIDE THE HOUSE.
I'M TO MEET WITH THE WIZARD LATER. YES, HE HAS A PLAN TO KILL MR. TERRIFIC AND HOP HARRIGAN WHILE AT THE SAME TIME SEIZING A SHIPMENT OF TREASURY BONDS.
OH.
DOWN, BOYS! DOWN! WHIZ BANGS OVERHEAD!
OVER THE TOP IN AN HOUR! WE'LL SHOW OLD FRITZ WHAT WE'VE GOT!
GOOD-BYE, DAD.

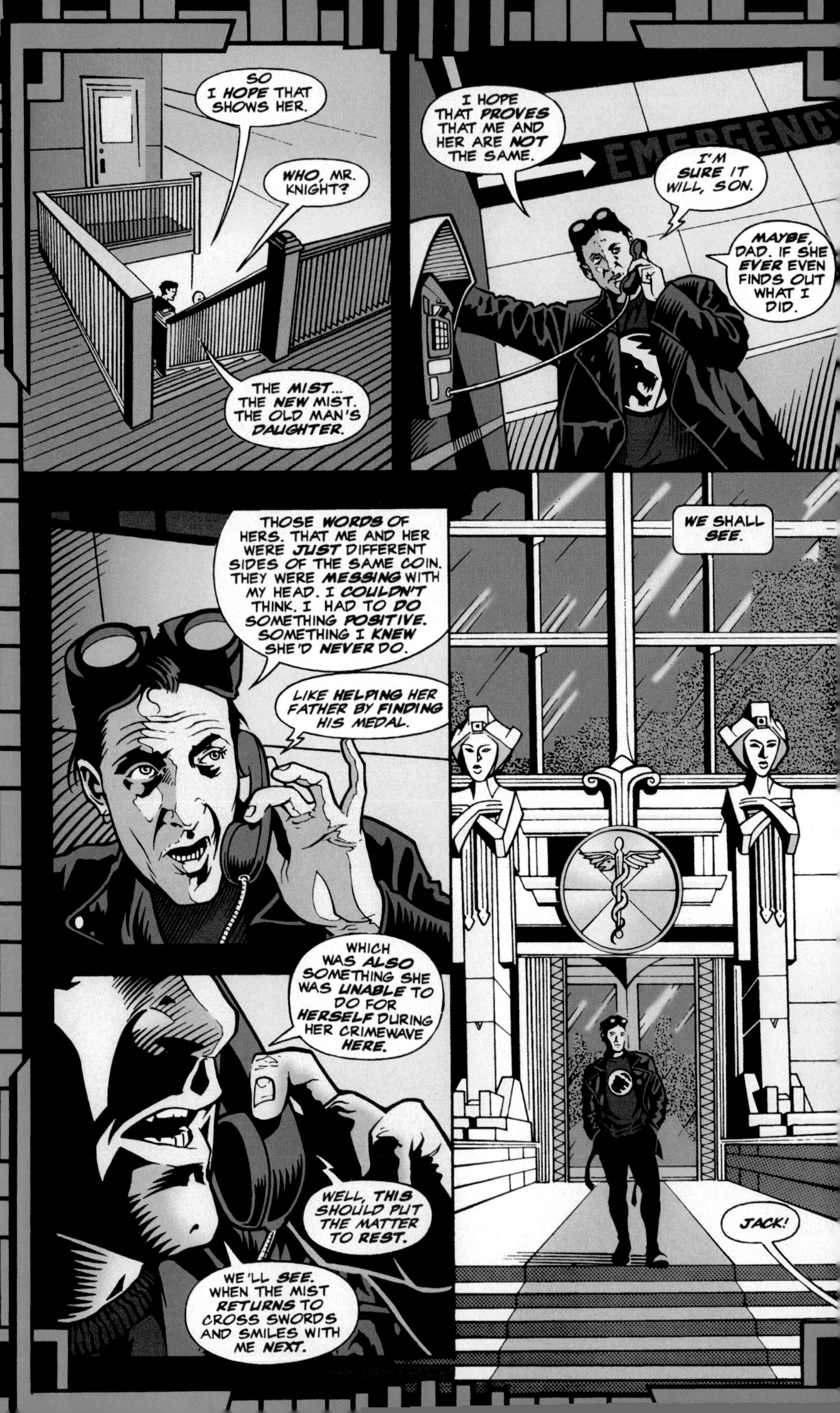
SO I HOPE THAT SHOWS HER.
WHO, MR. KNIGHT?
THE MIST... THE NEW MIST. THE OLD MAN'S DAUGHTER.
I HOPE THAT PROVES THAT ME AND HER ARE NOT THE SAME.
EMERGENCY
I'M SURE IT WILL, SON.
MAYBE, DAD. IF SHE EVER EVEN FINDS OUT WHAT I DID.
THOSE WORDS OF HERS. THAT ME AND HER WERE JUST DIFFERENT SIDES OF THE SAME COIN. THEY WERE MESSING WITH MY HEAD. I COULDN'T THINK. I HAD TO DO SOMETHING POSITIVE. SOMETHING I KNEW SHE'D NEVER DO.
LIKE HELPING HER FATHER BY FINDING HIS MEDAL.
WHICH WAS ALSO SOMETHING SHE WAS UNABLE TO DO FOR HERSELF DURING HER CRIMEWAVE HERE.
WELL, THIS SHOULD PUT THE MATTER TO REST.
WE'LL SEE. WHEN THE MIST RETURNS TO CROSS SWORDS AND SMILES WITH ME NEXT.
WE SHALL SEE.
JACK!

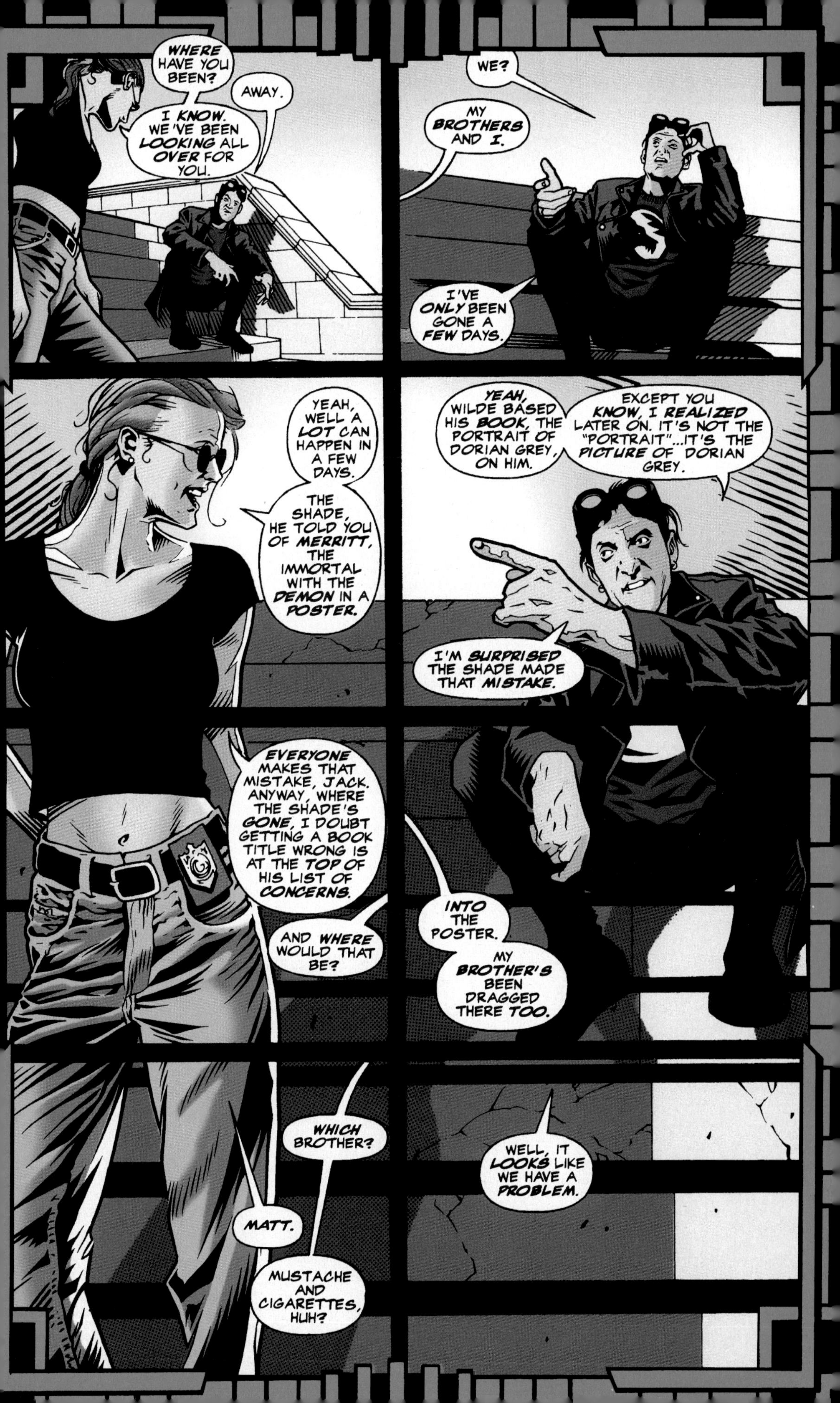
WHERE HAVE YOU BEEN?
AWAY.
I KNOW. WE'VE BEEN LOOKING ALL OVER FOR YOU.
WE?
MY BROTHERS AND I.
I'VE ONLY BEEN GONE A FEW DAYS.
YEAH, WELL A LOT CAN HAPPEN IN A FEW DAYS.
THE SHADE, HE TOLD YOU OF MERRITT, THE IMMORTAL WITH THE DEMON IN A POSTER.
YEAH, WILDE BASED HIS BOOK, THE PORTRAIT OF DORIAN GREY, ON HIM.
EXCEPT YOU KNOW, I REALIZED LATER ON. IT'S NOT THE "PORTRAIT"...IT'S THE PICTURE OF DORIAN GREY.
I'M SURPRISED THE SHADE MADE THAT MISTAKE.
EVERYONE MAKES THAT MISTAKE, JACK. ANYWAY, WHERE THE SHADE'S GONE, I DOUBT GETTING A BOOK TITLE WRONG IS AT THE TOP OF HIS LIST OF CONCERNS.
AND WHERE WOULD THAT BE?
INTO THE POSTER.
MY BROTHER'S BEEN DRAGGED THERE TOO.
WHICH BROTHER?
MATT.
MUSTACHE AND CIGARETTES, HUH?
WELL, IT LOOKS LIKE WE HAVE A PROBLEM.

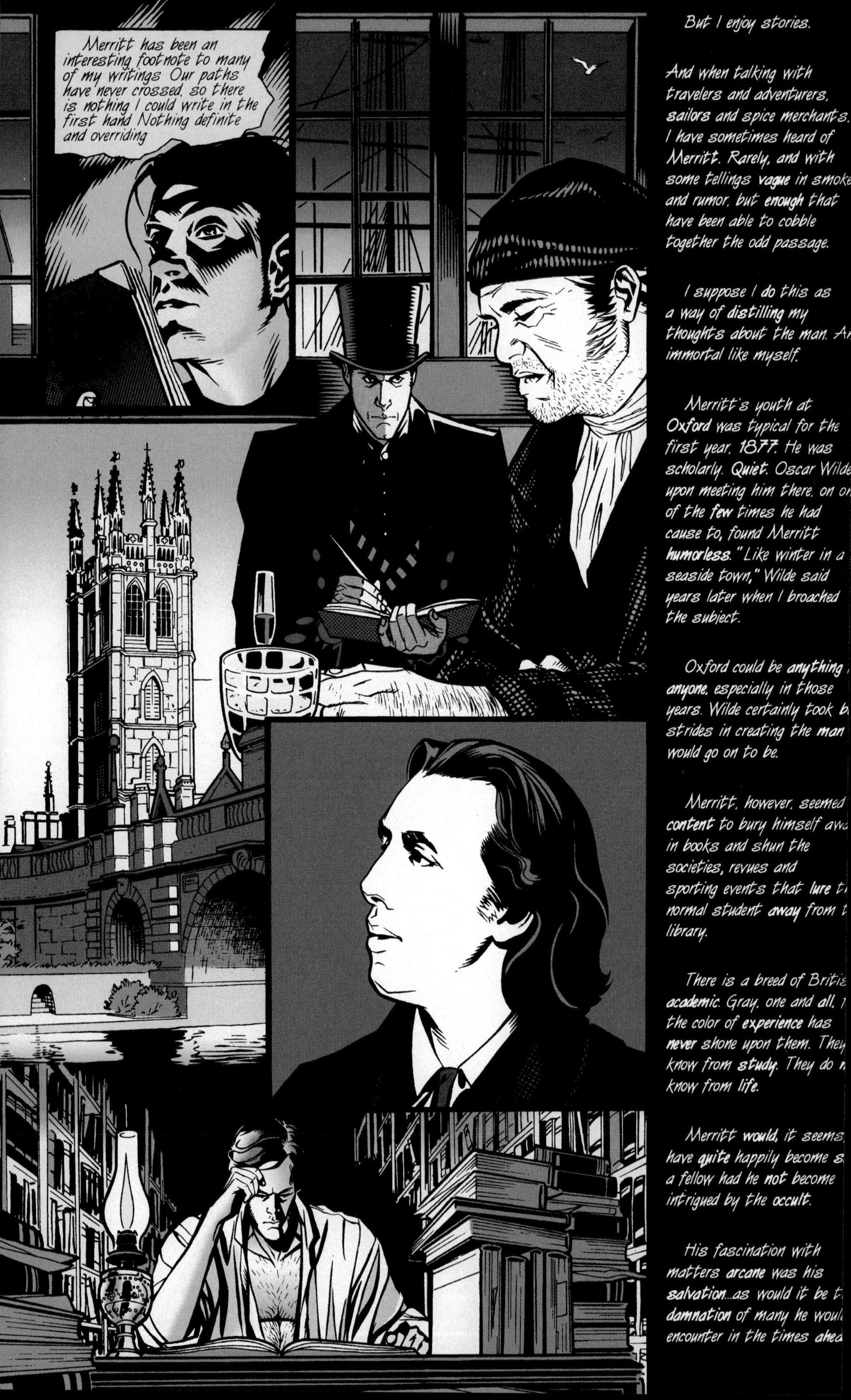
Merritt has been an interesting footnote to many of my writings Our paths have never crossed, so there is nothing I could write in the first hand Nothing definite and overriding

But I enjoy stories.

And when talking with travelers and adventurers, **sailors** and spice merchants, I have sometimes heard of Merritt. Rarely, and with some tellings **vague** in smoke and rumor, but **enough** that have been able to cobble together the odd passage.

I suppose I **do** this as a way of **distilling** my thoughts about the man. An immortal like myself.

Merritt's youth at **Oxford** was typical for the first year, **1877**. He was scholarly. **Quiet.** Oscar Wilde upon meeting him there, on on of the **few** times he had cause to, found Merritt **humorless.** "Like winter in a seaside town," Wilde said years later when I broached the subject.

Oxford could be **anything** anyone, especially in those years. Wilde certainly took b strides in creating the **man** would go on to be.

Merritt, however, seemed **content** to bury himself awa in books and shun the societies, revues and sporting events that **lure** t normal student **away** from t library.

There is a breed of Britis **academic**. Gray, one and **all**, t the color of **experience** has **never** shone upon them. They know from **study**. They do n know from **life**.

Merritt **would**, it seems, have **quite** happily become s a fellow had he **not** become intrigued by the **occult**.

His fascination with matters **arcane** was his **salvation**...as would it be t **damnation** of many he would encounter in the times ahea

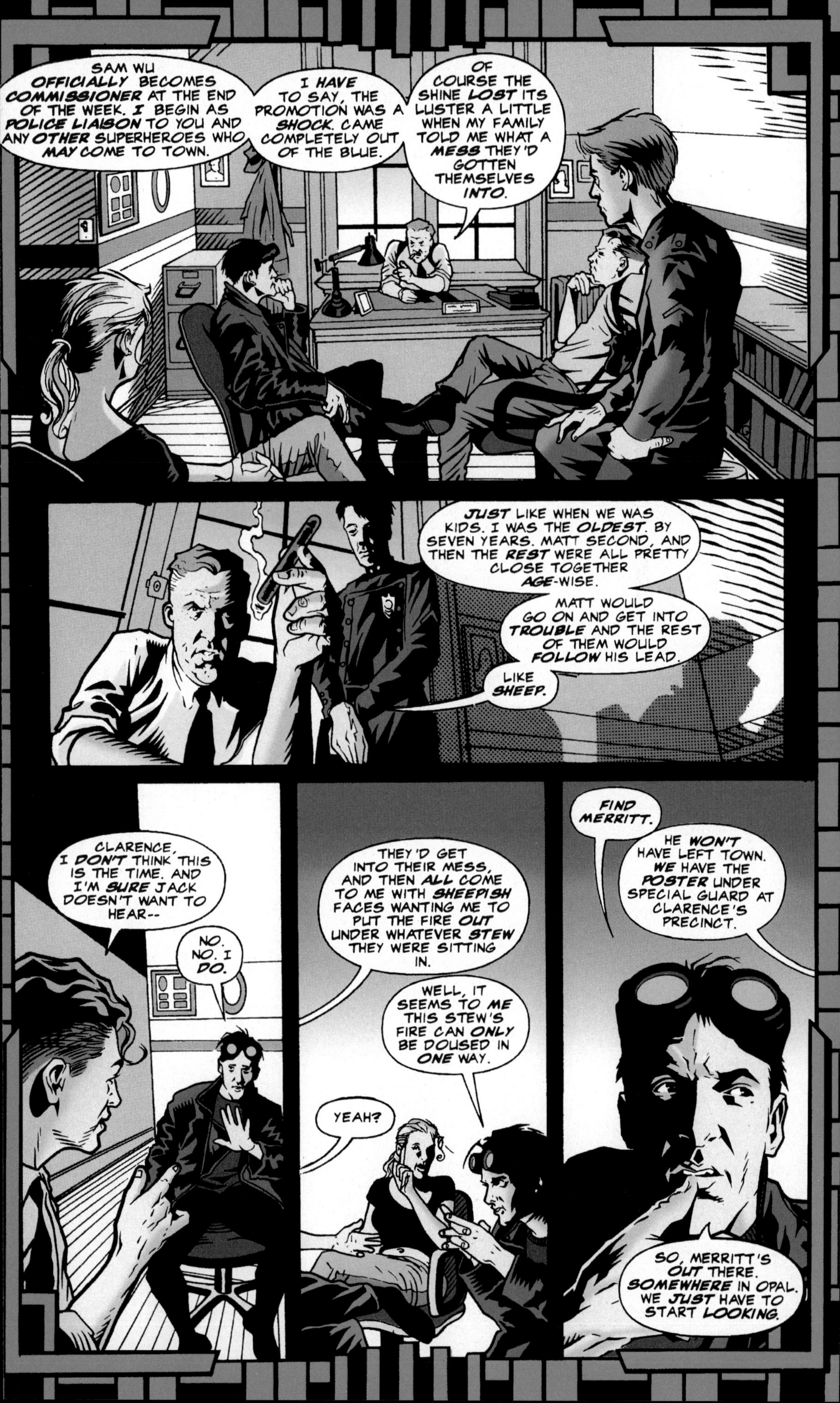
SAM WU OFFICIALLY BECOMES COMMISSIONER AT THE END OF THE WEEK. I BEGIN AS POLICE LIAISON TO YOU AND ANY OTHER SUPERHEROES WHO MAY COME TO TOWN.
I HAVE TO SAY, THE PROMOTION WAS A SHOCK. CAME COMPLETELY OUT OF THE BLUE.
OF COURSE THE SHINE LOST ITS LUSTER A LITTLE WHEN MY FAMILY TOLD ME WHAT A MESS THEY'D GOTTEN THEMSELVES INTO.
JUST LIKE WHEN WE WAS KIDS. I WAS THE OLDEST. BY SEVEN YEARS. MATT SECOND, AND THEN THE REST WERE ALL PRETTY CLOSE TOGETHER AGE-WISE.
MATT WOULD GO ON AND GET INTO TROUBLE AND THE REST OF THEM WOULD FOLLOW HIS LEAD.
LIKE SHEEP.
CLARENCE, I DON'T THINK THIS IS THE TIME. AND I'M SURE JACK DOESN'T WANT TO HEAR--
NO. NO. I DO.
THEY'D GET INTO THEIR MESS, AND THEN ALL COME TO ME WITH SHEEPISH FACES WANTING ME TO PUT THE FIRE OUT UNDER WHATEVER STEW THEY WERE SITTING IN.
WELL, IT SEEMS TO ME THIS STEW'S FIRE CAN ONLY BE DOUSED IN ONE WAY.
YEAH?
FIND MERRITT.
HE WON'T HAVE LEFT TOWN. WE HAVE THE POSTER UNDER SPECIAL GUARD AT CLARENCE'S PRECINCT.
SO, MERRITT'S OUT THERE. SOMEWHERE IN OPAL. WE JUST HAVE TO START LOOKING.

I have **yet** to learn the **name** of the demon Merritt summoned on that foggy evening in **1879**. I know that demons do have names and ranks and stations within Hell's **many** levels.

I'm **sure** this demon has **all** of the above. I'm sure he's a perfectly **nice** demon **too**. As demons go.

But demons from Hell and elsewhere, are all of them devilishly good (**excuse** the pun) at submitting **temptation** in such a menu as to seem the fools themselves.

They seem the guillible ones to offer something as **great** as whatever it is they bid, in **exchange** for something so **slight** as that **thing** they desire.

So it **was** with Merritt. **Immortality** in exchange for **custodianship**. **Everlasting** life in exchange for a **poster**.

And there was **more** to benefit Merritt in the demon's offer. At least Merritt saw it **so** and that his agreement was something of a **bargain**. It **seems** he knew the young man he was, and the old man he would **doubtless** become. A **gray** scholar.

There was a **part** of him that **knew** a world was **sweeter** for the living in it. Now, with a demon who required souls, and would have a **variety** of them, Merritt knew he would have to **lock** his timidity **away** in a cabin trunk and venture **forth** to procure.

A month into his **new** life everlasting, and Merritt wondered **how** he could have thought Oxford...nay, the **whole** of England's green and pleasant lands, could **ever** have been his **be**-all and end-all.

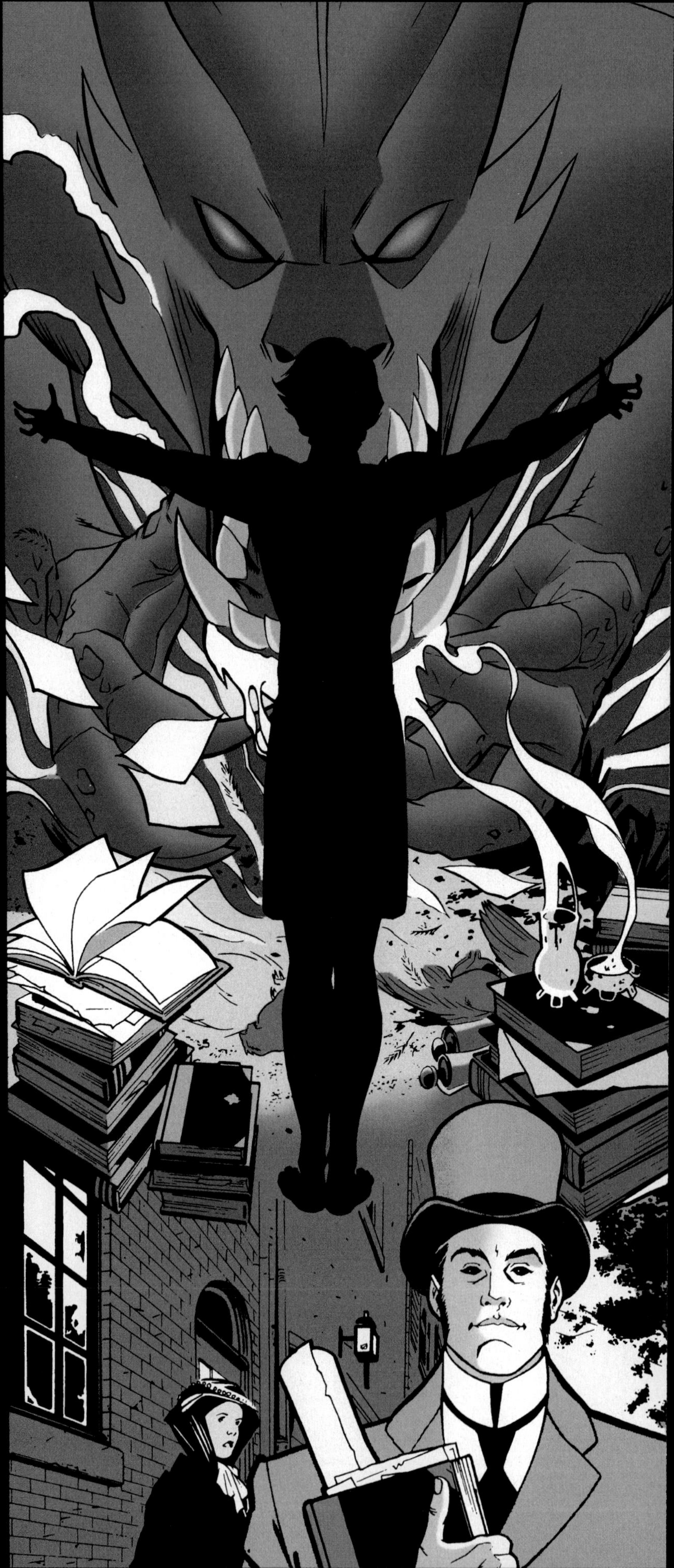

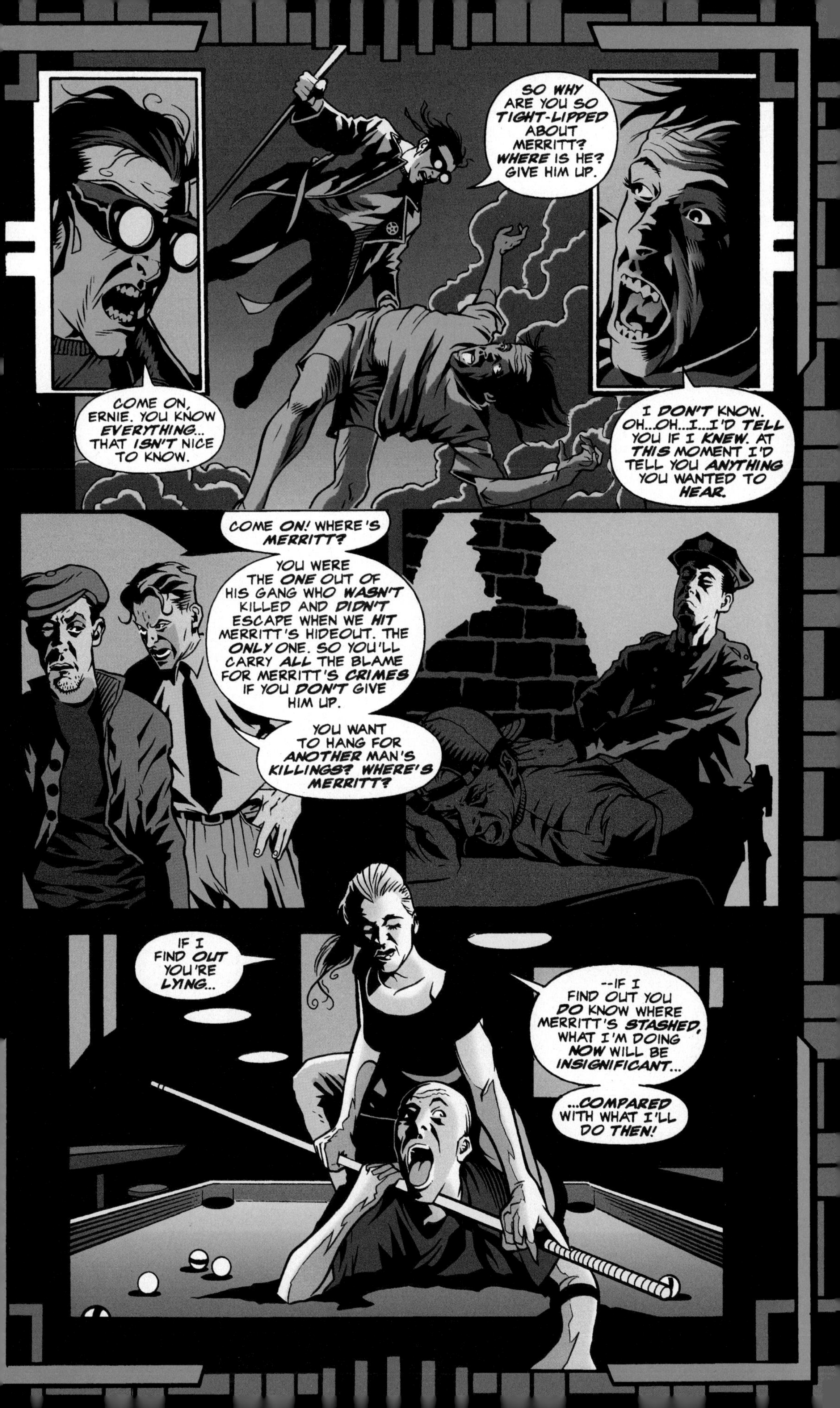
SO WHY ARE YOU SO TIGHT-LIPPED ABOUT MERRITT? WHERE IS HE? GIVE HIM UP.
COME ON, ERNIE. YOU KNOW EVERYTHING... THAT ISN'T NICE TO KNOW.
I DON'T KNOW. OH...OH...I...I'D TELL YOU IF I KNEW. AT THIS MOMENT I'D TELL YOU ANYTHING YOU WANTED TO HEAR.
COME ON! WHERE'S MERRITT?
YOU WERE THE ONE OUT OF HIS GANG WHO WASN'T KILLED AND DIDN'T ESCAPE WHEN WE HIT MERRITT'S HIDEOUT. THE ONLY ONE. SO YOU'LL CARRY ALL THE BLAME FOR MERRITT'S CRIMES IF YOU DON'T GIVE HIM UP.
YOU WANT TO HANG FOR ANOTHER MAN'S KILLINGS? WHERE'S MERRITT?
IF I FIND OUT YOU'RE LYING...
--IF I FIND OUT YOU DO KNOW WHERE MERRITT'S STASHED, WHAT I'M DOING NOW WILL BE INSIGNIFICANT...
...COMPARED WITH WHAT I'LL DO THEN!

Merritt sailed the high seas. He **advised** potentates. He **started** revolutions and uprisings. He **ended** one or two. He **spied** for the Dutch during the Boer War, and for the Turks in the Great War. He **found** gold in the Klondike and **lost** it on Wall Street. There is a street named after him in a suburb of Australia where he **spent** several relaxing years as a local politician, before boredom **dragged** him back to the world and five years with a rag tag theater troupe **touring** India and the East. He almost **lost his manhood** to Afghani tribesmen, but instead he **stayed** with the men for six months and in that time **took** a wife. In 1953 he **exhibited** paintings in a Belgian gallery. In 1919 he **sold** guns to the Black and Tans for a while, until things seemed fraught...at which point he happily **switched** sides and **sold** guns to Collins. The links to Ireland afforded him a whisky supplier when peace arrived. This whisky he **transported** to New York and Boston during prohibition. He **spent** 1891 as a riverboat gambler and 1931 **flying** mail planes in the Andes.

(It was there he **learned** the root of his magic. The root of the poster's power **stemmed** from lore first **gleaned** in those remote mountains. **Etching** a gateway to other levels of existence...to Hell and to Heaven...onto a flat portable plane. Few had **managed** to hone this skill, though tales of another who **did** such a thing upon a **Hawaiian Shirt** still **flutter** to my ears **now** and **once** a **few**.)

I **have** to say, his life **many** lifetimes long would have been one to envy. He **was** and **is**, quite possibly, the **greatest** adventurer of all.

If he **didn't** have that **annoying** habit of **putting** his poster on a wall and **having** the demon **emerge** from it to **devour** some passing innocent, I'd **admire** him slightly **more so**.

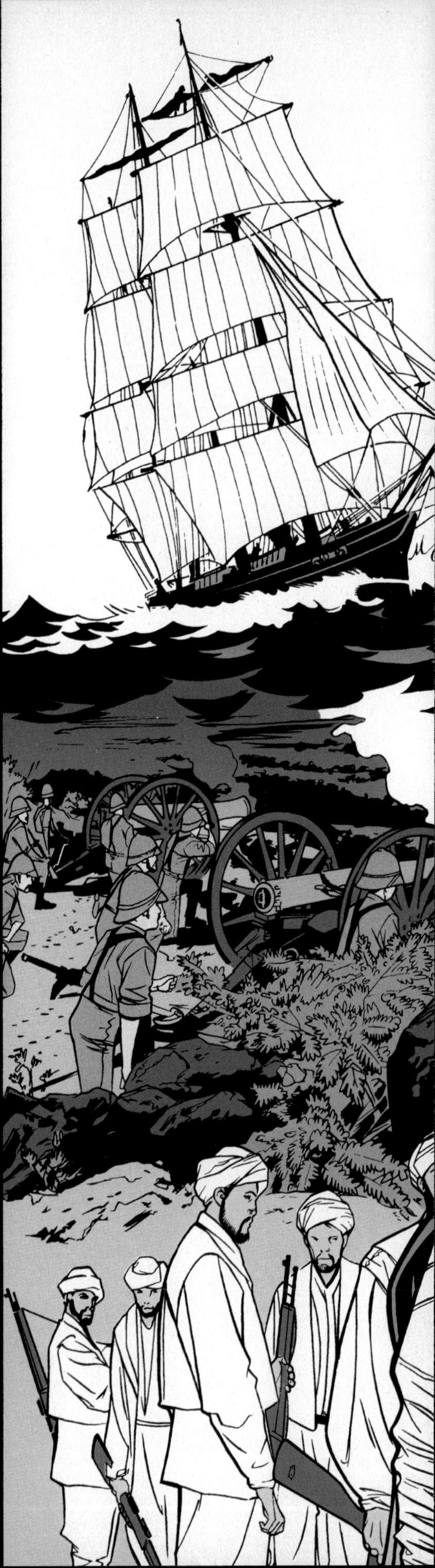

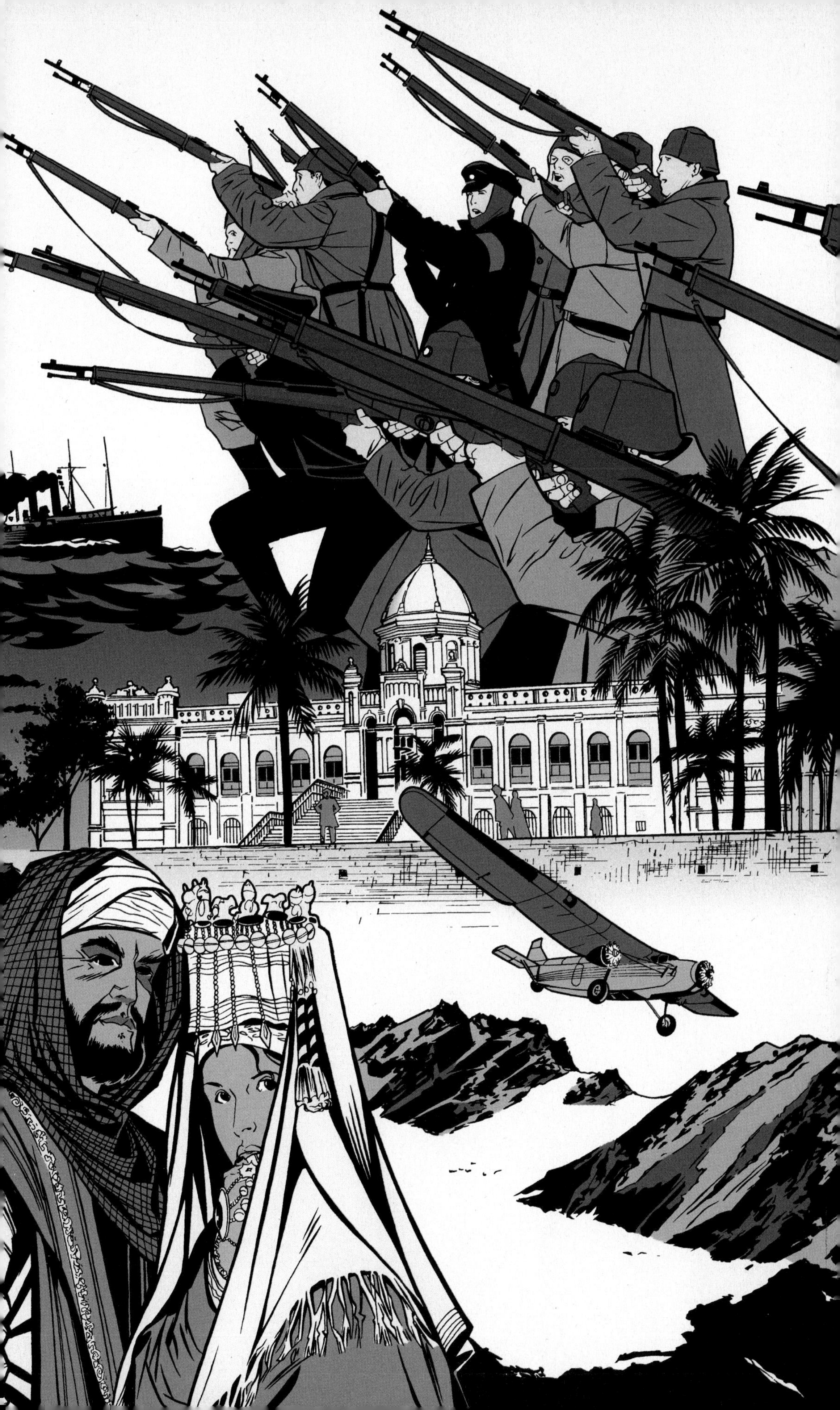

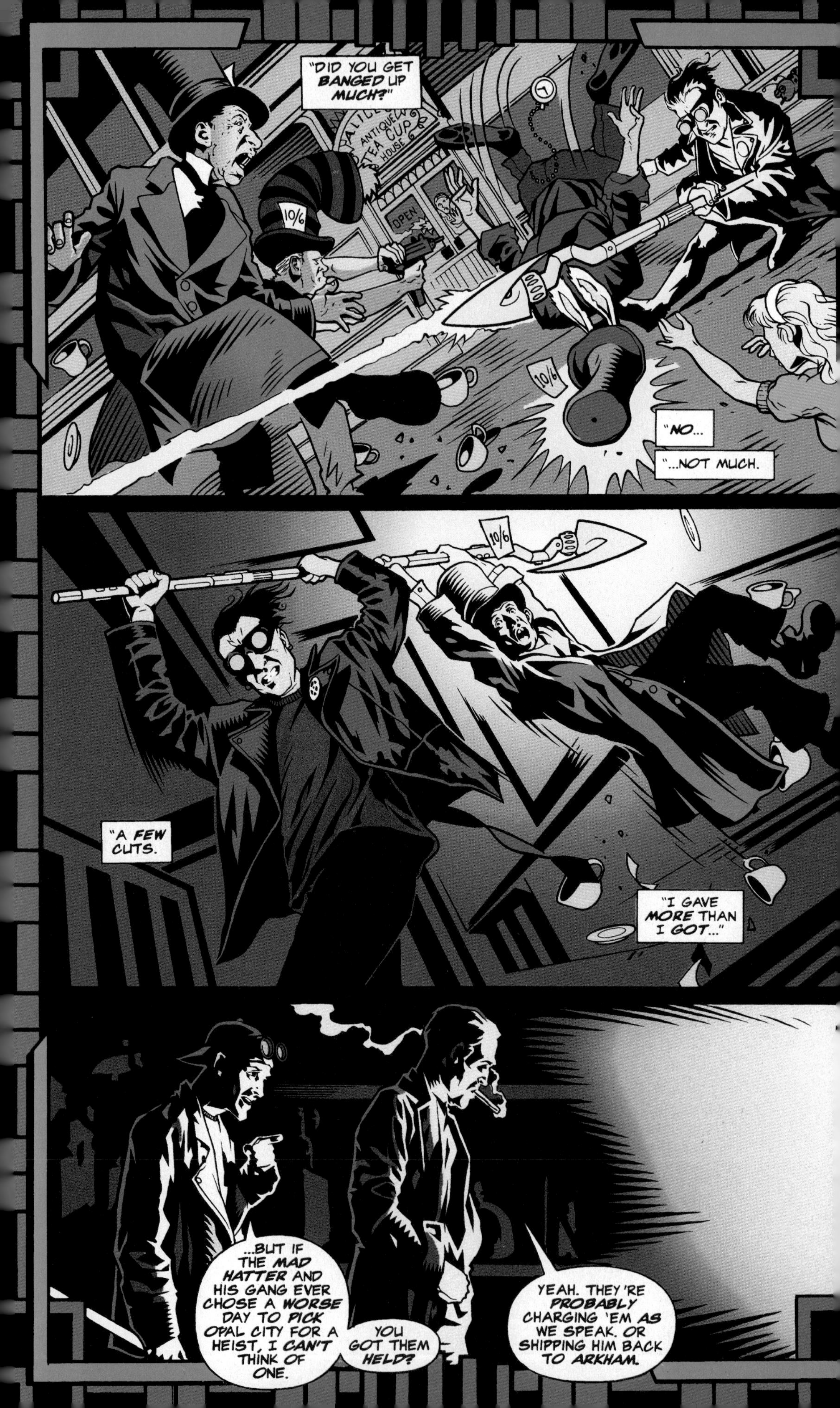
"DID YOU GET BANGED UP MUCH?"
ALICE'S ANTIQUE TEA CUP HOUSE
OPEN
10/6
"NO...
"...NOT MUCH.
10/6
"A FEW CUTS.
"I GAVE MORE THAN I GOT..."
...BUT IF THE MAD HATTER AND HIS GANG EVER CHOSE A WORSE DAY TO PICK OPAL CITY FOR A HEIST, I CAN'T THINK OF ONE.
YOU GOT THEM HELD?
YEAH. THEY'RE PROBABLY CHARGING 'EM AS WE SPEAK. OR SHIPPING HIM BACK TO ARKHAM.

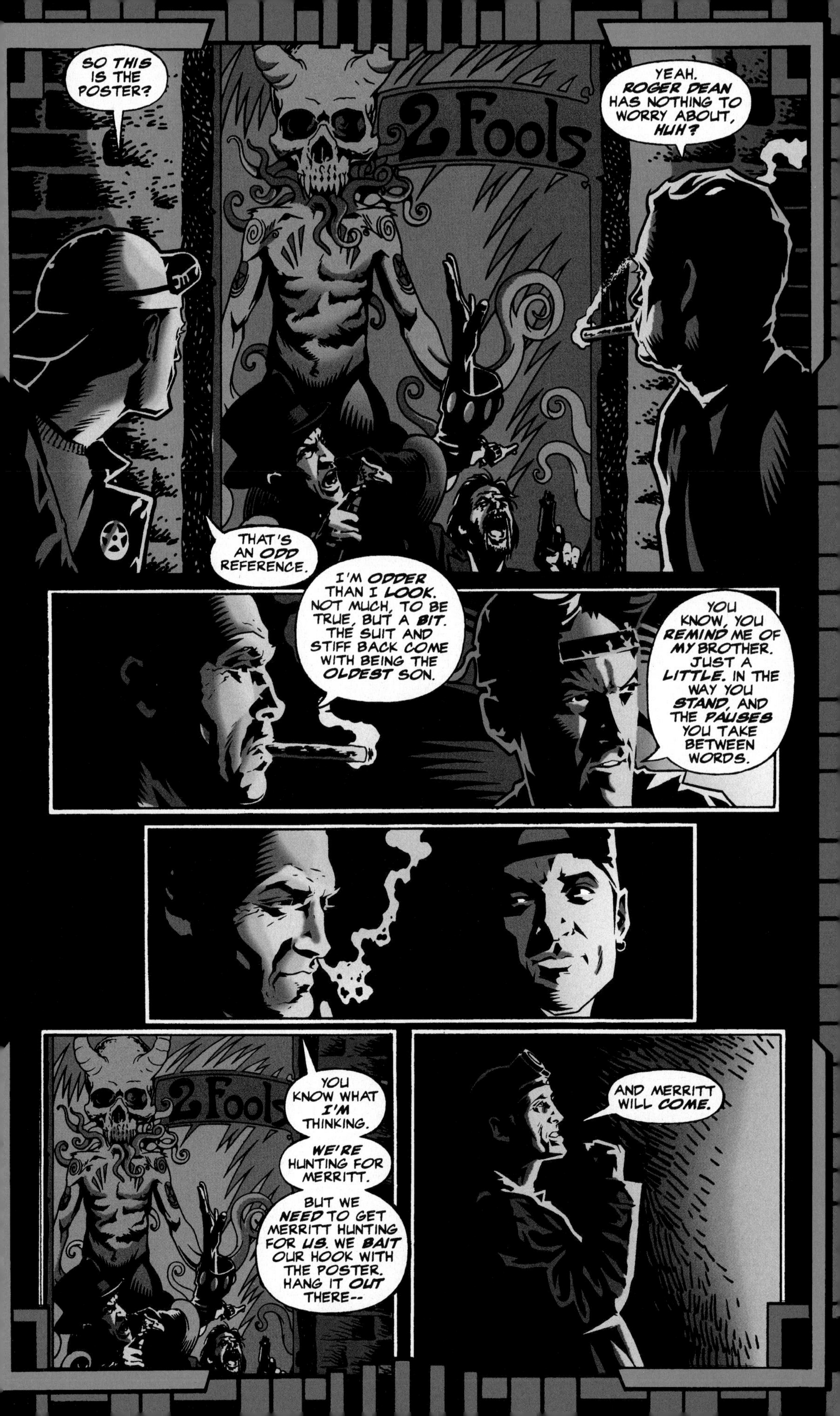
SO THIS IS THE POSTER?
2 Fools
YEAH. ROGER DEAN HAS NOTHING TO WORRY ABOUT, HUH?
THAT'S AN ODD REFERENCE.
I'M ODDER THAN I LOOK. NOT MUCH, TO BE TRUE, BUT A BIT. THE SUIT AND STIFF BACK COME WITH BEING THE OLDEST SON.
YOU KNOW, YOU REMIND ME OF MY BROTHER. JUST A LITTLE. IN THE WAY YOU STAND, AND THE PAUSES YOU TAKE BETWEEN WORDS.
2 Fools
YOU KNOW WHAT I'M THINKING.
WE'RE HUNTING FOR MERRITT.
BUT WE NEED TO GET MERRITT HUNTING FOR US. WE BAIT OUR HOOK WITH THE POSTER. HANG IT OUT THERE--
AND MERRITT WILL COME.

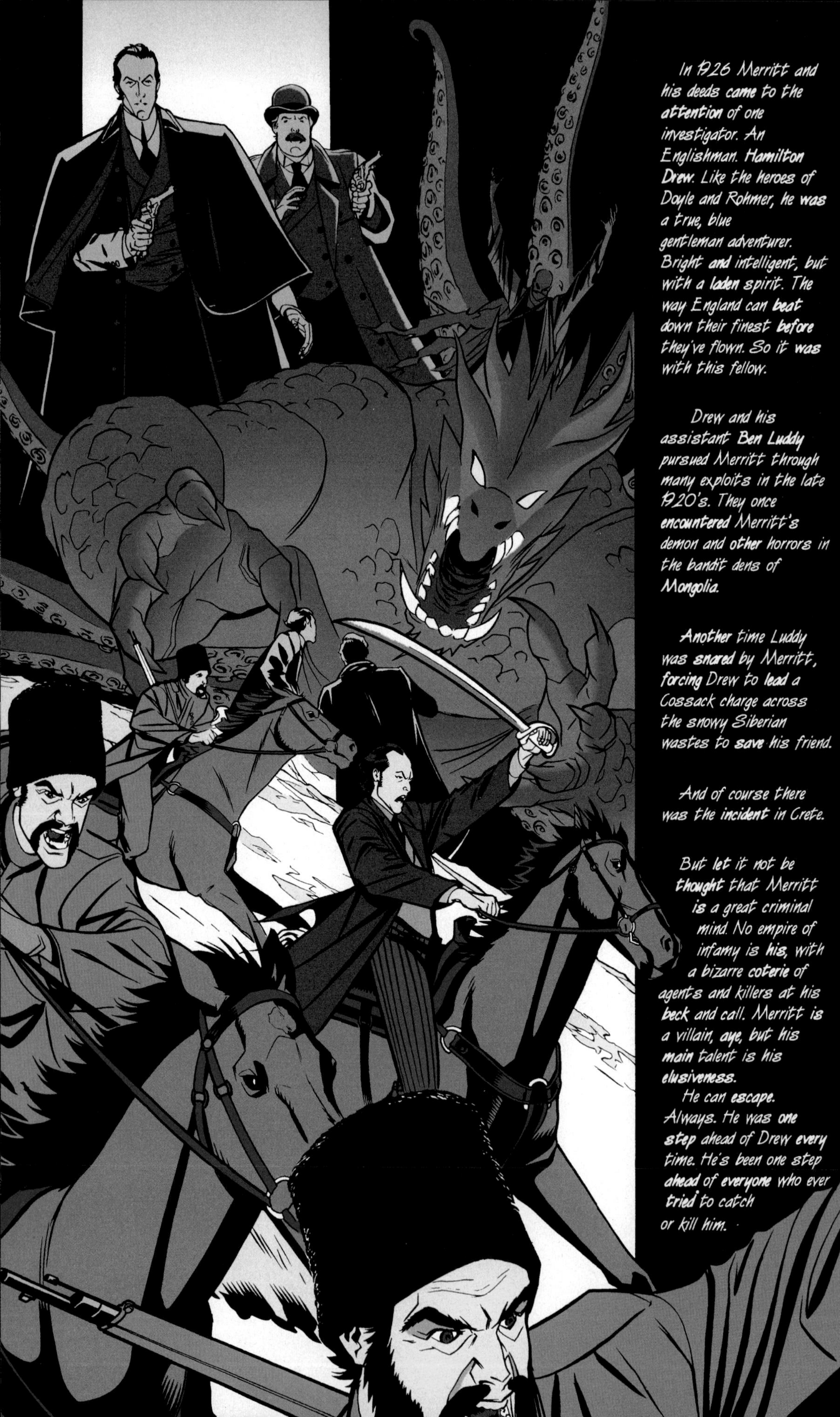
In 1926 Merritt and his deeds came to the attention of one investigator. An Englishman. Hamilton Drew. Like the heroes of Doyle and Rohmer, he was a true, blue gentleman adventurer. Bright and intelligent, but with a laden spirit. The way England can beat down their finest before they've flown. So it was with this fellow.
Drew and his assistant Ben Luddy pursued Merritt through many exploits in the late 1920's. They once encountered Merritt's demon and other horrors in the bandit dens of Mongolia.
Another time Luddy was snared by Merritt, forcing Drew to lead a Cossack charge across the snowy Siberian wastes to save his friend.
And of course there was the incident in Crete.
But let it not be thought that Merritt is a great criminal mind. No empire of infamy is his, with a bizarre coterie of agents and killers at his beck and call. Merritt is a villain, aye, but his main talent is his elusiveness.
He can escape. Always. He was one step ahead of Drew every time. He's been one step ahead of everyone who ever tried to catch or kill him.

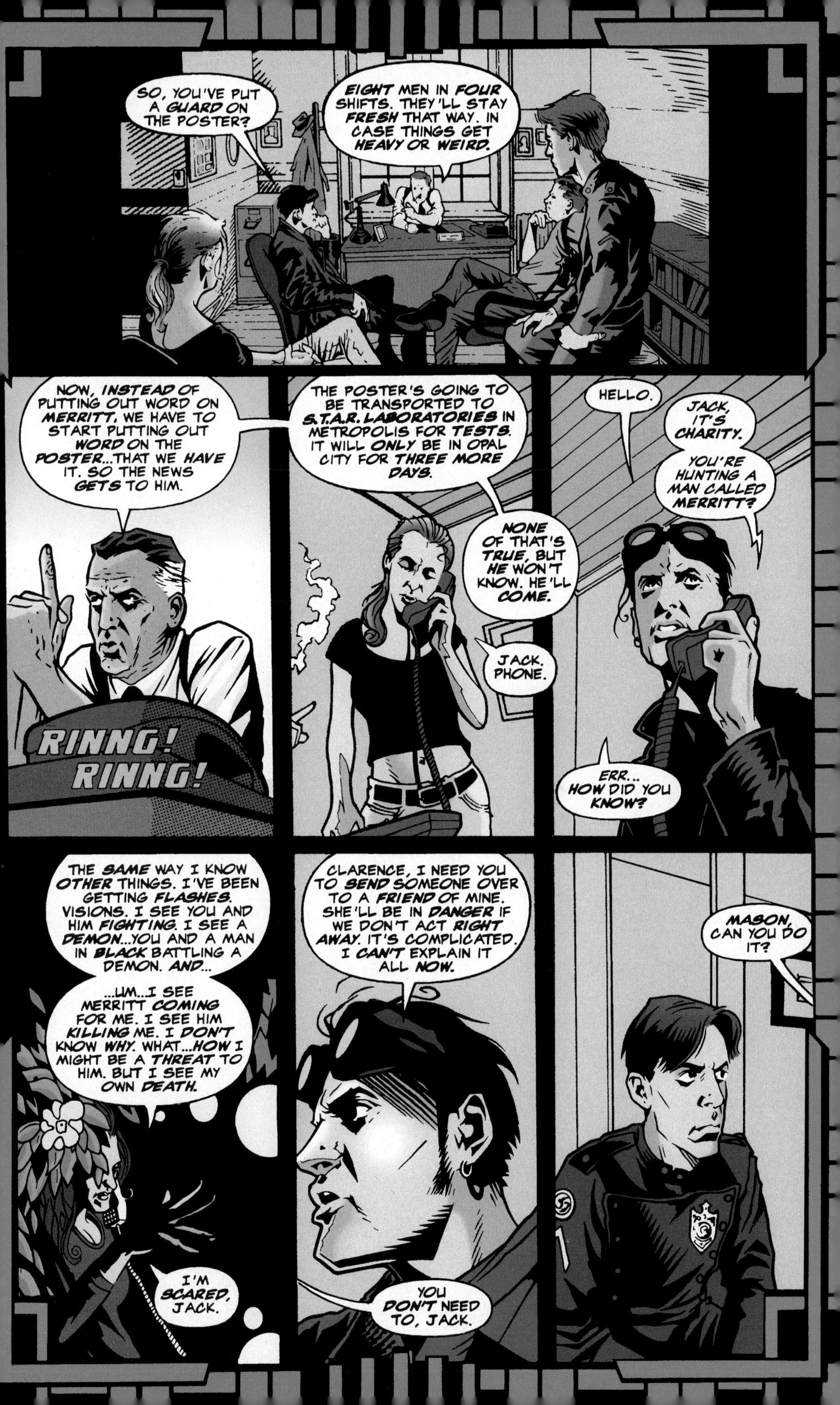
SO, YOU'VE PUT A GUARD ON THE POSTER?
EIGHT MEN IN FOUR SHIFTS. THEY'LL STAY FRESH THAT WAY. IN CASE THINGS GET HEAVY OR WEIRD.
NOW, INSTEAD OF PUTTING OUT WORD ON MERRITT, WE HAVE TO START PUTTING OUT WORD ON THE POSTER...THAT WE HAVE IT. SO THE NEWS GETS TO HIM.
RINNG! RINNG!
THE POSTER'S GOING TO BE TRANSPORTED TO S.T.A.R. LABORATORIES IN METROPOLIS FOR TESTS. IT WILL ONLY BE IN OPAL CITY FOR THREE MORE DAYS.
NONE OF THAT'S TRUE, BUT HE WON'T KNOW. HE'LL COME.
JACK. PHONE.
HELLO.
JACK, IT'S CHARITY.
YOU'RE HUNTING A MAN CALLED MERRITT?
ERR... HOW DID YOU KNOW?
THE SAME WAY I KNOW OTHER THINGS. I'VE BEEN GETTING FLASHES. VISIONS. I SEE YOU AND HIM FIGHTING. I SEE A DEMON...YOU AND A MAN IN BLACK BATTLING A DEMON. AND...
...UM...I SEE MERRITT COMING FOR ME. I SEE HIM KILLING ME. I DON'T KNOW WHY. WHAT...HOW I MIGHT BE A THREAT TO HIM. BUT I SEE MY OWN DEATH.
I'M SCARED, JACK.
CLARENCE, I NEED YOU TO SEND SOMEONE OVER TO A FRIEND OF MINE. SHE'LL BE IN DANGER IF WE DON'T ACT RIGHT AWAY. IT'S COMPLICATED. I CAN'T EXPLAIN IT ALL NOW.
YOU DON'T NEED TO, JACK.
MASON, CAN YOU DO IT?

The last **two reports** I **got** on Merritt were twenty years **after** Luddy ad been **committed** to the sylum and Drew had been dragged to Hell through the oster. The poster had been **snatching** from a street n **Chicago**. American nvestigator **Johnny Peril** got involved. He and the demon **skirmished**. Peril **survived**. The demon vanished. Peril never made the **link** from the demon to the oster it **emerged** from. Merritt **stole** away that ight to a **new** venue for is game. And Peril declared himself a victor, for what in reality was at best a **stalemate**.

And then **later** still, in Gotham City, the demon **fought** one of his **own** kind. **Another** stalemate. Although this a **fierier** one.

That was my **last** word n Merritt. My **last**.

Until today. A policeman aken. No signs. No clues. othing **overt**.

And **yet** I know. I know. **know**.

Merritt is in pal!

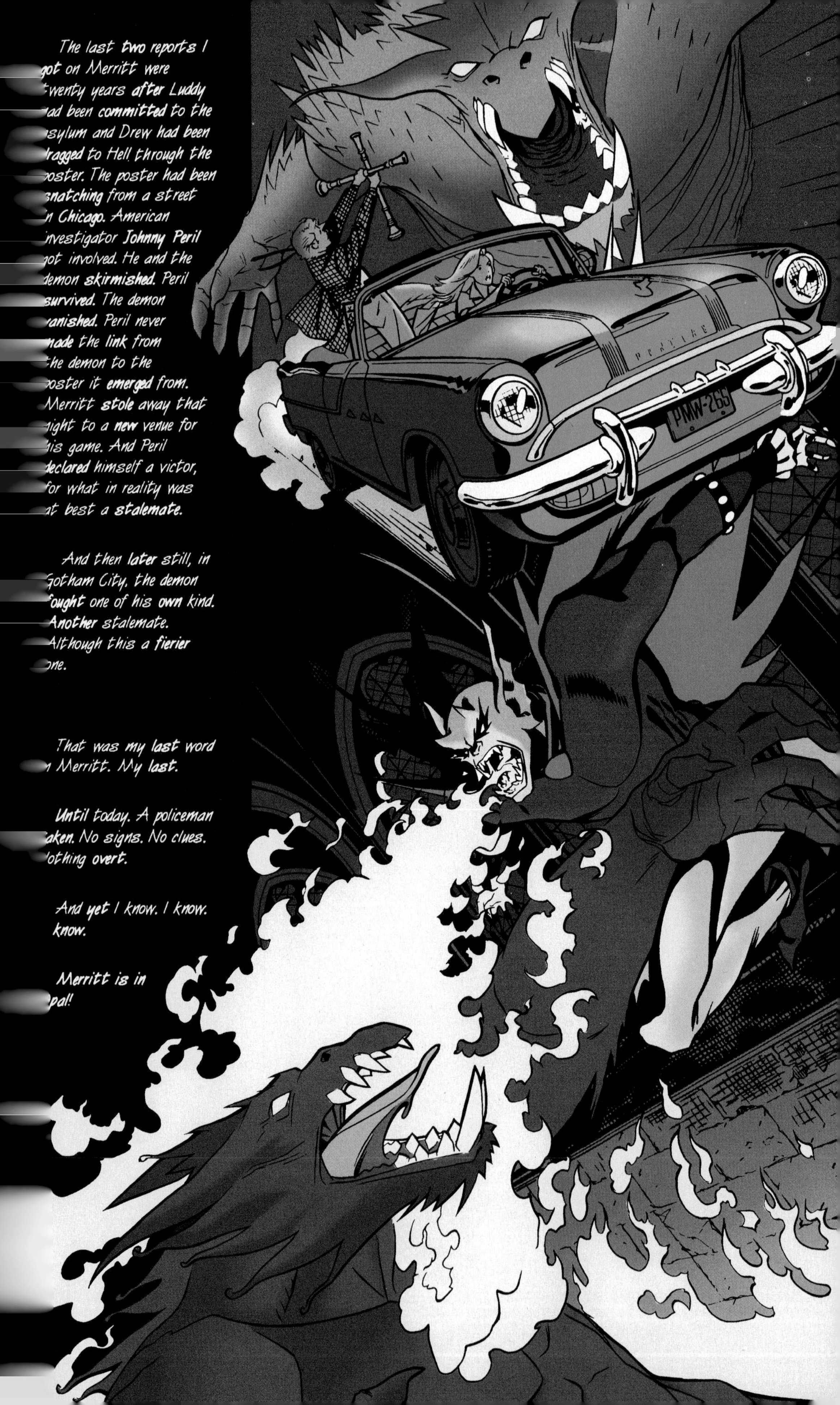
PMW-265

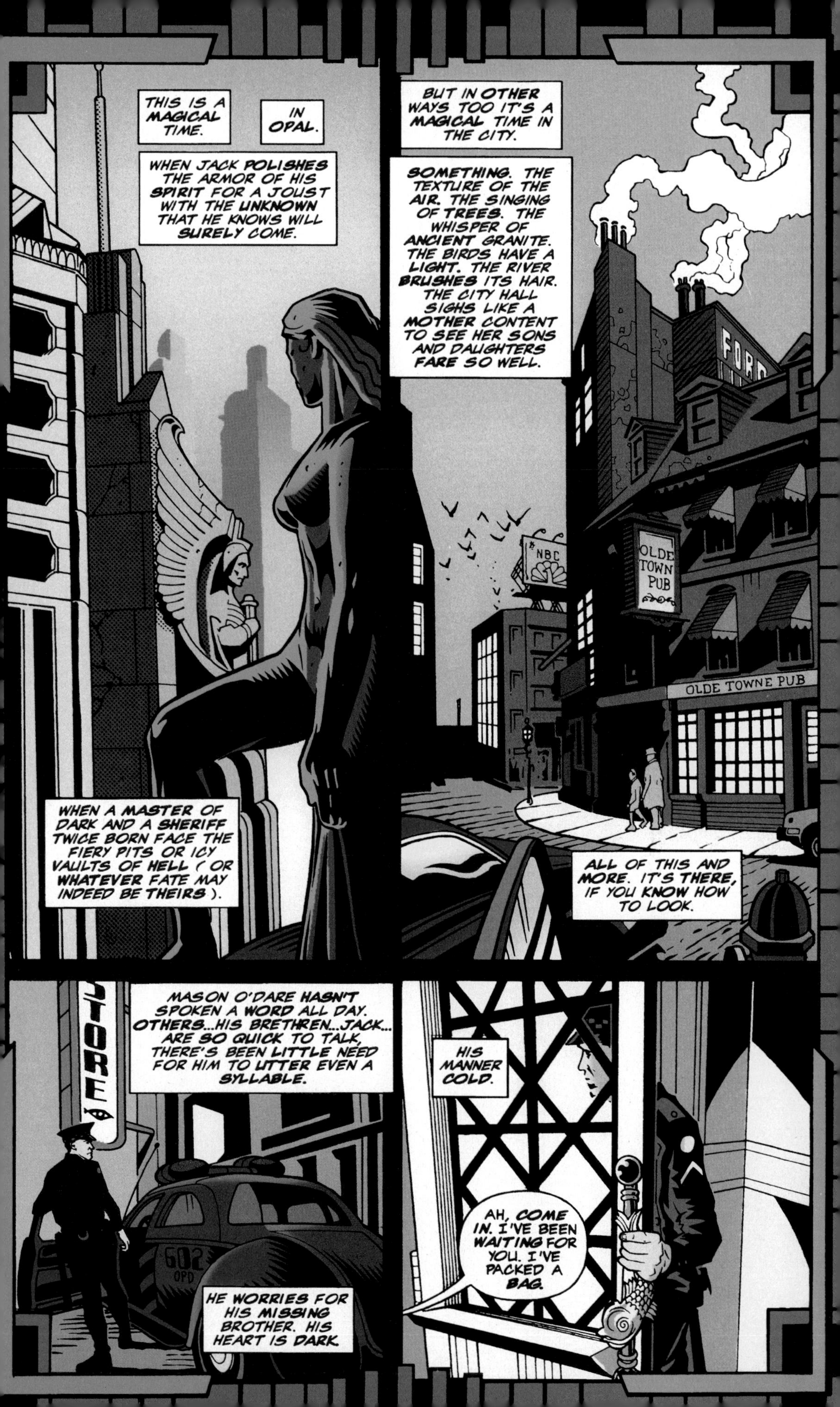
THIS IS A MAGICAL TIME.
IN OPAL.
WHEN JACK POLISHES THE ARMOR OF HIS SPIRIT FOR A JOUST WITH THE UNKNOWN THAT HE KNOWS WILL SURELY COME.
WHEN A MASTER OF DARK AND A SHERIFF TWICE BORN FACE THE FIERY PITS OR ICY VAULTS OF HELL (OR WHATEVER FATE MAY INDEED BE THEIRS).
BUT IN OTHER WAYS TOO IT'S A MAGICAL TIME IN THE CITY.
SOMETHING. THE TEXTURE OF THE AIR. THE SINGING OF TREES. THE WHISPER OF ANCIENT GRANITE. THE BIRDS HAVE A LIGHT. THE RIVER BRUSHES ITS HAIR. THE CITY HALL SIGHS LIKE A MOTHER CONTENT TO SEE HER SONS AND DAUGHTERS FARE SO WELL.
NBC
OLDE TOWN PUB
OLDE TOWNE PUB
ALL OF THIS AND MORE. IT'S THERE, IF YOU KNOW HOW TO LOOK.
MASON O'DARE HASN'T SPOKEN A WORD ALL DAY. OTHERS...HIS BRETHREN...JACK... ARE SO QUICK TO TALK, THERE'S BEEN LITTLE NEED FOR HIM TO UTTER EVEN A SYLLABLE.
STORE
602
OPD
HE WORRIES FOR HIS MISSING BROTHER. HIS HEART IS DARK.
HIS MANNER COLD.
AH, COME IN. I'VE BEEN WAITING FOR YOU. I'VE PACKED A BAG.

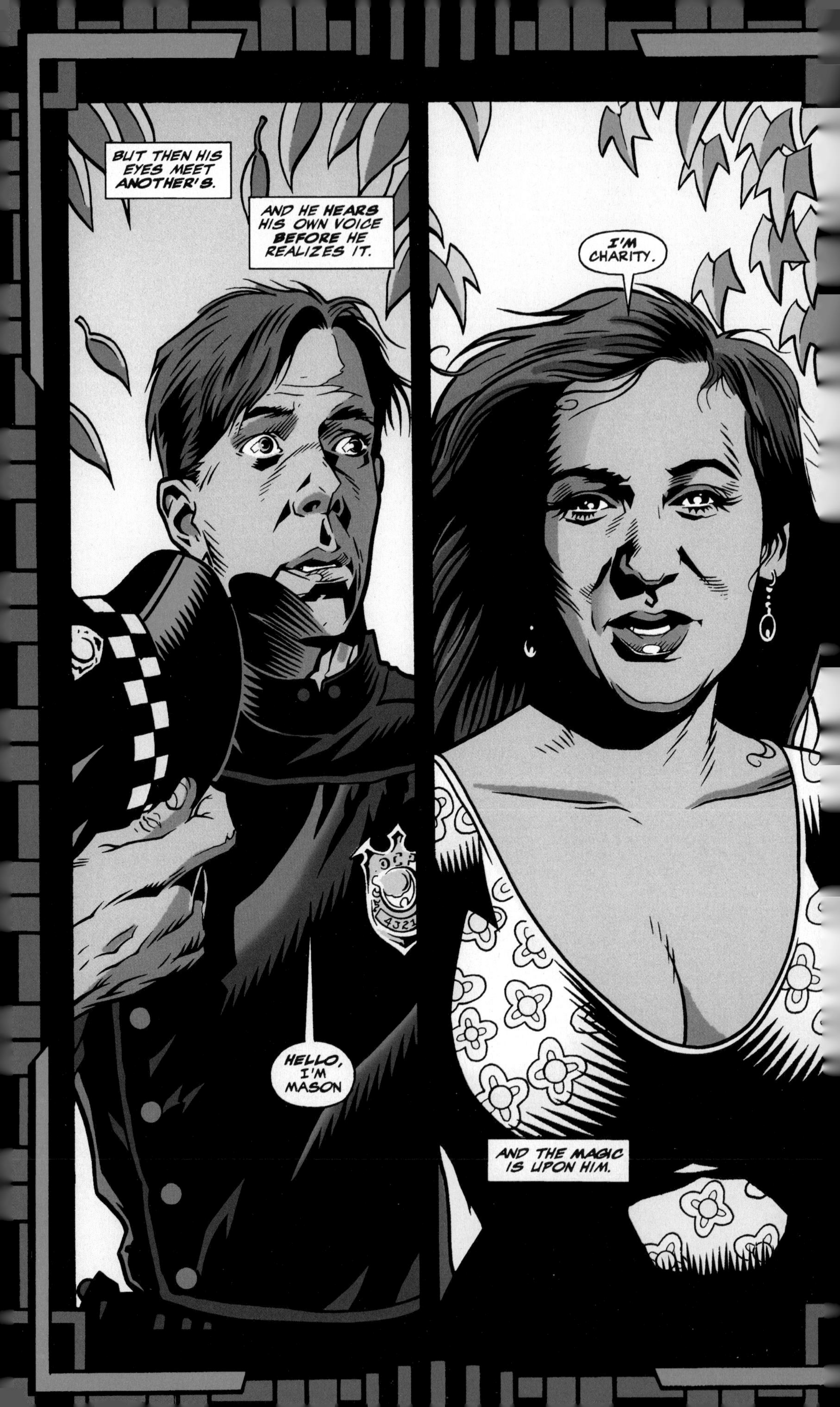
BUT THEN HIS EYES MEET ANOTHER'S.
AND HE HEARS HIS OWN VOICE BEFORE HE REALIZES IT.
HELLO, I'M MASON
I'M CHARITY.
AND THE MAGIC IS UPON HIM.

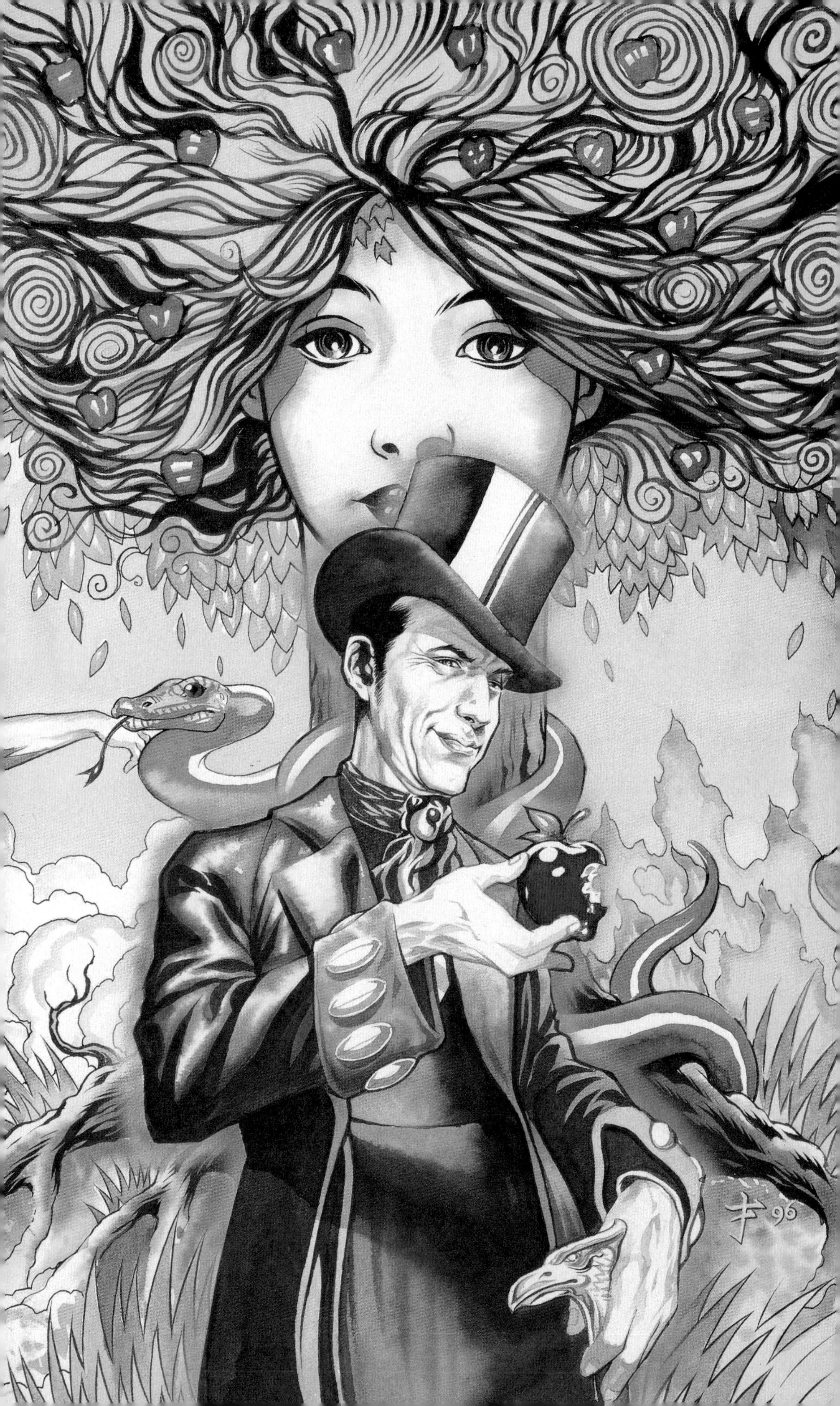

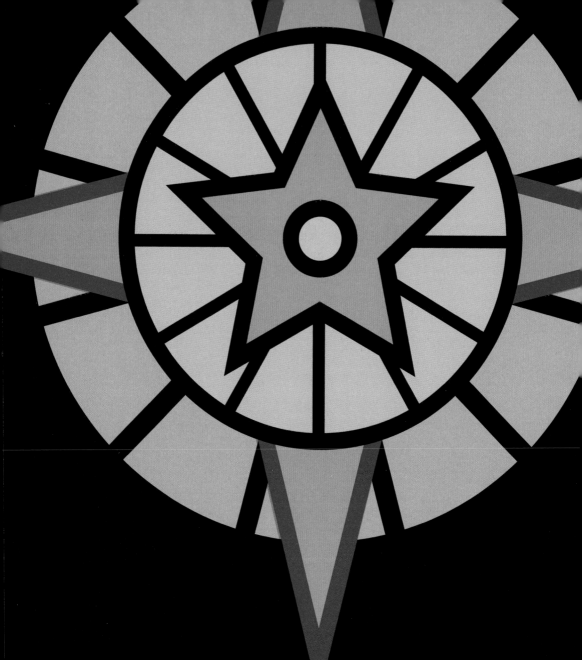

STARMAN 25

Cover by Tony Harris

Written by James Robinson

Pencils by Tony Harris

with inks by Wade von Grawbadger

and colors by Gregory Wright

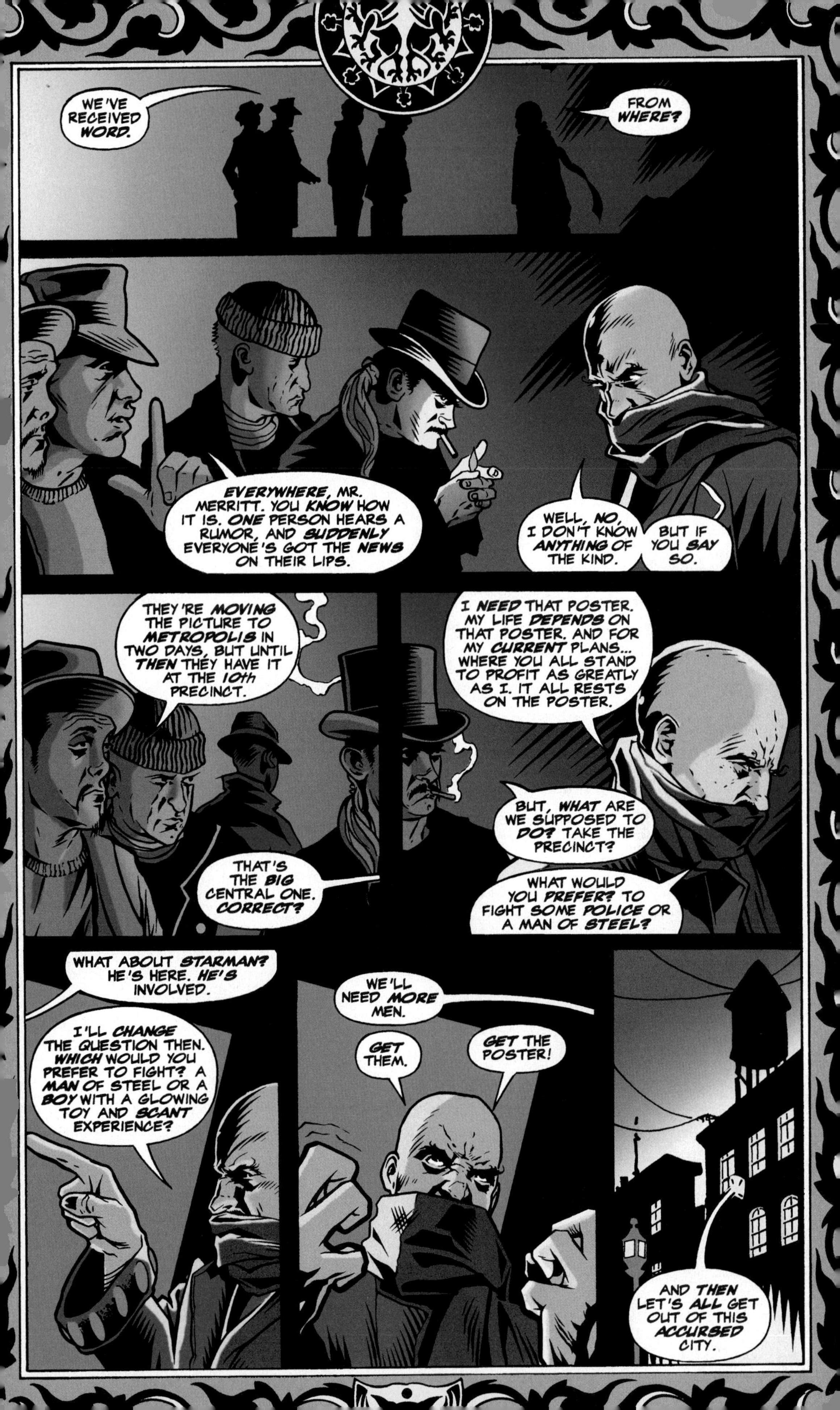

WE'VE RECEIVED WORD.
FROM WHERE?
EVERYWHERE, MR. MERRITT. YOU KNOW HOW IT IS. ONE PERSON HEARS A RUMOR, AND SUDDENLY EVERYONE'S GOT THE NEWS ON THEIR LIPS.
WELL, NO, I DON'T KNOW ANYTHING OF THE KIND.
BUT IF YOU SAY SO.
THEY'RE MOVING THE PICTURE TO METROPOLIS IN TWO DAYS, BUT UNTIL THEN THEY HAVE IT AT THE 10th PRECINCT.
THAT'S THE BIG CENTRAL ONE. CORRECT?
I NEED THAT POSTER. MY LIFE DEPENDS ON THAT POSTER. AND FOR MY CURRENT PLANS... WHERE YOU ALL STAND TO PROFIT AS GREATLY AS I. IT ALL RESTS ON THE POSTER.
BUT, WHAT ARE WE SUPPOSED TO DO? TAKE THE PRECINCT?
WHAT WOULD YOU PREFER? TO FIGHT SOME POLICE OR A MAN OF STEEL?
WHAT ABOUT STARMAN? HE'S HERE. HE'S INVOLVED.
I'LL CHANGE THE QUESTION THEN. WHICH WOULD YOU PREFER TO FIGHT? A MAN OF STEEL OR A BOY WITH A GLOWING TOY AND SCANT EXPERIENCE?
WE'LL NEED MORE MEN.
GET THEM.
GET THE POSTER!
AND THEN LET'S ALL GET OUT OF THIS ACCURSED CITY.

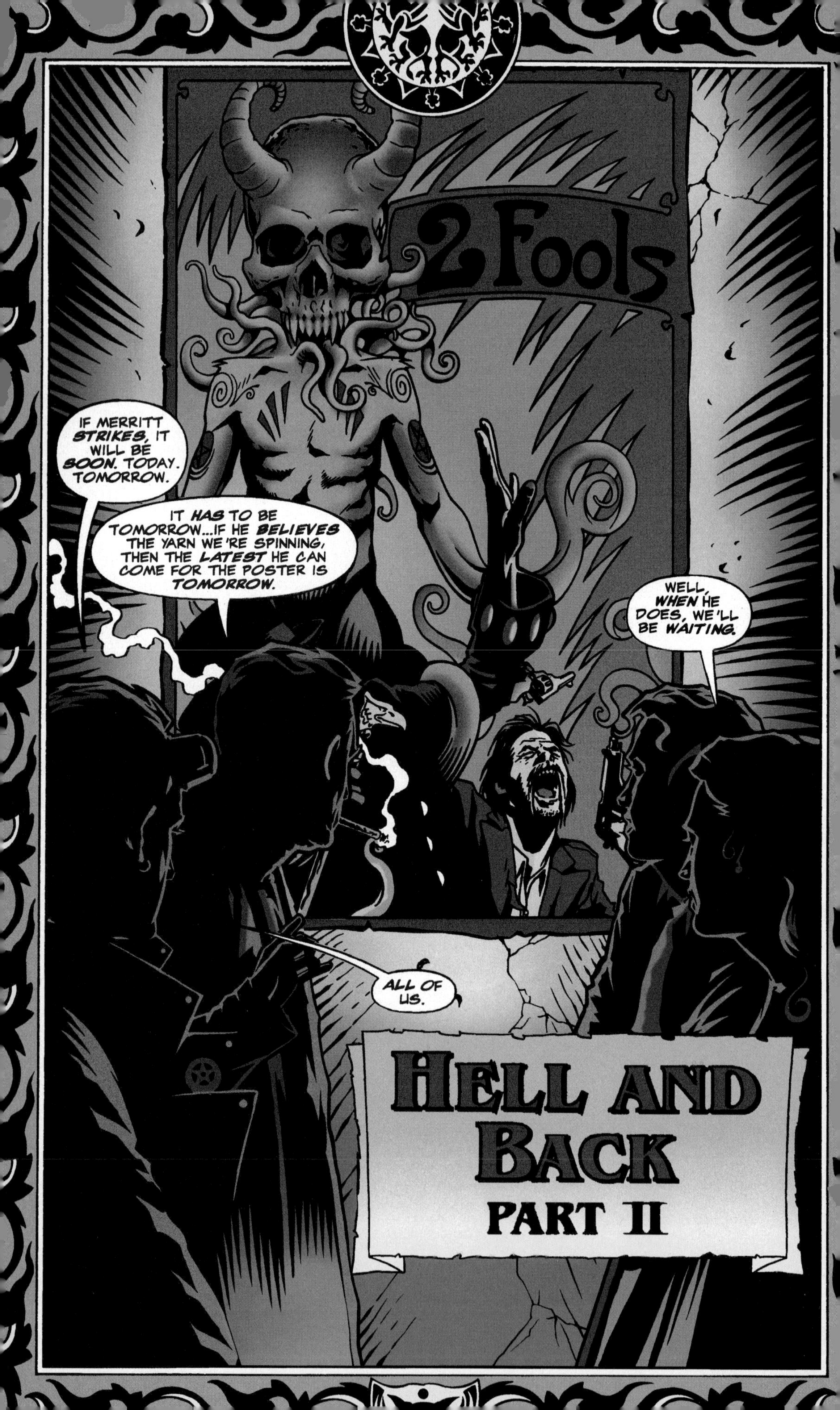
2 Fools
IF MERRITT STRIKES, IT WILL BE SOON. TODAY. TOMORROW.
IT HAS TO BE TOMORROW...IF HE BELIEVES THE YARN WE'RE SPINNING, THEN THE LATEST HE CAN COME FOR THE POSTER IS TOMORROW.
WELL, WHEN HE DOES, WE'LL BE WAITING.
ALL OF US.
HELL AND BACK
PART II

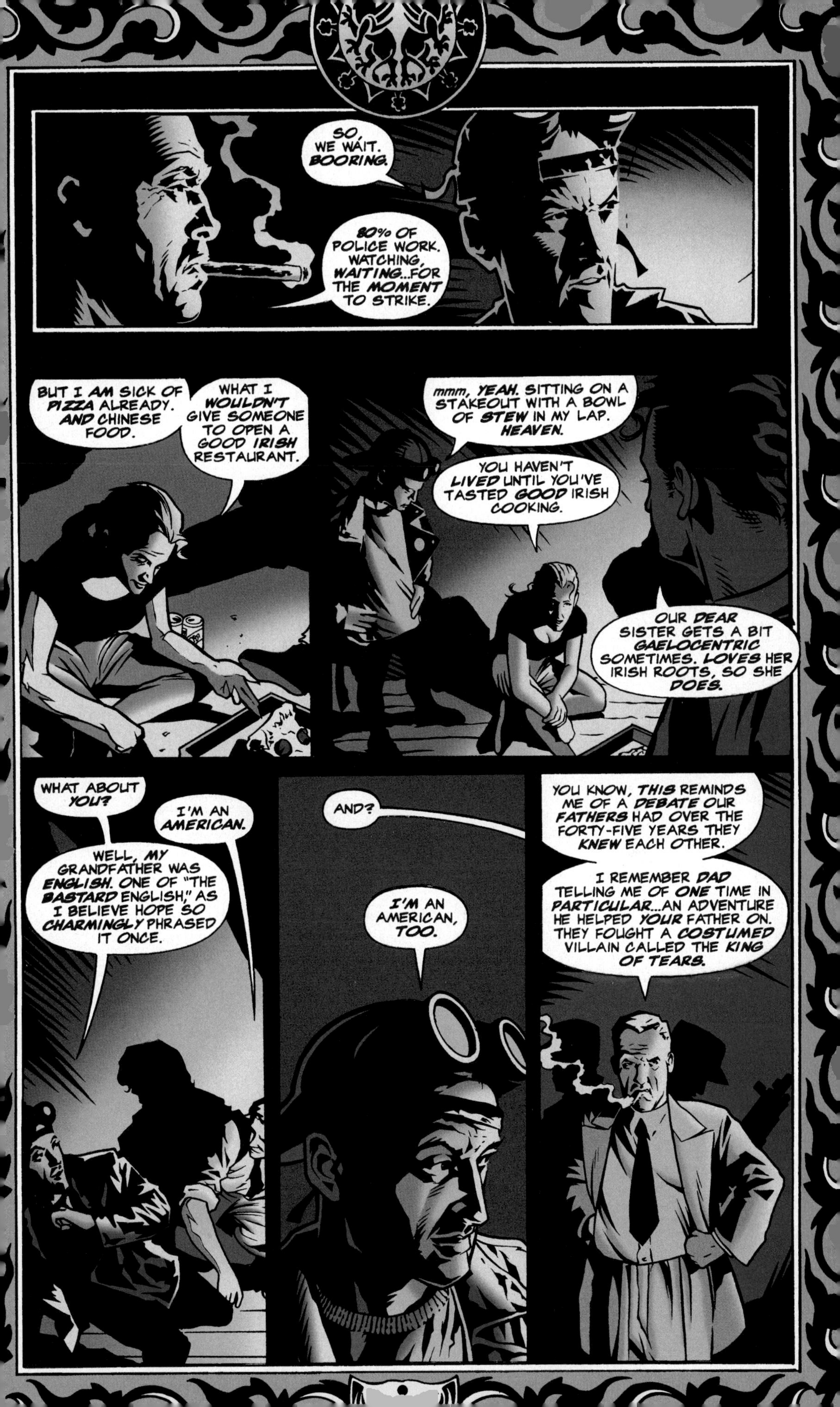
SO, WE WAIT. BOORING.
80% OF POLICE WORK. WATCHING, WAITING...FOR THE MOMENT TO STRIKE.
BUT I AM SICK OF PIZZA ALREADY. AND CHINESE FOOD.
WHAT I WOULDN'T GIVE SOMEONE TO OPEN A GOOD IRISH RESTAURANT.
mmm, YEAH. SITTING ON A STAKEOUT WITH A BOWL OF STEW IN MY LAP. HEAVEN.
YOU HAVEN'T LIVED UNTIL YOU'VE TASTED GOOD IRISH COOKING.
OUR DEAR SISTER GETS A BIT GAELOCENTRIC SOMETIMES. LOVES HER IRISH ROOTS, SO SHE DOES.
WHAT ABOUT YOU?
I'M AN AMERICAN.
WELL, MY GRANDFATHER WAS ENGLISH. ONE OF "THE BASTARD ENGLISH," AS I BELIEVE HOPE SO CHARMINGLY PHRASED IT ONCE.
AND?
I'M AN AMERICAN, TOO.
YOU KNOW, THIS REMINDS ME OF A DEBATE OUR FATHERS HAD OVER THE FORTY-FIVE YEARS THEY KNEW EACH OTHER.
I REMEMBER DAD TELLING ME OF ONE TIME IN PARTICULAR...AN ADVENTURE HE HELPED YOUR FATHER ON. THEY FOUGHT A COSTUMED VILLAIN CALLED THE KING OF TEARS.

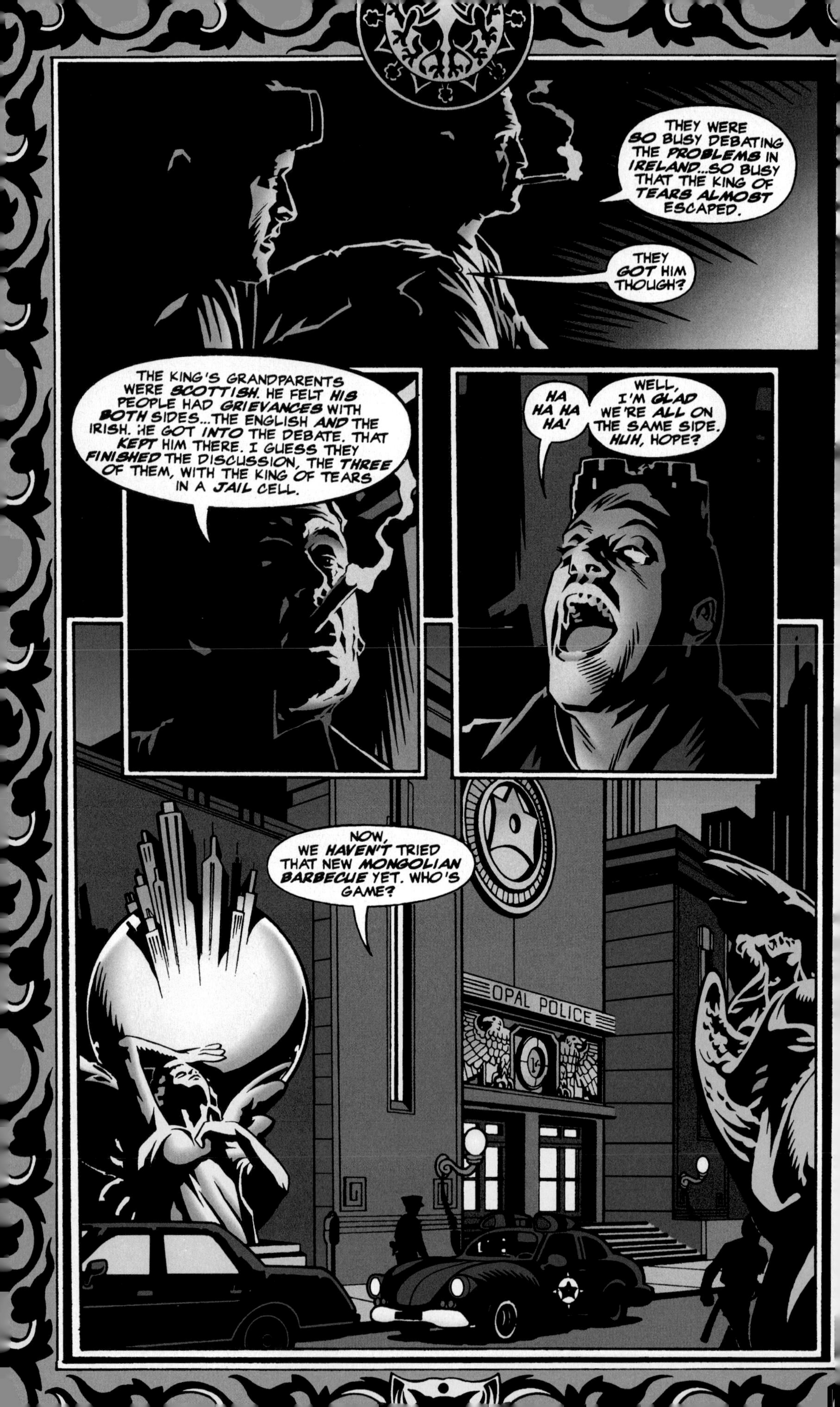
THEY WERE SO BUSY DEBATING THE PROBLEMS IN IRELAND...SO BUSY THAT THE KING OF TEARS ALMOST ESCAPED.
THEY GOT HIM THOUGH?
THE KING'S GRANDPARENTS WERE SCOTTISH. HE FELT HIS PEOPLE HAD GRIEVANCES WITH BOTH SIDES...THE ENGLISH AND THE IRISH. HE GOT INTO THE DEBATE. THAT KEPT HIM THERE. I GUESS THEY FINISHED THE DISCUSSION, THE THREE OF THEM, WITH THE KING OF TEARS IN A JAIL CELL.
HA HA HA HA!
WELL, I'M GLAD WE'RE ALL ON THE SAME SIDE. HUH, HOPE?
NOW, WE HAVEN'T TRIED THAT NEW MONGOLIAN BARBECUE YET. WHO'S GAME?
OPAL POLICE

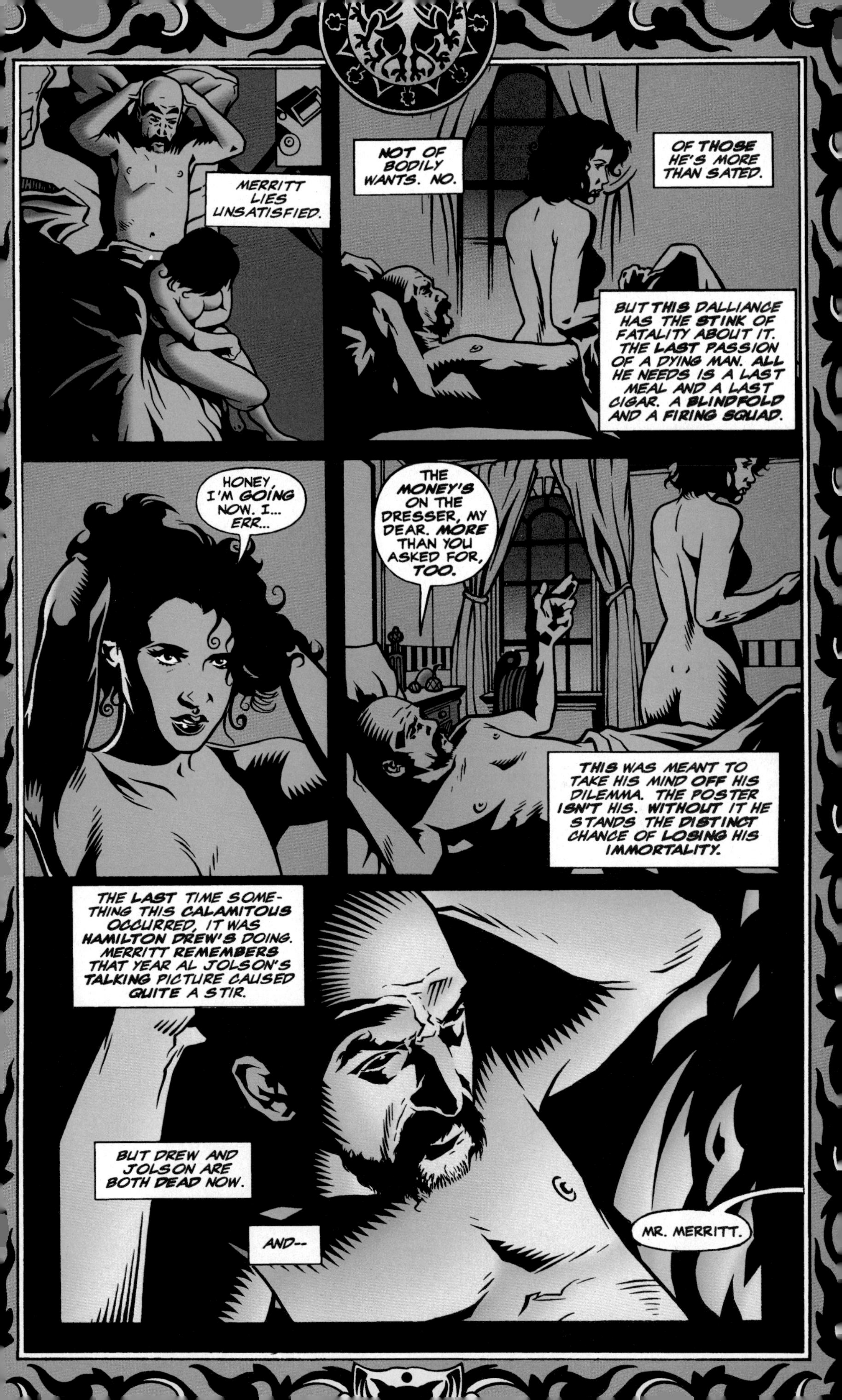
MERRITT LIES UNSATISFIED.
NOT OF BODILY WANTS. NO.
OF THOSE HE'S MORE THAN SATED.
BUT THIS DALLIANCE HAS THE STINK OF FATALITY ABOUT IT. THE LAST PASSION OF A DYING MAN. ALL HE NEEDS IS A LAST MEAL AND A LAST CIGAR. A BLINDFOLD AND A FIRING SQUAD.
HONEY, I'M GOING NOW. I... ERR...
THE MONEY'S ON THE DRESSER, MY DEAR. MORE THAN YOU ASKED FOR, TOO.
THIS WAS MEANT TO TAKE HIS MIND OFF HIS DILEMMA. THE POSTER ISN'T HIS. WITHOUT IT HE STANDS THE DISTINCT CHANCE OF LOSING HIS IMMORTALITY.
THE LAST TIME SOMETHING THIS CALAMITOUS OCCURRED, IT WAS HAMILTON DREW'S DOING. MERRITT REMEMBERS THAT YEAR AL JOLSON'S TALKING PICTURE CAUSED QUITE A STIR.
BUT DREW AND JOLSON ARE BOTH DEAD NOW.
AND--
MR. MERRITT.

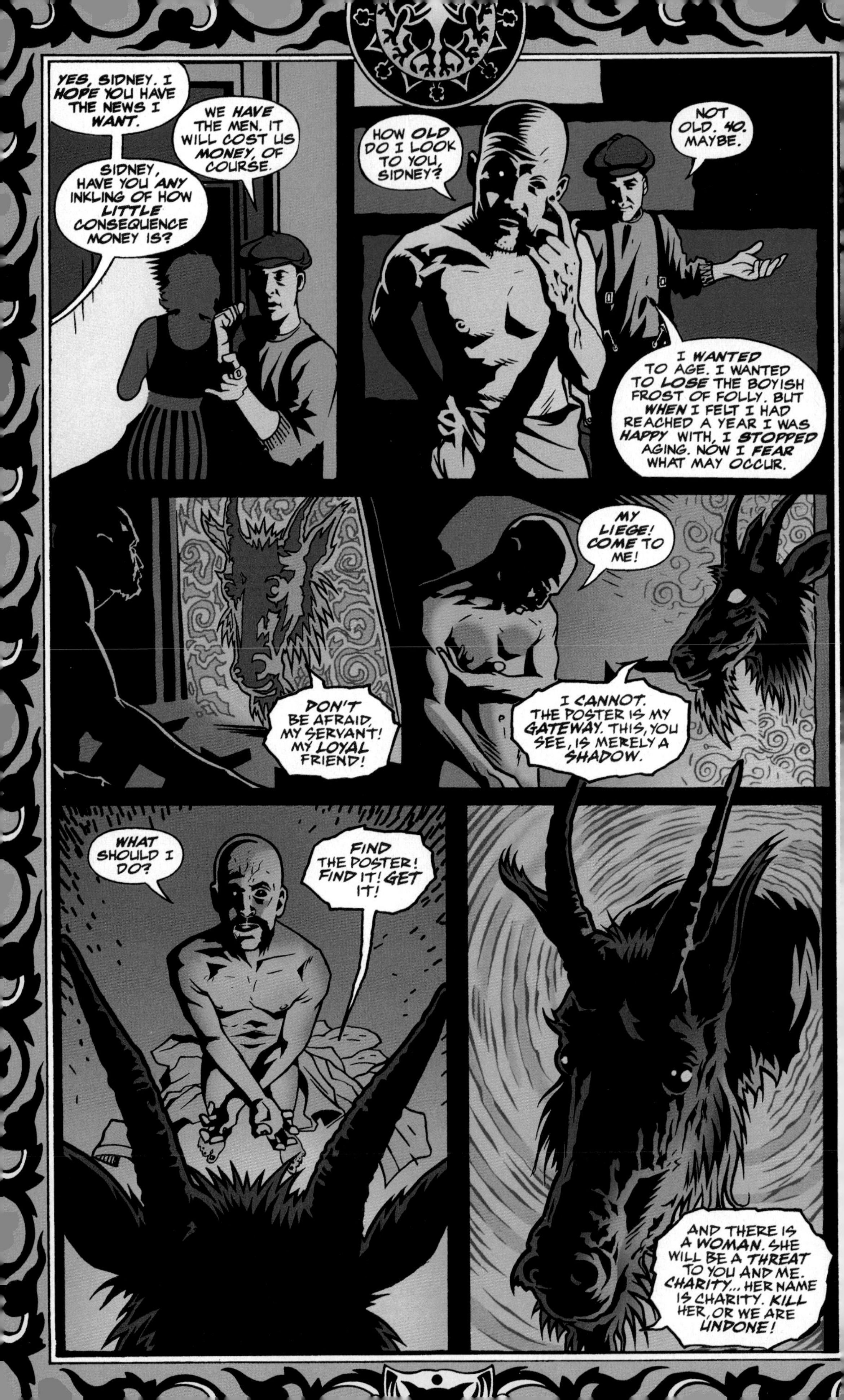
YES, SIDNEY. I HOPE YOU HAVE THE NEWS I WANT.
WE HAVE THE MEN. IT WILL COST US MONEY, OF COURSE.
SIDNEY, HAVE YOU ANY INKLING OF HOW LITTLE CONSEQUENCE MONEY IS?
HOW OLD DO I LOOK TO YOU, SIDNEY?
NOT OLD. 40. MAYBE.
I WANTED TO AGE. I WANTED TO LOSE THE BOYISH FROST OF FOLLY. BUT WHEN I FELT I HAD REACHED A YEAR I WAS HAPPY WITH, I STOPPED AGING. NOW I FEAR WHAT MAY OCCUR.
DON'T BE AFRAID, MY SERVANT! MY LOYAL FRIEND!
MY LIEGE! COME TO ME!
I CANNOT. THE POSTER IS MY GATEWAY. THIS, YOU SEE, IS MERELY A SHADOW.
WHAT SHOULD I DO?
FIND THE POSTER! FIND IT! GET IT!
AND THERE IS A WOMAN. SHE WILL BE A THREAT TO YOU AND ME. CHARITY... HER NAME IS CHARITY. KILL HER, OR WE ARE UNDONE!

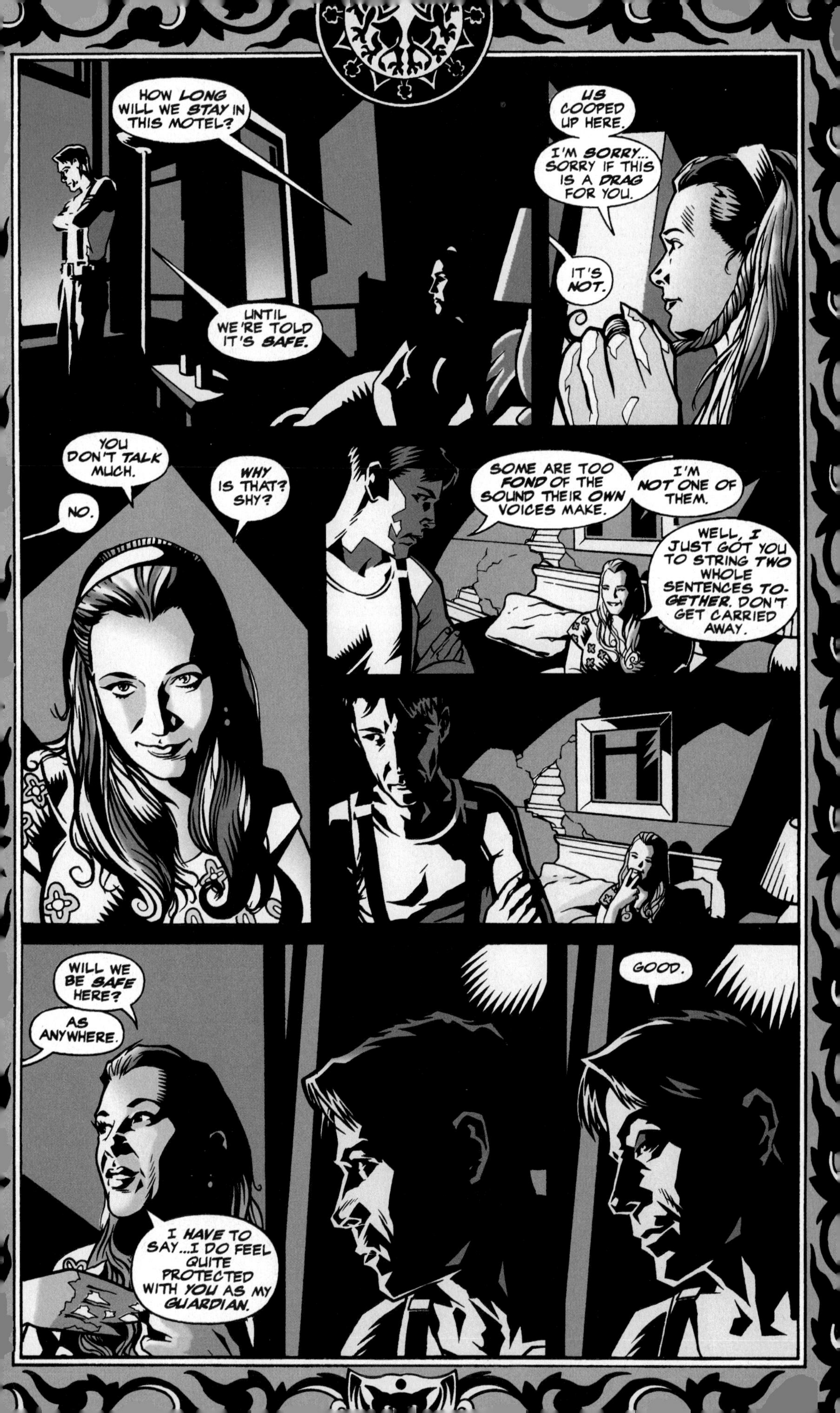

HOW LONG WILL WE STAY IN THIS MOTEL?
UNTIL WE'RE TOLD IT'S SAFE.
US COOPED UP HERE.
I'M SORRY... SORRY IF THIS IS A DRAG FOR YOU.
IT'S NOT.
YOU DON'T TALK MUCH.
NO.
WHY IS THAT? SHY?
SOME ARE TOO FOND OF THE SOUND THEIR OWN VOICES MAKE.
I'M NOT ONE OF THEM.
WELL, I JUST GOT YOU TO STRING TWO WHOLE SENTENCES TO-GETHER. DON'T GET CARRIED AWAY.
WILL WE BE SAFE HERE?
AS ANYWHERE.
I HAVE TO SAY...I DO FEEL QUITE PROTECTED WITH YOU AS MY GUARDIAN.
GOOD.

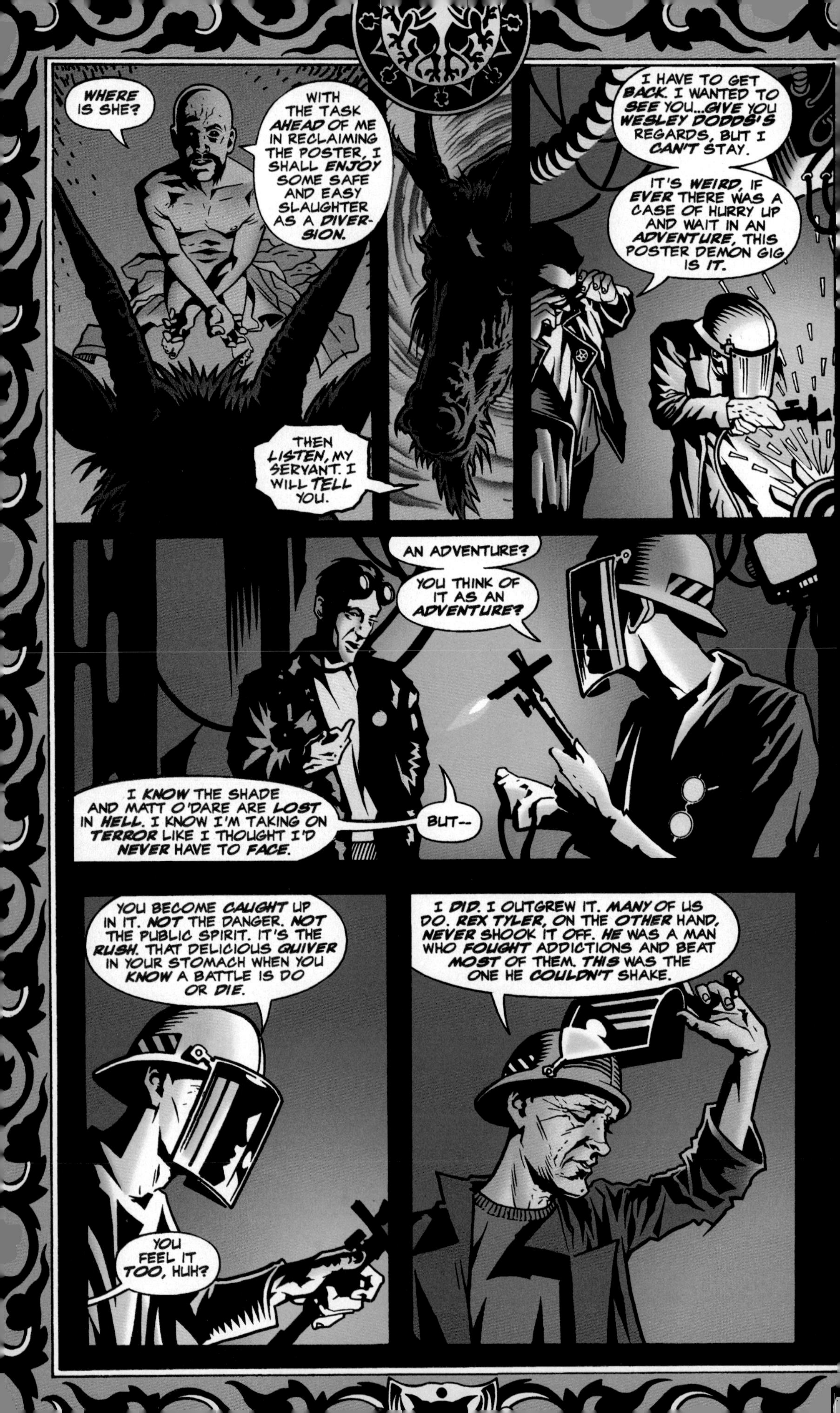
WHERE IS SHE?
WITH THE TASK AHEAD OF ME IN RECLAIMING THE POSTER, I SHALL ENJOY SOME SAFE AND EASY SLAUGHTER AS A DIVERSION.
THEN LISTEN, MY SERVANT. I WILL TELL YOU.
I HAVE TO GET BACK. I WANTED TO SEE YOU...GIVE YOU WESLEY DODDS'S REGARDS, BUT I CAN'T STAY.
IT'S WEIRD, IF EVER THERE WAS A CASE OF HURRY UP AND WAIT IN AN ADVENTURE, THIS POSTER DEMON GIG IS IT.
AN ADVENTURE?
YOU THINK OF IT AS AN ADVENTURE?
I KNOW THE SHADE AND MATT O'DARE ARE LOST IN HELL. I KNOW I'M TAKING ON TERROR LIKE I THOUGHT I'D NEVER HAVE TO FACE.
BUT--
YOU BECOME CAUGHT UP IN IT. NOT THE DANGER. NOT THE PUBLIC SPIRIT. IT'S THE RUSH. THAT DELICIOUS QUIVER IN YOUR STOMACH WHEN YOU KNOW A BATTLE IS DO OR DIE.
YOU FEEL IT TOO, HUH?
I DID. I OUTGREW IT. MANY OF US DO. REX TYLER, ON THE OTHER HAND, NEVER SHOOK IT OFF. HE WAS A MAN WHO FOUGHT ADDICTIONS AND BEAT MOST OF THEM. THIS WAS THE ONE HE COULDN'T SHAKE.

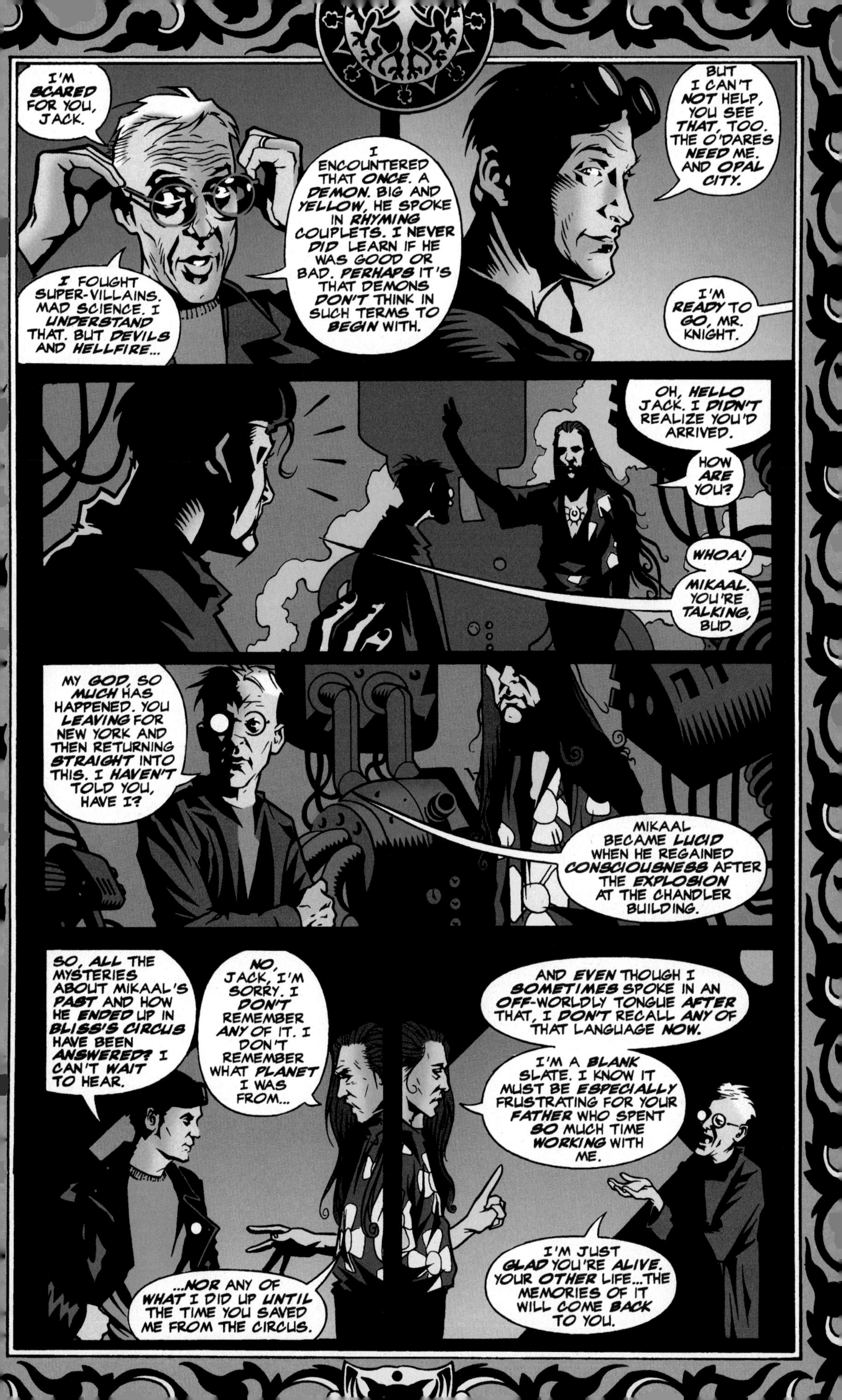
I'M SCARED FOR YOU, JACK.
I FOUGHT SUPER-VILLAINS. MAD SCIENCE. I UNDERSTAND THAT. BUT DEVILS AND HELLFIRE...
I ENCOUNTERED THAT ONCE. A DEMON. BIG AND YELLOW, HE SPOKE IN RHYMING COUPLETS. I NEVER DID LEARN IF HE WAS GOOD OR BAD. PERHAPS IT'S THAT DEMONS DON'T THINK IN SUCH TERMS TO BEGIN WITH.
BUT I CAN'T NOT HELP, YOU SEE THAT, TOO. THE O'DARES NEED ME. AND OPAL CITY.
I'M READY TO GO, MR. KNIGHT.
OH, HELLO JACK. I DIDN'T REALIZE YOU'D ARRIVED.
HOW ARE YOU?
WHOA!
MIKAAL. YOU'RE TALKING, BUD.
MY GOD, SO MUCH HAS HAPPENED. YOU LEAVING FOR NEW YORK AND THEN RETURNING STRAIGHT INTO THIS. I HAVEN'T TOLD YOU, HAVE I?
MIKAAL BECAME LUCID WHEN HE REGAINED CONSCIOUSNESS AFTER THE EXPLOSION AT THE CHANDLER BUILDING.
SO, ALL THE MYSTERIES ABOUT MIKAAL'S PAST AND HOW HE ENDED UP IN BLISS'S CIRCUS HAVE BEEN ANSWERED? I CAN'T WAIT TO HEAR.
NO, JACK, I'M SORRY. I DON'T REMEMBER ANY OF IT. I DON'T REMEMBER WHAT PLANET I WAS FROM...
...NOR ANY OF WHAT I DID UP UNTIL THE TIME YOU SAVED ME FROM THE CIRCUS.
AND EVEN THOUGH I SOMETIMES SPOKE IN AN OFF-WORLDLY TONGUE AFTER THAT, I DON'T RECALL ANY OF THAT LANGUAGE NOW.
I'M A BLANK SLATE. I KNOW IT MUST BE ESPECIALLY FRUSTRATING FOR YOUR FATHER WHO SPENT SO MUCH TIME WORKING WITH ME.
I'M JUST GLAD YOU'RE ALIVE. YOUR OTHER LIFE...THE MEMORIES OF IT WILL COME BACK TO YOU.

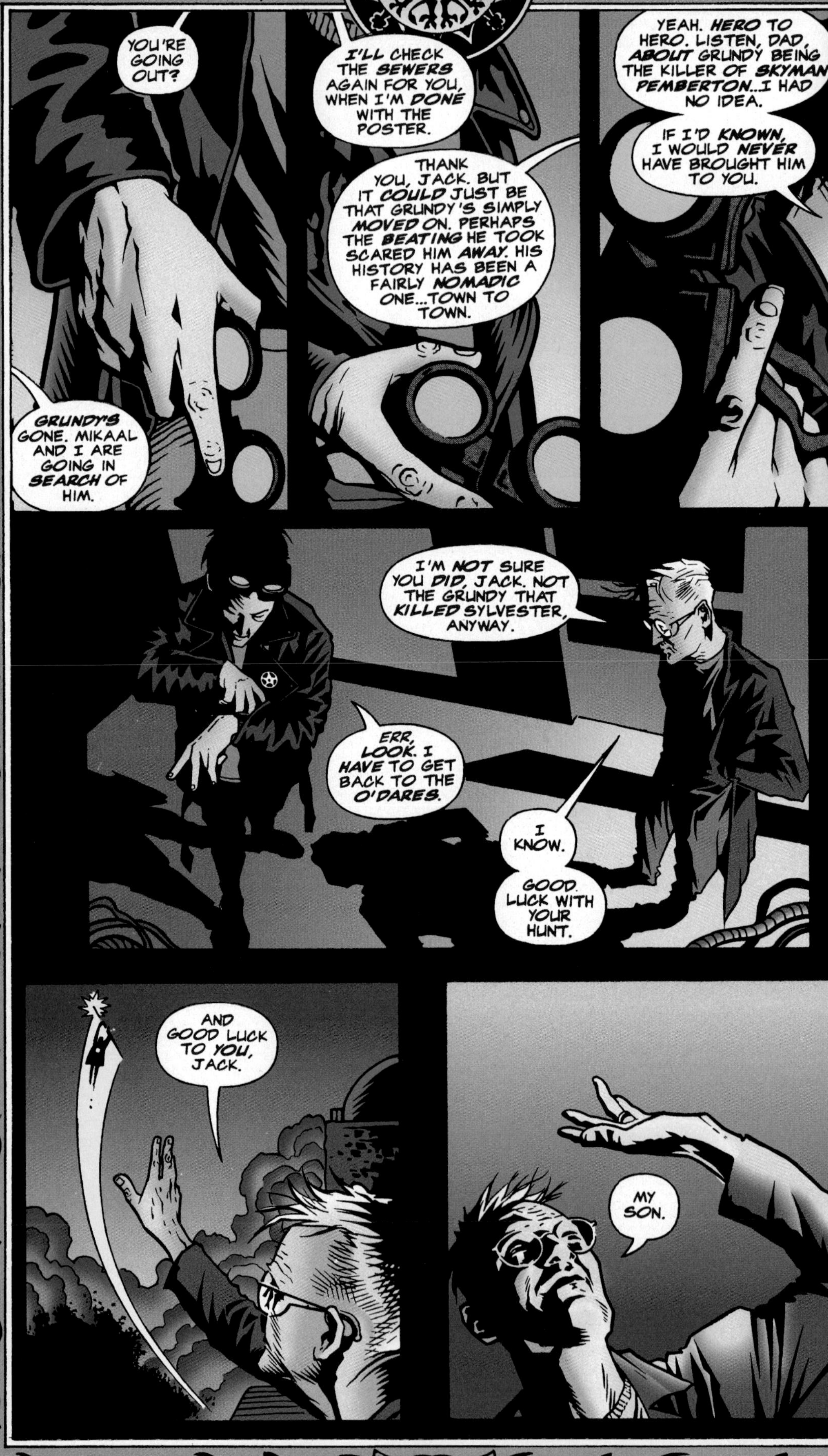
YOU'RE GOING OUT?
GRUNDY'S GONE. MIKAAL AND I ARE GOING IN SEARCH OF HIM.
I'LL CHECK THE SEWERS AGAIN FOR YOU, WHEN I'M DONE WITH THE POSTER.
THANK YOU, JACK. BUT IT COULD JUST BE THAT GRUNDY'S SIMPLY MOVED ON. PERHAPS THE BEATING HE TOOK SCARED HIM AWAY. HIS HISTORY HAS BEEN A FAIRLY NOMADIC ONE...TOWN TO TOWN.
YEAH. HERO TO HERO. LISTEN, DAD, ABOUT GRUNDY BEING THE KILLER OF SKYMAN PEMBERTON...I HAD NO IDEA.
IF I'D KNOWN, I WOULD NEVER HAVE BROUGHT HIM TO YOU.
I'M NOT SURE YOU DID, JACK. NOT THE GRUNDY THAT KILLED SYLVESTER, ANYWAY.
ERR, LOOK. I HAVE TO GET BACK TO THE O'DARES.
I KNOW.
GOOD. LUCK WITH YOUR HUNT.
AND GOOD LUCK TO YOU, JACK.
MY SON.

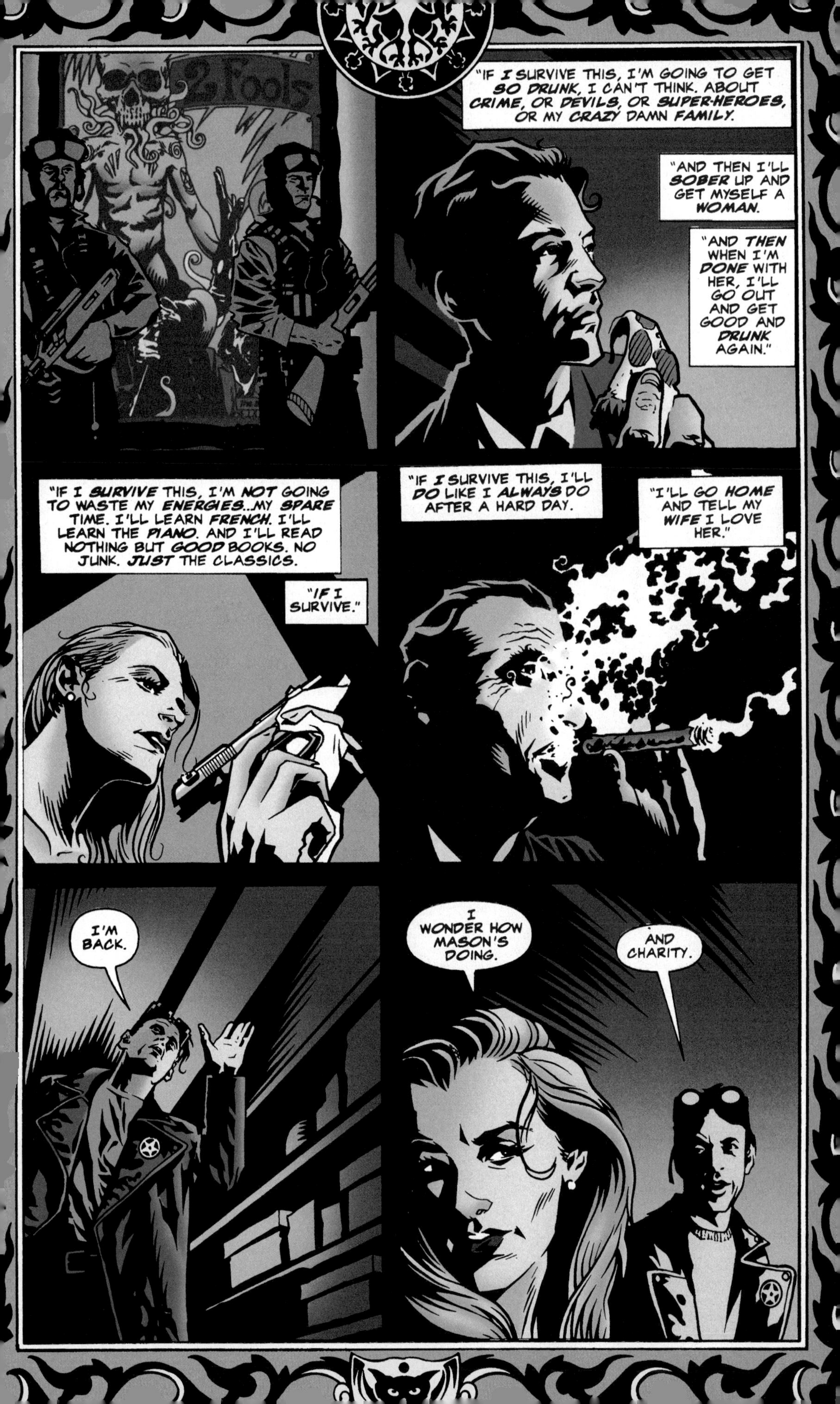
2 Fools
"IF I SURVIVE THIS, I'M GOING TO GET SO DRUNK, I CAN'T THINK. ABOUT CRIME, OR DEVILS, OR SUPER-HEROES, OR MY CRAZY DAMN FAMILY.
"AND THEN I'LL SOBER UP AND GET MYSELF A WOMAN.
"AND THEN WHEN I'M DONE WITH HER, I'LL GO OUT AND GET GOOD AND DRUNK AGAIN."
"IF I SURVIVE THIS, I'M NOT GOING TO WASTE MY ENERGIES...MY SPARE TIME. I'LL LEARN FRENCH. I'LL LEARN THE PIANO. AND I'LL READ NOTHING BUT GOOD BOOKS. NO JUNK. JUST THE CLASSICS.
"IF I SURVIVE."
"IF I SURVIVE THIS, I'LL DO LIKE I ALWAYS DO AFTER A HARD DAY.
"I'LL GO HOME AND TELL MY WIFE I LOVE HER."
I'M BACK.
I WONDER HOW MASON'S DOING.
AND CHARITY.

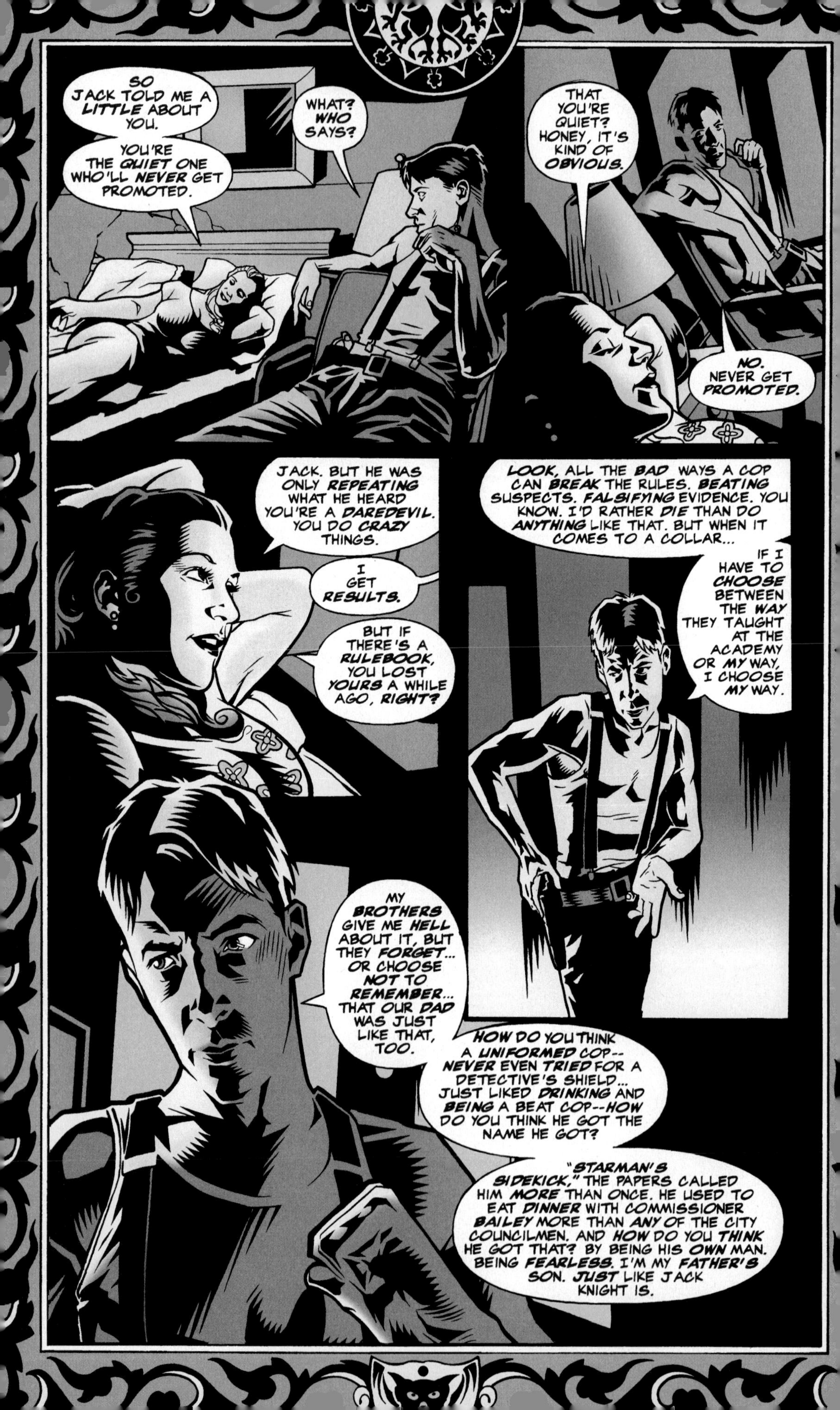

SO JACK TOLD ME A LITTLE ABOUT YOU.
YOU'RE THE QUIET ONE WHO'LL NEVER GET PROMOTED.
WHAT? WHO SAYS?
THAT YOU'RE QUIET? HONEY, IT'S KIND OF OBVIOUS.
NO. NEVER GET PROMOTED.
JACK. BUT HE WAS ONLY REPEATING WHAT HE HEARD YOU'RE A DAREDEVIL. YOU DO CRAZY THINGS.
I GET RESULTS.
BUT IF THERE'S A RULEBOOK, YOU LOST YOURS A WHILE AGO, RIGHT?
LOOK, ALL THE BAD WAYS A COP CAN BREAK THE RULES. BEATING SUSPECTS. FALSIFYING EVIDENCE. YOU KNOW. I'D RATHER DIE THAN DO ANYTHING LIKE THAT. BUT WHEN IT COMES TO A COLLAR...
IF I HAVE TO CHOOSE BETWEEN THE WAY THEY TAUGHT AT THE ACADEMY OR MY WAY, I CHOOSE MY WAY.
MY BROTHERS GIVE ME HELL ABOUT IT, BUT THEY FORGET... OR CHOOSE NOT TO REMEMBER... THAT OUR DAD WAS JUST LIKE THAT, TOO.
HOW DO YOU THINK A UNIFORMED COP-- NEVER EVEN TRIED FOR A DETECTIVE'S SHIELD... JUST LIKED DRINKING AND BEING A BEAT COP--HOW DO YOU THINK HE GOT THE NAME HE GOT?
"STARMAN'S SIDEKICK," THE PAPERS CALLED HIM MORE THAN ONCE. HE USED TO EAT DINNER WITH COMMISSIONER BAILEY MORE THAN ANY OF THE CITY COUNCILMEN. AND HOW DO YOU THINK HE GOT THAT? BY BEING HIS OWN MAN. BEING FEARLESS. I'M MY FATHER'S SON. JUST LIKE JACK KNIGHT IS.

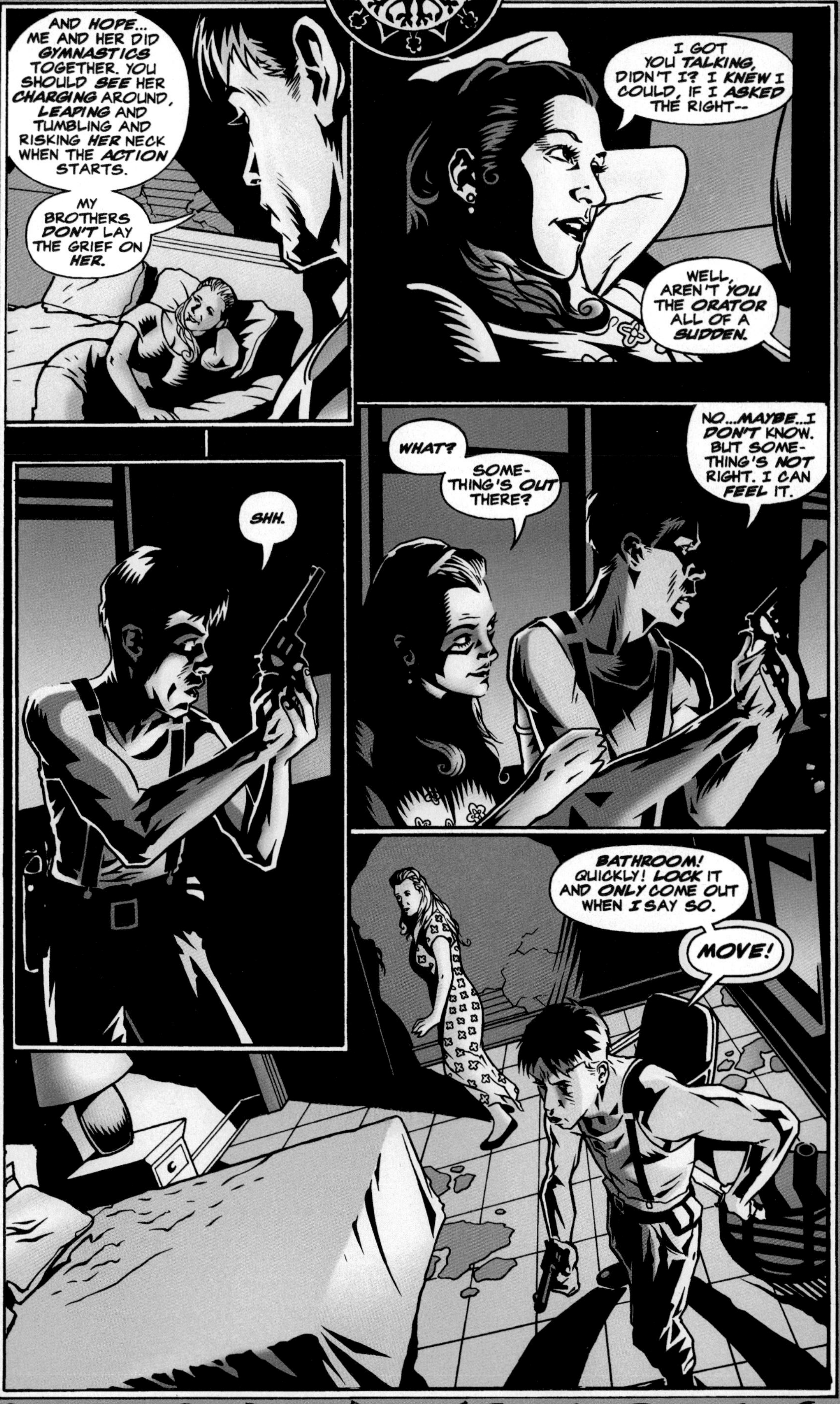
AND HOPE... ME AND HER DID GYMNASTICS TOGETHER. YOU SHOULD SEE HER CHARGING AROUND, LEAPING AND TUMBLING AND RISKING HER NECK WHEN THE ACTION STARTS.
MY BROTHERS DON'T LAY THE GRIEF ON HER.
I GOT YOU TALKING, DIDN'T I? I KNEW I COULD, IF I ASKED THE RIGHT--
WELL, AREN'T YOU THE ORATOR ALL OF A SUDDEN.
SHH.
WHAT?
SOME-THING'S OUT THERE?
NO...MAYBE...I DON'T KNOW. BUT SOME-THING'S NOT RIGHT. I CAN FEEL IT.
BATHROOM! QUICKLY! LOCK IT AND ONLY COME OUT WHEN I SAY SO.
MOVE!

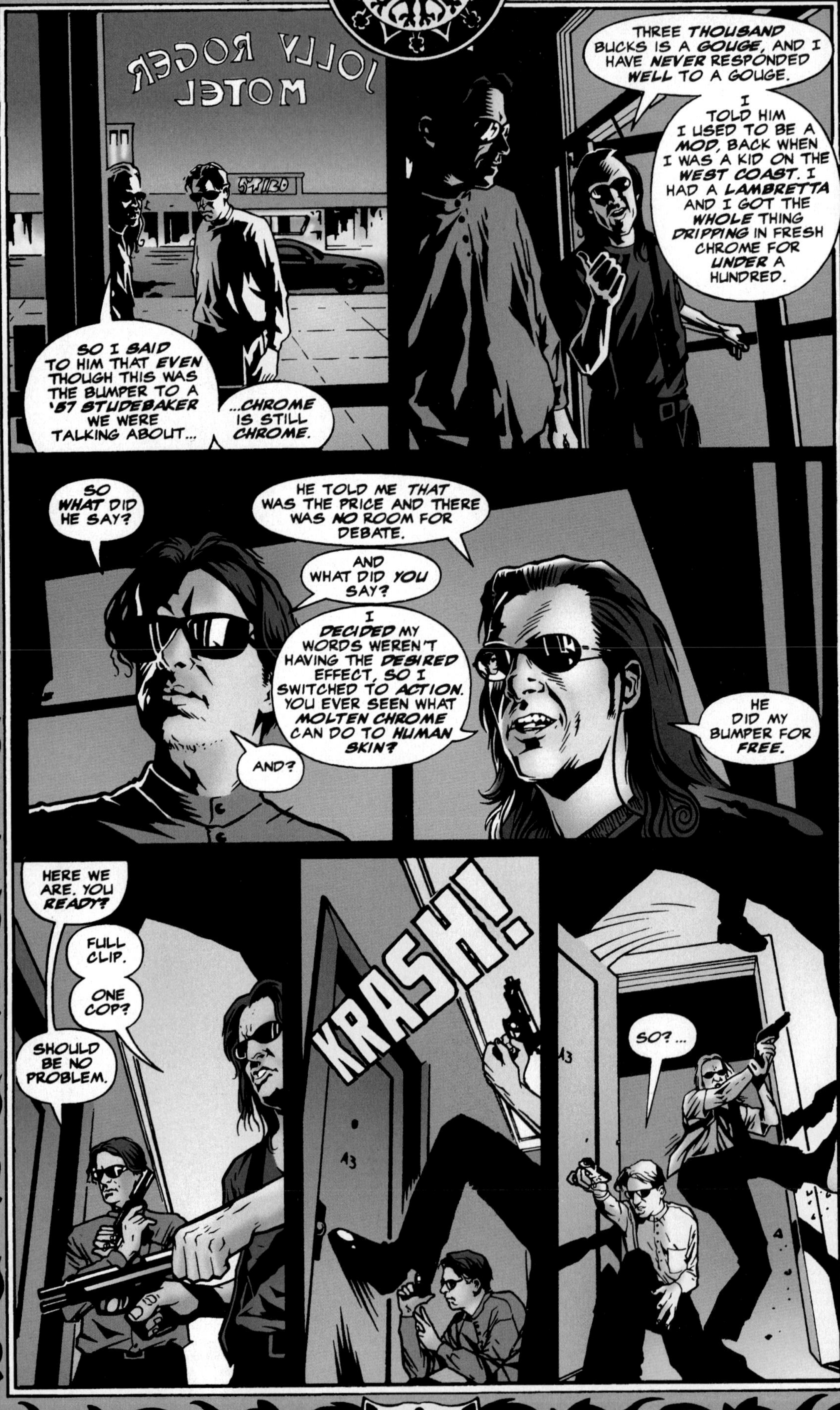

JOLLY ROGER MOTEL
SO I SAID TO HIM THAT EVEN THOUGH THIS WAS THE BUMPER TO A '57 STUDEBAKER WE WERE TALKING ABOUT...
...CHROME IS STILL CHROME.
THREE THOUSAND BUCKS IS A GOUGE, AND I HAVE NEVER RESPONDED WELL TO A GOUGE.
I TOLD HIM I USED TO BE A MOD, BACK WHEN I WAS A KID ON THE WEST COAST. I HAD A LAMBRETTA AND I GOT THE WHOLE THING DRIPPING IN FRESH CHROME FOR UNDER A HUNDRED.
SO WHAT DID HE SAY?
HE TOLD ME THAT WAS THE PRICE AND THERE WAS NO ROOM FOR DEBATE.
AND WHAT DID YOU SAY?
I DECIDED MY WORDS WEREN'T HAVING THE DESIRED EFFECT, SO I SWITCHED TO ACTION. YOU EVER SEEN WHAT MOLTEN CHROME CAN DO TO HUMAN SKIN?
AND?
HE DID MY BUMPER FOR FREE.
HERE WE ARE. YOU READY?
FULL CLIP.
ONE COP?
SHOULD BE NO PROBLEM.
KRASH!
SO?...

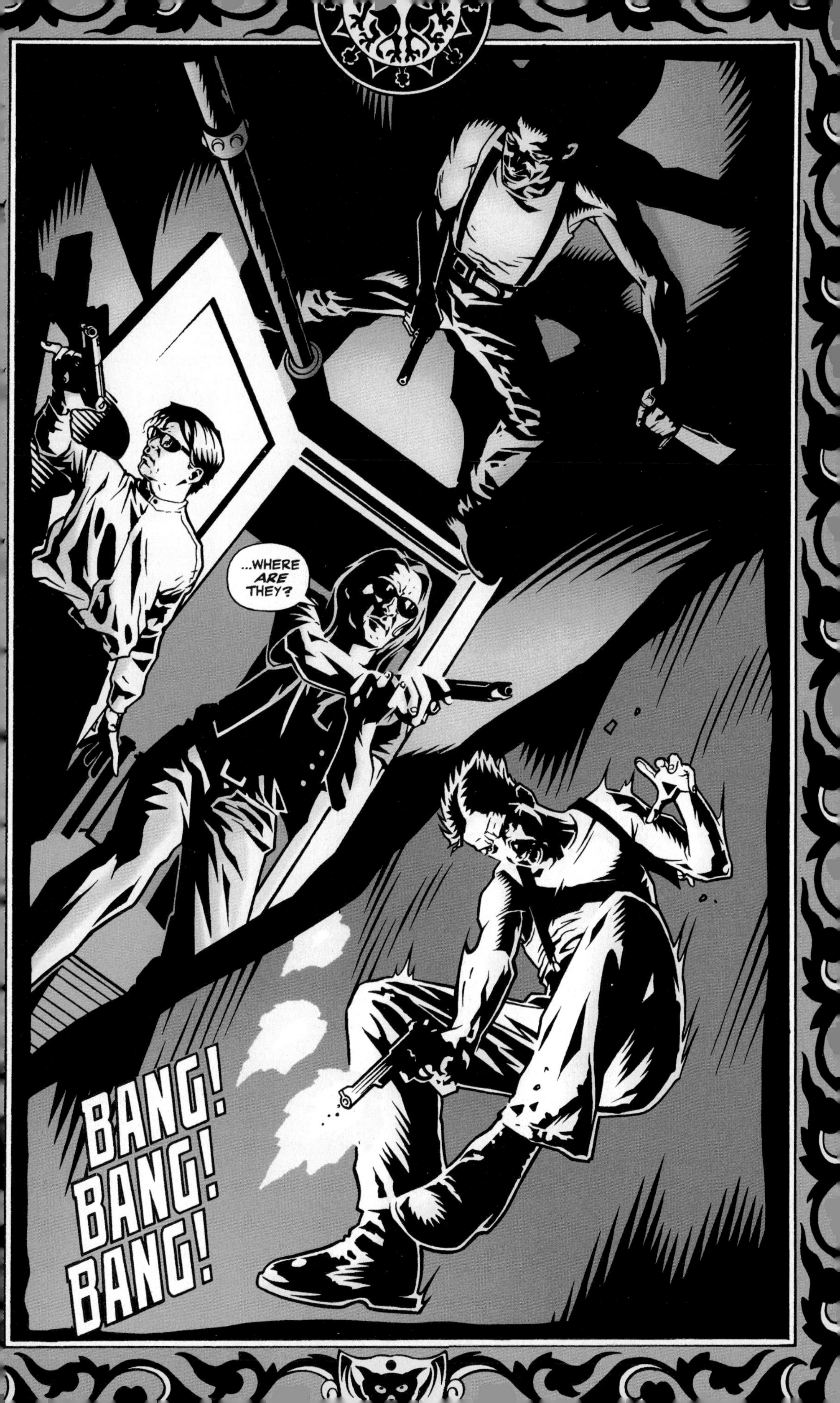
...WHERE *ARE* THEY?
BANG! BANG! BANG!

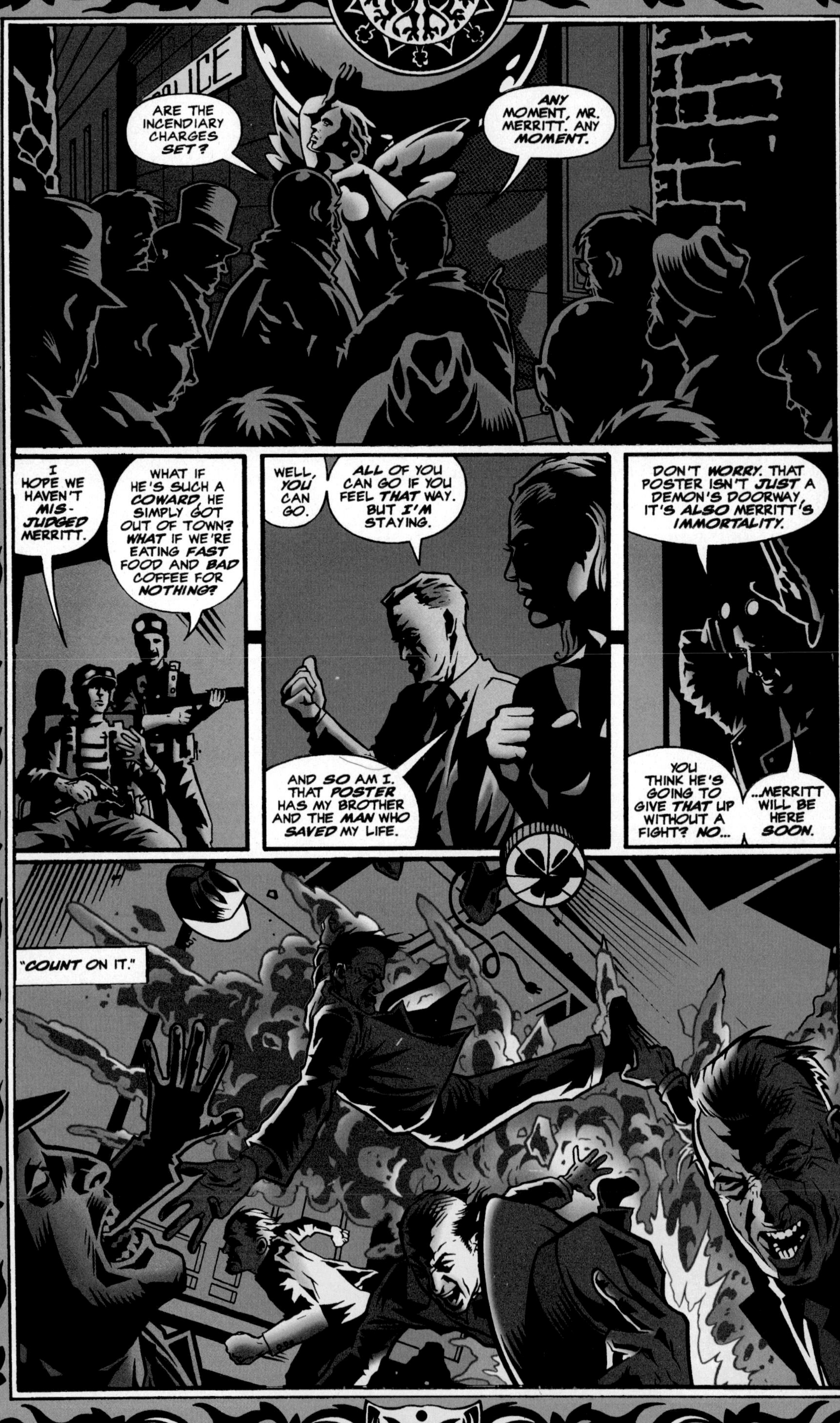

POLICE
ARE THE INCENDIARY CHARGES SET?
ANY MOMENT, MR. MERRITT. ANY MOMENT.
I HOPE WE HAVEN'T MIS-JUDGED MERRITT.
WHAT IF HE'S SUCH A COWARD, HE SIMPLY GOT OUT OF TOWN? WHAT IF WE'RE EATING FAST FOOD AND BAD COFFEE FOR NOTHING?
WELL, YOU CAN GO.
ALL OF YOU CAN GO IF YOU FEEL THAT WAY. BUT I'M STAYING.
AND SO AM I. THAT POSTER HAS MY BROTHER AND THE MAN WHO SAVED MY LIFE.
DON'T WORRY. THAT POSTER ISN'T JUST A DEMON'S DOORWAY. IT'S ALSO MERRITT'S IMMORTALITY.
YOU THINK HE'S GOING TO GIVE THAT UP WITHOUT A FIGHT? NO...
...MERRITT WILL BE HERE SOON.
"COUNT ON IT."

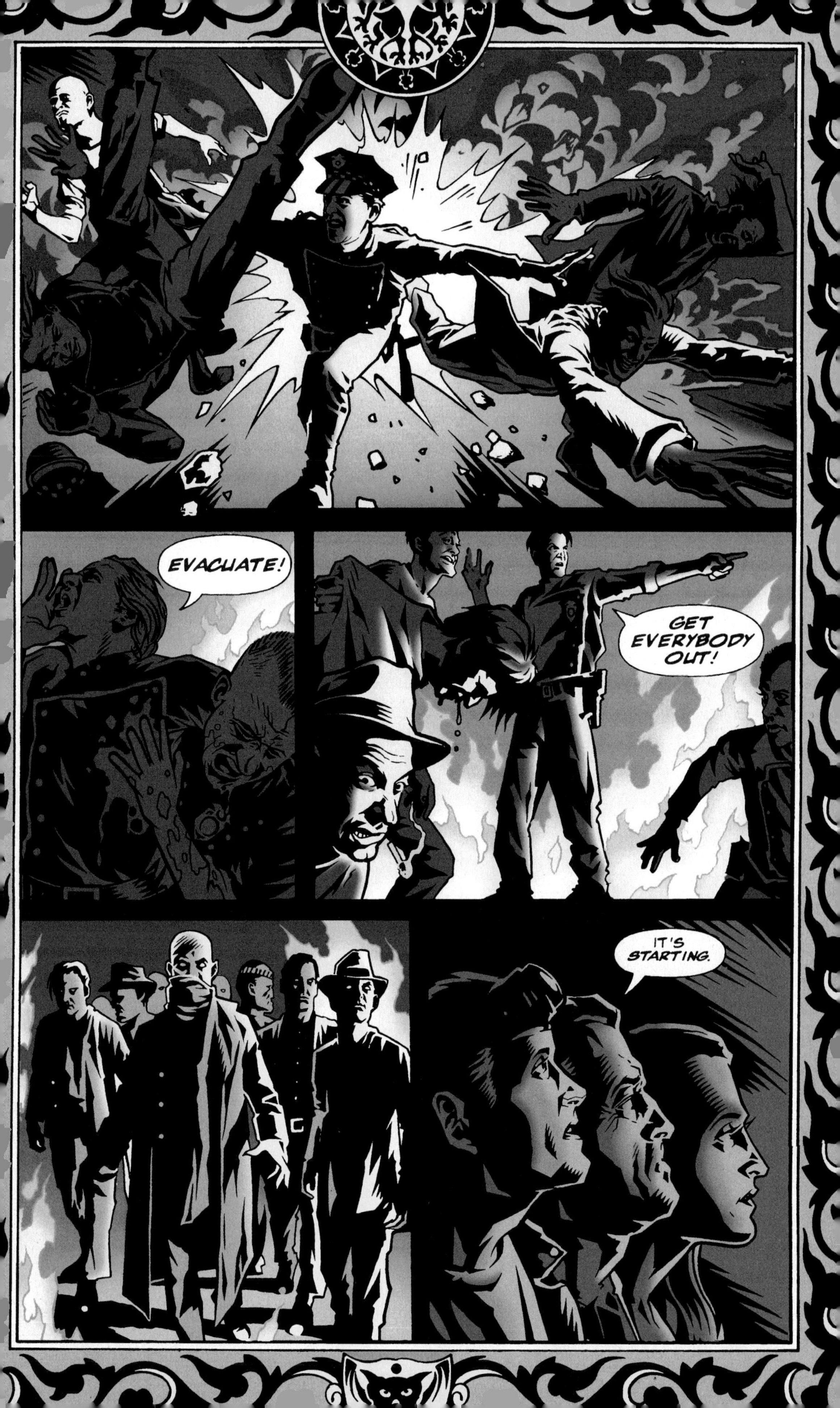
EVACUATE!
GET EVERYBODY OUT!
IT'S STARTING.

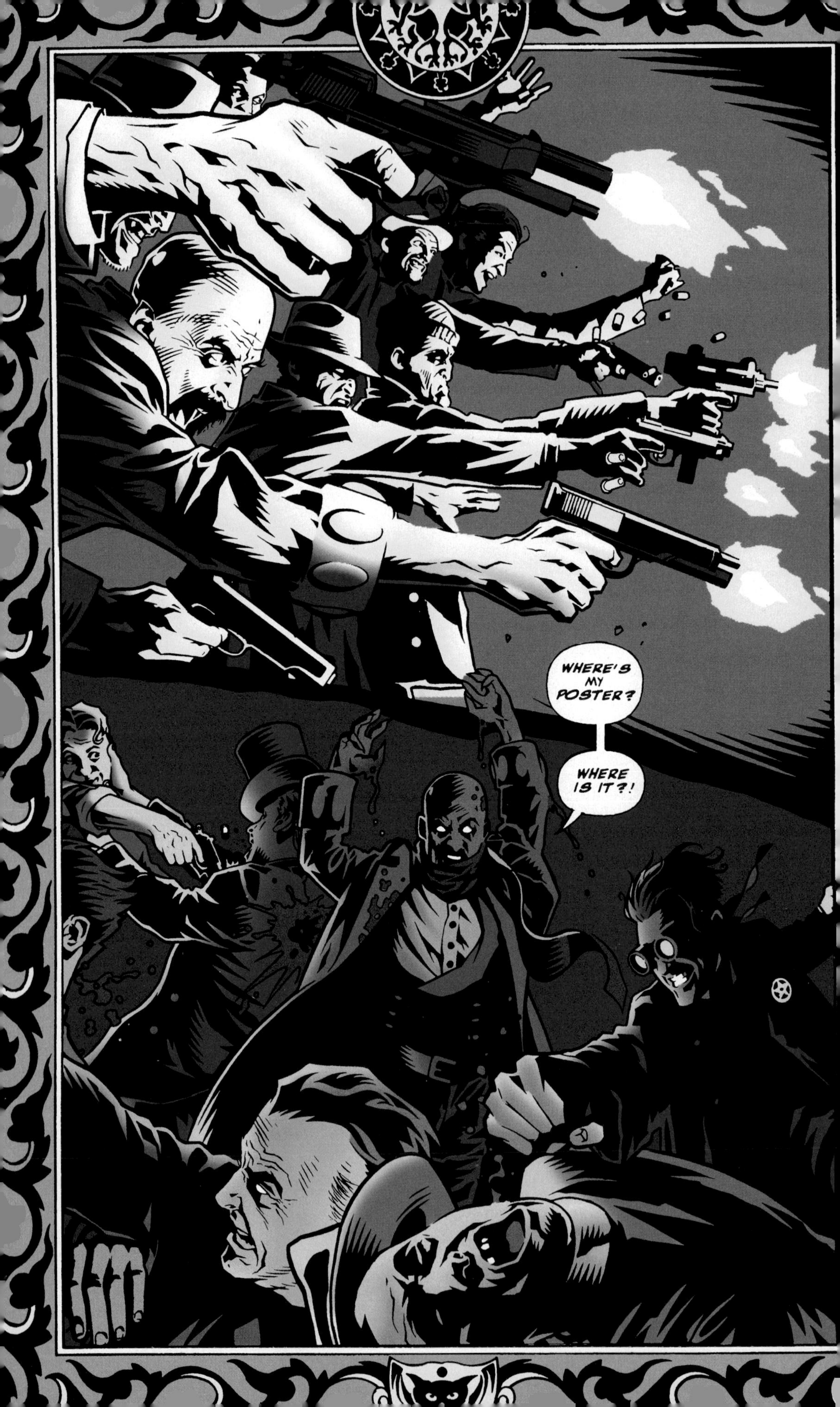
WHERE'S MY POSTER?
WHERE IS IT?!

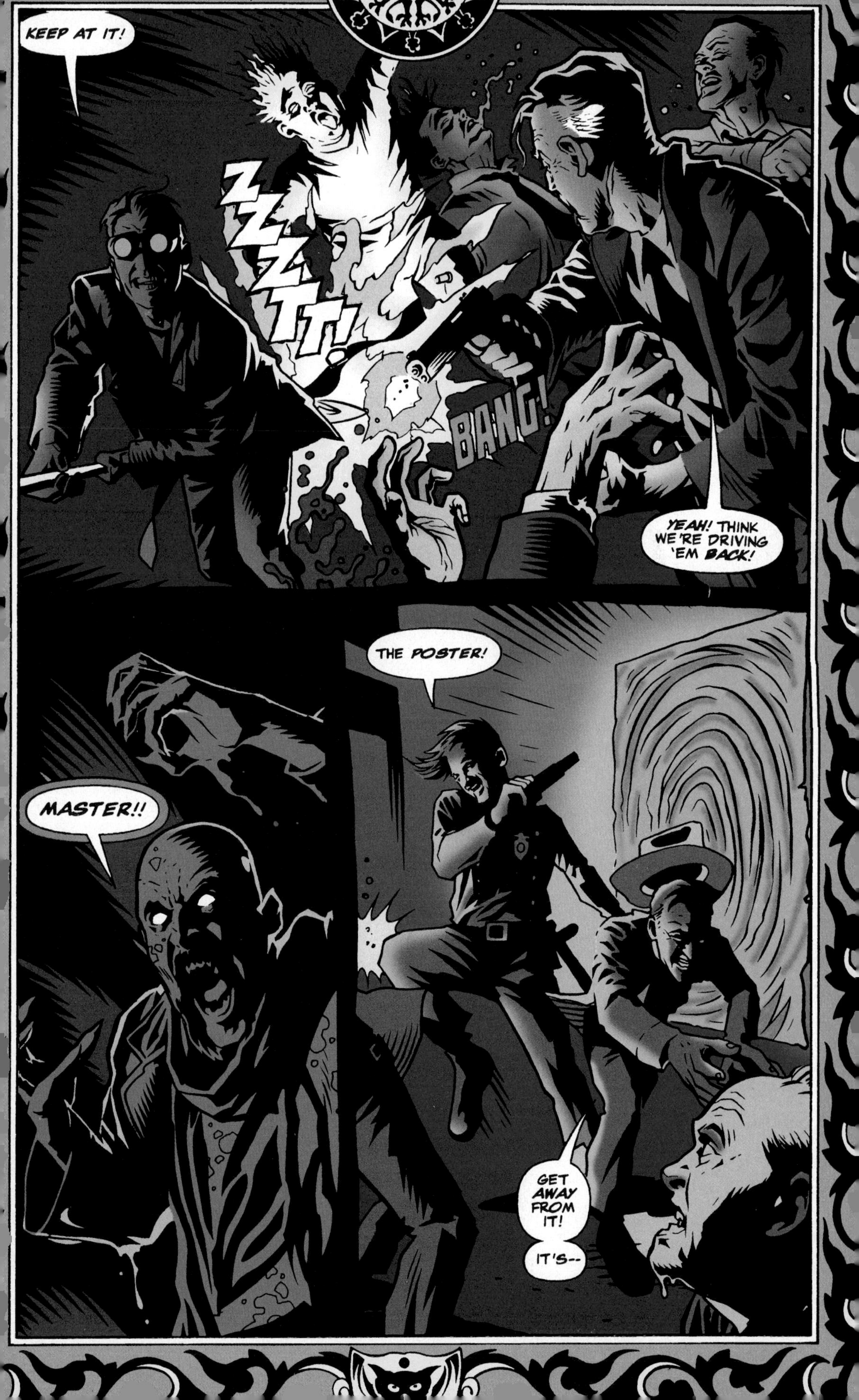
KEEP AT IT!
ZZZTT!
BANG!
YEAH! THINK WE'RE DRIVING 'EM BACK!
MASTER!!
THE POSTER!
GET AWAY FROM IT!
IT'S--

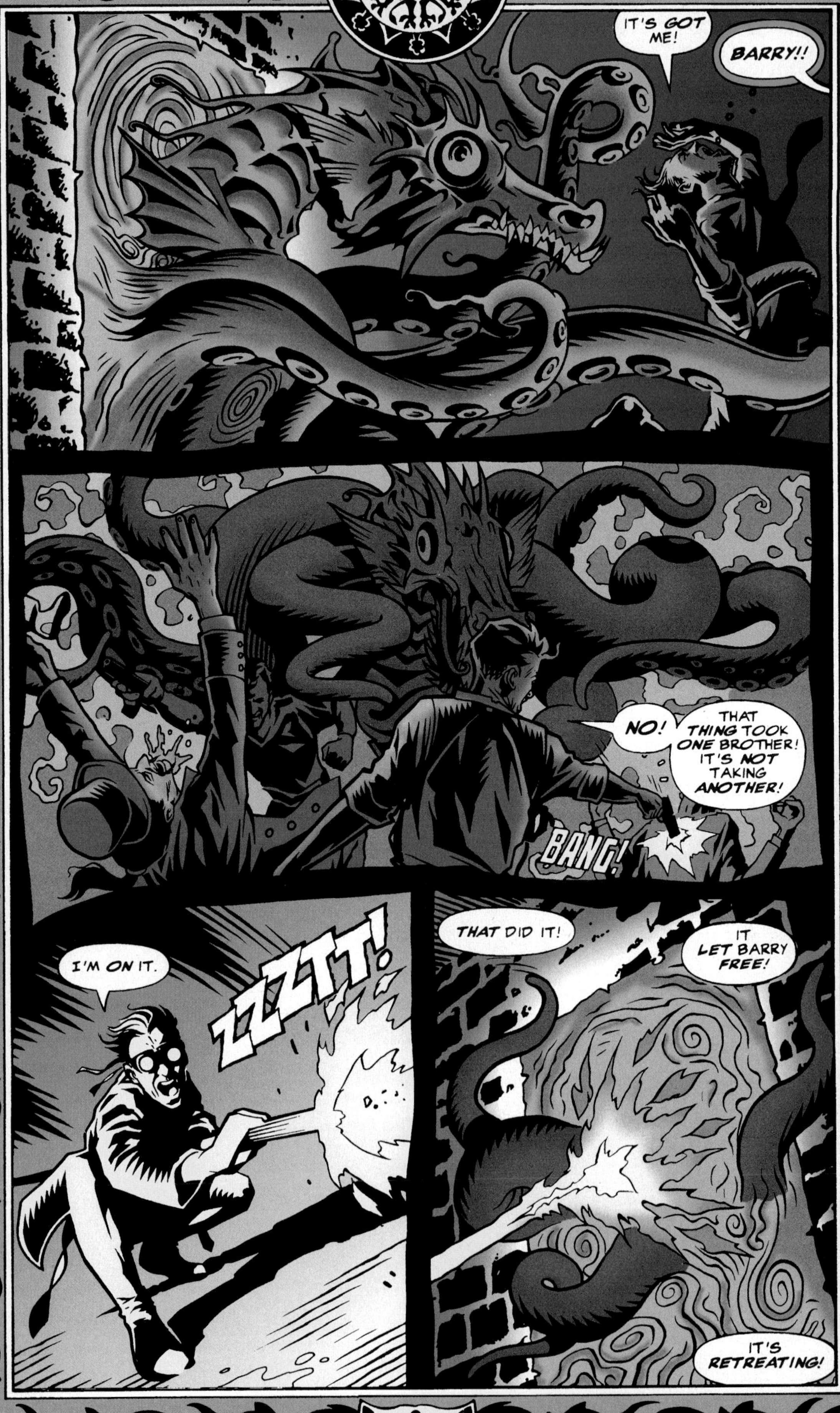

IT'S GOT ME!
BARRY!!
NO!
THAT THING TOOK ONE BROTHER! IT'S NOT TAKING ANOTHER!
BANG!
I'M ON IT.
ZZZZTT!
THAT DID IT!
IT LET BARRY FREE!
IT'S RETREATING!

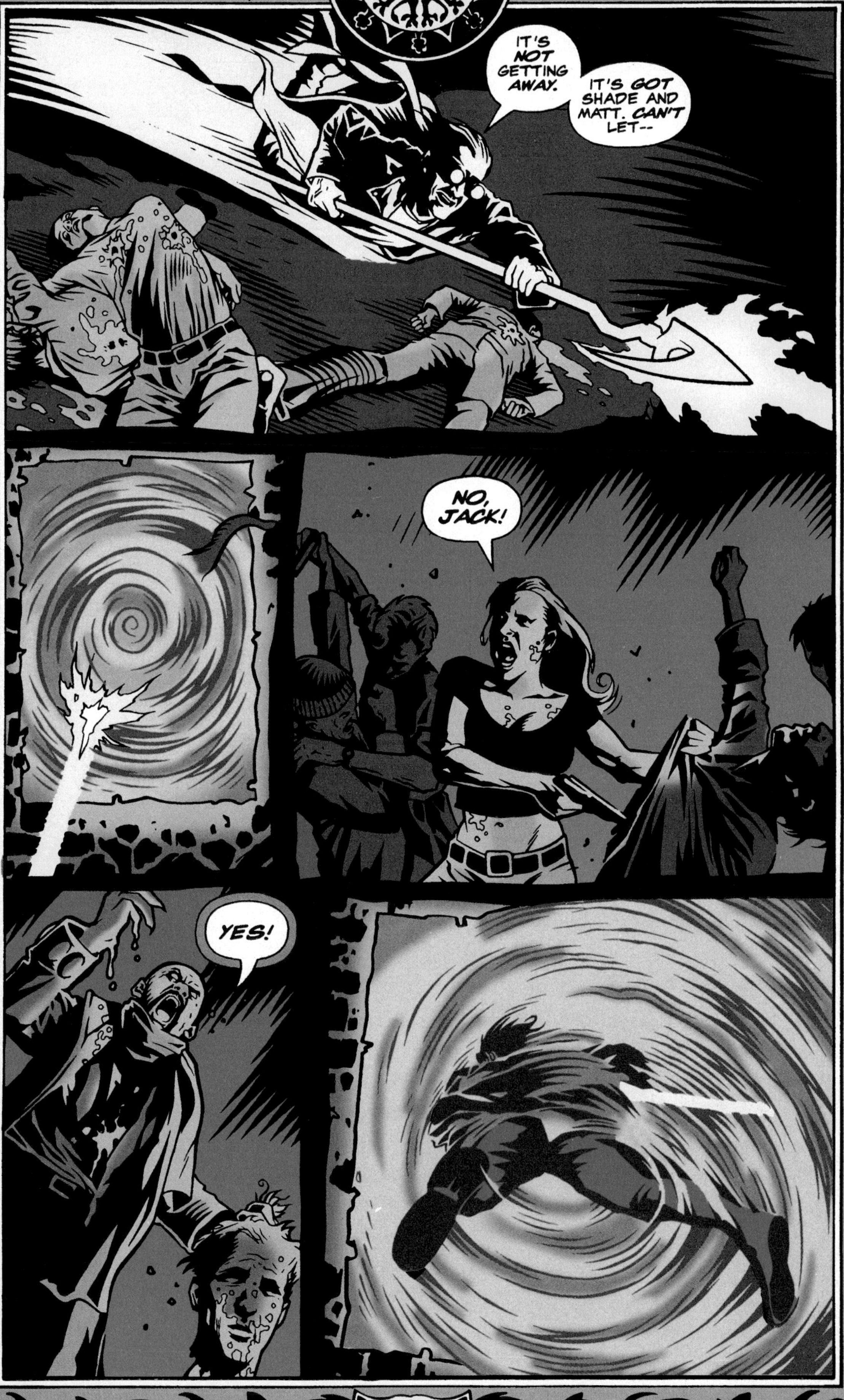
IT'S NOT GETTING AWAY.
IT'S GOT SHADE AND MATT. CAN'T LET--
NO, JACK!
YES!

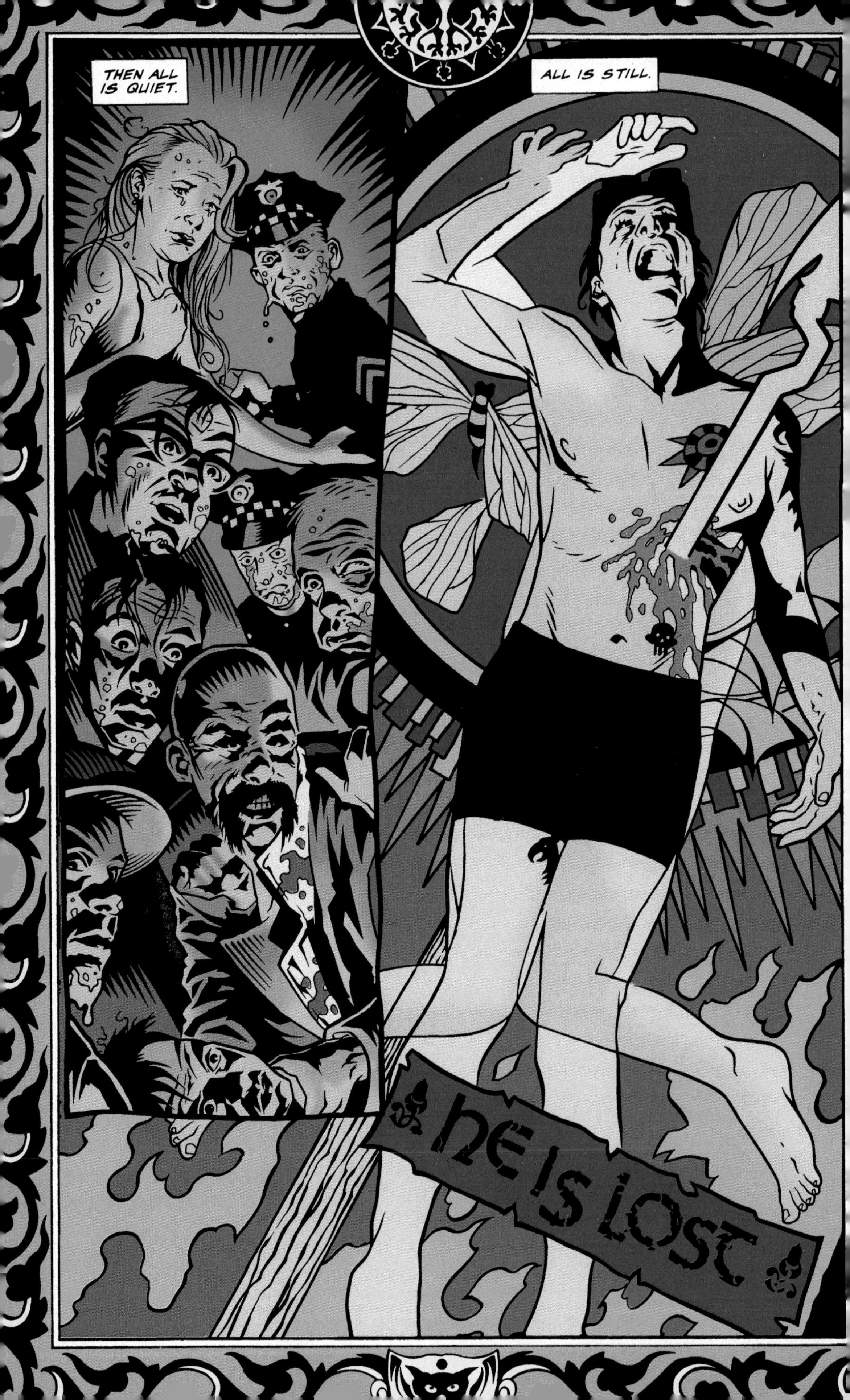
THEN ALL IS QUIET.
ALL IS STILL.
HE IS LOST

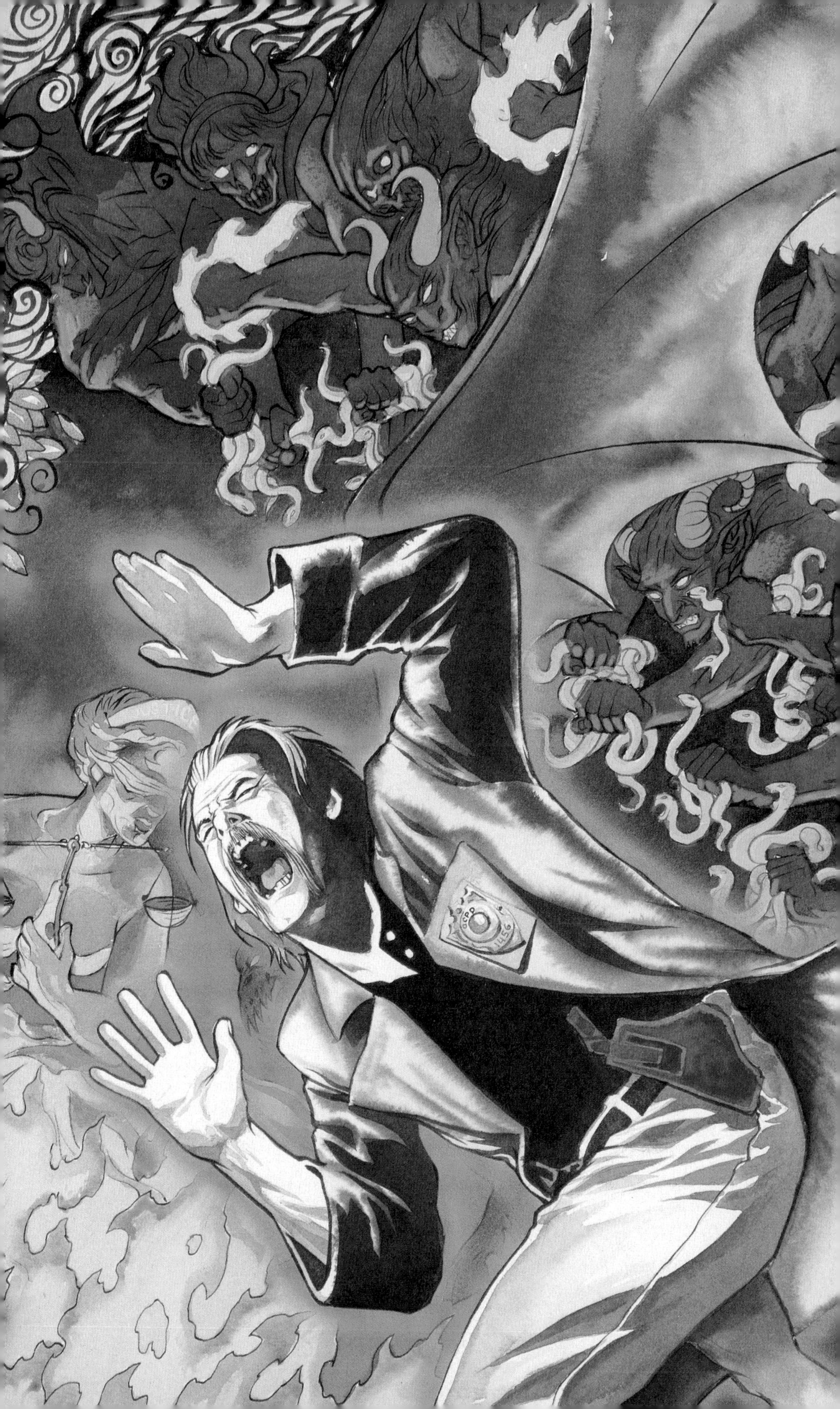
GCPD
1456

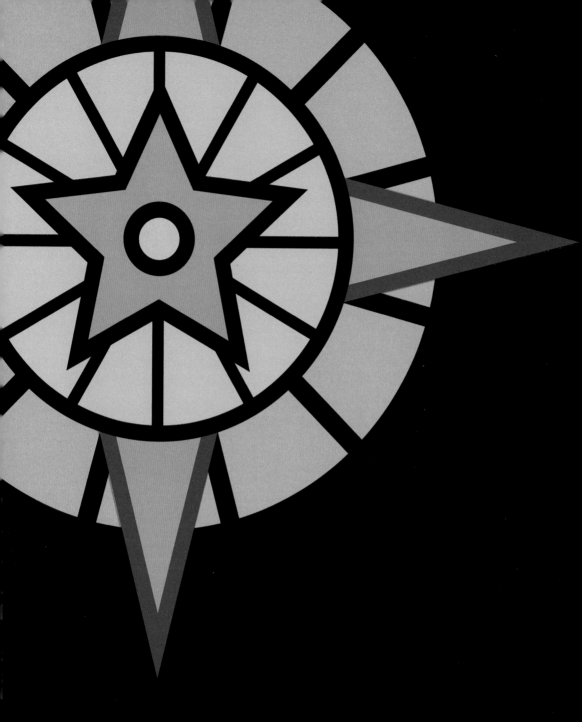

STARMAN 26

Cover by Tony Harris

Written by James Robinson

Art by Tony Harris & Wade von Grawbadger (pgs. 299-308, 311-312, 317-321)

J.H. Williams III & Mick Gray (pgs. 306-307, 309, 313-314, 317)

and Gary Erskine (pgs. 306-307, 310, 315-317)

with colors by Gregory Wright

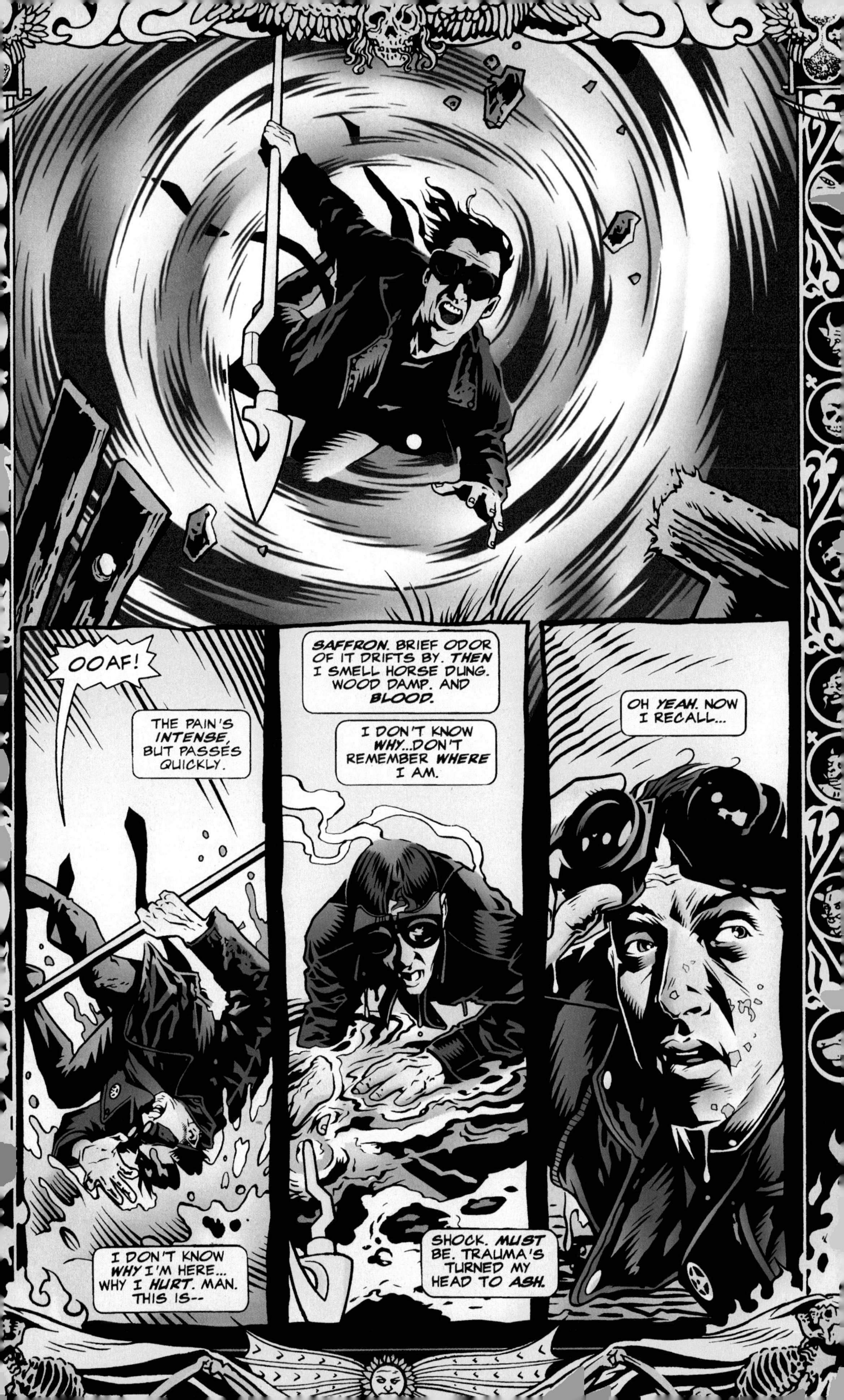
OOAF!
THE PAIN'S INTENSE, BUT PASSES QUICKLY.
I DON'T KNOW WHY I'M HERE... WHY I HURT. MAN. THIS IS--
SAFFRON. BRIEF ODOR OF IT DRIFTS BY. THEN I SMELL HORSE DUNG. WOOD DAMP. AND BLOOD.
I DON'T KNOW WHY...DON'T REMEMBER WHERE I AM.
SHOCK. MUST BE. TRAUMA'S TURNED MY HEAD TO ASH.
OH YEAH. NOW I RECALL...

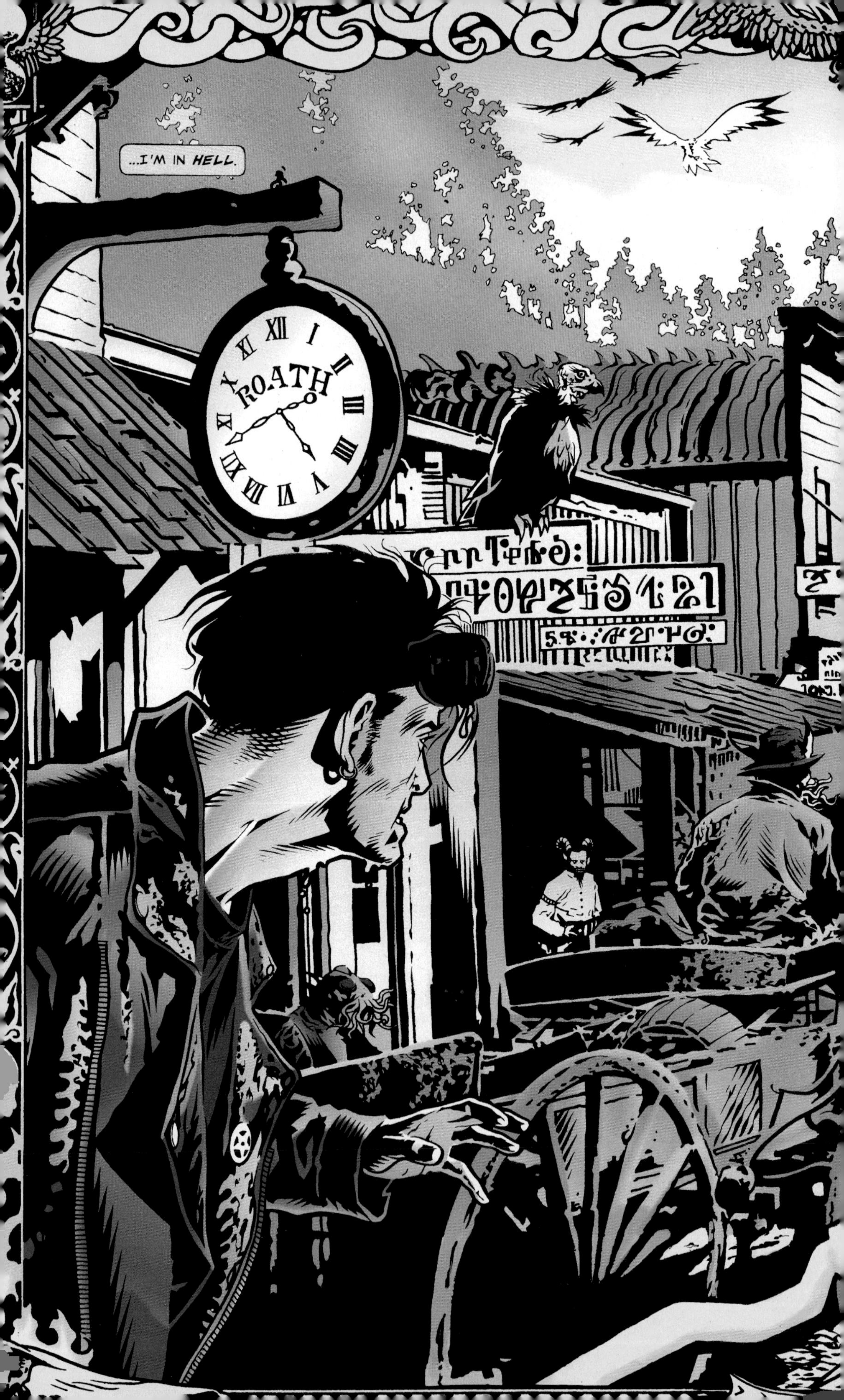
...I'M IN HELL.
ROATH

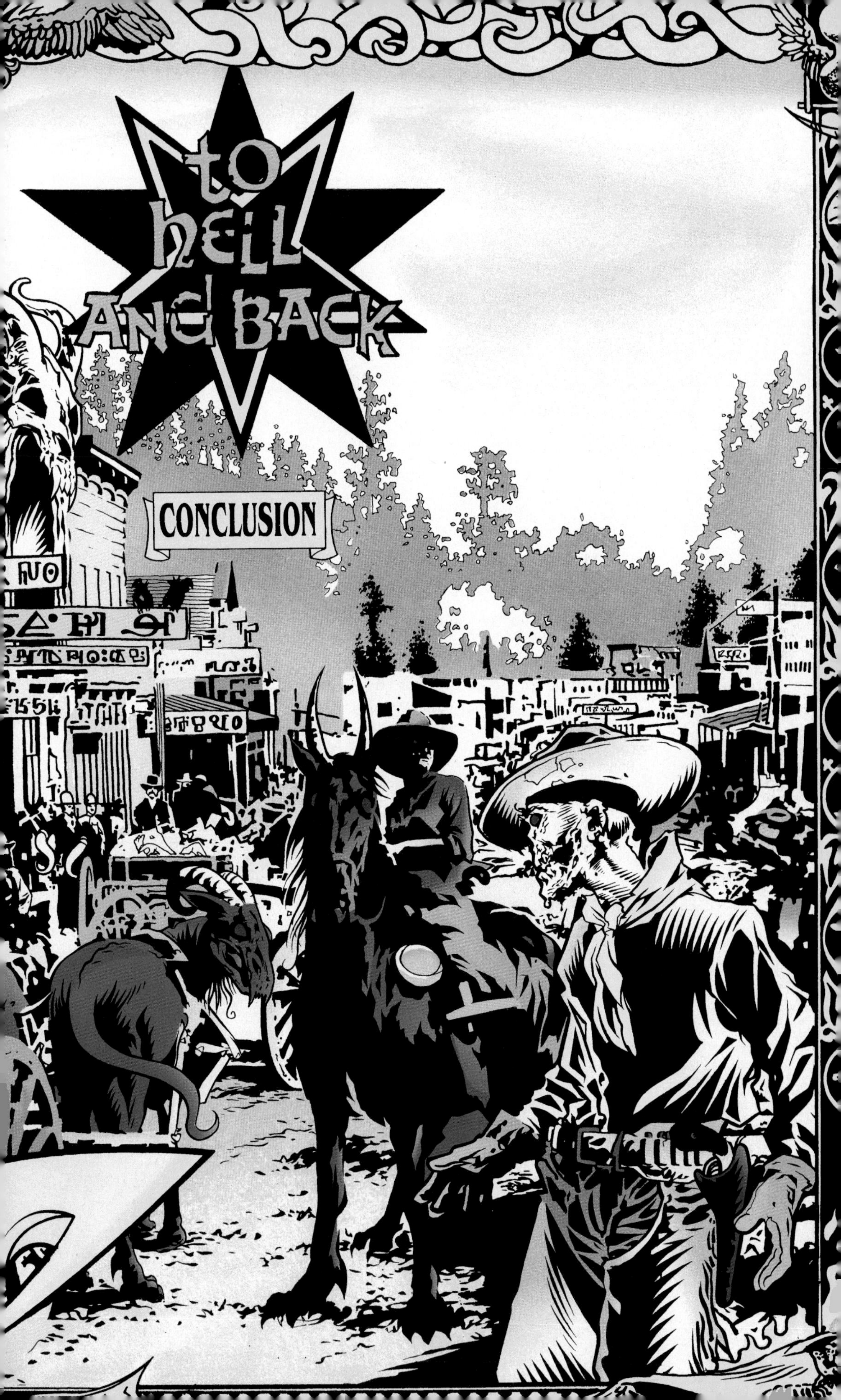
to hell and back
CONCLUSION

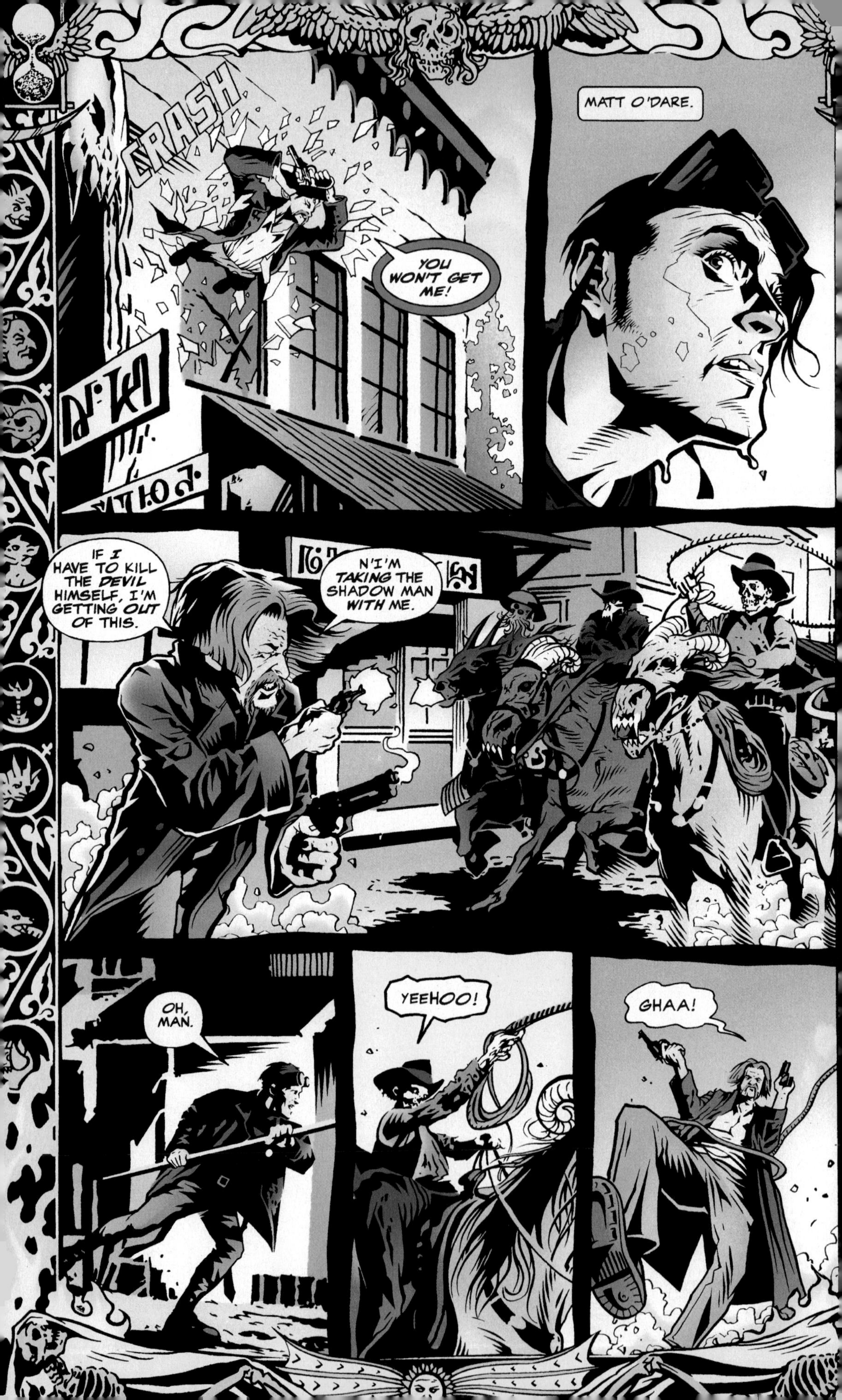

CRASH
YOU WON'T GET ME!
MATT O'DARE.
IF I HAVE TO KILL THE DEVIL HIMSELF, I'M GETTING OUT OF THIS.
N'I'M TAKING THE SHADOW MAN WITH ME.
OH, MAN.
YEEHOO!
GHAA!

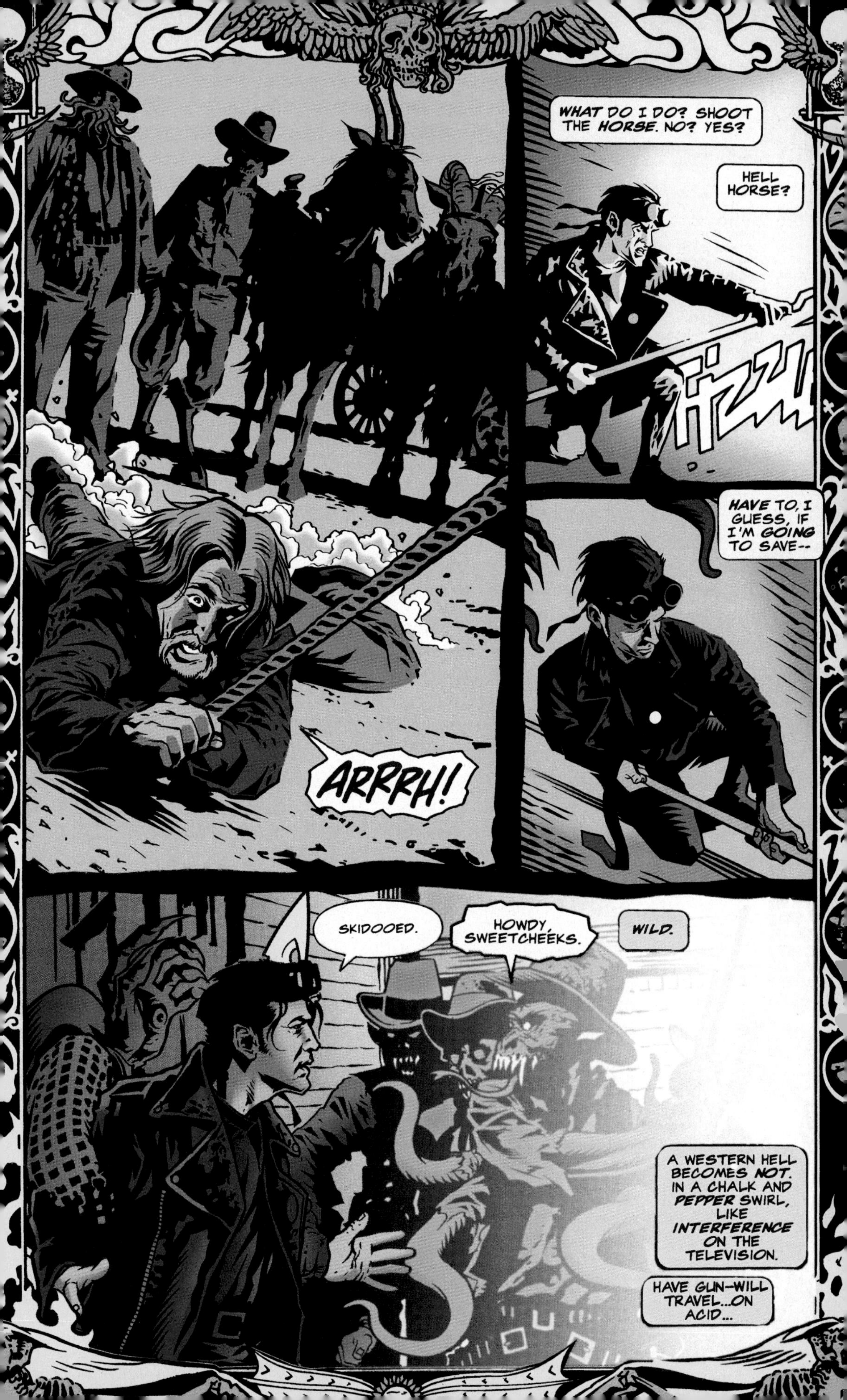

WHAT DO I DO? SHOOT THE HORSE. NO? YES?
HELL HORSE?
FIZZZ
ARRRH!
HAVE TO, I GUESS, IF I'M GOING TO SAVE--
SKIDOOED.
HOWDY, SWEETCHEEKS.
WILD.
A WESTERN HELL BECOMES NOT. IN A CHALK AND PEPPER SWIRL, LIKE INTERFERENCE ON THE TELEVISION.
HAVE GUN-WILL TRAVEL...ON ACID...

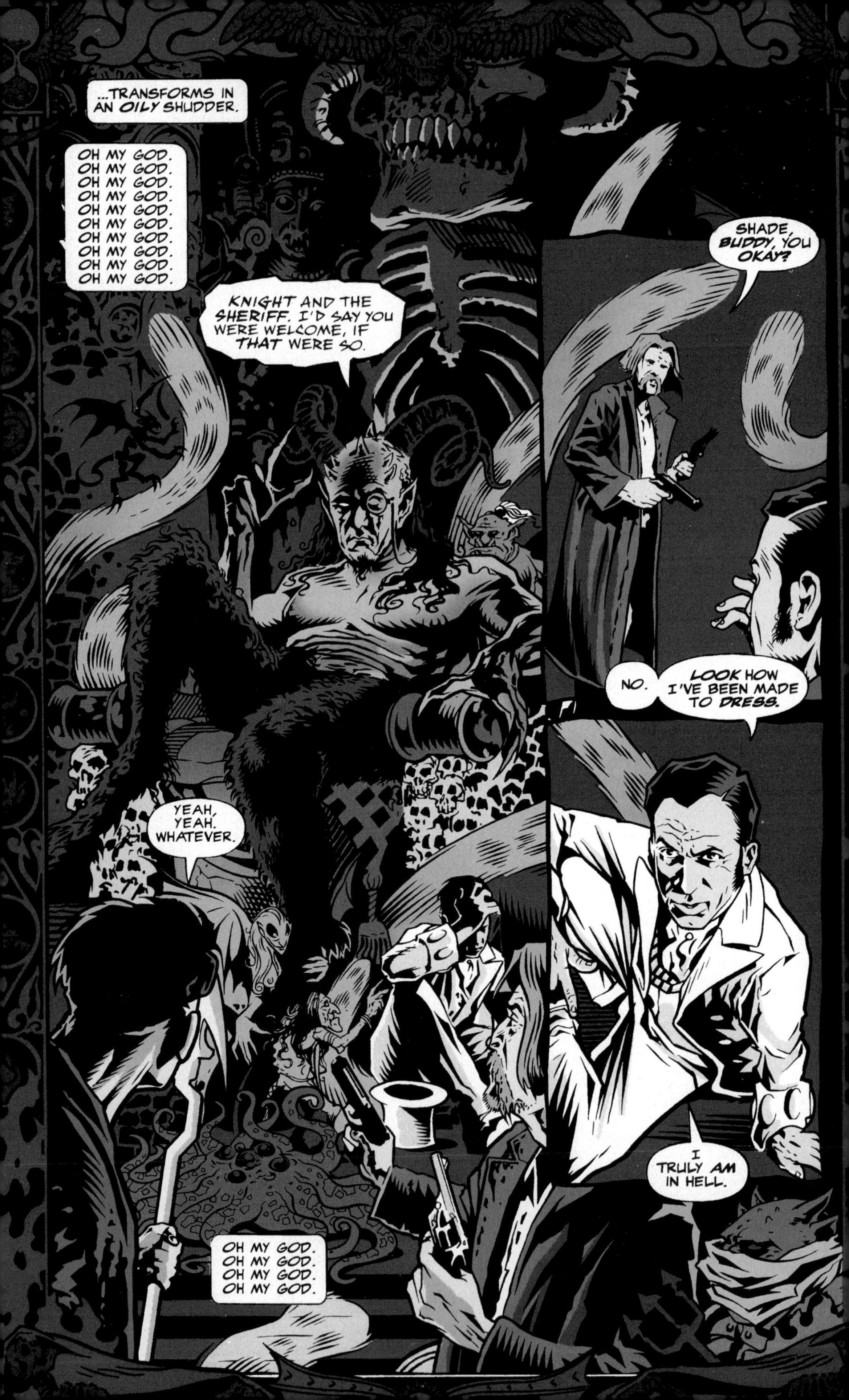
...TRANSFORMS IN AN OILY SHUDDER.
OH MY GOD. OH MY GOD. OH MY GOD. OH MY GOD. OH MY GOD. OH MY GOD. OH MY GOD. OH MY GOD. OH MY GOD. OH MY GOD.
KNIGHT AND THE SHERIFF. I'D SAY YOU WERE WELCOME, IF THAT WERE SO.
SHADE, BUDDY, YOU OKAY?
NO.
LOOK HOW I'VE BEEN MADE TO DRESS.
YEAH, YEAH. WHATEVER.
I TRULY AM IN HELL.
OH MY GOD. OH MY GOD. OH MY GOD. OH MY GOD.

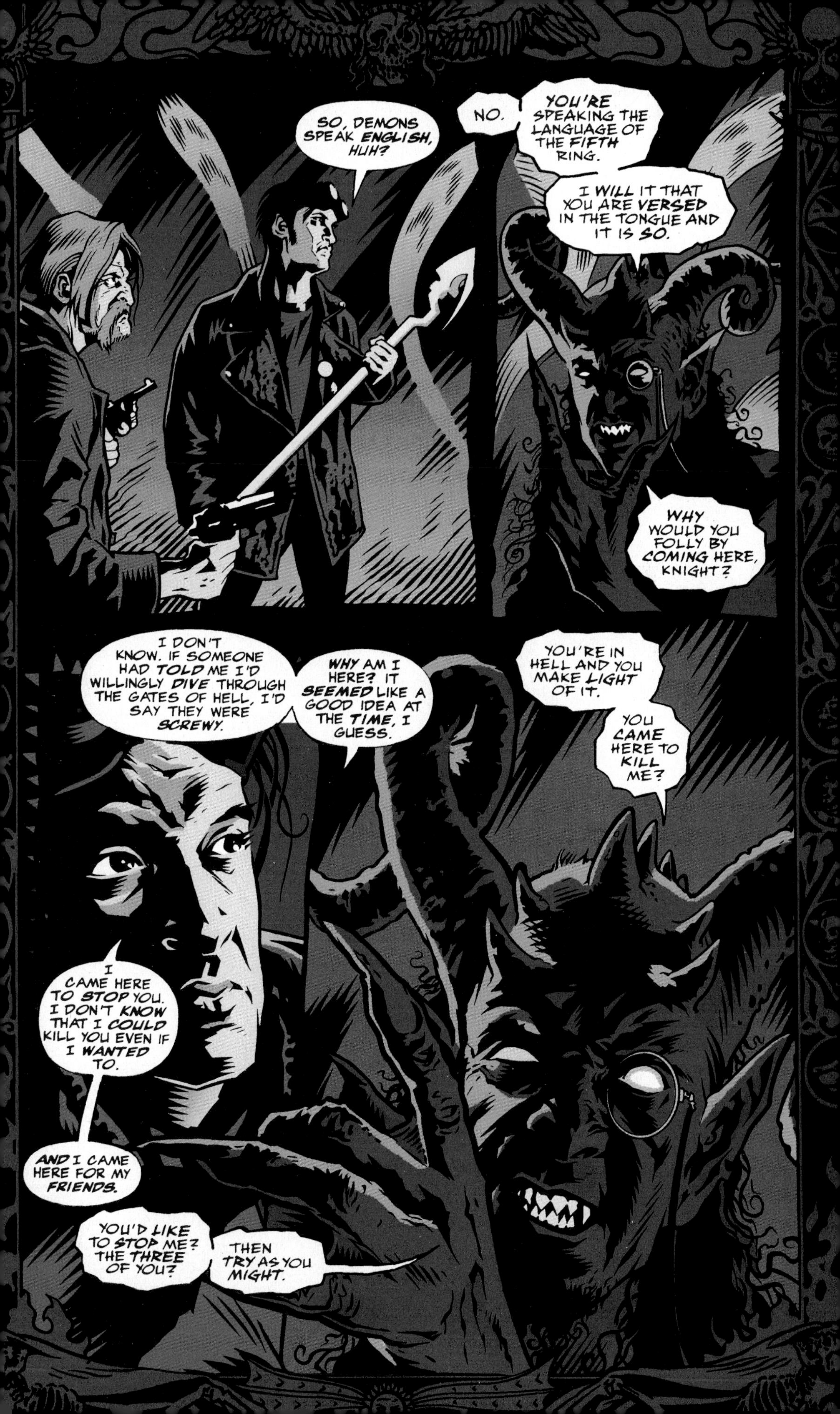
SO, DEMONS SPEAK ENGLISH, HUH?
NO.
YOU'RE SPEAKING THE LANGUAGE OF THE FIFTH RING.
I WILL IT THAT YOU ARE VERSED IN THE TONGUE AND IT IS SO.
WHY WOULD YOU FOLLY BY COMING HERE, KNIGHT?
I DON'T KNOW. IF SOMEONE HAD TOLD ME I'D WILLINGLY DIVE THROUGH THE GATES OF HELL, I'D SAY THEY WERE SCREWY.
WHY AM I HERE? IT SEEMED LIKE A GOOD IDEA AT THE TIME, I GUESS.
YOU'RE IN HELL AND YOU MAKE LIGHT OF IT.
YOU CAME HERE TO KILL ME?
I CAME HERE TO STOP YOU. I DON'T KNOW THAT I COULD KILL YOU EVEN IF I WANTED TO.
AND I CAME HERE FOR MY FRIENDS.
YOU'D LIKE TO STOP ME? THE THREE OF YOU?
THEN TRY AS YOU MIGHT.

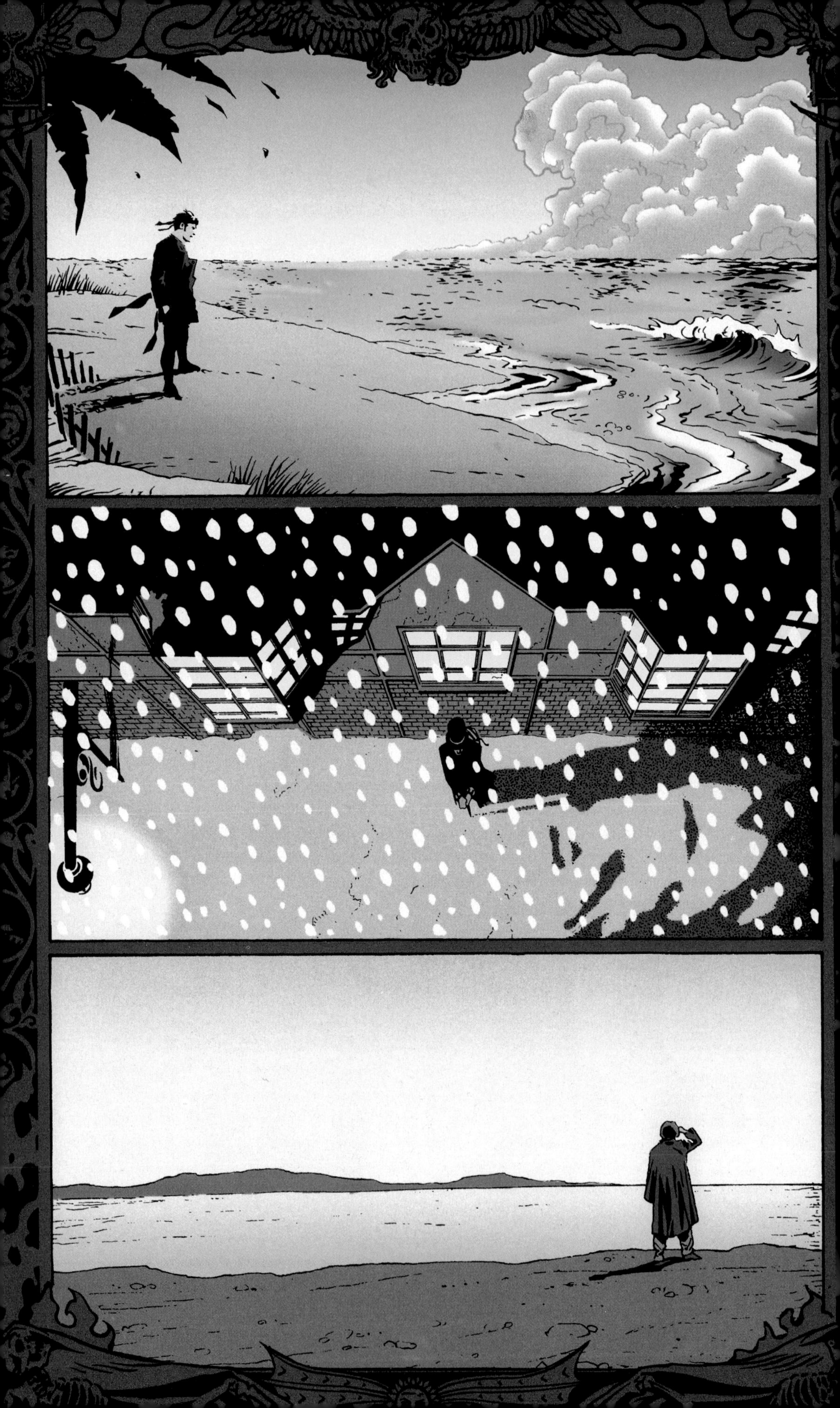

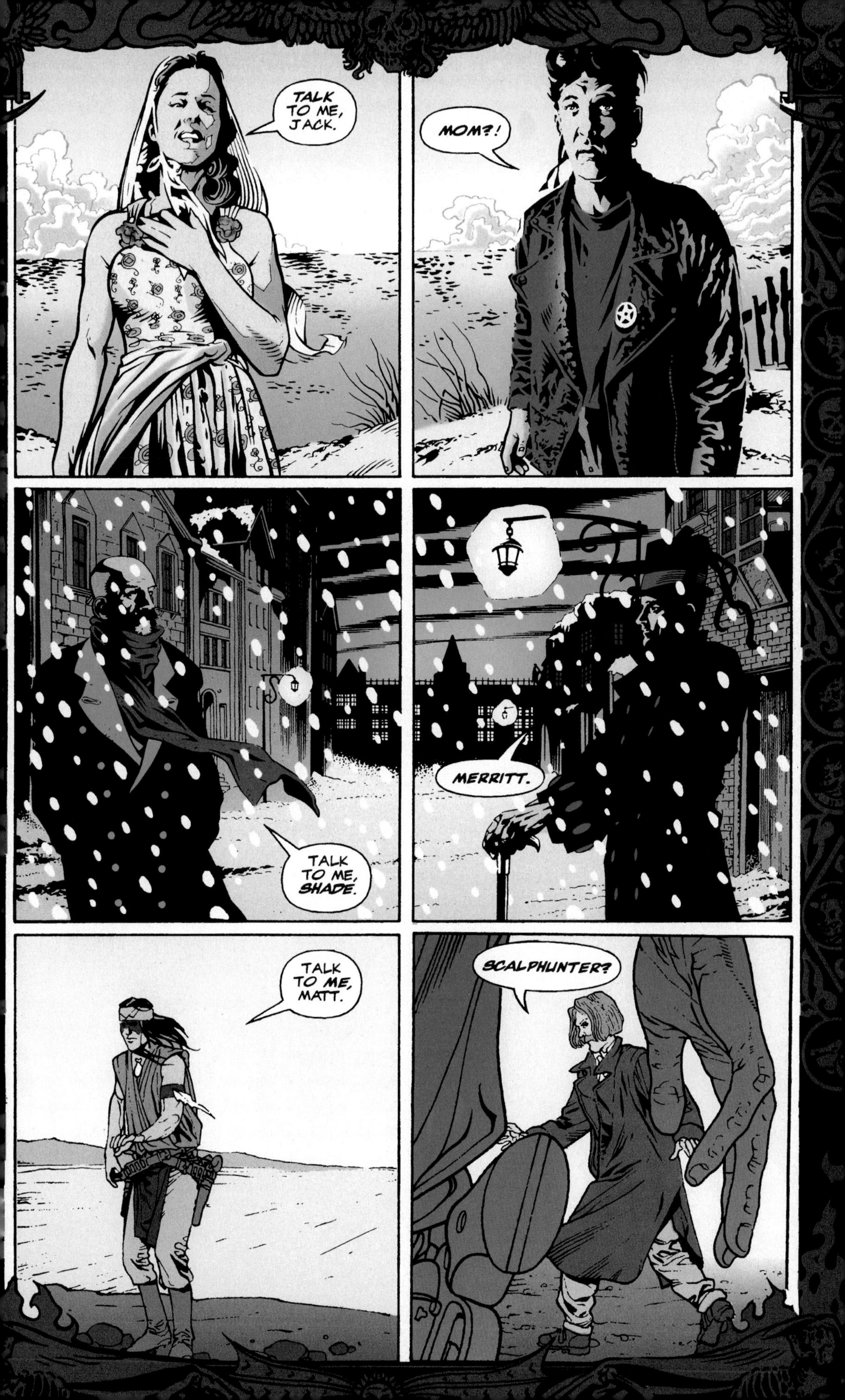
TALK TO ME, JACK.
MOM?!
TALK TO ME, SHADE.
MERRITT.
TALK TO ME, MATT.
SCALPHUNTER?

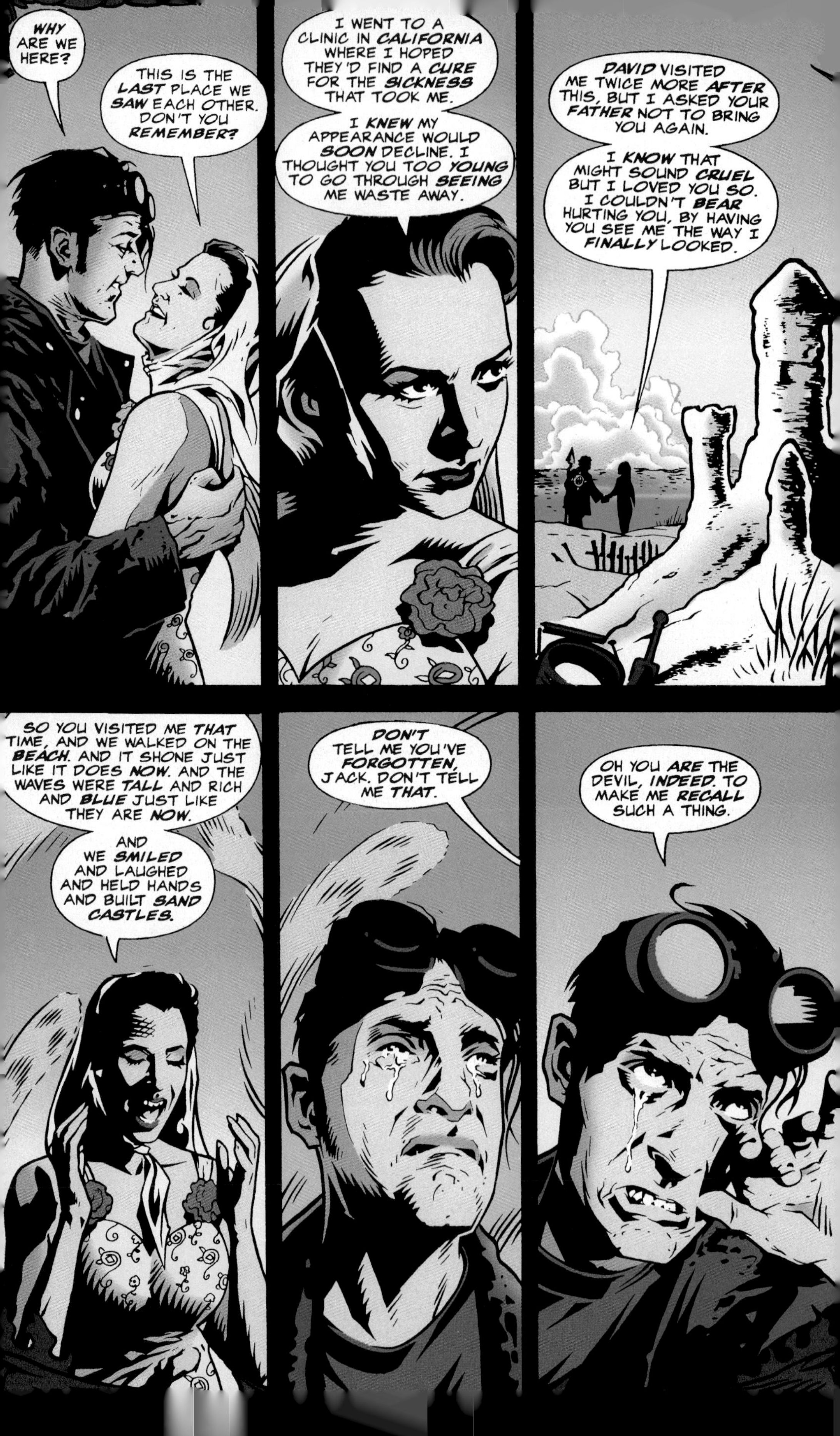
WHY ARE WE HERE?
THIS IS THE LAST PLACE WE SAW EACH OTHER. DON'T YOU REMEMBER?
I WENT TO A CLINIC IN CALIFORNIA WHERE I HOPED THEY'D FIND A CURE FOR THE SICKNESS THAT TOOK ME.
I KNEW MY APPEARANCE WOULD SOON DECLINE. I THOUGHT YOU TOO YOUNG TO GO THROUGH SEEING ME WASTE AWAY.
DAVID VISITED ME TWICE MORE AFTER THIS, BUT I ASKED YOUR FATHER NOT TO BRING YOU AGAIN.
I KNOW THAT MIGHT SOUND CRUEL BUT I LOVED YOU SO. I COULDN'T BEAR HURTING YOU, BY HAVING YOU SEE ME THE WAY I FINALLY LOOKED.
SO YOU VISITED ME THAT TIME, AND WE WALKED ON THE BEACH. AND IT SHONE JUST LIKE IT DOES NOW. AND THE WAVES WERE TALL AND RICH AND BLUE JUST LIKE THEY ARE NOW.
AND WE SMILED AND LAUGHED AND HELD HANDS AND BUILT SAND CASTLES.
DON'T TELL ME YOU'VE FORGOTTEN, JACK. DON'T TELL ME THAT.
OH YOU ARE THE DEVIL, INDEED. TO MAKE ME RECALL SUCH A THING.

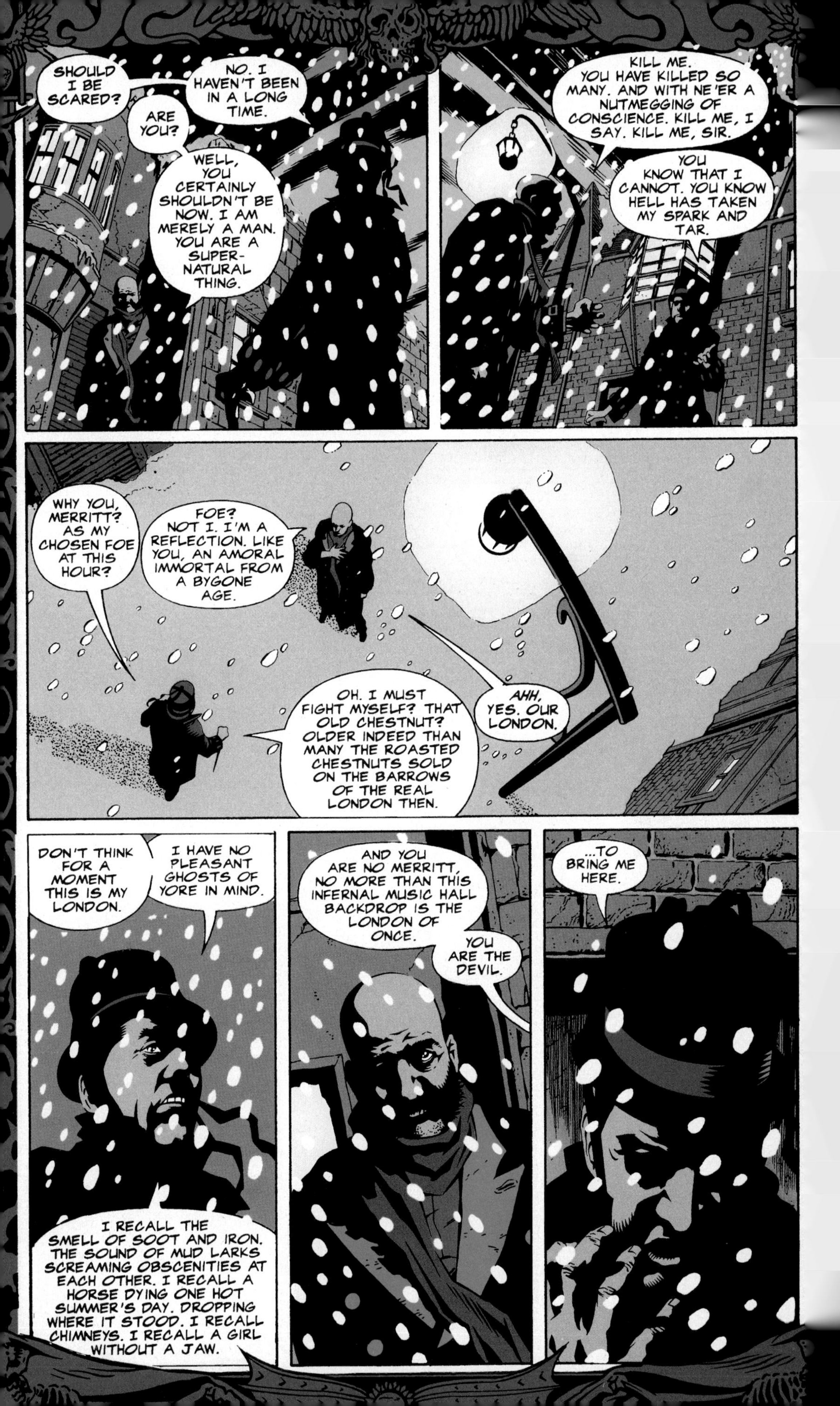
SHOULD I BE SCARED?
ARE YOU?
NO. I HAVEN'T BEEN IN A LONG TIME.
WELL, YOU CERTAINLY SHOULDN'T BE NOW. I AM MERELY A MAN. YOU ARE A SUPER-NATURAL THING.
KILL ME. YOU HAVE KILLED SO MANY. AND WITH NE'ER A NUTMEGGING OF CONSCIENCE. KILL ME, I SAY. KILL ME, SIR.
YOU KNOW THAT I CANNOT. YOU KNOW HELL HAS TAKEN MY SPARK AND TAR.
WHY YOU, MERRITT? AS MY CHOSEN FOE AT THIS HOUR?
FOE? NOT I. I'M A REFLECTION. LIKE YOU, AN AMORAL IMMORTAL FROM A BYGONE AGE.
OH. I MUST FIGHT MYSELF? THAT OLD CHESTNUT? OLDER INDEED THAN MANY THE ROASTED CHESTNUTS SOLD ON THE BARROWS OF THE REAL LONDON THEN.
AHH, YES. OUR LONDON.
DON'T THINK FOR A MOMENT THIS IS MY LONDON.
I HAVE NO PLEASANT GHOSTS OF YORE IN MIND.
I RECALL THE SMELL OF SOOT AND IRON. THE SOUND OF MUD LARKS SCREAMING OBSCENITIES AT EACH OTHER. I RECALL A HORSE DYING ONE HOT SUMMER'S DAY. DROPPING WHERE IT STOOD. I RECALL CHIMNEYS. I RECALL A GIRL WITHOUT A JAW.
AND YOU ARE NO MERRITT, NO MORE THAN THIS INFERNAL MUSIC HALL BACKDROP IS THE LONDON OF ONCE.
YOU ARE THE DEVIL.
...TO BRING ME HERE.

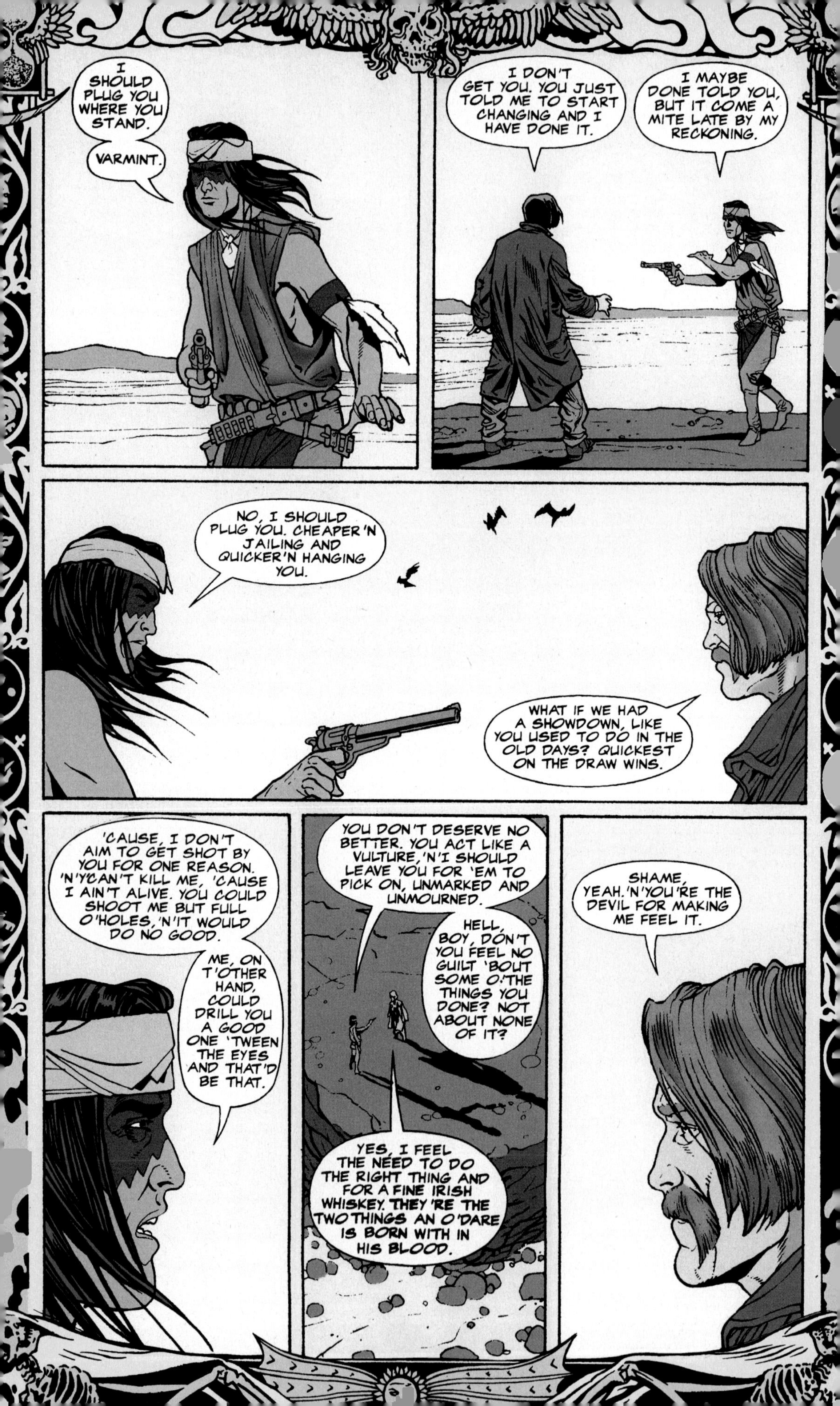
I SHOULD PLUG YOU WHERE YOU STAND.
VARMINT.
I DON'T GET YOU. YOU JUST TOLD ME TO START CHANGING AND I HAVE DONE IT.
I MAYBE DONE TOLD YOU, BUT IT COME A MITE LATE BY MY RECKONING.
NO, I SHOULD PLUG YOU. CHEAPER 'N JAILING AND QUICKER'N HANGING YOU.
WHAT IF WE HAD A SHOWDOWN, LIKE YOU USED TO DO IN THE OLD DAYS? QUICKEST ON THE DRAW WINS.
'CAUSE, I DON'T AIM TO GET SHOT BY YOU FOR ONE REASON. 'N'Y'CAN'T KILL ME, 'CAUSE I AIN'T ALIVE. YOU COULD SHOOT ME BUT FULL O'HOLES, 'N'IT WOULD DO NO GOOD.
ME, ON T'OTHER HAND, COULD DRILL YOU A GOOD ONE 'TWEEN THE EYES AND THAT'D BE THAT.
YOU DON'T DESERVE NO BETTER. YOU ACT LIKE A VULTURE, 'N'I SHOULD LEAVE YOU FOR 'EM TO PICK ON, UNMARKED AND UNMOURNED.
HELL, BOY, DON'T YOU FEEL NO GUILT 'BOUT SOME O' THE THINGS YOU DONE? NOT ABOUT NONE OF IT?
YES, I FEEL THE NEED TO DO THE RIGHT THING AND FOR A FINE IRISH WHISKEY. THEY'RE THE TWO THINGS AN O'DARE IS BORN WITH IN HIS BLOOD.
SHAME, YEAH. 'N'YOU'RE THE DEVIL FOR MAKING ME FEEL IT.

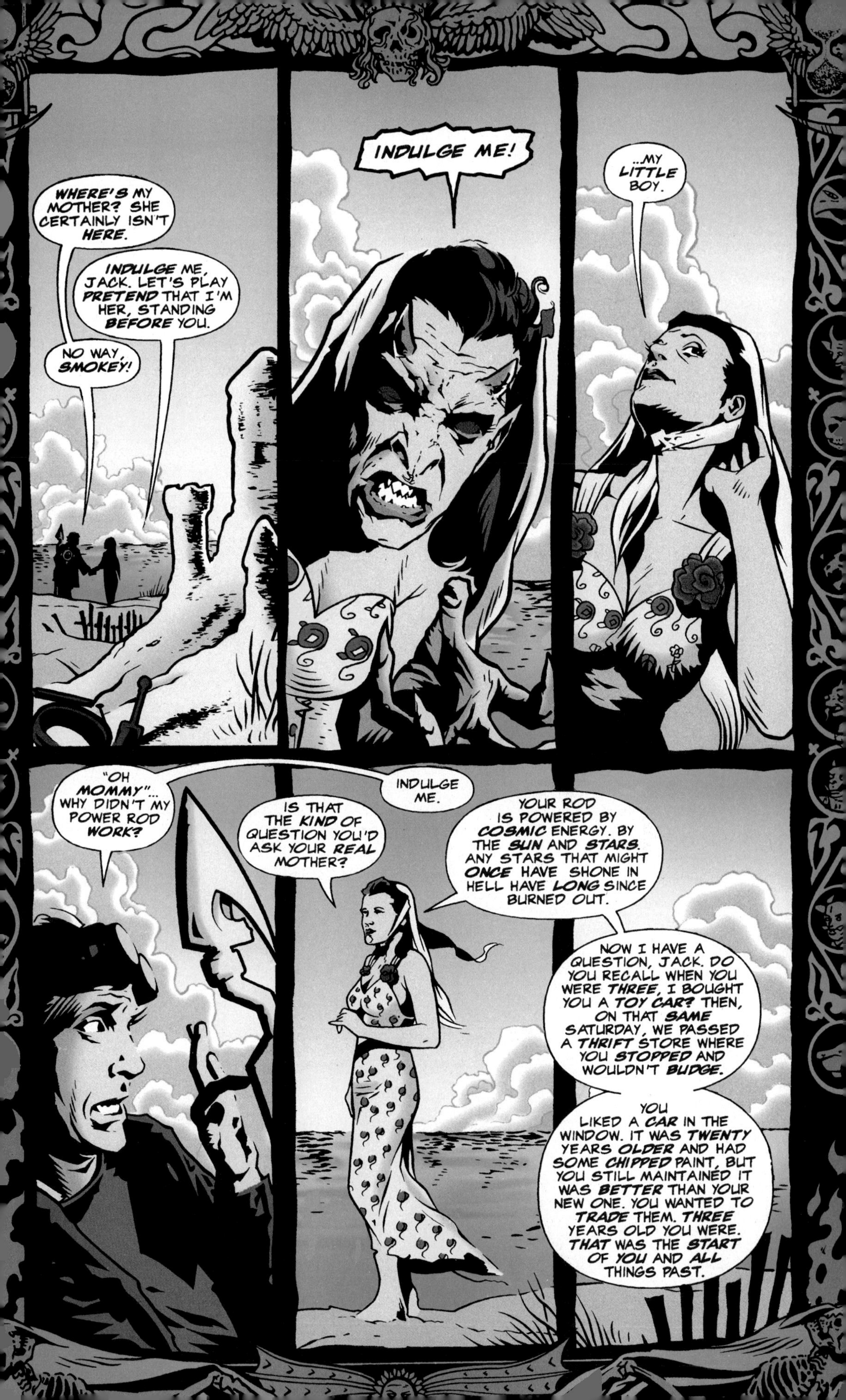
WHERE'S MY MOTHER? SHE CERTAINLY ISN'T HERE.
INDULGE ME, JACK. LET'S PLAY PRETEND THAT I'M HER, STANDING BEFORE YOU.
NO WAY, SMOKEY!
INDULGE ME!
...MY LITTLE BOY.
"OH MOMMY"... WHY DIDN'T MY POWER ROD WORK?
INDULGE ME.
IS THAT THE KIND OF QUESTION YOU'D ASK YOUR REAL MOTHER?
YOUR ROD IS POWERED BY COSMIC ENERGY. BY THE SUN AND STARS. ANY STARS THAT MIGHT ONCE HAVE SHONE IN HELL HAVE LONG SINCE BURNED OUT.
NOW I HAVE A QUESTION, JACK. DO YOU RECALL WHEN YOU WERE THREE, I BOUGHT YOU A TOY CAR? THEN, ON THAT SAME SATURDAY, WE PASSED A THRIFT STORE WHERE YOU STOPPED AND WOULDN'T BUDGE.
YOU LIKED A CAR IN THE WINDOW. IT WAS TWENTY YEARS OLDER AND HAD SOME CHIPPED PAINT, BUT YOU STILL MAINTAINED IT WAS BETTER THAN YOUR NEW ONE. YOU WANTED TO TRADE THEM. THREE YEARS OLD YOU WERE. THAT WAS THE START OF YOU AND ALL THINGS PAST.

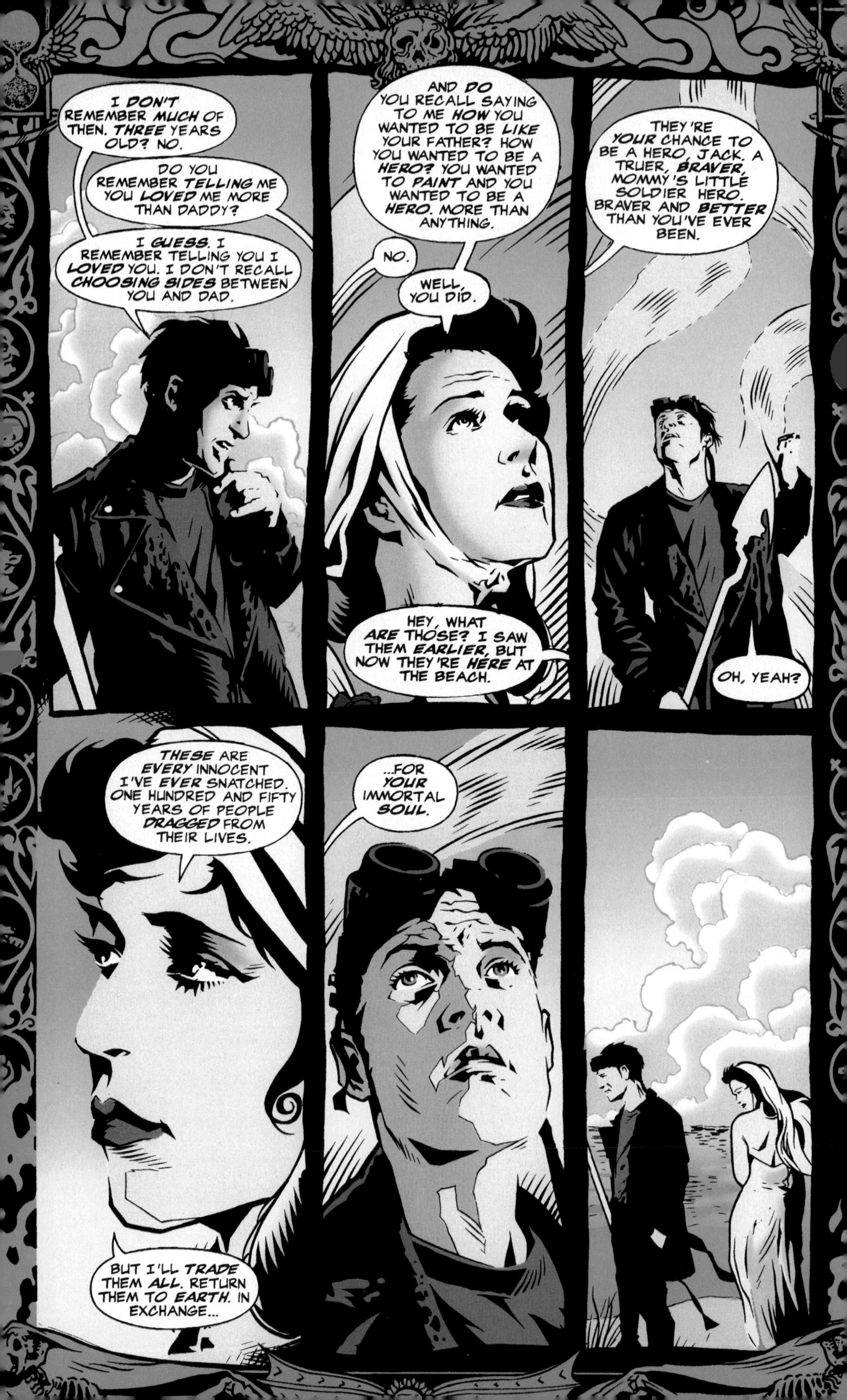
I DON'T REMEMBER MUCH OF THEN. THREE YEARS OLD? NO.
DO YOU REMEMBER TELLING ME YOU LOVED ME MORE THAN DADDY?
I GUESS. I REMEMBER TELLING YOU I LOVED YOU. I DON'T RECALL CHOOSING SIDES BETWEEN YOU AND DAD.
AND DO YOU RECALL SAYING TO ME HOW YOU WANTED TO BE LIKE YOUR FATHER? HOW YOU WANTED TO BE A HERO? YOU WANTED TO PAINT AND YOU WANTED TO BE A HERO. MORE THAN ANYTHING.
NO.
WELL, YOU DID.
HEY, WHAT ARE THOSE? I SAW THEM EARLIER, BUT NOW THEY'RE HERE AT THE BEACH.
THEY'RE YOUR CHANCE TO BE A HERO, JACK. A TRUER, BRAVER, MOMMY'S LITTLE SOLDIER HERO. BRAVER AND BETTER THAN YOU'VE EVER BEEN.
OH, YEAH?
THESE ARE EVERY INNOCENT I'VE EVER SNATCHED. ONE HUNDRED AND FIFTY YEARS OF PEOPLE DRAGGED FROM THEIR LIVES.
BUT I'LL TRADE THEM ALL. RETURN THEM TO EARTH. IN EXCHANGE...
...FOR YOUR IMMORTAL SOUL.

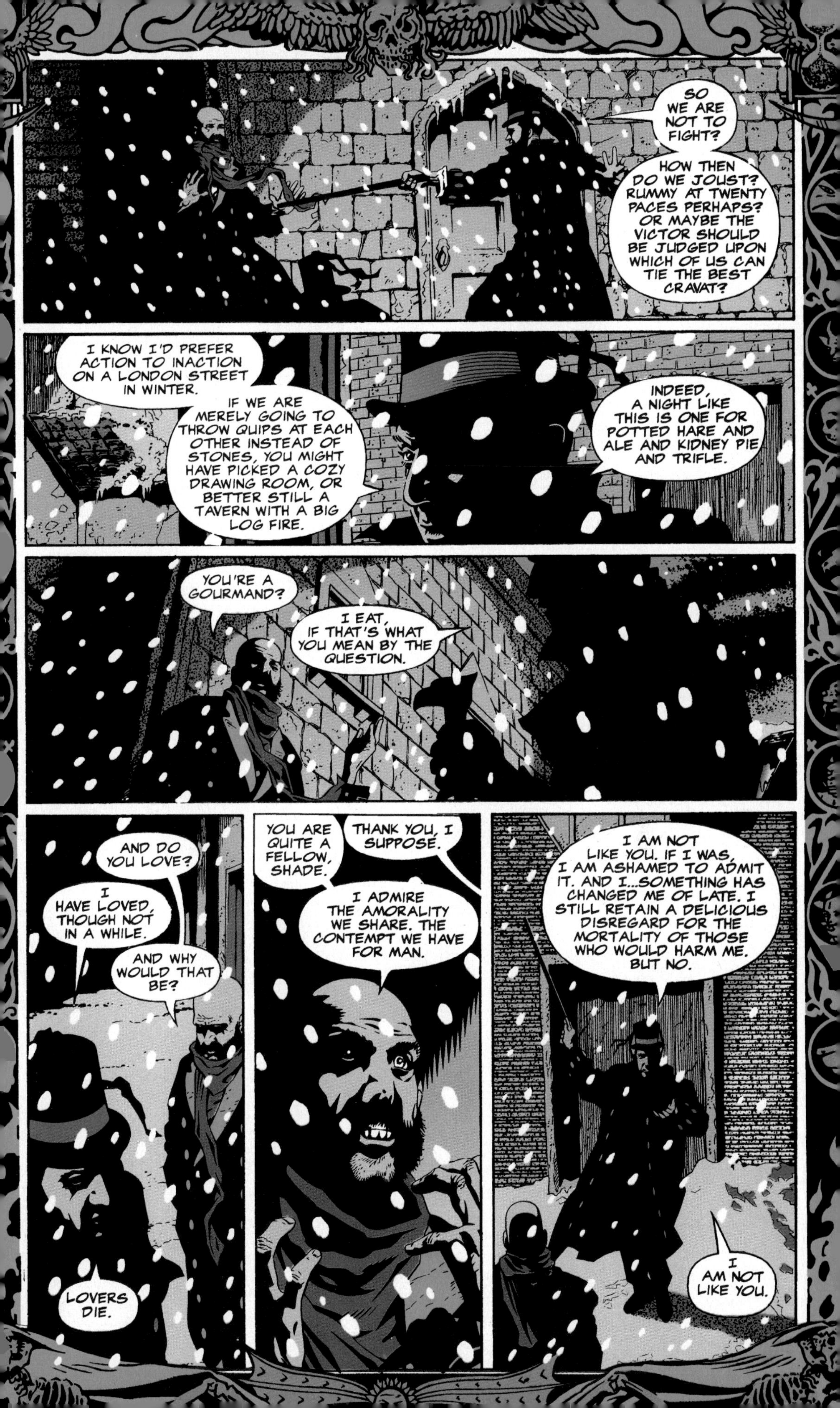
SO WE ARE NOT TO FIGHT?
HOW THEN DO WE JOUST? RUMMY AT TWENTY PACES PERHAPS? OR MAYBE THE VICTOR SHOULD BE JUDGED UPON WHICH OF US CAN TIE THE BEST CRAVAT?
I KNOW I'D PREFER ACTION TO INACTION ON A LONDON STREET IN WINTER.
IF WE ARE MERELY GOING TO THROW QUIPS AT EACH OTHER INSTEAD OF STONES, YOU MIGHT HAVE PICKED A COZY DRAWING ROOM, OR BETTER STILL A TAVERN WITH A BIG LOG FIRE.
INDEED, A NIGHT LIKE THIS IS ONE FOR POTTED HARE AND ALE AND KIDNEY PIE AND TRIFLE.
YOU'RE A GOURMAND?
I EAT, IF THAT'S WHAT YOU MEAN BY THE QUESTION.
AND DO YOU LOVE?
I HAVE LOVED, THOUGH NOT IN A WHILE.
AND WHY WOULD THAT BE?
LOVERS DIE.
YOU ARE QUITE A FELLOW, SHADE.
THANK YOU, I SUPPOSE.
I ADMIRE THE AMORALITY WE SHARE. THE CONTEMPT WE HAVE FOR MAN.
I AM NOT LIKE YOU. IF I WAS, I AM ASHAMED TO ADMIT IT. AND I...SOMETHING HAS CHANGED ME OF LATE. I STILL RETAIN A DELICIOUS DISREGARD FOR THE MORTALITY OF THOSE WHO WOULD HARM ME. BUT NO.
I AM NOT LIKE YOU.

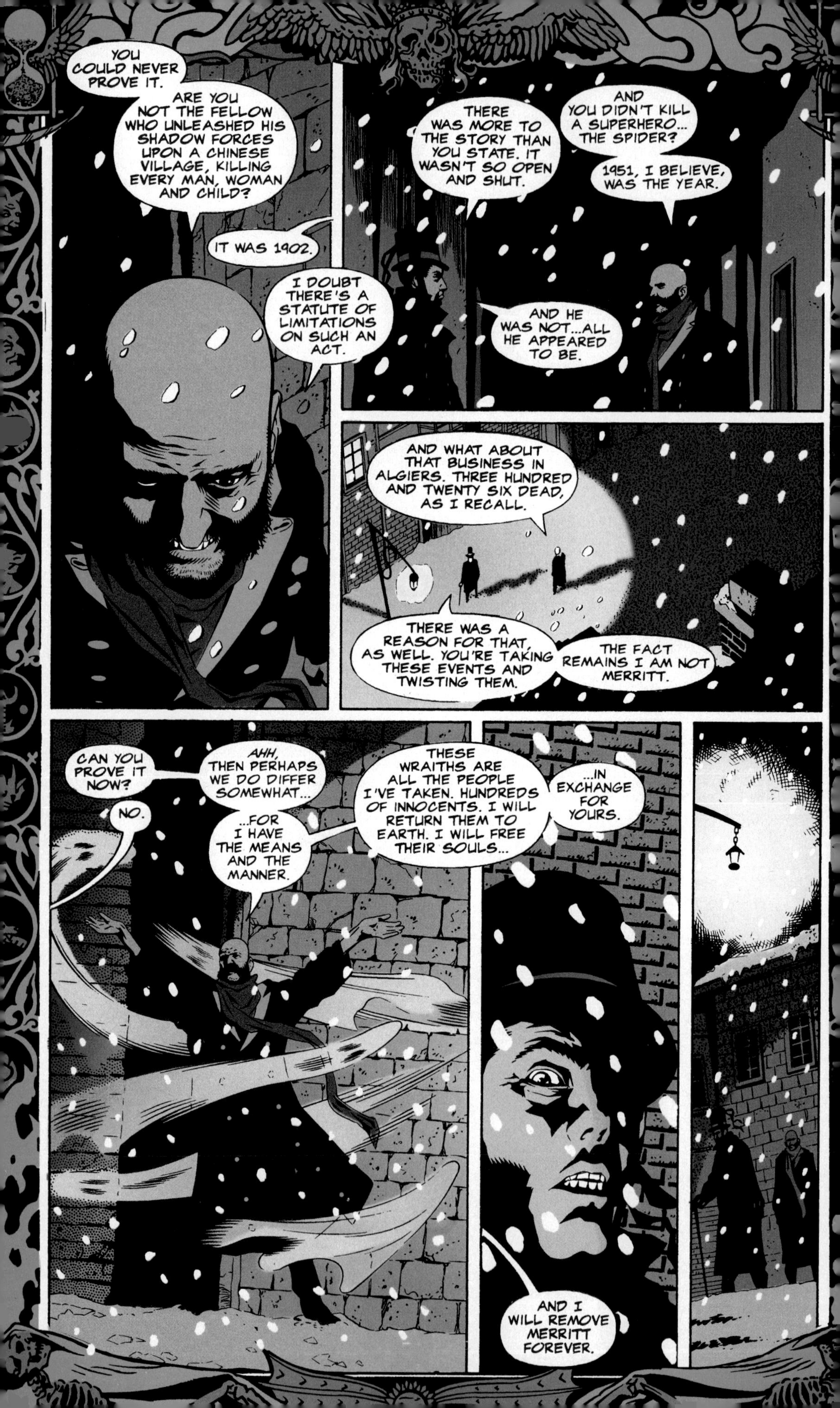

YOU COULD NEVER PROVE IT.
ARE YOU NOT THE FELLOW WHO UNLEASHED HIS SHADOW FORCES UPON A CHINESE VILLAGE, KILLING EVERY MAN, WOMAN AND CHILD?
IT WAS 1902.
I DOUBT THERE'S A STATUTE OF LIMITATIONS ON SUCH AN ACT.
THERE WAS MORE TO THE STORY THAN YOU STATE. IT WASN'T SO OPEN AND SHUT.
AND YOU DIDN'T KILL A SUPERHERO... THE SPIDER?
1951, I BELIEVE, WAS THE YEAR.
AND HE WAS NOT...ALL HE APPEARED TO BE.
AND WHAT ABOUT THAT BUSINESS IN ALGIERS. THREE HUNDRED AND TWENTY SIX DEAD, AS I RECALL.
THERE WAS A REASON FOR THAT, AS WELL. YOU'RE TAKING THESE EVENTS AND TWISTING THEM.
THE FACT REMAINS I AM NOT MERRITT.
CAN YOU PROVE IT NOW?
NO.
AHH, THEN PERHAPS WE DO DIFFER SOMEWHAT...
...FOR I HAVE THE MEANS AND THE MANNER.
THESE WRAITHS ARE ALL THE PEOPLE I'VE TAKEN. HUNDREDS OF INNOCENTS. I WILL RETURN THEM TO EARTH. I WILL FREE THEIR SOULS...
...IN EXCHANGE FOR YOURS.
AND I WILL REMOVE MERRITT FOREVER.

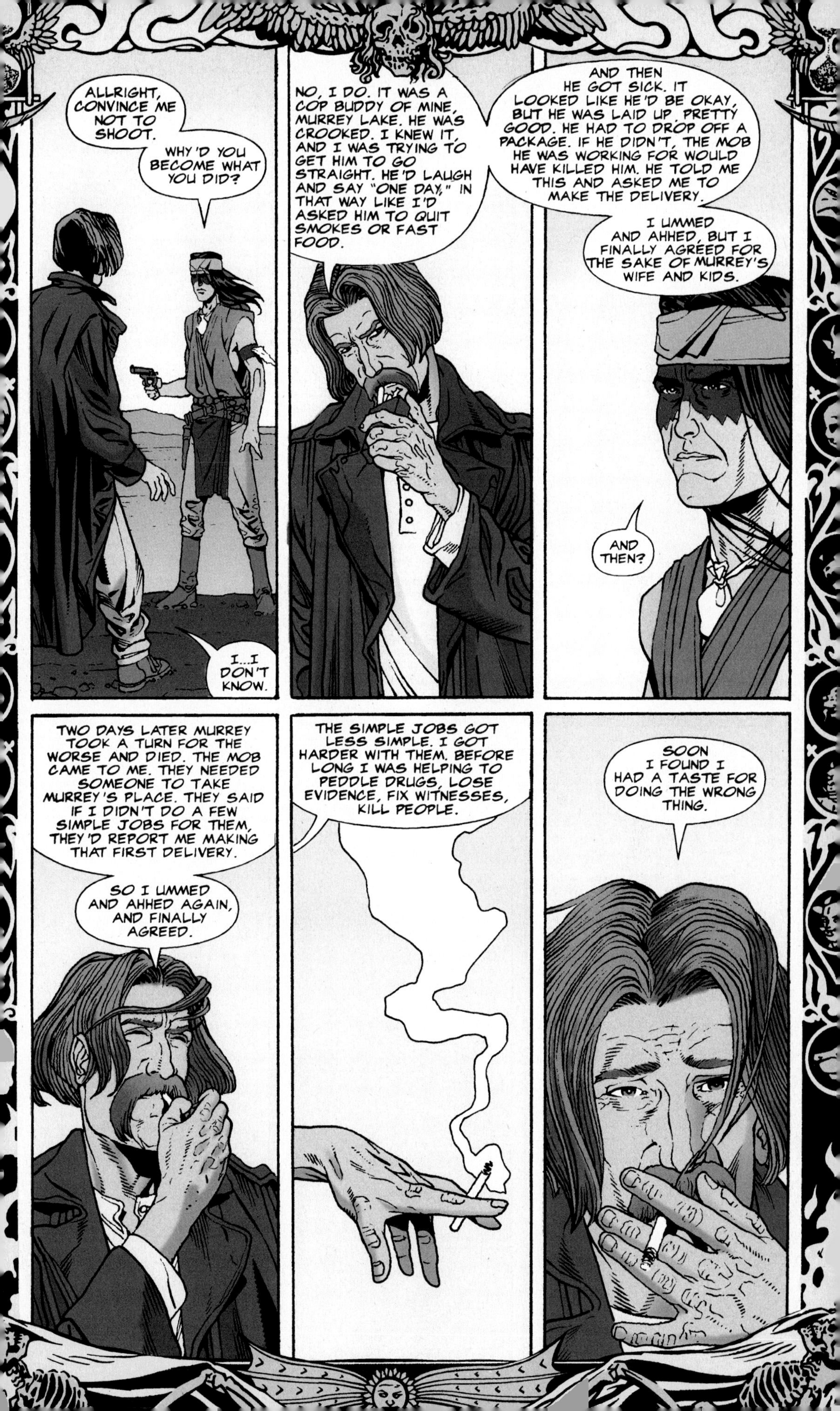
ALLRIGHT, CONVINCE ME NOT TO SHOOT.
WHY'D YOU BECOME WHAT YOU DID?
I...I DON'T KNOW.
NO, I DO. IT WAS A COP BUDDY OF MINE, MURREY LAKE. HE WAS CROOKED. I KNEW IT, AND I WAS TRYING TO GET HIM TO GO STRAIGHT. HE'D LAUGH AND SAY "ONE DAY," IN THAT WAY LIKE I'D ASKED HIM TO QUIT SMOKES OR FAST FOOD.
AND THEN HE GOT SICK. IT LOOKED LIKE HE'D BE OKAY, BUT HE WAS LAID UP PRETTY GOOD. HE HAD TO DROP OFF A PACKAGE. IF HE DIDN'T, THE MOB HE WAS WORKING FOR WOULD HAVE KILLED HIM. HE TOLD ME THIS AND ASKED ME TO MAKE THE DELIVERY.
I UMMED AND AHHED, BUT I FINALLY AGREED FOR THE SAKE OF MURREY'S WIFE AND KIDS.
AND THEN?
TWO DAYS LATER MURREY TOOK A TURN FOR THE WORSE AND DIED. THE MOB CAME TO ME. THEY NEEDED SOMEONE TO TAKE MURREY'S PLACE. THEY SAID IF I DIDN'T DO A FEW SIMPLE JOBS FOR THEM, THEY'D REPORT ME MAKING THAT FIRST DELIVERY.
SO I UMMED AND AHHED AGAIN, AND FINALLY AGREED.
THE SIMPLE JOBS GOT LESS SIMPLE. I GOT HARDER WITH THEM. BEFORE LONG I WAS HELPING TO PEDDLE DRUGS, LOSE EVIDENCE, FIX WITNESSES, KILL PEOPLE.
SOON I FOUND I HAD A TASTE FOR DOING THE WRONG THING.

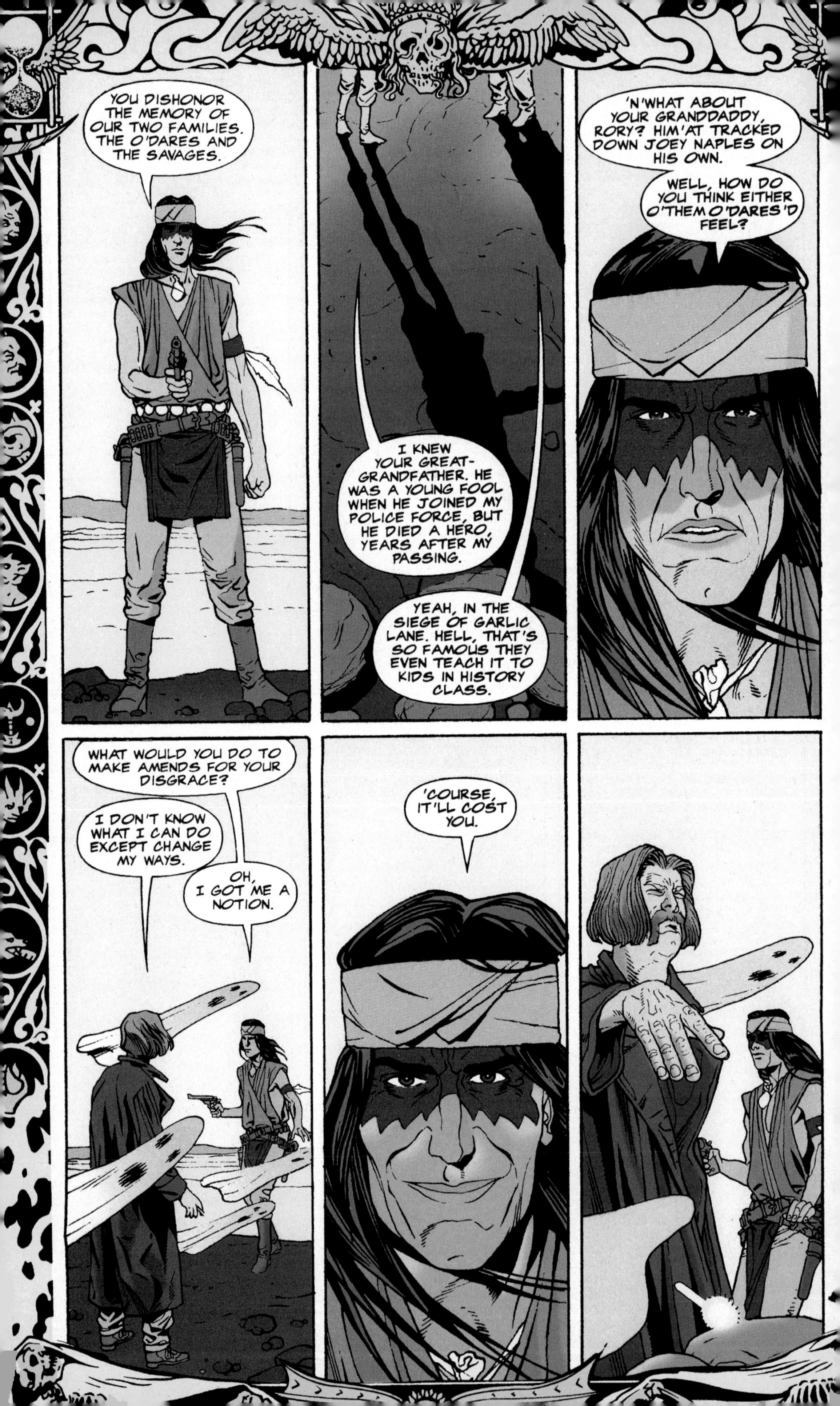
YOU DISHONOR THE MEMORY OF OUR TWO FAMILIES. THE O'DARES AND THE SAVAGES.
I KNEW YOUR GREAT-GRANDFATHER. HE WAS A YOUNG FOOL WHEN HE JOINED MY POLICE FORCE, BUT HE DIED A HERO, YEARS AFTER MY PASSING.
YEAH, IN THE SIEGE OF GARLIC LANE. HELL, THAT'S SO FAMOUS THEY EVEN TEACH IT TO KIDS IN HISTORY CLASS.
'N'WHAT ABOUT YOUR GRANDDADDY, RORY? HIM'AT TRACKED DOWN JOEY NAPLES ON HIS OWN.
WELL, HOW DO YOU THINK EITHER O'THEM O'DARES'D FEEL?
WHAT WOULD YOU DO TO MAKE AMENDS FOR YOUR DISGRACE?
I DON'T KNOW WHAT I CAN DO EXCEPT CHANGE MY WAYS.
OH, I GOT ME A NOTION.
'COURSE, IT'LL COST YOU.

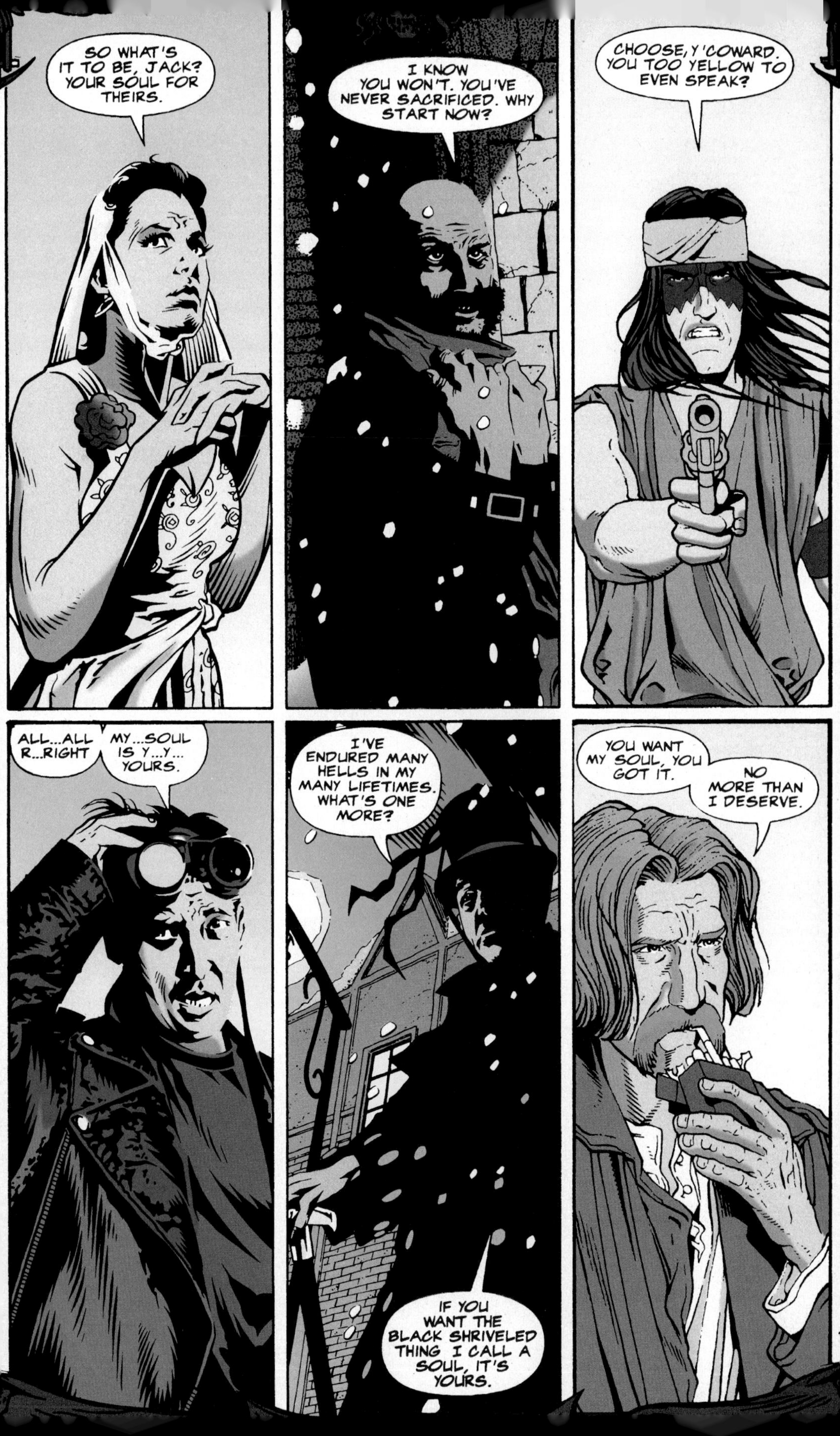

SO WHAT'S IT TO BE, JACK? YOUR SOUL FOR THEIRS.
I KNOW YOU WON'T. YOU'VE NEVER SACRIFICED. WHY START NOW?
CHOOSE, Y'COWARD. YOU TOO YELLOW TO EVEN SPEAK?
ALL...ALL R...RIGHT
MY...SOUL IS Y...Y... YOURS.
I'VE ENDURED MANY HELLS IN MY MANY LIFETIMES. WHAT'S ONE MORE?
IF YOU WANT THE BLACK SHRIVELED THING I CALL A SOUL, IT'S YOURS.
YOU WANT MY SOUL, YOU GOT IT.
NO MORE THAN I DESERVE.

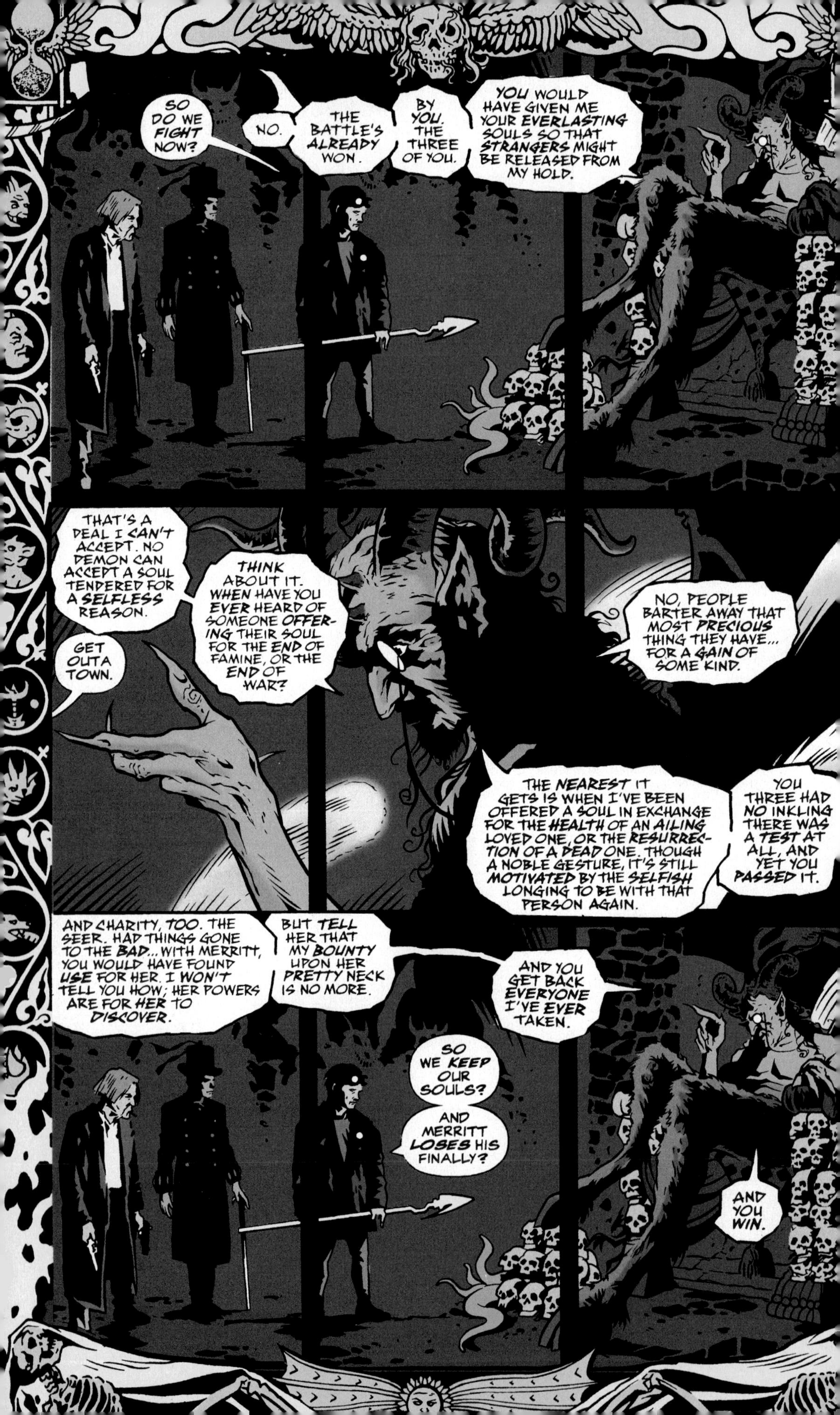

SO DO WE FIGHT NOW?
NO.
THE BATTLE'S ALREADY WON.
BY YOU. THE THREE OF YOU.
YOU WOULD HAVE GIVEN ME YOUR EVERLASTING SOULS SO THAT STRANGERS MIGHT BE RELEASED FROM MY HOLD.
THAT'S A DEAL I CAN'T ACCEPT. NO DEMON CAN ACCEPT A SOUL TENDERED FOR A SELFLESS REASON.
GET OUTA TOWN.
THINK ABOUT IT. WHEN HAVE YOU EVER HEARD OF SOMEONE OFFERING THEIR SOUL FOR THE END OF FAMINE, OR THE END OF WAR?
NO, PEOPLE BARTER AWAY THAT MOST PRECIOUS THING THEY HAVE... FOR A GAIN OF SOME KIND.
THE NEAREST IT GETS IS WHEN I'VE BEEN OFFERED A SOUL IN EXCHANGE FOR THE HEALTH OF AN AILING LOVED ONE, OR THE RESURRECTION OF A DEAD ONE. THOUGH A NOBLE GESTURE, IT'S STILL MOTIVATED BY THE SELFISH LONGING TO BE WITH THAT PERSON AGAIN.
YOU THREE HAD NO INKLING THERE WAS A TEST AT ALL, AND YET YOU PASSED IT.
AND CHARITY, TOO. THE SEER. HAD THINGS GONE TO THE BAD... WITH MERRITT, YOU WOULD HAVE FOUND USE FOR HER. I WON'T TELL YOU HOW; HER POWERS ARE FOR HER TO DISCOVER.
BUT TELL HER THAT MY BOUNTY UPON HER PRETTY NECK IS NO MORE.
AND YOU GET BACK EVERYONE I'VE EVER TAKEN.
SO WE KEEP OUR SOULS?
AND MERRITT LOSES HIS FINALLY?
AND YOU WIN.

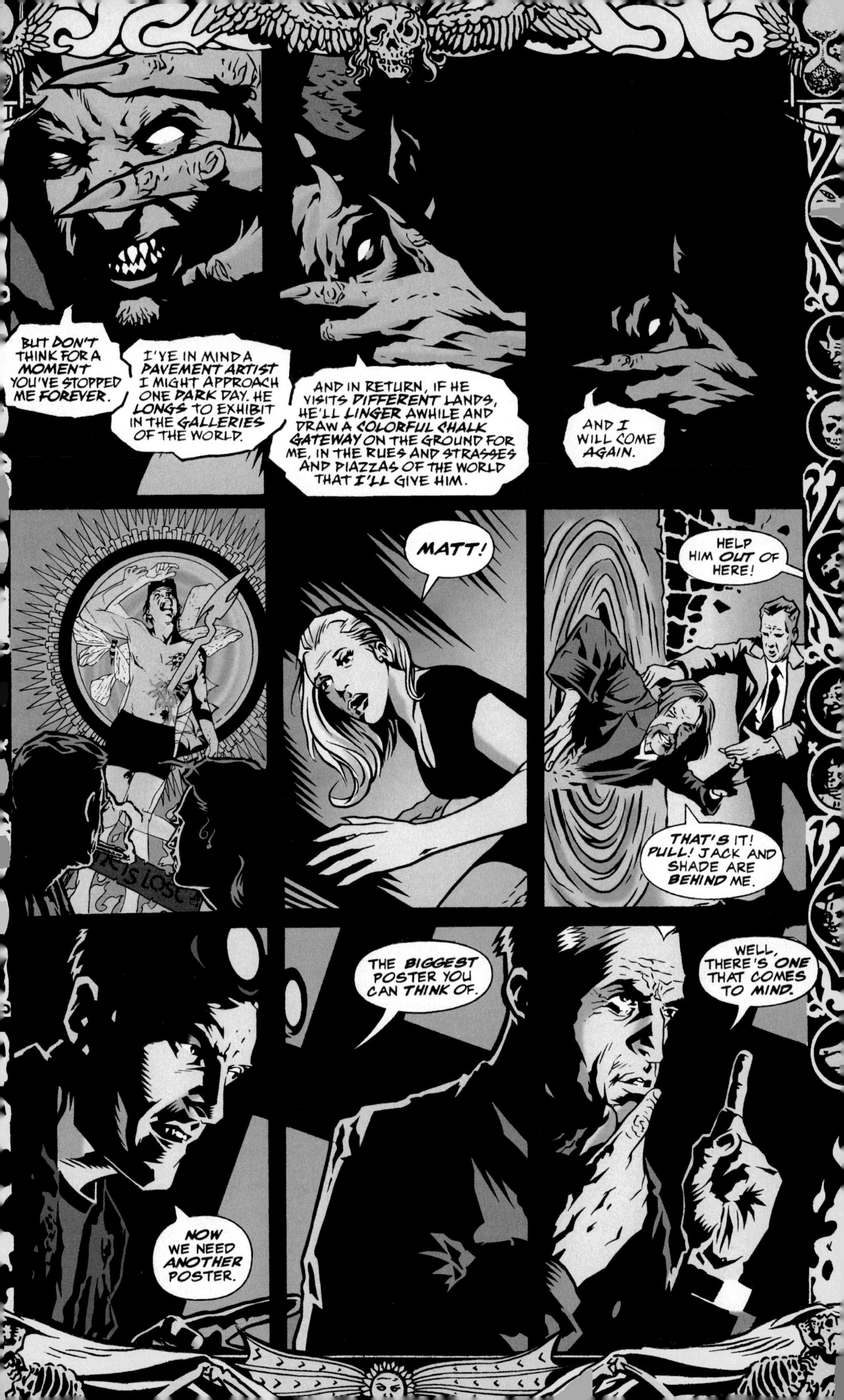
BUT DON'T THINK FOR A MOMENT YOU'VE STOPPED ME FOREVER.
I'VE IN MIND A PAVEMENT ARTIST I MIGHT APPROACH ONE DARK DAY. HE LONGS TO EXHIBIT IN THE GALLERIES OF THE WORLD.
AND IN RETURN, IF HE VISITS DIFFERENT LANDS, HE'LL LINGER AWHILE AND DRAW A COLORFUL CHALK GATEWAY ON THE GROUND FOR ME, IN THE RUES AND STRASSES AND PIAZZAS OF THE WORLD THAT I'LL GIVE HIM.
AND I WILL COME AGAIN.
MATT!
HELP HIM OUT OF HERE!
THAT'S IT! PULL! JACK AND SHADE ARE BEHIND ME.
NOW WE NEED ANOTHER POSTER.
THE BIGGEST POSTER YOU CAN THINK OF.
WELL, THERE'S ONE THAT COMES TO MIND.

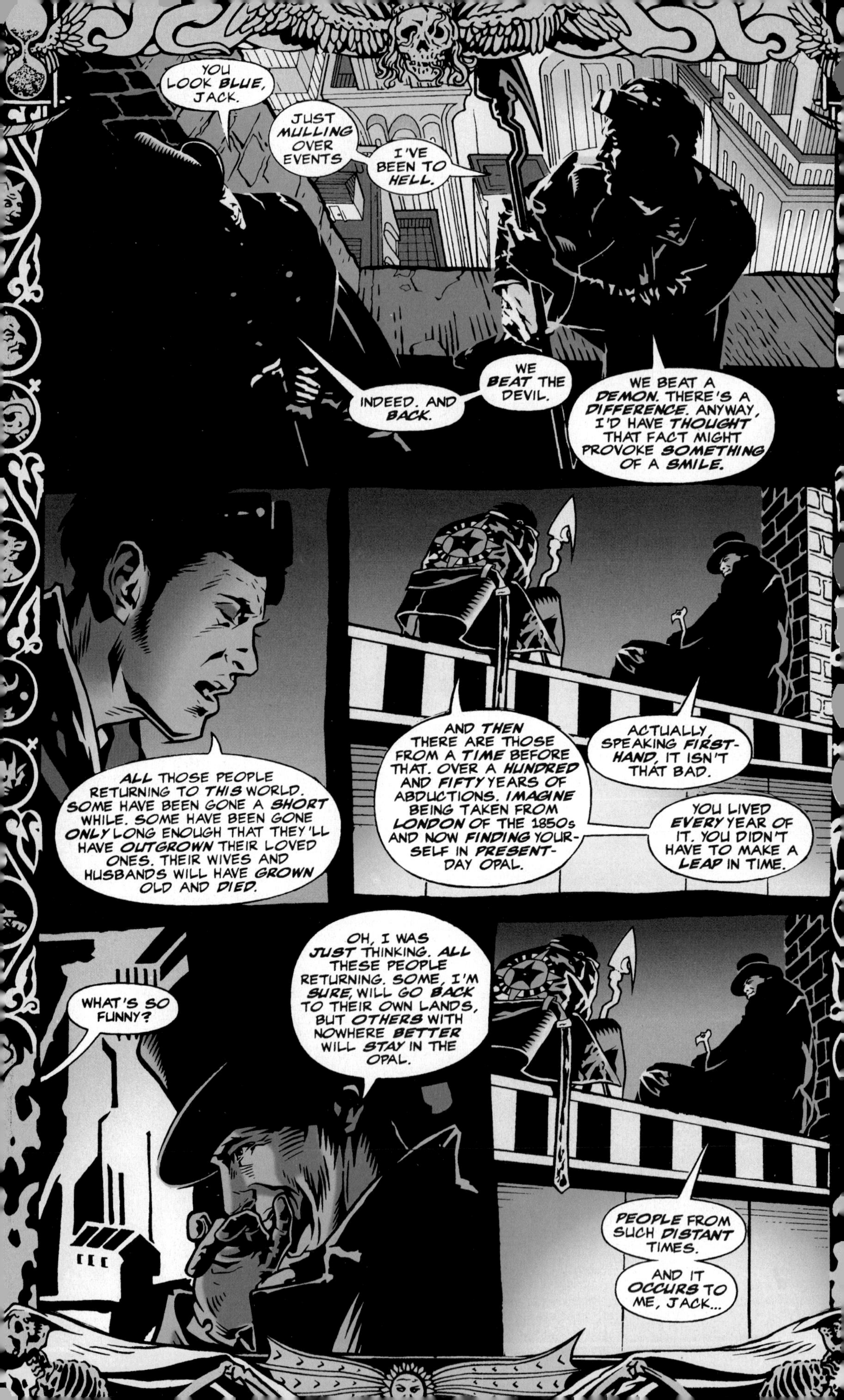
YOU LOOK BLUE, JACK.
JUST MULLING OVER EVENTS
I'VE BEEN TO HELL.
INDEED. AND BACK.
WE BEAT THE DEVIL.
WE BEAT A DEMON. THERE'S A DIFFERENCE. ANYWAY, I'D HAVE THOUGHT THAT FACT MIGHT PROVOKE SOMETHING OF A SMILE.
ALL THOSE PEOPLE RETURNING TO THIS WORLD. SOME HAVE BEEN GONE A SHORT WHILE. SOME HAVE BEEN GONE ONLY LONG ENOUGH THAT THEY'LL HAVE OUTGROWN THEIR LOVED ONES. THEIR WIVES AND HUSBANDS WILL HAVE GROWN OLD AND DIED.
AND THEN THERE ARE THOSE FROM A TIME BEFORE THAT. OVER A HUNDRED AND FIFTY YEARS OF ABDUCTIONS. IMAGINE BEING TAKEN FROM LONDON OF THE 1850s AND NOW FINDING YOURSELF IN PRESENT-DAY OPAL.
ACTUALLY, SPEAKING FIRST-HAND, IT ISN'T THAT BAD.
YOU LIVED EVERY YEAR OF IT. YOU DIDN'T HAVE TO MAKE A LEAP IN TIME.
WHAT'S SO FUNNY?
OH, I WAS JUST THINKING. ALL THESE PEOPLE RETURNING. SOME, I'M SURE, WILL GO BACK TO THEIR OWN LANDS, BUT OTHERS WITH NOWHERE BETTER WILL STAY IN THE OPAL.
PEOPLE FROM SUCH DISTANT TIMES.
AND IT OCCURS TO ME, JACK...

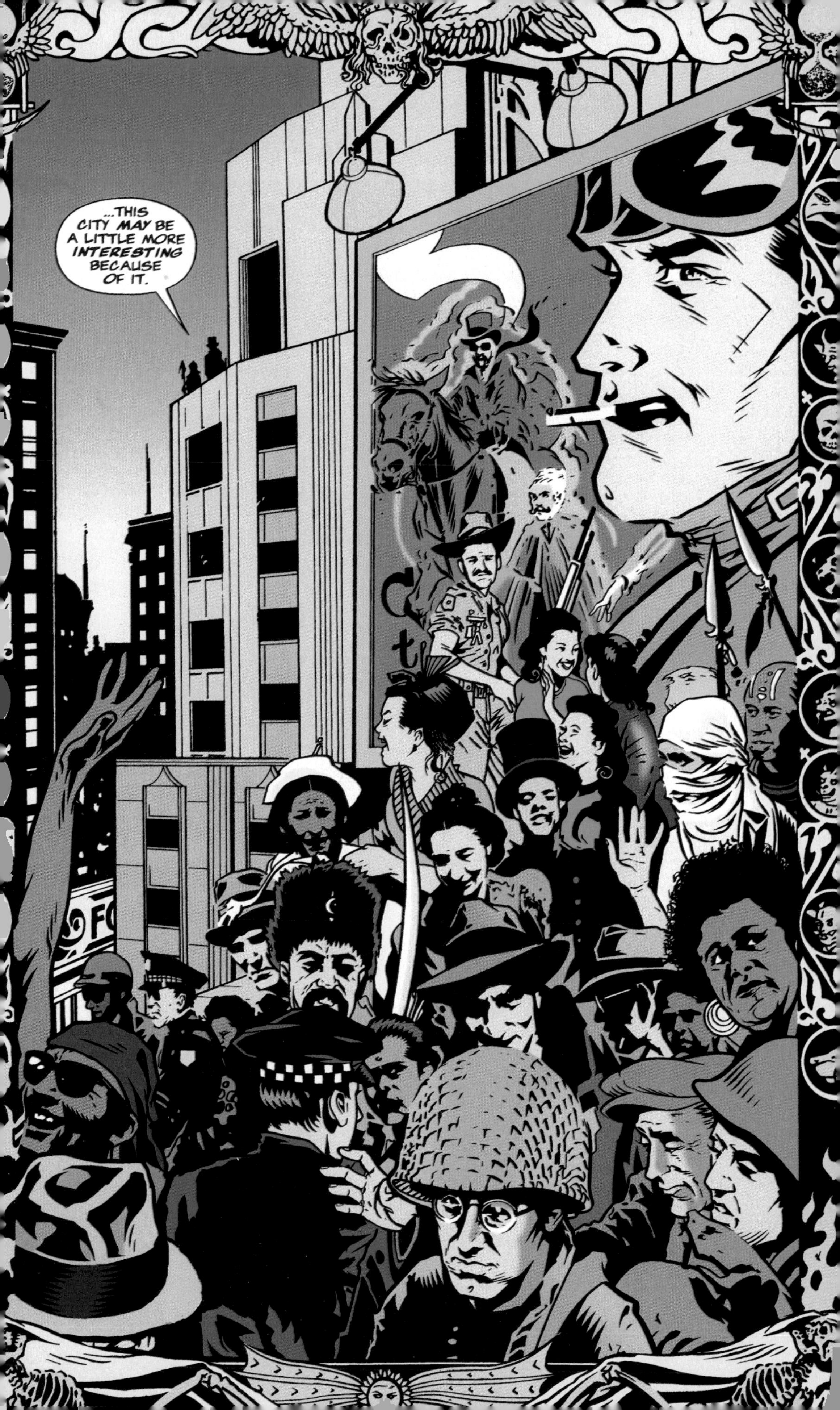
...THIS CITY MAY BE A LITTLE MORE INTERESTING BECAUSE OF IT.
FO

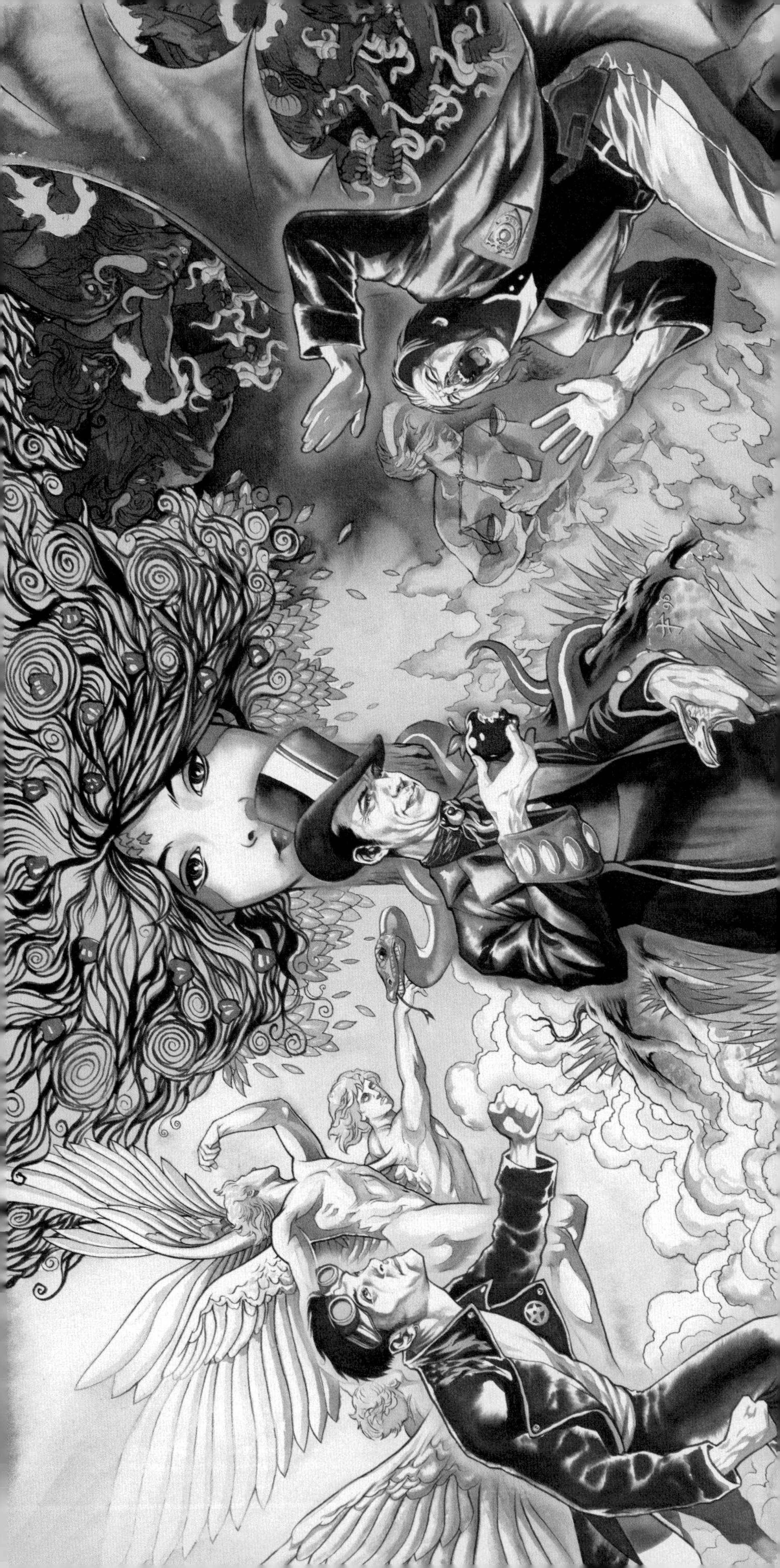

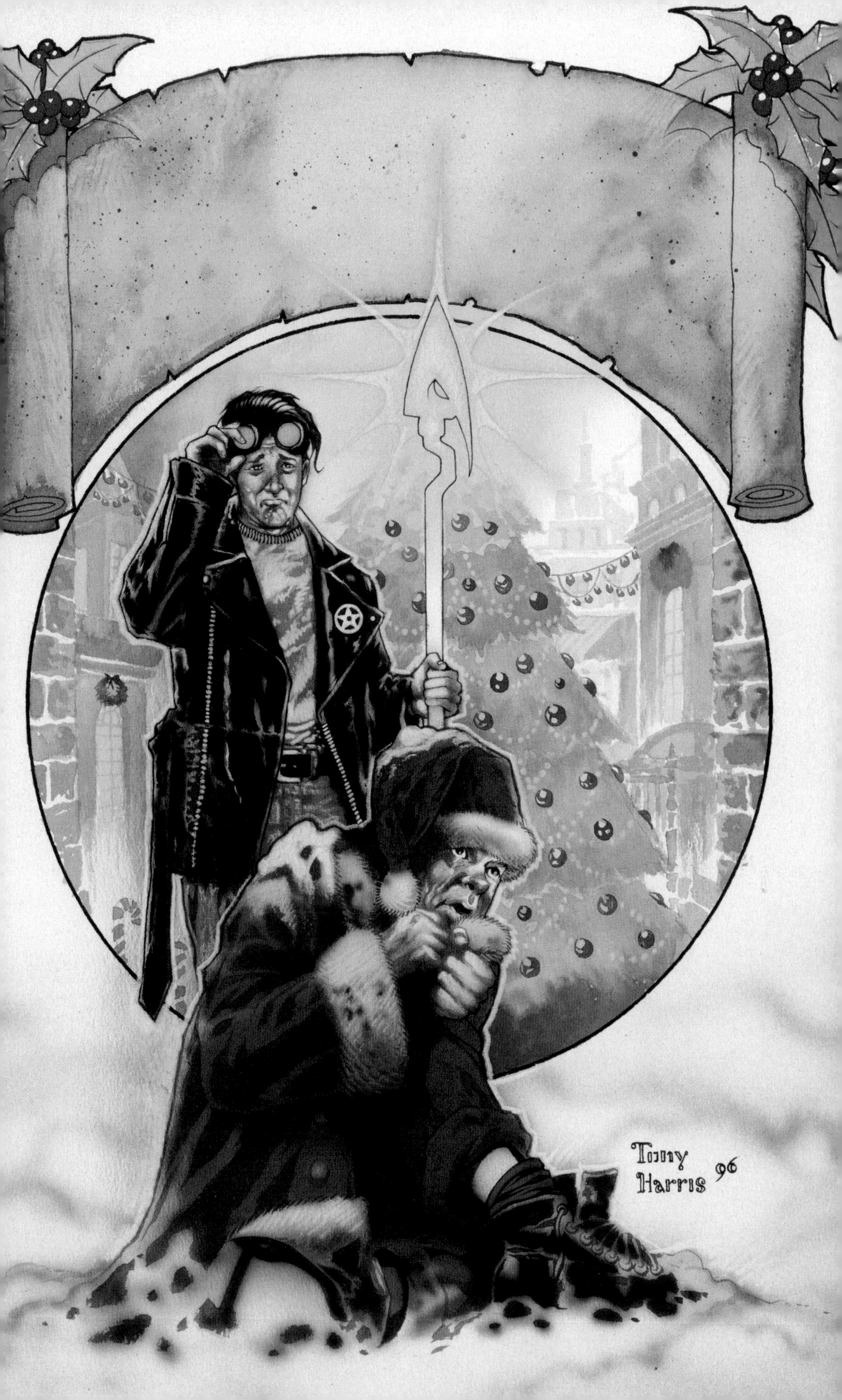
Tony Harris 96

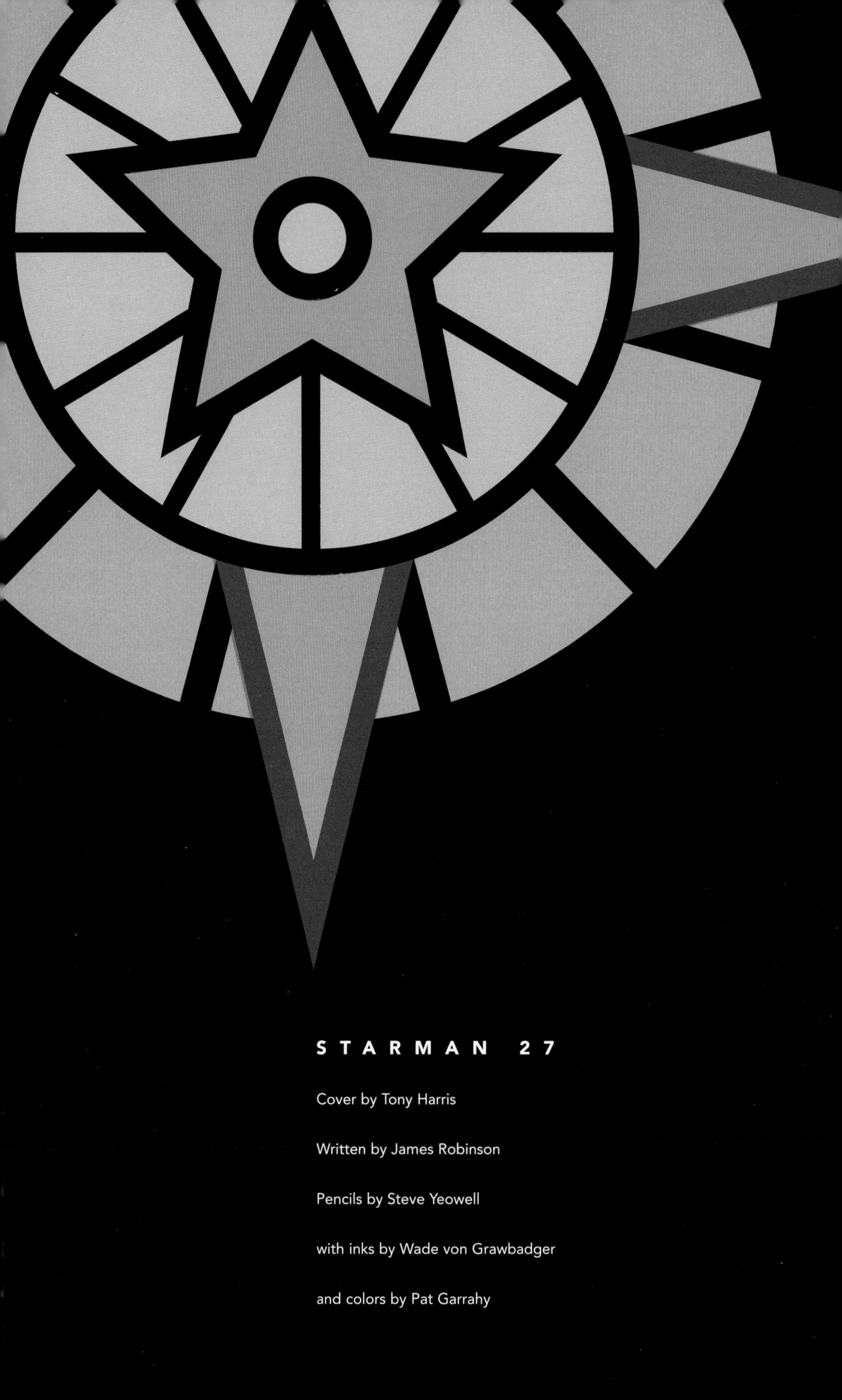

S T A R M A N   2 7

Cover by Tony Harris

Written by James Robinson

Pencils by Steve Yeowell

with inks by Wade von Grawbadger

and colors by Pat Garrahy

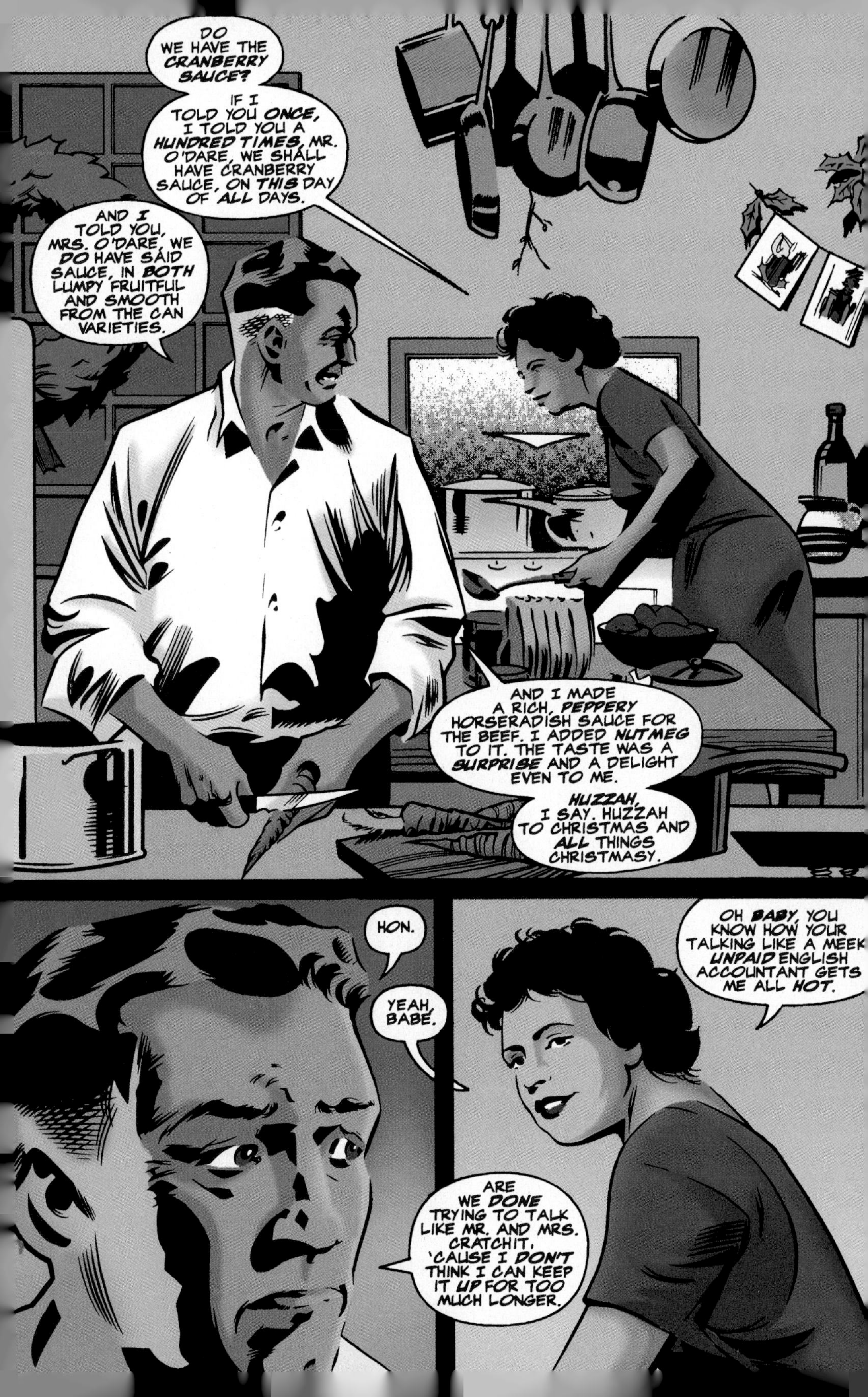
DO WE HAVE THE CRANBERRY SAUCE?
IF I TOLD YOU ONCE, I TOLD YOU A HUNDRED TIMES, MR. O'DARE, WE SHALL HAVE CRANBERRY SAUCE, ON THIS DAY OF ALL DAYS.
AND I TOLD YOU, MRS. O'DARE, WE DO HAVE SAID SAUCE, IN BOTH LUMPY FRUITFUL AND SMOOTH FROM THE CAN VARIETIES.
AND I MADE A RICH, PEPPERY HORSERADISH SAUCE FOR THE BEEF. I ADDED NUTMEG TO IT. THE TASTE WAS A SURPRISE AND A DELIGHT EVEN TO ME.
HUZZAH, I SAY. HUZZAH TO CHRISTMAS AND ALL THINGS CHRISTMASY.
HON.
YEAH, BABE.
OH BABY, YOU KNOW HOW YOUR TALKING LIKE A MEEK UNPAID ENGLISH ACCOUNTANT GETS ME ALL HOT.
ARE WE DONE TRYING TO TALK LIKE MR. AND MRS. CRATCHIT, 'CAUSE I DON'T THINK I CAN KEEP IT UP FOR TOO MUCH LONGER.

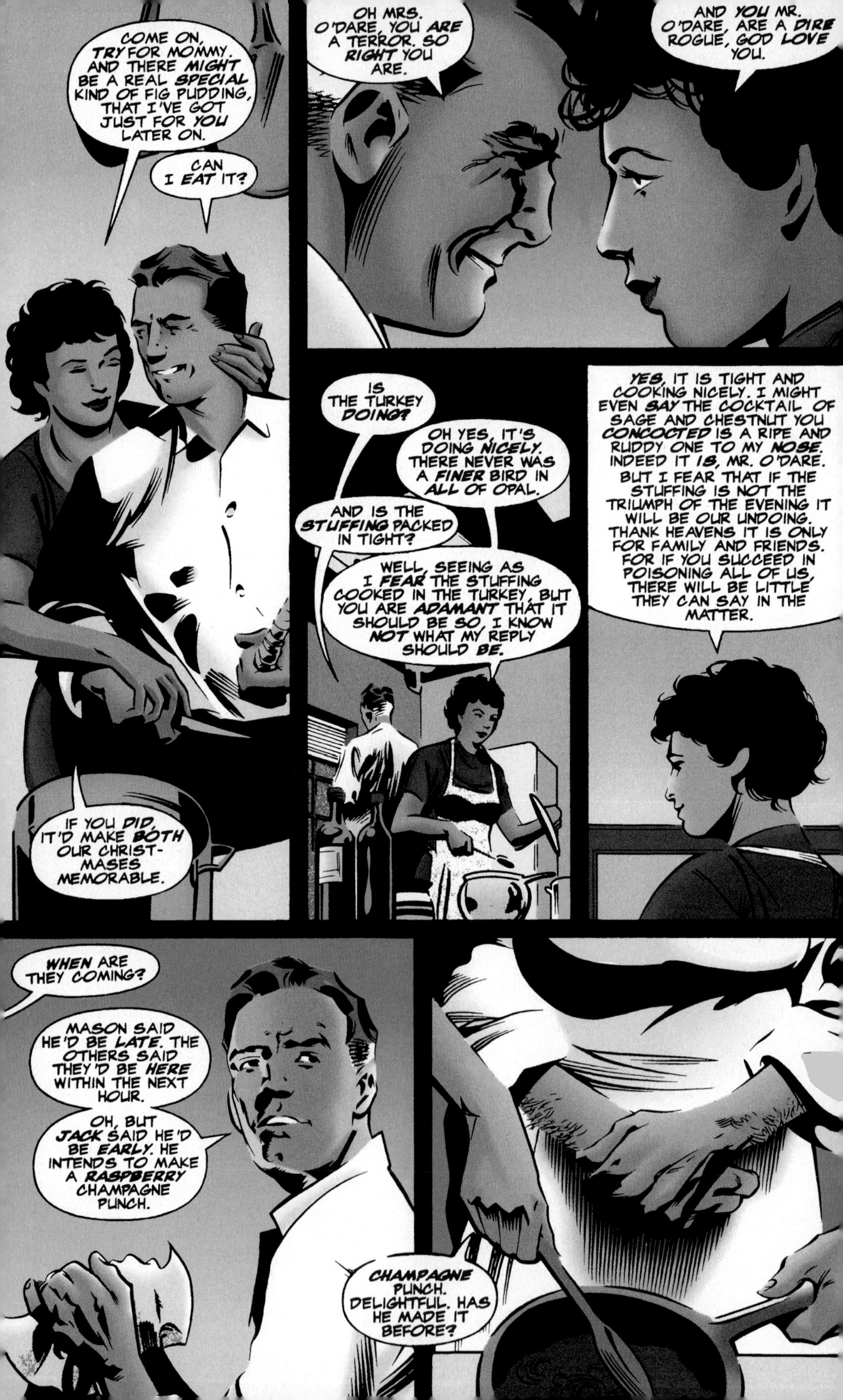

COME ON, TRY FOR MOMMY. AND THERE MIGHT BE A REAL SPECIAL KIND OF FIG PUDDING, THAT I'VE GOT JUST FOR YOU LATER ON.
CAN I EAT IT?
IF YOU DID, IT'D MAKE BOTH OUR CHRIST-MASES MEMORABLE.
OH MRS. O'DARE, YOU ARE A TERROR. SO RIGHT YOU ARE.
AND YOU MR. O'DARE, ARE A DIRE ROGUE, GOD LOVE YOU.
IS THE TURKEY DOING?
OH YES, IT'S DOING NICELY. THERE NEVER WAS A FINER BIRD IN ALL OF OPAL.
AND IS THE STUFFING PACKED IN TIGHT?
WELL, SEEING AS I FEAR THE STUFFING COOKED IN THE TURKEY, BUT YOU ARE ADAMANT THAT IT SHOULD BE SO, I KNOW NOT WHAT MY REPLY SHOULD BE.
YES, IT IS TIGHT AND COOKING NICELY. I MIGHT EVEN SAY THE COCKTAIL OF SAGE AND CHESTNUT YOU CONCOCTED IS A RIPE AND RUDDY ONE TO MY NOSE. INDEED IT IS, MR. O'DARE. BUT I FEAR THAT IF THE STUFFING IS NOT THE TRIUMPH OF THE EVENING IT WILL BE OUR UNDOING. THANK HEAVENS IT IS ONLY FOR FAMILY AND FRIENDS. FOR IF YOU SUCCEED IN POISONING ALL OF US, THERE WILL BE LITTLE THEY CAN SAY IN THE MATTER.
WHEN ARE THEY COMING?
MASON SAID HE'D BE LATE. THE OTHERS SAID THEY'D BE HERE WITHIN THE NEXT HOUR.
OH, BUT JACK SAID HE'D BE EARLY. HE INTENDS TO MAKE A RASPBERRY CHAMPAGNE PUNCH.
CHAMPAGNE PUNCH. DELIGHTFUL. HAS HE MADE IT BEFORE?

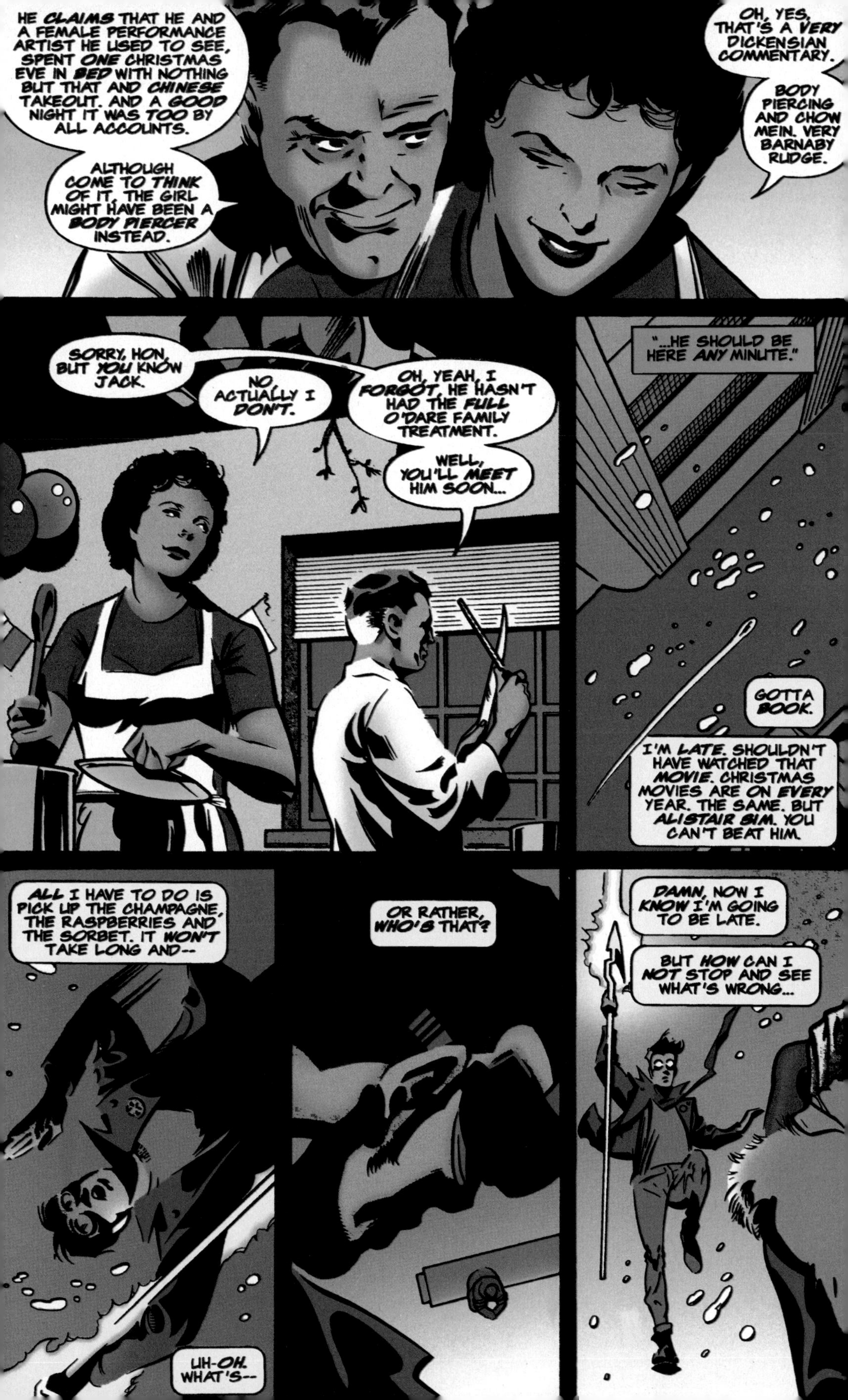
HE CLAIMS THAT HE AND A FEMALE PERFORMANCE ARTIST HE USED TO SEE, SPENT ONE CHRISTMAS EVE IN BED WITH NOTHING BUT THAT AND CHINESE TAKEOUT. AND A GOOD NIGHT IT WAS TOO BY ALL ACCOUNTS.
ALTHOUGH COME TO THINK OF IT, THE GIRL MIGHT HAVE BEEN A BODY PIERCER INSTEAD.
OH, YES, THAT'S A VERY DICKENSIAN COMMENTARY.
BODY PIERCING AND CHOW MEIN. VERY BARNABY RUDGE.
SORRY, HON, BUT YOU KNOW JACK.
NO, ACTUALLY I DON'T.
OH, YEAH, I FORGOT, HE HASN'T HAD THE FULL O'DARE FAMILY TREATMENT.
WELL, YOU'LL MEET HIM SOON...
"...HE SHOULD BE HERE ANY MINUTE."
GOTTA BOOK.
I'M LATE. SHOULDN'T HAVE WATCHED THAT MOVIE. CHRISTMAS MOVIES ARE ON EVERY YEAR. THE SAME. BUT ALISTAIR SIM. YOU CAN'T BEAT HIM.
ALL I HAVE TO DO IS PICK UP THE CHAMPAGNE, THE RASPBERRIES AND THE SORBET. IT WON'T TAKE LONG AND--
UH-OH. WHAT'S--
OR RATHER, WHO'S THAT?
DAMN, NOW I KNOW I'M GOING TO BE LATE.
BUT HOW CAN I NOT STOP AND SEE WHAT'S WRONG...

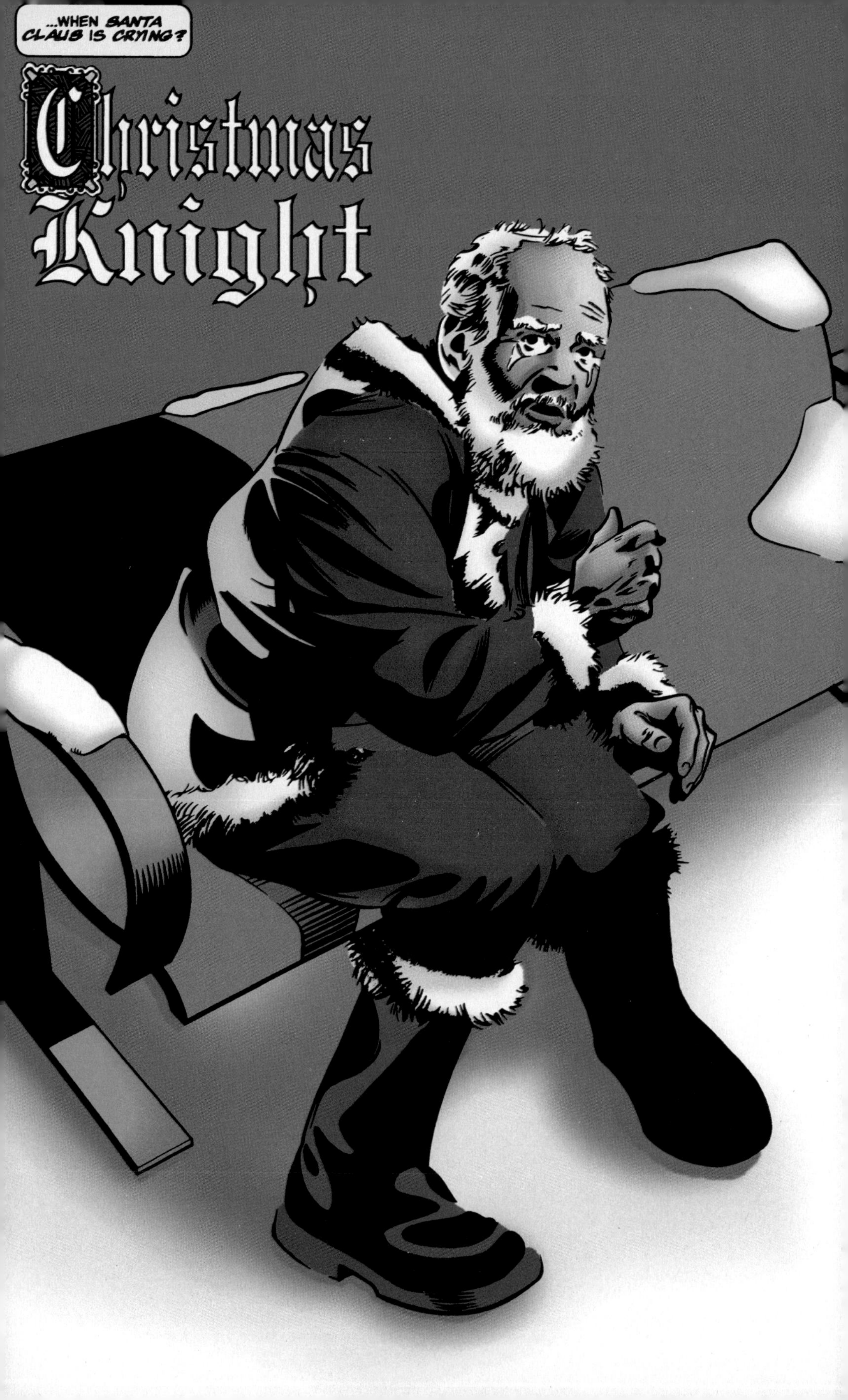
...WHEN SANTA CLAUS IS CRYING?
Christmas Knight

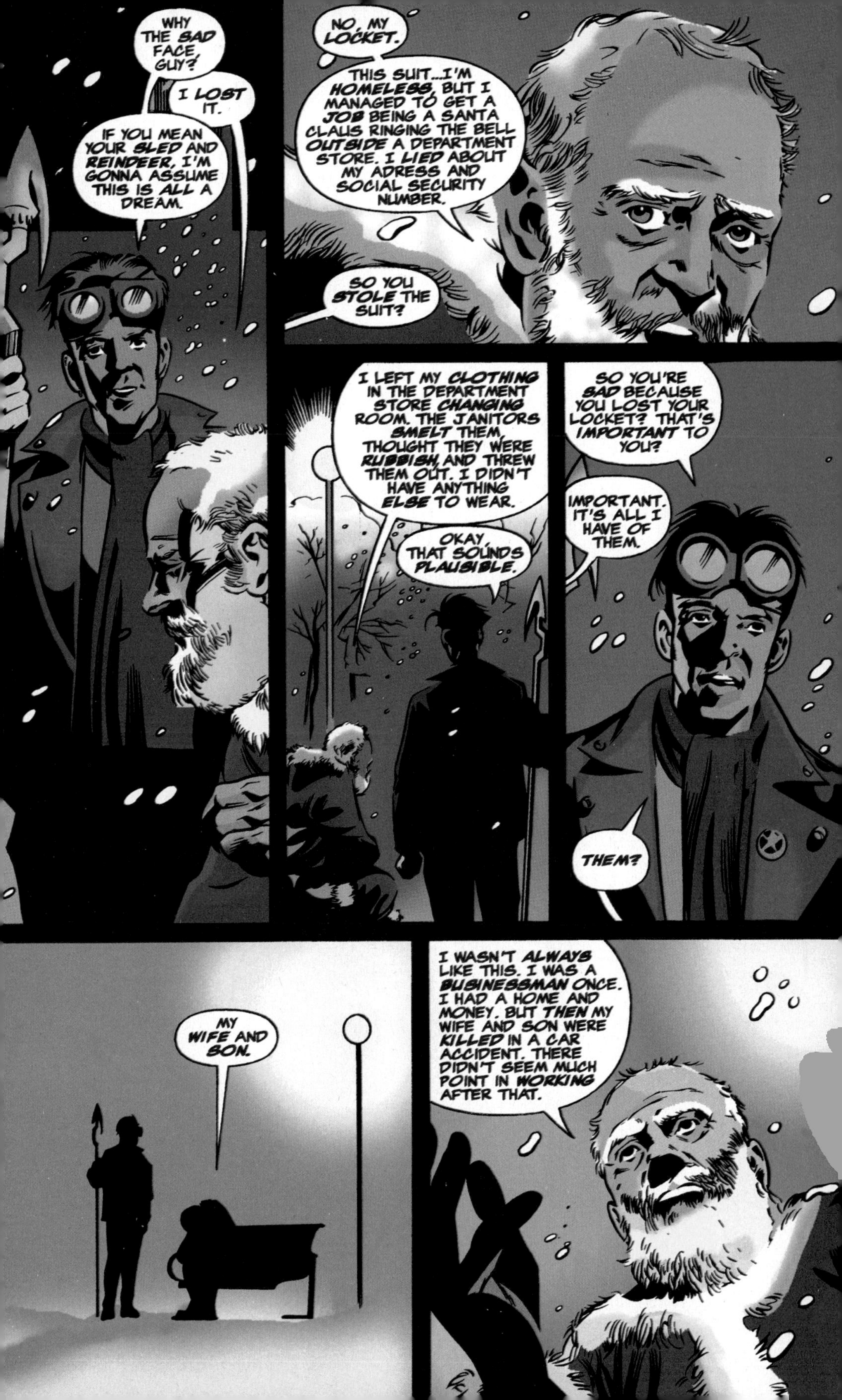
WHY THE SAD FACE, GUY?
I LOST IT.
IF YOU MEAN YOUR SLED AND REINDEER, I'M GONNA ASSUME THIS IS ALL A DREAM.
NO, MY LOCKET.
THIS SUIT...I'M HOMELESS, BUT I MANAGED TO GET A JOB BEING A SANTA CLAUS RINGING THE BELL OUTSIDE A DEPARTMENT STORE. I LIED ABOUT MY ADRESS AND SOCIAL SECURITY NUMBER.
SO YOU STOLE THE SUIT?
I LEFT MY CLOTHING IN THE DEPARTMENT STORE CHANGING ROOM. THE JANITORS SMELT THEM, THOUGHT THEY WERE RUBBISH, AND THREW THEM OUT. I DIDN'T HAVE ANYTHING ELSE TO WEAR.
OKAY, THAT SOUNDS PLAUSIBLE.
SO YOU'RE SAD BECAUSE YOU LOST YOUR LOCKET? THAT'S IMPORTANT TO YOU?
IMPORTANT. IT'S ALL I HAVE OF THEM.
THEM?
MY WIFE AND SON.
I WASN'T ALWAYS LIKE THIS. I WAS A BUSINESSMAN ONCE. I HAD A HOME AND MONEY. BUT THEN MY WIFE AND SON WERE KILLED IN A CAR ACCIDENT. THERE DIDN'T SEEM MUCH POINT IN WORKING AFTER THAT.

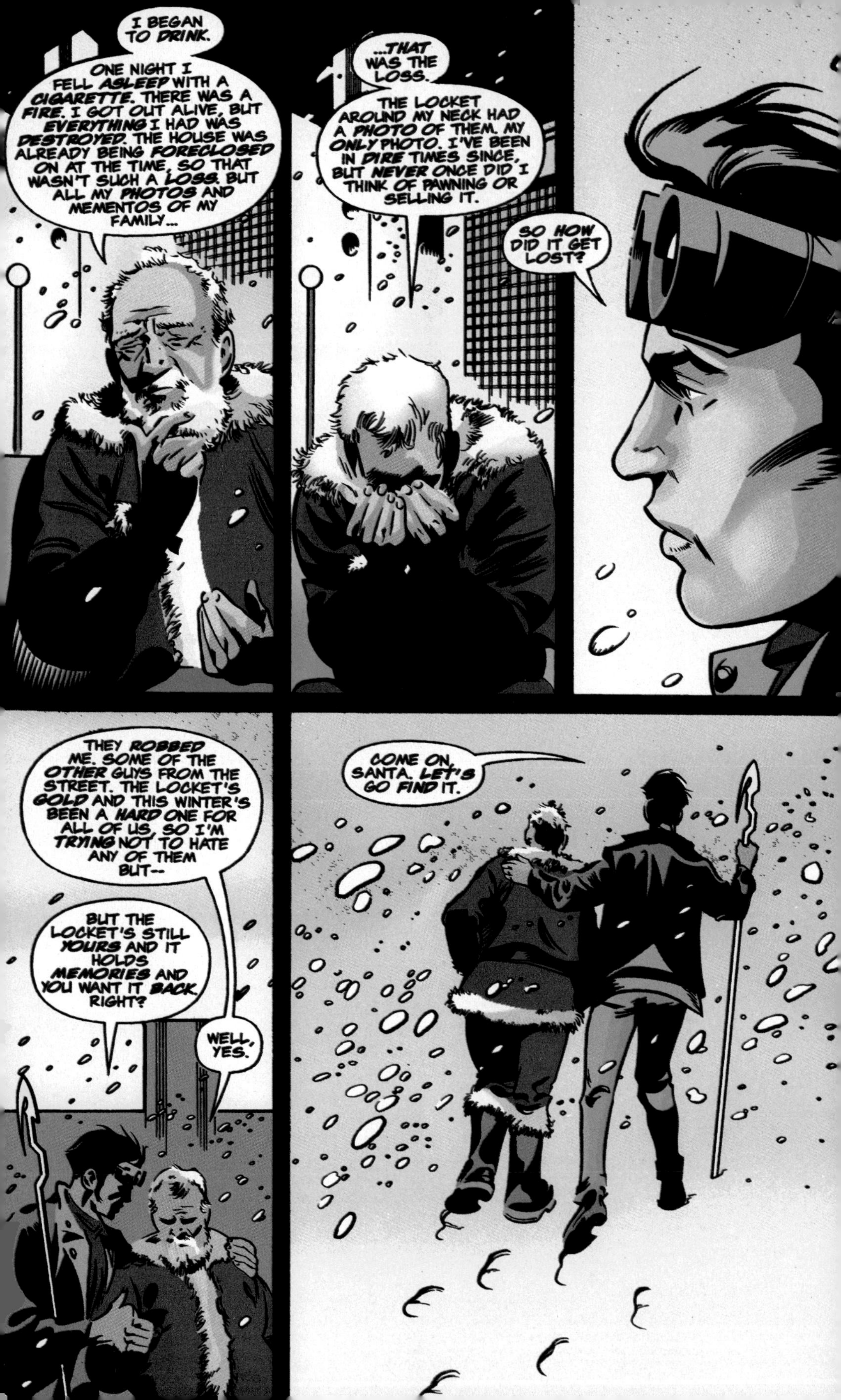
I BEGAN TO DRINK.
ONE NIGHT I FELL ASLEEP WITH A CIGARETTE. THERE WAS A FIRE. I GOT OUT ALIVE, BUT EVERYTHING I HAD WAS DESTROYED. THE HOUSE WAS ALREADY BEING FORECLOSED ON AT THE TIME, SO THAT WASN'T SUCH A LOSS. BUT ALL MY PHOTOS AND MEMENTOS OF MY FAMILY...
...THAT WAS THE LOSS.
THE LOCKET AROUND MY NECK HAD A PHOTO OF THEM. MY ONLY PHOTO. I'VE BEEN IN DIRE TIMES SINCE, BUT NEVER ONCE DID I THINK OF PAWNING OR SELLING IT.
SO HOW DID IT GET LOST?
THEY ROBBED ME. SOME OF THE OTHER GUYS FROM THE STREET. THE LOCKET'S GOLD AND THIS WINTER'S BEEN A HARD ONE FOR ALL OF US, SO I'M TRYING NOT TO HATE ANY OF THEM BUT--
BUT THE LOCKET'S STILL YOURS AND IT HOLDS MEMORIES AND YOU WANT IT BACK. RIGHT?
WELL, YES.
COME ON, SANTA. LET'S GO FIND IT.

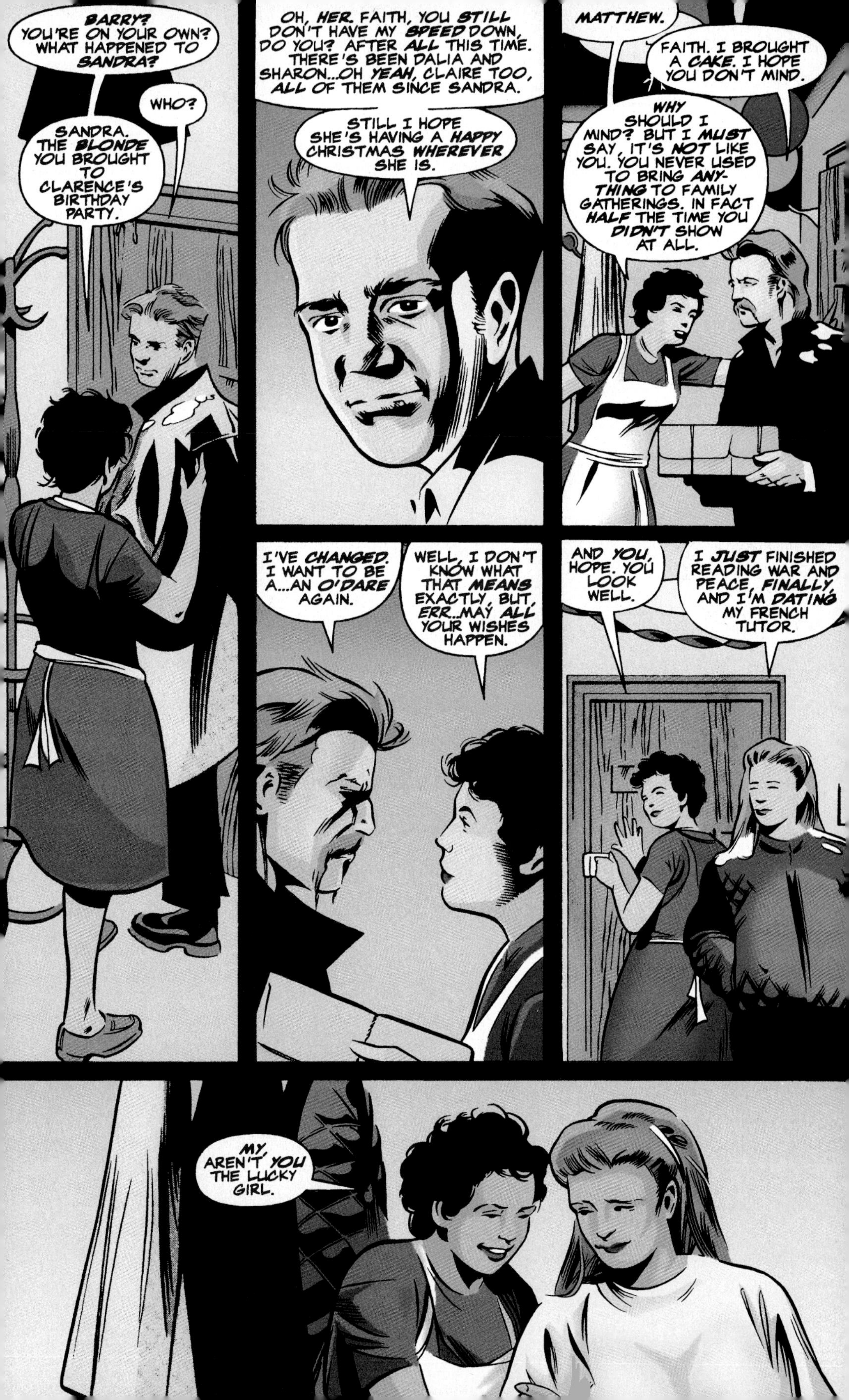
BARRY? YOU'RE ON YOUR OWN? WHAT HAPPENED TO SANDRA?
WHO?
SANDRA. THE BLONDE YOU BROUGHT TO CLARENCE'S BIRTHDAY PARTY.
OH, HER. FAITH, YOU STILL DON'T HAVE MY SPEED DOWN, DO YOU? AFTER ALL THIS TIME. THERE'S BEEN DALIA AND SHARON...OH YEAH, CLAIRE TOO, ALL OF THEM SINCE SANDRA.
STILL I HOPE SHE'S HAVING A HAPPY CHRISTMAS WHEREVER SHE IS.
MATTHEW.
FAITH. I BROUGHT A CAKE. I HOPE YOU DON'T MIND.
WHY SHOULD I MIND? BUT I MUST SAY, IT'S NOT LIKE YOU. YOU NEVER USED TO BRING ANY-THING TO FAMILY GATHERINGS. IN FACT HALF THE TIME YOU DIDN'T SHOW AT ALL.
I'VE CHANGED. I WANT TO BE A...AN O'DARE AGAIN.
WELL, I DON'T KNOW WHAT THAT MEANS EXACTLY, BUT, ERR..MAY ALL YOUR WISHES HAPPEN.
AND YOU, HOPE. YOU LOOK WELL.
I JUST FINISHED READING WAR AND PEACE, FINALLY, AND I'M DATING MY FRENCH TUTOR.
MY, AREN'T YOU THE LUCKY GIRL.

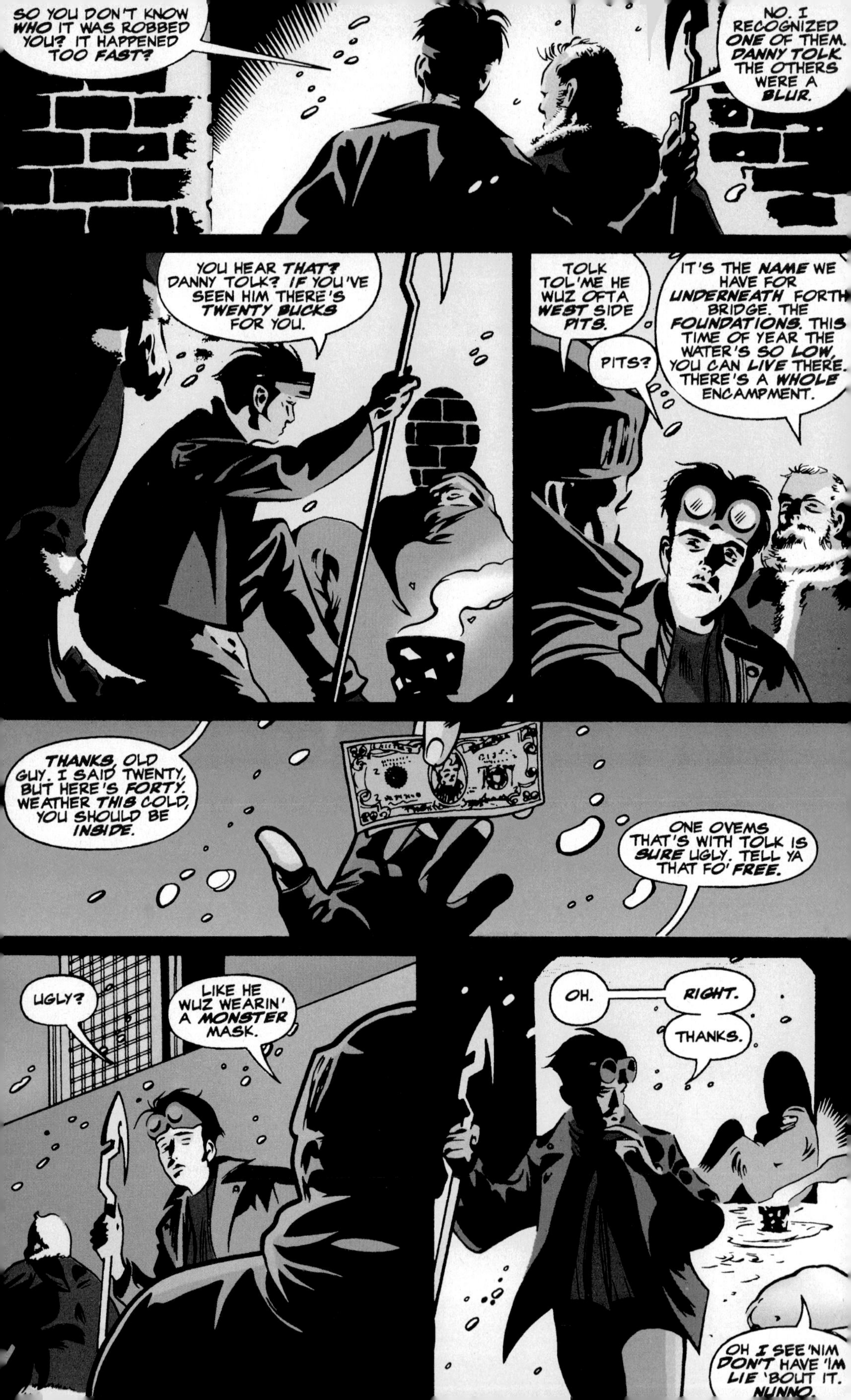
SO YOU DON'T KNOW WHO IT WAS ROBBED YOU? IT HAPPENED TOO FAST?
NO. I RECOGNIZED ONE OF THEM. DANNY TOLK. THE OTHERS WERE A BLUR.
YOU HEAR THAT? DANNY TOLK? IF YOU'VE SEEN HIM THERE'S TWENTY BUCKS FOR YOU.
TOLK TOL'ME HE WUZ OFTA WEST SIDE PITS.
PITS?
IT'S THE NAME WE HAVE FOR UNDERNEATH FORTH BRIDGE. THE FOUNDATIONS. THIS TIME OF YEAR THE WATER'S SO LOW, YOU CAN LIVE THERE. THERE'S A WHOLE ENCAMPMENT.
THANKS, OLD GUY. I SAID TWENTY, BUT HERE'S FORTY. WEATHER THIS COLD, YOU SHOULD BE INSIDE.
ONE OVEMS THAT'S WITH TOLK IS SURE UGLY. TELL YA THAT FO' FREE.
UGLY?
LIKE HE WUZ WEARIN' A MONSTER MASK.
OH.
RIGHT.
THANKS.
OH I SEE 'NIM DON'T HAVE 'IM LIE 'BOUT IT. NUNNO.

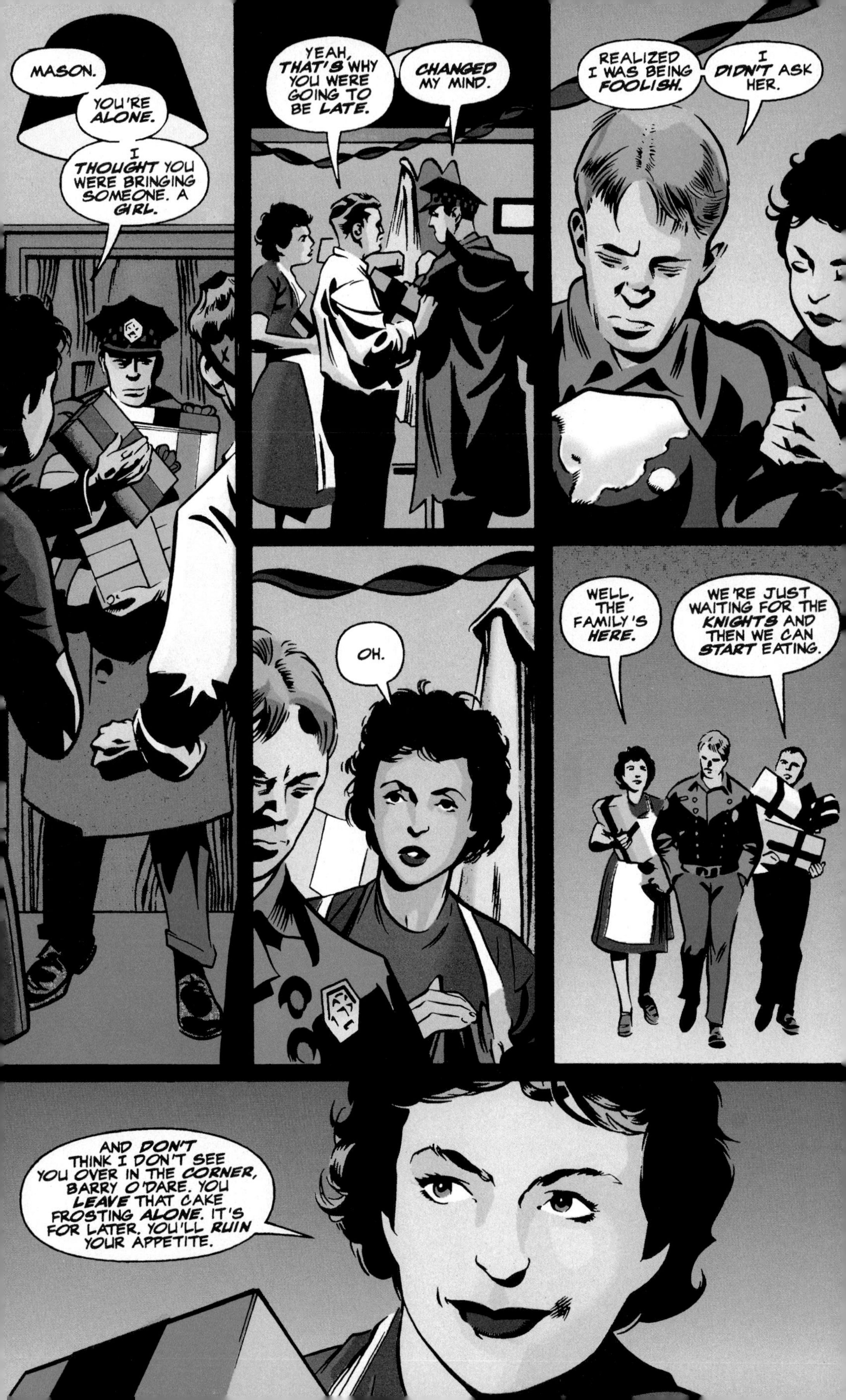
MASON.
YOU'RE ALONE.
I THOUGHT YOU WERE BRINGING SOMEONE. A GIRL.
YEAH, THAT'S WHY YOU WERE GOING TO BE LATE.
CHANGED MY MIND.
REALIZED I WAS BEING FOOLISH.
I DIDN'T ASK HER.
OH.
WELL, THE FAMILY'S HERE.
WE'RE JUST WAITING FOR THE KNIGHTS AND THEN WE CAN START EATING.
AND DON'T THINK I DON'T SEE YOU OVER IN THE CORNER, BARRY O'DARE. YOU LEAVE THAT CAKE FROSTING ALONE. IT'S FOR LATER. YOU'LL RUIN YOUR APPETITE.

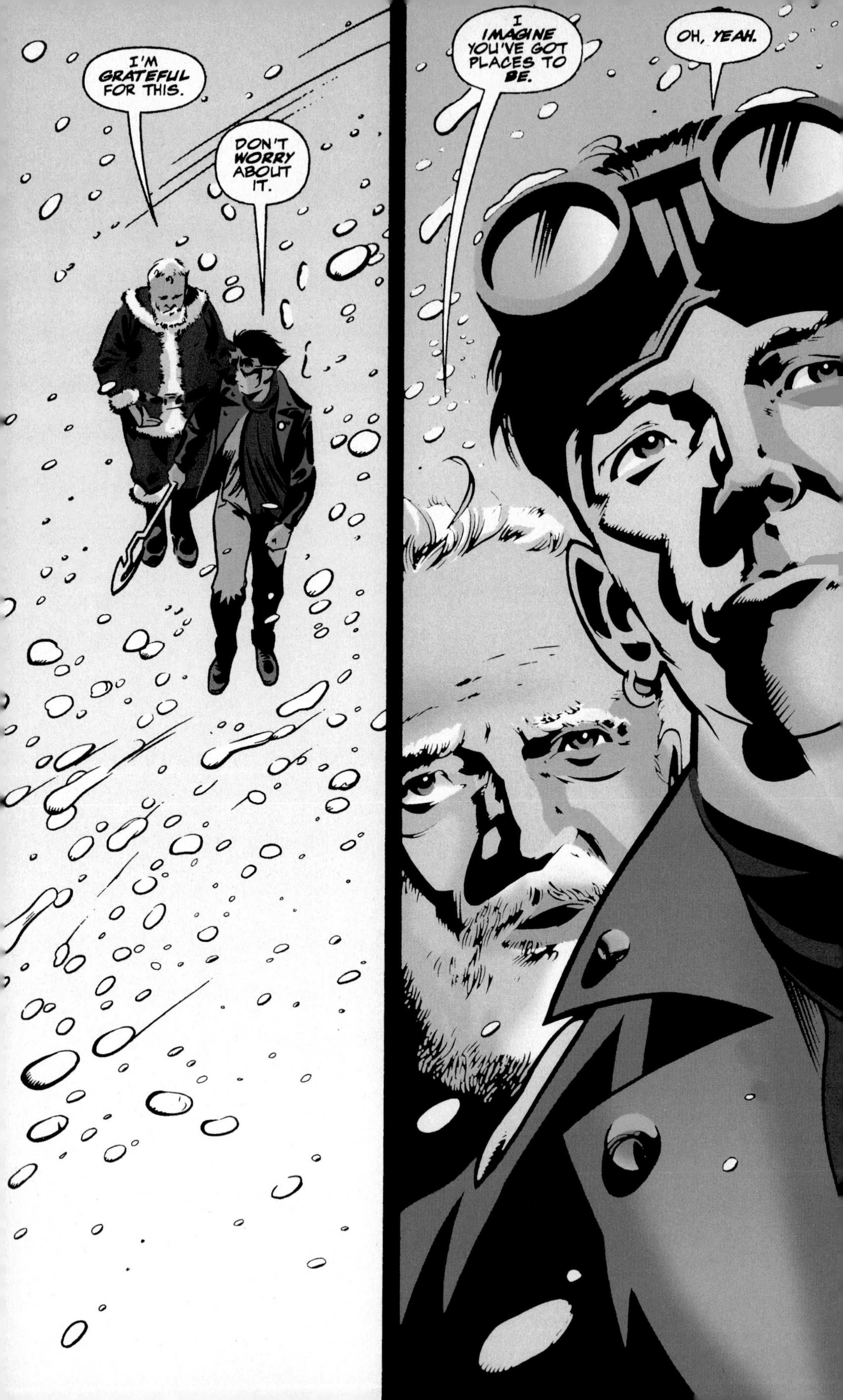

I'M GRATEFUL FOR THIS.
DON'T WORRY ABOUT IT.
I IMAGINE YOU'VE GOT PLACES TO BE.
OH, YEAH.

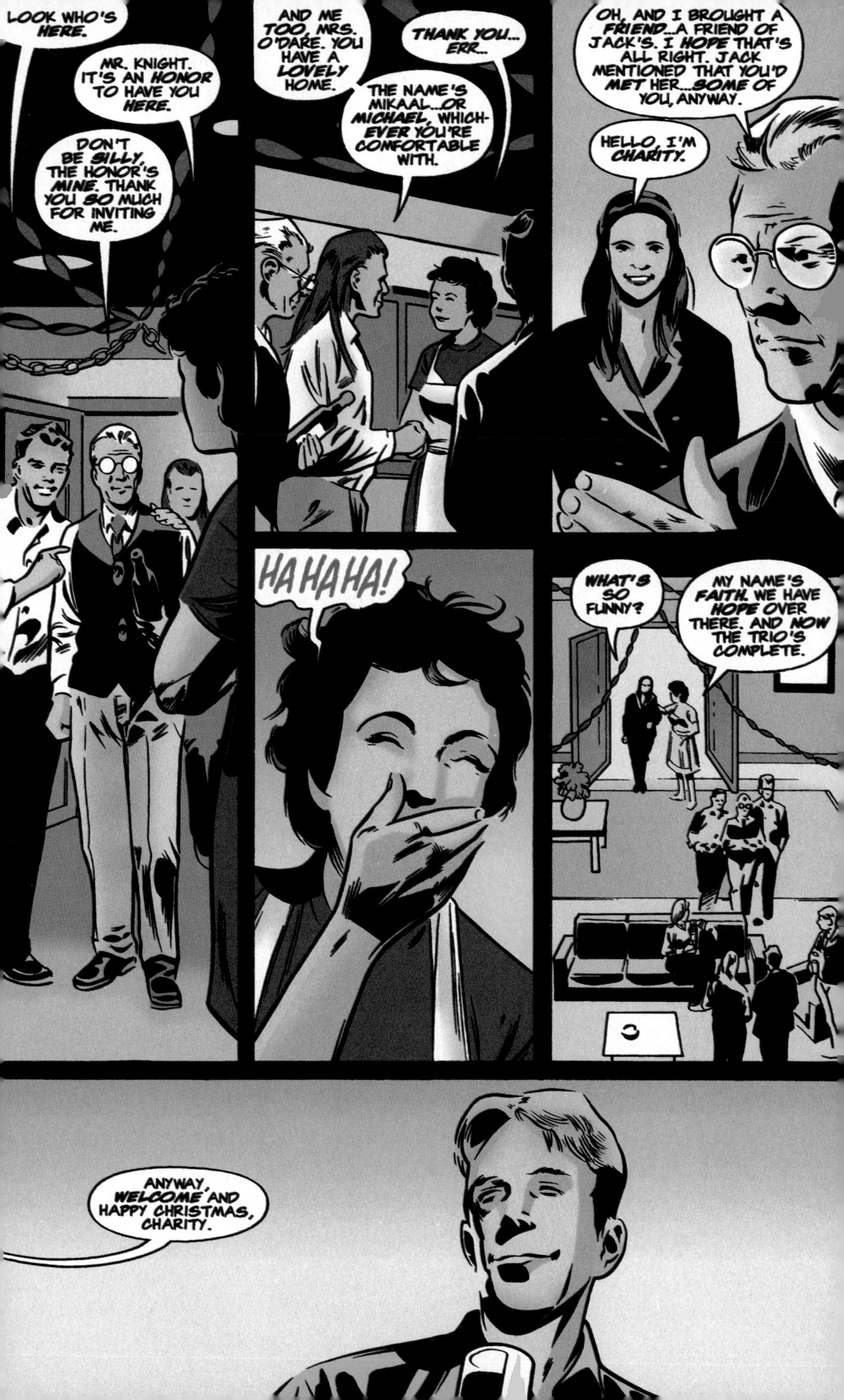
LOOK WHO'S HERE.
MR. KNIGHT. IT'S AN HONOR TO HAVE YOU HERE.
DON'T BE SILLY, THE HONOR'S MINE. THANK YOU SO MUCH FOR INVITING ME.
AND ME TOO, MRS. O'DARE. YOU HAVE A LOVELY HOME.
THANK YOU... ERR...
THE NAME'S MIKAAL...OR MICHAEL, WHICHEVER YOU'RE COMFORTABLE WITH.
OH, AND I BROUGHT A FRIEND...A FRIEND OF JACK'S. I HOPE THAT'S ALL RIGHT. JACK MENTIONED THAT YOU'D MET HER...SOME OF YOU, ANYWAY.
HELLO, I'M CHARITY.
HAHAHA!
WHAT'S SO FUNNY?
MY NAME'S FAITH. WE HAVE HOPE OVER THERE. AND NOW THE TRIO'S COMPLETE.
ANYWAY, WELCOME AND HAPPY CHRISTMAS, CHARITY.

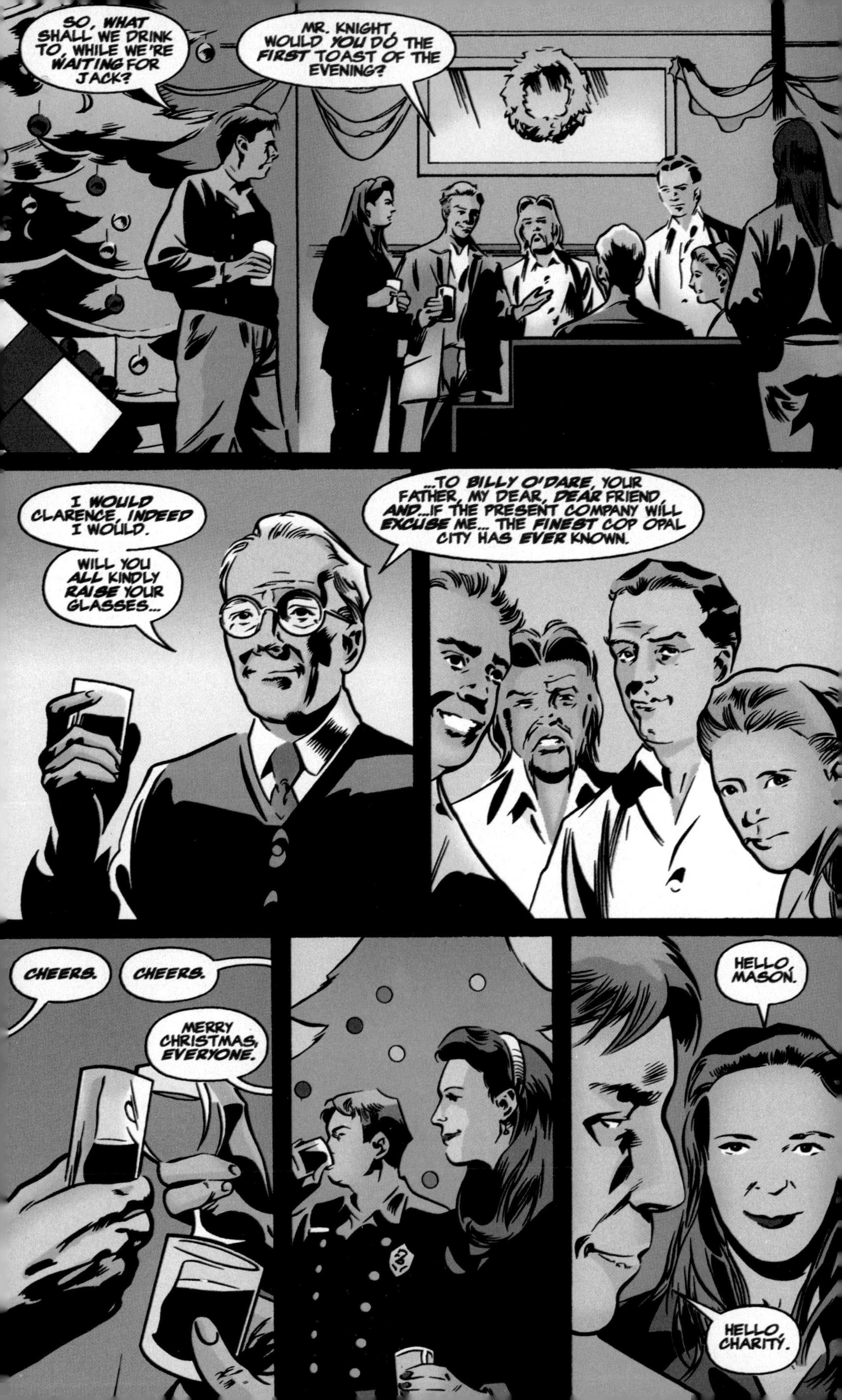

SO, WHAT SHALL WE DRINK TO, WHILE WE'RE WAITING FOR JACK?
MR. KNIGHT, WOULD YOU DO THE FIRST TOAST OF THE EVENING?
I WOULD CLARENCE, INDEED I WOULD.
WILL YOU ALL KINDLY RAISE YOUR GLASSES...
...TO BILLY O'DARE, YOUR FATHER, MY DEAR, DEAR FRIEND, AND...IF THE PRESENT COMPANY WILL EXCUSE ME... THE FINEST COP OPAL CITY HAS EVER KNOWN.
CHEERS.
CHEERS.
MERRY CHRISTMAS, EVERYONE.
HELLO, MASON.
HELLO, CHARITY.

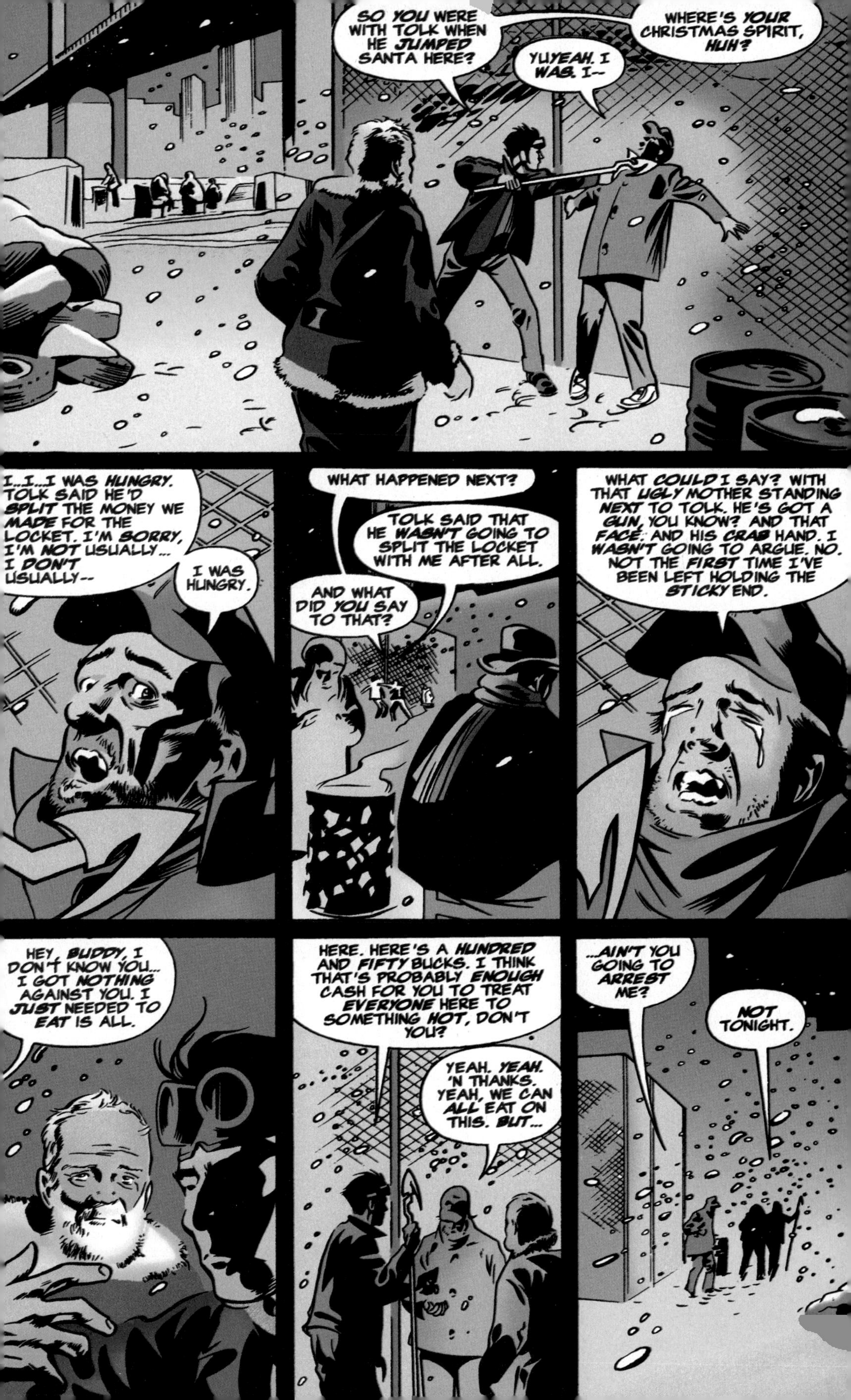

SO YOU WERE WITH TOLK WHEN HE JUMPED SANTA HERE?
WHERE'S YOUR CHRISTMAS SPIRIT, HUH?
YUYEAH. I WAS. I--
I...I...I WAS HUNGRY. TOLK SAID HE'D SPLIT THE MONEY WE MADE FOR THE LOCKET. I'M SORRY, I'M NOT USUALLY... I DON'T USUALLY--
I WAS HUNGRY.
WHAT HAPPENED NEXT?
TOLK SAID THAT HE WASN'T GOING TO SPLIT THE LOCKET WITH ME AFTER ALL.
AND WHAT DID YOU SAY TO THAT?
WHAT COULD I SAY? WITH THAT UGLY MOTHER STANDING NEXT TO TOLK. HE'S GOT A GUN, YOU KNOW? AND THAT FACE. AND HIS CRAB HAND. I WASN'T GOING TO ARGUE. NO. NOT THE FIRST TIME I'VE BEEN LEFT HOLDING THE STICKY END.
HEY, BUDDY, I DON'T KNOW YOU... I GOT NOTHING AGAINST YOU. I JUST NEEDED TO EAT IS ALL.
HERE. HERE'S A HUNDRED AND FIFTY BUCKS. I THINK THAT'S PROBABLY ENOUGH CASH FOR YOU TO TREAT EVERYONE HERE TO SOMETHING HOT, DON'T YOU?
YEAH. YEAH. 'N THANKS. YEAH, WE CAN ALL EAT ON THIS. BUT...
...AIN'T YOU GOING TO ARREST ME?
NOT TONIGHT.

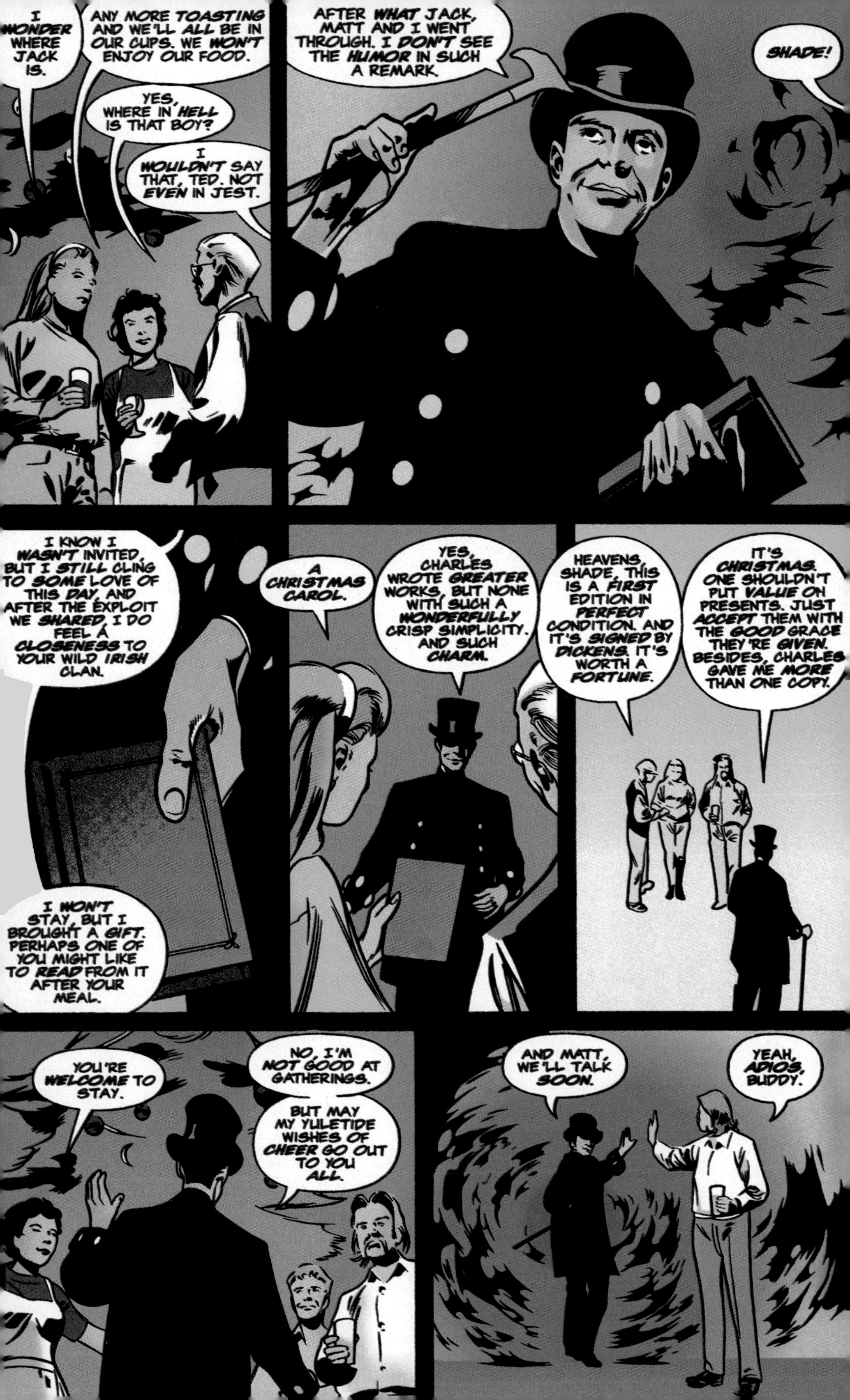
I WONDER WHERE JACK IS.
ANY MORE TOASTING AND WE'LL ALL BE IN OUR CUPS. WE WON'T ENJOY OUR FOOD.
YES, WHERE IN HELL IS THAT BOY?
I WOULDN'T SAY THAT, TED. NOT EVEN IN JEST.
AFTER WHAT JACK, MATT AND I WENT THROUGH, I DON'T SEE THE HUMOR IN SUCH A REMARK.
SHADE!
I KNOW I WASN'T INVITED, BUT I STILL CLING TO SOME LOVE OF THIS DAY, AND AFTER THE EXPLOIT WE SHARED, I DO FEEL A CLOSENESS TO YOUR WILD IRISH CLAN.
I WON'T STAY, BUT I BROUGHT A GIFT. PERHAPS ONE OF YOU MIGHT LIKE TO READ FROM IT AFTER YOUR MEAL.
A CHRISTMAS CAROL.
YES, CHARLES WROTE GREATER WORKS, BUT NONE WITH SUCH A WONDERFULLY CRISP SIMPLICITY. AND SUCH CHARM.
HEAVENS, SHADE, THIS IS A FIRST EDITION IN PERFECT CONDITION. AND IT'S SIGNED BY DICKENS. IT'S WORTH A FORTUNE.
IT'S CHRISTMAS. ONE SHOULDN'T PUT VALUE ON PRESENTS. JUST ACCEPT THEM WITH THE GOOD GRACE THEY'RE GIVEN. BESIDES, CHARLES GAVE ME MORE THAN ONE COPY.
YOU'RE WELCOME TO STAY.
NO, I'M NOT GOOD AT GATHERINGS.
BUT MAY MY YULETIDE WISHES OF CHEER GO OUT TO YOU ALL.
AND MATT, WE'LL TALK SOON.
YEAH, ADIOS, BUDDY.

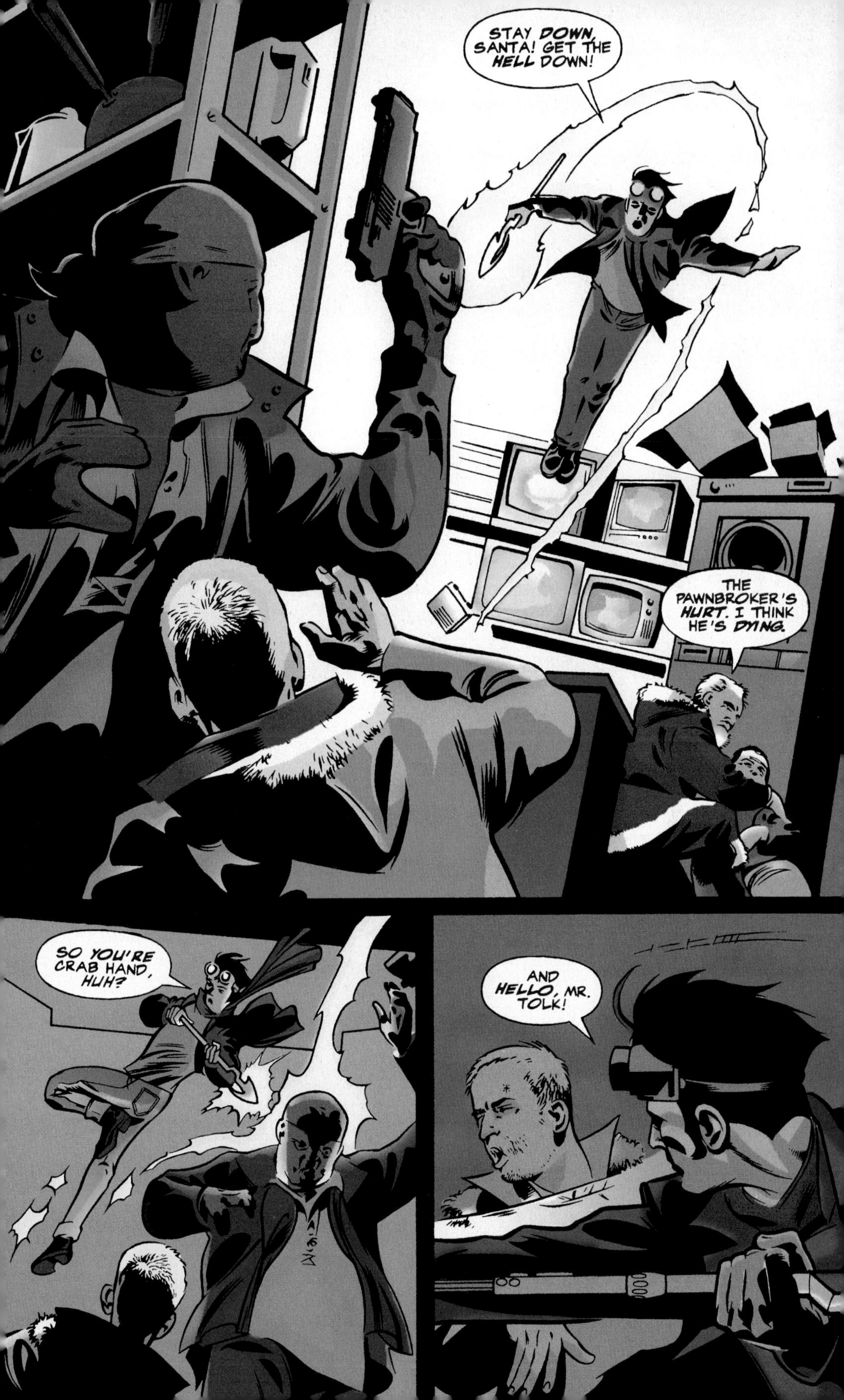
STAY DOWN, SANTA! GET THE HELL DOWN!
THE PAWNBROKER'S HURT. I THINK HE'S DYING.
SO YOU'RE CRAB HAND, HUH?
AND HELLO, MR. TOLK!

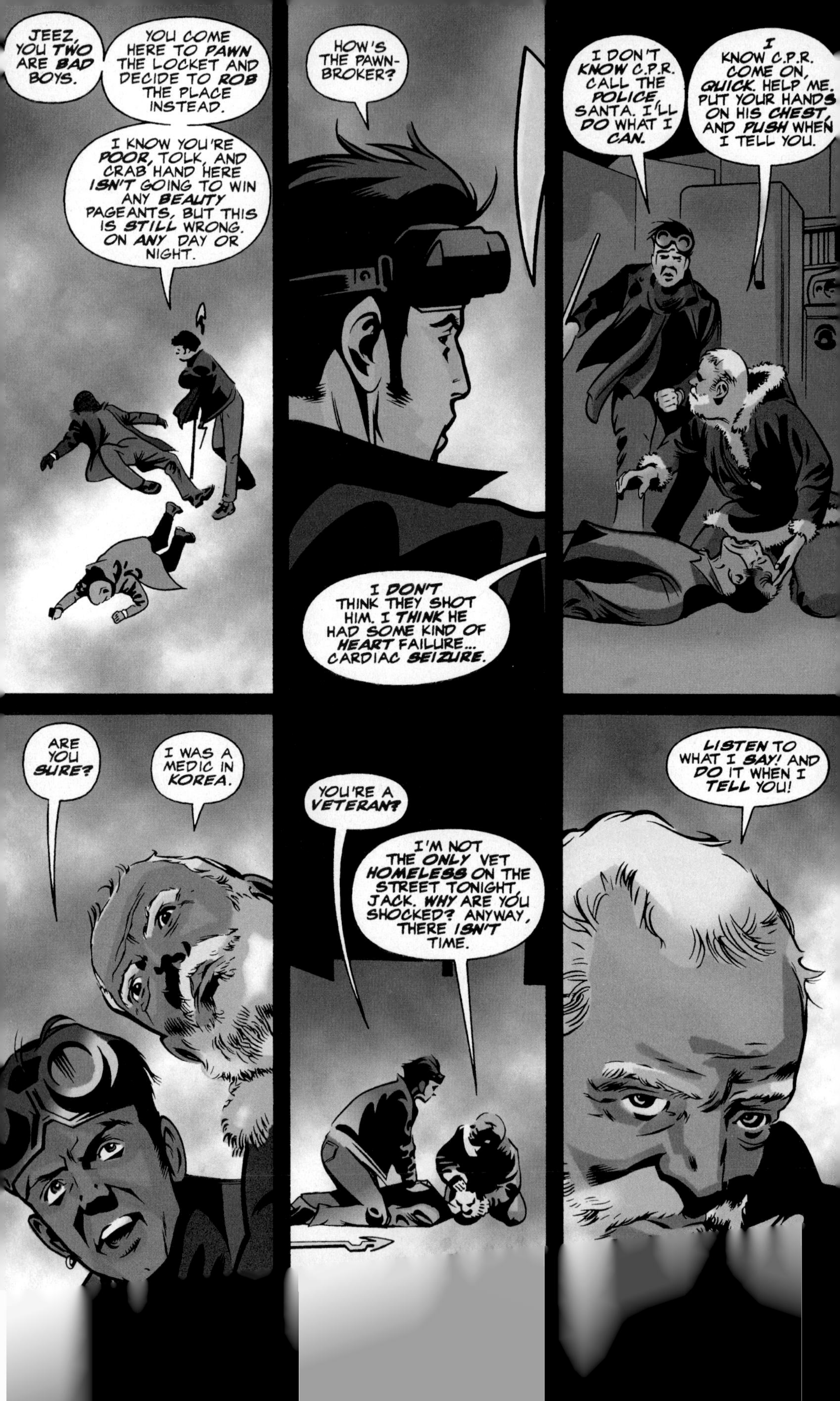
JEEZ, YOU TWO ARE BAD BOYS.
YOU COME HERE TO PAWN THE LOCKET AND DECIDE TO ROB THE PLACE INSTEAD.
I KNOW YOU'RE POOR, TOLK, AND CRAB HAND HERE ISN'T GOING TO WIN ANY BEAUTY PAGEANTS, BUT THIS IS STILL WRONG. ON ANY DAY OR NIGHT.
HOW'S THE PAWN-BROKER?
I DON'T THINK THEY SHOT HIM. I THINK HE HAD SOME KIND OF HEART FAILURE... CARDIAC SEIZURE.
I DON'T KNOW C.P.R. CALL THE POLICE, SANTA. I'LL DO WHAT I CAN.
I KNOW C.P.R. COME ON, QUICK. HELP ME. PUT YOUR HANDS ON HIS CHEST, AND PUSH WHEN I TELL YOU.
ARE YOU SURE?
I WAS A MEDIC IN KOREA.
YOU'RE A VETERAN?
I'M NOT THE ONLY VET HOMELESS ON THE STREET TONIGHT, JACK. WHY ARE YOU SHOCKED? ANYWAY, THERE ISN'T TIME.
LISTEN TO WHAT I SAY! AND DO IT WHEN I TELL YOU!

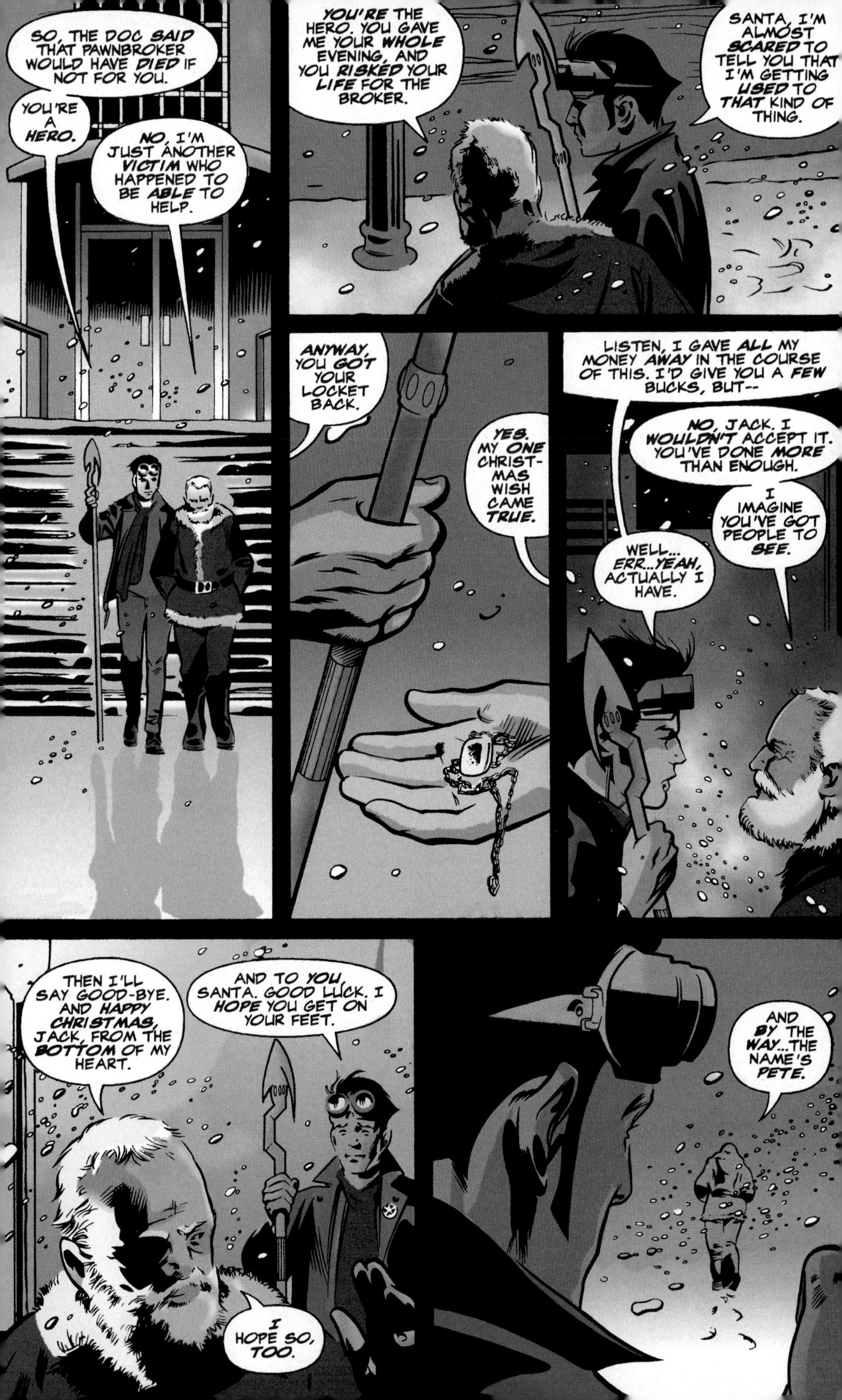
SO, THE DOC SAID THAT PAWNBROKER WOULD HAVE DIED IF NOT FOR YOU.
YOU'RE A HERO.
NO, I'M JUST ANOTHER VICTIM WHO HAPPENED TO BE ABLE TO HELP.
YOU'RE THE HERO. YOU GAVE ME YOUR WHOLE EVENING, AND YOU RISKED YOUR LIFE FOR THE BROKER.
SANTA, I'M ALMOST SCARED TO TELL YOU THAT I'M GETTING USED TO THAT KIND OF THING.
ANYWAY, YOU GOT YOUR LOCKET BACK.
YES. MY ONE CHRISTMAS WISH CAME TRUE.
LISTEN, I GAVE ALL MY MONEY AWAY IN THE COURSE OF THIS. I'D GIVE YOU A FEW BUCKS, BUT--
NO, JACK. I WOULDN'T ACCEPT IT. YOU'VE DONE MORE THAN ENOUGH.
I IMAGINE YOU'VE GOT PEOPLE TO SEE.
WELL... ERR...YEAH, ACTUALLY I HAVE.
THEN I'LL SAY GOOD-BYE. AND HAPPY CHRISTMAS, JACK, FROM THE BOTTOM OF MY HEART.
AND TO YOU, SANTA. GOOD LUCK. I HOPE YOU GET ON YOUR FEET.
I HOPE SO, TOO.
AND BY THE WAY...THE NAME'S PETE.

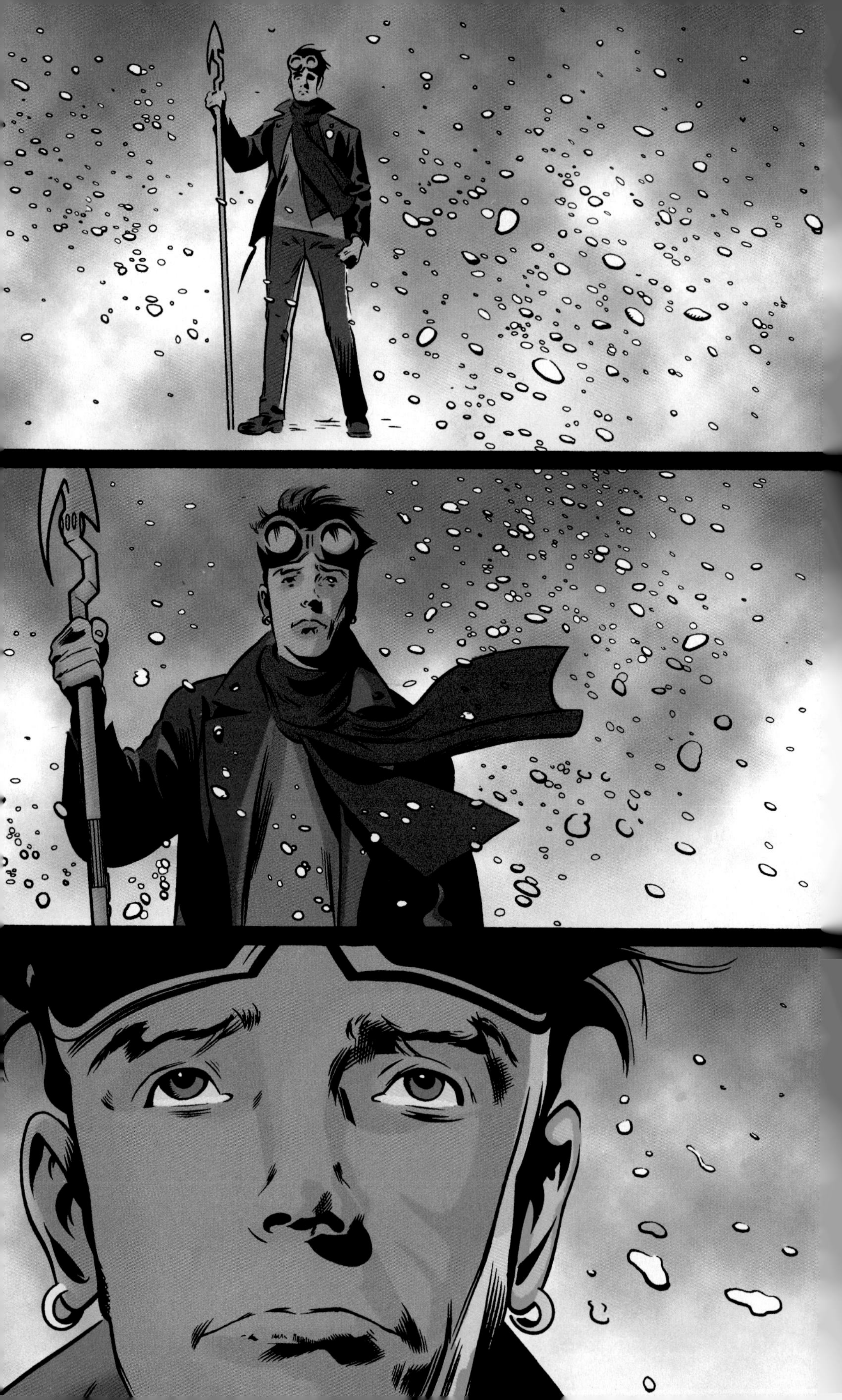

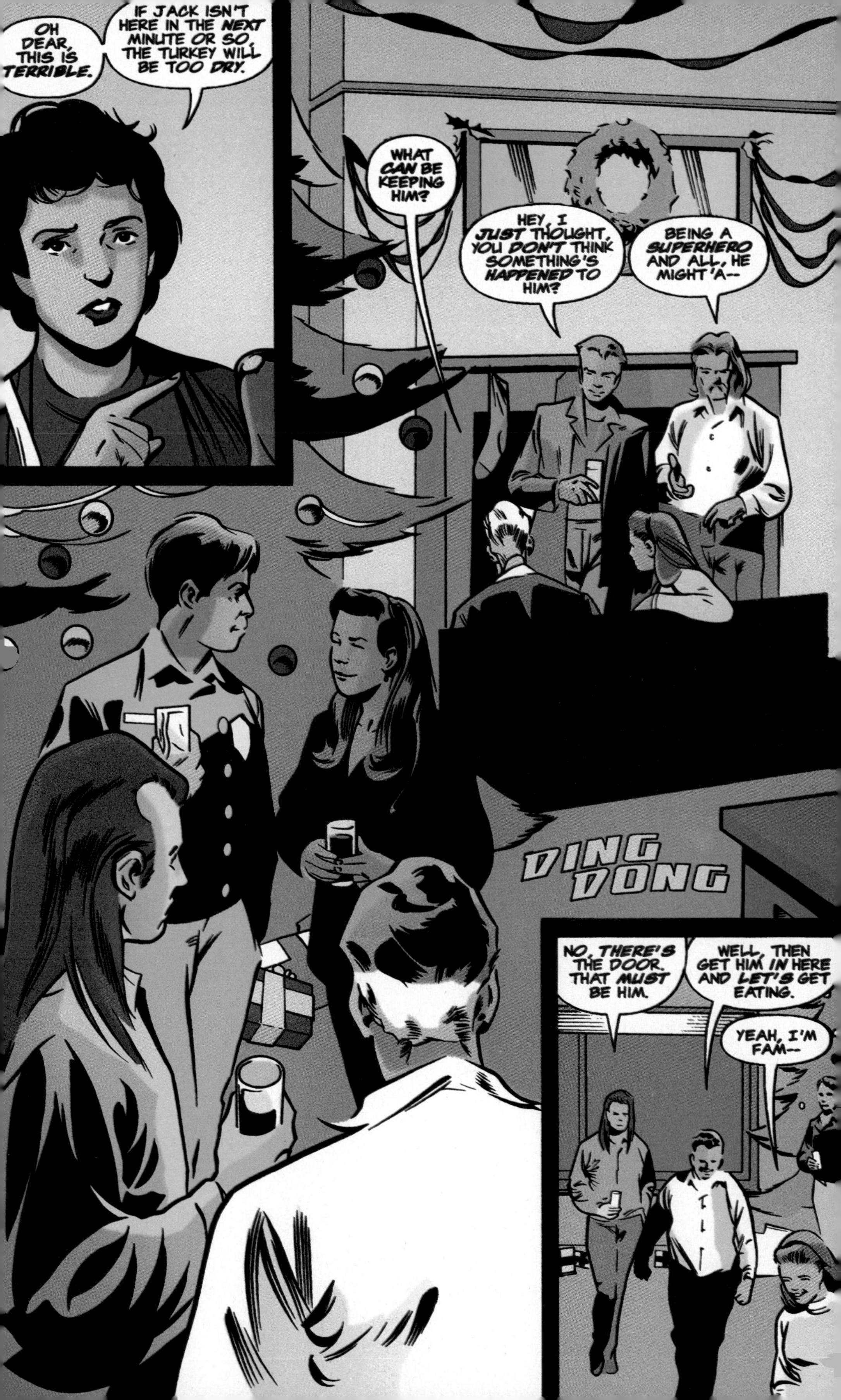

OH DEAR, THIS IS TERRIBLE.
IF JACK ISN'T HERE IN THE NEXT MINUTE OR SO, THE TURKEY WILL BE TOO DRY.
WHAT CAN BE KEEPING HIM?
HEY, I JUST THOUGHT, YOU DON'T THINK SOMETHING'S HAPPENED TO HIM?
BEING A SUPERHERO AND ALL, HE MIGHT 'A--
DING DONG
NO, THERE'S THE DOOR. THAT MUST BE HIM.
WELL, THEN GET HIM IN HERE AND LET'S GET EATING.
YEAH, I'M FAM--

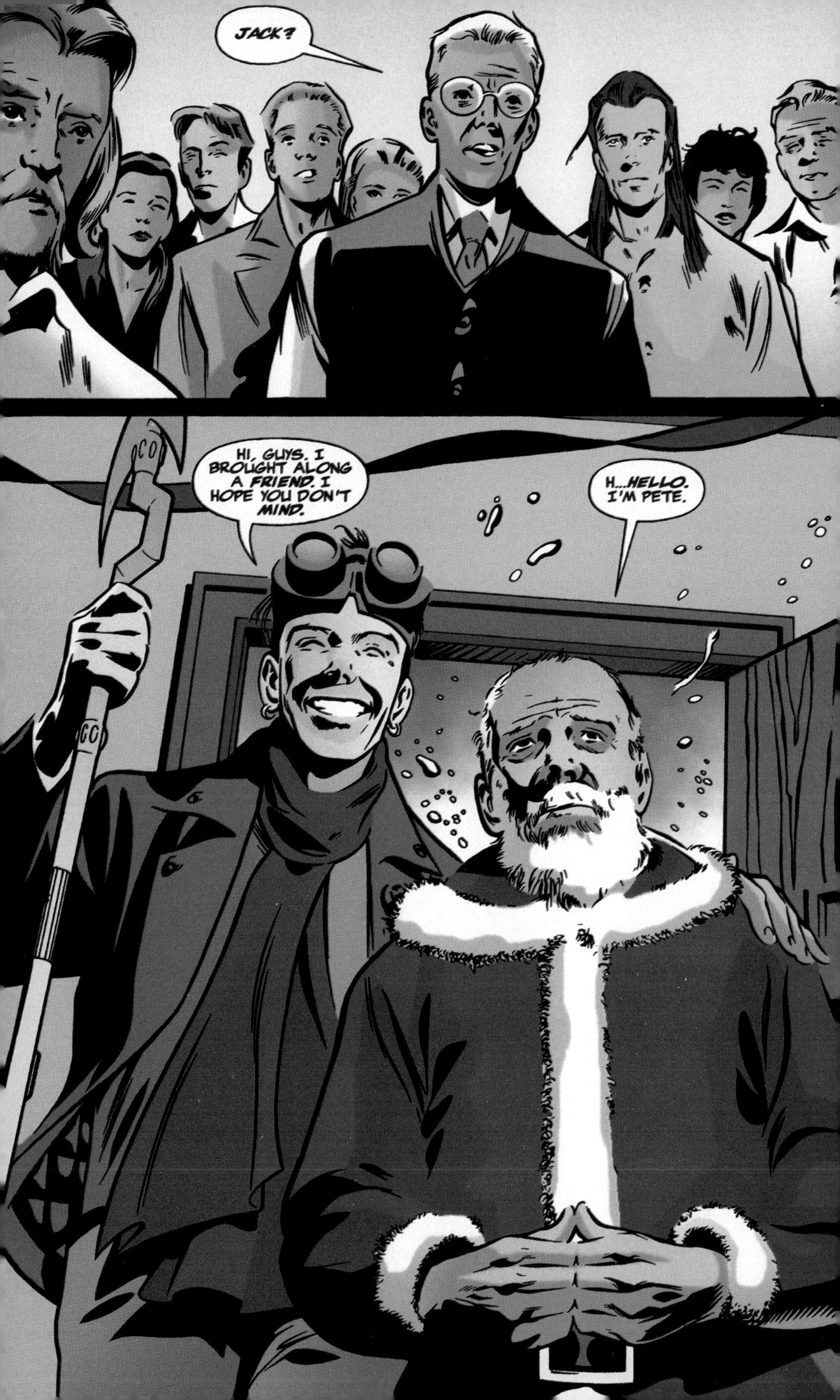
JACK?
HI, GUYS. I BROUGHT ALONG A FRIEND. I HOPE YOU DON'T MIND.
H...HELLO. I'M PETE.

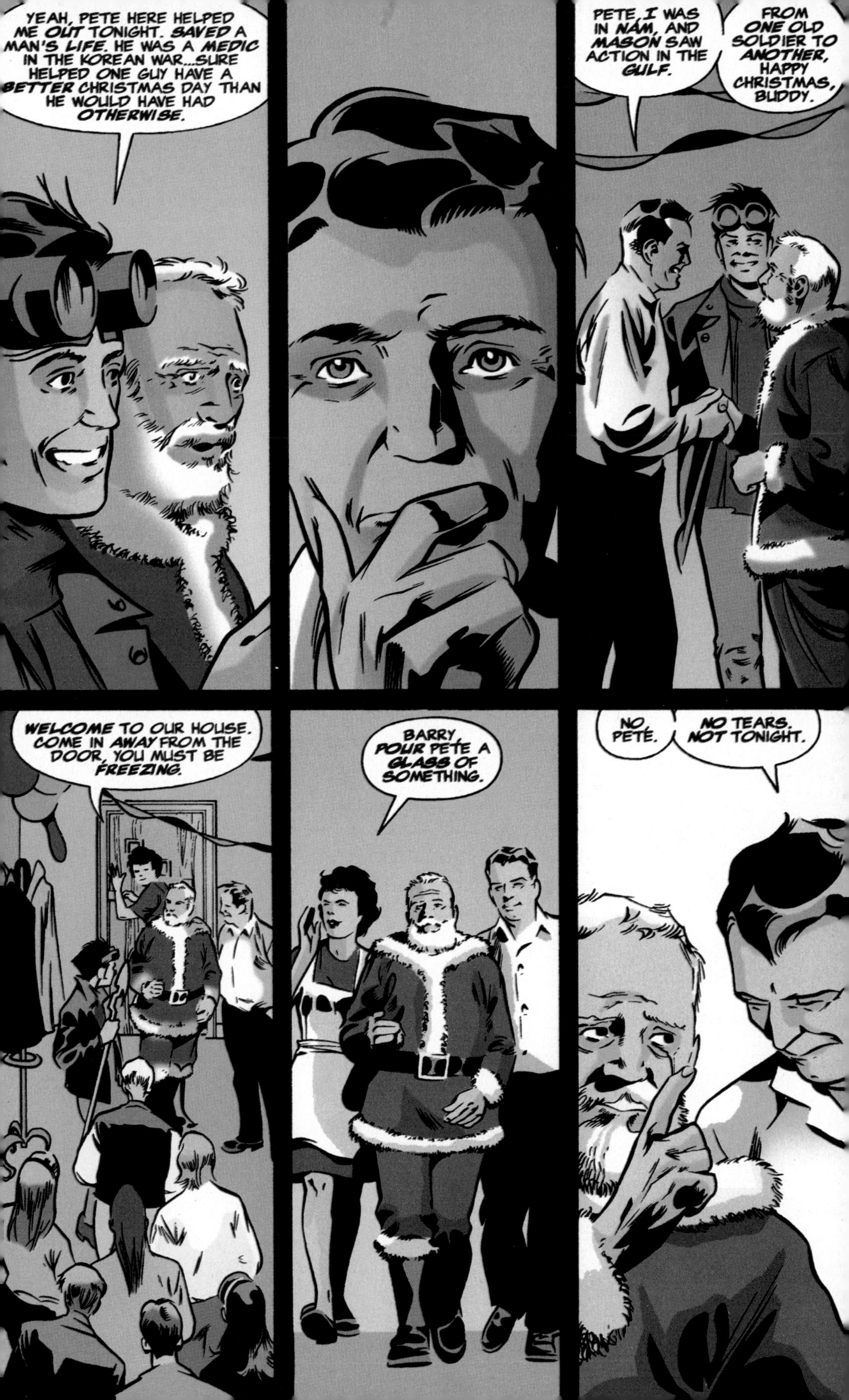
YEAH, PETE HERE HELPED ME OUT TONIGHT. SAVED A MAN'S LIFE. HE WAS A MEDIC IN THE KOREAN WAR...SURE HELPED ONE GUY HAVE A BETTER CHRISTMAS DAY THAN HE WOULD HAVE HAD OTHERWISE.
PETE, I WAS IN NAM, AND MASON SAW ACTION IN THE GULF.
FROM ONE OLD SOLDIER TO ANOTHER, HAPPY CHRISTMAS, BUDDY.
WELCOME TO OUR HOUSE. COME IN AWAY FROM THE DOOR, YOU MUST BE FREEZING.
BARRY, POUR PETE A GLASS OF SOMETHING.
NO, PETE.
NO TEARS. NOT TONIGHT.

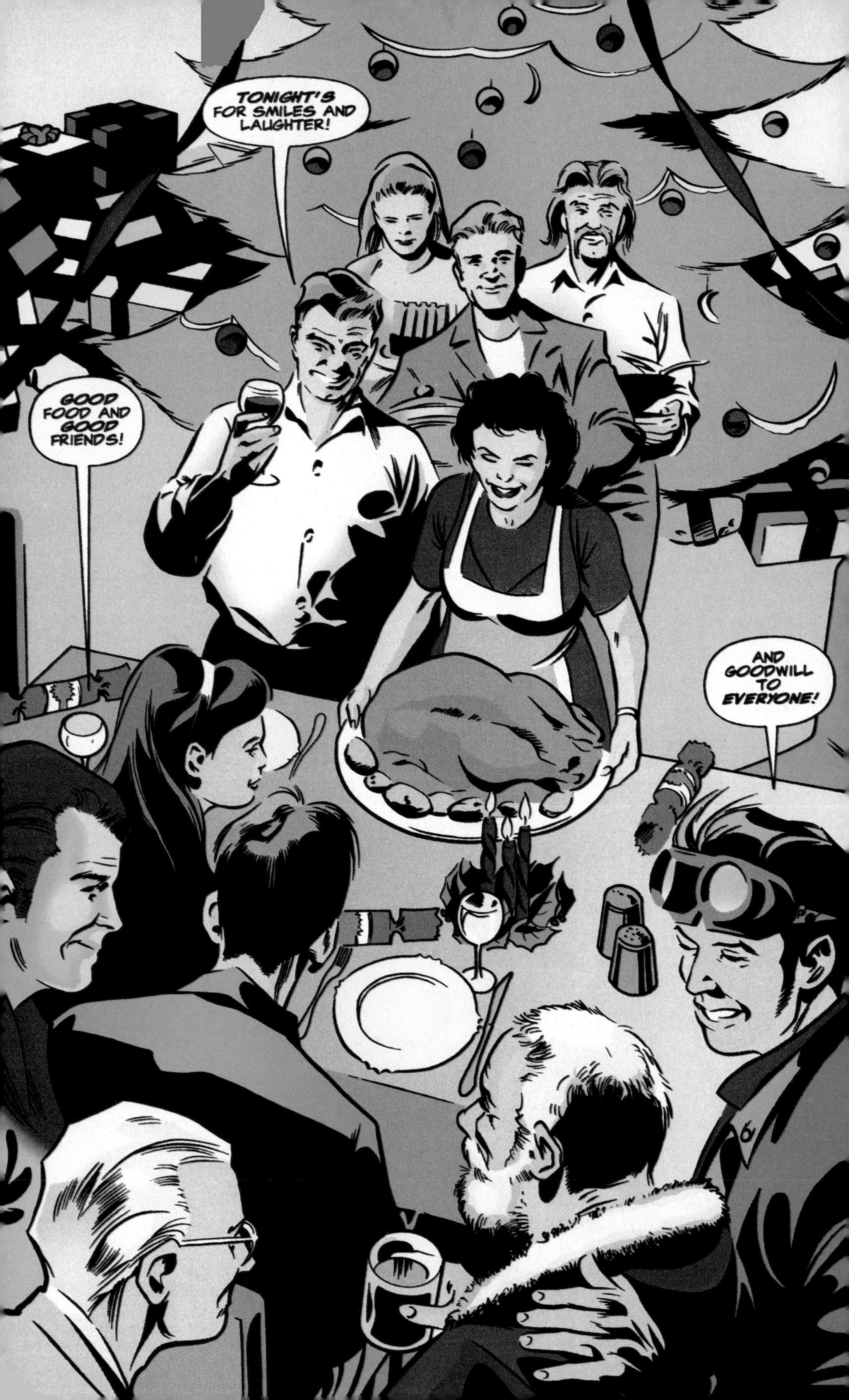
TONIGHT'S FOR SMILES AND LAUGHTER!
GOOD FOOD AND GOOD FRIENDS!
AND GOODWILL TO EVERYONE!

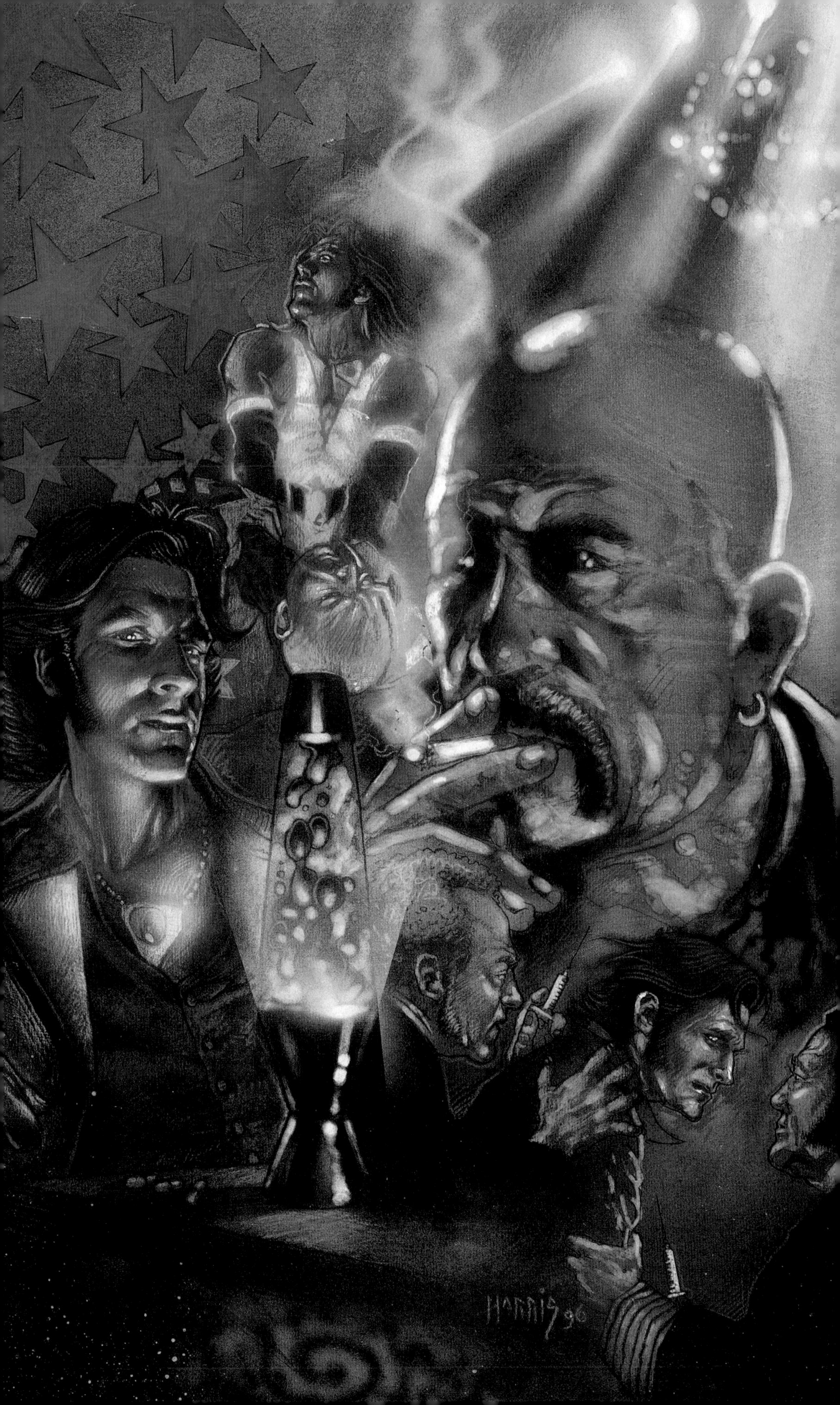
HARRIS 96

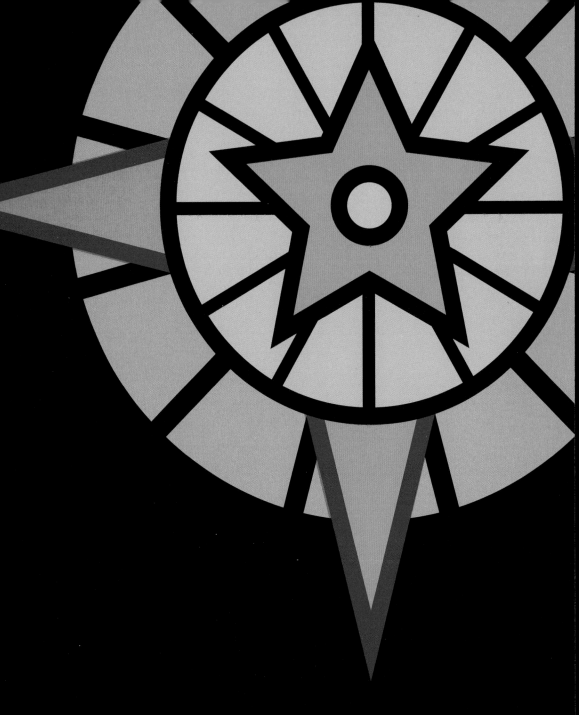

STARMAN 28

Cover by Tony Harris

Written by James Robinson

Pencils by Craig Hamilton

with inks by Ray Snyder

and colors by Gregory Wright

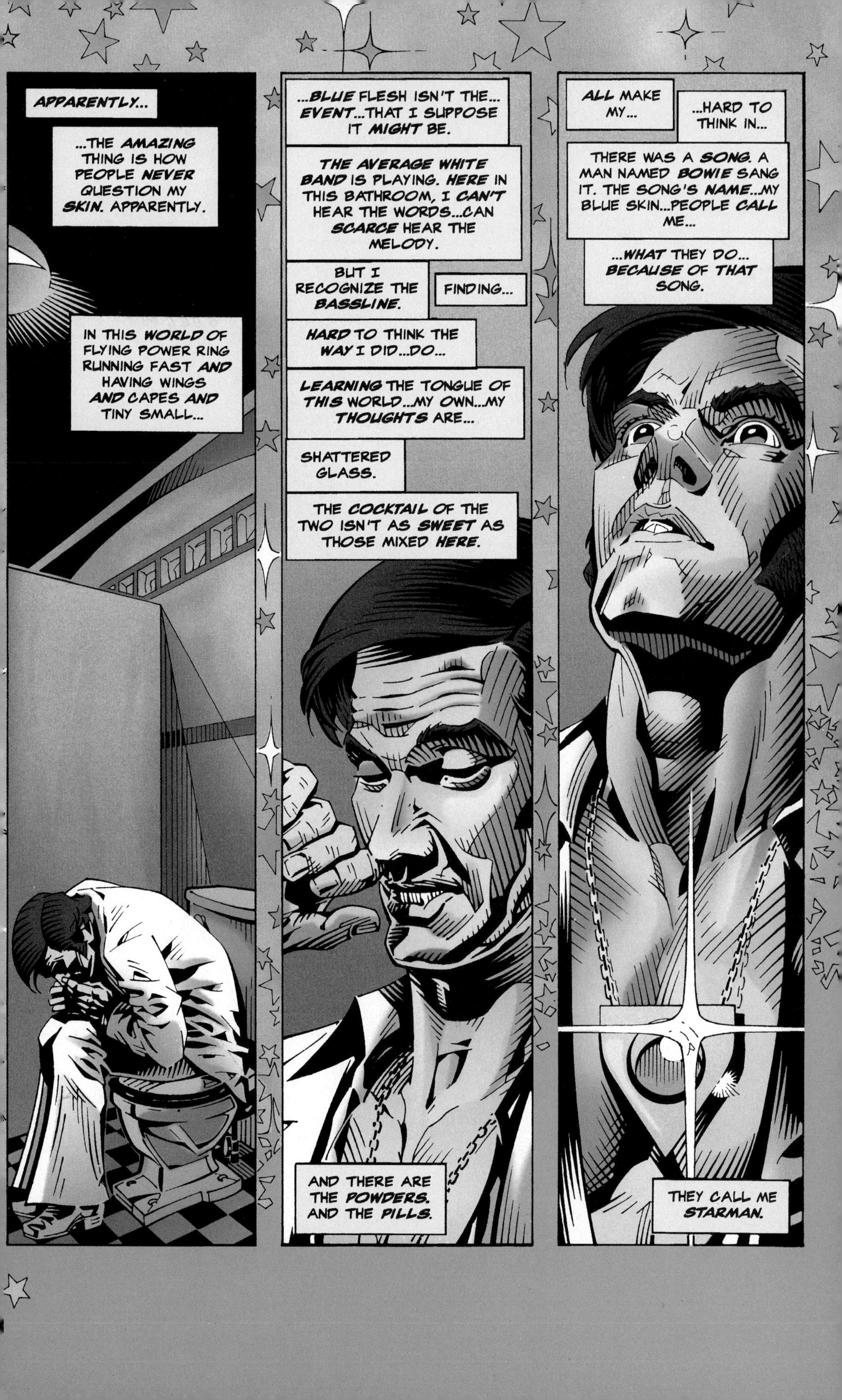

APPARENTLY...

...THE *AMAZING* THING IS HOW PEOPLE *NEVER* QUESTION MY *SKIN*. APPARENTLY.

IN THIS *WORLD* OF FLYING POWER RING RUNNING FAST *AND* HAVING WINGS AND CAPES AND TINY SMALL...

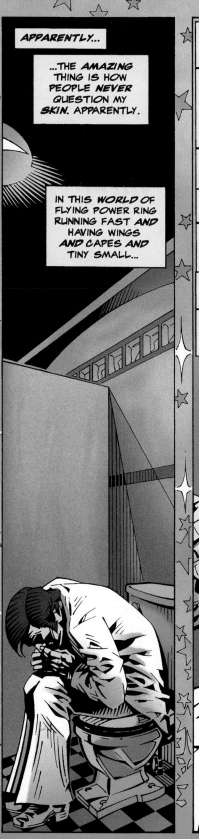

...*BLUE* FLESH ISN'T THE... *EVENT*...THAT I SUPPOSE IT *MIGHT* BE.

THE AVERAGE WHITE BAND IS PLAYING. *HERE* IN THIS BATHROOM, I *CAN'T* HEAR THE WORDS...CAN *SCARCE* HEAR THE MELODY.

BUT I RECOGNIZE THE *BASSLINE*.

FINDING...

HARD TO THINK THE WAY I DID...DO...

LEARNING THE TONGUE OF *THIS* WORLD...MY OWN...MY *THOUGHTS* ARE...

SHATTERED GLASS.

THE *COCKTAIL* OF THE TWO ISN'T AS *SWEET* AS THOSE MIXED *HERE*.

AND THERE ARE THE *POWDERS*. AND THE *PILLS*.

ALL MAKE MY...

...HARD TO THINK IN...

THERE WAS A *SONG*. A MAN NAMED *BOWIE* SANG IT. THE SONG'S *NAME*...MY BLUE SKIN...PEOPLE CALL ME...

...*WHAT* THEY DO... *BECAUSE OF THAT* SONG.

THEY CALL ME *STARMAN*.

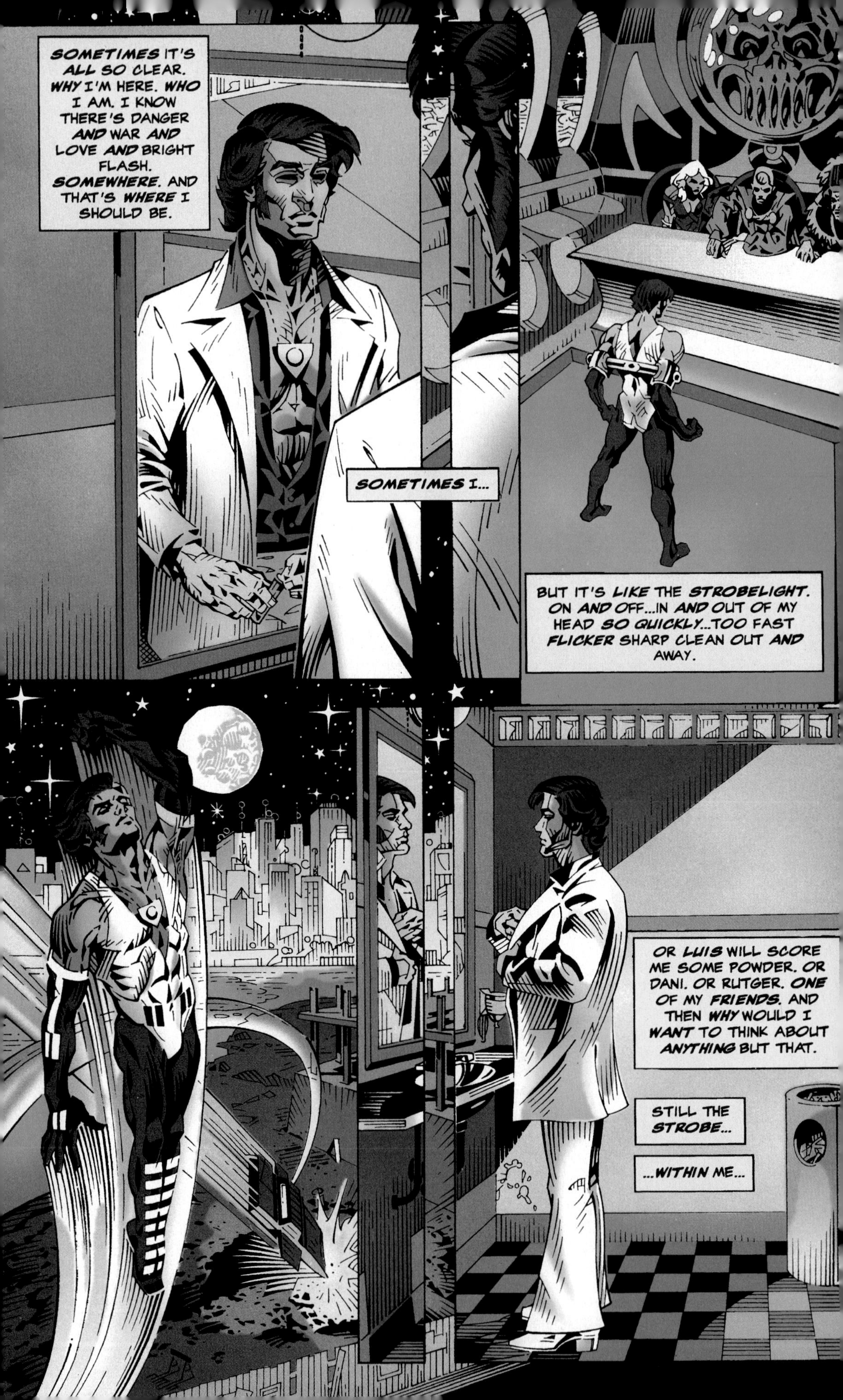
SOMETIMES IT'S ALL SO CLEAR. WHY I'M HERE. WHO I AM. I KNOW THERE'S DANGER AND WAR AND LOVE AND BRIGHT FLASH. SOMEWHERE. AND THAT'S WHERE I SHOULD BE.
SOMETIMES I...
BUT IT'S LIKE THE STROBELIGHT. ON AND OFF...IN AND OUT OF MY HEAD SO QUICKLY...TOO FAST FLICKER SHARP CLEAN OUT AND AWAY.
OR LUIS WILL SCORE ME SOME POWDER. OR DANI. OR RUTGER. ONE OF MY FRIENDS. AND THEN WHY WOULD I WANT TO THINK ABOUT ANYTHING BUT THAT.
STILL THE STROBE...
...WITHIN ME...

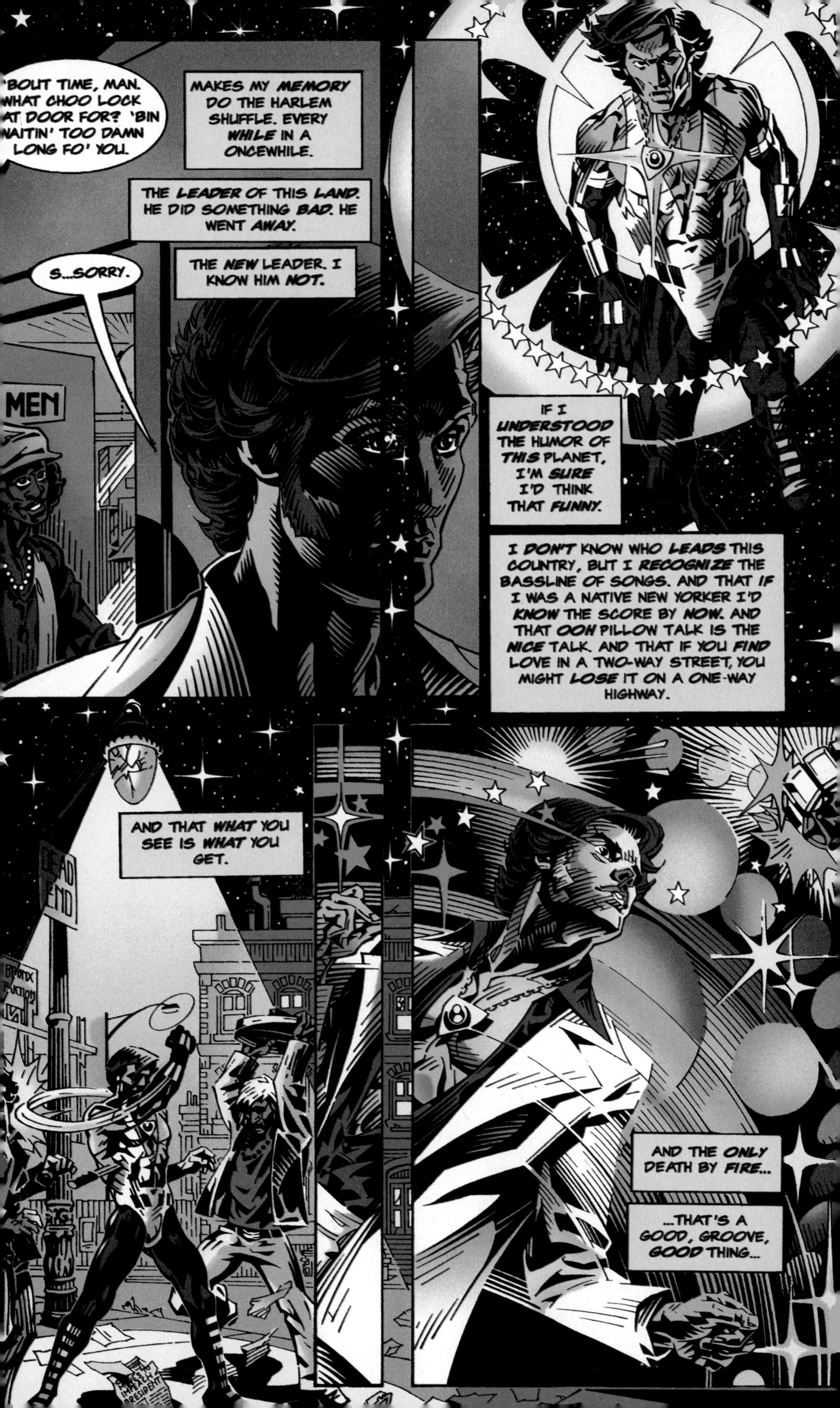

'BOUT TIME, MAN. WHAT CHOO LOCK AT DOOR FOR? 'BIN WAITIN' TOO DAMN LONG FO' YOU.
MAKES MY MEMORY DO THE HARLEM SHUFFLE. EVERY WHILE IN A ONCEWHILE.
THE LEADER OF THIS LAND. HE DID SOMETHING BAD. HE WENT AWAY.
S...SORRY.
THE NEW LEADER. I KNOW HIM NOT.
MEN
IF I UNDERSTOOD THE HUMOR OF THIS PLANET, I'M SURE I'D THINK THAT FUNNY.
I DON'T KNOW WHO LEADS THIS COUNTRY, BUT I RECOGNIZE THE BASSLINE OF SONGS. AND THAT IF I WAS A NATIVE NEW YORKER I'D KNOW THE SCORE BY NOW. AND THAT OOH PILLOW TALK IS THE NICE TALK. AND THAT IF YOU FIND LOVE IN A TWO-WAY STREET, YOU MIGHT LOSE IT ON A ONE-WAY HIGHWAY.
AND THAT WHAT YOU SEE IS WHAT YOU GET.
DEAD END
AND THE ONLY DEATH BY FIRE...
...THAT'S A GOOD, GROOVE, GOOD THING...

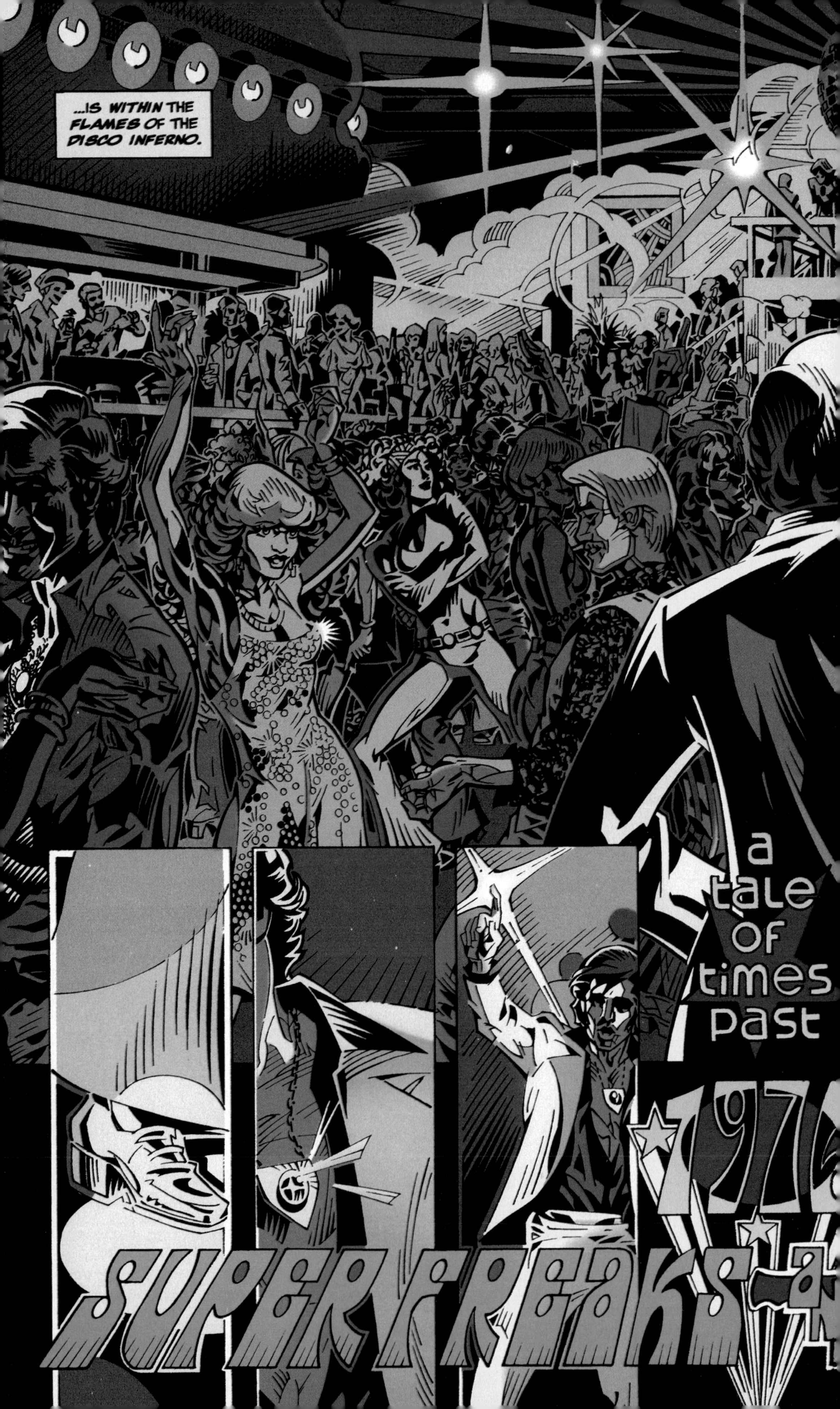
...IS WITHIN THE FLAMES OF THE DISCO INFERNO.
a tale of times past
1976
SUPERFREAKS

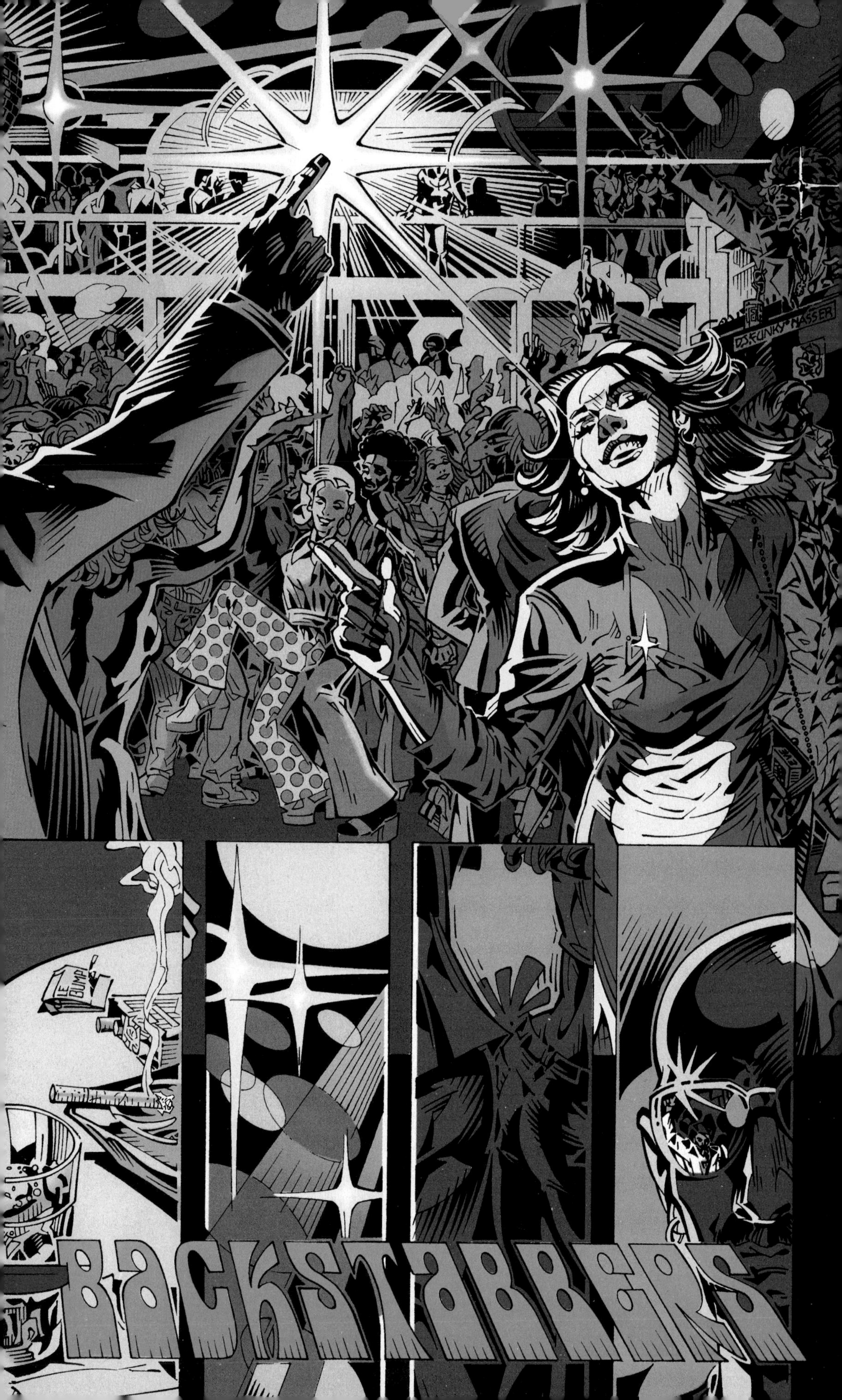
DJ FUNKY NASSER
LE BUMP
BACKSTABBERS

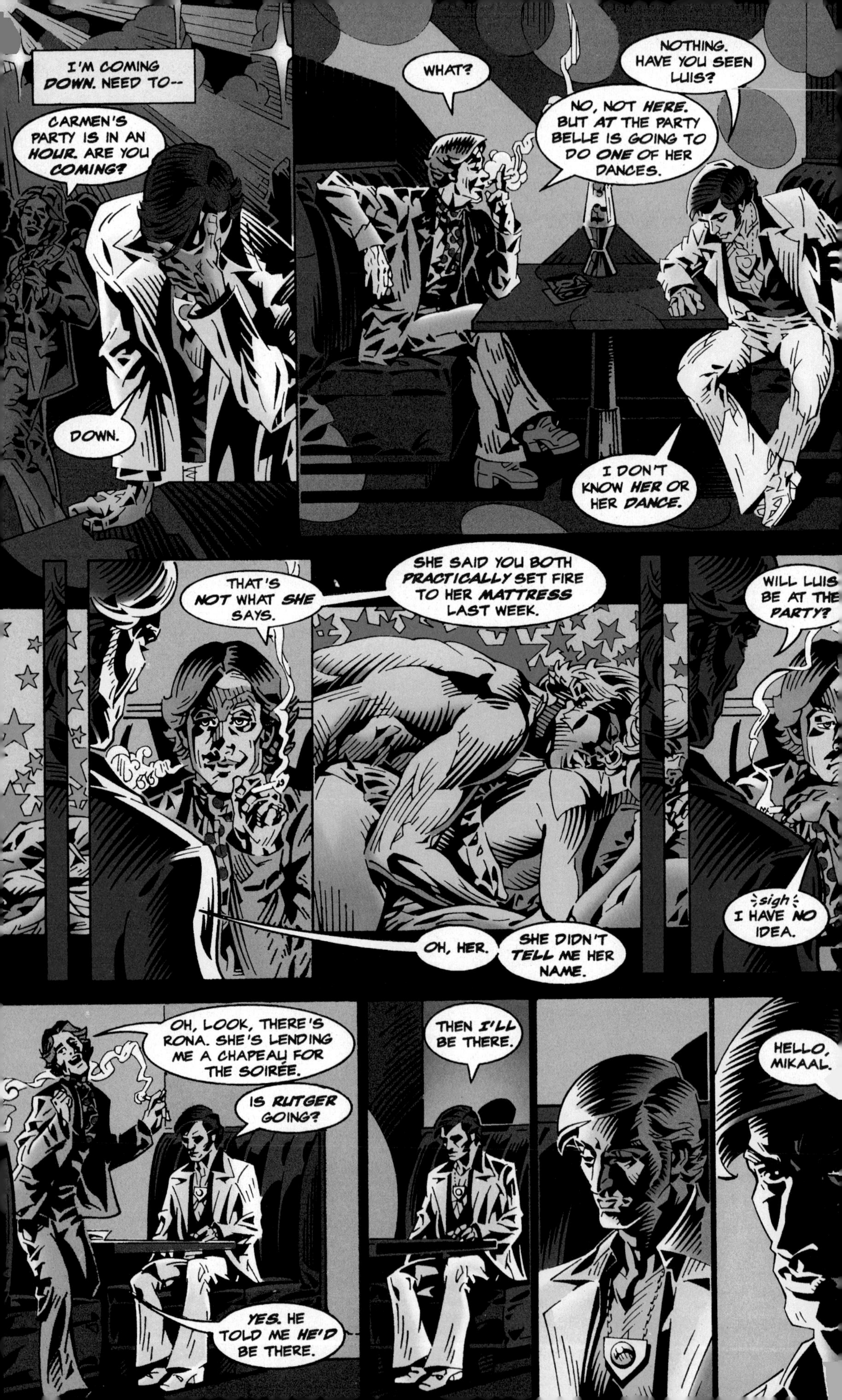
I'M COMING DOWN. NEED TO--
CARMEN'S PARTY IS IN AN HOUR. ARE YOU COMING?
DOWN.
WHAT?
NOTHING. HAVE YOU SEEN LUIS?
NO, NOT HERE. BUT AT THE PARTY BELLE IS GOING TO DO ONE OF HER DANCES.
I DON'T KNOW HER OR HER DANCE.
THAT'S NOT WHAT SHE SAYS.
SHE SAID YOU BOTH PRACTICALLY SET FIRE TO HER MATTRESS LAST WEEK.
OH, HER.
SHE DIDN'T TELL ME HER NAME.
WILL LUIS BE AT THE PARTY?
sigh
I HAVE NO IDEA.
OH, LOOK, THERE'S RONA. SHE'S LENDING ME A CHAPEAU FOR THE SOIRÉE.
IS RUTGER GOING?
YES. HE TOLD ME HE'D BE THERE.
THEN I'LL BE THERE.
HELLO, MIKAAL.

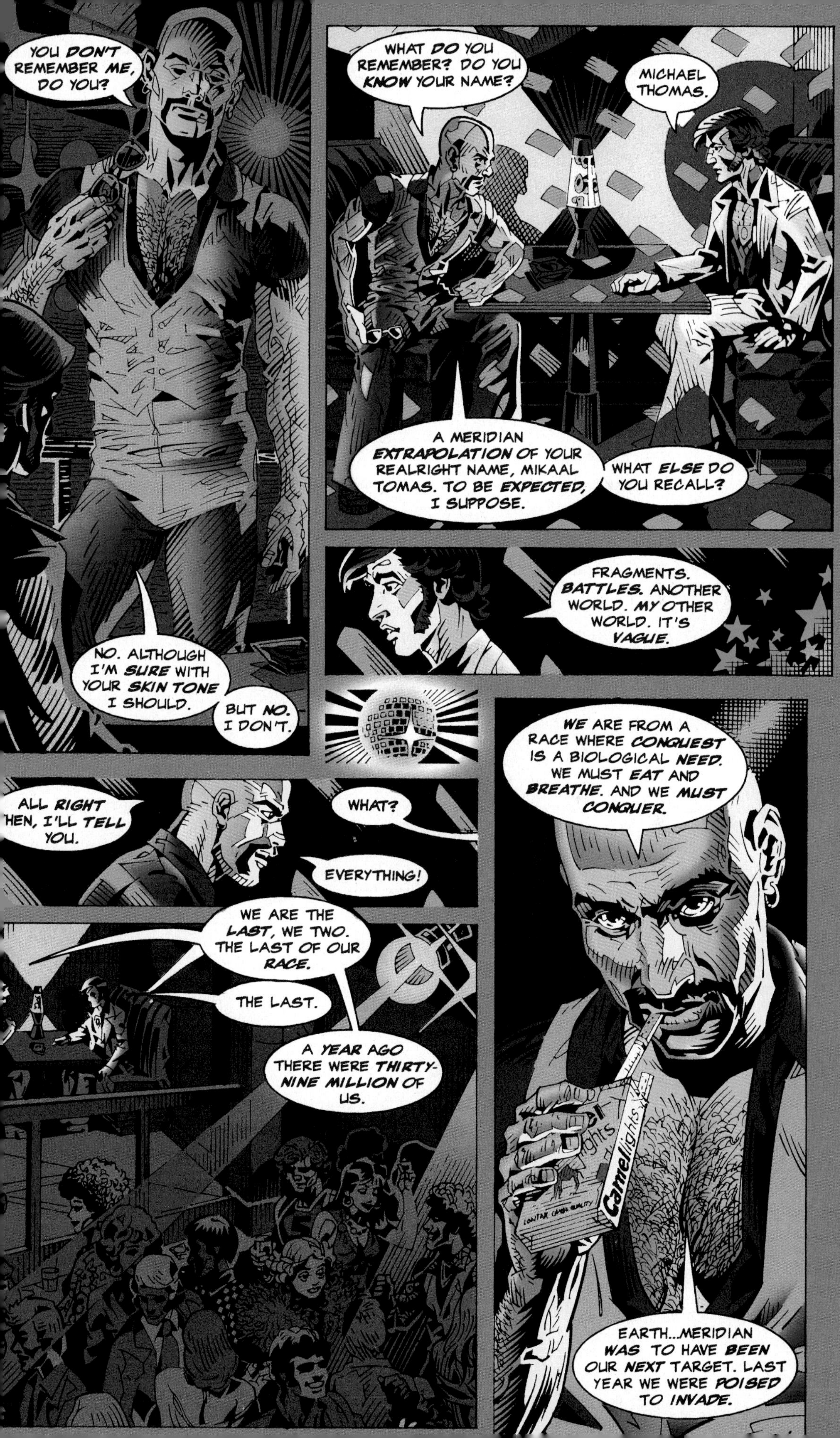
YOU DON'T REMEMBER ME, DO YOU?
NO. ALTHOUGH I'M SURE WITH YOUR SKIN TONE I SHOULD.
BUT NO. I DON'T.
WHAT DO YOU REMEMBER? DO YOU KNOW YOUR NAME?
MICHAEL THOMAS.
A MERIDIAN EXTRAPOLATION OF YOUR REALRIGHT NAME, MIKAAL TOMAS. TO BE EXPECTED, I SUPPOSE.
WHAT ELSE DO YOU RECALL?
FRAGMENTS. BATTLES. ANOTHER WORLD. MY OTHER WORLD. IT'S VAGUE.
ALL RIGHT HEN, I'LL TELL YOU.
WHAT?
EVERYTHING!
WE ARE THE LAST, WE TWO. THE LAST OF OUR RACE.
THE LAST.
A YEAR AGO THERE WERE THIRTY-NINE MILLION OF US.
WE ARE FROM A RACE WHERE CONQUEST IS A BIOLOGICAL NEED. WE MUST EAT AND BREATHE. AND WE MUST CONQUER.
EARTH...MERIDIAN WAS TO HAVE BEEN OUR NEXT TARGET. LAST YEAR WE WERE POISED TO INVADE.

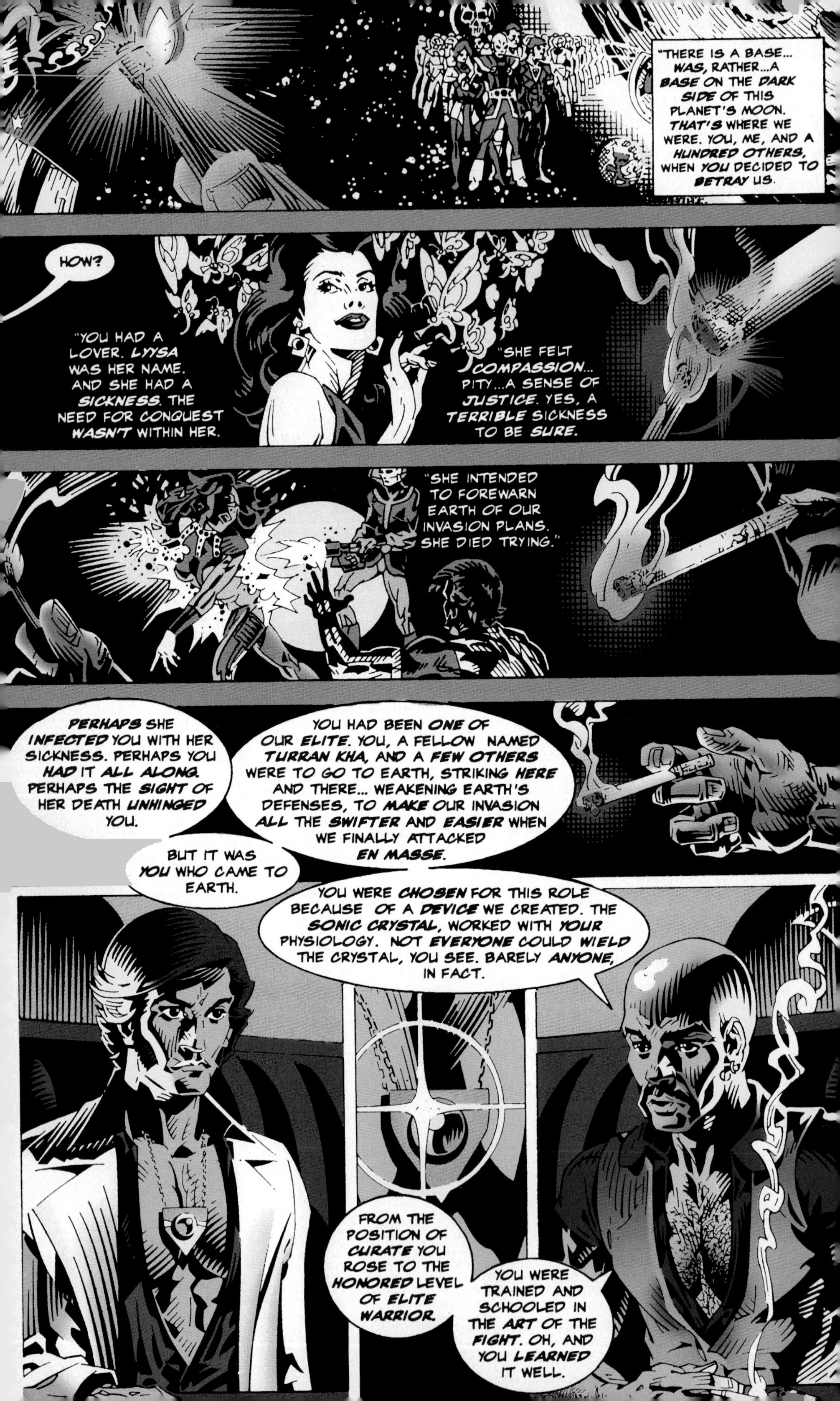
"THERE IS A BASE... WAS, RATHER...A BASE ON THE DARK SIDE OF THIS PLANET'S MOON. THAT'S WHERE WE WERE. YOU, ME, AND A HUNDRED OTHERS, WHEN YOU DECIDED TO BETRAY US.
HOW?
"YOU HAD A LOVER. LYYSA WAS HER NAME. AND SHE HAD A SICKNESS. THE NEED FOR CONQUEST WASN'T WITHIN HER.
"SHE FELT COMPASSION... PITY...A SENSE OF JUSTICE. YES, A TERRIBLE SICKNESS TO BE SURE.
"SHE INTENDED TO FOREWARN EARTH OF OUR INVASION PLANS. SHE DIED TRYING."
PERHAPS SHE INFECTED YOU WITH HER SICKNESS. PERHAPS YOU HAD IT ALL ALONG. PERHAPS THE SIGHT OF HER DEATH UNHINGED YOU.
YOU HAD BEEN ONE OF OUR ELITE. YOU, A FELLOW NAMED TURRAN KHA, AND A FEW OTHERS WERE TO GO TO EARTH, STRIKING HERE AND THERE... WEAKENING EARTH'S DEFENSES, TO MAKE OUR INVASION ALL THE SWIFTER AND EASIER WHEN WE FINALLY ATTACKED EN MASSE.
BUT IT WAS YOU WHO CAME TO EARTH.
YOU WERE CHOSEN FOR THIS ROLE BECAUSE OF A DEVICE WE CREATED. THE SONIC CRYSTAL, WORKED WITH YOUR PHYSIOLOGY. NOT EVERYONE COULD WIELD THE CRYSTAL, YOU SEE. BARELY ANYONE, IN FACT.
FROM THE POSITION OF CURATE YOU ROSE TO THE HONORED LEVEL OF ELITE WARRIOR.
YOU WERE TRAINED AND SCHOOLED IN THE ART OF THE FIGHT. OH, AND YOU LEARNED IT WELL.

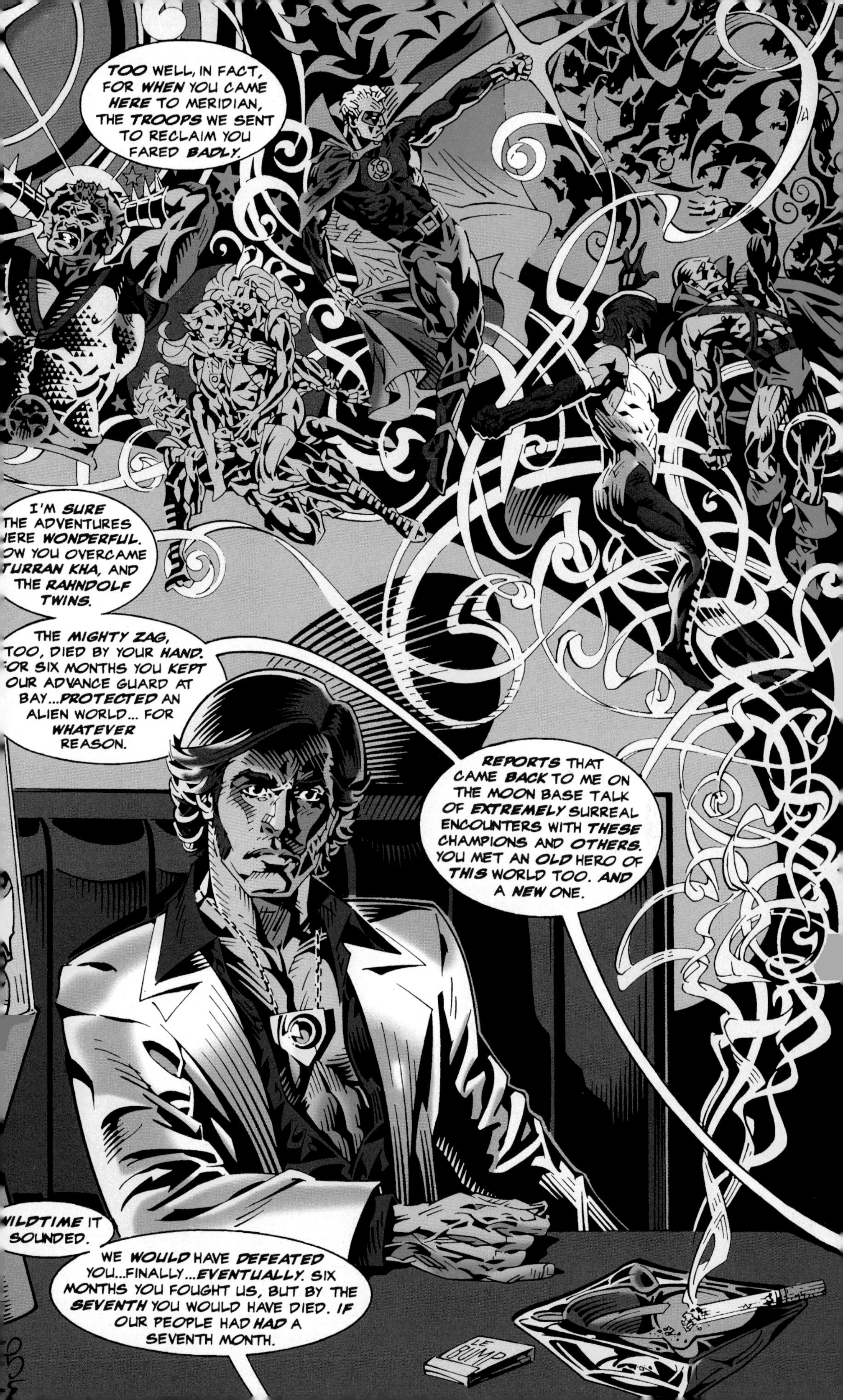
TOO WELL, IN FACT, FOR WHEN YOU CAME HERE TO MERIDIAN, THE TROOPS WE SENT TO RECLAIM YOU FARED BADLY.
I'M SURE THE ADVENTURES ERE WONDERFUL. OW YOU OVERCAME URRAN KHA, AND THE RAHNDOLF TWINS.
THE MIGHTY ZAG, TOO, DIED BY YOUR HAND. OR SIX MONTHS YOU KEPT OUR ADVANCE GUARD AT BAY...PROTECTED AN ALIEN WORLD... FOR WHATEVER REASON.
REPORTS THAT CAME BACK TO ME ON THE MOON BASE TALK OF EXTREMELY SURREAL ENCOUNTERS WITH THESE CHAMPIONS AND OTHERS. YOU MET AN OLD HERO OF THIS WORLD TOO. AND A NEW ONE.
ILDTIME IT SOUNDED.
WE WOULD HAVE DEFEATED YOU...FINALLY...EVENTUALLY. SIX MONTHS YOU FOUGHT US, BUT BY THE SEVENTH YOU WOULD HAVE DIED. IF OUR PEOPLE HAD HAD A SEVENTH MONTH.
LE BUMP

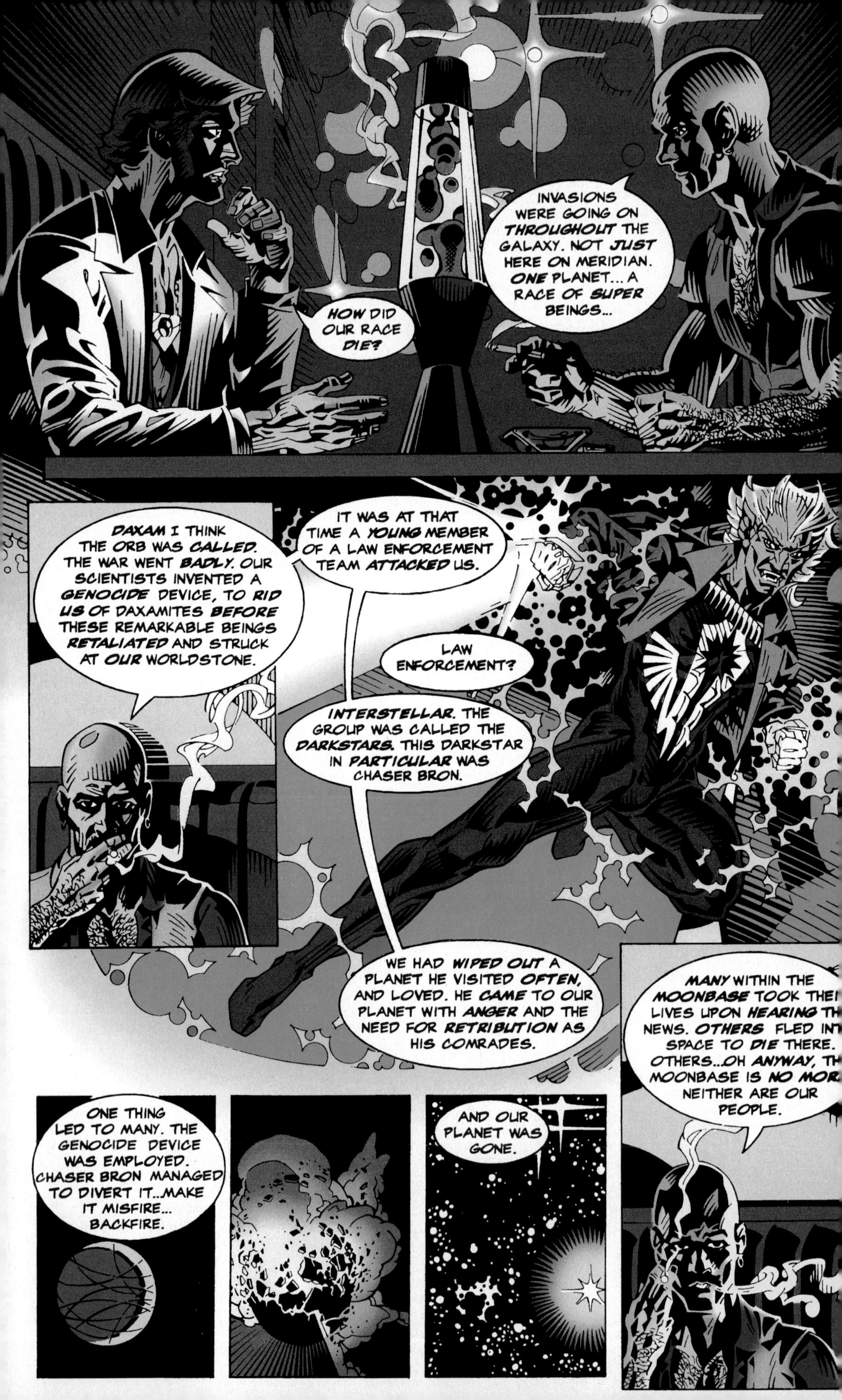

HOW DID OUR RACE DIE?
INVASIONS WERE GOING ON THROUGHOUT THE GALAXY. NOT JUST HERE ON MERIDIAN. ONE PLANET... A RACE OF SUPER BEINGS...
DAXAM I THINK THE ORB WAS CALLED. THE WAR WENT BADLY. OUR SCIENTISTS INVENTED A GENOCIDE DEVICE, TO RID US OF DAXAMITES BEFORE THESE REMARKABLE BEINGS RETALIATED AND STRUCK AT OUR WORLDSTONE.
IT WAS AT THAT TIME A YOUNG MEMBER OF A LAW ENFORCEMENT TEAM ATTACKED US.
LAW ENFORCEMENT?
INTERSTELLAR. THE GROUP WAS CALLED THE DARKSTARS. THIS DARKSTAR IN PARTICULAR WAS CHASER BRON.
WE HAD WIPED OUT A PLANET HE VISITED OFTEN, AND LOVED. HE CAME TO OUR PLANET WITH ANGER AND THE NEED FOR RETRIBUTION AS HIS COMRADES.
ONE THING LED TO MANY. THE GENOCIDE DEVICE WAS EMPLOYED. CHASER BRON MANAGED TO DIVERT IT...MAKE IT MISFIRE... BACKFIRE.
AND OUR PLANET WAS GONE.

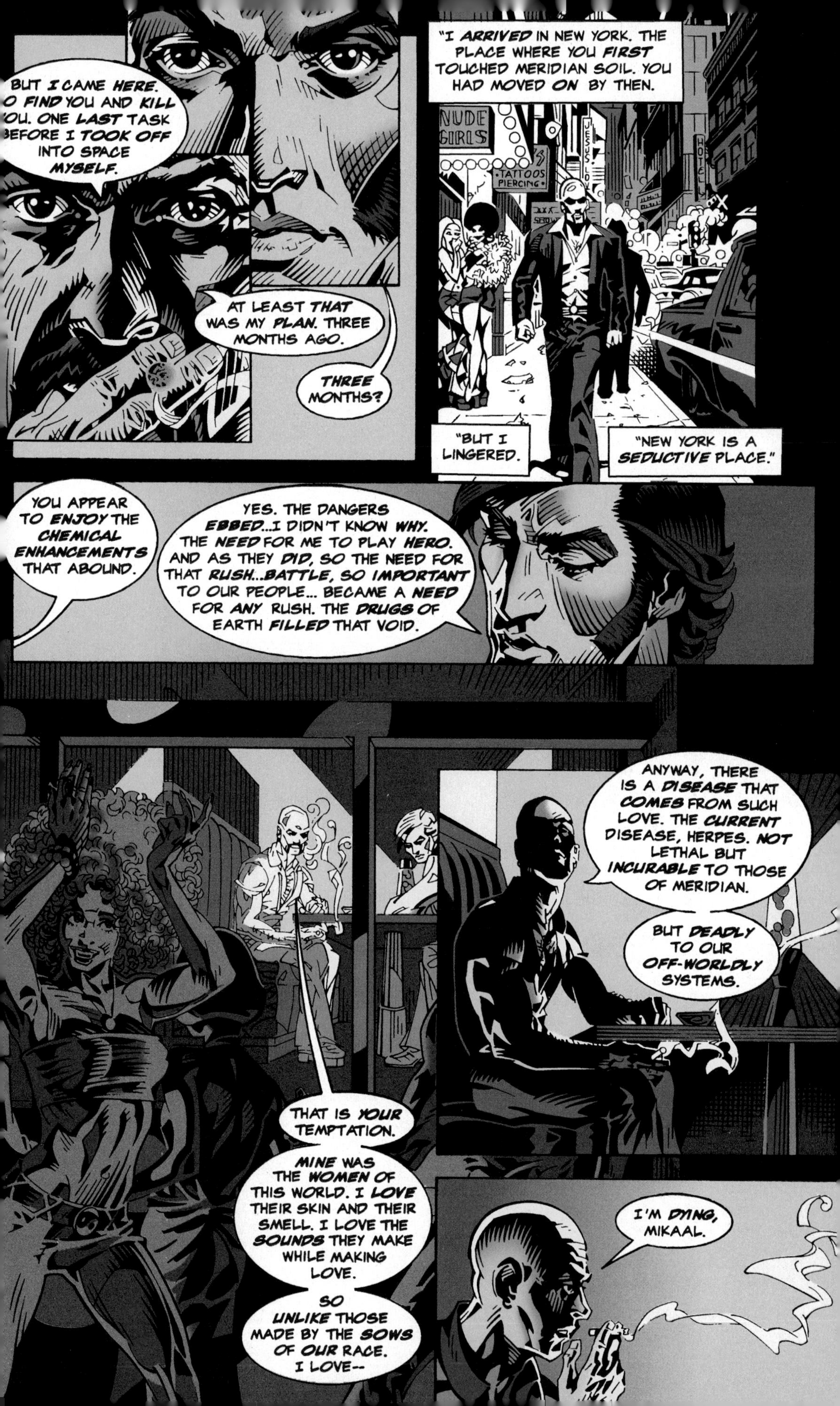
BUT I CAME HERE. O FIND YOU AND KILL OU. ONE LAST TASK BEFORE I TOOK OFF INTO SPACE MYSELF.
AT LEAST THAT WAS MY PLAN. THREE MONTHS AGO.
THREE MONTHS?
"I ARRIVED IN NEW YORK. THE PLACE WHERE YOU FIRST TOUCHED MERIDIAN SOIL. YOU HAD MOVED ON BY THEN.
NUDE GIRLS
TATTOOS PIERCING
HOTEL
"BUT I LINGERED.
"NEW YORK IS A SEDUCTIVE PLACE."
YOU APPEAR TO ENJOY THE CHEMICAL ENHANCEMENTS THAT ABOUND.
YES. THE DANGERS EBBED...I DIDN'T KNOW WHY. THE NEED FOR ME TO PLAY HERO. AND AS THEY DID, SO THE NEED FOR THAT RUSH...BATTLE, SO IMPORTANT TO OUR PEOPLE... BECAME A NEED FOR ANY RUSH. THE DRUGS OF EARTH FILLED THAT VOID.
THAT IS YOUR TEMPTATION.
MINE WAS THE WOMEN OF THIS WORLD. I LOVE THEIR SKIN AND THEIR SMELL. I LOVE THE SOUNDS THEY MAKE WHILE MAKING LOVE.
SO UNLIKE THOSE MADE BY THE SOWS OF OUR RACE. I LOVE--
ANYWAY, THERE IS A DISEASE THAT COMES FROM SUCH LOVE. THE CURRENT DISEASE, HERPES. NOT LETHAL BUT INCURABLE TO THOSE OF MERIDIAN.
BUT DEADLY TO OUR OFF-WORLDLY SYSTEMS.
I'M DYING, MIKAAL.

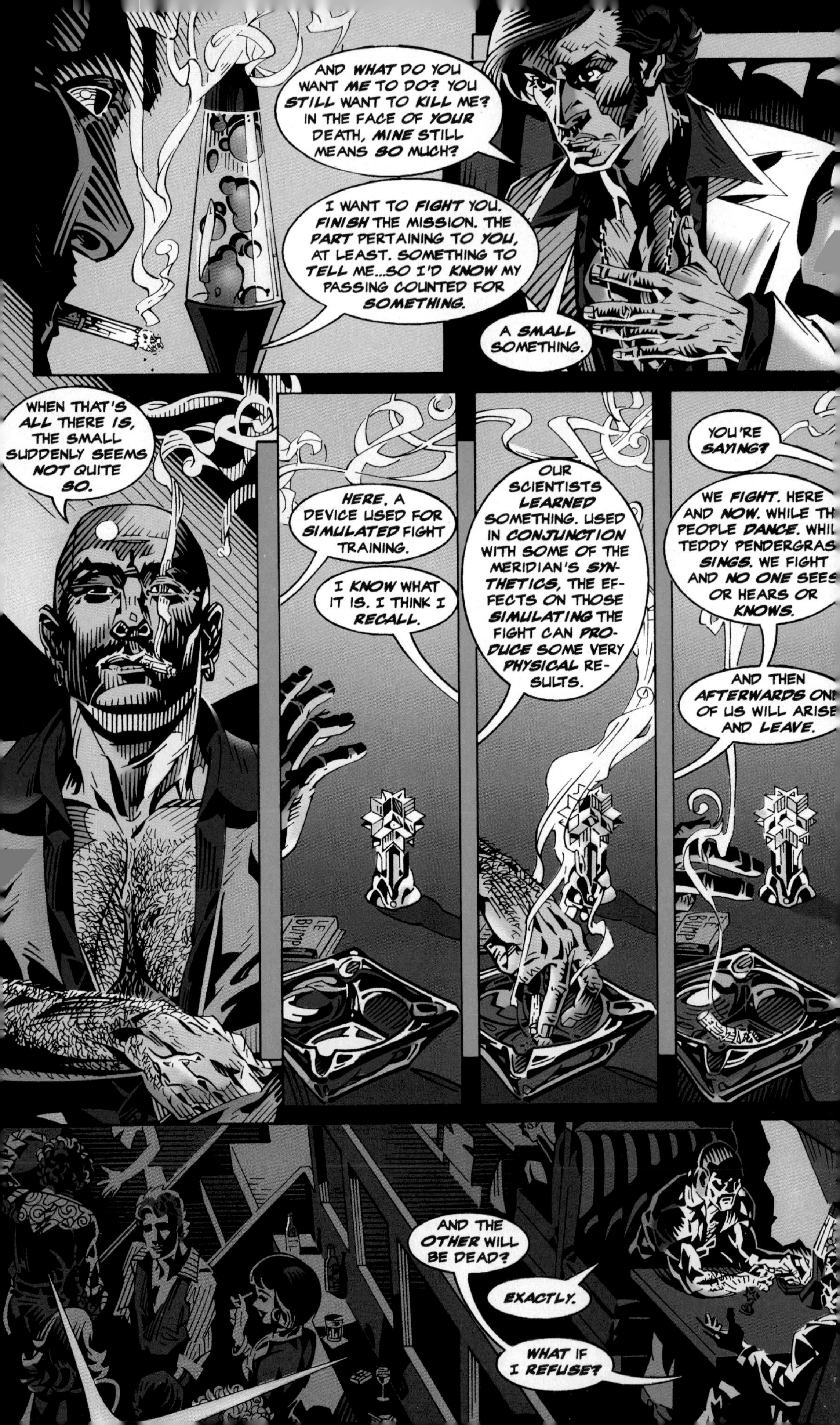
AND WHAT DO YOU WANT ME TO DO? YOU STILL WANT TO KILL ME? IN THE FACE OF YOUR DEATH, MINE STILL MEANS SO MUCH?
I WANT TO FIGHT YOU. FINISH THE MISSION. THE PART PERTAINING TO YOU, AT LEAST. SOMETHING TO TELL ME...SO I'D KNOW MY PASSING COUNTED FOR SOMETHING.
A SMALL SOMETHING.
WHEN THAT'S ALL THERE IS, THE SMALL SUDDENLY SEEMS NOT QUITE SO.
HERE. A DEVICE USED FOR SIMULATED FIGHT TRAINING.
I KNOW WHAT IT IS. I THINK I RECALL.
OUR SCIENTISTS LEARNED SOMETHING. USED IN CONJUNCTION WITH SOME OF THE MERIDIAN'S SYNTHETICS, THE EFFECTS ON THOSE SIMULATING THE FIGHT CAN PRODUCE SOME VERY PHYSICAL RESULTS.
YOU'RE SAYING?
WE FIGHT. HERE AND NOW. WHILE TH PEOPLE DANCE. WHIL TEDDY PENDERGRAS SINGS. WE FIGHT AND NO ONE SEES OR HEARS OR KNOWS.
AND THEN AFTERWARDS ON OF US WILL ARISE AND LEAVE.
AND THE OTHER WILL BE DEAD?
EXACTLY.
WHAT IF I REFUSE?

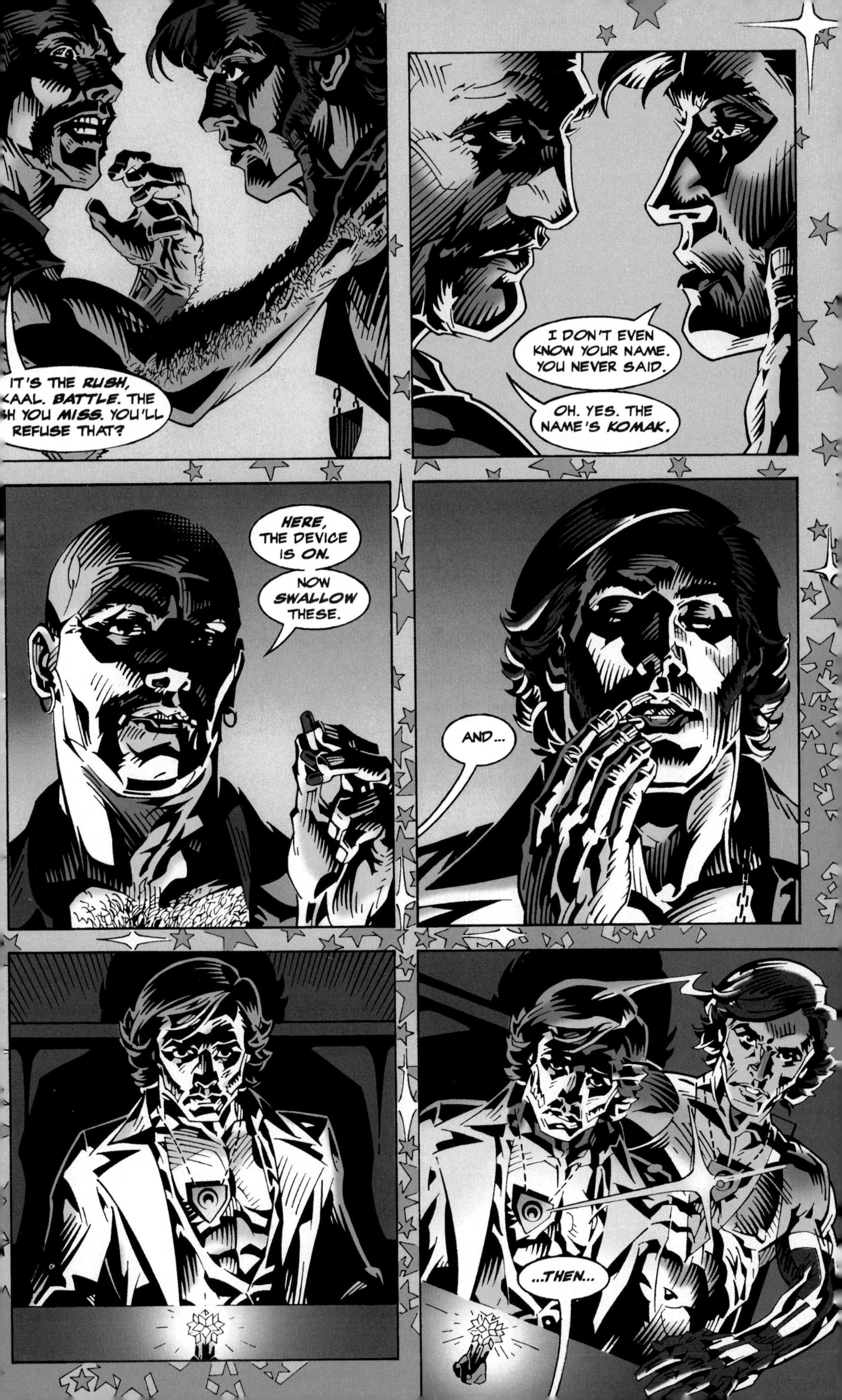
IT'S THE RUSH, KAAL. BATTLE. THE SH YOU MISS. YOU'LL REFUSE THAT?
I DON'T EVEN KNOW YOUR NAME. YOU NEVER SAID.
OH. YES. THE NAME'S KOMAK.
HERE, THE DEVICE IS ON.
NOW SWALLOW THESE.
AND...
...THEN...

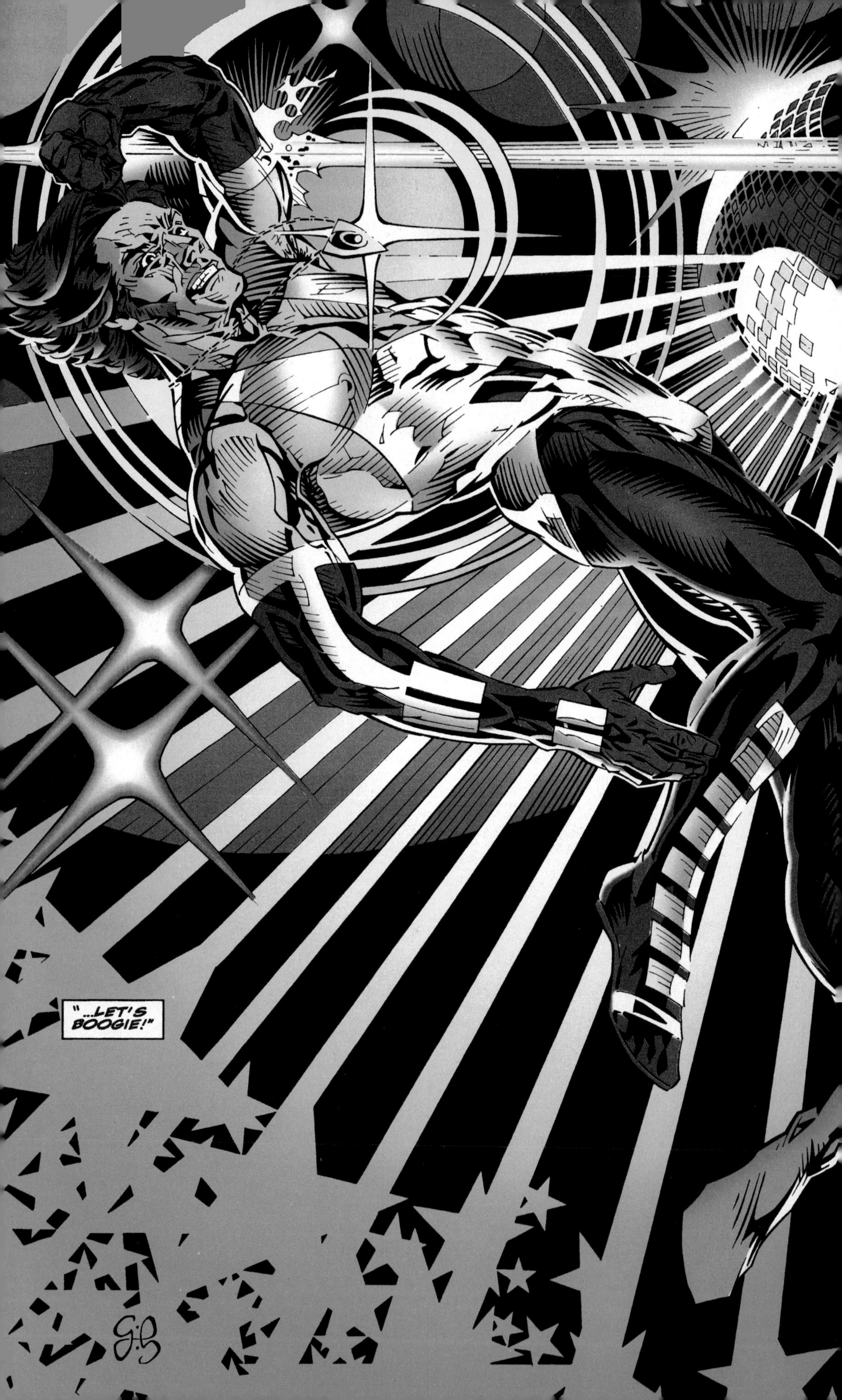
"...LET'S BOOGIE!"
G.B

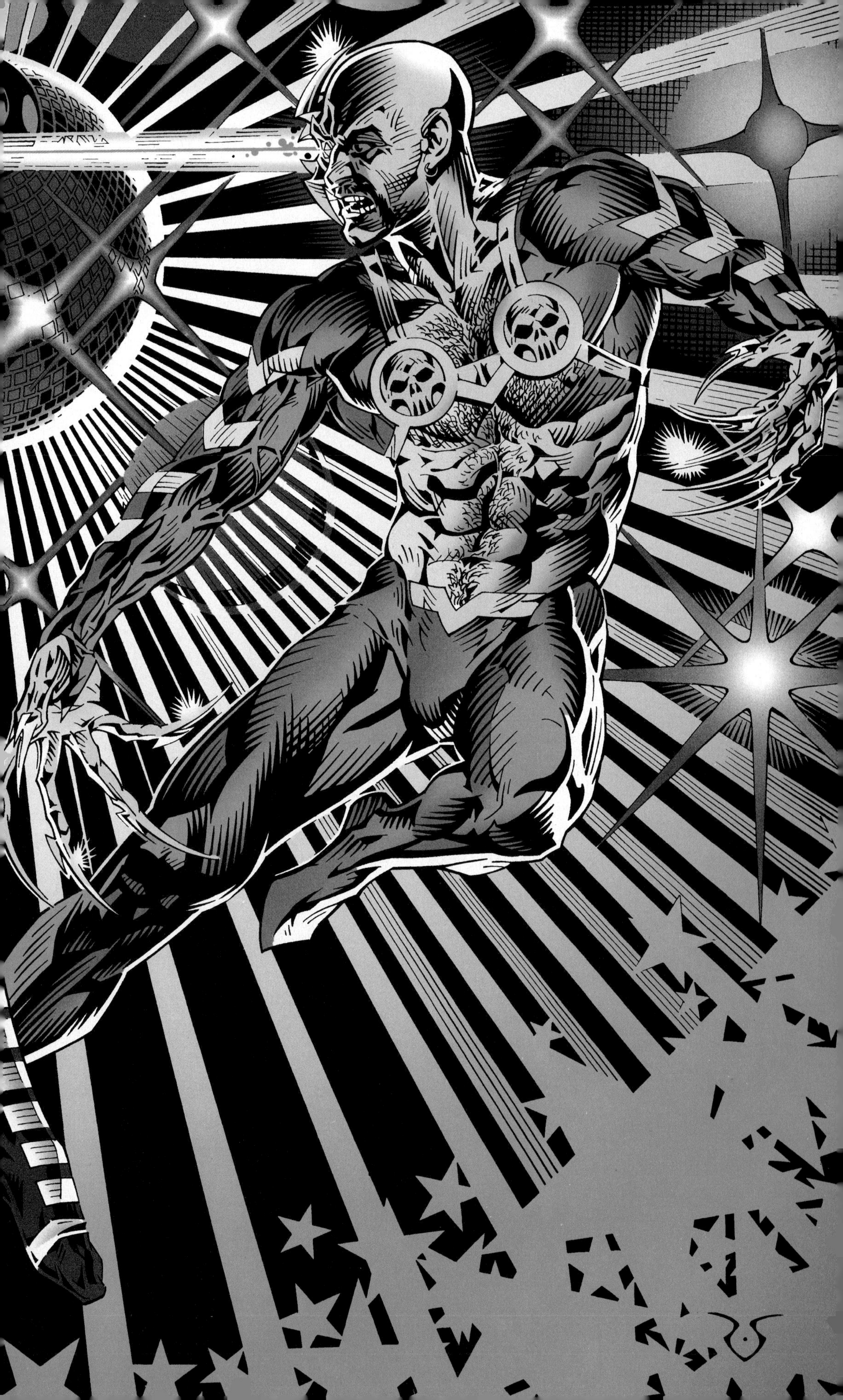

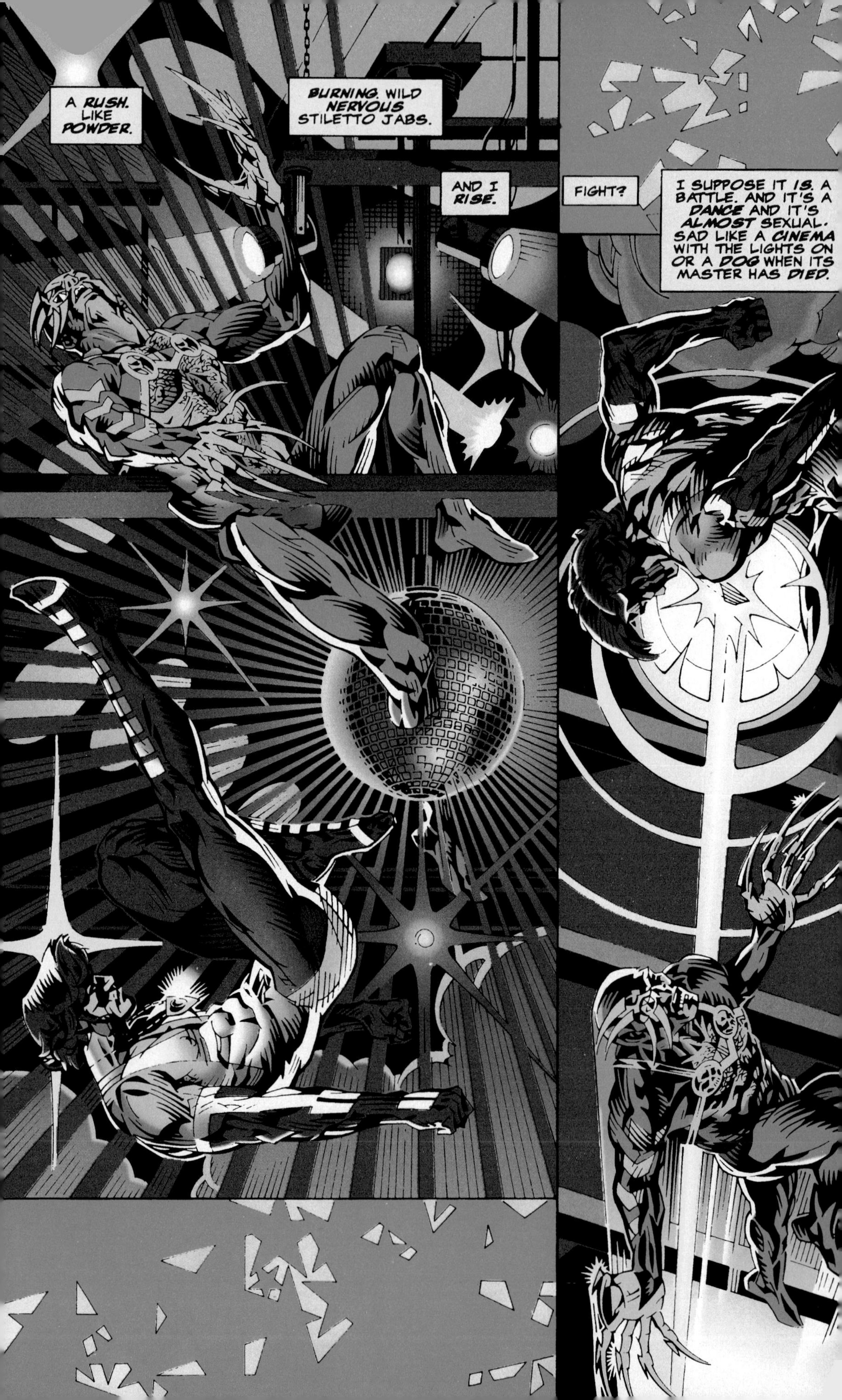
A RUSH. LIKE POWDER.
BURNING. WILD NERVOUS STILETTO JABS.
AND I RISE.
FIGHT?
I SUPPOSE IT IS. A BATTLE. AND IT'S A DANCE AND IT'S ALMOST SEXUAL. SAD LIKE A CINEMA WITH THE LIGHTS ON OR A DOG WHEN ITS MASTER HAS DIED.

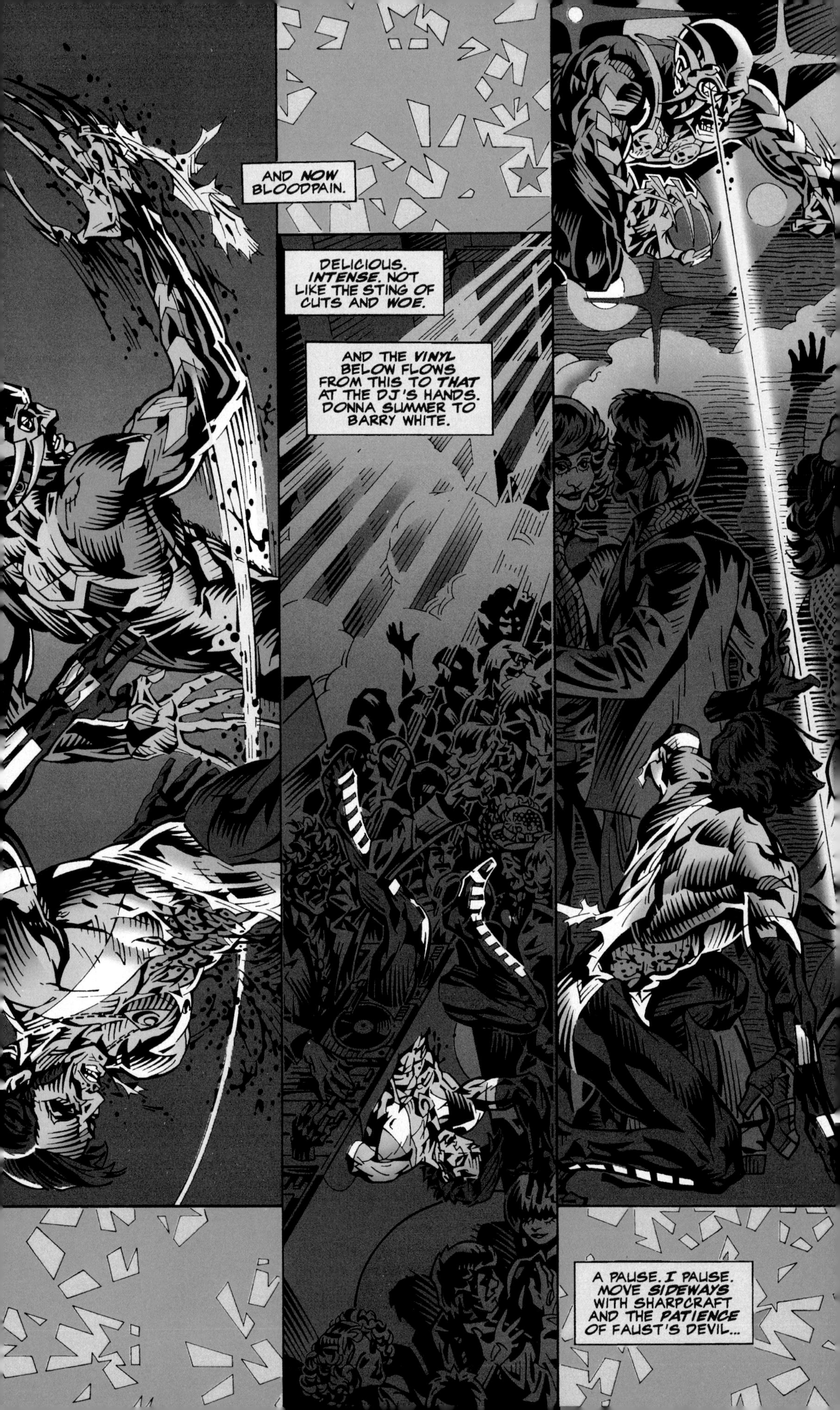
AND NOW BLOODPAIN.
DELICIOUS. INTENSE. NOT LIKE THE STING OF CUTS AND WOE.
AND THE VINYL BELOW FLOWS FROM THIS TO THAT AT THE DJ'S HANDS. DONNA SUMMER TO BARRY WHITE.
A PAUSE. I PAUSE. MOVE SIDEWAYS WITH SHARPCRAFT AND THE PATIENCE OF FAUST'S DEVIL...

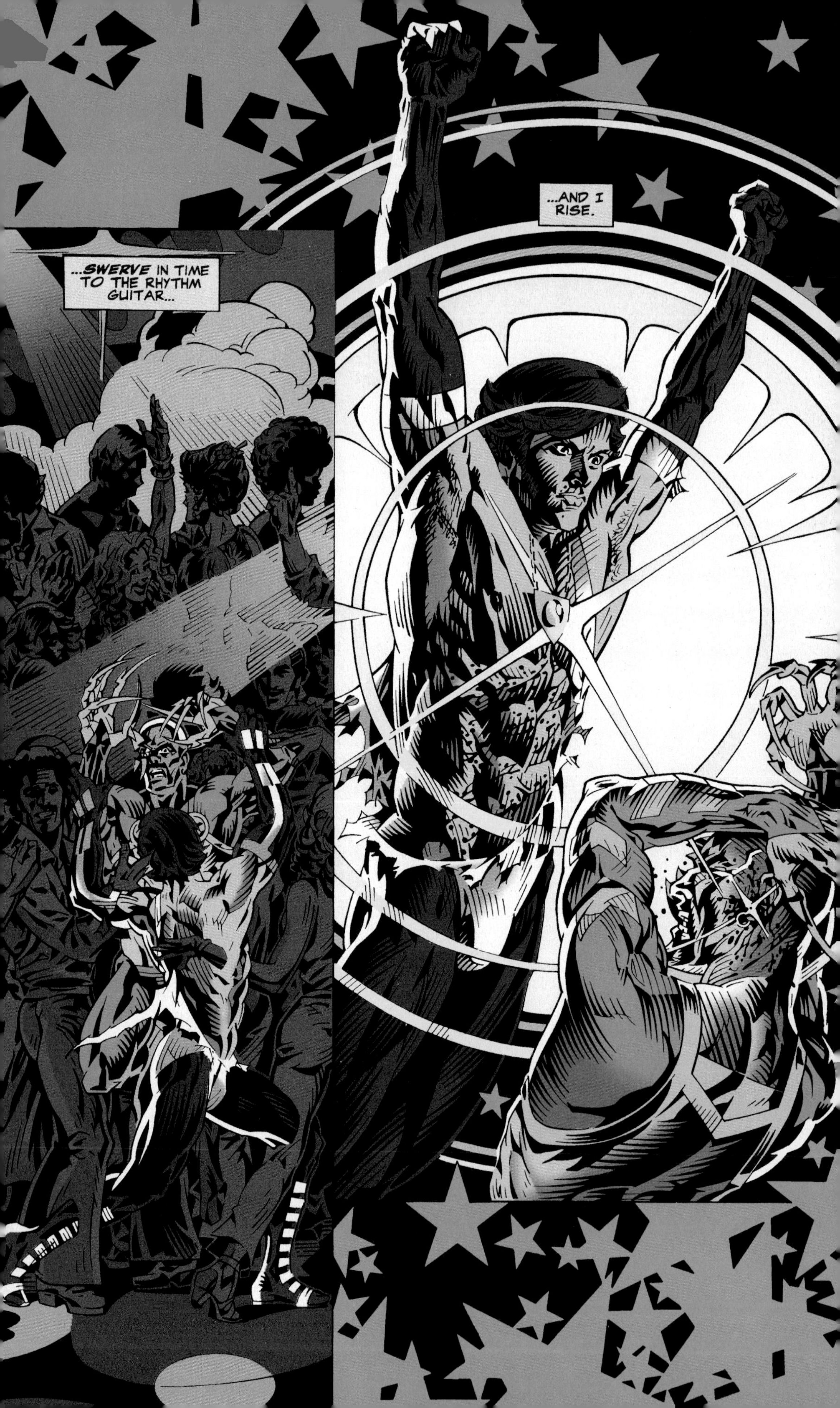
...SWERVE IN TIME TO THE RHYTHM GUITAR...
...AND I RISE.

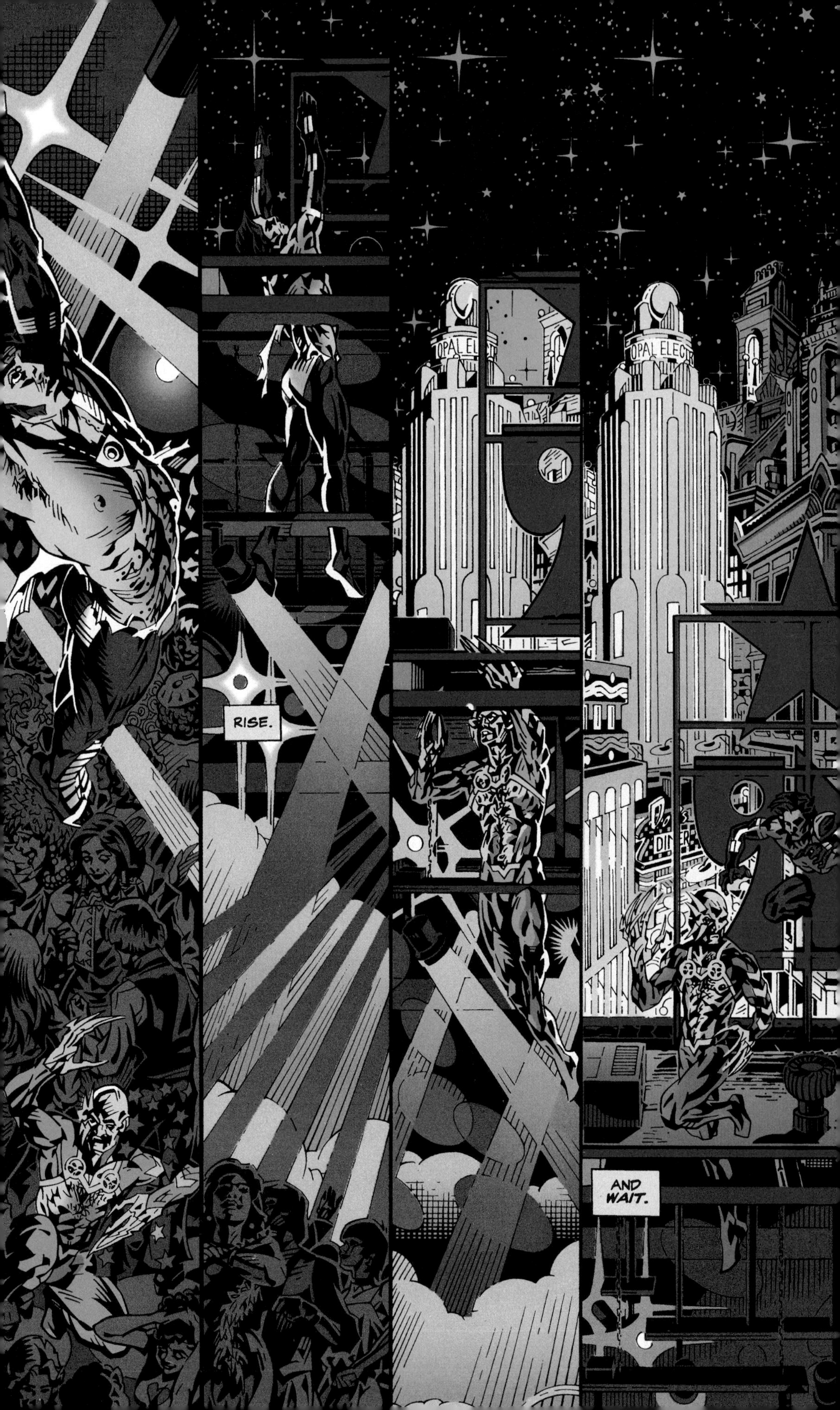
RISE.
OPAL ELECTR
OPAL ELECTR
DINER
AND WAIT.

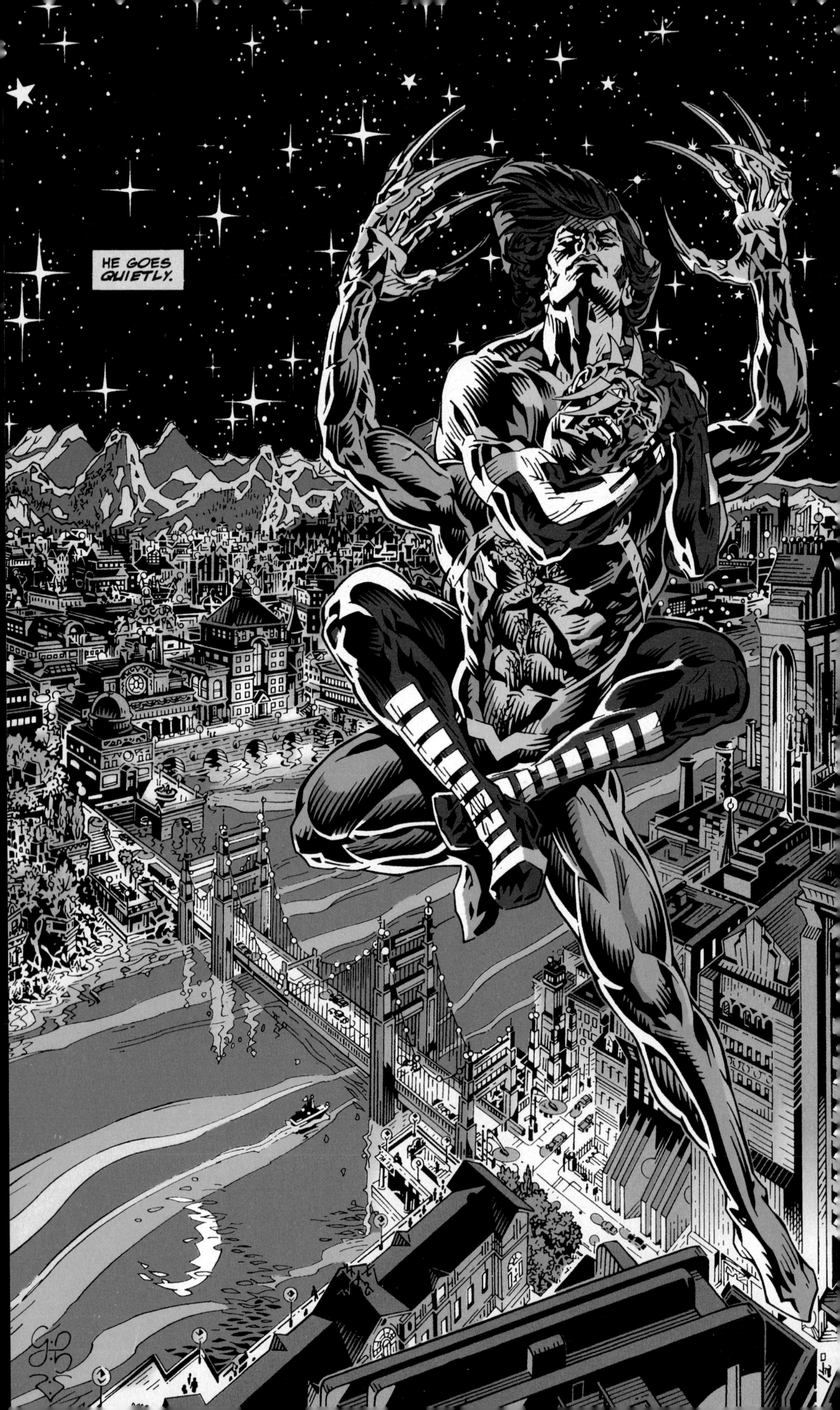
HE GOES
QUIETLY.

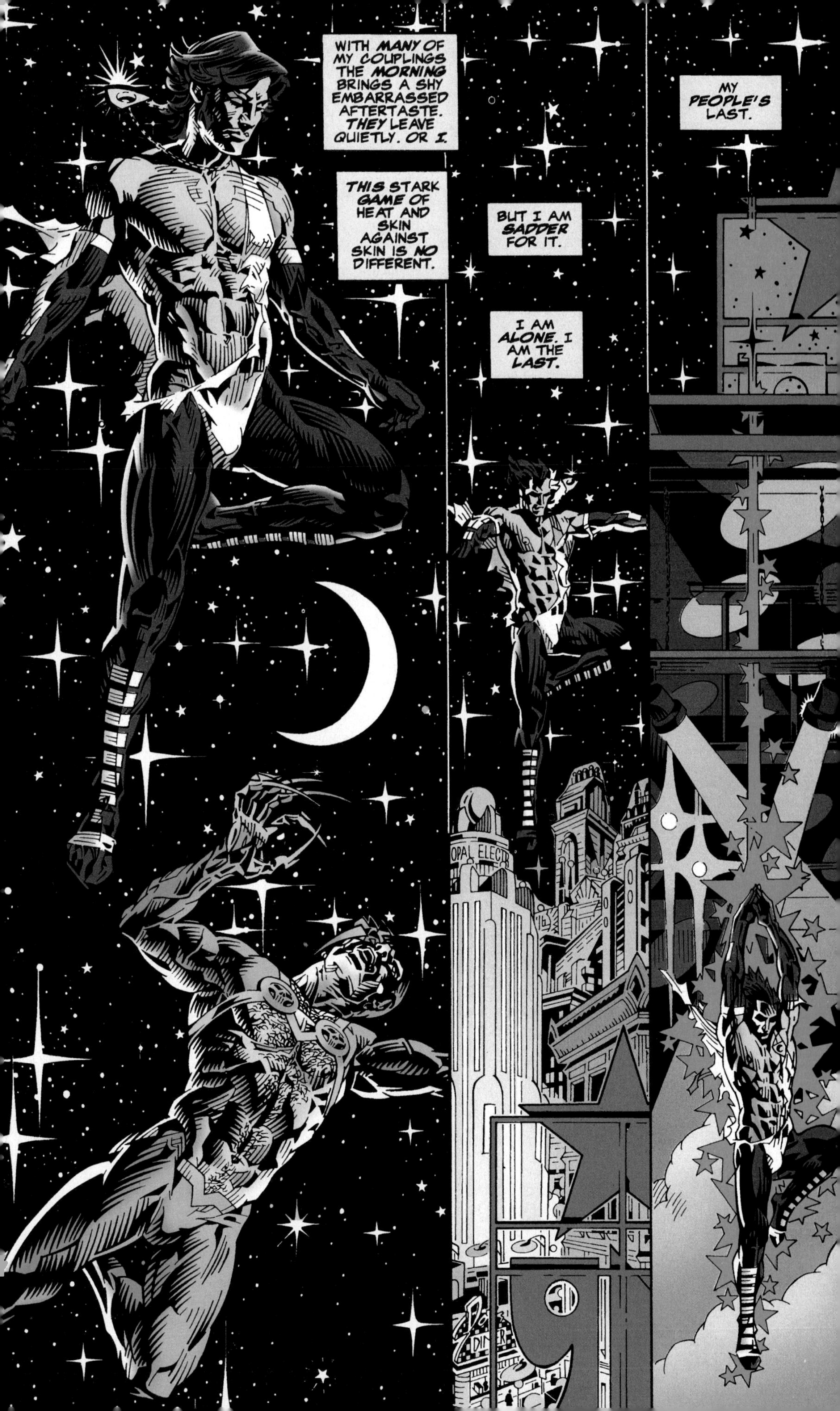
WITH MANY OF MY COUPLINGS THE MORNING BRINGS A SHY EMBARRASSED AFTERTASTE. THEY LEAVE QUIETLY. OR I.
THIS STARK GAME OF HEAT AND SKIN AGAINST SKIN IS NO DIFFERENT.
BUT I AM SADDER FOR IT.
I AM ALONE. I AM THE LAST.
MY PEOPLE'S LAST.
OPAL ELECT
DINER

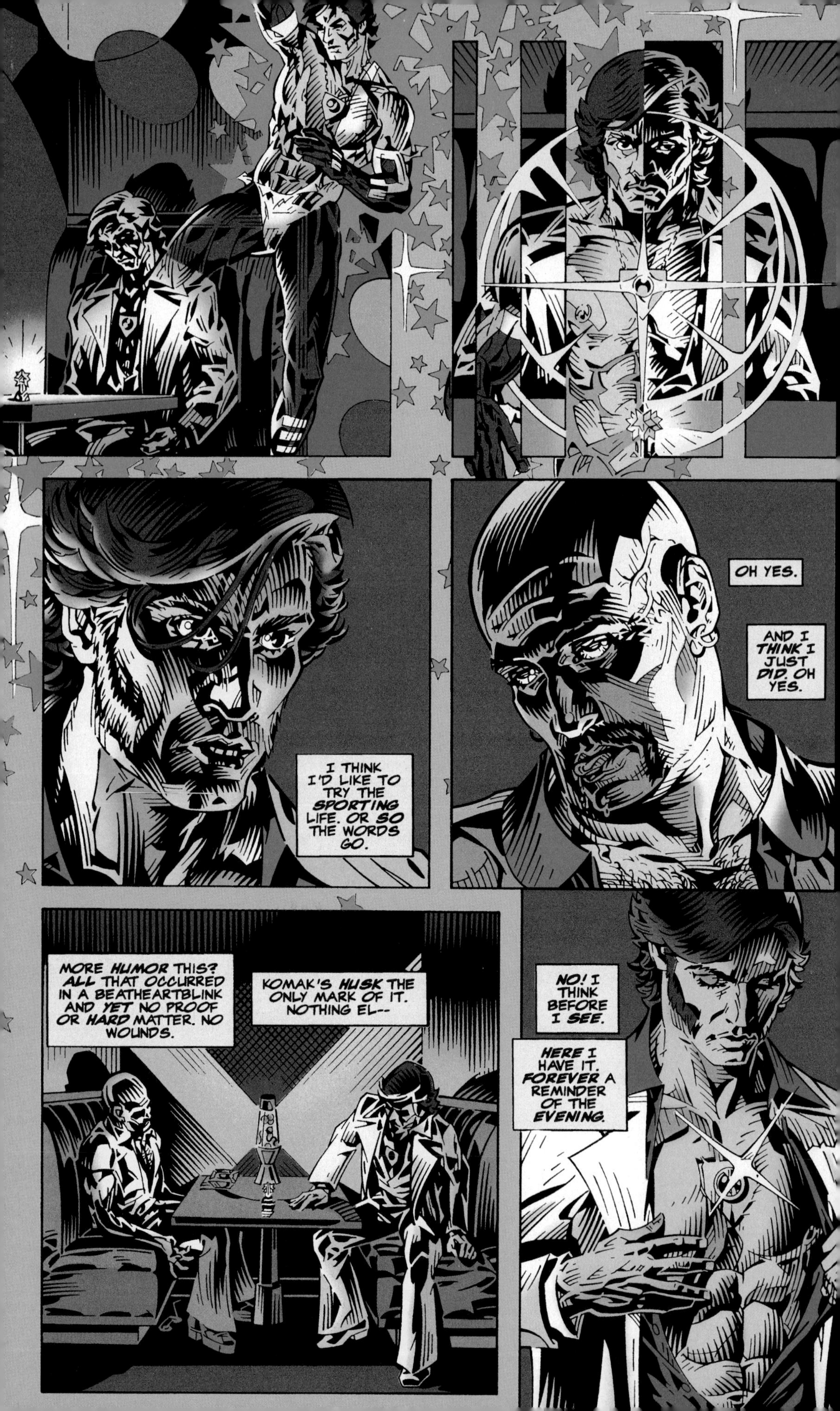
I THINK I'D LIKE TO TRY THE SPORTING LIFE. OR SO THE WORDS GO.
OH YES.
AND I THINK I JUST DID. OH YES.
MORE HUMOR THIS? ALL THAT OCCURRED IN A BEATHEARTBLINK AND YET NO PROOF OR HARD MATTER. NO WOUNDS.
KOMAK'S HUSK THE ONLY MARK OF IT. NOTHING EL--
NO! I THINK BEFORE I SEE.
HERE I HAVE IT. FOREVER A REMINDER OF THE EVENING.

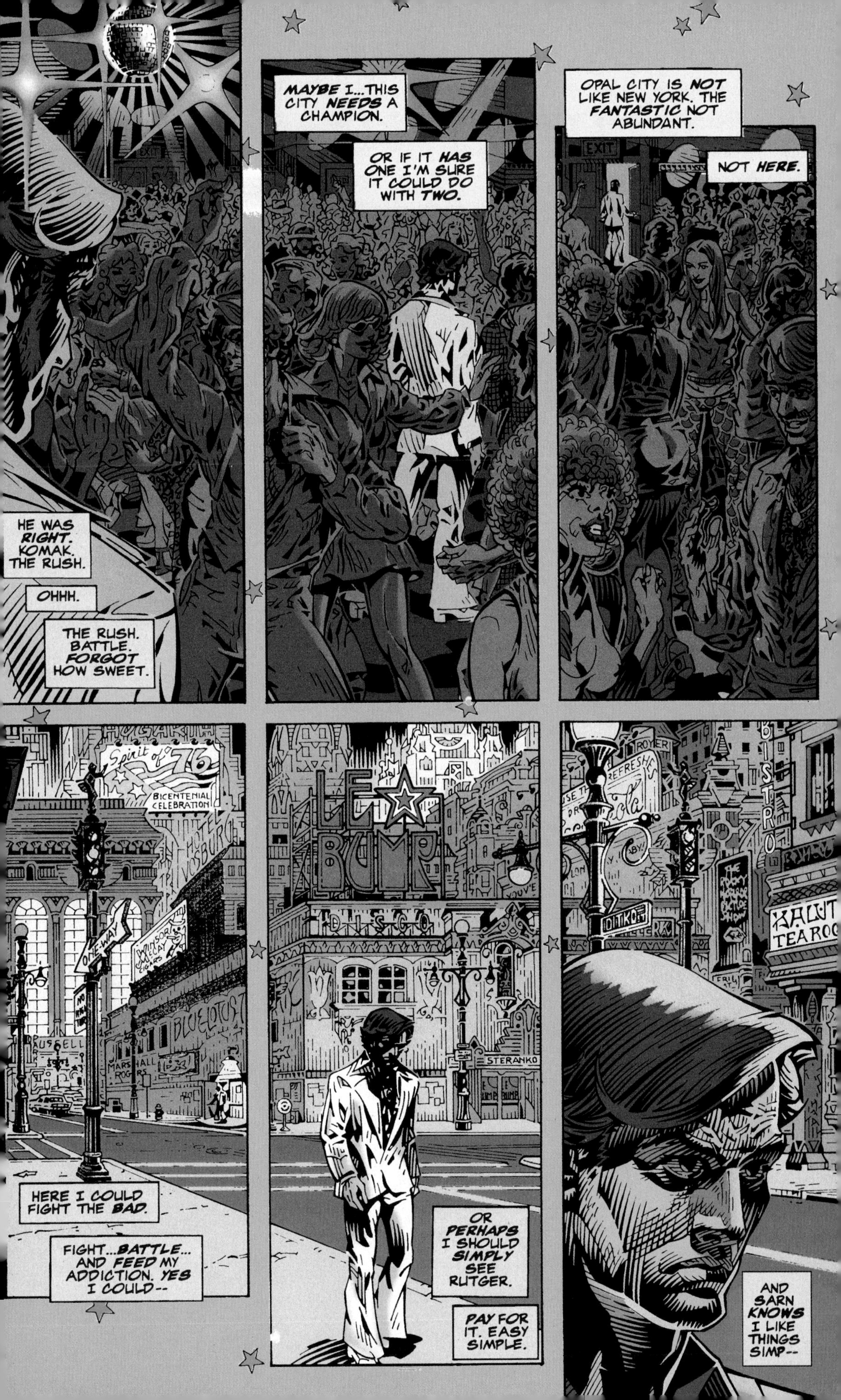
HE WAS RIGHT. KOMAK. THE RUSH.
OHHH.
THE RUSH. BATTLE. FORGOT HOW SWEET.
MAYBE I...THIS CITY NEEDS A CHAMPION.
OR IF IT HAS ONE I'M SURE IT COULD DO WITH TWO.
OPAL CITY IS NOT LIKE NEW YORK. THE FANTASTIC NOT ABUNDANT.
NOT HERE.
Spirit of '76
BICENTENIAL CELEBRATION
HOTEL VOSBURG
ONE-WAY
WINSOR McCAY CIGARS
BLUE LOTUS
RUSSELL
MARSHALL ROGERS
HERE I COULD FIGHT THE BAD.
FIGHT...BATTLE... AND FEED MY ADDICTION. YES I COULD--
LE BUMP
DISCO
STERANKO
OR PERHAPS I SHOULD SIMPLY SEE RUTGER.
PAY FOR IT. EASY SIMPLE.
ROYER
BISTRO
DITKO ST
TEAROO
AND SARN KNOWS I LIKE THINGS SIMP--

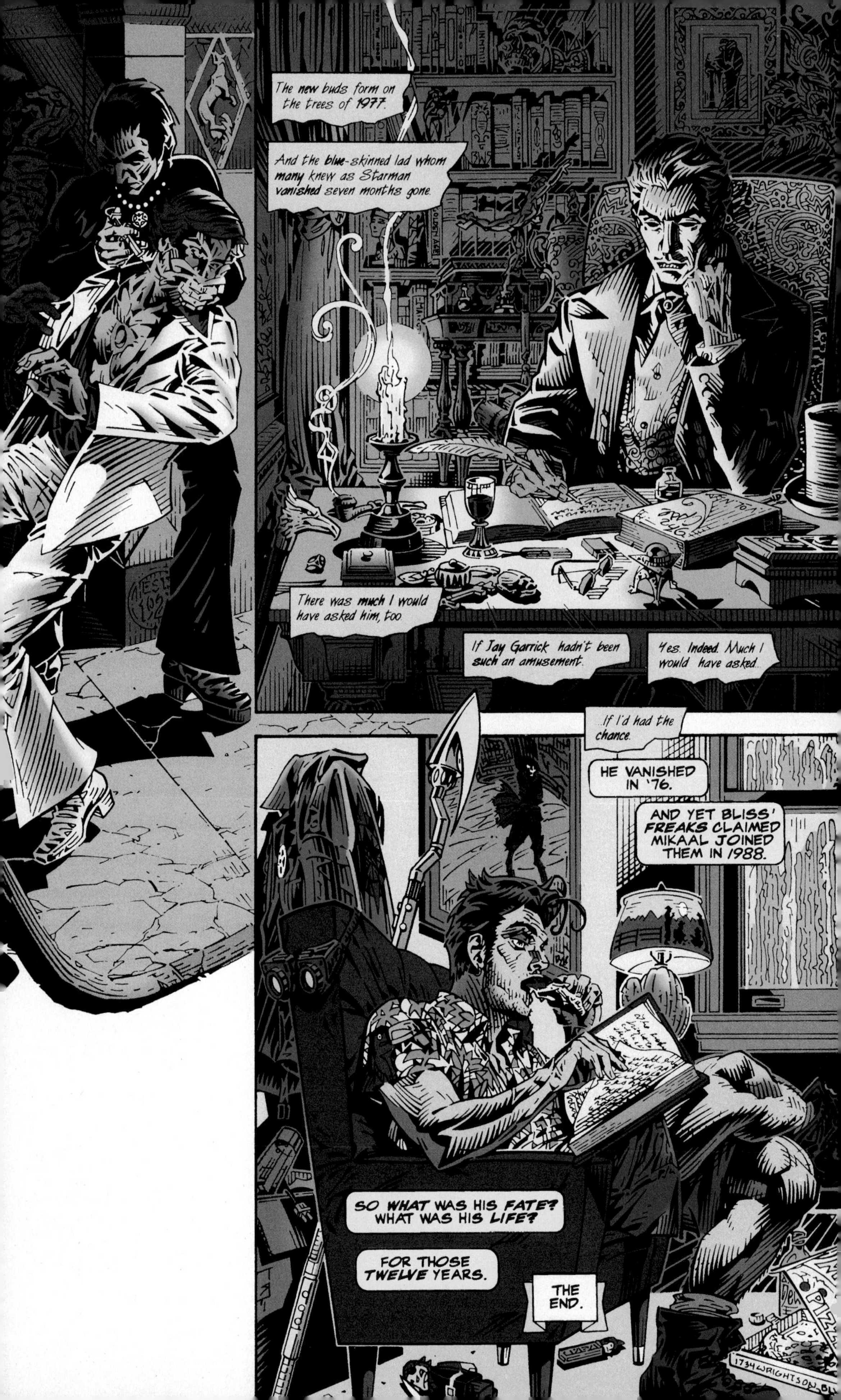

The new buds form on the trees of 1977.
And the blue-skinned lad whom many knew as Starman vanished seven months gone.
There was much I would have asked him, too.
If Jay Garrick hadn't been such an amusement.
Yes. Indeed. Much I would have asked...
...If I'd had the chance.
HE VANISHED IN '76.
AND YET BLISS' FREAKS CLAIMED MIKAAL JOINED THEM IN 1988.
SO WHAT WAS HIS FATE? WHAT WAS HIS LIFE?
FOR THOSE TWELVE YEARS.
THE END.

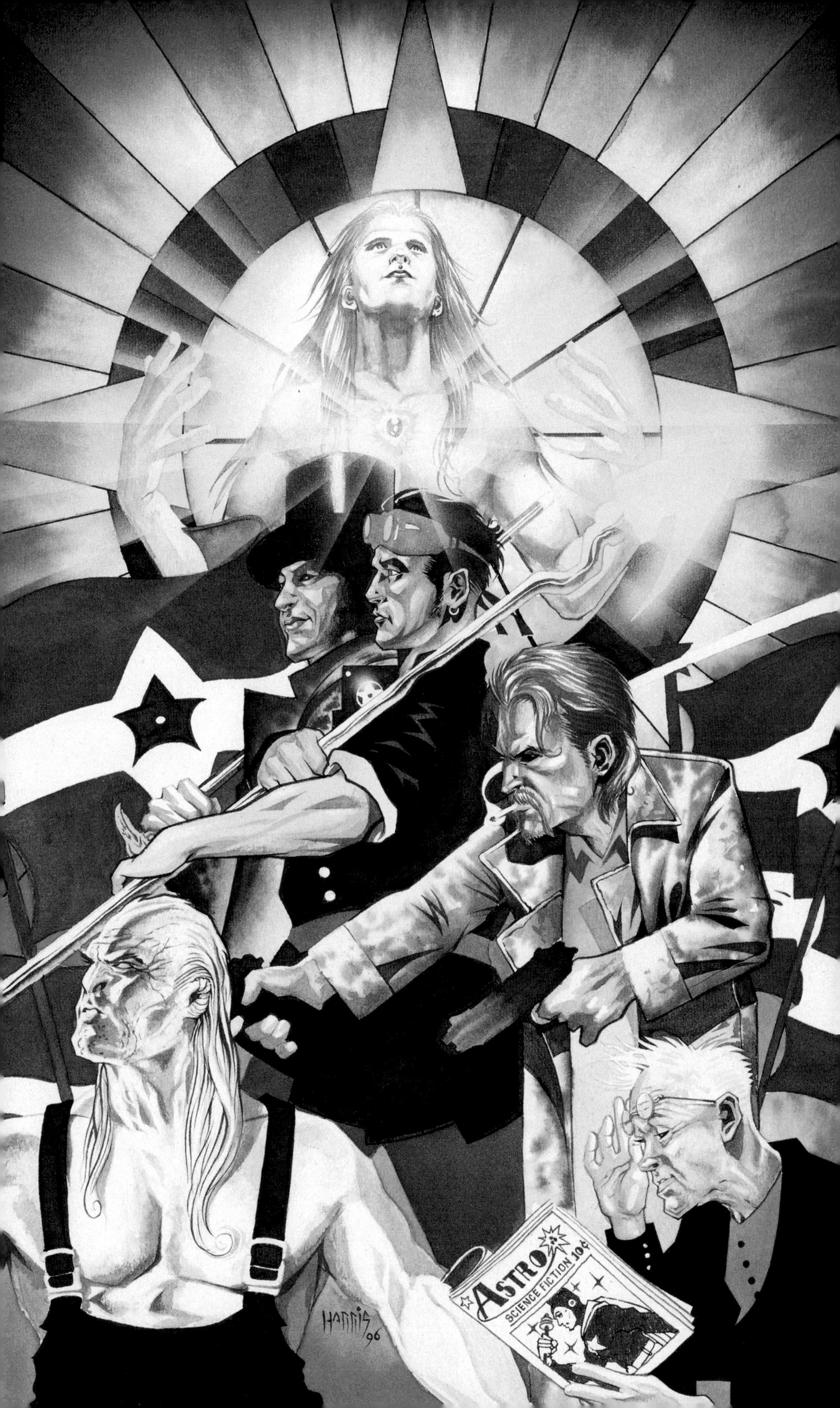
ASTRO
SCIENCE FICTION 10¢
HARRIS '96

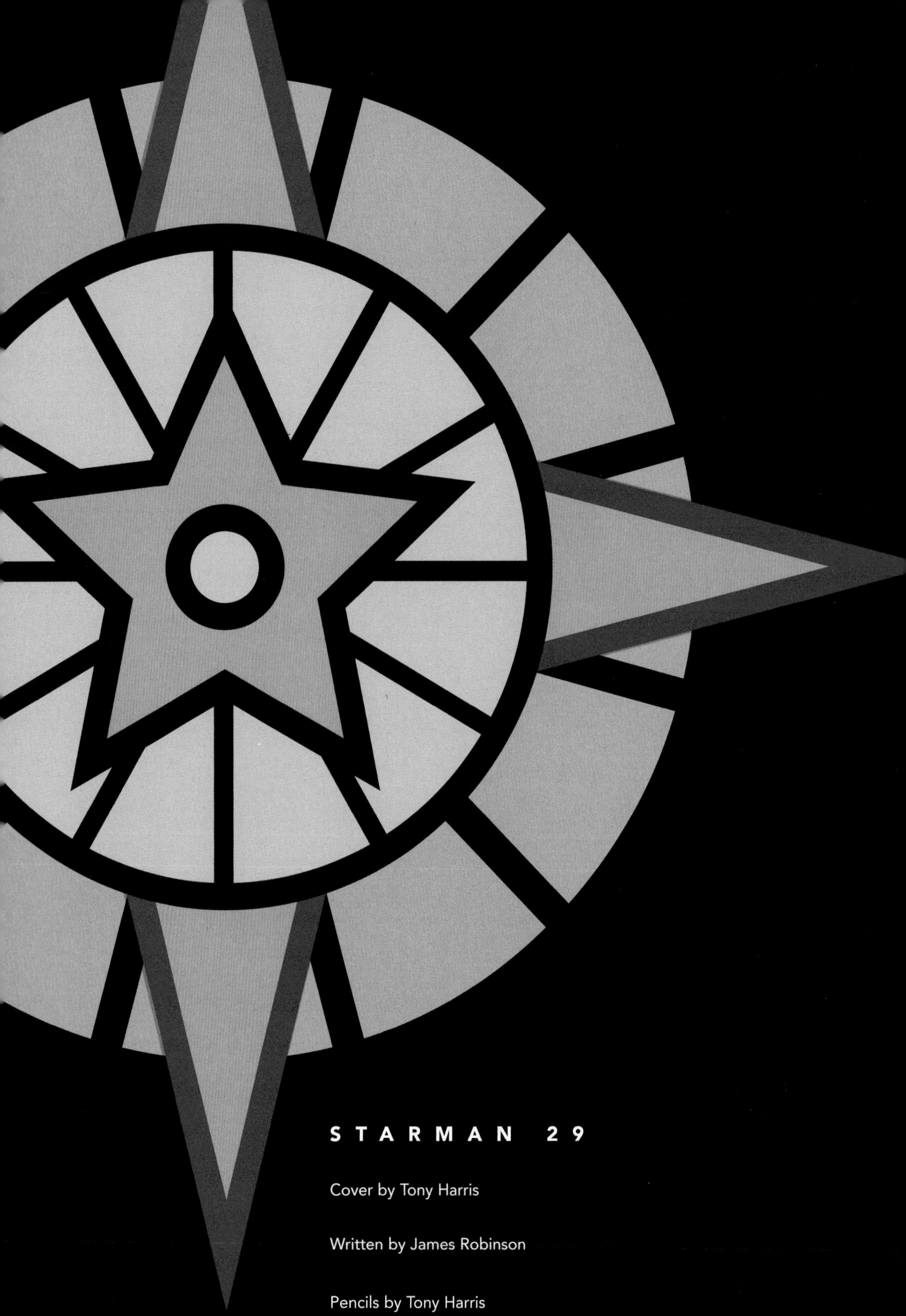

S T A R M A N   2 9

Cover by Tony Harris

Written by James Robinson

Pencils by Tony Harris

with inks by Wade von Grawbadger

and colors by Gregory Wright

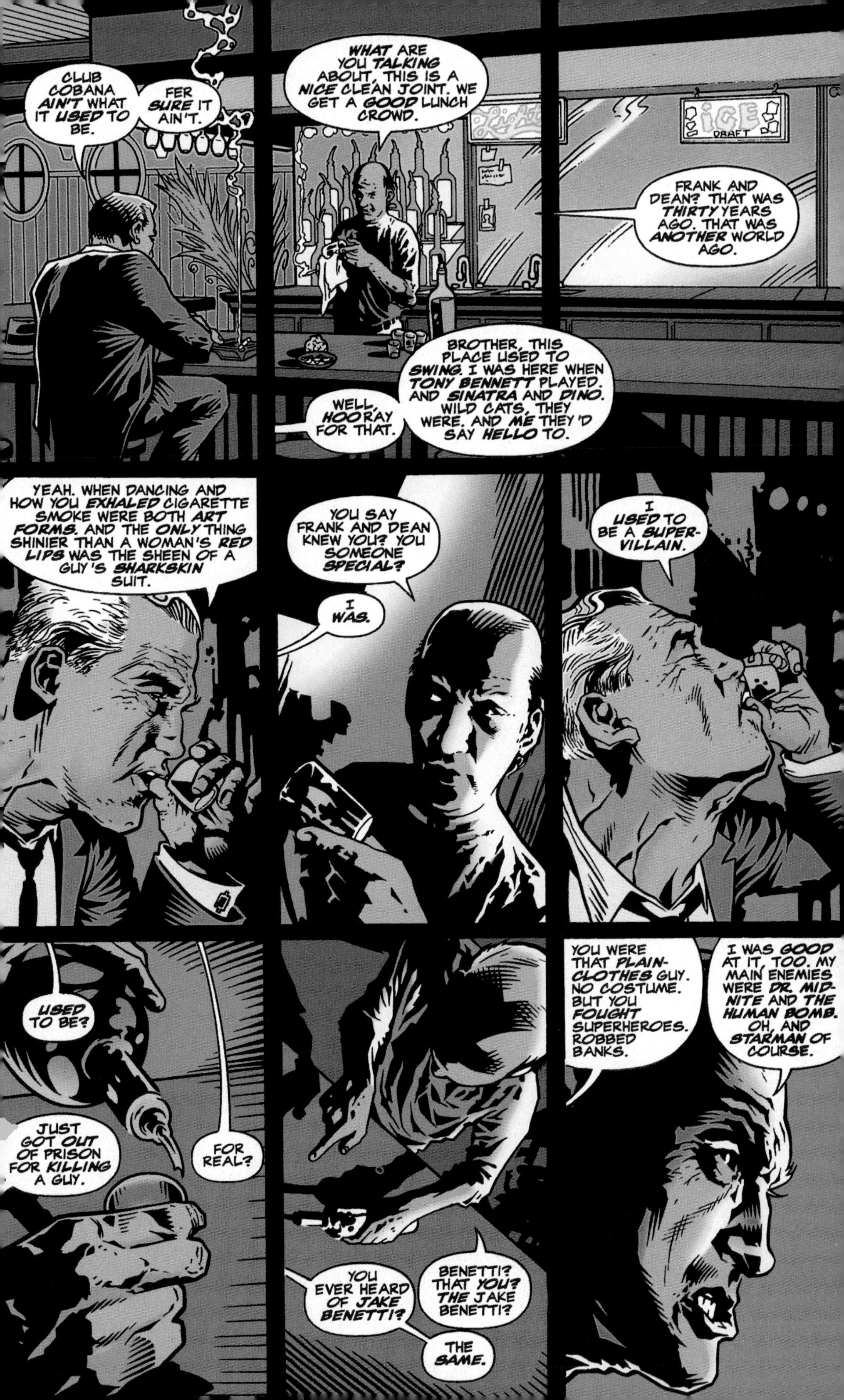
CLUB COBANA AIN'T WHAT IT USED TO BE.
FER SURE IT AIN'T.
WHAT ARE YOU TALKING ABOUT, THIS IS A NICE CLEAN JOINT. WE GET A GOOD LUNCH CROWD.
ICE DRAFT
FRANK AND DEAN? THAT WAS THIRTY YEARS AGO. THAT WAS ANOTHER WORLD AGO.
BROTHER, THIS PLACE USED TO SWING. I WAS HERE WHEN TONY BENNETT PLAYED. AND SINATRA AND DINO. WILD CATS, THEY WERE. AND ME THEY'D SAY HELLO TO.
WELL, HOORAY FOR THAT.
YEAH. WHEN DANCING AND HOW YOU EXHALED CIGARETTE SMOKE WERE BOTH ART FORMS. AND THE ONLY THING SHINIER THAN A WOMAN'S RED LIPS WAS THE SHEEN OF A GUY'S SHARKSKIN SUIT.
YOU SAY FRANK AND DEAN KNEW YOU? YOU SOMEONE SPECIAL?
I WAS.
I USED TO BE A SUPER-VILLAIN.
USED TO BE?
JUST GOT OUT OF PRISON FOR KILLING A GUY.
FOR REAL?
YOU EVER HEARD OF JAKE BENETTI?
BENETTI? THAT YOU? THE JAKE BENETTI?
THE SAME.
YOU WERE THAT PLAIN-CLOTHES GUY. NO COSTUME. BUT YOU FOUGHT SUPERHEROES. ROBBED BANKS.
I WAS GOOD AT IT, TOO. MY MAIN ENEMIES WERE DR. MID-NITE AND THE HUMAN BOMB. OH, AND STARMAN OF COURSE.

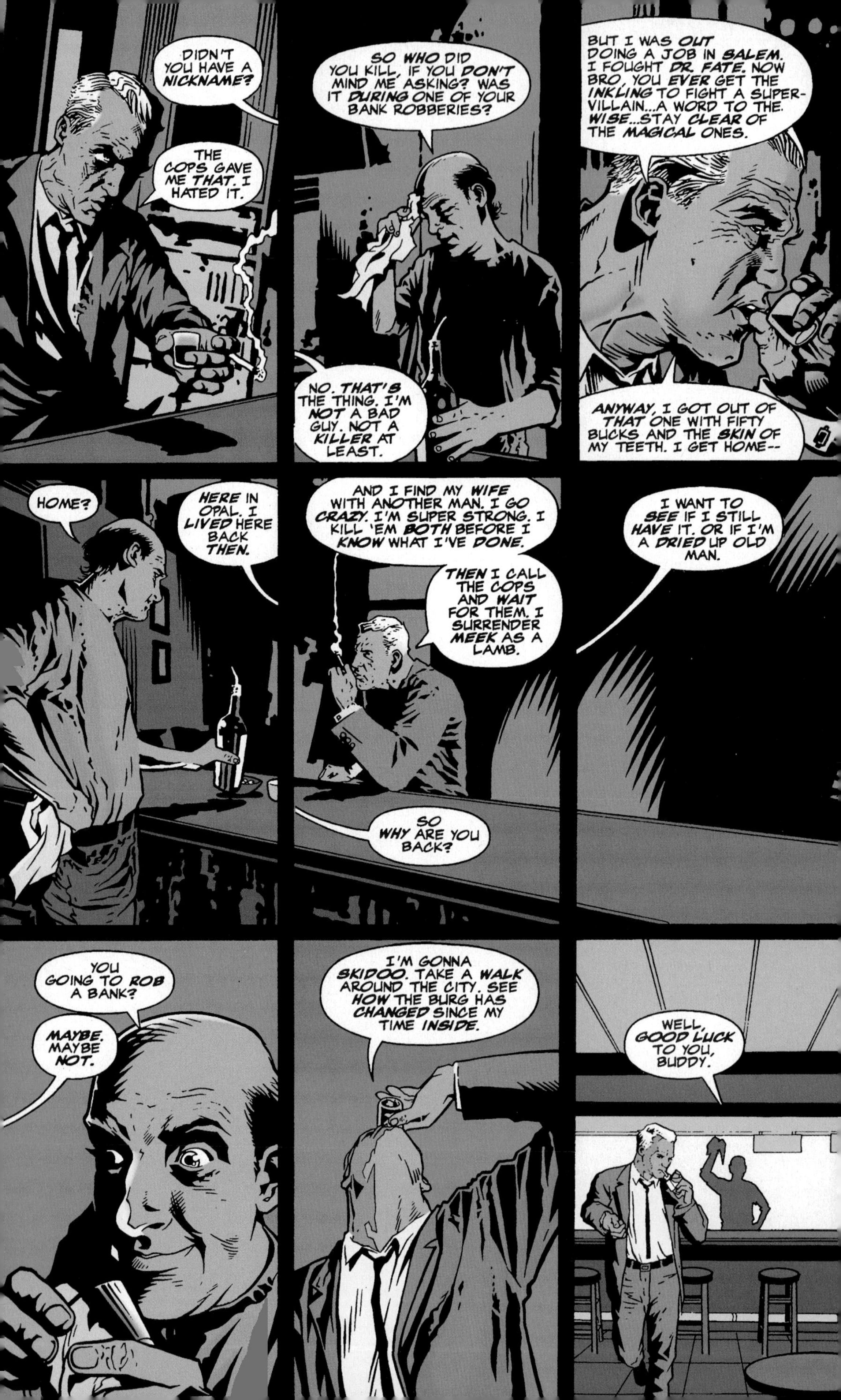

DIDN'T YOU HAVE A NICKNAME?
THE COPS GAVE ME THAT. I HATED IT.
SO WHO DID YOU KILL, IF YOU DON'T MIND ME ASKING? WAS IT DURING ONE OF YOUR BANK ROBBERIES?
NO. THAT'S THE THING. I'M NOT A BAD GUY. NOT A KILLER AT LEAST.
BUT I WAS OUT DOING A JOB IN SALEM. I FOUGHT DR. FATE. NOW BRO, YOU EVER GET THE INKLING TO FIGHT A SUPER-VILLAIN...A WORD TO THE WISE...STAY CLEAR OF THE MAGICAL ONES.
ANYWAY, I GOT OUT OF THAT ONE WITH FIFTY BUCKS AND THE SKIN OF MY TEETH. I GET HOME--
HOME?
HERE IN OPAL. I LIVED HERE BACK THEN.
AND I FIND MY WIFE WITH ANOTHER MAN. I GO CRAZY. I'M SUPER STRONG. I KILL 'EM BOTH BEFORE I KNOW WHAT I'VE DONE.
THEN I CALL THE COPS AND WAIT FOR THEM. I SURRENDER MEEK AS A LAMB.
SO WHY ARE YOU BACK?
I WANT TO SEE IF I STILL HAVE IT. OR IF I'M A DRIED UP OLD MAN.
YOU GOING TO ROB A BANK?
MAYBE. MAYBE NOT.
I'M GONNA SKIDOO. TAKE A WALK AROUND THE CITY. SEE HOW THE BURG HAS CHANGED SINCE MY TIME INSIDE.
WELL, GOOD LUCK TO YOU, BUDDY.

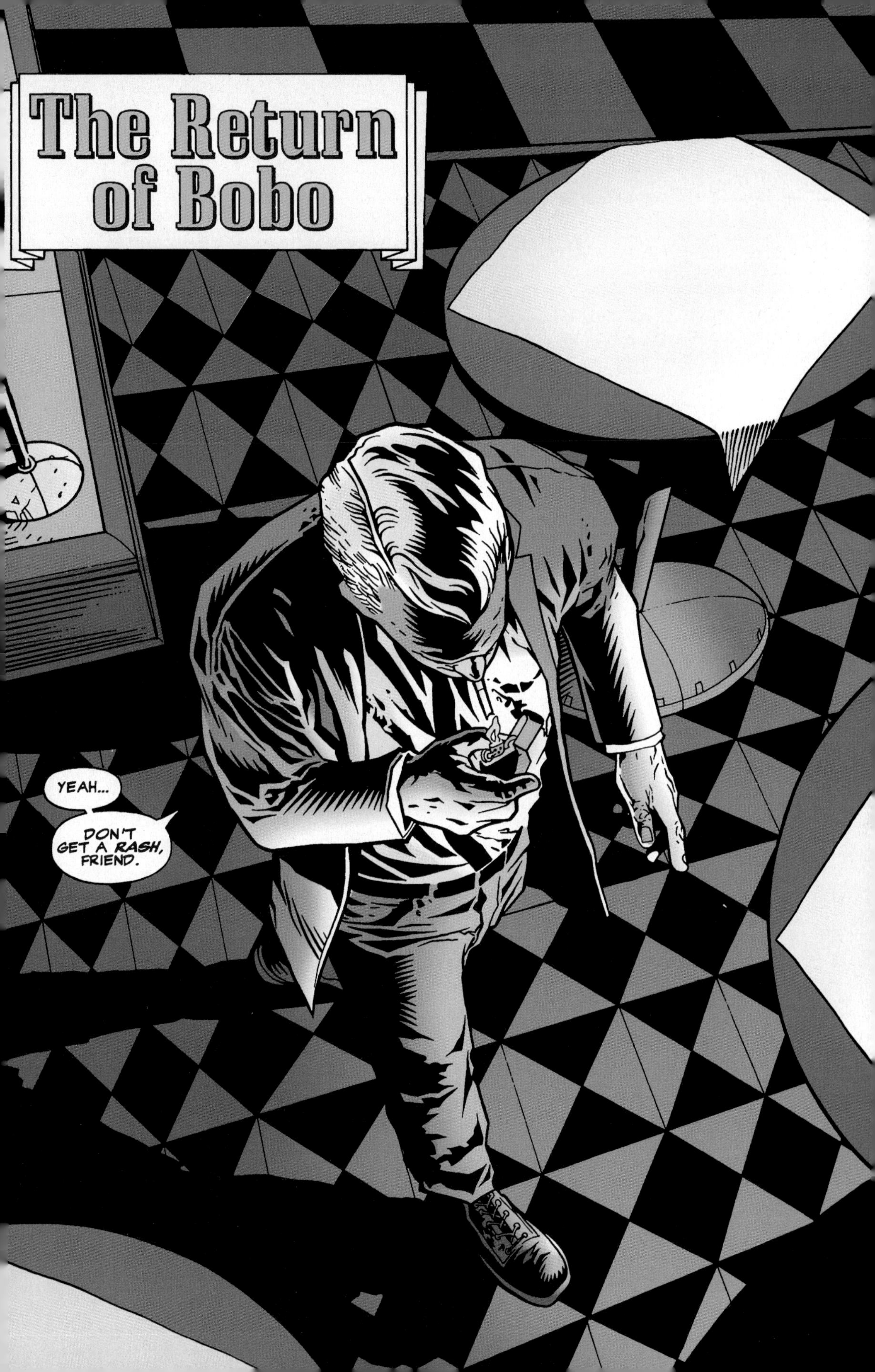
The Return of Bobo
YEAH...
DON'T GET A RASH, FRIEND.

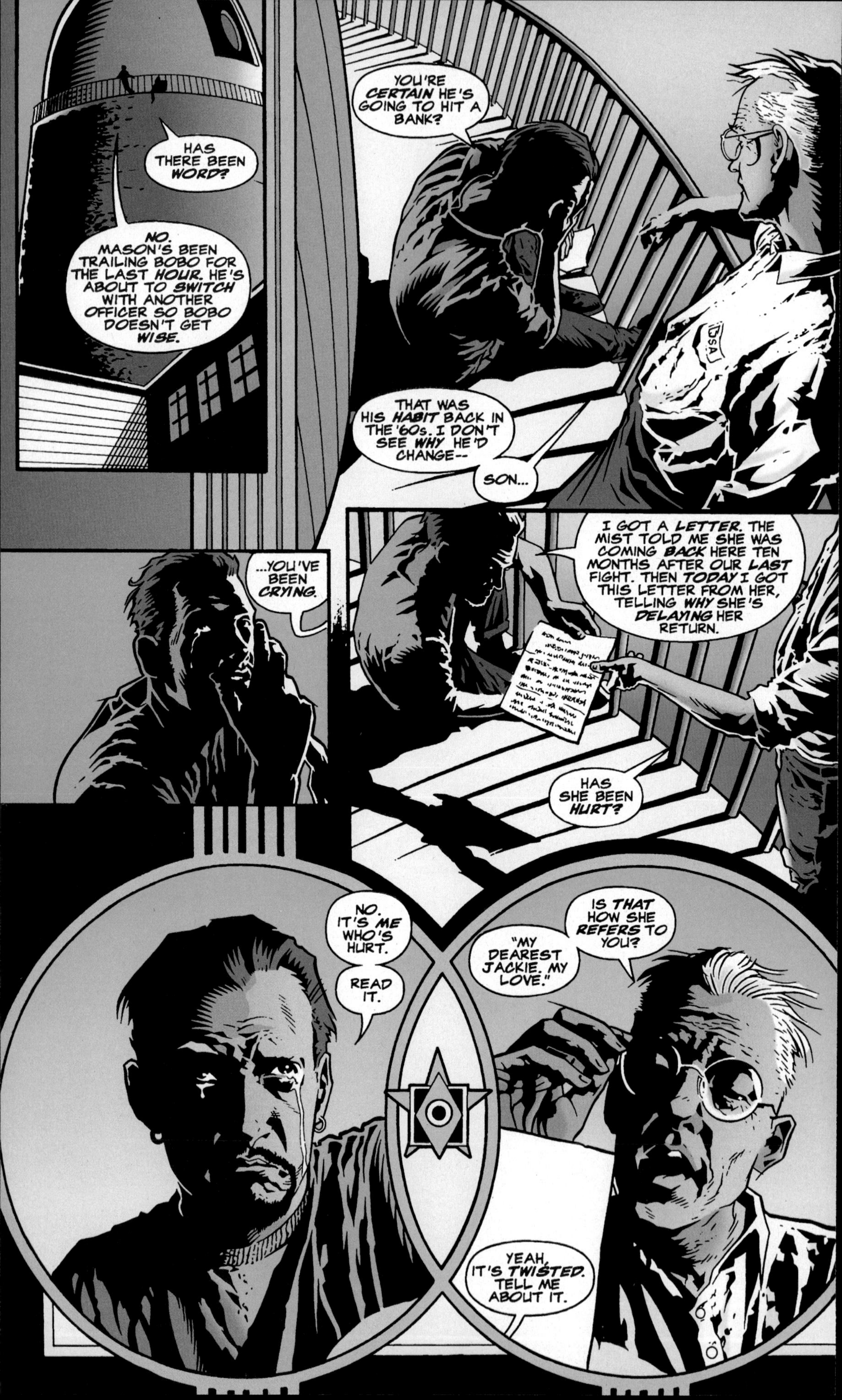
HAS THERE BEEN WORD?
NO. MASON'S BEEN TRAILING BOBO FOR THE LAST HOUR. HE'S ABOUT TO SWITCH WITH ANOTHER OFFICER SO BOBO DOESN'T GET WISE.
YOU'RE CERTAIN HE'S GOING TO HIT A BANK?
THAT WAS HIS HABIT BACK IN THE '60s. I DON'T SEE WHY HE'D CHANGE--
SON...
...YOU'VE BEEN CRYING.
I GOT A LETTER. THE MIST TOLD ME SHE WAS COMING BACK HERE TEN MONTHS AFTER OUR LAST FIGHT. THEN TODAY I GOT THIS LETTER FROM HER, TELLING WHY SHE'S DELAYING HER RETURN.
HAS SHE BEEN HURT?
NO. IT'S ME WHO'S HURT.
READ IT.
"MY DEAREST JACKIE. MY LOVE."
IS THAT HOW SHE REFERS TO YOU?
YEAH, IT'S TWISTED. TELL ME ABOUT IT.

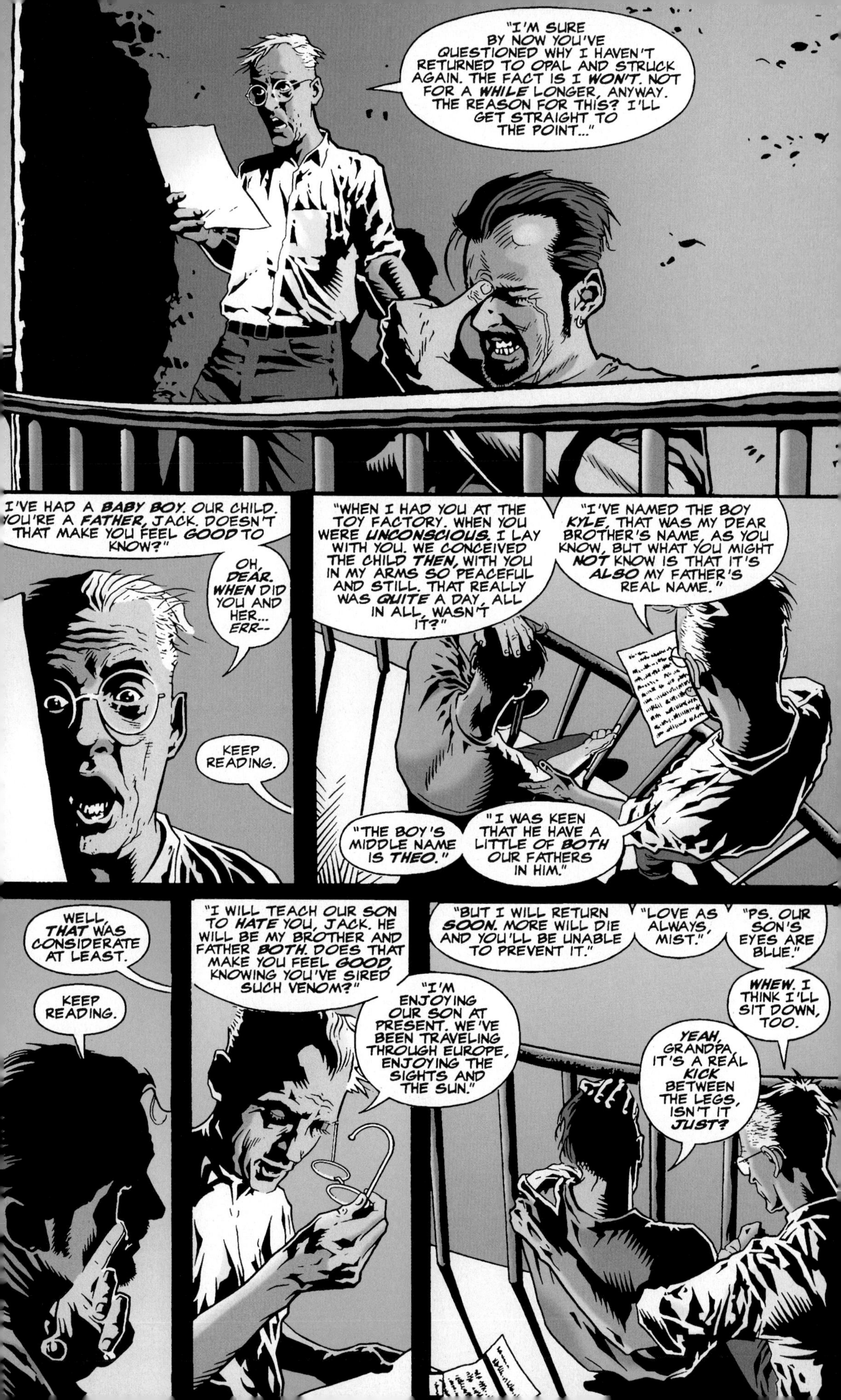
"I'M SURE BY NOW YOU'VE QUESTIONED WHY I HAVEN'T RETURNED TO OPAL AND STRUCK AGAIN. THE FACT IS I WON'T. NOT FOR A WHILE LONGER, ANYWAY. THE REASON FOR THIS? I'LL GET STRAIGHT TO THE POINT..."
I'VE HAD A BABY BOY. OUR CHILD. YOU'RE A FATHER, JACK. DOESN'T THAT MAKE YOU FEEL GOOD TO KNOW?"
OH, DEAR. WHEN DID YOU AND HER... ERR--
KEEP READING.
"WHEN I HAD YOU AT THE TOY FACTORY. WHEN YOU WERE UNCONSCIOUS. I LAY WITH YOU. WE CONCEIVED THE CHILD THEN, WITH YOU IN MY ARMS SO PEACEFUL AND STILL. THAT REALLY WAS QUITE A DAY, ALL IN ALL, WASN'T IT?"
"I'VE NAMED THE BOY KYLE. THAT WAS MY DEAR BROTHER'S NAME, AS YOU KNOW, BUT WHAT YOU MIGHT NOT KNOW IS THAT IT'S ALSO MY FATHER'S REAL NAME."
"THE BOY'S MIDDLE NAME IS THEO."
"I WAS KEEN THAT HE HAVE A LITTLE OF BOTH OUR FATHERS IN HIM."
WELL, THAT WAS CONSIDERATE AT LEAST.
KEEP READING.
"I WILL TEACH OUR SON TO HATE YOU, JACK. HE WILL BE MY BROTHER AND FATHER BOTH. DOES THAT MAKE YOU FEEL GOOD, KNOWING YOU'VE SIRED SUCH VENOM?"
"I'M ENJOYING OUR SON AT PRESENT. WE'VE BEEN TRAVELING THROUGH EUROPE, ENJOYING THE SIGHTS AND THE SUN."
"BUT I WILL RETURN SOON. MORE WILL DIE AND YOU'LL BE UNABLE TO PREVENT IT."
"LOVE AS ALWAYS, MIST."
"PS. OUR SON'S EYES ARE BLUE."
WHEW. I THINK I'LL SIT DOWN, TOO.
YEAH, GRANDPA, IT'S A REAL KICK BETWEEN THE LEGS, ISN'T IT JUST?

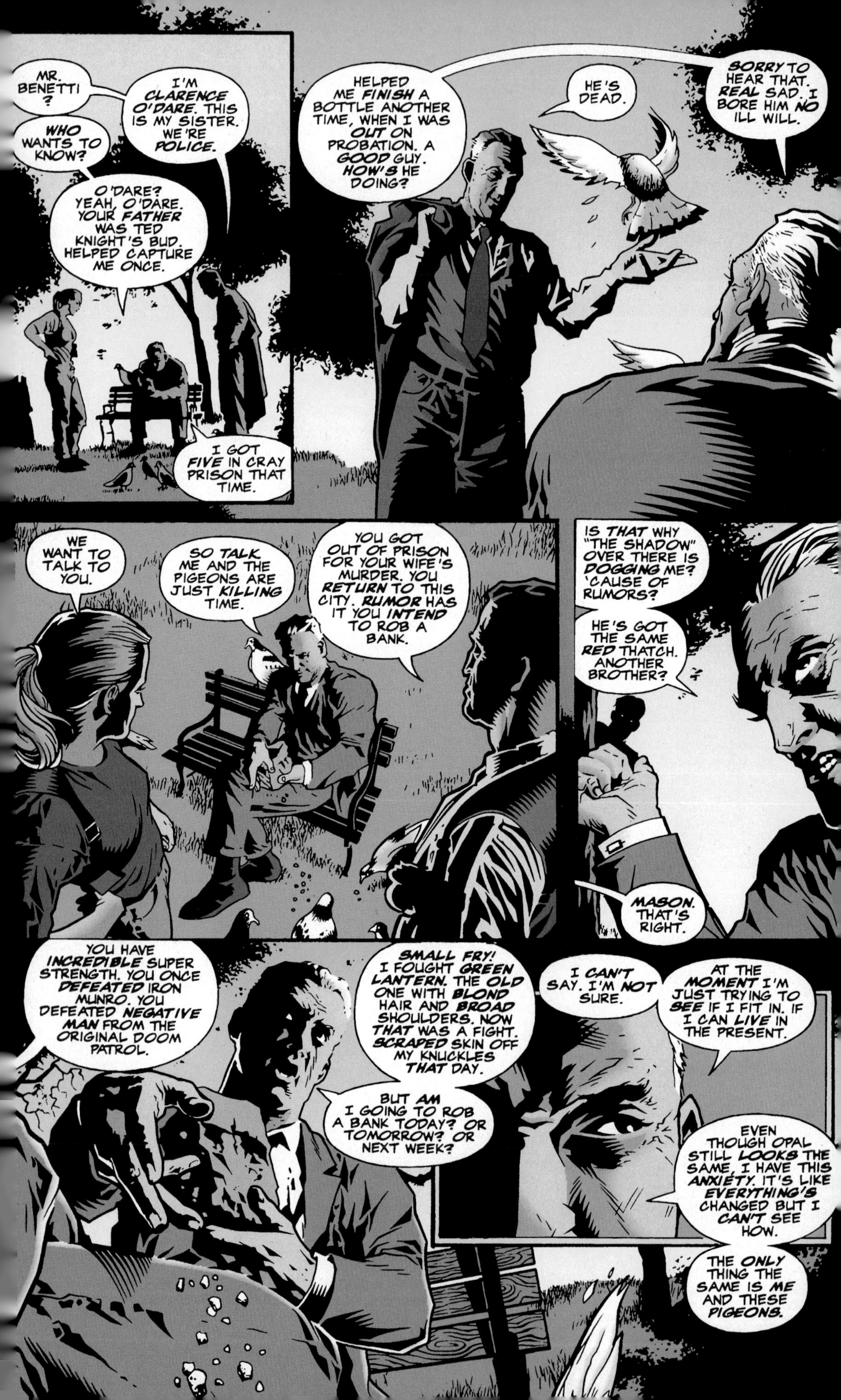

MR. BENETTI?
I'M CLARENCE O'DARE. THIS IS MY SISTER. WE'RE POLICE.
WHO WANTS TO KNOW?
O'DARE? YEAH, O'DARE. YOUR FATHER WAS TED KNIGHT'S BUD. HELPED CAPTURE ME ONCE.
I GOT FIVE IN CRAY PRISON THAT TIME.
HELPED ME FINISH A BOTTLE ANOTHER TIME, WHEN I WAS OUT ON PROBATION. A GOOD GUY. HOW'S HE DOING?
HE'S DEAD.
SORRY TO HEAR THAT. REAL SAD. I BORE HIM NO ILL WILL.
WE WANT TO TALK TO YOU.
SO TALK. ME AND THE PIGEONS ARE JUST KILLING TIME.
YOU GOT OUT OF PRISON FOR YOUR WIFE'S MURDER. YOU RETURN TO THIS CITY. RUMOR HAS IT YOU INTEND TO ROB A BANK.
IS THAT WHY "THE SHADOW" OVER THERE IS DOGGING ME? 'CAUSE OF RUMORS?
HE'S GOT THE SAME RED THATCH. ANOTHER BROTHER?
MASON. THAT'S RIGHT.
YOU HAVE INCREDIBLE SUPER STRENGTH. YOU ONCE DEFEATED IRON MUNRO. YOU DEFEATED NEGATIVE MAN FROM THE ORIGINAL DOOM PATROL.
SMALL FRY! I FOUGHT GREEN LANTERN. THE OLD ONE WITH BLOND HAIR AND BROAD SHOULDERS. NOW THAT WAS A FIGHT. SCRAPED SKIN OFF MY KNUCKLES THAT DAY.
BUT AM I GOING TO ROB A BANK TODAY? OR TOMORROW? OR NEXT WEEK?
I CAN'T SAY. I'M NOT SURE.
AT THE MOMENT I'M JUST TRYING TO SEE IF I FIT IN. IF I CAN LIVE IN THE PRESENT.
EVEN THOUGH OPAL STILL LOOKS THE SAME, I HAVE THIS ANXIETY. IT'S LIKE EVERYTHING'S CHANGED BUT I CAN'T SEE HOW.
THE ONLY THING THE SAME IS ME AND THESE PIGEONS.

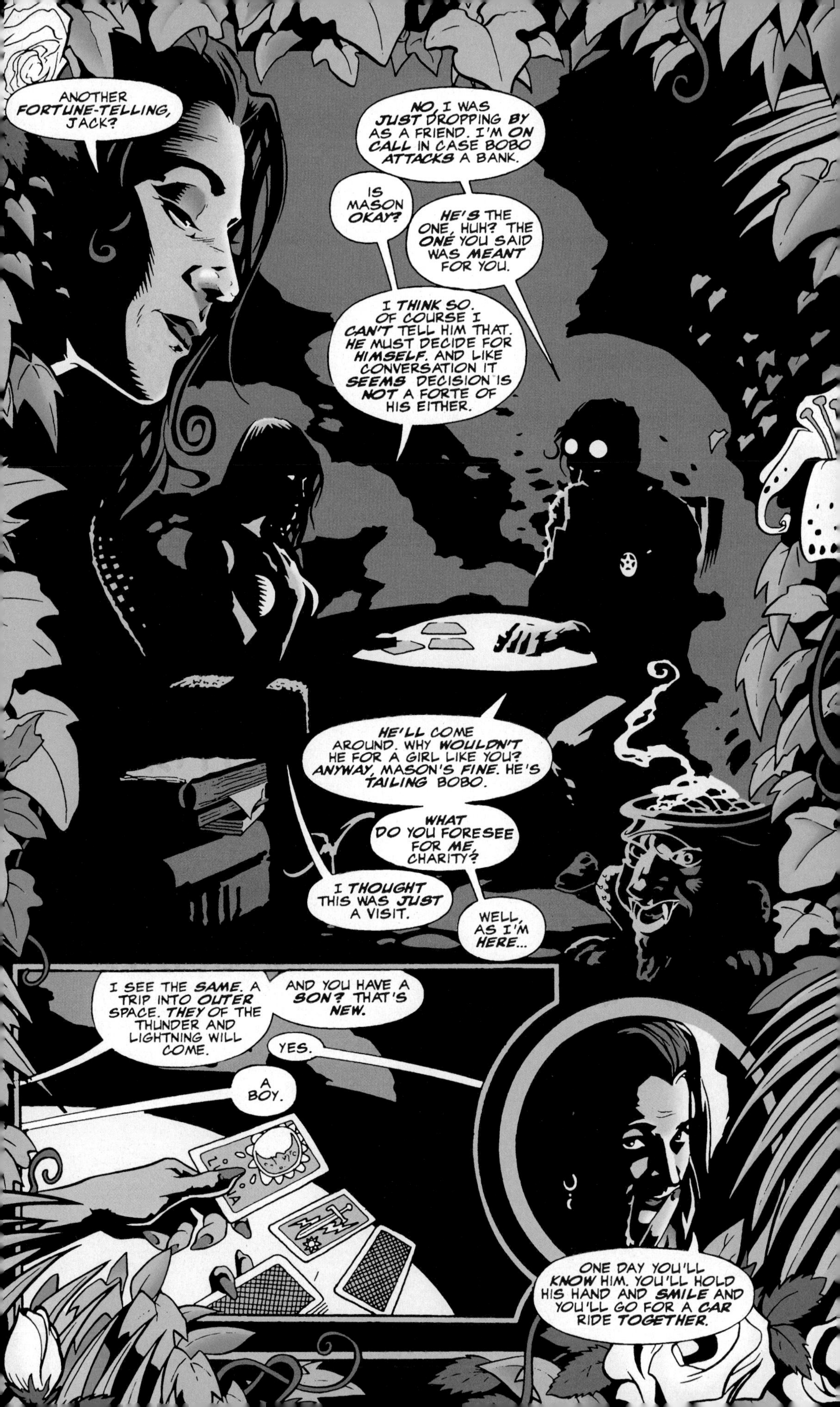

ANOTHER FORTUNE-TELLING, JACK?
NO, I WAS JUST DROPPING BY AS A FRIEND. I'M ON CALL IN CASE BOBO ATTACKS A BANK.
IS MASON OKAY?
HE'S THE ONE, HUH? THE ONE YOU SAID WAS MEANT FOR YOU.
I THINK SO. OF COURSE I CAN'T TELL HIM THAT. HE MUST DECIDE FOR HIMSELF. AND LIKE CONVERSATION IT SEEMS DECISION IS NOT A FORTE OF HIS EITHER.
HE'LL COME AROUND. WHY WOULDN'T HE FOR A GIRL LIKE YOU? ANYWAY, MASON'S FINE. HE'S TAILING BOBO.
WHAT DO YOU FORESEE FOR ME, CHARITY?
I THOUGHT THIS WAS JUST A VISIT.
WELL, AS I'M HERE...
I SEE THE SAME. A TRIP INTO OUTER SPACE. THEY OF THE THUNDER AND LIGHTNING WILL COME.
AND YOU HAVE A SON? THAT'S NEW.
YES.
A BOY.
ONE DAY YOU'LL KNOW HIM. YOU'LL HOLD HIS HAND AND SMILE AND YOU'LL GO FOR A CAR RIDE TOGETHER.

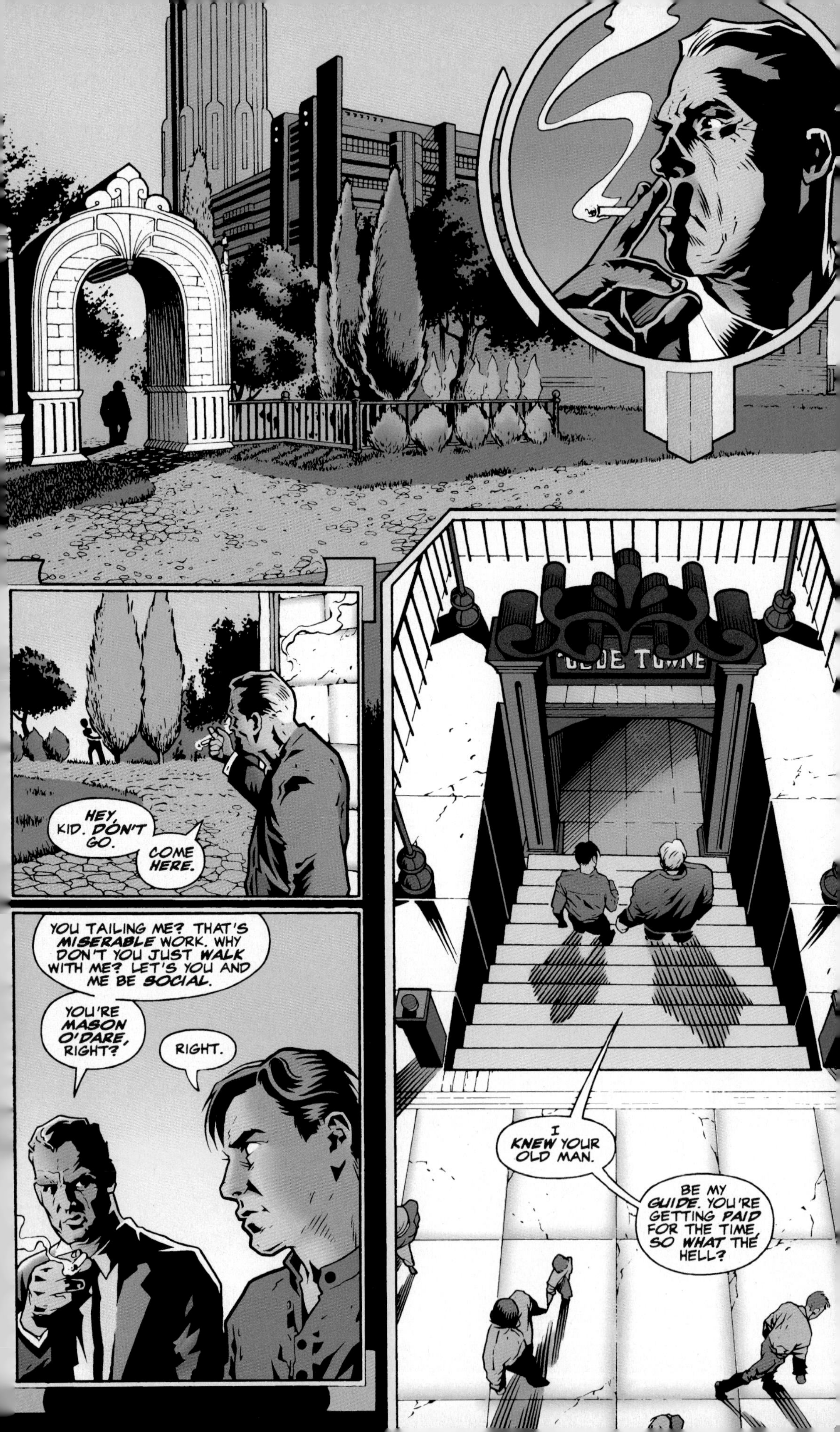
HEY, KID. DON'T GO.
COME HERE.
YOU TAILING ME? THAT'S MISERABLE WORK. WHY DON'T YOU JUST WALK WITH ME? LET'S YOU AND ME BE SOCIAL.
YOU'RE MASON O'DARE, RIGHT?
RIGHT.
OLDE TOWNE
I KNEW YOUR OLD MAN.
BE MY GUIDE. YOU'RE GETTING PAID FOR THE TIME, SO WHAT THE HELL?

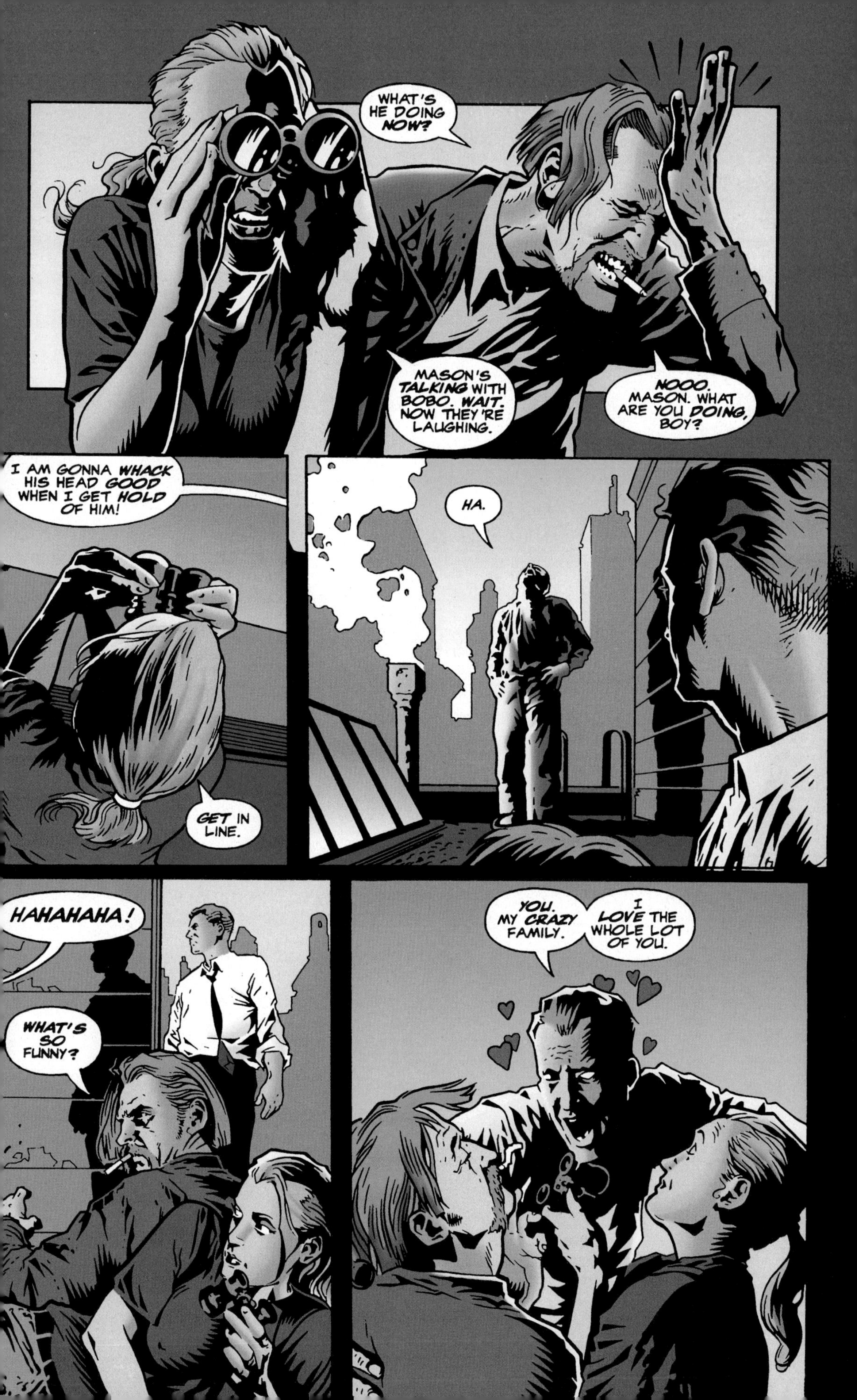
WHAT'S HE DOING NOW?
MASON'S TALKING WITH BOBO. WAIT. NOW THEY'RE LAUGHING.
NOOO. MASON. WHAT ARE YOU DOING, BOY?
I AM GONNA WHACK HIS HEAD GOOD WHEN I GET HOLD OF HIM!
GET IN LINE.
HA.
HAHAHAHA!
WHAT'S SO FUNNY?
YOU. MY CRAZY FAMILY.
I LOVE THE WHOLE LOT OF YOU.

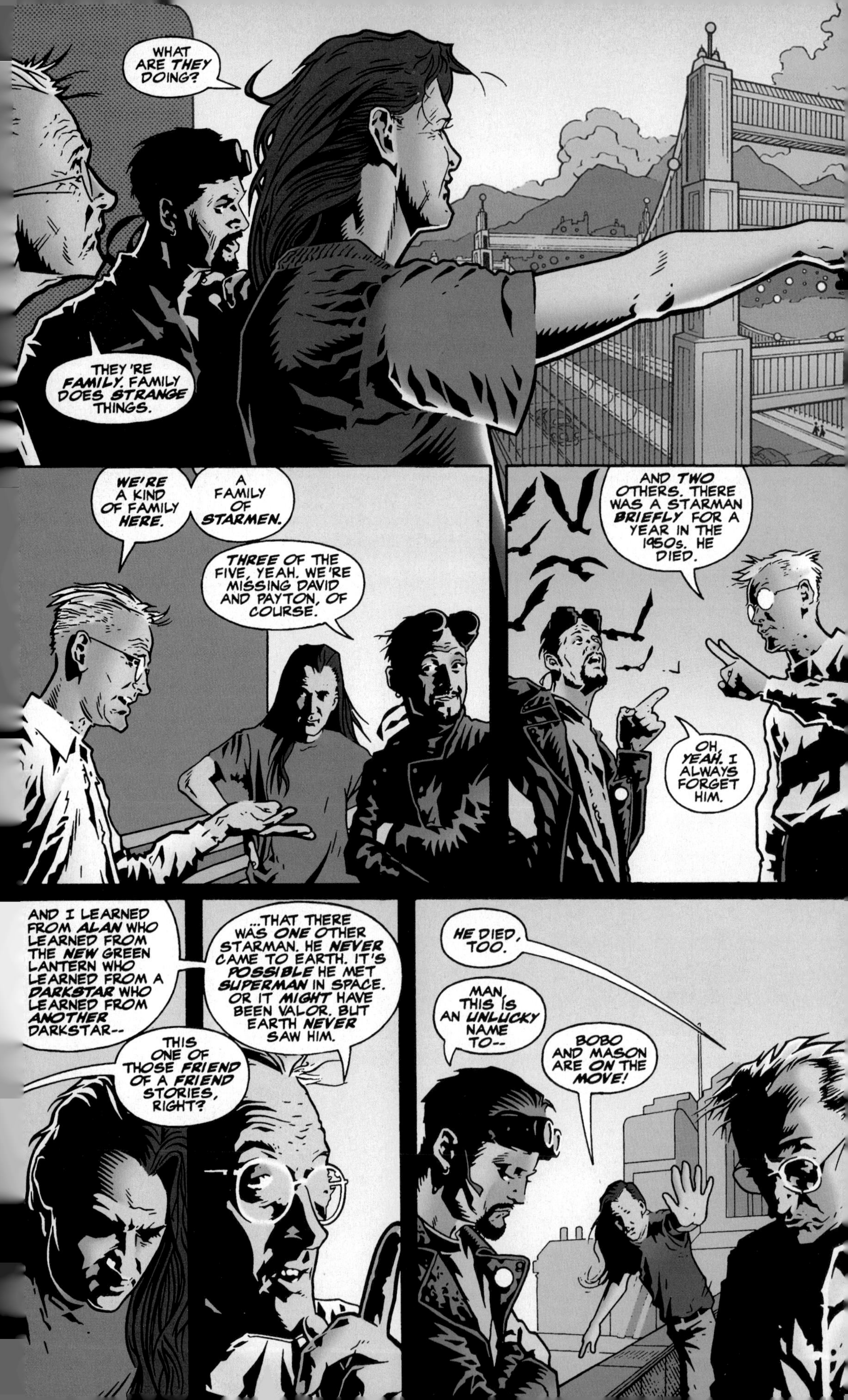
WHAT ARE THEY DOING?
THEY'RE FAMILY. FAMILY DOES STRANGE THINGS.
WE'RE A KIND OF FAMILY HERE.
A FAMILY OF STARMEN.
THREE OF THE FIVE, YEAH. WE'RE MISSING DAVID AND PAYTON, OF COURSE.
AND TWO OTHERS. THERE WAS A STARMAN BRIEFLY FOR A YEAR IN THE 1950s. HE DIED.
OH, YEAH. I ALWAYS FORGET HIM.
AND I LEARNED FROM ALAN WHO LEARNED FROM THE NEW GREEN LANTERN WHO LEARNED FROM A DARKSTAR WHO LEARNED FROM ANOTHER DARKSTAR--
...THAT THERE WAS ONE OTHER STARMAN. HE NEVER CAME TO EARTH. IT'S POSSIBLE HE MET SUPERMAN IN SPACE. OR IT MIGHT HAVE BEEN VALOR. BUT EARTH NEVER SAW HIM.
THIS ONE OF THOSE FRIEND OF A FRIEND STORIES, RIGHT?
HE DIED, TOO.
MAN, THIS IS AN UNLUCKY NAME TO--
BOBO AND MASON ARE ON THE MOVE!

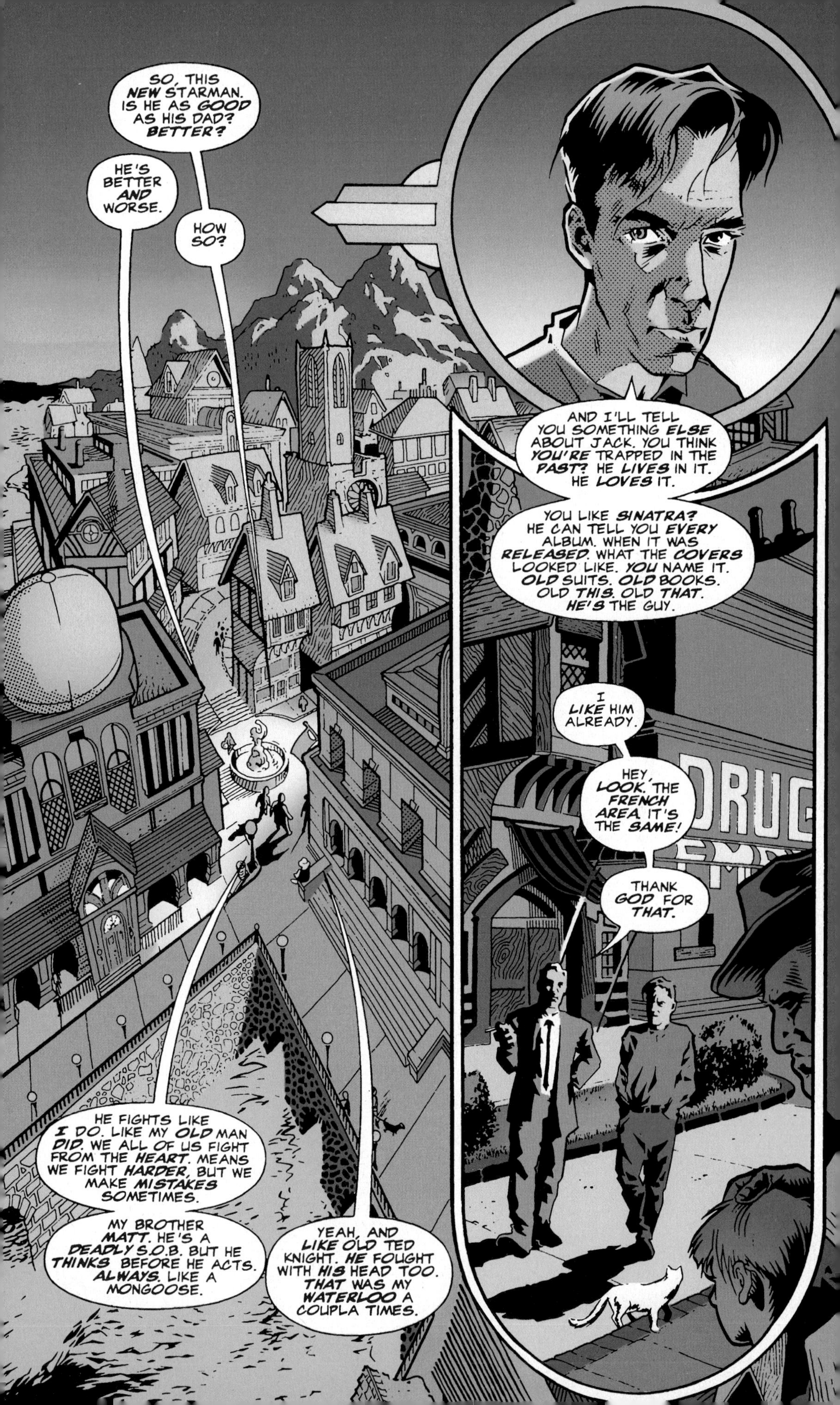
SO, THIS NEW STARMAN. IS HE AS GOOD AS HIS DAD? BETTER?
HE'S BETTER AND WORSE.
HOW SO?
HE FIGHTS LIKE I DO. LIKE MY OLD MAN DID. WE ALL OF US FIGHT FROM THE HEART. MEANS WE FIGHT HARDER, BUT WE MAKE MISTAKES SOMETIMES.
MY BROTHER MATT. HE'S A DEADLY S.O.B. BUT HE THINKS BEFORE HE ACTS. ALWAYS. LIKE A MONGOOSE.
YEAH, AND LIKE OLD TED KNIGHT. HE FOUGHT WITH HIS HEAD TOO. THAT WAS MY WATERLOO A COUPLA TIMES.
AND I'LL TELL YOU SOMETHING ELSE ABOUT JACK. YOU THINK YOU'RE TRAPPED IN THE PAST? HE LIVES IN IT. HE LOVES IT.
YOU LIKE SINATRA? HE CAN TELL YOU EVERY ALBUM. WHEN IT WAS RELEASED. WHAT THE COVERS LOOKED LIKE. YOU NAME IT. OLD SUITS. OLD BOOKS. OLD THIS. OLD THAT. HE'S THE GUY.
I LIKE HIM ALREADY.
HEY, LOOK. THE FRENCH AREA. IT'S THE SAME!
THANK GOD FOR THAT.
DRUG

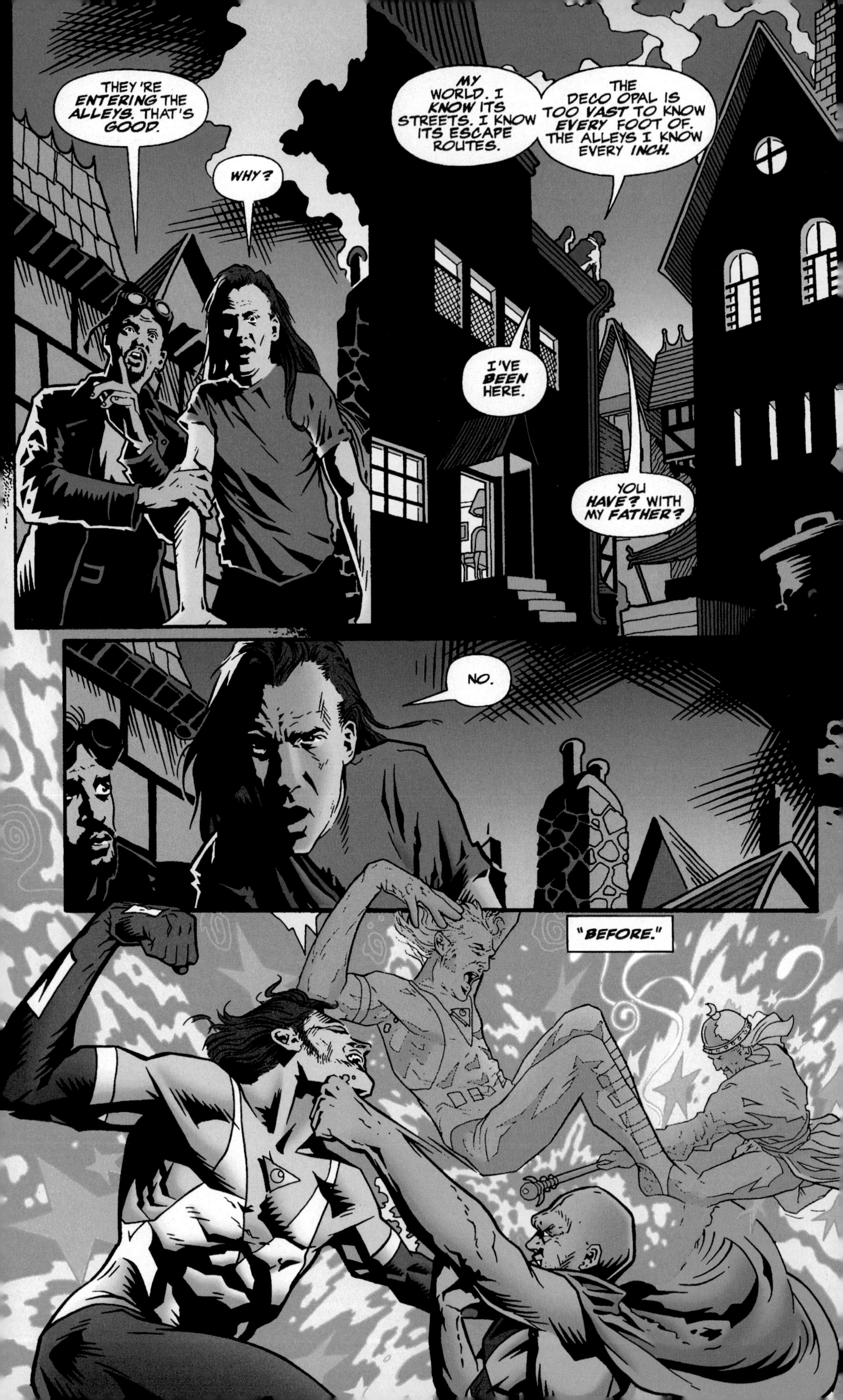

THEY'RE ENTERING THE ALLEYS. THAT'S GOOD.
WHY?
MY WORLD. I KNOW ITS STREETS. I KNOW ITS ESCAPE ROUTES.
THE DECO OPAL IS TOO VAST TO KNOW EVERY FOOT OF. THE ALLEYS I KNOW EVERY INCH.
I'VE BEEN HERE.
YOU HAVE? WITH MY FATHER?
NO.
"BEFORE."

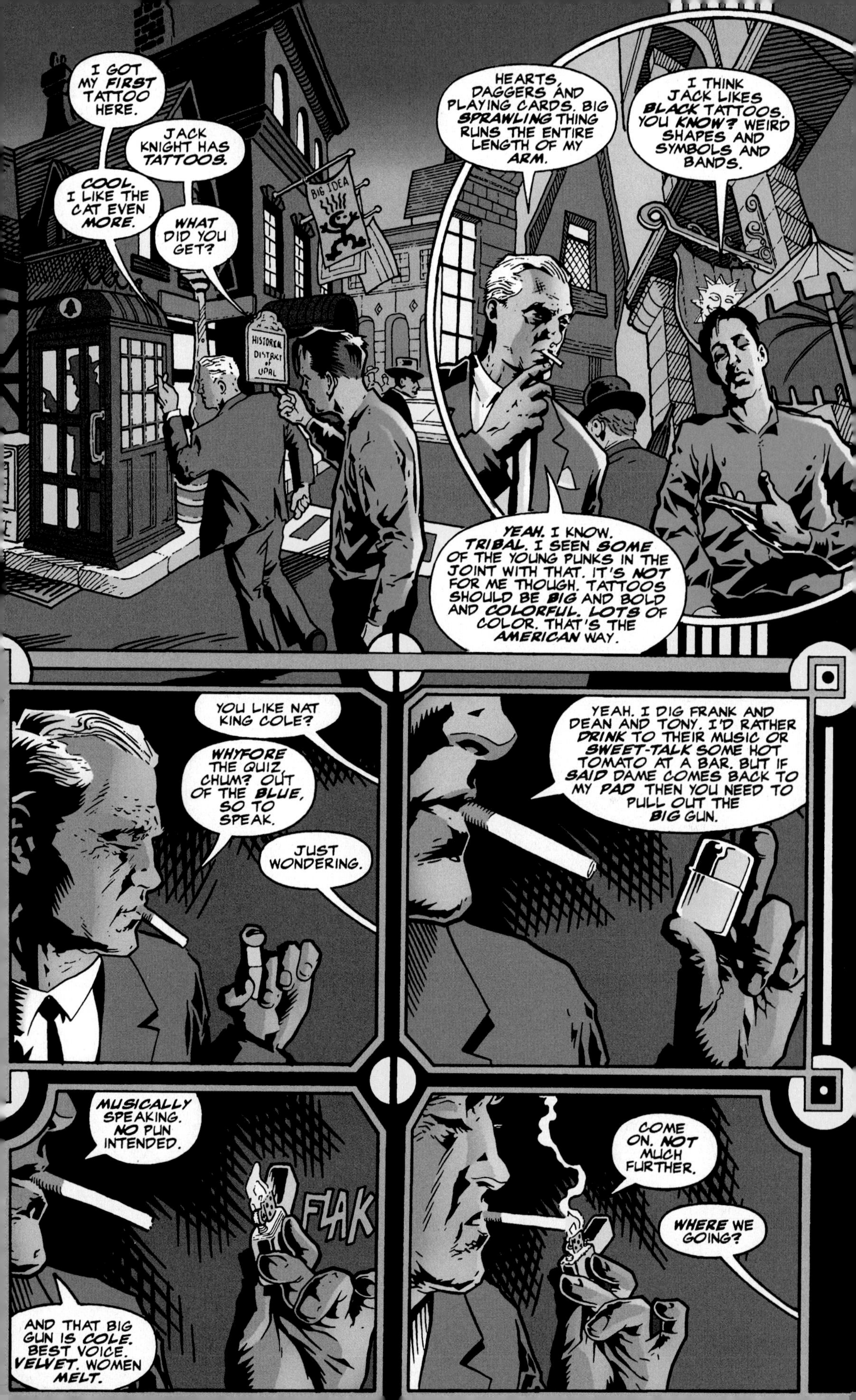
I GOT MY FIRST TATTOO HERE.
JACK KNIGHT HAS TATTOOS.
COOL. I LIKE THE CAT EVEN MORE.
WHAT DID YOU GET?
BIG IDEA
HISTORICAL DISTRICT of OPAL
HEARTS, DAGGERS AND PLAYING CARDS. BIG SPRAWLING THING RUNS THE ENTIRE LENGTH OF MY ARM.
I THINK JACK LIKES BLACK TATTOOS. YOU KNOW? WEIRD SHAPES AND SYMBOLS AND BANDS.
YEAH. I KNOW. TRIBAL. I SEEN SOME OF THE YOUNG PUNKS IN THE JOINT WITH THAT. IT'S NOT FOR ME THOUGH. TATTOOS SHOULD BE BIG AND BOLD AND COLORFUL. LOTS OF COLOR. THAT'S THE AMERICAN WAY.
YOU LIKE NAT KING COLE?
WHYFORE THE QUIZ, CHUM? OUT OF THE BLUE, SO TO SPEAK.
JUST WONDERING.
YEAH. I DIG FRANK AND DEAN AND TONY. I'D RATHER DRINK TO THEIR MUSIC OR SWEET-TALK SOME HOT TOMATO AT A BAR. BUT IF SAID DAME COMES BACK TO MY PAD THEN YOU NEED TO PULL OUT THE BIG GUN.
MUSICALLY SPEAKING. NO PUN INTENDED.
FLAK
AND THAT BIG GUN IS COLE. BEST VOICE. VELVET. WOMEN MELT.
COME ON. NOT MUCH FURTHER.
WHERE WE GOING?

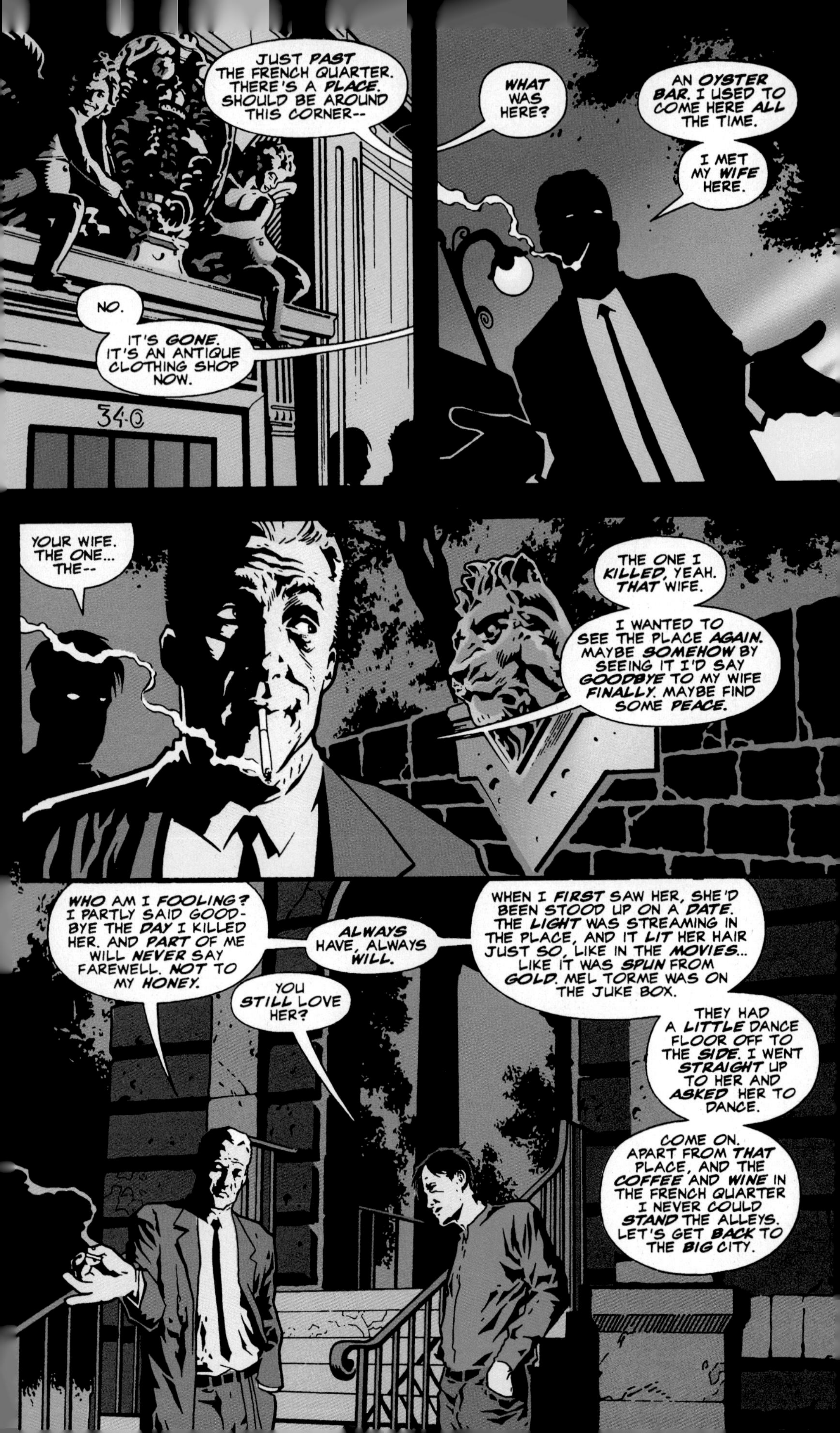
JUST PAST THE FRENCH QUARTER. THERE'S A PLACE. SHOULD BE AROUND THIS CORNER--
WHAT WAS HERE?
AN OYSTER BAR. I USED TO COME HERE ALL THE TIME.
I MET MY WIFE HERE.
NO.
IT'S GONE. IT'S AN ANTIQUE CLOTHING SHOP NOW.
340
YOUR WIFE. THE ONE... THE--
THE ONE I KILLED, YEAH. THAT WIFE.
I WANTED TO SEE THE PLACE AGAIN. MAYBE SOMEHOW BY SEEING IT I'D SAY GOODBYE TO MY WIFE FINALLY. MAYBE FIND SOME PEACE.
WHO AM I FOOLING? I PARTLY SAID GOOD-BYE THE DAY I KILLED HER. AND PART OF ME WILL NEVER SAY FAREWELL. NOT TO MY HONEY.
YOU STILL LOVE HER?
ALWAYS HAVE, ALWAYS WILL.
WHEN I FIRST SAW HER, SHE'D BEEN STOOD UP ON A DATE. THE LIGHT WAS STREAMING IN THE PLACE, AND IT LIT HER HAIR JUST SO, LIKE IN THE MOVIES... LIKE IT WAS SPUN FROM GOLD. MEL TORME WAS ON THE JUKE BOX.
THEY HAD A LITTLE DANCE FLOOR OFF TO THE SIDE. I WENT STRAIGHT UP TO HER AND ASKED HER TO DANCE.
COME ON. APART FROM THAT PLACE, AND THE COFFEE AND WINE IN THE FRENCH QUARTER I NEVER COULD STAND THE ALLEYS. LET'S GET BACK TO THE BIG CITY.

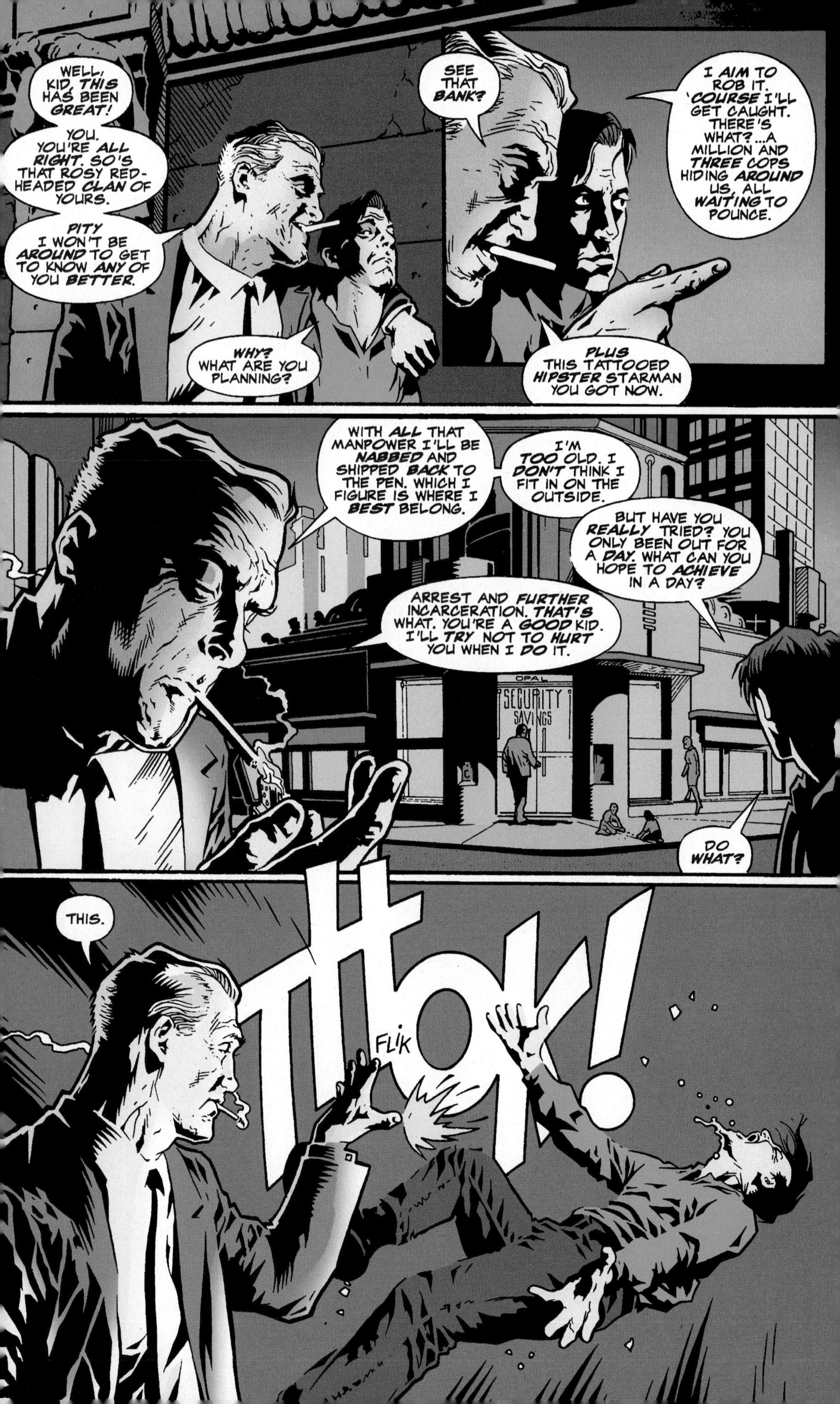
WELL, KID, THIS HAS BEEN GREAT!
YOU. YOU'RE ALL RIGHT. SO'S THAT ROSY RED-HEADED CLAN OF YOURS.
PITY I WON'T BE AROUND TO GET TO KNOW ANY OF YOU BETTER.
WHY? WHAT ARE YOU PLANNING?
SEE THAT BANK?
I AIM TO ROB IT. 'COURSE I'LL GET CAUGHT. THERE'S WHAT? ...A MILLION AND THREE COPS HIDING AROUND US, ALL WAITING TO POUNCE.
PLUS THIS TATTOOED HIPSTER STARMAN YOU GOT NOW.
WITH ALL THAT MANPOWER I'LL BE NABBED AND SHIPPED BACK TO THE PEN. WHICH I FIGURE IS WHERE I BEST BELONG.
I'M TOO OLD. I DON'T THINK I FIT IN ON THE OUTSIDE.
BUT HAVE YOU REALLY TRIED? YOU ONLY BEEN OUT FOR A DAY. WHAT CAN YOU HOPE TO ACHIEVE IN A DAY?
ARREST AND FURTHER INCARCERATION. THAT'S WHAT. YOU'RE A GOOD KID. I'LL TRY NOT TO HURT YOU WHEN I DO IT.
OPAL
SECURITY SAVINGS
DO WHAT?
THIS.
TTHOK!
FLIK

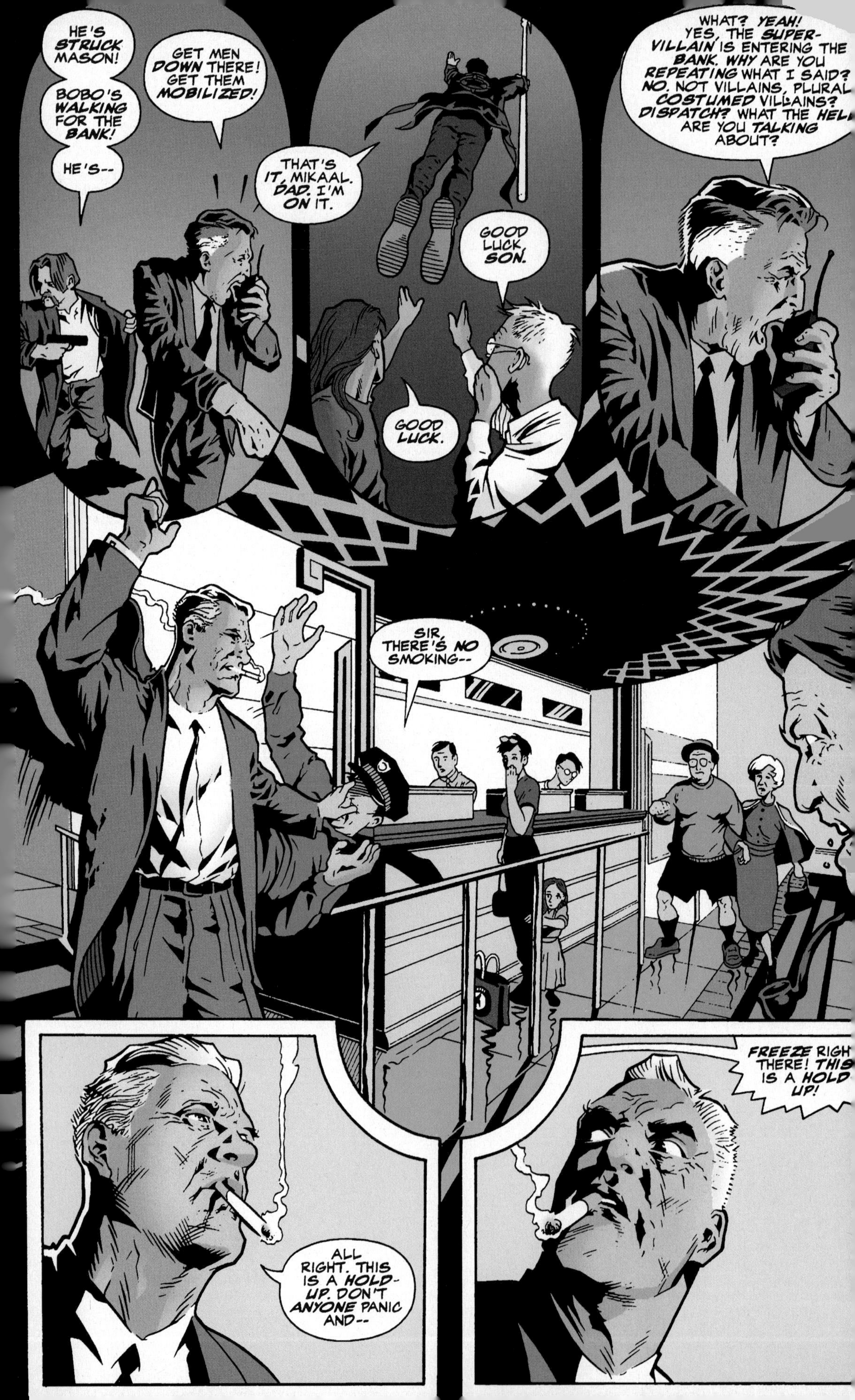
HE'S STRUCK MASON!
BOBO'S WALKING FOR THE BANK!
HE'S--
GET MEN DOWN THERE! GET THEM MOBILIZED!
THAT'S IT, MIKAAL. DAD. I'M ON IT.
GOOD LUCK, SON.
GOOD LUCK.
WHAT? YEAH! YES, THE SUPER-VILLAIN IS ENTERING THE BANK. WHY ARE YOU REPEATING WHAT I SAID? NO. NOT VILLAINS, PLURAL. COSTUMED VILLAINS? DISPATCH? WHAT THE HELL ARE YOU TALKING ABOUT?
SIR, THERE'S NO SMOKING--
ALL RIGHT. THIS IS A HOLD-UP. DON'T ANYONE PANIC AND--
FREEZE RIGHT THERE! THIS IS A HOLD UP!

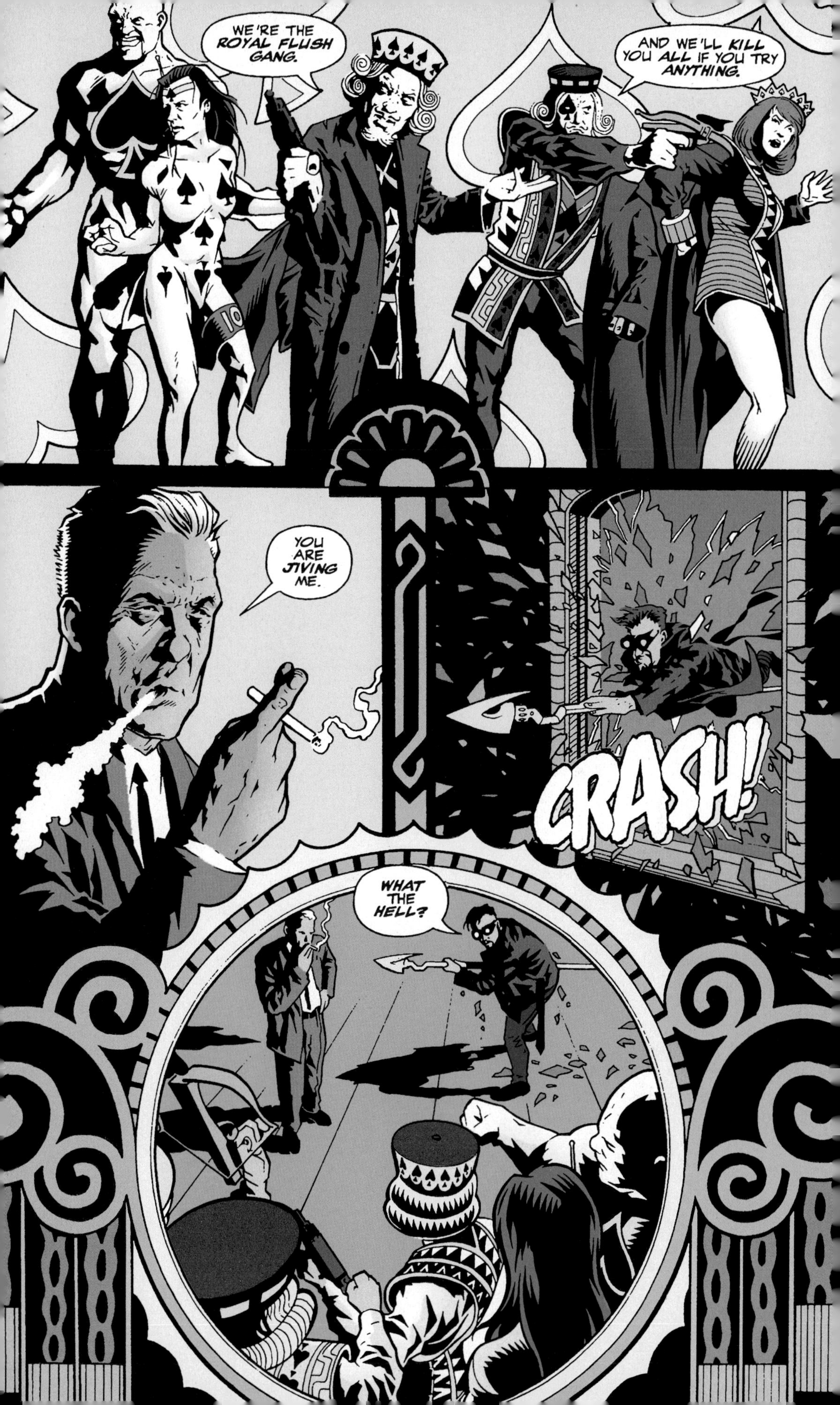
WE'RE THE ROYAL FLUSH GANG.
AND WE'LL KILL YOU ALL IF YOU TRY ANYTHING.
YOU ARE JIVING ME.
CRASH!
WHAT THE HELL?

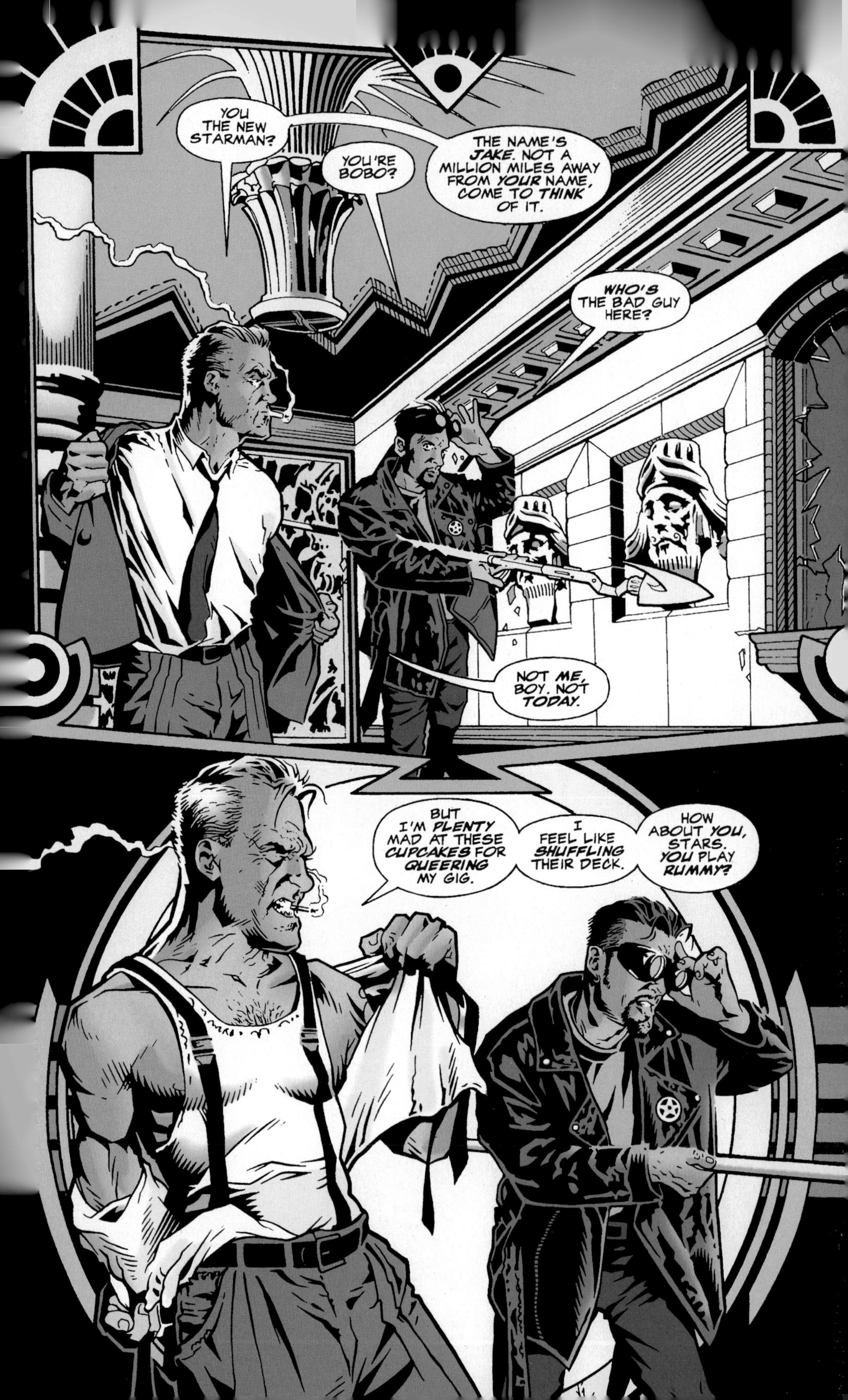
YOU THE NEW STARMAN?
YOU'RE BOBO?
THE NAME'S JAKE. NOT A MILLION MILES AWAY FROM YOUR NAME, COME TO THINK OF IT.
WHO'S THE BAD GUY HERE?
NOT ME, BOY. NOT TODAY.
BUT I'M PLENTY MAD AT THESE CUPCAKES FOR QUEERING MY GIG.
I FEEL LIKE SHUFFLING THEIR DECK.
HOW ABOUT YOU, STARS. YOU PLAY RUMMY?

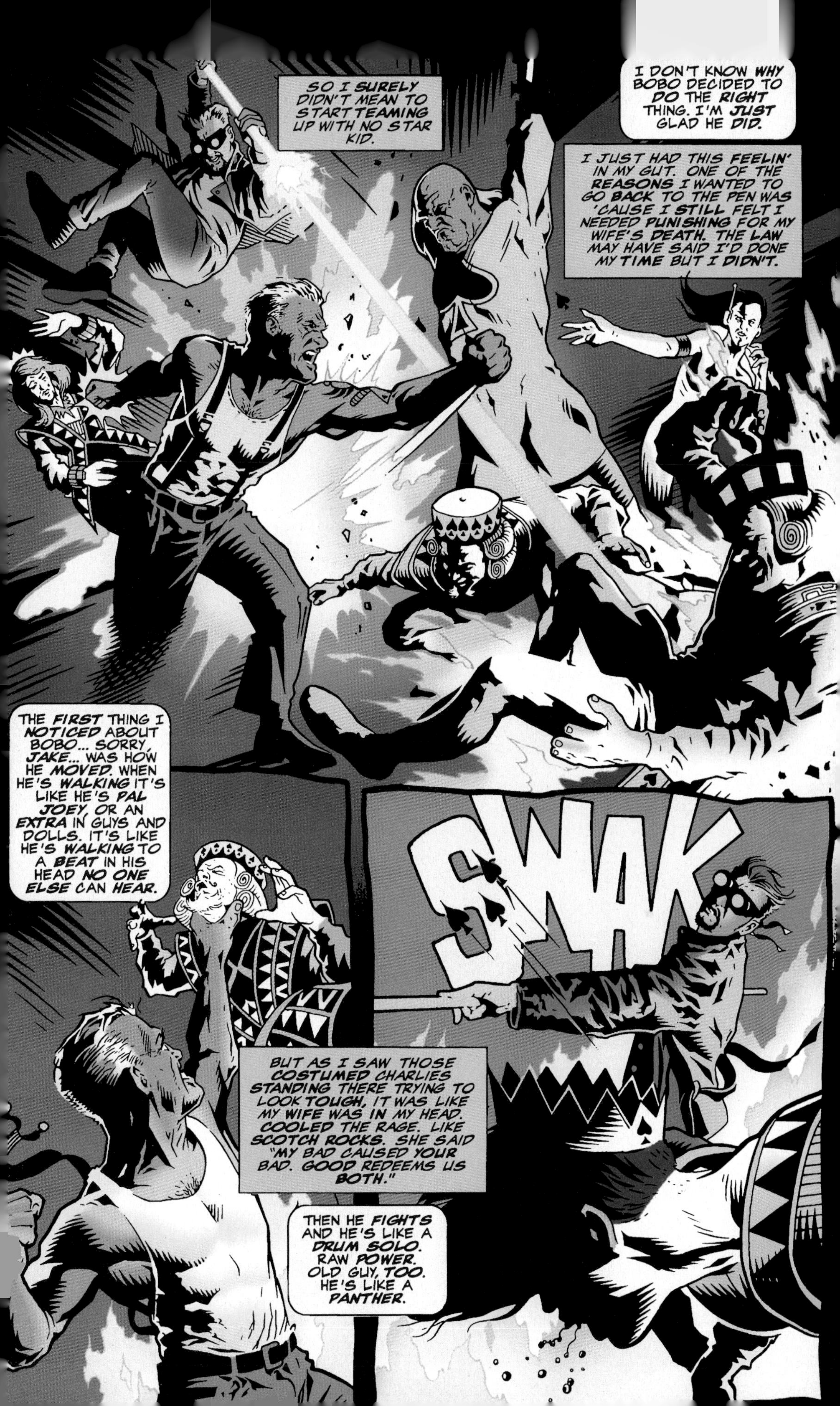
SO I SURELY DIDN'T MEAN TO START TEAMING UP WITH NO STAR KID.
I DON'T KNOW WHY BOBO DECIDED TO DO THE RIGHT THING. I'M JUST GLAD HE DID.
I JUST HAD THIS FEELIN' IN MY GUT. ONE OF THE REASONS I WANTED TO GO BACK TO THE PEN WAS 'CAUSE I STILL FELT I NEEDED PUNISHING FOR MY WIFE'S DEATH. THE LAW MAY HAVE SAID I'D DONE MY TIME BUT I DIDN'T.
THE FIRST THING I NOTICED ABOUT BOBO... SORRY, JAKE... WAS HOW HE MOVED. WHEN HE'S WALKING IT'S LIKE HE'S PAL JOEY, OR AN EXTRA IN GUYS AND DOLLS. IT'S LIKE HE'S WALKING TO A BEAT IN HIS HEAD NO ONE ELSE CAN HEAR.
SWAK
BUT AS I SAW THOSE COSTUMED CHARLIES STANDING THERE TRYING TO LOOK TOUGH, IT WAS LIKE MY WIFE WAS IN MY HEAD. COOLED THE RAGE. LIKE SCOTCH ROCKS. SHE SAID "MY BAD CAUSED YOUR BAD. GOOD REDEEMS US BOTH."
THEN HE FIGHTS AND HE'S LIKE A DRUM SOLO. RAW POWER. OLD GUY, TOO. HE'S LIKE A PANTHER.

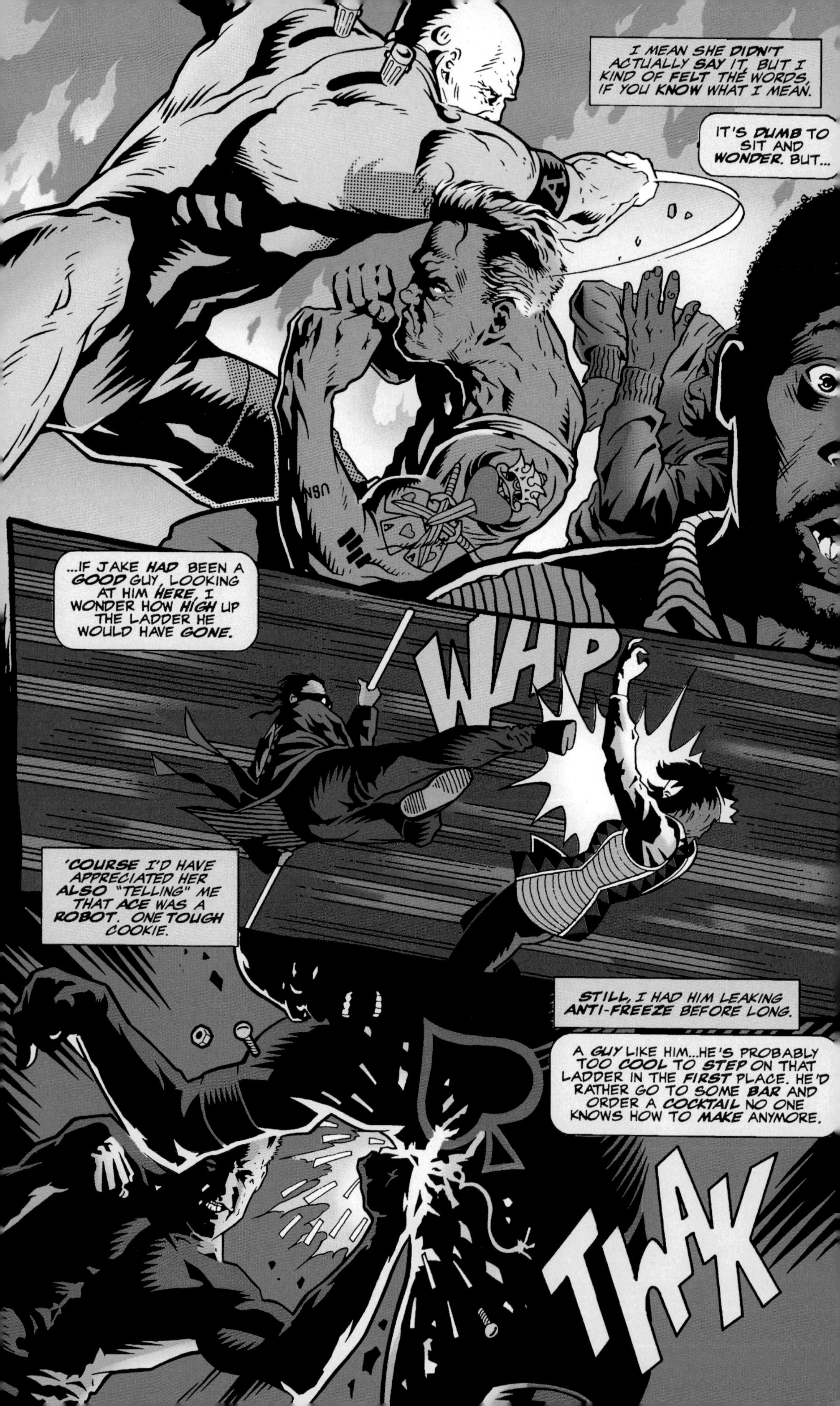
I MEAN SHE DIDN'T ACTUALLY SAY IT, BUT I KIND OF FELT THE WORDS, IF YOU KNOW WHAT I MEAN.
IT'S DUMB TO SIT AND WONDER. BUT...
...IF JAKE HAD BEEN A GOOD GUY, LOOKING AT HIM HERE, I WONDER HOW HIGH UP THE LADDER HE WOULD HAVE GONE.
WHP
'COURSE I'D HAVE APPRECIATED HER ALSO "TELLING" ME THAT ACE WAS A ROBOT. ONE TOUGH COOKIE.
STILL, I HAD HIM LEAKING ANTI-FREEZE BEFORE LONG.
A GUY LIKE HIM...HE'S PROBABLY TOO COOL TO STEP ON THAT LADDER IN THE FIRST PLACE. HE'D RATHER GO TO SOME BAR AND ORDER A COCKTAIL NO ONE KNOWS HOW TO MAKE ANYMORE.
THAK

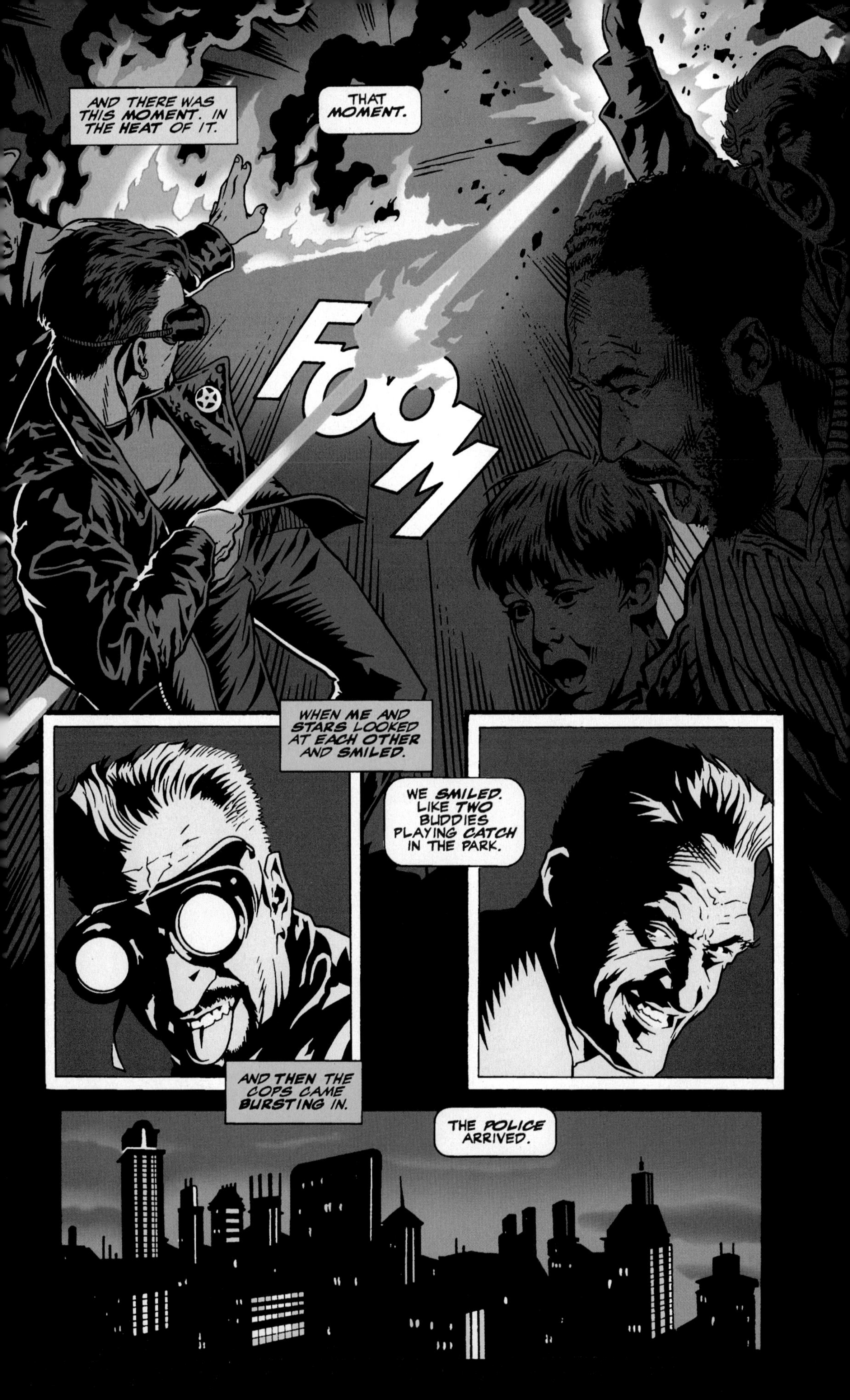
AND THERE WAS THIS MOMENT. IN THE HEAT OF IT.
THAT MOMENT.
FOOM
WHEN ME AND STARS LOOKED AT EACH OTHER AND SMILED.
WE SMILED. LIKE TWO BUDDIES PLAYING CATCH IN THE PARK.
AND THEN THE COPS CAME BURSTING IN.
THE POLICE ARRIVED.

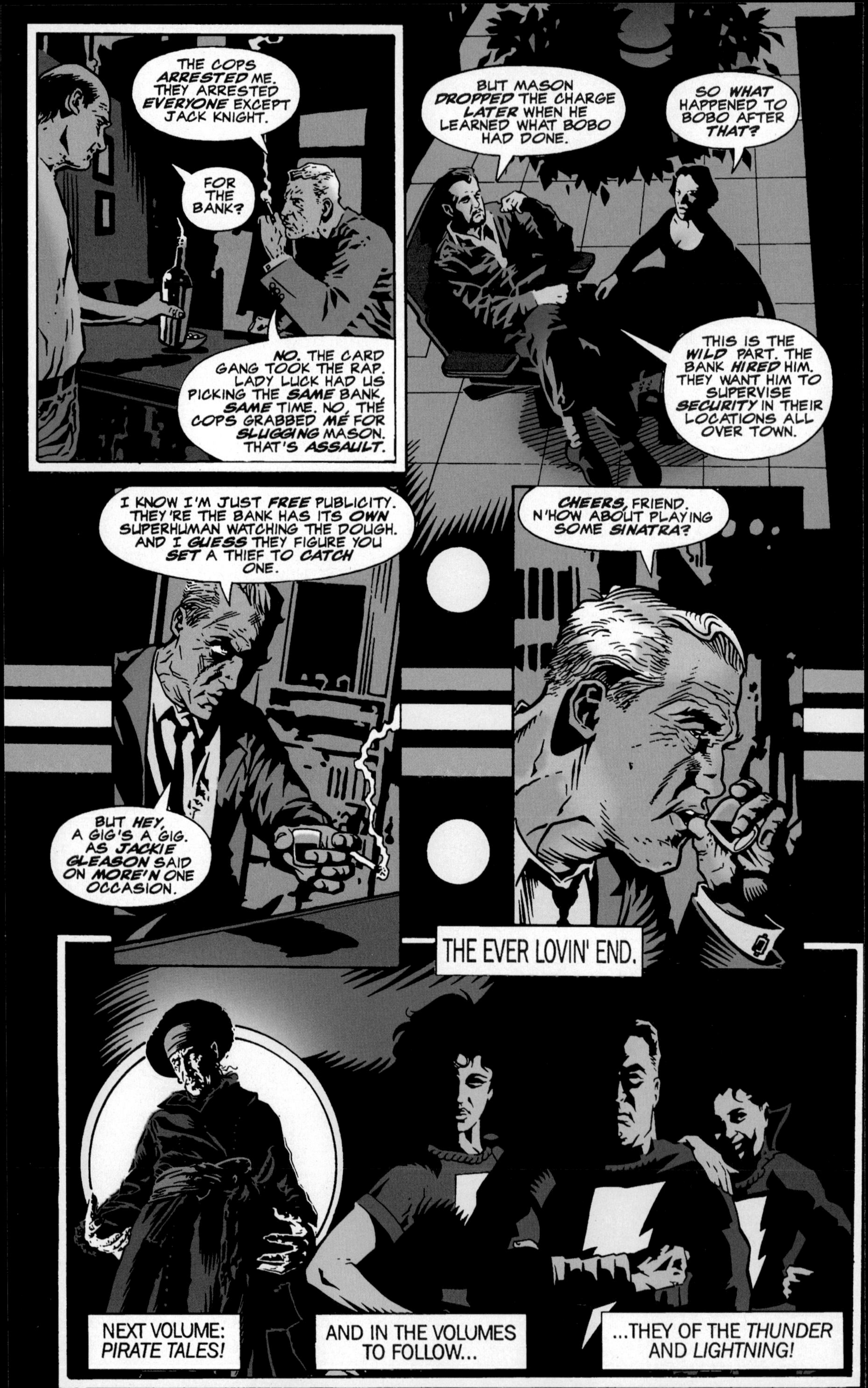
THE COPS ARRESTED ME. THEY ARRESTED EVERYONE EXCEPT JACK KNIGHT.
FOR THE BANK?
NO. THE CARD GANG TOOK THE RAP. LADY LUCK HAD US PICKING THE SAME BANK, SAME TIME. NO, THE COPS GRABBED ME FOR SLUGGING MASON. THAT'S ASSAULT.
BUT MASON DROPPED THE CHARGE LATER WHEN HE LEARNED WHAT BOBO HAD DONE.
SO WHAT HAPPENED TO BOBO AFTER THAT?
THIS IS THE WILD PART. THE BANK HIRED HIM. THEY WANT HIM TO SUPERVISE SECURITY IN THEIR LOCATIONS ALL OVER TOWN.
I KNOW I'M JUST FREE PUBLICITY. THEY'RE THE BANK HAS ITS OWN SUPERHUMAN WATCHING THE DOUGH. AND I GUESS THEY FIGURE YOU SET A THIEF TO CATCH ONE.
BUT HEY, A GIG'S A GIG. AS JACKIE GLEASON SAID ON MORE'N ONE OCCASION.
CHEERS, FRIEND. N'HOW ABOUT PLAYING SOME SINATRA?
THE EVER LOVIN' END.
NEXT VOLUME: PIRATE TALES!
AND IN THE VOLUMES TO FOLLOW...
...THEY OF THE THUNDER AND LIGHTNING!

From the Shade's Journal...

The problem with immortality is the memories.

Prolonged life means more events, which in turn means more recollections at a later date. And I have lived my life to the fullest. And there are so, so, so many events to recall.

Today there was nothing much occurring that I felt warranted inclusion in my journals. David Knight patrols the nighttime streets, and the city is Opal City. For this reason, with my book open on a blank white page, and my pen in my fingers, I feel compelled to write of the other times. Times past.

I remember London. Visiting it for the final time. Visiting Oscar too, at his Tite Street home. This was long before his fall from grace, thankfully. We ate a fine cream tea that afternoon, and I think this was not the first for Oscar, as his waistline was more than beginning to show. Not that it really mattered to me, I merely pause now to reflect.

Our time together was a delight. I sat and listened, mainly. Oscar's night before had been one of a fine port and rakishness, so he was slow to start with his wit. But, of course, he started eventually. And I listened and laughed as Oscar commented on "this" public figure or "that" bit of scandal. Indeed, that week there'd been a salacious new tale about Catherine Walters. "Skittles," as she was known, was one of London's more famous "grand horizontales." There had been talk of her and W.G. Grace, the famous cricket player. Oscar made a remark about "Dr. Grace getting a sticky wicket" that had me doubled over with laughter.

I'd just begin to realize, then, that perhaps, just perhaps, I was no longer going to age. This fact had crept up on me. It was with shock I realized that the week prior I'd turned sixty and yet still looked to be in my late thirties. And that day was when it really sank in. Oscar was beginning to show those signs of a misspent life that should have been mine also. Seeing the signs of wear and tear in my friend made me sad. And a little ashamed. Guilty.

Yes, looking back, perhaps that was why I never saw Oscar again. It was 1891, years after we'd last met in Opal City during his American tour. And years before his troubles with Queensbury and all the dreadfulness that followed. Poor Oscar, perhaps I should have been there for him in '95. But like many other friends, I was nowhere to be found.

Anyway, Oscar's evening was to be spent with Lord Alfred whom he'd recently met. Oscar was charmingly firm in telling me that I was not invited to accompany them.

And so we were alone that night, London and I.

My mood and the wind both had a sharp sting to them, and one or the other bid me to venture forth to Tiger Bay; down by the Thames where the air was foul and all good folk know never to go. But I am not, nor ever was, a good man. And so I went.

The opium dens and drinking clubs were full, with sailors, and doxies and Orientals. You could hear any language in the work. You could see and color skin too. London has always been a melting pot and on this night in Tiger Bay, the fire beneath that pot was burning fierce.

I walked into a deserted courtyard, on my way from one street to another, and there stumbled on a most singular occurrence; a large brown bear being clubbed to death by its owner. The beast was close to the end, from the many repeated blows his owner had given it with a sharp studded mallet. I inquired what terrible thing the beast had done, that it should be treated so, and the man replied that the bear was too old to perform anymore. The bear had been a street dancer and on weekends in Pitney Market and other parts, had made this fellow much coin. But now old, the bear was costing the owner more to feed than the animal brought in, and so the man had resolved to kill the beast and sell its flesh to the slaughterhouses.

Something about the scenario struck me as ludicrous. The man was small and weak and yet had somehow overcome this huge animal and with no regard or affection was now ending its existence merely for aging. I think my guilt over Oscar's aging might still have been affecting me. Perhaps.

Whatever. I killed the man.

"Well, Mr. Mild, I fear you have yet to learn that a little civility can go a long way," I responded. "Now, what is this about? Who is your employer? Why does he need me? And for that matter, how do you know so much about me that you knew your bullets would be useless against my shadow wraiths?"

"I'm paid a lot by my boss. I get them by doing my homework." Mild walked over to the man whom my wraiths had broken the back of. Crouching slightly, Mild placed the gun to the man's temple. The man groaned and closed his eyes.

"Sorry, Eddie," Mild whispered as he pulled back his gun's hammer. "You know how we do things."

"Yeah, I know," the wounded fellow whispered back. "See you, Sam."

Mild shot him.

He then turned away, with a coolness that impressed even me. It was as if he'd just gotten the mail, or swept a cobweb from the corners of his kitchen.

"Rules. The boss likes things done just so. Anyway, what were you asking? Oh yeah, there was this guy in St. Paul. Hubert Mason. A nutbox character. He had the crazy notion about you and the new breed of super-heroes and villains that's beginning to appear around the country. Flash and Human Bomb and Mr. Terrific. You know? Mason thought you were all a sign that the devil is taking hold of America. He thought you were all Satan's agents."

"Mr. Mason could be right," I said with a smile.

"Yeah, from the look of what you just did, he might indeed. But that's none of my business. My business was the information Mason had compiled on you. All of you. He intended to travel from state to state killing the lot of you. He'd killed a hero called the Clock already, when I caught up with him. His next target was to have been the Whip."

I smiled again. Mild did too. We broke out laughing together. "Yeah," Mild continued, "I guess he believed in starting small and working his way up to the big guys. Anyway, his true talent was information gathering. Don't ask me how he found out everything he did about you, but he knew a lot. That was how I learned bullets would be useless against your shadow demons. That was how I knew nothing can beat them."

"And where's this Mason chap now?"

"He fell asleep with a lit cigarette. Burned to death." Mild smiled again, wincing as he did, from the broken arm. " 'Course he didn't smoke until I made him."

"And your employer?"

"He's a big cheese in Hollywood. His life's in danger. Attacks. Supernatural creatures. Bizarre craziness. He needs you to sort it out. He'll pay well."

"Pay? Mild, do you realize that had you taken the trouble of a few words of explanation like this, I might have spared your men's lives."

Mild shrugged. "My boss is Howard Hughes."

"Howard Hughes, indeed. Hmmm. Well, I've never been to Hollywood, and I've always wanted to."

Mild nodded to his one surviving aide. "Dan, get the boys' wallets. We don't want them identified."

"What about the stuffed shirt?" Dan asked this, walking over to Spencer and nudging him with his toe.

Mild looked at me. His expression was sheepish. "Mr. Hughes doesn't want any witnesses."

Now it was my turn to shrug. "And I assume Mr. Hughes usually gets what he wants," I said, trying to look upset by this development.

Mild and I walked away, leaving Dan to kneel, gun drawn, by the fallen Spencer Kilne. We were already in the Ford as Dan's gunshot sounded. He came running out of Dart Street, a moment later, some of Spencer's blood wet on his pants leg, and hopped into the car.

"Is it warm in Los Angeles at this time of year?" I asked.

"Warmer than here," Mild replied.

"Good," I said, settling back. "Then I shall enjoy the weather if nothing else."

TO BE CONTINUED...

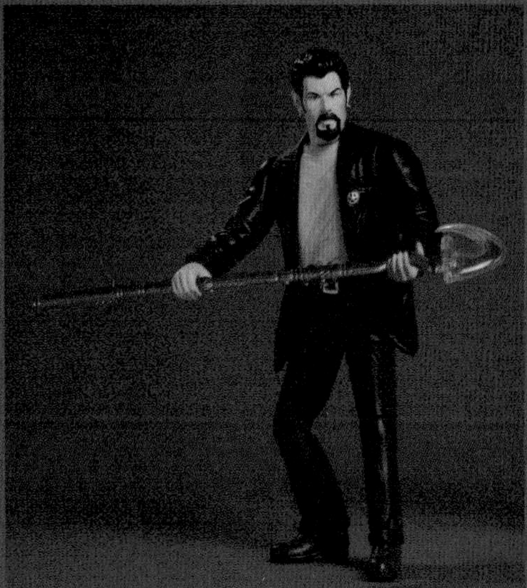

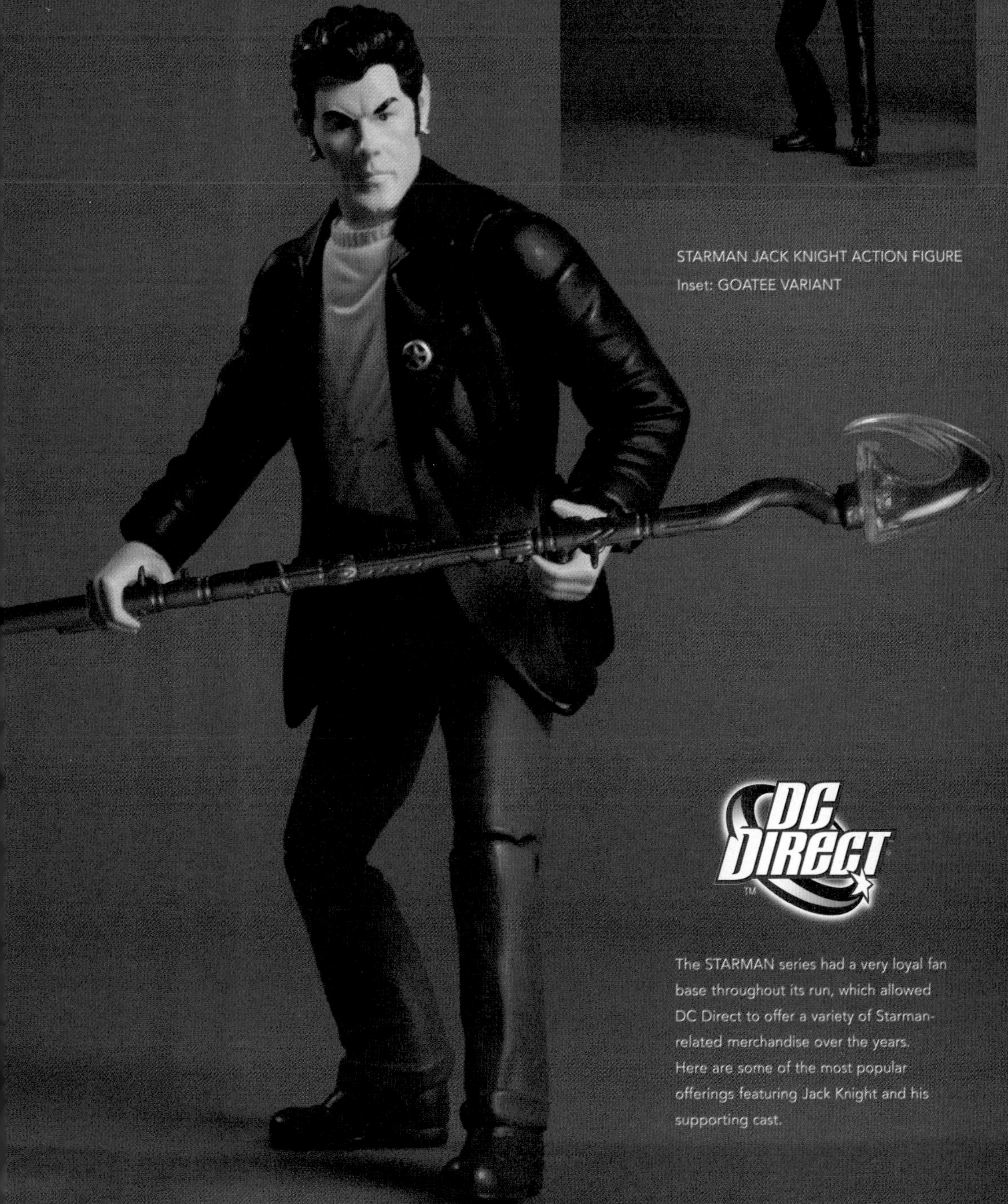

STARMAN JACK KNIGHT ACTION FIGURE
Inset: GOATEE VARIANT

DC DIRECT

The STARMAN series had a very loyal fan base throughout its run, which allowed DC Direct to offer a variety of Starman-related merchandise over the years. Here are some of the most popular offerings featuring Jack Knight and his supporting cast.

STARMAN STATUE sculpted by Tim Bruckner

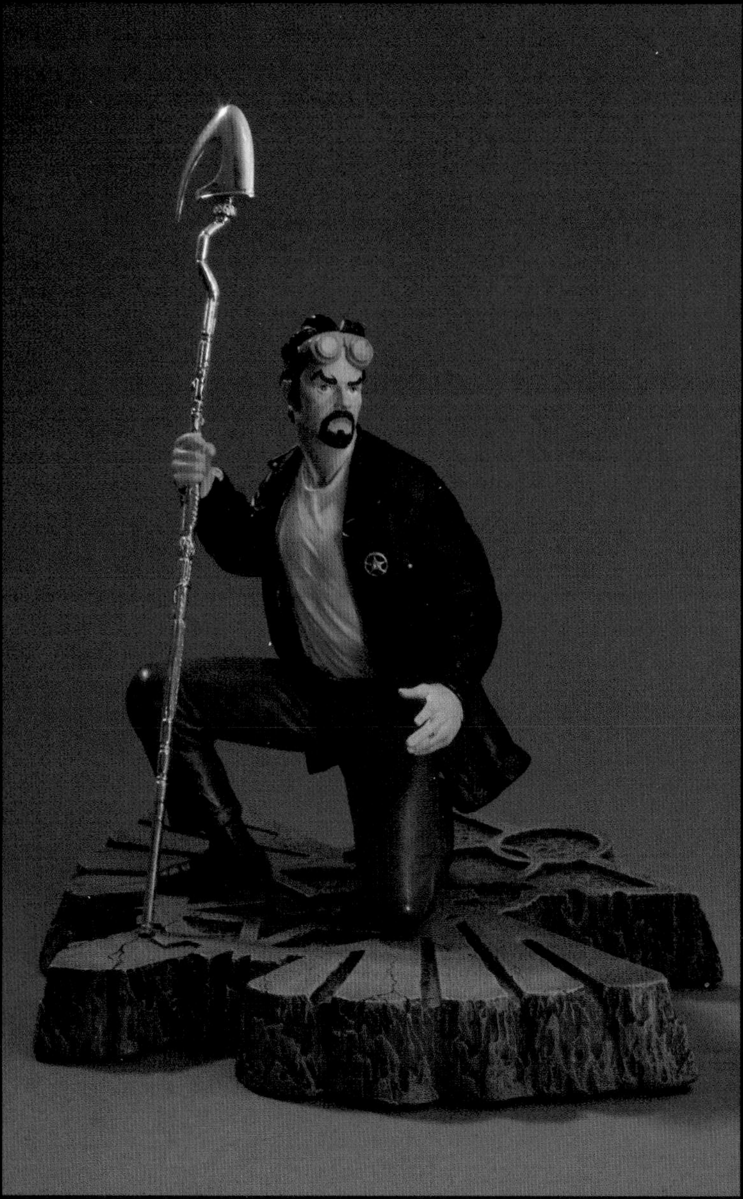

THE SHADE ACTION FIGURE

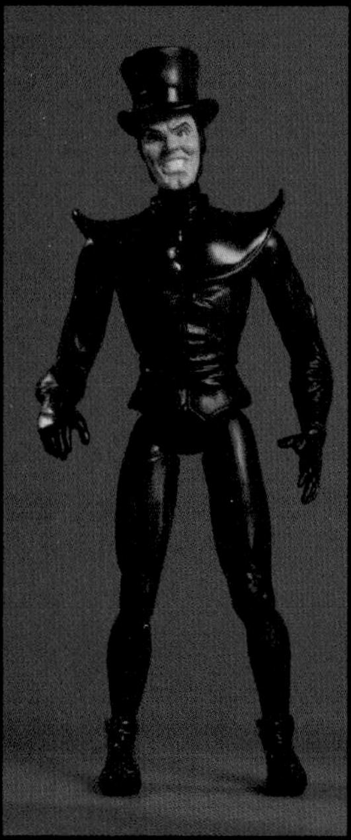

GOLDEN AGE STARMAN ACTION FIGURE

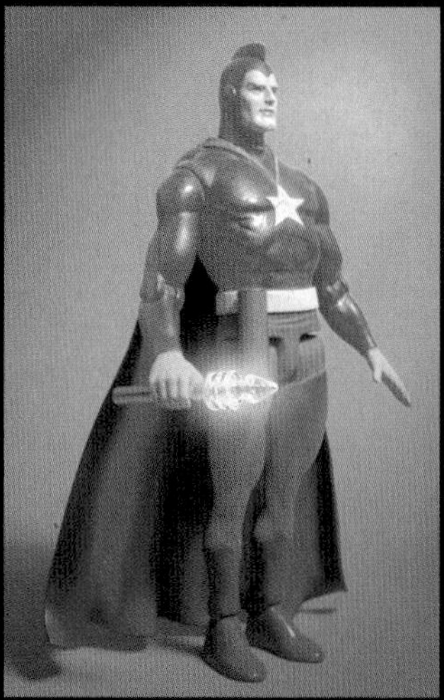

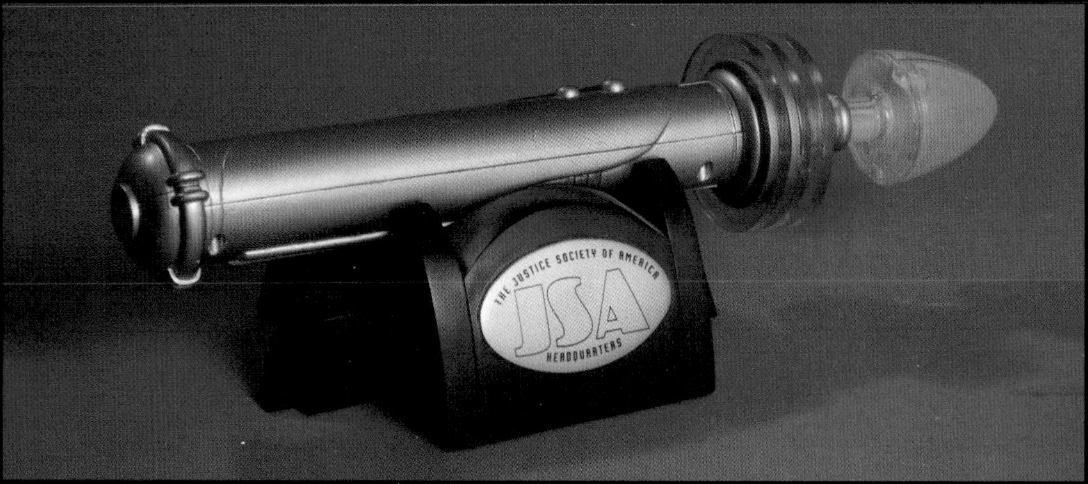
THE JUSTICE SOCIETY OF AMERICA
JSA
HEADQUARTERS

STARMAN COSMIC ROD PROP
This replica of Golden Age Starman Ted Knight's weapon made it to the development stage, but was never solicited or mass-produced. The only copy of it remains in the DC offices.

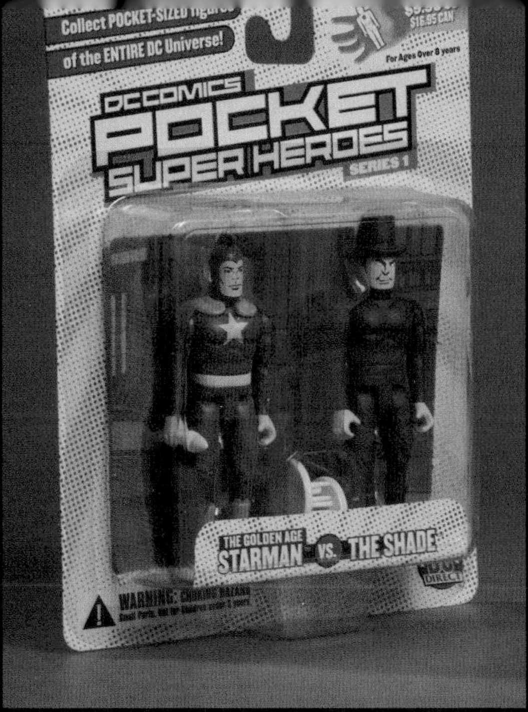
Collect POCKET-SIZED figures
of the ENTIRE DC Universe!
For Ages Over 8 years
DC COMICS
POCKET
SUPER HEROES
SERIES 1
THE GOLDEN AGE
STARMAN
VS.
THE SHADE
WARNING: CHOKING HAZARD

DC COMICS POCKET SUPER-HEROES:
GOLDEN AGE STARMAN AND THE SHADE

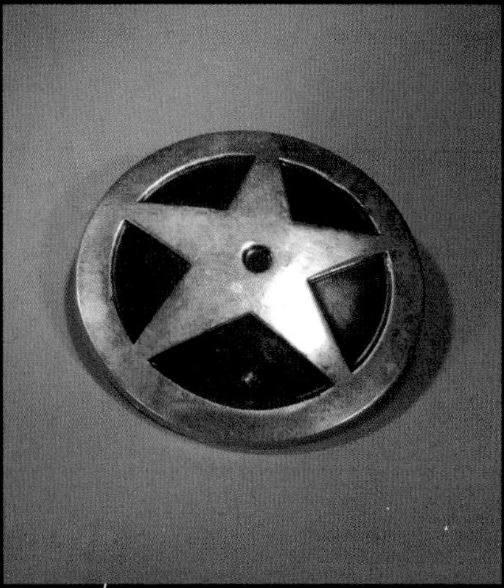

STARMAN PIN

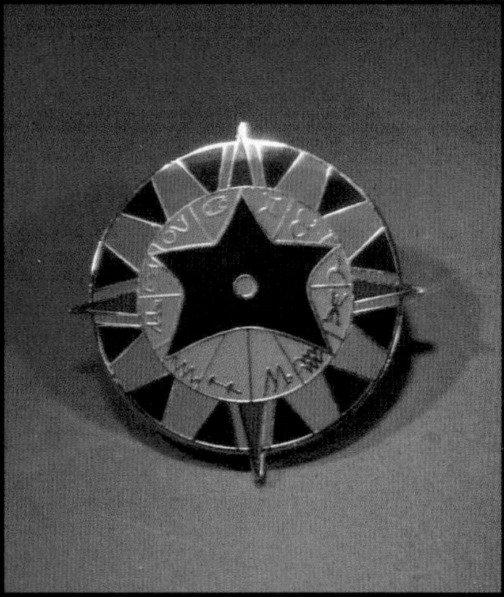

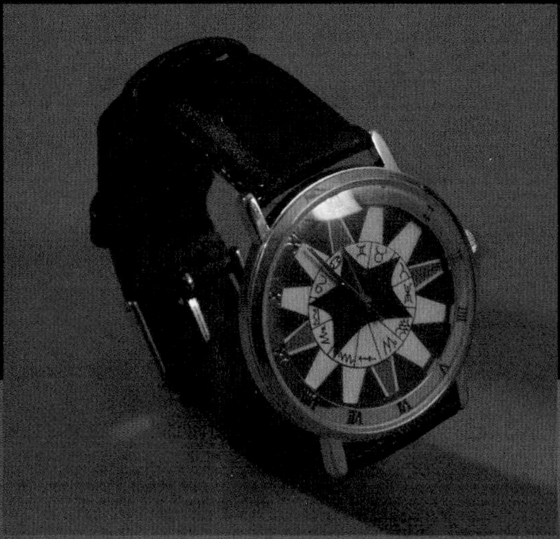

STARMAN WATCH

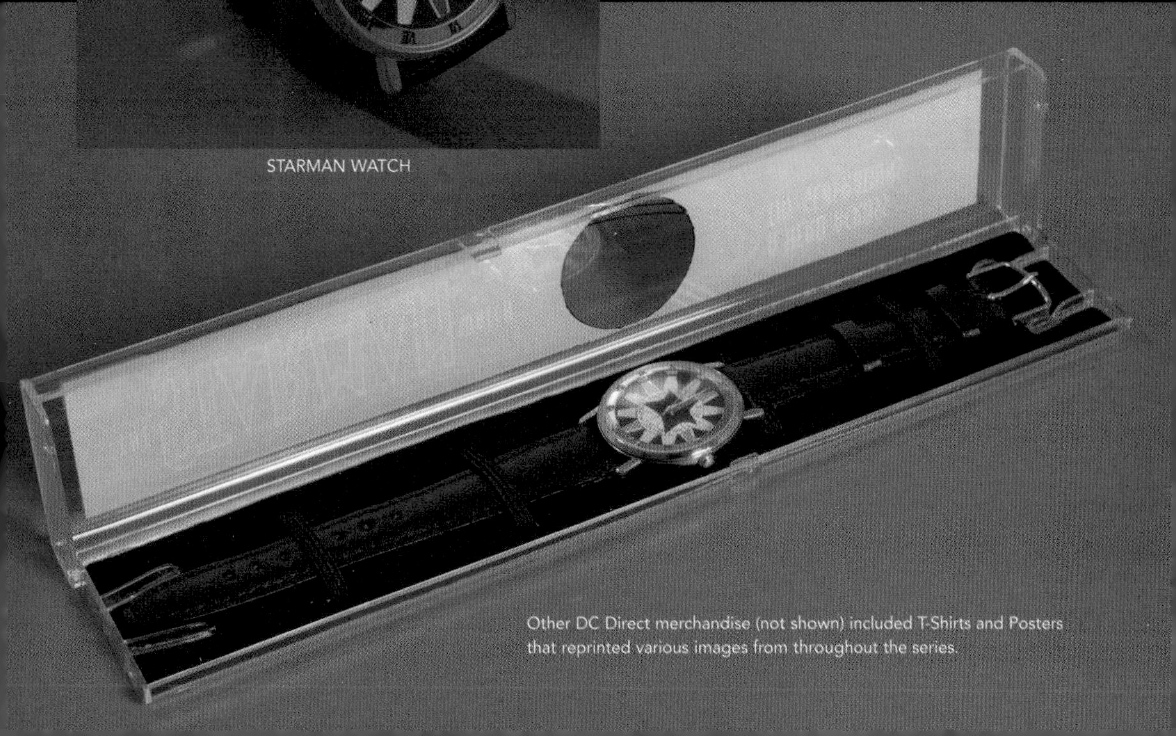

Other DC Direct merchandise (not shown) included T-Shirts and Posters that reprinted various images from throughout the series.

TIMES PAST An (ongoing) afterword

For those wise and/or lucky and/or foolhardy enough to get the last/first STARMAN OMNIBUS, you may recall I became the victim of a terrible case of (whatever the writer's written equivalent is of) verbal diarrhea. You got an intro and a very long and drawn-out frank accord of my youthful hubris, along with thoughts and recollections of the how, why and where of the conception of Starman. The one thing I didn't go into to any great degree in that first volume…was Tony Harris. This was for two reasons —

— Firstly, I knew then that Tony would be doing the introduction to this, the volume you now hold in your hands.

— And secondly, there really isn't as much to say about Tony's and my working relationship as one might expect. This isn't meant as a slight to him at all; merely that we had a good working relationship, at times bristly and at times smooth but with not as many ups and downs and arguments as many long-term creative teams.

My thoughts/memories on Tony as a whole are these.

I was convinced what Starman needed in terms of artistic representation was shadow. Obviously the sun is a star, so there's no reason Starman need restrict himself to the nighttime, but inspired by the Golden Age Starman à la Burnley and Meskin, who seemed to reserve most of Ted Knight's crime fighting for after dark, I felt this new Starman should be a light in the darkness too, not a bright shiny knight of the daytime. This required an artist who enjoyed drawing stark contrast.

I had had my eye on Tony Harris for some time. He'd done a couple of issues of Nightbreed for Marvel and his handling of light and shadow really caught my attention. Archie Goodwin liked him too. Our one concern was that Tony's speed wasn't up to doing a monthly book. However, our thought was that all we needed to do was get the first four issues out of him and then we could reexamine things from that point on.

Of course, Tony came through like a trooper and with a couple of "Times Past" issues a year to give him a little breathing room, he always met his deadlines and at the same time his art seemed to improve all the while, issue by issue. At no time did you feel he was skimping or cutting corners.

It was a pleasure to work with him. Even when we argued it was seldom, and always because of creative differences/for the betterment of the book rather than over some petty B.S.-driven ego.

In fact, the arguments we did have always helped the book, making us both try harder in an "I'll show him" kind of way.

We had an odd relationship. We spoke often enough, albeit from different sides of the country. I took an interest in his life and he too mine, to the degree two work colleagues do, but we never did become friends in that way workmates sometimes do. Tony was/is married and I was too at the time, but we never had a "couples dinner" at San Diego Con. In fact the only time I recall Tony and I sharing a meal at all was when we went out with Archie one afternoon. And yet when we'd sit and sign books together, we'd laugh and joke and have a lot of fun. I think it may have been both the distance between us and the fact that we both had a lot going on in our lives outside of comics. He had a marriage and children and all that goes along with that. I had a

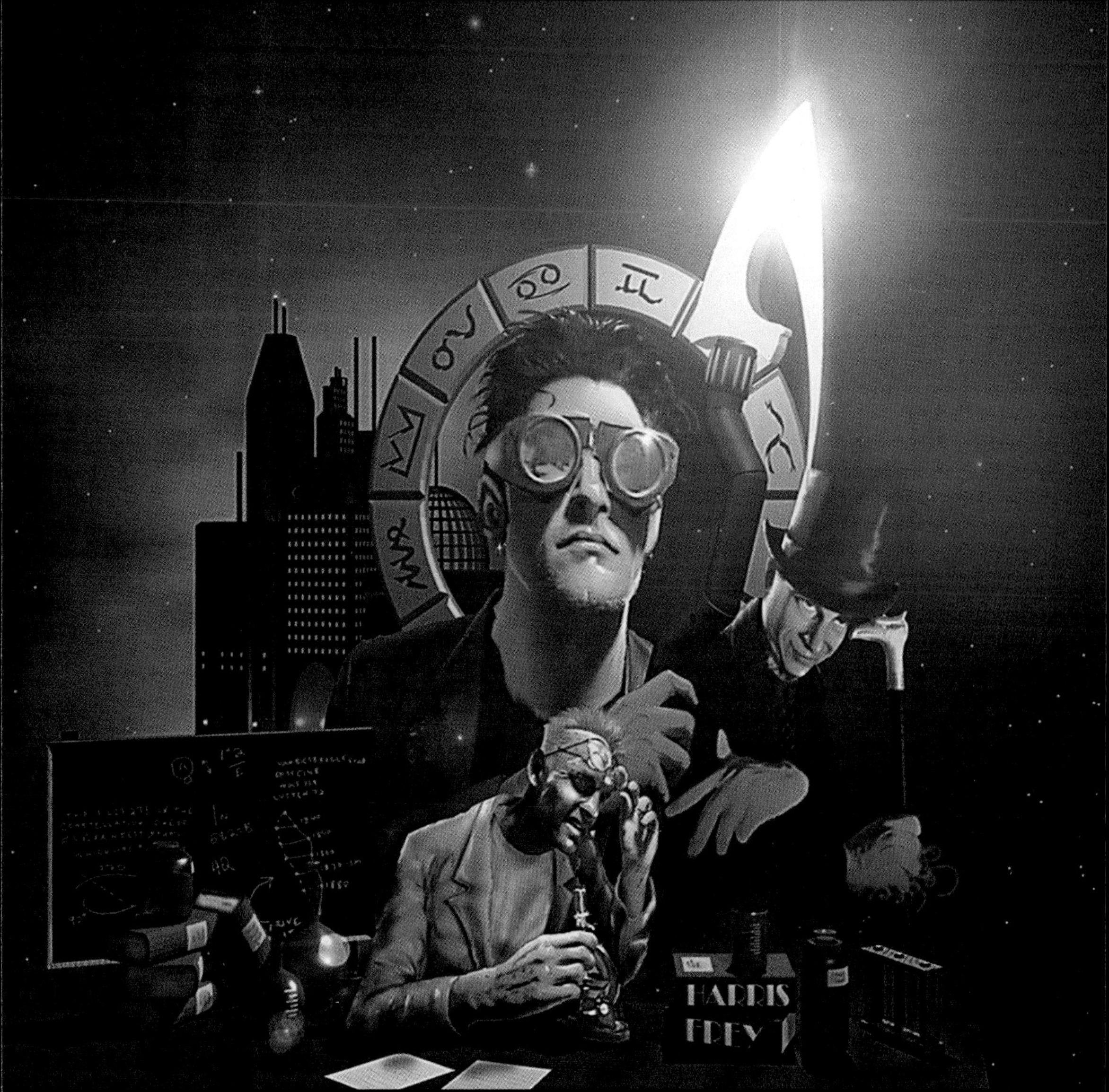
HARRIS
FREY

★ The cover to the STARMAN: SINS OF THE FATHER trade paperback by Tony Harris and Brian Frey.

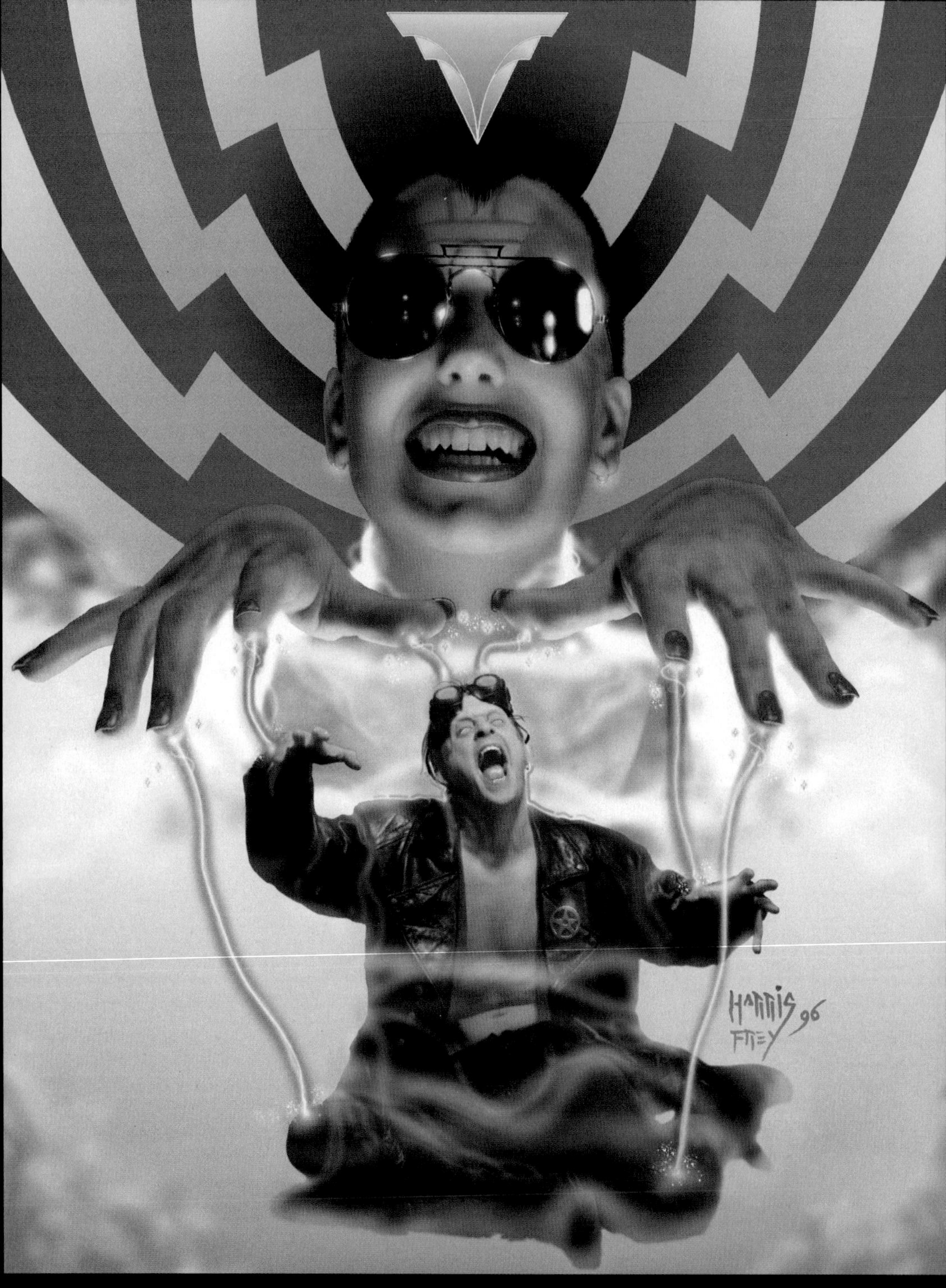
HARRIS 96
FREY

★ The cover to the STARMAN: NIGHT AND DAY trade paperback by Tony Harris and Brian Frey.

marriage that wasn't so good and all that goes along with that too. Still, some of the chats we'd have were long and fun and gossipy, so it wasn't all business.

Ironically, the only time Tony was truly upset with me was after he'd left the book. About nine months after Tony's departure I had opted (via a plot device that you'll need to read to fully understand) to divest Jack of his tattoos. [I guess I've let a future "plot cat" out of the bag (oops, sorry)]. These were the tattoos on Tony, each one on Jack mirroring his own. I think at first Tony thought this was malice on my part. It was actually something I didn't realize would be the logical upshot of what I'd done to Jack until after I'd written the cliffhanger last page of the issue before. Anyway Tony wasn't happy with me when I next saw him, but I think he finally began to see what I'd realized when I did it. It marked a passing of Tony from the book. Jack was changing as was I. It was truly a different time.

There's been talk of us getting back together to do a STARMAN graphic novel set in a prior point in Jack's life chronologically before Tony left the book and Jack became tattoo-less. At one point Tony, who has my sketchbook, said he was holding it for ransom until I wrote the script. However, in the last few years that talk has waned as Tony's career beyond STARMAN has taken off with EX MACHINA and now *War Heroes* and my career is whatever the Hell it now is. We may have spent too much time creatively away from each other. I don't know. And I do believe you should always get out while you're ahead, and leave a good-looking corpse. Yeah, I always think it's best to move on creatively. Don't look back. Never look back. The thought of Tony and I, a couple of old tarts prancing around trying to relearn half-forgotten dance steps might be a terrible, terrible thing. Or not. I don't know.

I do know I was lucky to work with Tony for as long as I did and I'm thankful and grateful he stuck with me and Jack until Jack went into the stars with issue #45. It was a great marriage of ideas and egos and the first half of Jack Knight's life wouldn't have been half as stellar without Tony Harris.

And Tony, if you read this — I want my sketchbook back.

★ ★ ★ ★ ★ ★

Part Two of this comprises a few thoughts/observations of the issues you've just read. Some will further reflect upon Tony — his and my working together, as well as the other artists who stepped up.

Issue #17. Thoughts/memories. Anyone who knows Tony will know of his love of pirates and of Howard Pyle, founder of the "Brandywine School" of Illustrative Art, whose most famous students include N.C. Wyeth, Frank Schoonover and Jessie Wilcox Smith. It was these two loves that inspired me to include The Black Pirate into the Byzantine plotline of Starman.

Oh, and another bit of Tony forcing me to think my way out of something narratively: When I decided to include Solomon Grundy in Starman I expected him to draw the typical Grundy. And had he done so, he would have appeared the first time he did and that would have been that. Instead, he gave me a gentle, chalky child-man, who in one form or another stayed around until the end of the series. In fact we eventually got to define/explain the many personas of Grundy, as you'll see in OMNIBUS VOL. 3.

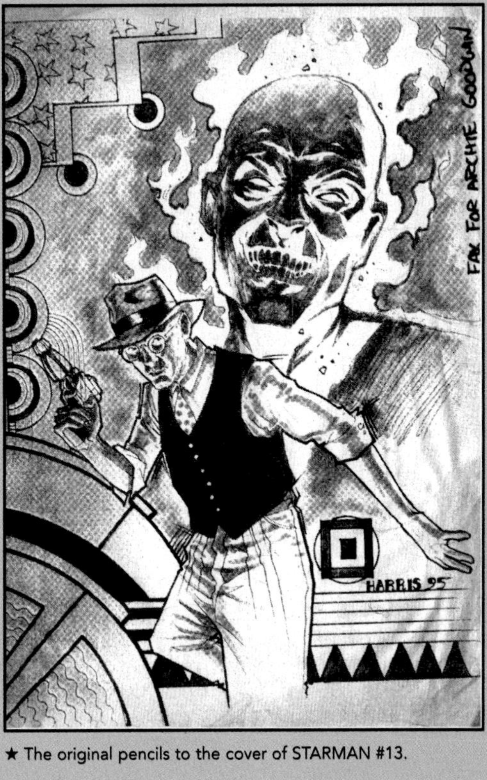
FAX FOR ARCHIE GOODWIN
HARRIS 95

★ The original pencils to the cover of STARMAN #13.

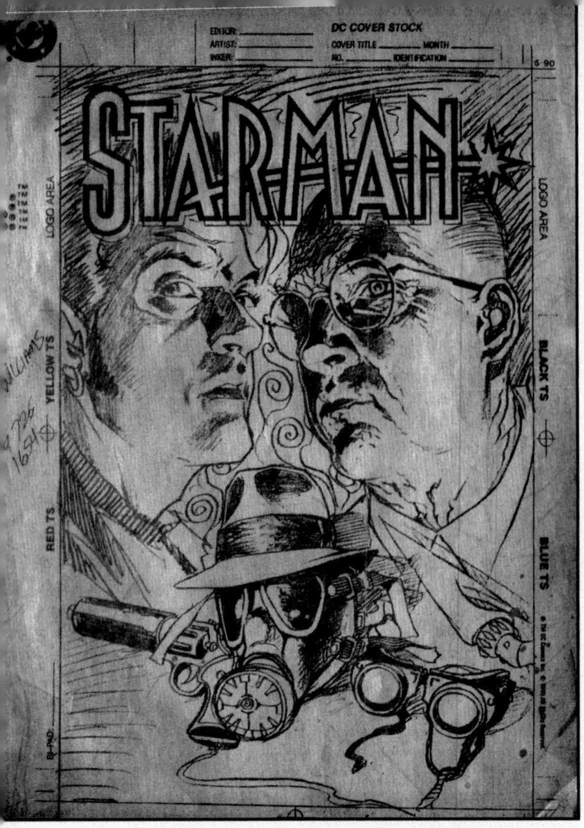
DC COVER STOCK
EDITOR:
ARTIST:
INKER:
COVER TITLE
MONTH
NO.
IDENTIFICATION
6-90
STARMAN
LOGO AREA
LOGO AREA
YELLOW TS
BLACK TS
RED TS
BLUE TS

★ The original pencils to the cover of STARMAN #22.

Issue #18. Not the best place for a "Times Past," but there you go. It was the first time I worked with John Watkiss, an artist I'd long admired. I recall John telling me years later he wasn't happy with the issue, but I thought he did great.

Issue #19. This was a gift to Tony. A chance for him to do more pirate stuff. "Talking With David" was always fun. The color or lack thereof was always exciting and the fact that it was just Jack and David goofing on each other.

Issues #20-23. I've never liked how some DC characters get lost forever to Vertigo. I think when you have supervillains raping hero's wives in the JLA satellite and alluding to taking cocaine, the line between "mature" and not is getting way blurred. Maybe it's time to make it all one big world again. Or maybe I'm morally bankrupt. Anyway, this was me continuing on somewhat the continuity from Matt Wagner's arc of SANDMAN MYSTERY THEATRE entitled "The Face." Matt and I loosely planned this together. It's not a big "you have to read it all" crossover, but I like the way it gently carries over from one storyline to the next. And it won me, Tony, Wade and Guy Davis the Eisner Award for best arc.

Issues #24-26. The Poster Demon. Merritt is the character referred to obliquely by Wilde in issue #6. The poster is a metaphor for Dorian Gray's picture.

It was also fun to do the Chris Sprouse pages in issue #24 — showing moments from the life of Hamilton Drew, my/Opal City's own version of Sherlock Holmes.

And in issue #26 it was fun dividing the pages/panels up between Tony, J.H. Williams and Gary Erskine. There's a lot more of that sort of thing done nowadays, but I recall at the time it was less seldom seen.

The end, with the people taken by Merritt's poster returning to Opal in the present was inspired by the end of *Close Encounters of the Third Kind.* I always found the most interesting thing about it was the people whom the aliens returned to Earth. I always wondered what their lives would be like. I've never seen the TV show *The 4400*, but I guess that covers some of the same ground.

Issue #27. Always a sucker for Christmas stories. And always a sucker for Steve Yeowell who I first worked with on a seldom seen, little-read GN for Epic Comics entitled 67 *Seconds.* You all probably know Steve better for his work with Grant on "Zenith" for *2000AD.* He's a great talent and a true gent. We haven't spoken in years for no reason except that people drift apart. A pity.

Issue #28. My first collaboration with Craig Hamilton. Always a pleasure. I was amazed, for the time, how much they let us get away with. Drug use, herpes, a homoerotic death scene and disco. Top that, Mr. Morrison.

Issue #29. Tony came back after a brief respite and together we introduced one of my favorite creations, Bobo Benetti. I don't exactly know where he came from. This was a special reintroduction issue, to get more readers. The idea of seeing Opal through the eyes of someone returning to the place after a long time away seemed a good way to reintroduce characters to new readers without that seeming so obvious.

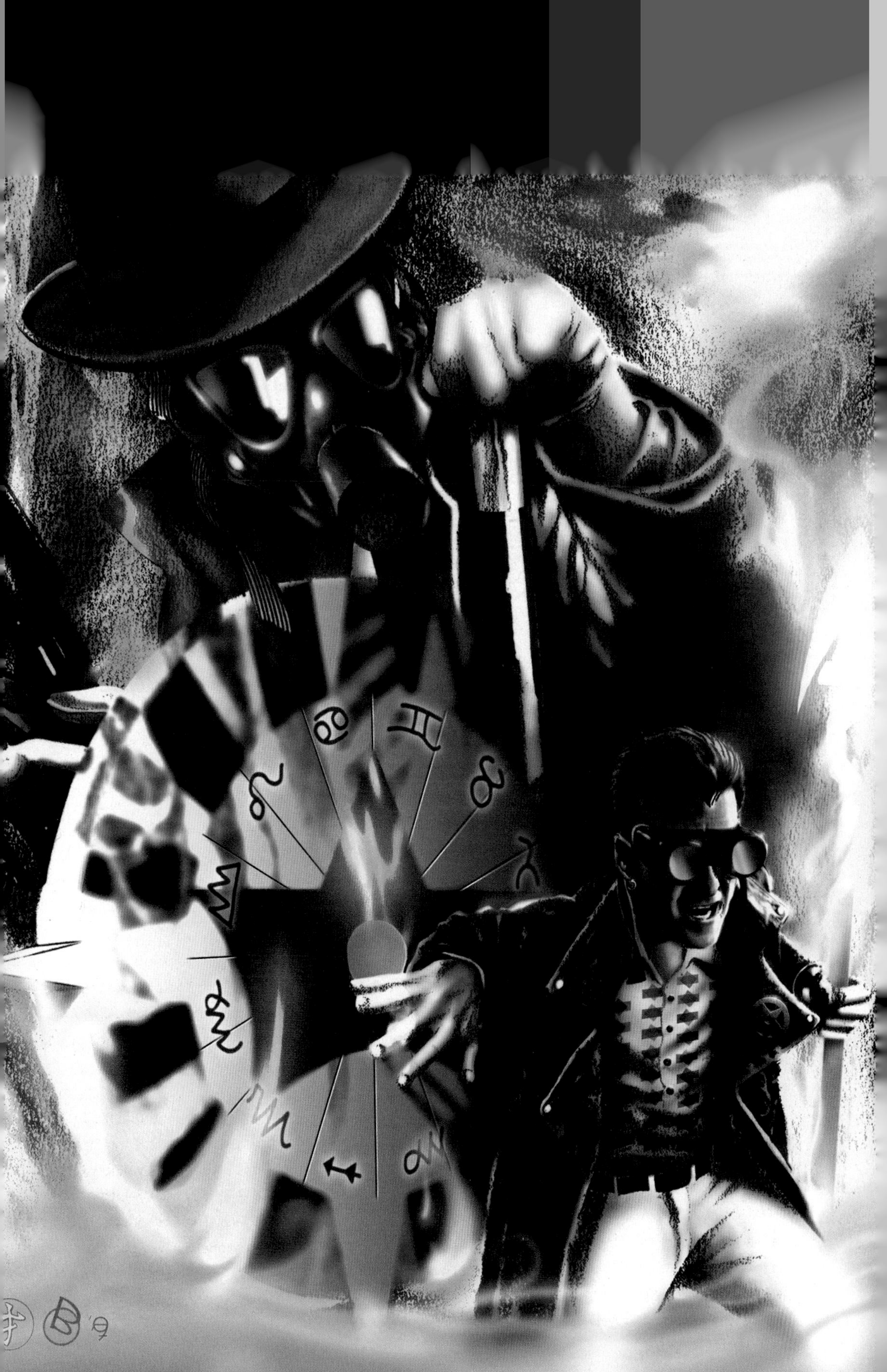

★ The cover to the STARMAN: A WICKED INCLINATION... trade paperback by Tony Harris and Brian Frey.

I know I was watching a lot of Scorsese at the time, but also reading some Herman Hesse. I think both elements of that are in Bobo. I have always had such fun writing him. I promise I will again someday.

Oh, and in this issue — Charity foretelling Jack's future — is where I first conceived the last page of Starman's last issue (#80), in terms of the big picture.

SHOWCASE '95 #12. My chance to work with Wade Von Grawbadger as an artist instead of as an inker. And the very first solo Shade story. Recalling it makes me remember Neal Pozner, SHOWCASE's editor who passed away. Man, I miss that guy.

SHOWCASE '96 #4-5. The Shade and Dr. Fate. This ties in with the magic that will be used to entrap Opal in Grand Guignol in the last Omnibus. I like the art by Matt Smith too. Matt's art is interesting in that it changed each time I worked with him (he had already done STARMAN #11, the second "Times Past" you will have already read in OMNIBUS VOL. 1.) He'd do one more "Times Past" later on, with his art different yet again. A good artist to work with.

And the ANNUAL #1. Lots of artists, lots of Starmen. Craig did the Shade framing sequence.

★ The cover to the STARMAN: TIMES PAST trade paperback by Brian Frey.

I recall him going to insane lengths, naming the children (drawn/colored as if each was a different descendant of an Opal City character — his idea not mine) and over-thinking stuff. But the dividend was beautiful art. The cityscapes are breathtaking.

Brett Blevins is another guy I've lost touch with. I loved his work on this issue. I felt it perfectly suited Prince Gavyn. And being a 1930s/40s movie buff, he understood perfectly when I said I wanted a suggestion of Ruritania (from *The Prisoner of Zenda*) to the uniforms and street scenes of Throneworld.

And this may or may not be my first gig with J.H. Williams. I confess I forget. We've worked together quite a bit on this thing or that. That beautiful art certainly suits the 1940s era the story is set in, though. And it's always such an easy time working with the guy.

And like Bobo, I have no idea how I came up with the Prairie Witch, but I am glad I was able to obliquely fold her into the whole Starman mythos by the end of the series (as those of you who haven't already read the comics shall all one day see.)

So there you have it. For now.

Thank you one and all for buying this tome. And please buy the next. Which I promise won't be as long coming out as this one was.

Don't get a rash.

James Robinson
Hollywood, California
October, 2008